Fundamentals of Business Law

6th Edition

Roger LeRoy Miller
Institute for University Studies
Arlington, Texas

Gaylord A. Jentz
Herbert D. Kelleher
Emeritus Professor in Business Law
University of Texas at Austin

THOMSON

SOUTH-WESTERN

WEST

Australia · Canada · Mexico · Singapore · Spain · United Kingdom · United States

THOMSON

SOUTH-WESTERN

WEST

Fundamentals of Business Law
6TH EDITION

Roger LeRoy Miller
Institute for University Studies
Arlington, Texas

Gaylord A. Jentz
Herbert D. Kelleher
Emeritus Professor in Business Law
University of Texas at Austin

**Vice President and
Editorial Director:**
Jack Calhoun

**Vice President and
Editor-in-Chief:**
George Werthman

**Publisher, Business Law
and Accounting:**
Rob Dewey

Senior Developmental Editor:
Jan Lamar

Marketing Manager:
Steve Silverstein

Production Manager:
Bill Stryker

Media Developmental Editor:
Christine A. Wittmer

Media Production Editor:
Amy Wilson

Manufacturing Coordinator:
Rhonda Utley

Compositor:
Parkwood Composition Service
New Richmond, WI

Printer:
West Group

Sr. Design Project Manager:
Michelle Kunkler

Internal Designer:
Bill Stryker

Cover Designer:
Kathy Heming
Cincinnati, OH

Cover Image:
© Thinkstock

**Library of Congress Control
Number:** 2003114935

ISBN 0-324-27094-1

Contents in Brief

Contents

ix

Preface to the Instructor

Now, more than ever before, a fundamental knowledge of the tenets of business law is crucial for anyone contemplating a career in business. Consequently, we have written *Fundamentals of Business Law,* Sixth Edition, with this goal in mind: to present a clear and comprehensive treatment of what every student should know about commercial law. While some of this law may change, the fundamentals rarely do—and that's what students reading this text will acquire.

Emphasis on Internet Law

Fundamentals of Business Law, Sixth Edition, is truly up to date and reflects current law to the fullest extent possible. We have included throughout the text, whenever relevant, sections discussing the most recent developments in the law as it is being applied to Internet transactions and e-commerce. For example, in Chapter 5, which focuses on intellectual property, we point out how traditional laws—and some newly enacted laws—are being applied to online issues relating to *copyrights, trademarks, patents,* and *trade secrets.* Other chapters in the text include sections on *privacy rights* in the online world, *jurisdictional issues* as they arise in cyberspace, *cyber torts* and *cyber crimes, online securities offerings,* and a number of other topics relating to the online legal environment. We have also included an entire chapter (Chapter 13) devoted solely to the topic of *electronic contracts,* or e-contracts.

The Internet Connection

In addition to incorporating cyberlaw throughout the basic text of the book, the Sixth Edition offers several other components focusing on technology.

FUNDAMENTALS OF BUSINESS LAW ON THE WEB

When your students visit our Web site at **http://fundamentals.westbuslaw.com**, they will find, at a minimum, the following:

- Interactive quizzes for every chapter in this text. (These are included in the Interactive Study Center.)

- Internet exercises for each chapter in this text as well as selected Web sources of information relevant to each chapter. (These are included in the Interactive Study Center.)

- Answers to the end-of-chapter *Case Problem with Sample Answer* problems. (These can be accessed through the Interactive Study Center.)

- Court case updates, which present summaries of new cases from various West legal publications, all linked to this text.

- Links to legal resources available for free on the Web.

- A "Talk to the Authors" feature that allows you and your students to e-mail your questions about *Fundamentals of Business Law* to the authors.

- A "Statutes" page offering links to selected statutes referenced in this text.

- Videos with accompanying video questions (discussed in more detail later in this preface).

WESTLAW® CAMPUS

Westlaw® Campus is now available to students using West Legal Studies in Business texts. Westlaw Campus is derived from Westlaw®, the preferred computer-assisted legal research database of legal professionals. It can be bundled with your text, at an outstanding discount, for every student through a passcode. (Students who purchase used books may buy access to Westlaw Campus at **http://campus.westbuslaw.com**.)

In addition to primary legal materials (federal and state cases, statutes, and administrative law), Westlaw Campus offers secondary resources, such as *American Law Reports (ALR), American Jurisprudence 2d (Am.Jur.2d),* and law reviews. These materials can greatly enhance research assignments, critical thinking exercises, and term papers.

ONLINE LEGAL RESEARCH GUIDE

With every new book, your students will receive a free copy of the *Online Legal Research Guide.* This is the most complete brief guide to using the Internet that exists today. Text co-author Roger LeRoy Miller developed and wrote this supplement, which has been updated for the Sixth Edition, especially to accompany *Fundamentals of Business Law.* There is even an appendix on how to evaluate information obtained from the Internet.

CYBERLAW FEATURES AND PEDAGOGY

We have included in many chapters in this text a special feature, titled *Business Law in the Online World,* to inform your students about how technological developments are affecting specific areas of law. Additionally, the following special features and pedagogy in the Sixth Edition of *Fundamentals of Business Law* are designed to acquaint your students with the broad array of legal resources available on the Web.

- *URLs for cases*—Whenever possible, we have included URLs that can be used to access the cases presented in the text. When a URL is available, it appears just below the case citation, and a footnote to the URL explains to the student how to navigate the accessed site to find the specific case.

- *Accessing the Internet*—These end-of-chapter features list specific Internet addresses, or URLs, that students can use to access online information concerning a topic being discussed in the text.

- *Online Legal Research*—To familiarize your students with online legal resources and help them learn to navigate the Internet, we have included at the end of every chapter, just following the URLs listed in the *Accessing the Internet* features, at least two Internet exercises. These exercises refer students to Internet activities presented in the "Interactive Study Center" section of the *Fundamentals of Business Law* Web site at **http://fundamentals. westbuslaw.com**.

- *Before the Test*—At the end of every chapter, just following the *Online Legal Research* section, students are directed to online quizzes available on the *Fundamentals of Business Law* Web site.

A Special Case Format

In each chapter, we present cases that have been selected to illustrate the principles of law discussed in the text. The cases are numbered sequentially for easy referencing in class discussions, homework assignments, and examinations. In choosing the cases to be included in this edition, our goal has been to present not only cases that reflect the most current law but also cases that constitute significant precedents in case law.

Each case is presented in the following special format:

- *Case title and full case citation* (including all parallel citations and, when possible, a URL and an explanatory note indicating how the case can be accessed online).

- *Facts.*

- *Issue.*

- *Decision.*

- *Reason.*

In addition, each case concludes with a *For Critical Analysis* section, which consists of a question that requires the student to think critically about a particular issue raised by the case. The section addresses the AACSB's curriculum requirements by focusing on how particular aspects of the dispute or the court's decision relate to ethical, international, technological, cultural, or other types of issues.

For the Sixth Edition of *Fundamentals of Business Law,* we have given special emphasis to landmark and classic cases by setting these off with a special heading and logo. Additionally, a *Comment* section at the end of each landmark or classic case stresses the importance of the court's decision in the case to the evolution of the law concerning the issue.

Emphasis on Ethics and Corporate Accountability

For the Sixth Edition of *Fundamentals of Business Law,* we have included a virtually rewritten chapter on ethics and social responsibility (Chapter 3). The chapter now presents a more practical approach to this topic, including a case study examining the scandal surrounding the Enron Corporation's actions in the early 2000s. In addition to this chapter on ethics, one chapter in each unit contains a question entitled *A Question of Ethics and Social Responsibility* at the end of the *Questions and Case Problems* section.

In the Sixth Edition, we also refer to the Sarbanes-Oxley Act of 2002 and the corporate scandals that led to the passage of that legislation. For example, in Chapter 3, which focuses on ethics and social responsibility, we refer to the requirements of the Sarbanes-Oxley Act relating to confidential reporting systems. In Chapter 27, we look at some of the key provisions of the act relating to corporate accountability with respect to securities transactions. In Chapter 31, we again examine the provisions of this act as they relate to public accounting firms and accounting practices.

Finally, for an additional cost, users of this text can access a special Web project focusing on Enron, entitled "Inside Look." This project is on the Web at **http://insidelook. westbuslaw.com**. There you will find in-depth articles and expert analysis concerning the events leading to Enron's collapse and the continuing investigation of that company. "Inside Look" provides analysis from all angles by using an interdisciplinary approach emphasizing accounting, business law, and management disciplines.

Other Features and Pedagogy

In addition to the components of the teaching/learning package accompanying *Fundamentals of Business Law,* Sixth Edition, that we have described above, the text offers a number of other special features and pedagogy.

FEATURES

As well as the *Business Law in the Online World* feature, which we have already discussed, one chapter in each unit of this text now includes a feature entitled *Management Perspective.* In this feature, your students can read about issues facing managers in today's business world and how the courts have dealt with those issues. Each feature concludes with a section summarizing the implications of the courts' decisions for managers and business owners.

PEDAGOGICAL DEVICES IN EACH CHAPTER

- Chapter Objectives.
- Exhibits and forms (about one hundred).
- Highlighted, numbered examples to illustrate important points of law.

CHAPTER-ENDING PEDAGOGY

- *Terms and Concepts* (with appropriate page references).
- *Chapter Summary* (in graphic format with page references).
- *For Review* (the questions set forth in the chapter-opening *Chapter Objectives* section are again presented to aid the student in reviewing the chapter).
- *Questions and Case Problems* (including hypotheticals and case problems).
- *Case Problem with Sample Answer* (each chapter contains one of these case problems, for which the answers have been provided on the text's Web site).
- *A Question of Ethics and Social Responsibility* (in selected chapters).
- *Video Question* (in selected chapters, as discussed next).
- *Accessing the Internet.*
- *Online Legal Research.*
- *Before the Test.*

VIDEO QUESTIONS

For this edition of *Fundamentals of Business Law,* we have added special new *Video Questions* at the ends of selected chapters. Each of these questions directs students to the text's Web site (at **http://fundamentals.westbuslaw.com**) to view a video relevant to a topic covered in the chapter. This instruction is followed by a series of questions based on the video. The questions are again repeated on the Web site, when the student accesses the video. An access code for the videos is available with each new copy of this textbook, when requested. (Students who purchase used books may buy access to the digital video library at **http://digitalvideolibrary. westbuslaw.com**.)

These videos can be used as homework assignments, discussion starters, or classroom demonstrations. By watching a video and answering the questions, students will gain an understanding of how the legal concepts they have studied in the chapter apply to the real-life situation portrayed in the video. **Suggested answers for all of the video questions are given in both the *Instructor's Manual* and the *Answer's Manual*** that accompany this text. The videos are part of the *West's Digital Video Library,* a compendium of fifty-five video scenarios and explanations.

UNIT-ENDING PEDAGOGY

Concluding each unit is a two-page feature called *Focus on Legal Reasoning,* which examines a specific court case relating to a topic covered in the unit. Each feature opens with an introductory section, which discusses the background and significance of the case being presented. Then we provide excerpts from the court's majority opinion as well as from a dissenting opinion in the case. The feature concludes with a series of questions, under the heading *Legal Reasoning and Analysis,* that prompt the student to think critically about the legal, ethical, economic, international, or general business implications of the case. In the *Going Online* section that follows, the student is directed to one or more Web sites at which the case itself or further information on the case can be found.

Appendices

Because the majority of students keep their business law text as a reference source, we have included at the end of the book the following full set of appendices (Appendix C has been modified for the Sixth Edition):

A. How to Brief a Case and Analyze Case Problems.
B. The Constitution of the United States.

C. The Uniform Commercial Code (Excerpts), including Article 1, Article 2, excerpts from the 2003 amendments to Article 2, Article 2A, the revised Articles 3 and 4, Article 4A, and the revised Article 9.

D. Spanish Equivalents for Important Legal Terms in English.

A Flexible Teaching/Learning Package

We realize that different people have different teaching philosophies and learning goals. We believe that the Sixth Edition of *Fundamentals of Business Law* and its extensive supplements offer business law instructors a flexible teaching/learning package. For example, although we have attempted to make the materials flow from chapter to chapter, most of the chapters are self-contained. In other words, you can use the chapters in any order you wish.

Additionally, the extensive number of supplements accompanying *Fundamentals of Business Law* allows instructors to choose those supplements that will most effectively complement classroom instruction. These supplementary materials, including printed and multimedia supplements, all contribute to the goal of making *Fundamentals of Business Law* a flexible teaching/learning package.

Supplemental Teaching Materials

This edition of *Fundamentals of Business Law* is accompanied by an expansive number of teaching and learning supplements. Individually and in conjunction with a number of our colleagues, we have developed supplementary teaching materials that we believe are the best available today. Each component of the supplements package is listed below.

SUPPLEMENTS FOR INSTRUCTORS

- *Instructor's Resource CD-ROM*—Includes the following supplements: Instructor's Manual, Answers Manual, Test Bank, ExamView, Case Printouts, Case-Problem Cases, and PowerPoint Slides.

- *Instructor's Manual*—Includes answers to all *For Critical Analysis* questions in the features. Also available on the IRCD.

- *Test Bank*—Includes three multiple-choice questions for each *Focus on Legal Reasoning* section. Also available on the IRCD.

- *ExamView*—Also available on the IRCD.

- *Answers Manual (Answers to Questions and Case Problems and Alternate Problem Sets with Answers)*—Includes answers to the *Questions and Case Problems,* answers to the *For Critical Analysis* questions in the features, and alternate problem sets with answers. Also available on the IRCD.

- *PowerPoint Slides*—Also available on the IRCD.

- *Transparency Acetates.*

- *Video Library*—Including Court TV®, the *Legal Conflicts in Business* videos, and the *Drama of the Law* video series. (For further information on video supplements, go to http://videos.westbuslaw.com.)

- *Instructor's Manual* for the *Drama of the Law* video series.

- *Westlaw®*—To qualified adopters.

- *WebTutor™ ToolBox.*

SUPPLEMENTS FOR STUDENTS

- *Online Legal Research Guide* (free with every new copy of this text).

- *Study Guide.*

- *Handbook of Landmark Cases and Statutes in Business Law and the Legal Environment.*

- *Guide to Personal Law.*

- *Handbook on Critical Thinking and Writing in Business Law and the Legal Environment.*

- *Westlaw® Campus.*

A Special Note to Users of the Fifth Edition

We thought that those of you who have been using *Fundamentals of Business Law* would like to know some of the major changes that have been made for the Sixth Edition. The book is basically the same, but we think that we have improved it greatly, thanks in part to the many letters, e-mails, telephone calls, and reviews that we have received.

EXPANDED COVERAGE OF INTERNET LAW

For the Sixth Edition of *Fundamentals of Business Law,* we have expanded the coverage of cyberlaw as it relates to topics covered in the chapters. The text now includes more material on jurisdictional issues in cyberspace, a thoroughly updated discussion of intellectual property rights in the online environment, new sections discussing online securities offerings and online securities fraud, an expanded discussion of privacy rights in the employment context, an updated chapter on e-contracts, and more.

An Improved Presentation of Ethics and Corporate Accountability

As noted earlier in this preface, the chapter on ethics and social responsibility (Chapter 3) has been virtually rewritten for the Sixth Edition. As mentioned, the chapter now presents a more real-world examination of ethical issues in the legal environment, including a case study of the Enron Corporation and the consequences resulting from its unethical actions for that firm. Congress responded to the ethical scandals of the early 2000s by passing the Sarbanes-Oxley Act of 2002. As also noted earlier, we discuss this act and some of its key provisions in Chapter 3, in the context of ethics; in Chapter 27, in the context of securities transactions; and again in Chapter 31, in the context of professional liability.

Incorporation of Revised Article 9 Provisions

The chapter on secured transactions has been updated and, in many sections, completely rewritten to base the coverage of this topic on the revised Article 9 of the Uniform Commercial Code (UCC). Additionally, the revised Article 9 is now included in Appendix C, which presents excerpts from the UCC.

Reference to the 2003 Amendments to UCC Article 2

In the chapters covering sales and lease contracts, we have added footnotes discussing the 2003 amendments to UCC Article 2 whenever they significantly alter the law. Excerpts from the 2003 amendments to Article 2 have also been included in Appendix C, just following Article 2.

New Features and Pedagogy

For the Sixth Edition of *Fundamentals of Business Law*, we have added the following entirely new elements:

- *Business Law in the Online World* features.
- *Management Perspective* features.
- A *Comment* section concluding each landmark and classic case.
- *Case Problem with Sample Answer* problems (in the *Questions and Case Problems* section), for which model answers are provided on the text's Web site.
- *Video Questions* (in selected chapters).

Significantly Revised Chapters

Each chapter of the Sixth Edition has been revised as necessary to incorporate new developments in the law or to streamline the presentations. Other major changes and additions made for this edition include those described below.

- **Chapter 1 (Sources of Business Law and the Global Legal Environment)**—The section on the commerce clause now includes a subsection (and a feature) discussing the dormant commerce clause. Cyberlaw issues, including online speech, are now covered in this chapter. The section titled "Finding and Analyzing the Law" has been moved from this chapter to an appendix just following Chapter 1.

- **Chapter 2 (Traditional and Online Dispute Resolution)**—This chapter now includes a discussion of the types of jurisdictional issues that have been raised by Internet transactions, including international transactions, and how the courts have dealt with these issues. In addition, several sections have been added to this chapter, including sections covering electronic filing, the courts' use of Web sites, cyber courts, online dispute resolution, and the difficulty parties sometimes face in enforcing court judgments.

- **Chapter 3 (Ethics and Social Responsibility)**—As noted earlier in this preface, this chapter has been virtually rewritten to address ethical concerns in today's legal environment. The chapter now includes sections on how to set an ethical tone in a business environment, the Enron scandal, and the requirements of the Sarbanes-Oxley Act of 2002 with respect to corporate compliance. Generally, the revised chapter offers a more practical approach to business and ethical decision making.

- **Chapter 4 (Torts and Cyber Torts)**—A final section in the chapter now covers cyber torts, including defamation online and spamming.

- **Chapter 5 (Intellectual Property and Internet Law)**—The materials on intellectual property rights in the online environment have been thoroughly revised and updated. They have also been integrated into the discussions of each form of intellectual property covered in the chapter.

- **Chapter 6 (Criminal Law and Cyber Crimes)**—The section on crimes affecting business has been reorganized and rewritten to streamline the presentation. New to the chapter is a discussion of cyber crimes, including cyber theft, cyber-stalking, hacking, cyber terrorism, the difficulty of prosecuting cyber crime, and the Computer Fraud and Abuse Act.

- **Chapter 13 (E-Contracts)**—This chapter has been thoroughly revised. It now opens with a discussion of what should be included in online offers and the nature of online acceptances. Because of its significance in today's legal environment, the coverage of the Uniform Electronic Transactions Act has been greatly expanded.

- **Chapters 14 through 17 (on sales and lease contracts)**—Throughout this unit, text or footnotes have been added, whenever relevant, to indicate how the 2003 amendments to Article 2 of the Uniform Commercial Code (UCC) alter existing law.

- **Chapters 18 and 19 (on negotiable instruments)**—Whenever relevant, footnotes have been added to clarify how the 2002 amendments to Articles 3 and 4 of the UCC affect existing law. Chapter 19 (Checks, the Banking System, and E-Money) now includes sections discussing e-money, online banking, and the Uniform Money Services Act.

- **Chapter 20 (Secured Transactions)**—This chapter was virtually rewritten to base it on the revised version of Article 9 of the UCC. Existing exhibits have been replaced as necessary to reflect concepts and requirements set forth in the revised Article 9.

- **Chapter 23 (Employment Law)**—This chapter has been revised to include recent developments in employment-related areas, including disability-based discrimination, sexual harassment, electronic performance monitoring, affirmative action, and the virtual workplace.

- **Chapter 27 (Investor Protection and Online Securities Offerings)**—This chapter was revised as necessary to reflect the relevant provisions of the Sarbanes-Oxley Act of 2002. Also included is a full-page exhibit describing some of the key provisions of this act that relate to corporate accountability with respect to securities transactions. The chapter now concludes with sections discussing online securities offerings and online securities fraud.

- **Chapter 29 (Real Property)**—Sections discussing environmental takings and takings for private development have been added to this chapter.

- **Chapter 31 (Professional Liability)**—This chapter now includes a discussion (and an exhibit) on the provisions of the Sarbanes-Oxley Act of 2002 that concern public accounting firms and accounting practices.

WHAT ELSE IS NEW?

In addition to the changes noted above, you will find a number of other new items or features in *Fundamentals of Business Law*, Sixth Edition, as listed below.

- An expanded number of Internet exercises—there are now at least two of these exercises for each chapter, most of which have been newly created.

- New cases, including many cases from 2002 and 2003.

- New case problems, many of which are from 2002 or 2003.

- New exhibits.

- Revised Appendix C, as noted earlier.

- Answers to the *For Critical Analysis* questions in the features in both the *Instructor's Manual* and the *Answers Manual*.

- Three multiple-choice questions in the *Test Bank* for each *Focus on Legal Reasoning* feature.

NEW SUPPLEMENTS AND OTHER SPECIAL RESOURCES

- Westlaw® Campus (allowing your students to access any case presented or cited in this text using their Westlaw Campus account).

- "Inside Look" (Web project on ethics, available at an additional cost at http://insidelook.westbuslaw.com).

- A "Statutes" page on the text's Web site (at http://www.fundamentals.westbuslaw.com) containing links to selected statutes referenced in this text.

- New interactive quizzes on the text's Web site. For each chapter in the text, there are now at least twenty interactive questions, many of which have been newly created.

- Model answers on the text's Web site for the *Case Problem with Sample Answer* problems presented in the *Questions and Case Problems* sections.

- West's Digital Video Library, a collection of 55 video scenarios to illustrate the application of legal concepts to business situations. Many of these videos have discussion questions on the text's web site.

Acknowledgments

Kenneth Anderson
Mott Community College

Janie Blankenship
Del Mar College

Daniel R. Cahoy
The Pennsylvania State University

Len Callahan
Embry-Riddle Aeronautical University

Anniken Davenport
Harrisburg Area Community College

Philip E. De Marco
Mission College

Carol Docan
California State University, Northridge

James T. Foster
Florence Darlington Technical College

Frank Giesber
Texas Lutheran University

Thomas F. Goldman
Bucks County Community College

Edward M. Kissling
Ocean County College

Percy L. Lambert
Borough of Manhattan Community College

Daniel A. Levin
University of Colorado, Boulder

Jane A. Malloy
Delaware County Community College

John F. Mastriani
El Paso Community College

Russell A. Meade
Gardner-Webb University

Michael W. Pearson
Arizona State University

Steven M. Platau
The University of Tampa

Lee Ruck
George Mason University

Gayle L. Terry
Mary Washington College

Sheila Vagle
Northwest Technical College

Alan L. Weldy
Goshen College

John O. Wheeler
University of Virginia

Paula York
Northern Maine Technical College

We are greatly indebted to the many individuals at West/ South-Western who worked on this project. We especially wish to thank Rob Dewey and Jan Lamar for their helpful advice and guidance. Christine Wittmer, our media developmental editor, and Amy Wilson, our media production editor, deserve a special note of appreciation for their masterful work on the Web site. Our long-time production editor at West, Bill Stryker, made sure that we came out with an error-free edition on time. We will always be in his debt. We also thank Ann Borman for her assistance.

Additionally, we thank William Eric Hollowell, co-author of the *Instructor's Manual, Study Guide,* and *Test Bank,* for his contributions to this edition. We also must thank Lavina Leed Miller, who provided expert research, editing, and proofing services for the project, as well as Gregory Scott, who provided valuable assistance to the authors. The copy-editing and proofreading skills of Suzie Franklin DeFazio and Pat Lewis, respectively, will not go unnoticed. Finally, our appreciation goes to Roxanna Lee and Suzanne Jasin for their many special efforts on the project.

We know that we are not perfect. If you or your students find something you don't like or want us to change, you can contact us easily using the "Talk to the Authors" feature on this text's accompanying Web site at **http://fundamentals. com**. Your comments can help us make *Fundamentals of Business Law* an even better book in the future.

Roger LeRoy Miller
Gaylord A. Jentz

Dedication

To Paul Jack,
Your enthusiasm pervades your
every sentence and activity.
While I might not always be able
to keep up with you, I will continue
trying. Good luck on your new venture!
R.L.M.

To my wife, JoAnn; to my children,
Kathy, Gary, Lori, and Rory; and to
my grandchildren, Erin,
Megan, Eric, Emily, Michelle,
Javier, Carmen, and Steve.
G.A.J.

UNIT 1

The Legal Environment of Business

1

Sources of Business Law and the Global Legal Environment

CHAPTER OBJECTIVES

After reading this chapter, you should be able to answer the following questions:

① What is the common law tradition?

② What is a precedent? When might a court depart from precedent?

③ What is the difference between remedies at law and remedies in equity?

④ What are some important classifications of law?

⑤ How does the U.S. Constitution affect business activities in the United States?

Law is of interest to all persons, not just to lawyers. Those entering the world of business will find themselves subject to numerous laws and government regulations. A basic knowledge of these laws and regulations is beneficial—if not essential—to anyone contemplating a successful career in the business world of today.

In this introductory chapter, after a brief look at the nature of law, we examine the common law tradition of the United States and some of the major sources and classifications of American law. The chapter concludes with a discussion of the U.S. Constitution as it affects business.

The Nature of Law

There have been and will continue to be different definitions of *law*. The Greek philosopher Aristotle (384–322 B.C.E.) saw law as a "pledge that citizens of a state will do justice to one another." Aristotle's mentor, Plato (427–347 B.C.E.), believed that law was a form of social control. The Roman orator and politician Cicero (106–43 B.C.E.) contended that law was the agreement of reason and nature, the distinction between the just and the unjust. The British jurist Sir William Blackstone (1723–1780) described law as "a rule of civil conduct prescribed by the supreme power in a state, commanding what is right, and prohibiting what is wrong." In America, the eminent jurist Oliver Wendell Holmes, Jr. (1841–1935), asserted that law was a set of rules that allowed one to predict how a court would resolve a particular dispute—"the prophecies of what the courts will do in fact, and nothing more pretentious, are what I mean by the law."

Although these definitions vary in their particulars, they all are based on the following general observation: **law** consists of enforceable rules governing relationships among individuals and between individuals and their society. In the study of law, often referred to as **jurisprudence**, this very broad statement about the nature of law is the point of departure for all legal scholars and philosophers.

The Common Law Tradition

How jurists view the law is particularly important in a legal system in which judges play a paramount role, as they do in the American legal system. Because of our colonial heritage, much of American law is based on the English legal system. A knowledge of this tradition is necessary to an understanding of the nature of our legal system today.

EARLY ENGLISH COURTS OF LAW

After the Normans conquered England in 1066, William the Conqueror and his successors began the process of unifying the country under their rule. One of the means they used was the establishment of the king's courts, or *curiae regis*. Before the Norman Conquest, disputes had been settled according to the local legal customs and traditions in various regions of the country. The king's courts sought to establish a uniform set of rules for the country as a whole. What evolved in these courts was the beginning of the **common law**—a body of general legal principles that eventually was applied throughout the entire English realm.

Courts developed the common law rules from the principles underlying judges' decisions in actual legal controversies. Judges attempted to be consistent, and whenever possible, they based their decisions on the principles suggested by earlier cases. They sought to decide similar cases in a similar way and considered new cases with care, because they knew that their decisions would make new law. Each interpretation became part of the law on the subject and served as a legal **precedent**—that is, a decision that furnished an example or authority for deciding subsequent cases involving similar legal principles or facts.

In the early years of the common law, there was no single place or publication where court opinions, or written decisions, could be found. Beginning in the late thirteenth and early fourteenth centuries, however, each year portions of significant decisions of that year were gathered together and recorded in *Year Books*. The *Year Books* were useful references for lawyers and judges. In the sixteenth century, the *Year Books* were discontinued, and other reports of cases became available. (See the appendix to this chapter for a discussion of how cases are reported, or published, in the United States today.)

STARE DECISIS

The practice of deciding new cases by referring to former decisions, or precedents, eventually became a cornerstone of the English and American judicial systems. The practice forms a doctrine called *stare decisis*[1] ("to stand on decided cases").

The Importance of Precedents in Judicial Decision Making. The doctrine of *stare decisis* means that once a court has set forth a principle of law as applicable to a certain set of facts, that court and courts of lower rank must adhere to that principle and apply it in future cases involving similar fact patterns.

● **EXAMPLE #1** Suppose that the lower state courts in California have reached conflicting conclusions on whether drivers are liable for accidents they cause while merging into freeway traffic, even though the drivers looked and did not see any oncoming traffic and even though witnesses (passengers in their cars) testified to that effect. To settle the law on this issue, the California Supreme Court decides to review a case involving this fact pattern. The court rules that in such a situation, the driver who is merging into traffic is liable for any accidents caused by the driver's failure to yield to freeway traffic, regardless of whether the driver looked carefully and did not see an approaching vehicle. The California Supreme Court's decision on the matter will influence the outcome of all future cases on this issue brought before the California state courts.●

Similarly, a decision on a given issue by the United States Supreme Court (the nation's highest court) is binding on all inferior courts. Controlling precedents in a jurisdiction (an area in which a court or courts have the power to apply the law—see Chapter 2) are referred to as binding authorities. A **binding authority** is any source of law that a court must follow when deciding a case. Binding authorities include

---

[1] Pronounced *ster-ay* dih-si-ses.

constitutions, statutes, and regulations that govern the issue being decided, as well as court decisions that are controlling precedents within the jurisdiction.

Stare Decisis and Legal Stability. The doctrine of *stare decisis* helps the courts to be more efficient, because if other courts have carefully reasoned through a similar case, their legal reasoning and opinions can serve as guides. *Stare decisis* also makes the law more stable and predictable. If the law on a given subject is well settled, someone bringing a case to court can usually rely on the court to make a decision based on what the law has been.

Departures from Precedent. Sometimes a court will depart from the rule of precedent if it decides that a given precedent should no longer be followed. If a court decides that a precedent is simply incorrect or that technological or social changes have rendered the precedent inapplicable, the court might rule contrary to the precedent. Cases that overturn precedent often receive a great deal of publicity. ● EXAMPLE #2 In *Brown v. Board of Education of Topeka*,[2] the United States Supreme Court expressly overturned precedent when it concluded that separate educational facilities for whites and blacks, which had been upheld as constitutional in numerous previous cases,[3] were inherently unequal. The Supreme Court's departure from precedent in *Brown* received a tremendous amount of publicity as people began to realize the ramifications of this change in the law. ●

When There Is No Precedent. At times, courts hear cases for which there are no precedents within their jurisdictions on which to base their decisions. When hearing such cases, called "cases of first impression," courts often look to precedents set in other jurisdictions for guidance. Precedents from other jurisdictions, because they are not binding on the court, are called **persuasive authorities.** A court may also consider a number of factors, including legal principles and policies underlying previous court decisions or existing statutes, fairness, social values and customs, public policy, and data and concepts drawn from the social sciences.

EQUITABLE REMEDIES AND COURTS OF EQUITY

A **remedy** is the means given to a party to enforce a right or to compensate for the violation of a right. ● EXAMPLE #3 Suppose that Shem is injured because of Rowan's wrongdo-

ing. A court may order Rowan to compensate Shem for the harm by paying Shem a certain amount of money. ●

In the early king's courts of England, the kinds of remedies that could be granted were severely restricted. If one person wronged another, the king's courts could award as compensation either money or property, including land. These courts became known as *courts of law*, and the remedies were called *remedies at law*. Even though this system introduced uniformity in the settling of disputes, when plaintiffs wanted a remedy other than economic compensation, the courts of law could do nothing, so "no remedy, no right."

Remedies in Equity. *Equity* refers to a branch of the law, founded in justice and fair dealing, that seeks to supply a fairer and more adequate remedy when no remedy is available at law. In medieval England, when individuals could not obtain an adequate remedy in a court of law, they petitioned the king for relief. Most of these petitions were decided by an adviser to the king called the *chancellor*. The chancellor was said to be the "keeper of the king's conscience." When the chancellor thought that the claim was a fair one, new and unique remedies were granted. In this way, a new body of rules and remedies came into being, and eventually formal *chancery courts,* or *courts of equity,* were established. The remedies granted by these courts were called *remedies in equity*. Thus, two distinct court systems were created, each having a different set of judges and a different set of remedies.

Plaintiffs (those bringing lawsuits) had to specify whether they were bringing an "action at law" or an "action in equity," and they chose their courts accordingly. ● EXAMPLE #4 A plaintiff might ask a court of equity to order a **defendant** (a person against whom a lawsuit is brought) to perform within the terms of a contract. A court of law could not issue such an order, because its remedies were limited to payment of money or property as compensation for damages. A court of equity, however, could issue a decree for *specific performance*—an order to perform what was promised. A court of equity could also issue an *injunction*, directing a party to do or refrain from doing a particular act. In certain cases, a court of equity could allow for the *rescission* (cancellation) of the contract so that the parties would be returned to the positions that they held before the contract was formed. ● Equitable remedies will be discussed in greater detail in Chapter 12.

The Merging of Law and Equity. Today, in most states, the courts of law and equity are merged, and thus the distinction between the two courts has largely disappeared. A plaintiff may now request both legal and equitable remedies in the same action, and the trial court judge may grant either form—or both forms—of relief. The merging of law

---

[2] 347 U.S. 483, 74 S.Ct. 686, 98 L.Ed. 873 (1954). (See the appendix at the end of this chapter for an explanation of how to read legal citations.)
[3] See, for example, *Plessy v. Ferguson*, 163 U.S. 537, 16 S.Ct. 1138, 41 L.Ed. 256 (1896).

and equity, however, does not diminish the importance of distinguishing legal remedies from equitable remedies. To request the proper remedy, a businessperson (or his or her attorney) must know what remedies are available for the specific kinds of harms suffered. Today, as a rule, courts will grant an equitable remedy only when the remedy at law (money damages) is inadequate.

Sources of American Law

There are numerous sources of American law. **Primary sources of law,** or sources that establish the law, include the following:

- The U.S. Constitution and the constitutions of the various states.
- Statutes, or laws, passed by Congress and by state legislatures.
- Regulations created by administrative agencies, such as the federal Food and Drug Administration.
- Case law (court decisions).

We describe each of these important primary sources of law in the following pages. (See the appendix at the end of this chapter for a discussion of how to find statutes, regulations, and case law.)

Secondary sources of law are books and articles that summarize and clarify the primary sources of law. Legal encyclopedias, compilations (such as *Restatements of the Law*—to be discussed later in this chapter), official comments to statutes, treatises, articles in law reviews published by law schools, and articles in other legal journals are examples of secondary sources of law. Courts often refer to secondary sources of law for guidance in interpreting and applying the primary sources of law discussed here.

CONSTITUTIONAL LAW

The federal government and the states have separate written constitutions that set forth the general organization, powers, and limits of their respective governments. **Constitutional law** is the law as expressed in these constitutions.

The U.S. Constitution is the supreme law of the land. As such, it is the basis of all law in the United States. A law in violation of the Constitution, no matter what its source, will be declared unconstitutional and will not be enforced. Because of its paramount importance in the American legal system, we examine the U.S. Constitution in detail later in this chapter and present the complete text of the Constitution in Appendix B.

The Tenth Amendment to the U.S. Constitution, which defines the powers of and limitations on the federal government, reserves all powers not granted to the federal government to the states. Each state in the union has its own constitution. Unless they conflict with the U.S. Constitution or a federal law, state constitutions are supreme within their respective borders.

STATUTORY LAW

Statutes enacted by legislative bodies at any level of government make up another source of law, which is generally referred to as **statutory law.**

Federal Statutes. Federal statutes are laws that are enacted by the U.S. Congress. As mentioned, any law—including a federal statute—that violates the U.S. Constitution will be held unconstitutional.

Federal statutes that affect business operations include laws regulating the purchase and sale of securities (corporate stocks and bonds—discussed in Chapter 27) and statutes prohibiting employment discrimination (discussed in Chapter 23). Whenever a particular statute is mentioned in this text, we usually provide a footnote showing its **citation** (a reference to a publication in which a legal authority—such as a statute or a court decision—or other source can be found). In the appendix following this chapter, we explain how you can use these citations to find statutory law.

State and Local Statutes and Ordinances. State statutes are laws enacted by state legislatures. Any state law that is found to conflict with the U.S. Constitution, with federal laws enacted by Congress, or with the state's constitution will be deemed unconstitutional. Statutory law also includes the ordinances passed by cities and counties, none of which can violate the U.S. Constitution, the relevant state constitution, or federal or state laws.

State statutes include state criminal statutes (discussed in Chapter 6), state corporation statutes (discussed in Chapters 25 through 27), state laws governing wills and trusts (discussed in Chapter 30), and state versions of the Uniform Commercial Code (to be discussed shortly). Local ordinances include zoning ordinances and local laws regulating housing construction and such matters as the overall appearance of a community.

A federal statute, of course, applies to all states. A state statute, in contrast, applies only within the state's borders. State laws thus vary from state to state.

Uniform Laws. The differences among state laws were particularly notable in the 1800s, when conflicting state statutes frequently created problems for the rapidly developing trade and commerce among the states. To counter these problems, a group of legal scholars and lawyers formed the National Conference of Commissioners on Uniform State Laws (NCCUSL) in 1892 to draft uniform ("model") statutes for adoption by the states. The NCCUSL still exists today and continues to issue uniform statutes.

Adoption of a uniform law is a state matter, and a state may reject all or part of the statute or rewrite it as the state legislature wishes. Hence, even when a uniform law is said to have been adopted in many states, those states' laws may not be entirely "uniform." Once adopted by a state legislature, a uniform act becomes a part of the statutory law of that state.

The earliest uniform law, the Uniform Negotiable Instruments Law, was completed by 1896 and was adopted in every state by the early 1920s (although not all states used exactly the same wording). Over the following decades, other acts were drawn up in a similar manner. In all, over two hundred uniform acts have been issued by the NCCUSL since its inception. Recent uniform acts issued by the NCCUSL include the Uniform Electronic Transactions Act. This act, which addresses some of the specific legal needs created by e-commerce, will be discussed at length in Chapter 13, in the context of electronic contracts. The most ambitious uniform act of all, however, was the Uniform Commercial Code.

The Uniform Commercial Code (UCC). The Uniform Commercial Code (UCC), which was created through the joint efforts of the NCCUSL and the American Law Institute,[4] was first issued in 1952. The UCC has been adopted in all fifty states,[5] the District of Columbia, and the Virgin Islands. The UCC facilitates commerce among the states by providing a uniform, yet flexible, set of rules governing commercial transactions. The UCC assures businesspersons that their contracts, if validly entered into, normally will be enforced.

Because of its importance in the area of commercial law, we cite the UCC frequently in this text. We also present excerpts from the latest version of the UCC in Appendix C.

ADMINISTRATIVE LAW

Another important source of American law consists of **administrative law**—the rules, orders, and decisions of administrative agencies. An **administrative agency** is a federal, state, or local government agency established to perform a specific function. Rules issued by various administrative

agencies now affect virtually every aspect of a business's operations, including the firm's capital structure and financing, its hiring and firing procedures, its relations with employees and unions, and the way it manufactures and markets its products.

Types of Agencies. At the national level, numerous **executive agencies** exist within the cabinet departments of the executive branch. For example, the Food and Drug Administration is within the Department of Health and Human Services. Executive agencies are subject to the authority of the president, who has the power to appoint and remove officers of federal agencies. There are also major **independent regulatory agencies** at the federal level, including the Federal Trade Commission, the Securities and Exchange Commission, and the Federal Communications Commission. The president has less power over independent agencies; their officers serve for fixed terms and cannot be removed without just cause.

There are administrative agencies at the state and local levels as well. Commonly, a state agency (such as a state pollution-control agency) is created as a parallel to a federal agency (such as the Environmental Protection Agency). Just as federal statutes take precedence over conflicting state statutes, so do federal agency regulations take precedence over conflicting state regulations. Because the rules of state and local agencies vary widely, we focus here exclusively on federal administrative law.

Agency Creation. Because Congress cannot possibly oversee the actual implementation of all the laws it enacts, it must delegate such tasks to others, particularly when the issues concern highly technical areas, such as air and water pollution. Congress creates an administrative agency by enacting **enabling legislation**, which specifies the name, composition, purpose, and powers of the agency being created.

● **EXAMPLE #5** The Federal Trade Commission (FTC) was created in 1914 by the Federal Trade Commission Act.[6] This act prohibits unfair and deceptive trade practices. It also describes the procedures the agency must follow to charge persons or organizations with violations of the act, and it provides for judicial review (review by the courts) of agency orders. Other portions of the act grant the agency powers to "make rules and regulations for the purpose of carrying out the Act," to conduct investigations of business practices, to obtain reports from interstate corporations regarding their business practices, to investigate possible violations of the act, to publish findings of its investiga-

---

[4] This institute was formed in the 1920s and consists of practicing attorneys, legal scholars, and judges.

[5] Louisiana has adopted only Articles 1, 3, 4, 5, 7, 8, and 9.

---

[6] 15 U.S.C. Sections 45–58.

tions, and to recommend new legislation. The act also empowers the FTC to hold trial-like hearings and to **adjudicate** (resolve judicially) certain kinds of trade disputes that involve FTC regulations.●

Note that the FTC's grant of power incorporates functions associated with the legislative branch of government (rulemaking), the executive branch (investigation and enforcement), and the judicial branch (adjudication). Taken together, these functions constitute what has been termed **administrative process**, which is the administration of law by administrative agencies.

CASE LAW AND COMMON LAW DOCTRINES

The body of law that was first developed in England and that is still used today in the United States consists of the rules of law announced in court decisions. These rules of law include interpretations of constitutional provisions, of statutes enacted by legislatures, and of regulations created by administrative agencies. Today, this body of law is referred to variously as the common law, judge-made law, or **case law.**

The common law—the doctrines and principles embodied in case law—governs all areas not covered by statutory law (or agency regulations issued to implement various statutes). ● EXAMPLE #6 In disputes concerning contracts for the sale of goods, the Uniform Commercial Code (statutory law) applies when one of its provisions supersedes the common law of contracts. Similarly, in a dispute concerning a particular employment practice, a statute regulating that practice will apply rather than the common law doctrine governing employment relationships that applied before the enactment of the statute.●

The Relationship between the Common Law and Statutory Law. The body of statutory law has expanded greatly since the beginning of this nation, and this expansion has resulted in a proportionate reduction in the applicability of common law doctrines. Nonetheless, there is a significant overlap between statutory law and the common law, and thus common law doctrines remain a significant source of legal authority.

Many statutes essentially codify existing common law rules, so the courts, in interpreting the statutes, often rely on the common law as a guide to what the legislators intended. Additionally, how the courts interpret a particular statute determines how that statute will be applied. Thus, if you wanted to learn about the coverage and applicability of a particular statute, you would, of course, need to locate the statute and study it. You would also need to see how the courts in your jurisdiction have interpreted the statute—in other words, what precedents have been established in regard to that statute. Often, the applicability of a newly enacted statute does not become clear until a body of case law develops to clarify how, when, and to whom the statute applies.

Restatements of the Law. The American Law Institute (ALI) has drafted and published compilations of the common law called *Restatements of the Law*, which generally summarize the common law rules followed by most states. There are *Restatements of the Law* in many areas of the law, including contracts, torts, agency, trusts, property, restitution, security, judgments, and conflict of laws. Although the *Restatements*, like other secondary sources of law, do not in themselves have the force of law, they are an important source of legal analysis and opinion on which judges often rely in making their decisions.

The ALI periodically revises the *Restatements*, and many of them are now in their second or third editions. For instance, as you will read in Chapter 17, the ALI has recently published the first volume of the third edition of the *Restatement of the Law of Torts*.

We refer to the *Restatements* frequently in subsequent chapters of this text, indicating in parentheses the edition to which we are referring. For example, we refer to the second edition of the *Restatement of the Law of Contracts* simply as the *Restatement (Second) of Contracts*.

Classifications of Law

The huge body of the law may be broken down according to several classification systems. For example, one classification system divides law into **substantive law** (all laws that define, describe, regulate, and create legal rights and obligations) and **procedural law** (all laws that establish the methods of enforcing the rights established by substantive law). Other classification systems divide law into federal law and state law, private law (dealing with relationships between persons) and public law (addressing the relationship between persons and their government), and so on.

We look below at two broad classifications. One divides the law into criminal and civil law; the other divides the law into national and international law.

CIVIL LAW AND CRIMINAL LAW

Civil law spells out the rights and duties that exist between persons and between persons and their governments, and the relief available when a person's rights are violated. Typically, in a civil case, a private party sues another private party (although the government can also sue a party for a civil law violation) to make that other party comply with a duty or pay for the damage caused by the failure to comply with a duty. • EXAMPLE #7 If a seller fails to perform a contract with a buyer, the buyer may bring a lawsuit against the seller. The purpose of the lawsuit will be either to compel the seller to perform as promised or, more commonly, to obtain money damages for the seller's failure to perform. •

Much of the law that we discuss in this text is civil law. Contract law, for example, which we discuss in Chapters 7 through 13, is civil law. The whole body of tort law (see Chapter 4) is civil law. Note that *civil law* is not the same as a *civil law system*. As you will read shortly, in the subsection discussing international law, a civil law system is a legal system based on a written code of laws.

Criminal law has to do with wrongs committed against society for which society demands redress (see Chapter 6). Criminal acts are proscribed by local, state, or federal government statutes. Criminal defendants are thus prosecuted by public officials, such as a district attorney (D.A.), on behalf of the state, not by their victims or other private parties. Whereas in a civil case the object is to obtain remedies (such as money damages) to compensate the injured party, in a criminal case the object is to punish the wrongdoer in an attempt to deter others from similar actions. Penalties for violations of criminal statutes consist of fines and/or imprisonment—and, in some cases, death. We will discuss the differences between civil and criminal law in greater detail in Chapter 6.

NATIONAL AND INTERNATIONAL LAW

Although the focus of this book is U.S. business law, increasingly businesspersons in this country engage in transactions that extend beyond our national borders. In these situations, the laws of other nations or the laws governing relationships among nations may come into play. For this reason, those who pursue a career in business today should have an understanding of the global legal environment.

National Law. The law of a particular nation, such as the United States or Sweden, is **national law**. National law, of course, varies from country to country, because each nation's law reflects the interests, customs, activities, and values that are unique to its particular culture. Even though the laws and legal systems of various countries differ substantially, broad similarities do exist.

Basically, there are two legal systems in today's world. One of these systems is the common law system of England and the United States, which we have already discussed. The other system is based on Roman civil law, or "code

law." The term *civil law,* as used here, refers not to civil as opposed to criminal law but to codified law—an ordered grouping of legal principles enacted into law by a legislature or governing body. In a **civil law system**, the primary source of law is a statutory code, and case precedents are not judicially binding, as they normally are in a common law system. Although judges in a civil law system commonly refer to previous decisions as sources of legal guidance, they are not bound by precedent; in other words, the doctrine of *stare decisis* does not apply.

Generally, countries that were once colonies of Great Britain retained their English common law heritage after they achieved their independence. Similarly, the civil law system, which is followed in most of the continental European countries, was retained in the Latin American, African, and Asian countries that were once colonies of those nations. Japan and South Africa also have civil law systems, and ingredients of the civil law system are found in the Islamic courts of predominantly Muslim countries. In the United States, the state of Louisiana, because of its historical ties to France, has in part a civil law system. The legal systems of Puerto Rico, Québec, and Scotland are similarly characterized as having elements of the civil law system.

International Law. In contrast to national law, international law applies to more than one nation. **International law** can be defined as a body of written and unwritten laws observed by independent nations and governing the acts of individuals as well as governments. International law is an intermingling of rules and constraints derived from a variety of sources, including the laws of individual nations, the customs that have evolved among nations in their relations with one another, and treaties and international organizations. In essence, international law is the result of centuries-old attempts to reconcile the traditional need of each nation to be the final authority over its own affairs with the desire of nations to benefit economically from trade and harmonious relations with one another.

The key difference between national law and international law is that national law can be enforced by government authorities. If a nation violates an international law, however, the most that other countries or international organizations can do (if persuasive tactics fail) is to resort to coercive actions against the violating nation. Coercive actions range from the severance of diplomatic relations and boycotts to, at the last resort, war. Of increasing importance in regulating international activities, however, are treaties and international organizations.

Treaties. A treaty is an agreement between two or more nations that creates rights and duties binding on the parties to the treaty, just as a private contract creates rights and duties binding on the parties to the contract. To give effect to a treaty, the supreme power of each nation that is a party to the treaty must ratify it. For example, the U.S. Constitution requires approval by two-thirds of the Senate before a treaty executed by the president will be binding on the U.S. government.

Bilateral agreements, as the term implies, occur when only two nations form an agreement that will govern their commercial exchanges or other relations with one another. Multilateral agreements are those formed by several nations. The European Union (EU), for example, which regulates commercial activities among its twenty-five member nations, is the result of a multilateral trade agreement. The North American Free Trade Agreement (NAFTA), which regulates trade among Canada, the United States, and Mexico, is another example of a multilateral trade agreement.

One treaty of particular significance to the international legal environment of business is the United Nations 1980 Convention on Contracts for the International Sale of Goods (CISG). Essentially, the CISG is to international sales transactions what the Uniform Commercial Code is to domestic sales transactions. The CISG governs the international sale of goods between firms or individuals located in different countries, providing that the countries involved have ratified the CISG. We examine the CISG and its provisions more closely in Chapter 14, when we discuss the law governing the sale of goods.

International Organizations.

International organizations and conferences also play an important role in the international legal arena. International organizations and conferences adopt resolutions, declarations, and other types of standards that often require a particular behavior of nations. The General Assembly of the United Nations, for example, has adopted numerous resolutions and declarations that embody principles of international law and has sponsored conferences that have led to the formation of international agreements. The United States is a member of more than one hundred multilateral and bilateral organizations, including at least twenty through the United Nations.

Commercial Contracts in an International Setting.

Language and legal differences among nations can create special problems for parties to international contracts when disputes arise. It is possible to avoid these problems by including in a contract special provisions designating the official language of the contract, the legal forum (court or place) in which disputes under the contract will be settled, and the substantive law that will be applied in settling any disputes. Parties to international contracts should also state in their contracts what acts or events will excuse the parties from performance under the contract and whether disputes under the contract will be arbitrated or litigated.

Choice of Language. A deal struck between a U.S. company and a company in another country normally involves two languages. The complex contractual terms involved may not be understood by one party in the other party's language. Typically, many phrases in one language are not readily translatable into another. To make sure that no disputes arise out of this language problem, an international sales contract should have a **choice-of-language clause** designating the official language by which the contract will be interpreted in the event of disagreement.

Choice of Forum. When several countries are involved, litigation may be sought in courts in different nations. There are no universally accepted rules regarding the jurisdiction of a particular court over subject matter or parties to a dispute. Consequently, parties to an international transaction should always include in the contract a **forum-selection clause** stating what court, jurisdiction, or tribunal will decide any disputes arising under the contract. It is especially important to indicate specifically what court will have jurisdiction. The forum does not necessarily have to be within the geographical boundaries of either of the parties' nations.

Choice of Law. A contractual provision designating the applicable law—such as the law of Germany or England or California—is called a **choice-of-law clause.** Every international contract typically includes a choice-of-law clause. At common law (and in European civil law systems), parties are allowed to choose the law that will govern their contractual relationship provided that the law chosen is the law of a jurisdiction that has a substantial relationship to the parties and to the international business transaction.

Under Section 1–105 of the Uniform Commercial Code, parties may choose the law that will govern the contract as long as the choice is "reasonable." Article 6 of the United Nations Convention on Contracts for the International Sale of Goods (discussed in Chapter 14), however, imposes no limitation on the parties in their choice of what law will govern the contract. The 1986 Hague Convention on the Law Applicable to Contracts for the International Sale of Goods—often referred to as the Choice-of-Law Convention—allows unlimited autonomy in the choice of law. The Hague Convention states that whenever a choice of law is not specified in a contract, the governing law is that of the country in which the *seller's* place of business is located.

The Constitution As It Affects Business

Each of the sources of law just discussed helps to frame the legal environment of business. Because laws that govern business have their origin in the lawmaking authority granted by the U.S. Constitution, we examine that document more closely here. The Constitution provides the legal basis for both state and federal (national) powers. It is the supreme law in this country, and any law that conflicts with the Constitution, if challenged in court, will be declared invalid by the court.

THE COMMERCE CLAUSE

To prevent states from establishing laws and regulations that would interfere with trade and commerce among the states, the Constitution expressly delegated to the national government the power to regulate interstate commerce. Article I, Section 8, of the U.S. Constitution expressly permits Congress "[t]o regulate Commerce with foreign Nations, and among the several States, and with the Indian Tribes." This clause, referred to as the **commerce clause**, has had a greater impact on business than any other provision in the Constitution.

For some time, the power based on the commerce clause was interpreted as being limited to *interstate* commerce (commerce among the states) and not applicable to *intrastate* commerce (commerce within the states). In 1824,

however, in *Gibbons v. Ogden,*[7] the United States Supreme Court held that commerce within states could also be regulated by the national government as long as the commerce *substantially affected* commerce involving more than one state.

The Commerce Clause and the Expansion of National Powers. In *Gibbons v. Ogden,* the commerce clause was expanded to regulate activities that "substantially affect interstate commerce." As the nation grew and faced new kinds of problems, the commerce clause became a vehicle for the additional expansion of the national government's regulatory powers. Even activities that seemed purely local came under the regulatory reach of the national government if those activities were deemed to substantially affect interstate commerce. ● EXAMPLE #8 In 1942, in *Wickard v. Filburn,*[8] the Supreme Court held that wheat production by an individual farmer intended wholly for consumption on his own farm was subject to federal regulation. The Court reasoned that the home consumption of wheat reduced the demand for wheat and thus could have a substantial effect on interstate commerce. ●

The following landmark case involved a challenge to the scope of the national government's constitutional authority to regulate local activities.

---

[7] 22 U.S. (9 Wheat.) 1, 6 L.Ed. 23 (1824).
[8] 317 U.S. 111, 63 S.Ct. 82, 87 L.Ed. 122 (1942).

Landmark and Classic Cases

CASE 1.1   Heart of Atlanta Motel v. United States

Supreme Court of the United States, 1964.
379 U.S. 241,
85 S.Ct. 348,
13 L.Ed.2d 258.
http://supct.law.cornell.edu/supct/cases/name. htm[a]

---

a. This is the "Historic Supreme Court Decisions—by Party Name" page within the "Caselists" collection of the Legal Information Institute available at its site on the Web. Click on the "H" link or scroll down the list of cases to the entry for the *Heart of Atlanta* case. Click on the case name. When the link opens, click on one of the choices to read the "Syllabus," the "Full Decision," or the "Edited Decision."

FACTS The owner of the Heart of Atlanta Motel, in violation of the Civil Rights Act of 1964, refused to rent rooms to African Americans. The motel owner brought an action in a federal district court to have the Civil Rights Act declared unconstitutional, alleging that Congress had exceeded its constitutional authority to regulate commerce by enacting the act. The owner argued that his motel was not engaged in interstate commerce but was "of a purely local character." The motel, however, was accessible to state and interstate highways. The owner advertised nationally, maintained billboards throughout the state, and accepted convention trade from outside the state (75 percent of the guests were residents of other states). The court sustained the constitutionality of the

CASE 1.1—Continued

act and enjoined (prohibited) the owner from discriminating on the basis of race. The owner appealed. The case ultimately went to the United States Supreme Court.

ISSUE Did Congress exceed its constitutional power to regulate interstate commerce by enacting the Civil Rights Act of 1964?

DECISION No. The United States Supreme Court upheld the constitutionality of the act.

REASON The Court noted that the act was passed to correct "the deprivation of personal dignity" accompanying the denial of equal access to "public establishments." Testimony before Congress leading to the passage of the act indicated that African Americans in particular experienced substantial discrimination in attempting to secure lodging while traveling. This discrimination impeded interstate travel and thus

impeded interstate commerce. As for the owner's argument that his motel was "of a purely local character," the Court said that even if this was true, "if it is interstate commerce that feels the pinch, it does not matter how local the operation that applies the squeeze." Therefore, under the commerce clause, "the power of Congress to promote interstate commerce also includes the power to regulate the local incidents thereof, including local activities."

COMMENT *If the Supreme Court had invalidated the Civil Rights Act of 1964, the legal landscape of the United States would be much different today. The act prohibited discrimination based on race, color, national origin, religion, or gender in all "public accommodations" and discrimination in employment based on these criteria. Although state laws now prohibit many of these forms of discrimination as well, the protections available vary from state to state—and it is not certain when (and if) such laws would have been passed had the 1964 federal Civil Rights Act been deemed unconstitutional.*

The Commerce Power Today. Today, at least theoretically, the power over commerce authorizes the national government to regulate every commercial enterprise in the United States. Federal (national) legislation governs virtually every major activity conducted by businesses—from hiring and firing decisions to workplace safety, competitive practices, and financing.

In the last decade, however, the Supreme Court has begun to curb somewhat the national government's regulatory authority under the commerce clause. In 1995, the Court held—for the first time in sixty years—that Congress had exceeded its regulatory authority under the commerce clause. The Court stated that the Gun-Free School Zones Act of 1990, which banned the possession of guns within one thousand feet of any school, was unconstitutional because it attempted to regulate an area that had "nothing to do with commerce."[9]

Two years later, in 1997, the Court struck down portions of the Brady Handgun Violence Prevention Act of 1993, which obligated state and local law enforcement officers to do background checks on prospective handgun buyers until a national instant check system could be implemented. The Court stated that Congress lacked the power to "dragoon" state employees into federal service through an unfunded mandate of this kind.[10] In 2000, the Court invalidated key

portions of the federal Violence Against Women Act of 1994, which allowed women to sue in federal court when they were victims of gender-motivated violence, such as rape. According to the Court, the commerce clause did not justify national regulation of noneconomic, criminal conduct.[11] Nonetheless, the commerce clause continues to serve as the constitutional backbone for national laws regulating a broad number of activities.

The Regulatory Powers of the States. As part of their inherent sovereignty, state governments have the authority to regulate affairs within their borders. This authority stems in part from the Tenth Amendment to the Constitution, which reserves all powers not delegated to the national government to the states. State regulatory powers are often referred to as **police powers.** The term encompasses not only criminal law enforcement but also the right of state governments to regulate private activities to protect or promote the public order, health, safety, morals, and general welfare. Fire and building codes, antidiscrimination laws, parking regulations, zoning restrictions, licensing requirements, and thousands of other state statutes covering virtually every aspect of life have been enacted pursuant to a state's police powers. Local governments, including cities, also exercise police powers.[12]

---

[9] *United States v. Lopez,* 514 U.S. 549, 115 S.Ct. 1624, 131 L.Ed.2d 626 (1995).

[10] *Printz v. United States,* 521 U.S. 898, 117 S.Ct. 2365, 138 L.Ed.2d 914 (1997).

[11] *United States v. Morrison,* 529 U.S. 598, 120 S.Ct. 1740, 146 L.Ed.2d 658 (2000).

[12] Local governments derive their authority to regulate their communities from the state, because they are creatures of the state. In other words, they cannot come into existence unless authorized by the state to do so.

The "Dormant" Commerce Clause. The United States Supreme Court has interpreted the commerce clause to mean that the national government has the *exclusive* authority to regulate commerce that substantially affects trade and commerce among the states. This express grant of authority to the national government, which is often referred to as the "positive" aspect of the commerce clause, implies a negative aspect—that the states do *not* have the authority to regulate interstate commerce. This negative aspect of the commerce clause is often referred to as the **dormant** (implied) **commerce clause**.

The dormant commerce clause comes into play when state regulations impinge on interstate commerce. In this situation, the courts normally weigh the state's interest in regulating a certain matter against the burden that the state's regulation places on interstate commerce. ● EXAMPLE #9   In one case, the United States Supreme Court invalidated state regulations that, in the interest of promoting traffic safety, limited the length of trucks traveling on the state's highways. The Court invalidated the regulations, concluding that although they imposed a "substantial burden on interstate commerce," they failed to "make more than the most speculative contribution to highway safety."[13]● Because courts balance the interests involved, it is extremely difficult to predict the outcome in a particular case.

An emerging issue related to state laws that impinge on interstate commerce involves the Internet. For some examples of how commerce clause principles are being applied in cases involving the sale of wine via the Internet, see this chapter's *Business Law in the Online World* feature.

BUSINESS AND THE BILL OF RIGHTS

The importance of a written declaration of the rights of individuals eventually caused the First Congress of the United States to submit twelve amendments to the Constitution to the states for approval. The first ten of these amendments, commonly known as the **Bill of Rights**, were adopted in 1791 and embody a series of protections for the individual against various types of interference by the federal government.[14] Some constitutional protections apply to business entities as well. For example, corporations exist as separate legal entities, or legal persons, and enjoy many

of the same rights and privileges as natural persons do. Summarized here are the protections guaranteed by these ten amendments (see the Constitution in Appendix B for the complete text of each amendment):

① The First Amendment guarantees the freedoms of religion, speech, and the press and the rights to assemble peaceably and to petition the government.

② The Second Amendment guarantees the right to keep and bear arms.

③ The Third Amendment prohibits, in peacetime, the lodging of soldiers in any house without the owner's consent.

④ The Fourth Amendment prohibits unreasonable searches and seizures of persons or property.

⑤ The Fifth Amendment guarantees the rights to indictment by grand jury, to due process of law, and to fair payment when private property is taken for public use. The Fifth Amendment also prohibits compulsory self-incrimination and double jeopardy (trial for the same crime twice).

⑥ The Sixth Amendment guarantees the accused in a criminal case the right to a speedy and public trial by an impartial jury and with counsel. The accused has the right to cross-examine witnesses against him or her and to solicit testimony from witnesses in his or her favor.

⑦ The Seventh Amendment guarantees the right to a trial by jury in a civil case involving at least twenty dollars.[15]

⑧ The Eighth Amendment prohibits excessive bail and fines, as well as cruel and unusual punishment.

⑨ The Ninth Amendment establishes that the people have rights in addition to those specified in the Constitution.

⑩ The Tenth Amendment establishes that those powers neither delegated to the federal government nor denied to the states are reserved for the states.

As originally intended, the Bill of Rights limited only the powers of the national government. Over time, however, the Supreme Court "incorporated" most of these rights into the protections against state actions afforded by the Fourteenth Amendment to the Constitution. That amendment, passed in 1868 after the Civil War, provides in part that "[n]o State shall . . . deprive any person of life, liberty, or property, without due process of law." Starting in 1925, the Supreme Court began to define various rights and liberties guaranteed in the national Constitution as constituting "due process of law," which was required of state

---

[13] *Raymond Motor Transportation, Inc. v. Rice,* 434 U.S. 429, 98 S.Ct. 787, 54 L.Ed.2d 664 (1978).

[14] One of these proposed amendments was ratified 203 years later (in 1992) and became the Twenty-seventh Amendment to the Constitution. See Appendix B.

[15] Twenty dollars was forty days' pay for the average person when the Bill of Rights was written.

BUSINESS LAW IN THE ONLINE WORLD
Internet Wine Sales and the Constitution

In the past decade, the Internet has come to be widely used for direct sales to consumers, including direct sales of wine. Yet a number of state statutes effectively prohibit consumers from purchasing and receiving wine directly from out-of-state sellers. In a series of recent cases, plaintiffs have alleged that such statutes violate the commerce clause of the Constitution. As mentioned elsewhere, the commerce clause implies a negative, or "dormant," aspect: the states do not have the authority to regulate interstate commerce. Here we look at how the dormant commerce clause applies to state regulations affecting the sale and purchase of wine via the Internet.

For example, in *Dickerson v. Bailey,*[a] the plaintiffs—Texas residents who wanted to receive wine shipments directly from out-of-state suppliers—claimed that a Texas statute prohibiting such purchases violated the dormant commerce clause. The statute prohibited Texans from importing for their personal use more than three gallons of wine without a permit unless the resident "personally accompan[ies] the wine or liquor as it enters the state." A federal court held that the statute violated the dormant commerce clause. In effect, the law discriminated against interstate commerce by prohibiting out-of-state wineries from shipping wines to Texas residents while allowing local Texas wineries or retailers to do so.

ENTER THE TWENTY-FIRST AMENDMENT In the Texas case, and in other recent cases involving the same issue, one of the arguments made by state authorities is that their liquor regulations are justified by Section 2 of the Twenty-first Amendment.[b] That section reads, "The transportation or importation into any State, Territory, or possession of the United States for delivery or use therein of intoxicating liquors, *in violation of the laws thereof,* is hereby prohibited." [Emphasis added.]

DOES THE TWENTY-FIRST AMENDMENT TRUMP THE DORMANT COMMERCE CLAUSE? Does the Twenty-first Amendment create an exception to the normal operation of the commerce clause? The courts are giving different answers to this question. In the Texas case, for example, the court held that the amendment did not create such an exception. The court did note that substantial deference is given to a state's power to regulate the sale and distribution of liquor within its boundaries when the goal of the regulation is "to combat the perceived evils of an unrestricted traffic in liquor." The court concluded, however, that no temperance (abstinence from alcohol) goal was served by the Texas statute because residents of that state could "become as drunk on local wines" as they could on wines that were effectively "kept out of the state by the statute." Because the goal of the Texas law was primarily to protect the economic interests of in-state wine producers and distributors, the law was not entitled to such deference and violated the commerce clause.

The first federal appellate court to rule on this issue reached a different conclusion. In *Bridenbaugh v. Freeman-Wilson,*[c] Indiana residents challenged the constitutionality of a state statute making it unlawful for persons in another state or country to ship alcoholic beverages directly to Indiana residents. The court concluded that the primary purpose of the Twenty-first Amendment was not necessarily to promote temperance; rather, it was designed to close a "loophole" created by the dormant commerce clause. This loophole allowed direct shipments from out-of-state sellers to consumers to "bypass state regulatory (and tax) systems." The Indiana statute did not involve any substantial discrimination against interstate commerce; it merely enabled the state "to collect its excise tax equally from in-state and out-of-state sellers."

FOR CRITICAL ANALYSIS

Suppose that a state passed a law prohibiting direct sales of tobacco products via the Internet to in-state consumers. Would such a law necessarily violate the commerce clause? Why or why not?

a. 87 F.Supp.2d 691 (S.D.Tex. 2000).
b. Section 1 of the Twenty-first Amendment (ratified in 1933) repealed the Eighteenth Amendment (ratified in 1919), which had made the manufacture, sale, or transportation of alcoholic beverages illegal. Section 2 of the Twenty-first Amendment effectively left the regulation of such activity up to the states.

c. 227 F.3d 848 (7th Cir. 2000).

governments under the Fourteenth Amendment. Today, most of the rights and liberties set forth in the Bill of Rights apply to state governments as well as the national government.

We will look closely at several of the amendments in the above list in Chapter 6, in the context of criminal law and procedures. Here we examine two important guarantees of the First Amendment—freedom of speech and freedom of religion. These and other First Amendment freedoms (of the press, assembly, and petition) have all been applied to the states through the due process clause of the Fourteenth Amendment. As you read through the following pages, keep in mind that none of these (or other) constitutional freedoms confers an absolute right. Ultimately, it is the United States Supreme Court, as the final interpreter of the Constitution, that gives meaning to these rights and determines their boundaries.

The First Amendment—Freedom of Speech. Freedom of speech is the most prized freedom that Americans have. Indeed, it forms the basis for our democratic form of government, which could not exist if people were unable to express their political opinions freely and criticize government actions or policies. Because of its importance, the courts traditionally have protected this right to the fullest extent possible.

The courts also protect **symbolic speech**—gestures, movements, articles of clothing, and other forms of nonverbal expressive conduct. ● EXAMPLE #10 In 1989, the Supreme Court held that the burning of the American flag to protest government policies is a constitutionally protected form of expression.[16] In a subsequent case, the Supreme Court ruled that a city statute banning bias-motivated disorderly conduct (including, in this case, the placing of a burning cross in another's front yard as a gesture of hate) was an unconstitutional restriction of speech.[17] ●

Corporate Political Speech. Political speech by corporations also falls under the protection of the First Amendment. ● EXAMPLE #11 In *First National Bank of Boston v. Bellotti*,[18] national banking associations and business corporations sought United States Supreme Court review of a Massachusetts statute that prohibited corporations from making political contributions or expenditures

that individuals were permitted to make. The Court ruled that the Massachusetts law was unconstitutional because it violated the right of corporations to freedom of speech. ● Similarly, the Court has held that a law prohibiting a corporation from using bill inserts to express its views on controversial issues violates the First Amendment.[19] Although a more conservative Supreme Court subsequently reversed this trend somewhat,[20] corporate political speech continues to be given significant protection under the First Amendment.

Commercial Speech. The courts also give substantial protection to "commercial" speech, which consists of speech and communications—primarily advertising—made by business firms. The protection given to commercial speech under the First Amendment is not as extensive as that afforded to noncommercial speech, however. A state may restrict certain kinds of advertising, for example, in the interest of protecting consumers from being misled by the advertising practices. States also have a legitimate interest in the beautification of roadsides, and this interest allows states to place restraints on billboard advertising.

Generally, a restriction on commercial speech will be considered valid as long as it meets the following three criteria: (1) it must seek to implement a substantial government interest, (2) it must directly advance that interest, and (3) it must go no further than necessary to accomplish its objective. ● EXAMPLE #12 The South Carolina Supreme Court held that a state statute banning ads for video gambling violated the First Amendment because the statute did not directly advance a substantial government interest. Although the court acknowledged that the state had a substantial interest in minimizing gambling, there was no evidence that a reduction in video gambling ads would result in a reduction in gambling.[21] ●

The court in the following case applied these principles to determine the constitutionality of a county ordinance that regulated video games based on their content—the ordinance applied only to "graphically violent" video games.

---

[16] See *Texas v. Johnson*, 491 U.S. 397, 109 S.Ct. 2533, 105 L.Ed.2d 342 (1989).
[17] *R.A.V. v. City of St. Paul, Minnesota*, 505 U.S. 377, 112 S.Ct. 2538, 120 L.Ed.2d 305 (1992).
[18] 435 U.S. 765, 98 S.Ct. 1407, 55 L.Ed.2d 707 (1978).

[19] *Consolidated Edison Co. v. Public Service Commission*, 447 U.S. 530, 100 S.Ct. 2326, 65 L.Ed.2d 319 (1980).
[20] See *Austin v. Michigan Chamber of Commerce*, 494 U.S. 652, 110 S.Ct. 1391, 108 L.Ed.2d 652 (1990), in which the Court upheld a state law prohibiting corporations from using general corporate funds for independent expenditures in state political campaigns.
[21] *Evans v. State*, 344 S.C. 60, 543 S.E.2d 547 (2001).

CASE 1.2   Interactive Digital Software Association v. St. Louis County, Missouri

United States Court of Appeals,
Eighth Circuit, 2003.
329 F.3d 954.

FACTS St. Louis County, Missouri, passed an ordinance that made it unlawful for any person knowingly to sell, rent, or make available "graphically violent" video games to minors, or to "permit the free play of" such games by minors, without a parent's or guardian's consent.[a] Interactive Digital Software Association, and others that create or provide the public with video games and related software, filed a suit against the county in a federal district court. The plaintiffs asserted that the ordinance violated the First Amendment. The county argued that the ordinance forwarded the compelling state interest of protecting the "psychological well-being of minors" by reducing the harm suffered by children who play violent video games. A psychologist, a high school principal, and other experts offered their conclusions that playing violent video games leads to aggressive behavior, but the county did not provide proof of a link between the games and any psychological harm. The court dismissed the case. The plaintiffs appealed to the U.S. Court of Appeals for the Eighth Circuit.

ISSUE Are video games entitled to the same First Amendment protection as other types of speech?

a. St. Louis County Revised Ordinances Sections 602.425 through 602.460.

DECISION Yes. The U.S. Court of Appeals for the Eighth Circuit reversed the judgment of the lower court and remanded the case for the entry of an injunction against the county's enforcement of its ordinance. The defendants failed to present the evidence of harm required to uphold a law threatening protected speech.

REASON The appellate court reasoned that "[i]f the First Amendment is versatile enough to shield the painting of Jackson Pollock, music of Arnold Schoenberg, or Jabberwocky verse of Lewis Carroll, we see no reason why the pictures, graphic design, concept art, sounds, music, stories, and narrative present in video games are not entitled to a similar protection. * * * [V]ideo games contain stories, imagery, age-old themes of literature, and messages, even an ideology, just as books and movies do." With video games, "players may skip the expressive parts of the game and proceed straight to the player-controlled action. But the same could be said of action-packed movies." Also, "there is no justification for disqualifying video games as speech simply because they are constructed to be interactive." The court noted that some books, "in which the reader makes choices that determine the plot of the story, * * * can be every bit as interactive." Because video games are entitled to protection, "the County must come forward with empirical support for its belief that violent video games cause psychological harm to minors. In this case, * * * the County has failed to present the substantial supporting evidence of harm that is required."

FOR CRITICAL ANALYSIS—Political Consideration
In determining whether a medium of speech is entitled to constitutional protection, should a court consider the messages communicated by that medium?

Unprotected Speech. The United States Supreme Court has made it clear that certain types of speech will not be given any protection under the First Amendment. Speech that harms the good reputation of another, or defamatory speech (see Chapter 4), will not be protected. Speech that violates criminal laws (such as threatening speech) is not constitutionally protected. Other unprotected speech includes "fighting words," or words that are likely to incite others to respond violently.

The Supreme Court has also held that obscene speech is not protected by the First Amendment. The Court has grappled from time to time with the problem of trying to establish an objective definition of obscene speech. In a 1973

case, *Miller v. California,*[22] the Supreme Court created a test for legal obscenity, which involved a set of requirements that must be met for material to be legally obscene. Under this test, material is obscene if (1) the average person finds that it violates contemporary community standards; (2) the work taken as a whole appeals to a prurient interest in sex; (3) the work shows patently offensive sexual conduct; and (4) the work lacks serious redeeming literary, artistic, political, or scientific merit.

Because community standards vary widely, the *Miller* test has had inconsistent applications, and obscenity

22 413 U.S. 15, 93 S.Ct. 2607, 37 L.Ed.2d 419 (1973).

remains a constitutionally unsettled issue. Numerous state and federal statutes make it a crime to disseminate obscene materials, however, and such laws have often been upheld by the Supreme Court, including laws prohibiting the sale and possession of child pornography.[23]

Online Obscenity. A significant problem facing the courts and lawmakers today is how to control obscenity and child pornography that are disseminated via the Internet. Congress first attempted to protect minors from pornographic materials on the Internet with the Communications Decency Act of 1996.[24] The act was challenged by civil liberties groups as an unconstitutional restraint on speech. The United States Supreme Court ultimately ruled that the act was improperly applied to a great deal of nonpornographic material with serious educational or literary value. Moreover, the "community standards" criterion used to define "patently offensive" materials was not properly applied.[25]

Some of the later attempts by Congress to curb pornography on the Internet also encountered constitutional stumbling blocks. For example, the Child Online Protection Act (COPA)[26] of 1998 banned material "harmful to minors" distributed without an age-verification system to separate adult and minor users. In 2002, the Supreme Court upheld a lower court injunction suspending the COPA, but narrowed the grounds on which it could be found unconstitutional.[27] In 2000, Congress enacted the Children's Internet Protection Act (CIPA),[28] which requires public schools and libraries to block adult content from access by children by installing **filtering software**. Such software is designed to prevent persons from viewing selected Web sites. The CIPA was also challenged on constitutional grounds, but in 2003 the Supreme Court held that the act did not violate the First Amendment. The Court concluded that because libraries can disable the filters for any patrons who ask, the system was reasonably flexible and did not burden free speech to an unconstitutional extent.[29]

Other Forms of Online Speech. Extreme hate speech appears on the Internet, including racist materials and Holocaust denials. Can the federal government restrict this type of speech? Should it? Are there other forms of speech that the government should restrict?[30] Content restrictions can be difficult to enforce. Also, U.S. federal law is only "local" law in cyberspace—fewer than half of the users of the Internet are in the United States. What if other countries attempt to impose their speech-restricting laws on U.S. Web sites? In 2001, a federal district court found that French laws banning the display of Nazi memorabilia could not be enforced against Yahoo in the United States.[31]

The First Amendment—Freedom of Religion. The First Amendment states that the government may neither establish any religion nor prohibit the free exercise of religious practices. The first part of this constitutional provision is referred to as the **establishment clause**, and the second part is known as the **free exercise clause**. Government action, both federal and state, must be consistent with this constitutional mandate.

The establishment clause prohibits the government from establishing a state-sponsored religion, as well as from passing laws that promote (aid or endorse) religion or that show a preference for one religion over another. The establishment clause does not require a complete separation of church and state, however. On the contrary, it requires the government to accommodate religions.[32] The Supreme Court has held that for a government law or policy to be constitutional, it must be secular in aim, must not have the primary effect of advancing or inhibiting religions, and must not create "an excessive government entanglement with religion."[33] Generally, federal or state regulation that does not promote religion or place a significant burden on religion is constitutional even if it has some impact on religion.

● **EXAMPLE #13** "Sunday closing laws" make the performance of some commercial activities on Sunday illegal. These statutes, also known as "blue laws" (from the color of the paper on which an early Sunday law was written), have been upheld on the ground that it is a legitimate function of government to provide a day of rest. The United States Supreme Court has held that the closing laws, although originally of a religious character, have taken on the secular

---

[23] See, for example, *Osborne v. Ohio*, 495 U.S. 103, 110 S.Ct. 1691, 109 L.Ed.2d 98 (1990).

[24] 47 U.S.C. Section 223(a)(1)(B)(ii).

[25] *Reno v. American Civil Liberties Union*, 521 U.S. 844, 117 S.Ct. 2329, 138 L.Ed.2d 874 (1997).

[26] 47 U.S.C. Section 231.

[27] *Ashcroft v. American Civil Liberties Union*, 535 U.S. 564, 122 S.Ct. 1700, 152 L.Ed.2d 771 (2002).

[28] 17 U.S.C. Sections 1701–1741.

[29] *United States v. American Library Association*, ___U.S, ___, 123 S.Ct. 2297, 156 L.Ed.2d. 221 (2003).

[30] The content of some speech is regulated to a certain extent by tort law, copyright law, trademark law, and other statutes. See Chapters 4 and 5 for a discussion of these topics.

[31] *Yahoo! Inc. v. La Ligue Contre le Racisme et l'Antisemitisme*, 169 F.Supp.2d 1181 (N.D.Cal. 2001). We present the original case, tried in France, in Chapter 2.

[32] *Zorach v. Clauson*, 343 U.S. 306, 72 S.Ct. 679, 96 L.Ed. 954 (1952).

[33] *Lemon v. Kurtzman*, 403 U.S. 602, 91 S.Ct. 2105, 29 L.Ed.2d 745 (1971).

purpose of promoting the health and welfare of workers.[34] Even though Sunday closing laws admittedly make it easier for Christians to attend religious services, the Court has viewed this effect as an incidental, not a primary, purpose of Sunday closing laws. ●

The free exercise clause guarantees that a person can hold any religious belief that she or he wants; or a person can have no religious belief. When religious practices work against public policy and the public welfare, however, the government can act. For example, regardless of a child's or parent's religious beliefs, the government can require certain types of vaccinations. For business firms, an important issue involves the accommodation that businesses must make for the religious beliefs of their employees. We will look further at this issue in Chapter 23, in the context of employment discrimination.

Due Process. Both the Fifth and the Fourteenth Amendments provide that no person shall be deprived "of life, liberty, or property, without due process of law." The **due process clause** of each of these constitutional amendments has two aspects—procedural and substantive.

Procedural Due Process. Procedural due process requires that any government decision to take life, liberty, or property must be made fairly. For example, fair procedures must be used in determining whether a person will be subjected to punishment or have some burden imposed on him or her. Fair procedure has been interpreted as requiring that the person have at least an opportunity to object to a proposed action before a fair, neutral decision maker (which need not be a judge). Thus, for example, if a driver's license is construed as a property interest, some sort of opportunity

---

[34] *McGowan v. Maryland,* 366 U.S. 420, 81 S.Ct. 1101, 6 L.Ed.2d 393 (1961).

to object to its suspension or termination by the state must be provided.

Substantive Due Process. Substantive due process focuses on the content, or substance, of legislation. If a law or other governmental action limits a *fundamental right,* it will be held to violate substantive due process unless it promotes a compelling or overriding state interest. Fundamental rights include interstate travel, privacy, voting, and all First Amendment rights. Compelling state interests could include, for example, the public's safety. ● EXAMPLE #14 Laws designating speed limits may be upheld even though they affect interstate travel, if they are shown to reduce highway fatalities, because the state has a compelling interest in protecting the lives of its citizens. ●

In situations not involving fundamental rights, a law or action does not violate substantive due process if it rationally relates to any legitimate governmental end. It is almost impossible for a law or action to fail the "rationality" test. Under this test, virtually any business regulation will be upheld as reasonable—the United States Supreme Court has sustained insurance regulations, price and wage controls, banking controls, and controls of unfair competition and trade practices against substantive due process challenges.

● EXAMPLE #15 If a state legislature enacted a law imposing a fifteen-year term of imprisonment without a trial on all businesspersons who appeared in their own television commercials, the law would be unconstitutional on both substantive and procedural grounds. Substantive review would invalidate the legislation because it abridges freedom of speech. Procedurally, the law is unfair because it imposes the penalty without giving the accused a chance to defend her or his actions. ● The lack of procedural due process will cause a court to invalidate any statute or prior court decision. Similarly, a denial of substantive due process requires courts to overrule any state or federal law that violates the Constitution.

Terms and Concepts

adjudicate 7	choice-of-law clause 9	defendant 4
administrative agency 6	citation 5	dormant commerce clause 12
administrative law 6	civil law 7	due process clause 17
administrative process 7	civil law system 8	enabling legislation 6
Bill of Rights 12	commerce clause 10	establishment clause 16
binding authority 3	common law 3	executive agency 6
case law 7	constitutional law 5	filtering software 16
choice-of-language clause 9	criminal law 8	forum-selection clause 9

free exercise clause   16
independent regulatory
  agency   6
international law   8
International organizations   9
jurisprudence   3
law   3

national law   8
persuasive authority   4
plaintiff   4
police powers   11
precedent   3
primary source of law   5
procedural law   7

remedy   4
secondary source of law   5
stare decisis   3
statutory law   5
substantive law   7
symbolic speech   14
treaty   8

Chapter Summary	Sources of Business Law and the Global Legal Environment
The Nature of Law (See pages 2–3.)	Law can be defined as a body of rules of conduct with legal force and effect, prescribed by the controlling authority (the government) of a society.
The Common Law Tradition (See pages 3–5.)	1. *Common law*—Law that originated in medieval England with the creation of the king's courts, or *curiae regis,* and the development of a body of rules that were common to (or applied throughout) the land. 2. *Stare decisis*—A doctrine under which judges "stand on decided cases"—or follow the rule of precedent—in deciding cases. *Stare decisis* is the cornerstone of the common law tradition. 3. *Remedies*— a. Remedies at law—Money or something else of value. b. Remedies in equity—Remedies that are granted when the remedies at law are unavailable or inadequate. Equitable remedies include specific performance, an injunction, and contract rescission (cancellation).
Sources of American Law (See pages 5–7.)	1. *Constitutional law*—The law as expressed in the U.S. Constitution and the various state constitutions. The U.S. Constitution is the supreme law of the land. State constitutions are supreme within state borders to the extent that they do not violate the U.S. Constitution or a federal law. 2. *Statutory law*—Laws or ordinances created by federal, state, and local legislatures and governing bodies. None of these laws can violate the U.S. Constitution or the relevant state constitutions. Uniform laws, when adopted by a state legislature, become statutory law in that state. 3. *Administrative law*—The rules, orders, and decisions of federal or state government administrative agencies. Federal administrative agencies are created by enabling legislation enacted by the U.S. Congress. Agency functions include rulemaking, investigation and enforcement, and adjudication. 4. *Case law and common law doctrines*—Judge-made law, including interpretations of constitutional provisions, statutes enacted by legislatures, and regulations created by administrative agencies. The common law—the doctrines and principles embodied in case law—governs all areas not covered by statutory law (or agency regulations issued to implement various statutes).
Classifications of Law (See pages 7–9.)	The law may be broken down according to several classification systems, such as substantive or procedural law, federal or state law, and private or public law. Two broad classifications are civil and criminal law, and national and international law.

Chapter Summary	Sources of Business Law and the Global Legal Environment—Continued
The Constitution as It Affects Business (See pages 10–17.)	1. *Commerce clause*—Expressly permits Congress to regulate commerce. That power authorizes the national government, at least theoretically, to regulate every commercial enterprise in the United States. Under their police powers, state governments may regulate private activities to protect or promote the public order, health, safety, morals, and general welfare. 2. *Bill of Rights*—The first ten amendments to the U.S. Constitution. They embody a series of protections for individuals—and in some cases, business entities—against various types of interference by the federal government. One of the freedoms guaranteed by the Bill of Rights that affects businesses is the freedom of speech guaranteed by the First Amendment. Also important are the protections of the Fifth and the Fourteenth Amendments, which provide that no person shall be deprived of "life, liberty, or property, without due process of law."

For Review

① What is the common law tradition?

② What is a precedent? When might a court depart from precedent?

③ What is the difference between remedies at law and remedies in equity?

④ What are some important classifications of law?

⑤ How does the U.S. Constitution affect business activities in the United States?

Questions and Case Problems

1–1. Legal Systems. What are the key differences between a common law system and a civil law system? Why do some countries have common law systems and others have civil law systems?

1–2. Sources of American Law. This chapter discussed a number of sources of American law. Which source of law takes priority in the following situations, and why?

  (a) A federal statute conflicts with the U.S. Constitution.

  (b) A federal statute conflicts with a state constitution.

  (c) A state statute conflicts with the common law of that state.

  (d) A state constitutional amendment conflicts with the U.S. Constitution.

  (e) A federal administrative regulation conflicts with a state constitution.

1–3. *Stare Decisis*. In the text of this chapter, we stated that the doctrine of *stare decisis* "became a cornerstone of the English and American judicial systems." What does *stare decisis* mean, and why has this doctrine been so fundamental to the development of our legal tradition?

1–4. Binding versus Persuasive Authority. A county court in Illinois is deciding a case involving an issue that has never been addressed before in that state's courts. The Iowa Supreme Court, however, recently decided a case involving a very similar fact pattern. Is the Illinois court obligated to follow the Iowa Supreme Court's decision on the issue? If the United States Supreme Court had decided a similar case, would that decision be binding on the Illinois court? Explain.

1–5. Freedom of Speech. A mayoral election is about to be held in a large U.S. city. One of the candidates is Luis Delgado, and his campaign supporters want to post campaign signs on lampposts and utility posts throughout the city. A city ordinance, however, prohibits the posting of any signs on public property. Delgado's supporters contend that the city ordinance is unconstitutional, because it violates their rights to free speech. What factors might a court consider in determining the constitutionality of this ordinance?

1–6. Commerce Clause. Suppose that Georgia enacts a law requiring the use of contoured rear-fender mudguards on trucks and trailers operating within the state. The statute further makes it illegal for trucks and trailers to use straight mudguards. In thirty-five other states, straight mudguards are legal. Moreover, in the neighboring state of Florida, straight mudguards are explicitly required by law. There is some evidence suggesting that contoured mudguards might be a little safer than straight mudguards. Discuss whether this Georgia statute would violate the commerce clause of the U.S. Constitution.

1–7. Freedom of Speech. The members of Greater New Orleans Broadcasting Association, Inc., operate radio and television stations in New Orleans. They wanted to broadcast ads for private, for-profit casinos that are legal in Louisiana. A federal statute banned casino advertising, but other federal statutes exempted ads for tribal, government, nonprofit, and "occasional and ancillary" commercial casinos. The association filed a suit in a federal district court against the federal government, asking the court to hold that the statute, as it applied to their ads, violated the First Amendment. The government argued that the ban should be upheld, because "[u]nder appropriate conditions, some broadcast signals from Louisiana broadcasting stations may be heard in neighboring states including Texas and Arkansas," where private casino gambling is unlawful. What is the test for determining whether a regulation of commercial speech violates the First Amendment? How might it apply in this case? How should the court rule? [*Greater New Orleans Broadcasting Association, Inc. v. United States,* 527 U.S. 173, 199 S.Ct. 1923, 144 L.Ed.2d 161 (1999)]

CASE PROBLEM WITH SAMPLE ANSWER

1–8. Thomas worked in the nonmilitary operations of a large firm that produced both military and nonmilitary goods. When the company discontinued the production of nonmilitary goods, Thomas was transferred to a plant producing military equipment. Thomas left his job, claiming that it violated his religious principles to participate in the manufacture of goods to be used in destroying life. In effect, he argued, the transfer to the war-materials plant forced him to quit his job. He was denied unemployment compensation by the state because he had not been effectively "discharged" by the employer but had voluntarily terminated his employment. Did the state's denial of unemployment benefits to Thomas violate the free exercise clause of the First Amendment? Explain. [*Thomas v. Review Board of the Indiana Employment Security Division,* 450 U.S. 707, 101 S.Ct. 1425, 67 L.Ed.2d 624 (1981)]

▶ To view a sample answer for this case problem, go to this book's Web site at **http://fundamentals.westbuslaw.com** and click on "Interactive Study Center."

1–9. Freedom of Speech. The Telephone Consumer Protection Act (TCPA) of 1991 made it unlawful for any person "to use any telephone facsimile machine, computer, or other device to send an unsolicited advertisement to a telephone facsimile machine." In enacting the TCPA, Congress did not consider any studies or empirical data estimating the cost of receiving a fax or the number of unsolicited fax ads that an average business receives in a day. American Blast Fax, Inc. (ABFI), provides fax ad services in Missouri. Between July 2000 and June 2001, the office of Jeremiah Nixon, the Missouri attorney general, received 229 unsolicited faxes, some of which were ads. Nixon filed a suit in a federal district court against ABFI and others, alleging in part violations of the TCPA. ABFI filed a motion to dismiss, asserting that the TCPA provision on unsolicited fax ads was unconstitutional. Nixon claimed that the ads shifted costs from advertisers to recipients and tied up recipients' fax machines, but he offered no evidence of the cost in money or time. What is the test for considering a restriction on commercial speech? Is the TCPA provision valid? Explain. [*Nixon v. American Blast Fax, Inc.,* 196 F.Supp.2d 920 (E.D.Mo. 2002)]

1–10. Free Speech. Henry Mishkoff is a Web designer whose firm does business as "Webfeats." When Taubman Co. began building a mall called "The Shops at Willow Bend" near Mishkoff's home, Mishkoff registered the domain name "shopsatwillowbend.com" and created a Web site with that address. The site featured information about the mall, a disclaimer indicating that Mishkoff's site was unofficial, and a link to the mall's official site. Taubman discovered Mishkoff's site and filed a suit in a federal district court against him. Mishkoff then registered other names, including "taubmansucks.com," with links to a site documenting his battle with Taubman. (A Web name with a "sucks.com" moniker attached to it is known as a "complaint name," and the process of registering and using such names is known as "cybergriping.") Taubman asked the court to order Mishkoff to stop using all of these names. Should the court grant Taubman's request? On what basis might the court protect Mishkoff's use of the names? [*Taubman Co. v. Webfeats,* 319 F.3d 770 (6th Cir. 2003)]

SOURCES OF BUSINESS LAW AND THE GLOBAL LEGAL ENVIRONMENT

Today, business law professors and students can go online to access information on virtually every topic covered in this text. A good point of departure for online legal research is this text's Web site at

http://fundamentals.westbuslaw.com

There you will find numerous materials relevant to this text and to business law generally, including links to various legal resources on the Web. Additionally, every chapter in this text ends with an *Accessing the Internet* feature that contains selected Web addresses.

You can access many of the sources of law discussed in Chapter 1 at the FindLaw Web site, which is probably the most comprehensive source of free legal information on the Internet. Go to

http://www.findlaw.com

The Legal Information Institute (LII) at Cornell Law School, which offers extensive information about U.S. law, is also a good starting point for legal research. The URL for this site is

http://www.law.cornell.edu

The Library of Congress offers extensive links to state and federal government resources at

http://www.loc.gov

The Virtual Law Library Index, created and maintained by the Indiana University School of Law, provides an index of legal sources categorized by subject at

http://www.law.indiana.edu/v-lib

For an online version of the Constitution that provides hypertext links to amendments and other changes, go to

http://www.law.cornell.edu/constitution/constitution.table.html

To learn the founders' views on federalism, a good source is *The Federalist Papers,* a series of essays written by Alexander Hamilton, James Madison, and John Jay. You can access these essays online at

http://www.law.emory.edu/FEDERAL/federalist

For discussions of current issues involving the rights and liberties contained in the Bill of Rights, go to the Web site of the American Civil Liberties Union at

http://www.aclu.org

Summaries and the full texts of constitutional law decisions by the United States Supreme Court are included at the Oyez site, which also has audio clips of arguments before the Court:

http://www.oyez.org/oyez/frontpage

Online Legal Research

The text's Web site also offers online research exercises. These exercises will help you find and analyze specific types of legal information available at specific Web sites. There is at least one of these exercises for each chapter in *Fundamentals of Business Law,* Sixth Edition. To access these exercises, go to this book's Web site at **http://fundamentals.westbuslaw.com** and click on "Interactive Study Center." When that page opens, select the relevant chapter to find the exercises relating to topics in that chapter. The following activities will direct you to some of the topics discussed in Chapter 1.

Activity 1–1: LEGAL PERSPECTIVE—Internet Sources of Law
Activity 1–2: MANAGEMENT PERSPECTIVE—Online Assistance from Government
            Agencies
Activity 1–3: SOCIAL PERSPECTIVE—Flag Burning

Before the Test

Go to the *Fundamentals of Business Law* home page at **http://fundamentals. westbuslaw.com**. Click on "Interactive Quizzes." You will find at least twenty interactive questions relating to this chapter.

Westlaw® Campus

If your textbook provided for a subscription to Westlaw® Campus, or if you have otherwise purchased access to the Westlaw Campus database, you can access any of the cases presented or cited in this chapter by using your Westlaw Campus account.

Appendix to Chapter 1

Finding and Analyzing the Law

The statutes, agency regulations, and case law referred to in this text establish the rights and duties of businesspersons engaged in various types of activities. The cases presented in this text provide you with concise, real-life illustrations of how the courts interpret and apply these laws. Because of the importance of knowing how to find statutory, administrative, and case law, this appendix offers a brief introduction to how these laws are published and to the legal "shorthand" used in referencing these legal sources.

Finding Statutory and Administrative Law

When Congress passes laws, they are collected in a publication titled *United States Statutes at Large*. When state legislatures pass laws, they are collected in similar state publications. Most frequently, however, laws are referred to in their codified form—that is, the form in which they appear in the federal and state codes.

In these codes, laws are compiled by subject. The *United States Code* (U.S.C.) arranges all existing federal laws of a public and permanent nature by subject. Each of the fifty subjects into which the U.S.C. arranges the laws is given a title and a title number. For example, laws relating to commerce and trade are collected in Title 15, which is titled "Commerce and Trade." Titles are subdivided by sections. A citation to the U.S.C. includes title and section numbers. Thus, a reference to "15 U.S.C. Section 1" means that the statute can be found in Section 1 of Title 15. ("Section" may also be designated by the symbol §, and "Sections" by §§.)

Sometimes a citation includes the abbreviation *et seq.*—as in "15 U.S.C. Sections 1 *et seq.*" The term is an abbreviated form of *et sequitur,* which in Latin means "and the following"; when used in a citation, it refers to sections that concern the same subject as the numbered section and follow it in sequence.

State codes follow the U.S.C. pattern of arranging law by subject. The state codes may be called codes, revisions, compilations, consolidations, general statutes, or statutes, depending on the preference of the states. In some codes, subjects are designated by number. In others, they are designated by name. For example, "13 Pennsylvania Consolidated Statutes Section 1101" means that the statute can be found in Title 13, Section 1101, of the Pennsylvania code. "California Commercial Code Section 1101" means that the statute can be found under the subject heading "Commercial Code" of the California code in Section 1101. Abbreviations may be used. For example, "13 Pennsylvania Consolidated Statutes Section 1101" may be abbreviated "13 Pa. C.S. § 1101," and "California Commercial Code Section 1101" may be abbreviated "Cal. Com. Code § 1101."

Rules and regulations adopted by federal administrative agencies are compiled in the *Code of Federal Regulations* (C.F.R.). Like the U.S.C., the C.F.R. is divided into fifty titles. Rules within each title are assigned section numbers. A full citation to the C.F.R. includes title and section numbers. For example, a reference to "17 C.F.R. Section 230.504" means that the rule can be found in Section 230.504 of Title 17.

Commercial publications of these laws and regulations are available and are widely used. For example, West Group publishes the *United States Code Annotated* (U.S.C.A.). The U.S.C.A. contains the complete text of laws included in the

U.S.C., as well as notes of court decisions that interpret and apply specific sections of the statutes, plus the text of presidential proclamations and executive orders. The U.S.C.A. also includes research aids, such as cross-references to related statutes, historical notes, and library references. A citation to the U.S.C.A. is similar to a citation to the U.S.C.: "15 U.S.C.A. Section 1."

Finding Case Law

Before discussing the case reporting system, we need to look briefly at the court system (which will be discussed in detail in Chapter 2). There are two types of courts in the United States, federal courts and state courts. Both the federal and state court systems consist of several levels, or tiers, of courts. *Trial courts,* in which evidence is presented and testimony given, are on the bottom tier (which also includes lower courts handling specialized issues). Decisions from a trial court can be appealed to a higher court, which commonly would be an intermediate *court of appeals,* or an *appellate court.* Decisions from these intermediate courts of appeals may be appealed to an even higher court, such as a state supreme court or the United States Supreme Court.

STATE COURT DECISIONS

Most state trial court decisions are not published. Except in New York and a few other states that publish selected opinions of their trial courts, decisions from state trial courts are merely filed in the office of the clerk of the court, where the decisions are available for public inspection. Written decisions of the appellate, or reviewing, courts, however, are published and distributed. As you will note, most of the state court cases presented in this book are from state appellate courts. The reported appellate decisions are published in volumes called *reports* or *reporters,* which are numbered consecutively. State appellate court decisions are found in the state reporters of that particular state.

Additionally, state court opinions appear in regional units of the *National Reporter System,* published by West Group. Most lawyers and libraries have the West reporters because they report cases more quickly and are distributed more widely than the state-published reports. In fact, many states have eliminated their own reporters in favor of West's National Reporter System. The National Reporter System divides the states into the following geographic areas: *Atlantic* (A. or A.2d), *South Eastern* (S.E. or S.E.2d), *South Western* (S.W., S.W.2d, or S.W.3d), *North Western* (N.W. or N.W.2d), *North Eastern* (N.E. or N.E.2d), *Southern* (So. or

So.2d), and *Pacific* (P., P.2d, or P.3d). (The 2d and 3d in the abbreviations refer to *Second Series* and *Third Series,* respectively.) The states included in each of these regional divisions are shown in Exhibit 1A–1, which illustrates West's National Reporter System.

After appellate decisions have been published, they are normally referred to (cited) by the name of the case; the volume, name, and page number of the state's official reporter (if different from West's National Reporter System); the volume, unit, and page number of the *National Reporter;* and the volume, name, and page number of any other selected reporter. This information is included in the *citation.* (Citing a reporter by volume number, name, and page number, in that order, is common to all citations.) When more than one reporter is cited for the same case, each reference is called a *parallel citation.* For example, consider the following case: *Davidson v. Microsoft Corp.,* 143 Md.App. 43, 792 A.2d 336 (2001). We see that the opinion in this case may be found in Volume 143 of the official *Maryland Appellate Reports,* on page 43. The parallel citation is to Volume 792 of the *Atlantic Reporter, Second Series,* on page 336. In presenting appellate opinions in this text, in addition to the reporter, we give the name of the court hearing the case and the year of the court's decision.

A few states—including those with intermediate appellate courts, such as California, Illinois, and New York—have more than one reporter for opinions issued by their courts. Sample citations from these courts, as well as others, are listed and explained in Exhibit 1A–2 on pages 26 through 28.

FEDERAL COURT DECISIONS

Federal district court decisions are published unofficially in West's *Federal Supplement* (F.Supp. or F.Supp.2d), and opinions from the circuit courts of appeals (federal reviewing courts) are reported unofficially in West's *Federal Reporter* (F., F.2d, or F.3d). Cases concerning federal bankruptcy law are published unofficially in West's *Bankruptcy Reporter* (Bankr.). The official edition of United States Supreme Court decisions is the *United States Reports* (U.S.), which is published by the federal government. Unofficial editions of Supreme Court cases include West's *Supreme Court Reporter* (S.Ct.) and the *Lawyers' Edition of the Supreme Court Reports* (L.Ed. or L.Ed.2d). Sample citations for federal court decisions are also listed and explained in Exhibit 1A–2.

UNPUBLISHED OPINIONS

Many court opinions that are not yet published or that are not intended for publication can be accessed through Westlaw® (abbreviated in citations as "WL"), an online

EXHIBIT 1A–1 NATIONAL REPORTER SYSTEM—REGIONAL/FEDERAL

Regional Reporters	Coverage Beginning	Coverage
(A. or A.2d)	1885	Connecticut, Delaware, Maine, Maryland, New Hampshire, New Jersey, Pennsylvania, Rhode Island, Vermont, and District of Columbia.
(N.E. or N.E.2d)	1885	Illinois, Indiana, Massachusetts, New York, and Ohio.
(N.W. or N.W.2d)	1879	Iowa, Michigan, Minnesota, Nebraska, North Dakota, South Dakota, and Wisconsin.
(P., P.2d, or P.3d)	1883	Alaska, Arizona, California, Colorado, Hawaii, Idaho, Kansas, Montana, Nevada, New Mexico, Oklahoma, Oregon, Utah, Washington, and Wyoming.
(S.E. or S.E.2d)	1887	Georgia, North Carolina, South Carolina, Virginia, and West Virginia.
(S.W., S.W.2d, or S.W.3d)	1886	Arkansas, Kentucky, Missouri, Tennessee, and Texas.
(So. or So.2d)	1887	Alabama, Florida, Louisiana, and Mississippi.

Federal Reporters		
(F., F.2d, or F.3d)	1880	U.S. Circuit Court from 1880 to 1912; U.S. Commerce Court from 1911 to 1913; U.S. District Courts from 1880 to 1932; U.S. Court of Claims (now called U.S. Court of Federal Claims) from 1929 to 1932 and since 1960; U.S. Courts of Appeals since 1891; U.S. Court of Customs and Patent Appeals since 1929; U.S. Emergency Court of Appeals since 1943.
(F.Supp. or F.Supp.2d)	1932	U.S. Court of Claims from 1932 to 1960; U.S. District Courts since 1932; and U.S. Customs Court since 1956.
(F.R.D.)	1939	U.S. District Courts involving the Federal Rules of Civil Procedure since 1939 and Federal Rules of Criminal Procedure since 1946.
(S.Ct.)	1882	U.S. Supreme Court since the October term of 1882.
(Bankr.)	1980	Bankruptcy decisions of U.S. Bankruptcy Courts, U.S. District Courts, U.S. Courts of Appeals, and U.S. Supreme Court.
(M.J.)	1978	U.S. Court of Military Appeals and Courts of Military Review for the Army, Navy, Air Force, and Coast Guard.

NATIONAL REPORTER SYSTEM MAP

Legend:
- Pacific
- North Western
- South Western
- North Eastern
- Atlantic
- South Eastern
- Southern

EXHIBIT 1A–2 **HOW TO READ CITATIONS**

State Courts

263 Neb. 881, 644 N.W.2d 128 (2002)[a]

> *N.W.* is the abbreviation for West's publication of state court decisions rendered in the *North Western Reporter* of the National Reporter System. *2d* indicates that this case was included in the *Second Series* of that reporter. The number 644 refers to the volume number of the reporter; the number 128 refers to the first page in that volume on which this case can be found.

> *Neb.* is an abbreviation for *Nebraska Reports,* Nebraska's official reports of the decisions of its highest court, the Nebraska Supreme Court.

98 Cal.App.4th 892, 120 Cal.Rptr.2d 576 (2002)

> *Cal.Rptr.* is the abbreviation for West's unofficial reports—titled *California Reporter*—of the decisions of the California Supreme Court and California appellate courts.

97 N.Y.2d 463, 768 N.E.2d 1121, 742 N.Y.S.2d 182 (2002)

> *N.Y.S.* is the abbreviation for West's unofficial reports—titled *New York Supplement*—of the decisions of New York courts.

> *N.Y.* is the abbreviation for *New York Reports,* New York's official reports of the decisions of its court of appeals. The New York Court of Appeals is the state's highest court, analogous to other states' supreme courts. (In New York, a supreme court is a trial court.)

253 Ga.App. 639, 560 S.E.2d 40 (2002)

> *Ga.App.* is the abbreviation for *Georgia Appeals Reports,* Georgia's official reports of the decisions of its court of appeals.

Federal Courts

534 U.S. 184, 122 S.Ct. 681, 151 L.Ed.2d 615 (2002)

> *L.Ed.* is an abbreviation for *Lawyers' Edition of the Supreme Court Reports,* an unofficial edition of decisions of the United States Supreme Court.

> *S.Ct.* is the abbreviation for West's unofficial reports— titled *Supreme Court Reporter*—of decisions of the United States Supreme Court.

> *U.S.* is the abbreviation for *United States Reports,* the official edition of the decisions of the United States Supreme Court.

---

a. The case names have been deleted from these citations to emphasize the publications. It should be kept in mind, however, that the name of a case is as important as the specific numbers of the volumes in which it is found. If a citation is incorrect, the correct citation may be found in a publication's index of case names. The date of a case is also important because, in addition to providing a check on error in citations, the value of a recent case as an authority is likely to be greater than that of an earlier case.

EXHIBIT 1A–2 **HOW TO READ CITATIONS (CONTINUED)**

Federal Courts (continued)

287 F.3d 122 (2d Cir. 2002)

> *2d Cir.* is an abbreviation denoting that this case was decided in the United States Court of Appeals for the Second Circuit.

187 F.Supp.2d 1288 (D.Colo. 2002)

> *D.Colo.* is an abbreviation indicating that the United States District Court for the District of Colorado decided this case.

English Courts

9 Exch. 341, 156 Eng.Rep. 145 (1854)

> *Eng.Rep.* is an abbreviation for *English Reports, Full Reprint,* a series of reports containing selected decisions made in English courts between 1378 and 1865.

> *Exch.* is an abbreviation for *English Exchequer Reports,* which included the original reports of cases decided in England's Court of Exchequer.

Statutory and Other Citations

18 U.S.C. Section 1961(1)(A)

> *U.S.C.* denotes *United States Code,* the codification of *United States Statutes at Large.* The number 18 refers to the statute's U.S.C. title number and 1961 to its section number within that title. The number 1 refers to a subsection within the section and the letter A to a subdivision within the subsection.

UCC 2–206(1)(b)

> *UCC* is an abbreviation for *Uniform Commercial Code.* The first number 2 refers to an article of the UCC and 206 to a section within that article. The number 1 refers to a subsection within the section and the letter b to a subdivision within the subsection.

Restatement (Second) of Contracts, Section 162

> *Restatement (Second) of Contracts* refers to the second edition of the American Law Institute's *Restatement of the Law of Contracts.* The number 162 refers to a specific section.

17 C.F.R. Section 230.505

> *C.F.R.* is an abbreviation for *Code of Federal Regulations,* a compilation of federal administrative regulations. The number 17 designates the regulation's title number, and 230.505 designates a specific section within that title.

EXHIBIT 1A–2 HOW TO READ CITATIONS (CONTINUED)

Westlaw® Citations[b]

2004 WL 10238

WL is an abbreviation for Westlaw®. The number 2004 is the year of the document that can be found with this citation in the Westlaw® database. The number 10238 is a number assigned to a specific document. A higher number indicates that a document was added to the Westlaw® database later in the year.

Uniform Resource Locators (URLs)

http://www.westlaw.com[c]

The suffix *com* is the top-level domain (TLD) for this Web site. The TLD *com* is an abbreviation for "commercial," which means that normally a for-profit entity hosts (maintains or supports) this Web site.

westlaw is the host name—the part of the domain name selected by the organization that registered the name. In this case, West Group registered the name. This Internet site is the Westlaw database on the Web.

www is an abbreviation for "World Wide Web." The Web is a system of Internet servers that support documents formatted in *HTML* (hypertext markup language). HTML supports links to text, graphics, and audio and video files.

http://www.uscourts.gov

This is "The Federal Judiciary Home Page." The host is the Administrative Office of the U.S. Courts. The TLD *gov* is an abbreviation for "government." This Web site includes information and links from, and about, the federal courts.

http://www.law.cornell.edu/index.html

This part of a URL points to a Web page or file at a specific location within the host's domain. This page is a menu with links to documents within the domain and to other Internet resources.

This is the host name for a Web site that contains the Internet publications of the Legal Information Institute (LII), which is a part of Cornell Law School. The LII site includes a variety of legal materials and links to other legal resources on the Internet. The TLD *edu* is an abbreviation for "educational institution" (a school or a university).

http://www.ipl.org/div/subject

div/subject refers to "Subject Collections," a list of the topics into which the links at this Web site have been categorized.

ipl is an abbreviation for "Internet Public Library," which is an online service that provides reference resources and links to other information services on the Web. The IPL is supported chiefly by the School of Information at the University of Michigan. The TLD *org* is an abbreviation for "organization (normally nonprofit)."

b. Many court decisions that are not yet published or that are not intended for publication can be accessed through Westlaw®, an online legal database.

c. The basic form for a URL is "service://hostname/path." The Internet service for all of the URLs in this text is *http* (hypertext transfer protocol). Most Web browsers will add this prefix automatically when a user enters a host name or a hostname/path.

legal database maintained by West Group. When no citation to a published reporter is available for cases cited in this text, we give the WL citation (see Exhibit 1A–2 for an example).

OLD CASE LAW

On a few occasions, this text cites opinions from old, classic cases dating to the nineteenth century or earlier; some of these are from the English courts. The citations to these cases appear not to conform to the descriptions given above because the reporters in which they were published have since been replaced.

Reading and Understanding Case Law

The cases in this text have been condensed from the full text of the courts' opinions and paraphrased by the authors. For those wishing to review court cases for future research projects or to gain additional legal information, the following sections will provide useful insights into how to read and understand case law.

CASE TITLES AND TERMINOLOGY

The title of a case, such as *Adams v. Jones,* indicates the names of the parties to the lawsuit. The *v.* in the case title stands for *versus,* which means "against." In the trial court, Adams was the plaintiff—the person who filed the suit. Jones was the defendant. If the case is appealed, however, the appellate court will sometimes place the name of the party appealing the decision first, so the case may be called *Jones v. Adams.* Because some reviewing courts retain the trial court order of names, it is often impossible to distinguish the plaintiff from the defendant in the title of a reported appellate court decision. You must carefully read the facts of each case to identify the parties.

The following terms and phrases are frequently encountered in court opinions and legal publications. Because it is important to understand what these terms and phrases mean, we define and discuss them here.

Plaintiffs and Defendants. As mentioned in Chapter 1, the plaintiff in a lawsuit is the party that initiates the action. The defendant is the party against which a lawsuit is brought. Lawsuits frequently involve more than one plaintiff and/or defendant.

Appellants and Appellees. The *appellant* is the party that appeals a case to another court or jurisdiction from the court or jurisdiction in which the case was originally brought. Sometimes, an appellant that appeals a judgment is referred to as the *petitioner.* The *appellee* is the party against which the appeal is taken. Sometimes, the appellee is referred to as the *respondent.*

Judges and Justices. The terms *judge* and *justice* are usually synonymous and represent two designations given to judges in various courts. All members of the United States Supreme Court, for example, are referred to as justices. *Justice* is the formal title usually given to judges of appellate courts as well, although this is not always the case. In New York, a justice is a judge of the trial court (which is called the Supreme Court), and a member of the Court of Appeals (the state's highest court) is called a judge. The term *justice* is commonly abbreviated to J., and *justices* to JJ. A Supreme Court case might refer to Justice O'Connor as O'Connor, J., or to Chief Justice Rehnquist as Rehnquist, C.J.

Decisions and Opinions. Most decisions reached by reviewing, or appellate, courts are explained in written *opinions.* The opinion contains the court's reasons for its decision, the rules of law that apply, and the judgment. When all judges or justices unanimously agree on an opinion, the opinion is written for the entire court and can be deemed a *unanimous opinion.* When there is not a unanimous opinion, a *majority opinion* is written, outlining the views of the majority of the judges or justices deciding the case.

Often, a judge or justice who feels strongly about making or emphasizing a point that was not made or emphasized in the unanimous or majority opinion will write a *concurring opinion.* That means the judge or justice agrees (concurs) with the judgment given in the unanimous or majority opinion but for different reasons. In other than unanimous opinions, a *dissenting opinion* is usually written by a judge or justice who does not agree with the majority. (See the *Focus on Legal Reasoning* feature following Chapter 3 for an example of a dissenting opinion.) The dissenting opinion is important because it may form the basis of the arguments used years later in overruling the precedential majority opinion. Occasionally, a court issues a *per curiam* (Latin for "of the court") opinion, which does not indicate which judge or justice authored the opinion.

A SAMPLE COURT CASE

Knowing how to read and analyze a court opinion is an essential step in undertaking accurate legal research. A further step involves "briefing" the case. Legal researchers routinely brief cases by summarizing and reducing the texts of the opinions to their essential elements. (For instructions on how to brief a case, see Appendix A at the end of this text.) The cases contained within the chapters of this book have already been analyzed and briefed by the authors, and the essential aspects of each case are presented in a convenient format consisting of four basic sections: *Facts, Issue, Decision,* and *Reason,* as shown in Exhibit 1A–3, which has

also been annotated to illustrate the kind of information that is contained in each section.

As you can see in Exhibit 1A–3, each case is followed by a brief section entitled *For Critical Analysis,* which presents a question regarding some issue raised by the case.

EXHIBIT 1A-3 **A SAMPLE COURT CASE**

❶ **Williams v. Dominion Technology Partners, L.L.C.**
❷ Virginia Supreme Court, 2003.
❸ 576 S.E.2d 752.
❹ **http://www.courts.state.va.us/txtndex.htm**[a]

❺ **FACTS** Dominion Technology Partners, L.L.C., is an employment firm specializing in recruiting and placing computer consultants on a temporary basis. Stihl, Inc., a power-tool manufacturing firm, sought a consultant to oversee the installation of new software on computer systems at Stihl's facilities in Virginia Beach, Virginia. Dominion recruited Donald Williams to fill the position as an at-will employee. In January 1999, Stihl contracted to employ Williams for three months. The installation was completed on time, and Stihl retained Williams in a support and maintenance role for an indeterminate period on a monthly basis. More than a year later, when Stihl was considering a further software upgrade, Williams indicated that he would prefer to continue working at Stihl under a direct agreement, and resigned as an employee of Dominion. When Dominion learned that Williams was continuing to work at Stihl, Dominion filed a suit in a Virginia state court against Williams, alleging breach of fiduciary duty, among other things. The court entered a judgment in Dominion's favor. Williams appealed to the Virginia Supreme Court.

❻ **ISSUE** Did Williams breach his duty of loyalty to Dominion?

❼ **DECISION** No. The Virginia Supreme Court reversed the judgment of the lower court and entered a judgment for Williams.

❽ **REASON** The state supreme court acknowledged that an at-will employee "owes a fiduciary duty of loyalty to his employer during his employment. * * * Nonetheless, in the absence of a contract restriction regarding this duty of loyalty, an employee has the right to make arrangements during his employment to compete with his employer after resigning his post." Here, "Dominion had not sought a non-compete agreement from Williams * * * . In such circumstances, it cannot be said that Williams' conduct to safeguard his own interests was either disloyal or unfair to Dominion. * * * Dominion's contracts provided it with nothing more than a subjective belief or hope that the business relationships would continue and merely a possibility that future economic benefit would accrue to it." By providing reasonable notice of his intent to resign, "Williams allowed Dominion to receive all the benefits for which it had bargained. Dominion's disappointment that its hopes did not bear the expected additional benefit it might have obtained under a different * * * agreement * * * does not translate into a breach of any fiduciary duty."

❾ **FOR CRITICAL ANALYSIS—Technological Consideration** *Could Stihl's plan to further upgrade its software be considered a "trade secret" that Williams misappropriated, thereby violating his duty of loyalty to Dominion?*

---

a. This is a page on a Web site maintained by the state of Virginia. Scroll to the name of the case and click on the number to access the opinion.

REVIEW OF THE SAMPLE COURT CASE

❶ The name of the case is *Williams v. Dominion Technology Partners, L.L.C.* (*L.L.C.* is an abbreviation for *limited liability company,* which is a particular form of business enterprise that limits the liability of its owners for the firm's debts and other obligations. See Chapter 24.) Donald Williams is the plaintiff, or petitioner, and Dominion is the respondent.

❷ The court deciding this case is the Virginia Supreme Court.

❸ The citation is to Volume 576 of the official *South Eastern Reporter,* Second Series, page 752.

❹ The case citation includes a citation to a page on the Web where the case can be found. This page is an index to the state of Virginia's online collection of Virginia Supreme Court opinions. A footnote to the citation offers information about the Web location of this opinion.

❺ The *Facts* section identifies the parties to the suit, describes the events leading up to it and the allegations made by the respondent in the initial suit, and (because this case is an appellate court decision) indicates the lower court's ruling and the party appealing the ruling. The appellant's contention on appeal is also sometimes included here.

❻ The *Issue* section presents the central issue (or issues) to be decided by the court. In this case, the Virginia Supreme Court is reviewing the lower court's judgment for an error of law, as argued by Williams on appeal. Cases frequently involve more than one issue.

❼ The *Decision* section, as the term indicates, contains the court's decision on the issue or issues before the court. The decision reflects the opinion of the majority of the judges or justices hearing the case. Decisions by appellate courts are frequently phrased in reference to the lower court's decision; that is, the appellate court may "affirm" the lower court's ruling or "reverse" it. In this particular case, the Virginia Supreme Court reversed the judgment of the lower court and entered a judgment in favor of the appellant.

❽ The *Reason* section indicates what relevant laws and judicial principles were applied in forming the particular conclusion arrived at in the case at bar ("before the court"). In this case, the relevant common law principles involved the employment-at-will doctrine and an employee's duty of loyalty to his or her employer. The court determined that in the absence of a contract to the contrary, an employee has the right to arrange, during his or her employment, to work for another employer after resigning his or her position.

❾ The *For Critical Analysis—Technological Consideration* section raises a question to be considered in relation to the case just presented. Here the question involves a "technological" consideration. In other cases presented in this text, the "consideration" may involve a cultural, economic, environmental, ethical, international, political, social, or technological consideration.

2

Traditional and Online Dispute Resolution

CHAPTER OBJECTIVES

After reading this chapter, you should be able to answer the following questions:

① What is judicial review? How and when was the power of judicial review established?

② Before a court can hear a case, it must have jurisdiction. Over what must it have jurisdiction? How are the courts applying traditional jurisdictional concepts to cases involving Internet transactions?

③ What is the difference between a trial court and an appellate court?

④ In a lawsuit, what are the pleadings? What is discovery? What is electronic filing?

⑤ How are online forums being used to resolve disputes?

Ultimately, we are all affected by what the courts say and do. This is particularly true in the business world—nearly every businessperson faces either a potential or an actual lawsuit at some time or another in her or his career. For this reason, anyone contemplating a career in business will benefit from an understanding of American court systems, including the mechanics of lawsuits.

In this chapter, after examining the judiciary's overall role in the American governmental scheme, we discuss some basic requirements that must be met before a party may bring a lawsuit before a particular court. We then look at the court systems of the United States in some detail and, to clarify judicial procedures, follow a hypothetical case through a state court system. Even though there are fifty-two court systems—one for each of the fifty states and one for the District of Columbia, plus a federal system—similarities abound. Keep in mind that the federal courts are not superior to the state courts; they are simply an independent system of courts, which derives its authority from Article III, Section 2, of the U.S. Constitution. The chapter concludes with an overview of some alternative methods of settling disputes, including methods for settling disputes in online forums.

Note that technological developments are affecting court procedures just as they are affecting all other areas of the law.

In this chapter, we will also describe how court doctrines and procedures, as well as alternative methods of dispute settlement, are being adapted to the needs of a cyber age.

The Judiciary's Role in American Government

As you learned in Chapter 1, the body of American law includes the federal and state constitutions, statutes passed by legislative bodies, administrative law, and the case decisions and legal principles that form the common law. These laws would be meaningless, however, without courts to interpret and apply them. This is the essential role of the judiciary—the courts—in the American governmental system: to interpret and apply the law.

As the branch of government entrusted with interpreting the laws, the judiciary can decide, among other things, whether the laws or actions of the other two branches are constitutional. The process for making such a determination is known as **judicial review**. The power of judicial review enables the judicial branch to act as a check on the other two branches of government, in line with the checks-and-balances system established by the U.S. Constitution.

The power of judicial review was not mentioned in the Constitution, but the concept was not new at the time the nation was founded. The doctrine of judicial review was not legally established, however, until 1803, when the United States Supreme Court rendered its decision in *Marbury v. Madison.*[1] In that case, the Supreme Court stated, "It is emphatically the province and duty of the Judicial Department to say what the law is. . . . If two laws conflict with each other, the courts must decide on the operation of each. . . . So if the law be in opposition to the Constitution . . . [t]he Court must determine which of these conflicting rules governs the case. This is the very essence of judicial duty." Since the *Marbury v. Madison* decision, the power of judicial review has remained unchallenged. Today, this power is exercised by both federal and state courts.

Basic Judicial Requirements

Before a court can hear a lawsuit, certain requirements must first be met. These requirements relate to jurisdiction, venue, and standing to sue. We examine each of these important concepts here.

[1] 5 U.S. (1 Cranch) 137, 2 L.Ed. 60 (1803).

JURISDICTION

In Latin, *juris* means "law," and *diction* means "to speak." Thus, "the power to speak the law" is the literal meaning of the term **jurisdiction**. Before any court can hear a case, it must have jurisdiction over the person against whom the suit is brought or over the property involved in the suit. The court must also have jurisdiction over the subject matter.

Jurisdiction over Persons. Generally, a court can exercise personal jurisdiction (*in personam* jurisdiction) over residents of a certain geographic area. A state trial court, for example, normally has jurisdictional authority over residents of a particular area of the state, such as a county or district. A state's highest court (often called the state supreme court)[2] has jurisdictional authority over all residents within the state.

In some cases, under the authority of a state **long arm statute**, a court can exercise personal jurisdiction over nonresident defendants as well. Before a court can exercise jurisdiction over a nonresident under a long arm statute, though, it must be demonstrated that the nonresident had sufficient contacts, or *minimum contacts,* with the state to justify the jurisdiction.[3] ● **EXAMPLE #1** If an individual has committed a wrong within the state, such as causing an automobile injury or selling defective goods, a court can usually exercise jurisdiction even if the person causing the harm is located in another state. Similarly, a state may exercise personal jurisdiction over a nonresident defendant who is sued for breaching a contract that was formed within the state. ●

In regard to corporations,[4] the minimum-contacts requirement is usually met if the corporation does business within the state. ● **EXAMPLE #2** Suppose that a corporation incorporated under the laws of Maine and headquartered in that state has a branch office or manufacturing plant in Georgia. Does this corporation have sufficient minimum contacts with the state of Georgia to allow a Georgia court to exercise jurisdiction over the Maine corporation? Yes, it does. If the Maine corporation advertises and sells its products in Georgia, those activities may suffice to meet the minimum-contacts requirement. ●

[2] As will be discussed shortly, a state's highest court is often referred to as the state supreme court, but there are exceptions. For example, in New York, the supreme court is a trial court.

[3] The minimum-contacts standard was established in *International Shoe Co. v. State of Washington,* 326 U.S. 310, 66 S.Ct. 154, 90 L.Ed. 95 (1945).

[4] In the eyes of the law, corporations are "legal persons"—entities that can sue and be sued. See Chapter 25.

Jurisdiction over Property. A court can also exercise jurisdiction over property that is located within its boundaries. This kind of jurisdiction is known as *in rem* jurisdiction, or "jurisdiction over the thing." ● EXAMPLE #3 Suppose that a dispute arises over the ownership of a boat in dry dock in Fort Lauderdale, Florida. The boat is owned by an Ohio resident, over whom a Florida court normally cannot exercise personal jurisdiction. The other party to the dispute is a resident of Nebraska. In this situation, a lawsuit concerning the boat could be brought in a Florida state court on the basis of the court's *in rem* jurisdiction. ●

Jurisdiction over Subject Matter. Jurisdiction over subject matter is a limitation on the types of cases a court can hear. In both the federal and state court systems, there are courts of *general* (unlimited) *jurisdiction* and courts of *limited jurisdiction*. An example of a court of general jurisdiction is a state trial court or a federal district court. An example of a state court of limited jurisdiction is a probate court. **Probate courts** are state courts that handle only matters relating to the transfer of a person's assets and obligations after that person's death, including matters relating to the custody and guardianship of children. An example of a federal court of limited subject-matter jurisdiction is a bankruptcy court. **Bankruptcy courts** handle only bankruptcy proceedings, which are governed by federal bankruptcy law (discussed in Chapter 21). In contrast, a court of general jurisdiction can decide a broad array of cases.

A court's jurisdiction over subject matter is usually defined in the statute or constitution creating the court. In both the federal and state court systems, a court's subject-matter jurisdiction can be limited not only by the subject of the lawsuit but also by the amount of money in controversy, by whether a case is a felony (a more serious type of crime) or a misdemeanor (a less serious type of crime), or by whether the proceeding is a trial or an appeal.

Original and Appellate Jurisdiction. The distinction between courts of original jurisdiction and courts of appellate jurisdiction normally lies in whether the case is being heard for the first time. Courts having original jurisdiction are courts of the first instance, or trial courts—that is, courts in which lawsuits begin, trials take place, and evidence is presented. In the federal court system, the *district courts* are trial courts. In the various state court systems, the trial courts are known by various names, as will be discussed shortly.

The key point here is that, normally, any court having original jurisdiction is known as a trial court. Courts having appellate jurisdiction act as reviewing courts, or appellate courts. In general, cases can be brought before appellate courts only on appeal from an order or a judgment of a trial court or other lower court.

Jurisdiction of the Federal Courts. Because the federal government is a government of limited powers, the jurisdiction of the federal courts is limited. Article III of the U.S. Constitution establishes the boundaries of federal judicial power. Section 2 of Article III states that "[t]he judicial Power shall extend to all Cases, in Law and Equity, arising under this Constitution, the Laws of the United States, and Treaties made, or which shall be made, under their Authority."

Whenever a plaintiff's cause of action is based, at least in part, on the U.S. Constitution, a treaty, or a federal law, then a **federal question** arises, and the case comes under the judicial power of the federal courts. Any lawsuit involving a federal question can originate in a federal court. People who claim that their rights under the U.S. Constitution have been violated can begin their suits in a federal court.

Federal district courts can also exercise original jurisdiction over cases involving **diversity of citizenship**. Such cases may arise between (1) citizens of different states, (2) a foreign country and citizens of a state or of different states, or (3) citizens of a state and citizens or subjects of a foreign country. The amount in controversy must be more than $75,000 before a federal court can take jurisdiction in such cases. For purposes of diversity jurisdiction, a corporation is a citizen of both the state in which it is incorporated and the state in which its principal place of business is located. A case involving diversity of citizenship can be filed in the appropriate federal district court, or, if the case starts in a state court, it can sometimes be transferred to a federal court. A large percentage of the cases filed in federal courts each year are based on diversity of citizenship.

Note that in a case based on a federal question, a federal court will apply federal law. In a case based on diversity of citizenship, however, a federal court will apply the relevant state law (which is often the law of the state in which the court sits).

Exclusive versus Concurrent Jurisdiction. When both federal and state courts have the power to hear a case, as is true in suits involving diversity of citizenship, **concurrent jurisdiction** exists. When cases can be tried only in federal courts or only in state courts, exclusive jurisdiction exists. Federal courts have **exclusive jurisdiction** in cases involving federal crimes, bankruptcy, patents, and copyrights; in suits against the United States; and in some areas of admiralty law (law governing transportation on the seas and ocean waters). States also have exclusive jurisdiction in certain subject matters—for example, in divorce and adoption. The concepts of exclusive and concurrent jurisdiction are illustrated in Exhibit 2–1.

When concurrent jurisdiction exists, a party has a choice of whether to bring a suit in, for example, a federal or a state court. The party's lawyer will consider several factors in coun-

EXHIBIT 2–1   EXCLUSIVE AND CONCURRENT JURISDICTION

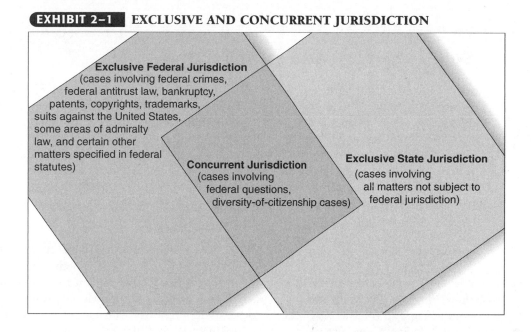

Exclusive Federal Jurisdiction
(cases involving federal crimes, federal antitrust law, bankruptcy, patents, copyrights, trademarks, suits against the United States, some areas of admiralty law, and certain other matters specified in federal statutes)

Concurrent Jurisdiction
(cases involving federal questions, diversity-of-citizenship cases)

Exclusive State Jurisdiction
(cases involving all matters not subject to federal jurisdiction)

seling the party as to which choice is preferable. The lawyer may prefer to litigate the case in a state court because he or she is more familiar with the state court's procedures, or perhaps the attorney believes that the state's judge or jury would be more sympathetic to the client and the case. Alternatively, the lawyer may advise the client to sue in federal court. Perhaps the state court's **docket** (the court's schedule listing the cases to be heard) is crowded, and the case could be brought to trial sooner in a federal court. Perhaps some feature of federal practice or procedure could offer an advantage in the client's case. Other important considerations include the law in an available jurisdiction, how that law has been applied in the jurisdiction's courts, and what the results in similar cases have been in that jurisdiction.

JURISDICTION IN CYBERSPACE

The Internet's capacity to bypass political and geographic boundaries undercuts the traditional basic limitations on a court's authority to exercise jurisdiction. These limits include a party's contacts with a court's geographic jurisdiction. As already discussed, for a court to compel a defendant to come before it, there must be at least minimum contacts—the presence of a salesperson within the state, for example. Are there sufficient minimum contacts if the only connection to a jurisdiction is an ad on the Web originating from a remote location?

The "Sliding-Scale" Standard. Gradually, the courts are developing a standard—called a "sliding-scale" standard— for determining when the exercise of jurisdiction over an

out-of-state defendant is proper. In developing this standard, the courts have identified three types of Internet business contacts. (1) substantial business conducted over the Internet (with contracts, sales, and so on); (2) some interactivity through a Web site; and (3) passive advertising. Jurisdiction is proper for the first category, improper for the third, and may or may not be appropriate for the second.[5] (For a discussion of whether a single e-mail can constitute "minimum contacts," see this chapter's *Business Law in the Online World* feature on the next page.)

International Jurisdictional Issues. Because the Internet is international in scope, international jurisdictional issues understandably have come to the fore. What seems to be emerging in the world's courts is a standard that echoes the requirement of "minimum contacts" applied by the U.S. courts. Most courts are indicating that minimum contacts— doing business within the jurisdiction, for example—are enough to compel a defendant to appear and that a physical presence is not necessary.[6] The effect of this standard is that a business firm has to comply with the laws in any jurisdiction in which it targets customers for its products.

---

[5] For a leading case on this issue, see *Zippo Manufacturing Co. v. Zippo Dot Com, Inc.,* 952 F.Supp. 1119 (W.D.Pa. 1997).

[6] An international conference is currently developing the Hague Convention on Jurisdiction, a proposed treaty that would make civil judgments enforceable across national borders. One issue in the negotiations is whether to require that all disputes be settled in the country of the seller or the country of the buyer. It has also been suggested that mandatory jurisdiction provisions be left out of the treaty.

BUSINESS LAW IN THE ONLINE WORLD
Web Contacts and Jurisdiction

In virtually every area of the law, the use of the Internet to conduct business activities has raised new legal questions—or, more often, new variations on old questions. This is certainly true with respect to jurisdiction. To be sure, the courts are coming to some consensus as to when jurisdiction over a Web site owner or operator in another state is proper. Yet cases continue to come before the courts that do not readily fit into the categories and rules being developed by case law.

Consider a case that recently came before a federal court sitting in Mississippi. The case involved a lawsuit brought by Internet Doorway, Inc., an Internet service provider based in Mississippi, against Connie Davis, a Texas resident. Internet Doorway alleged that Davis had sent an unsolicited e-mail message, advertising a pornographic Web site, to persons all over the world, including Mississippi residents. The problem for Internet Doorway was that Davis had falsified the "from" header to make the e-mail appear to have been sent from an Internet Doorway account. In its suit, Internet Doorway claimed that Davis had committed the tort (civil wrong—see Chapter 4) of trespass to chattels, or personal property—the property in this case consisting of Internet Doorway's name and Internet accounts. Internet Doorway claimed that its reputation and goodwill in the community had been harmed as a result of Davis's action. Davis asked the court to dismiss the case for lack of personal jurisdiction.

THE MINIMUM-CONTACTS REQUIREMENT Years

ago, in *International Shoe Co. v. State of Washington*,[a] the United States Supreme Court made it clear that before a state can exercise jurisdiction over a nonresident, the nonresident must have some minimum contacts with the state. If there were no minimum-contacts requirement, the exercise of personal jurisdiction "would offend traditional notions of fair play and substantial justice" mandated by the due process clause of the Fourteenth Amendment (see Chapter 1). Generally, the courts have concluded that a defendant's conduct in connection with the forum state (the state in which a lawsuit is initiated) must be such that she or he should reasonably anticipate "being haled into court" in that state.

DOES ONE E-MAIL CONSTITUTE "MINIMUM CONTACTS"? In determining whether jurisdiction over

Davis was proper, the federal court in Mississippi had to decide, among other things, whether Davis's single e-mail to Mississippi residents satisfied the minimum-contacts requirement for jurisdiction over an out-of-state defendant. The court held that "even a single contact" could satisfy the minimum-contacts requirement in certain situations, including this one.

In its reasoning, the court distinguished between "active" and "passive" Internet communications. In this case, the message was not posted on a "passive" Web site, which people would have to voluntarily access in order to read the message. Rather, the message was sent via "active" e-mail to specific recipients. The court further noted that exercising jurisdiction over Davis did not offend any notions of fair play and substantial justice. The court concluded that Davis, by sending her e-mail solicitation "to the far reaches of the earth," had done so "at her own peril." She should reasonably have expected that she could be "haled into court in a distant jurisdiction to answer for the ramifications of that [e-mail]."[b]

FOR CRITICAL ANALYSIS

What if Internet Doorway had never become aware of Davis's action? Davis would still have committed a tort, but who would file a suit?

a. 326 U.S. 310, 66 S.Ct. 154, 90 L.Ed. 95 (1945).

b. *Internet Doorway, Inc. v. Parks*, 138 F.Supp.2d 773 (S.D.Miss. 2001).

The question then arises as to whether, in light of current technology, it is possible to do business over the Internet in one jurisdiction but not in another. If a company provides a link on its Web site through which a person in one country can do business with the firm, is it technically possible for that company to block access to persons in other countries? This question was one of the issues in the following widely publicized case.

CASE 2.1   International League Against Racism and Antisemitism v. Yahoo! Inc.

Tribunal de Grande Instance de Paris, 2000.

FACTS Yahoo! Inc. operates a "Yahoo Auctions" Web site (at **http://auctions.yahoo.com**) that is directed principally at customers in the United States. Items offered for sale have included objects representing symbols of Nazi ideology. In France, the act of displaying such objects is a crime and is also subject to civil liability. The International League Against Racism and Antisemitism and others filed a suit in the Tribunal de Grande Instance de Paris (a French court) against Yahoo and others, seeking an injunction and damages. The court ordered Yahoo to, among other things, "take all necessary measures to dissuade and make impossible any access [by persons in France or French territory] via yahoo.com to the auction service for Nazi merchandise as well as to any other site or service that may be construed as an apology for Nazism or contesting the reality of Nazi crimes." Two months later, Yahoo returned to the court, arguing in part that the court did not have jurisdiction and that even if it did, Yahoo could not do technically what the court ordered.

ISSUE Does a business firm have to comply with the laws of a jurisdiction in which it targets business?

DECISION Yes. The court affirmed the injunction, reasoning that the "combination of [the] technical measures at [Yahoo's] disposal" rendered compliance possible. The court gave Yahoo three months to comply, after which it would be fined 100,000 francs (approximately $14,000) for each day that it failed to do so. The court also ordered Yahoo to pay each plaintiff 10,000 francs.

REASON First, the court reasoned that because "YAHOO is aware that it is addressing French parties," as evidenced by the Web site's advertising banners in French, "a sufficient basis is thus established in this case for a connecting link with France, which renders our jurisdiction perfectly competent to rule in this matter." Next, on the technical questions, the court found that "it is possible to determine the physical location of a surfer from the IP address" and that Yahoo "already carries out geographical identification of French surfers or surfers operating out of French territory and visiting its auctions site." Surfers "whose IP address is ambiguous" can be asked "to provide a declaration of nationality, * * * when the home page is reached, or when a search is initiated for Nazi objects * * * before the request is processed by the search engine." These techniques "would enable a filtering success rate approaching 90%." Also, Yahoo "would know the place of delivery, and would be in a position to prevent the delivery from taking place if the delivery address was located in France."

FOR CRITICAL ANALYSIS—Technological Consideration
With this case in mind, how is the technology that underlies the Internet likely to change?

COMMENT *As you read in Chapter 1, Yahoo filed a suit in a U.S. federal court, arguing that the French court's order was not enforceable in the United States on the ground that the order presented a "real and immediate threat" to Yahoo's constitutional right to free speech. The federal court agreed and refused to recognize the French court's order. See* Yahoo!, Inc. v. La Ligue Contre le Racisme et L'Antisemitisme, *169 F.Supp.2d 1181 (N.D.Cal. 2001).*

VENUE

Jurisdiction has to do with whether a court has authority to hear a case involving specific persons, property, or subject matter. **Venue**[7] is concerned with the most appropriate location for a trial. Two state courts (or two federal courts) may have the authority to exercise jurisdiction over a case, but it may be more appropriate or convenient to hear the case in one court than in the other.

Basically, the concept of venue reflects the policy that a court trying a suit should be in the geographic neighbor-

hood (usually the county) where the incident leading to the lawsuit occurred or where the parties involved in the lawsuit reside. Pretrial publicity or other factors, though, may require a change of venue to another community, especially in criminal cases in which the defendant's right to a fair and impartial jury has been impaired. ● **EXAMPLE #4** A change of venue from Oklahoma City to Denver, Colorado, was ordered for the trials of Timothy McVeigh and Terry Nichols, who had been indicted in connection with the 1995 bombing of the Alfred P. Murrah Federal Building in Oklahoma City. (At trial, both McVeigh and Nichols were convicted. McVeigh received the death penalty and was put to death by lethal injection in early 2001. Nichols was sentenced to life imprisonment.)●

---

[7] Pronounced *ven-yoo.*

STANDING TO SUE

Before a person can bring a lawsuit before a court, the party must have **standing to sue**, or a sufficient "stake" in a matter to justify seeking relief through the court system. In other words, a party must have a legally protected and tangible interest at stake in the litigation in order to have standing. The party bringing the lawsuit must have suffered a harm, or have been threatened by a harm, as a result of the action about which she or he complained. At times, a person will have standing to sue on behalf of another person. ● EXAMPLE #5 Suppose that a child suffered serious injuries as a result of a defectively manufactured toy. Because the child is a minor, a lawsuit could be brought on his or her behalf by another person, such as the child's parent or legal guardian.●

Standing to sue also requires that the controversy at issue be a **justiciable**[8] **controversy**—a controversy that is real and substantial, as opposed to hypothetical or academic. ● EXAMPLE #6 In the above example, the child's parent could not sue the toy manufacturer merely on the ground that the toy was defective. The issue would become justiciable only if the child had actually been injured due to the defect in the toy as marketed. In other words, the parent normally could not ask the court to determine, for example, what damages might be obtained if the child had been injured, because this would be merely a hypothetical question.●

[8] Pronounced jus-*tish*-uh-bul.

The State and Federal Court Systems

As mentioned earlier in this chapter, each state has its own court system. Additionally, there is a system of federal courts. Although state court systems differ, Exhibit 2–2 illustrates the basic organizational structure characteristic of the court systems in many states and how the federal court system is structured. The exhibit also shows how federal and state administrative agencies relate to the judicial structure. Decisions made during adjudication by federal administrative agencies may be appealed to a federal court. Similarly, decisions made by state administrative agencies may be appealed to a state court. We turn now to an examination of the federal and state court systems, beginning with the state courts.

STATE COURT SYSTEMS

Typically, a state court system will include several levels, or tiers, of courts. As shown in Exhibit 2–2, state courts may include (1) trial courts of limited jurisdiction, (2) trial courts of general jurisdiction, (3) appellate courts, and (4) the state's highest court (often called the state supreme court). Generally, any person who is a party to a lawsuit has the opportunity to plead the case before a trial court and then, if he or she loses, before at least one level of appellate court. Finally, if a federal statute or federal constitutional issue is involved in the decision of the state supreme court, that decision may be further appealed to the United States Supreme Court.

EXHIBIT 2–2 ▌ **FEDERAL AND STATE COURT SYSTEMS**

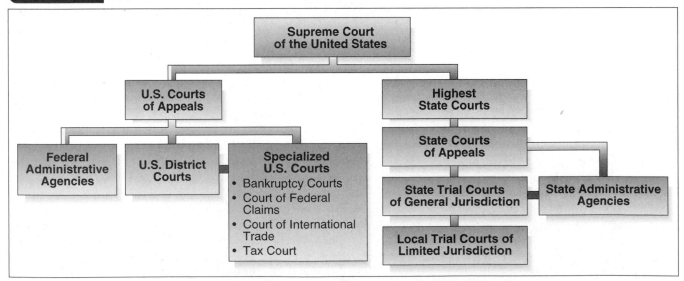

Judges in the state court system are usually elected by the voters for a specified term. In contrast, as you will read shortly, judges in the federal court system are appointed by the president of the United States and, if they are confirmed by the Senate, hold office for life—unless they engage in blatantly illegal conduct.

Trial Courts. Trial courts are exactly what their name implies—courts in which trials are held and testimony taken. State trial courts have either general or limited jurisdiction. Trial courts that have general jurisdiction as to subject matter may be called county, district, superior, or circuit courts.[9] The jurisdiction of these courts is often determined by the size of the county in which the court sits. State trial courts of general jurisdiction have jurisdiction over a wide variety of subjects, including both civil disputes and criminal prosecutions. In some states, trial courts of general jurisdiction may hear appeals from courts of limited jurisdiction.

Some courts of limited jurisdiction are called special inferior trial courts or minor judiciary courts. **Small claims courts** are inferior trial courts that hear only civil cases involving claims of less than a certain amount, such as $5,000 (the amount varies from state to state). Suits brought in small claims courts are generally conducted informally, and lawyers are not required. In a minority of states, lawyers are not even allowed to represent people in small claims courts for most purposes. Another example of an inferior trial court is a local municipal court that hears mainly traffic cases. Decisions of small claims courts and municipal courts may be appealed to a state trial court of general jurisdiction.

Other courts of limited jurisdiction as to subject matter include domestic relations courts, which handle only divorce actions and child-custody cases, and probate courts, as mentioned earlier.

Courts of Appeals. Every state has at least one court of appeals (appellate court, or reviewing court), which may be an intermediate appellate court or the state's highest court. About three-fourths of the states have intermediate appellate courts. Generally, courts of appeals do not conduct new trials, in which evidence is submitted to the court and witnesses are examined. Rather, an appellate court panel of three or more judges reviews the record of the case on appeal, which includes a transcript of the trial proceedings, and determines whether the trial court committed an error.

Usually, appellate courts do not look at questions of *fact* (such as whether a party did, in fact, commit a certain action, such as burning a flag) but at questions of *law* (such as whether the act of flag-burning is a form of speech protected by the First Amendment to the Constitution). Only a judge, not a jury, can rule on questions of law. Appellate courts normally defer to a trial court's findings on questions of fact because the trial court judge and jury were in a better position to evaluate testimony—by directly observing witnesses' gestures, demeanor, and nonverbal behavior during the trial. At the appellate level, the judges review the written transcript of the trial, which does not include these nonverbal elements.

An appellate court will challenge a trial court's finding of fact only when the finding is clearly erroneous (that is, when it is contrary to the evidence presented at trial) or when there is no evidence to support the finding. ● **EXAMPLE #7** If a jury concluded that a manufacturer's product harmed the plaintiff but no evidence was submitted to the court to support that conclusion, the appellate court would hold that the trial court's decision was erroneous.● The options exercised by appellate courts will be further discussed later in this chapter.

State Supreme (Highest) Courts. The highest appellate court in a state is usually called the supreme court but may be called by some other name. For example, in both New York and Maryland, the highest state court is called the court of appeals. The decisions of each state's highest court on all questions of state law are final. Only when issues of federal law are involved can a decision made by a state's highest court be overruled by the United States Supreme Court.

THE FEDERAL COURT SYSTEM

The federal court system is basically a three-tiered model consisting of (1) U.S. district courts (trial courts of general jurisdiction) and various courts of limited jurisdiction, (2) U.S. courts of appeals (intermediate courts of appeals), and (3) the United States Supreme Court.

Unlike state court judges, who are usually elected, federal court judges—including the justices of the Supreme Court—are appointed by the president of the United States and confirmed by the U.S. Senate. All federal judges receive lifetime appointments (because under Article III they "hold their offices during Good Behavior").

U.S. District Courts. At the federal level, the equivalent of a state trial court of general jurisdiction is the district court. There is at least one federal district court in every state. The

---

[9] The name in Ohio is court of common pleas; the name in New York is supreme court.

number of judicial districts can vary over time, primarily owing to population changes and corresponding caseloads. Currently, there are ninety-four federal judicial districts.

U.S. district courts have original jurisdiction in federal matters. Federal cases typically originate in district courts. There are other courts with original, but special (or limited), jurisdiction, such as the federal bankruptcy courts and others shown in Exhibit 2–2 on page 38.

U.S. Courts of Appeals. In the federal court system, there are thirteen U.S. courts of appeals—also referred to as U.S. circuit courts of appeals. The federal courts of appeals for twelve of the circuits, including the U.S. Court of Appeals for the District of Columbia Circuit, hear appeals from the federal district courts located within their respective judicial circuits. The Court of Appeals for the Thirteenth Circuit, called the Federal Circuit, has national appellate jurisdiction over certain types of cases, such as cases involving patent law and cases in which the U.S. government is a defendant.

The decisions of the circuit courts of appeals are final in most cases, but appeal to the United States Supreme Court is possible. Exhibit 2–3 shows the geographic boundaries of the U.S. circuit courts of appeals and the boundaries of the U.S. district courts within each circuit.

The United States Supreme Court. The highest level of the three-tiered model of the federal court system is the United States Supreme Court. According to the language of Article III of the U.S. Constitution, there is only one national Supreme Court. All other courts in the federal system are considered "inferior." Congress is empowered to create other inferior courts as it deems necessary. The inferior courts that Congress has created include the second tier in our model—the U.S. courts of appeals—as well as the district courts and any other courts of limited, or specialized, jurisdiction.

The United States Supreme Court consists of nine justices. Although the Supreme Court has original, or trial, jurisdiction in rare instances (set forth in Article III, Section 2), most of its work is as an appeals court. The Supreme Court can review any case decided by any of the federal courts of appeals, and it also has appellate authority over some cases decided in the state courts.

EXHIBIT 2–3   U.S. COURTS OF APPEALS AND U.S. DISTRICT COURTS

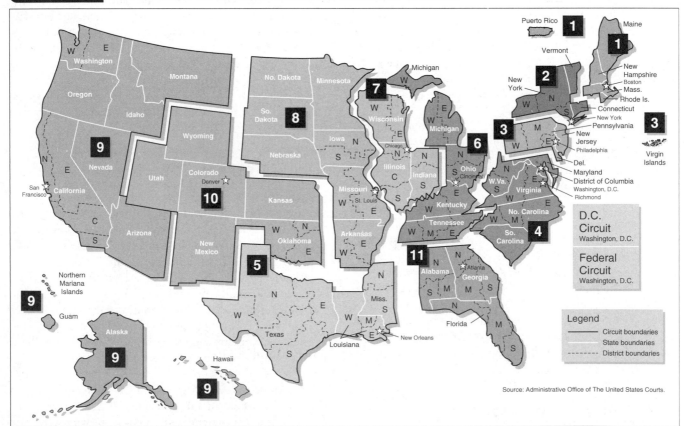

Source: Administrative Office of The United States Courts.

Appeals to the Supreme Court. To bring a case before the Supreme Court, a party requests the Court to issue a writ of *certiorari*. A **writ of *certiorari***[10] is an order issued by the Supreme Court to a lower court requiring the latter to send it the record of the case for review. The Court will not issue a writ unless at least four of the nine justices approve of it. This is called the **rule of four**. Whether the Court will issue a writ of *certiorari* is entirely within its discretion. The Court is not required to issue one, and most petitions for writs are denied. (Thousands of cases are filed with the Supreme Court each year, yet it hears, on average, fewer than one hundred of these cases.)[11] A denial is not a decision on the merits of a case, nor does it indicate agreement with the lower court's opinion. Furthermore, a denial of the writ has no value as a precedent.

Petitions Granted by the Court. Typically, the petitions granted by the Court involve cases that raise important constitutional questions or cases that conflict with other state or federal court decisions. Similarly, if federal appellate courts are rendering inconsistent opinions on an important issue, the Supreme Court may review the case and issue a decision to define the law on the matter. The justices, however, never explain their reasons for hearing certain cases and not others, so it is difficult to predict which type of case the Court might select.

Certainly, many legal scholars were surprised when the Court, in the confusing aftermath of the 2000 elections, decided to review the Florida Supreme Court's decision that the votes in selected Florida counties could be manually recounted. Many observers had predicted that, given the Court's tendency to support states' rights and its traditional reluctance to get involved in "political questions," it would deny *certiorari* in that case. The Court, however, concluded that the case raised an important constitutional question—whether manually counting votes in some counties but not others violated the equal protection clause—and thus reviewed (and overturned) the Florida court's decision.[12]

Following a State Court Case

To illustrate the procedures that would be followed in a civil lawsuit brought in a state court, we present a hypothetical case and follow it through the state court system. The case involves an automobile accident in which Kevin Anderson, driving a Mercedes, struck Lisa Marconi, driving a Ford Taurus. The accident occurred at the intersection of Wilshire Boulevard and Rodeo Drive in Beverly Hills, California. Marconi suffered personal injuries, incurring medical and hospital expenses as well as lost wages for four months. Anderson and Marconi are unable to agree on a settlement, and Marconi sues Anderson. Marconi is the plaintiff, and Anderson is the defendant. Both are represented by lawyers.

During each phase of the **litigation** (the process of working a lawsuit through the court system), Marconi and Anderson will be required to observe strict procedural requirements. A large body of law—procedural law—establishes the rules and standards for determining disputes in courts. Procedural rules are very complex, and they vary from court to court. There is a set of federal rules of procedure as well as various sets of rules for state courts. Additionally, the applicable procedures will depend on whether the case is a civil or criminal proceeding. Generally, the Marconi-Anderson civil lawsuit will involve the procedures discussed in the following subsections. Keep in mind that attempts to settle the case may be ongoing throughout the trial.

THE PLEADINGS

The complaint and answer (and the counterclaim and reply)—all of which are discussed below—taken together are called the **pleadings**. The pleadings inform each party of the other's claims and specify the issues (disputed questions) involved in the case.

The Plaintiff's Complaint. Marconi's suit against Anderson begins when her lawyer files a **complaint** with the appropriate court. The complaint contains a statement alleging (asserting to the court, in a pleading) the facts necessary for the court to take jurisdiction, a brief summary of the facts necessary to show that the plaintiff is entitled to a remedy, and a statement of the remedy the plaintiff is seeking. Exhibit 2–4 on the next page illustrates how the complaint might read in the Marconi-Anderson case. Complaints may be lengthy or brief, depending on the complexity of the case.

After the complaint has been filed, the sheriff, a deputy of the county, or another *process server* (one who delivers a complaint and summons) serves a **summons** and a copy of the complaint on defendant Anderson. The summons notifies Anderson that he must file an answer to the complaint with both the court and the plaintiff's attorney within a specified time period (usually twenty to thirty days). The summons also informs Anderson that failure to answer may

---

[10] Pronounced sur-shee-uh-*rah*-ree.
[11] From the mid-1950s through the early 1990s, the Supreme Court reviewed more cases per year than it has in the last few years. In the Court's 1982–1983 term, for example, the Court issued opinions in 151 cases. In contrast, in its 2002–2003 term, the Court issued opinions in only 80 cases.
[12] *Bush v. Gore,* 531 U.S. 98, 121 S.Ct. 525, 148 L.Ed.2d 388 (2000).

EXHIBIT 2–4   **EXAMPLE OF A TYPICAL COMPLAINT**

IN THE LOS ANGELES MUNICIPAL COURT
FOR THE LOS ANGELES JUDICIAL DISTRICT

CIVIL NO. 8–1026

Lisa Marconi
        Plaintiff

v.

                                                              COMPLAINT

Kevin Anderson
        Defendant

Comes now the plaintiff and for her cause of action against the defendant alleges and states as follows:

1. The jurisdiction of this court is based on Section 86 of the California Civil Code.
2. This action is between plaintiff, a California resident living at 1434 Palm Drive, Anaheim, California, and defendant, a California resident living at 6950 Garrison Avenue, Los Angeles, California.
3. On September 10, 2004, plaintiff, Lisa Marconi, was exercising good driving habits and reasonable care in driving her car through the intersection of Rodeo Drive and Wilshire Boulevard when defendant, Kevin Anderson, negligently drove his vehicle through a red light at the intersection and collided with plaintiff's vehicle. Defendant was negligent in the operation of the vehicle as to:

     a. Speed,
     b. Lookout,
     c. Management and control.

4. As a result of the collision plaintiff suffered severe physical injury that prevented her from working and property damage to her car. The costs she incurred included $10,000 in medical bills, $9,000 in lost wages, and $5,000 for automobile repairs.

WHEREFORE, plaintiff demands judgment against the defendant for the sum of $24,000 plus interest at the maximum legal rate and the costs of this action.

By _____*Roger Harrington*_____
Roger Harrington
Attorney for the Plaintiff
800 Orange Avenue
Anaheim, CA 91426

result in a **default judgment** for the plaintiff, meaning the plaintiff will be awarded the damages alleged in her complaint.

How service of process occurs depends on the rules of the court or jurisdiction in which the lawsuit is brought. Under the Federal Rules of Civil Procedure (FRCP), service of process in federal court cases may be effected by anyone who is not a party to the lawsuit and who is at least eighteen years of age. In state courts, the process server is often a county sheriff. Usually, the server effects the service by handing the summons to the defendant personally or by leaving it at the defendant's residence or place of business. In a few states, a summons can be served by mail if the defendant so agrees. When the defendant cannot be reached, special rules sometimes permit the summons to be served by leaving it with a designated person, such as the state's secretary of state.

In the following case, the issue was whether service of process could be accomplished via e-mail.

CASE 2.2 Rio Properties, Inc. v. Rio International Interlink

United States Court of Appeals,
Ninth Circuit, 2002.
284 F.3d 1007.

FACTS Rio International Interlink (RII) is a Costa Rican entity that participates in an Internet sports gambling operation, doing business as Rio International Sportsbook, Rio Online Sportsbook, or Rio International Sports, at **http:// www.riosports.com**. RII grosses an estimated $3 million annually. Rio Properties, Inc. (Rio), owns a gambling casino in Las Vegas, Nevada. When Rio became aware of RII's operation, Rio demanded that RII stop infringing Rio's trademark. RII disabled the "riosports" site but soon activated **http:// www.betrio.com** to host an identical operation. Rio filed a suit in a federal district court against RII, alleging trademark infringement. To effect service of process, Rio attempted to locate RII, but its U.S. address housed only its international courier, which was not authorized to accept service on RII's behalf, and RII did not have an address in Costa Rica. RII advertised that it preferred communication through its e-mail address, **email@betrio.com**. Unable to serve RII by traditional means, Rio filed a motion for alternative service of process, asking the court for permission to serve RII via its e-mail address. The court granted the motion. When RII later failed to comply with the court's orders for discovery (discovery is discussed later in this chapter), the court entered a default judgment against RII. RII appealed to the U.S. Court of Appeals for the Ninth Circuit, alleging in part that the service of process was insufficient.

ISSUE Was the service of process by e-mail sufficient?

DECISION Yes. The U.S. Court of Appeals for the Ninth Circuit upheld the lower court's order for service of process via e-mail.

REASON Because RII did not have an address in the United States or Costa Rica at which service could be accomplished through traditional means, and RII advertised that it preferred contact through its e-mail address, service by e-mail was proper. E-mail was also "the method of service most likely to reach RII." The court also pointed out that the "Constitution does not require any particular means of service of process, only that the method selected be reasonably calculated to provide notice and an opportunity to respond. In proper circumstances, this broad constitutional principle unshackles the federal courts from anachronistic methods of service and permits them entry into the technological renaissance. * * * Indeed, when faced with an international e-business scofflaw [habitual violator], playing hide-and-seek with the federal court, e-mail may be the only means of effecting service of process. Certainly in this case, it was a means reasonably calculated to apprise RII of * * * the lawsuit, and the Constitution requires nothing more."

FOR CRITICAL ANALYSIS—Technological Consideration
Suppose that there had been a reasonable alternative to e-mail for service of process against RII. Would that mean that service by e-mail was not reasonable? Would the availability of such an alternative have altered the court's reasoning and decision in this case?

The Defendant's Answer. The defendant's **answer** either admits the statements or allegations set forth in the complaint or denies them and outlines any defenses that the defendant may have. If Anderson admits to all of Marconi's allegations in his answer, the court will enter a judgment for Marconi. If Anderson denies any of Marconi's allegations, the litigation will go forward.

Anderson can deny Marconi's allegations and set forth his own claim that Marconi was in fact negligent and therefore owes him money for damages to his Mercedes. This is appropriately called a **counterclaim**. If Anderson files a

counterclaim, Marconi will have to answer it with a pleading, normally called a **reply**, which has the same characteristics as an answer.

Anderson can also admit the truth of Marconi's complaint but raise new facts that may result in dismissal of the action. This is called raising an affirmative defense. For example, Anderson could assert the expiration of the time period under the relevant statute of limitations (a state or federal statute that sets the maximum time period during which a certain action can be brought or rights enforced) as an affirmative defense.

Motion to Dismiss. A motion to dismiss requests the court to dismiss the case for stated reasons. A defendant often makes a motion to dismiss before filing an answer to the plaintiff's complaint. Grounds for dismissal of a case include improper delivery of the complaint and summons, improper venue, and the plaintiff's failure to state a claim for which a court could grant relief (a remedy). For example, if Marconi had suffered no injuries or losses as a result of Anderson's negligence, Anderson could move to have the case dismissed because Marconi had not stated a claim for which relief could be granted.

If the judge grants the motion to dismiss, the plaintiff generally is given time to file an amended complaint. If the judge denies the motion, the suit will go forward, and the defendant must then file an answer. Note that if Marconi wishes to discontinue the suit because, for example, an out-of-court settlement has been reached, she can likewise move for dismissal. The court can also dismiss the case on its own motion.

PRETRIAL MOTIONS

Either party may attempt to get the case dismissed before trial through the use of various pretrial motions. We have already mentioned the motion to dismiss. Two other important pretrial motions are the motion for judgment on the pleadings and the motion for summary judgment.

At the close of the pleadings, either party may make a **motion for judgment on the pleadings**, or on the merits of the case. The judge will grant the motion only when there is no dispute over the facts of the case and the only issue to be resolved is a question of law. In deciding on the motion, the judge may consider only the evidence contained in the pleadings.

In contrast, in a **motion for summary judgment** the court may consider evidence outside the pleadings, such as sworn statements (affidavits) by parties or witnesses or other documents relating to the case. A motion for summary judgment can be made by either party. As with the motion for judgment on the pleadings, a motion for summary judgment will be granted only if there are no genuine questions of fact and the only question is a question of law.

DISCOVERY

Before a trial begins, each party can use a number of procedural devices to obtain information and gather evidence about the case from the other party or from third parties. The process of obtaining such information is known as **discovery**. Discovery includes gaining access to witnesses, documents, records, and other types of evidence.

The Federal Rules of Civil Procedure and similar rules in the states set forth the guidelines for discovery activity. The rules governing discovery are designed to make sure that a witness or a party is not unduly harassed, that privileged material (communications that need not be presented in court) is safeguarded, and that only matters relevant to the case at hand are discoverable.

Discovery prevents surprises at trial by giving parties access to evidence that might otherwise be hidden. This allows both parties to learn as much as they can about what to expect at a trial before they reach the courtroom.[13] It also serves to narrow the issues so that trial time is spent on the main questions in the case.

Depositions and Interrogatories. Discovery can involve the use of depositions or interrogatories, or both. **Depositions** are sworn testimony by a party to the lawsuit or any witness. The person being deposed (the deponent) answers questions asked by the attorneys, and the questions and answers are recorded by an authorized court official and sworn to and signed by the deponent. (Occasionally, written depositions are taken when witnesses are unable to appear in person.) The answers given to depositions will, of course, help the attorneys prepare their cases. They can also be used in court to impeach (challenge the credibility of) a party or a witness who changes testimony at the trial. In addition, the answers given in a deposition can be used as testimony if the witness is not available at trial.

Interrogatories are written questions for which written answers are prepared and then signed under oath. The main difference between interrogatories and written depositions is that interrogatories are directed to a party to the lawsuit (the plaintiff or the defendant), not to a witness, and the party can prepare answers with the aid of an attorney. The scope of interrogatories is broader, because parties are obligated to answer questions, even if it means disclosing information from their records and files.

Other Information. A party can serve a written request to the other party for an admission of the truth of matters relating to the trial. Any matter admitted under such a request is conclusively established for the trial. For example, Marconi can ask Anderson to admit that he was driving at a speed of forty-five miles an hour. A request for admission saves time at trial, because the parties will not have to spend time proving facts on which they already agree.

---

[13] This is particularly evident in the Federal Rules of Civil Procedure, as revised in 1993. The rules provide that each party must disclose to the other, on an ongoing basis, the types of evidence that will be presented at trial, the names of witnesses that may or will be called, and so on.

A party can also gain access to documents and other items not in her or his possession in order to inspect and examine them. Likewise, a party can gain "entry upon land" to inspect the premises. Anderson's attorney, for example, normally can gain permission to inspect and duplicate Marconi's car repair bills.

When the physical or mental condition of one party is in question, the opposing party can ask the court to order a physical or mental examination. If the court is willing to make the order, which it will do only if the need for the information outweighs the right to privacy of the person to be examined, the opposing party can obtain the results of the examination.

Electronic Discovery and Compliance Costs. Any relevant material, including information stored electronically, may be the object of a discovery request. As individuals and businesses have increased their use of computers to create and store documents, make deals, and exchange e-mail, the universe of discoverable material has expanded exponentially. The more information there is to discover, however, the more expensive it is to unearth all of the relevant data.

Generally, the party responding to a discovery request must pay the expenses involved in obtaining the asked-for materials. A court can limit the scope of a request, however, if compliance would be too burdensome or the cost would be too high. When compliance becomes too arduous or too expensive, a court may also shift the costs of discovery to the requesting party. A contentious issue has been the point at which such "cost shifting" should occur. In the following case, which involved the discovery of electronic data, the court developed a new set of factors for determining when discovery costs should be shifted to the requester.

CASE 2.3   Zubulake v. UBS Warburg, LLC

United States District Court,
Southern District of New York, 2003.
__ F.Supp.2d __.

FACTS UBS Warburg, LLC, an investment sales firm, hired Laura Zubulake in August 1999 as a director and senior salesperson in a department managed by Dominic Vail. Zubulake was told that she would be considered for Vail's position if it became vacant. In December 2000, however, when the position opened, she was not even interviewed—UBS hired Matthew Chapin instead. Less than eight months later, Zubulake filed a charge with the Equal Employment Opportunity Commission, alleging that Chapin had, among other things, excluded her from employment-related activities with male co-workers and clients.[a] Less than eight weeks later, she was fired. She filed a suit in a federal district court against UBS, alleging violations of antidiscrimination laws. As part of a discovery request, Zubulake asked UBS for "[a]ll documents concerning any communication by or between UBS employees concerning Plaintiff," including "without limitation, electronic or computerized data compilations." UBS produced one hundred pages of e-mail but refused to search further, claiming that the cost would be too high.

ISSUE Should the costs of discovery of electronic data be shifted to the requesting party when that data is relatively inaccessible?

DECISION Yes. The court set out a new seven-factor test for determining this issue. Based on the test, the court ordered UBS to retrieve all data from easily accessible media at its own expense. The court also ordered the defendant to retrieve, from a "relatively inaccessible" medium, certain sample data, the expense and content of which the court would review to decide whether the plaintiff should pay the cost of retrieving more.

REASON The court identified a three-step analysis for deciding disputes over discovery costs. "*First,* it is necessary to thoroughly understand the responding party's computer system, both with respect to active and stored data. For data that is kept in an accessible format, the usual rules of discovery apply: the responding party should pay the costs of producing responsive data. A court should consider cost-shifting *only* when electronic data is relatively inaccessible * * * . *Second,* * * * it is necessary to determine what data may be found on the inaccessible media. Requiring the responding party to restore and produce responsive documents from a small sample of the requested [medium] is a sensible approach in most cases. *Third,* * * * the following factors should be considered, weighted more-or-less in the following

---

a. This allegation and Zubulake's other charges are related to employment discrimination, which is discussed in detail in Chapter 23.

(Continued)

CASE 2.3—Continued

order:" the extent to which the request is specifically tailored, the availability of the information from other sources, the total cost of production compared to the amount in controversy, the total cost of production compared to the resources available to each party, the relative ability of each party to control costs, the importance of the issues at stake, and the relative benefits to the parties of obtaining the information.

FOR CRITICAL ANALYSIS—Economic Consideration
Should cost shifting be considered in every case involving the discovery of electronic data?

PRETRIAL CONFERENCE

Either party or the court can request a pretrial conference, or hearing. Usually, the hearing consists of an informal discussion between the judge and the opposing attorneys after discovery has taken place. The purpose of the hearing is to explore the possibility of a settlement without trial and, if this is not possible, to identify the matters that are in dispute and to plan the course of the trial.

JURY SELECTION

A trial can be held with or without a jury. The Seventh Amendment to the U.S. Constitution guarantees the right to a jury trial for cases in federal courts when the amount in controversy exceeds $20. Most states have similar guarantees in their own constitutions (although the threshold dollar amount is higher than $20). The right to a trial by jury does not have to be exercised, and many cases are tried without a jury. In most states and in federal courts, one of the parties must request a jury, or the right is presumed to be waived.

Before a jury trial commences, a jury must be selected. The jury selection process is known as *voir dire*.[14] In most jurisdictions, *voir dire* consists of oral questions that attorneys for the plaintiff and the defendant ask prospective jurors to determine whether a potential jury member is biased or has any connection with a party to the action or with a prospective witness.

During *voir dire*, a party may challenge a certain number of prospective jurors *peremptorily*—that is, ask that an individual not be sworn in as a juror without providing any reason. Alternatively, a party may challenge a prospective juror *for cause*—that is, provide a reason why an individual should not be sworn in as a juror. If the judge grants the challenge, the individual is asked to step down. A prospective juror may not be excluded from the jury by the use of discriminatory challenges, however, such as those based on racial criteria[15] or gender.[16]

AT THE TRIAL

At the beginning of the trial, the attorneys present their opening arguments, setting forth the facts that they expect to prove during the trial. Then the plaintiff's case is presented. In our hypothetical case, Marconi's lawyer would introduce evidence (relevant documents, exhibits, and the testimony of witnesses) to support Marconi's position. The defendant has the opportunity to challenge any evidence introduced and to cross-examine any of the plaintiff's witnesses.

At the end of the plaintiff's case, the defendant's attorney has the opportunity to ask the judge to direct a verdict for the defendant on the ground that the plaintiff has presented no evidence that would justify the granting of the plaintiff's remedy. This is called a **motion for a directed verdict** (known in federal courts as a *motion for judgment as a matter of law*). In considering the motion, the judge looks at the evidence in the light most favorable to the plaintiff and grants the motion only if there is insufficient evidence to raise an issue of fact. If the motion is not granted (it seldom is), the defendant's attorney then presents the evidence and witnesses for the defendant's case. At the conclusion of the defendant's case, the defendant's attorney has another opportunity to make a motion for a directed verdict. The plaintiff's attorney can challenge any evidence introduced and cross-examine the defendant's witnesses.

After the defense concludes its presentation, the attorneys present their closing arguments, each urging a verdict in favor of her or his client. The judge instructs the jury in the law that applies to the case (these instructions are often called *charges*), and the jury retires to the jury room to

---

[14] Pronounced vwahr *deehr.* These Old French verbs mean "to speak the truth." In legal language, the phrase refers to the process of interrogating prospective jurors to learn about their backgrounds, attitudes, and so on.

[15] *Batson v. Kentucky,* 476 U.S. 79, 106 S.Ct. 1712, 90 L.Ed.2d 69 (1986).
[16] *J.E.B. v. Alabama ex rel. T.B.,* 511 U.S. 127, 114 S.Ct. 1419, 128 L.Ed.2d 89 (1994). (*Ex rel.* is Latin for *ex relatione.* The phrase refers to an action brought on behalf of the state, by the attorney general, at the instigation of an individual who has a private interest in the matter.)

deliberate a verdict. In the Marconi-Anderson case, the jury will not only decide for the plaintiff or for the defendant but, if it finds for the plaintiff, will also decide on the amount of the **award** (the money to be paid to her).

POSTTRIAL MOTIONS

After the jury has rendered its verdict, either party may make a posttrial motion. If Marconi wins, and Anderson's attorney has previously moved for a directed verdict, Anderson's attorney may make a **motion for judgment n.o.v.** (from the Latin *non obstante veredicto,* which means "notwithstanding the verdict"—called a *motion for judgment as a matter of law* in the federal courts) in Anderson's favor on the ground that the jury verdict in favor of Marconi was unreasonable and erroneous. If the judge decides that the jury's verdict was reasonable in light of the evidence presented at trial, the motion will be denied. If the judge agrees with Anderson's attorney, then he or she will set the jury's verdict aside and enter a judgment in favor of Anderson.

Alternatively, Anderson could make a **motion for a new trial,** requesting the judge to set aside the adverse verdict and to hold a new trial. The motion will be granted if the judge is convinced, after looking at all the evidence, that the jury was in error but does not feel it is appropriate to grant judgment for the other side. A new trial may also be granted on the ground of newly discovered evidence, misconduct by the participants or the jury during the trial, or error by the judge.

THE APPEAL

Assume here that any posttrial motion is denied and that Anderson appeals the case. (If Marconi wins but receives a smaller money award than she sought, she can appeal as well.) A notice of appeal must be filed with the clerk of the trial court within a prescribed time. Anderson now becomes the appellant, or petitioner, and Marconi becomes the appellee, or respondent.

Filing the Appeal. Anderson's attorney files with the appellate court the record on appeal, which includes the pleadings, the trial transcript, the judge's rulings on motions made by the parties, and other trial-related documents. Anderson's attorney will also provide a condensation of the record, known as an abstract, which is filed with the reviewing court along with the brief. The **brief** is a formal legal document outlining the facts and issues of the case, the judge's rulings or jury's findings that should be reversed or modified, the applicable law, and arguments on Anderson's behalf (citing applicable statutes and relevant cases as precedents).

Marconi's attorney will file an answering brief. Anderson's attorney can file a reply to Marconi's brief, although it is not required. The reviewing court then considers the case.

Appellate Review. As mentioned earlier, a court of appeals does not hear evidence. Rather, it reviews the record for errors of law. Its decision concerning a case is based on the record on appeal, the abstracts, and the attorneys' briefs. The attorneys can present oral arguments, after which the case is taken under advisement. In general, appellate courts do not reverse findings of fact unless the findings are unsupported or contradicted by the evidence.

If the reviewing court believes that an error was committed during the trial or that the jury was improperly instructed, the judgment will be *reversed.* Sometimes the case will be *remanded* (sent back to the court that originally heard the case) for a new trial.

● EXAMPLE #8 A case may be remanded for several reasons. For instance, if the appellate court decides that a judge improperly granted summary judgment, the case will be remanded for trial. If the appellate court decides that the trial judge erroneously applied the law, the case will be remanded for a new trial, with instructions to the trial court to apply the law as clarified by the appellate court. If the appellate court decides that the trial jury's award of damages was too high, the case will be remanded with instructions to reduce the damages award.● In most cases, the judgment of the lower court is *affirmed,* resulting in the enforcement of the court's judgment or decree.

Most of the state court opinions presented in this book are from state appellate courts. In part, this is because most state trial court decisions are not published in reporters (see the appendix to Chapter 1) and are thus not readily available. Also important, however, is the fact that appellate courts decide questions of law, and all trial courts within that jurisdiction will be obligated to follow the appellate court's opinion with respect to a particular issue. Thus, appellate court decisions have a broader reach and more final authority than decisions rendered by trial courts. Even when a case is remanded to a trial court for further proceedings, the appellate court normally spells out how the relevant law should be interpreted and applied to the case. Thus, you may not learn about the ultimate disposition of a case after it has been remanded, but you will discover the relevant legal principles and laws that apply to the case.

Appeal to a Higher Appellate Court. If the reviewing court is an intermediate appellate court, the losing party normally may appeal to the state supreme court (the highest state court). Such a petition corresponds to a petition for a writ of *certiorari* from the United States Supreme Court. If the petition is granted (in some states, a petition is automatically granted), new briefs must be filed before the state supreme court, and the attorneys may be allowed or requested to present oral arguments. Like the intermediate appellate courts, the supreme court may reverse or affirm the appellate court's decision or remand the case. If the state supreme court affirms the appellate court's ruling, the case has reached its end—unless a federal question is at issue.

ENFORCING THE JUDGMENT

The uncertainties of the litigation process are compounded by the lack of guarantees that any judgment will be enforceable. Even if a plaintiff wins an award of damages in court, the defendant may not have sufficient assets or insurance to cover that amount. Usually, one of the factors considered before a lawsuit is initiated is whether the defendant has sufficient assets to cover the amount of damages sought, should the plaintiff win the case.

The Courts Adapt to the Online World

We have already mentioned how the courts have attempted to adapt traditional jurisdictional concepts to the online world. Not surprisingly, the Internet has also brought about changes in court procedures and practices, including new methods for filing pleadings and other documents and issuing decisions and opinions. Several courts are experimenting with electronic delivery, using the Internet or CD-ROM. Some jurisdictions are exploring the possibility of cyber courts, in which legal proceedings could be conducted totally online.

ELECTRONIC FILING

The federal court system first experimented with an electronic filing system in January 1996, in an asbestos case heard by the U.S. District Court for the Northern District of Ohio. Currently, a number of federal courts permit attorneys to file documents electronically in certain types of cases. By May 2003, documents in more than seven million cases had been filed electronically in federal courts. The Administrative Office of the U.S. Courts expects that electronic filing will be available for all federal courts by 2005.

State and local courts are also setting up electronic court filing systems. Since the late 1990s, the court system in Pima County, Arizona, has been accepting pleadings via e-mail. The supreme court of the state of Washington also now accepts online filings of litigation documents. Electronic filing projects are also being developed in other states, including California, Idaho, Kansas, Maryland, Michigan, Mississippi, Texas, Utah, and Virginia. Notably, the judicial branch of the state of Colorado has implemented the first statewide court e-filing system in the United States. E-filing is now an option in three hundred courts in that state. In California, Florida, and some other states, some court clerks offer docket information and other searchable databases online.

Typically, when electronic filing is made available, it is optional. In 2001, however, a trial court judge in the District of Columbia launched a pilot project that *required* attorneys to file electronically all documents relating to certain types of civil cases.

COURTS ONLINE

Most courts today have sites on the Web. Of course, it is up to each court to decide what to make available at its site. Some courts display only the names of court personnel and office phone numbers. Others add court rules and forms. Some include judicial decisions, although generally the sites do not feature archives of old decisions. Instead, decisions are available online for only a limited time. For example, California keeps opinions online for only sixty days.

Appellate court decisions are often posted online immediately after they are rendered. Recent decisions of the U.S. courts of appeals, for example, are available online at their Web sites. The United States Supreme Court has also launched an official Web site and publishes its opinions there immediately after they are announced to the public.

CYBER COURTS AND PROCEEDINGS

Someday, litigants may be able to use cyber courts, in which judicial proceedings take place only on the Internet. The parties to a case could meet online to make their arguments and present their evidence. This might be done with e-mail submissions, via video cameras, in designated "chat" rooms, at closed sites, or through the use of other Internet facilities. These courtrooms could be efficient and economical. We might also see the use of virtual lawyers, judges, and juries—and possibly the replacement of court personnel with computers or software.

The governor of Michigan recently proposed that separate cyber courts be created for cases involving technology and high-tech businesses. In these courts, everything would be done using computers and the Internet, rather than in a courtroom. The state of Maryland is also planning a separate judicial division for cases involving high-tech businesses. Many lawyers predict that other states will do likewise.

The courts may also use the Internet in other ways. In a ground-breaking decision in early 2001, for example, a

Florida county court granted "virtual" visitation rights in a couple's divorce proceeding. Although the court granted custody rights to the father of the couple's ten-year-old daughter, the court also ordered each parent to buy a computer and a videoconferencing system so that the mother could "visit" with her child via the Internet at any time.[17]

Alternative Dispute Resolution

Litigation is expensive. It is also time consuming. Because of the backlog of cases pending in many courts, several years may pass before a case is actually tried. For these and other reasons, more and more businesspersons are turning to **alternative dispute resolution (ADR)** as a means of settling their disputes.

Methods of ADR range from neighbors sitting down over a cup of coffee in an attempt to work out their differences to huge multinational corporations agreeing to resolve a dispute through a formal hearing before a panel of experts. The great advantage of ADR is its flexibility. Normally, the parties themselves can control how the dispute will be settled, what procedures will be used, and whether the decision reached (either by themselves or by a neutral third party) will be legally binding or nonbinding.

Today, about 95 percent of cases are settled before trial through some form of ADR. Indeed, the majority of the states either require or encourage parties to undertake ADR prior to trial. Several federal courts have instituted ADR programs as well. In the following pages, we examine various forms of ADR. Keep in mind, though, that ADR is an ongoing experiment. In other words, new methods of ADR—or new combinations of existing methods—are continuously being devised and employed. In recent years, several organizations have been offering dispute-resolution services via the Internet. After looking at traditional forms of ADR, we examine some of the ways in which disputes are being resolved in various online forums.

NEGOTIATION

One of the simplest forms of ADR is **negotiation**, a process in which the parties attempt to settle their dispute informally, with or without attorneys to represent them.

---

[17] For a discussion of this case, see Shelley Emling, "After the Divorce, Internet Visits?" *Austin American-Statesman,* January 30, 2001, pp. A1 and A10.

Attorneys frequently advise their clients to negotiate a settlement voluntarily rather than proceed to trial.

Negotiation traditionally involves just the parties themselves and (typically) their attorneys. The attorneys, though, are advocates—they are obligated to put their clients' interests first. Often, parties find it helpful to have the opinion and guidance of a neutral (unbiased) third party when deciding whether or how to negotiate a settlement of their dispute. The methods of ADR discussed next all involve neutral third parties.

MEDIATION

In the **mediation** process, the parties themselves attempt to negotiate an agreement, but with the assistance of a neutral third party, a mediator. In mediation, the mediator talks with the parties separately as well as jointly. The mediator emphasizes points of agreement, helps the parties evaluate their positions, and proposes solutions. The mediator, however, does not make a decision on the matter being disputed. The mediator, who need not be a lawyer, usually charges a fee for his or her services (which can be split between the parties). States that require parties to undergo ADR before trial often offer mediation as one of the ADR options or (as in Florida) the only option.

Mediation is not adversarial in nature, as lawsuits are. In litigation, the parties "do battle" with each other in the courtroom, while the judge is the neutral party. Because of its nonadversarial nature, the mediation process tends to reduce the antagonism between the disputants and to allow them to resume their former relationship. For this reason, mediation is often the preferred form of ADR for disputes involving business partners, employers and employees, or other parties involved in long-term relationships.

● EXAMPLE #9 Suppose that two business partners have a dispute over how the profits of their firm should be distributed. If the dispute is litigated, the parties will be adversaries, and their respective attorneys will emphasize how the parties' positions differ, not what they have in common. In contrast, when a dispute is mediated, the mediator emphasizes the common ground shared by the parties and helps them work toward agreement.●

In a recent development in ADR, characteristics of mediation are being combined with those of arbitration (to be discussed next). In *binding mediation,* for example, the parties agree that if they cannot resolve the dispute, the mediator can make a legally binding decision on the issue. In *mediation-arbitration,* or "med-arb," the parties agree to first attempt to settle their dispute through mediation. If no settlement is reached, the dispute will be arbitrated.

ARBITRATION

A more formal method of ADR is **arbitration**, in which an arbitrator (a neutral third party or a panel of experts) hears a dispute and renders a decision. The key difference between arbitration and the forms of ADR just discussed is that in arbitration, the parties typically agree that the third party's decision will be *legally binding*. Parties can also agree to *nonbinding* arbitration, however. Additionally, when a court refers a case for arbitration, the arbitrator's decision is not binding on the parties. If the parties do not agree with the arbitrator's decision, they can go forward with the lawsuit.

In some respects, formal arbitration resembles a trial, although usually the procedural rules are much less restrictive than those governing litigation. In the typical hearing format, the parties present opening arguments to the arbitrator and state what remedies should or should not be granted. Next, evidence is presented, and witnesses may be called and examined by both sides. The arbitrator then renders a decision, which is called an *award*.

An arbitrator's award is usually the final word on the matter. Although the parties may appeal an arbitrator's decision, a court's review of the decision will be much more restricted in scope than an appellate court's review of a trial court's decision. The general view is that because the parties were free to frame the issues and set the powers of the arbitrator at the outset, they cannot complain about the results. The award will be set aside only if the arbitrator's conduct or "bad faith" substantially prejudiced the rights of one of the parties, if the award violates an established public policy, or if the arbitrator exceeded her or his powers (arbitrated issues that the parties did not agree to submit to arbitration).

Arbitration Clauses and Statutes. Virtually any commercial matter can be submitted to arbitration. Frequently, parties include an **arbitration clause** in a contract (a written agreement—see Chapter 7); the clause provides that any dispute that arises under the contract will be resolved through arbitration rather than through the court system. Parties can also agree to arbitrate a dispute after a dispute arises.

Most states have statutes (often based in part on the Uniform Arbitration Act of 1955) under which arbitration clauses will be enforced, and some state statutes compel arbitration of certain types of disputes, such as those involving public employees. At the federal level, the Federal Arbitration Act (FAA), enacted in 1925, enforces arbitration clauses in contracts involving maritime activity and inter-state commerce. Because of the breadth of the commerce clause (see Chapter 1), arbitration agreements involving transactions only slightly connected to the flow of interstate commerce may fall under the FAA.

The Issue of Arbitrability. When a dispute arises over whether the parties have agreed in an arbitration clause to submit a particular matter to arbitration, one party may file suit to compel arbitration. The court before which the suit is brought will decide not the basic controversy but rather the issue of arbitrability—that is, whether the matter is one that must be resolved through arbitration. If the court finds that the subject matter in controversy is covered by the agreement to arbitrate, then a party may be compelled to arbitrate the dispute. Even when a claim involves a violation of a statute passed to protect a certain class of people, such as employees, a court may determine that the parties must nonetheless abide by their agreement to arbitrate the dispute. Usually, a court will allow the claim to be arbitrated if the court, in interpreting the statute, can find no legislative intent to the contrary.

A significant question in the last several years has concerned mandatory arbitration clauses in employment contracts. Many claim that employees' rights are not sufficiently protected when they are forced, in order to be hired, to agree to arbitrate all disputes and thus to waive their rights under statutes specifically designed to protect employees. The Supreme Court, however, has generally held that mandatory arbitration clauses in employment contracts are enforceable.[18]

No party, however, will be ordered to submit a particular dispute to arbitration unless the court is convinced that the party has consented to do so.[19] Additionally, the courts will not compel arbitration if it is clear that the prescribed arbitration rules and procedures are inherently unfair to one of the parties. (For a further discussion of this issue, see this chapter's *Management Perspective* feature on page 52.)

By the early 2000s, at issue was whether the Federal Arbitration Act even applied to employment contracts. Some lower courts claimed that Congress, when passing the FAA, intended to exempt such contracts from coverage. In the following case, the Supreme Court addressed this issue.

---

[18] *Gilmer v. Interstate/Johnson Lane Corp.*, 500 U.S. 20, 111 S.Ct. 1647, 114 L.Ed.2d 26 (1991).

[19] See, for example, *Wright v. Universal Maritime Service Corp.*, 525 U.S. 70, 119 S.Ct. 391, 142 L.Ed.2d 361 (1998).

CASE 2.4 Circuit City Stores, Inc. v. Adams

Supreme Court of the United States, 2001.
532 U.S. 105,
121 S.Ct. 1302,
149 L.Ed.2d 234.
http://www.findlaw.com/casecode/
supreme.html[a]

FACTS Saint Clair Adams applied for a job at Circuit City Stores, Inc. Adams signed an employment application that contained a clause requiring the arbitration of any employment-related disputes, including claims under federal and state law. Adams was hired as a sales counselor in a Circuit City store in Santa Rosa, California. Two years later, Adams filed a suit in a California state court against Circuit City, alleging employment discrimination in violation of state law. Circuit City immediately filed a suit against Adams in a federal district court, asking the court to compel arbitration of Adams's claim. Adams argued that Section 1 of the Federal Arbitration Act (FAA), which excludes from coverage "contracts of employment of seamen, railroad employees, or any other class of workers engaged in foreign or interstate commerce," excluded all employment contracts. The court entered an order in favor of Circuit City. Adams appealed to the U.S. Court of Appeals for the Ninth Circuit, which held that the arbitration agreement between Adams and Circuit City was contained in a "contract of employment" and thus was not subject to the FAA. The court interpreted the language in Section 1 to exclude all employment contracts. Circuit City appealed to the United States Supreme Court.

ISSUE Are all employment contracts excluded from coverage under the FAA?

DECISION No. The United States Supreme Court reversed the judgment of the lower court and remanded the case, holding that the FAA applies to most employment contracts (excluding only those involving interstate transportation workers).

REASON The Supreme Court found that the federal appellate court's decision to exclude all employment contracts was inconsistent with the Court's previous decisions. The Court also reasoned that interpreting "the residual phrase to exclude all employment contracts fails to give independent effect to the statute's enumeration of the specific categories of workers which precedes it; there would be no need for Congress to use the phrases 'seamen' and 'railroad employees' if those same classes of workers were subsumed within the meaning of the 'engaged in * * * commerce' residual clause. * * * [W]here general words follow specific words in a statutory enumeration, the general words are construed to embrace only objects similar in nature to those objects enumerated by the preceding specific words. Under this rule of construction the residual clause should be read to give effect to the terms 'seamen' and 'railroad employees,' and should itself be controlled and defined by reference to the enumerated categories of workers which are recited just before it."

FOR CRITICAL ANALYSIS—Cultural Consideration
What does the decision in this case indicate about the courts' interpretation of the phrases used in statutes?

---

a. Click on "2001 Decisions." In the result, click on the name of the case to access the opinion. This site is maintained by FindLaw.

OTHER TYPES OF ADR

The three forms of ADR just discussed are the oldest and traditionally the most commonly used forms. In recent years, a variety of new types of ADR have emerged, some of which were mentioned earlier in the discussion of mediation. Other ADR forms that are used today are sometimes referred to as "assisted negotiation" because they involve a third party in what is essentially a negotiation process. For example, in **early neutral case evaluation,** the parties select a neutral third party (generally an expert in the subject matter of the dispute) to evaluate their respective positions. The parties explain their posi-

tions to the case evaluator in any manner they choose. The case evaluator then assesses the strengths and weaknesses of the parties' positions, and this evaluation forms the basis for negotiating a settlement.

Another form of assisted negotiation that is often used by business parties is the **mini-trial,** in which each party's attorney briefly argues the party's case before representatives of each firm who have the authority to settle the dispute. Typically, a neutral third party (usually an expert in the area being disputed) acts as an adviser. If the parties fail to reach an agreement, the adviser renders an opinion as to how a court would likely decide the issue. The proceeding assists the parties in determining whether they

MANAGEMENT PERSPECTIVE
Arbitration Clauses in Employment Contracts

MANAGEMENT FACES A LEGAL ISSUE Arbitration is normally simpler, speedier, and less costly than litigation. For that reason, business owners and managers today often include arbitration clauses in their contracts, including employment contracts. What happens, though, if a job candidate whom you wish to hire (or an existing employee whose contract is being renewed) objects to one or more of the provisions in an arbitration clause? If you insist that signing the agreement to arbitrate future disputes is a mandatory condition of employment, will such a clause be enforceable?

WHAT THE COURTS SAY As stated elsewhere in this chapter, the United States Supreme Court has consistently taken the position that because the Federal Arbitration Act (FAA) favors the arbitration of disputes, arbitration clauses in employment contracts should generally be enforced. Nonetheless, some courts have held that arbitration clauses in employment contracts should not be enforced if they are too one sided and unfair to the employee.

In one case, for example, a court held that an employee did not have to submit her claim to arbitration when the arbitration agreement let the employer establish the procedure and rules of the arbitration.[a]

a. *Hooters of America, Inc. v. Phillips,* 173 F.3d 933 (4th Cir. 1999).

In another case, the U.S. Court of Appeals for the Ninth Circuit refused to enforce an arbitration clause on the ground that the agreement was *unconscionable*—so one-sided and unfair as to be unenforceable under "ordinary principles of state contract law." The agreement was a standard form contract drafted by the employer (the party with superior bargaining power), and the employee had to sign it without any modification as a prerequisite to employment. Moreover, only the employees were required to arbitrate their disputes, while the employer remained free to litigate any claims it had against its employees in court. Among other things, the contract also severely limited the relief that was available to employees. For these reasons, the court held the entire arbitration agreement unenforceable.[b]

IMPLICATIONS FOR MANAGERS Although the United States Supreme Court has made it clear that arbitration clauses in employment contracts are enforceable under the FAA, business owners and managers would be wise to exercise caution when drafting such clauses. It is especially important to make sure that the terms of the agreement are not so one sided that a court could declare the entire agreement unconscionable.

b. *Circuit City Stores, Inc. v. Adams,* 279 F.3d 889 (9th Cir. 2002). (This was the Ninth Circuit's decision, on remand, after the United States Supreme Court reviewed the case—see Case 2.4 on the previous page.)

---

should negotiate a settlement of the dispute or take it to court.

Today's courts are also experimenting with a variety of ADR alternatives to speed up (and reduce the cost of) justice. Numerous federal courts now hold **summary jury trials (SJTs),** in which the parties present their arguments and evidence and the jury renders a verdict. The jury's verdict is not binding, but it does act as a guide to both sides in reaching an agreement during the mandatory negotiations that immediately follow the trial. Other alternatives being employed by the courts include summary procedures for commercial litigation and the appointment of special masters to assist judges in deciding complex issues.

PROVIDERS OF ADR SERVICES

ADR services are provided by both government agencies and private organizations. The American Arbitration Association (AAA), which was founded in 1926, is a major provider of ADR services. Currently, about 200,000 disputes are submitted to the AAA for resolution each year in its numerous offices in the United States and other countries. Most of the largest U.S. law firms are members of this nonprofit association.

Cases brought before the AAA are heard by an expert or a panel of experts in the subject matter of the dispute and are usually settled quickly. Generally, about half of the panel members are lawyers. To cover its costs, the AAA charges a fee, paid by the party filing the claim. In addition, each party to the dispute pays a specified amount for each hearing day, as well as a special additional fee for cases involving personal injuries or property loss.

Hundreds of for-profit firms around the country also provide various forms of dispute-resolution services. Typically, these firms hire retired judges to conduct arbitration hearings or otherwise help parties settle their disputes. The judges follow procedures similar to those of the federal courts and use similar rules. Usually, each party to the dispute pays a filing fee and a designated fee for a hearing session or conference.

Online Dispute Resolution

An increasing number of companies and organizations offer dispute-resolution services using the Internet. The settlement of disputes in these online forums is known as **online dispute resolution (ODR)**. To date, the disputes resolved in these forums have most commonly involved disagreements over the rights to domain names (Web site addresses) and disagreements over the quality of goods sold via the Internet, including goods sold through Internet auction sites.

Currently, ODR may be best for resolving small- to medium-sized business liability claims, which may not be worth the expense of litigation or traditional methods of alternative dispute resolution. Rules being developed in online forums, however, may ultimately become a code of conduct for all of those who do business in cyberspace. Most online forums do not automatically apply the law of any specific jurisdiction. Instead, results are often based on general, universal legal principles. As with offline methods of dispute resolution, any party may appeal to a court at any time.

NEGOTIATION AND MEDIATION SERVICES

The online negotiation of a dispute is generally simpler and more practical than litigation. Typically, one party files a complaint, and the other party is notified by e-mail. Password-protected access is possible twenty-four hours a day, seven days a week. Fees are sometimes nominal and otherwise low (often 2 to 4 percent, or less, of the disputed amount).

CyberSettle.com, Inc., clickNsettle.com, and other Web-based firms offer online forums for negotiating monetary settlements. The parties to a dispute may agree to submit offers; if the offers fall within a previously agreed-on range, they will end the dispute, and the parties will split the difference. Special software keeps secret any offers that are not within the range. If there is no agreed-on range, typically an offer includes a deadline within which the other party must respond before the offer expires. The parties can drop the negotiations at any time.

Mediation providers have also tried resolving disputes online. SquareTrade, one of the mediation providers that has been used by eBay, the online auction site, mediates disputes involving $100 or more among eBay customers, currently for no charge. SquareTrade, which also resolves disputes among other parties, uses automated Web-based software that walks participants through a five-step e-resolution process. Negotiation between the parties occurs on a secure page within SquareTrade's Web site. The parties may consult a mediator. The entire process takes as little as ten to fourteen days, and there is no fee unless the parties use a mediator.

ARBITRATION PROGRAMS

A number of organizations and companies offer online arbitration programs. The Internet Corporation for Assigned Names and Numbers (ICANN), a nonprofit corporation that the federal government set up to oversee the distribution of domain names, has issued special rules for the resolution of domain name disputes.[20] ICANN has also authorized several organizations to arbitrate domain name disputes in accordance with ICANN's rules. The American Arbitration Association now provides technology-based arbitration services as well.

Resolution Forum, Inc. (RFI), a nonprofit organization associated with the Center for Legal Responsibility at South Texas College of Law, offers arbitration services through its CAN-WIN conferencing system. Using standard browser software and an RFI password, the parties to a dispute access an online conference room. When multiple parties are involved, private communications and breakout sessions are possible via private messaging facilities. RFI also offers mediation services.

The Virtual Magistrate Project (VMAG) is affiliated with the American Arbitration Association, Chicago-Kent College of Law, Cyberspace Law Institute, National Center for Automated Information Research, and other organizations. VMAG offers arbitration for disputes involving users of online systems; victims of wrongful messages, postings, and files; and system operators subject to complaints or similar demands. VMAG also arbitrates intellectual property, personal property, real property, and tort disputes

---

[20] ICANN's Rules for Uniform Domain Name Dispute Resolution Policy are online at **http://www.icann.org/udrp/udrp-rules-24oct99.htm**. Domain names will be discussed in more detail in Chapter 5, in the context of trademark law.

related to online contracts. VMAG attempts to resolve a dispute within seventy-two hours. The proceedings occur in a password-protected online newsgroup setting, and private e-mail among the participants is possible. A VMAG arbitrator's decision is issued in a written opinion. A party may appeal the outcome to a court.

Terms and Concepts

alternative dispute resolution (ADR) 49

answer 43

arbitration 50

arbitration clause 50

award 47

bankruptcy court 34

brief 47

complaint 41

concurrent jurisdiction 34

counterclaim 43

default judgment 42

deposition 44

discovery 44

diversity of citizenship 34

docket 35

early neutral case evaluation 51

exclusive jurisdiction 34

federal question 34

interrogatories 44

judicial review 33

jurisdiction 33

justiciable controversy 38

litigation 41

long arm statute 33

mediation 49

mini-trial 51

motion for a directed verdict 46

motion for a new trial 47

motion for judgment *n.o.v.* 47

motion for judgment on the pleadings 44

motion for summary judgment 44

motion to dismiss 44

negotiation 49

online dispute resolution (ODR) 53

pleadings 41

probate court 34

reply 43

rule of four 41

small claims court 39

standing to sue 38

summary jury trial (SJT) 52

summons 41

venue 37

voir dire 46

writ of *certiorari* 41

Chapter Summary   Traditional and Online Dispute Resolution

The Judiciary's Role in American Government (See page 33.)	The role of the judiciary—the courts—in the American system of government is to interpret and apply the law. Through the process of judicial review—determining the constitutionality of laws—the judicial branch acts as a check on the executive and legislative branches of government.
Basic Judicial Requirements (See pages 33–38.)	1. *Jurisdiction*—Before a court can hear a case, it must have jurisdiction over the person against whom the suit is brought or the property involved in the suit, as well as jurisdiction over the subject matter. a. Limited versus general jurisdiction—Limited jurisdiction exists when a court is limited to a specific subject matter, such as probate or divorce. General jurisdiction exists when a court can hear any kind of case. b. Original versus appellate jurisdiction—Original jurisdiction exists with courts that have authority to hear a case for the first time (trial courts). Appellate jurisdiction exists with courts of appeals, or reviewing courts; generally, appellate courts do not have original jurisdiction. c. Federal jurisdiction—Arises (1) when a federal question is involved (when the plaintiff's cause of action is based, at least in part, on the U.S. Constitution, a treaty, or a federal law) or (2) when a case involves diversity of citizenship (citizens of different states, for example) and the amount in controversy exceeds $75,000.

Chapter Summary	Traditional and Online Dispute Resolution—Continued
Basic Judicial Requirements— continued	d. Concurrent versus exclusive jurisdiction—Concurrent jurisdiction exists when two different courts have authority to hear the same case. Exclusive jurisdiction exists when only state courts or only federal courts have authority to hear a case.
	2. *Jurisdiction in cyberspace*—Because the Internet does not have physical boundaries, traditional jurisdictional concepts have been difficult to apply in cases involving activities conducted via the Web. Gradually, the courts are developing standards to use in determining when jurisdiction over a Web owner or operator in another state is proper.
	3. *Venue*—Venue has to do with the most appropriate location for a trial, which is usually the geographic area where the event leading to the dispute took place or where the parties reside.
	4. *Standing to sue*—A requirement that a party must have a legally protected and tangible interest at stake sufficient to justify seeking relief through the court system. The controversy at issue must also be a justiciable controversy—one that is real and substantial, as opposed to hypothetical or academic.
The State and Federal Court Systems (See pages 38–41.)	1. *Trial courts*—Courts of original jurisdiction, in which legal actions are initiated.
	a. State—Courts of general jurisdiction can hear any case; courts of limited jurisdiction include divorce courts, probate courts, traffic courts, small claims courts, and so on.
	b. Federal—The federal district court is the equivalent of the state trial court. Federal courts of limited jurisdiction include the U.S. Tax Court, the U.S. Bankruptcy Court, and the U.S. Court of Federal Claims.
	2. *Intermediate appellate courts*—Courts of appeals, or reviewing courts; generally without original jurisdiction. Many states have an intermediate appellate court; in the federal court system, the U.S. circuit courts of appeals are the intermediate appellate courts.
	3. *Supreme (highest) courts*—Each state has a supreme court, although it may be called by some other name, from which appeal to the United States Supreme Court is possible only if a federal question is involved. The United States Supreme Court is the highest court in the federal court system and the final arbiter of the Constitution and federal law.
Following a State Court Case (See pages 41–48.)	Rules of procedure prescribe the way in which disputes are handled in the courts. Rules differ from court to court, and separate sets of rules exist for federal and state courts, as well as for criminal and civil cases. A sample civil court case in a state court would involve the following procedures:
	1. *The pleadings*—
	a. Complaint—Filed by the plaintiff with the court to initiate the lawsuit; served with a summons on the defendant.
	b. Answer—Admits or denies allegations made by the plaintiff; may assert a counterclaim or an affirmative defense.
	c. Motion to dismiss—A request to the court to dismiss the case for stated reasons, such as the plaintiff's failure to state a claim for which relief can be granted.
	2. *Pretrial motions (in addition to the motion to dismiss)*—
	a. Motion for judgment on the pleadings—May be made by either party; will be granted if the parties agree on the facts and the only question is how the law applies to the facts. The judge bases the decision solely on the pleadings.

(Continued)

Chapter Summary	**Traditional and Online Dispute Resolution—Continued**
Following a State Court Case— continued	b. Motion for summary judgment—May be made by either party; will be granted if the parties agree on the facts. The judge applies the law in rendering a judgment. The judge can consider evidence outside the pleadings when evaluating the motion.
	3. *Discovery*—The process of gathering evidence concerning the case. Discovery involves depositions (sworn testimony by a party to the lawsuit or any witness), interrogatories (written questions and answers to these questions made by parties to the action with the aid of their attorneys), and various requests (for admissions, documents, medical examination, and so on).
	4. *Pretrial conference*—Either party or the court can request a pretrial conference to identify the matters in dispute after discovery has taken place and to plan the course of the trial.
	5. *Trial*—Following jury selection (*voir dire*), the trial begins with opening statements from both parties' attorneys. The following events then occur:
	a. The plaintiff's introduction of evidence (including the testimony of witnesses) supporting the plaintiff's position. The defendant's attorney can challenge evidence and cross-examine witnesses.
	b. The defendant's introduction of evidence (including the testimony of witnesses) supporting the defendant's position. The plaintiff's attorney can challenge evidence and cross-examine witnesses.
	c. Closing arguments by attorneys in favor of their respective clients, the judge's instructions to the jury, and the jury's verdict.
	6. *Posttrial motions*—
	a. Motion for judgment *n.o.v.* ("notwithstanding the verdict")—Will be granted if the judge is convinced that the jury was in error.
	b. Motion for a new trial—Will be granted if the judge is convinced that the jury was in error; can also be granted on the grounds of newly discovered evidence, misconduct by the participants during the trial, or error by the judge.
	7. *Appeal*—Either party can appeal the trial court's judgment to an appropriate court of appeals. After reviewing the record on appeal, the abstracts, and the attorneys' briefs, the appellate court holds a hearing and renders its opinion.
The Courts Adapt to the Online World (See pages 48–49.)	A number of state and federal courts now allow parties to file litigation-related documents with their courts via the Internet or other electronic means. The federal courts are gradually implementing electronic filing systems. Virtually every court now has a Web page offering information about the court and its procedures, and an increasing number of courts publish their opinions online. In the future, we may see "cyber courts," in which all trial proceedings are conducted online.
Alternative Dispute Resolution (See pages 49–53.)	1. *Negotiation*—The parties come together, with or without attorneys to represent them, and try to reach a settlement without the involvement of a third party.
	2. *Mediation*—The parties themselves reach an agreement with the help of a neutral third party, called a mediator, who proposes solutions. At the parties' request, a mediator may make a legally binding decision.
	3. *Arbitration*—A more formal method of ADR in which the parties submit their dispute to a neutral third party, the arbitrator, who renders a decision. The decision may or may not be legally binding, depending on the circumstances.

Chapter Summary	Traditional and Online Dispute Resolution—Continued
Alternative Dispute Resolution—continued	4. *Other types of ADR*—These include early neutral case evaluation, mini-trials, and summary jury trials (SJTs); generally, these are forms of "assisted negotiation."
	5. *Providers of ADR services*—The leading nonprofit provider of ADR services is the American Arbitration Association. Hundreds of for-profit firms also provide ADR services.
Online Dispute Resolution (See pages 53–54.)	A number of organizations and firms are now offering negotiation, mediation, and arbitration services through online forums. To date, these forums have been a practical alternative for the resolution of domain name disputes and e-commerce disputes in which the amount in controversy is relatively small.

For Review

① What is judicial review? How and when was the power of judicial review established?

② Before a court can hear a case, it must have jurisdiction. Over what must it have jurisdiction? How are the courts applying traditional jurisdictional concepts to cases involving Internet transactions?

③ What is the difference between a trial court and an appellate court?

④ In a lawsuit, what are the pleadings? What is discovery? What is electronic filing?

⑤ How are online forums being used to resolve disputes?

Questions and Case Problems

2–1. Appellate Process. If a judge enters a judgment on the pleadings, the losing party can usually appeal but cannot present evidence to the appellate court. Does this seem fair? Explain.

2–2. Arbitration. In an arbitration proceeding, the arbitrator need not be a judge or even a lawyer. How, then, can the arbitrator's decision have the force of law and be binding on the parties involved?

2–3. Appellate Process. Sometimes on appeal there are questions concerning whether the facts presented in the trial court support the conclusion reached by the judge or the jury. An appellate court, however, normally defers to the trial court's decision with regard to the facts. Can you see any reason for this?

2–4. Jurisdiction. Marya Callais, a citizen of Florida, was walking near a busy street in Tallahassee one day when a large crate flew off a passing truck and hit her, resulting in numerous injuries to Callais. She incurred a great deal of pain and suffering plus numerous medical expenses, and she could not work for six months. She wishes to sue the trucking firm for $300,000 in damages. The firm's headquarters are in Georgia, although the company does business in Florida. In what court may Callais bring suit—a Florida state court, a Georgia state court, or a federal court? What factors might influence her decision?

2–5. Jurisdiction. Shem and Nadine Maslov, who live in Massachusetts, saw a national hotel chain's advertisement for vacationers in the *Boston Globe:* "Stay in Maximum Inns's beachfront hotel in Puerto Rico for one week for only $800; continental breakfast included." The Maslovs decided to accept the offer and spent a week at the hotel. On the last day, Nadine fell on a wet floor in the hotel lobby and sustained multiple fractures to her left ankle and hip. Because of her injuries, which were subsequently complicated by infections, she was unable to work at her job as an airline flight attendant for ten months. The hotel chain does not do business in Massachusetts. If Nadine sues Maximum Inns in a Massachusetts state court, can the court exercise jurisdiction over Maximum Inns? What factors should the court consider in deciding this jurisdictional issue?

2–6. Arbitration. Randall Fris worked as a seaman on an Exxon Shipping Co. oil tanker for eight years without incident. One night, he boarded the ship for duty while drunk, in violation of company policy. This policy allowed Exxon to fire employees who were intoxicated and thus unfit for work. Exxon discharged Fris. Under a contract with Fris's union, the discharge was submitted to arbitration. The arbitrators ordered Exxon to reinstate Fris on an oil tanker. Exxon filed a suit against the union, challenging the award as contrary to public policy, which opposes having intoxicated persons operate seagoing vessels. Can a court set aside an arbitration award on the ground that the award violates public policy? Should the court set aside the award in this case? Explain. [*Exxon Shipping Co. v. Exxon Seamen's Union,* 11 F.3d 1189 (3d Cir. 1993)]

2–7. Jurisdiction. George Noonan, a Boston police detective and a devoted nonsmoker, has spent most of his career educating Bostonians about the health risks of tobacco use. In 1992, an ad for Winston cigarettes featuring Noonan's image appeared in several French magazines. Some of the magazines were on sale at newsstands in Boston. Noonan filed a suit in a federal district court against The Winston Co., Lintas:Paris (the French agency that created the ads), and others. Lintas:Paris and the other French defendants claimed that they did not know the magazines would be sold in Boston and filed a motion to dismiss the suit for lack of personal jurisdiction. Does the court have jurisdiction? Why or why not? [*Noonan v. The Winston Co.,* 135 F.3d 85 (1st Cir. 1998)]

2–8. Standing. Blue Cross and Blue Shield insurance companies (the Blues) provide 68 million Americans with health-care financing. The Blues have paid billions of dollars for care attributable to illnesses related to tobacco use. In an attempt to recover some of this amount, the Blues filed a suit in a federal district court against tobacco companies and others, alleging fraud, among other things. The Blues claimed that beginning in 1953, the defendants conspired to addict millions of Americans, including members of Blue Cross plans, to cigarettes and other tobacco products. The conspiracy involved misrepresentation about the safety of nicotine and its addictive properties, marketing efforts targeting children, and agreements not to produce or market safer cigarettes. Their success caused lung, throat, and other cancers, as well as heart disease, stroke, emphysema, and other illnesses. The defendants asked the court to dismiss the case on the ground that the plaintiffs did not have standing to sue. Do the Blues have standing in this case? [*Blue Cross and Blue Shield of New Jersey, Inc. v. Philip Morris, Inc.,* 36 F.Supp.2d 560 (E.D.N.Y. 1999)]

2–9. Discovery. Advance Technology Consultants, Inc. (ATC), contracted with RoadTrac, L.L.C., to provide software and client software systems for products utilizing global positioning satellite (GPS) technology being developed by RoadTrac. RoadTrac agreed to provide ATC with hardware with which ATC's software would interface. Problems soon arose, however. ATC claimed that RoadTrac's hardware was defective, making it difficult to develop the software. RoadTrac contended that its hardware was fully functional and that ATC simply failed to provide supporting software. ATC told RoadTrac that it considered their contract terminated. RoadTrac filed a suit in a Georgia state court against ATC, charging, among other things, breach of contract. During discovery, RoadTrac requested ATC's customer lists and marketing procedures. Before producing this material, ATC asked the court to limit RoadTrac's use of the information. Meanwhile, RoadTrac and ATC had become competitors in the GPS industry. How should the court rule regarding RoadTrac's discovery request? [*Advance Technology Consultants, Inc. v. RoadTrac, L.L.C.,* 236 Ga.App. 582, 512 S.E.2d 27 (1999)]

CASE PROBLEM WITH SAMPLE ANSWER

2–10. Ms. Thompson filed a suit in a federal district court against her employer, Altheimer & Gray, seeking damages for alleged racial discrimination in violation of federal law. During *voir dire,* the judge asked the prospective jurors whether "there is something about this kind of lawsuit for money damages that would start any of you leaning for or against a particular party?" Ms. Leiter, one of the prospective jurors, raised her hand and explained that she had "been an owner of a couple of businesses and am currently an owner of a business, and I feel that as an employer and owner of a business that will definitely sway my judgment in this case." She explained, "I am constantly faced with people that want various benefits or different positions in the company or better contacts or, you know, a myriad of issues that employers face on a regular basis, and I have to decide whether or not that person should get them." Asked by Thompson's lawyer whether "you believe that people file lawsuits just because they don't get something they want," Leiter answered, "I believe there are some people that do." In answer to another question, she said, "I think I bring a lot of background to this case, and I can't say that it's not going to cloud my judgment. I can try to be as fair as I can, as I do every day." Thompson filed a motion to strike Leiter for cause. Should the judge grant the motion? Explain. [*Thompson v. Altheimer & Gray,* 248 F.3d 621 (7th Cir. 2001)]

▶ To view a sample answer for this case problem, go to this book's Web site at **http://fundamentals.westbuslaw.com** and click on "Interactive Study Center."

2–11. Motion for a Directed Verdict. Gerald Adams worked as a cook for Uno Restaurants, Inc., at Warwick Pizzeria Uno Restaurant & Bar in Warwick, Rhode Island. One night, shortly after Adams's shift began, he noticed that the kitchen floor was saturated with a foul-smelling liquid coming from the drains and backing up water onto the floor. He complained of illness and went home, where he contacted the state health department. A department representative visited the restaurant and closed it for the night, leaving instructions to sanitize the kitchen and clear the drains. Two days later, in the restaurant, David Badot, the manager, shouted at Adams in the presence of other employees. When Adams shouted back, Badot fired Adams and had him arrested. Adams filed a suit in a Rhode Island state court against Uno, alleging that he had been unlawfully terminated for contacting the health department. Arguing that Adams had been fired for threatening Badot, Uno filed a motion for a directed verdict. What does a court weigh in considering whether to grant such a motion? Should the court grant the motion in this case? Why or why not? [*Adams v. Uno Restaurants, Inc.,* 794 A.2d 489 (R.I. 2002)]

2–12. Jurisdiction. Kazaa BV was a company formed under the laws of the Netherlands. Kazaa distributed Kazaa Media Desktop (KMD) software, which enabled users to exchange, via a peer-to-peer transfer network, digital media, including movies and music. Kazaa also operated the Kazaa.com Web site, through which it distributed the KMD software to millions of California residents and other users. Metro-Goldwyn-Mayer Studios, Inc., and other parties in the entertainment industries based in California, filed a suit in a federal district court against Kazaa and others, alleging copyright infringement. Kazaa filed a counterclaim, but while legal action was pending, the firm passed its assets and its Web site to Sharman Networks, Ltd., a company organized under the laws of Vanuatu (an island republic east of Australia) and doing business principally in Australia. Sharman explicitly disclaimed the assumption of any of Kazaa's liabilities. When the plaintiffs added Sharman as a defendant, Sharman filed a motion to dismiss on the ground that the court did not have jurisdiction. Would it be fair to subject Sharman to suit in this case? Explain. [*Metro-Goldwyn-Mayer Studios, Inc. v. Grokster, Ltd.*, 243 F.Supp.2d.1073 (C.D.Cal. 2003)]

VIDEO QUESTION

2–13. Go to this text's Web site at **http://fundamentals.westbuslaw.com** and click on "Video Questions." Select "Chapter 2" and view the video titled *Jurisdiction in Cyberspace*. Then answer the following questions:

1. What standard would a court apply to determine whether it has jurisdiction over the out-of-state computer firm in the video?
2. What factors is a court likely to consider in assessing whether sufficient contacts existed when the only connection to the jurisdiction is through a Web site?
3. How do you think the court would resolve the issue in this case?

TRADITIONAL AND ONLINE DISPUTE RESOLUTION

For updated links to resources available on the Web, as well as a variety of other materials, visit this text's Web site at

http://fundamentals.westbuslaw.com

For the decisions of the United States Supreme Court, as well as information about the Supreme Court, go to

http://supremecourtus.gov

The Web site for the federal courts offers information on the federal court system and links to all federal courts at

http://www.uscourts.gov

The National Center for State Courts (NCSC) offers links to the Web pages of all state courts. Go to

http://www.ncsconline.org

For information on alternative dispute resolution, go to the American Arbitration Association's Web site at

http://www.adr.org

To learn more about online dispute resolution, go to the following Web sites:

http://clicknsettle.com
http://cybersettle.com
http://squaretrade.com

For an example of a typical set of state rules governing attorney conduct, you can access Idaho's Rules of Professional Conduct Governing Lawyers at

http://www2.state.id.us/isb/rules/irpc/irpc.htm

Picking the "right" jury can be an important part of litigation strategy, and several firms now specialize in jury consulting services. To learn more about this topic, go to the Jury Research Institute Web site at

http://www.jri-inc.com

Smith & Johnson, P.C., a Michigan law firm, offers a summary of Michigan's proposed cyber court legislation at

http://www.smith-johnson.com/businesslaw/cybercourt.htm

Online Legal Research

Go to the *Fundamentals of Business Law* home page at **http://fundamentals. westbuslaw.com**. Select "Interactive Study Center" and then click on "Chapter 2." There you will find the following Internet research exercises that you can perform to learn more about topics covered in this chapter.

Activity 2–1: LEGAL PERSPECTIVE—**Alternative Dispute Resolution**
Activity 2–2: MANAGEMENT PERSPECTIVE—**Small Claims Court**
Activity 2–3: TECHNOLOGICAL PERSPECTIVE—**Virtual Courtrooms**

Before the Test

Go to the *Fundamentals of Business Law* home page at **http://fundamentals. westbuslaw.com**. Click on "Interactive Quizzes." You will find at least twenty interactive questions relating to this chapter.

Westlaw® Campus

If your textbook provided for a subscription to Westlaw® Campus, or if you have otherwise purchased access to the Westlaw Campus database, you can access any of the cases presented or cited in this chapter by using your Westlaw Campus account.

CHAPTER OBJECTIVES

After reading this chapter, you should be able to answer the following questions:

① What is ethics? What is business ethics? Why is business ethics important?

② What steps can business leaders take to ensure that their companies behave legally and ethically?

③ How do duty-based ethical standards differ from outcome-based ethical standards?

④ What is corporate social responsibility? What are some different theories of social responsibility?

⑤ What is the difference between maximum profits and optimum profits?

Just because business ethics scandals have been in the news during the early part of the 2000s does not mean that the subject was unimportant before then. Nor does it mean that as soon as the current scandals subside, businesspersons can go back to "business as usual." Few today would doubt that ethically run businesses will survive in the long run, while companies whose officers and directors act with little regard for established ethical norms will fail.

Certainly, those responsible for grossly inflating the reported profits at WorldCom, Inc., ended up not only destroying shareholder value in a great company but also facing possible prison terms. Those officers and directors at Enron Corporation who utilized a system of complicated off-the-books transactions to inflate current earnings saw their company go bankrupt—the largest bankruptcy in U.S. history. They harmed not only their employees and share-holders but also the communities in which they worked—and themselves (some of them may be serving prison sentences when you read this). The officers and directors of Tyco International who used corporate funds to pay for lav-ish personal lifestyles also ended up in court. The share-holders of that company suffered dearly, too.

Ethical business decision making is not just theory. It is practical, useful, and essential. While a good understanding of business law and the legal environment is critical, it is not enough. Understanding how one should act in her or his business dealings is equally—if not more—important in today's business arena. How one should act in business is the focus of this chapter.

Business Ethics

Before we look at business ethics, we need to discuss what is meant by ethics generally. **Ethics** can be defined as the study of what constitutes right or wrong behavior. It is the branch of philosophy that focuses on morality and the way in which moral principles are derived or the way in which a given set of moral principles applies to one's conduct in daily life. Ethics has to do with questions relating to the fairness, justness, rightness, or wrongness of an action. What is fair? What is just? What is the right thing to do in this situation? These are essentially ethical questions.

WHAT IS BUSINESS ETHICS?

Business ethics focuses on what constitutes right or wrong behavior in the business world and on how moral and ethical principles are applied by businesspersons to situations that arise in their daily activities in the workplace. Note that business ethics is not a separate *kind* of ethics. The ethical

standards that guide our behavior as, say, mothers, fathers, or students apply equally well to our activities as businesspersons. Business decision makers, though, must often address more complex ethical issues and conflicts in the workplace than they face in their personal lives.

WHY IS BUSINESS ETHICS IMPORTANT?

Why is business ethics important? The answer to this question is clear from this chapter's introduction. A keen and in-depth understanding of business ethics is important to the long-run viability of a corporation. A thorough knowledge of business ethics is also important to the well-being of the individual officers and directors of the corporation, as well as to the welfare of the firm's employees.

Note that questions about ethical and responsible behavior are not confined to the corporate context. In a business partnership, for example, partners owe a fiduciary duty (a duty to act primarily for another's benefit) to each other and to their firm. This duty can sometimes conflict with what a partner sees as his or her own best interest. Partners who act solely in their own interests may violate their duties to the other partners and the firm, however. By violating this duty, they may end up paying steep penalties—as the following case illustrates.

CASE 3.1   Time Warner Entertainment Co. v. Six Flags Over Georgia, L.L.C.

Georgia Court of Appeals, 2002.
254 Ga.App. 598,
563 S.E.2d 178.
**http://www.ganet.org/appeals/opinions/
index.cgi**[a]

FACTS The Six Flags Over Georgia theme park in Atlanta, Georgia, was developed in 1967 as a limited partnership known as Six Flags Over Georgia, L.L.C. (Flags). The sole limited partner was Six Flags Fund, Limited (Fund). The general partner was Six Flags Over Georgia, Inc. (SFOG). In 1991, Time Warner Entertainment Company (TWE) became the majority shareholder of SFOG. The next year, TWE secretly bought 13.7 acres of land next to the park, limiting the park's expansion opportunities. Over the next couple of years, using confidential business information from the park, TWE began plans to develop a competing park. Meanwhile, TWE installed

no major new attractions at the park, deferred basic maintenance, withheld financial information from Fund (the limited partner), and began signing future employment contracts with SFOG officers. TWE also charged Flags for unrelated expenses, including over $4 million for lunches in New York City and luxury automobiles for TWE officers. Flags and Fund filed a suit in a Georgia state court against TWE and SFOG, alleging, among other things, breach of fiduciary duty. A jury awarded the plaintiffs $197,296,000 in compensatory damages and $257,000,000 in punitive damages.[b] TWE appealed to a state intermediate appellate court, alleging in part that the amount of the punitive damages was excessive.

ISSUE Was the amount of punitive damages excessive?

DECISION No. The state intermediate appellate court affirmed the judgment of the lower court.

---

a. This Web site is sponsored by the state of Georgia. At the search screen, click on "Search Court of Appeals Opinions." On the appellate court's screen, set the search year to "all." You can go to a case most directly if you use as key words the full name of a party—for example, "six flags over georgia llc."

b. Damages that are intended to punish the wrongdoer and deter others from similar wrongdoing—see Chapter 4.

CASE 3.1—Continued

REASON The appellate court held that the award of punitive damages was not excessive, considering the amount of compensatory damages ("the ratio of compensatory to punitive damages is 1 to 1.3"), the defendants' financial status "with collective assets measured in billions of dollars," and "reprehensible" (wrongful) conduct toward the plaintiffs. The appellate court stated, "In examining the degree of reprehensibility of a defendant's conduct, [there are] a number of aggravating factors [to consider], including whether the harm was more than purely economic in nature, and whether the defendant's behavior evinced indifference to or reckless disregard for the health and safety of others. Here, although the harm to Flags and Fund was primarily economic, it was caused by conduct we find especially reprehensible.

Appellants' intentional breach of its fiduciary duty revealed a callous indifference to the financial well-being of its limited partners and their individual investors." The court concluded that "[a]ppellants' conduct was, in short, the kind of behavior we find deserving of reproof, rebuke, or censure; blameworthy—the very definition of reprehensible. * * * Trickery and deceit are reprehensible wrongs, especially when done intentionally through affirmative acts of misconduct."

FOR CRITICAL ANALYSIS—Ethical Consideration
If TWE had proceeded with its plans to build a competing park but had not otherwise acted "reprehensibly" toward Flags and Fund, would the decision in this case likely have been different?

Setting the Right Ethical Tone

Many unethical business decisions are made simply because they *can* be made. In other words, the decision makers not only have the opportunity to make such decisions but also are not too concerned about being seriously sanctioned for their unethical actions. Perhaps one of the most difficult challenges for business leaders today is to create the right "ethical tone" in their workplaces in order to deter unethical conduct.

THE IMPORTANCE OF ETHICAL LEADERSHIP

Talking about ethical business decision making means nothing if management does not set standards. Moreover, managers must apply those standards to themselves and to the employees in the company.

Attitude of Top Management. One of the most important factors in creating and maintaining an ethical workplace is the attitude of top management. Managers who are not totally committed to maintaining an ethical workplace will rarely succeed in creating one. Surveys of business executives indicate that management's behavior, more than anything else, sets the ethical tone of a firm. In other words, employees take their cue from management. If a firm's managers adhere to obvious ethical norms in their business dealings, employees will likely follow their example. In contrast, if managers act unethically, employees will see no reason not to do so themselves. For example, if an employee observes a manager cheating on her expense account, the employee quickly understands that such behavior is acceptable.

Looking the Other Way. A manager who looks the other way when he knows about an employee's unethical behavior also sets an example—one indicating that ethical transgressions will be accepted. Managers must show that they will not tolerate unethical business behavior. Although this may seem harsh, managers have found that discharging even one employee for ethical reasons has a tremendous impact as a deterrent to unethical behavior in the workplace.

Creating Realistic Goals Helps. Managers can reduce the probability that employees will act unethically by setting realistic production or sales goals. If a sales quota, for example, can be met only through high-pressure, unethical sales tactics, employees trying to act "in the best interests of the firm" may think that management is implicitly asking them to behave unethically.

Periodic Evaluation. Some companies require their managers to meet individually with employees and to grade them on their ethical (or unethical) behavior. ● **EXAMPLE #1** One company asks its employees to fill out ethical checklists each week and return them to their supervisors. This practice serves two purposes: First, it demonstrates to employees that ethics matters. Second, employees have an opportunity to reflect on how well they have measured up in terms of ethical performance.●

CREATING ETHICAL CODES OF CONDUCT

One of the most effective ways to set a tone of ethical behavior within an organization is to create an ethical code of conduct. A well-written code of ethics explicitly states a company's ethical priorities.

A Necessity—Clear Communication to Employees. For an ethical code to be effective, its provisions must be clearly communicated to employees. Most large companies have implemented ethics training programs, in which management discusses with employees on a face-to-face basis the firm's policies and the importance of ethical conduct. Some firms hold periodic ethics seminars during which employees can openly discuss any ethical problems that they may be experiencing and learn how the firm's ethical policies apply to those specific problems.

Johnson & Johnson—An Example of Web-Based Ethics Training. Creating a code of conduct and implementing it are two different activities. In many companies, codes of conduct are simply documents that have very little relevance to day-to-day operations. When Johnson & Johnson wanted to do "better" than other companies with respect to ethical business decision making, it created a Center for Legal and Credo Awareness. (Its code of ethical conduct is called its credo.)

The center created a Web-based set of instructions designed to enhance the corporation's efforts to train employees in the importance of its code of conduct. Given that Johnson & Johnson has over 120,000 employees throughout the world, reinforcing its code of conduct and its values has not been easy, but Web-based training has helped. The company established a Web-based legal and compliance center, which consists of a set of interactive modules to train employees in the areas of law and ethics.

CORPORATE COMPLIANCE PROGRAMS

In large corporations, ethical codes of conduct are usually just one part of a comprehensive corporate compliance program. Other components of such a program, some of which were already mentioned, include a corporation's ethics committee, ethical training programs, and internal audits to monitor compliance with applicable laws and the company's standards of ethical conduct.

The Sarbanes-Oxley Act and Web-Based Reporting Systems. The Sarbanes-Oxley Act of 2002[1] requires that companies set up confidential systems so that employees and others may "raise red flags" about suspected illegal or unethical auditing and accounting practices. The act required publicly traded companies to have such systems in

place by April 2003. At least one Web-based reporting system was put in place in 2002. Employees can click on an icon on their computer that anonymously links them with Ethicspoint, an organization based in Vancouver, Washington. Through Ethicspoint, employees may report suspicious accounting practices, sexual harassment, and other possibly unethical behavior. Ethicspoint, in turn, alerts management personnel or the audit committee at the designated company to the possible problem. Those who have used the system say that it is less inhibiting than calling a company's 800 number.

Compliance Programs Must Be Integrated. To be effective, a compliance program must be integrated throughout the firm. For large corporations, such integration is essential. Ethical policies and programs need to be coordinated and monitored by a committee that is separate from various corporate departments. Otherwise, unethical behavior in one department can easily escape the attention of those in control of the corporation or the corporate officials responsible for implementing and monitoring the company's compliance program.

CONFLICTS AND TRADE-OFFS

Management constantly faces ethical trade-offs, some of which may lead to legal problems. As mentioned earlier, firms have implied ethical (and legal) duties to a number of groups, including shareholders and employees.

When a company decides to reduce costs by downsizing and restructuring, the decision may benefit shareholders, but it will harm those employees who are laid off or fired. When downsizing occurs, which employees should be laid off first? Cost-cutting considerations might dictate firing the most senior employees, who generally have higher salaries, and retaining less senior employees, whose salaries are much lower. A company does not necessarily act illegally when it does so. Yet the decision to be made by management clearly involves an important ethical question: Which group's interests—those of the shareholders or those of employees who have been loyal to the firm for a long period of time—should take priority in this situation?

Selling information can bolster a company's profits, which may satisfy the firm's duty to its owners, but when the data is personal, its sale may violate an ethical or legal duty. In what circumstances might a party who sells information about someone else have a duty to that other party with respect to the sale of the information? This question arose in the following case.

---

[1] 15 U.S.C. Sections 7201 *et seq.* This act, which became effective on August 29, 2002, will be discussed in Chapter 27.

CASE 3.2 Remsburg v. Docusearch, Inc.

New Hampshire Supreme Court, 2003.
816 A.2d 1001.
http://www.courts.state.nh.us/supreme/
opinions/index.htm[a]

FACTS Docusearch, Inc., operates Docusearch.com, an Internet-based investigation and information service. In July 1999, Liam Youens, a resident of New Hampshire, contacted Docusearch through its Web site and requested information about Amy Boyer, another New Hampshire resident. Youens provided his name, address, and phone number, and paid Docusearch's fee by credit card. Docusearch provided Boyer's home address, birth date, and Social Security number. Youens asked for Boyer's workplace address. To obtain this information, Michele Gambino, a Docusearch subcontractor, placed a "pretext" phone call to Boyer. Gambino lied about who she was and the purpose of her call. On October 15, Youens drove to Boyer's workplace and fatally shot her, and then shot and killed himself. The police discovered Youens's Web site, which referred to stalking and killing Boyer. Helen Remsburg, Boyer's mother, filed a suit in a federal district court against Docusearch and others, claiming the defendants acted wrongfully. The court asked the New Hampshire Supreme Court about the parties' duties under the state's common law.

a. When the page opens, click on "February 2003." In the "February 18, 2003" section, click on the name of the case to access the opinion. This is a page within a Web site maintained by the Judicial Branch of the State of New Hampshire.

ISSUE Does a person who sells information about someone else have a duty to that other party with respect to the sale?

DECISION Yes. The New Hampshire Supreme Court held that an information broker who sells to a client information about a third person has a duty to exercise reasonable care in disclosing the information.

REASON The court explained that a "party who realizes or should realize that his conduct has created a condition which involves an unreasonable risk of harm to another has a duty to exercise reasonable care to prevent the risk from occurring." In determining whether a risk of criminal misconduct is foreseeable to an investigator and an information broker, the court examined "two risks of information disclosure implicated by this case: stalking and identity theft. It is undisputed that stalkers, in seeking to locate and track a victim, sometimes use an investigator to obtain personal information about the victim. * * * Not only is stalking itself a crime, but it can lead to more violent crimes, including assault, rape or homicide." Identity theft, "the use of one person's identity by another, is an increasingly common risk associated with the disclosure of personal information. * * * Victims of identity theft risk the destruction of their good credit histories. This often destroys a victim's ability to obtain credit from any source and may, in some cases, render the victim unemployable or even cause the victim to be incarcerated."

FOR CRITICAL ANALYSIS—Technological Consideration *What might the defendants in this case have done to satisfy their legal and ethical duties?*

Defying the Rules: The Enron Case

For years to come, the Enron debacle—the single largest bankruptcy in the history of U.S. business—will remain a symbol of the cost of unethical behavior to management, employees, suppliers, shareholders, the community, society, and indeed the world. Shareholders lost $62 billion of value in a very short period of time in the early 2000s. This case study of "cooking the books," conflicts of interest, and deviation from accepted ethical standards of business has all of the trappings of an epic novel. Unfortunately, for the thousands of employees who lost millions of dollars and for the millions of shareholders who lost billions of dollars, the Enron story was not fiction.

THE GROWTH OF ENRON IN A NUTSHELL

In the 1990s, two gas-pipeline companies, Houston Natural Gas Corporation and InterNorth, Inc., merged to create a very large energy trading company, Enron Corporation. It was a "first mover" in a deregulated electricity market and enjoyed impressive growth. By 1998, Enron was the largest energy trader in the world. Then it entered the online energy trading market. By December 2000, a share of its stock was selling at $85. Most Enron employees had a large part or even all of their retirement packages tied up in the company's stock.

When competition in energy trading increased, Enron diversified into water, power plants in Brazil and India, and finally fiber optics and high-speed Internet transmission.

ACCOUNTING ISSUES

According to the rules of the Financial Accounting Standards Board, energy traders such as Enron could include in *current* earnings profits that they *anticipated* on energy contracts. Herein lay the beginning of a type of accounting "fudging" that increased over time as the company struggled to improve its reported current earnings. By 2000, 50 percent of Enron's $1.4 billion of reported pretax profits consisted of "anticipated" future earnings on energy contracts.

Because Enron's managers received bonuses based on whether they met earnings goals, they had an incentive to inflate the anticipated earnings on such contracts. Some of the contracts extended as long as twenty years in the future. In retrospect, the temptation to management was too great, and common norms of both ethical and legal business decision making were violated as managers overestimated future earnings in order to inflate current earnings.

OFF-THE-BOOKS TRANSACTIONS

To artificially maintain and even increase its reported earnings, Enron also created a complex network of subsidiaries that enabled it to move losses from the core company to the subsidiaries—companies that did not show up on Enron's books. When it created the subsidiaries, Enron transferred assets to them, assigning a value to the assets that was much greater than their actual market value. The effect was to increase Enron's apparent net worth. Consider one example: Enron sold its unused fiber optic cable capacity to a subsidiary for $30 million in cash and a $70 million promissory note. This transaction added $53 million to Enron's reported earnings for just one quarter. The value of the unused fiber optic cable would soon be negligible, however.

For several years, Enron transferred assets from its books, along with the accompanying debt, to partnerships outside the main corporation. Many of these transactions were carried out in the Cayman Islands, a haven for those seeking corporate secrecy as well as a way to avoid federal income taxes.

SELF-DEALING

Enron's chief executive officer (CEO) frequently did business with companies owned by his son and his daughter. The son created a company that was later bought by Enron. The son was then hired as an executive with a guaranteed pay package of $1 million over three years and 20,000 Enron stock options. The CEO's daughter owned a Houston travel agency that received over $10 million—50 percent of the agency's total revenues—from Enron during a three-year period.

THE CORPORATE CULTURE

The many transgressions just described could not have happened without a corporate culture that fostered unethical and, in many instances, illegal business decision making. This case study of unethical behavior is sufficiently important that West Legal Studies in Business has created a project titled "Inside Look," accessible on the Web at **http://insidelook. westbuslaw.com**. There you will discover how, on numerous occasions, Enron management was informed, both by insiders and outsiders, that a "house of cards" had been created. Nonetheless, upper management more often than not refused to investigate and reveal to the public (or to shareholders and employees) the financial improprieties that had occurred over the previous three years.

Business Ethics and the Law

Today, legal compliance is regarded as a **moral minimum**—the minimum acceptable standard for ethical business behavior. Had Enron Corporation strictly complied with existing laws and generally accepted accounting practices, very likely the "Enron scandal" would never have happened. Simply obeying the law does not fulfill all business ethical obligations, however. In the interests of preserving personal freedom, as well as for practical reasons, the law does not—and cannot—codify all ethical requirements. No law says, for example, that it is illegal to lie to one's family, but it may be unethical to do so.

Likewise, in the business world, numerous actions may be unethical but not necessarily illegal. Even though it may be convenient for businesspersons merely to comply with the law, such an approach may not always yield ethical outcomes. ● **EXAMPLE #2** A pharmaceutical company may be banned from marketing a particular drug in the United States because of the drug's possible adverse side effects. Yet no law prohibits the company from selling the drug in foreign markets—even though some consumers in those markets may suffer serious health problems as a result of using the drug. At issue here is not whether it would be legal to market the drug in other countries but whether it would be *ethical* to do so.●

It may seem that determining the legality of a given action should be simple. Either something is legal or it is not. In fact, one of the major challenges businesspersons face is that the legality of a particular action is not always clear. In part, this is because there are so many laws regulating business that a firm may violate one of them without realizing it. The law also contains numerous "gray areas," making it difficult to predict with certainty how a court will apply a given law to a particular action.

LAWS REGULATING BUSINESS

Today's business firms are subject to extensive government regulation. As mentioned in Chapter 1, virtually every action a firm undertakes—from the initial act of going into business to hiring and firing personnel to selling products in the marketplace—is subject to statutory law and to numerous rules and regulations issued by administrative agencies. Furthermore, these rules and regulations are changed or supplemented frequently.

Determining whether a planned action is legal thus requires that decision makers keep abreast of the law. Normally, large business firms have attorneys on their staffs to assist them in making key decisions. Small firms must also seek legal advice before making important business decisions because the consequences of just one violation of a regulatory rule may be costly.

Ignorance of the law will not excuse a business owner or manager from liability for violating a statute or regulation. ● EXAMPLE #3 In one case, the court imposed criminal fines, as well as imprisonment, on a company's supervisory employee for violating a federal environmental act—even though the employee was completely unaware of what was required under the provisions of that act.[2]●

"GRAY AREAS" IN THE LAW

In many situations, business firms can predict with a fair amount of certainty whether a given action would be legal. For example, firing an employee solely because of that per-

son's race or gender clearly violates federal laws prohibiting employment discrimination. In some situations, though, the legality of a particular action may be less clear.

● EXAMPLE #4 Suppose that a firm decides to launch a new advertising campaign. How far can the firm go in making claims for its products or services? Federal and state laws prohibit businesses from engaging in "deceptive advertising." At the federal level, the test for deceptive advertising normally used by the Federal Trade Commission is whether an advertising claim would deceive a "reasonable consumer." At what point, though, would a reasonable consumer be deceived by a particular ad?●

Another gray area in the law has to do with product misuse. Product liability laws (see Chapter 17) require manufacturers and sellers to warn consumers of the kinds of injuries that might result from the foreseeable misuse of their products. An exception to this rule is made when a risk associated with a product is "open and obvious." Sharp knives, for example, can obviously injure their users. Sometimes, though, a business has no way of predicting whether a court will decide that a particular risk is open and obvious or that consumers should be warned of the risk.

In short, business decision makers need to proceed with caution and evaluate an action and its consequences from an ethical perspective. Generally, if a company can demonstrate that it acted in good faith and responsibly in the circumstances, it has a better chance of successfully defending its action in court or before an administrative law judge.

Even courts often disagree on certain issues. In the following case, for example, the trial court and the appellate court arrived at different conclusions on whether a warning on an aerosol can of butane adequately alerted consumers to the danger of inhaling the contents of the can.

---

[2] *United States v. Hanousek*, 176 F.3d 1116 (9th Cir. 1999). This case is presented in Chapter 6 as Case 6.1.

CASE 3.3   Pavlik v. Lane Ltd./Tobacco Exporters International

United States Court of Appeals,
Third Circuit, 1998.
135 F.3d 876.
**http://www.findlaw.com/casecode/courts/
3rd.html[a]**

FACTS Butane is a fuel for cigarette lighters. Zeus brand butane is distributed in small aerosol cans by Lane Limited/Tobacco Exporters International (Lane). On each can

is the warning "DO NOT BREATHE SPRAY." Twenty-year-old Stephen Pavlik died from intentionally inhaling the contents of one of the cans. His father, George Pavlik, filed a suit in a federal district court against Lane and others, claiming in part that the statement on the can did not adequately warn users of the hazards of butane inhalation. The court issued a summary judgment in the defendants' favor, reasoning in part that Stephen must have been aware of the dangers of inhaling butane and that a more specific warning would not have affected his conduct. George Pavlik appealed to the U.S. Court of Appeals for the Third Circuit.

---

a. In the "Browsing" section, select "1998." Then, under "Select Month," choose "February" and click on "search." When that page opens, scroll down the list to the *Pavlik* case name and click on it to access the opinion.

(Continued)

CASE 3.3—Continued

ISSUE Was it clear that Stephen was fully aware of the dangers of inhaling butane, based on the label on the Zeus cans?

DECISION No. The U.S. Court of Appeals for the Third Circuit reversed the judgment of the lower court and remanded the case for trial.

REASON The U.S. Court of Appeals for the Third Circuit acknowledged that a distributor may not be held liable for injuries resulting from the use of a product if it includes an adequate warning of "latent dangers." In this case, the court

did not find the Zeus warning to be adequate as a matter of law. The court pointed out that the warning gave Pavlik "no notice of the serious nature of the danger posed by inhalation, intentional or otherwise." The court, however, did not find the Zeus warning to be inadequate as a matter of law, either, "and so we must leave the question for the jury."

FOR CRITICAL ANALYSIS—Cultural Consideration
Would it have made any difference to the outcome in this case if Stephen's parents had warned him of the dangers of inhaling butane?

TECHNOLOGICAL DEVELOPMENTS AND LEGAL UNCERTAINTIES

Uncertainties about how particular laws may apply to specific factual situations have been compounded in the cyber age. As noted in Chapter 2, the widespread use of the Internet has given rise to situations never before faced by the courts.

The case presented next is illustrative. The case involved an airline pilot who claimed that defamatory, gender-based messages made by her co-workers in an online forum created a hostile working environment. Federal law prohibits

harassment in the workplace, including "hostile-environment harassment," which occurs when an employee is subjected to sexual conduct or comments that he or she perceives as offensive (see Chapter 23). Generally, employers are expected to take immediate and appropriate corrective action in response to employees' complaints of sexual harassment or abuse. Otherwise, they may be held liable for the harassing actions of an employee's co-workers or supervisors. At issue in the case was whether the online forum could be considered part of the "workplace" over which the employer had control.

CASE 3.4 **Blakey v. Continental Airlines, Inc.**

New Jersey Supreme Court, 2000.
751 A.2d 538.
http://lawlibrary.rutgers.edu/search.shtml[a]

FACTS CompuServe, Inc., a subsidiary of America Online, Inc., provided Internet services for Continental Airlines, Inc., including a "Crew Members Forum." The Forum was used by pilots and crew members to exchange ideas and information. Tammy Blakey, a pilot for Continental Airlines since 1984, was the airline's first female captain—and one of only five Continental pilots—to fly an Airbus aircraft. Shortly after qualifying to be a captain on the Airbus A300, Blakey complained

about pornographic photos and vulgar gender-based comments directed at her in her plane's cockpit and other work areas by her male co-employees. Blakey pursued claims against Continental with the Equal Employment Opportunity Commission, the federal agency that administers federal laws prohibiting employment discrimination, and in a federal district court.[b] Meanwhile, Continental pilots published a series of harassing, gender-based, defamatory messages about Blakey on the online forum. When the court refused to consider these messages, Blakey filed a complaint against Continental and others in a New Jersey state court. She alleged, in part, gender-based harassment arising from a hostile work environment. Continental filed a motion for summary judgment on this claim, which the court granted. A state intermediate appellate court upheld the summary

---

a. This page includes a search box for a database of the recent opinions of the New Jersey state courts. In the box, type "Blakey" and click on the "Search" link. When the results appear, scroll down the list and click on the *Blakey* case name to access the opinion. This Web site is maintained by Rutgers School of Law in Camden, New Jersey.

b. In 1997, the federal court ruled in favor of Blakey on a claim of gender-based harassment, awarding her $480,000 in back pay, $15,000 in front pay, and $250,000 for emotional distress, pain, and suffering. The court also found that Blakey had failed to mitigate damages (reduce her damages—by finding other work, for example) and subtracted $120,000 from her back pay award.

CASE 3.4—Continued

judgment, and Blakey appealed to the New Jersey Supreme Court.

ISSUE Can an employees' online forum be such an integral part of the workplace that harassment on it may be regarded as an extension of a pattern of harassment in the workplace?

DECISION Yes. The New Jersey Supreme Court reversed the judgment of the lower court and remanded the case for further proceedings. The state supreme court indicated that the trial court was to determine, among other things, which messages were harassing, whether Continental had notice of those messages, and the severity or pervasiveness of the harassing conduct.

REASON The state supreme court explained that "[o]ur common experience tells us how important are the extensions of the workplace where the relations among employees are cemented or sometimes sundered. If an 'old boys' network' continued, in an after-hours setting, the belittling con-

duct that edges over into harassment, what exactly is the outsider (whether black, Latino, or woman) to do? Keep swallowing the abuse or give up the chance to make the team? We believe that severe or pervasive harassment in a work-related setting that continues a pattern of harassment on the job is sufficiently related to the workplace that an informed employer who takes no effective measures to stop it, sends the harassed employee the message that the harassment is acceptable and that the management supports the harasser." The court compared CompuServe's role to "that of a company that builds an old-fashioned bulletin board. If the maker of an old-fashioned bulletin board provided a better bulletin board by setting aside space on it for employees to post messages, we would have little doubt that messages on the company bulletin board would be part of the workplace setting."

FOR CRITICAL ANALYSIS—Social Consideration
Does the holding in the Blakey *case mean that employers have a duty to monitor their employees' e-mail and other online communications?*

Approaches to Ethical Reasoning

Each individual, when faced with a particular ethical dilemma, engages in **ethical reasoning**—that is, a reasoning process in which the individual examines the situation at hand in light of her or his moral convictions or ethical standards. Businesspersons do likewise when making decisions with ethical implications.

How do business decision makers decide whether a given action is the "right" one for their firms? What ethical standards should be applied? Broadly speaking, ethical reasoning in business traditionally has been characterized by two fundamental approaches. One approach defines ethical behavior in terms of duty, which also implies certain rights. The other approach determines what is ethical in terms of the consequences, or outcome, of any given action. We examine each of these approaches here.

DUTY-BASED ETHICS

Duty-based ethical standards often are derived from revealed truths, such as religious precepts. They can also be derived through philosophical reasoning.

Religious Ethical Standards. In the Judeo-Christian tradition, which is the dominant religious tradition in the United States, the Ten Commandments of the Old

Testament establish fundamental rules for moral action. Other religions have their own sources of revealed truth. Religious rules generally are absolute with respect to the behavior of their adherents. For example, the commandment "Thou shalt not steal" is an absolute mandate for a person, such as a Jew or a Christian, who believes that the Ten Commandments reflect revealed truth. Even a benevolent motive for stealing (such as Robin Hood's) cannot justify the act because the act itself is inherently immoral and thus wrong.

Ethical standards based on religious teachings also involve an element of *compassion.* ● **EXAMPLE #5** Even though it might be profitable for a firm to lay off a less productive employee, if that employee would find it difficult to find employment elsewhere and his or her family would suffer as a result, this potential suffering would be given substantial weight by the decision makers.● Compassionate treatment of others is also mandated—to a certain extent, at least—by the Golden Rule of the ancients ("Do unto others as you would have them do unto you"), which has been adopted by most religions.

Kantian Ethics. Duty-based ethical standards may also be derived solely from philosophical reasoning. The German philosopher Immanuel Kant (1724–1804), for example, identified some general guiding principles for moral behavior based on what he believed to be the fundamental nature of human beings. Kant held that it is rational to assume that human beings are qualitatively different from other physical objects occupying space. Persons are endowed with moral integrity and the capacity to reason and conduct their affairs rationally. Therefore, their thoughts and actions should be respected. When human beings are treated merely as a means to an end, they are being treated as the equivalent of objects and are being denied their basic humanity.

A central postulate in Kantian ethics is that individuals should evaluate their actions in light of the consequences that would follow if *everyone* in society acted in the same way. This **categorical imperative** can be applied to any action. ● **EXAMPLE #6** Suppose that you are deciding whether to cheat on an examination. If you have adopted Kant's categorical imperative, you will decide not to cheat because if everyone cheated, the examination would be meaningless. ●

The Principle of Rights. Because a duty cannot exist without a corresponding right, duty-based ethical standards imply that human beings have basic rights. For example, the commandment "Thou shalt not kill" implies that individuals have a right to live. Additionally, religious ethics may involve a rights component because of the belief—characteristic of some religions—that an individual is "made in the image of God." This belief confers on the individual great dignity as a person. For one who holds this belief, not to respect that dignity—and the rights and status that flow from it—would be morally wrong. Kantian ethics also implies fundamental rights based on the personal dignity of each individual. Just as individuals have a duty not to treat others as a means to an end, so individuals have a right to have their status and moral integrity as human beings treated with respect.

The principle that human beings have certain fundamental rights (to life, freedom, and the pursuit of happiness, for example) is deeply embedded in Western culture. The *natural law* tradition embraces the concept that certain actions (such as killing another person) are morally wrong because they are contrary to nature (the natural desire to continue living). Those who adhere to this **principle of rights,** or "rights theory," believe that a key factor in determining whether a business decision is ethical is how that decision affects the rights of others. These others include the firm's owners, its employees, the consumers of its products or services, its suppliers, the community in which it does business, and society as a whole.

Which Rights Are Most Important? A potential dilemma for those who support rights theory, however, is that they may disagree on which rights are most important. When considering all those affected by a business decision, for example, how much weight should be given to employees relative to shareholders, customers relative to the community, or employees relative to society as a whole?

In general, rights theorists believe that whichever right is stronger in a particular circumstance takes precedence. ● **EXAMPLE #7** Suppose that a firm can either shut down a plant to avoid dumping pollutants in a river that would affect the health of thousands of people or save the jobs of the twelve workers in the plant. In this situation, a rights theorist can easily choose which group to favor. (Not all choices are so clear-cut, however.) ●

OUTCOME-BASED ETHICS: UTILITARIANISM

"Thou shalt act so as to generate the greatest good for the greatest number." This is a paraphrase of the major premise of the utilitarian approach to ethics. **Utilitarianism** is a philosophical theory developed by Jeremy Bentham (1748–1832) and then advanced, with some modifications, by John Stuart Mill (1806–1873)—both British philosophers. In contrast to duty-based ethics, utilitarianism is outcome oriented. It focuses on the consequences of an action, not on the nature of the action itself or on any set of preestablished moral values or religious beliefs.

Under a utilitarian model of ethics, an action is morally correct, or "right," when, among the people it affects, it produces the greatest amount of good for the greatest number. When an action affects the majority adversely, it is morally wrong. Applying the utilitarian theory thus requires (1) a determination of which individuals will be affected by the action in question; (2) a **cost-benefit analysis,** which involves an assessment of the negative and positive effects of alternative actions on these individuals; and (3) a choice among alternative actions that will produce maximum societal utility (the greatest positive net benefits for the greatest number of individuals).

The utilitarian approach to decision making commonly is employed by businesses, as well as by individuals. Weighing the consequences of a decision in terms of its costs and benefits for everyone affected by it is a useful analytical tool in the decision-making process. At the same time, utilitarianism is often criticized because its objective, calculated approach to problems tends to reduce the welfare of human beings to plus and minus signs on a cost-benefit worksheet and to "justify" human costs that many find totally unacceptable.

Corporate Social Responsibility

At one time businesses had few ethical requirements other than complying with the law. Generally, if an action was legal, it was regarded as ethical—no more, no less. By the 1960s, however, this attitude had begun to change significantly. Groups concerned with civil rights, employee safety and welfare, consumer protection, environmental preservation, and other causes began to pressure corporate America to behave in a more responsible manner with respect to these causes. Thus was born the concept of **corporate social responsibility**—the idea that corporations can and should act ethically and be accountable to society for their actions.

VIEWS ON CORPORATE SOCIAL RESPONSIBILITY

Just what constitutes corporate social responsibility has been debated for some time. No one contests the claim that corporations have duties to their shareholders, employees, and product or service users (consumers). Many of these duties are written into law—that is, they are legal duties. The nature of a corporation's duties to other groups and to society at large, however, is not so clear. Today, there are a number of views on this issue.

Profit Maximization. Corporate directors and officers have a duty to act in the shareholders' interest. The law holds directors and officers to a high standard of care in business decision making (see Chapter 26).

In the traditional view, this duty to shareholders takes precedence over all other corporate duties, and the primary goal of corporations should be profit maximization. Those who accept this position argue that a firm can best contribute to society by generating profits. Society benefits because a firm realizes profits only when it markets products or services that are desired by society. These products and services enhance the standard of living, and the profits accumulated by successful business firms generate national wealth. Because our society regards income and wealth as ethical goals, corporations, by contributing to income and wealth, automatically are acting ethically.

The Stakeholder Approach. Another view of corporate social responsibility stresses that a corporation's duty to its shareholders should be weighed against its duties to other *stakeholders*—employees, customers, creditors, suppliers, and the community. The reasoning behind this approach is that in some circumstances, one or more of these other groups may have a greater stake in company decisions than the shareholders do.

● **EXAMPLE #8** A heavily indebted corporation is facing imminent bankruptcy. The shareholder-investors have little to lose in this situation because their stock is already next to worthless. The corporation's creditors will be first in line for any corporate assets remaining. In this situation the creditors have the greatest "stake" in the corporation, and under the stakeholder view, corporate directors and officers should give greater weight to the creditors' interests than to those of the shareholders. ●

Corporate Citizenship. Another theory of social responsibility argues that corporations should actively promote goals that society deems worthwhile and take positive steps toward solving social problems. Because so much of the wealth and power of this country is controlled by business, business in turn has a responsibility to society to use that wealth and power in socially beneficial ways. To be sure, corporations have long contributed some of their shareholders' wealth to meet social needs. Virtually all large corporations today have established nonprofit foundations. Yet corporate citizenship requires more than just making donations to worthwhile causes. Under the corporate citizenship view, companies are also judged on employment discrimination, human rights, environmental concerns, and so on.

Critics of this approach believe that it is inappropriate to use the power of business to promote social causes. Determinations about what is in society's best interest are political; therefore, the public, through the political process, should make those determinations. The legislature—not the corporate board room—is the appropriate forum for such decisions.

THE ROLE OF PUBLIC OPINION

Complicating business ethical decision making is the increasingly important role played by public opinion in determining whether business behavior is ethical. In the last two decades, the actions of business firms have been more closely scrutinized by the media and various interest groups (groups supporting human rights, animal rights, the environment, consumers, employees, and so on) than they were in the past. "Corporate watch" groups report on their Web sites corporate activities that the groups deem unethical. Usually, the groups also urge those who access the site to take action—by printing out and sending a prepared letter to the offending firm, for example. Numerous Web sites have been set up to protest against specific companies' products or services—a topic discussed in this chapter's *Business Law in the Online World* feature on the next page.)

If a corporation undertakes or continues an action deemed to be unethical by one or more interest groups, the firm's "unethical" behavior may become widely known. To maintain their good reputations and their profitability, business firms therefore pay attention to public opinion. As a manager, you might personally be convinced that there is nothing unethical about a certain business action. If a vocal interest group believes otherwise, though, you might want to reassess your decision with a view toward preserving the firm's goodwill and reputation in the community. If you decide to pursue the action regardless of public opinion, you may violate your ethical (and legal) duty to act in the firm's best interests.

BUSINESS LAW IN THE ONLINE WORLD
Cybergriping

In today's online world, a recurring challenge for businesses is how to deal with cybergripers—those who complain in cyberspace about corporate products, services, or activities. For trademark owners, the issue becomes particularly thorny when cybergriping sites add the word "sucks" or "stinks" or some other disparaging term to the domain name of particular companies. These sites, sometimes referred to collectively as "sucks" sites, are established solely for the purpose of criticizing the products or services sold by the companies that own the marks. Can businesses do anything to ward off these cyber attacks on their reputations and goodwill?

TRADEMARK PROTECTION VERSUS FREE SPEECH RIGHTS

A number of companies have sued the owners of "sucks" sites for trademark infringement (see Chapter 5) in the hope that a court or an arbitrating panel will order the owner of that site to cease using the domain name. To date, however, companies have had little success pursuing this alternative. In one case, for example, Bally Total Fitness Holding Corporation sued Andrew Faber, who had established a "Bally sucks" site for the purpose of criticizing Bally's health clubs and business practices. Bally claimed that Faber had infringed on its trademark. The court did not agree, holding that the "speech"—consumer commentary—on Faber's Web site was protected by the First Amendment. According to the court, "The explosion of the Internet is not without its growing pains. It is an efficient means for business to disseminate information, but it also affords critics of those businesses an equally efficient means of disseminating commen-

tary." In short, Bally could not look to trademark law for a remedy against cyber critics.[a]

Generally, the courts have been reluctant to hold that the use of a business's domain name for a "sucks" site infringes on the trademark owner's rights. After all, one of the primary reasons trademarks are protected under U.S. law is to prevent customers from becoming confused over the origins of the goods for sale—and a cybergriping site would certainly not create such confusion. Furthermore, American courts give extensive protection to free speech rights, including the right to express opinions about companies and their products.

PREVENTIVE TACTICS

Many businesses have concluded that while they cannot control what people say about them, they can make it more difficult for it to be said—by buying up insulting domain names before the cybergripers can register them. For example, United Parcel Service (UPS) recently bought UPSstinks.com, IHateUPS.com, UPSBites.com, and a number of similar names. This has now become standard procedure for many firms. Indeed, a study by Company Sleuth of domain name registrations revealed that in just one month (August 2000), nearly 250 companies had registered domain names containing "stinks," "bites," "sucks," or similarly disparaging words. Wal-Mart alone registered more than two hundred anti–Wal-Mart names.[b]

FOR CRITICAL ANALYSIS

Do you believe that cybergriping sites help to improve the ethical performance of the businesses they criticize?

a. *Bally Total Fitness Holding Corp. v. Faber,* 29 F.Supp.2d 1161 (C.D.Cal. 1998).
b. David Stretfield, "Making Bad Names for Themselves: Firms Preempt Critics with Nasty Domains," *The Washington Post,* September 8, 2000, p. A1.

MAXIMUM VERSUS OPTIMUM PROFITS

Today's corporate decision makers are, in a sense, poised between profitability and ethical responsibility. If they emphasize profits at the expense of perceived ethical responsibilities to other groups, they may become the target of negative media exposure and even lawsuits. If they go too

far in the other direction (for example, keep an unprofitable plant open so that employees do not lose their jobs), their profits will suffer, and they may even have to go out of business.

Striking the right balance is difficult, and usually some profits must be sacrificed in the process. Instead of maximum profits, many firms today aim for **optimum profits**—

the maximum profits a firm can realize while staying within legal *and* ethical limits.

Business Ethics on a Global Level

Given the various cultures and religions existing throughout the world, one should not be surprised if frequent conflicts in ethics arise between foreign and U.S. businesspersons. ● EXAMPLE #9 In certain countries the consumption of alcohol and specific foods is forbidden for religious reasons. Under such circumstances, it would be thoughtless and imprudent for a U.S. businessperson to invite a local business contact out for a drink.●

The role played by women in other countries may also present some difficult ethical problems for firms doing business internationally. Equal employment opportunity is a fundamental public policy in the United States, and Title VII of the Civil Rights Act of 1964 prohibits discrimination against women in the employment context (see Chapter 23). Some other countries, however, offer little protection for women against gender discrimination in the workplace, including sexual harassment.

We look here at how laws governing workers in other countries, particularly developing countries, have created some especially difficult ethical problems for U.S. sellers of goods manufactured in foreign countries. We also examine some of the ethical ramifications of a U.S. law that prohibits U.S. businesspersons from bribing foreign officials to obtain favorable business contracts.

MONITORING THE EMPLOYMENT PRACTICES OF FOREIGN SUPPLIERS

Many U.S. businesses now contract with companies in developing nations to produce goods, such as shoes and clothing, because the wage rates in those nations are significantly lower than in the United States. Yet what if a foreign company exploits its workers—by hiring women and children at below-minimum-wage rates, for example, or by requiring its employees to work long hours in a workplace full of health hazards? What if the company's supervisors routinely engage in workplace conduct that is offensive to women?

Given today's global communications network, few companies can assume that their actions in other nations will go unnoticed by "corporate watch" groups that discover and publicize unethical corporate behavior. As a result, U.S. businesses today usually take steps to avoid such adverse publicity—either by refusing to deal with certain suppliers or by making arrangements to monitor their suppliers' workplaces to make sure that the workers are not being mistreated.

THE FOREIGN CORRUPT PRACTICES ACT

Another ethical problem in international business dealings has to do with the legitimacy of certain side payments to government officials. In the United States, the majority of contracts are formed within the private sector. In many foreign countries, however, decisions on most major construction and manufacturing contracts are made by government officials because of extensive government regulation and control over trade and industry. Side payments to government officials in exchange for favorable business contracts are not unusual in such countries, nor are they considered to be unethical. In the past, U.S. corporations doing business in these countries largely followed the dictum, "When in Rome, do as the Romans do."

In the 1970s, however, the U.S. press, and government officials as well, uncovered a number of business scandals involving large side payments by U.S. corporations—such as Lockheed Aircraft—to foreign representatives to secure advantageous international trade contracts. In response to this unethical behavior, in 1977 Congress passed the Foreign Corrupt Practices Act (FCPA), which prohibits U.S. businesspersons from bribing foreign officials to secure advantageous contracts.

Prohibition against the Bribery of Foreign Officials. The first part of the FCPA applies to all U.S. companies and their directors, officers, shareholders, employees, and agents. This part prohibits the bribery of most officials of foreign governments if the purpose of the payment is to get the official to act in his or her official capacity to provide business opportunities.

The FCPA does not prohibit payment of substantial sums to minor officials whose duties are ministerial. These payments are often referred to as "grease," or facilitating payments. They are meant to accelerate the performance of administrative services that might otherwise be carried out at a slow pace. Thus, for example, if a firm makes a payment to a minor official to speed up an import licensing process, the firm has not violated the FCPA. Generally, the act, as amended, permits payments to foreign officials if such payments are lawful within the foreign country. The act also does not prohibit payments to private foreign companies or other third parties unless the U.S. firm knows that the payments will be passed on to a foreign government in violation of the FCPA.

Accounting Requirements. In the past, bribes were often concealed in corporate financial records. Thus, the second part of the FCPA is directed toward accountants. All companies must keep detailed records that "accurately and fairly" reflect the company's financial activities. In addition, all companies must have an accounting system that provides "reasonable assurance" that all transactions entered into by the company are accounted for and legal. These requirements assist in detecting illegal bribes. The FCPA further prohibits any person from making false statements to accountants or false entries in any record or account.

Penalties for Violations. In 1988, the FCPA was amended to provide that business firms that violate the act may be fined up to $2 million. Individual officers or directors who violate the FCPA may be fined up to $100,000 (the fine cannot be paid by the company) and may be imprisoned for up to five years.

OTHER NATIONS DENOUNCE BRIBERY

For twenty years, the FCPA was the only law of its kind in the world, despite attempts by U.S. political leaders to convince other nations to pass similar legislation. That situation is now changing. In 1997, the Organization for Economic Cooperation and Development, to which twenty-six of the world's leading industrialized nations belong, adopted a convention (treaty) that made the bribery of foreign public officials a serious crime. Each signatory is obligated to enact legislation within its nation in accordance with the treaty. The agreement may not only improve the ethical climate in international trade but will also level the playing field for U.S. businesspersons.

Terms and Concepts

business ethics 62	ethical reasoning 69	optimum profits 72
categorical imperative 70	ethics 62	principle of rights 70
corporate social responsibility 71	moral minimum 66	utilitarianism 70
cost-benefit analysis 70		

Chapter Summary   Ethics and Social Responsibility

Business Ethics (See pages 62–63.)	Ethics can be defined as the study of what constitutes right or wrong behavior. Business ethics focuses on how moral and ethical principles are applied in the business context.
Setting the Right Ethical Tone (See pages 63–65.)	1. *Role of management*—Management's commitment and behavior are essential in creating an ethical workplace. Most large firms have ethical codes or policies and corporate compliance programs to help staff members determine whether certain actions are ethical. 2. *Ethical trade-offs*—Management constantly faces ethical trade-offs because firms have ethical and legal duties to a number of groups, including shareholders and employees.
Defying the Rules: The Enron Case (See pages 65–66.)	The Enron debacle—the largest bankruptcy in U.S. history—can serve as a case study of a corporate culture that fostered unethical and, in part, illegal business decision making.
Business Ethics and the Law (See pages 66–69.)	1. *The moral minimum*—Lawful behavior is a moral minimum. The law has its limits, though, and some actions may be legal but not ethical. 2. *Legal uncertainties*—It may be difficult to predict with certainty whether particular actions are legal given the numerous and frequently changing laws regulating business and the "gray areas" in the law.
Approaches to Ethical Reasoning (See pages 69–70.)	1. *Duty-based ethics*—Ethics based on religious beliefs; philosophical reasoning, such as that of Immanuel Kant; and the basic rights of human beings (the principle of rights). 2. *Outcome-based ethics (utilitarianism)*—Ethics based on philosophical reasoning, such as that of John Stuart Mill.
Corporate Social Responsibility (See pages 70–73.)	Corporate social responsibility means that corporations can and should act ethically and be accountable to society for their actions. Different views on what constitutes social responsibility include:

Chapter Summary	Ethics and Social Responsibility—Continued
Corporate Social Responsibility— continued	1. *Profit maximization*—The only concern of corporations should be to maximize profits while operating within legal limits so that the shareholders and society in general benefit from increased wealth.
	2. *Stakeholder view*—A corporation has other stakeholders besides shareholders (including employees, consumers, suppliers, and creditors), and the interests of shareholders should be balanced against the interests of other stakeholders in corporate decision making.
	3. *Corporate citizenship*—Corporations, through philanthropy and their own conduct, should promote social goals (equal opportunity for women, minority groups, and persons with disabilities; protect the human rights of employees; and so on).
Business Ethics on a Global Level (See pages 73–74.)	There are many cultural, religious, and legal differences among nations. Notable differences relate to the role of women in society, employment laws governing workplace conditions, and the practice of giving side payments to foreign officials to secure favorable contracts.

For Review

① What is ethics? What is business ethics? Why is business ethics important?

② What steps can business leaders take to ensure that their companies behave legally and ethically?

③ How do duty-based ethical standards differ from outcome-based ethical standards?

④ What is corporate social responsibility? What are some different theories of social responsibility?

⑤ What is the difference between maximum profits and optimum profits?

Questions and Case Problems

3–1. Business Ethics. Some business ethicists maintain that whereas personal ethics has to do with "right" or "wrong" behavior, business ethics is concerned with "appropriate" behavior. In other words, ethical behavior in business has less to do with moral principles than with what society deems to be appropriate behavior in the business context. Do you agree with this distinction? Do personal and business ethics ever overlap? Should personal ethics play any role in business ethical decision making?

3–2. Business Ethics. If a firm engages in "ethical" behavior solely for the purpose of gaining profits from the goodwill it generates, the "ethical" behavior is essentially a means toward a self-serving end (profits and the accumulation of wealth). In this situation, is the firm acting unethically in any way? Should motive or conduct carry greater weight on the ethical scales in this situation?

3–3. Ethical Reasoning. Susan Whitehead serves on the city planning commission. The city is planning to build a new subway system, and Susan's brother-in-law, Jerry, who owns the Custom Transportation Co., has submitted the lowest bid for the system. Susan knows that Jerry could complete the job for the estimated amount, but she also knows that once Jerry completes this job, he will probably sell his company and quit working. Susan is con-

cerned that Custom Transportation's subsequent management might not be as easy to work with if revisions need to be made on the subway system after its completion. She is torn as to whether she should tell the city about the potential changes in Custom Transportation's management. If the city knew about the instability of Custom Transportation, it might prefer to give the contract to one of Jerry's competitors, whose bid was only slightly higher than Jerry's. Does Susan have an ethical obligation to disclose the information about Jerry to the city planning commission? How would you apply duty-based ethical standards to this question? What might be the outcome of a utilitarian analysis? Discuss fully.

3–4. Ethical Decision Making. Assume that you are a high-level manager for a shoe manufacturer. You know that your firm could increase its profit margin by producing shoes in Indonesia, where you could hire women for $40 a month to assemble them. You also know, however, that human rights advocates recently accused a competing shoe manufacturer of engaging in exploitative labor practices because the manufacturer sold shoes made by Indonesian women working for similarly low wages. You personally do not believe that paying $40 a month to Indonesian women is unethical because you know that in that impoverished country, $40 a month is a better-than-average wage rate. Assuming that the decision is yours to make, should you have the shoes manufactured in Indonesia and make higher profits for your company? Or should you avoid the risk of negative publicity and the consequences of that publicity for the firm's reputation and subsequent profits? Are there other alternatives? Discuss fully.

3–5. Ethical Decision Making. Shokun Steel Co. owns many steel plants. One of its plants is much older than the others. Equipment at the old plant is outdated and inefficient, and the costs of production at that plant are now twice as high as at any of Shokun's other plants. Shokun cannot increase the price of its steel because of competition, both domestic and international. The plant is located in Twin Firs, Pennsylvania, which has a population of about 45,000, and currently employs over a thousand workers. Shokun is contemplating whether to close the plant. What factors should the firm consider in making its decision? Will the firm violate any ethical duties if it closes the plant? Analyze these questions from the two basic perspectives on ethical reasoning discussed in this chapter.

CASE PROBLEM WITH SAMPLE ANSWER

3–6. Isuzu Motors America, Inc., does not warn its customers of the danger of riding unrestrained in the cargo beds of its pickup trucks. Seventeen-year-old Donald Josue was riding unrestrained in the bed of an Isuzu truck driven by Iaone Frias. When Frias lost control of the truck, it struck a concrete center divider. Josue was ejected and his consequent injuries rendered him a paraplegic. Josue filed a suit in a Hawaii state court against Isuzu, asserting a variety of legal claims based on its failure to warn of the danger of riding in the bed of the truck. Should Isuzu be held liable for Josue's injuries? Why or why not? [*Josue v. Isuzu Motors America, Inc.*, 87 Haw. 413, 958 P.2d 535 (1998)]

♦ To view a sample answer for this case problem, go to this book's Web site at **http://fundamentals.westbuslaw.com** and click on "Interactive Study Center."

3–7. Ethical Conduct. Richard Fraser was an "exclusive career insurance agent" under a contract with Nationwide Mutual Insurance Co. Fraser leased computer hardware and software from Nationwide for his business. During a dispute between Nationwide and the Nationwide Insurance Independent Contractors Association, an organization representing Fraser and other exclusive career agents, Fraser prepared a letter to Nationwide's competitors asking whether they were interested in acquiring the represented agents' policyholders. Nationwide obtained a copy of the letter and searched its electronic file server for e-mail indicating that the letter had been sent. It found a stored e-mail that Fraser had sent to a coworker indicating that the letter had been sent to at least one competitor. The e-mail was retrieved from the co-worker's file of already received and discarded messages stored on the receiver. When Nationwide canceled its contract with Fraser, he filed a suit in a federal district court against the firm, alleging, among other things, violations of various federal laws that

prohibit the interception of electronic communications during transmission. In whose favor should the court rule, and why? In any case, did Nationwide act ethically in retrieving the e-mail? [*Fraser v. Nationwide Mutual Insurance Co.*, 135 F.Supp.2d 623 (E.D.Pa. 2001)]

3–8. Ethical Conduct. EF Cultural Travel BV is a travel agency whose principal clients are students. EF requires some employees to sign an agreement that prohibits them from using confidential information obtained during their employment to compete with EF. In the spring of 2000, several former EF employees started Explorica, Inc., to compete with EF. Explorica hired Zefer Corp. to build a scraper to "scrape" EF's prices from its Web site. (A scraper is a computer program that accesses information contained in a succession of Web pages and downloads it to the user's computer.) At the time, there was no statement on EF's site restricting the use of scrapers. After receiving the data from Zefer, Explorica set its prices to undersell EF. When EF discovered Explorica's use of the scraper, EF filed a suit in a federal district court against Zefer and others, seeking in part an injunction against the use of the scraper. Have any of the defendants violated an ethical or legal duty? In particular, on what basis might Zefer be ordered to stop scraping EF's site? Explain. [*EF Cultural Travel BV v. Zefer Corp.*, 318 F.3d 58 (1st Cir. 2003)]

A QUESTION OF ETHICS AND SOCIAL RESPONSIBILITY

3–9. Hazen Paper Co. manufactured paper and paperboard for use in such products as cosmetic wrap, lottery tickets, and pressure-sensitive items. Walter Biggins, a chemist hired by Hazen in 1977, developed a water-based paper coating that was both environmentally safe and of superior quality. By the mid-1980s, the company's sales had increased dramatically as a result of its extensive use of "Biggins Acrylic." Because of this, Biggins thought he deserved a substantial raise in salary, and from 1984 to 1986, Biggins's persistent requests for a raise became a bone of contention between him and his employers. Biggins ran a business on the side, which involved cleaning up hazardous wastes for various companies. Hazen told Biggins that unless he signed a "confidentiality agreement" promising to restrict his outside activities during the time he was employed by Hazen and for a limited time afterward, he would be fired. Biggins said he would sign the agreement only if Hazen raised his salary to $100,000. Hazen refused to do so, fired Biggins, and hired a younger man to replace him. At the time of his discharge in 1986, Biggins was sixty-two years old, had worked for the company nearly ten years, and was just a few weeks away from being entitled to pension rights worth about $93,000. In view of these circumstances, evaluate and answer the following questions. [*Hazen Paper Co. v. Biggins*, 507 U.S. 604, 113 S.Ct. 1701, 123 L.Ed.2d 338 (1993)]

1. Did the company owe an ethical duty to Biggins to increase his salary, given that its sales increased dramatically as a result of Biggins's efforts and ingenuity in developing the

coating? If you were one of the company's executives, would you have raised Biggins's salary? Why or why not?

2. Generally, what public policies come into conflict in cases involving employers who, for reasons of cost and efficiency of operations, fire older, higher-paid workers and replace them with younger, lower-paid workers? If you were an employer facing the need to cut back on personnel to save costs, what would you do, and on what ethical premises would you justify your decision?

VIDEO QUESTION

3–10. Go to this text's Web site at **http://fundamentals.westbuslaw.com** and click on "Video Questions." Select "Chapter 3" and view the video titled *Ethics: Business Ethics an Oxymoron?* Then answer the following questions:

1. According to the instructor in the video, what is the primary reason why businesses act ethically?

2. Of the two approaches to ethical reasoning that were discussed in the chapter, which approach does the instructor seem to be more influenced by in the discussion of how business activities are related to societies? Explain your answer.

3. The instructor asserts that "[i]n the end, it is the unethical behavior that becomes costly, and conversely ethical behavior creates its own competitive advantage." Do you agree with this statement? Why or why not?

ETHICS AND SOCIAL RESPONSIBILITY

For updated links to resources available on the Web, as well as a variety of other materials, visit this text's Web site at

http://fundamentals.westbuslaw.com

You can find articles on shareholders and corporate accountability at the Corporate Governance Web site. Go to

http://www.corpgov.net

Global Exchange offers information on global business activities, including some of the ethical issues stemming from those activities, at

http://www.globalexchange.org

Online Legal Research

Go to the *Fundamentals of Business Law* home page at **http://fundamentals.westbuslaw.com**. Select "Interactive Study Center" and then click on "Chapter 3." There you will find the following Internet research exercises that you can perform to learn more about topics covered in this chapter.

Activity 3–1: LEGAL PERSPECTIVE—Ethics in Business
Activity 3–2: MANAGEMENT PERSPECTIVE—Environmental Self-Audits

Before the Test

Go to the *Fundamentals of Business Law* Web site at **http://fundamentals.westbuslaw.com**. Click on "Interactive Quizzes." You will find at least twenty interactive questions relating to this chapter.

Westlaw® Campus

If your textbook provided for a subscription to Westlaw® Campus, or if you have otherwise purchased access to the Westlaw Campus database, you can access any of the cases presented or cited in this chapter by using your Westlaw Campus account.

Kasky v. Nike, Inc.

INTRODUCTION

In Chapter 1, we discussed the principles governing commercial speech under the First Amendment to the Constitution. In this *Focus on Legal Reasoning,* we examine *Kasky v. Nike, Inc.,*[1] a case in which the California Supreme Court considered whether certain statements constituted commercial speech.

CASE BACKGROUND

Nike, Inc., makes and sells athletic shoes and apparel. Subcontractors in China, Vietnam, and Indonesia make

_____
1. 27 Cal.4th 939, 45 P.3d 243, 119 Cal.Rptr.2d 296 (2002). This case was appealed to the United States Supreme Court, which granted *cert.* After hearing oral arguments, however, the Court decided not to issue a ruling. *Nike, Inc. v. Kasky,* ___ U.S. ___, 123 S.Ct. 2554, 156 L.Ed.2d 580 (2003).

most of Nike's products. In October 1996, the media began to publicize allegations that in the factories where Nike products are made, workers were paid less than the local minimum wage; were required to work overtime; were allowed and encouraged to work more hours than local laws permitted; were subjected to physical, verbal, and sexual abuse; and were exposed to toxic chemicals, noise, heat, and dust without adequate safety equipment, in violation of local health and safety regulations.

Nike responded that workers who make its products are protected from physical and sexual abuse, that they are paid in accordance with local laws governing wages, that they receive free meals and health care, and that their working conditions comply with local regulations. Nike made these statements in press releases; in full-page newspaper ads; and in letters to newspapers, university presidents, and athletic directors.

Marc Kasky, a California resident, filed a suit in a California state court against Nike, alleging in part that these statements were false and misleading in violation of state law. Kasky asked the court to order Nike to "disgorge all monies . . . acquired by means of any act found . . . to be an unlawful and/or unfair business practice" and to begin corrective advertising. Nike asserted in part that the relief Kasky sought "is absolutely barred by the First Amendment." The court dismissed the suit. On Kasky's appeal, a state intermediate appellate court affirmed the dismissal. Kasky petitioned the California Supreme Court for review, arguing in part that Nike's statements were entitled to less protection under the First Amendment because they constituted commercial speech.

MAJORITY OPINION

KENNARD, J. [Justice]

* * * *

The United States Supreme Court has not adopted an all-purpose test to distinguish commercial from noncommercial speech under the First Amendment * * * . A close reading of the high court's commercial speech decisions [including *Bolger v. Young Drug Products Corp.,* 463 U.S. 60, 103 S.Ct. 2875, 77 L.Ed.2d 469 (1983)] suggests, however, that it is possible to formulate a limited-purpose test. We conclude, therefore, that when a court must decide whether particular speech may be subjected to laws aimed at preventing false advertising or other forms of commercial deception, *categorizing a particular statement as commercial or noncommercial speech requires consideration of three elements: the speaker, the intended audience, and the content of the message.* [Emphasis added.]

In typical commercial speech cases, the *speaker* is likely to be someone engaged in commerce—that is, generally, the production, distribution, or sale of goods or services—or someone acting on behalf of a person so engaged, and the *intended audience* is likely to be actual or potential buyers or customers of the speaker's goods or services, or persons acting for actual or potential buyers or customers, or persons (such as reporters or reviewers) likely to repeat the message to or otherwise influence actual or potential buyers or customers. * * *

* * * *

Finally, the factual content of the message should be commercial in character. In the context of regulation of false or misleading advertising, this typically means that the speech consists of representations of fact about the business operations, products, or services of the speaker * * * , made for the purpose of promoting sales of, or other commercial transactions in, the speaker's products or services * * * .

* * * *

Here, the first element—a commercial speaker—is satisfied because the speakers—Nike and its officers and directors—are engaged in commerce. Specifically, they manufacture, import, distribute, and sell consumer goods in the form of athletic shoes and apparel.

The second element—an intended commercial audience—is also satisfied. [For example,] Nike's letters to university presidents and directors of athletic departments were addressed directly to actual and potential purchasers of Nike's products, because college and university athletic departments are major purchasers of athletic shoes and apparel. * * *

The third element—representations of fact of a commercial nature—is also present. In describing its own labor policies, and the practices and working conditions in factories where its products are made, Nike was making factual representations about its own business operations. * * *

* * * *

The judgment of the Court of Appeals is reversed, and the matter is remanded to that court for further proceedings consistent with this opinion.

DISSENTING OPINION
BROWN, J. [Justice]
* * * *

* * * [T]he majority's test for commercial speech contravenes long-standing principles of First Amendment law.

First, the test flouts the very essence of the distinction between commercial and noncommercial speech * * * . If commercial speech is to be distinguished, it must be distinguished by its content. * * * [T]he majority distinguishes commercial from noncommercial speech using two criteria wholly unrelated to the speech's content: the identity of the speaker and the intended audience. * * *

Second, the test contravenes a fundamental tenet of First Amendment jurisprudence by making the identity of the speaker potentially dispositive [decisive]. * * * [T]he identity of the speaker is not decisive in determining whether speech is protected, and speech does not lose its protection because of the corporate identity of the speaker. This is because corporations and other speakers engaged in commerce contribute to the discussion, debate, and the dissemination of information and ideas that the First Amendment seeks to foster. Thus, the inherent worth of the speech in terms of its capacity for informing the public does not depend upon the identity of its source, whether corporation, association, union, or individual. * * *

Third, the test violates the First Amendment by stifling the ability of speakers engaged in commerce, such as corporations, to participate in debates over public issues. * * * Speech on public issues occupies the highest rung of the hierarchy of First Amendment values, and is entitled to special protection because such speech is more than self-expression; it is the essence of self-government. The * * * [First] Amendment remove[s] governmental restraints from the arena of public discussion, putting the decision as to what views shall be voiced largely into the hands of each of us, in the hope that use of such freedom will ultimately produce a more capable citizenry and more perfect polity [nation or government] * * * .

LEGAL REASONING AND ANALYSIS

❶ **Legal Analysis.** Find the *Bolger v. Young Drug Products Corp.* case (see the *Accessing the Internet* section at the end of Chapter 2 for instructions on how to access federal court opinions). Compare the facts and issues in that case to the facts and issues of the Kasky case. How are they similar? How are they different?

Why did the court refer to this case in its opinion?

❷ **Legal Reasoning.** Contrast the conclusion of the majority with that of the dissent. What arguments did the dissent make to support its assertion that the majority's conclusion was incorrect? What legal sources did the dissent cite to justify its position?

❸ **Implications for the Business Manager.** What effect might the holding in this case have on businesses that are, or may be, subject to negative allegations about their operations?

❹ **Case Briefing Assignment.** Using the guidelines for briefing cases given in Appendix A of this text, brief the *Kasky* case.

This text's Web site, at **http://fundamentals.westbuslaw.com**, offers links to West's Court Case Updates, as well as to other online research sources. You can also locate court cases at the Web sites listed in the *Accessing the Internet* section at the end of Chapter 2. The United States Supreme Court commonly issues opinions in cases involving the Constitution, including disputes concerning commercial speech and the First Amendment. Supreme Court cases are online at a number of sites, including **http://www.findlaw.com**. FindLaw, Inc., a part of West Group, maintains this Web site.

UNIT 2

Torts and Crimes

CHAPTER

4

Torts and Cyber Torts

CHAPTER OBJECTIVES

After reading this chapter, you should be able to answer the following questions:

① What is a tort?

② What is the purpose of tort law? What are two basic categories of torts?

③ What are the four elements of negligence?

④ What is meant by strict liability? In what circumstances is strict liability applied?

⑤ What is a cyber tort, and how are tort theories being applied in cyberspace?

Torts are wrongful actions.[1] Through tort law, society compensates those who have suffered injuries as a result of the wrongful conduct of others. Although some torts, such as assault and trespass, originated in the English common law, the field of tort law continues to expand. As new ways to commit wrongs are discovered, such as the use of the Internet to carry out injurious acts, the courts are extending tort law to cover these wrongs.

As you will see in later chapters of this book, many of the lawsuits brought by or against business firms are based on the tort theories discussed in this chapter. Some of the torts examined here can occur in any context, including the business environment. Others traditionally have been

referred to as **business torts,** which are defined as wrongful interferences with the business rights of others. Included in business torts are such vaguely worded concepts as *unfair competition* and *wrongfully interfering with the business relations of others.* Torts committed via the Internet are sometimes referred to as **cyber torts.** We look at how the courts have applied traditional tort law to wrongful actions in the online environment in the concluding pages of this chapter.

The Basis of Tort Law

Two notions serve as the basis of all torts: wrongs and compensation. Tort law recognizes that some acts are wrong because they cause injuries to others. In a tort action, one

---

[1] The word *tort* is French for "wrong."

person or group brings a personal suit against another person or group to obtain compensation (money **damages**) or other relief for the harm suffered.

Generally, the purpose of tort law is to provide remedies for the invasion of various *protected interests*. Society recognizes an interest in personal physical safety, and tort law provides remedies for acts that cause physical injury or that interfere with physical security and freedom of movement. Society recognizes an interest in protecting real and personal property, and tort law provides remedies for acts that cause destruction or damage to property. Society also recognizes an interest in protecting certain intangible interests, such as personal privacy, family relations, reputation, and dignity, and tort law provides remedies for invasion of these protected interests.

There are two broad classifications of torts: *intentional torts* and *unintentional torts* (torts involving negligence). The classification of a particular tort depends largely on how the tort occurs (intentionally or negligently) and the surrounding circumstances.

Intentional Torts against Persons

An **intentional tort**, as the term implies, requires *intent*. The **tortfeasor** (the one committing the tort) must intend to commit an act, the consequences of which interfere with the personal or business interests of another in a way not permitted by law. An evil or harmful motive is not required—in fact, the actor may even have a beneficial motive for committing what turns out to be a tortious act. In tort law, intent means only that the actor intended the consequences of his or her act or knew with substantial certainty that certain consequences would result from the act. The law generally assumes that individuals intend the *normal* consequences of their actions. Thus, forcefully pushing another—even if done in jest and without any evil motive—is an intentional tort (if injury results), because the object of a strong push can ordinarily be expected to go flying.

This section discusses intentional torts against persons, which include assault and battery, false imprisonment, infliction of emotional distress, defamation, invasion of the right to privacy, appropriation, misrepresentation, and wrongful interference.

ASSAULT AND BATTERY

Any intentional, unexcused act that creates in another person a reasonable apprehension or fear of immediate harmful or offensive contact is an **assault**. Apprehension is not the same as fear. If a contact is such that a reasonable person would want to avoid it, and if there is a reasonable basis for believing that the contact will occur, then the plaintiff suffers apprehension whether or not he or she is afraid. The interest protected by tort law regarding assault is the freedom from having to expect harmful or offensive contact. The occurrence of apprehension is enough to justify compensation.

The *completion* of the act that caused the apprehension, if it results in harm to the plaintiff, is a **battery**, which is defined as an unexcused and harmful or offensive physical contact *intentionally* performed. For example, suppose that Ivan threatens Jean with a gun, then shoots her. The pointing of the gun at Jean is an assault; the firing of the gun (if the bullet hits Jean) is a battery. The interest protected by tort law concerning battery is the right to personal security and safety. The contact can be harmful, or it can be merely offensive (such as an unwelcome kiss). Physical injury need not occur. The contact can involve any part of the body or anything attached to it—for example, a hat or other item of clothing, a purse, or a chair or an automobile in which one is sitting. Whether the contact is offensive or not is determined by the *reasonable person standard*.[2] The contact can be made by the defendant or by some force the defendant sets in motion—for example, a rock thrown, food poisoned, or a stick swung.

Compensation. If the plaintiff shows that there was contact, and the jury agrees that the contact was offensive, the plaintiff has a right to compensation. There is no need to show that the defendant acted out of malice; the person could have just been joking or playing around. The underlying motive does not matter, only the intent to bring about the harmful or offensive contact to the plaintiff. In fact, proving a motive is never necessary (but is sometimes relevant). A plaintiff may be compensated for the emotional harm or loss of reputation resulting from a battery, as well as for physical harm.

Defenses to Assault and Battery. A number of legally recognized **defenses** (reasons why plaintiffs should not obtain what they are seeking) can be raised by a defendant who is sued for assault or battery, or both:

① *Consent.* When a person consents to the act that damages her or him, there is generally no liability (legal responsibility) for the damage done.

---

[2] The reasonable person standard is an objective test of how a reasonable person would have acted under the same circumstances. See "The Duty of Care and Its Breach" later in this chapter.

② *Self-defense.* An individual who is defending his or her life or physical well-being can claim self-defense. In situations of both *real* and *apparent* danger, a person may use whatever force is *reasonably* necessary to prevent harmful contact.

③ *Defense of others.* An individual can act in a reasonable manner to protect others who are in real or apparent danger.

④ *Defense of property.* Reasonable force may be used in attempting to remove intruders from one's home, although force that is likely to cause death or great bodily injury can never be used merely to protect property.

FALSE IMPRISONMENT

False imprisonment is defined as the intentional confinement or restraint of another person's activities without justification. False imprisonment interferes with the freedom to move without restriction. The confinement can be accomplished through the use of physical barriers, physical restraint, or threats of physical force. Moral pressure or threats of future harm do not constitute false imprisonment. It is essential that the person being held not comply with the restraint willingly.

Businesspersons are often confronted with suits for false imprisonment after they have attempted to confine a suspected shoplifter for questioning. Under the "privilege to detain" granted to merchants in some states, a merchant can use the defense of *probable cause* to justify delaying a suspected shoplifter. Probable cause exists when the evidence to support the belief that a person is guilty outweighs the evidence against that belief. Although laws governing false imprisonment vary from state to state, generally they require that any detention be conducted in a *reasonable* manner and for only a *reasonable* length of time.

INFLICTION OF EMOTIONAL DISTRESS

The tort of *infliction of emotional distress* can be defined as an intentional act that amounts to extreme and outrageous conduct resulting in severe emotional distress to another. ● EXAMPLE #1 A prankster telephones an individual and says that the individual's spouse has just been in a horrible accident. As a result, the individual suffers intense mental pain or anxiety. The caller's behavior is deemed to be extreme and outrageous conduct that exceeds the bounds of decency accepted by society and is therefore **actionable** (capable of serving as the ground for a lawsuit). ●

The tort of infliction of emotional distress poses several problems for the courts. One problem is the difficulty of proving the existence of emotional suffering. For this rea-

son, courts in some jurisdictions require that the emotional distress be evidenced by some physical symptom or illness or some emotional disturbance that can be documented by a psychiatric consultant or other medical professional.

Another problem is that emotional distress claims must be subject to some limitation, or they could flood the courts with lawsuits. A society in which individuals are rewarded if they are unable to endure the normal emotional stresses of day-to-day living is obviously undesirable. Therefore, the law usually holds that indignity or annoyance alone is not enough to support a lawsuit based on infliction of emotional distress. Repeated annoyances (such as those experienced by a person who is being stalked), however, coupled with threats, are enough. In the business context, the repeated use of extreme methods to collect a delinquent account may be actionable.

DEFAMATION

Defamation of character involves wrongfully hurting a person's good reputation. The law has imposed a general duty on all persons to refrain from making false, defamatory statements about others. Breaching this duty orally involves the tort of **slander**; breaching it in writing involves the tort of **libel**. The tort of defamation also arises when a false statement is made about a person's product, business, or title to property. We deal with these torts later in the chapter.

The common law defines four types of false utterances that are considered slander *per se* (meaning that no proof of injury or harm is required for these false utterances to be actionable):

① A statement that another has a loathsome communicable disease.

② A statement that another has committed improprieties while engaging in a profession or trade.

③ A statement that another has committed or has been imprisoned for a serious crime.

④ A statement that a woman is unchaste.

The Publication Requirement. The basis of the tort of defamation is the publication of a statement or statements that hold an individual up to contempt, ridicule, or hatred. *Publication* here means that the defamatory statements are communicated to persons other than the defamed party. ● EXAMPLE #2 If Thompson writes Andrews a private letter accusing him of embezzling funds, the action does not constitute libel. If Peters calls Gordon dishonest, unattractive, and incompetent when no one else is around, the action does not constitute slander. In neither case was the message communicated to a third party. ●

The courts have generally held that even dictating a letter to a secretary may constitute publication. Moreover, if a third party overhears defamatory statements by chance, the courts usually hold that this also constitutes publication. Defamatory statements made via the Internet are also actionable. Note further that any individual who republishes or repeats defamatory statements is liable even if that person reveals the source of such statements.

Defenses against Defamation. Truth is normally an absolute defense against a defamation charge. In other words, if the defendant in a defamation suit can prove that his or her allegedly defamatory statements were true, the defendant will not be liable.

Another defense that is sometimes raised is that the statements were **privileged** communications, and thus the defendant is immune from liability. Privileged communications are of two types: absolute and qualified. Only in judicial proceedings and certain legislative proceedings is *absolute* privilege granted. For example, statements made in the courtroom by attorneys and judges during a trial are absolutely privileged. So are statements made by legislators during congressional floor debate, even if the legislators make such statements maliciously—that is, knowing them to be untrue. An absolute privilege is granted in these situations because judicial and legislative personnel deal with matters that are so much in the public interest that the parties involved should be able to speak out fully and freely without restriction.

In general, false and defamatory statements that are made about *public figures* (public officials who exercise substantial governmental power and any persons in the public limelight) and that are published in the press are privileged if they are made without **actual malice**.[3] To be made with actual malice, a statement must be made with *either knowledge of falsity or a reckless disregard of the truth.* Statements made about public figures, especially when they are made via a public medium, are usually related to matters of general public interest; they are made about people who substantially affect all of us. Furthermore, public figures generally have some access to a public medium for answering disparaging (belittling, discrediting) falsehoods about themselves. Private individuals do not. For these reasons, public figures have a greater burden of proof in defamation cases (they must prove actual malice) than do private individuals.

INVASION OF THE RIGHT TO PRIVACY

A person has a right to solitude and freedom from prying public eyes—in other words, to privacy. As discussed in Chapter 1, the Supreme Court has held that a fundamental

right to privacy is also implied by various amendments to the U.S. Constitution. Some state constitutions explicitly provide for privacy rights. In addition, a number of federal and state statutes have been enacted to protect individual rights in specific areas. Tort law also safeguards these rights through the tort of *invasion of privacy*. Four acts qualify as an invasion of privacy:

① *The use of a person's name, picture, or other likeness for commercial purposes without permission.* We will examine this tort, which is usually referred to as the tort of *appropriation,* shortly.

② *Intrusion in an individual's affairs or seclusion.* For example, invading someone's home or illegally searching someone's briefcase is an invasion of privacy. The tort has been held to extend to eavesdropping by wiretap, the unauthorized scanning of a bank account, compulsory blood testing, and window peeping.

③ *Publication of information that places a person in a false light.* This could be a story attributing to the person ideas not held or actions not taken by the person. (Publishing such a story could involve the tort of defamation as well.)

④ *Public disclosure of private facts about an individual that an ordinary person would find objectionable.* A newspaper account of a private citizen's sex life or financial affairs could be an actionable invasion of privacy.

A pressing issue in today's online world has to do with the privacy rights of Internet users. This is particularly true with respect to personal information collected not only by government agencies but by online merchants. Internet users also face significant privacy issues in the employment context.

APPROPRIATION

The use by one person of another person's name, likeness, or other identifying characteristic, without permission and for the benefit of the user, constitutes the tort of **appropriation.** Under the law, an individual's right to privacy normally includes the right to the exclusive use of her or his identity.

● **EXAMPLE #3** Vanna White, the hostess of the popular television game show *Wheel of Fortune,* brought a case against Samsung Electronics America, Inc. Without White's permission, Samsung included in an advertisement for its videocassette recorders (VCRs) a depiction of a robot dressed in a wig, gown, and jewelry, posed in a scene that resembled the *Wheel of Fortune* set, in a stance for which White is famous. The court held in White's favor, holding that the tort of appropriation does not require the use of a celebrity's name or likeness. The court stated that

---

[3] *New York Times Co. v. Sullivan,* 376 U.S. 254, 84 S.Ct. 710, 11 L.Ed.2d 686 (1964).

Samsung's robot ad left "little doubt" as to the identity of the celebrity whom the ad was meant to depict.[4]●

Cases of wrongful appropriation, or misappropriation, may also involve the rights of those who invest time and money in the creation of a special system, such as a method of broadcasting sports events. Commercial misappropriation may also occur when a person takes and uses the property of another for the sole purpose of capitalizing unfairly on the goodwill or reputation of the property owner.

MISREPRESENTATION (FRAUD)

A misrepresentation leads another to believe in something that is different from what actually exists. This is often accomplished through a false or an incorrect statement. Misrepresentations may be innocently made by someone who is unaware of the existing facts, but the tort of **fraudulent misrepresentation**, or fraud, involves intentional deceit for personal gain. The tort includes several elements:

① Misrepresentation of facts or conditions with knowledge that they are false or with reckless disregard for the truth.

② Intent to induce another to rely on the misrepresentation.

③ Justifiable reliance by the deceived party.

④ Damages suffered as a result of the reliance.

⑤ Causal connection between the misrepresentation and the injury suffered.

For fraud to occur, more than mere **puffery**, or *seller's talk*, must be involved. Fraud exists only when a person represents as a fact something he or she knows is untrue. For example, it is fraud to claim that a building does not leak when one knows it does. Facts are objectively ascertainable, whereas seller's talk is not. "I am the best accountant in town" is seller's talk. The speaker is not trying to represent something as fact, because the term *best* is a subjective, not an objective, term.[5]

Normally, the tort of misrepresentation or fraud occurs only when there is reliance on a *statement of fact*. Sometimes, however, reliance on a *statement of opinion* may involve the tort of misrepresentation if the individual making the statement of opinion has a superior knowledge of the subject matter. For example, when a lawyer makes a statement of opinion about the law in a state in which the

lawyer is licensed to practice, a court would construe reliance on such a statement to be equivalent to reliance on a statement of fact. We examine fraudulent misrepresentation in further detail in Chapter 10, in the context of contract law.

WRONGFUL INTERFERENCE

Business torts involving wrongful interference are generally divided into two categories: wrongful interference with a contractual relationship and wrongful interference with a business relationship.

Wrongful Interference with a Contractual Relationship. The body of tort law relating to *intentional interference with a contractual relationship* has expanded greatly in recent years. A landmark nineteenth-century case involved an opera singer, Joanna Wagner, who was under contract to sing for a man named Lumley for a specified period of years. Another man, Gye, who knew of this contract, nonetheless "enticed" Wagner to refuse to carry out the agreement, and Wagner began to sing for Gye. Gye's action constituted a tort because it wrongfully interfered with the contractual relationship between Wagner and Lumley.[6] (Of course, Wagner's refusal to carry out the agreement also entitled Lumley to sue Wagner for breach of contract.)

Three elements are necessary for wrongful interference with a contractual relationship to occur:

① A valid, enforceable contract must exist between two parties.

② A third party must know that this contract exists.

③ The third party must *intentionally* cause either of the two parties to breach the contract.

The contract may be between a firm and its employees or a firm and its customers. Sometimes a competitor of a firm draws away one of the firm's key employees. If the original employer can show that the competitor induced the breach—that is, that the former employee would not otherwise have broken the contract—damages can be recovered from the competitor.

The following case illustrates the elements of the tort of wrongful interference with a contractual relationship in the context of a contract between an independent sales representative and his agent (agency relationships are discussed in Chapter 22). The case was complicated by the existence of a second contract between the sales representative and the third party.

---

[4] *White v. Samsung Electronics America, Inc.*, 971 F.2d 1395 (9th Cir. 1992).

[5] In contracts for the sale of goods, Article 2 of the Uniform Commercial Code distinguishes, for warranty purposes, between statements of opinion ("puffery") and statements of fact. See Chapter 17 for a further discussion of this issue.

---

[6] *Lumley v. Gye*, 118 Eng.Rep. 749 (1853).

CASE 4.1   Mathis v. Liu

United States Court of Appeals,
Eighth Circuit, 2002.
276 F.3d 1027.

FACTS Ching and Alex Liu own Pacific Cornetta, Inc. In 1997, Pacific Cornetta entered into a contract with Lawrence Mathis, under which Mathis agreed to solicit orders for Pacific Cornetta's products from Kmart Corporation for a commission of 5 percent on net sales. Under the terms, either party could terminate the contract at any time. The next year, Mathis entered into a one-year contract with John Evans, under which Evans agreed to serve as Mathis's agent to solicit orders from Kmart for the product lines that Mathis represented, including Pacific Cornetta, for a commission of 1 percent on net sales. Under the terms of this contract, either party could terminate it only on six months' written notice. A few months later, Pacific Cornetta persuaded Evans to break his contract with Mathis and enter into a contract with Pacific Cornetta to be its sales representative to Kmart. Evans terminated his contract with Mathis without notice. Two days later, Pacific Cornetta terminated its contract with Mathis. Mathis filed a suit in a federal district court against the Lius and Pacific Cornetta, alleging in part wrongful interference with a contractual relationship. The court issued a judgment that included a ruling in Mathis's favor on this claim, but Mathis appealed the amount of damages to the U.S. Court of Appeals for the Eighth Circuit.

ISSUE Had the defendants wrongfully interfered with Mathis's contract with Evans?

DECISION Yes. The appellate court affirmed the lower court's judgment, holding that the defendants had wrongfully interfered with Mathis's contractual relationship with Evans.

REASON Factors used "to determine whether a defendant's interference is improper" include "the nature of the actor's conduct[,] * * * the actor's motive[,] * * * the interests of the other with which the actor's conduct interferes[,] * * * the interests sought to be advanced by the actor[,] * * * the social interests in protecting the freedom of action of the actor and the contractual interests of the other[,] * * * the proximity or remoteness of the actor's conduct to the interference[,] and * * * the relations between the parties." Evans's contract with Mathis "did not create a simple at-will arrangement [a legal doctrine under which a contract can be terminated at any time by either party for any, or no, reason] because Mr. Evans could terminate it only after giving Mr. Mathis six months' notice of his intention to do so. In these circumstances, we think that the jury was entitled to conclude that Pacific Cornetta's blandishments [enticements] were improper, especially since inducing a breach of contract absent compelling justification is, in and of itself, improper." Evans's sales of Pacific Cornetta products after Pacific Cornetta terminated its contract with Mathis did not furnish a basis for damages on this claim, however, because the contract with Mathis was terminable at will.

FOR CRITICAL ANALYSIS—Ethical Consideration
Does the ruling in this case mean that Mathis is entirely without recourse? Could he sue Evans for anything?

Wrongful Interference with a Business Relationship. Businesspersons devise countless schemes to attract customers, but they are forbidden by the courts to interfere unreasonably with another's business in their attempts to gain a share of the market. There is a difference between competitive methods and **predatory behavior**—actions undertaken with the intention of unlawfully driving competitors completely out of the market.

The distinction usually depends on whether a business is attempting to attract customers in general or to solicit only those customers who have shown an interest in a similar product or service of a specific competitor. If a shopping center contains two shoe stores, an employee of Store A cannot be positioned at the entrance of Store B to divert customers to Store A. This type of activity constitutes the tort of wrongful interference with a business relationship, which is commonly considered to be an unfair trade practice. If this type of activity were permitted, Store A would reap the benefits of Store B's advertising.

Defenses to Wrongful Interference. A person will not be liable for the tort of wrongful interference with a contractual or business relationship if it can be shown that the interference was justified, or permissible. Bona fide competitive behavior is a permissible interference even if it results in the breaking of a contract. ● **EXAMPLE #4** If Antonio's Meats advertises so effectively that it induces Beverly's Restaurant Chain to break its contract with Otis Meat Company, Otis Meat Company will be unable to recover against Antonio's Meats on a wrongful interference theory. After all, the public policy that favors free competition in advertising outweighs any possible instability that such competitive activity might cause in contractual relations.●

Intentional Torts against Property

Intentional torts against property include trespass to land, trespass to personal property, conversion, and disparagement of property. These torts are wrongful actions that interfere with individuals' legally recognized rights to their land or personal property. The law distinguishes real property from personal property (see Chapters 28 and 29). *Real property* is land and things "permanently" attached to the land. *Personal property* consists of all other items, which are basically movable. Thus, a house and lot are real property, whereas the furniture inside a house is personal property. Money, stocks, and bonds are also personal property.

TRESPASS TO LAND

A **trespass to land** occurs whenever a person, without permission, enters onto, above, or below the surface of land that is owned by another; causes anything to enter onto the land; remains on the land; or permits anything to remain on it. Actual harm to the land is not an essential element of this tort because the tort is designed to protect the right of an owner to exclusive possession of his or her property. Common types of trespass to land include walking or driving on the land, shooting a gun over the land, throwing rocks at a building that belongs to someone else, building a dam across a river and thus causing water to back up on someone else's land, and placing part of one's building on an adjoining landowner's property.

Trespass Criteria, Rights, and Duties. Before a person can be a trespasser, the owner of the real property (or other person in actual and exclusive possession of the property) must establish that person as a trespasser. For example, "posted" trespass signs expressly establish as a trespasser a person who ignores these signs and enters onto the property. A guest in your home is not a trespasser—unless she or he has been asked to leave but refuses. Any person who enters onto your property to commit an illegal act (such as a thief entering a lumberyard at night to steal lumber) is established impliedly as a trespasser, even if no signs are posted.

At common law, a trespasser is liable for damages caused to the property and generally cannot hold the owner liable for injuries sustained on the premises. This common law rule is being abandoned in many jurisdictions in favor of a "reasonable duty of care" rule that varies depending on the status of the parties. For example, a landowner may have a duty to post a notice that the property is patrolled by guard dogs. Furthermore, under the "attractive nuisance" doctrine, children do not assume the risks of the premises if they are attracted to the premises by some object, such as a swimming pool, an abandoned building, or a sand pile. Trespassers normally can be removed from the premises through the use of reasonable force without the owner's being liable for assault and battery.

Defenses against Trespass to Land. Trespass to land involves wrongful interference with another person's real property rights. A defense exists if it can be shown that the trespass was warranted, however, such as when a trespasser enters to assist someone in danger. Another defense exists when the trespasser can show that he or she had a license to come onto the land. A *licensee* is one who is invited (or allowed to enter) onto the property of another for the licensee's benefit. A person who enters another's property to read an electric meter, for example, is a licensee. When you purchase a ticket to attend a movie or sporting event, you are licensed to go onto the property of another to view that movie or event. Note that licenses to enter onto another's property are *revocable* by the property owner. If a property owner asks a meter reader to leave and the meter reader refuses to do so, the meter reader at that point becomes a trespasser.

TRESPASS TO PERSONAL PROPERTY

Whenever any individual unlawfully harms the personal property of another or otherwise interferes with the personal property owner's right to exclusive possession and enjoyment of that property, **trespass to personal property**—also called *trespass to personalty*[7]—occurs. If a student takes another student's business law book as a practical joke and hides it so that the owner is unable to find it for several days before a final examination, the student has engaged in trespass to personal property.

If it can be shown that trespass to personal property was warranted, then a complete defense exists. Most states, for example, allow automobile repair shops to hold a customer's car (under what is called an *artisan's lien,* discussed in Chapter 21) when the customer refuses to pay for repairs already completed.

CONVERSION

Whenever personal property is wrongfully taken from its rightful owner or possessor and placed in the service of another, the act of **conversion** occurs. Conversion is defined

---

[7] Pronounced *per-sun-ul-tee.*

as any act depriving an owner of personal property without that owner's permission and without just cause. When conversion occurs, the lesser offense of trespass to personal property usually occurs as well. If the initial taking of the property was unlawful, there is trespass; retention of that property is conversion. If the initial taking of the property was permitted by the owner or for some other reason is not a trespass, failure to return it may still be conversion. Conversion is the civil side of theft crimes. A store clerk who steals merchandise from the store commits a crime and engages in the tort of conversion at the same time.

Even if a person mistakenly believed that she or he was entitled to the goods, the tort of conversion may occur. In other words, good intentions are not a defense against conversion; in fact, conversion can be an entirely innocent act. Someone who buys stolen goods, for example, is guilty of conversion even if he or she did not know that the goods were stolen. If the true owner brings a tort action against the buyer, the buyer must either return the property to the owner or pay the owner the full value of the property, despite having already paid money to the thief.

A successful defense against the charge of conversion is that the purported owner does not in fact own the property or does not have a right to possess it that is superior to the right of the holder. Necessity is another possible defense against conversion. ● **EXAMPLE #5** If Abrams takes Mendoza's cat, Abrams is guilty of conversion. If Mendoza sues Abrams, Abrams must return the cat or pay damages. If, however, the cat has rabies and Abrams took the cat to protect the public, Abrams has a valid defense—necessity (and perhaps even self-defense, if he can prove that he was in danger because of the cat).● Conversion was one of the claims in the following case.

CASE 4.2   Pearl Investments, LLC v. Standard I/O, Inc.

United States District Court,
District of Maine, 2003.
257 F.Supp.2d 326.

FACTS Pearl Investments, LLC, operates automated stock-trading computer systems (ATS) in Portland, Maine. Standard I/O, Inc., provides custom software programming services. Jesse Chunn owns Standard. In April 2000, Pearl hired Standard to develop software for Pearl's ATS. Standard installed the software on several of Pearl's servers, including one Pionex server, at a computer facility maintained by On-Site Trading, Inc., in New York. In March 2001, with Pearl's consent, Chunn opened an account with On-Site. Chunn bought and delivered a Pionex server to On-Site, and told it to maintain the server apart from Pearl's equipment. In November, On-Site sold its assets to A.B. Watley, Inc. (ABW). Pearl asked ABW to install a new operating system on Pearl's Pionex server, but ABW mistakenly installed the system on Chunn's server, which ABW found connected to Pearl's network. Dennis Daudelin, Pearl's chief executive officer, removed the server from ABW's facility. After repeated demands, Daudelin returned the server on January 9, 2002, and its hard disk drive on October 24. Pearl filed a suit in a federal district court against Standard and Chunn, alleging, among other things, misappropriation of trade secrets. Chunn filed a counterclaim against Pearl, alleging conversion.

ISSUE Is Pearl liable to Chunn for conversion?

DECISION Yes. The court denied the plaintiffs' motions for summary judgment and granted summary judgment to Chunn on his counterclaim for conversion against Pearl. The court ordered a trial for a determination as to the amount of damages. The court also ordered that other issues, including some of the plaintiffs' claims, be submitted for trial (adding, however, that Pearl could not base any claim on the contents of Chunn's server).

REASON The court stated that "[t]he necessary elements to make out a claim for conversion are: (1) a showing that the person claiming that his property was converted has a property interest in the property; (2) that he had the right to possession at the time of the alleged conversion; and (3) that the party with the right to possession made a demand for its return that was denied by the holder." In this case, "Daudelin seized Chunn's server from ABW without Chunn's knowledge or permission and * * * Daudelin and Pearl were unwilling to return the server, despite demand." The court acknowledged Daudelin and Pearl's arguments "that the server was discovered to have been connected to Pearl's [network] without its authorization and that Daudelin's intent was solely to preserve evidence for any later claim against whomever owned the server." The court pointed out, however, that "good faith is not a defense" to a charge of conversion.

FOR CRITICAL ANALYSIS—Technological Consideration
How might Daudelin and Pearl successfully assert necessity as a defense to Chunn's charge?

DISPARAGEMENT OF PROPERTY

Disparagement of property occurs when economically injurious falsehoods are made not about another's reputation but about another's product or property. Disparagement of property is a general term for torts that can be more specifically referred to as *slander of quality* or *slander of title*.

Slander of Quality. Publication of false information about another's product, alleging that it is not what its seller claims, constitutes the tort of **slander of quality,** or **trade libel.** The plaintiff must prove that actual damages proximately resulted from the slander of quality. In other words, the plaintiff must show not only that a third person refrained from dealing with the plaintiff because of the improper publication but also that there were associated damages. The economic calculation of such damages—they are, after all, conjectural—is often extremely difficult.

An improper publication may be both a slander of quality and a defamation. For example, a statement that disparages the quality of a product may also, by implication, disparage the character of the person who would sell such a product. In one case, for instance, the claim that a product that was marketed as a sleeping aid contained "habit-forming drugs" was held to constitute defamation.[8]

During the 1990s, at least thirteen states enacted special statutes to protect against disparagement of perishable food products. Food producers began to push for such laws in 1991 after Washington state apple growers, using traditional libel and product-disparagement laws, failed to win a lawsuit against CBS News for a *60 Minutes* broadcast on the growth regulator Alar. Food-disparagement laws received national media attention when a group of Texas cattle ranchers sued talk-show host Oprah Winfrey for saying on one of her shows that the fear of "mad cow" disease "stopped her cold from eating a hamburger." The ranchers claimed that Winfrey had defamed their product, beef, in violation of the Texas food-disparagement statute. In 1998, the federal judge hearing the case held that the cattle ranchers had failed to make a case under the Texas statute.

Slander of Title. When a publication denies or casts doubt on another's legal ownership of any property, and when this results in financial loss to that property's owner, the tort of **slander of title** may exist. Usually, this is an intentional tort in which someone knowingly publishes an untrue statement about property with the intent of discouraging a third

person from dealing with the person slandered. For example, it would be difficult for a car dealer to attract customers after competitors published a notice that the dealer's stock consisted of stolen autos.

Unintentional Torts (Negligence)

The tort of **negligence** occurs when someone suffers injury because of another's failure to live up to a required *duty of care*. In contrast to intentional torts, in torts involving negligence, the tortfeasor neither wishes to bring about the consequences of the act nor believes that they will occur. The actor's conduct merely creates a *risk* of such consequences. If no risk is created, there is no negligence.

Many of the actions discussed in the section on intentional torts constitute negligence if the element of intent is missing. ● **EXAMPLE #6** If Juarez intentionally shoves Natsuyo, who falls and breaks an arm as a result, Juarez will have committed the intentional tort of assault and battery. If Juarez carelessly bumps into Natsuyo, however, and she falls and breaks an arm as a result, Juarez's action will constitute negligence. In either situation, Juarez has committed a tort. ●

In examining a question of negligence, one should ask four questions:

① Did the defendant owe a duty of care to the plaintiff?

② Did the defendant breach that duty?

③ Did the plaintiff suffer a legally recognizable injury as a result of the defendant's breach of the duty of care?

④ Did the defendant's breach cause the plaintiff's injury?

Each of these elements of negligence is discussed in this section.

THE DUTY OF CARE AND ITS BREACH

The concept of a **duty of care** arises from the notion that if we are to live in society with other people, some actions can be tolerated and some cannot; some actions are right and some are wrong; and some actions are reasonable and some are not. The basic principle underlying the duty of care is that people are free to act as they please so long as their actions do not infringe on the interests of others.

When someone fails to comply with the duty of exercising reasonable care, a potentially tortious act may have been committed. Failure to live up to a standard of care may be an act (accidentally setting fire to a building) or an omission (neglecting to put out a campfire). It may be a careless act or a carefully performed but nevertheless dangerous act that results in injury. It may even be an unwitting or accidental

---

[8] *Harwood Pharmacal Co. v. National Broadcasting Co.*, 9 N.Y.2d 460, 174 N.E.2d 602, 214 N.Y.S.2d 725 (1961).

MANAGEMENT PERSPECTIVE
Evidence Spoliation as a Tort

MANAGEMENT FACES A LEGAL ISSUE According to an age-old legal maxim, when a party loses or destroys evidence relating to a lawsuit, the presumption arises that the evidence was harmful to the "spoliator"—the party that lost or destroyed the evidence. Courts may impose sanctions—including fines, the dismissal of a lawsuit, or the entry of a default judgment for the opposing party—for evidence spoliation. In addition, some states now allow the injured party to file a separate tort action against the spoliator to recover money damages.

WHAT THE COURTS SAY Traditionally, courts have imposed sanctions for evidence spoliation only when evidence is *intentionally* destroyed. Increasingly, however, courts are imposing sanctions even when the evidence was *accidentally* destroyed. In one case, for example, a federal court of appeals sanctioned the plaintiff by dismissing his lawsuit because, through no fault of his own, he had failed to preserve evidence (a defective landing gear) for the defendant's inspection.[a]

Some state courts are going even further to punish those who destroy or lose evidence. Consider a case that came before the Ohio Supreme Court in 2001. In that case, the plaintiff sued Wal-Mart for the wrongful death of her husband, a fork lift operator and employee who was killed when the driver of the truck he was loading pulled away. The jury found for the plaintiff and awarded her damages. After the trial was over, the plaintiff's attorney requested and the trial court awarded additional interest because of Wal-Mart's failure to make a good faith effort to settle the case. During this posttrial proceeding, the plaintiff discovered evidence indicating that Wal-Mart employees had given false and misleading testimony during depositions prior to trial and that certain documents (weekly accident reports) were not produced. The plaintiff filed another tort action for spoliation.

The trial court granted Wal-Mart's motion for summary judgment on the ground that the plaintiff's complaints against Wal-Mart had already been determined by the jury. Ultimately, however, the Ohio Supreme Court[b] held that "[c]oncealing, destroying, misrepresenting or intentionally interfering with evidence" during a trial may give rise to a separate tort action if the evidence spoliation is not discovered until after the conclusion of the trial.

IMPLICATIONS FOR MANAGERS As a practical matter, business owners and managers should take great care to preserve any evidence that may be necessary to bring or defend against a lawsuit. Courts may impose sanctions even if the evidence was lost or destroyed accidentally, or by someone who was working for you. Moreover, in some states losing or destroying evidence may subject you to tort liability and even punitive damages. Businesspersons should also be aware that failure to produce documents and evidence during the discovery process may be interpreted by some courts as evidence spoliation.

a. *Miller v. Mid-Continent Aircraft Service, Inc.*, 139 F.3d 912 (10th Cir. 1998).

b. *Davis v. Wal-Mart Stores, Inc.*, 93 Ohio St.3d 488, 756 N.E.2d 657 (2001).

destruction of evidence—see, for example, this chapter's *Management Perspective*. Courts consider the nature of the act (whether it is outrageous or commonplace), the manner in which the act is performed (cautiously versus carelessly), and the nature of the injury (whether it is serious or slight) in determining whether the duty of care has been breached.

The Reasonable Person Standard. Tort law measures duty by the **reasonable person standard**. In determining whether a duty of care has been breached, the courts ask how a reasonable person would have acted in the same circumstances. The reasonable person standard is said to be (though in an absolute sense it cannot be) objective. It is not necessarily how a particular person would act. It is society's judgment on how people *should* act. If the so-called reasonable person existed, he or she would be careful, conscientious, even tempered, and honest. This hypothetical reasonable person is frequently used by the courts in decisions involving other areas of law as well.

That individuals are required to exercise a reasonable standard of care in their activities is a pervasive concept in business law, and many of the issues dealt with in subsequent chapters of this text have to do with this duty. What constitutes reasonable care varies, of course, with the circumstances.

The Duty of Landowners. Landowners are expected to exercise reasonable care to protect persons coming onto their property from harm. As mentioned earlier, in some jurisdictions, landowners are held to owe a duty to protect even trespassers against certain risks. Landowners who rent or lease premises to tenants (see Chapter 29) are expected to exercise reasonable care to ensure that the tenants and their guests are not harmed in common areas, such as stairways, entryways, laundry rooms, and the like.

Retailers and other firms that explicitly or implicitly invite persons to come onto their premises are usually charged with a duty to exercise reasonable care to protect those persons, who are considered **business invitees**. For example, if you entered a supermarket, slipped on a wet floor, and sustained injuries as a result, the owner of the supermarket would be liable for damages if at the time you slipped there was no sign warning that the floor was wet. A court would hold that the business owner was negligent because the owner failed to exercise a reasonable degree of care in protecting the store's

customers against foreseeable risks about which the owner knew or *should have known*. That a patron might slip on the wet floor and be injured as a result was a foreseeable risk, and the owner should have taken care to avoid this risk or to warn the customer of it. The landowner also has a duty to discover and remove any hidden dangers that might injure a customer or other invitee.

Some risks, of course, are so obvious that the owner need not warn of them. For instance, a business owner does not need to warn customers to open a door before attempting to walk through it. Other risks, however, even though they may seem obvious to a business owner, may not be so in the eyes of another, such as a child. For example, a hardware store owner may not think it is necessary to warn customers that a stepladder leaning against the back wall of the store could fall down and harm them. It is possible, though, that a child could tip the ladder over and be hurt as a result and that the store could be held liable.

In the following case, the court had to decide whether a store owner should be held liable for a customer's injury on the premises. The question was whether the owner had notice of the condition that led to the customer's injury.

CASE 4.3   Martin v. Wal-Mart Stores, Inc.

United States Court of Appeals, Eighth Circuit, 1999. 183 F.3d 770. http://www.findlaw.com/casecode/courts/8th.html[a]

FACTS Harold Martin was shopping in the sporting goods department of a Wal-Mart store. There was one employee in the department at that time. In front of the sporting goods section, in the store's main aisle (which the employees referred to as "action alley"), there was a large display of stacked cases of shotgun shells. On top of the cases were individual boxes of shells. Shortly after the sporting goods employee walked past the display, Martin did so, but Martin slipped on some loose shotgun shell pellets and fell to the floor. He immediately lost feeling in, and control of, his legs. Sensation and control returned, but during the next week, he lost the use of his legs several times for periods of ten to fifteen minutes. Eventually, sensation and control did not return to the front half of his left foot. Doctors diagnosed the condi-

tion as permanent. Martin filed a suit against Wal-Mart in a federal district court, seeking damages for his injury. The jury found in his favor, and the court denied Wal-Mart's motion for a directed verdict. Wal-Mart appealed to the U.S. Court of Appeals for the Eighth Circuit.

ISSUE Should Wal-Mart be held liable for Martin's injury?

DECISION Yes. The U.S. Court of Appeals for the Eighth Circuit affirmed the judgment of the lower court.

REASON The appellate court stated, "The traditional rule * * * required a plaintiff in a slip and fall case to establish that the defendant store had either actual or constructive notice[b] of the dangerous condition." The court, however, explained that this case involved the self-service store exception to the traditional slip-and-fall rule. A self-service store has notice that certain dangers arising through customer involvement are likely to occur and has a duty to anticipate them. Part of this duty is to "warn customers or protect them from the danger." Here, Wal-Mart had constructive notice of the

---
a. This URL will take you to a page maintained by FindLaw. When you access the page, enter "Wal-Mart" in the "Party Name Search" box and then click on "Search." Scroll down the list on the page that opens and select the link to "Harold Martin v. Wal-Mart Stores."

b. *Constructive notice* is notice that is implied by law, in view of the circumstances.

CASE 4.3—Continued

pellets on the floor in the main aisle. "Martin slipped on pellets next to a large display of shotgun shells immediately abutting the sporting goods department. The chance that merchandise will wind up on the floor (or merchandise will be spilled on the floor) in the department in which that merchandise is sold or displayed is exactly the type of foreseeable risk" that is part of the self-service store exception.

FOR CRITICAL ANALYSIS—Ethical Consideration

Why do the courts impose constructive notice requirements on owners of self-service stores but not on owners of other stores?

The Duty of Professionals. If an individual has knowledge, skill, or intelligence superior to that of an ordinary person, the individual's conduct must be consistent with that status. Professionals—including physicians, dentists, psychiatrists, architects, engineers, accountants, lawyers, and others—are required to have a standard minimum level of special knowledge and ability. Therefore, in determining what constitutes reasonable care in the case of professionals, their training and expertise are taken into account. In other words, an accountant cannot defend against a lawsuit for negligence by stating, "But I was not familiar with that principle of accounting."

If a professional violates her or his duty of care toward a client, the professional may be sued for **malpractice**. For example, a patient might sue a physician for *medical malpractice*. A client might sue an attorney for *legal malpractice*.

THE INJURY REQUIREMENT AND DAMAGES

For a tort to have been committed, the plaintiff must have suffered a *legally recognizable* injury. To recover damages (receive compensation), the plaintiff must have suffered some loss, harm, wrong, or invasion of a protected interest. Essentially, the purpose of tort law is to compensate for legally recognized injuries resulting from wrongful acts. If no harm or injury results from a given negligent action, there is nothing to compensate—and no tort exists.

● **EXAMPLE #7** If you carelessly bump into a passerby, who stumbles and falls as a result, you may be liable in tort if the passerby is injured in the fall. If the person is unharmed, however, there normally could be no suit for damages, because no injury was suffered. Although the passerby might be angry and suffer emotional distress, few courts recognize negligently inflicted emotional distress as a tort unless it results in some physical disturbance or dysfunction.●

As already mentioned, the purpose of tort law is not to punish people for tortious acts but to compensate the injured parties for damages suffered. Occasionally, however, damages awarded in tort lawsuits include both **compensatory damages** (which are intended to reimburse a plaintiff for actual losses—to make the plaintiff whole) and **punitive damages** (which are intended to punish the wrongdoer and deter others from similar wrongdoing).

CAUSATION

Another element necessary to a tort is *causation*. If a person fails in a duty of care and someone suffers injury, the wrongful activity must have caused the harm for a tort to have been committed. In deciding whether there is causation, the court must address two questions:

① *Is there causation in fact?* Did the injury occur because of the defendant's act, or would it have occurred anyway? If an injury would not have occurred without the defendant's act, then there is causation in fact. **Causation in fact** can usually be determined by the use of the *but for* test: "but for" the wrongful act, the injury would not have occurred. Theoretically, causation in fact is limitless. One could claim, for example, that "but for" the creation of the world, a particular injury would not have occurred. Thus, as a practical matter, the law has to establish limits, and it does so through the concept of proximate cause.

② *Was the act the proximate cause of the injury?* **Proximate cause**, or legal cause, exists when the connection between an act and an injury is strong enough to justify imposing liability. ● **EXAMPLE #8** Ackerman carelessly leaves a campfire burning. The fire not only burns down the forest but also sets off an explosion in a nearby chemical plant that spills chemicals into a river, killing all the fish for a hundred miles downstream and ruining the economy of a tourist resort. Should Ackerman be liable to the resort owners? To the tourists whose vacations were ruined? These are questions of proximate cause that a court must decide.●

Foreseeability. The courts use *foreseeability* as the test for proximate cause. If the victim of the harm or the consequences of the harm done are unforeseeable, there is no proximate cause. It is difficult to predict when a court will say that something is foreseeable and when it will decide that something is not. How far a court stretches foreseeability is determined in part by the extent to which the court is willing to stretch the defendant's duty of care.

Superseding Cause. An independent intervening force may break the connection between a wrongful act and an injury to another. If so, it acts as a *superseding cause*—that is, the intervening force or event sets aside, or replaces, the original wrongful act as the cause of the injury. ● **EXAMPLE #9** Suppose that Derrick keeps a can of gasoline in the trunk of his car. The presence of the gasoline creates a foreseeable risk and is thus a negligent act. If Derrick's car skids and crashes into a tree, causing the gasoline can to explode, Derrick would be liable for injuries sustained by passing pedestrians because of his negligence. If the explosion had been caused by lightning striking the car, however, the lightning would supersede Derrick's original negligence as a cause of the damage, because the lightning was not foreseeable. ●

In negligence cases, the negligent party will often attempt to show that some act has intervened after his or her action and that this second act was the proximate cause of injury. Typically, in cases in which an individual takes a defensive action, such as swerving to avoid an oncoming car, the original wrongdoer will not be relieved of liability even if the injury actually resulted from the attempt to escape harm. The same is true under the "danger invites rescue" doctrine. Under this doctrine, if Lemming commits an act that endangers Salter, and Yokem sustains an injury trying to protect Salter, then Lemming will be liable for Yokem's injury, as well as for any injuries Salter may sustain. Rescuers can injure themselves, or the person rescued, or even a stranger, but the original wrongdoer will still be liable.

DEFENSES TO NEGLIGENCE

Defendants often defend against negligence claims by asserting that the plaintiffs failed to prove the existence of one or more of the required elements for negligence. A defendant may also assert that an intervening force should be deemed a superseding cause, thus relieving the defendant of liability. Additionally, there are three basic *affirmative* defenses in negligence cases (defenses that defendants can use to avoid liability even if the facts are as the plaintiffs state). These defenses are (1) assumption of risk and (2) contributory and comparative negligence.

Assumption of Risk. A plaintiff who voluntarily enters into a risky situation, knowing the risk involved, will not be allowed to recover. This is the defense of **assumption of risk.** The requirements of this defense are (1) knowledge of the risk and (2) voluntary assumption of the risk.

The risk can be assumed by express agreement, or the assumption of risk can be implied by the plaintiff's knowledge of the risk and subsequent conduct. For example, a driver entering a race knows that there is a risk of being killed or injured in a crash. Of course, the plaintiff does not assume a risk different from or greater than the risk normally carried by the activity. In our example, the race driver would not assume the risk that the banking in the curves of the racetrack will give way during the race because of a construction defect.

Risks are not deemed to be assumed in situations involving emergencies. Neither are they assumed when a statute protects a class of people from harm and a member of the class is injured by the harm. For example, employees are protected by statute from dangerous working conditions and therefore do not assume the risks associated with the workplace. If an employee is injured, he or she will generally be compensated regardless of fault under state workers' compensation statutes (discussed in Chapter 23).

Contributory and Comparative Negligence. All individuals are expected to exercise a reasonable degree of care in looking out for themselves. In a few jurisdictions, recovery for injury resulting from negligence is prevented if the plaintiff was also negligent (failed to exercise a reasonable degree of care). This is the defense of **contributory negligence.** Under the common law doctrine of contributory negligence, no matter how insignificant the plaintiff's negligence is relative to the defendant's negligence, the plaintiff will be precluded from recovering any damages.

An exception to the doctrine of contributory negligence may apply if the defendant failed to take advantage of an opportunity to avoid causing the damage. Under the "last clear chance" rule, the plaintiff may recover full damages despite her or his own negligence. (Note that in those states that have adopted the comparative negligence rule, discussed next, the last clear chance doctrine does not apply.) ● **EXAMPLE #10** Murphy is walking across the street against the light, and Lewis, a motorist, sees her in time to avoid hitting her but hits her anyway. In this situation, Lewis (the defendant) is not permitted to use Murphy's (the plaintiff's) prior negligence as a defense. The defendant negligently missed the opportunity to avoid injuring the plaintiff. ●

The majority of states now allow recovery based on the doctrine of **comparative negligence.** This doctrine enables both the plaintiff's and the defendant's negligence to be computed and the liability for damages distributed accordingly. Some jurisdictions have adopted a "pure" form of comparative negligence that allows the plaintiff to recover, even if the extent of his or her fault is greater than that of the defendant. For example, if the plaintiff was 80 percent at fault and the defendant 20 percent at fault, the plaintiff may recover 20 percent of his or her damages. Many states' comparative negligence statutes, however, contain a "50 percent" rule by which the plaintiff recovers nothing if she or he was more than 50 percent at fault.

SPECIAL NEGLIGENCE DOCTRINES AND STATUTES

There are a number of special doctrines and statutes relating to negligence. We examine a few of them here.

Res Ipsa Loquitur.   Generally, in lawsuits involving negligence, the plaintiff has the burden of proving that the defendant was negligent. In certain situations, however, when negligence is very difficult or impossible to prove, the courts may infer that negligence has occurred; then, the burden of proof rests on the defendant—to prove he or she was not negligent. The inference of the defendant's negligence is known as the doctrine of *res ipsa loquitur,*[9] which translates as "the facts speak for themselves."

This doctrine is applied only when the event creating the damage or injury is one that ordinarily would occur only as a result of negligence. ● **EXAMPLE #11** If a person undergoes knee surgery and following the surgery has a severed nerve in the knee area, that person can sue the surgeon under a theory of *res ipsa loquitur.* In this case, the injury would not have occurred but for the surgeon's negligence.[10]● For the doctrine of *res ipsa loquitur* to apply, the event must have been within the defendant's power to control, and it must not have been due to any voluntary action or contribution on the part of the plaintiff.

Negligence *Per Se.*   Certain conduct, whether it consists of an action or a failure to act, may be treated as **negligence** *per se* (*per se* means "in or of itself"). Negligence *per se* may occur if an individual violates a statute or an ordinance providing for a criminal penalty and that violation causes another to be injured. The injured person must prove (1) that the statute clearly sets out what standard of conduct is expected, when and where it is expected, and of whom it is expected; (2) that he or she is in the class intended to be protected by the statute; and (3) that the statute was designed to prevent the type of injury that he or she suffered. The standard of conduct required by the statute is the duty that the defendant owes to the plaintiff, and a violation of the statute is the breach of that duty.

● **EXAMPLE #12**   A statute may require a landowner to keep a building in safe condition and may also subject the landowner to a criminal penalty, such as a fine, if the building is not kept safe. The statute is meant to protect those who are rightfully in the building. Thus, if the owner, without a sufficient excuse, violates the statute and a tenant is thereby injured, a majority of courts will hold that the owner's unexcused violation of the statute conclusively establishes a breach of a duty of care—that is, that the owner's violation is negligence *per se.* ●

Special Negligence Statutes.   A number of states have enacted statutes prescribing duties and responsibilities in certain circumstances. For example, most states now have what are called **Good Samaritan statutes.**[11] Under these statutes, persons who are aided voluntarily by others cannot turn around and sue the "Good Samaritans" for negligence. These laws were passed largely to protect physicians and medical personnel who voluntarily render their services in emergency situations to those in need, such as individuals hurt in car accidents.

Many states have also passed **dram shop acts,** under which a tavern owner or bartender may be held liable for injuries caused by a person who became intoxicated while drinking at the bar or who was already intoxicated when served by the bartender. In some states, statutes impose liability on *social hosts* (persons hosting parties) for injuries caused by guests who became intoxicated at the hosts' homes. Under these statutes, it is unnecessary to prove that the tavern owner, bartender, or social host was negligent.

Strict Liability

Another category of torts is called **strict liability,** or *liability without fault.* Intentional torts and torts of negligence involve acts that depart from a reasonable standard of care and cause injuries. Under the doctrine of strict liability, liability for injury is imposed for reasons other than fault. Strict liability for damages proximately caused by an abnormally dangerous or exceptional activity is one application of this doctrine. Courts apply the doctrine of strict liability in such cases because of the extreme risk of the activity. Even if blasting with dynamite is performed with all reasonable care, there is still a risk of injury. Balancing that risk against the potential for harm, it seems reasonable to ask the person

---

[9] Pronounced *rihz ihp-*suh *low-*kwuh-duhr.
[10] *Edwards v. Boland,* 41 Mass.App.Ct. 375, 670 N.E.2d 404 (1996).

[11] These laws derive their name from the Good Samaritan story in the Bible. In the story, a traveler who had been robbed and beaten lay along the roadside, ignored by those passing by. Eventually, a man from the country of Samaria (the "Good Samaritan") stopped to render assistance to the injured person.

engaged in the activity to pay for injuries caused by that activity. Although there is no fault, there is still responsibility because of the dangerous nature of the undertaking.

There are other applications of the strict liability principle. Persons who keep dangerous animals, for example, are strictly liable for any harm inflicted by the animals. A significant application of strict liability is in the area of *product liability*—liability of manufacturers and sellers for harmful or defective products. Liability here is a matter of social policy and is based on two factors: (1) the manufacturing company can better bear the cost of injury, because it can spread the cost throughout society by increasing prices of goods and services; and (2) the manufacturing company is making a profit from its activities and therefore should bear the cost of injury as an operating expense. We will discuss product liability in greater detail in Chapter 17.

Cyber Torts

A significant issue that has come before the courts in recent years involves the question of who should be held liable for *cyber torts,* or torts committed in cyberspace. For example, who should be held liable when someone posts a defamatory message online? Should an Internet service provider (ISP), such as Yahoo or America Online (AOL), be liable for the remark if the ISP was unaware that it was being made?

Other questions involve issues of proof. How, for example, can it be proved that an online defamatory remark was "published" (which requires that a third party see or hear it)? How can the identity of the person who made the remark be discovered? Can an ISP be forced to reveal the source of an anonymous comment? We explore some of these questions in this section, as well as some of the legal issues that have arisen with respect to bulk e-mail advertising.

DEFAMATION ONLINE

Online forums allow anyone—customers, employees, or crackpots—to complain about a business firm's personnel, policies, practices, or products. Regardless of whether the complaint is justified or whether it is true, it may have an impact on the business of the firm. One of the early questions in the online legal arena was whether the providers of such forums could be held liable for defamatory statements made in those forums.

Liability of Internet Service Providers. Newspapers, magazines, and television and radio stations may be held liable for defamatory remarks that they disseminate, even if those remarks are prepared or created by others. Under the Communications Decency Act of 1996, however, Internet service providers (ISPs), or "interactive computer service providers," are not liable for such material.[12] An ISP typically provides access to the Internet through a local phone number and may provide other services, including access to databases available only to the ISP's subscribers. (See this chapter's *Business Law in the Online World* feature for a further discussion of the immunity of interactive service providers.)

Piercing the Veil of Anonymity. A threshold barrier to anyone who seeks to bring an action for online defamation is discovering the identity of the person who posted the defamatory message online. ISPs can disclose personal information about their customers only when ordered to do so by a court. Because of this, businesses and individuals are increasingly resorting to lawsuits against "John Does." Then, using the authority of the courts, they can obtain from the ISPs the identities of the persons responsible for the messages. ● EXAMPLE #13 Eric Hvide, a former chief executive of a company called Hvide Marine, sued a number of "John Does" who had posted allegedly defamatory statements about his company on various online message boards. Hvide, who eventually lost his job, sued the John Does for libel in a Florida court. The court ruled that Yahoo and AOL had to reveal the identities of the defendant Does.[13] ●

SPAM

Bulk, unsolicited e-mail ("junk" e-mail) sent to all of the users on a particular e-mailing list is often called **spam**.[14] Typical spam consists of a product ad sent to all of the users on an e-mailing list or all of the members of a newsgroup.

Spam can waste user time and network bandwidth (the amount of data that can be transmitted within a certain time). It can also impose a burden on an ISP's equipment. ● EXAMPLE #14 In one case, Cyber Promotions, Inc., sent bulk e-mail to subscribers of CompuServe, Inc., an ISP. CompuServe subscribers complained to the service about ads, and many canceled their subscriptions. Handling the ads also placed a tremendous burden on CompuServe's equipment. CompuServe told Cyber Promotions to stop

---

[12] 47 U.S.C. Section 230.
[13] *Does v. Hvide,* 770 So.2d 1237 (Fla.App.3d 2000).
[14] The term *spam* is said to come from a Monty Python song with the lyrics, "Spam spam spam spam, spam spam spam spam, lovely spam, wonderful spam." Like these lyrics, spam online is often judged to be a repetition of worthless text.

BUSINESS LAW IN THE ONLINE WORLD
Interactive Service Providers and Tort Liability

Recall from the discussion of defamation earlier in this chapter that one who repeats or otherwise republishes a defamatory statement is subject to liability as if he or she had originally published it. Thus, publishers generally can be held liable for defamatory contents in the books and periodicals that they publish.

Before the passage of the Communications Decency Act (CDA) of 1996, the courts grappled on several occasions with the question of whether Internet service providers (ISPs) should be regarded as publishers and thus held liable for defamatory messages made by users of their services. The CDA resolved the issue by stating that "[n]o provider or user of an interactive computer service shall be treated as the publisher or speaker of any information provided by another information content provider." Although portions of the CDA were held unconstitutional by the United States Supreme Court (the provisions prohibiting the transmission of materials harmful to minors—see Chapter 1), the provision regarding the liability of ISPs was not.

THE CDA SHIELDS ISPS FROM LIABILITY In a number of key cases, the ISP provisions of the CDA have been invoked to shield ISPs from liability for defamatory postings on their bulletin boards. In a leading case, decided the year after the CDA was enacted, America Online, Inc. (AOL), was not held liable even though it did not promptly remove defamatory messages of which it had been made aware. In upholding a district court's ruling in AOL's favor, a federal appellate court stated that the CDA "plainly immunizes computer service providers like AOL from liability for information that originates with third parties." The court explained that the purpose of the statute is "to maintain the robust nature of Internet communication and, accordingly, to keep government interference in the medium to a minimum." The court added, "None of this means, of course, that the

original culpable party who posts defamatory messages would escape accountability."[a]

EXTENDING CDA IMMUNITY TO ONLINE AUCTION SERVICES Most of the cases concerning ISP immunity under the CDA have involved bulletin boards and other forums provided by ISPs. In 2000, however, a California state court extended the CDA further into the realm of e-commerce when it ruled that eBay, the online auction house, could not be held liable for the sale of pirated sound recordings on its Web site. In *Stoner v. eBay, Inc.*,[b] the plaintiff alleged that eBay had knowingly reaped "massive profits" from the sale of pirated sound recordings in violation of a California statute prohibiting unfair business practices. A California state court, however, concluded that there was nothing to indicate that eBay's function should be transformed from that of an interactive service provider to that of a seller responsible for items sold on the site. The court noted that "a principal objective of the immunity provision [of the CDA] is to encourage commerce over the Internet by ensuring that interactive computer service providers are not held responsible for how third parties use their services."

FOR CRITICAL ANALYSIS

Although publishers traditionally have been held liable for defamatory contents in the books and periodicals that they publish, distributors (libraries, bookstores, newsstands, and the like) have not—unless it can be shown that a distributor was aware of the defamatory nature of a particular work and distributed it anyway. Can you think of any reason why the drafters of the CDA decided to grant virtually total immunity to ISPs instead of treating them as "distributors"? Explain.

a. *Zeran v. America Online, Inc.*, 129 F.3d 327 (4th Cir. 1997); *cert.* denied, 524 U.S. 934, 118 S.Ct. 2341, 141 L.Ed.2d 712 (1998).
b. Cal.Super.Ct. 2000. For further details on this unpublished decision, see "California Judge Finds eBay Immune under CDA," *e-commerce Law & Strategy*, November 2000, p. 9.

using CompuServe's equipment to process and store the ads—in effect, to stop sending the ads to CompuServe subscribers. Ignoring the demand, Cyber Promotions stepped up the volume of its ads. After CompuServe attempted

unsuccessfully to block the flow with screening software, it filed a suit against Cyber Promotions in a federal district court, seeking an injunction on the ground that the ads constituted trespass to personal property. The court agreed and ordered Cyber Promotions to stop sending its ads to e-mail addresses maintained by CompuServe.[15]●

Because of the problems associated with spam, some states have taken steps to prohibit or regulate its use. For example, a few states, such as Washington, prohibit unsolicited e-mail promoting goods, services, or real estate for sale or lease. In California, an unsolicited e-mail ad must state in its subject line that it is an ad ("ADV:"). The ad must also include a toll-free phone number or return e-mail address through which the recipient can contact the sender to request that no more ads be e-mailed.[16] An ISP can bring a successful suit in a California state court against a spammer who violates the ISP's policy prohibiting or restricting unsolicited e-mail ads. The court can award damages of up to $25,000 per day.[17] The Internet is a public forum, however. Thus, free speech issues may be involved—see Chapter 1.

---

[15] *CompuServe, Inc. v. Cyber Promotions, Inc.*, 962 F.Supp. 1015 (S.D.Ohio 1997).

[16] Ca. Bus. & Prof. Code Section 17538.4.
[17] Ca. Bus. & Prof. Code Section 17538.45.

Terms and Concepts

actionable 84	defamation 84	puffery 86
actual malice 85	defense 83	punitive damages 93
appropriation 85	disparagement of property 90	reasonable person standard 91
assault 83	dram shop act 95	*res ipsa loquitur* 95
assumption of risk 94	duty of care 90	slander 84
battery 83	fraudulent misrepresentation 86	slander of quality 90
business invitee 92	Good Samaritan statute 95	slander of title 90
business tort 82	intentional tort 83	spam 96
causation in fact 93	libel 84	strict liability 95
comparative negligence 94	malpractice 93	tort 82
compensatory damages 93	negligence 90	tortfeasor 83
contributory negligence 94	negligence *per se* 95	trade libel 90
conversion 88	predatory behavior 87	trespass to land 88
cyber tort 82	privilege 85	trespass to personal property 88
damages 83	proximate cause 93	

Chapter Summary   Torts and Cyber Torts

Intentional Torts against Persons (See pages 83–88.)	1. *Assault and battery*—An assault is an unexcused and intentional act that causes another person to be apprehensive of immediate harm. A battery is an assault that results in physical contact.
	2. *False imprisonment*—The intentional confinement or restraint of another person's movement without justification.
	3. *Infliction of emotional distress*—An intentional act that amounts to extreme and outrageous conduct resulting in severe emotional distress to another.
	4. *Defamation (libel or slander)*—A false statement of fact, not made under privilege, that is communicated to a third person and that causes damage to a person's reputation. For public figures, the plaintiff must also prove actual malice.
	5. *Invasion of the right to privacy*—The use of a person's name or likeness for commercial purposes without permission, wrongful intrusion into a person's private activities, publication of information that places a person in a false light, or disclosure of private facts that an ordinary person would find objectionable.

Chapter Summary	Torts and Cyber Torts—Continued
Intentional Torts against Persons—continued	6. *Appropriation*—The use of another person's name, likeness, or other identifying characteristic, without permission and for the benefit of the user. 7. *Misrepresentation (fraud)*—A false representation made by one party, through misstatement of facts or through conduct, with the intention of deceiving another and on which the other reasonably relies to his or her detriment. 8. *Wrongful interference*—The knowing, intentional interference by a third party with an enforceable contractual relationship or an established business relationship between other parties for the purpose of advancing the economic interests of the third party.
Intentional Torts against Property (See pages 88–90.)	1. *Trespass to land*—The invasion of another's real property without consent or privilege. Specific rights and duties apply once a person is expressly or impliedly established as a trespasser. 2. *Trespass to personal property*—Unlawfully damaging or interfering with the owner's right to use, possess, or enjoy his or her personal property. 3. *Conversion*—A wrongful act in which personal property is taken from its rightful owner or possessor and placed in the service of another. 4. *Disparagement of property*—Any economically injurious falsehood that is made about another's product or property; an inclusive term for the torts of *slander of quality* and *slander of title*.

Unintentional Torts—Negligence (See pages 90–95.)	1. *Negligence*—The careless performance of a legally required duty or the failure to perform a legally required act. Elements that must be proved are that a legal duty of care exists, that the defendant breached that duty, and that the breach caused damage or injury to another.
	
	2. *Defenses to negligence*—The basic affirmative defenses in negligence cases are (a) assumption of risk, (b) superseding cause, and (c) contributory and comparative negligence.
	
	3. *Special negligence doctrines and statutes*—
	
	  a. *Res ipsa loquitur*—A doctrine under which a plaintiff need not prove negligence on the part of the defendant in certain circumstances because "the facts speak for themselves."
	
	  b. Negligence *per se*—A type of negligence that may occur if a person violates a statute or an ordinance providing for a criminal penalty and the violation causes another to be injured.
	
	  c. Special negligence statutes—State statutes that prescribe duties and responsibilities in certain circumstances, the violation of which will impose civil liability. Dram shop acts and Good Samaritan statutes are examples of special negligence statutes.

Strict Liability (See page 95–96.)	Under the doctrine of strict liability, a person may be held liable, regardless of the degree of care exercised, for damages or injuries caused by her or his product or activity. Strict liability includes liability for harms caused by abnormally dangerous activities, by dangerous animals, and by defective products (product liability).
Cyber Torts (See pages 96–98.)	General tort principles are being extended to cover cyber torts, or torts that occur in cyberspace, such as online defamation or spamming (which may constitute trespass to personal property). Federal and state statutes may also apply to certain forms of cyber torts. For example, under the federal Communications Decency Act of 1996, Internet service providers (ISPs) are not liable for defamatory messages posted by their subscribers. Some states restrict the use of unsolicited e-mail advertising, or spam.

For Review

① What is a tort?

② What is the purpose of tort law? What are two basic categories of torts?

③ What are the four elements of negligence?

④ What is meant by strict liability? In what circumstances is strict liability applied?

⑤ What is a cyber tort, and how are tort theories being applied in cyberspace?

Questions and Case Problems

4–1. Defenses to Negligence. Corinna was riding her bike on a city street. While she was riding, she frequently looked back to verify that the books that she had fastened to the rear part of her bike were still attached. On one occasion while she was looking behind her, she failed to notice a car that was entering an intersection just as she was crossing it. The car hit her, causing her to sustain numerous injuries. Three eyewitnesses stated that the driver of the car had failed to stop at the stop sign before entering the intersection. Corinna sued the driver of the car for negligence. What defenses might the defendant driver raise in this lawsuit? Discuss fully.

4–2. Liability to Business Invitees. Kim went to Ling's Market to pick up a few items for dinner. It was a rainy, windy day, and the wind had blown water through the door of Ling's Market each time the door opened. As Kim entered through the door, she slipped and fell in the approximately one-half inch of rainwater that had accumulated on the floor. The manager knew of the weather conditions but had not posted any sign to warn customers of the water hazard. Kim injured her back as a result of the fall and sued Ling's for damages. Can Ling's be held liable for negligence in this situation? Discuss.

4–3. Negligence. In which of the following situations will the acting party be liable for the tort of negligence? Explain fully.

(a) Mary goes to the golf course on Sunday morning, eager to try out a new set of golf clubs she has just purchased. As she tees off on the first hole, the head of her club flies off and injures a nearby golfer.

(b) Mary's doctor gives her some pain medication and tells her not to drive after she takes it because the medication induces drowsiness. In spite of the doctor's warning, Mary decides to drive to a store while on the medication. Owing to her lack of alertness, she fails to stop at a traffic light and crashes into another vehicle, injuring a passenger.

4–4. Causation. Ruth carelessly parks her car on a steep hill, leaving the car in neutral and failing to engage the parking brake. The car rolls down the hill, knocking down an electric line. The sparks from the broken line ignite a grass fire. The fire spreads until it reaches a barn one mile away. The barn houses dynamite, and the burning barn explodes, causing part of the roof to fall on and injure a passing motorist, Jim. Can Jim recover from Ruth? Why or why not?

4–5. Wrongful Interference. Jennings owns a bakery shop. He has been trying to obtain a long-term contract with the owner of Julie's Tea Salon for some time. Jennings starts a local advertising campaign on radio and television and in the newspaper. The campaign is so persuasive that Julie decides to break the contract she has had for several years with Orley's Bakery so that she can patronize Jennings's bakery. Is Jennings liable to Orley's Bakery for the tort of wrongful interference with a contractual relationship? Is Julie liable for this tort? For anything?

4–6. Negligence *Per Se*. A North Carolina Department of Transportation regulation prohibits the placement of telephone booths within public rights-of-way. Despite this regulation, GTE South, Inc., placed a booth in the right-of-way near the intersection of Hillsborough and Sparger Roads in Durham County. Laura Baldwin was using the booth when an accident at the intersection caused a dump truck to cross the right-of-way and smash into the booth. To recover for her injuries, Baldwin filed a suit in a North Carolina state court against GTE and others. Was Baldwin within the class of persons protected by the regulation? If so, did GTE's placement of the booth constitute negligence *per se*? [*Baldwin v. GTE South, Inc.,* 335 N.C. 544, 439 S.E.2d 108 (1995)]

4–7. Duty to Business Invitees. Flora Gonzalez visited a Wal-Mart store. While walking in a busy aisle from the store's cafeteria toward a refrigerator, Gonzalez stepped on some macaroni that came from the cafeteria. She slipped and fell, sustaining injuries to her back, shoulder, and knee. She filed a suit in a Texas state court against Wal-Mart, alleging that the store was negligent. She presented evidence that the macaroni had "a lot of dirt" and tracks through it and testified that the macaroni "seemed like it had been there awhile." What duty does a business have to protect its patrons from dangerous conditions? In Gonzalez's case, should Wal-Mart be held liable for a breach of that duty? Why or why not? [*Wal-Mart Stores, Inc. v. Gonzalez,* 968 S.W.2d 934 (Tex.Sup. 1998)]

4–8. Misappropriation. The United States Golf Association (USGA) was founded in 1894. In 1911, the USGA developed the Handicap System, which was designed to enable individual golfers of different abilities to compete fairly with one another. The USGA revised the system and implemented new handicap formulas between 1987 and 1993. The USGA permits any entity to use the system free of charge as long as it complies with the USGA's procedure for peer review through authorized golf associations of the handicaps issued to individual golfers. In 1991, Arroyo Software Corp. began marketing software known as EagleTrak, which incorporated the USGA's system, and used the USGA's name in the software's ads without permission. Arroyo's EagleTrak did not incorporate any means for obtaining peer review of handicap computations. The USGA filed a suit in a California state court against Arroyo, alleging, among other things, misappropriation. The USGA asked the court to stop Arroyo's use of its system. Should the court grant the injunction? Why or why not? [*United States Golf Association v. Arroyo Software Corp.,* 69 Cal.App.4th 607, 81 Cal.Rptr.2d 708 (1999)]

CASE PROBLEM WITH SAMPLE ANSWER

4–9. America Online, Inc. (AOL), provides services to its customers (members), including the transmission of e-mail to and from other members and across the Internet. To become a member, a person must agree not to use AOL's computers to send bulk, unsolicited, commercial e-mail (spam). AOL uses filters to block spam, but bulk e-mailers sometimes use other software to thwart the filters. National Health Care Discount, Inc. (NHCD), sells discount optical and dental service plans. To generate leads for NHCD's products, sales representatives, who included AOL members, sent more than 300 million spam messages through AOL's computer system. Each item cost AOL an estimated $.00078 in equipment expenses. Some of the spam used false headers and other methods to hide the source. After receiving more than 150,000 complaints, AOL asked NHCD to stop. When the spam continued, AOL filed a suit in a federal district court against NHCD, alleging in part trespass to chattels—an unlawful interference with another's rights to possess personal property. AOL asked the court for a summary judgment on this claim. Did the spamming constitute trespass to chattels? Explain. [*America Online, Inc. v. National Health Care Discount, Inc.,* 121 F.Supp.2d 1255 (N.D.Iowa 2000)]

▶ To view a sample answer for this case problem, go to this book's Web site at **http://fundamentals.westbuslaw.com** and click on "Interactive Study Center."

4–10. Invasion of Privacy. During the spring and summer of 1999, Edward and Geneva Irvine received numerous "hang-up" phone calls, including three calls in the middle of the night. With the help of their local phone company, the Irvines learned that many of the calls were from the telemarketing department of the *Akron Beacon Journal* in Akron, Ohio. The *Beacon's* sales force was equipped with an automatic dialing machine. During business hours, the dialer was used to maximize productivity by calling multiple phone numbers at once and connecting a call to a sales representative only after it was answered. After business hours, the dialer was used to dial a list of disconnected numbers to determine whether they had been reconnected. If the dialer detected a ring, it recorded the information and dropped the call. If the automated dialing system crashed, which it did frequently, it redialed the entire list. The Irvines filed a suit in an Ohio state court against the *Beacon* and others, alleging in part an invasion of privacy. In whose favor should the court rule, and why? [*Irvine v. Akron Beacon Journal,* 147 Ohio App.3d 428, 770 N.E.2d 1105 (9 Dist. 2002)]

VIDEO QUESTION

4–11. Go to this text's Web site at **http://fundamentals.westbuslaw.com** and click on "Video Questions." Select "Chapter 4" and view the video titled *Negligence and Assumption of Risk.* Then answer the following questions.

1. According to the chapter, what standard of care does the supermarket in the video owe to Maria?
2. Did Vinny, the employee of the supermarket, act as a reasonable person would have acted under the circumstances? Why or why not? Why is this determination important?
3. What was the proximate cause of Maria's injuries? Should the supermarket be liable for damages?
4. What defenses, other than assumption of the risk, might be raised in this scenario?

TORTS AND CYBER TORTS

For updated links to resources available on the Web, as well as other materials, visit this text's Web site at

http://fundamentals.westbuslaw.com

You can find cases and articles on torts, including business torts, at the Internet Law Library's Web site at

http://www.lawguru.com/ilawlib/110.htm

For information on the *Restatements of the Law*, including the *Restatement (Second) of Torts* and the *Restatement (Third) of Torts: Product Liability,* go to the Web site of the American Law Institute at

http://www.ali.org

Online Legal Research

Go to the *Fundamentals of Business Law* home page at **http://fundamentals. westbuslaw.com**. Select "Interactive Study Center" and then click on "Chapter 4." There you will find the following Internet research exercises that you can perform to learn more about topics covered in this chapter.

Activity 4–1: LEGAL PERSPECTIVE—Negligence and the *Titanic*
Activity 4–2: MANAGEMENT PERSPECTIVE—Legal and Illegal Uses of Spam

Before the Test

Go to the *Fundamentals of Business Law* home page at **http://fundamentals. westbuslaw.com**. Click on "Interactive Quizzes." You will find at least twenty interactive questions relating to this chapter.

Westlaw® Campus

If your textbook provided for a subscription to Westlaw® Campus, or if you have otherwise purchased access to the Westlaw Campus database, you can access any of the cases presented or cited in this chapter by using your Westlaw Campus account.

Intellectual Property and Internet Law

CHAPTER OBJECTIVES

After reading this chapter, you should be able to answer the following questions:

① What is intellectual property?

② Why are trademarks and patents protected by the law?

③ What laws protect authors' rights in the works they generate?

④ What are trade secrets, and what laws offer protection for this form of intellectual property?

⑤ What steps have been taken to protect intellectual property rights in today's digital age?

Of significant concern to businesspersons today is the need to protect their rights in intellectual property. **Intellectual property** is any property resulting from intellectual, creative processes—the products of an individual's mind. Although it is an abstract term for an abstract concept, intellectual property is nonetheless wholly familiar to virtually everyone. The information contained in books and computer files is intellectual property. The software you use, the movies you see, and the music you listen to are all forms of intellectual property. In fact, in today's information age, it should come as no surprise that the value of the world's intellectual property now exceeds the value of physical property, such as machines and houses.

The need to protect creative works was voiced by the framers of the U.S. Constitution over two hundred years

ago: Article I, Section 8, of the Constitution authorized Congress "[t]o promote the Progress of Science and useful Arts, by securing for limited Times to Authors and Inventors the exclusive Right to their respective Writings and Discoveries." Laws protecting patents, trademarks, and copyrights are explicitly designed to protect and reward inventive and artistic creativity. Exhibit 5–1 on the following two pages offers a comprehensive summary of these forms of intellectual property, as well as intellectual property that consists of *trade secrets*.

An understanding of intellectual property law is important because intellectual property has taken on increasing significance, not only in the United States but globally as well. Today, ownership rights in intangible intellectual property are more important to the prosperity of many U.S. companies

EXHIBIT 5–1   FORMS OF INTELLECTUAL PROPERTY

	PATENT	COPYRIGHT	TRADEMARKS (SERVICE MARKS AND TRADE DRESS)	TRADE SECRETS
Definition	A grant from the government that gives an inventor exclusive rights to an invention.	An intangible property right granted to authors and originators of a literary work or artistic production that falls within specified categories.	Any distinctive word, name, symbol, or device (image or appearance), or combination thereof, that an entity uses to identify and distinguish its goods or services from those of others.	Any information (including formulas, patterns, programs, devices, techniques, and processes) that a business possesses and that gives the business an advantage over competitors who do not know the information or processes.
Requirements	An invention must be: 1. Novel. 2. Not obvious. 3. Useful.	Literary or artistic works must be: 1. Original. 2. Fixed in a durable medium that can be perceived, reproduced, or communicated. 3. Within a copyrightable category.	Trademarks, service marks, and trade dresses must be sufficiently distinctive (or must have acquired a secondary meaning) to enable consumers and others to distinguish the manufacturer's, seller's, or business user's products or services from those of competitors.	Information and processes that have commercial value, that are not known or easily ascertainable by the general public or others, and that are reasonably protected from disclosure.
Types or Categories	1. Utility (general). 2. Design. 3. Plant (flowers, vegetables, and so on).	1. Literary works (including computer programs). 2. Musical works. 3. Dramatic works. 4. Pantomime and choreographic works. 5. Pictorial, graphic, and sculptural works. 6. Films and audiovisual works. 7. Sound recordings.	1. Strong, distinctive marks (such as fanciful, arbitrary, or suggestive marks). 2. Marks that have acquired a secondary meaning by use. 3. Other types of marks, including certification marks and collective marks. 4. Trade dress (such as a distinctive decor, menu, or style or type of service).	1. Customer lists. 2. Research and development. 3. Plans and programs. 4. Pricing information. 5. Production techniques. 6. Marketing techniques. 7. Formulas. 8. Compilations.
How Acquired	By filing a patent application with the U.S. Patent and Trademark Office and receiving that office's approval.	Automatic (once in tangible form).	1. At common law, ownership is created by use of mark. 2. Registration (either with the U.S. Patent and Trademark Office or with the appropriate state office) gives constructive notice of date of use.	Through the originality and development of information and processes that are unique to a business, that are unknown by others, and that would be valuable to

EXHIBIT 5–1	FORMS OF INTELLECTUAL PROPERTY—CONTINUED

	PATENT	COPYRIGHT	TRADEMARKS (SERVICE MARKS AND TRADE DRESS)	TRADE SECRETS
How Acquired— continued			3. Federal registration is permitted if the mark is currently in use or if the applicant intends use within six months (period can be extended to three years). 4. Federal registration can be renewed between the fifth and sixth years and, thereafter, every ten years.	competitors if they knew of the information and processes.
Rights	An inventor has the right to make, use, sell, assign, or license the invention during the duration of the patent's term. The first to invent has patent rights.	The author or originator has the exclusive right to reproduce, distribute, display, license, or transfer a copyrighted work.	The owner has the right to use the mark or trade dress and to exclude others from using it. The right of use can be licensed or sold (assigned) to another.	The owner has the right to sole and exclusive use of the trade secrets and the right to use legal means to protect against misappropriation of the trade secrets by others. The owner can license or assign a trade secret.
Duration	Twenty years from the date of application; for design patents, fourteen years.	1. For authors: the life of the author, plus 70 years. 2. For publishers: 95 years after the date of publication or 120 years after creation.	Unlimited, as long as it is in use. To continue notice by registration, the registration must be renewed by filing.	Unlimited, as long as not revealed to others. (Once revealed to others, they are no longer trade secrets.)
Civil Remedies for Infringement	Monetary damages, which include reasonable royalties and lost profits, *plus* attorneys' fees. (Treble damages are available for intentional infringement.)	Actual damages, plus profits received by the infringer; *or* statutory damages of not less than $500 and not more than $20,000 ($100,000, if infringement is willful); *plus* costs and attorneys' fees.	1. Injunction prohibiting future use of mark. 2. Actual damages, plus profits received by the infringer (can be increased to three times the actual damages under the Lanham Act). 3. Impoundment and destruction of infringing articles. 4. *Plus* costs and attorneys' fees.	Monetary damages for misappropriation (the Uniform Trade Secrets Act permits punitive damages up to twice the amount of actual damages for willful and malicious misappropriation); *plus* costs and attorneys' fees.

than are their tangible assets. As you will read in this chapter, protecting these assets in today's online world has proved particularly challenging. This is because the Internet's capability is profoundly different from anything we have had in the past.

Trademarks and Related Property

A **trademark** is a distinctive mark, motto, device, or emblem that a manufacturer stamps, prints, or otherwise affixes to the goods it produces so that they may be identified on the market and their origin vouched for. At common law, the person who used a symbol or mark to identify a business or product was protected in the use of that trademark. Clearly, by using another's trademark, a business could lead consumers to believe that its goods were made by the other business. The law seeks to avoid this kind of confusion. In the following famous case concerning Coca-Cola, the defendants argued that the Coca-Cola trademark was entitled to no protection under the law, because the term did not accurately represent the product.

Landmark and Classic Cases

CASE 5.1   **The Coca-Cola Co. v. Koke Co. of America**

Supreme Court of the United States, 1920.
254 U.S. 143,
41 S.Ct. 113,
65 L.Ed. 189.
http://www.findlaw.com/casecode/supreme.html[a]

FACTS The Coca-Cola Company brought an action in a federal district court to enjoin other beverage companies from using the words "Koke" and "Dope" for the defendants' products. The defendants contended that the Coca-Cola trademark was a fraudulent representation and that Coca-Cola was therefore not entitled to any help from the courts. By use of the Coca-Cola name, the defendants alleged, the Coca-Cola Company represented that the beverage contained cocaine (from coca leaves). The district court granted the injunction, but the federal appellate court reversed. The Coca-Cola Company appealed to the United States Supreme Court.

ISSUE Did the marketing of products called Koke and Dope by the Koke Company of America and other firms constitute an infringement on Coca-Cola's trademark?

DECISION Yes for Koke, but no for Dope. The Supreme Court enjoined the competing beverage companies from

calling their products Koke, but did not prevent them from calling their products Dope.

REASON The Court noted that, to be sure, prior to 1900 the Coca-Cola beverage had contained a small amount of cocaine, but this ingredient had been deleted from the formula by 1906 at the latest, and the Coca-Cola Company had advertised to the public that no cocaine was present in its drink. Coca-Cola was a widely popular drink "to be had at almost any soda fountain." Because of the public's widespread familiarity with Coca-Cola, the retention of the name of the beverage (referring to coca leaves and kola nuts) was not misleading: "Coca-Cola probably means to most persons the plaintiff's familiar product to be had everywhere rather than a compound of particular substances." The name Coke was found to be so common a term for the trademarked product Coca-Cola that the defendants' use of the similar-sounding Koke as a name for their beverages was disallowed. The Court could find no reason to restrain the defendants from using the name Dope, however.

COMMENT *In this classic case, the United States Supreme Court made it clear that trademarks and trade names (and nicknames for those marks and names, such as the nickname "Coke" for "Coca-Cola") that are in common use receive protection under the common law. This holding is significant historically because the federal statute later passed to protect trademark rights (the Lanham Trade-Mark Act of 1946, to be discussed shortly) in many ways represented a codification of common law principles governing trademarks.*

a. This is the "U.S. Supreme Court Opinions" page within the Web site of the "FindLaw Internet Legal Resources" database. This page provides several options for accessing an opinion. Because you know the citation for this case, you can go to the "Citation Search" box, type in the appropriate volume and page numbers for the *United States Reports* ("254" and "143," respectively, for the *Coca-Cola* case), and click on "Get It."

STATUTORY PROTECTION OF TRADEMARKS

Statutory protection of trademarks and related property is provided at the federal level by the Lanham Trade-Mark Act of 1946.[1] The Lanham Act was enacted in part to protect manufacturers from losing business to rival companies that used confusingly similar trademarks. The Lanham Act incorporates the common law of trademarks and provides remedies for owners of trademarks who wish to enforce their claims in federal court.

Many states also have trademark statutes. In 1995, Congress amended the Lanham Act by passing the Federal Trademark Dilution Act,[2] which extended the protection available to trademark owners by creating a federal cause of action for trademark *dilution*. Until the passage of this amendment, federal trademark law only prohibited the unauthorized use of the same mark on competing—or on noncompeting but "related"—goods or services when such use would likely confuse consumers as to the origin of those goods and services. Trademark dilution laws, which about half of the states have also enacted, protect "distinctive" or "famous" trademarks (such as Jergens, McDonald's, RCA, and Macintosh) from certain unauthorized uses of the marks *regardless* of a showing of competition or a likelihood of confusion.

A famous mark may be diluted not only by the use of an *identical* mark but also by the use of a *similar* mark. ● **EXAMPLE #1** Ringling Bros.–Barnum & Bailey, Combined Shows, Inc., brought a suit against the state of Utah, claiming that Utah's use of the slogan "The Greatest Snow on Earth"—to attract visitors to the state's recreational and scenic resorts—diluted the distinctiveness of the circus's famous trademark, "The Greatest Show on Earth." Utah moved to dismiss the suit, arguing that the 1995 provisions protect owners of famous trademarks only against the unauthorized use of identical marks. A federal court disagreed and refused to grant Utah's motion to dismiss the case.[3] ●

TRADEMARK REGISTRATION

Trademarks may be registered with the state or with the federal government. To register for protection under federal trademark law, a person must file an application with the U.S. Patent and Trademark Office in Washington, D.C. Under current law, a mark can be registered (1) if it is currently in commerce or (2) if the applicant intends to put the mark into commerce within six months.

Under extenuating circumstances, the six-month period can be extended by thirty months, giving the applicant a total of three years from the date of notice of trademark approval to make use of the mark and file the required use statement. Registration is postponed until the mark is actually used. Nonetheless, during this waiting period, any applicant can legally protect his or her trademark against a third party who previously has neither used the mark nor filed an application for it. Registration is renewable between the fifth and sixth years after the initial registration and every ten years thereafter (every twenty years for trademarks registered before 1990).

TRADEMARK INFRINGEMENT

Registration of a trademark with the U.S. Patent and Trademark Office gives notice on a nationwide basis that the trademark belongs exclusively to the registrant. The registrant is also allowed to use the symbol ® to indicate that the mark has been registered. Whenever that trademark is copied to a substantial degree or used in its entirety by another, intentionally or unintentionally, the trademark has been *infringed* (used without authorization). When a trademark has been infringed, the owner of the mark has a cause of action against the infringer. A person need not have registered a trademark in order to sue for trademark infringement, but registration does furnish proof of the date of inception of the trademark's use.

Only those trademarks that are deemed sufficiently distinctive from all competing trademarks will be protected, however. The trademarks must be sufficiently distinct to enable consumers to identify the manufacturer of the goods easily and to differentiate among competing products.

Strong Marks. Fanciful, arbitrary, or suggestive trademarks are generally considered to be the most distinctive (strongest) trademarks, because they are normally taken from outside the context of the particular product and thus provide the best means of distinguishing one product from another.

● **EXAMPLE #2** Fanciful trademarks include invented words, such as "Xerox" for one manufacturer's copiers and "Kodak" for another company's photographic products. Arbitrary trademarks include actual words that have no literal connection to the product, such as "English Leather" used as a name for an after-shave lotion (and not for leather processed in England). Suggestive trademarks are those that suggest something about a product without describing the product directly. For example, "Dairy Queen" suggests an association between its products and milk, but it does not directly describe ice cream. ●

---

[1] 15 U.S.C. Sections 1051–1128.
[2] 15 U.S.C. Section 1125.
[3] *Ringling Bros.–Barnum & Bailey, Combined Shows, Inc. v. Utah Division of Travel Development*, 935 F.Supp. 763 (E.D.Va. 1996).

Secondary Meaning. Descriptive terms, geographic terms, and personal names are not inherently distinctive and do not receive protection under the law until they acquire a secondary meaning. A secondary meaning may arise when customers begin to associate a specific term or phrase, such as "London Fog," with specific trademarked items (coats with "London Fog" labels). Whether a secondary meaning becomes attached to a term or name usually depends on how extensively the product is advertised, the market for the product, the number of sales, and other factors. The United States Supreme Court has held that even a color can qualify for trademark protection.[4] Once a secondary meaning is attached to a term or name, a trademark is considered distinctive and is protected.

Generic Terms. Generic terms (general, commonly used terms that refer to an entire class of products, such as *bicycle* or *computer*) receive no protection, even if they acquire secondary meanings. A particularly thorny problem arises when a trademark acquires generic use. For example, *aspirin* and *thermos* were originally trademarked products, but today the words are used generically. Other examples are *escalator, trampoline, raisin bran, dry ice, lanolin, linoleum, nylon,* and *corn flakes.* Even so, the courts will not allow another firm to use those marks in such a way as to deceive a potential consumer.

SERVICE, CERTIFICATION, AND COLLECTIVE MARKS

A **service mark** is similar to a trademark but is used to distinguish the services of one person or company from those of another. For example, each airline has a particular mark or symbol associated with its name. Titles and character names used in radio and television are frequently registered as service marks.

Other marks protected by law include certification marks and collective marks. A *certification mark* is used by one or more persons other than the owner to certify the region, materials, mode of manufacture, quality, or accuracy of the owner's goods or services. When used by members of a cooperative, association, or other organization, it is referred to as a *collective mark.* ● EXAMPLE #3 Certification marks include such marks as "Good Housekeeping Seal of Approval" and "UL Tested." Collective marks appear at the ends of the credits of movies to indicate the various associations and organizations that participated in making the movie. The union marks found on the tags of certain products are also collective marks.●

TRADE NAMES

Trademarks apply to *products*. The term **trade name** is used to indicate part or all of a business's name, whether the business is a sole proprietorship, a partnership, or a corporation. Generally, a trade name is directly related to a business and its goodwill. Trade names may be protected as trademarks if the trade name is the same as the company's trademarked product—for example, Coca-Cola. Unless also used as a trademark or service mark, a trade name cannot be registered with the federal government. Trade names are protected under the common law, however. As with trademarks, words must be unusual or fancifully used if they are to be protected as trade names. The word *Safeway,* for example, was held by the courts to be sufficiently fanciful to obtain protection as a trade name for a food-store chain.[5]

TRADE DRESS

The term **trade dress** refers to the image and overall appearance of a product. Basically, trade dress is subject to the same protection as trademarks. ● EXAMPLE #4 The distinctive decor, menu, layout, and style of service of a particular restaurant may be regarded as the restaurant's trade dress. Similarly, if a golf course is distinguished from other golf courses by prominent features, those features may be considered the golf course's trade dress.● In cases involving trade dress infringement, as in trademark infringement cases, a major consideration is whether consumers are likely to be confused by the allegedly infringing use.

Cyber Marks

In cyberspace, trademarks are sometimes referred to as **cyber marks.** We turn now to a discussion of trademark-related issues in cyberspace and how new laws and the courts are addressing these issues. One concern relates to the rights of a trademark's owner to use the mark as part of a domain name (Internet address). Other issues have to do with cybersquatting, meta tags, and trademark dilution on the Web. The use of licensing as a way to avoid liability for infringing on another's intellectual property rights in cyberspace will be discussed later in this chapter.

---

[4] *Qualitex Co. v. Jacobson Products Co.,* 514 U.S. 159, 115 S.Ct. 1300, 131 L.Ed.2d 248 (1995).

[5] *Safeway Stores v. Suburban Foods,* 130 F.Supp. 249 (E.D.Va. 1955).

DOMAIN NAMES

In the past, one enterprise could often use the same name as another without causing any conflict, particularly if the firms were small, their goods or services were different, and the areas where they did business were separate. In the online world, however, there is only one area of business—cyberspace. Disputes between parties over which one has the right to use a particular domain name therefore emerged during the 1990s. A **domain name** is part of an Internet address, such as "westlaw.com." The top level domain (TLD) is the part of the name to the right of the period, such as *com*. The second level domain (to the left of the period) is chosen by the business or individual registering the domain name.

By using the same, or a similar, domain name, parties have attempted to profit from the goodwill of a competitor, to sell pornography, to offer for sale another party's domain name, and otherwise infringe on others' trademarks. As noted in Chapter 2, the Internet Corporation for Assigned Names and Numbers (ICANN) has played a leading role in settling domain name disputes worldwide.

ANTICYBERSQUATTING LEGISLATION

In the late 1990s, Congress passed legislation prohibiting another practice that had given rise to numerous disputes over domain names: cybersquatting. **Cybersquatting** occurs when a person registers a domain name that is the same as, or confusingly similar to, the trademark of another and then offers to sell the domain name back to the trademark owner. During the 1990s, cybersquatting became a contentious issue and led to much litigation. Often in dispute in these cases was whether cybersquatting constituted a commercial use of the mark so as to violate federal trademark law. Additionally, it was not always easy to separate cybersquatting from legitimate business activity. Although no clear rules emerged from this litigation, many courts held that cybersquatting violated trademark law.[6]

In 1999, Congress addressed this issue by passing the Anticybersquatting Consumer Protection Act (ACPA), which amended the Lanham Act—the federal law protecting trademarks, discussed earlier in this chapter. The ACPA makes it illegal for a person to "register, traffic in, or use" a domain name (1) if the name is identical or confusingly similar to the trademark of another and (2) if the one registering, trafficking in, or using the domain name has a "bad faith intent" to profit from that trademark. The act does not define what constitutes bad faith. Instead, it lists several factors that courts can consider in deciding whether bad faith exists. Some of these factors are the trademark rights of the other person, whether there is an intent to divert consumers in a way that could harm the goodwill represented by the trademark, whether there is an offer to transfer or sell the domain name to the trademark owner, and whether there is an intent to use the domain name to offer goods and services.

The ACPA applies to all domain name registrations of trademarks, even domain names registered before the passage of the act. Successful plaintiffs in suits brought under the act can collect actual damages and profits, or they can elect to receive statutory damages of from $1,000 to $100,000. The question in the following case was whether the ACPA applied to reregistrations of domain names containing family names that were initially registered before the effective date of the act.

---

[6] See, for example, *Panavision International, L.P. v. Toeppen*, 141 F.3d 1316 (9th Cir. 1998).

CASE 5.2   Schmidheiny v. Weber

United States Court of Appeals, Third Circuit, 2003.
319 F.3d 581.

FACTS In February 1999, Steven Weber registered the domain name *schmidheiny.com*. The Anticybersquatting Consumer Protection Act (ACPA) took effect nine months later, on November 29. Weber reregistered the name on behalf of Famology.com, Inc., in June 2000, with a different registrar. Weber is the president and treasurer of Famology.com and the administrative and technical contact for the *schmidheiny.com* domain. The following November, Weber sent an e-mail to Stephan Schmidheiny, offering to sell him the name. With a net worth of $3.1 billion, Schmidheiny is among the wealthiest individuals in the world. Schmidheiny filed a suit in a federal district court against Weber and Famology.com, alleging violations of the ACPA. The court granted summary judgment to the defendants. Schmidheiny appealed to the U.S. Court of Appeals for the Third Circuit.

(Continued)

CASE 5.2—Continued

ISSUE Does a domain name's reregistration qualify as a "registration" for purposes of the ACPA?

DECISION Yes. The U.S. Court of Appeals for the Third Circuit reversed the judgment of the lower court, and remanded the case for further proceedings consistent with this opinion.

REASON The appellate court reasoned that a domain name's "creation date" (the date when a domain name is initially created) does not "control whether a registration is subject to the Anticybersquatting Act, and we believe that the plain meaning of the word 'registration,'" as used in the

ACPA, "is not limited to 'creation registration.' The words 'initial' and 'creation' appear nowhere in [the ACPA] and Congress did not add an exception for 'non-creation registrations.' * * * We hold that the word 'registration' includes a new contract at a different registrar and to a different registrant. In this case, with respect to Famology.com—that occurs after the effective date of the Anticybersquatting Act. To conclude otherwise would permit the domain names of living persons to be sold and purchased without the living persons' consent, *ad infinitum,* so long as the name was first registered before the effective date of the Act."

FOR CRITICAL ANALYSIS—Social Consideration
Should all legislation be presumed to apply retroactively?

META TAGS

Search engines compile their results by looking through a Web site's key-words field. *Meta tags,* or key words, may be inserted into this field to increase the frequency of a site's inclusion in search engine results, even though the site has nothing to do with the inserted words. Using this same technique, one site may appropriate the key words of other sites with more frequent hits, so that the appropriating site appears in the same search engine results as the more popular sites. Using another's trademark in a meta tag without the owner's permission, however, constitutes trademark infringement.

• **EXAMPLE #5** An early case concerning meta tags involved Calvin Designer Label's use of "Playboy," "Playboy magazine," and "Playmate"—marks that were all owned by Playboy Enterprises, Inc. (PEI)—as meta tags for its Web sites on the Internet. As tags, the terms were invisible to viewers, but they caused the Web sites to be returned at the top of the list of a search engine query for "Playboy" or "Playmate." PEI sued Calvin Designer Label, alleging, among other things, trademark infringement. The court granted PEI's motion for summary judgment and ordered Calvin Designer Label to stop using PEI's trademarks.[7] •

DILUTION IN THE ONLINE WORLD

As discussed earlier, trademark *dilution* occurs when a trademark is used, without authorization, in a way that diminishes the distinctive quality of the mark. Unlike trademark infringement, a dilution cause of action does not require proof that consumers are likely to be confused by a connec-

tion between the unauthorized use and the mark. For this reason, the products involved do not have to be similar. In the first case alleging dilution on the Web, a court precluded the use of "candyland.com" as the URL for an adult site. The suit was brought by the maker of the "Candyland" children's game and owner of the "Candyland" mark.[8]

In one case, a court issued an injunction on the ground that spamming under another's logo is trademark dilution. In that case, Hotmail, Inc., provided e-mail services and worked to dissociate itself from spam. Van$ Money Pie, Inc., and others spammed thousands of e-mail customers, using Hotmail as a return address. The court ordered the defendants to stop.[9]

Patents

A **patent** is a grant from the government that gives an inventor the exclusive right to make, use, and sell an invention for a period of twenty years from the date of filing the application for a patent. Patents for designs, as opposed to inventions, are given for a fourteen-year period. For either a regular patent or a design patent, the applicant must demonstrate to the satisfaction of the U.S. Patent and Trademark Office that the invention, discovery, process, or design is genuine, novel, useful, and not obvious in light of current technology. A patent holder gives notice to all that an article or design is patented by placing on it the word

---

[7] *Playboy Enterprises, Inc. v. Calvin Designer Label,* 985 F.Supp.2d 1220 (N.D.Cal. 1997).

[8] *Hasbro, Inc. v. Internet Entertainment Group, Ltd.,* 1996 WL 84853 (W.D.Wash. 1996).

[9] *Hotmail Corp. v. Van$ Money Pie, Inc.,* 47 U.S.P.Q.2d 1020 (N.D.Cal. 1998). For a further discussion of this case, see the *Business Law in the Online World* feature in Chapter 10.

Patent or *Pat.* plus the patent number. In contrast to patent law in other countries, in the United States patent protection is given to the first person to invent a product or process, even though someone else may have been the first to file for a patent on that product or process.

At one time, it was difficult for developers and manufacturers of software to obtain patent protection because many software products simply automate procedures that can be performed manually. In other words, the computer programs do not meet the "novel" and "not obvious" requirements previously mentioned. Also, the basis for software is often a mathematical equation or formula, which is not patentable. In 1981, however, the United States Supreme Court held that it is possible to obtain a patent for a *process* that incorporates a computer program—providing, of course, that the process itself is patentable.[10] Subsequently, many patents have been issued for software-related inventions.

A significant development relating to patents is the availability online of the world's patent databases. The Web site of the U.S. Patent and Trademark Office provides searchable databases covering U.S. patents granted since 1976. The Web site of the European Patent Office maintains databases covering all patent documents in sixty-five nations and the legal status of patents in twenty-two of those countries.

PATENT INFRINGEMENT

If a firm makes, uses, or sells another's patented design, product, or process without the patent owner's permission, it commits the tort of patent infringement. Patent infringement may exist even though the patent owner has not put the patented product in commerce. Patent infringement may also occur even though not all features or parts of an invention are copied. (With respect to a patented process, however, all steps or their equivalent must be copied for infringement to exist.)

Often, litigation for patent infringement is so costly that the patent holder will instead offer to sell to the infringer a license to use the patented design, product, or process—licensing is discussed later in this chapter. Indeed, in many cases the costs of detection, prosecution, and monitoring are so high that patents are valueless to their owners; the owners cannot afford to protect them.

BUSINESS PROCESS PATENTS

Traditionally, patents have been granted to inventions that are "new and useful processes, machines, manufactures, or compositions of matter, or any new and useful improve-

ments thereof." The U.S. Patent and Trademark Office routinely rejected computer systems and software applications because they were deemed not to be useful processes, machines, articles of manufacture, or compositions of matter. They were simply considered to be mathematical algorithms, abstract ideas, or "methods of doing business." In a landmark 1998 case, however, *State Street Bank & Trust Co. v. Signature Financial Group, Inc.,*[11] the U.S. Court of Appeals for the Federal Circuit ruled that only three categories of subject matter will always remain unpatentable: (1) the laws of nature, (2) natural phenomena, and (3) abstract ideas. This decision meant, among other things, that business processes were patentable.

After this decision, numerous technology firms applied for business process patents. Walker Digital applied for a business process patent for its "Dutch auction" system, which allowed consumers to make offers for airline tickets on the Internet and led to the creation of Priceline.com. About.com obtained a patent for its "Elaborative Internet Data Mining System," which creates and pulls together the Web content of a large range of topics onto a single Web site. Amazon.com obtained a business process patent for its "one-click" ordering system, a method of processing credit-card orders securely without asking for the customer's card number or other personal information, such as the customer's name and address, more than once. Indeed, since the *State Street* decision, the number of Internet-related patents issued by the U.S. Patent and Trademark Office has increased more than 800 percent.

Copyrights

A **copyright** is an intangible property right granted by federal statute to the author or originator of certain literary or artistic productions. Currently, copyrights are governed by the Copyright Act of 1976,[12] as amended. Works created after January 1, 1978, are automatically given statutory copyright protection for the life of the author plus 70 years. For copyrights owned by publishing houses, the copyright expires 95 years from the date of publication or 120 years from the date of creation, whichever is first. For works by more than one author, the copyright expires 70 years after the death of the last surviving author.[13]

Copyrights can be registered with the U.S. Copyright Office in Washington, D.C. A copyright owner no longer

---

[10] *Diamond v. Diehr,* 450 U.S. 175, 101 S.Ct. 1048, 67 L.Ed.2d 155 (1981).

[11] 149 F.3d 1368 (Fed. Cir. 1998).

[12] 17 U.S.C. Sections 101 *et seq.*

[13] These time periods reflect the extensions set forth in the Sonny Bono Copyright Term Extension Act of 1998.

needs to place a © or *Copr.* or *Copyright* on the work, however, to have the work protected against infringement. Chances are that if somebody created it, somebody owns it.

WHAT IS PROTECTED EXPRESSION?

Works that are copyrightable include books, records, films, artworks, architectural plans, menus, music videos, product packaging, and computer software. To obtain protection under the Copyright Act, a work must be original and fall into one of the following categories: (1) literary works; (2) musical works; (3) dramatic works; (4) pantomimes and choreographic works; (5) pictorial, graphic, and sculptural works; (6) films and other audiovisual works; and (7) sound recordings. To be protected, a work must be "fixed in a durable medium" from which it can be perceived, reproduced, or communicated. Protection is automatic. Registration is not required.

Section 102 of the Copyright Act specifically excludes copyright protection for any "idea, procedure, process, system, method of operation, concept, principle, or discovery, regardless of the form in which it is described, explained, illustrated, or embodied." Note that it is not possible to copyright an *idea*. The underlying ideas embodied in a work may be freely used by others. What is copyrightable is the particular way in which an idea is expressed. Whenever an idea and an expression are inseparable, the expression cannot be copyrighted. Generally, anything that is not an original expression will not qualify for copyright protection. Facts widely known to the public are not copyrightable. Page numbers are not copyrightable, because they follow a sequence known to everyone. Mathematical calculations are not copyrightable.

Compilations of facts, however, are copyrightable. Section 103 of the Copyright Act defines a compilation as "a work formed by the collection and assembling of preexisting materials of data that are selected, coordinated, or arranged in such a way that the resulting work as a whole constitutes an original work of authorship." The key requirement for the copyrightability of a compilation is originality. ● EXAMPLE #6 The White Pages of a telephone directory do not qualify for copyright protection when the information that makes up the directory (names, addresses, and telephone numbers) is not selected, coordinated, or arranged in an original way.[14] In one case, even the Yellow Pages of a telephone directory did not qualify for copyright protection.[15] ●

---

[14] *Feist Publications, Inc. v. Rural Telephone Service Co.,* 499 U.S. 340, 111 S.Ct. 1282, 113 L.Ed.2d 358 (1991).
[15] *Bellsouth Advertising & Publishing Corp. v. Donnelley Information Publishing, Inc.,* 999 F.2d 1436 (11th Cir. 1993).

COPYRIGHT INFRINGEMENT

Whenever the form or expression of an idea is copied, an infringement of copyright occurs. The reproduction does not have to be exactly the same as the original, nor does it have to reproduce the original in its entirety.

Penalties or remedies can be imposed on those who infringe copyrights. These range from actual damages (damages based on the actual harm caused to the copyright holder by the infringement) or statutory damages (damages provided for under the Copyright Act, not to exceed $150,000) to criminal proceedings for willful violations (which may result in fines and/or imprisonment).

An exception to liability for copyright infringement is made under the "fair use" doctrine. In certain circumstances, a person or organization can reproduce copyrighted material without paying royalties (fees paid to the copyright holder for the privilege of reproducing the copyrighted material). Section 107 of the Copyright Act provides as follows:

> [T]he fair use of a copyrighted work, including such use by reproduction in copies or phonorecords or by any other means specified by [Section 106 of the Copyright Act,] for purposes such as criticism, comment, news reporting, teaching (including multiple copies for classroom use), scholarship, or research, is not an infringement of copyright. In determining whether the use made of a work in any particular case is a fair use the factors to be considered shall include—
>
> (1) the purpose and character of the use, including whether such use is of a commercial nature or is for nonprofit educational purposes;
> (2) the nature of the copyrighted work;
> (3) the amount and substantiality of the portion used in relation to the copyrighted work as a whole; and
> (4) the effect of the use upon the potential market for or value of the copyrighted work.

Because these guidelines are very broad, the courts determine whether a particular use is fair on a case-by-case basis. Thus, anyone reproducing copyrighted material may be committing a violation.

COPYRIGHT PROTECTION FOR SOFTWARE

In 1980, Congress passed the Computer Software Copyright Act, which amended the Copyright Act of 1976 to include computer programs in the list of creative works protected by federal copyright law. The 1980 statute, which classifies computer programs as "literary works," defines a computer program as a "set of statements or instructions to be used directly or indirectly in a computer in order to bring about a certain result."

Because of the unique nature of computer programs, the courts had many problems applying and interpreting the 1980 act. Generally, though, the courts have held that copyright protection extends not only to those parts of a computer program that can be read by humans, such as the high-level language of a source code, but also to the binary-language object code of a computer program, which is readable only by the computer.[16] Additionally, such elements as the overall structure, sequence, and organization of a program were deemed copyrightable.[17] The courts have disagreed on the issue of whether the "look and feel"—the general appearance, command structure, video images, menus, windows, and other screen displays—of computer programs should also be protected by copyright. The courts have tended, however, not to extend copyright protection to look-and-feel aspects of computer programs.

COPYRIGHTS IN DIGITAL INFORMATION

Copyright law is probably the most important form of intellectual property protection on the Internet. This is because much of the material on the Internet consists of works of authorship (including multimedia presentations, software, and database information), which are the traditional focus of copyright law. Copyright law is also important because the nature of the Internet requires that data be "copied" to be transferred online. Copies are a significant part of the traditional controversies arising in this area of the law. (For an example of one controversy concerning unauthorized copies of copyrighted materials, see this chapter's *Business Law in the Online World* feature on page 115.)

The Copyright Act of 1976. When Congress drafted the principal U.S. law governing copyrights, the Copyright Act of 1976, cyberspace did not exist for most of us. The threat to copyright owners was posed not by computer technology but by unauthorized *tangible* copies of works and the sale of rights to movies, television, and other media.

Some of the issues that were unimagined when the Copyright Act was drafted have posed thorny questions for the courts. For example, to sell a copy of a work, permission of the copyright holder is necessary. Because of the nature of cyberspace, however, one of the early controversies was determining at what point an intangible, electronic "copy" of a work has been made. The courts have held that loading a file or program into a computer's random access memory, or RAM, constitutes the making of a "copy" for purposes of copyright law.[18] RAM is a portion of a computer's memory into which a file, for example, is loaded so that it can be accessed (read or written over). Thus, a copyright is infringed when a party downloads software into RAM without owning the software or otherwise having a right to download it.[19]

Other rights, including those relating to the revision of "collective works" such as magazines, were acknowledged thirty years ago but were considered to have only limited economic value. Today, technology has made some of those rights vastly more significant. How does the old law apply to these rights? That was one of the questions in the following case.

---

[16] See *Stern Electronics, Inc. v. Kaufman*, 669 F.2d 852 (2d Cir. 1982); and *Apple Computer, Inc. v. Franklin Computer Corp.*, 714 F.2d 1240 (3d Cir. 1983).

[17] *Whelan Associates, Inc. v. Jaslow Dental Laboratory, Inc.*, 797 F.2d 1222 (3d Cir. 1986).

[18] *MAI Systems Corp. v. Peak Computer, Inc.*, 991 F.2d 511 (9th Cir. 1993).

[19] *DSC Communications Corp. v. Pulse Communications, Inc.*, 170 F.3d 1354 (Fed. Cir. 1999).

CASE 5.3   **New York Times Co. v. Tasini**

Supreme Court of the United States, 2001.
533 U.S. 483,
121 S.Ct. 2381,
150 L.Ed.2d 500.
http://supct.law.cornell.edu:8080/supct[a]

FACTS Magazines and newspapers, including the *New York Times*, buy and publish articles written by freelance writers. Besides circulating hard copies of their periodicals, these publishers sell the contents to e-publishers for inclusion in online

and other electronic databases. Jonathan Tasini and other freelance writers filed a suit in a federal district court against The New York Times Company and additional publishers, including the e-publishers, contending that the e-publication of the articles violated the Copyright Act. The publishers responded, among other things, that the Copyright Act gave them a right to produce "revisions" of their publications. The writers argued that the Copyright Act did not cover electronic "revisions." The court granted a summary judgment in the publishers' favor, which was reversed on the writers' appeal to the U.S. Court of Appeals for the Second Circuit. The publishers appealed to the United States Supreme Court.

---

a. In the "Search" box at the top of the screen, type in "Tasini" and select "all current and historic decisions." Then click on "Submit." On the page that opens, click on the appropriate link to access the opinion.

(Continued)

CASE 5.3—Continued

ISSUE To put the contents of periodicals into e-databases and onto CD-ROMs, do publishers need to obtain the permission of the writers whose contributions are included in the periodicals?

DECISION Yes. The United States Supreme Court affirmed the lower court's judgment. The Supreme Court remanded the case for a determination regarding how the writers should be compensated.

REASON The Court pointed out that databases are "vast domain[s] of diverse texts," consisting of "thousands or millions of files containing individual articles from thousands of collective works." The Court found that these databases have little relationship to the articles' original publication. The data-

bases are not "revisions," as the publishers argued, because the databases reproduce and distribute articles "clear of the context provided by the original periodical editions"—not "as part of that particular collective work" to which the author contributed, not "as part of * * * any revision," and not "as part of * * * any later collective work in the same series," as the Copyright Act provides. The Court reasoned that a database composed of such articles was no more a revision of an original work than "a 400-page novel quoting a sonnet in passing would represent a 'revision' of that poem."

FOR CRITICAL ANALYSIS—Economic Consideration
When technology creates a situation in which rights such as those in this case become more valuable, should the law be changed to redistribute the economic benefit of those rights?

Further Developments in Copyright Law. In the last several years, Congress has enacted legislation designed specifically to protect copyright holders in a digital age. For example, prior to 1997, criminal penalties under copyright law could be imposed only if unauthorized copies were exchanged for financial gain. Yet much piracy of copyrighted materials was "altruistic" in nature; that is, unauthorized copies were made and distributed not for financial gain but simply for reasons of generosity—to share the copies with others.

To combat altruistic piracy and for other reasons, Congress passed the No Electronic Theft (NET) Act of 1997. This act extends criminal liability for the piracy of copyrighted materials to persons who exchange unauthorized copies of copyrighted works, such as software, even though they realize no profit from the exchange. The act also imposes penalties on those who make unauthorized electronic copies of books, magazines, movies, or music for *personal* use, thus altering the traditional "fair use" doctrine. The criminal penalties for violating the act are steep; they include fines as high as $250,000 and incarceration for up to five years.

The Digital Millennium Copyright Act of 1998. In 1996, the World Intellectual Property Organization (WIPO) enacted a treaty to upgrade global standards of copyright protection, particularly for the Internet. In 1998, Congress implemented the provisions of the WIPO treaty by updating U.S. copyright law. The new law—the Digital Millennium Copyright Act of 1998—is a landmark step in the protection of copyright owners and, because of the leading position of the United States in the creative industries, serves as a model for other nations. Among other things, the act created civil and criminal penalties for anyone who circumvents (bypasses, or gets around—

through clever maneuvering, for example) encryption software or other technological antipiracy protection. Also prohibited are the manufacture, import, sale, and distribution of devices or services for circumvention.

The act provides for exceptions to fit the needs of libraries, scientists, universities, and others. In general, the law does not restrict the "fair use" of circumvention methods for educational and other noncommercial purposes. For example, circumvention is allowed to test computer security, to conduct encryption research, to protect personal privacy, and to enable parents to monitor their children's use of the Internet. The exceptions are to be reconsidered every three years.

The 1998 act also limited the liability of Internet service providers (ISPs). Under the act, an ISP is not liable for any copyright infringement by its customer *unless* the ISP is aware of the subscriber's violation. An ISP may be held liable only if it fails to take action to shut the subscriber down after learning of the violation. A copyright holder has to act promptly, however, by pursuing a claim in court, or the subscriber has the right to be restored to online access.

MP3 and File-Sharing Technology. At one time, music fans swapped compact discs (CDs) and recorded the songs that they liked from others' CDs onto their own cassettes. This type of "file-sharing" was awkward at best. Soon after the Internet became popular, a few enterprising programmers created software to compress large data files, particularly those that store music. The reduced file sizes make transmitting music over the Internet feasible. The most widely known compression and decompression system is MP3, which enables music fans to download songs or entire CDs onto their computers or onto a portable listening device, such as

BUSINESS LAW IN THE ONLINE WORLD
DVD "Piracy"—The Courts Speak

Digital versatile disks (DVDs) provide many advantages over traditional videocassettes. For one thing, they are more compact. They also offer superior audio and video quality. Additionally, they provide for such enhancements as directors' commentaries, separate foreign language audio tracks, and multiple foreign language subtitles. Not surprisingly, the owners of motion picture copyrights have a vested interest in preventing renters and owners of DVDs from making the contents of those DVDs available on the Internet. All DVDs include an encryption system created to protect against the unauthorized copying of the contents.

Almost as soon as encryption technology was used to safeguard the contents of DVDs, however, the code was cracked by a group of hackers, including nineteen-year-old Norwegian Jon Johansen. His decryption program, called DeCCS, was quickly made available at various sites on the Internet, including 2600.com, owned by Ed Corly. Almost immediately after DeCCS was posted, a group of movie companies, including Disney and Twentieth Century-Fox, filed suit.

VIOLATION OF THE DIGITAL MILLENNIUM COPYRIGHT ACT
In what was seen as a victory for the motion picture industry, a federal district court ruled, in *Universal City Studios, Inc. v. Reimerdes,*[a] that DeCCS violated the Digital Millennium Copyright Act of 1998. As you will read elsewhere in this chapter, this act essentially prohibits individuals from breaking encryption programs put in place to protect digital versions of intellectual property such as movies, music, and the like. After all, reasoned the court, since the posting of DeCCS,

along with a separate video-compression program known as Divx, the pirating of movies had become increasingly common on the Internet.

The defendants argued that software programs designed to break encryption schemes were simply a form of constitutionally protected speech. The court, however, rejected the free speech argument. "Computer code is not purely expressive any more than the assassination of a political figure is purely a political statement. . . . The Constitution, after all, is a framework for building a just and democratic society. It is not a suicide pact," stated the court.

NEW FORMS OF ENCRYPTION MAY CURB DVD PIRACY
New forms of encryption and copyright protection now being developed may at least slow down the amount of piracy on the Internet. New DVD-Audio discs contain a digital "watermark" that can be tracked. In this way, if pirated copies of the watermarked DVD-Audio disc are found, record labels can better pursue the originator of the pirated copies. Additionally, DVD-Audio discs that are copied have much poorer sound quality than the originals do.

New versions of Microsoft's Media Player software allow digital restrictions dictated by copyright holders. The software scrambles the digital output so that it cannot be recorded. Finally, IBM is developing an encryption system designed to prevent DVD piracy.

If the past is any predictor of the future, however, no matter how well a copyrighted work is encrypted, skilled programmers will be able to "crack" the encryption code, thereby allowing pirated copies to resurface.

FOR CRITICAL ANALYSIS
Will the decision in the Universal City Studios *case have any practical effect, given that literally thousands of copies of DeCCS already existed on the Internet before the decision was issued?*

a. 111 F.Supp.2d 294 (S.D.N.Y. 2000).

Rio. The MP3 system also made it possible for music fans to access other music fans' files by file-sharing via the Internet.

File-sharing over the Internet can be accomplished through what is known as **peer-to-peer (P2P) networking**. The concept is simple. Rather than going through a central Web server, P2P involves numerous personal computers

(PCs) that are connected to the Internet. Files stored on one PC can be accessed by others who run the same networking software. Sometimes this is called a **distributed network**. In other words, parts of the network are distributed all over the country or the world. File-sharing software allows an unlimited number of uses for distributed networks.

Currently, for example, many researchers permit their home computers' computing power to be accessed through file-sharing software so that very large mathematical problems can be solved quickly. Additionally, persons scattered throughout the country or the world can work together on the same project by using file-sharing programs.

When file-sharing is used to download others' stored music files, however, copyright issues arise. Recording artists and their labels stand to lose large amounts of royalties and revenues if relatively few CDs are purchased and then made available on distributed networks, from which everyone can get them for free. In the following widely pub-

licized case, several firms in the recording industry sued Napster, Inc., the owner of the then-popular Napster Web site. The firms alleged that Napster was contributing to copyright infringement by those who downloaded CDs from other computers in the Napster file-sharing system. At issue was whether Napster could be held vicariously liable for the infringement.[20]

---

[20] Vicarious (indirect) liability exists when one person is subject to liability for another's actions. A common example occurs in the employment context, when an employer is held vicariously liable by third parties for torts committed by employees in the course of their employment.

CASE 5.4   A&M Records, Inc. v. Napster, Inc.

United States Court of Appeals, Ninth Circuit, 2001.
239 F.3d 1004.
http://www.findlaw.com/casecode/courts/9th.html[a]

FACTS Napster, Inc. (http://www.napster.com), facilitated the transmission of MP3 files among the users of its Web site through a process called "peer-to-peer" file-sharing. Napster allowed users to transfer exact copies of the contents of MP3 files from one computer to another via the Internet. This was made possible by Napster's MusicShare software, available free of charge from Napster's site, and Napster's network servers and server-side software. Napster also provided technical support. A&M Records, Inc., and others engaged in the commercial recording, distribution, and sale of copyrighted musical compositions and sound recordings, filed a suit in a federal district court against Napster, alleging copyright infringement. The court issued a preliminary injunction ordering Napster to stop "facilitating others in copying, downloading, uploading, transmitting, or distributing plaintiffs' copyrighted musical compositions and sound recordings, * * * without express permission of the rights owner." Napster appealed to the U.S. Court of Appeals for the Ninth Circuit.

ISSUE Did Napster's failure to obtain permission before facilitating the transmission of copyrighted material via its Web site constitute copyright infringement?

DECISION Yes. The U.S. Court of Appeals for the Ninth Circuit affirmed the lower court's decision that Napster was obligated to police its own system and had likely infringed the plaintiffs' copyrights. Holding that the injunction was "overbroad," however, the appellate court remanded the case for a clarification of Napster's responsibility to determine whether music on its Web site was copyrighted.

REASON The U.S. Court of Appeals for the Ninth Circuit pointed out that "[i]n the context of copyright law, vicarious liability extends * * * to cases in which a defendant has the right and ability to supervise the infringing activity and also has a direct financial interest in such activities." The court found that "plaintiffs have demonstrated that Napster retains the right to control access to its system." To avoid liability, "the reserved right to police must be exercised to its fullest extent." Napster "failed to exercise that right to prevent the exchange of copyrighted material." The court explained that Napster "has the ability to locate infringing material listed on its search indices, and the right to terminate users' access to the system," even though the file names "may not match copyrighted material exactly (for example, the artist or song could be spelled wrong)." Napster's failure to police its system, "combined with a showing that Napster financially benefits from the continuing availability of infringing files on its system, leads to the imposition of vicarious liability."

FOR CRITICAL ANALYSIS—Technological Consideration
How might the Napster system be put to commercially significant but noninfringing uses?

---

a. This URL will take you to a Web site maintained by FindLaw, which is now a part of West Group. When you access the site, enter "Napster" in the "Party Name Search" box and then click on "Search." Select the first *Napster* case in the list (dated "02/12/2001") on the page that opens.

COMMENT *The court's ruling in this case forced Napster to stop supporting the free downloading of music. In 2002, Napster filed for bankruptcy after a brief attempt to provide for-fee downloads. Note, however, that there are numerous sites on the Web today that offer similar services.*

Trade Secrets

Some business processes and information that are not or cannot be patented, copyrighted, or trademarked are nevertheless protected against appropriation by a competitor as trade secrets. **Trade secrets** consist of customer lists, plans, research and development, pricing information, marketing techniques, production methods, and generally anything that makes an individual company unique and that would have value to a competitor.

Unlike copyright and trademark protection, protection of trade secrets extends both to ideas and to their expression. (For this reason, and because a trade secret involves no registration or filing requirements, trade secret protection may be well suited for software.) Of course, the secret formula, method, or other information must be disclosed to some persons, particularly to key employees. Businesses generally attempt to protect their trade secrets by having all employees who use the process or information agree in their contracts, or in confidentiality agreements, never to divulge it.

STATE AND FEDERAL LAW ON TRADE SECRETS

In the past, virtually all law with respect to trade secrets was common law. In an effort to reduce the unpredictability of the common law in this area, a model act, the Uniform Trade Secrets Act, was presented to the states for adoption in 1979. Parts of the act have been adopted in more than twenty states. Typically, a state that has adopted parts of the act has adopted only those parts that encompass its own existing common law. Additionally, in 1996 Congress passed the Economic Espionage Act, which made the theft of trade secrets a federal crime. We will examine the provisions and significance of this act in Chapter 6, in the context of crimes related to business.

TRADE SECRETS IN CYBERSPACE

The nature of new computer technology undercuts a business firm's ability to protect its confidential information, including trade secrets.[21] For example, a dishonest employee could e-mail trade secrets stored in a company's computer to a competitor or a future employer. If e-mail is not an option, the employee might walk out with the information on a computer disk. Dissatisfied former employees have resorted to other options as well. ● **EXAMPLE #7** In one case, a former employee of Intel Corporation, Ken Hamidi,

using a list of employees that he had obtained from a company directory, sent massive quantities of e-mail to current Intel employees. Unable to block the disruptive messages, Intel sued Hamidi for trespass to personal property. The court refused to grant Intel an injunction, however, because Intel failed to show that the e-mail damaged or impaired the functioning of its computer system.[22] ●

Licensing

One of the ways to make use of another's trademark, copyright, patent, or trade secret, while avoiding litigation, is to obtain a license to do so. A license in this context is basically an agreement to permit the use of a trademark, copyright, patent, or trade secret for certain purposes.

LICENSING CONTRACTS

Licensing agreements are essentially contracts and are thus governed by contract law. A licensing agreement with a firm calls for a payment of royalties on some basis—such as so many cents per unit produced or a certain percentage of the profits from units sold in a particular geographic territory. ● **EXAMPLE #8** The Coca-Cola Bottling Company licenses firms worldwide to use (and keep confidential) its secret formula for the syrup used in its soft drink, in return for a percentage of the income gained from the sale of Coca-Cola by those companies.●

BENEFITS OF LICENSING ARRANGEMENTS

The licensing of intellectual property rights benefits all parties to the transaction. The firm that receives the license can take advantage of an established reputation for quality. The company that grants the license receives income from the sales of its products. In the global marketplace, licensing also allows a business to establish its reputation worldwide. Once a firm's trademark is known around the world, the demand for other products manufactured or sold by that firm may also increase, which is another advantage of licensing.

International Protection for Intellectual Property

For many years, the United States has been a party to various international agreements covering intellectual property rights. For example, the Paris Convention of 1883, to which

---

[21] Note that in one case, the court indicated that customers' e-mail addresses may constitute trade secrets. See *T-N-T Motorsports, Inc. v. Hennessey Motorsports, Inc.*, 965 S.W.2d 18 (Tex.App.—Hous. [1 Dist.] 1998), rehearing overruled (1998), petition dismissed (1998).

[22] *Intel Corp. v. Hamidi*, 30 Cal.4th 1342, 71 P.3d 296, 1 Cal.Rptr.3d 32 (2003).

about ninety countries are signatory, allows parties in one country to file for patent and trademark protection in any of the other member countries. Other international agreements include the Berne Convention and the TRIPS agreement.

THE BERNE CONVENTION

Under the Berne Convention of 1886, an international copyright agreement, if an American writes a book, her or his copyright in the book must be recognized by every country that has signed the convention. Also, if a citizen of a country that has not signed the convention first publishes a book in a country that has signed, all other countries that have signed the convention must recognize that author's copyright. Copyright notice is not needed to gain protection under the Berne Convention for works published after March 1, 1989.

This convention and other international agreements have given some protection to intellectual property on a worldwide level. None of them, however, has been as significant and far-reaching in scope as the agreement on Trade-Related Aspects of Intellectual Property Rights, or, more simply, TRIPS.

THE TRIPS AGREEMENT

The TRIPS agreement was signed by representatives from over one hundred nations in 1994. The agreement established, for the first time, standards for the international protection of intellectual property rights, including patents, trademarks, and copyrights for movies, computer programs, books, and music.

Prior to the agreement, U.S. sellers of intellectual property in the international market faced difficulties because many other countries had no laws protecting intellectual property rights or failed to enforce existing laws. To address this problem, the TRIPS agreement provides that each member country must include in its domestic laws broad intellectual property rights and effective remedies (including civil and criminal penalties) for violations of those rights.

Generally, the TRIPS agreement provides that each member nation must not discriminate (in the administration, regulation, or adjudication of intellectual property rights) against foreign owners of such rights. In other words, a member nation cannot give its own nationals (citizens) favorable treatment without offering the same treatment to nationals of all member countries. For example, if a U.S. software manufacturer brings a suit for the infringement of intellectual property rights under a member country's national laws, the U.S. manufacturer is entitled to receive the same treatment as a domestic manufacturer. Each member nation must also ensure that legal procedures are available for parties who wish to bring actions for infringement of intellectual property rights. Additionally, in a related document, a mechanism was established for settling disputes among member nations.

Particular provisions of the TRIPS agreement refer to patent, trademark, and copyright protection for intellectual property. The agreement specifically provides copyright protection for computer programs by stating that compilations of data, databases, or other materials are "intellectual creations" and that they are to be protected as copyrightable works. Other provisions relate to trade secrets and the rental of computer programs and cinematographic works.

Terms and Concepts

copyright 111	intellectual property 103	trade name 108
cyber mark 108	patent 110	trade secret 117
cybersquatting 109	peer-to-peer (P2P) networking 115	trademark 106
distributed network 115	service mark 108	
domain name 109	trade dress 108	

Chapter Summary	**Intellectual Property and Internet Law**
Trademarks and Related Property (See pages 106–108.)	1. A *trademark* is a distinctive mark, motto, device, or emblem that a manufacturer stamps, prints, or otherwise affixes to the goods it produces so that they may be identified on the market and their origin vouched for.
	2. The major federal statutes protecting trademarks and related property are the Lanham Trade-Mark Act of 1946 and the Federal Trademark Dilution Act of 1995. Generally, to be protected, a trademark must be sufficiently distinctive from all competing trademarks.
	3. *Trademark infringement* occurs when one uses a mark that is the same as, or confusingly similar to, the protected trademark, service mark, trade name, or trade dress of another without permission when marketing goods or services.
Cyber Marks (See pages 108–110.)	A *cyber mark* is a trademark in cyberspace. Trademark infringement in cyberspace occurs when one person uses a name that is the same as, or confusingly similar to, the protected mark of another in a domain name or in meta tags.
Patents (See pages 110–111.)	1. A *patent* is a grant from the government that gives an inventor the exclusive right to make, use, and sell an invention for a period of twenty years from the date of filing the application for a patent. To be patentable, an invention (or a discovery, process, or design) must be genuine, novel, useful, and not obvious in light of current technology. Computer software may be patented.
	2. *Patent infringement* occurs when one uses or sells another's patented design, product, or process without the patent owner's permission.
Copyrights (See pages 111–116.)	1. A *copyright* is an intangible property right granted by federal statute to the author or originator of certain literary or artistic productions. Computer software may be copyrighted.
	2. *Copyright infringement* occurs whenever the form or expression of an idea is copied without the permission of the copyright holder. An exception applies if the copying is deemed a "fair use."
	3. Copyrights are governed by the Copyright Act of 1976, as amended. To protect copyrights in digital information, Congress passed the No Electronic Theft Act of 1997 and the Digital Millennium Copyright Act of 1998.
Trade Secrets (See page 117.)	*Trade secrets* include customer lists, plans, research and development, pricing information, and so on. Trade secrets are protected under the common law and, in some states, under statutory law against misappropriation by competitors. The Economic Espionage Act of 1996 made the theft of trade secrets a federal crime (see Chapter 6).
Licensing (See pages 117–118.)	In the context of intellectual property rights, a *license* is an agreement in which the owner of a trademark, copyright, patent, or trade secret permits another person or entity to use that property for certain purposes.
International Protection (See page 118.)	International protection for intellectual property exists under various international agreements. A landmark agreement is the 1994 agreement on Trade-Related Aspects of Intellectual Property Rights (TRIPS), which provides for enforcement procedures in all countries signatory to the agreement.

For Review

① What is intellectual property?

② Why are trademarks and patents protected by the law?

③ What laws protect authors' rights in the works they generate?

④ What are trade secrets, and what laws offer protection for this form of intellectual property?

⑤ What steps have been taken to protect intellectual property rights in today's digital age?

Questions and Case Problems

5–1. Copyright Infringement. In which of the following situations would a court likely hold Maruta liable for copyright infringement?

(a) At the library, Maruta photocopies ten pages from a scholarly journal relating to a topic on which she is writing a term paper.

(b) Maruta makes leather handbags and sells them in her small leather shop. She advertises her handbags as "Vutton handbags," hoping that customers might mistakenly assume that they were made by Vuitton, the well-known maker of high-quality luggage and handbags.

(c) Maruta owns a video store. She purchases one copy of all the latest videos from various video manufacturers. Then, using blank videotapes, she makes copies to rent or sell to her customers.

5–2. Trademark Infringement. Alpha Software, Inc., announced a new computer operating system to be marketed under the name McSoftware. McDonald's Corp. wrote Alpha a letter stating that the use of this name infringed on the McDonald's family of trademarks characterized by the prefix "Mc" attached to a generic term. Alpha claimed that "Mc" had come into generic use as a prefix and therefore McDonald's had no trademark rights to the prefix itself. Alpha filed an action seeking a declaratory judgment from the court that the mark McSoftware did not infringe on the McDonald's federally registered trademarks or common law rights to its marks and would not constitute an unfair trade practice. What factors must the court consider in deciding this issue? What will be the probable outcome of the case? Explain.

5–3. Patent Infringement. John and Andrew Doney invented a hard-bearing device for balancing rotors. Although they registered their invention with the U.S. Patent and Trademark Office, it was never used as an automobile wheel balancer. Some time later, Exetron Corp. produced an automobile wheel balancer that used a hard-bearing device with a support plate similar to that of the Doneys. Given the fact that the Doneys had not used their device for automobile wheel balancing, does Exetron's use of a similar hard-bearing device infringe on the Doneys' patent?

5–4. Copyright Infringement. Max plots a new Batman adventure and carefully and skillfully imitates the art of DC Comics to create an authentic-looking Batman comic. Max is not affiliated with the owners of the copyright to Batman. Can Max publish the comic without infringing on the owners' copyright?

5–5. Trademark Infringement. Elvis Presley Enterprises, Inc. (EPE), owns all of the trademarks of the Elvis Presley estate. None of these marks is registered for use in the restaurant business. Barry Capece registered "The Velvet Elvis" as a service mark for a restaurant and tavern with the U.S. Patent and Trademark Office. Capece opened a nightclub called "The Velvet Elvis" with a menu, décor, advertising, and promotional events that evoked Elvis Presley and his music. EPE filed a suit in a federal district court against Capece and others, claiming, among other things, that "The Velvet Elvis" service mark infringed on EPE's trademarks. During the trial, witnesses testified that they thought the bar was associated with Elvis Presley. Should Capece be ordered to stop using "The Velvet Elvis" mark? Why or why not? [*Elvis Presley Enterprises, Inc. v. Capece,* 141 F.3d 188 (5th Cir. 1998)]

5–6. Copyrights. Webbworld operates a Web site called Neptics, Inc. The site accepts downloads of certain images from third parties and makes these images available to any user who accesses the site. Before being allowed to view the images, however, the user must pay a subscription fee of $11.95 per month. Over a period of several months, images were available that were originally created by or for Playboy Enterprises, Inc. (PEI). The images were displayed at Neptics's site without PEI's permission. PEI filed a suit in a federal district court against Webbworld, alleging copyright infringement. Webbworld argued in part that it should not be held liable because, like an Internet service provider that furnishes access to the Internet, it did not create or control the content of the information available to its subscribers. Do you agree with Webbworld? Why or why not? [*Playboy Enterprises, Inc. v. Webbworld,* 968 F.Supp. 1171 (N.D.Tex. 1997)]

5–7. Trademark Infringement. A&H Sportswear, Inc., a swimsuit maker, obtained a trademark for its MIRACLESUIT in 1992. The MIRACLESUIT design makes the wearer appear slimmer. The MIRACLESUIT was widely advertised and discussed in the media. The MIRACLESUIT was also sold for a brief time in the Victoria's Secret (VS) catalogue, which is published by Victoria's Secret Catalogue, Inc. In 1993, Victoria's Secret Stores, Inc., began selling a cleavage-enhancing bra, which was named THE MIRACLE BRA and for which a trademark was obtained. The next year, THE MIRACLE BRA swimwear debuted in the VS catalogue and stores. A&H filed a suit in a federal district court against VS Stores and VS Catalogue, alleging in part that THE MIRACLE BRA mark, when applied to swimwear, infringed on the MIRACLESUIT mark. A&H argued that there was a "possibility of confusion" between the marks. The VS entities contended that the appropriate standard was "likelihood of confusion" and that, in this case, there was no likelihood of confusion. In whose favor will the court rule, and why? [*A&H Sportswear, Inc. v. Victoria's Secret Stores, Inc.,* 166 F.3d 197 (3d Cir. 1999)]

 5–8. In 1999, Steve and Pierce Thumann and their father, Fred, created Spider Webs, Ltd., a partnership, to, according to Steve, "develop Internet address names." Spider Webs registered nearly two thousand Internet domain names for an average of $70 each, including the names of cities, the names of buildings, names related to a business or trade (such as air conditioning or plumbing), and the names of famous companies. It offered many of the names for sale on its Web site and through eBay.com. Spider Webs registered the domain name "ERNESTANDJULIOGALLO.COM" in Spider Webs's name. E. and J. Gallo Winery filed a suit against Spider Webs, alleging, in part, violations of the Anticybersquatting Consumer Protection Act (ACPA). Gallo asked the court for, among other things, statutory damages. Gallo also sought to have the domain name at issue transferred to Gallo. During the suit, Spider Webs published anticorporate articles and opinions, and discussions of the suit, at the URL "ERNESTANDJULIOGALLO.COM." Should the court rule in Gallo's favor? Why or why not? [*E. & J. Gallo Winery v. Spider Webs, Ltd.,* 129 F.Supp.2d 1033 (S.D. Tex. 2001)]

◗ To view a sample answer for this case problem, go to this book's Web site at **http://fundamentals.westbuslaw.com** and click on "Interactive Study Center."

5–9. Fair Use Doctrine. Leslie Kelly is a professional photographer who has copyrighted many of his images of the American West. Some of the images can be seen on Kelly's Web site or other sites with which Kelly has a contract. Arriba Soft Corp. operates an Internet search engine that displays its results in the form of small pictures (thumbnails) rather than text. The thumbnails consist of images copied from other sites and reduced in size. By clicking on one of the thumbnails, a user can view a large version of the picture within the context of an Arriba Web page. Arriba displays the large picture by inline linking (importing the image from the other site without copying it onto Arriba's site). When Kelly discovered that his photos were displayed through Arriba's site without his permission, he filed a suit in a federal district court against Arriba, alleging copyright infringement. Arriba claimed that its use of Kelly's images was a "fair use." Considering the factors courts weigh to determine whether a use is fair, do Arriba's thumbnails qualify? Does Arriba's use of the larger images infringe on Kelly's copyright? Explain. [*Kelly v. Arriba Soft Corp.,* 280 F.3d 934 (9th Cir. 2002)]

A QUESTION OF ETHICS AND SOCIAL RESPONSIBILITY

5–10. Texaco, Inc., conducts research to develop new products and technology in the petroleum industry. As part of the research, Texaco employees routinely photocopy articles from scientific and medical journals without the permission of the copyright holders. The publishers of the journals brought a copyright infringement action against Texaco in a federal district court. The court ruled that the copying was not a fair use. The U.S. Court of Appeals for the Second Circuit affirmed this ruling "primarily because the dominant purpose of the use is 'archival'—to assemble a set of papers for future reference, thereby serving the same purpose for which additional subscriptions are normally sold, or . . . for which photocopying licenses may be obtained." [*American Geophysical Union v. Texaco, Inc.,* 37 F.3d 881 (2d Cir. 1994)]

1. Do you agree with the court's decision that the copying was not a fair use? Why or why not?
2. Do you think that the law should impose a duty on every person to obtain permission to photocopy or reproduce any article under any circumstance? What would be some of the implications of such a duty for society? Discuss fully.

VIDEO QUESTION

5–11. Go to this text's Web site at **http://fundamentals.westbuslaw.com** and click on "Video Questions." Select "Chapter 5" and view the video titled *Choosing a Business Name and a Domain Name.* Then answer the following questions:

1. Which form of intellectual property is a domain name?
2. Can a Web-based business register and use a domain name that is identical to the business name of a firm located in a distant state?
3. If Caleb and Anna in the video chose to use the name "Wizard for Hire" and were sued for infringement, would it make any difference to the court whether a consumer was likely to be confused between the two computer businesses? What would the court focus on in analyzing the infringement claim in this situation?

INTELLECTUAL PROPERTY AND INTERNET LAW

For updated links to resources available on the Web, as well as a variety of other materials, visit this text's Web site at

http://fundamentals.westbuslaw.com

An excellent overview of the laws governing various forms of intellectual property is available at FindLaw's Web site. Go to

http://profs.lp.findlaw.com

You can find answers to common questions about trademark and patent law—and links to registration forms, statutes, international patent and trademark offices, and numerous other related materials—at the Web site of the U.S. Patent and Trademark Office. Go to

http://www.uspto.gov

For information on invalid and improperly granted patents, go to

http://www.bustpatents.com

You can also access information on various topics relating to intellectual property at the following Internet site:

http://www.patents.com

For information on copyrights, go to the U.S. Copyright Office at

http://www.loc.gov/copyright

You can find extensive information on copyright law—including United States Supreme Court decisions in this area and the texts of the Berne Convention and other international treaties on copyright issues—at the Web site of the Legal Information Institute at Cornell University's School of Law. Go to

http://www.law.cornell.edu/topics/copyright.html

Online Legal Research

Go to the *Fundamentals of Business Law* home page at **http://fundamentals. westbuslaw.com**. Select "Interactive Study Center" and then click on "Chapter 5." There you will find the following Internet research exercises that you can perform to learn more about topics covered in this chapter.

Activity 5–1: LEGAL PERSPECTIVE—**Unwarranted Legal Threats**
Activity 5–2: MANAGEMENT PERSPECTIVE—**Protecting Intellectual Property across Borders**
Activity 5–3: TECHNOLOGICAL PERSPECTIVE—**File-Sharing**

Before the Test

Go to the *Fundamentals of Business Law* home page at **http://fundamentals. westbuslaw.com**. Click on "Interactive Quizzes." You will find at least twenty interactive questions relating to this chapter.

Westlaw® Campus

If your textbook provided for a subscription to Westlaw® Campus, or if you have otherwise purchased access to the Westlaw Campus database, you can access any of the cases presented or cited in this chapter by using your Westlaw Campus account.

CHAPTER
6
Criminal Law and Cyber Crimes

CHAPTER OBJECTIVES

After reading this chapter, you should be able to answer the following questions:

① What two elements must exist before a person can be held liable for a crime? Can a corporation be liable for crimes?

② What are five broad categories of crimes? What is white-collar crime?

③ What defenses might be raised by criminal defendants to avoid liability for criminal acts?

④ What constitutional safeguards exist to protect persons accused of crimes? What are the basic steps in the criminal process?

⑤ What is cyber crime? What laws apply to crimes committed in cyberspace?

Various sanctions are used to bring about a society in which individuals engaging in business can compete and flourish. These sanctions include damages for various types of tortious conduct (as discussed in Chapter 4), damages for breach of contract (to be discussed in Chapter 12), and the equitable remedies discussed in Chapter 1. Additional sanctions are imposed under criminal law. Many statutes regulating business provide for criminal as well as civil sanctions. Therefore, criminal law joins civil law as an important element in the legal environment of business.

In this chapter, following a brief summary of the major differences between criminal and civil law, we look at how crimes are classified and what elements must be present for criminal liability to exist. We then examine various cate-

gories of crime, the defenses that can be raised to avoid liability for criminal actions, and criminal procedural law. Criminal procedural law attempts to ensure that a criminal defendant's right to the Fourteenth Amendment's guarantee of "due process of law" is enforced.

Since the advent of computer networks and, more recently, the Internet, new types of crimes or new variations of traditional crimes have been committed in cyberspace. For that reason, they are often referred to as **cyber crime**. Generally, cyber crime refers more to the way particular crimes are committed than to a new category of crimes. We devote the concluding pages of this chapter to a discussion of this increasingly significant area of criminal activity.

Civil Law and Criminal Law

Remember from Chapter 1 that *civil law* spells out the duties that exist between persons or between persons and their governments, excluding the duty not to commit crimes. Contract law, for example, is part of civil law. The whole body of tort law, which deals with the infringement by one person on the legally recognized rights of another, is also an area of civil law.

Criminal law, in contrast, has to do with crime. A **crime** can be defined as a wrong against society proclaimed in a statute and, if committed, punishable by society through fines and/or imprisonment—and, in some cases, even death. As mentioned in Chapter 1, because crimes are *offenses against society as a whole,* they are prosecuted by a public official, such as a district attorney (D.A.), not by victims.

KEY DIFFERENCES BETWEEN CIVIL LAW AND CRIMINAL LAW

Because the state has extensive resources at its disposal when prosecuting criminal cases, there are numerous procedural safeguards to protect the rights of defendants. One of these safeguards is the higher standard of proof that applies in a criminal case. As you can see in Exhibit 6–1, which summarizes some of the key differences between civil law and criminal law, in a civil case the plaintiff usually must prove his or her case by a *preponderance of the evidence.* Under this standard, the plaintiff must convince the court that, based on the evidence presented by both parties, it is more likely than not that the plaintiff's allegation is true.

In a criminal case, in contrast, the state must prove its case **beyond a reasonable doubt.** Every juror in a criminal case must be convinced, beyond a reasonable doubt, of the defendant's guilt. The higher standard of proof in criminal cases reflects a fundamental social value—a belief that it is worse to convict an innocent individual than to let a guilty person go free. We will look at other safeguards later in the chapter, in the context of criminal procedure.

CIVIL LIABILTY FOR CRIMINAL ACTS

Those who commit crimes may be subject to both civil and criminal liability. ● **EXAMPLE #1** Joe is walking down the street, minding his own business, when suddenly a person attacks him. In the ensuing struggle, the attacker stabs Joe several times, seriously injuring him. A police officer restrains and arrests the wrongdoer. In this situation, the attacker may be subject both to criminal prosecution by the state and to a tort lawsuit brought by Joe.● Exhibit 6–2 illustrates how the same act can result in both a tort action and a criminal action against the wrongdoer.

Classification of Crimes

Depending on their degree of seriousness, crimes are classified as felonies or misdemeanors. **Felonies** are serious crimes punishable by death or by imprisonment in a federal or state penitentiary for more than a year. The Model Penal Code[1] provides for four degrees of felony: (1) capital offenses, for which the maximum penalty is death; (2) first degree felonies, punishable by a maximum penalty of life imprison-

---

[1] The American Law Institute issued the Official Draft of the Model Penal Code in 1962. The Model Penal Code is not a uniform code. Uniformity of criminal law among the states is not as important as uniformity in other areas of the law. Types of crimes vary with local circumstances, and it is appropriate that punishments vary accordingly. The Model Penal Code contains four parts: (1) general provisions, (2) definitions of special crimes, (3) provisions concerning treatment and corrections, and (4) provisions on the organization of corrections.

EXHIBIT 6–1 CIVIL AND CRIMINAL LAW COMPARED

ISSUE	CIVIL LAW	CRIMINAL LAW
Area of concern	Rights and duties between individuals and between persons and their government	Offenses against society as a whole
Wrongful act	Harm to a person or to a person's property	Violation of a statute that prohibits some type of activity
Party who brings suit	Person who suffered harm	The state
Standard of proof	Preponderance of the evidence	Beyond a reasonable doubt
Remedy	Damages to compensate for the harm, or a decree to achieve an equitable result	Punishment (fine, removal from public office, imprisonment, or death)

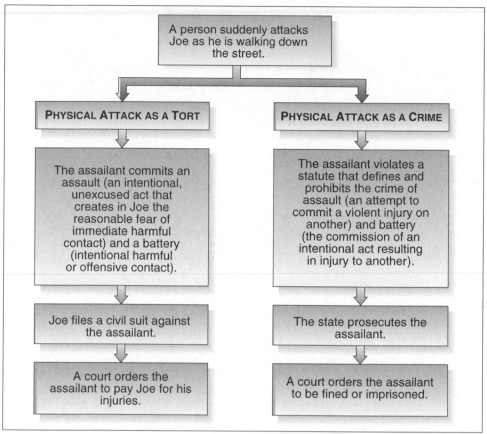

EXHIBIT 6–2 TORT LAWSUIT AND CRIMINAL PROSECUTION FOR THE SAME ACT

A person suddenly attacks Joe as he is walking down the street.

PHYSICAL ATTACK AS A TORT

The assailant commits an assault (an intentional, unexcused act that creates in Joe the reasonable fear of immediate harmful contact) and a battery (intentional harmful or offensive contact).

Joe files a civil suit against the assailant.

A court orders the assailant to pay Joe for his injuries.

PHYSICAL ATTACK AS A CRIME

The assailant violates a statute that defines and prohibits the crime of assault (an attempt to commit a violent injury on another) and battery (the commission of an intentional act resulting in injury to another).

The state prosecutes the assailant.

A court orders the assailant to be fined or imprisoned.

ment; (3) second degree felonies, punishable by a maximum of ten years' imprisonment; and (4) third degree felonies, punishable by a maximum of five years' imprisonment.

Under federal law and in most states, any crime that is not a felony is considered a **misdemeanor**. Misdemeanors are crimes punishable by a fine or by confinement for up to a year. If incarcerated (imprisoned), the guilty party goes to a local jail instead of a prison. Disorderly conduct and trespass are common misdemeanors. Some states have different classes of misdemeanors. For example, in Illinois misdemeanors are either Class A (confinement for up to a year), Class B (not more than six months), or Class C (not more than thirty days). Whether a crime is a felony or a misdemeanor can also determine whether the case is tried in a magistrate's court (for example, by a justice of the peace) or in a general trial court.

In most jurisdictions, **petty offenses** are considered to be a subset of misdemeanors. Petty offenses are minor violations, such as driving faster than the posted speed limit or violating a building code. Even for petty offenses, however,

a guilty party can be put in jail for a few days, fined, or both, depending on state or local law.

Criminal Liability

Two elements must exist simultaneously for a person to be convicted of a crime: (1) the performance of a prohibited act and (2) a specified state of mind or intent on the part of the actor. Every criminal statute prohibits certain behavior. Most crimes require an act of *commission;* that is, a person must *do* something in order to be accused of a crime.[2] In some cases, an act of *omission* can be a crime, but only when a person has a legal duty to perform the omitted act. Failure to file a tax return is an example of an omission that is a crime.

The *guilty act* requirement is based on one of the premises of criminal law—that a person is punished for harm

---

[2] Called the *actus reus* (pronounced *ak*-tuhs *ray*-uhs), or "guilty act."

done to society. Thinking about killing someone or about stealing a car may be wrong, but the thoughts do no harm until they are translated into action. Of course, a person can be punished for attempting murder or robbery, but normally only if he or she took substantial steps toward the criminal objective.

A *wrongful mental state*[3] is as necessary as a wrongful act in establishing criminal liability. What constitutes such a mental state varies according to the wrongful action. For murder, the act is the taking of a life, and the mental state is the intent to take life. For theft, the guilty act is the taking of another person's property, and the mental state involves both the knowledge that the property belongs to another and the intent to deprive the owner of it.

Criminal liability typically arises for actions that violate state criminal statutes. Federal criminal jurisdiction is limited to crimes that occur outside the jurisdiction of any state, crimes involving interstate commerce or communications, crimes that interfere with the operation of the federal government or its agents, and crimes directed at citizens or property located outside the United States. Federal jurisdiction also exists if a federal law or a federal government agency (such as the U.S. Department of Justice or the federal Environmental Protection Agency) defines a certain type of action as a crime. Today, businesspersons are subject to criminal penalties under numerous federal laws and regulations. We will examine many of these laws in later chapters of this text.

Corporate Criminal Liability

At one time, it was thought that a corporation could not incur criminal liability because, although a corporation is a legal person, it can act only through its agents (corporate

directors, officers, and employees). Therefore, the corporate entity itself could not "intend" to commit a crime. Under modern criminal law, however, a corporation may be held liable for crimes. Obviously, corporations cannot be imprisoned, but they can be fined or denied certain legal privileges (such as a license). Today, corporations are normally liable for the crimes committed by their agents and employees within the course and scope of their employment.

Corporate directors and officers are personally liable for the crimes they commit, regardless of whether the crimes were committed for their personal benefit or on the corporation's behalf. Additionally, corporate directors and officers may be held liable for the actions of employees under their supervision. Under what has become known as the "responsible corporate officer" doctrine, a court may impose criminal liability on a corporate officer regardless of whether she or he participated in, directed, or even knew about a given criminal violation.

● **EXAMPLE #2** In *United States v. Park,*[4] the chief executive officer of a national supermarket chain was held personally liable for sanitation violations in corporate warehouses in which the food was exposed to contamination by rodents. The court imposed personal liability on the corporate officer not because he intended the crime or even knew about it, but because he was in a "responsible relationship" to the corporation and had the power to prevent the violation.● Since the *Park* decision, courts have applied this "responsible corporate officer" doctrine on a number of occasions to hold corporate officers liable for their employees' statutory violations. The following case illustrates that corporate officers and supervisors who oversee operations causing environmental harm may be held liable under the criminal provisions of environmental statutes.

---

[3] Called the *mens rea* (pronounced mehns *ray*-uh), or "evil intent."

[4] 421 U.S. 658, 95 S.Ct. 1903, 44 L.Ed.2d 489 (1975).

CASE 6.1   United States v. Hanousek

United States Court of Appeals,
Ninth Circuit, 1999.
176 F.3d 1116.
http://www.ca9.uscourts.gov[a]

---

a. The U.S. Court of Appeals for the Ninth Circuit maintains this Web site. Click on the "Opinions" box. On the left-hand side of the page, select "Opinions by date." From that page, click on the "1999" icon, and when the menu opens, select "March." Scroll down to "USA V HANOUSEK" (decided on 03/19/99) and click on the case name to access the case.

FACTS Edward Hanousek worked for Pacific & Arctic Railway and Navigation Company (P&A) as a roadmaster of the White Pass & Yukon Railroad in Alaska. Hanousek was responsible "for every detail of the safe and efficient maintenance and construction of track, structures, and marine facilities of the entire railroad," including special projects. One project was a rock quarry, known as "6-mile," above the Skagway River. Next to the quarry, and just beneath the surface, ran a high-pressure oil pipeline owned by Pacific & Arctic Pipeline, Inc., P&A's sister company. Hanousek aban-

CASE 6.1—Continued

doned pipeline protection measures that had been implemented by previous supervisors. When the quarry's backhoe operator punctured the pipeline, an estimated 1,000 to 5,000 gallons of oil were discharged into the river. Hanousek was charged with, among other things, negligently discharging a harmful quantity of oil into a navigable water of the United States in violation of the criminal provisions of the Clean Water Act (CWA). After a trial in a federal district court, a jury convicted Hanousek, and the court imposed a sentence of six months' imprisonment, six months in a halfway house, six months' supervised release, and a fine of $5,000. Hanousek appealed to the U.S. Court of Appeals for the Ninth Circuit, arguing in part that the statute under which he was convicted violated his right to due process because he was not aware of what the CWA required.

ISSUE Were Hanousek's due process rights violated?

DECISION No. The U.S. Court of Appeals for the Ninth Circuit affirmed Hanousek's conviction.

REASON A corporate manager who has responsibility for operations with the potential to cause harm can be held criminally liable for harm that results even if he or she does not actually know of the specific statute under which liability may be imposed. The CWA is public-welfare legislation, which "is designed to protect the public from potentially harmful or injurious items and may render criminal a type of conduct that a reasonable person should know is subject to stringent public regulation." The court stated, "[I]t is well established that a public-welfare statute may subject a person to criminal liability for his or her ordinary negligence without violating due process." When "dangerous or deleterious [harmful] devices or products or obnoxious waste materials are involved, the probability of regulation is so great that anyone who is aware that he is in possession of them or dealing with them must be presumed to be aware of the regulation." Hanousek knew about the pipeline and the danger that a puncture would pose. "Therefore, Hanousek should have been alerted to the probability of strict regulation."

FOR CRITICAL ANALYSIS—Environmental Consideration *If corporate actors were able to avoid responsibility for violations of environmental statutes of which they were unaware, what might result?*

Types of Crimes

The number of acts that are defined as criminal is nearly endless. Federal, state, and local laws provide for the classification and punishment of hundreds of thousands of different criminal acts. Traditionally, though, crimes have been grouped into five broad categories, or types: violent crime (crimes against persons), property crime, public order crime, white-collar crime, and organized crime. Cyber crime—which consists of crimes committed in cyberspace with the use of computers—is, as mentioned earlier, less a category of crime than a new way to commit crime. We will examine cyber crime later in this chapter.

VIOLENT CRIME

Crimes against persons, because they cause others to suffer harm or death, are referred to as *violent crimes.* Murder is a violent crime. So is sexual assault, or rape. Assault and battery, which were discussed in Chapter 4 in the context of tort law, are also classified as violent crimes. **Robbery**—defined as the taking of money, personal property, or any other article of value from a person by means of force or fear—is also a violent crime. Typically, states have more severe penalties for *aggravated robbery*—robbery with the use of a deadly weapon.

Each of these violent crimes is further classified by degree, depending on the circumstances surrounding the criminal act. These circumstances include the intent of the person committing the crime, whether a weapon was used, and (in cases other than murder) the level of pain and suffering experienced by the victim.

PROPERTY CRIME

The most common type of criminal activity is property crime—violations in which the goal of the offender is some form of economic gain or the damaging of property. Robbery is a form of property crime, as well as a violent crime, because the offender seeks to gain the property of another. We look here at a number of other wrongs that fall within the general category of property crime.

Burglary. Traditionally, **burglary** was defined under the common law as breaking and entering the dwelling of another at night with the intent to commit a felony. Originally, the definition was aimed at protecting an individual's home and its occupants. Most state statutes have eliminated some of the requirements found in the common law definition. The time at which the breaking and entering occurs, for example, is usually immaterial. State statutes frequently omit the element of breaking, and some states do not require that the building be a dwelling. Aggravated burglary, which is defined as burglary with the use of a deadly weapon, burglary of a dwelling, or both, incurs a greater penalty.

Larceny. Any person who wrongfully or fraudulently takes and carries away another person's personal property is guilty of **larceny**. Larceny includes the fraudulent intent to deprive an owner permanently of property. Many business-related larcenies entail fraudulent conduct. Whereas robbery involves force or fear, larceny does not. Therefore, picking pockets is larceny. Similarly, taking company products and supplies home for personal use, if one is not authorized to do so, is larceny.

In most states, the definition of property that is subject to larceny statutes has expanded. Stealing computer programs may constitute larceny even though the "property" consists of magnetic impulses. Stealing computer time can also constitute larceny. So, too, can the theft of natural gas. Trade secrets can be subject to larceny statutes. Obtaining another's phone-card number and then using that number, without authorization, to place long-distance calls is a form of property theft. These types of larceny are covered by "theft of services" statutes in many jurisdictions.

The common law distinguishes between grand and petit larceny depending on the value of the property taken. Many states have abolished this distinction, but in those that have not, grand larceny is a felony and petit larceny, a misdemeanor.

Obtaining Goods by False Pretenses. It is a criminal act to obtain goods by means of false pretenses—for example, buying groceries with a check, knowing that one has insufficient funds to cover it. Statutes dealing with such illegal activities vary widely from state to state.

Receiving Stolen Goods. It is a crime to receive stolen goods. The recipient of such goods need not know the true identity of the owner or the thief. All that is necessary is that the recipient knows or should have known that the goods are stolen, which implies an intent to deprive the owner of those goods.

Arson. The willful and malicious burning of a building (and in some states, personal property) owned by another is the crime of **arson**. At common law, arson traditionally applied only to burning down another person's house. The

law was designed to protect human life. Today, arson statutes have been extended to cover the destruction of any building, regardless of ownership, by fire or explosion.

Every state has a special statute that covers a person's burning a building for the purpose of collecting insurance. ● **EXAMPLE #3** If Smith owns an insured apartment building that is falling apart and sets fire to it himself or pays someone else to do so, he is guilty not only of arson but also of defrauding insurers, which is an attempted larceny.● Of course, the insurer need not pay the claim when insurance fraud is proved.

Forgery. The fraudulent making or altering of any writing in a way that changes the legal rights and liabilities of another is **forgery**. If, without authorization, Severson signs Bennett's name to the back of a check made out to Bennett, Severson is committing forgery. Forgery also includes changing trademarks, falsifying public records, counterfeiting, and altering a legal document.

PUBLIC ORDER CRIME

Historically, societies have always outlawed activities that are considered to be contrary to public values and morals. Today, the most common public order crimes include public drunkenness, prostitution, gambling, and illegal drug use. These crimes are sometimes referred to as victimless crimes because they frequently harm only the offender. From a broader perspective, however, they are deemed detrimental to society as a whole because they might create an environment that gives rise to property and violent crimes.

WHITE-COLLAR CRIME

Crimes that typically occur only in the business context are commonly referred to as **white-collar crimes**. Although there is no official definition of white-collar crime, the term is popularly used to mean an illegal act or series of acts committed by an individual or business entity using some nonviolent means. Usually, this kind of crime is committed in the course of a legitimate occupation. Corporate crimes fall into this category.

Embezzlement. When a person entrusted with another person's property or money fraudulently appropriates it, **embezzlement** occurs. Typically, embezzlement involves an employee who steals funds. Banks face this problem, and so do a number of businesses in which corporate officers or accountants "jimmy" the books to cover up the fraudulent conversion of funds for their own benefit. Embezzlement is not larceny, because the wrongdoer does not physically take the property from the possession of another, and it is not robbery, because force or fear is not used.

It does not matter whether the accused takes the funds from the victim or from a third person. If, as the financial officer of a large corporation, Saunders pockets a certain number of checks from third parties that were given to her to deposit into the corporate account, she is embezzling.

Ordinarily, an embezzler who returns what has been taken does not face prosecution, because the owner usually will not take the time to make a complaint, give depositions, and appear in court. That the accused intended eventually to return the embezzled property, however, does not constitute a sufficient defense to the crime of embezzlement.

Mail and Wire Fraud. One of the most potent weapons against white-collar criminals is the Mail Fraud Act of 1990.[5] Under this act, it is a federal crime (mail fraud) to use the mails to defraud the public. Illegal use of the mails must involve (1) mailing or causing someone else to mail a writing—something written, printed, or photocopied—for the purpose of executing a scheme to defraud and (2) a contemplated or an organized scheme to defraud by false pretenses. If, for example, Johnson advertises by mail the sale of a cure for cancer that he knows to be fraudulent because it has no medical validity, he can be prosecuted for fraudulent use of the mails.

Federal law also makes it a crime (wire fraud) to use wire (for example, the telephone), radio, or television transmissions to defraud.[6] Violators may be fined up to $1,000, imprisoned for up to five years, or both. If the violation affects a financial institution, the violator may be fined up to $1 million, imprisoned for up to thirty years, or both.

Bribery. Basically, three types of bribery are considered crimes: bribery of public officials, commercial bribery, and bribery of foreign officials. The attempt to influence a public official to act in a way that serves a private interest is a crime. As an element of this crime, intent must be present and proved. The bribe can be anything the recipient considers to be valuable. Realize that *the crime of bribery occurs when the bribe is offered*. It does not matter whether the person to whom the bribe is offered accepts the bribe or agrees to perform whatever action is desired by the person offering the bribe. *Accepting a bribe* is a separate crime.

Typically, people make commercial bribes to obtain proprietary information, cover up an inferior product, or secure new business. Industrial espionage sometimes involves commercial bribes. For example, a person in one firm may offer an employee in a competing firm some type of payoff in exchange for trade secrets or pricing schedules. So-called kickbacks, or payoffs for special favors or services, are a form of commercial bribery in some situations.

Bribing foreign officials to obtain favorable business contracts is a crime. The Foreign Corrupt Practices Act of 1977, which was described in Chapter 3, was passed to curb the use of bribery by American businesspersons in securing foreign contracts.

Bankruptcy Fraud. Today, federal bankruptcy law (see Chapter 21) allows individuals and businesses to be relieved of oppressive debt through bankruptcy proceedings. Numerous white-collar crimes may be committed during the many phases of a bankruptcy proceeding. A creditor, for example, may file a false claim against the debtor, which is a crime. Also, a debtor may fraudulently transfer assets to favored parties before or after the petition for bankruptcy is filed. For example, a company-owned automobile may be "sold" at a bargain price to a trusted friend or relative. Closely related to the crime of fraudulent transfer of property is the crime of fraudulent concealment of property, such as hiding gold coins.

The Theft of Trade Secrets. As discussed in Chapter 5, trade secrets constitute a form of intellectual property that for many businesses can be extremely valuable. The Economic Espionage Act of 1996[7] made the theft of trade secrets a federal crime. The act also made it a federal crime to buy or possess trade secrets of another person, knowing that the trade secrets were stolen or otherwise acquired without the owner's authorization.

Violations of the act can result in steep penalties. An individual who violates the act can be imprisoned for up to ten years and fined up to $500,000. If a corporation or other organization violates the act, it can be fined up to $5 million. Additionally, the law provides that any property acquired as a result of the violation and any property used in the commission of the violation are subject to criminal *forfeiture*—meaning that the government can take the property. A theft of trade secrets conducted via the Internet, for example, could result in the forfeiture of every computer, printer, or other device used to commit or facilitate the violation.

Insider Trading. An individual who obtains "inside information" about the plans of a publicly listed corporation can often make stock-trading profits by using the information to guide decisions relating to the purchase or sale of

---

[5] 18 U.S.C. Sections 1341–1342.
[6] 18 U.S.C. Section 1343.

[7] 18 U.S.C. Sections 1831–1839.

corporate securities. **Insider trading** is a violation of securities law and will be considered more fully in Chapter 27. At this point, it may be said that one who possesses inside information and who has a duty not to disclose it to outsiders may not profit from the purchase or sale of securities based on these facts until the information is available to the public.

ORGANIZED CRIME

As mentioned, white-collar crime takes place within the confines of the legitimate business world. *Organized crime,* in contrast, operates *illegitimately* by, among other things, providing illegal goods and services. For organized crime, the traditional preferred markets are gambling, prostitution, illegal narcotics, pornography, and loan sharking (lending money at higher-than-legal interest rates), along with more recent ventures into counterfeiting and credit-card scams.

Money Laundering. The profits from illegal activities amount to billions of dollars a year, particularly the profits from illegal drug transactions and, to a lesser extent, from racketeering, prostitution, and gambling. Under federal law, banks, savings and loan associations, and other financial institutions are required to report currency transactions involving more than $10,000. Consequently, those who engage in illegal activities face difficulties in depositing their cash profits from unlawful transactions.

As an alternative to simply storing cash from illegal transactions in a safe-deposit box, wrongdoers and racketeers have invented ways to launder "dirty" money to make it "clean." This **money laundering** is done through legitimate businesses.

● **EXAMPLE #4** Matt, a successful drug dealer, becomes a partner with a restaurateur. Little by little, the restaurant shows an increasing profit. As partner in the restaurant, Matt is able to report the "profits" of the restaurant as legitimate income on which he pays federal and state taxes. He can then spend those monies without worrying that his lifestyle may exceed the level possible with his reported income.●

The Federal Bureau of Investigation estimates that organized crime has invested tens of billions of dollars in as many as a hundred thousand business establishments in the United States for the purpose of money laundering. Globally, it is estimated that more than $500 billion in ill-gained money moves through the world banking system every year.

The Racketeer Influenced and Corrupt Organizations Act. In 1970, in an effort to curb the apparently increasing entry of organized crime into the legitimate business world,

Congress passed the Racketeer Influenced and Corrupt Organizations Act (RICO).[8] This legislation, which was enacted as part of the Organized Crime Control Act, makes it a federal crime to (1) use income obtained from racketeering activity to purchase any interest in an enterprise, (2) acquire or maintain an interest in an enterprise through racketeering activity, (3) conduct or participate in the affairs of an enterprise through racketeering activity, or (4) conspire to do any of the preceding activities.

Racketeering activity is not a new type of substantive crime created by RICO; rather, RICO incorporates by reference twenty-six separate types of federal crimes and nine types of state felonies[9] and declares that if a person commits two of these offenses, he or she is guilty of "racketeering activity." Additionally, RICO is more often used today as an effective tool to attack white-collar crimes rather than organized crime.

In the event of a violation, the statute permits the government to seek civil penalties, including the divestiture of a defendant's interest in a business (called forfeiture) or the dissolution of the business. Perhaps the most controversial aspect of RICO is that, in some cases, private individuals are allowed to recover three times their actual losses (treble damages), plus attorneys' fees, for business injuries caused by a violation of the statute. Under criminal provisions of RICO, any individual found guilty of a violation is subject to a fine of up to $25,000 per violation, imprisonment for up to twenty years, or both. Additionally, the statute provides that those who violate RICO may be required to forfeit (give up) any assets, in the form of property or cash, that were acquired as a result of the illegal activity or that were "involved in" or an "instrumentality of" the activity.

Defenses to Criminal Liability

Among the most important defenses to criminal liability are infancy, intoxication, insanity, mistake, consent, duress, justifiable use of force, entrapment, and the statute of limitations. Many of these defenses involve assertions that the intent requirement for criminal liability is lacking. Also, in some cases, defendants are given immunity and thus are relieved, at least in part, of criminal liability for crimes they committed. We look at each of these defenses here.

Note that procedural violations, such as obtaining evidence without a valid search warrant, may operate as defenses also. As you will read later in this chapter, evidence obtained in violation of a defendant's constitutional

---

[8] 18 U.S.C. Sections 1961–1968.
[9] See 18 U.S.C. Section 1961(1)(A).

rights normally may not be admitted in court. If the evidence is suppressed, then there may be no basis for prosecuting the defendant.

INFANCY

The term *infant,* as used in the law, refers to any person who has not yet reached the age of majority (see Chapter 9). In all states, certain courts handle cases involving children who are alleged to have violated the law. In some states, juvenile courts handle children's cases exclusively. In other states, however, courts that handle children's cases may also have jurisdiction over other matters.

Originally, juvenile court hearings were informal, and lawyers were rarely present. Since 1967, however, when the United States Supreme Court ordered that a child charged with delinquency must be allowed to consult with an attorney before being committed to a state institution,[10] juvenile court hearings have become more formal. In some states, a child may be treated as an adult and tried in a regular court if she or he is above a certain age (usually fourteen) and is guilty of a felony, such as rape or murder.

INTOXICATION

The law recognizes two types of intoxication, whether from drugs or from alcohol: *involuntary* and *voluntary.* Involuntary intoxication occurs when a person either is physically forced to ingest or inject an intoxicating substance or is unaware that a substance contains drugs or alcohol. Involuntary intoxication is a defense to a crime if its effect was to make a person incapable of obeying the law or incapable of understanding that the act committed was wrong. Voluntary intoxication is rarely a defense, but it may be effective in cases in which the defendant was *extremely* intoxicated when committing the wrong.

INSANITY

Just as a child is often judged incapable of the state of mind required to commit a crime, so also may be someone suffering from a mental illness. Thus, insanity may be a defense to a criminal charge. The courts have had difficulty deciding what the test for legal insanity should be, however, and psychiatrists as well as lawyers are critical of the tests used. Almost all federal courts and some states use the relatively liberal standard set forth in the Model Penal Code:

> A person is not responsible for criminal conduct if at the time of such conduct as a result of mental disease or defect he lacks

substantial capacity either to appreciate the wrongfulness of his conduct or to conform his conduct to the requirements of the law.

Some states use the *M'Naghten* test,[11] under which a criminal defendant is not responsible if, at the time of the offense, he or she did not know the nature and quality of the act or did not know that the act was wrong. Other states use the irresistible-impulse test. A person operating under an irresistible impulse may know an act is wrong but cannot refrain from doing it.

MISTAKE

Everyone has heard the saying "Ignorance of the law is no excuse." Ordinarily, ignorance of the law or a mistaken idea about what the law requires is not a valid defense. In some states, however, that rule has been modified. Criminal defendants who claim that they honestly did not know that they were breaking a law may have a valid defense if (1) the law was not published or reasonably made known to the public or (2) the defendant relied on an official statement of the law that was erroneous.

A *mistake of fact,* as opposed to a *mistake of law,* operates as a defense if it negates the mental state necessary to commit a crime. ● **EXAMPLE #5** If Oliver Wheaton mistakenly walks off with Julie Tyson's briefcase because he thinks it is his, there is no theft. Theft requires knowledge that the property belongs to another. (If Wheaton's act causes Tyson to incur damages, however, Wheaton may be subject to liability for trespass to personal property or conversion, torts that were discussed in Chapter 4.)●

CONSENT

What if a victim consents to a crime or even encourages the person intending a criminal act to commit it? The law allows **consent** as a defense if the consent cancels the harm that the law is designed to prevent. In each case, the question is whether the law forbids an act that was committed against the victim's will or forbids the act without regard to the victim's wish. The law forbids murder, prostitution, and drug use regardless of whether the victim consents to it. Also, if the act causes harm to a third person who has not consented, there is no escape from criminal liability. Consent or forgiveness given after a crime has been committed is not really a defense, though it can affect the likelihood of prosecution. Consent operates most successfully as a defense in crimes against property.

---

[10] *In re Gault,* 387 U.S. 1, 87 S.Ct. 1428, 18 L.Ed.2d 527 (1967).

[11] A rule derived from *M'Naghten's Case,* 8 Eng.Rep. 718 (1843).

DURESS

Duress exists when the *wrongful threat* of one person induces another person to perform an act that she or he would not otherwise perform. In such a situation, duress is said to negate the mental state necessary to commit a crime. For duress to qualify as a defense, the following requirements must be met:

① The threat must be of serious bodily harm or death.

② The harm threatened must be greater than the harm caused by the crime.

③ The threat must be immediate and inescapable.

④ The defendant must have been involved in the situation through no fault of his or her own.

JUSTIFIABLE USE OF FORCE

Probably the most well-known defense to criminal liability is **self-defense.** Other situations, however, also justify the use of force: the defense of one's dwelling, the defense of other property, and the prevention of a crime. In all of these situations, it is important to distinguish between the use of deadly and nondeadly force. *Deadly force* is likely to result in death or serious bodily harm. *Nondeadly force* is force that reasonably appears necessary to prevent the imminent use of criminal force.

Generally speaking, people can use the amount of nondeadly force that seems necessary to protect themselves, their dwellings, or other property or to prevent the commission of a crime. Deadly force can be used in self-defense if there is a *reasonable belief* that imminent death or grievous bodily harm will otherwise result, if the attacker is using unlawful force (an example of lawful force is that exerted by a police officer), and if the defender has not initiated or provoked the attack. Deadly force normally can be used to defend a dwelling only if the unlawful entry is violent and the person believes deadly force is necessary to prevent imminent death or great bodily harm or—in some jurisdictions—if the person believes deadly force is necessary to prevent the commission of a felony (such as arson) in the dwelling.

ENTRAPMENT

Entrapment is a defense designed to prevent police officers or other government agents from encouraging crimes in order to apprehend persons wanted for criminal acts. In the typical entrapment case, an undercover agent suggests that a crime be committed and somehow pressures or induces an individual to commit it. The agent then arrests the individual for the crime.

For entrapment to be considered a defense, both the suggestion and the inducement must take place. The defense is intended not to prevent law enforcement agents from setting a trap for an unwary criminal but rather to prevent them from pushing the individual into it. The crucial issue is whether a person who committed a crime was predisposed to commit the crime or did so because the agent induced it.

STATUTE OF LIMITATIONS

With some exceptions, such as for the crime of murder, statutes of limitations apply to crimes just as they do to civil wrongs. In other words, criminal cases must be prosecuted within a certain number of years. If a criminal action is brought after the statutory time period has expired, the accused person can raise the statute of limitations as a defense.

IMMUNITY

At times, the state may wish to obtain information from a person accused of a crime. Accused persons are understandably reluctant to give information if it will be used to prosecute them, and they cannot be forced to do so. The privilege against self-incrimination is granted by the Fifth Amendment to the Constitution, which reads, in part, "nor shall [any person] be compelled in any criminal case to be a witness against himself." In cases in which the state wishes to obtain information from a person accused of a crime, the state can grant *immunity* from prosecution or agree to prosecute for a less serious offense in exchange for the information. Once immunity is given, the person can no longer refuse to testify on Fifth Amendment grounds because he or she now has an absolute privilege against self-incrimination.

Often, a grant of immunity from prosecution for a serious crime is part of the **plea bargaining** between the defendant and the prosecuting attorney. The defendant may be convicted of a lesser offense, while the state uses the defendant's testimony to prosecute accomplices for serious crimes carrying heavy penalties.

Constitutional Safeguards and Criminal Procedures

Criminal law brings the power of the state, with all its resources, to bear against the individual. Criminal procedures are designed to protect the constitutional rights of individuals and to prevent the arbitrary use of power on the part of the government.

The U.S. Constitution provides specific safeguards for those accused of crimes. Most of these safeguards protect individuals against state government actions, as well as federal government actions, by virtue of the due process clause of the Fourteenth Amendment. These safeguards are set forth in the Fourth, Fifth, Sixth, and Eighth Amendments.

FOURTH AMENDMENT PROTECTIONS

The Fourth Amendment protects the "right of the people to be secure in their persons, houses, papers, and effects." Before searching or seizing private property, law enforcement officers must obtain a **search warrant**—an order from a judge or other public official authorizing the search or seizure.

Search Warrants and Probable Cause. To obtain a search warrant, the officers must convince a judge that they have reasonable grounds, or **probable cause**, to believe a search will reveal a specific illegality. Probable cause requires law enforcement officials to have trustworthy evidence that would convince a reasonable person that the proposed search or seizure is more likely justified than not. Furthermore, the Fourth Amendment prohibits general warrants. It requires a particular description of that which is to be searched or seized. General searches through a person's belongings are impermissible. The search cannot extend beyond what is described in the warrant.

There are exceptions to the requirement of a search warrant, as when it is likely that the items sought will be removed before a warrant can be obtained. For example, if a police officer has probable cause to believe an automobile contains evidence of a crime and it is likely that the vehicle will be unavailable by the time a warrant is obtained, the officer can search the vehicle without a warrant.

Searches and Seizures in the Business Context. Constitutional protection against unreasonable searches and seizures is important to businesses and professionals. As federal and state regulation of commercial activities increased, frequent and unannounced government inspections were conducted to ensure compliance with the regulations. Such inspections were extremely disruptive at times. In *Marshall v. Barlow's, Inc.*,[12] the United States Supreme Court held that government inspectors do not have the right to enter business premises without a warrant, although the standard of probable cause is not the same as that required in nonbusiness contexts. The existence of a general and neutral enforcement plan will justify issuance of the warrant.

Lawyers and accountants frequently possess the business records of their clients, and inspecting these documents while they are out of the hands of their true owners also requires a warrant. No warrant is required, however, for seizures of spoiled or contaminated food. Nor are warrants required for searches of businesses in such highly regulated industries as liquor, guns, and strip mining. General manufacturing is not considered to be one of these highly regulated industries, however.

Of increasing concern to many employers is how to maintain a safe and efficient workplace without jeopardizing the Fourth Amendment rights of employees "to be secure in their persons." Requiring employees to undergo random drug tests, for example, may be held to violate the Fourth Amendment.

FIFTH AMENDMENT PROTECTIONS

The Fifth Amendment offers significant protections for accused persons. One is the guarantee that no one can be deprived of "life, liberty, or property without due process of law." Two other important Fifth Amendment provisions protect persons against double jeopardy and self-incrimination.

Due Process of Law. Remember from Chapter 1 that *due process of law* has both procedural and substantive aspects. Procedural due process requirements underlie criminal procedures. Basically, the law must be carried out in a fair and orderly way. In criminal cases, due process means that defendants should have an opportunity to object to the charges against them before a fair, neutral decision maker, such as a judge. Defendants must also be given the opportunity to confront and cross-examine witnesses and accusers and to present their own witnesses.

Double Jeopardy. The Fifth Amendment also protects persons from **double jeopardy** (being tried twice for the same criminal offense). The prohibition against double jeopardy means that once a criminal defendant is acquitted (found "not guilty") of a particular crime, the government may not reindict the person and retry him or her for the same crime.

The prohibition against double jeopardy does not preclude the crime victim from bringing a civil suit against the same person to recover damages, however. Additionally, a state's prosecution of a crime will not prevent a separate federal prosecution relating to the same activity, and vice versa. ● **EXAMPLE #6** A person found "not guilty" of assault and battery in a criminal case may be sued by the victim in a civil tort case for damages. A person who is prosecuted for assault and battery in a state court may be prosecuted in a

---

[12] 436 U.S. 307, 98 S.Ct. 1816, 56 L.Ed.2d 305 (1978).

federal court for civil rights violations resulting from the same action. ●

Self-Incrimination. The Fifth Amendment guarantees that no person "shall be compelled in any criminal case to be a witness against himself." Thus, in any criminal proceeding, an accused person cannot be compelled to give testimony that might subject her or him to any criminal prosecution.

The Fifth Amendment's guarantee against **self-incrimination** extends only to natural persons. Because a corporation is a legal entity and not a natural person, the privilege against self-incrimination does not apply to it. Similarly, the business records of a partnership do not receive Fifth Amendment protection.[13] When a partnership is required to produce these records, it must do so even if the information incriminates the persons who constitute the business entity. Sole proprietors and sole practitioners (those who fully own their businesses) who have not incorporated cannot be compelled to produce their business records. These individuals have full protection against self-incrimination, because they function in only one capacity; there is no separate business entity (see Chapter 24).

PROTECTIONS UNDER THE SIXTH AND EIGHTH AMENDMENTS

The Sixth Amendment guarantees several important rights for criminal defendants: the right to a speedy trial, the right to a jury trial, the right to a public trial, the right to con-

---

[13] The privilege has been applied to some small family partnerships. See *United States v. Slutsky*, 352 F.Supp. 1005 (S.D.N.Y. 1972).

front witnesses, and the right to counsel. The Eighth Amendment prohibits excessive bail and fines, and cruel and unusual punishment.

THE EXCLUSIONARY RULE AND THE *MIRANDA* RULE

Two other procedural protections for criminal defendants are the exclusionary rule and the *Miranda* rule.

The Exclusionary Rule. Under what is known as the **exclusionary rule**, all evidence obtained in violation of the constitutional rights spelled out in the Fourth, Fifth, and Sixth Amendments normally must be excluded from the trial, as well as all evidence derived from the illegally obtained evidence. Evidence derived from illegally obtained evidence is known as the "fruit of the poisonous tree." For example, if a confession is obtained after an illegal arrest, the arrest is "the poisonous tree," and the confession, if "tainted" by the arrest, is the "fruit."

The purpose of the exclusionary rule is to deter police from conducting warrantless searches and from engaging in other misconduct. The rule is sometimes criticized because it can lead to injustice. Many a defendant has "gotten off on a technicality" because law enforcement personnel failed to observe procedural requirements. Even though a defendant may be obviously guilty, if the evidence of that guilt was obtained improperly (without a valid search warrant, for example), it normally cannot be used against the defendant in court.

In the following case, the court considered whether certain evidence had been obtained improperly and should be excluded as "fruit of the poisonous tree."

CASE 6.2   **People v. McFarlan**

New York Supreme Court, 2002.[a]
191 Misc.2d 531,
744 N.Y.S.2d 287.

FACTS In May 2001, Lisa Kordes saw two men picking pockets on a Lexington Avenue bus in Manhattan, in New York City. Based on Kordes's description of the men, a police department computer produced a six-photo array of possible suspects. Kordes selected a photo of Kevin McFarlan as one of the men she had seen. Five days later, on a bus, Neal

Ariano, a police officer, arrested McFarlan after seeing him bump an elderly woman while placing his hand near her pocketbook. At the police station, Kordes viewed a lineup including McFarlan and identified him as the man she had seen on the Lexington Avenue bus. McFarlan was charged in a New York state court with various crimes. The printout of the computer-generated photo array that Kordes had been shown was lost, but the "People" (the state of New York) introduced into evidence a second printout to show what Kordes had seen. McFarlan argued, among other things, that the first printout was the original photo array and that because that printout had been lost, the court should presume the photo-array procedure had been illegal. Thus, McFarlan's arrest and Kordes's identification of him in the lineup should be excluded as "fruit of the poisonous tree."

---

a. In New York, a supreme court is a trial court.

CASE 6.2—Continued

ISSUE Should the second printout of the photo array be considered "fruit of the poisonous tree" and thus inadmissible?

DECISION No. The New York state court held that the second printout of the photo array was not "fruit of the poisonous tree" and could be properly accepted into evidence.

REASON The court concluded that "as both printouts were generated in the same format, there can be no prejudice from the fact that the defendant was selected from the first printout and that a second identical printout was later [introduced into evidence]. Each is identical and conveys the full recoverable information. To decide * * * to the contrary * * * is absurd. Where, for example, a witness is shown only the screen display, what must the People [public prose-

cutor] keep? For on such an analysis the printout of the screen could not be the 'original.' The purpose of requiring the preservation of a record is clear. Concern for the integrity of information has always led the Courts to prefer the original, and has led to many rules to bar or limit the use of non-'original' material. Here the original array was in electronic form in the computer memory, the testimony was unequivocal that [both] printout[s] * * * were generated in the same manner. * * * [A]s a result, defendant's argument crumbles."

FOR CRITICAL ANALYSIS—Technological Consideration
When a record is stored on a computer, which should be considered the "original" record—the version on the computer or a printout of the computer version?

The *Miranda* Rule. In *Miranda v. Arizona,*[14] a case decided in 1966, the United States Supreme Court established the rule that individuals who are arrested must be informed of certain constitutional rights, including their Fifth Amendment right to remain silent and their Sixth Amendment right to counsel. If the arresting officers fail to inform a criminal suspect of these constitutional rights, any statements the suspect makes normally will not be admissible in court.

The Supreme Court's *Miranda* decision was controversial, and in 1968 Congress attempted to overrule the decision when it enacted Section 3501 of the Omnibus Crime Control Act of that year. Essentially, Section 3501 reinstated the rule that had been in effect for 180 years before *Miranda*—namely, that statements by defendants can be used against them as long as the statements are made voluntarily. The U.S. Justice Department immediately disavowed Section 3501 as unconstitutional, however, and the section has never been enforced. Although the U.S. Court of Appeals for the Fourth Circuit attempted to enforce the provision in 1999, the court's decision was reversed by the United States Supreme Court in 2000. The Supreme Court held that the *Miranda* rights enunciated by the Court in the 1966 case were constitutionally based and thus could not be overruled by a legislative act.[15]

Over time the United States Supreme Court has carved out several exceptions to the *Miranda* rule. In 1984, for example, the Court recognized a "public safety" exception to the *Miranda* rule. The need to protect the public war-

ranted the admissibility of statements made by the defendant (in this case, indicating where he placed the gun) as evidence in a trial, even when the defendant had not been informed of his *Miranda* rights.[16] In this situation and in certain other circumstances, juries are able to consider confessions, even if they are not voluntary.

Criminal Process

As mentioned, a criminal prosecution differs significantly from a civil case in several respects. These differences reflect the desire to safeguard the rights of the individual against the state. Exhibit 6–3 on the next page summarizes the major procedural steps in a criminal case. We discuss three phases of the criminal process—arrest, indictment or information, and trial—in more detail below.

ARREST

Before a warrant for arrest can be issued, there must be probable cause for believing that the individual in question has committed a crime. As discussed earlier, *probable cause* can be defined as a substantial likelihood that the person has committed or is about to commit a crime. Note that probable cause involves a *likelihood*, not just a possibility. Arrests may sometimes be made without a warrant if there is no time to get one, as when a police officer observes a crime taking place, but the action of the arresting officer is still judged by the standard of probable cause.

---

[14] 384 U.S. 436, 86 S.Ct. 1602, 16 L.Ed.2d 694 (1966).
[15] *Dickerson v. United States,* 530 U.S. 428, 120 S.Ct. 2326, 147 L.Ed.2d 405 (2000).

[16] *New York v. Quarles,* 467 U.S. 649, 104 S.Ct. 2626, 81 L.Ed.2d 550 (1984).

EXHIBIT 6–3 MAJOR PROCEDURAL STEPS IN A CRIMINAL CASE

ARREST

Police officer takes suspect into custody. Most arrests are made without a warrant. After the arrest, the officer searches the suspect, who is then taken to the police station.

BOOKING

At the police station, the suspect is searched again, photographed, fingerprinted, and allowed at least one telephone call. After the booking, charges are reviewed, and if they are not dropped,[a] a complaint is filed and a magistrate reviews the case for probable cause.

INITIAL APPEARANCE

The suspect appears before the magistrate, who informs the suspect of the charges and of his or her rights. If the suspect requires a lawyer, one is appointed. The magistrate sets bail (conditions under which a suspect can obtain release pending disposition of the case).

GRAND JURY

A grand jury determines if there is probable cause to believe that the defendant committed the crime. The federal government and about half of the states require grand jury indictments for at least some felonies.

PRELIMINARY HEARING

In a court proceeding, a prosecutor presents evidence, and the judge determines if there is probable cause to hold the defendant over for trial.

INDICTMENT

An indictment is the charging instrument issued by the grand jury.

INFORMATION

An information is the charging instrument issued by the prosecutor.

ARRAIGNMENT

The suspect is brought before the trial court, informed of the charges, and asked to enter a plea.

PLEA BARGAIN

A plea bargain is a prosecutor's promise to make concessions (or promise to seek concessions) in return for a suspect's guilty plea. Concessions may include a reduced charge or a lesser sentence.

GUILTY PLEA

In many jurisdictions, most cases that reach the arraignment stage do not go to trial but are resolved by a guilty plea, often as a result of a plea bargain. The judge sets the case for sentencing.

TRIAL

Generally, most felony trials are jury trials, and most misdemeanor trials are bench trials (trials before judges). If the verdict is "guilty," the judge sets the case for sentencing. Everyone convicted of a crime has the right to an appeal.

a. At any point in the processing of a criminal case, charges may be reduced or dismissed.

INDICTMENT OR INFORMATION

Individuals must be formally charged with having committed specific crimes before they can be brought to trial. If issued by a grand jury, this charge is called an **indictment**.[17] A **grand jury** usually consists of more jurors than the ordinary trial jury. A grand jury does not determine the guilt or innocence of an accused party; rather, its function is to determine, after hearing the state's evidence, whether a reasonable basis (probable cause) exists for believing that a crime has been committed and whether a trial ought to be held.

Usually, grand juries are used in cases involving serious crimes, such as murder. For lesser crimes, an individual may be formally charged with a crime by what is called an **information**, or criminal complaint. An information will be issued by a government prosecutor if the prosecutor determines that there is sufficient evidence to justify bringing the individual to trial.

TRIAL

At a criminal trial, the accused person does not have to prove anything; the entire burden of proof is on the prosecutor (the state). As mentioned earlier, the prosecution must show that, based on all the evidence presented, the defendant's guilt is established *beyond a reasonable doubt*. If there is any reasonable doubt as to whether a criminal defendant did, in fact, commit the crime with which she or he has been charged, then the verdict must be "not guilty." Note that giving a verdict of "not guilty" is not the same as stating that the defendant is innocent; it merely means that not enough evidence was properly presented to the court to prove guilt beyond all reasonable doubt.

Courts have complex rules about what types of evidence may be presented and how the evidence may be brought out in criminal cases. These rules are designed to ensure that evidence presented in trials is relevant, reliable, and not prejudicial to the defendant.

---

[17] Pronounced in-*dyte*-ment.

SENTENCING GUIDELINES

Traditionally, persons who had committed the same crime might have received very different sentences, depending on the judge hearing the case, the jurisdiction in which it was heard, and many other factors. Today, however, court judges typically must follow state or federal guidelines when sentencing convicted persons.

At the federal level, the Sentencing Reform Act created the U.S. Sentencing Commission, which was charged with the task of standardizing sentences for federal crimes. The commission fulfilled its task, and since 1987 its sentencing guidelines for all federal crimes have been applied by federal court judges. The guidelines establish a range of possible penalties for each federal crime. Depending on the defendant's criminal record, the seriousness of the offense, and other factors specified in the guidelines (see this chapter's *Business Law in the Online World* feature on page 139 for a factor considered in one case), federal judges must select a sentence from within this range.

The commission also created specific guidelines for the punishment of crimes committed by corporate employees (white-collar crimes). These guidelines established stiffer penalties for criminal violations of securities laws (see Chapter 27), antitrust laws, employment laws (see Chapter 23), mail and wire fraud, commercial bribery and kickbacks, and money laundering. The guidelines allow federal judges to take into consideration a number of factors when selecting from the range of possible penalties for a specified crime. These factors include the defendant company's history of past violations, the magnitude of management's cooperation with federal investigators, and the extent to which the firm has undertaken specific programs and procedures to prevent criminal activities by its employees.

In imposing a sentence, a judge may depart from the guidelines only if the defendant has some notice of this possibility and thus can prepare to argue against it. Does the same notice requirement apply to unusual conditions of supervised release, or probation? That was the question in the following case.

CASE 6.3 **United States v. Scott**

United States Court of Appeals,
Seventh Circuit, 2003.
316 F.3d 733.

FACTS Todd Scott was charged in a federal district court with fraud, and he pleaded guilty. Based on his conduct and previous crimes, the court imposed the maximum sentence—twenty-four months' imprisonment followed by three years'

supervised release. During the sentencing, the prosecutor suggested that because a police search of a computer in Scott's office turned up a few images of child pornography, Scott's access to the Internet should be limited as part of the supervised release. The court agreed, and ordered that Scott "shall be prohibited from access to any Internet services without prior approval of the probation officer." Scott appealed this order to the U.S. Court of Appeals for the Seventh Circuit,

(Continued)

CASE 6.3—Continued

contending in part that he should have received notice of this condition so that he could have offered an alternative at the sentencing.

ISSUE Is a defendant entitled to notice of unusual conditions that may be imposed as a condition of supervised release?

DECISION Yes. The U.S. Court of Appeals for the Seventh Circuit vacated the judgment of the lower court and remanded the case for a new sentencing proceeding at which Scott could offer alternatives to a total ban on post-imprisonment access to the Internet.

REASON The appellate court explained that "the surprise addition of the Internet-access condition made it impossible for Scott's lawyer to formulate [alternative] proposals." The court reasoned that "[k]nowledge that a condition of this kind was in prospect would have enabled the parties to discuss

such options intelligently. Notice also would have afforded defense counsel time to * * * remind the district judge * * * that special conditions of supervised release must entail no greater deprivation of liberty than is reasonably necessary for the purposes of sentencing * * * . If Scott had used the Internet extensively to commit the crime of conviction, then perhaps a ban might be justified. But here the only justification was misbehavior that neither resulted in a conviction nor was treated as relevant conduct, making an outright ban difficult to justify." A defendant is entitled to "notice of terms that are out of the ordinary, and thus unexpected—and the United States does not contend that Scott should have foreseen that Internet access would be a subject of discussion at sentencing. So Scott is entitled to a new proceeding, at which he can offer alternatives to a flat ban."

FOR CRITICAL ANALYSIS—Technological Consideration
Are limitations on a convicted criminal's access to the Internet ever justified?

Cyber Crime

Some years ago, the American Bar Association defined **computer crime** as any act that is directed against computers and computer parts, that uses computers as instruments of crime, or that involves computers and constitutes abuse. Today, because much of the crime committed with the use of computers occurs in cyberspace, many computer crimes fall under the broad label of cyber crime.

As we mentioned earlier, most cyber crimes are not "new" crimes. Rather, they are existing crimes in which the Internet is the instrument of wrongdoing. The challenge for law enforcement is to apply traditional laws—which were designed to protect persons from physical harm or to safeguard their physical property—to crimes committed in cyberspace. Here we look at several types of activity that constitute cyber crimes against persons or property. Other cyber crimes will be discussed in later chapters of this text as they relate to particular topics, such as banking or consumer law.

CYBER THEFT

In cyberspace, thieves are not subject to the physical limitations of the "real" world. A thief can steal data stored in a networked computer with dial-in access from anywhere on the globe. Only the speed of the connection and the thief's

computer equipment limit the quantity of data that can be stolen.

Financial Crimes. Computer networks also provide opportunities for employees to commit crimes that can involve serious economic losses. For example, employees of a company's accounting department can transfer funds among accounts with little effort and often with less risk than that involved in transactions evidenced by paperwork.

Generally, the dependence of businesses on computer operations has left firms vulnerable to sabotage, fraud, embezzlement, and the theft of proprietary data, such as trade secrets or other intellectual property. As noted in Chapter 5, the piracy of intellectual property via the Internet is one of the most serious legal challenges facing lawmakers and the courts today.

Identity Theft. A form of cyber theft that has become particularly troublesome in recent years is **identity theft.** Identity theft occurs when the wrongdoer steals a form of identification—such as a name, date of birth, or Social Security number—and uses the information to access the victim's financial resources. This crime existed to a certain extent before the widespread use of the Internet. Thieves would "steal" calling-card numbers by watching people using public telephones, or they would rifle through garbage to find bank account or credit-card numbers. The identity thieves would then use the calling-card or credit-

BUSINESS LAW IN THE ONLINE WORLD
Web Site Ads and the Sentencing Guidelines

The Internet is a boon for advertisers. Ads offering goods for sale can be disseminated quickly and inexpensively to hundreds of millions of people throughout the world. Yet the same characteristics that make the Internet a valuable tool in today's commerce also allow unscrupulous individuals to reap profits by defrauding innocent victims. As you will read shortly, attempts to prosecute cyber crimes have raised new types of questions—including questions related to sentencing offenders convicted of cyber fraud.

A CASE OF WIRE FRAUD Consider, for example, a case that came before the U.S. Court of Appeals for the Ninth Circuit in 2001. Michael Pirello posted a series of ads on a Web site known as *Excite Classifieds* (at **http://classifieds.excite.com**) offering computers for sale. In the ads, Pirello described the computers at great length, including details about their operating systems, monitors, memory capacities, modems, weights, processors, and the like. In fact, the ads were part of a fraudulent scheme whereby Pirello would induce prospective buyers to send him money for computers that he never intended to deliver. Over the course of three months, Pirello received checks totaling more than $4,000 for the nonexistent computers.

Ultimately, Pirello was convicted of, among other things, three counts of wire fraud. For this crime, the U.S. Sentencing Guidelines instruct district courts to enhance a defendant's sentence by two levels if the offense was committed through "mass-marketing." The guidelines define mass-marketing as "a plan, program, promotion, or campaign that is conducted through *solicitation by* telephone, mail, *the Internet,* or other means to induce a large number of persons to . . .

purchase goods or services." (Emphasis added.) The judge concluded that Pirello's fraud was committed through mass-marketing and applied the enhanced penalty.

DOES ADVERTISING ON A WEB SITE CONSTITUTE "MASS-MARKETING"? One of Pirello's arguments on appeal was that his actions could not have constituted mass-marketing because his ads did not amount to "solicitation by . . . the Internet." Mass-marketing in the Internet context, claimed Pirello, occurs only where the seller actively solicits a large number of purchasers by circulating mass e-mail to a purchased list of e-mail addresses. The appellate court did not agree. The court noted that Pirello's use of a classified ad arguably enabled him to solicit even more people than would have been possible with a mass e-mail. While mass e-mail is sent to a finite number of people, there is no similar limitation on the number of people who can be exposed to an ad on a Web site accessible by the public.

One of the appellate court judges dissented from this reasoning. According to the dissenting judge, solicitation involves more than simply advertising goods for sale and suggests "some sort of one-on-one importuning [requesting or demanding]." Pirello's passive placement of an ad on a Web site did not, in this judge's mind, constitute the "solicitation by . . . the Internet" required by the sentencing guidelines for the enhanced penalty.[a]

FOR CRITICAL ANALYSIS

The outcome of this case clearly hinged on how the court interpreted the phrase "solicitation by . . . the Internet." Do you agree with the majority's interpretation of the phrase or with the dissenting judge's interpretation? Explain.

a. *United States v. Pirello,* 255 F.3d 728 (9th Cir. 2001).

---

card numbers or would withdraw funds from the victims' accounts.

The Internet, however, has turned identity theft into perhaps the fastest-growing financial crime in the United States. From the identity thief's perspective, the Internet provides those who steal information offline with an easy medium for using items such as stolen credit-card numbers or e-mail addresses while protected by anonymity. An

estimated 500,000 Americans are victims of identity theft each year.

CYBER STALKING

California enacted the first stalking law in 1990, in response to the murders of six women—including Rebecca Schaeffer, a television star—by men who had harassed them. The law made it a crime to harass or follow a person while making a "credible threat" that puts that person in reasonable fear for his or her safety or the safety of the person's immediate family.[18] Most other states have also enacted stalking laws, yet in about half of the states these laws require a physical act (following the victim). **Cyber stalkers** (stalkers who commit their crimes in cyberspace), however, find their victims through Internet chat rooms, Usenet newsgroups or other bulletin boards, or e-mail. To close this "loophole" in existing stalking laws, more than three-fourths of the states now have laws specifically designed to combat cyber stalking and other forms of online harassment.

HACKING

Persons who use one computer to break into another are sometimes referred to as **hackers**. Hackers who break into computers without authorization often commit cyber theft. Sometimes, however, their principal aim is to prove how smart they are by gaining access to others' password-protected computers and causing random data errors or making unpaid-for telephone calls.[19]

The Computer Crime and Security Survey polled 538 companies and large government institutions and found that 85 percent had experienced security breaches through computer-based means in 2000. It is difficult to know, however, just how frequently hackers succeed in breaking into databases across the United States. The Federal Bureau of Investigation (FBI) estimates that only 25 percent of all corporations that suffer such security breaches report the incident to a law enforcement agency. For one thing, corporations do not want it to become publicly known that the security of their data has been breached. For another, admitting to a breach would be admitting to a certain degree of incompetence, which could damage corporate reputations.

CYBER TERRORISM

Cyber terrorists are hackers who, rather than trying to gain attention, strive to remain undetected so that they can exploit computers for a serious impact. Just as "real" terrorists destroyed the World Trade Center towers and a portion of the Pentagon in September 2001, cyber terrorists might explode "logic bombs" to shut down central computers. Such activities can pose a danger to national secu-

rity. After an American surveillance airplane collided with a Chinese military jet in 2001, hackers from China bombarded American Web sites with messages such as "Hack the USA" and "For our pilot Wang." Over a period of several weeks, these hackers were able to destroy or deface hundreds of Web sites, including some from the White House, the FBI, and NASA.

Businesses may also be targeted by cyber terrorists. The goals of a hacking operation might include a wholesale theft of data, such as a merchant's customer files, or the monitoring of a computer to discover a business firm's plans and transactions. A cyber terrorist might also want to insert false codes or data. For example, the processing control system of a food manufacturer could be changed to alter the levels of ingredients so that consumers of the food would become ill. A cyber terrorist attack on a major financial institution such as the New York Stock Exchange or a large bank could leave securities or money markets in flux and seriously affect the daily lives of millions of citizens. Similarly, any prolonged disruption of computer, cable, satellite, or telecommunications systems due to the actions of expert hackers would have serious repercussions on business operations—and national security—on a global level. Computer viruses are another tool that can be used by cyber terrorists to cripple communications networks.

PROSECUTING CYBER CRIMES

The "location" of cyber crime (cyberspace) has raised new issues in the investigation of crimes and the prosecution of offenders. A threshold issue is, of course, jurisdiction. A person who commits an act against a business in California, where the act is a cyber crime, might never have set foot in California but might instead reside in New York, or even in Canada, where the act may not be a crime. If the crime was committed via e-mail, the question arises as to whether the e-mail would constitute sufficient "minimum contacts" (see Chapter 2) for the victim's state to exercise jurisdiction over the perpetrator.

Identifying the wrongdoers can also be difficult. Cyber criminals do not leave physical traces, such as fingerprints or DNA samples, as evidence of their crimes. Even electronic "footprints" can be hard to find and follow. For example, e-mail may be sent through a remailer, an online service that guarantees that a message cannot be traced to its source.

For these reasons, laws written to protect physical property are difficult to apply in cyberspace. Nonetheless, governments at both the state and federal levels have taken significant steps toward controlling cyber crime, both by applying existing criminal statutes and by enacting new laws that specifically address wrongs committed in cyberspace.

---

[18] Cal. Penal Code Section 646.9.

[19] The total cost of crime on the Internet is estimated to be several billion dollars annually, but two-thirds of that total is said to consist of unpaid-for toll calls.

The Computer Fraud and Abuse Act. Perhaps the most significant federal statute specifically addressing cyber crime is the Counterfeit Access Device and Computer Fraud and Abuse Act of 1984 (commonly known as the Computer Fraud and Abuse Act, or CFAA). This act, as amended by the National Information Infrastructure Protection Act of 1996,[20] provides, among other things, that a person who accesses a computer online, without authority, to obtain classified, restricted, or protected data, or attempts to do so, is subject to criminal prosecution. Such data could include financial and credit records, medical records, legal files, military and national security files,

and other confidential information in government or private computers. The crime has two elements: accessing a computer without authority and taking the data.

This theft is a felony if it is committed for a commercial purpose or for private financial gain, or if the value of the stolen data (or computer time) exceeds $5,000. Penalties include fines and imprisonment for up to twenty years. A victim of computer theft can also bring a civil suit against the violator to obtain damages, an injunction, and other relief.

The CFAA defines *damage* as a "loss aggregating at least $5,000 in value during any one-year period to one or more individuals." At issue in the following case was whether the term *individuals* in this definition included a corporation.

---

[20] 18 U.S.C. Section 1030.

CASE 6.4 United States v. Middleton

United States Court of Appeals, Ninth Circuit, 2000. 231 F.3d 1207.

FACTS Nicholas Middleton worked as the personal computer administrator for Slip.net, an Internet service provider. His responsibilities included installing software and hardware on the company's computers and providing technical support to its employees. He had extensive knowledge of Slip.net's internal computer system. Dissatisfied with his job, Middleton quit. Through various subterfuges, he obtained access to a computer that the company had named "Lemming." Slip.net used Lemming to perform internal administrative functions and to host customers' Web sites. Lemming also contained the software for a new billing system. Middleton changed all the administrative passwords, altered the computer's registry, and deleted the entire billing system and two internal databases. Correcting the damage cost Slip.net more than 150 worker-hours, in addition to the expense of an outside consultant and new software. Middleton was convicted of intentionally causing damage to a "protected computer" without authorization, in violation of the CFAA. He appealed to the U.S. Court of Appeals for the Ninth Circuit, arguing that the term *individuals,* as used in the statute, did not include a corporation.

ISSUE Does the CFAA's use of the term *individuals* include a corporation?

DECISION Yes. The U.S. Court of Appeals for the Ninth Circuit affirmed Middleton's conviction. He was sentenced to

three years' probation, subject to a condition of 180 days in community confinement, and ordered to pay $9,147 in restitution.

REASON The U.S. Court of Appeals for the Ninth Circuit noted that Congress amended the CFAA in 1996, altering the definition of damage to read, "loss aggregating at least $5,000 in value during any one-year period to one or more individuals." Although the court found no explanation for this change, "[w]e do not believe * * * that this change evidences an intent to limit the statute's reach. To the contrary, Congress has consciously broadened the statute consistently since its original enactment." The court pointed out, for example, that a Senate report on the 1996 amendments noted that "the interaction between the provision that prohibits conduct causing damage and the provision that defines damage will prohibit a hacker from stealing passwords from an existing log-on program, when this conduct requires 'all system users to change their passwords, and requires the system administrator to devote resources to resecuring the system.'" The court reasoned that "if Congress intended to limit the definition of the crime to conduct causing financial damage to a natural person only, its report would not use the example of a 'system administrator' devoting resources to fix a computer problem as illustrative of the 'damage' to be prevented and criminalized."

FOR CRITICAL ANALYSIS—Technological Consideration
How might Middleton's employer have avoided the damage to its computer systems?

Other Federal Statutes. The federal wire fraud statute, the Economic Espionage Act of 1996, and RICO, all of which were discussed earlier in this chapter, extend to crimes committed in cyberspace as well. Other federal statutes that may apply include the Electronic Fund Transfer Act of 1978,[21] which makes the unauthorized access to an electronic fund transfer system a crime; the Anticounterfeiting Consumer Protection Act of 1996,[22] which increased penal-

ties for stealing copyrighted or trademarked property; and the National Stolen Property Act of 1988, which concerns the interstate transport of stolen property.[23] In later chapters of this text, you will read about other federal statutes and regulations that are designed to address wrongs committed in cyberspace in specific areas of the law.

[21] 15 U.S.C. Section 1693.
[22] 17 U.S.C. Section 603(c) and 18 U.S.C. Section 2318.

[23] The relevant portion of the act is collected in 18 U.S.C. 2314.

Terms and Concepts

arson 128	embezzlement 128	larceny 128
beyond a reasonable doubt 124	entrapment 132	misdemeanor 125
burglary 127	exclusionary rule 134	money laundering 130
computer crime 138	felony 124	petty offense 125
consent 131	forgery 128	plea bargaining 132
crime 124	grand jury 137	probable cause 133
cyber crime 123	hacker 140	robbery 127
cyber stalker 140	identity theft 138	search warrant 133
cyber terrorist 140	indictment 137	self-defense 132
double jeopardy 133	information 137	self-incrimination 134
duress 132	insider trading 130	white-collar crime 128

Chapter Summary   Criminal Law and Cyber Crimes

Civil Law and Criminal Law (See page 124.)	1. *Civil law*—Spells out the duties that exist between persons or between citizens and their governments, excluding the duty not to commit crimes.
	2. *Criminal law*—Has to do with crimes, which are defined as wrongs against society proclaimed in statutes and, if committed, punishable by society through fines and/or imprisonment—and, in some cases, death. Because crimes are *offenses against society as a whole,* they are prosecuted by a public official, not by victims.
	3. *Key differences*—An important difference between civil and criminal law is that the standard of proof is higher in criminal cases (see Exhibit 6–1 for other differences between criminal and civil laws).
	4. *Civil liability for criminal acts*—A criminal act may give rise to both criminal liability and civil liability (see Exhibit 6–2 for an example of criminal and tort liability for the same act).
Classification of Crimes (See pages 124–125.)	1. *Felonies*—Serious crimes punishable by death or by imprisonment in a penitentiary for more than one year.
	2. *Misdemeanors*—Under federal law and in most states, any crimes that are not felonies.

Chapter Summary	Criminal Law and Cyber Crimes—Continued
Criminal Liability (See pages 125–126.)	1. *Guilty act*—In general, some form of harmful act must be committed for a crime to exist.
	2. *Intent*—An intent to commit a crime, or a wrongful mental state, is required for a crime to exist.
Corporate Criminal Liability (See pages 126–127.)	1. *Liability of corporations*—Corporations normally are liable for the crimes committed by their agents and employees within the course and scope of their employment. Corporations cannot be imprisoned, but they can be fined or denied certain legal privileges.
	2. *Liability of corporate officers and directors*—Corporate directors and officers are personally liable for the crimes they commit and may be held liable for the actions of employees under their supervision.
Types of Crimes (See pages 127–130.)	1. *Violent crime*—Crimes that cause others to suffer harm or death. Examples include murder, assault and battery, rape, and robbery.
	2. *Property crime*—Crimes in which the goal of the offender is some form of economic gain or the damaging of property. Examples include burglary, larceny, arson, receiving stolen goods, forgery, and obtaining goods by false pretenses.
	3. *Public order crime*—Crimes contrary to public values and morals. Examples include public drunkenness, prostitution, gambling, and illegal drug use.
	4. *White-collar crime*—Nonviolent crimes committed in the course of a legitimate occupation to obtain a personal or business advantage. Examples include embezzlement, mail and wire fraud, bribery, bankruptcy fraud, insider trading, and the theft of trade secrets.
	5. *Organized crime*—Crime committed by groups operating illegitimately to satisfy the public's demand for illegal goods and services (such as narcotics or pornography). Often, organized crime involves money laundering—the establishment of legitimate enterprises through which "dirty" money obtained through criminal activities can be "laundered" and made to appear as legitimate income. The Racketeer Influenced and Corrupt Organizations Act (RICO) of 1970, which prohibits racketeering activity, was passed, in part, to control organized crime.
Defenses to Criminal Liability (See pages 130–132.)	1. *Infancy.* 6. *Duress.* 2. *Intoxication.* 7. *Justifiable use of force.* 3. *Insanity.* 8. *Entrapment.* 4. *Mistake.* 9. *Statute of limitations.* 5. *Consent.* 10. *Immunity.*
Constitutional Safeguards and Criminal Procedures (See pages 132–135.)	1. *Fourth Amendment*—Provides protection against unreasonable searches and seizures and requires that probable cause exist before a warrant for a search or an arrest can be issued.
	2. *Fifth Amendment*—Requires due process of law, prohibits double jeopardy, and protects against self-incrimination.
	3. *Sixth Amendment*—Provides guarantees of a speedy trial, a trial by jury, a public trial, the right to confront witnesses, and the right to counsel.
	4. *Eighth Amendment*—Prohibits excessive bail and fines, and cruel and unusual punishment.

(Continued)

Chapter Summary	Criminal Law and Cyber Crimes—Continued
Constitutional Safeguards and Criminal Procedures—continued	5. *Exclusionary rule*—A criminal procedural rule that prohibits the introduction at trial of all evidence obtained in violation of constitutional rights, as well as any evidence derived from the illegally obtained evidence. 6. *Miranda rule*—A rule set forth by the Supreme Court in *Miranda v. Arizona* that individuals who are arrested must be informed of certain constitutional rights, including their right to counsel.
Criminal Process (See pages 135–138.)	1. *Arrest, indictment, and trial*—Procedures governing arrest, indictment, and trial for a crime are designed to safeguard the rights of the individual against the state. See Exhibit 6–3 for the steps involved in prosecuting a criminal case. 2. *Sentencing guidelines*—Both the federal government and the states have established sentencing laws or guidelines. The federal sentencing guidelines indicate a range of penalties for each federal crime; federal judges generally must abide by these guidelines when imposing sentences on those convicted of federal crimes.
Cyber Crime (See pages 138–142.)	Cyber crime is any crime that occurs in cyberspace. Examples include cyber theft (financial crimes committed with the aid of computers, as well as identity theft), cyber stalking, hacking, and cyber terrorism. Significant federal statutes addressing cyber crimes include the Electronic Fund Transfer Act of 1978 and the Computer Fraud and Abuse Act of 1984, as amended by the National Information Infrastructure Protection Act of 1996.

For Review

① What two elements must exist before a person can be held liable for a crime? Can a corporation be liable for crimes?

② What are five broad categories of crimes? What is white-collar crime?

③ What defenses might be raised by criminal defendants to avoid liability for criminal acts?

④ What constitutional safeguards exist to protect persons accused of crimes? What are the basic steps in the criminal process?

⑤ What is cyber crime? What laws apply to crimes committed in cyberspace?

Questions and Case Problems

6–1. Criminal versus Civil Trials. In criminal trials, the defendant must be proved guilty beyond a reasonable doubt, whereas in civil trials, the defendant need only be proved guilty by a preponderance of the evidence. Discuss why a higher standard of proof is required in criminal trials.

6–2. Types of Crimes. The following situations are similar (all involve the theft of Makoto's television set), yet they represent three different crimes. Identify the three crimes, noting the differences among them.

(a) While passing Makoto's house one night, Sarah sees a portable television set left unattended on Makoto's lawn. Sarah takes the television set, carries it home, and tells everyone she owns it.

(b) While passing Makoto's house one night, Sarah sees Makoto outside with a portable television set. Holding Makoto at gunpoint, Sarah forces him to give up the set. Then Sarah runs away with it.

(c) While passing Makoto's house one night, Sarah sees a portable television set in a window. Sarah breaks the front-door lock, enters, and leaves with the set.

6–3. Types of Crimes. Which, if any, of the following crimes necessarily involve illegal activity on the part of more than one person?

(a) Bribery.

(b) Forgery.

(c) Embezzlement.

(d) Larceny.

(e) Receiving stolen property.

6–4. Double Jeopardy. Armington, while robbing a drugstore, shot and seriously injured Jennings, a drugstore clerk. Armington was subsequently convicted in a criminal trial of armed robbery and assault and battery. Jennings later brought a civil tort suit against Armington for damages. Armington contended that he could not be tried again for the same crime, as that would constitute double jeopardy, which is prohibited by the Fifth Amendment to the Constitution. Is Armington correct? Explain.

6–5. Receiving Stolen Property. Rafael stops Laura on a busy street and offers to sell her an expensive wristwatch for a fraction of its value. After some questioning by Laura, Rafael admits that the watch is stolen property, although he says he was not the thief. Laura pays for and receives the wristwatch. Has Laura committed any crime? Has Rafael? Explain.

6–6. Defenses to Criminal Liability. The Child Protection Act of 1984 makes it a crime to receive knowingly through the mails sexually explicit depictions of children. After this act was passed, government agents found Keith Jacobson's name on a bookstore's mailing list. (Jacobson previously had ordered and received from a bookstore two *Bare Boys* magazines containing photographs of nude preteen and teen-age boys.) To test Jacobson's willingness to break the law, government agencies sent mail to him, through five fictitious organizations and a bogus pen pal, over a period of two and a half years. Many of these "organizations" claimed that they had been founded to protect sexual freedom, freedom of choice, and so on. Jacobson eventually ordered a magazine. He testified at trial that he ordered the magazine because he was curious about "all the trouble and the hysteria over pornography and I wanted to see what the material was." When the magazine was delivered, he was arrested for violating the 1984 act. What defense discussed in this chapter might Jacobson raise to avoid criminal liability under the act? Explain fully. [*Jacobson v. United States*, 503 U.S. 540, 112 S.Ct. 1535, 118 L.Ed.2d 174 (1992)]

6–7. Searches and Seizures. The city of Ferndale enacted an ordinance regulating massage parlors. Among other things, the ordinance provided for periodic inspections of the establishments by "[t]he chief of police or other authorized inspectors from the City." Operators and employees of massage parlors in Ferndale filed a suit in a Michigan state court against the city. The plaintiffs pointed out that the ordinance did not require a warrant to conduct a search and argued in part that this was a violation of the Fourth Amendment. On what ground might the court uphold the ordinance? Do massage parlors qualify on this ground? Why or why not? [*Gora v. City of Ferndale*, 456 Mich. 704, 576 N.W.2d 141 (1998)]

6–8. Fifth Amendment. The federal government was investigating a corporation and its employees. The alleged criminal wrongdoing, which included the falsification of corporate books and records, occurred between 1993 and 1996 in one division of the corporation. In 1999, the corporation pleaded guilty and agreed to cooperate in an investigation of the individuals who might have been involved in the improper corporate activities. "Doe I," "Doe II," and "Doe III" were officers of the corporation during the period when the illegal activities occurred and worked in the division where the wrongdoing took place. They were no longer employed by the corporation, however, when, as part of the subsequent investigation, the government asked them to provide specific corporate documents in their possession. All three asserted the Fifth Amendment privilege against self-incrimination. The government asked a federal district court to order the three to produce the records. Corporate employees can be compelled to produce corporate records in a criminal proceeding because they hold the records as representatives of the corporation, to which the Fifth Amendment privilege against self-incrimination does not apply. Should *former* employees also be compelled to produce corporate records in their possession? Why or why not? [*In re Three Grand Jury Subpoenas* Duces Tecum *Dated January 29, 1999*, 191 F.3d 173 (2d Cir. 1999)]

CASE PROBLEM WITH SAMPLE ANSWER

6–9. The District of Columbia Lottery Board licensed Soo Young Bae, a Washington, D.C., merchant, to operate a terminal that prints and dispenses lottery tickets for sale. Bae used the terminal to generate tickets with a face value of $525,586, for which he did not pay. The winning tickets among these had a total redemption value of $296,153, of which Bae successfully obtained all but $72,000. Bae pleaded guilty to computer fraud, and the court sentenced him to eighteen months in prison. In sentencing a defendant for fraud, a federal court must make a reasonable estimate of the victim's loss. The court determined that the value of the loss due to the fraud was $503,650—the market value of the tickets less the commission Bae would have received from the lottery board had he sold those tickets. Bae appealed, arguing that "[a]t the instant any lottery ticket is printed," it is worth whatever value the lottery drawing later assigns to it; that is, losing tickets have no value. Bae thus calculated the loss at $296,153, the value of his winning tickets. Should the U.S. Court of Appeals for the District of Columbia Circuit affirm or reverse Bae's sentence? Why? [*United States v. Bae*, 250 F.3d 774 (C.A.D.C. 2001)]

◆ To view a sample answer for this case problem, go to this book's Web site at **http://fundamentals.westbuslaw.com** and click on "Interactive Study Center."

6–10. Theft of Trade Secrets. Four Pillars Enterprise Co. is a Taiwanese company owned by Pin Yen Yang. Avery Dennison, Inc., a U.S. corporation, is one of Four Pillars's chief competitors in the manufacture of adhesives. In 1989, Victor Lee, an Avery employee, met Yang and Yang's daughter Hwei Chen. They agreed to pay Lee $25,000 a year to serve as a consultant to Four Pillars. Over the next eight years, Lee supplied the Yangs with confidential Avery reports, including information that Four Pillars used to make a new adhesive that had been developed by Avery. The Federal Bureau of Investigation (FBI) confronted Lee, and he agreed to cooperate in an operation to catch the Yangs. When Lee next met the Yangs, he showed them documents provided by the FBI. The documents bore "confidential" stamps, and Lee said that they were Avery's confidential property. The FBI arrested the Yangs with the documents in their possession. The Yangs and Four Pillars were charged with, among other crimes, the attempted theft of trade secrets. The defendants argued in part that it was impossible for them to have committed this crime because the documents were not actually trade secrets. Should the court acquit them? Why or why not? [*United States v. Yang*, 281 F.3d 534 (6th Cir. 2002)]

CRIMINAL LAW AND CYBER CRIMES

For updated links to resources available on the Web, as well as other materials, visit this text's Web site at

http://fundamentals.westbuslaw.com

The Bureau of Justice Statistics in the U.S. Department of Justice offers an impressive collection of statistics on crime at the following Web site:

http://www.ojp.usdoj.gov/bjs

For summaries of famous criminal cases and documents relating to these trials, go to Court TV's Web site at

http://www.courttv.com/index.html

Many criminal codes are now online. To find your state's code, go to

http://www.findlaw.com

and select "State" under the link to "Laws: Cases and Codes."

You can learn about some of the constitutional questions raised by various criminal laws and procedures by going to the Web site of the American Civil Liberties Union at

http://www.aclu.org

Online Legal Research

Go to the *Fundamentals of Business Law* home page at **http://fundamentals. westbuslaw.com**. Select "Interactive Study Center" and then click on "Chapter 6." There you will find the following Internet research exercises that you can perform to learn more about topics covered in this chapter.

Activity 6–1: LEGAL PERSPECTIVE—Revisiting *Miranda*
Activity 6–2: MANAGEMENT PERSPECTIVE—Hackers
Activity 6–3: INTERNATIONAL PERSPECTIVE—Fighting Cyber Crime Worldwide

Before the Test

Go to the *Fundamentals of Business Law* home page at **http://fundamentals. westbuslaw.com**. Click on "Interactive Quizzes." You will find at least twenty interactive questions relating to this chapter.

Westlaw® Campus

If your textbook provided for a subscription to Westlaw® Campus, or if you have otherwise purchased access to the Westlaw Campus database, you can access any of the cases presented or cited in this chapter by using your Westlaw Campus account.

Pinsonneault v. Merchants & Farmers Bank & Trust Co.

INTRODUCTION

In Chapter 4, we discussed the common law principles of negligence. In this *Focus on Legal Reasoning*, we examine *Pinsonneault v. Merchants & Farmers Bank & Trust Co.,*[1] a decision that applied those principles in the context of a fatal shooting during a robbery.

CASE BACKGROUND

On October 28, 1992, Lawson Strickland and Christian Boyd escaped from jail in Vernon Parish, Louisiana.[2] In need of money, they planned a rob-

---

1. 816 So.2d 270 (La. 2002).
2. A *parish* is a geographic and political division within the state of Louisiana that corresponds to a county in other states.

---

bery. They chose the branch of the Merchants & Farmers Bank & Trust Company in Leesville for the cover it afforded, hoping to escape through the woods behind the bank. On the night of November 3, they hid atop a hill behind a McDonald's restaurant next to the bank and waited.

At 1:30 A.M., Jesse Pinsonneault, the twenty-three-year-old assistant manager of Sambino's Pizza, left work and drove to the bank to deposit $64.06, the evening's receipts and operating cash. The bank's night deposit box was on the McDonald's side of the bank under a canopy that extended over the drive-through lanes. As Pinsonneault's car approached, Strickland ran down the hill and hid behind the bank. When Pinsonneault got out of his car and

walked up to the night deposit box, Strickland confronted him, brandished a gun, and demanded money. In the ensuing struggle, Strickland shot Pinsonneault, who died at a hospital nine hours later.

Pinsonneault's parents and brother filed a suit in a Louisiana state court against the bank and others, alleging in part that the bank negligently failed to provide adequate security to customers using the night depository. After a trial, the court issued a judgment in favor of the defendants. The Pinsonneaults appealed to a state intermediate appellate court, which reversed the trial court's judgment and awarded damages of more than $1 million to the plaintiffs. The defendants appealed to the Louisiana Supreme Court.

MAJORITY OPINION

WEIMER, Justice.

* * * *

* * * In *Posecai v. Wal-Mart Stores, Inc.,* 752 So.2d 762 (La. 1999), we held that while business owners generally have no duty to protect others from the criminal acts of third persons, "they do have a duty to implement reasonable measures to protect their patrons from criminal acts when those acts are foreseeable." Determining when a crime is foreseeable is a critical inquiry in the duty equation. This inquiry is answered employing a balancing test. * * * The foreseeability of the crime risk on the defendant's property and the gravity of the risk determine the existence and the extent of the defendant's duty. *The greater the foreseeability and gravity of the harm, the greater the duty of care that will be imposed on the business.* * * * [Emphasis added.]

* * * *

In the instant case, there had been two armed robberies of this particular branch of Merchants Bank in the fourteen-year period prior to the attack on Jesse. The first occurred in 1984, during regular banking hours, when robbers absconded with cash from the bank. No customers were robbed. The perpetrators escaped using a helicopter they landed on the bank's front lawn. The second robbery took place in 1989. Again, this was a daytime robbery, during regular operating hours. No patrons were robbed. In this incident, the lone perpetrator escaped to the woods behind the bank through the northeast corner of the bank's property.

* * * *

Given these facts, it appears that night deposit customers at Merchants Bank faced a very low crime risk. Therefore, we con-

cur with the trial court and find that Merchants Bank * * * did not possess the requisite [required] foreseeability for the imposition of a duty to employ heightened security measures for the protection of patrons of its night depository.

This finding does not end our inquiry with respect to the bank's duty, however. * * * [O]ther factors, such as the location, nature, and condition of the property should also be taken into account. * * *

In this case, * * * not only did the bank recognize a duty to its patrons through the adoption of a written security plan, it took affirmative steps in furtherance of that plan, providing lighting at its nighttime depository, erecting fencing along vulnerable perimeters, and setting up a schedule for the installation of modern surveillance cameras at each of its branches.

Thus, we have no difficulty determining the defendant bank had a duty to implement reasonable security measures. Whether a defendant has breached a duty is a question of fact.

* * * *

[In this case] there is a reasonable factual basis for determining the lighting was adequate. There is a reasonable factual basis for determining the lack of security cameras was not a deterrent. The height of the shrubs was disputed as was the role of the shrubs in this incident. Fencing existed and the need for additional fencing and the deterrent effect of additional fencing was disputed. * * * [W]e find the decision of the trial court was reasonable * * *.

* * * *

(Continued)

We find that the Court of Appeal erred in * * * substituting its own conclusions for those of the trial court. Therefore, we reverse the Court of Appeal's judgment in favor of plaintiffs.

DISSENTING OPINION

JOHNSON, J. [Justice], dissents and assigns reasons.

I would affirm the decision of the court of appeal, assessing the bank with liability for the death of plaintiff's decedent, Jesse Pinsonneault. I agree with the court of appeal that, in accordance with * * * *Posecai v. Wal-Mart Stores, Inc.*, the bank had foreseeability of harm to its patrons sufficient to impose a duty to add adequate security measures. The bank's failure to provide such measures constitutes a breach of this duty.

* * * *

The court of appeal correctly found that although the prior crimes [at the bank] lacked similarity to the instant assault, they were nevertheless "predatory offenses which convey a risk of harm to both employees and customers of the bank." In addition, the record reveals that the bank had been informed of the hazards posed by the nature of its business through a banking newsletter, the *Advisor*, which repeatedly reported night deposit crimes and advised of the need to formulate security procedures and to install protective security measures.

* * * *

[Finally, the] record supports the court of appeal's conclusion that the bank "possessed the requisite foreseeability to impose a duty to implement, at the very least, security measures such as installation of improved lighting and functional surveillance cameras, installing fencing which would have enclosed the entire property and shielded the property from the adjacent wooded area, and trimming and maintaining the shrubbery at a level which would not facilitate hiding."

LEGAL REASONING AND ANALYSIS

1 Legal Analysis. Find the *Posecai v. Wal-Mart Stores, Inc.* case (see the appendix to Chapter 1 for instructions on how to find state court opinions). Compare the facts and issues in that case to the facts and issues of the *Pinsonneault* case. How are they similar?

How are they different? Why did the court refer to this case in its opinion?

2 Legal Reasoning. Compare the conclusions of the majority and the dissent. What is the basis for their disagreement about the outcome of this case?

3 Implications for the Business Owner. What does the holding in this case indicate about the responsibility of a business to take precautions against the risk of crime?

4 Case Briefing Assignment. Using the guidelines for briefing cases given in Appendix A of this text, brief the *Pinsonneault* case.

This text's Web site, at **http://fundamentals.westbuslaw.com**, offers links to West's Court Case Updates, as well as to other online research sources. You can also locate court cases at the Web sites listed in the *Accessing the Internet* section at the end of Chapter 2.

For more information on tort law, including overviews of the subject and background on current litigation, Jurist provides an index of links to online resources at **http://jurist.law.pitt. edu/sg_torts.htm**. The University of Pittsburgh School of Law in Pittsburgh, Pennsylvania, maintains this Web site.

UNIT 3

Contracts

UNIT CONTENTS

CHAPTER

7

Nature and Classification

(**CHAPTER OBJECTIVES**

After reading this chapter, you should be able to answer the following questions:

① What is a contract? What is the objective theory of contracts?

② What are the four basic elements necessary to the formation of a valid contract?

③ What is the difference between an implied-in-fact contract and an implied-in-law contract (quasi contract)?

④ What is a void contract? How does it differ from a voidable contract? What is an unenforceable contract?

⑤ What rules guide the courts in interpreting contracts?

Keeping promises is important to a stable social order. Contract law deals with, among other things, the formation and keeping of promises. A **promise** is a declaration that something either will or will not happen in the future.

Like other types of law, contract law reflects our social values, interests, and expectations at a given point in time. It shows, for example, what kinds of promises our society thinks should be legally binding. It displays what excuses our society accepts for breaking such promises. Additionally, it signifies what promises are considered to be contrary to public policy, or against the interests of society, and therefore legally void. If a promise goes against the interests of society as a whole, it will be invalid. Also, if it was made by a child or a mentally incompetent person, or

on the basis of false information, a question will arise as to whether the promise should be enforced. Resolving such questions is the essence of contract law.

In the business world, questions and disputes concerning contracts arise daily. Although aspects of contract law vary from state to state, much of it is based on the common law. In 1932, the American Law Institute compiled the *Restatement of the Law of Contracts.* This work is a nonstatutory, authoritative exposition of the present law on the subject of contracts and is currently in its second edition (although a third edition is in the process of being drafted). Throughout the following chapters on contracts, we will refer to the second edition of the *Restatement of the Law of Contracts* as simply the *Restatement (Second) of Contracts.*

The Uniform Commercial Code (UCC), which governs contracts and other transactions relating to the sale and lease of goods, occasionally departs from common law contract rules. Generally, the different treatment of contracts falling under the UCC stems from the general policy of encouraging commerce. The ways in which the UCC changes common law contract rules will be discussed extensively in later chapters. In this unit covering the common law of contracts (Chapters 7 through 13), we only indicate briefly or in footnotes those common law rules that have been altered significantly by the UCC for sales and lease contracts.

The Function of Contracts

No aspect of modern life is entirely free of contractual relationships. You acquire rights and obligations, for example, when you borrow funds, when you buy or lease a house, when you procure insurance, when you form a business, when you purchase goods or services—the list goes on. Contract law is designed to provide stability and predictability for both buyers and sellers in the marketplace.

Contract law assures the parties to private agreements that the promises they make will be enforceable. Clearly, many promises are kept because the parties involved feel a moral obligation to do so or because keeping a promise is in their mutual self-interest, not because the **promisor** (the person making the promise) or the **promisee** (the person to whom the promise is made) is conscious of the rules of contract law. Nevertheless, the rules of contract law are often followed in business agreements to avoid potential problems.

By supplying procedures for enforcing private agreements, contract law provides an essential condition for the existence of a market economy. Without a legal framework of reasonably assured expectations within which to plan and venture, businesspersons would be able to rely only on the good faith of others. Duty and good faith are usually sufficient, but when dramatic price changes or adverse economic conditions make it costly to comply with a promise, these elements may not be enough. Contract law is necessary to ensure compliance with a promise or to entitle the innocent party to some form of relief.

Definition of a Contract

A **contract** is an agreement that can be enforced in court. It is formed by two or more parties who agree to perform or to refrain from performing some act now or in the future. Generally, contract disputes arise when there is a promise of future performance. If the contractual promise is not ful-

filled, the party who made it is subject to the sanctions of a court (see Chapter 12). That party may be required to pay money damages for failing to perform the contractual promise; in limited instances, the party may be required to perform the promised act.

In determining whether a contract has been formed, the element of intent is of prime importance. In contract law, intent is determined by what is referred to as the **objective theory of contracts,** not by the personal or subjective intent, or belief, of a party. The theory is that a party's intention to enter into a contract is judged by outward, objective facts as interpreted by a reasonable person, rather than by the party's own secret, subjective intentions. Objective facts include (1) what the party said when entering into the contract, (2) how the party acted or appeared, and (3) the circumstances surrounding the transaction. As will be discussed later in this chapter, in the section on express versus implied contracts, intent to form a contract may be manifested not only in words, oral or written, but also by conduct.

Requirements of a Contract

The following list describes the four requirements that must be met before a valid contract exists. Each item will be explained more fully in the chapter indicated. Although we pair these requirements in subsequent chapters (for example, agreement and consideration are treated in Chapter 8), it is important to stress that each requirement is separate and independent. They are paired merely for reasons of space.

① *Agreement.* An agreement includes an offer and an acceptance. One party must offer to enter into a legal agreement, and another party must accept the terms of the offer (Chapter 8).

② *Consideration.* Any promises made by parties must be supported by legally sufficient and bargained-for consideration (something of value received or promised, to convince a person to make a deal) (Chapter 8).

③ *Contractual capacity.* Both parties entering into the contract must have the contractual capacity to do so; the law must recognize them as possessing characteristics that qualify them as competent parties (Chapter 9).

④ *Legality.* The contract's purpose must be to accomplish some goal that is legal and not against public policy (Chapter 9).

If any of these four elements is lacking, no contract will have been formed. Even if all of these elements exist, however, a contract may be unenforceable if the following requirements are not met. These requirements typically are raised as *defenses* to the enforceability of an otherwise valid contract.

①　*Genuineness of assent.* The apparent consent of both parties must be genuine (Chapter 10).

②　*Form.* The contract must be in whatever form the law requires; for example, some contracts must be in writing to be enforceable (Chapter 10).

Freedom of Contract and Freedom from Contract

As a general rule, the law recognizes everyone's ability to enter freely into contractual arrangements. This recognition is called *freedom of contract,* a freedom protected by the U.S. Constitution in Article I, Section 10. Because freedom of contract is a fundamental public policy of the United States, courts rarely interfere with contracts that have been voluntarily made.

Of course, as in other areas of the law, there are many exceptions to the general rule that contracts voluntarily negotiated will be enforced. For example, illegal bargains, agreements that unreasonably restrain trade, and certain unfair contracts made between one party with a great amount of bargaining power and another with little power are generally not enforced. In addition, as you will read in Chapter 9, certain contracts and clauses may not be enforceable if they are contrary to public policy, fairness, and justice. (For an example of a clause that was held to be contrary to public policy, see this chapter's *Business Law in the Online World* feature on page 154.) These exceptions provide freedom from contract for persons who may have been forced into making contracts unfavorable to themselves.

Types of Contracts

There are numerous types of contracts. They are categorized based on legal distinctions as to formation, enforceability, or performance. The best way to explain each type of contract is to compare one type with another.

BILATERAL VERSUS UNILATERAL CONTRACTS

Every contract involves at least two parties. The **offeror** is the party making the offer. The **offeree** is the party to whom the offer is made. The offeror always promises to do or not to do something and thus is also a promisor. Whether the contract is classified as *unilateral* or *bilateral* depends on what the offeree must do to accept the offer and bind the offeror to a contract.

Bilateral Contracts. If to accept the offer the offeree must only promise to perform, the contract is a **bilateral contract.** Hence, a bilateral contract is a "promise for a promise." An example of a bilateral contract is a contract in which one person agrees to buy another person's automobile for a specified price. No performance, such as the payment of money or delivery of goods, need take place for a bilateral contract to be formed. The contract comes into existence at the moment the promises are exchanged.

Unilateral Contracts. If the offer is phrased so that the offeree can accept only by completing the contract performance, the contract is a **unilateral contract.** Hence, a unilateral contract is a "promise for an act." ● **EXAMPLE #1** Joe says to Celia, "If you drive my car from New York to Los Angeles, I'll give you $1,000." Only on Celia's completion of the act—bringing the car to Los Angeles—does she fully accept Joe's offer to pay $1,000. If she chooses not to accept the offer to bring the car to Los Angeles, there are no legal consequences.●

Contests, lotteries, and other competitions offering prizes are also examples of offers for unilateral contracts. If a person complies with the rules of the contest—such as by submitting the right lottery number at the right place and time—a unilateral contract is formed, binding the organization offering the prize to a contract to perform as promised in the offer.

Can a school's, or an employer's, letter of tentative acceptance to a prospective student, or a possible employee, qualify as a unilateral contract? That was the issue in the following case.

CASE 7.1　**Ardito v. City of Providence**

United States District Court,
District of Rhode Island, 2003.
263 F.Supp.2d 358.

FACTS　In 2001, the City of Providence, Rhode Island, decided to begin hiring police officers to fill vacancies in its

police department. Because only individuals who had graduated from the Providence Police Academy were eligible, the city also decided to conduct two training sessions, the "60th and 61st Police Academies." To be admitted, an applicant had to pass a series of tests and be deemed qualified by members of the department after an interview. The applicants judged most qualified were sent a letter informing them that they had

CASE 7.1—Continued

been selected to attend the academy if they successfully completed a medical checkup and a psychological examination. The letter for the applicants for the 61st Academy, dated October 15, stated that it was "a conditional offer of employment." Meanwhile, a new chief of police, Dean Esserman, decided to revise the selection process, an act that caused some of those who had received the letter to be rejected. Derek Ardito and thirteen other newly rejected applicants filed a suit in a federal district court against the city, seeking a halt to the 61st Academy unless they were allowed to attend. They alleged in part that the city was in breach of contract.

ISSUE Was the October 15 letter a unilateral offer that the plaintiffs had accepted by passing the required medical and psychological examinations?

DECISION Yes. The court issued an injunction to prohibit the city from conducting the 61st Police Academy unless the plaintiffs were included.

REASON The court found the October 15 letter to be "a classic example of an offer to enter into a unilateral contract.

The October 15 letter expressly stated that it was a 'conditional offer of employment' and the message that it conveyed was that the recipient would be admitted into the 61st Academy if he or she successfully completed the medical and psychological examinations." The court contrasted the letter with "notices sent to applicants by the City at earlier stages of the selection process. Those notices merely informed applicants that they had completed a step in the process and remained eligible to be considered for admission into the Academy. Unlike the October 15 letter, the prior notices did not purport to extend a 'conditional offer' of admission." The court concluded that "[t]he plaintiffs accepted the City's offer of admission into the Academy by satisfying the specified conditions. Each of the plaintiffs submitted to and passed lengthy and intrusive medical and psychological examinations."

FOR CRITICAL ANALYSIS—Social Consideration
How might the city have phrased the October 15 letter to avoid its being considered a unilateral contract?

Revocation of Offers for Unilateral Contracts. A problem arises in unilateral contracts when the promisor attempts to *revoke* (cancel) the offer after the promisee has begun performance but before the act has been completed. ● **EXAMPLE #2** Suppose that Roberta offers to buy Ed's sailboat, moored in San Francisco, on delivery of the boat to Roberta's dock in Newport Beach, three hundred miles south of San Francisco. Ed rigs the boat and sets sail. Shortly before his arrival at Newport Beach, Ed receives a radio message from Roberta withdrawing her offer. Roberta's offer is an offer for a unilateral contract, and only Ed's delivery of the sailboat at her dock is an acceptance.●

In contract law, offers are normally *revocable* (capable of being taken back, or canceled) until accepted. Under the traditional view of unilateral contracts, Roberta's revocation would terminate the offer. Because of the harsh effect on the offeree of the revocation of an offer to form a unilateral contract, the modern-day view is that once performance has been *substantially* undertaken, the offeror cannot revoke the offer. Thus, in our example, even though Ed has not yet accepted the offer by complete performance, Roberta is prohibited from revoking it. Ed can deliver the boat and bind Roberta to the contract.

EXPRESS VERSUS IMPLIED CONTRACTS

An **express contract** is one in which the terms of the agreement are fully and explicitly stated in words, oral or written. A signed lease for an apartment or a house is an express written contract. If a classmate accepts your offer to sell your textbooks from last semester for $50, an express oral contract has been made.

A contract that is implied from the conduct of the parties is called an **implied-in-fact contract**, or an implied contract. This type of contract differs from an express contract in that the *conduct* of the parties, rather than their words, creates and defines at least some of the terms of the contract. ● **EXAMPLE #3** Suppose that you need an accountant to fill out your tax return this year. You look through the Yellow Pages and find an accounting firm located in your neighborhood. You drop by the firm's office, explain your problem to an accountant, and learn what fees will be charged. The next day you return and give the receptionist all of the necessary information and documents, such as canceled checks, W-2 forms, and so on. Then you walk out the door without saying anything expressly to the receptionist. In this situation, you have entered into an

BUSINESS LAW IN THE ONLINE WORLD
Forum-Selection Clauses and Public Policy

Parties to contracts frequently include clauses in their contracts relating to how any disputes that arise may be resolved. For example, as you read in Chapter 2, parties often include arbitration clauses in contracts, stipulating that any dispute will be resolved through arbitration proceedings rather than litigation. A contract may also include a *forum-selection clause,* specifying the forum (such as the court or jurisdiction) in which the dispute will be resolved.

FORUM SELECTION AND ONLINE CONTRACTS

Because parties to contracts formed online may be located in physically distant sites, online sellers of goods and services often include forum-selection clauses in their contracts. This helps to prevent problems for the online sellers, who might otherwise end up being haled into court in many distant jurisdictions. Recall from Chapter 2 that under a state long arm statute, a state may exercise jurisdiction over an out-of-state defendant if the defendant had "minimum contacts" with the state.

As mentioned elsewhere in this chapter, the courts rarely refuse to enforce clauses or contracts to which parties have voluntarily agreed, and this principle extends to online contracts as well. Exceptions to this rule are made, however, as America Online, Inc. (AOL), the Internet service provider, learned in 2001.

THE CASE AGAINST AOL

In a case against AOL, the plaintiffs—Al Mendoza and other former AOL subscribers living in California—sought compensatory and punitive damages. They claimed that AOL had continued to debit their credit cards for monthly service fees, without authorization, for some time after they had terminated their subscriptions. AOL moved to dismiss the action on the basis of the forum-selection clause in its "Terms of Service" agreement with subscribers. That clause required all lawsuits under the agreement to be brought in Virginia, AOL's home state. At issue in the case was whether the clause was enforceable.

A California trial court held that it was not. The court based its conclusion on the finding that the clause, among other things, was contained in a standard form and was not readily identifiable by subscribers because of its small type and location at the end of the agreement. According to the court, the clause was "unfair and unreasonable," and public policy was best served by denying enforceability to the clause. A California appellate court affirmed the lower court's ruling and also gave another reason why the clause should not be enforced. The appellate court noted that Virginia law provides "significantly less" consumer protection than California law, and therefore enforcing the forum-selection clause would violate the "strong California public policy" expressed in the state's consumer protection statutes.[a]

Be aware that this case may mark an exception to the rule that forum-selection clauses in online contracts are generally enforceable. Yet different courts have reached different conclusions on this issue, so businesspersons forming online contracts would be wise to take special care in drafting such clauses. As one court held (in a case challenging the enforceability of the forum-selection clause in Microsoft Network's online agreement), "If a forum-selection clause is clear in its purport and has been presented to the party to be bound in a fair and forthright fashion, no consumer fraud policies or principles have been violated."[b]

FOR CRITICAL ANALYSIS

Do you believe that the outcome in the case against AOL would have been different if the forum-selection clause had been conspicuous and easily identifiable by those agreeing to AOL's Terms of Service? Why or why not?

a. *America Online, Inc. v. Superior Court,* 90 Cal.App.4th 1, 108 Cal.Rptr.2d 699 (2001).
b. *Caspi v. Microsoft Network, LLC,* 323 N.J.Super. 118, 732 A.2d 528 (1999).

---

implied-in-fact contract to pay the accountant the usual and reasonable fees for the accounting services. The contract is implied by your conduct. The accountant expects to be paid for completing your tax return. By bringing in the records the accountant will need to do the work, you have implied an intent to pay for the services.● For a discussion of implied contracts in the employment context, see this chapter's *Management Perspective* on page 156.

The following three steps establish an implied-in-fact contract:

① The plaintiff furnished some service or property.

② The plaintiff expected to be paid for that service or property, and the defendant knew or should have known that payment was expected (by using the objective-theory-of-contracts test, discussed previously).

③ The defendant had a chance to reject the services or property and did not.

In the following case, the question before the court was whether a contract for electrical work had come into existence, given the absence of any written agreement.

CASE 7.2   Homer v. Burman

Indiana Court of Appeals, 2001.
743 N.E.2d 1144.
http://www.IN.gov/judiciary/opinions/
search.html[a]

FACTS Dave and Annette Homer owned a rental house in Marion, Indiana. When their tenant, Stephanie Clevenger, complained of malfunctioning lights, the Homers paid Burman Electric Service $2,650 to rewire the house. The parties did not sign a written contract. After the work was supposedly done, the Homers discovered, among other things, holes in the ceiling, plaster damage around electrical outlets, and exposed wires along aluminum siding on the outside of the house. When the power was reconnected, Clevenger's television, VCR, satellite receiver, and Playstation were destroyed. Over the next two months, her hair dryers, clocks, and lamps repeatedly burned out. The Homers filed a suit against Burman in an Indiana state court, alleging breach of contract. The court ruled against the Homers, who appealed to a state intermediate appellate court.

---

a. This page is maintained by the state of Indiana. To find this case, put a check only in the "Appeals Court" box, enter "Homer" into the search field, and click on "search." *Homer v. Burman* should be the first case on the resulting list.

ISSUE Despite the absence of a written agreement, did the parties have a contract?

DECISION Yes. The state intermediate appellate court reversed the decision of the lower court and remanded the case to determine the amount of damages and attorneys' fees to be awarded to the Homers.

REASON The appellate court stated, "An offer, acceptance, plus consideration make up the basis for a contract. A mutual assent or a meeting of the minds on all essential elements or terms must exist in order to form a binding contract. Assent to the terms of a contract may be expressed by acts which manifest acceptance." The court concluded that the parties had a contract even though they did not put anything in writing. The court explained that "the Homers paid Burman Electric $2,650.00 to rewire their home. Burman Electric accepted the payment and began work. Therefore, because we have an offer, acceptance, consideration, and a manifestation of mutual assent, an implied-in-fact contract was in existence."

FOR CRITICAL ANALYSIS—Social Consideration
What might be the most important term of an implied contract to perform work?

QUASI CONTRACTS—CONTRACTS IMPLIED IN LAW

Quasi contracts, or contracts *implied in law,* are wholly different from actual contracts. Express contracts and implied-in-fact contracts are actual, or true, contracts. The word *quasi* is Latin for "as if" or "analogous to." Quasi contracts are thus not true contracts. They do not arise from any agreement, express or implied, between the parties themselves. Rather, quasi contracts are fictional contracts imposed on parties by courts "as if" the parties had entered into an actual contract. Usually, quasi contracts are imposed to avoid the *unjust enrichment* of one party at the expense of another. The doctrine of unjust enrichment is based on the theory that individuals should not be allowed to profit or enrich themselves inequitably at the expense of others.

● **EXAMPLE #4** Suppose that a vacationing physician is driving down the highway and encounters Emerson, who is lying unconscious on the side of the road. The physician renders medical aid that saves Emerson's life. Although the injured, unconscious Emerson did not solicit the medical aid and was not aware that the aid had been rendered, Emerson received a valuable benefit, and the requirements for a quasi contract were fulfilled. In such a situation, the law normally will impose a quasi contract, and Emerson will have to pay the physician for the reasonable value of the medical services rendered. ●

Limitations on Quasi-Contractual Recovery. Although quasi contracts exist to prevent unjust enrichment, in some

MANAGEMENT PERSPECTIVE
Employment Manuals and Implied Contracts

MANAGEMENT FACES A LEGAL ISSUE It is a common practice today for large companies or other organizations to create and distribute to their employees an employment manual, or handbook, setting forth the conditions of employment. Yet when drafting and distributing such manuals to employees, business owners and managers must consider the following question: Will statements made in an employee handbook constitute "promises" in an implied-in-fact employment contract?

WHAT THE COURTS SAY Increasingly, courts are holding that promises made in an employment manual may create an implied-in-fact employment contract. For example, if an employment handbook states that employees will only be fired for "good cause," the employer may be held to that promise.[a]

This is possible even if, under state law, employment is "at will." Under the employment-at-will doctrine, employers may hire and terminate employees at will, with or without cause. The at-will doctrine will not apply, however, if the terms of employment are subject to a contract between the employer and the employee. If a court holds that an implied employment contract exists, on the basis of promises made in an employment manual, the employer will be bound by the contract and liable for damages for breaching the contract. Generally, the key consideration in determining whether an employment manual creates an implied contractual obligation is the reasonable expectations of employees.[b]

IMPLICATIONS FOR MANAGERS To avoid being contractually bound by terms in an employment manual, you should avoid making definite statements (such as "employees will only be terminated for good cause") that would cause employees to reasonably believe that those statements are contractual promises. You should also inform employees, when initially giving them the handbook or discussing its contents with them, that it is not intended as a contract. A conspicuous written disclaimer to this effect should also be included in the employment manual. The disclaimer might read as follows: "This policy manual describes the basic personnel policies and practices of our Company. You should understand that the manual does not modify our Company's 'at will' employment doctrine or provide employees with any kind of contractual rights."

a. See, for example, *Pepe v. Rival Co.*, 85 F.Supp.2d 349 (D.N.J. 1999).

b. *Doll v. Port Authority Trans-Hudson Corp.*, 92 F.Supp.2d 416 (D.N.J. 2000).

situations the party who obtains a benefit will not be deemed to have been unjustly enriched. Basically, the quasi-contractual principle cannot be invoked by a party who has conferred a benefit on someone else unnecessarily or as a result of misconduct or negligence.

● **EXAMPLE #5** You take your car to the local car wash and ask to have it run through the washer and to have the gas tank filled. While your car is being washed, you go to a nearby shopping center for two hours. In the meantime, one of the workers at the car wash mistakenly assumes that your car is the one that he is supposed to hand wax. When you come back, you are presented with a bill for a full tank of gas, a wash job, and a hand wax. Clearly, you have received a benefit, but this benefit was conferred because of a mistake by the car wash employee. You have not been unjustly enriched under these circumstances. People normally cannot be forced to pay for benefits "thrust" on them.●

When a Contract Already Exists. The doctrine of quasi contract generally cannot be used when an actual contract covers the area in controversy.[1] This is because a remedy already exists if a party is unjustly enriched as a result of a breach of contract: the nonbreaching party can sue the breaching party for breach of contract. No quasi contract need be imposed by the court in this instance to achieve justice.

FORMAL VERSUS INFORMAL CONTRACTS

Formal contracts require a special form or method of creation (formation) to be enforceable. They include (1) contracts under seal, (2) recognizances, (3) negotiable instruments, and (4) letters of credit.[2] *Contracts under seal*

[1] See, for example, *Industrial Lift Truck Service Corp. v. Mitsubishi International Corp.*, 104 Ill.App.3d 357, 432 N.E.2d 999, 60 Ill.Dec. 100 (1982).
[2] *Restatement (Second) of Contracts*, Section 6.

are formalized writings with a special seal attached.[3] The significance of the seal has lessened, although about ten states require no consideration when a contract is under seal. A *recognizance* is an acknowledgment in court by a person that he or she will perform some specified obligation or pay a certain sum if he or she fails to perform. One form of recognizance is the surety bond.[4] Another is the personal recognizance bond used as bail in a criminal matter. As will be discussed at length in subsequent chapters, *negotiable instruments* include checks, notes, drafts, and certificates of deposit; *letters of credit* are agreements to pay contingent on the purchaser's receipt of invoices and bills of lading (documents evidencing receipt of, and title to, goods shipped).

Informal contracts (also called *simple contracts*) include all other contracts. No special form is required (except for certain types of contracts that must be in writing), as the contracts are usually based on their substance rather than their form. Typically, businesspersons put their contracts in writing to ensure that there is some proof of a contract's existence should problems arise.

EXECUTED VERSUS EXECUTORY CONTRACTS

Contracts are also classified according to their state of performance. A contract that has been fully performed on both sides is called an **executed contract.** A contract that has not been fully performed on either side is called an **executory contract.** If one party has fully performed but the other has not, the contract is said to be executed on the one side and executory on the other, but the contract is still classified as executory.

● **EXAMPLE #6** Assume that you agree to buy ten tons of coal from Western Coal Company. Further assume that Western has delivered the coal to your steel mill, where it is now being burned. At this point, the contract is an executory contract—it is executed on the part of Western and executory on your part. After you pay Western for the coal, the contract will be executed on both sides.●

VALID, VOID, VOIDABLE, AND UNENFORCEABLE CONTRACTS

A **valid contract** has the four elements necessary for contract formation: (1) an agreement (offer and acceptance) (2) supported by legally sufficient consideration (3) for a legal purpose and (4) made by parties who have the legal capacity to enter into the contract. As mentioned, we will discuss each of these elements in the following chapters.

A **void contract** is no contract at all. The terms *void* and *contract* are contradictory. None of the parties has any legal obligations if a contract is void. A contract can be void because, for example, one of the parties was adjudged by a court to be legally insane (and thus lacked the legal capacity to enter into a contract) or because the purpose of the contract was illegal.

A **voidable contract** is a *valid* contract but one that can be avoided at the option of one or both of the parties. The party having the option can elect either to avoid any duty to perform or to *ratify* (make valid) the contract. If the contract is avoided, both parties are released from it. If it is ratified, both parties must fully perform their respective legal obligations.

As you will read in Chapter 9, contracts made by minors, insane persons, and intoxicated persons may be voidable. As a general rule, for example, contracts made by minors are voidable at the option of the minor. Additionally, contracts entered into under fraudulent conditions are voidable at the option of the defrauded party. Contracts entered into under legally defined duress or undue influence are voidable (see Chapter 10).

An **unenforceable contract** is one that cannot be enforced because of certain legal defenses against it. It is not unenforceable because a party failed to satisfy a legal requirement of the contract; rather, it is a valid contract rendered unenforceable by some statute or law. For example, some contracts must be in writing (see Chapter 10), and if they are not, they will not be enforceable except in certain exceptional circumstances.

Interpretation of Contracts

Common law rules of contract interpretation have evolved over time. These rules provide the courts with guidelines for deciding disputes regarding how contract terms or provisions should be interpreted.

THE PLAIN-MEANING RULE

When the writing is clear and unequivocal, a court will enforce the contract according to its plain terms (what is clearly stated in the contract), and there is no need for the court to interpret the language of the contract. The meaning of the terms must be determined from the *face of the instrument*—from the written document alone. This is sometimes referred to as the *plain-meaning rule*. Under this rule, if a contract's words appear to be clear and unambiguous, a court cannot consider *extrinsic evidence*, which is any

---

[3] A seal may be actual (made of wax or some other durable substance), impressed on the paper, or indicated simply by the word *seal* or the letters *L.S.* at the end of the document. L.S. stands for *locus sigilli* and means "the place for the seal."
[4] An obligation of a party who guarantees that he or she will pay a second party if a third party does not perform.

evidence not contained in the document itself. Admissibility of extrinsic evidence can significantly affect how a court interprets ambiguous contractual provisions and thus can affect the outcome of litigation.

OTHER RULES OF INTERPRETATION

When the writing contains ambiguous or unclear terms, a court will interpret the language to give effect to the parties' intent as *expressed in their contract*. This is the primary purpose of the rules of interpretation—to determine the parties' intent from the language used in their agreement and to give effect to that intent. A court normally will not make or remake a contract, nor will it normally interpret the language according to what the parties *claim* their intent was when they made it. The courts use the following rules in interpreting ambiguous contractual terms:

1. Insofar as possible, a reasonable, lawful, and effective meaning will be given to all of a contract's terms.

2. A contract will be interpreted as a whole; individual, specific clauses will be considered subordinate to the contract's general intent. All writings that are a part of the same transaction will be interpreted together.

3. Terms that were the subject of separate negotiation will be given greater consideration than standardized terms and terms that were not negotiated separately.

4. A word will be given its ordinary, commonly accepted meaning, and a technical word or term will be given its technical meaning, unless the parties clearly intended something else.

5. Specific and exact wording will be given greater consideration than general language.

6. Written or typewritten terms prevail over preprinted terms.

7. Because a contract should be drafted in clear and unambiguous language, a party that uses ambiguous expressions is held to be responsible for the ambiguities. Thus, when the language has more than one meaning, it will be interpreted against the party that drafted the contract.

8. Evidence of trade usage, prior dealing, and course of performance may be admitted to clarify the meaning of an ambiguously worded contract. (We define and discuss these terms in Chapter 14.) What each of the parties does pursuant to the contract will be interpreted as consistent with what the other does and with any relevant usage of trade and course of dealing or performance. Express terms (terms expressly stated in the contract) are given the greatest weight, followed by course of performance, course of dealing, and custom and usage of trade—in that order. When considering custom and usage, a court will look at the trade customs and usage common to the particular business or industry and to the locale in which the contract was made or is to be performed.

In the following case, the court applied "common sense" to interpret a disputed contract term.

CASE 7.3 Dispatch Automation, Inc. v. Richards

United States Court of Appeals,
Seventh Circuit, 2002.
280 F.3d 1116.
http://www.ca7.uscourts.gov[a]

FACTS Tony Richards is a software developer who, in 1982, wrote a computer program—RiMS Version 1.0—to help police and fire departments with records management and vehicle dispatch. In 1993, Richards and his wife formed Dispatch Automation, Inc., with Gary Hagar and his wife. Hagar was to market the product, and Richards was to con-

tinue developing it. Successive versions of the software culminated in RiMS 2000, also known as RiMS Version 8.0, in 1999. Under an agreement between the Richardses and the Hagars when Dispatch Automation was formed, the proceeds from the sales of "the RiMS group of computer-aided dispatch and records management software products" were to accrue to Dispatch Automation, which was to continue to "develop" the product, but Richards alone owned the rights to it and only licensed it to the corporation.[b] In February 2001, the couples had a falling out. Richards canceled Dispatch Automation's license to market RiMS, and he and his wife resigned as employees of the corporation. Dispatch

---

a. In the left column, select "Case Information," and then, on the same page, click on "Opinions." On the next page, in the "Last Name or Corporation" box, enter "Dispatch," select "Begins," and click on "Search for Person." Click on the number next to the name of the case in the result to access the opinion. The U.S. Court of Appeals for the Seventh Circuit maintains this Web site.

b. This is unusual in the software industry. Ordinarily, an employer insists on owning all the software that its employees develop. Richards, however, was not an ordinary employee but, with his wife, was a half owner of Dispatch Automation, which was built around his technology.

CASE 7.3—Continued

Automation filed a suit in a federal district court against the Richardses for breach of contract, contending that Richards did not own RiMS 2000. The corporation argued that "develop[ments]," as used in the parties' agreement, referred to "small, incremental changes" and that RiMS 2000 was so different from the earlier versions that it was a new product. The court issued a summary judgment for the defendants (the Richardses). Dispatch Automation appealed to the U.S. Court of Appeals for the Seventh Circuit.

ISSUE Was summary judgment in favor of the Richardses appropriate?

DECISION Yes. The U.S. Court of Appeals for the Seventh Circuit affirmed the lower court's summary judgment in favor of the Richardses. Richards, not Dispatch Automation, owned RiMS 2000. Therefore, the Richardses' actions did not constitute a breach of the contract with the Hagars.

REASON According to the court, "[i]t would have been contrary to Dispatch Automation's own interests as they * * * appeared [when the corporation was formed] for the parties to have agreed that Richards would own successive versions [of RiMS] provided they made only incremental improvements over their predecessors but that he would have no rights to a successive version that made a real breakthrough. That would have given him an incentive to pull his punches, or to quit the company if he thought he was on the brink of a breakthrough * * * . Since the corporation received the entire income * * * from the sale of programs licensed to it by Richards, it had every reason to encourage him to make breakthroughs. * * * When a contractual interpretation makes no economic sense, that's an admissible and, in the limit, a compelling reason for rejecting it. The presumption in commercial contracts is that the parties were trying to accomplish something rational." Also, the court concluded that although RiMS 2000 was faster, more stable, and more user friendly than its predecessors, and "has some new bells and whistles," the software was sufficiently similar to its predecessors to fit within the contractual term "the RiMS group of * * * software programs."

FOR CRITICAL ANALYSIS—Economic Consideration *Suppose that Richards had signed an agreement giving to Dispatch Automation all software that he developed during the time that Dispatch Automation employed him. What effect might that have had on the outcome of this case?*

Terms and Concepts

bilateral contract   152
contract   151
executed contract   157
executory contract   157
express contract   153
formal contract   156
implied-in-fact contract   153

informal contract   157
objective theory of contracts   151
offeree   152
offeror   152
promise   150
promisee   151
promisor   151

quasi contract   155
unenforceable contract   157
unilateral contract   152
valid contract   157
void contract   157
voidable contract   157

Chapter Summary   Nature and Classification

The Function of Contracts (See page 151.)	Contract law establishes what kinds of promises will be legally binding and supplies procedures for enforcing legally binding promises, or agreements.
Definition of a Contract (See page 151.)	A contract is an agreement that can be enforced in court. It is formed by two or more competent parties who agree to perform or to refrain from performing some act now or in the future.
Requirements of a Contract (See pages 151–152.)	1. *Elements of a valid contract*—Agreement, consideration, contractual capacity, and legality. 2. *Possible defenses to the enforcement of a contract*—Genuineness of assent and form.

(Continued)

Chapter Summary	Nature and Classification—Continued
Types of Contracts (See pages 152–157.)	1. *Bilateral*—A promise for a promise. 2. *Unilateral*—A promise for an act (acceptance is the completed—or substantial—performance of the contract by the offeree). 3. *Express*—Formed by words (oral, written, or a combination). 4. *Implied in fact*—Formed at least in part by the conduct of the parties. 5. *Quasi contract (contract implied in law)*—Imposed by law to prevent unjust enrichment. 6. *Formal*—Requires a special form for creation. 7. *Informal*—Requires no special form for creation. 8. *Executed*—A fully performed contract. 9. *Executory*—A contract not yet fully performed. 10. *Valid*—A contract that has the necessary contractual elements of offer and acceptance, consideration, parties with legal capacity, and having been made for a legal purpose. 11. *Void*—No contract exists, or there is a contract without legal obligations. 12. *Voidable*—A contract in which a party has the option of avoiding or enforcing the contractual obligation. 13. *Unenforceable*—A valid contract that cannot be enforced because of a legal defense.
Interpretation of Contracts (See pages 157–159.)	When the terms of a contract are unambiguous, a court will enforce the contract according to its plain terms, the meaning of which must be determined from the written document alone. (Plain-language laws enacted by the federal government and the majority of the states require contracts to be clearly written and easily understandable.) When the terms of a contract are ambiguous, the courts use the following rules in interpreting the terms: 1. A reasonable, lawful, and effective meaning will be given to all contract terms. 2. A contract will be interpreted as a whole, specific clauses will be considered subordinate to the contract's general intent, and all writings that are a part of the same transaction will be interpreted together. 3. Terms that were negotiated separately will be given greater consideration than standardized terms and terms not negotiated separately. 4. Words will be given their commonly accepted meanings and technical words their technical meanings, unless the parties clearly intended otherwise. 5. Specific wording will be given greater consideration than general language. 6. Written or typewritten terms prevail over preprinted terms. 7. A party that uses ambiguous expressions is held to be responsible for the ambiguities. 8. Evidence of prior dealing, course of performance, or usage of trade is admissible to clarify an ambiguously worded contract. In these circumstances, express terms are given the greatest weight, followed by course of performance, course of dealing, and custom and usage of trade—in that order.

For Review

① What is a contract? What is the objective theory of contracts?

② What are the four basic elements necessary to the formation of a valid contract?

③ What is the difference between an implied-in-fact contract and an implied-in-law contract (quasi contract)?

④ What is a void contract? How does it differ from a voidable contract? What is an unenforceable contract?

⑤ What rules guide the courts in interpreting contracts?

Questions and Case Problems

7–1. Express versus Implied Contracts. Suppose that a local businessperson, McDougal, is a good friend of Krunch, the owner of a nearby candy store. Every day on his lunch hour McDougal goes into Krunch's candy store and spends about five minutes looking at the candy. After examining Krunch's candy and talking with Krunch, McDougal usually buys one or two candy bars. One afternoon, McDougal goes into Krunch's candy shop, looks at the candy, and picks up a $1 candy bar. Seeing that Krunch is very busy, he waves the candy bar at Krunch without saying a word and walks out. Is there a contract? If so, classify it within the categories presented in this chapter.

7–2. Contractual Promises. Rosalie, a wealthy widow, invited an acquaintance, Jonathan, to her home for dinner. Jonathan accepted the offer and, eager to please her, spent lavishly in preparing for the evening. His purchases included a new blazer, new shoes, an expensive floral arrangement, and champagne. At the appointed time, Jonathan arrived at Rosalie's house only to find that she had left for the evening. Jonathan wants to sue Rosalie to recover some of his expenses. Can he? Why or why not?

7–3. Contract Classification. Jennifer says to her neighbor, Gordon, "On your completion of mowing my lawn, I'll pay you $25." Gordon orally accepts her offer. Is there a contract? Is Jennifer's offer intended to create a bilateral or a unilateral contract? What is the legal significance of the distinction?

7–4. Contract Classification. High-Flying Advertising, Inc., contracted with Burger Baby Restaurants to fly an advertisement above the Connecticut beaches. The advertisement offered $5,000 to any person who could swim from the Connecticut beaches to Long Island across the Long Island Sound in less than a day. McElfresh saw the streamer and accepted the challenge. He started his marathon swim that same day at 10 A.M. After he had been swimming for four hours and was about halfway across the sound, McElfresh saw another plane pulling a streamer that read, "Burger Baby revokes." Is there a contract between McElfresh and Burger Baby? If there is a contract, what type(s) of contract is (are) formed?

7–5. Bilateral versus Unilateral Contracts. Nichols is the principal owner of Samuel Nichols, Inc., a real estate firm. Nichols signed an exclusive brokerage agreement with Molway to find a purchaser for Molway's property within ninety days.

This type of agreement entitles the broker to a commission if the property is sold to any purchaser to whom the property is shown during the ninety-day period. Molway tried to cancel the brokerage agreement before the ninety-day term had expired. Nichols had already advertised the property, put up a "for sale" sign, and shown the property to prospective buyers. Molway claimed that the brokerage contract was unilateral and that she could cancel the contract at any time before Nichols found a buyer. Nichols claimed the contract was bilateral and that Molway's cancellation breached the contract. Discuss who should prevail at trial. [*Samuel Nichols, Inc. v. Molway*, 25 Mass.App. 913, 515 N.E.2d 598 (1987)]

7–6. Recovery for Services Rendered. After Walter Washut had suffered a heart attack and could no longer take care of himself, he asked Eleanor Adkins, a friend who had previously refused Washut's proposal to marry him, to move to his ranch. For the next twelve years, Adkins lived with Washut, although she retained ownership of her own house and continued to work full-time at her job. Adkins took care of Washut's personal needs, cooked his meals, cleaned and maintained his house, cared for the livestock, and handled other matters for Washut. According to Adkins, Washut told her on numerous occasions that "everything would be taken care of" and that she would never have to leave the ranch. After Washut's death, Adkins sought to recover in quasi contract for the value of the services she had rendered to Washut. Adkins stated in her deposition that she performed the services because she loved Washut, not because she expected to be paid for them. What will the court decide, and why? [*Adkins v. Lawson*, 892 P.2d 128 (Wyo. 1995)]

7–7. Interpretation of Contracts. Jerilyn Dawson hired Michael Shaw of the law firm of Jones, Waldo, Holbrook & McDonough to represent her in her divorce. Dawson signed an agreement to pay the attorneys' fees. The agreement did not include an estimate of how much the divorce would cost. When Dawson failed to pay, the firm filed a suit in a Utah state court to collect, asking for an award of more than $43,000. During the trial, Shaw testified that he had told Dawson the divorce would cost "something in the nature of $15,000 to $18,000." The court awarded the firm most—but not all—of what it sought. Both parties appealed: Dawson contended that the award was too high, and the firm complained that it was too low. What rule of interpretation discussed in this chapter might the appellate court apply in deciding the appropriate amount of damages in this case? If this rule is applied, what will the court likely decide? Explain. [*Jones, Waldo, Holbrook & McDonough v. Dawson,* 923 P.2d 1366 (Utah 1996)]

7–8. Implied Contract. Thomas Rinks and Joseph Shields developed Psycho Chihuahua, a caricature of a Chihuahua dog with a "do-not-back-down" attitude. They promoted and marketed the character through their company, Wrench, L.L.C. Ed Alfaro and Rudy Pollak, representatives of Taco Bell Corp., learned of Psycho Chihuahua and met with Rinks and Shields to talk about using the character as a Taco Bell "icon." Wrench sent artwork, merchandise, and marketing ideas to Alfaro, who promoted the character within Taco Bell. Alfaro asked Wrench to propose terms for Taco Bell's use of Psycho Chihuahua. Taco Bell did not accept Wrench's terms, but Alfaro continued to promote the character within the company. Meanwhile, Taco Bell hired a new advertising agency, which proposed an advertising campaign involving a Chihuahua. When Alfaro learned of this proposal, he sent the Psycho Chihuahua materials to the agency. Taco Bell made a Chihuahua the focus of its marketing but paid nothing to Wrench. Wrench filed a suit against Taco Bell in a federal district court, claiming in part that it had an implied contract with Taco Bell, which the latter breached. Do these facts satisfy the requirements for an implied contract? Why or why not? [*Wrench L.L.C. v. Taco Bell Corp.,* 51 F.Supp.2d 840 (W.D.Mich. 1999)]

CASE PROBLEM WITH SAMPLE ANSWER

7–9. Professor Dixon was an adjunct professor at Tulsa Community College (TCC) in Tulsa, Oklahoma. Each semester, near the beginning of the term, the parties executed a written contract that always included the following provision: "It is agreed that this agreement may be cancelled by the Administration or the instructor at any time before the first class session." In the spring semester of Dixon's seventh year, he filed a complaint with TCC alleging that one of his students, Meredith Bhuiyan, had engaged in disruptive classroom conduct. He gave her an incomplete grade and asked TCC to require her to apologize as a condition of receiving a final grade. TCC later claimed, and Dixon denied, that he was told to assign Bhuiyan a grade if he wanted to teach in the fall. Toward the end of the semester, Dixon was told which classes he would teach in the fall, but the parties did not sign a written contract. The Friday before classes began, TCC terminated him. Dixon filed a suit in an Oklahoma state court against TCC and others, alleging breach of contract. Did the parties have a contract? If so, did TCC breach it? Explain. [*Dixon v. Bhuiyan,* 10 P.3d 888 (Okla. 2000)]

▶ To view a sample answer for this case problem, go to this book's Web site at **http://fundamentals.westbuslaw.com** and click on "Interactive Study Center."

7–10. Bilateral versus Unilateral Contracts. D.L. Peoples Group (D.L.) placed an ad in a Missouri newspaper to recruit admissions representatives, who were hired to enlist Missouri residents to attend D.L.'s college in Florida. Donald Hawley responded to the ad, his interviewer recommended him for the job, and he signed, in Missouri, an "Admissions Representative Agreement," which was mailed to D.L.'s president, who signed it in his office in Florida. The agreement provided in part that Hawley would devote exclusive time and effort to the business in his assigned territory in Missouri and that D.L. would pay Hawley a commission if he successfully recruited students for the school. While attempting to make one of his first calls on his new job, Hawley was accidentally shot and killed. On the basis of his death, a claim was filed in Florida for workers' compensation. (Under Florida law, when an accident occurs outside Florida, workers' compensation benefits are payable only if the employment contract was made in Florida.) Is this admissions representative agreement a bilateral or a unilateral contract? What are the consequences of the distinction in this case? Explain. [*D.L. Peoples Group, Inc. v. Hawley,* 804 So.2d 561 (Fla.App. 1 Dist. 2002)]

VIDEO QUESTION

7–11. Go to this text's Web site at **http://fundamentals.westbuslaw.com** and click on "Video Questions." Select "Chapter 7" and view the video titled *Nature and Classification of Contracts: Unilateral Contract.* Then answer the following questions:

1. In the example of a bilateral contract given by the instructor in the video, suppose that the teen shows up and mows the lawn on Friday instead of Thursday. Has the teen breached the contract?

2. Now consider the second example given by the instructor in the video, which involved a unilateral contract. According to the chapter materials, if the teen showed up on Thursday evening and mowed half of the instructor's lawn, intending to finish the next day, could the instructor revoke his offer?

3. Suppose that the teen involved in the unilateral contract did not finish mowing the lawn until Saturday morning. The instructor was home at the time and knew that the teen was mowing his lawn. When the job was complete, the instructor refused to pay because the teen had not mowed the lawn "before" Saturday. Discuss whether there are any other types of contracts discussed in this chapter under which the teen might be entitled to payment?

NATURE AND CLASSIFICATION

For updated links to resources available on the Web, as well as other materials, visit this text's Web site at

http://fundamentals.westbuslaw.com

The 'Lectric Law Library provides information on contract law, including a definition of a contract and the elements required for a contract. Go to

http://www.lectlaw.com/lay.html

and scroll down to "Contracts."

For easy-to-understand definitions of legal terms, including those relating to contracts, go to

http://dictionary.law.com

Online Legal Research

Go to the *Fundamentals of Business Law* home page at **http://fundamentals. westbuslaw.com**. Select "Interactive Study Center" and then click on "Chapter 7." There you will find the following Internet research exercises that you can perform to learn more about contract law:

Activity 7–1: LEGAL PERSPECTIVE—**Contracts and Contract Provisions**
Activity 7–2: MANAGEMENT PERSPECTIVE—**Implied Employment Contracts**
Activity 7–3: HISTORICAL PERSPECTIVE—**Contracts in Ancient Mesopotamia**

Before the Test

Go to the *Fundamentals of Business Law* home page at **http://fundamentals. westbuslaw.com**. Click on "Interactive Quizzes." You will find at least twenty interactive questions relating to this chapter.

Westlaw® Campus

If your textbook provided for a subscription to Westlaw® Campus, or if you have otherwise purchased access to the Westlaw Campus database, you can access any of the cases presented or cited in this chapter by using your Westlaw Campus account.

8
Agreement and Consideration

CHAPTER OBJECTIVES

After reading this chapter, you should be able to answer the following questions:

① What elements are necessary for an effective offer? What are some examples of nonoffers?

② In what circumstances will an offer be irrevocable?

③ What are the elements that are necessary for an effective acceptance?

④ What is consideration? What is required for consideration to be legally sufficient?

⑤ In what circumstances might a promise be enforced despite a lack of consideration?

In Chapter 7, we pointed out that promises and agreements, and the knowledge that certain of those promises and agreements will be legally enforced, are essential to civilized society. The homes we live in, the food we eat, the clothes we wear, the cars we drive, the books we read, the videos and recordings we watch and listen to—all of these have been purchased through contractual agreements. Contract law developed over time, through the common law tradition, to meet society's need to know with certainty what kinds of promises, or contracts, will be enforced and the point at which a valid and binding contract is formed.

For a contract to be considered valid and enforceable, the requirements listed in Chapter 7 must be met. In this chapter, we look closely at two of these requirements, *agreement* and *consideration*. As you read through this chapter, keep in mind that the requirements of agreement and consideration apply to all contracts, regardless of how they are formed. Many contracts continue to be formed in the traditional way—through the exchange of paper documents. Increasingly, contracts are also being formed online—through the exchange of electronic messages or documents. Although we discuss online contracts to a limited extent in this chapter, we will look at them more closely in Chapter 13.

Agreement

An essential element for contract formation is **agreement**— the parties must agree on the terms of the contract. Ordinarily, agreement is evidenced by two events: an *offer* and an *acceptance*. One party offers a certain bargain to another party, who then accepts that bargain.

Because words often fail to convey the precise meaning intended, the law of contracts generally adheres to the *objective theory of contracts,* as discussed in Chapter 7. Under this theory, a party's words and conduct are held to mean whatever a reasonable person in the offeree's position would think they meant. The court will give words their usual meanings even if "it were proved by twenty bishops that [the] party . . . intended something else."[1]

REQUIREMENTS OF THE OFFER

An **offer** is a promise or commitment to perform or refrain from performing some specified act in the future. As discussed in Chapter 7, the party making an offer is called the *offeror,* and the party to whom the offer is made is called the *offeree.*

Three elements are necessary for an offer to be effective:

① The offeror must have a serious intention to become bound by the offer.

② The terms of the offer must be reasonably certain, or definite, so that the parties and the court can ascertain the terms of the contract.

③ The offer must be communicated to the offeree.

Once an effective offer has been made, the offeree's acceptance of that offer creates a legally binding contract

---

[1] Judge Learned Hand in *Hotchkiss v. National City Bank of New York,* 200 F. 287 (2d Cir. 1911), aff'd 231 U.S. 50, 34 S.Ct. 20, 58 L.Ed. 115 (1913). (The term *aff'd* is an abbreviation for *affirmed;* an appellate court can affirm a lower court's judgment, decree, or order, thereby declaring that it is valid and must stand as rendered.)

(providing the other essential elements for a valid and enforceable contract are present).

In today's e-commerce world, offers are frequently made online. Essentially, the requirements for traditional offers apply to online offers as well, as you will read in Chapter 13.

Intention. The first requirement for an effective offer to exist is a serious, objective intention on the part of the offeror. Intent is not determined by the *subjective* intentions, beliefs, or assumptions of the offeror. Rather, it is determined by what a reasonable person in the offeree's position would conclude the offeror's words and actions meant. Offers made in obvious anger, jest, or undue excitement do not meet the serious-and-objective-intent test. Because these offers are not effective, an offeree's acceptance does not create an agreement.

● **EXAMPLE #1** You and three classmates ride to school each day in Julio's new automobile, which has a market value of $18,000. One cold morning the four of you get into the car, but Julio cannot get it started. He yells in anger, "I'll sell this car to anyone for $500!" You drop $500 in his lap. A reasonable person, taking into consideration Julio's frustration and the obvious difference in value between the car's market price and the purchase price, would declare that Julio's offer was not made with serious and objective intent and that you do not have an agreement.● In the subsections that follow, we examine the concept of intention further as we look at the distinctions between offers and nonoffers.

Lucy v. Zehmer, presented below, is a classic case in the area of contractual agreement. The case involved a business transaction in which boasts, brags, and dares "after a few drinks" resulted in a contract to sell certain property. The sellers claimed that the offer had been made in jest and that, in any event, the contract was voidable at their option because they were intoxicated when the offer was made and thus lacked contractual capacity (see Chapter 9). The court, however, looked to the words and actions of the parties— not their secret intentions—to determine whether a contract had been formed.

Landmark and Classic Cases

CASE 8.1   Lucy v. Zehmer

Supreme Court of Appeals of Virginia, 1954.
196 Va. 493,
84 S.E.2d 516.

FACTS Lucy and Zehmer had known each other for fifteen or twenty years. For some time, Lucy had been wanting to buy Zehmer's farm. Zehmer had always told Lucy that he was

(Continued)

CASE 8.1—Continued

not interested in selling. One night, Lucy stopped in to visit with the Zehmers at a restaurant they operated. Lucy said to Zehmer, "I bet you wouldn't take $50,000 for that place." Zehmer replied, "Yes, I would, too; you wouldn't give fifty." Throughout the evening, the conversation returned to the sale of the farm. At the same time, the parties were drinking whiskey. Eventually, Zehmer wrote up an agreement, on the back of a restaurant check, for the sale of the farm, and he asked his wife to sign it—which she did. When Lucy brought an action in a Virginia state court to enforce the agreement, Zehmer argued that he had been "high as a Georgia pine" at the time and that the offer had been made in jest: "two dog-goned drunks bluffing to see who could talk the biggest and say the most." Lucy claimed that he had not been intoxicated and did not think Zehmer had been, either, given the way Zehmer handled the transaction. The trial court ruled in favor of the Zehmers, and Lucy appealed.

ISSUE Can the agreement be avoided on the basis of intoxication?

DECISION No. The agreement to sell the farm was binding.

REASON The opinion of the court was that the evidence given about the nature of the conversation, the appearance and completeness of the agreement, and the signing all tended to show that a serious business transaction, not a casual jest, was intended. The court had to look into the objective meaning of the words and acts of the Zehmers: "An agreement or mutual assent is of course essential to a valid contract, but the law imputes to a person an intention corresponding to the reasonable meaning of his words and acts. If his words and acts, judged by a reasonable standard, manifest an intention to agree, it is immaterial what may be the real but unexpressed state of mind."

COMMENT *This is a classic case in contract law because it illustrates so clearly the objective theory of contracts with respect to determining whether an offer was intended. Today, the objective theory of contracts continues to be applied by the courts, and* Lucy v. Zehmer *is routinely cited as a significant precedent in this area. Note that in cases involving contracts formed online, the issue of contractual intent rarely arises. Perhaps this is because an online offer is, by definition, "objective" in the sense that it consists of words only—the offeror's physical actions and behavior are not evidenced.*

Expressions of Opinion. An expression of opinion is not an offer. It does not evidence an intention to enter into a binding agreement. ● EXAMPLE #2 In *Hawkins v. McGee*,[2] Hawkins took his son to McGee, a doctor, and asked McGee to operate on the son's hand. McGee said that the boy would be in the hospital three or four days and that the hand would *probably* heal a few days later. The son's hand did not heal for a month, but nonetheless the father did not win a suit for breach of contract. The court held that McGee did not make an offer to heal the son's hand in three or four days. He merely expressed an opinion regarding when the hand would heal. ●

Statements of Intention. A statement of an *intention* to do something in the future is not an offer. ● EXAMPLE #3 If Ari says "I *plan* to sell my stock in Novation, Inc., for $150 per share," a contract is not created if John "accepts" and tenders the $150 per share for the stock. Ari has merely expressed his intention to enter into a future contract for the sale of the stock. If John accepts and tenders the $150 per share, no contract is formed, because a reasonable per-

son would conclude that Ari was only *thinking about* selling his stock, not promising to sell it. ●

Preliminary Negotiations. A request or invitation to negotiate is not an offer; it only expresses a willingness to discuss the possibility of entering into a contract. Examples are statements such as "Will you sell Forest Acres?" and "I wouldn't sell my car for less than $1,000." A reasonable person in the offeree's position would not conclude that such a statement evidenced an intention to enter into a binding obligation. Likewise, when the government and private firms need to have construction work done, contractors are invited to submit bids. The *invitation* to submit bids is not an offer, and a contractor does not bind the government or private firm by submitting a bid. (The bids that the contractors submit are offers, however, and the government or private firm can bind the contractor by accepting the bid.)

Advertisements, Catalogues, and Circulars. In general, advertisements, mail-order catalogues, price lists, and circular letters (meant for the general public) are treated as invitations to negotiate, not as offers to form a contract.[3]

---

[2] 84 N.H. 114, 146 A. 641 (1929).

[3] *Restatement (Second) of Contracts*, Section 26, Comment b.

● **EXAMPLE #4** Suppose that you put an ad in the classified section of your local newspaper offering to sell your guitar for $75. Seven people call and "accept" your "offer" before you can remove the ad from the newspaper. If the ad were truly an offer, you would be bound by seven contracts to sell your guitar. Because *initial* advertisements are treated as *invitations* to make offers rather than offers, however, you will have seven offers to choose from, and you can accept the best one without incurring any liability for the six you reject.● On some occasions, though, courts have construed advertisements to be offers because the ads contained definite terms that invited acceptance (such as an ad offering a reward for the return of a lost dog).[4]

Price lists are another form of invitation to negotiate or trade. A seller's price list is not an offer to sell at that price; it merely invites the buyer to offer to buy at that price. In fact, the seller usually puts "prices subject to change" on the price list. Only in rare circumstances will a price quotation be construed as an offer.[5]

Auctions. In an auction, a seller "offers" goods for sale through an auctioneer. This is not, however, an offer for purposes of contract. The seller is really expressing only a willingness to sell. Unless the terms of the auction are explicitly stated to be *without reserve*, the seller (through the auctioneer) may withdraw the goods at any time before the auctioneer closes the sale by announcement or by fall of the hammer. The seller's right to withdraw the goods characterizes an auction with reserve; all auctions are assumed to be of this type unless a clear statement to the contrary is made.[6] At auctions without reserve, the goods cannot be withdrawn and must be sold to the highest bidder.

In an auction with reserve, there is no obligation to sell, and the seller may refuse the highest bid. The bidder is actually the offeror. Before the auctioneer strikes the hammer, which constitutes acceptance of the bid, a bidder may revoke her or his bid, or the auctioneer may reject that bid or all bids. Typically, an auctioneer will reject a bid that is below the price the seller is willing to accept. When the auctioneer accepts a higher bid, he or she rejects all previous bids. Because rejection terminates an offer (as will be pointed out later), those bids represent offers that have been terminated. Thus, if the highest bidder withdraws his or her bid before the hammer falls, none of the previous bids is reinstated. If the bid is not withdrawn or rejected,

the contract is formed when the auctioneer announces, "Going once, going twice, sold!" (or something similar) and lets the hammer fall.

Alternatively, in auctions with reserve, the seller may reserve the right to confirm or reject the sale even after "the hammer has fallen." In this situation, the seller is obligated to notify those attending the auction that sales of goods made during the auction are not final until confirmed by the seller.

Agreements to Agree. Traditionally, agreements to agree—that is, agreements to agree to the material terms of a contract at some future date—were not considered to be binding contracts. The modern view, however, is that agreements to agree may be enforceable agreements (contracts) if it is clear that the parties intend to be bound by the agreements. In other words, under the modern view the emphasis is on the parties' intent rather than on form.

● **EXAMPLE #5** When the Pennzoil Company discussed with the Getty Oil Company the possible purchase of Getty's stock, a memorandum of agreement was drafted to reflect the terms of the conversations. After more negotiations over the price, both companies issued press releases announcing an agreement in principle on the terms of the memorandum. The next day, Texaco, Inc., offered to buy all of Getty's stock at a higher price. The day after that, Getty's board of directors voted to accept Texaco's offer, and Texaco and Getty signed a merger agreement. When Pennzoil sued Texaco for tortious interference with its "contractual" relationship with Getty, a jury concluded that Getty and Pennzoil had intended to form a binding contract, with only the details left to be worked out, before Texaco made its offer. Texaco was held liable for wrongfully interfering with this contract.[7]●

Definiteness. The second requirement for an effective offer involves the definiteness of its terms. An offer must have reasonably definite terms so that a court can determine if a breach has occurred and provide an appropriate remedy.[8]

An offer may invite an acceptance to be worded in such specific terms that the contract terms are made definite.

---

[4] See, for example, *Lefkowitz v. Great Minneapolis Surplus Store, Inc.,* 251 Minn. 188, 86 N.W.2d 689 (1957).

[5] See, for example, *Fairmount Glass Works v. Grunden-Martin Woodenware Co.,* 106 Ky. 659, 51 S.W. 196 (1899).

[6] See UCC 2–328.

[7] *Texaco, Inc. v. Pennzoil Co.,* 729 S.W.2d 768 (Tex.App.—Houston [1st Dist.] 1987, writ ref'd n.r.e.). (Generally, a complete Texas Court of Appeals citation includes the writ of error history showing the Texas Supreme Court's disposition of the case. In this case, *writ ref'd n.r.e.* is an abbreviation for "writ refused, no reversible error," which means that Texas's highest court refused to grant the appellant's request to review the case, because the court did not think there was any reversible error.)

[8] *Restatement (Second) of Contracts,* Section 33. The UCC has relaxed the requirements regarding the definiteness of terms in contracts for the sale of goods. See UCC 2–204(3).

● **EXAMPLE #6** Suppose that Marcus Business Machines contacts your corporation and offers to sell "from one to ten MacCool copying machines for $1,600 each; state number desired in acceptance." Your corporation agrees to buy two copiers. Because the quantity is specified in the acceptance, the terms are definite, and the contract is enforceable.●

Courts sometimes are willing to supply a missing term in a contract when the parties have clearly manifested an intent to form a contract. If, in contrast, the parties have attempted to deal with a particular term of the contract but their expression of intent is too vague or uncertain to be given any precise meaning, the court will not supply a "reasonable" term because to do so might conflict with the intent of the parties. In other words, the court will not rewrite the contract.

If the essential terms are spelled out, however, a court may find that an enforceable contract exists even though the parties failed to specify other terms. The following case illustrates this point.

CASE 8.2 **Satellite Entertainment Center, Inc. v. Keaton**

Superior Court of New Jersey,
Appellate Division, 2002.
347 N.J.Super. 268,
789 A.2d 662.

FACTS In 1993, John Keaton decided to open a barbecue restaurant in Jersey City, New Jersey, and entered into a six-year lease with George Williams to occupy a portion of Williams's building. After Williams died, Morris Winograd, the owner of Satellite Entertainment Center, Inc., bought the building that included Keaton's restaurant. Winograd planned to renovate the entire premises to open a new restaurant and bar. In September 1995, Winograd asked Keaton how much it would cost to buy his business. Keaton named a price of $175,000. Keaton later claimed, as corroborated by witnesses, that Winograd said he would pay that amount, that he wanted Keaton out by the end of the year, and that he wanted Keaton to manage the new enterprise. Keaton vacated the premises by December. In January, Winograd began paying Keaton a salary, but did not pay him the $175,000, despite repeated requests. In April 1997, Winograd terminated Keaton. In a subsequent claim in a New Jersey state court against Satellite and Winograd, Keaton sought the $175,000. Winograd denied agreeing to pay Keaton anything. The court ruled in Keaton's favor. Winograd appealed to a state intermediate appellate court, claiming in part that the alleged agreement should not be enforced because it did not include the essential terms of an enforceable contract.

ISSUE Did the agreement include the essential terms of an enforceable contract?

DECISION Yes. The state intermediate appellate court affirmed the judgment of the lower court on Keaton's claim for $175,000. The essential terms of the agreement for the sale of Keaton's business could be determined, and thus there was an enforceable contract between the parties.

REASON The court explained, "First, the price was firm: it was $175,000. So too was the description of what Winograd was purchasing. He was buying all of Keaton's business, including whatever tangible assets, inventory or 'good will' might be involved. However, * * * none of those assets were particularly significant to Winograd. Thus, it is not surprising that the parties did not, for example, itemize with specificity the inventory or the furniture of Keaton's business which was to be turned over to Winograd. To Winograd, those details were unimportant. The critical point, and the real reason for Winograd's payment of $175,000, was Keaton's agreement to vacate the property by the end of 1995, which he did." Any missing incidental terms can be implied. "And that is particularly true when there has been part performance of the contract, or—as here—where one of the parties (Keaton) has fully performed his part of the bargain."

FOR CRITICAL ANALYSIS—Social Consideration
Suppose that the assets, inventory, and "good will" belonging to Keaton's business had been important to Winograd. In this situation, would the court have held that an enforceable contract existed?

Communication. A third requirement for an effective offer is communication—the offer must be communicated to the offeree. ● **EXAMPLE #7** Suppose that Tolson advertises a reward for the return of her lost cat. Dirlik, not knowing of the reward, finds the cat and returns it to Tolson. Ordinarily, Dirlik cannot recover the reward because an essential element of a reward contract is that the one who claims the reward must have known it was offered. A few states would allow recovery of the reward, but not on contract principles—Dirlik would be allowed to recover on the basis that it would be unfair to deny him the reward just because he did not know about it.●

TERMINATION OF THE OFFER

The communication of an effective offer to an offeree gives the offeree the power to transform the offer into a binding, legal obligation (a contract) by an acceptance. This power of acceptance, however, does not continue forever. It can be terminated by action of the parties or by operation of law.

Termination by Action of the Parties. An offer can be terminated by the action of the parties in any of three ways: by revocation, by rejection, or by counteroffer.

Revocation of the Offer by the Offeror. The offeror's act of withdrawing an offer is referred to as **revocation**. Unless an offer is irrevocable, the offeror usually can revoke the offer (even if he or she has promised to keep the offer open), as long as the revocation is communicated to the offeree before the offeree accepts. Revocation may be accomplished by an express repudiation of the offer (for example, with a statement such as "I withdraw my previous offer of October 17") or by the performance of acts that are inconsistent with the existence of the offer and that are made known to the offeree.

● **EXAMPLE #8** Geraldine offers to sell some land to Gary. A week passes, and Gary, who has not yet accepted the offer, learns from his friend Konstantine that Geraldine has in the meantime sold the property to Nunan. Gary's knowledge of Geraldine's sale of the land to Nunan, even though he learned of it through a third party, effectively revokes Geraldine's offer to sell the land to Gary. Geraldine's sale of the land to Nunan is inconsistent with the continued existence of the offer to Gary, and thus the offer to Gary is revoked.●

The general rule followed by most states is that a revocation becomes effective when the offeree or offeree's agent (a person who acts on behalf of another) actually receives it. Therefore, a letter of revocation mailed on April 1 and delivered at the offeree's residence or place of business on April 3 becomes effective on April 3.

An offer made to the general public can be revoked in the same manner in which the offer was originally communicated. ● **EXAMPLE #9** Suppose that a department store offers a $10,000 reward to anyone giving information leading to the apprehension of the persons who burglarized its downtown store. The offer is published in three local papers and in four papers in neighboring communities. To revoke the offer, the store must publish the revocation in all seven papers for the same number of days it published the

offer. The revocation is then accessible to the general public, and the offer is revoked even if some particular offeree does not know about the revocation.●

Irrevocable Offers. Although most offers are revocable, some can be made irrevocable. Increasingly, courts refuse to allow an offeror to revoke an offer when the offeree has changed position because of justifiable reliance on the offer (under the doctrine of detrimental reliance, or promissory estoppel, discussed later in the chapter). In some circumstances, "firm offers" made by merchants may also be considered irrevocable. We discuss these offers in Chapter 14.

Another form of irrevocable offer is an option contract. An **option contract** is created when an offeror promises to hold an offer open for a specified period of time in return for a payment (consideration) given by the offeree. An option contract takes away the offeror's power to revoke an offer for the period of time specified in the option. If no time is specified, then a reasonable period of time is implied. ● **EXAMPLE #10** Suppose that you are in the business of writing movie scripts. Your agent contacts the head of development at New Line Cinema and offers to sell New Line your new movie script. New Line likes your script and agrees to pay you $5,000 for a six-month option. In this situation, you (through your agent) are the offeror, and New Line is the offeree. You cannot revoke your offer to sell New Line your script for the next six months. If after six months no contract has been formed, however, New Line loses the $5,000, and you are free to sell the script to another firm.●

Option contracts are also frequently used in conjunction with the sale of real estate. ● **EXAMPLE #11** You might agree with a landowner to lease a home and include in the lease contract a clause stating that you will pay $2,000 for an option to purchase the home within a specified period of time. If you decide not to purchase the home after the specified period has lapsed, you lose the $2,000, and the landlord is free to sell the property to another buyer.●

Rejection of the Offer by the Offeree. An offer may be rejected by the offeree, in which case the offer is terminated. Any subsequent attempt by the offeree to accept will be construed as a new offer, giving the original offeror (now the offeree) the power of acceptance. A rejection is ordinarily accomplished by words or by conduct evidencing an intent not to accept the offer.

As with revocation, rejection of an offer is effective only when it is actually received by the offeror or the offeror's agent. ● **EXAMPLE #12** Suppose that Growgood Farms mails a letter to Campbell Soup Company offering to sell carrots at ten cents a pound. Campbell Soup Company could reject the offer by sending or faxing a letter to Growgood Farms expressly rejecting the offer, or by mailing the offer back to Growgood, evidencing an intent to reject it. Alternatively, Campbell could offer to buy the carrots at eight cents per pound (a counteroffer), necessarily rejecting the original offer.●

Merely inquiring about the offer does not constitute rejection. ●**EXAMPLE #13** A friend offers to buy your CD-ROM library for $300. You respond, "Is this your best offer?" or "Will you pay me $375 for it?" A reasonable person would conclude that you did not reject the offer but merely made an inquiry for further consideration of the offer. You can still accept and bind your friend to the $300 purchase price. When the offeree merely inquires as to the firmness of the offer, there is no reason to presume that she or he intends to reject it.●

Counteroffer by the Offeree. A **counteroffer** is a rejection of the original offer and the simultaneous making of a new offer. ●**EXAMPLE #14** Suppose that Burke offers to sell his home to Lang for $170,000. Lang responds, "Your price is too high. I'll offer to purchase your house for $165,000." Lang's response is called a counteroffer because it rejects Burke's offer to sell at $170,000 and creates a new offer by Lang to purchase the home at a price of $165,000.●

At common law, the **mirror image rule** requires that the offeree's acceptance match the offeror's offer exactly. In other words, the terms of the acceptance must "mirror" those of the offer. If the acceptance materially changes or adds to the terms of the original offer, it will be considered not an acceptance but a counteroffer—which, of course, need not be accepted. The original offeror can, however, accept the terms of the counteroffer and create a valid contract.[9]

Termination by Operation of Law. The offeree's power to transform an offer into a binding, legal obligation can be terminated by operation of law if any of four conditions occur: lapse of time, destruction of the specific subject matter, death or incompetence of the offeror or offeree, or supervening illegality of the proposed contract.

Lapse of Time. An offer terminates automatically when the time specified in it has passed. This time begins to run when the offeree receives the offer, not when the offer is sent. If the communication of an offer is delayed because of something the offeror does (such as writing the wrong

address on the envelope), and the offeree knows or should know about this, the delay does not affect the moment at which the offer lapses. If, however, the offeree is not aware of the delay and has no reason to be aware of it, then the moment at which the offer lapses may be different, but the length of time within which the offeree can accept the offer remains the same.[10]

●**EXAMPLE #15** Suppose that Beth offers to sell her boat to Jonah, stating that the offer will remain open until May 20. Unless Jonah accepts the offer by midnight on May 20, the offer will lapse (terminate). Now suppose that Beth writes a letter to Jonah, offering to sell him her boat if Jonah accepts the offer within twenty days of the letter's date, which is May 1. Jonah must accept within twenty days after May 1, or the offer will terminate. The same rule would apply even if Beth had used improper postage when mailing the offer, and Jonah received the letter ten days after May 1, knowing of the improper mailing. If, however, Jonah did not know about the improper mailing, and he would otherwise have received the offer on May 3, he may have until May 27 to accept.●

If no time for acceptance is specified in the offer, the offer terminates at the end of a *reasonable* period of time. A reasonable period of time is determined by the subject matter of the contract, business and market conditions, and other relevant circumstances. An offer to sell farm produce, for example, will terminate sooner than an offer to sell farm equipment, because farm produce is perishable and subject to greater fluctuations in market value.

Destruction of the Subject Matter. An offer is automatically terminated if the specific subject matter of the offer is destroyed before the offer is accepted. For example, if Bekins offers to sell his prize cow to Yatsen, but the cow is struck by lightning and dies before Yatsen can accept, the offer is automatically terminated.

Death or Incompetence of the Offeror or Offeree. An offeree's power of acceptance is terminated when the offeror or offeree dies or is deprived of legal capacity to enter into the proposed contract, *unless the offer is irrevocable.*[11] An offer is personal to both parties and normally cannot pass to the decedent's heirs, guardian, or estate. This rule applies whether or not one party had notice of the death or incompetence of the other party.

---

[9] The mirror image rule has been greatly modified in regard to sales contracts. Section 2–207 of the UCC provides that a contract is formed if the offeree makes a definite expression of acceptance (such as signing the form in the appropriate location), even though the terms of the acceptance modify or add to the terms of the original offer (see Chapter 14).

[10] *Restatement (Second) of Contracts,* Section 49.

[11] *Restatement (Second) of Contracts,* Section 48. If the offer is irrevocable, it is not terminated when the offeror dies. Also, if the offer is such that it can be accepted by the performance of a series of acts, and those acts began before the offeror died, the offeree's power of acceptance is not terminated.

Supervening Illegality of the Proposed Contract. A statute or court decision that makes an offer illegal will automatically terminate the offer. ● **EXAMPLE #16** If Acme Finance Corporation offers to lend Jack $20,000 at 15 percent annually, and the state legislature enacts a statute prohibiting loans at interest rates greater than 12 percent before Jack can accept, the offer is automatically terminated. (If the statute is enacted after Jack accepts the offer, a valid contract is formed, but the contract may still be unenforceable—see Chapter 9.)●

ACCEPTANCE

An **acceptance** is a voluntary act by the offeree that shows assent, or agreement, to the terms of an offer. The offeree's act may consist of words or conduct. The acceptance must be unequivocal and must be communicated to the offeror.

Who Can Accept? Generally, a third person cannot substitute for the offeree and effectively accept the offer. After all, the identity of the offeree is as much a condition of a bargaining offer as any other term contained therein. Thus, except in special circumstances, only the person to whom the offer is made or that person's agent can accept the offer and create a binding contract. For example, Lottie makes an offer to Paul. Paul is not interested, but Paul's friend José accepts the offer. No contract is formed.

Unequivocal Acceptance. To exercise the power of acceptance effectively, the offeree must accept unequivocally. This is the *mirror image rule* previously discussed. If the acceptance is subject to new conditions or if the terms of the acceptance materially change the original offer, the acceptance may be deemed a counteroffer that implicitly rejects the original offer.

Certain terms, when added to an acceptance, will not qualify the acceptance sufficiently to constitute rejection of the offer. ● **EXAMPLE #17** Suppose that in response to a person offering to sell a painting by a well-known artist, the offeree replies, "I accept; please send a written contract." The offeree is requesting a written contract but is not making it a condition for acceptance. Therefore, the acceptance is effective without the written contract. If the offeree replies, "I accept *if* you send a written contract," however, the acceptance is expressly conditioned on the request for a writing, and the statement is not an acceptance but a counteroffer. (Notice how important each word is!)[12]●

Silence as Acceptance. Ordinarily, silence cannot constitute acceptance, even if the offeror states, "By your silence and inaction, you will be deemed to have accepted this offer." This general rule applies because an offeree should not be put under a burden of liability to act affirmatively in order to reject an offer. No consideration—that is, nothing of value—has passed to the offeree to impose such a liability.

In some instances, however, the offeree does have a duty to speak, in which case his or her silence or inaction will operate as an acceptance. Silence may be an acceptance when an offeree takes the benefit of offered services even though he or she had an opportunity to reject them and knew that they were offered with the expectation of compensation. ● **EXAMPLE #18** Suppose that John, a college student who earns extra income by washing store windows, taps on the window of a store and catches the attention of the store's manager. John points to the window and raises his cleaner, signaling that he will be washing the window. The manager does nothing to stop him. Here, the store manager's silence constitutes an acceptance, and an implied-in-fact contract is created. The store is bound to pay a reasonable value for John's work.●

Silence can also operate as acceptance when the offeree has had prior dealings with the offeror. If a merchant, for example, routinely receives shipments from a supplier and in the past has always notified the supplier of rejection of defective goods, then silence constitutes acceptance. Also, if a person solicits an offer specifying that certain terms and conditions are acceptable, and the offeror makes the offer in response to the solicitation, the offeree has a duty to reject—that is, a duty to tell the offeror that the offer is not acceptable. Failure to reject (silence) would operate as an acceptance.

Communication of Acceptance. Whether the offeror must be notified of the acceptance depends on the nature of the contract. In a bilateral contract, communication of acceptance is necessary, because acceptance is in the form of a promise (not performance), and the contract is formed when the promise is made (rather than when the act is performed). Communication of acceptance is not necessary, however, if the offer dispenses with the requirement. Also, if the offer can be accepted by silence, no communication is necessary.[13]

In a unilateral contract, the full performance of some act is called for; therefore, acceptance is usually evident, and

---

[12] As noted in footnote 9, in regard to sales contracts, the UCC provides that an acceptance may still be effective even if some terms are added. The new terms are simply treated as proposals for additions to the contract, unless both parties are merchants—in which case the additional terms (with some exceptions) become part of the contract [UCC 2–207(2)].

[13] Under the UCC, an order or other offer to buy goods that are to be promptly shipped may be treated as either a bilateral or a unilateral offer and can be accepted by a promise to ship or by actual shipment. See UCC 2–206(1)(b).

notification is unnecessary. Exceptions do exist, however. When the offeror requests notice of acceptance or has no adequate means of determining whether the requested act has been performed, or when the law requires such notice of acceptance, then notice is necessary.[14]

Mode and Timeliness of Acceptance. The general rule is that acceptance in a bilateral contract is timely if it is effected within the duration of the offer. Problems arise, however, when the parties involved are not dealing face to face. In such situations, the offeree may use an authorized mode of communication.

The Mailbox Rule. Acceptance takes effect, thus completing formation of the contract, at the time the offeree sends or delivers the communication via the mode expressly or impliedly authorized by the offeror. This is the so-called **mailbox rule**, also called the "deposited acceptance rule," which the majority of courts uphold. Under this rule, if the authorized mode of communication is the mail, an acceptance becomes valid when it is dispatched (placed in the control of the U.S. Postal Service)—*not* when it is received by the offeror.

The mailbox rule was formed to prevent the confusion that arises when an offeror sends a letter of revocation but, before it arrives, the offeree sends a letter of acceptance. Thus, whereas a revocation becomes effective only when it is *received* by the offeree, an acceptance becomes effective on *dispatch* (even if it is never received), provided that an *authorized* means of communication is used.

Authorized Means of Communication. Authorized means of communicating an acceptance can be either expressly authorized—that is, expressly stipulated in the offer—or impliedly authorized by facts or law.[15] An acceptance sent by means not expressly or impliedly authorized is normally not effective until it is received by the offeror.

When an offeror specifies how acceptance should be made (for example, by first-class mail or express delivery), *express authorization* is said to exist. Moreover, both the offeror and the offeree are bound in contract the moment that such means of acceptance are employed. Most offerors do not expressly specify the means by which the offeree is

to accept. Thus, the common law recognizes the following implied authorized means of acceptance:[16]

① The choice of a particular means by the offeror in making the offer implies that the offeree is authorized to use the same or a faster means for acceptance.

② When two parties are at a distance, mailing is impliedly authorized.

Exceptions. There are three basic exceptions to the rule that a contract is formed when acceptance is sent by authorized means:

① If the acceptance is not properly dispatched (if a letter is incorrectly addressed, for example, or is without the proper postage), in most states it will not be effective until it is received by the offeror.

② The offeror can specifically condition her or his offer on the receipt of an acceptance by a certain time; in this case, to be effective, the acceptance must be received prior to the end of the specified time period.

③ Sometimes an offeree sends a rejection first, then later changes his or her mind and sends an acceptance. Obviously, this chain of events could cause confusion and even detriment to the offeror, depending on whether the rejection or the acceptance arrived first. In such situations, the law cancels the rule of acceptance on dispatch, and the first communication received by the offeror determines whether a contract is formed. If the rejection arrives first, there is no contract.[17]

Technology and Acceptances. Technology, and particularly the Internet, has all but eliminated the need for the mailbox rule because online acceptances typically are communicated instantaneously to the offeror. As you will learn in Chapter 13, while online offers are not significantly different from traditional offers contained in paper documents, online acceptances have posed some unusual problems. (For an example of one such problem, see this chapter's *Business Law in the Online World* feature.)

Consideration and Its Requirements

In every legal system, some promises will be enforced, and some promises will not be enforced. The simple fact that a party has made a promise, then, does not mean the promise

---

[14] UCC 2–206(2).

[15] *Restatement (Second) of Contracts*, Section 30, provides that an offer invites acceptance "by any medium reasonable in the circumstances," unless the offer is specific about the means of acceptance. Under Section 65, a medium is reasonable if it is one used by the offeror or one customary in similar transactions, unless the offeree knows of circumstances that would argue against the reasonableness of a particular medium (the need for speed because of rapid price changes, for example).

[16] Note that UCC 2–206(1)(a) states specifically that an acceptance of an offer for the sale of goods can be made by any medium that is reasonable under the circumstances.

[17] *Restatement (Second) of Contracts*, Section 40.

BUSINESS LAW IN THE ONLINE WORLD
Click-On Acceptances Must Be Reasonable

Online offers normally invite offerees to indicate their acceptance of the terms of the offer by clicking on an "I agree" or "I accept" box on the computer screen. For example, suppose that you wish to download software from a Web site. Typically, you will be presented with a "Terms of Service" agreement, or offer, by the licensor (the party licensing, or permitting, you to use the software under certain conditions) and asked to indicate your assent by clicking on an "I agree" box or icon (or something similar). Suppose, however, that you are not presented with any such agreement until *after* you have downloaded the software. Further suppose that the software damages your computer system and files. If you click "I agree" after having downloaded the software, are you bound by the terms of the contract (license)?

IS THERE A CONTRACT? Whether a contract had been formed in such a situation was essentially the question at issue in a case brought by Mark Williams and other Massachusetts residents against America Online, Inc. (AOL). Williams and the other plaintiffs sought damages for the harms caused to their computer systems after they downloaded AOL's Version 5.0 software. The plaintiffs claimed that the installation of the software caused unauthorized changes to the configuration of their computers. Because of these changes, they could no longer access other Internet service providers, run e-mail programs other than AOL's program, or access personal information and files.

When Williams and the others sued AOL in a Massachusetts state court, AOL moved for dismissal. AOL argued that the contract to which the plaintiffs had

agreed contained a forum-selection clause[a] specifying that any disputes under the contract would have to be brought in Virginia courts. Therefore, contended AOL, the plaintiffs could not bring their suit against AOL in a Massachusetts court.

The court, however, concluded that the damage complained of occurred before the plaintiffs were given the opportunity to accept or reject the agreement's terms. The plaintiffs' injuries were thus precontractual in nature, and they could obtain redress for their injuries in a Massachusetts court. In other words, they were not bound by the contract's forum-selection clause.

AN UNREASONABLE PROCESS The court also took issue with the way AOL invited acceptance of its terms. Once the installation was complete, the user had the option of choosing between "I agree" or "Read now," with the default being set to "I agree." If a user chose to "Read now," a second choice between the default "I agree" and "Read now" was presented. In other words, to read the text of the agreement, the user had to overcome two defaults. Even then, if a user declined to accept the agreement, it was too late to reverse the harm already caused to his or her computer system. The court refused to accept this process as reasonable.[b]

FOR CRITICAL ANALYSIS
Do you agree with the court that AOL's method of acceptance was unreasonable? Why or why not?

a. As noted in Chapter 7, a forum-selection clause specifies the forum (court or jurisdiction) in which any contract dispute will be resolved. Forum-selection clauses are commonly included in contracts, particularly when the parties are at a distance from one another.
b. *Williams v. America Online, Inc.*, 2001 WL 135825 (Mass.Super. 2001).

---

is enforceable. Under the common law, a primary basis for the enforcement of promises is consideration. **Consideration** is usually defined as the value given in return for a promise. We look here at the basic elements of consideration and then at some other contract doctrines relating to consideration.

ELEMENTS OF CONSIDERATION

Often, consideration is broken down into two parts: (1) something of *legally sufficient value* must be given in exchange for the promise, and (2) there must be a *bargained-for exchange*.

Legal Value. The "something of legally sufficient value" may consist of (1) a promise to do something that one has no prior legal duty to do, (2) the performance of an action that one is otherwise not obligated to undertake, or (3) the refraining from an action that one has a legal right to undertake (called a *forbearance*). Consideration in bilateral contracts normally consists of a promise in return for a promise, as explained in Chapter 7. ● **EXAMPLE #19** Suppose that in a contract for the sale of goods, the seller promises to ship specific goods to the buyer, and the buyer promises to pay for those goods when they are received. Each of these promises constitutes consideration for the contract.●

In contrast, unilateral contracts involve a promise in return for a performance. ● EXAMPLE #20 Suppose that Anita says to her neighbor, "When you finish painting the garage, I will pay you $100." Anita's neighbor paints the garage. The act of painting the garage is the consideration that creates Anita's contractual obligation to pay her neighbor $100.●

Bargained-for Exchange. The second element of consideration is that it must provide the basis for the bargain struck between the contracting parties. The promise given by the promisor must induce the promisee to incur a legal detriment either now or in the future, and the detriment incurred must induce the promisor to make the promise. This element of bargained-for exchange distinguishes contracts from gifts.

● EXAMPLE #21 Suppose that Jerry says to his son, "In consideration of the fact that you are not as wealthy as your brothers, I will pay you $500." This promise is not enforceable because Jerry's son has not given any return consideration for the $500 promised.[18] The son (the promisee) does not have to promise anything or undertake (or refrain from undertaking) any action to receive the $500. Here, Jerry has simply stated his motive for giving his son a gift. The fact that the word *consideration* is used does not, by itself, mean that consideration has been given.●

LEGAL SUFFICIENCY AND ADEQUACY OF CONSIDERATION

Legal sufficiency of consideration involves the requirement that consideration be something of value in the eyes of the law. Adequacy of consideration involves "how much" consideration is given. Essentially, adequacy of consideration concerns the fairness of the bargain. On the surface, fairness would appear to be an issue when the items exchanged are of unequal value. In general, however, courts do not question the adequacy of consideration if the consideration is legally sufficient. Under the doctrine of freedom of contract, parties are usually free to bargain as they wish. If people could sue merely because they had entered into an unwise contract, the courts would be overloaded with frivolous suits.

In extreme cases, however, a court of law may look to the amount or value (the adequacy) of the consideration because apparently inadequate consideration can indicate that fraud, duress, or undue influence was involved or that a gift was made (if a father "sells" a $100,000 house to his daughter for only $1, for example). Additionally, in cases in which the consideration is grossly inadequate, the courts may declare the contract unenforceable on the ground that it is *unconscionable*[19]—that is, generally speaking, it is so one sided under the circumstances as to be clearly unfair. (Unconscionability will be discussed further in Chapter 9.)

At issue in the following case was whether an agreement between company executives was void for lack of consideration.

---

[18] See *Fink v. Cox*, 18 Johns. 145, 9 Am.Dec. 191 (N.Y. 1820).

[19] Pronounced un-*kon*-shun-uh-bul.

CASE 8.3 Powell v. MVE Holdings, Inc.

Minnesota Court of Appeals, 2001.
626 N.W.2d 451.
http://www.lawlibrary.state.mn.us/archive[a]

FACTS CAIRE, Inc., in Burnsville, Minnesota, is a subsidiary of MVE Holdings, Inc., and manufactures home health-care products. R. Edwin Powell worked for CAIRE for thirteen years before becoming its chief executive officer (CEO) and presi-

---

a. In the "Court of Appeals Opinions" box, click on "Index by Case Name (First Party)." When the page opens, in the "Published" section, click on "P–R." On that page, scroll to the case name and click on the docket number to access the opinion. The Minnesota State Law Library in St. Paul, Minnesota, maintains this database.

---

dent. In 1996, a group of investors became the primary owners of MVE by buying a majority of its stock for $125.456 per share. In January 1997, David O'Halloran, MVE's CEO and president, met with Powell. O'Halloran asked Powell to resign as CAIRE's CEO and president, but to continue to attend trade-association board meetings and lobby Congress on MVE's behalf. O'Halloran also asked Powell to tell CAIRE's key customers and industry contacts that his resignation was voluntary. Powell later claimed that, in return, O'Halloran offered that MVE would pay Powell $125.456 per share for his MVE stock. Powell did as O'Halloran asked until April, when O'Halloran asked him to stop. When MVE refused to pay Powell $125.456 per share for his stock, he filed a suit in a Minnesota state court against MVE, alleging breach of contract. The court ruled in Powell's favor. MVE appealed to a

CASE 8.3—Continued

state intermediate appellate court, arguing in part that any alleged agreement between O'Halloran and Powell was void for lack of consideration.

ISSUE Was there consideration for an agreement between O'Halloran and Powell?

DECISION Yes. The state intermediate appellate court affirmed the decision of the lower court, upholding the award to Powell of nearly $3.5 million for his MVE stock.

REASON The state intermediate appellate court acknowledged that "[w]hen a contract is not supported by consideration, no valid contract is formed." Consideration is "something of value given in return for a performance or promise of

performance," and "requires that a contractual promise be the product of a bargain." The court emphasized that Powell performed lobbying efforts and "other tasks" on MVE's behalf at O'Halloran's request. MVE argued that many of these tasks "were of no value." The court pointed out, however, that it "will not examine the adequacy of consideration so long as something of value has passed between the parties. Although the consideration that Powell furnished may not have been as significant as the benefits that [MVE] promised to confer, Powell provided adequate consideration, and the agreement between Powell and [MVE] is not void for lack of consideration."

FOR CRITICAL ANALYSIS—Economic Consideration
Why might a corporation refuse to honor an agreement entered into by its president?

CONTRACTS THAT LACK CONSIDERATION

Sometimes, one of the parties (or both parties) to a contract may think that they have exchanged consideration when in fact they have not. Here we look at some situations in which the parties' promises or actions do not qualify as contractual consideration.

Preexisting Duty. Under most circumstances, a promise to do what one already has a legal duty to do does not constitute legally sufficient consideration.[20] The preexisting legal duty may be imposed by law or may arise out of a previous contract. A sheriff, for example, cannot collect a reward for information leading to the capture of a criminal if the sheriff already has a legal duty to capture the criminal. Likewise, if a party is already bound by contract to perform a certain duty, that duty cannot serve as consideration for a second contract.

● **EXAMPLE #22** Suppose that Bauman-Bache, Inc., begins construction on a seven-story office building and after three months demands an extra $75,000 on its contract. If the extra $75,000 is not paid, it will stop working. The owner of the land, having no one else to complete construction, agrees to pay the extra $75,000. The agreement is not enforceable because it is not supported by legally sufficient consideration; Bauman-Bache had a preexisting contractual duty to complete the building.●

Unforeseen Difficulties. The rule regarding preexisting duty is meant to prevent extortion and the so-called holdup game. What happens, though, when an honest contractor,

who has made a deal with a landowner to build a house, runs into extraordinary difficulties that were totally unforeseen at the time the contract was formed? In the interests of fairness and equity, the courts sometimes allow exceptions to the preexisting duty rule. In the example just mentioned, if the landowner agrees to pay extra compensation to the contractor for overcoming the unforeseen difficulties (such as having to use dynamite and special equipment to remove an unexpected rock formation to excavate for a basement), the court may refrain from applying the preexisting duty rule and enforce the agreement. When the "unforeseen difficulties" that give rise to a contract modification are the types of risks ordinarily assumed in business, however, the courts will usually assert the preexisting duty rule.[21]

Rescission and New Contract. The law recognizes that two parties can mutually agree to rescind their contract, at least to the extent that it is executory (still to be carried out). Rescission[22] is defined as the unmaking of a contract so as to return the parties to the positions they occupied before the contract was made. When rescission and the making of a new contract take place at the same time, the courts frequently are given a choice of applying the preexisting duty rule or allowing rescission and letting the new contract stand.

Past Consideration. Promises made in return for actions or events that have already taken place are unenforceable. These promises lack consideration in that the element of

---

[20] See *Foakes v. Beer*, 9 App.Cas. 605 (1884).

[21] Note that under the UCC, any agreement modifying a contract within Article 2 on Sales needs no consideration to be binding. See UCC 2–209(1).

[22] Pronounced reh-*sih*-zhen.

bargained-for exchange is missing. In short, you can bargain for something to take place now or in the future but not for something that has already taken place. Therefore, **past consideration** is no consideration.

● EXAMPLE #23 Suppose that Elsie, a real estate agent, does her friend Judy a favor by selling Judy's house and not charging any commission. Later, Judy says to Elsie, "In return for your generous act, I will pay you $3,000." This promise is made in return for past consideration and is thus unenforceable; in effect, Judy is stating her intention to give Elsie a gift.●

Illusory Promises. If the terms of the contract express such uncertainty of performance that the promisor has not definitely promised to do anything, the promise is said to be *illusory*—without consideration and unenforceable.

● EXAMPLE #24 The president of Tuscan Corporation says to his employees, "All of you have worked hard, and if profits continue to remain high, a 10 percent bonus at the end of the year will be given—if management thinks it is warranted." This is an *illusory promise,* or no promise at all, because performance depends solely on the discretion of the president (the management). There is no bargained-for consideration. The statement declares merely that management may or may not do something in the future.●

Option-to-cancel clauses in contracts for specified time periods sometimes present problems in regard to consideration. ● EXAMPLE #25 Abe contracts to hire Chris for one year at $5,000 per month, reserving the right to cancel the contract at any time. On close examination of these words, you can see that Abe has not actually agreed to hire Chris, as Abe could cancel without liability before Chris started performance. Abe has not given up the opportunity of hiring someone else. This contract is therefore illusory. Now suppose that Abe contracts to hire Chris for a one-year period at $5,000 per month, reserving the right to cancel the contract at any time after Chris has begun performance by giving Chris thirty days' notice. Abe, by saying that he will give Chris thirty days' notice, is relinquishing the opportunity (legal right) to hire someone else instead of Chris for a thirty-day period. If Chris works for one month, at the end of which Abe gives him thirty days' notice, Chris has a valid and enforceable contractual claim for $10,000 in salary.●

SETTLEMENT OF CLAIMS

Businesspersons or others can settle legal claims in several ways. It is important to understand the nature of consideration given in these kinds of settlement agreements, or contracts. A common means of settling a claim is through an *accord and satisfaction,* in which a debtor offers to pay a lesser amount than the creditor purports to be owed. Two

other methods that are commonly used to settle claims are the *release* and the *covenant not to sue.*

Accord and Satisfaction. In an **accord and satisfaction,** a debtor offers to pay, and a creditor accepts, a lesser amount than the creditor originally purported to be owed. Thus, in an accord and satisfaction, the obligor attempts to extinguish an obligation. The *accord* is the agreement under which one of the parties undertakes to give or perform, and the other to accept, in satisfaction of a claim, something other than that on which the parties originally agreed. *Satisfaction* may take place when the accord is executed. A basic rule is that there can be no satisfaction unless there is first an accord.

For accord and satisfaction to occur, the amount of the debt *must be in dispute.* If a debt is *liquidated,* accord and satisfaction cannot take place. A liquidated debt is one whose amount has been ascertained, fixed, agreed on, settled, or exactly determined. An example of a liquidated debt would be a loan contract in which the borrower agrees to pay a stipulated amount every month until the amount of the loan is paid. In the majority of states, acceptance of (an accord for) a lesser sum than the entire amount of a liquidated debt is not satisfaction, and the balance of the debt is still legally owed. The rationale for this rule is that the debtor has given no consideration to satisfy the obligation of paying the balance to the creditor—because the debtor has a preexisting legal obligation to pay the entire debt.

An *unliquidated debt* is the opposite of a liquidated debt. Here, reasonable persons may differ over the amount owed. It is not settled, fixed, agreed on, ascertained, or determined. In these circumstances, acceptance of payment of the lesser sum operates as a satisfaction, or discharge, of the debt. One argument to support this rule is that the parties give up a legal right to contest the amount in dispute, and thus consideration is given.

Release. A **release** is a contract in which one party forfeits the right to pursue a legal claim against the other party. Releases will generally be binding if they are (1) given in good faith, (2) stated in a signed writing (required by many states), and (3) accompanied by consideration.[23] Clearly, persons are better off if they know the extent of their injuries or damages before signing releases.

● EXAMPLE #26 Suppose that you are involved in an automobile accident caused by Raoul's negligence. Raoul offers to give you $1,000 if you will release him from further liability resulting from the accident. You believe that this amount will cover your damages, so you agree to and sign the release. Later you discover that it will cost $1,200

---

[23] Under the UCC, a written, signed waiver or renunciation by an aggrieved party discharges any further liability for a breach, even without consideration [UCC 1–107].

to repair your car. Can you collect the balance from Raoul? The answer is normally no; you are limited to the $1,000 in the release. Why? The reason is that a valid contract existed. You and Raoul both assented to the bargain (hence, agreement existed), and sufficient consideration was present. Your consideration for the contract was the legal detriment you suffered (by releasing Raoul from liability, you forfeited your right to sue to recover damages, should they be more than $1,000). This legal detriment was induced by Raoul's promise to give you the $1,000. Raoul's promise was, in turn, induced by your promise not to pursue your legal right to sue him for damages.●

Covenant Not to Sue. A covenant not to sue, unlike a release, does not always bar further recovery. The parties simply substitute a contractual obligation for some other type of legal action based on a valid claim. Suppose (following the earlier example) that you agree with Raoul not to sue for damages in a tort action if he will pay for the damage to your car. If Raoul fails to pay, you can bring an action for breach of contract.

PROMISES ENFORCEABLE WITHOUT CONSIDERATION—PROMISSORY ESTOPPEL

Sometimes, individuals rely on promises, and such reliance may form a basis for contract rights and duties. Under the doctrine of **promissory estoppel** (also called *detrimental reliance*), a person who has reasonably relied on the promise of another can often hope to obtain some measure of recovery. When the doctrine of promissory estoppel is applied, the promisor (the offeror) is **estopped** (barred, or impeded) from revoking the promise. For the doctrine of promissory estoppel to be applied, the following elements are required:

① There must be a clear and definite promise.

② The promisee must justifiably rely on the promise.

③ The reliance normally must be of a substantial and definite character.

④ Justice will be better served by the enforcement of the promise.

●**EXAMPLE #27** Your uncle tells you, "I'll pay you $150 a week so you won't have to work anymore." In reliance on your uncle's promise, you quit your job, but your uncle refuses to pay you. Under the doctrine of promissory estoppel, you may be able to enforce his promise.[24] Now your uncle makes a promise to give you $10,000 with which to buy a car. If you buy the car with your own funds and he does not pay you, you may once again be able to enforce the promise under this doctrine.●

---

[24] *Ricketts v. Scothorn*, 57 Neb. 51, 77 N.W. 365 (1898).

Terms and Concepts

Chapter Summary　Agreement and Consideration

AGREEMENT	
Requirements of the Offer (See pages 165–169.)	1. *Intent*—There must be a serious, objective intention by the offeror to become bound by the offer. Nonoffer situations include (a) expressions of opinion; (b) statements of intention; (c) preliminary negotiations; (d) generally, advertisements, catalogues, price lists, and circulars; (e) solicitations for bids made by an auctioneer; and (f) traditionally, agreements to agree in the future.

(Continued)

Chapter Summary	Agreement and Consideration—Continued
Requirements of the Offer—continued	2. *Definiteness*—The terms of the offer must be sufficiently definite to be ascertainable by the parties or by a court. 3. *Communication*—The offer must be communicated to the offeree.

Termination of the Offer
(See pages 169–171.)
	1. *By action of the parties*—
	
	  a. Revocation—Unless the offer is irrevocable, it can be revoked at any time before acceptance without liability. Revocation is not effective until received by the offeree or the offeree's agent. Some offers, such as the merchant's firm offer and option contracts, are irrevocable.
	
	  b. Rejection—Accomplished by words or actions that demonstrate a clear intent not to accept the offer; not effective until received by the offeror or the offeror's agent.
	
	  c. Counteroffer—A rejection of the original offer and the making of a new offer.
	
	2. *By operation of law*—
	
	  a. Lapse of time—The offer terminates (1) at the end of the time period specified in the offer or (2) if no time period is stated in the offer, at the end of a reasonable time period.
	
	  b. Destruction of the specific subject matter of the offer—Automatically terminates the offer.
	
	  c. Death or incompetence—Terminates the offer unless the offer is irrevocable.
	
	  d. Illegality—Supervening illegality terminates the offer.

Acceptance
(See pages 171–172.)
	1. Can be made only by the offeree or the offeree's agent.
	
	2. Must be unequivocal. Under the common law (mirror image rule), if new terms or conditions are added to the acceptance, it will be considered a counteroffer.
	
	3. Acceptance of a unilateral offer is effective on full performance of the requested act. Generally, no communication is necessary.
	
	4. Acceptance of a bilateral offer can be communicated by the offeree by any authorized mode of communication and is effective on dispatch. Unless the mode of communication is expressly specified by the offeror, the following methods are impliedly authorized:
	
	  a. The same mode used by the offeror or a faster mode.
	
	  b. Mail, when the two parties are at a distance.
	
	  c. In sales contracts, by any reasonable medium.

	CONSIDERATION
Elements of Consideration (See pages 173–174.)	Consideration is broken down into two parts: (1) something of *legally sufficient value* must be given in exchange for the promise, and (2) there must be a *bargained-for exchange*. To be legally sufficient, consideration must involve doing (or refraining from doing) something that one had no prior legal duty to do (or to refrain from doing).
Legal Sufficiency and Adequacy of Consideration (See pages 174–175.)	Legal sufficiency of consideration relates to the first element of consideration just mentioned—something of legal value must be given in exchange for a promise. Adequacy of consideration relates to "how much" consideration is given and whether a fair bargain was reached. Courts will inquire into the adequacy of consideration (if the consideration is legally sufficient) only when fraud, undue influence, duress, or unconscionability may be involved.

Chapter Summary	Agreement and Consideration—Continued
Contracts That Lack Consideration (See pages 175–176.)	Consideration is lacking in the following situations: 1. *Preexisting duty*—Consideration is not legally sufficient if someone is, either by law or by contract, under a preexisting duty to perform the action being offered as consideration for a new contract. 2. *Past consideration*—Actions or events that have already taken place do not constitute legally sufficient consideration. 3. *Illusory promises*—When the nature or extent of performance is too uncertain, the promise is rendered illusory (without consideration and unenforceable).
Settlement of Claims (See pages 176–177.)	1. *Accord and satisfaction*—An *accord* is an agreement in which a debtor offers to pay a lesser amount than the creditor purports to be owed. *Satisfaction* may take place when the accord is executed. 2. *Release*—An agreement by which, for consideration, a party is barred from further recovery beyond the terms specified in the release. 3. *Covenant not to sue*—An agreement not to sue on a present, valid claim.
Promises Enforceable without Consideration— Promissory Estoppel (See page 177.)	Under the doctrine of promissory estoppel (also called detrimental reliance), a person who has justifiably relied on the promise of another may, in some circumstances, obtain relief. The promise must be clear and definite, the reliance must be reasonable and substantial, and justice must be better served by enforcing the promise.

For Review

① What elements are necessary for an effective offer? What are some examples of nonoffers?

② In what circumstances will an offer be irrevocable?

③ What are the elements that are necessary for an effective acceptance?

④ What is consideration? What is required for consideration to be legally sufficient?

⑤ In what circumstances might a promise be enforced despite a lack of consideration?

Questions and Case Problems

8–1. Offer. Chernek, the sole owner of a small business, has a large piece of used farm equipment for sale. He offers to sell the equipment to Bollow for $10,000. Discuss the legal effects of the following events on the offer.

(a) Chernek dies prior to Bollow's acceptance, and at the time she accepts, Bollow is unaware of Chernek's death.

(b) The night before Bollow accepts, a fire destroys the equipment.

(c) Bollow pays $100 for a thirty-day option to purchase the equipment. During this period Chernek dies, and Bollow accepts the offer, knowing of Chernek's death.

(d) Bollow pays $100 for a thirty-day option to purchase the equipment. During this period Bollow dies, and Bollow's estate accepts Chernek's offer within the stipulated time period.

8–2. Offers versus Nonoffers. On June 1, Jason placed an ad in a local newspaper, to be run on the following Sunday, June 5, offering a reward of $100 to anyone who found his wallet. When his wallet had not been returned by June 12, he purchased another wallet and took steps to obtain duplicates of his driver's license, credit cards, and other items that he had lost. On June 15, Sharith, who had seen Jason's ad in the paper, found Jason's wallet, returned it to Jason, and asked for the $100. Is Jason obligated to pay Sharith the $100? Why or why not?

8–3. Offer and Acceptance. Carrie offered to sell a set of legal encyclopedias to Antonio for $300. Antonio said that he would think about her offer and let her know his decision the next day. Norvel, who had overheard the conversation between Carrie and Antonio, said to Carrie, "I accept your offer" and gave her $300. Carrie gave Norvel the books. The next day,

Antonio, who had no idea that Carrie had already sold the books to Norvel, told Carrie that he accepted her offer. Has Carrie breached a valid contract with Antonio? Explain.

8–4. Consideration. Ben hired Lewis to drive his race car in a race. Tuan, a friend of Lewis, promised to pay Lewis $3,000 if he won the race. Lewis won the race, but Tuan refused to pay the $3,000. Tuan contended that no legally binding contract had been formed because he had received no consideration from Lewis for his promise to pay the $3,000. Lewis sued Tuan for breach of contract, arguing that winning the race was the consideration given in exchange for Tuan's promise to pay the $3,000. What rule of law discussed in this chapter supports Tuan's claim? Explain.

8–5. Acceptance. On Saturday, Arthur mailed Tanya an offer to sell his car to her for $2,000. On Monday, having changed his mind and not having heard from Tanya, Arthur sent her a letter revoking his offer. On Wednesday, before she had received Arthur's letter of revocation, Tanya mailed a letter of acceptance to Arthur. When Tanya demanded that Arthur sell his car to her as promised, Arthur claimed that no contract existed because he had revoked his offer prior to Tanya's acceptance. Is Arthur correct? Explain.

8–6. Preexisting Duty. New England Rock Services, Inc., agreed to work as a subcontractor on a sewer project on which Empire Paving, Inc., was the general contractor. For drilling and blasting a certain amount of rock, Rock Services was to be paid $29 per cubic yard or on a time-and-materials basis, whichever was less. From the beginning, Rock Services experienced problems. The primary obstacle was a heavy concentration of water, which, according to the custom in the industry, Empire should have controlled but did not. Rock Services was compelled to use more costly and time-consuming methods than anticipated, and it was unable to complete the work on time. The subcontractor asked Empire to pay for the rest of the project on a time-and-materials basis. Empire signed a modification of the original agreement. On completion of the work, Empire refused to pay Rock Services the balance due under the modification. Rock Services filed a suit in a Connecticut state court against Empire. Empire claimed that the modification lacked consideration and was thus not valid and enforceable. Is Empire right? Why or why not? [*New England Rock Services, Inc. v. Empire Paving, Inc.,* 53 Conn.App. 771, 731 A.2d 784 (1999)]

CASE PROBLEM WITH SAMPLE ANSWER

8–7. In 1995, Helikon Furniture Co. appointed Gaede as its independent sales agent for the sale of its products in parts of Texas. The parties signed a one-year contract that specified, among other things, the commissions that Gaede would receive. Over a year later, although the parties had not signed a new contract, Gaede was still representing Helikon when it was acquired by a third party. Helikon's new management allowed Gaede to continue to perform for the same commissions and

sent him a letter stating that it would make no changes in its sales representatives "for at least the next year." Three months later, in December 1997, the new managers sent Gaede a letter proposing new terms for a contract. Gaede continued to sell Helikon products until May 1997, when he received a letter effectively reducing the amount of his commissions. Gaede filed a suit in a Texas state court against Helikon, alleging breach of contract. Helikon argued in part that there was no contract because there was no consideration. In whose favor should the court rule, and why? [*Gaede v. SK Investments, Inc.,* 38 S.W.3d 753 (Tex.App.—Houston [14 Dist.] 2001)]

▸ To view a sample answer for this case problem, go to this book's Web site at **http://fundamentals.westbuslaw.com** and click on "Interactive Study Center."

8–8. Definiteness of Terms. Southwick Homes, Ltd., develops and markets residential subdivisions. William McLinden and Ronald Coco are the primary owners of Southwick Homes. Coco is also the president of Mutual Development Co. Whiteco Industries, Inc., wanted to develop lots and sell homes in Schulien Woods, a subdivision in Crown Point, Indiana. In September 1996, Whiteco sent McLinden a letter enlisting Southwick Homes to be the project manager for developing and marketing the finished lots (lots where roads had been built and on which utility installation and connections to water and sewer lines were complete); the letter set out the roles and expectations of each of the parties, including the terms of payment. In October 1997, Whiteco sent Coco a letter naming Mutual Development the developer and general contractor for the houses to be built on the finished lots. A few months later, Coco told McLinden that he would not share the profits from the construction of the houses. McLinden and others filed a suit in an Indiana state court against Coco and others, claiming, in part, a breach of fiduciary duty. The defendants responded that the letter to McLinden lacked such essential terms as to render it unenforceable. What terms must an agreement include to be an enforceable contract? Did the McLinden letter include these terms? In whose favor should the court rule? Explain. [*McLinden v. Coco,* 765 N.E.2d 606 (Ind.App. 2002)]

8–9. Settlement of Claims. Shoreline Towers Condominium Owners Association in Gulf Shores, Alabama, authorized Resort Development, Inc. (RDI), to manage Shoreline's property. On Shoreline's behalf, RDI obtained a property-insurance policy from Zurich American Insurance Co. In October 1995, Hurricane Opal struck Gulf Shores. RDI filed claims with Zurich regarding damage to Shoreline's property. Zurich determined that the cost of the damage was $334,901. Zurich then subtracted an applicable $40,000 deductible, and sent checks to RDI totaling $294,901. RDI disputed the amount. Zurich eventually agreed to issue a check for an additional $86,000 in return for RDI's signing a "Release of All Claims." Later, contending that the deductible had been incorrectly applied and that this was a breach of contract, among other things, Shoreline filed a suit against Zurich in a federal district court. How, if at all, should the agreement reached by RDI and Zurich affect

Shoreline's claim? Explain. [*Shoreline Towers Condominium Owners Association, Inc. v. Zurich American Insurance Co.,* 196 F.Supp.2d 1210 (S.D.Ala. 2002)]

VIDEO QUESTION

8–10. Go to this text's Web site at **http:// fundamentals.westbuslaw.com** and click on "Video Questions." Select "Chapter 8" and view the video titled *Offer and Acceptance.* Then answer the following questions:

1. On the video, Vinny indicates that he can't sell his car to Oscar for four thousand dollars, and then says, "maybe five . . . " Discuss whether Vinny has made an offer or counteroffer?

2. Oscar then says to Vinny, "Okay, I'll take it. But you gotta let me pay you four thousand now and the other thousand in two weeks." According to the chapter, do Oscar and Vinny have an agreement? Why or why not?

3. When Maria later says to Vinny, I'll take it," has she accepted an offer? Why or why not?

AGREEMENT AND CONSIDERATION

For updated links to resources available on the Web, as well as other materials, visit this text's Web site at

http://fundamentals.westbuslaw.com

To learn what kinds of clauses are included in typical contracts, you can explore the collection of example contracts made available by FindLaw at

http://contracts.corporate.findlaw.com/index.html

You can find contract cases decided by the United States Supreme Court and federal appellate courts (as well as federal statutory law on contracts) at Cornell University's School of Law site:

http://www.law.cornell.edu/topics/contracts.html

The New Hampshire Consumer's Sourcebook provides information on contract law, including consideration, from a consumer's perspective. You can access this site at

http://www.state.nh.us/nhdoj/Consumer/cpb.html

Online Legal Research

Go to the *Fundamentals of Business Law* home page at **http://fundamentals. westbuslaw.com**. Select "Interactive Study Center" and then click on "Chapter 8." There you will find the following Internet research exercises that you can perform to learn more about topics covered in this chapter.

Activity 8–1: ETHICAL PERSPECTIVE—Offers and Advertisements
Activity 8–2: MANAGEMENT PERSPECTIVE—Promissory Estoppel
Activity 8–3: INTERNATIONAL PERSPECTIVE—Contract Consideration in Canada

Before the Test

Go to the *Fundamentals of Business Law* home page at **http://fundamentals. westbuslaw.com**. Click on "Interactive Quizzes." You will find at least twenty interactive questions relating to this chapter.

Westlaw® Campus

If your textbook provided for a subscription to Westlaw® Campus, or if you have otherwise purchased access to the Westlaw Campus database, you can access any of the cases presented or cited in this chapter by using your Westlaw Campus account.

9
Capacity and Legality

CHAPTER OBJECTIVES

After reading this chapter, you should be able to answer the following questions:

① What are some exceptions to the rule that a minor can disaffirm any contract?

② Under what circumstances does intoxication make a contract voidable?

③ Does mental incompetence necessarily render a contract void?

④ Under what circumstances will a covenant not to compete be enforceable? When will such covenants not be enforced?

⑤ What is an exculpatory clause? In what circumstances might exculpatory clauses be enforced? When will they not be enforced?

Courts generally want contracts to be enforceable, and much of the law is devoted to aiding the enforceability of contracts. Nonetheless, not all people can make legally binding contracts at all times. Contracts entered into by persons lacking the capacity to do so may be unenforceable. Similarly, contracts calling for the performance of an illegal act are illegal and thus void—they are not contracts at all.

In this chapter, we examine contractual capacity and some aspects of illegal bargains. As you read through the chapter, keep in mind that contractual capacity and legality are not inherently related other than that they are both contract requirements. We treat these topics in one chapter merely for convenience and reasons of space.

Contractual Capacity

Contractual capacity is the legal ability to enter into a contractual relationship. Courts generally presume the existence of contractual capacity, but in some situations, capacity is lacking or may be questionable. A person *adjudged by a court* to be mentally incompetent, for example, cannot form a legally binding contract with another party. In other situations, a party may have the capacity to enter into a valid contract but also have the right to avoid liability under it. For example, minors—or *infants,* as they are commonly referred to by the law—usually are not legally bound by contracts. In this section, we look at the effect of youth, intoxication, and mental incompetence on contractual capacity.

MINORS

Today, in virtually all states, the *age of majority* (when a person is no longer a minor) for contractual purposes is eighteen years for both genders. (The age of majority may still be twenty-one for other purposes, however, such as the purchase and consumption of alcohol.) In addition, some states provide for the termination of minority on marriage. Subject to certain exceptions, the contracts entered into by a minor are voidable at the option of that minor.

The general rule is that a minor can enter into any contract an adult can, provided that the contract is not one prohibited by law for minors (for example, the sale of alcoholic beverages or tobacco). Although minors have the right to avoid their contracts, there are exceptions (to be discussed shortly).

Disaffirmance. To exercise the option to avoid a contract, a minor need only manifest an intention not to be bound by it. The minor "avoids" the contract by disaffirming it. **Disaffirmance** is the legal avoidance, or setting aside, of a contractual obligation. Words or conduct may serve to express this intent. The contract can ordinarily be disaffirmed at any time during minority or for a reasonable time after the minor comes of age. If a minor disaffirms a contract, the *entire* contract must be disaffirmed. The minor cannot decide to keep part of the goods contracted for and return the remainder.

Keep in mind that an adult who enters into a contract with a minor cannot avoid his or her contractual duties on the ground that the minor can do so. Unless the minor exercises the option to disaffirm the contract, the adult party normally is bound by it.

A Minor's Obligations on Disaffirmance. All state laws permit minors to disaffirm contracts (with certain exceptions), including executed contracts. States differ, however, on the extent of a minor's obligations on disaffirmance. Courts in a majority of states hold that the minor need only return the goods (or other consideration) subject to the contract, provided the goods are in the minor's possession or control. ● **EXAMPLE #1** Jim Garrison, a seventeen-year-old, purchases a computer from Radio Shack. While transporting the computer to his home, Garrison, through no fault of his own, is involved in a car accident. As a result of the accident, the plastic casing of the computer is broken. The next day, he returns the computer to Radio Shack and disaffirms the contract. Under the majority view, this return fulfills Garrison's duty even though the computer is now damaged. Garrison is entitled to receive a refund of the purchase price (if paid in cash) or to be relieved of any further obligations under an agreement to purchase the computer on credit.●

A growing number of states, either by statute or by court decision, place an additional duty on the minor—the duty to restore the adult party to the position he or she held before the contract was made. In the example just given, Garrison would be required not only to return the computer but also to pay Radio Shack for the damage to the unit.

In the following case, the Tennessee Supreme Court faced the issue of whether a minor should be held responsible for damage, ordinary wear and tear, and depreciation of goods used by the minor prior to his disaffirmance of the contract. The case illustrates the trend among today's courts in regard to this issue.

CASE 9.1   Dodson v. Shrader

Supreme Court of Tennessee, 1992.
824 S.W.2d 545.

FACTS When Joseph Dodson was sixteen years old, he bought a used pickup truck for $4,900 from Shrader's Auto, which was owned by Burns and Mary Shrader. Nine months later, the truck developed mechanical problems. A mechanic informed Dodson that the problem might be a burnt valve. Without having the truck repaired, Dodson continued to drive it. One month later, the truck's engine "blew up," and the

truck was rendered inoperable. Dodson disaffirmed the contract and sought to return the truck to the Shraders and obtain a full refund of the purchase price. The Shraders refused to refund the purchase price and would not accept possession of the truck. Later, while parked in Dodson's front yard, the pickup was hit by an unknown driver. Dodson filed suit against the Shraders to compel a refund of the purchase price. Although the Shraders claimed that the truck's value had been reduced to $500, the trial court granted rescission (canceled the contract) and ordered the Shraders to refund

(Continued)

CASE 9.1—Continued

the full $4,900 purchase price to Dodson on Dodson's delivery of the truck to them. The Shraders appealed.

ISSUE Are the Shraders legally obligated to refund the full purchase price of the truck to Dodson?

DECISION No. The Supreme Court of Tennessee adopted a rule that required the seller to be compensated for the depreciated value—not the purchase price—of the pickup and remanded the case for a determination of the fairness of the contract and the fair market value of the vehicle.

REASON The court concluded that if the minor "has not been overreached in any way, and there has been no undue influence, and the contract is a fair and reasonable one, and the minor has actually paid money on the purchase price, and taken and used the article purchased, [then] he ought not to be permitted to recover the amount actually paid, without allowing the vendor of the goods reasonable compensation for the use of, depreciation, and willful or negligent damage to the article purchased, while in his hands." The court recognized "modern conditions under which minors * * * transact a great deal of business for themselves, long before they have reached the age of legal majority." To rule otherwise, explained the court, "can only lead to the corruption of principles and encourage young people in habits of trickery and dishonesty."

FOR CRITICAL ANALYSIS—Ethical Consideration
Do you believe that the goal of protecting minors from the consequences of unwise contracts should ever outweigh the goal of encouraging minors to behave in a responsible manner?

Disaffirmance and Misrepresentation of Age. Suppose that a minor tells a seller she is twenty-one years old when she is really seventeen. Ordinarily, the minor can disaffirm the contract even though she has misrepresented her age. Moreover, in certain jurisdictions the minor is not liable for the tort of fraud for such misrepresentation, the rationale being that such a tort judgment might indirectly force the minor to perform the contract.

Many jurisdictions, however, do find circumstances under which a minor can be bound by a contract when the minor has misrepresented his or her age. First, several states have enacted statutes for precisely this purpose. In these states, misrepresentation of age is enough to prohibit disaffirmance. Other statutes prohibit disaffirmance by a minor who has engaged in business as an adult. Second, some courts refuse to allow minors to disaffirm executed (fully performed) contracts unless they can return the consideration received. The combination of the minors' misrepresentations and their unjust enrichment has persuaded these courts to *estop* (prevent) the minors from asserting contractual incapacity.

Third, some courts allow a misrepresenting minor to disaffirm the contract, but they hold the minor liable for damages in tort. Here, the defrauded party may sue the minor for misrepresentation or fraud. Authority is split on this point because some courts, as previously noted, have recognized that allowing a suit in tort is equivalent to indirectly enforcing the minor's contract.

Liability for Necessaries, Insurance, and Loans. A minor who enters into a contract for necessaries may disaffirm the contract but remains liable for the reasonable value of the goods used. **Necessaries** are basic needs, such as food, clothing, shelter, and medical services, at a level of value required to maintain the minor's standard of living or financial and social status. Thus, what will be considered a necessary for one person may be a luxury for another. Additionally, what is considered a necessary depends on whether the minor is under the care or control of his or her parents, who are required by law to provide necessaries for the minor. If a minor's parents provide the minor with shelter, for example, then a contract to lease shelter (such as an apartment) normally will not be classified as a contract for necessaries.

Generally, then, to qualify as a contract for necessaries, (1) the item contracted for must be necessary to the minor's existence, (2) the value of the necessary item may be up to a level required to maintain the minor's standard of living or financial and social status, and (3) the minor must not be under the care of a parent or guardian who is required to supply this item. Unless these three criteria are met, the minor can disaffirm the contract *without* being liable for the reasonable value of the goods used.

Traditionally, insurance has not been viewed as a necessary, so minors can ordinarily disaffirm their insurance contracts and recover all premiums paid. Some jurisdictions, however, prohibit the right to disaffirm insurance contracts—for example, when minors contract for life insurance on their own lives. Financial loans are seldom considered to be necessaries, even if the minor spends the money borrowed on necessaries. If, however, a lender makes a loan to a minor for the express purpose of enabling the minor to purchase necessaries, and the lender personally makes sure the money is so spent, the minor normally is obligated to repay the loan.

Ratification. In contract law, **ratification** is the act of accepting and giving legal force to an obligation that previously was not enforceable. A minor who has reached the age of majority can ratify a contract expressly or impliedly.

Express ratification occurs when the minor expressly states, orally or in writing, that she or he intends to be bound by the contract. Implied ratification exists when the conduct of the minor is inconsistent with disaffirmance (as when the minor enjoys the benefits of the contract) or when the minor fails to disaffirm an executed (fully performed) contract within a reasonable time after reaching the age of majority. If the contract is still executory (not yet performed or only partially performed), however, failure to disaffirm the contract will not necessarily imply ratification.

Generally, the courts base their determination on whether the minor, after reaching the age of majority, has had ample opportunity to consider the nature of the contractual obligations he or she entered into as a minor and the extent to which the adult party to the contract has performed.

Parents' Liability. As a general rule, parents are not liable for the contracts made by minor children acting on their own, except contracts for necessaries, which the parents are legally required to provide. This is why businesses ordinarily require parents to cosign any contract made with a minor. The parents then become personally obligated under the contract to perform the conditions of the contract, even if their child avoids liability.

Generally, a minor is held personally liable for the torts he or she commits. Therefore, minors cannot disaffirm their liability for their tortious conduct. The parents of the minor can *also* be held liable under certain circumstances. For example, if the minor commits a tort under the direction of a parent or while performing an act requested by a parent, the injured party can hold the parent liable. In addition, in many states parents are liable up to a statutory amount for malicious torts committed by a minor child living in their home.

Emancipation. Minority status may also be terminated by a minor's **emancipation**, which occurs when a child's parent or legal guardian relinquishes the legal right to exercise control over the child. Normally, a minor who leaves home to support himself or herself is considered emancipated. As mentioned, some states provide for emancipation on marriage. Several jurisdictions permit minors to petition a court for emancipation themselves. For business purposes, a minor may petition a court to be treated as an adult.

INTOXICATED PERSONS

Contractual capacity also becomes an issue when a contract is formed by a person who claims to have been intoxicated at the time the agreement was made. The general rule is that if a person who is sufficiently intoxicated to lack mental capacity enters into a contract, the contract is voidable at the option of that person. This is true even if the intoxication was purely voluntary. For the contract to be voidable, it must be proved that the intoxicated person's reason and judgment were impaired to the extent that she or he did not comprehend the legal consequences of entering into the contract. In addition, to avoid the contract in the majority of states, the person claiming intoxication must be able to return all consideration received. If the person was intoxicated but understood the legal consequences, the contract is enforceable.

Simply because the terms of the contract are foolish or are obviously favorable to the other party does not mean the contract is voidable (unless the other party fraudulently induced the person to become intoxicated). Problems often arise in determining whether a party was sufficiently intoxicated to avoid legal duties. Generally, courts rarely permit contracts to be avoided on the ground of intoxication.

MENTALLY INCOMPETENT PERSONS

If a person has been adjudged mentally incompetent by a court of law and a guardian has been appointed, any contract made by the mentally incompetent person is void—no contract exists. Only the guardian can enter into a binding contract on behalf of the mentally incompetent person.

If a mentally incompetent person not previously so adjudged by a court enters into a contract, the contract may be *voidable* if the person does not know he or she is entering into the contract or lacks the mental capacity to comprehend its nature, purpose, and consequences. In such situations, the contract is voidable at the option of the mentally incompetent person but not the other party. The contract may then be disaffirmed or ratified. To disaffirm the contract, the person claiming mental incompetence must return any consideration received. Ratification can only occur after the person has regained mental competence or after a guardian is appointed and ratifies the contract. Mentally incompetent persons are liable for the reasonable value of any necessaries they receive.

A contract entered into by a mentally incompetent (but not previously so adjudged by a court) person may also be deemed valid and enforceable if the contract was entered into during a lucid interval. For such a contract to be valid, it must be shown that the person was able to comprehend the nature, purpose, and consequences of the contract *at the time the contract was formed.*

Legality

To this point, we have discussed three of the requirements for a valid contract to exist—agreement, consideration, and contractual capacity. Now we examine a fourth—legality. For a contract to be valid and enforceable, it must be formed for a legal purpose. A contract to do something that is prohibited by federal or state statutory law is illegal and, as such, void from the outset and thus unenforceable. Additionally, a contract to commit a tortious act or to commit an action that is contrary to public policy is illegal and unenforceable.

CONTRACTS CONTRARY TO STATUTE

Statutes sometimes prescribe the terms of contracts. We examine here several ways in which contracts may be contrary to a statute and thus illegal.

Usury. Virtually every state has a statute that sets the maximum rate of interest that can be charged for different types of transactions, including ordinary loans. A lender who makes a loan at an interest rate above the lawful maximum commits **usury**. The maximum rate of interest varies from state to state.

Although usury statutes place a ceiling on allowable rates of interest, exceptions have been made to facilitate business transactions. For example, many states exempt corporate loans from the usury laws. In addition, almost all states have adopted special statutes allowing much higher interest rates on small loans to help those borrowers who need funds and who could not otherwise obtain loans.

The consequences of a usurious loan differ from state to state. A number of states allow the lender to recover only the principal of a loan along with interest up to the legal maximum. In effect, the lender is denied recovery of the excess interest. In other states, the lender can recover the principal amount of the loan but not the interest. In a few states, a usurious loan is a void transaction, and the lender cannot recover either the principal or the interest.

Gambling. In general, gambling contracts are illegal and thus void. All states have statutes that regulate gambling— defined as any scheme that involves the distribution of property by chance among persons who have paid valuable consideration for the opportunity (chance) to receive the property.[1] Gambling is the creation of risk for the purpose of assuming it.

In some states, such as Nevada, New Jersey, and Louisiana, casino gambling is legal. In other states, certain other forms of gambling are legal. California, for example, has not defined draw poker as a crime, although criminal statutes prohibit numerous other types of gambling games. Several states allow horse racing, and many states have legalized state-operated lotteries, as well as lotteries (such as bingo) conducted for charitable purposes. Gambling is allowed on many Indian reservations.

Sometimes it is difficult to distinguish a gambling contract from the risk sharing inherent in almost all contracts. ● **EXAMPLE #2** In one case, each of five co-workers received a free lottery ticket from a customer and agreed to split the winnings if one of the tickets turned out to be the winning one. At first glance, this may seem entirely legal. The court, however, noted that the oral contract in this case "was an exchange of promises to share winnings from the parties' individually owned lottery tickets upon the happening of the uncertain event" that one of the tickets would win. Consequently, concluded the court, the agreement at issue was "founded on a gambling consideration" and therefore void.[2] ●

Sabbath (Sunday) Laws. Statutes called Sabbath (Sunday) laws prohibit the formation or performance of certain contracts on a Sunday. Under the common law, such contracts are legal in the absence of this statutory prohibition. Under some state and local laws, all contracts entered into on a Sunday are illegal. Laws in other states or municipalities prohibit only the sale of certain types of merchandise, such as alcoholic beverages, on a Sunday.

As noted in Chapter 1, these laws, which date back to colonial times, are often called **blue laws**. Blue laws get their name from the blue paper on which New Haven, Connecticut, printed its new town ordinance in 1781. The ordinance prohibited all work on Sunday and required all shops to close on the "Lord's Day." A number of states and municipalities enacted laws forbidding the carrying on of "all secular labor and business on the Lord's Day." Exceptions to Sunday laws permit contracts for necessities

---

[1] See *Wishing Well Club v. Akron*, 66 Ohio Law Abs. 406, 112 N.E.2d 41 (1951).
[2] *Dickerson v. Deno*, 770 So.2d 63 (Ala. 2000).

(such as food) and works of charity. Additionally, a fully performed (executed) contract that was entered into on a Sunday normally cannot be rescinded (canceled).

Sunday laws are often not enforced, and some of these laws have been held to be unconstitutional on the ground that they are contrary to the freedom of religion. Nonetheless, as a precaution, business owners contemplating doing business in a particular locality should check to see if any Sunday statutes or ordinances will affect their business activities.

Licensing Statutes. All states require that members of certain professions obtain licenses allowing them to practice. Physicians, lawyers, real estate brokers, architects, electricians, and stockbrokers are but a few of the people who must be licensed. Some licenses are obtained only after extensive schooling and examinations, which indicate to the public that a special skill has been acquired. Others require only that the particular person be of good moral character.

Generally, business licenses provide a means of regulating and taxing certain businesses and protecting the public against actions that could threaten the general welfare. For example, in nearly all states, a stockbroker must be licensed and must file a bond with the state to protect the public from fraudulent stock transactions. Similarly, a plumber must be licensed and bonded to protect the public against incompetent plumbers and to protect the public health. Only persons or businesses possessing the qualifications and complying with the conditions required by statute are entitled to licenses. Typically, for example, an owner of a saloon or tavern must sell food as a condition of obtaining a license to sell liquor for consumption on the premises.

When a person enters into a contract with an unlicensed individual, the contract may still be enforceable, depending on the nature of the licensing statute. Some states expressly provide that the lack of a license in certain occupations bars the enforcement of work-related contracts. If the statute does not expressly state this, one must look to the underlying purpose of the licensing requirements for a particular occupation. If the goal is to protect the public from unauthorized practitioners, a contract involving an unlicensed individual is illegal and unenforceable. If, however, the underlying purpose of the statute is to raise government revenues, a contract with an unlicensed practitioner is enforceable—although the unlicensed person is usually fined.

Contracts Contrary to Public Policy

Although contracts involve private parties, some are not enforceable because of the negative impact they would have on society. These contracts are said to be *contrary to public*

policy. Examples include a contract to commit an immoral act (such as a surrogate-parenting contract, which several courts and state statutes equate with "baby selling") and a contract that prohibits marriage. ● **EXAMPLE #3** Everett offers a young man $10,000 if he refrains from marrying Everett's daughter. Even if the young man accepts, no contract is formed (the contract is void) because it is contrary to public policy. Thus, if the man marries Everett's daughter, Everett cannot sue him for breach of contract. ● Business contracts that may be contrary to public policy include contracts in restraint of trade and unconscionable contracts or clauses.

Contracts in Restraint of Trade. Contracts in restraint of trade (anticompetitive agreements) usually adversely affect the public policy that favors competition in the economy. Typically, such contracts also violate one or more federal or state statutes.[3] An exception is recognized when the restraint is reasonable and is *ancillary* to (is a subsidiary part of) a contract, such as a contract for the sale of a business or an employment contract. Many such exceptions involve a type of restraint called a *covenant not to compete,* or a restrictive covenant.

Covenants Not to Compete and the Sale of an Ongoing Business. Covenants not to compete are often contained in contracts concerning the sale of an ongoing business. A covenant not to compete is created when a seller agrees not to open a new store in a certain geographic area surrounding the old store. Such an agreement, when it is ancillary to a sales contract and reasonable in terms of time and geographic area, enables the seller to sell, and the purchaser to buy, the "goodwill" and "reputation" of an ongoing business. If, for example, a well-known merchant sells his or her store and opens a competing business a block away, many of the merchant's customers will likely do business at the new store. This renders valueless the good name and reputation sold to the other merchant for a price. If a covenant not to compete is not ancillary to a sales agreement, however, it will be void, because it unreasonably restrains trade and is contrary to public policy.

Covenants Not to Compete in Employment Contracts. Agreements not to compete can also be contained in employment contracts. People in middle-level and upper-level management positions commonly agree not to work for competitors or not to start a competing business for a

---

[3] Federal statutes prohibiting anticompetitive agreements include the Sherman Antitrust Act of 1890, the Clayton Act of 1914, and the Federal Trade Commission Act of 1914.

specified period of time after terminating employment. Such agreements are generally legal so long as the specified period of time is not excessive in duration and the geographic restriction is reasonable. Basically, the restriction on competition must be reasonable—that is, not any greater than necessary to protect a legitimate business interest. The following case illustrates those requirements. (For a discussion of what time and geographic restrictions are "reasonable" in the online environment, see this chapter's *Business Law in the Online World* feature.)

CASE 9.2   Moore v. Midwest Distribution, Inc.

Court of Appeals of Arkansas, 2002.
76 Ark.App. 397,
65 S.W.3d 490.
http://courts.state.ar.us/opinions/opinions.html[a]

FACTS Ronnie Moore began working in the product display business in 1997 for Hubb Group (HG), in Memphis, Tennessee. In 1999, HG terminated his contract. Moore moved to Fort Smith, Arkansas, to work for Midwest Distribution, Inc., which also set up product displays as a contractor for HG. Midwest asked Moore to sign a "Service Work for Hire Agreement" under which Moore agreed that, for one year after the termination of his employment, he would not "provide, or solicit or offer to provide to any present or former Customer of Contractor, or become directly or indirectly interested in any person or entity which provides, or solicits or offers to provide, any services to such Customers." The agreement applied "to those geographical areas in which the Contractee acts as independent contractor including, but not limited to, the State of Arkansas, Illinois, Iowa, Kansas, Missouri, Nebraska, New Mexico, Oklahoma, Texas, and any other state that contractor has granted a contract or agreement within." Moore quit this job to work for Jay Godwin, who also contracted with HG. Midwest Distribution filed a suit in an Arkansas state court against Moore, seeking to enjoin (prevent) him from providing services to Godwin. The court issued a temporary injunction. Moore appealed to a state intermediate appellate court.

---

a. In the "Search Cases by Party Name" section, enter "Moore" in the "Party Name" box and select "Search by Date Range." For the date range, choose "From January 2002" and "To February 2002," and click on "Search." From the list of results, click on the name of the case that includes "Reversed" to access the opinion. The Arkansas judiciary maintains this Web site.

ISSUE Is Midwest Distribution's covenant not to compete with Moore enforceable?

DECISION No. The state intermediate appellate court reversed the judgment of the lower court. The appellate court concluded that the covenant not to compete was unenforceable because it did not protect a legitimate interest of Midwest Distribution and the geographic scope of the agreement was unreasonably broad.

REASON The court pointed out that "[t]he test of reasonableness of contracts in restraint of trade is that the restraint imposed upon one party must not be greater than is reasonably necessary for the protection of the other and not so great as to injure a public interest. Where a covenant not to compete grows out of an employment relationship, the courts have found an interest sufficient to warrant enforcement of the covenant only in those cases where the covenantee provided special training, or made available trade secrets, confidential business information, or customer lists, and then only if it is found that the covenantee was able to use information so obtained to gain an unfair competitive advantage." Moore had not been given any special training, trade secrets, confidential information, or customer lists, and was not using "any information to gain an unfair competitive advantage over" Midwest Distribution. As for the geographic restriction, Midwest "did not conduct any business in Oklahoma. We find that it is not reasonable to restrict appellant from working in a state he never worked in before."

FOR CRITICAL ANALYSIS—Ethical Consideration
What did the court mean by the statement that a restraint should not be "so great as to injure a public interest"? What public interest might be injured by an overbroad covenant not to compete?

Enforcement Problems. The laws governing the enforceability of covenants not to compete vary significantly from state to state. In some states, such as Texas, such a covenant will not be enforced unless the employee has received some benefit in return for signing the noncompete agreement. This is true even if the covenant is reasonable as to time and area. If the employee receives no benefit, the covenant will be deemed void. California prohibits the enforcement of covenants not to compete altogether.

Occasionally, depending on the jurisdiction, courts will *reform* covenants not to compete. If a covenant is found to be unreasonable in time or geographic area, the court may

BUSINESS LAW IN THE ONLINE WORLD
Covenants Not to Compete in the Internet Context

For some companies today, particularly those in high-tech industries, trade secrets are their most valuable assets. Often, to prevent departing employees from disclosing trade secrets to competing employers, business owners and managers have their key employees sign covenants not to compete. A question of growing significance to employers—and the courts—today is how to adapt traditional requirements relating to such covenants to a cyber age.

RESTRICTIONS MUST BE REASONABLE As mentioned elsewhere in this chapter, in a covenant not to compete the employee typically agrees not to set up a competing business, or work for a competitor, in a specified geographic area for a certain period of time. Generally, the time and geographic restrictions must be "reasonable." For example, while a time restriction of one year may be upheld by a court as reasonable, a time restriction of two, three, or five years may not be. For quite a while, attorneys typically have advised their business clients to restrict the noncompete period to one year for this reason.

Yet can time and space restrictions that have been deemed reasonable in the past serve as a guide to what might constitute reasonable restrictions in today's changing legal landscape? After all, in the Internet environment there are no physical borders, so geographic restrictions are no longer relevant. Similarly, given the rapid pace of development within the information technology industry, restricting an employee from working in the area for one year could seriously affect the employee's career.

DEFINING "REASONABILITY" IN THE INTERNET CONTEXT In view of the dynamic nature and the global reach of the Internet, some courts have begun to redefine what constitute "reasonable" restrictions in covenants not to compete. A case decided by a federal district court in New York is instructive in this respect. The case involved Mark Schlack, who worked as a Web site manager and vice president for EarthWeb, Inc. EarthWeb provides products and services to business professionals in the information technology industry. When he was hired by EarthWeb, Schlack signed a covenant not to compete stating that, on termination of his employment, he would not work for any competing company for one year. When Schlack later accepted an offer from another company to design a Web site, EarthWeb sued to enforce the covenant not to compete.

The court refused to enforce the covenant, in part because there was no evidence that Schlack had misappropriated any of EarthWeb's trade secrets or solicited EarthWeb's clients, as EarthWeb had claimed. The court also stated, "When measured against the information technology industry in the Internet environment, a one-year hiatus [break] from the work force is several generations, if not an eternity." In effect, concluded the court, the covenant prohibited Schlack from working for a competing company located anywhere in the world for one year—because the Internet lacks physical borders.[a]

IMPLICATIONS FOR HIGH-TECH INDUSTRIES What are the implications of this case—and some similar cases[b]—for employers in high-tech industries? The consensus among legal specialists in this area is that employees who sign covenants not to compete should be given some counterbalancing benefits—such as a continuation of salary and/or other benefits during the specified period of noncompetition. Generally, a court will be much more likely to enforce a noncompete agreement if it contains fair and reasonable counterbalancing provisions. Additionally, because for Web-based work the geographic restriction can be worldwide in scope, the time restriction should be narrowed considerably to compensate for the extensive geographic restriction.[c]

FOR CRITICAL ANALYSIS

Other than having their employees sign covenants not to compete, what actions might companies in high-tech industries take to encourage their employees to keep trade secrets confidential?

a. *EarthWeb, Inc. v. Schlack,* 71 F.Supp.2d 299 (S.D.N.Y. 1999).
b. See, for example, *National Business Services, Inc. v. Wright,* 2 F.Supp.2d 701 (E.D.Pa. 1998).
c. For other guidelines for high-tech companies to consider when forming noncompete covenants, see Beverly Garofalo and Mitchell L. Fishberg, "Trade Secrets: Noncompete Agreements," *The National Law Journal,* January 17, 2000.

convert the terms into reasonable ones and then enforce the reformed covenant. This presents a problem, however, in that the judge, implicitly, has become a party to the contract. Consequently, contract **reformation** is usually carried out by a court only when necessary to prevent undue burdens or hardships.

Unconscionable Contracts or Clauses. Ordinarily, a court does not look at the fairness or equity of a contract; for example, a court normally will not inquire into the adequacy of consideration. Persons are assumed to be reasonably intelligent, and the courts do not come to their aid just because they have made unwise or foolish bargains. In certain circumstances, however, bargains are so oppressive that the courts relieve innocent parties of part or all of their duties. Such a bargain is called an **unconscionable contract** (or **unconscionable clause**). Both the Uniform Commercial Code (UCC) and the Uniform Consumer Credit Code (UCCC) embody the unconscionability concept—the former with regard to the sale of goods and the latter with regard to consumer loans and the waiver of rights.[4]

Procedural Unconscionability. Procedural unconscionability has to do with how a term becomes part of a contract and relates to factors bearing on a party's lack of knowledge or understanding of the contract terms because of inconspicuous print, unintelligible language ("legalese"), lack of opportunity to read the contract or ask questions about its meaning, and other factors. Procedural unconscionability sometimes relates to purported lack of voluntariness because of a disparity in bargaining power between the two parties. Contracts entered into because of one party's vastly superior bargaining power may be deemed unconscionable. These situations usually involve an **adhesion contract**, which is a contract drafted by the dominant party and then presented to the other—the adhering party—on a "take-it-or-leave-it" basis.[5]

Substantive Unconscionability. Substantive unconscionability characterizes those contracts, or portions of contracts, that are oppressive or overly harsh. Courts generally focus on provisions that deprive one party of the benefits of the agreement or leave that party without remedy for nonperformance by the other. For example, suppose that a welfare recipient with a fourth-grade education agrees to purchase a refrigerator for $2,000 and signs a two-year installment contract. The same type of refrigerator usually sells for $400 on the market. Some courts have held this type of contract to be unconscionable, despite the general rule that the courts will not inquire into the adequacy of the consideration, because the contract terms are so oppressive as to "shock the conscience" of the court.[6]

Exculpatory Clauses. Often closely related to the concept of unconscionability are **exculpatory clauses**, defined as clauses that release a party from liability in the event of monetary or physical injury, *no matter who is at fault.* Indeed, some courts refer to such clauses in terms of unconscionability. ● **EXAMPLE #4** Suppose, for example, that Madison Manufacturing Company hires a laborer and has him sign a contract containing the following clause:

> Said employee hereby agrees with employer, in consideration of such employment, that he will take upon himself all risks incident to his position and will in no case hold the company liable for any injury or damage he may sustain, in his person or otherwise, by accidents or injuries in the factory, or which may result from defective machinery or carelessness or misconduct of himself or any other employee in service of the employer.

This contract provision attempts to remove Madison's potential liability for injuries occurring to the employee, and it would usually be held contrary to public policy.[7] ● Additionally, exculpatory clauses found in agreements to lease commercial property are also, in the majority of cases, held to be contrary to public policy, and such clauses are almost universally held to be illegal and unenforceable when they are included in residential property leases.

Generally, an exculpatory clause will not be enforced if the party seeking its enforcement is involved in a business that is important to the public interest. These businesses include public utilities, common carriers, and banks. Because of the essential nature of these services, the companies offering them have an advantage in bargaining strength and could insist that anyone contracting for their services agree not to hold them liable. With no potential liability, the companies might be less careful, and the number of injuries could increase.

Exculpatory clauses may be enforced, however, when the parties seeking their enforcement are not involved in businesses considered important to the public interest. These

---

[4] See, for example, UCC Sections 2–302 and 2–719 (discussed in Chapters 14 and 16, respectively) and UCCC Sections 5.108 and 1.107.
[5] See, for example, *Henningsen v. Bloomfield Motors, Inc.,* 32 N.J. 358, 161 A.2d 69 (1960).

[6] See, for example, *Jones v. Star Credit Corp.,* 59 Misc.2d 189, 298 N.Y.S.2d 264 (1969). This case is presented in Chapter 14 as Case 14.3.
[7] For a case with similar facts, see *Little Rock & Fort Smith Railway Co. v. Eubanks,* 48 Ark. 460, 3 S.W. 808 (1887). In such a case, the exculpatory clause may also be illegal because it violates a state workers' compensation law.

businesses have included health clubs, amusement parks, horse-rental operations, golf-cart concessions, and skydiving organizations. Because these services are not essential, the firms offering them are sometimes regarded as having no relative advantage in bargaining strength, and anyone contracting for their services is considered to do so voluntarily. In the following case, the question was whether an exculpatory clause could be enforced against a racer who, although she was likely aware of the organizers' requirement that she sign the clause, somehow participated in the race without signing it.

CASE 9.3　Beaver v. Grand Prix Karting Association, Inc.

United States Court of Appeals, Seventh Circuit, 2001.
246 F.3d 905.
http://www.ca7.uscourts.gov/op3.fwx[a]

FACTS Dorothy Beaver began racing go-karts in 1985. Many of the races required her to sign an exculpatory clause to participate. In 1993, she signed a clause to participate in the annual Elkhart Grand Prix, a series of races in Elkhart, Indiana, organized by Grand Prix Karting Association, Inc., and others. The next year, she returned for another Grand Prix. During the event in which she drove, a piece of foam padding used as a course barrier was torn from its base and ended up on the track. A portion of the padding struck Beaver in the head, and another portion was thrown into oncoming traffic, causing a multikart collision during which she sustained severe injuries. She and her husband, Stacy, filed a suit in federal district court against the organizers and others on various tort grounds. The organizers could not find an exculpatory clause signed by Beaver for the 1994 race, but argued in part that even if she had not signed one, her actions showed her intent to be bound by its terms. When the court entered a judgment in favor of the organizers, Beaver appealed to the U.S. Court of Appeals for the Seventh Circuit.

_____

a. In the "Last Name or Corporation" section, click on "Begins," enter "Beaver" in the box, and click on "Search for Person." When the result appears, click on the docket number to access the opinion. The U.S. Court of Appeals for the Seventh Circuit maintains this Web site.

ISSUE Can an individual, by participating in an event that requires the execution of an exculpatory clause, be bound to its terms even if she or he has not signed it?

DECISION Yes. The U.S. Court of Appeals for the Seventh Circuit affirmed the decision of the lower court, binding Beaver to the terms of the clause.

REASON The U.S. Court of Appeals for the Seventh Circuit pointed out that "courts repeatedly have held that assent to a contract—and that, in essence, is what [an exculpatory clause] is—may be established by acts which manifest acceptance." A "manifestation or expression of assent necessary to form a contract may be by work, act, or conduct which evinces the intention of the parties to contract." In other words, exculpatory clauses "are governed by the same rules as other contracts." Thus, assent "may be assumed where a knowledgeable party enters into the contract, aware of the limitation and its legal effect, without indicating non-acquiescence to those terms." The court noted that "[b]ased on the evidence presented, the jury reasonably concluded that it is the custom and practice of the go kart industry, as well as the Elkhart Grand Prix, to require race participants to execute releases. The jury further reasonably concluded that Beaver was well aware of this requirement and chose to participate in the 1994 race anyway. * * * [T]hese facts sufficiently establish Beaver's assent to the release."

FOR CRITICAL ANALYSIS—Economic Consideration
Why would the organizers of a race require that all participants sign exculpatory clauses?

THE EFFECT OF ILLEGALITY

As a general rule, a court will not enforce or rescind (cancel) an illegal contract. In other words, a court will not aid either party. In most illegal contracts, both parties are considered to be equally at fault—*in pari delicto*. If the contract is executory (not yet fulfilled), neither party can enforce it. If it is executed, there can be neither contractual nor quasi-contractual recovery.

That one wrongdoer in an illegal contract is unjustly enriched at the expense of the other is of no concern to the law—except under certain circumstances (to be discussed shortly). The major justification for this hands-off attitude is that it is improper to place the machinery of justice at the disposal of a plaintiff who has broken the law by entering into an illegal bargain. Another justification is the hoped-for deterrent effect of this general rule. A plaintiff who suffers a loss because of an illegal bargain will presumably be deterred from entering into similar illegal bargains in the future.

There are exceptions to the general rule that neither party to an illegal bargain can sue for breach and neither can recover for performance rendered. We look at these exceptions here.

Justifiable Ignorance of the Facts. When one of the parties to a contract is relatively innocent (has no knowledge or any reason to know that the contract is illegal), that party can often obtain restitution or recovery of benefits conferred in a partially executed contract. The courts do not enforce the contract but do allow the parties to return to their original positions.

It is also possible for an innocent party who has fully performed under the contract to enforce the contract against the guilty party. For example, if a party engages in an illegal act by selling certain goods in violation of the law and contracts with a trucking firm to deliver the goods for $1,000, the trucking firm, as an innocent party, will be entitled to collect the $1,000 once the delivery is made.

Members of Protected Classes. When a statute protects a specific class of people, a member of that class can enforce an illegal contract even though the other party cannot. For example, statutes prohibit certain employees (such as flight attendants) from working more than a specified number of hours per month. These employees thus constitute a class protected by statute. An employee who is required to work more than the maximum can recover for those extra hours of service.

Another example of statutes designed to protect a particular class of people are **blue sky laws**, which are state laws that regulate and supervise investment companies for the protection of the public. (The phrase *blue sky laws* dates to a 1917 decision by the United States Supreme Court in which the Court declared that the purpose of such laws was to prevent "speculative schemes which have no more basis than so many feet of 'blue sky.'")[8] These laws are intended to stop the sale of stock in fly-by-night concerns, such as visionary oil wells and distant and perhaps nonexistent gold mines. Investors are protected as a class and can sue to recover the purchase price of stock issued in violation of such laws.

Most states also have statutes regulating the sale of insurance. If an insurance company violates a statute when selling insurance, the purchaser can nevertheless enforce the policy and recover from the insurer.

Withdrawal from an Illegal Agreement. If the illegal part of a bargain has not yet been performed, the party tendering performance can withdraw from the bargain and recover the performance or its value. ● **EXAMPLE #5** Suppose that Martha and Andy decide to wager (illegally) on the outcome of a boxing match. Each deposits money with a stakeholder, who agrees to pay the winner of the bet. At this point, each party has performed part of the agreement, but the illegal part of the contract will not occur until the money is paid to the winner. Before such payment occurs, either party is entitled to withdraw from the agreement by giving notice to the stakeholder of his or her withdrawal. ●

Fraud, Duress, or Undue Influence. Whenever a plaintiff has been induced to enter into an illegal bargain as a result of fraud, duress, or undue influence, she or he can either enforce the contract or recover for its value.

---

[8] *Hall v. Geiger-Jones Co.*, 242 U.S. 539, 37 S.Ct. 217, 61 L.Ed. 480 (1917).

Chapter Summary   Capacity and Legality

CONTRACTUAL CAPACITY	
Minors (See pages 183–185.)	A minor is a person who has not yet reached the age of majority. In most states, the age of majority is eighteen for contract purposes. Contracts with minors are voidable at the option of the minor.

Chapter Summary	Capacity and Legality—Continued

Minors—continued	1. *Disaffirmance*—Defined as the legal avoidance of a contractual obligation.
	
	  a. Disaffirmance can take place (in most states) at any time during minority and within a reasonable time after the minor has reached the age of majority.
	
	  b. If a minor disaffirms part of a contract, the entire contract must be disaffirmed.
	
	  c. When disaffirming executed contracts, the minor has a duty to return received goods if they are still in the minor's control or (in some states) to pay their reasonable value.
	
	  d. A minor who has committed an act of fraud (such as misrepresentation of age) will be denied the right to disaffirm by some courts.
	
	  e. A minor may disaffirm a contract for necessaries but remains liable for the reasonable value of the goods.
	
	2. *Ratification*—Defined as the acceptance, or affirmation, of a legal obligation; may be express or implied.
	
	  a. Express ratification—Exists when the minor, through a writing or an oral agreement, explicitly assumes the obligations imposed by the contract.
	
	  b. Implied ratification—Exists when the conduct of the minor is inconsistent with disaffirmance or when the minor fails to disaffirm an executed contract within a reasonable time after reaching the age of majority.
	
	3. *Parents' liability*—Generally, except for contracts for necessaries, parents are not liable for the contracts made by minor children acting on their own, nor are parents liable for minors' torts except in certain circumstances.
	
	4. *Emancipation*—Occurs when a child's parent or legal guardian relinquishes the legal right to exercise control over the child. Normally, a minor who leaves home to support himself or herself is considered emancipated. In some jurisdictions, minors themselves are permitted to petition for emancipation for limited purposes.

Intoxicated Persons (See page 185.)	1. A contract entered into by an intoxicated person is voidable at the option of the intoxicated person if the person was sufficiently intoxicated to lack mental capacity, even if the intoxication was voluntary. 2. A contract with an intoxicated person is enforceable if, despite being intoxicated, the person understood the legal consequences of entering into the contract.
Mentally Incompetent Persons (See pages 185–186.)	1. A contract made by a person adjudged by a court to be mentally incompetent is void. 2. A contract made by a mentally incompetent person not adjudged by a court to be mentally incompetent is voidable at the option of the mentally incompetent person.
LEGALITY	
Contracts Contrary to Statute (See pages 186–187.)	1. *Usury*—Usury occurs when a lender makes a loan at an interest rate above the lawful maximum. The maximum rate of interest varies from state to state. 2. *Gambling*—Gambling contracts that contravene (go against) state statutes are deemed illegal and thus void. 3. *Sabbath (Sunday) laws*—These laws prohibit the formation or the performance of certain contracts on Sunday. Such laws vary widely from state to state, and many states do not enforce them.

(Continued)

Chapter Summary	Capacity and Legality—Continued
Contracts Contrary to Statute— continued	4. *Licensing statutes*—Contracts entered into by persons who do not have a license, when one is required by statute, will not be enforceable *unless* the underlying purpose of the statute is to raise government revenues (and not to protect the public from unauthorized practitioners).
Contracts Contrary to Public Policy (See pages 187–191.)	1. *Contracts in restraint of trade*—Contracts to reduce or restrain free competition are illegal. Most such contracts are now prohibited by statutes. An exception is a *covenant not to compete*. It is usually enforced by the courts if the terms are ancillary to a contract (such as a contract for the sale of a business or an employment contract) and are reasonable as to time and area of restraint. Courts tend to scrutinize covenants not to compete closely. If a covenant is overbroad, a court may either reform the covenant to fall within reasonable constraints and then enforce the reformed contract or declare the covenant void and thus unenforceable.
	2. *Unconscionable contracts and clauses*—When a contract or contract clause is so unfair that it is oppressive to one party, it can be deemed unconscionable; as such, it is illegal and cannot be enforced.
	3. *Exculpatory clauses*—An exculpatory clause is a clause that releases a party from liability in the event of monetary or physical injury, no matter who is at fault. In certain situations, exculpatory clauses may be contrary to public policy and thus unenforceable.
Effect of Illegality (See pages 191–192.)	In general, an illegal contract is void, and the courts will not aid either party when both parties are considered to be equally at fault *(in pari delicto)*. If the contract is executory, neither party can enforce it. If the contract is executed, there can be neither contractual nor quasi-contractual recovery. Exceptions (situations in which recovery is allowed):
	1. When one party to the contract is relatively innocent.
	2. When one party to the contract is a member of a group of persons protected by statute.
	3. When either party seeks to recover consideration given for an illegal contract before the illegal act is performed.
	4. When one party was induced to enter into an illegal bargain through fraud, duress, or undue influence.

For Review

① What are some exceptions to the rule that a minor can disaffirm any contract?

② Under what circumstances does intoxication make a contract voidable?

③ Does mental incompetence necessarily render a contract void?

④ Under what circumstances will a covenant not to compete be enforceable? When will such covenants not be enforced?

⑤ What is an exculpatory clause? In what circumstances might exculpatory clauses be enforced? When will they not be enforced?

Questions and Case Problems

9–1. Contracts by Minors. Kalen is a seventeen-year-old minor who has just graduated from high school. He is attending a university two hundred miles from home and has contracted to rent an apartment near the university for one year at $500 per month. He is working at a convenience store to earn enough income to be self-supporting. After living in the apartment and paying monthly rent for four months, he becomes involved in a dispute with his landlord. Kalen, still a minor, moves out and returns the key to the landlord. The landlord wants to hold Kalen liable for the balance of the payments due under the lease. Discuss fully Kalen's liability in this situation.

9–2. Covenants Not to Compete. Joseph, who owns the only pizza parlor in Middletown, learns that Giovanni is about to open a competing pizza parlor in the same small town, just a few blocks from Joseph's restaurant. Joseph offers Giovanni $10,000 in return for Giovanni's promise not to open a pizza parlor in the Middletown area. Giovanni accepts the $10,000 but goes ahead with his plans, in spite of the agreement. When Giovanni opens his restaurant for business, Joseph sues to enjoin (prevent) Giovanni's continued operation of his restaurant or to recover the $10,000. The court denies recovery. On what basis?

9–3. Intoxication. After Katie has several drinks one night, she sells Emily a valuable fur stole for $10. The next day, Katie offers the $10 to Emily and requests the return of her stole. Emily refuses, claiming that they had a valid contract of sale. Katie states that she was intoxicated at the time the bargain was made, and thus the contract is voidable at her option. Who is right? Explain.

9–4. Mental Incompetence. Jermal has been the owner of a car dealership for a number of years. One day, Jermal sold one of his most expensive cars to Kessler. At the time of the sale, Jermal thought Kessler acted in a peculiar manner, but he gave the matter no further thought until four months later, when Kessler's court-appointed guardian appeared at Jermal's office, tendered back the car, and demanded Kessler's money back. The guardian informed Jermal that Kessler had been adjudicated mentally incompetent two months earlier by a proper court.

(a) Discuss the rights of the parties in this situation.
(b) If Kessler had been adjudicated mentally incompetent before the contract was formed, what would be the legal effect of the contract?

9–5. Licensing Statutes. State X requires that persons who prepare and serve liquor in the form of drinks at commercial establishments be licensed by the state to do so. The only requirement for obtaining a yearly license is that the person be at least twenty-one years old. Mickey, aged thirty-five, is hired as a bartender for the Southtown Restaurant. Gerald, a staunch alumnus of a nearby university, brings twenty of his friends to the restaurant to celebrate a football victory one afternoon. Gerald orders four rounds of drinks, and the bill is nearly $200. On learning that Mickey has failed to renew his bartender's license, Gerald refuses to pay, claiming that the contract is unenforceable. Discuss whether Gerald is correct.

9–6. Usury. Tony's Tortilla Factory, Inc., had two checking accounts with First Bank. Due to financial difficulties, Tony's wrote a total of 2,165 checks (totaling $88,000) for which there were insufficient funds in the accounts. First Bank paid the overdrawn checks but imposed an "NSF" (nonsufficient funds) fee of $20 for each check paid. The owners of Tony's sued First Bank and one of its officers, alleging, among other

things, that the $20-per-check fee was essentially "interest" charged by the bank for Tony's use of the bank's funds (the funds the bank advanced to cover the bad checks); because the rate of "interest" charged by the bank ($20 per check) exceeded the rate allowed by law, it was usurious. First Bank claimed that its NSF fees were not interest but fees charged to cover its costs in processing checks drawn on accounts with insufficient funds. How should the court decide this issue? Discuss fully. [*First Bank v. Tony's Tortilla Factory, Inc.,* 877 S.W.2d 285 (Tex. 1994)]

9–7. Minority. Sergei Samsonov is a Russian and one of the top hockey players in the world. When Samsonov was seventeen years old, he signed a contract to play hockey for two seasons with the Central Sports Army Club, a Russian club known by the abbreviation CSKA. Before the start of the second season, Samsonov learned that because of a dispute among CSKA coaches, he would not be playing in Russia's premier hockey league. Samsonov hired Athletes and Artists, Inc. (A&A), an American sports agency, to make a deal with a U.S. hockey team. Samsonov signed a contract to play for the Detroit Vipers (whose corporate name was, at the time, Arena Associates, Inc.). Neither A&A nor Arena knew about the CSKA contract. CSKA filed a suit in a federal district court against Arena and others, alleging, among other things, wrongful interference with a contractual relationship. What effect will Samsonov's age have on the outcome of this suit? [*Central Sports Army Club v. Arena Associates, Inc.,* 952 F.Supp. 181 (S.D.N.Y. 1997)]

9–8. Exculpatory Clause. Norbert Eelbode applied for a job with Travelers Inn in the state of Washington. As part of the application process, Eelbode was sent to Laura Grothe, a physical therapist at Chec Medical Centers, Inc., for a preemployment physical exam. Before the exam, Eelbode signed a document that stated in part, "I hereby release Chec and the Washington Readicare Medical Group and its physicians from all liability arising from any injury to me resulting from my participation in the exam." During the exam, Grothe asked Eelbode to lift an item while bending from the waist using only his back with his knees locked. Eelbode experienced immediate sharp and burning pain in his lower back and down the back of his right leg. Eelbode filed a suit in a Washington state court against Grothe and Chec, claiming that he was injured because of an improperly administered back torso strength test. Citing the document that Eelbode signed, Grothe and Chec filed a motion for summary judgment. Should the court grant the motion? Why or why not? [*Eelbode v. Chec Medical Centers, Inc.,* 984 P.2d 436 (Wash.App. 1999)]

CASE PROBLEM WITH SAMPLE ANSWER

9–9. In 1993, Mutual Service Casualty Insurance Co. and its affiliates (collectively, MSI) hired Thomas Brass as an insurance agent. Three years later, Brass entered into a career agent's contract with MSI. This contract contained provisions regarding Brass's activities after termination. These provisions stated that, for a period of not less than one year, Brass could not solicit any MSI customers to "lapse, cancel, or replace" any insurance contract in force with MSI in an effort to take that business to a competitor. If he did, MSI could at any time refuse to pay the commissions that it otherwise owed him. The contract also restricted Brass from working for American National Insurance Co. for three years after termination. In 1998, Brass quit MSI and immediately went to work for American National, soliciting MSI customers. MSI filed a suit in a Wisconsin state court against Brass, claiming that he had violated the noncompete terms of his MSI contract. Should the court enforce the covenant not to compete? Why or why not? [*Mutual Service Casualty Insurance Co. v. Brass,* 625 N.W.2d 648 (Wis.App. 2001)]

▶ To view a sample answer for this case problem, go to this book's Web site at **http://fundamentals.westbuslaw.com** and click on "Interactive Study Center."

9–10. Unconscionability. Frank Rodziewicz was driving a Volvo tractor-trailer on Interstate 90 in Lake County, Indiana, when he struck a concrete barrier. His tractor-trailer became stuck on the barrier, and the Indiana State Police contacted Waffco Heavy Duty Towing, Inc., to assist in the recovery of the truck. Before beginning work, Waffco told Rodziewicz that it would cost $275 to tow the truck. There was no discussion of labor or any other costs. Rodziewicz told Waffco to take the truck to a local Volvo dealership. Within a few minutes, Waffco pulled the truck off the barrier and towed it to Waffco's nearby towing yard. Rodziewicz was soon notified that, in addition to the $275 towing fee, he would have to pay $4,070 in labor costs and that Waffco would not release the truck until payment was made. Rodziewicz paid the total amount. Disputing the labor charge, however, he filed a suit in an Indiana state court against Waffco, alleging in part breach of contract. Was the towing contract unconscionable? Would it make a difference if the parties had discussed the labor charge before the tow? Explain. [*Rodziewicz v. Waffco Heavy Duty Towing, Inc.,* 763 N.E.2d 491 (Ind.App. 2002)]

CAPACITY AND LEGALITY

For updated links to resources available on the Web, as well as other materials, visit this text's Web site at

http://fundamentals.westbuslaw.com

For an example of state statutory provisions governing the emancipation of minors, you can view Wyoming's statutes at

http://legisweb.state.wy.us/statutes/sub14.htm

Online Legal Research

Go to the *Fundamentals of Business Law* home page at **http://fundamentals. westbuslaw.com**. Select "Interactive Study Center" and then click on "Chapter 9." There you will find the following Internet research exercises that you can perform to learn more about topics covered in this chapter.

Activity 9–1: LEGAL PERSPECTIVE—Covenants Not to Compete
Activity 9–2: MANAGEMENT PERSPECTIVE—Minors and the Law
Activity 9–3: SOCIAL PERSPECTIVE—Online Gambling

Before the Test

Go to the *Fundamentals of Business Law* home page at **http://fundamentals. westbuslaw.com**. Click on "Interactive Quizzes." You will find at least twenty interactive questions relating to this chapter.

Westlaw® Campus

If your textbook provided for a subscription to Westlaw® Campus, or if you have otherwise purchased access to the Westlaw Campus database, you can access any of the cases presented or cited in this chapter by using your Westlaw Campus account.

(CHAPTER OBJECTIVES

After reading this chapter, you should be able to answer the following questions:

① In what types of situations might genuineness of assent to a contract's terms be lacking?

② What is the difference between a mistake of value or quality and a mistake of fact?

③ What elements must exist for fraudulent misrepresentation to occur?

④ What contracts must be in writing to be enforceable?

⑤ What is parol evidence? When is it admissible to clarify the terms of a written contract?

An otherwise valid contract may still be unenforceable if the parties have not genuinely assented to its terms. As mentioned in Chapter 7, lack of genuine assent is a *defense* to the enforcement of a contract. The law seeks to ensure that the citizens of a state will do justice to one another. If the law were to enforce contracts not genuinely assented to by the contracting parties, injustice would result. The first part of this chapter focuses on the kinds of factors that indicate that genuineness of assent to a contract may be lacking.

A contract that is otherwise valid may also be unenforceable if it is not in the proper form. For example, if a contract is required by law to be in writing and there is no written evidence of the agreement, it may not be enforce-able. In the second part of this chapter, we examine the kinds of contracts that require a writing under what is called the *Statute of Frauds*. The chapter concludes with a discussion of the parol evidence rule, under which courts determine the admissibility at trial of evidence extraneous (external) to written contracts.

Genuineness of Assent

Genuineness of assent may be lacking because of mistake, fraudulent misrepresentation, undue influence, or duress. Generally, a party who demonstrates that he or she did not genuinely assent to the terms of a contract can choose either to carry out the contract or to rescind (cancel) it and thus avoid the entire transaction.

MISTAKES

We all make mistakes, so it is not surprising that mistakes are made when contracts are created. In certain circumstances, contract law allows a contract to be avoided on the basis of mistake. Realize, though, that the concept of mistake in contract law has to do with mistaken assumptions relating to contract formation. For example, the error you make when you send your monthly bank loan payment to your plumber "by mistake" is totally different from the kind of mistake that we are discussing here. In contract law, a mistake may be a defense to the enforcement of a contract if it can be proved that the parties entered into the contract under differing assumptions about the subject matter of the contract.

Courts have considerable difficulty in specifying the circumstances that justify allowing a mistake to invalidate a contract. Generally, though, courts distinguish between *mistakes as to judgment of market value or conditions* and *mistakes as to fact*. Only the latter normally have legal significance. ● EXAMPLE #1 Jud Wheeler contracts to buy ten acres of land because he believes that he can resell the land at a profit to Bart. Can Jud escape his contractual obligations if it later turns out that he was mistaken? Not likely. Jud's overestimation of the value of the land or of Bart's interest in it is an ordinary risk of business for which a court normally will not provide relief. Now suppose that Jud purchases a painting of a landscape from Roth's Gallery. Both Jud and Roth believe that the painting is by the artist van Gogh. Jud later discovers that the painting is a very clever fake. Because neither Jud nor Roth was aware of this fact when they made their deal, Jud can normally rescind the contract and recover the purchase price of the painting. ●

Mistakes occur in two forms—*unilateral* and *bilateral* (*mutual*). A unilateral mistake is made by only one of the contracting parties; a mutual mistake is made by both.

Unilateral Mistakes. A unilateral mistake occurs when only one party is mistaken as to a *material fact*—that is, a fact important to the subject matter of the contract. Generally, a unilateral mistake does not afford the mistaken party any right to relief from the contract. In other words, the contract normally is enforceable against the mistaken party. ● EXAMPLE #2 Ellen intends to sell her motor home for $17,500. When she learns that Chin is interested in buying a used motor home, she types a letter offering to sell her vehicle to him. When typing the letter, however, she mis-

takenly keys in the price of $15,700. Chin writes back, accepting Ellen's offer. Even though Ellen intended to sell her motor home for $17,500, she has made a unilateral mistake and is bound by contract to sell the vehicle to Chin for $15,700. ●

There are at least two exceptions to this rule.[1] First, if the *other* party to the contract knows or should have known that a mistake of fact was made, the contract may not be enforceable. In the above example, if Chin knew that Ellen intended to sell her motor home for $17,500, then Ellen's unilateral mistake (stating $15,700 in her offer) may render the resulting contract unenforceable. The second exception arises when a unilateral mistake of fact was due to a significant mathematical error in addition, subtraction, division, or multiplication and was made inadvertently and without gross (extreme) negligence. If a contractor's bid was low because he or she made a substantial mistake in addition when totaling the estimated costs, any contract resulting from the bid normally may be rescinded. Of course, in both situations, the mistake must still involve some *material fact*.

Bilateral (Mutual) Mistakes. When both parties are mistaken about the same material fact, the contract can be rescinded by either party.[2] Note that, as with unilateral mistakes, the mistake must be about a *material fact* (one that is important and central to the contract—as was the one concerning the "van Gogh" painting in Example #1). If, instead, a mutual mistake concerns the later market value or quality of the object of the contract, the contract normally can be enforced by either party. This rule is based on the theory that both parties assume certain risks when they enter into a contract. Without this rule, almost any party who did not receive what she or he considered a fair bargain could argue bilateral mistake.

A word or term in a contract may be subject to more than one reasonable interpretation. In that situation, if the parties to the contract attach materially different meanings to the term, their mutual misunderstanding may allow the contract to be rescinded. ● EXAMPLE #3 In *Raffles v. Wichelhaus*,[3] a classic case involving a mutual mistake, Wichelhaus purchased a shipment of cotton from Raffles to arrive on a ship called the *Peerless* from Bombay, India. Wichelhaus meant a ship called the *Peerless* sailing from Bombay in October; Raffles

---

[1] The *Restatement (Second) of Contracts*, Section 153, liberalizes the general rule to take into account the modern trend of allowing avoidance in some circumstances even though only one party has been mistaken.
[2] *Restatement (Second) of Contracts*, Section 152.
[3] 159 Eng.Rep. 375 (1864).

meant another ship called the *Peerless* sailing from Bombay in December. When the goods arrived on the December *Peerless*, Raffles delivered them to Wichelhaus. By that time, however, Wichelhaus was no longer willing to accept them. The British court hearing the case stated, "There is nothing on the face of the contract to show that any particular ship called the 'Peerless' was meant; but the moment it appears that two ships called the 'Peerless' were about to sail from Bombay there is a latent ambiguity. . . . That being so, there was no consensus . . . and therefore no binding contract." ●

FRAUDULENT MISREPRESENTATION

Although fraud is a tort, the presence of fraud also affects the genuineness of the innocent party's consent to a contract. When an innocent party consents to a contract with fraudulent terms, the contract usually can be avoided because he or she has not *voluntarily* consented to the terms.[4] Normally, the innocent party can either rescind (cancel) the contract and be restored to his or her original position or enforce the contract and seek damages for injuries resulting from the fraud.

Typically, fraud involves three elements:

① A misrepresentation of a material fact must occur.

② There must be an intent to deceive.

③ The innocent party must justifiably rely on the misrepresentation.

---

[4] *Restatement (Second) of Contracts*, Sections 163 and 164.

Additionally, to collect damages, a party must have been injured as a result of the misrepresentation.

Fraudulent misrepresentation can also occur in the online environment—see, for example, the case discussed in this chapter's *Business Law in the Online World* feature on page 201.

Misrepresentation Must Occur. The first element of proving fraud is to show that misrepresentation of a material fact has occurred. This misrepresentation can take the form of words or actions. For example, an art gallery owner's statement "This painting is a Picasso" is a misrepresentation of fact if the painting was done by another artist.

A statement of opinion is generally not subject to a claim of fraud. For example, claims such as "This computer will never break down" and "This car will last for years and years" are statements of opinion, not fact, and contracting parties should recognize them as such and not rely on them. A fact is objective and verifiable; an opinion is usually subject to debate. Therefore, a seller is allowed to "huff and puff his wares" without being liable for fraud. In certain cases, however, particularly when a naïve purchaser relies on an expert's opinion, the innocent party may be entitled to rescission or reformation (an equitable remedy granted by a court in which the terms of a contract are altered to reflect the true intentions of the parties).

In the following classic case, the court addressed the issue of whether statements made by instructors at a dancing school to one of the school's dance students qualified as statements of opinion or statements of fact.

Landmark and Classic Cases

CASE 10.1   **Vokes v. Arthur Murray, Inc.**

District Court of Appeal of Florida, Second District, 1968. 212 So.2d 906.

FACTS Audrey Vokes was a fifty-one-year-old widow. While she was attending a dance party at Davenport's School of Dancing, an Arthur Murray dancing school, an instructor sold her eight half-hour dance lessons for the sum of $14.50. Thereafter, over a period of less than sixteen months, she was sold a total of fourteen dance courses, which amounted to 2,302 hours of dancing lessons for a total cash outlay of $31,090.45 (in 2003, this would amount to more than

$125,000). All of these lessons were sold to her by salespersons who continually assured her that she was very talented, that she was progressing in her lessons, that she had great dance potential, and that they were "developing her into a beautiful dancer." Vokes contended that, in fact, she was not progressing in her dancing ability, had no "dance aptitude," and had difficulty even "hearing the musical beat." She filed suit against the school in a Florida state court, seeking rescission of her contract on the ground of fraudulent misrepresentation. When the trial court dismissed her complaint, she appealed.

(Continued)

CASE 10.1—Continued

ISSUE Could Vokes's contract be rescinded because the salespersons misrepresented her dancing ability?

DECISION Yes. The Florida appellate court reinstated Vokes's complaint and remanded the case to the trial court for further proceedings consistent with the appellate court's opinion.

REASON The court held that Vokes could avoid the contract because it was procured by false representations that she had a promising career in dancing. The court acknowledged that ordinarily, to be grounds for rescission, a misrepresentation must be one of fact rather than of opinion. The court concluded that "[a] statement of a party having * * *

superior knowledge may be regarded as a statement of fact although it would be considered as opinion if the parties were dealing on equal terms. It could be reasonably supposed here that defendants [the dance studio] had 'superior knowledge' as to whether plaintiff had 'dance potential.' "

COMMENT *This case has become a classic in contract law because it so clearly illustrates an important principle. The general rule (that a misrepresentation must be one of fact rather than one of opinion to be actionable) does not apply when the parties do not deal at arm's length or when the person to whom representations are made (such as Vokes, in this case) does not have an equal opportunity to become aware of the truth or falsity of the fact represented.*

Misrepresentation by Conduct. Misrepresentation can occur by conduct, as well as through express oral or written statements. For example, if a seller, by her or his actions, prevents a buyer from learning of some fact that is material to the contract, such an action constitutes misrepresentation by conduct.[5] ● EXAMPLE #4 Cummings contracts to purchase a racehorse from Garner. The horse is blind in one eye, but when Garner shows the horse, he skillfully conceals this fact by keeping the horse's head turned so that Cummings does not see the defect. The concealment constitutes fraud.● Another example of misrepresentation by conduct is the false denial of knowledge or information concerning facts that are material to the contract when such knowledge or information is requested.

Misrepresentation of Law. Misrepresentation of law does not *ordinarily* entitle a party to be relieved of a contract. ● EXAMPLE #5 Debbie has a parcel of property that she is trying to sell to Barry. Debbie knows that a local ordinance prohibits building anything higher than three stories on the property. Nonetheless, she tells Barry, "You can build a condominium fifty stories high if you want to." Barry buys the land and later discovers that Debbie's statement is false. Normally, Barry cannot avoid the contract because under the common law, people are assumed to know state and local laws.● Exceptions to this rule occur, however, when the misrepresenting party is in a profession known to require greater knowledge of the law than the average citizen possesses. If Debbie, in the preceding example, had been a lawyer or a real estate agent, her misrepresentation of the area's zoning status would probably have constituted fraud.

Misrepresentation by Silence. Ordinarily, neither party to a contract has a duty to come forward and disclose facts, and a contract normally will not be set aside because certain pertinent information has not been volunteered. ● EXAMPLE #6 Suppose that you are selling a car that has been in an accident and has been repaired. You do not need to volunteer this information to a potential buyer. If, however, the purchaser asks you if the car has had extensive body work and you lie, you have committed a fraudulent misrepresentation.●

Generally, if a major defect or a potentially serious problem is known to the seller but cannot reasonably be suspected to be known by the buyer, the seller may have a duty to speak. ● EXAMPLE #7 Suppose that a city fails to disclose to bidders for sewer-construction contracts the fact that subsoil conditions will cause great expense in constructing the sewer. In this situation, the city has committed fraud.[6]● Also, when the parties are in a *fiduciary relationship* (one of trust, such as partners, physician and patient, or attorney and client), there is a duty to disclose material facts; failure to do so may constitute fraud.

Intent to Deceive. The second element of fraud is knowledge on the part of the misrepresenting party that facts have been misrepresented. This element, normally called *scienter*,[7] or "guilty knowledge," generally signifies that there was an intent to deceive. *Scienter* clearly exists if a party knows that a fact is not as stated. *Scienter* also exists if a party makes a statement that he or she believes not to

---

[5] *Restatement (Second) of Contracts*, Section 160.

[6] *City of Salinas v. Souza & McCue Construction Co.*, 66 Cal.2d 217, 424 P.2d 921, 57 Cal.Rptr. 337 (1967). Normally, the seller must disclose only "latent" defects—that is, defects that would not readily be discovered. Thus, termites in a house would not be a latent defect, because a buyer could normally discover their presence.

[7] Pronounced sy-*en*-ter.

BUSINESS LAW IN THE ONLINE WORLD
Hotmail versus the Spammers

Hotmail Corporation provides free e-mail service to more than eighty million subscribers. To obtain the service, a prospective subscriber goes to Hotmail's Web site and clicks on an "I accept" button to indicate agreement to Hotmail's "Terms of Service." These terms prohibit a subscriber from using the service to send spam—unsolicited bulk e-mail similar to junk mail sent through the U.S. Postal Service. What if a subscriber, after agreeing to the Terms of Service, uses Hotmail's service to send spam? Does Hotmail have a cause of action against the subscriber?

This issue came before the court in a case brought by Hotmail against Van$ Money Pie, Inc., and others (the defendants) after they began using Hotmail's service to send spam offering to sell pornography, "get-rich-quick" schemes, and other items. Hotmail was soon inundated with hundreds of thousands of misdirected responses to the spam, including complaints from subscribers and returned e-mail that had been sent to nonexistent or incorrect addresses. The flood of replies took up a substantial amount of Hotmail's computer capacity, threatened to adversely affect subscribers' ability to send and receive e-mail, and resulted in significant costs to Hotmail for increased personnel to sort and respond to the complaints. Hotmail sued the defendants for, among other things, fraud and breach of contract and asked the court to enjoin (prohibit) the defendants from using Hotmail's service.

THE FRAUD ISSUE The court concluded that Hotmail had presented enough evidence of fraud to warrant the granting of a preliminary injunction against the defen-

dants' further use of Hotmail's service. The evidence indicated that the defendants had promised to abide by the Terms of Service without any intention of doing so and had suppressed the fact that such accounts were created for the purpose of facilitating a spamming operation. Furthermore, Hotmail had relied on the misrepresentations to allow e-mails to be transmitted over its services and to take up storage space on its computers.

BREACH OF CONTRACT A threshold issue in this case was whether Hotmail's online service agreement, with its click-on acceptance button, was an enforceable contract. Significantly, the court held that it was (for an examination of the evolution of the law regarding click-on acceptances, see Chapter 13). The court also held that the evidence indicated that the defendants had breached this contract by using their Hotmail accounts to send spam. The court concluded that "if defendants are not enjoined they will continue to create such accounts in violation of the Terms of Service."[a]

FOR CRITICAL ANALYSIS

What if the defendants claimed that they had not read the Terms of Service before they clicked on the "I accept" button? Would this claim affect the enforceability of the contract?

a. *Hotmail Corp. v. Van$ Money Pie, Inc.,* 1998 WL 388389 (N.D.Cal. 1998).

be true or makes a statement recklessly, without regard to whether it is true or false. Finally, this element is met if a party says or implies that a statement is made on some basis, such as personal knowledge or personal investigation, when it is not.

● **EXAMPLE #8** Suppose that Rolando, when selling a house to Cariton, tells Cariton that the plumbing pipe is of a certain quality. Rolando knows nothing about the quality of the pipe but does not believe it to be what she is representing it to be (and in fact it is not what she says it is). Rolando's statement induces Cariton to buy the house.

Rolando's statement is a fraudulent misrepresentation because she does not believe that what she says is true and because she knows that she does not have any basis for making the statement. Cariton can avoid the contract.●

Reliance on the Misrepresentation. The third element of fraud is *justifiable reliance* on the misrepresentation of fact. The deceived party must have a justifiable reason for relying on the misrepresentation, and the misrepresentation must be an important factor (but not necessarily the sole factor) in inducing the party to enter into the contract.

Reliance is not justified if the innocent party knows the true facts or relies on obviously extravagant statements. ● **EXAMPLE #9** If a used-car dealer tells you, "This old Cadillac will get over sixty miles to the gallon," you normally would not be justified in relying on this statement. Suppose, however, that Merkel, a bank director, induces O'Connell, a co-director, to sign a statement that the bank's assets will satisfy its liabilities by telling O'Connell, "We have plenty of assets to satisfy our creditors." This statement is false. If O'Connell

knows the true facts or, as a bank director, should know the true facts, he is not justified in relying on Merkel's statement. If O'Connell does not know the true facts, however, *and has no way of finding them out*, he may be justified in relying on the statement. ●

In the following case, a buyer claimed that he had relied on certain representations by the owner of a business in deciding whether to become a partner with the owner and ultimately buy the business.

CASE 10.2   Foley v. Parlier

Court of Appeals of Texas,
Fort Worth, 2002.
68 S.W.3d 870.

FACTS Diane Foley owned Finishes, a commercial tile business in Dallas and Fort Worth, Texas. Rick Parlier operated a residential tile business in California. In 1999, Foley and Parlier negotiated the terms of a potential partnership and purchase by Parlier of Foley's business. Parlier said that he needed to earn at least $6,000 a month to make it feasible to move to Texas. Foley assured Parlier that he would be able to make "well over [that] amount." She gave him a list of five purported contracts and represented that he would receive $8,500 per month under the contracts if he bought into the business. In a letter, she sent him photocopies of checks, claiming that they represented work done for customers. Parlier shut down his business and moved to Texas. They entered into a contract, under which Parlier was to become a partner with Foley, receive a share of the profits, be paid for certain expenses, and eventually buy the business. When Parlier did not receive any money and hired an accountant to review the firm's records, Foley terminated their relationship. Parlier filed a suit in a Texas state court against Foley, alleging in part fraud in misrepresenting what Parlier would receive. The jury ruled in Parlier's favor, and the court awarded him damages of $55,750. Foley appealed to a state intermediate

appellate court, arguing in part that there was insufficient evidence to support the jury's finding.

ISSUE Were Foley's representations sufficient to support a finding of fraud?

DECISION Yes. The state intermediate appellate court affirmed the judgment of the lower court. The appellate court concluded that there was sufficient evidence to support the jury's finding of fraud.

REASON The appellate court stated that there was "more than a scintilla [tiny amount] of evidence" to support the jury's finding of fraud. The court emphasized, "Parlier's testimony reveals that Foley utilized the checks to misrepresent the company's monthly profit. Parlier testified that when he asked if he would make more than $6,000 per month, Foley assured him he would be able to make over $6,000 a month." About the photocopied checks, Parlier said, "Well, * * * those checks show large amounts of money. $15-, $30-, $40-, $65,000, one was for $80,000, and these were monthly income checks. So looking at that, I'm thinking, well this is a very, very good business."

FOR CRITICAL ANALYSIS—Economic Consideration
Could Parlier have verified the nature of Foley's business more thoroughly before moving to Texas?

Injury to the Innocent Party. Most courts do not require a showing of injury when the action is to *rescind* (cancel) the contract—these courts hold that because rescission returns the parties to the positions they held before the contract was made, a showing of injury to the innocent party is unnecessary.[8]

For a person to recover damages caused by fraud, however, proof of an injury is universally required. The measure of damages is ordinarily equal to the property's value had it been delivered as represented, less the actual price paid for the property. In actions based on fraud, courts often award *punitive,* or *exemplary, damages,* which are granted to a plaintiff over and above the proved, actual compensation for the loss. As pointed out in Chapter 4, punitive damages are based on the public-policy consideration of punishing

---

8 See, for example, *Kaufman v. Jaffe*, 244 App.Div. 344, 279 N.Y.S. 392 (1935).

UNDUE INFLUENCE

Undue influence arises from relationships in which one party can greatly influence another party, thus overcoming that party's free will. Minors and elderly people, for example, are often under the influence of guardians. If a guardian induces a young or elderly ward (a person placed by a court under the care of a guardian) to enter into a contract that benefits the guardian, the guardian may have exerted undue influence.

Undue influence can arise from a number of confidential or fiduciary relationships, including attorney-client, physician-patient, guardian-ward, parent-child, husband-wife, and trustee-beneficiary relationships. The essential feature of undue influence is that the party being taken advantage of does not, in reality, exercise free will in entering into a contract. A contract entered into under excessive or undue influence lacks genuine assent and is therefore voidable.[9]

DURESS

Assent to the terms of a contract is not genuine if one of the parties is forced into the agreement. Forcing a party to enter into a contract because of the fear created by threats is referred to as *duress*.[10] In addition, inducing consent to a contract through blackmail or extortion constitutes duress. Duress is both a defense to the enforcement of a contract and a ground for rescission, or cancellation, of a contract. Therefore, a party who signs a contract under duress can choose to carry out the contract or to avoid the entire transaction. (The wronged party usually has this choice in cases in which assent is not real or genuine.)

Economic need is generally not sufficient to constitute duress, even when one party exacts a very high price for an item the other party needs. If the party exacting the price also creates the need, however, economic duress may be found. ● **EXAMPLE #10** The Internal Revenue Service (IRS) assessed a large tax and penalty against Weller. Weller retained Eyman to resist the assessment. Two days before the deadline for filing a reply with the IRS, Eyman declined to represent Weller unless he agreed to pay a very high fee for Eyman's services. The agreement was held to be unenforceable.[11] Although Eyman had threatened only to with-draw his services, something that he was legally entitled to do, he was responsible for delaying his withdrawal until the last two days. Because Weller was forced into either signing the contract or losing his right to challenge the IRS assessment, the agreement was secured under duress.●

The Statute of Frauds— Requirement of a Writing

Today, every state has a statute that stipulates what types of contracts must be in writing. In this text, we refer to such statutes as the **Statute of Frauds.** The primary purpose of the statute is to ensure that, for certain types of contracts, there is reliable evidence of the contracts and their terms. These types of contracts are those deemed historically to be important or complex. Although the statutes vary slightly from state to state, the following types of contracts are normally required to be in writing or evidenced by a written memorandum:

① Contracts involving interests in land.

② Contracts that cannot by their terms be performed within one year from the day after the date of formation.

③ Collateral contracts, such as promises to answer for the debt or duty of another.

④ Promises made in consideration of marriage.

⑤ Contracts for the sale of goods priced at $500 or more.

Agreements or promises that fit into one or more of these categories are said to "fall under" or "fall within" the Statute of Frauds. (Certain exceptions are made to the applicability of the Statute of Frauds in some circumstances, however, as you will read later in this section.)

The actual name of the Statute of Frauds is misleading because it does not apply to fraud. Rather, the statute denies enforceability to certain contracts that do not comply with its requirements. The name derives from an English act passed in 1677.

CONTRACTS INVOLVING INTERESTS IN LAND

Land is a form of *real property,* or real estate, which includes not only land but all physical objects that are permanently attached to the soil, such as buildings, plants, trees, and the soil itself. A contract for the sale of land ordinarily involves the entire interest in the real property, including buildings, growing crops, vegetation, minerals, timber, and anything else affixed to the land. Therefore, a *fixture* (personal property so affixed or so used as to become a part of the realty—see Chapter 29) is treated as real property.

---

[9] *Restatement (Second) of Contracts,* Section 177.

[10] *Restatement (Second) of Contracts,* Sections 174 and 175.

[11] *Thompson Crane & Trucking Co. v. Eyman,* 123 Cal.App.2d 904, 267 P.2d 1043 (1954).

Under the Statute of Frauds, a contract involving an interest in land, to be enforceable, must be evidenced by a writing.[12] If Carol, for example, contracts orally to sell Seaside Shelter to Axel but later decides not to sell, Axel cannot enforce the contract. Similarly, if Axel refuses to close the deal, Carol cannot force Axel to pay for the land by bringing a lawsuit. The Statute of Frauds is a *defense* to the enforcement of this type of oral contract.

The Statute of Frauds requires written contracts not just for the sale of land but also for the transfer of other interests in land, such as mortgages and leases. We describe these other interests in Chapter 29.

THE ONE-YEAR RULE

Contracts that cannot, *by their own terms,* be performed within one year from the day after the contract is formed must be in writing to be enforceable. Because disputes over such contracts are unlikely to occur until some time after the contracts are made, resolution of these disputes is difficult unless the contract terms have been put in writing. The one-year period begins to run *the day after the contract is formed.* Exhibit 10–1 illustrates the one-year rule.

Normally, the test for determining whether an oral contract is enforceable under the one-year rule of the Statute of Frauds is not whether the agreement is *likely* to be performed within one year from the date of contract formation but whether performance within a year is *possible.* When performance of a contract is objectively impossible during the one-year period, the oral contract will be unenforceable.

---

[12] In some states, the contract will be enforced, however, if each party admits to the existence of the oral contract in court or admits to its existence during discovery before trial (see Chapter 2).

COLLATERAL PROMISES

A **collateral promise,** or secondary promise, is one that is ancillary (subsidiary) to a principal transaction or primary contractual relationship. In other words, a collateral promise is one made by a third party to assume the debts or obligations of a primary party to a contract if that party does not perform. Any collateral promise of this nature falls under the Statute of Frauds and therefore must be in writing to be enforceable. To understand this concept, it is important to distinguish between primary and secondary promises and obligations.

Primary versus Secondary Obligations. As a general rule, a contract in which a party assumes a primary obligation does not need to be in writing to be enforceable. ● **EXAMPLE #11** Suppose that Kenneth orally contracts with Joanne's Floral Boutique to send his mother a dozen roses for Mother's Day. Kenneth promises to pay the boutique when he receives the bill for the flowers. Kenneth is a direct party to this contract and has incurred a *primary* obligation under the contract. Because he is a party to the contract and has a primary obligation to Joanne's Floral Boutique, this contract does not fall under the Statute of Frauds and does not have to be in writing to be enforceable. If Kenneth fails to compensate the florist and the florist sues him for payment, Kenneth cannot claim that the contract is unenforceable because it was not in writing.●

In contrast, a contract in which a party assumes a secondary obligation does have to be in writing to be enforceable. ● **EXAMPLE #12** Suppose that Kenneth's mother borrows $1,000 from the Medford Trust Company on a promissory note payable six months later. Kenneth promises the bank officer handling the loan that he will pay the $1,000 *if his mother does not pay the loan on time.* Kenneth, in this situation, becomes what is known as a *guarantor* on

EXHIBIT 10–1 THE ONE-YEAR RULE

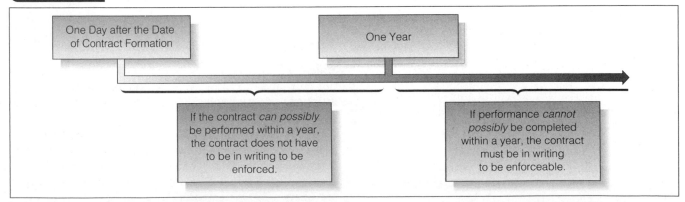

the loan; that is, he is guaranteeing to the bank (the creditor) that he will pay the loan if his mother fails to do so. This kind of collateral promise, in which the guarantor states that he or she will become responsible only if the primary party does not perform, must be in writing to be enforceable.● We return to the concept of guaranty and the distinction between primary and secondary obligations in Chapter 21, in the context of creditors' rights.

An Exception—The "Main Purpose" Rule. An oral promise to answer for the debt of another is covered by the Statute of Frauds unless the guarantor's purpose in accepting secondary liability is to secure a personal benefit. Under the "main purpose" rule, this type of contract need not be in writing.[13] The assumption is that a court can infer from the circumstances of a case whether a "leading objective" of the promisor was to secure a personal benefit.

●▐EXAMPLE #13▌ Oswald contracts with Machine Manufacturing Company to have some machines custom-made for Oswald's factory. She promises Allrite Materials Supply Company, Machine Manufacturing's supplier, that if Allrite continues to deliver materials to Machine Manufacturing, she will guarantee payment. This promise need not be in writing, even though the effect may be to pay the debt of another, because Oswald's main purpose is to secure a benefit for herself.[14]●

Another typical application of the so-called main purpose doctrine is the situation in which one creditor guarantees the debtor's debt to another creditor to forestall litigation. This allows the debtor to remain in business long enough to generate profits sufficient to pay *both* creditors. In this situation, the guaranty does not need to be in writing to be enforceable.

PROMISES MADE IN CONSIDERATION OF MARRIAGE

A unilateral promise to pay a sum of money or to give property in consideration of marriage must be in writing. If Mr. Baumann promises to pay Joe Villard $10,000 if Villard marries Baumann's daughter, the promise must be in writing to be enforceable. The same rule applies to **prenuptial agreements**—agreements made before marriage (also called *antenuptial agreements*) that define each partner's ownership rights in the other partner's property. For example, a prospective wife or husband may wish to limit the amount the prospective spouse can obtain if the marriage ends in

divorce. Prenuptial agreements made in consideration of marriage must be in writing to be enforceable.

Generally, courts tend to give more credence to prenuptial agreements that are accompanied by consideration. ●▐EXAMPLE #14▌ Maureen, who has little money, marries Kaiser, who has a net worth of $300 million. Kaiser has several children, and he wants them to receive most of his wealth on his death. Prior to their marriage, Maureen and Kaiser draft and sign a prenuptial agreement in which Kaiser promises to give Maureen $100,000 per year for the rest of her life should they divorce. As consideration for consenting to this amount, Kaiser offers Maureen $500,000. If Maureen consents to the agreement and accepts the $500,000, very likely a court would hold this to be a valid prenuptial agreement should the agreement ever be contested.●

CONTRACTS FOR THE SALE OF GOODS

The Uniform Commercial Code (UCC) contains Statute of Frauds provisions that require written evidence of a contract. Section 2–201 contains the major provision, which generally requires a writing or memorandum for the sale of goods priced at $500 or more ($5,000 or more under the 2003 Amendments to the UCC—see Chapter 14). A writing that will satisfy the UCC requirement need only state the quantity term; other terms agreed on need not be stated "accurately" in the writing, as long as they adequately reflect both parties' intentions. The contract will not be enforceable, however, for any quantity greater than that set forth in the writing. In addition, the writing must be signed by the person against whom enforcement is sought. Beyond these two requirements, the writing need not designate the buyer or the seller, the terms of payment, or the price.

EXCEPTIONS TO THE STATUTE OF FRAUDS

Exceptions to the applicability of the Statute of Frauds are made in certain situations. We describe those situations here.

Partial Performance. In cases involving contracts relating to the transfer of interests in land, if the purchaser has paid part of the price, taken possession, and made valuable improvements to the property, and if the parties cannot be returned to the positions they held prior to the contract, a court may grant *specific performance* (performance of the contract according to its precise terms). Whether a court will enforce an oral contract for an interest in land when partial performance has taken place is usually determined by the degree of injury that would be suffered if the court chose *not* to enforce the oral contract. In some states, mere reliance on certain types of oral contracts is enough to

---

[13] *Restatement (Second) of Contracts*, Section 116.
[14] See *Kampman v. Pittsburgh Contracting and Engineering Co.*, 316 Pa. 502, 175 A. 396 (1934).

remove them from the Statute of Frauds. Under the UCC, an oral contract for goods priced at $500 or more is enforceable to the extent that a seller accepts payment or a buyer accepts delivery of the goods.[15]

[15] UCC 2–201(3)(c). As mentioned, the 2003 amendments to the UCC increased this amount to $5,000—see Chapter 14.

In the following case, a dispute arose over irrigation water rights. The question was whether oral agreements for the rights were outside the Statute of Frauds because the agreements had been partially performed by the parties who claimed that the rights should be theirs.

CASE 10.3 Spears v. Warr

Supreme Court of Utah, 2002.
2002 UT 24,
44 P.3d 742.
http://www.utcourts.gov/opinions[a]

FACTS Edward and Hazel Warr bought approximately 110 acres of land in Tooele County, Utah, to sell in five-acre parcels as the Rocky Top Subdivision beginning in 1986. The Warrs also owned an interest in water from Rose Spring that they planned to use to irrigate the subdivision. During negotiations with prospective buyers, the Warrs represented that water rights were included in the price of the lots. The deeds conveying title to the lots did not convey water rights, however. The new owners repeatedly asked why water was not yet being provided. The Warrs responded that they intended to provide water as soon as possible. Eventually, the Warrs began installing a pipeline to channel water to the lots. Some of the owners helped pay for, and participated in, the installation of the pipe. In 1994, the Warrs asked the owners to pay $2,500 to $5,000 each for the water rights. The owners refused, contending that they had already paid. Melvin Spears and other owners filed a suit in a Utah state court against the Warrs, demanding that they convey (transfer) the water rights. The court ruled in the plaintiffs' favor. The Warrs appealed to the Utah Supreme Court, insisting in part that the Statute of Frauds barred enforcement of the alleged oral contracts for water.

ISSUE Were the oral contracts for water rights enforceable?

a. In the "Supreme Court Opinions" section, in the "By Date" row, click on "2002." From the list of results, scroll to the name of the case and click on it to access the opinion. The Utah state courts maintain this Web site.

DECISION Yes. The Utah Supreme Court affirmed the trial court's conclusion that the plaintiffs paid for the water rights at the time they paid for the lots, and that the parties orally agreed that the water rights would be transferred after the land-purchase transaction. These oral contracts were outside the Statute of Frauds based on the doctrine of partial performance.

REASON The doctrine of partial performance requires that "[1] the oral contract and its terms must be clear and definite; [2] the acts done in performance of the contract must be equally clear and definite; and [3] the acts must be in reliance on the contract. Such acts in reliance must be such that (a) they would not have been performed had the contract not existed, and (b) the failure to perform on the part of the promisor would result in fraud on the performer who relied, since damages would be inadequate." The court concluded, "First, the oral contract and its terms are clear and definite. * * * [T]he inclusion of irrigation water in the purchase price of the plaintiffs' lots was a basis of the bargain [to buy the lots]. * * * Second, the acts done in performance of the contract are equally clear and definite. * * * [T]he parties paid money for the irrigation water at the time they paid for their lots. * * * Third, the plaintiffs' acts were done in reliance on the contract. * * * Payment * * * would not have been made if the oral agreements had not existed." Also, "failure by the Warrs to perform their obligation would result in fraud on the plaintiffs."

FOR CRITICAL ANALYSIS—Economic Consideration
Given that Tooele County is entirely located in a desert, would anyone be likely to buy Tooele County land that did not include water rights?

Admissions. In some states, if a party against whom enforcement of an oral contract is sought admits in pleadings, testimony, or otherwise in court proceedings that a contract for sale was made, the contract will be enforceable.[16] A contract subject to the UCC will be enforceable, but only

[16] *Restatement (Second) of Contracts*, Section 133.

to the extent of the quantity admitted.[17] Thus, if the president of Ajax Corporation admits under oath that an oral agreement was made with Cloney, Inc., for the twenty crates of bleach, the agreement will be enforceable to that extent.

[17] UCC 2–201(3)(b). See Chapter 14.

Promissory Estoppel. In some states, an oral contract that would otherwise be unenforceable under the Statute of Frauds may be enforced under the doctrine of promissory estoppel, or detrimental reliance. Recall from Chapter 8 that if a promisor makes a promise on which the promisee justifiably relies to her or his detriment, a court may *estop* (prevent) the promisor from denying that a contract exists. Section 139 of the *Restatement (Second) of Contracts* provides that in these circumstances, an oral promise can be enforceable notwithstanding the Statute of Frauds if the reliance was foreseeable to the person making the promise and if injustice can be avoided only by enforcing the promise.

Special Exceptions under the UCC. Special exceptions to the applicability of the Statute of Frauds exist for sales contracts. Oral contracts for customized goods may be enforced in certain circumstances. Another exception has to do with oral contracts between merchants that have been confirmed in writing. We will examine these exceptions in Chapter 14.

The Statute of Frauds— Sufficiency of the Writing

A written contract will satisfy the writing requirement of the Statute of Frauds. A *written memorandum* (written evidence of the oral contract) signed by the party against whom enforcement is sought will also satisfy the writing requirement.[18] The signature need not be placed at the end of the document but can be anywhere in the writing; it can even be initials rather than the full name.

A significant issue in today's business world has to do with how "signatures" can be created and verified on electronic contracts and other documents. We will examine electronic signatures in Chapter 13.

WHAT CONSTITUTES A WRITING?

A writing can consist of any confirmation, invoice, sales slip, check, or fax—or such items in combination. The written contract need not consist of a single document to constitute an enforceable contract. One document may incorporate another document by expressly referring to it. Several documents may form a single contract if they are physically attached such as by staple, paper clip, or glue. Several documents may form a single contract even if they are only placed in the same envelope.

● **EXAMPLE #15** Sam orally agrees to sell to Terry some land next to a shopping mall. Sam gives Terry an unsigned memo that contains a legal description of the property, and Terry gives Sam an unsigned first draft of their contract. Sam sends Terry a signed letter that refers to the memo and to the first and final drafts of the contract. Terry sends Sam an unsigned copy of the final draft of the contract with a signed check stapled to it. Together, the documents can constitute a writing sufficient to satisfy the Statute of Frauds and bind both parties to the terms of the contract as evidenced by the writings.●

WHAT MUST BE CONTAINED IN THE WRITING?

A memorandum evidencing the oral contract need only contain the essential terms of the contract. Under most provisions of the Statute of Frauds, the writing must name the parties, subject matter, consideration, and quantity. With respect to contracts for the sale of land, some states require that the memorandum also set forth the essential terms of the contract, such as location and price, with sufficient clarity to allow the terms to be determined from the memo itself, without reference to any outside sources.[19] Under the UCC, in regard to the sale of goods, the writing need only name the quantity term and be signed by the party against whom enforcement is sought.

Because only the party against whom enforcement is sought need have signed the writing, a contract may be enforceable by one of its parties but not by the other. ● **EXAMPLE #16** Rock orally agrees to buy Devlin's lake house and lot for $150,000. Devlin writes Rock a letter confirming the sale by identifying the parties and the essential terms of the sales contract—price, method of payment, and legal address—and signs the letter. Devlin has made a written memorandum of the oral land contract. Because she signed the letter, she normally can be held to the oral contract by Rock. Rock, however, because he has not signed or entered into a written contract or memorandum, can plead the Statute of Frauds as a defense, and Devlin cannot enforce the contract against him.●

The Parol Evidence Rule

The **parol evidence rule** prohibits the introduction at trial of evidence of the parties' prior negotiations, previous agreements, or contemporaneous oral agreements if that evidence contradicts or varies the terms of the parties' written contract. The written contract is ordinarily assumed to be the complete embodiment of the parties' agreement. Because of the rigidity of the parol evidence rule, however, courts make several exceptions:

---

[18] As mentioned earlier, under the UCC Statute of Frauds, a writing is required only for contracts for the sale of goods priced at $500 or more (increased to $5,000 or more by the 2003 Amendments to the UCC—see Chapter 14).

[19] *Rhodes v. Wilkins*, 83 N.M. 782, 498 P.2d 311 (1972).

① Evidence of a *subsequent modification* of a written contract can be introduced in court. Keep in mind that the oral modifications may not be enforceable if they come under the Statute of Frauds—for example, if they increase the price of the goods for sale to $500 or more or increase the term for performance to more than one year. Also, oral modifications will not be enforceable if the original contract provides that any modification must be in writing.[20]

② Oral evidence can be introduced in all cases to show that the contract was voidable or void (for example, induced by mistake, fraud, or misrepresentation). In this situation, if deception led one of the parties to agree to the terms of a written contract, oral evidence indicating fraud should not be excluded. Courts frown on bad faith and are quick to allow the introduction at trial of parol evidence when it establishes fraud.

③ When the terms of a written contract are ambiguous, evidence is admissible to show the meaning of the terms.

④ Evidence is admissible when the written contract is incomplete in that it lacks one or more of the essential terms. The courts allow evidence to "fill in the gaps" in the contract.

⑤ Under the UCC, evidence can be introduced to explain or supplement a written contract by showing a prior dealing, course of performance, or usage of trade.[21] We discuss these terms in further detail in Chapter 14, in the context of sales contracts. Here, it is sufficient to say that when buyers and sellers deal with each other over extended periods of time, certain customary practices develop. These practices are often overlooked in the writing of the contract, so courts allow the introduction of evidence to show how the parties have acted in the past. Usage of trade—practices and customs generally followed in a particular industry—can also shed light on the meaning of certain contract provisions, and thus evidence of trade usage may be admissible.

⑥ The parol evidence rule does not apply if the existence of the entire written contract is subject to an orally agreed-on condition. Proof of the condition does not alter or modify the written terms but affects the *enforceability* of the written contract. ● **EXAMPLE #17** Jelek agrees to purchase Armand's car for $4,000, but only if Jelek's mechanic, Frank, inspects the car and approves of the purchase. Armand agrees to this condition, but because he is leaving town for the weekend and Jelek wants to use the car (if he buys it) before Armand returns, Jelek drafts a contract of sale, and they both sign it. Frank, the mechanic, does not approve of the purchase, and when Jelek does not buy the car, Armand sues him, alleging that he breached the contract. In this case, Jelek's oral agreement did not alter or modify the terms of the written agreement but concerned whether the contract existed at all. Therefore, the parol evidence rule does not apply.●

⑦ When an *obvious* or *gross* clerical (or typographic) error exists that clearly would not represent the agreement of the parties, parol evidence is admissible to correct the error. ● **EXAMPLE #18** Sharon agrees to lease 1,000 square feet of office space at the current monthly rate of $3 per square foot from Stone Enterprises. The signed written lease provides for a monthly lease payment of $300 rather than the $3,000 agreed to by the parties. Because the error is obvious, Stone Enterprises would be allowed to admit parol evidence to correct the mistake.●

The determination of whether evidence will be allowed basically depends on whether the written contract is intended to be a complete and final embodiment of the terms of the agreement. If it is so intended, it is referred to as an **integrated contract**, and extraneous evidence is excluded. If the contract is only partially integrated, evidence of consistent additional terms is admissible to supplement the written agreement.[22]

As the following case illustrates, however, a court will not apply any of these exceptions merely when a party's "subjective expectations [are] thwarted by a bad bargain."

---

[20] UCC 2–209(2), (3). See Chapter 14.
[21] UCC 1–205, 2–202. See Chapter 14.

[22] *Restatement (Second) of Contracts*, Section 216.

CASE 10.4 **APJ Associates, Inc. v. North American Philips Corp.**

United States Court of Appeals,
Sixth Circuit, 2003.
317 F.3d 610.
**http://pacer.ca6.uscourts.gov/opinions/
main.php**[a]

a. This is a page within the Web site of the U.S. Court of Appeals for the Sixth Circuit. In the left-hand column, click on "Opinions Search." In the "Short Title contains" box, type "APJ" and click "Submit Query." In the "Opinion" box corresponding to the name of the case, click on the number to access the opinion.

CASE 10.4—Continued

FACTS North American Philips Corporation, a microprocessor supplier that makes electronic components for automobile cruise control systems, wanted to become a supplier to General Motors Corporation (GMC) and hired APJ Associates, Inc., to develop a business relationship between Philips and GMC. APJ and Philips signed a contract that provided that "[e]ither party may terminate the agreement for its convenience upon at least thirty (30) days prior written notice," with no commissions to be paid on posttermination sales. The contract also stated that it "constitutes the entire Agreement between the parties * * * and supersedes and replaces all prior or contemporaneous agreements, written and verbal." The parties signed three subsequent one-year contracts with the same clauses. Each time, Jim Alexander, APJ's president, objected, but Philips refused to make any changes. After GMC chose Philips to develop a cruise control module, Philips gave APJ notice that it was terminating their contract and sent APJ a check for $2,649.43. APJ filed a suit in a federal district court against Philips, seeking commissions on future sales. The court issued a summary judgment in Philips's favor. APJ appealed to the U.S. Court of Appeals for the Sixth Circuit.

ISSUE Was APJ bound to the written terms of the contracts that it signed with Philips?

DECISION Yes. The U.S. Court of Appeals for the Sixth Circuit affirmed the judgment of the lower court. The written terms of the contracts between APJ and Philips were clear and unambiguous.

REASON The appellate court explained that "[t]he much-discussed thirty-day termination clause, included over Alexander's repeated objections and ratified in the three subsequent agreements, does not indicate any question as to whether the relationship could be terminated at the will of either party. The very fact that Alexander protested the clause every year shows that he was only too well aware of its implications. * * * Nor do the provisions for the payment of commissions introduce any ambiguity in the agreement upon which [APJ] can base its claims. The written agreements unequivocally bar the payment of any posttermination commissions." The court added that "each agreement contained an integration clause," which "conclusively establishes that the parties intended the written contract to be the complete expression of their agreement, and the parol evidence rule bars the use of extrinsic evidence to contradict the terms of a written contract intended to be the final and complete expression of the contracting parties' agreement."

FOR CRITICAL ANALYSIS—Social Consideration
Could promissory estoppel serve as a basis for awarding commissions on future sales to APJ?

Terms and Concepts

Chapter Summary   Defenses against Contract Enforceability

GENUINENESS OF ASSENT	
Mistakes (See pages 198–199.)	1. *Unilateral*—Generally, the mistaken party is bound by the contract *unless* (a) the other party knows or should have known of the mistake or (b) the mistake is an inadvertent mathematical error—such as an error in addition or subtraction—committed without gross negligence. 2. *Bilateral (mutual)*—When both parties are mistaken about the same material fact, such as identity, either party can avoid the contract. If the mistake concerns value or quality, either party can enforce the contract.
Fraudulent Misrepresentation (See pages 199–203.)	When fraud occurs, usually the innocent party can enforce or avoid the contract. The elements necessary to establish fraud are as follows: 1. A misrepresentation of a material fact must occur.

(Continued)

Chapter Summary | Defenses against Contract Enforceability—Continued

Fraudulent Misrepresentation— continued	2. There must be an intent to deceive. 3. The innocent party must justifiably rely on the misrepresentation.
Undue Influence (See page 203.)	Undue influence arises from special relationships, such as fiduciary or confidential relationships, in which one party's free will has been overcome by the undue influence exerted by the other party. Usually, the contract is voidable.
Duress (See page 203.)	Duress is defined as the tactic of forcing a party to enter a contract under the fear of a threat—for example, the threat of violence or serious economic loss. The party forced to enter the contract can rescind the contract.
	FORM
The Statute of Frauds—Requirement of a Writing (See pages 203–207.)	*Applicability*—The following types of contracts fall under the Statute of Frauds and must be in writing to be enforceable: 1. *Contracts involving interests in land*—The statute applies to any contract for an interest in realty, such as a sale, a lease, or a mortgage. 2. *Contracts whose terms cannot be performed within one year*—The statute applies only to contracts objectively impossible to perform fully within one year from (the day after) the contract's formation. 3. *Collateral promises*—The statute applies only to express contracts made between the guarantor and the creditor whose terms make the guarantor secondarily liable. *Exception:* the "main purpose" rule. 4. *Promises made in consideration of marriage*—The statute applies to promises to pay money or give property in consideration of a promise to marry and to prenuptial agreements made in consideration of marriage. 5. *Contracts for the sale of goods priced at $500 or more*—Under the UCC Statute of Frauds provision in UCC 2–201. *Exceptions*—Partial performance, admissions, and promissory estoppel.
The Statute of Frauds—Sufficiency of the Writing (See page 207.)	To constitute an enforceable contract under the Statute of Frauds, a writing must be signed by the party against whom enforcement is sought, must name the parties, must identify the subject matter, and must state with reasonable certainty the essential terms of the contract. In a sale of land, the price and a description of the property may need to be stated with sufficient clarity to allow them to be determined without reference to outside sources. Under the UCC, a contract for the sale of goods is not enforceable beyond the quantity of goods shown in the contract.
The Parol Evidence Rule (See pages 207–209.)	The parol evidence rule prohibits the introduction at trial of evidence of the parties' prior negotiations, prior agreements, or contemporaneous oral agreements that contradicts or varies the terms of the parties' written contract. The written contract is assumed to be the complete embodiment of the parties' agreement. Exceptions are made in the following circumstances: 1. To show that the contract was subsequently modified. 2. To show that the contract was voidable or void. 3. To clarify the meaning of ambiguous terms. 4. To clarify the terms of the contract when the written contract lacks one or more of its essential terms.

Chapter Summary	Defenses against Contract Enforceability—Continued
The Parol Evidence Rule— continued	5. Under the UCC, to explain the meaning of contract terms in light of a prior dealing, course of performance, or usage of trade. 6. To show that the entire contract is subject to an orally agreed-on condition. 7. When an obvious clerical or typographic error was made.

For Review

① In what types of situations might genuineness of assent to a contract's terms be lacking?

② What is the difference between a mistake of value or quality and a mistake of fact?

③ What elements must exist for fraudulent misrepresentation to occur?

④ What contracts must be in writing to be enforceable?

⑤ What is parol evidence? When is it admissible to clarify the terms of a written contract?

Questions and Case Problems

10–1. Genuineness of Assent. Jerome is an elderly man who lives with his nephew, Philip. Jerome is totally dependent on Philip's support. Philip tells Jerome that unless Jerome transfers a tract of land he owns to Philip for a price 30 percent below market value, Philip will no longer support and take care of him. Jerome enters into the contract. Discuss fully whether Jerome can set aside this contract.

10–2. Collateral Promises. Gemma promises a local hardware store that she will pay for a lawn mower that her brother is purchasing on credit if the brother fails to pay the debt. Must this promise be in writing to be enforceable? Why or why not?

10–3. Fraudulent Misrepresentation. Larry offered to sell Stanley his car and told Stanley that the car had been driven only 25,000 miles and had never been in an accident. Stanley hired Cohen, a mechanic, to appraise the condition of the car, and Cohen said that the car most likely had at least 50,000 miles on it and most likely had been in an accident. In spite of this information, Stanley still thought the car would be a good buy for the price, so he purchased it. Later, when the car developed numerous mechanical problems, Stanley sought to rescind the contract on the basis of Larry's fraudulent misrepresentation of the auto's condition. Will Stanley be able to rescind his contract? Discuss.

10–4. Collateral Promises. Jeffrey took his mother on a special holiday to Mountain Air Resort. Jeffrey was a frequent patron of the resort and was well known by its manager. The resort required each of its patrons to make a large deposit to ensure payment for the room. Jeffrey asked the manager to waive the requirement for his mother and told the manager that if his mother for any reason failed to pay the resort for her stay there, he would cover the charges. Relying on Jeffrey's promise, the manager waived the deposit requirement for

Jeffrey's mother. After she returned home from her holiday, Jeffrey's mother refused to pay the resort bill. The resort manager tried to collect the sum from Jeffrey, but Jeffrey also refused to pay, stating that his promise was not enforceable under the Statute of Frauds. Is Jeffrey correct? Explain.

10–5. Misrepresentation. W. B. McConkey owned commercial property, including a building that, as McConkey knew, had experienced flooding problems for years. McConkey painted the building, replaced damaged carpeting, and sold the property to M&D, Inc., on an "as is" basis. M&D did not ask whether there were flooding problems, and McConkey said nothing about them. M&D leased the property to Donmar, Inc., to operate a pet supplies store. Two months after the store opened, the building flooded following heavy rain. M&D and Donmar filed a suit in a Michigan state court against McConkey and others, claiming in part that McConkey had committed misrepresentation by silence. Based on this claim, will the court hold McConkey liable? Why or why not? [*M&D, Inc. v. McConkey*, 585 N.W.2d 33 (Mich.App. 1998)]

10–6. The Parol Evidence Rule. Vision Graphics, Inc., provides printing services to customers such as Milton Bradley Co. To perform its services, Vision agreed to buy or lease parts of a computer software system from E. I. du Pont de Nemours & Co. Vision needed the system to accept files written in "PostScript," a computer language used in the printing industry. Du Pont orally represented to Vision that with three upgrades, its system would be completely "postscriptable." None of the parties' written contracts included any promises regarding postscriptability. Each contract, however, included an integration clause stating that the contract contained the entire agreement of the parties. Before the three upgrades were complete, du Pont determined that for financial reasons, it could no longer support its system and told Vision that the software would not be made postscriptable. Vision lost customers and could not attract new accounts, and its reputation in the industry was damaged. Vision filed a suit in a federal district court against du Pont, alleging, among other things, breach of contract on the basis of the oral promises. Du Pont filed a motion for summary judgment, arguing that whether it breached any oral agreement was "immaterial." Will the court agree? Why or why not? [*Vision Graphics, Inc. v. E. I. du Pont de Nemours & Co.,* 41 F.Supp.2d 93 (D.Mass. 1999)]

10–7. Oral Contracts. Sierra Bravo, Inc., and Shelby's, Inc., entered into a written "Waste Disposal Agreement" under which Shelby's allowed Sierra to deposit on Shelby's land waste products, deleterious (harmful) materials, and debris removed by Sierra in the construction of a highway. Later, Shelby's asked Sierra why it had not constructed a waterway and a building pad suitable for a commercial building on the property, as they had orally agreed. Sierra denied any such agreement. Shelby's filed a suit in a Missouri state court against Sierra, alleging breach of contract. Sierra contended that any oral agreement was unenforceable under the Statute of Frauds. Sierra argued that because the right to *remove* minerals from land is considered a contract for the sale of an interest in land to which the Statute of Frauds applies, the Statute of Frauds should apply to the right to *deposit* soil on another person's property. How should the court rule, and why? [*Shelby's, Inc. v. Sierra Bravo, Inc.,* 68 S.W.3d 604 (Mo.App.S.D. 2002)]

10–8. Fraudulent Misrepresentation. United Parcel Service Co. and United Parcel Service of America, Inc., are together known as "UPS." In 1987, UPS decided to change its parcel delivery business from relying on contract carriers to establishing its own airline. During the transition, which took sixteen months, UPS hired 811 pilots. At the time, UPS expressed a desire to hire pilots who remained throughout that period with its contract carriers, which included Orion Air. A UPS representative met with more than fifty Orion pilots and made promises of future employment. John Rickert, a captain with Orion, was one of the pilots. Orion ceased operation after the UPS transition, and UPS did not hire Rickert, who obtained employment about six months later as a second officer with American Airlines, but at a lower salary. Rickert filed a suit in a Kentucky state court against UPS, claiming, in part, fraud based on the promises made by the UPS representative. UPS filed a motion for a directed verdict. What are the elements for a cause of action based on fraudulent misrepresentation? In whose favor should the court rule in this case, and why? [*United Parcel Service, Inc. v. Rickert,* 996 S.W.2d 464 (Ky. 1999)]

10–9. Fraudulent Misrepresentation. William Meade, Leland Stewart, Doug Vierkant, and David Girard applied for, and were offered, jobs at the El-Jay Division of Cedarapids, Inc., in Eugene, Oregon. During the interviews, each applicant asked about El-Jay's future. They were told, among other things, that El-Jay was a stable company with few downsizings and layoffs,

sales were up and were expected to increase, and production was expanding. Cedarapids management had already planned to close El-Jay, however. Each applicant signed an at-will employment agreement. To take the job at El-Jay, each new employee either quit the job he was doing or passed up other employment opportunities. Each employee and his family then moved to Eugene. When El-Jay closed soon after they started their new jobs, Meade and the others filed a suit in a federal district court against Cedarapids, alleging, in part, fraudulent misrepresentation. Were the plaintiffs justified in relying on the statements made to them during their job interviews? Explain. [*Meade v. Cedarapids, Inc.,* 164 F.3d 1218 (9th Cir. 1999)]

CASE PROBLEM WITH SAMPLE ANSWER

 10–10. Robert Pinto, doing business as Pinto Associates, hired Richard MacDonald as an independent contractor in March 1992. The parties orally agreed on the terms of employment, including payment to MacDonald of a share of the company's income, but they did not put anything in writing. In March 1995, MacDonald quit. Pinto then told MacDonald that he was entitled to $9,602.17—25 percent of the difference between the accounts receivable and the accounts payable as of MacDonald's last day. MacDonald disagreed and demanded more than $83,500—25 percent of the revenue from all invoices, less the cost of materials and outside processing, for each of the years that he worked for Pinto. Pinto refused. MacDonald filed a suit in a Connecticut state court against Pinto, alleging breach of contract. In Pinto's response and at the trial, he testified that the parties had an oral contract under which MacDonald was entitled to 25 percent of the difference between accounts receivable and payable as of the date of MacDonald's termination. Did the parties have an enforceable contract? How should the court rule, and why? [*MacDonald v. Pinto,* 62 Conn.App. 317, 771 A.2d 156 (2001)]

▶ To view a sample answer for this case problem, go to this book's Web site at **http://fundamentals.westbuslaw.com** and click on "Interactive Study Center."

 ### VIDEO QUESTION
10–11. Go to this text's Web site at **http://fundamentals.westbuslaw.com** and click on "Video Questions." Select "Chapter 10" and view the video titled *Mistake.* Then answer the following questions:

1. What kind of mistake is involved in the dispute shown on the video (mutual or unilateral, mistake of fact or mistake of value)?
2. According to the chapter, in what two situations would the supermarket be able to rescind a contract to sell peppers to Melnick at the incorrectly advertised price?
3. Does it matter if the price that was advertised was a reasonable price for the peppers? Why or why not?

DEFENSES AGAINST CONTRACT ENFORCEABILITY

For updated links to resources available on the Web, as well as a variety of other materials, visit this text's Web site at

http://fundamentals.westbuslaw.com

For a discussion of fraudulent misrepresentation, go to the Web site of attorney Owen Katz at

http://www.katzlawoffice.com/misrep.html

The online version of UCC Section 2–201 on the Statute of Frauds includes links to definitions of certain terms used in the section. To access this site, go to

http://www.law.cornell.edu/ucc/2/2-201.html

To read a summary of a case concerning whether the exchange of e-mails satisfied the writing requirement of the Statute of Frauds, go to

http://www.phillipsnizer.com/library/topics/statute_frauds.cfm

Online Legal Research

Go to the *Fundamentals of Business Law* home page at **http://fundamentals. westbuslaw.com**. Select "Interactive Study Center" and then click on "Chapter 10." There you will find the following Internet research exercises that you can perform to learn more about topics covered in this chapter.

Activity 10–1: ECONOMIC PERSPECTIVE—**Economic Duress**
Activity 10–2: LEGAL PERSPECTIVE—**Promissory Estoppel and the Statute of Frauds**
Activity 10–3: MANAGEMENT PERSPECTIVE—**"Get It in Writing"**

Before the Test

Go to the *Fundamentals of Business Law* home page at **http://fundamentals. westbuslaw.com**. Click on "Interactive Quizzes." You will find at least twenty interactive questions relating to this chapter.

Westlaw® Campus

If your textbook provided for a subscription to Westlaw® Campus, or if you have otherwise purchased access to the Westlaw Campus database, you can access any of the cases presented or cited in this chapter by using your Westlaw Campus account.

CHAPTER
11
Third Party Rights and Discharge

CHAPTER OBJECTIVES

After reading this chapter, you should be able to answer the following questions:

① What is the difference between an assignment and a delegation?

② What rights can be assigned despite a contract clause expressly prohibiting assignment?

③ What factors indicate that a third party beneficiary is an intended beneficiary?

④ How are most contracts discharged?

⑤ What is a contractual condition, and how might a condition affect contractual obligations?

Because a contract is a private agreement between the parties who have entered into it, it is fitting that these parties alone should have rights and liabilities under the contract. This concept is referred to as **privity of contract**, and it establishes the basic principle that third parties have no rights in contracts to which they are not parties.

You are probably convinced by now that for every rule of contract law there seems to be an exception. As times change, so must the laws. When justice cannot be served by adherence to a rule of law, exceptions to the rule must be made. In this chapter, we look at some exceptions to the rule of privity of contract. We also examine how a contract is *discharged*. Normally, contract discharge is accomplished when both parties have performed the acts promised in the contract. In the latter part of this chapter, we look at the degree of perform-

ance required to discharge a contractual obligation, as well as at some other ways in which contract discharge can occur.

Assignments and Delegations

When third parties acquire rights or assume duties arising from contracts to which they were not parties, the rights are transferred to them by *assignment,* and the duties are transferred by *delegation.*

ASSIGNMENTS

In a bilateral contract, normally one party has a right to require the other to perform some task, and the other has a duty to perform it. The transfer of *rights* to a third person is

214

known as an **assignment**. When rights under a contract are assigned unconditionally, the rights of the **assignor** (the party making the assignment) are extinguished.[1] The third party (the **assignee**, or party receiving the assignment) has a right to demand performance from the other original party to the contract (the *obligor*). ● EXAMPLE #1 Brent owes Alex $1,000, and Alex assigns to Carmen the right to receive the $1,000. Here, a valid assignment of a debt exists. Carmen, the assignee, can enforce the contract against Brent if Brent fails to perform.● Exhibit 11–1 illustrates assignment relationships.

The assignee takes only those rights that the assignor originally had. Furthermore, the assignee's rights are subject to the defenses that the obligor has against the assignor. ● EXAMPLE #2 Brent owes Alex $1,000 under a contract in which Brent agreed to buy Alex's computer work station. Alex assigns his right to receive the $1,000 to Carmen. Brent, in deciding to purchase the work station, relied on Alex's fraudulent misrepresentation that the computer's hard drive had a storage capacity of 120 gigabytes. When Brent discovers that the computer can store only 20 gigabytes, he tells Alex that he is going to return the work station to him and

cancel the contract. Even though Alex has assigned his "right" to receive the $1,000 to Carmen, Brent need not pay Carmen the $1,000—Brent can raise the defense of Alex's fraudulent misrepresentation to avoid payment.●

The Importance of Assignments in the Business Context. Assignments are important because they are utilized in much business financing. Lending institutions, for example, such as banks, frequently assign the rights to receive payments under their loan contracts to other firms, which pay for those rights. If you obtain a loan from your local bank to purchase a car, you might later receive in the mail a notice stating that your bank has transferred (assigned) its rights to receive payments on the loan to another company and that, when the time comes to repay your loan, you must make the payments to that other firm.

Lenders that make *mortgage loans* (loans to allow prospective home buyers to purchase land or a home) often assign their rights to collect the mortgage payments to a third party, such as GMAC Mortgage Corporation. Following an assignment, the home buyer is notified that future payments must be made not to the lender that loaned the funds but to the third party. Many millions of dollars change hands daily in the business world in the form of assignments of rights in

---

[1] *Restatement (Second) of Contracts*, Section 317.

EXHIBIT 11–1 **ASSIGNMENT RELATIONSHIPS**

In the assignment relationship illustrated here, Alex assigns his *rights* under a contract that he made with Brent to a third party, Carmen. Alex thus becomes the *assignor* and Carmen the *assignee* of the contractual rights. Brent, the *obligor* (the party owing performance under the contract), now owes performance to Carmen instead of Alex. Alex's original contract rights are extinguished after assignment.

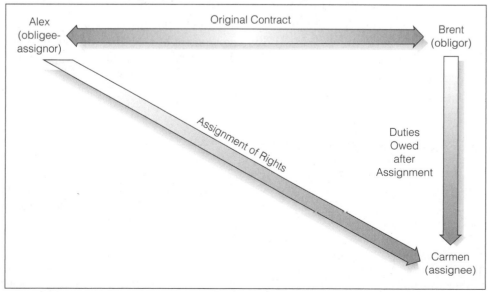

contracts. If it were not possible to transfer (assign) contractual rights, many businesses could not continue to operate.

Rights That Cannot Be Assigned. As a general rule, all rights can be assigned. Exceptions are made, however, in the following special circumstances:

① If a statute expressly prohibits assignment, the particular right in question cannot be assigned. ● EXAMPLE #3 Marn is a new employee of CompuFuture, Inc. CompuFuture is an employer under workers' compensation statutes (see Chapter 23) in this state, and thus Marn is a covered employee. Marn has a relatively high-risk job. In need of a loan, Marn borrows some money from Stark, assigning to Stark all workers' compensation benefits due her should she be injured on the job. The assignment of *future* workers' compensation benefits is prohibited by state statute, and thus such rights cannot be assigned. ●

② When a contract is for personal services, the rights under the contract normally cannot be assigned unless all that remains is a money payment.[2] ● EXAMPLE #4 Brent signs a contract to be a tutor for Alex's children. Alex then attempts to assign to Carmen his right to Brent's services. Carmen cannot enforce the contract against Brent. Brent may not like Carmen's children or may for some other reason not want to tutor them. Because personal services are unique to the person rendering them, rights to receive personal services cannot be assigned. ●

③ A right cannot be assigned if assignment will materially increase or alter the risk or duties of the obligor.[3] ● EXAMPLE #5 Alex has a hotel, and to insure it, he takes out a policy with Northwest Insurance Company. The policy insures against fire, theft, floods, and vandalism. Alex attempts to assign the insurance policy to Carmen, who also owns a hotel. The assignment is ineffective because it may substantially alter the insurance company's duty of performance and the risk that the company undertakes. An insurance company evaluates the particular risk of a certain party and tailors its policy to fit that risk. If the policy is assigned to a third party, the insurance risk is materially altered. ●

④ If a contract stipulates that the right cannot be assigned, then *ordinarily* it cannot be assigned. ● EXAMPLE #6 Brent agrees to build a house for Alex. The contract between Brent and Alex states, "This contract cannot be assigned by Alex without Brent's consent. Any assignment without such consent renders this contract void, and all rights hereunder will thereupon terminate." Alex then assigns his rights to Carmen, without first obtaining Brent's consent. Carmen cannot enforce the contract against Brent. ●

The fourth rule has several exceptions:

① A contract cannot prevent an assignment of the right to receive money. This exception exists to encourage the free flow of money and credit in modern business settings.

② The assignment of ownership rights in real estate often cannot be prohibited because such a prohibition is contrary to public policy in most states. Prohibitions of this kind are called restraints against **alienation** (the voluntary transfer of land ownership).

③ The assignment of negotiable instruments (see Chapter 18) cannot be prohibited.

④ In a contract for the sale of goods, the right to receive damages for breach of contract or for payment of an account owed may be assigned even though the sales contract prohibits such assignment.[4]

In the following case, both parties had violated an anti-assignment clause. The question before the court was how one party's violation affected that party's recovery for the other party's violation.

---

[2] *Restatement (Second) of Contracts*, Sections 317 and 318.
[3] See UCC 2–210(2).

[4] UCC 2–210(2).

CASE 11.1 **Forest Commodity Corp. v. Lone Star Industries, Inc.**

Court of Appeals of Georgia, 2002.
564 S.E.2d 755.

FACTS Forest Commodity Corporation (FCC) owns an ocean terminal facility where ships unload and store bulk cargo. FCC, which has no employees or equipment, leases the facility to Woodchips Export Corporation (WEC). Construction Aggregates, Limited, owned by Lone Star Industries, Inc. (jointly referred to as CAL), mines and ships aggregate stone. FCC and CAL entered into a three-year contract under which FCC agreed to provide terminal space for unloading aggregate stone, which FCC would then store, reload onto trucks, and weigh for further shipment. CAL promised to unload a minimum of 150,000 tons per year or pay a higher price. The contract prohibited its assignment without the other party's

CASE 11.1—Continued

consent. FCC transferred its obligations under this contract to WEC without CAL's consent. About a year later, after CAL had shipped nearly 200,000 tons, Martin Marietta Materials, Inc., acquired CAL and offered to accept its obligations under the contract with FCC, but FCC refused. At the same time, FCC and Martin Marietta entered into a separate, but substantially similar, contract. The total aggregate shipped under both contracts over a three-year period was 484,868 tons. FCC filed a suit in a Georgia state court against CAL for breach of contract, alleging that CAL had failed to ship the agreed minimum. The court issued a summary judgment in CAL's favor. FCC appealed to a state intermediate appellate court.

ISSUE Was FCC's breach of the antiassignment clause a material breach of the agreement with CAL, which would prevent FCC from holding CAL to the contract?

DECISION Yes. The state intermediate appellate court affirmed the lower court's judgment. FCC breached its contract with CAL by violating the antiassignment clause, and this breach precluded FCC from enforcing the contract.

REASON The court explained that "a party's refusal to abide by a contract provision prohibiting assignment * * *

is properly considered a repudiation of the contract amounting to an anticipatory breach. Such a repudiation of the agreement estops FCC from seeking to enforce other provisions of the agreement." FCC claimed that any breach of the antiassignment clause was not material, because "the fundamental purpose of the agreement—to provide CAL with a place to discharge and store its aggregate cargo [stone]—was satisfied." The court responded, "FCC's own refusal of CAL's request for consent to an assignment of the agreement to Martin Marietta * * * shows that FCC thought the identity of the parties to the agreement was important or it would have accepted CAL's proposed assignment. In addition, the agreement creates a bailment relationship between FCC and CAL, wherein CAL entrusts aggregate to FCC's safekeeping.[a] Certainly, the uniqueness and identity of the parties is a material term in such a relationship."

FOR CRITICAL ANALYSIS—Economic Consideration
Given that FCC has no employees or equipment, why might it be organized as a corporation separate from WEC?

---

a. In a bailment relationship, the property of one party is entrusted to another, who is obligated to return the property or otherwise dispose of it as instructed. See Chapter 28.

Notice of Assignment. Once a valid assignment of rights has been made to a third party, the third party should notify the obligor of the assignment (for example, in Exhibit 11–1, Carmen should notify Brent). Giving notice is not legally necessary to establish the validity of the assignment, because an assignment is effective immediately, whether or not notice is given. Two major problems arise, however, when notice of the assignment is *not* given to the obligor:

① If the assignor assigns the same right to two different persons, the question arises as to which one has priority—that is, which one has the right to the performance by the obligor. Although the rule most often observed in the United States is that the first assignment in time is the first in right, some states follow the English rule, which basically gives priority to the first assignee who gives notice. ● **EXAMPLE #7** Brent owes Alex $5,000 on a contractual obligation. On May 1, Alex assigns this monetary claim to Carmen. Carmen gives no notice of the assignment to Brent. On June 1, for services Dorman has rendered to Alex, Alex assigns the same monetary claim (to collect $5,000 from Brent) to Dorman. Dorman immediately notifies Brent of the assignment. In the majority of states, Carmen would

have priority, because the assignment to her was first in time. In some states, however, Dorman would have priority, because he gave first notice. ●

② Until the obligor has notice of assignment, the obligor can discharge his or her obligation by performance to the assignor, and performance by the obligor to the assignor constitutes a discharge to the assignee. Once the obligor receives proper notice, only performance to the assignee can discharge the obligor's obligations. ● **EXAMPLE #8** In the above example, Alex assigns to Carmen his right to collect $5,000 from Brent. Carmen does not give notice to Brent. Brent subsequently pays Alex the $5,000. Although the assignment was valid, Brent's payment to Alex was a discharge of the debt, and Carmen's failure to notify Brent of the assignment caused her to lose the right to collect the money from Brent. If Carmen had given Brent notice of the assignment, however, Brent's payment to Alex would not have discharged the debt. ●

In the following case, the issue was whether the right to buy advertising space in certain publications at a steep discount was validly assigned from the original owner to companies that he later formed.

CASE 11.2 Gold v. Ziff Communications Co.

Appellate Court of Illinois, First District, 2001.
322 Ill.App.3d 32,
748 N.E.2d 198,
254 Ill.Dec. 752.
http://state.il.us/court/default.htm[a]

FACTS In 1982, Ziff Communications Company, a publisher of specialty magazines, bought *PC Magazine* from its founder, Anthony Gold, for more than $10 million. As part of the deal, Ziff gave Gold, or a company that he "controlled," "ad/list rights"—rights to advertise at an 80 percent discount on a limited number of pages in Ziff publications and free use of Ziff's subscriber lists. In 1983, Gold formed Software Communications, Inc. (SCI), a mail-order software business that he wholly owned, to use the ad/list rights. In 1987 and 1988, he formed two new mail-order companies, Hanson & Connors, Inc., and PC Brand, Inc. Gold told Ziff that he was allocating his ad/list rights to Hanson & Connors, which took over most of SCI's business, and to PC Brand, of which Gold owned 90 percent. Ziff's other advertisers complained about this "allocation." Ziff refused to run large ads for Hanson & Connors or to release its subscriber lists to the company. Ziff also declared PC Brand ineligible for the ad discount because it "was not controlled by Gold." Gold and his companies filed a suit in an Illinois state court against Ziff, alleging breach of

---

a. On this page, click on "Appellate Court of Illinois." On the next page, in the "Appellate Court Documents" section, click on "Appellate Court opinions." In the result, in the "Appellate Court" section, click on "2001." On the next page, in the "First District" section, click on "March." Finally, scroll to the bottom of the chart and click on the case name to access the opinion. The state of Illinois maintains this Web site.

contract. The court ordered Ziff to pay the plaintiffs more than $88 million in damages and interest. Ziff appealed to an intermediate state appellate court, arguing in part that Gold had not properly assigned the ad/list rights to Hanson & Connors and PC Brand.

ISSUE Was there a valid assignment of rights from Gold and SCI to Hanson & Connors and PC Brand?

DECISION Yes. The state intermediate appellate court affirmed the lower court's decision on this issue. The appellate court remanded the case, however, for a new trial on the amount of the damages, reasoning that some parts of the award "were not within the reasonable contemplation of the parties."

REASON The court explained, "We agree with plaintiffs that assignments can be implied from circumstances. No particular mode or form * * * is necessary to effect a valid assignment, and any acts or words are sufficient which show an intention of transferring or appropriating the owner's interest. In the instant case, it is undisputed that Gold owned 100 [percent] of SCI. In a letter dated May 13, 1988, Gold, as president of SCI, instructed Ziff that he was allocating the ad/list rights to Hanson and PC Brand. Additionally, SCI stopped using the ad/list rights when PC Brand and Hanson were formed. * * * Gold's behavior toward his companies and his conduct toward the obligor, Ziff, implied that the ad/list rights were assigned to PC Brand and Hanson."

FOR CRITICAL ANALYSIS—Social Consideration
Would the assignments in this case have been valid if Gold had not notified Ziff?

DELEGATIONS

Just as a party can transfer rights to a third party through an assignment, a party can also transfer duties. Duties are not assigned, however; they are *delegated*. Normally, a **delegation of duties** does not relieve the party making the delegation (the **delegator**) of the obligation to perform in the event that the party to whom the duty has been delegated (the **delegatee**) fails to perform. No special form is required to create a valid delegation of duties. As long as the delegator expresses an intention to make the delegation, it is effective; the delegator need not even use the word *delegate*. Exhibit 11–2 graphically illustrates delegation relationships.

Duties That Cannot Be Delegated. As a general rule, any duty can be delegated. This rule has some exceptions, however. Delegation is prohibited in the following circumstances:

① When performance depends on the personal skill or talents of the obligor.

② When special trust has been placed in the obligor.

③ When performance by a third party will vary materially from that expected by the obligee (the one to whom performance is owed) under the contract.

④ When the contract expressly prohibits delegation.

EXHIBIT 11–2 DELEGATION RELATIONSHIPS

In the delegation relationship illustrated here, Brent delegates his *duties* under a contract that he made with Alex to a third party, Carmen. Brent thus becomes the *delegator* and Carmen the *delegatee* of the contractual duties. Carmen now owes performance of the contractual duties to Alex. Note that a delegation of duties normally does not relieve the delegator (Brent) of liability if the delegatee (Carmen) fails to perform the contractual duties.

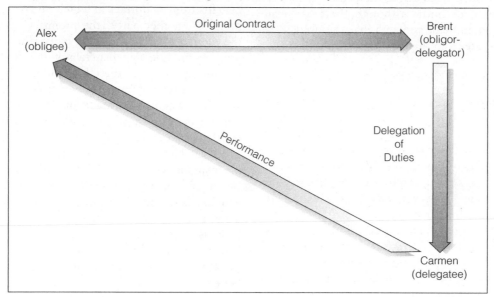

The following examples will help to clarify the kinds of duties that can and cannot be delegated:

① Brent contracts with Alex to tutor Alex in various aspects of financial underwriting and investment banking. Brent, an experienced businessperson known for his expertise in finance, delegates his duties to a third party, Carmen. This delegation is ineffective because Brent contracted to render a service that is founded on Brent's *expertise,* and the delegation changes Alex's expectancy under the contract.

② Brent contracts with Alex to *personally* mow Alex's lawn during June, July, and August. Then Brent decides that he would rather spend the summer at the beach. Brent delegates his lawn-mowing duties to Carmen, who is in the business of mowing lawns and doing other landscaping work to earn income to pay for college. No matter how competent Carmen is, the delegation is not effective without Alex's consent. The contract was for *personal* performance.

③ Brent contracts with Alex to pick up and deliver heavy construction machinery to Alex's property. Brent delegates this duty to Carmen, who is in the business of delivering heavy machinery. This delegation is effective.

The performance required is of a routine and nonpersonal nature, and the delegation does not change Alex's expectations under the contract.

Effect of a Delegation. If a delegation of duties is enforceable, the *obligee* (the one to whom performance is owed) must accept performance from the delegatee (the one to whom the duties are delegated). ● EXAMPLE #9 In the third example in the above list, Brent delegates his duty (to pick up and deliver heavy construction machinery to Alex's property) to Carmen. In that situation, Alex (the obligee) must accept performance from Carmen (the delegatee), because the delegation was effective. The obligee can legally refuse performance from the delegatee only if the duty is one that cannot be delegated. ●

A valid delegation of duties does not relieve the delegator of obligations under the contract.[5] In the above example, if Carmen (the delegatee) fails to perform, Brent (the delegator) is still liable to Alex (the obligee). The obligee can also hold the delegatee liable if the delegatee made a promise of performance that will directly benefit the

---

[5] *Crane Ice Cream Co. v. Terminal Freezing & Heating Co.,* 147 Md. 588, 128 A. 280 (1925).

obligee. In this situation, there is an "assumption of duty" on the part of the delegatee, and breach of this duty makes the delegatee liable to the obligee. For example, if Carmen (the delegatee) promises Brent (the delegator), in a contract, to pick up and deliver the construction equipment to Alex's property but fails to do so, Alex (the obligee) can sue Brent, Carmen, or both. Although there are many exceptions, the general rule today is that the obligee can sue both the delegatee and the delegator.

"ASSIGNMENT OF ALL RIGHTS"

Sometimes, a contract provides for an "assignment of all rights." The traditional view was that under this type of assignment, the assignee did not assume any duties. This view was based on the theory that the assignee's agreement to accept the benefits of the contract was not sufficient to imply a promise to assume the duties of the contract.

Modern authorities, however, take the view that the probable intent in using such general words is to create both an assignment of rights and an assumption of duties.[6] Therefore, when general words are used (for example, "I assign the contract" or "all my rights under the contract"), the contract is construed as implying both an assignment of rights and an assumption of duties.

Third Party Beneficiaries

As mentioned earlier in this chapter, to have contractual rights, a person normally must be a party to the contract. In other words, privity of contract must exist. An exception to the doctrine of privity exists when the original parties to the contract intend, at the time of contracting, that the contract performance directly benefit a third person. In this situation, the third person becomes a **third party beneficiary** of the contract. As an **intended beneficiary** of the contract, the third party has legal rights and can sue the promisor directly for breach of the contract.

Who, though, is the promisor? In bilateral contracts, both parties to the contract are promisors because they both make promises that can be enforced. In third party beneficiary contracts, courts determine the identity of the promisor by asking which party made the promise that benefits the third party; the answer indicates which person is the promisor. Allowing the third party to sue the promisor directly in effect circumvents the "middle person" (the promisee) and thus reduces the burden on the courts. Otherwise, the third party would sue the promisee, who would then sue the promisor.

TYPES OF INTENDED BENEFICIARIES

The law distinguishes between *intended* beneficiaries and *incidental* beneficiaries. Only intended beneficiaries acquire legal rights in a contract. One type of intended beneficiary is a *creditor beneficiary*. A creditor beneficiary is one who benefits from a contract in which one party (the promisor) promises another party (the promisee) to pay a debt that the promisee owes to a third party (the creditor beneficiary). As an intended beneficiary, the creditor beneficiary can sue the promisor directly to enforce the contract.

Another type of intended beneficiary is a *donee* beneficiary. When a contract is made for the express purpose of giving a *gift* to a third party, the third party (the donee beneficiary) can sue the promisor directly to enforce the promise.[7] The most common donee beneficiary contract is a life insurance contract. ● **EXAMPLE #10** Akins (the promisee) pays premiums to Standard Life, a life insurance company, and Standard Life (the promisor) promises to pay a certain amount of money on Akins's death to anyone Akins designates as a beneficiary. The designated beneficiary is a donee beneficiary under the life insurance policy and can enforce the promise made by the insurance company to pay him or her on Akins's death. ●

As the law concerning third party beneficiaries evolved, numerous cases arose in which the third party beneficiary did not fit readily into either category—creditor beneficiary or donee beneficiary. Thus, the modern view, and the one adopted by the *Restatement (Second) of Contracts,* does not draw such clear lines and distinguishes only between intended beneficiaries (who can sue to enforce contracts made for their benefit) and incidental beneficiaries (who cannot sue, as will be discussed shortly).

WHEN THE RIGHTS OF AN INTENDED BENEFICIARY VEST

An intended third party beneficiary cannot enforce a contract against the original parties until the rights of the third party have *vested,* which means the rights have taken effect and cannot be taken away. Until these rights have vested, the original parties to the contract—the promisor and the promisee—can modify or rescind the contract without the consent of the third party. When do the rights of third parties vest? Generally, the rights vest when one of the following occurs:

① When the third party demonstrates manifest assent to the contract, such as sending a letter or note acknowl-

---

[6] See UCC 2–210(1), (4); and *Restatement (Second) of Contracts,* Section 328.

[7] *Seaver v. Ransom,* 224 N.Y. 233, 120 N.E. 639 (1918).

edging awareness of and consent to a contract formed for her or his benefit.

② When the third party materially alters his or her position in detrimental reliance on the contract, such as when a donee beneficiary contracts to have a home built in reliance on the receipt of funds promised to him or her in a donee beneficiary contract.

③ When the conditions for vesting mature. For example, the rights of a beneficiary under a life insurance policy vest when the insured person dies.

If the contract expressly reserves to the contracting parties the right to cancel, rescind, or modify the contract, the rights of the third party beneficiary are subject to any changes that result. In such a situation, the vesting of the third party's rights does not terminate the power of the original contracting parties to alter their legal relationships.[8]

INCIDENTAL BENEFICIARIES

The benefit that an **incidental beneficiary** receives from a contract between two parties is unintentional. Therefore, an incidental beneficiary cannot enforce a contract to which he or she is not a party. • EXAMPLE #11 In one case, spectators of a Mike Tyson boxing fight in which Tyson was disqualified for biting his opponent's ear sued Tyson and the fight's promoters for a refund of their money on the basis of breach of contract. The spectators claimed that they had standing to sue the defendants as third party beneficiaries of the contract between Tyson and the fight's promoters. The court, however, held that the spectators did not have standing to sue because they were not in contractual privity with any of the defendants. Furthermore, any benefits they received from the contract were incidental to the contract.

The court noted that the spectators got what they paid for: "the right to view whatever event transpired."[9] • (For another illustration of the rule that incidental beneficiaries cannot enforce contracts to which they are not parties, see this chapter's *Business Law in the Online World* feature on page 223.)

INTENDED VERSUS INCIDENTAL BENEFICIARIES

In determining whether a third party beneficiary is an intended or an incidental beneficiary, the courts generally use the *reasonable person* test. That is, a beneficiary will be considered an intended beneficiary if a reasonable person in the position of the beneficiary would believe that the promisee *intended* to confer on the beneficiary the right to bring suit to enforce the contract. In determining whether a party is an intended or an incidental beneficiary, the courts also look at a number of other factors. The presence of one or more of the following factors strongly indicates that the third party is an intended (rather than an incidental) beneficiary to the contract:

① Performance is rendered directly to the third party.

② The third party has the right to control the details of performance.

③ The third party is expressly designated as a beneficiary in the contract.

Is a party who borrows money to build a house an intended beneficiary of a contract between the lender and a party whom the lender hires to monitor the progress of the home's construction? That was the question in the following case.

---

[8] Defenses raised against third party beneficiaries are given in *Restatement (Second) of Contracts*, Section 309.

[9] *Castillo v. Tyson*, 268 A.D.2d 336, 701 N.Y.S.2d 423 (Sup.Ct.App.Div. 2000).

CASE 11.3 **Vogan v. Hayes Appraisal Associates, Inc.**

Supreme Court of Iowa, 1999.
588 N.W.2d 420.
http://www.judicial.state.ia.us[a]

FACTS Susan and Rollin Vogan wanted to build a home in West Des Moines, Iowa. They met with builder Gary Markley of Char Enterprises, Inc., who agreed to build the home for $169,633.59. The Vogans obtained a $170,000 construction loan from MidAmerica Savings Bank, which hired Hayes Appraisal Associates, Inc., to monitor the progress of the construction. MidAmerica was to disburse payments to Markley based on Hayes's reports. There were cost overruns on the job, and after three months, less than $2,000 of the initial loan remained. Markley said that it would take another $70,000 to finish the house. The Vogans borrowed $42,050

---

a. This Web site is maintained by the state of Iowa. In the left column, click on "Supreme Court." On that page, again in the left column, click on "Opinions Archive." When the archive opens, click on "1999," and in that list, next to "January 21, 1999," click on "Index." Scroll down the list of cases to the *Vogan* case and click on the case name to access the opinion.

(Continued)

CASE 11.3—Continued

more, added some of their own money, and gave it to the bank to continue payments to Markley based on Hayes's reports. A few weeks later, Hayes reported that the house was 90 percent complete. Seven months later, with the house still unfinished, Markley ceased working on the job. Another contractor estimated that completion would cost an additional $60,000. The Vogans filed a suit in an Iowa state court against Hayes, based in part on Hayes's contract with MidAmerica. Hayes answered in part that the Vogans were not third party beneficiaries of that contract. The court issued a judgment in favor of the Vogans. Hayes appealed to a state intermediate appellate court, which reversed the judgment. The Vogans then appealed to the Iowa Supreme Court.

ISSUE Were the Vogans intended third party beneficiaries of the contract between Hayes and MidAmerica?

DECISION Yes. The Iowa Supreme Court held that the Vogans were intended third party beneficiaries of the contract between Hayes and MidAmerica, as evidenced by the state-

ments in the contract. The state supreme court vacated the decision of the state intermediate appellate court and affirmed the judgment of the trial court.

REASON The court stated that "the primary question in a third-party beneficiary case is whether the contract manifests an intent to benefit a third party. However, this intent need not be to benefit a third party directly." The court reasoned that in this case, "[t]he promised performance of Hayes Appraisal to MidAmerica will be of pecuniary benefit to the Vogans, and the contract is so expressed as to give Hayes reason to know that such benefit is contemplated by MidAmerica as one of the motivating causes of making the contract. * * * [In] these circumstances, the Vogans qualify as [intended] third-party beneficiaries of the agreement between MidAmerica and Hayes Appraisal."

FOR CRITICAL ANALYSIS—Social Consideration
If the Vogans could not recover as third party beneficiaries of the Hayes-MidAmerica contract, would they have any legal recourse? If so, against whom?

Contract Discharge

The most common way to **discharge**, or terminate, one's contractual duties is by the **performance** of those duties. The duty to perform under a contract may be *conditioned* on the occurrence or nonoccurrence of a certain event, or the duty may be *absolute*. In addition to performance, a contract can be discharged in numerous other ways, including discharge by agreement of the parties and discharge by operation of law.

CONDITIONS OF PERFORMANCE

In most contracts, promises of performance are not expressly conditioned or qualified. Instead, they are *absolute promises*. They must be performed, or the party promising the act will be in breach of contract. ● EXAMPLE #12 JoAnne contracts to sell Alfonso a painting for $10,000. The parties' promises are unconditional: JoAnne's transfer of the painting to Alfonso and Alfonso's payment of $10,000 to JoAnne. The payment does not have to be made if the painting is not transferred. ●

In some situations, however, contractual promises are conditioned. A **condition** is a possible future event, the occurrence or nonoccurrence of which will trigger the performance of a legal obligation or terminate an existing obligation under a contract. If the condition is not satisfied, the

obligations of the parties are discharged. ● EXAMPLE #13 Suppose that Alfonso, in the above example, offers to purchase JoAnne's painting only if an independent appraisal indicates that it is worth at least $10,000. JoAnne accepts Alfonso's offer. Their obligations (promises) are conditioned on the outcome of the appraisal. Should this condition not be satisfied (for example, if the appraiser deems the value of the painting to be only $5,000), their obligations to each other are discharged and cannot be enforced. ●

We look here at three types of conditions that can be present in any given contract: conditions precedent, conditions subsequent, and concurrent conditions.

Conditions Precedent. A condition that must be fulfilled before a party's promise becomes absolute is called a **condition precedent**. The condition precedes the absolute duty to perform. ● EXAMPLE #14 In the JoAnne-Alfonso example just given, Alfonso's promise is subject to the condition precedent that the appraised value of the painting be at least $10,000. Until the condition is fulfilled, Alfonso's promise is not absolute. Insurance contracts frequently specify that certain conditions, such as passing a physical examination, must be met before the insurance company will be obligated to perform under the contract. ●

Conditions Subsequent. When a condition operates to terminate a party's absolute promise to perform, it is called

BUSINESS LAW IN THE ONLINE WORLD
Beneficiaries of Contracts for Internet Services

As you will read elsewhere in this chapter, the courts generally consider several factors when deciding whether a party is an *intended* third party beneficiary of a contract or only an *incidental* third party beneficiary of the contract. One of these factors is whether the third party is expressly designated as a beneficiary in the contract.

HOW SPECIFIC MUST THE DESIGNATION OF A THIRD PARTY BENEFICIARY BE?

Suppose that a contract between an Internet service provider (ISP) and a subscriber states that the subscriber will not use the services of the ISP to, among other things, "infringe on the rights of others." If, in violation of this contract, a subscriber does infringe on the rights of others, do "others" have the right, as intended third party beneficiaries, to sue the ISP? Do the "others" referred to in this contract constitute incidental or intended beneficiaries of the contract?

This question came before a court in a case that arose when subscribers of two ISPs offered for sale over the Internet videotapes of intercollegiate athletes in various states of undress. The athletes were videotaped, without their knowledge or consent, by hidden cameras in rest rooms, locker rooms, and showers. Among other things,

the athletes contended that they were intended third party beneficiaries of the contracts between the ISPs and the subscribers. The contracts provided that the subscribers would not use the services of the ISPs "to violate federal or state law, or infringe [on] the rights of others, or distribute child pornography or obscenity over the Internet." The athletes argued that they qualified as "others" and thus were intended third party beneficiaries.

"OTHERS" IS NOT SPECIFIC ENOUGH

The court held that the athletes did not acquire the status of third party beneficiaries merely because they qualified as "others." Said the court, "This is insufficient to state a claim as an intended third party beneficiary. Plaintiffs [the athletes] must allege express language in the contract identifying the third party beneficiary or imply a showing where the implication that the contract applies to third parties is so strong as to be practically an express declaration." Because the plaintiffs failed to accomplish this, they failed to state a claim as third party beneficiaries.[a]

FOR CRITICAL ANALYSIS

Why did the athletes sue the ISPs as third party beneficiaries under contract law? Did they have recourse against the subscribers' actions under any other legal theory?

a. *Doe v. Franco Productions*, 2000 WL 816779 (N.D.Ill. 2000).

---

a **condition subsequent.** The condition follows, or is subsequent to, the absolute duty to perform. If the condition occurs, the party need not perform any further. ● EXAMPLE #15 A law firm hires Julia Darby, a recent law school graduate and a newly licensed attorney. Their contract provides that the firm's obligation to continue employing Darby is discharged if Darby fails to maintain her license to practice law. This is a condition subsequent because a failure to maintain the license will discharge a duty that has already arisen.[10] ●

Generally, conditions precedent are common, while conditions subsequent are rare. The *Restatement (Second) of Contracts* deletes the terms *condition subsequent* and *condition precedent* and refers to both simply as "conditions."[11]

Concurrent Conditions. When each party's absolute duty to perform is conditioned on the other party's absolute duty to perform, **concurrent conditions** are present. These conditions exist only when the parties expressly or impliedly are to perform their respective duties *simultaneously*. ● EXAMPLE #16 If a buyer promises to pay for goods when they are delivered by the seller, each party's absolute duty to perform is conditioned on the other party's absolute duty to perform. The buyer's duty to pay for the goods does not become absolute until the seller either delivers or attempts to deliver the goods.

---

[10] The difference between conditions precedent and conditions subsequent is relatively unimportant from a substantive point of view but very important procedurally. Usually, the plaintiff must prove conditions precedent because typically it is the plaintiff who claims that there is a duty to be performed. Similarly, the defendant must normally prove conditions subsequent because typically it is the defendant who claims that a duty no longer exists.

[11] *Restatement (Second) of Contracts*, Section 224.

Likewise, the seller's duty to deliver the goods does not become absolute until the buyer pays or attempts to pay for the goods. Therefore, neither can recover from the other for breach without first tendering performance.●

DISCHARGE BY PERFORMANCE

The contract comes to an end when both parties fulfill their respective duties by performance of the acts they have promised. Performance can also be accomplished by tender. **Tender** is an unconditional offer to perform by a person who is ready, willing, and able to do so. Therefore, a seller who places goods at the disposal of a buyer has tendered delivery and can demand payment according to the terms of the agreement. A buyer who offers to pay for goods has tendered payment and can demand delivery of the goods.

Once performance has been tendered, the party making the tender has done everything possible to carry out the terms of the contract. If the other party then refuses to perform, the party making the tender can consider the duty discharged and sue for **breach of contract**.

Complete versus Substantial Performance. Normally, conditions expressly stated in the contract must fully occur in all aspects for *complete performance* (strict performance) of the contract to occur. Any deviation breaches the contract and discharges the other party's obligations to perform. Although in most contracts the parties fully discharge their obligations by complete performance, sometimes a party fails to fulfill all of the duties or completes the duties in a manner contrary to the terms of the contract. The issue then arises as to whether the performance was nonetheless sufficiently substantial to discharge the contractual obligations.

To qualify as *substantial performance,* the performance must not vary greatly from the performance promised in the contract, and it must create substantially the same benefits as those promised in the contract. If performance is substantial, the other party's duty to perform remains absolute (less damages, if any, for the minor deviations).

●**EXAMPLE #17** A couple contracts with a construction company to build a house. The contract specifies that Brand X plasterboard be used for the walls. The builder cannot obtain Brand X plasterboard, and the buyers are on holiday in the mountains of Peru and virtually unreachable. The builder decides to install Brand Y instead, which he knows is identical in quality and durability to Brand X plasterboard. All other aspects of construction conform to the contract. Does this deviation constitute a breach of contract? Can the buyers avoid their contractual obligation to pay the builder because Brand Y plasterboard was used instead of Brand X? Very likely, a court would hold that the builder had substantially performed his end of the bargain,

and therefore the couple will be obligated to pay the builder.●

What if the plasterboard substituted for Brand X was not of the same quality as Brand X, and the value of the house was reduced by $10,000? Again, a court would likely hold that the contract was substantially performed and that the contractor should be paid the price agreed on in the contract, less that $10,000.

Performance to the Satisfaction of Another. Contracts often state that completed work must personally satisfy one of the parties or a third person. The question is whether this satisfaction becomes a condition precedent, requiring actual personal satisfaction or approval for discharge, or whether the test of satisfaction is performance that would satisfy a *reasonable person* (substantial performance).

When the subject matter of the contract is personal, a contract to be performed to the satisfaction of one of the parties is conditioned, and performance must actually satisfy that party. For example, contracts for portraits, works of art, and tailoring are considered personal. Therefore, only the personal satisfaction of the party fulfills the condition—unless a jury finds the party is expressing dissatisfaction only to avoid payment or otherwise is not acting in good faith.

Contracts that involve mechanical fitness, utility, or marketability need be performed only to the satisfaction of a reasonable person unless they *expressly state otherwise.* When such contracts require performance to the satisfaction of a third party (for example, "to the satisfaction of Robert Ames, the supervising engineer"), the courts are divided. A majority of courts require the work to be satisfactory to a reasonable person, but some courts hold that the personal satisfaction of the third party designated in the contract (Robert Ames, in this example) must be met. Again, the personal judgment must be made honestly, or the condition will be excused.

Material Breach of Contract. When a breach of contract is *material*[12]—that is, when performance is not deemed substantial—the nonbreaching party is excused from the performance of contractual duties and has a cause of action to sue for damages caused by the breach. If the breach is *minor* (not material), the nonbreaching party's duty to perform may sometimes be suspended until the breach is remedied, but the duty is not entirely excused. Once the minor breach is cured, the nonbreaching party must resume performance of the contractual obligations that had been undertaken.

A breach entitles the nonbreaching party to sue for damages, but only a material breach discharges the nonbreach-

---

[12] *Restatement (Second) of Contracts,* Section 241.

ing party from the contract. The policy underlying these rules is that contracts should go forward when only minor problems occur, but contracts should be terminated if major problems arise.[13]

Anticipatory Repudiation of a Contract. Before either party to a contract has a duty to perform, one of the parties may refuse to fulfill her or his contractual obligations. This is called **anticipatory repudiation**.[14] When anticipatory repudiation occurs, it is treated as a material breach of contract, and the nonbreaching party is permitted to bring an action for damages immediately, even though the scheduled time for performance under the contract may still be in the future.[15] Until the nonbreaching party treats this early repudiation as a breach, however, the breaching party can retract the anticipatory repudiation by proper notice and restore the parties to their original obligations.[16]

An anticipatory repudiation is treated as a present, material breach for two reasons. First, the nonbreaching party should not be required to remain ready and willing to perform when the other party has already repudiated the contract. Second, the nonbreaching party should have the opportunity to seek a similar contract elsewhere and may have the duty to do so to minimize his or her loss.

Quite often, an anticipatory repudiation occurs when a sharp fluctuation in market prices creates a situation in which performance of the contract would be extremely unfavorable to one of the parties. ● EXAMPLE #18 Shasta Manufacturing Company contracts to manufacture and sell 100,000 personal computers to New Age, Inc., a computer retailer with 500 outlet stores. Delivery is to be made two months from the date of the contract. One month later, three suppliers of computer parts raise their prices to Shasta. Because of these higher prices, Shasta stands to lose $500,000 if it sells the computers to New Age at the contract price. Shasta writes to New Age, informing New Age that it cannot deliver the 100,000 computers at the agreed-on contract price. Even though you might sympathize with Shasta, its letter is an anticipatory repudiation of the contract, allowing New Age the option of treating the repudiation as a material breach and proceeding immediately to

pursue remedies, even though the contract delivery date is still a month away.[17]●

DISCHARGE BY AGREEMENT

Any contract can be discharged by the agreement of the parties. The agreement can be contained in the original contract, or the parties can form a new contract for the express purpose of discharging the original contract.

Discharge by Rescission. As discussed in an earlier chapter, rescission is the process in which the parties cancel the contract and are returned to the positions they occupied prior to the contract's formation. For *mutual rescission* to take place, the parties must make another agreement that also satisfies the legal requirements for a contract—there must be an *offer,* an *acceptance,* and *consideration.* Ordinarily, if the parties agree to rescind the original contract, their promises not to perform those acts promised in the original contract will be legal consideration for the second contract.

Mutual rescission can occur in this manner when the original contract is executory on both sides (that is, neither party has completed performance). The agreement to rescind an executory contract is generally enforceable, even if it is made orally and even if the original agreement was in writing.[18] When one party has fully performed, however, an agreement to rescind the original contract usually is not enforceable unless additional consideration or restitution is made.[19]

Discharge by Novation. The process of **novation** substitutes a third party for one of the original parties. Essentially, the parties to the original contract and one or more new parties all get together and agree to the substitution. The requirements of a novation are as follows:

① The existence of a previous, valid obligation.

② Agreement by all of the parties to a new contract.

③ The extinguishing of the old obligation (discharge of the prior party).

④ A new, valid contract.

---

[13] See UCC 2–612, which deals with installment contracts for the sale of goods.

[14] *Restatement (Second) of Contracts,* Section 253; and UCC 2–610.

[15] The doctrine of anticipatory repudiation first arose in the landmark case of *Hochster v. De La Tour,* 2 Ellis and Blackburn Reports 678 (1853), when the English court recognized the delay and expense inherent in a rule requiring a nonbreaching party to wait until the time of performance before suing on an anticipatory repudiation.

[16] See UCC 2–611.

---

[17] Another illustration can be found in *Reliance Cooperage Corp. v. Treat,* 195 F.2d 977 (8th Cir. 1952).

[18] Agreements to rescind contracts involving transfers of realty, however, must be evidenced by a writing. Another exception has to do with the sale of goods under the UCC, when the sales contract requires written rescission.

[19] Under UCC 2–209(1), however, no consideration is needed to modify a contract for a sale of goods. See Chapter 14. Also see UCC 1–107.

An important distinction between an assignment or delegation and a novation is that a novation involves a new contract, and an assignment or delegation involves the old contract.

● **EXAMPLE #19** Suppose that you contract with A. Logan Enterprises to sell it your office equipment business. Logan later learns that it should not expand at this time but knows of another party, MBI Corporation, that is interested in purchasing your business. All three of you get together and agree to a novation. As long as the new contract is supported by consideration, the novation discharges the original contract between you and Logan and replaces it with the new contract between you and MBI Corporation. Logan prefers the novation to an assignment because the novation discharges all the contract liabilities stemming from Logan's contract with you. If the original contract had been an installment sales contract requiring twelve monthly payments, and Logan had merely assigned the contract (assigned its rights and delegated its duties under the contract) to MBI Corporation, Logan would have remained liable to you for the payments if MBI Corporation defaulted.●

Discharge by Accord and Satisfaction. As discussed in Chapter 8, in an *accord and satisfaction,* the parties agree to accept performance different from the performance originally promised. An *accord* is an executory contract (one that has not yet been performed) to perform some act in order to satisfy an existing contractual duty that is not yet discharged.[20] A *satisfaction* is the performance of the accord agreement. An *accord* and its *satisfaction* discharge the original contractual obligation.

Once the accord has been made, the original obligation is merely suspended until the accord agreement is fully performed. If it is not performed, the party to whom performance is owed can bring an action on the original obligation or for breach of the accord. ● **EXAMPLE #20** Shea obtains a judgment against Marla for $4,000. Later, both parties agree that the judgment can be satisfied by Marla's transfer of her automobile to Shea. This agreement to accept the auto in lieu of $4,000 in cash is the accord. If Marla transfers her automobile to Shea, the accord agreement is fully performed, and the $4,000 debt is discharged. If Marla refuses to transfer her car, the accord is breached. Because the original obligation is merely suspended, Shea can bring an action to enforce the judgment for $4,000 in cash or bring an action for breach of the accord.●

DISCHARGE BY OPERATION OF LAW

Under some circumstances, contractual duties may be discharged by operation of law. These circumstances include material alteration of the contract, the running of the relevant statute of limitations, bankruptcy, and impossibility of performance.

Contract Alteration. To discourage parties from altering written contracts, the law operates to allow an innocent party to be discharged when one party has materially altered a written contract without the knowledge or consent of the other party. For example, if a party alters a material term of the contract—such as the quantity term or the price term—without the knowledge or consent of the other party, the party who was unaware of the alteration can treat the contract as discharged or terminated.

Statutes of Limitations. As mentioned earlier in this text, statutes of limitations limit the period during which a party can sue on a particular cause of action. After the applicable limitations period has passed, a suit can no longer be brought. For example, the limitations period for bringing suits for breach of oral contracts is usually two to three years; for written contracts, four to five years; and for recovery of amounts awarded in judgment, ten to twenty years, depending on state law. Suits for breach of a contract for the sale of goods must be brought within four years after the cause of action has accrued. By original agreement, the parties can reduce this four-year period to a one-year period. They cannot, however, extend it beyond the four-year limitations period.

Bankruptcy. A proceeding in bankruptcy attempts to allocate the assets the debtor owns to the creditors in a fair and equitable fashion. Once the assets have been allocated, the debtor receives a *discharge in bankruptcy*—see Chapter 21. A discharge in bankruptcy will ordinarily bar enforcement of most of a debtor's contracts by the creditors.

When Performance Is Impossible. After a contract has been made, performance may become impossible in an objective sense. This is known as **impossibility of performance** and may discharge the contract.[21]

Objective Impossibility. *Objective impossibility* ("It can't be done") must be distinguished from subjective impossibility ("I'm sorry, I simply can't do it"). An example of subjective impossibility is a contract in which funds cannot be paid on time because the bank is closed.[22] In effect, the nonperforming party is saying, "It is impossible for *me* to perform," rather than "It is impossible for *anyone* to perform."

---

[20] *Restatement (Second) of Contracts,* Section 281.

[21] *Restatement (Second) of Contracts,* Section 261.
[22] *Ingham Lumber Co. v. Ingersoll & Co.,* 93 Ark. 447, 125 S.W. 139 (1910).

Accordingly, such excuses do not discharge a contract, and the nonperforming party is normally held in breach of contract. Four basic types of situations will generally qualify as grounds for the discharge of contractual obligations based on impossibility of performance:[23]

① *When a party whose personal performance is essential to the completion of the contract dies or becomes incapacitated prior to performance.* ● EXAMPLE #21 Fred, a famous dancer, contracts with Ethereal Dancing Guild to play a leading role in its new ballet. Before the ballet can be performed, Fred becomes ill and dies. His personal performance was essential to the completion of the contract. Thus, his death discharges the contract and his estate's liability for his nonperformance.●

② *When the specific subject matter of the contract is destroyed.* ● EXAMPLE #22 A-1 Farm Equipment agrees to sell Gudgel the green tractor on its lot and promises to have it ready for Gudgel to pick up on Saturday. On Friday night, however, a truck veers off the nearby highway and smashes into the tractor, destroying it beyond repair. Because the contract was for this specific tractor, A-1's performance is rendered impossible owing to the accident.●

③ *When a change in the law renders performance illegal.* An example is a contract to build an apartment building, when the zoning laws are changed to prohibit the construction of residential rental property at this location. This change renders the contract impossible to perform.

④ *When performance becomes commercially impracticable.* The inclusion of this type of "impossibility" as a basis for contract discharge results from a growing trend to allow parties to discharge contracts in which the originally contemplated performance turns out to be much more difficult or expensive than anticipated. In such situations, courts may excuse parties from their performance obligations under the doctrine of *commercial impracticability.* For example, in one case, a court held that a contract could be discharged because a party would have to pay ten times more than the original estimate to excavate a certain amount of gravel.[24]

Temporary Impossibility. An occurrence or event that makes performance temporarily impossible operates to suspend performance until the impossibility ceases. Then, ordinarily, the parties must perform the contract as originally planned. If, however, the lapse of time and the change in circumstances surrounding the contract make it substantially more burdensome for the parties to perform the promised acts, the contract is discharged.

● EXAMPLE #23 The leading case on the subject, *Autry v. Republic Productions,*[25] involved an actor who was drafted into the army in 1942. Being drafted rendered the actor's contract temporarily impossible to perform, and it was suspended until the end of the war. When the actor got out of the army, the purchasing power of the dollar had so changed that performance of the contract would have been substantially burdensome to him. Therefore, the contract was discharged.●

---

[23] *Restatement (Second) of Contracts,* Sections 262–266; and UCC 2–615.

[24] *Mineral Park Land Co. v. Howard,* 172 Cal. 289, 156 P. 458 (1916).
[25] 30 Cal.2d 144, 180 P.2d 888 (1947).

Terms and Concepts

Chapter Summary	**Third Party Rights and Discharge**

THIRD PARTY RIGHTS	

Assignments
(See pages 214–218.)
	1. An assignment is the transfer of rights under a contract to a third party. The person assigning the rights is the *assignor,* and the party to whom the rights are assigned is the *assignee.* The assignee has a right to demand performance from the other original party to the contract.
	
	2. Generally, all rights can be assigned, except in the following circumstances:
	
	  a. When assignment is expressly prohibited by statute (for example, workers' compensation benefits).
	
	  b. When a contract calls for the performance of personal services.
	
	  c. When the assignment will materially increase or alter the risks or duties of the obligor (the party that is obligated to perform).
	
	  d. When the contract itself stipulates that the rights cannot be assigned (with some exceptions).
	
	3. The assignee should give notice of the assignment to the obligor.
	
	  a. If the assignor assigns the same right to two different persons, generally the first assignment in time is the first in right, although in some states the first assignee to give notice takes priority.
	
	  b. Until the obligor is notified of the assignment, the obligor can tender performance to the assignor; and if performance is accepted by the assignor, the obligor's duties under the contract are discharged without benefit to the assignee.

Delegations
(See pages 218–220.)
	1. A delegation is the transfer of duties under a contract to a third party (the *delegatee*), who then assumes the obligation of performing the contractual duties previously held by the one making the delegation (the *delegator*).
	
	2. As a general rule, any duty can be delegated, except in the following circumstances:
	
	  a. When performance depends on the personal skill or talents of the obligor.
	
	  b. When special trust has been placed in the obligor.
	
	  c. When performance by a third party will vary materially from that expected by the obligee (the one to whom the duty is owed) under the contract.
	
	  d. When the contract expressly prohibits delegation.
	
	3. A valid delegation of duties does not relieve the delegator of obligations under the contract. If the delegatee fails to perform, the delegator is still liable to the obligee.
	
	4. An "assignment of all rights" or an "assignment of contract" is often construed to mean that both the rights and the duties arising under the contract are transferred to a third party.

Third Party Beneficiaries (See pages 220–222.)	A third party beneficiary contract is one made for the purpose of benefiting a third party. 1. *Intended beneficiary*—One for whose benefit a contract is created. When the promisor (the one making the contractual promise that benefits a third party) fails to perform as promised, the third party can sue the promisor directly. Examples of third party beneficiaries are creditor and donee beneficiaries. 2. *Incidental beneficiary*—A third party who indirectly (incidentally) benefits from a contract but for whose benefit the contract was not specifically intended. Incidental beneficiaries have no rights to the benefits received and cannot sue to have the contract enforced.

Chapter Summary	Third Party Rights and Discharge—Continued

CONTRACT DISCHARGE	
Conditions of Performance (See pages 222–224.)	Contract obligations may be subject to the following types of conditions: 1. *Condition precedent*—A condition that must be fulfilled before a party's promise becomes absolute. 2. *Condition subsequent*—A condition that operates to terminate a party's absolute promise to perform. 3. *Concurrent conditions*—In this case, each party's absolute duty to perform is conditioned on the other party's absolute duty to perform.
Discharge by Performance (See pages 224–225.)	A contract may be discharged by complete (strict) performance or by substantial performance. In some cases, performance must be to the satisfaction of another. Totally inadequate performance constitutes a material breach of contract. An anticipatory repudiation of a contract allows the other party to sue immediately for breach of contract.
Discharge by Agreement (See pages 225–226.)	Parties may agree to discharge their contractual obligations in several ways: 1. *By rescission*—The parties mutually agree to rescind (cancel) the contract. 2. *By novation*—A new party is substituted for one of the primary parties to a contract. 3. *By accord and satisfaction*—The parties agree to render and accept performance different from that on which they originally agreed.
Discharge by Operation of Law (See pages 226–227.)	Parties' obligations under contracts may be discharged by operation of law owing to one of the following: 1. Contract alteration. 2. Statutes of limitations. 3. Bankruptcy. 4. Impossibility of performance.

For Review

① What is the difference between an assignment and a delegation?

② What rights can be assigned despite a contract clause expressly prohibiting assignment?

③ What factors indicate that a third party beneficiary is an intended beneficiary?

④ How are most contracts discharged?

⑤ What is a contractual condition, and how might a condition affect contractual obligations?

Questions and Case Problems

11–1. Substantial Performance. Complete performance is full performance according to the terms of a contract. Discuss the effect on the parties if there is less than full performance.

11–2. Third Party Beneficiaries. Wilken owes Rivera $2,000. Howie promises Wilken that he will pay Rivera the $2,000 in return for Wilken's promise to give Howie's children guitar lessons. Is Rivera an intended beneficiary of the Howie-Wilken contract? Explain.

11–3. Assignments. Aron, a college student, signs a one-year lease agreement that runs from September 1 to August 31. The lease agreement specifies that the lease cannot be assigned without the landlord's consent. In late May, Aron decides not to go to summer school and assigns the balance of the lease (three months) to a close friend, Erica. The landlord objects to the assignment and denies Erica access to the apartment. Aron claims that Erica is financially sound and should be allowed the full rights and privileges of an assignee. Discuss fully whether the landlord or Aron is correct.

11–4. Novation versus Accord and Satisfaction. Doug owes creditor Cartwright $1,000, which is due and payable on June 1. Doug has a car accident, misses several months of work, and consequently does not have the funds to pay Cartwright on June 1. Doug's father, Bert, offers to pay Cartwright $1,100 in four equal installments if Cartwright will discharge Doug from any further liability on the debt. Cartwright accepts. Is the transaction a novation or an accord and satisfaction? Explain.

11–5. Impossibility of Performance. Millie contracted to sell Frank 1,000 bushels of corn to be grown on Millie's farm. Owing to a drought during the growing season, Millie's yield was much less than anticipated, and she could deliver only 250 bushels to Frank. Frank accepted the lesser amount but sued Millie for breach of contract. Can Millie defend successfully on the basis of objective impossibility of performance? Explain.

11–6. Performance. Steven McPheters, a house builder and developer, hired Terry Tentinger, who did business as New Horizon Construction, to do some touching up and repainting on one of McPheters's new houses. Tentinger worked two days, billed McPheters $420 (a three-man crew for fourteen hours at $30 per hour), and offered to return to the house to remedy any defects in his work at no cost. McPheters objected to the number of hours on the bill—although he did not express dissatisfaction with the work—and offered Tentinger $250. Tentinger refused to accept this sum and filed a suit in an Idaho state court to collect the full amount. McPheters filed a counterclaim, alleging that Tentinger failed to perform the job in a skilled manner, resulting in $2,500 in damages, which it would cost $500 to repair. Tentinger's witnesses testified that although some touch-up work needed to be done, the job had been performed in a skilled manner. McPheters presented testimony indicating that the work was so defective as to render it commercially unreasonable. On what basis could the court rule in Tentinger's favor? Explain fully. [*Tentinger v. McPheters*, 132 Idaho 620, 977 P.2d 234 (Idaho App. 1999)]

CASE PROBLEM WITH SAMPLE ANSWER

11–7. In May 1996, O'Brien-Shiepe Funeral Home, Inc., in Hempstead, New York, hired Teramo & Co. to build an addition to O'Brien's funeral home. The parties' contract did not specify a date for the completion of the work. The city of Hempstead issued a building permit for the project on June 14, and Teramo began work about two weeks later. There was some delay in construction because O'Brien asked that no work be done during funeral services, but by the end of March 1997, the work was substantially complete. The city of Hempstead issued a "Certificate of Completion" on April 15. During the construction, O'Brien made periodic payments to Teramo, but there was a balance due of $17,950, which O'Brien did not pay. To recover this amount, Teramo filed a suit in a New York state court against O'Brien. O'Brien filed a counterclaim to recover lost profits for business allegedly lost due to the time Teramo took

to build the addition, and for $6,180 spent to correct problems caused by poor work. Which, if any, party is entitled to an award in this case? Explain. [*Teramo & Co. v. O'Brien-Shiepe Funeral Home, Inc.*, 725 N.Y.S.2d 87 (A.D. 2 Dept. 2001)]

▶ **To view a sample answer for this case problem, go to this book's Web site at <u>http://fundamentals.westbuslaw.com</u> and click on "Interactive Study Center."**

11–8. Third Party Beneficiary. Acciai Speciali Terni USA, Inc. (AST), hired a carrier to ship steel sheets and coils from Italy to the United States on the *M/V Berane*. The ship's receipt for the goods included a forum-selection clause, which stated that any dispute would be "decided in the country where the carrier has his principal place of business." The receipt also contained a "Himalaya" clause, which extended "every right, exemption from liability, defense and immunity" that the carrier enjoyed to those acting on the carrier's behalf. Transcom Terminals, Ltd., was the U.S. stevedore—that is, Transcom off-loaded the vessel and stored the cargo for eventual delivery to AST. Finding the cargo damaged, AST filed a suit in a federal district court against Transcom and others, charging in part negligence in the off-loading. Transcom filed a motion to dismiss on the basis of the forum-selection clause. Transcom argued that it was an intended third party beneficiary of this provision through the Himalaya clause. Is Transcom correct? What should the court rule? Explain. [*Acciai Speciali Terni USA, Inc. v. M/V Berane*, 181 F.Supp.2d 458 (D.Md. 2002)]

11–9. Substantial Performance. Adolf and Ida Krueger contracted with Pisani Construction, Inc., to erect a metal building as an addition to an existing structure. The two structures were to share a common wall, and the frames and panel heights of the new building were to match those of the existing structure. Shortly before completion of the project, however, it was apparent that the roof line of the new building was approximately three inches higher than that of the existing structure. Pisani modified the ridge caps of the buildings to blend the roof lines. The discrepancy had other consequences, however, including misalignment of the gutters and windows of the two buildings, which resulted in an icing problem in the winter. The Kruegers occupied the new structure, but refused to make the last payment under the contract. Pisani filed a suit in a Connecticut state court to collect. Did Pisani substantially perform its obligations? Should the Kruegers be ordered to pay? Why or why not? [*Pisani Construction, Inc. v. Krueger*, 68 Conn.App. 361, 791 A.2d 634 (2002)]

A QUESTION OF ETHICS AND SOCIAL RESPONSIBILITY

11–10. Bath Iron Works (BIW) offered a job to Thomas Devine, contingent on Devine's passing a drug test. The testing was conducted by NorDx, a subcontractor of Roche Biomedical Laboratories. When NorDx found that Devine's urinalysis showed the presence of opiates, a result confirmed by Roche, BIW refused to offer Devine permanent employment. Devine claimed that the ingestion of poppy seeds can lead to a positive result and that he tested positive for opiates only because of his daily consumption of poppy seed muffins. In Devine's suit against Roche, Devine argued, among other things, that he was a third party beneficiary of the contract between his employer (BIW) and NorDx (Roche). Given this factual background, consider the following questions. [*Devine v. Roche Biomedical Laboratories,* 659 A.2d 868 (Me. 1995)]

1. Is Devine an intended third party beneficiary of the BIW–NorDx contract? In deciding this issue, should the court focus on the nature of the promises made in the contract itself or on the consequences of the contract for Devine, a third party?

2. Should employees whose job security and reputation have suffered as a result of false test results be allowed to sue the drug-testing labs for the tort of negligence? In such situations, do drug-testing labs have a duty to the employees to exercise reasonable care in conducting the tests?

VIDEO QUESTION

11–11. Go to this text's Web site at **http://fundamentals.westbuslaw.com** and click on "Video Questions." Select "Chapter 11" and view the video titled *Third Party Beneficiaries.* Then answer the following questions:

1. Discuss whether a valid contract was formed when Oscar and Vinny bet on the outcome of a football game. Would Vinny be able to enforce the contract in court?
2. Is the Fresh Air Fund an incidental or intended beneficiary? Why?
3. Can Maria sue to enforce Vinny's promise to donate Oscar's winnings to the Fresh Air Fund?

THIRD PARTY RIGHTS AND DISCHARGE

For updated links to resources available on the Web, as well as other materials, visit this text's Web site at

http://fundamentals.westbuslaw.com

You can find a *New York Law Journal* article that discusses third party beneficiaries and other topics covered in this chapter at

http://www6.law.com/ny/links/150sterk.html

Online Legal Research

Go to the *Fundamentals of Business Law* home page at **http://fundamentals.westbuslaw.com**. Select "Interactive Study Center" and then click on "Chapter 11." There you will find the following Internet research exercises that you can perform to learn more about topics covered in this chapter.

Activity 11–1: MANAGEMENT PERSPECTIVE—**Professional Liability to Third Parties**
Activity 11–2: ECONOMIC PERSPECTIVE—**Commercial Impracticability**

Before the Test

Go to the *Fundamentals of Business Law* home page at **http://fundamentals.westbuslaw.com**. Click on "Interactive Quizzes." You will find at least twenty interactive questions relating to this chapter.

Westlaw® Campus

If your textbook provided for a subscription to Westlaw® Campus, or if you have otherwise purchased access to the Westlaw Campus database, you can access any of the cases presented or cited in this chapter by using your Westlaw Campus account.

12 Breach and Remedies

After reading this chapter, you should be able to answer the following questions:

① What is the difference between compensatory damages and consequential damages? What are nominal damages, and when might they be awarded by a court?

② What is the usual measure of damages on a breach of contract for a sale of goods?

③ Under what circumstances will the remedy of rescission and restitution be available?

④ When might specific performance be granted as a remedy?

⑤ What is the rationale underlying the doctrine of election of remedies?

Normally, a person enters into a contract with another to secure an advantage. When it is no longer advantageous for a party to fulfill his or her contractual obligations, breach of contract may result. As discussed in Chapter 11, a *breach of contract* occurs when a party fails to perform part or all of the required duties under a contract.[1] Once a party fails to perform or performs inadequately, the other party—the nonbreaching party—can choose one or more of several remedies.

The most common remedies available to a nonbreaching party under contract law include damages, rescission and restitution, specific performance, and reformation. As discussed in Chapter 1, courts distinguish between *remedies at law* and *remedies in equity*. Today, the remedy at law is normally money damages. We discuss this remedy in the first part of this chapter. Equitable remedies include rescission and restitution, specific performance, and reformation, all of which we examine later in the chapter. Usually, a court will not award an equitable remedy unless the remedy at law is inadequate. In the final pages of this chapter, we look at some special legal doctrines and concepts relating to remedies.

Damages

A breach of contract entitles the nonbreaching party to sue for money damages. As you read in Chapter 4, damages are designed to compensate a party for harm suffered as a result

---

[1] *Restatement (Second) of Contracts*, Section 235(2).

of another's wrongful act. In the context of contract law, damages are designed to compensate the nonbreaching party for the loss of the bargain. Often, courts say that innocent parties are to be placed in the position they would have occupied had the contract been fully performed.[2]

TYPES OF DAMAGES

There are basically four kinds of damages: compensatory, consequential, punitive, and nominal damages.

Compensatory Damages. As discussed in Chapter 4, *compensatory damages* compensate an injured party for injuries or damages actually sustained by that party. The nonbreaching party must prove that the actual damages arose directly from the loss of the bargain caused by the breach of contract. The amount of compensatory damages is the difference between the value of the breaching party's promised performance under the contract and the value of her or his actual performance. This amount is reduced by any loss that the injured party has avoided, however.

● **EXAMPLE #1** You contract with Marinot Industries to perform certain personal services exclusively for Marinot during August for a payment of $3,500. Marinot cancels the contract and is in breach. You are able to find another job during August but can earn only $1,000. You normally can sue Marinot for breach and recover $2,500 as compensatory damages. You may also recover from Marinot the amount that you spent to find the other job.● Expenses that are directly incurred because of a breach of contract—such as those incurred to obtain performance from another source—are called *incidental damages.*

The measurement of compensatory damages varies by type of contract. Certain types of contracts deserve special mention—contracts for the sale of goods, contracts for the sale of land, and construction contracts.

Sale of Goods. In a contract for the sale of goods, the usual measure of compensatory damages is an amount equal to the difference between the contract price and the market price.[3] ● **EXAMPLE #2** MediQuick Laboratories contracts with Cal Computer Industries to purchase ten model X-15 computer work stations for $8,000 each. If Cal Computer fails to deliver the ten work stations, and the current market price of the work stations is $8,150, MediQuick's measure of damages is $1,500 (10 × $150).● When the buyer breaches and the seller has not yet produced the goods, compensatory damages normally equal the lost profits on the sale rather than the difference between the contract price and the market price.

Sale of Land. The measure of damages in a contract for the sale of land is ordinarily the same as it is for contracts involving the sale of goods—that is, the difference between the contract price and the market price of the land. The majority of states follow this rule regardless of whether the buyer or the seller breaches the contract.

Construction Contracts. With construction contracts, the measure of damages often varies depending on which party breaches and at what stage the breach occurs. See Exhibit 12–1 for illustrations.

---

[2] *Restatement (Second) of Contracts,* Section 347; and UCC 1–106(1).

[3] That is, the difference between the contract price and the market price at the time and place at which the goods were to be delivered or tendered. See UCC 2–708, 2–713, and 2–715(1) (discussed in Chapter 16).

EXHIBIT 12–1 **MEASUREMENT OF DAMAGES—BREACH OF CONSTRUCTION CONTRACTS**

PARTY IN BREACH	TIME OF BREACH	MEASUREMENT OF DAMAGES
Owner	Before construction begins	Profits (contract price less cost of materials and labor)
Owner	After construction begins	Profits plus costs incurred up to time of breach
Owner	After construction is completed	Contract price
Contractor	Before construction is completed	Generally, all costs incurred by owner to complete construction

Consequential Damages. Foreseeable damages that result from a party's breach of contract are referred to as **consequential damages**, or *special damages*. Consequential damages differ from compensatory damages in that they are caused by special circumstances beyond the contract itself. When a seller does not deliver goods, knowing that a buyer is planning to use or resell those goods immediately, consequential damages are awarded for the loss of profits from the planned resale.

● EXAMPLE #3 Gilmore contracts to have a specific item shipped to her—one that she desperately needs to repair her printing press. In her contract with the shipper, Gilmore states that she must receive the item by Monday or she will not be able to print her paper and will lose $950. If the shipper is late, Gilmore normally can recover the consequential damages caused by the delay (that is, the $950 in losses). ●

For a nonbreaching party to recover consequential damages, the breaching party must know (or have reason to know) that special circumstances will cause the nonbreaching party to suffer an additional loss.[4] This rule was enunciated in *Hadley v. Baxendale,*[5] a case decided in England in 1854; today the rule still applies. When damages are awarded, compensation is given only for those injuries that the defendant *could reasonably have foreseen* as a probable result of the usual course of events following a breach. If the injury complained of is outside the usual and foreseeable course of events, the plaintiff must show specifically that the defendant had reason to know the facts and foresee the injury.

Punitive Damages. Recall from Chapter 4 that punitive damages are designed to punish a wrongdoer and set an example to deter similar conduct in the future. Punitive damages, which are also referred to as *exemplary damages,* are generally not recoverable in an action for breach of contract. Such damages have no legitimate place in contract law because they are, in essence, penalties, and a breach of contract is not unlawful in a criminal sense. A contract is simply a civil relationship between the parties. The law may compensate one party for the loss of the bargain—no more and no less.

In a few situations, a person's actions can cause both a breach of contract and a tort. For example, the parties can establish by contract a certain reasonable standard or duty of care. Failure to live up to that standard is a breach of contract, and the act itself may constitute negligence. An intentional tort (such as fraud) may also be tied to a breach of contract. In such a situation, it is possible for the nonbreaching party to recover punitive damages for the tort in addition to compensatory and consequential damages for the breach of contract.

Nominal Damages. Damages that are awarded to an innocent party when only a technical injury is involved and no actual damage (no financial loss) has been suffered are called **nominal damages**. Nominal damage awards are often small, such as one dollar, but they do establish that the defendant acted wrongfully. Most lawsuits for nominal damages are brought as a matter of principle under the theory that a breach has occurred and some damages must be imposed regardless of actual loss.

● EXAMPLE #4 Parrott contracts to buy potatoes at fifty cents a pound from Lentz. Lentz breaches the contract and does not deliver the potatoes. Meanwhile, the price of potatoes falls. Parrott is able to buy them in the open market at half the price he agreed to pay Lentz. Parrott is clearly better off because of Lentz's breach. Thus, in a suit for breach of contract, Parrott may be awarded only nominal damages for the technical injury he sustained, as no monetary loss was involved. ●

MITIGATION OF DAMAGES

In most situations, when a breach of contract occurs, the injured party is held to a duty to mitigate, or reduce, the damages that he or she suffers. Under this doctrine of **mitigation of damages**, the required action depends on the nature of the situation.

For example, some states require a landlord to use reasonable means to find a new tenant if a tenant abandons the premises and fails to pay rent. If an acceptable tenant becomes available, the landlord is required to lease the premises to the tenant to mitigate the damages recoverable from the former tenant. The former tenant is still liable for the difference between the amount of the rent under the original lease and the rent received from the new tenant. If the landlord has not used the reasonable means necessary to find a new tenant, presumably a court can reduce any award by the amount of rent the landlord could have received had such reasonable means been used.

In the majority of states, wrongfully terminated employees have a duty to mitigate damages suffered by their employers' breach. The damages they will be awarded are their salaries less the incomes they would have received in similar jobs obtained by reasonable means. The employer has the burden of proving that such jobs existed and that the employee could have been hired. An employee is, of course, under no duty to take a job that is not of the same type and rank as the one that he or she lost.

Whether a business firm failed to mitigate its damages was at issue in the following case.

---

[4] UCC 2–715(2). See Chapter 16.
[5] 156 Eng.Rep. 145 (1854).

CASE 12.1   Fujitsu, Ltd. v. Federal Express Corp.

United States Court of Appeals,
Second Circuit, 2001.
247 F.3d 423.

FACTS On May 30, 1996, Fujitsu, Ltd., shipped a container of silicon wafers (computer chips) from Narita, Japan, to Ross Technologies, Inc., in Austin, Texas, using Federal Express (FedEx) as the carrier. The next day, the container arrived in Austin and was held for clearance by the U.S. Customs Service. (FedEx cannot release imported goods until the Customs Service has approved delivery and all applicable taxes have been paid.) Meanwhile, Ross told FedEx that it was rejecting the shipment and that FedEx should return the goods to Fujitsu at Ross's expense.**ᵃ** The goods left Austin in good condition, but when they arrived in Japan, Fujitsu found the outer container broken and covered with an oily substance that had permeated some of the interior boxes and coated the sealed aluminum bags containing the wafers. Fujitsu reported the damage, which FedEx acknowledged, and on the instructions of Fujitsu's insurance company, disposed of the container and the wafers without opening any of the bags. Fujitsu filed a suit in a federal district court against FedEx, alleging, in part, breach of contract. The court found FedEx liable for damages in the amount of $726,640. FedEx appealed to the U.S. Court of Appeals for the Second Circuit, arguing that Fujitsu failed to mitigate its damages.

---

a. It was not clear from the trial court's records why Ross was rejecting the shipment.

ISSUE Did Fujitsu fail to mitigate its damages by not opening the bags and attempting to salvage at least some of the wafers?

DECISION No. The U.S. Court of Appeals for the Second Circuit affirmed the judgment of the lower court.

REASON The appellate court acknowledged, "FedEx is correct that the record contains no evidence that the wafers themselves were damaged," but found that "the shipment was a total loss because the residue on the outer packaging made it impossible to access the wafers." The court explained that "the bags containing the wafers could only be opened in a specially designed and maintained 'clean room' so as to prevent dust contamination. However, because the bags themselves were coated with the oily residue, they could not be brought into a clean room for inspection, as the residue itself would contaminate the clean room." Consequently, even if the wafers had been undamaged, "Fujitsu was unable to extract them from the bags in an operable condition." The court concluded that there is "no difference between damage rendering the wafers inoperable and damage that prevents otherwise operable wafers from being used or salvaged." The court added that "efforts to salvage the wafers would have been prohibitively expensive."

FOR CRITICAL ANALYSIS—Ethical Consideration
Should Fujitsu have been sanctioned for its "spoliation of the evidence" (its disposal of the container and wafers on the instructions of its insurance company)?

LIQUIDATED DAMAGES VERSUS PENALTIES

A **liquidated damages** provision in a contract specifies that a certain dollar amount is to be paid in the event of a future default or breach of contract. (*Liquidated* means determined, settled, or fixed.) Liquidated damages differ from penalties. A **penalty** specifies a certain amount to be paid in the event of a default or breach of contract and is designed to punish the breaching party. Liquidated damages provisions normally are enforceable. In contrast, if a court finds that a provision is a penalty provision, the agreement as to the amount will not be enforced, and recovery will be limited to actual damages.[6]

To determine whether a particular provision is for liquidated damages or for a penalty, the court must answer two questions: First, at the time the contract was formed, was it difficult to estimate the potential damages that would be incurred if the contract was not performed on time? Second, was the amount set as damages a reasonable estimate of those potential damages and not excessive?[7] If the answers to both questions are yes, the provision normally will be enforced. If either answer is no, the provision will normally not be enforced. In a construction contract, it is difficult to estimate the amount of damages that might be caused by a delay in completing construction, so liquidated damages clauses are often used.

The court in the following case answered the liquidated damages questions in the context of a provision in an agreement for the lease of a hotel.

---

[6] This is also the rule under the Uniform Commercial Code. See UCC 2–718(1).

[7] *Restatement (Second) of Contracts*, Section 356(1).

CASE 12.2   Green Park Inn, Inc. v. Moore

North Carolina Court of Appeals, 2002.
562 S.E.2d 53.
http://www.aoc.state.nc.us/www/public/
html/opinions.htm[a]

FACTS Allen and Pat McCain own Green Park Inn, Inc.,
which operates the Green Park Inn. In 1996, they leased the
Inn to GMAFCO, LLC, which is owned by Gary and Gail
Moore. The lease agreement provided that, in case of a
default by GMAFCO, Green Park Inn, Inc., would be entitled
to $500,000 as "liquidated damages." GMAFCO defaulted on
the February 2000 rent. Green Park Inn, Inc., gave GMAFCO
an opportunity to cure the default, but GMAFCO made no
further payments and returned possession of the property to
the lessor. When Green Park Inn, Inc., sought the "liquidated
damages," the Moores refused to pay. Green Park Inn, Inc.,
filed a suit in a North Carolina state court against the Moores,
GMAFCO, and their bank to obtain the $500,000. The defen-
dants contended in part that the lease clause requiring payment of "liquidated damages" was an unenforceable penalty
provision. The court ordered the defendants to pay Green
Park Inn, Inc. The defendants appealed to a state intermediate appellate court.

ISSUE Did the liquidated damages provision in the lease
agreement amount to an unenforceable penalty clause?

---

a. In the "Court of Appeals Opinions" section, click on "2002." On
the next page, scroll to the "2 April 2002" section and click on the
name of the case to access the opinion. The North Carolina
Appellate Division Reporter maintains this Web site.

DECISION No. The state intermediate appellate court
affirmed the decision of the lower court.

REASON The appellate court quoted from the lease agreement's liquidated damages clause, which listed such items to
be included in the lessor's damages as "restoration of the
physical plant," "lost lease payments," and "harm to the reputation of the hotel." The clause also stated that the McCains
were "retired to Florida" and "would have to relocate back to
Blowing Rock" if they were "forced out of retirement to take
over the operation of the hotel." The lease stated that
$500,000 was "a fair and reasonable estimate and measure
of the damages to be suffered by lessor in the event of
default by lessee." The court held that these provisions satisfied the two-part test for liquidated damages: the amount of
the damages would have been difficult to determine at the
time that the lease was signed, and the estimate of the damages was reasonable. The court acknowledged that "some of
the items listed in the liquidated damages provision are not
indefinite or uncertain," but found that "others, such as the
harm to the hotel's reputation or the cost to the McCains of
being forced out of retirement, clearly would have been difficult to ascertain at the time the Lease Agreement was
signed." The court also pointed out that after McCain and his
wife came out of retirement and were again operating the
hotel, he testified that $500,000 was "a fair and reasonable
estimate to measure the damages" and that the Moores did
not attempt to show that this amount was unreasonable.

FOR CRITICAL ANALYSIS—Economic Consideration
*If the lease had specified $3 million in damages, would the
result in this case have been different? If so, why?*

Rescission and Restitution

As discussed in Chapter 11, *rescission* is essentially an
action to undo, or cancel, a contract—to return nonbreaching parties to the positions that they occupied prior to the
transaction. When fraud, mistake, duress, or failure of consideration is present, rescission is available. The failure of
one party to perform under a contract entitles the other
party to rescind the contract.[8] The rescinding party must
give prompt notice to the breaching party. Furthermore,

both parties must make **restitution** to each other by returning goods, property, or funds previously conveyed.[9] If the
physical property or goods can be returned, they must be.
If the property or goods have been consumed, restitution
must be made in an equivalent dollar amount.

Essentially, restitution involves the recapture of a benefit
conferred on the defendant that has unjustly enriched her or
him. ● **EXAMPLE #5** Andrea pays $12,000 to Myles in return
for his promise to design a house for her. The next day, Myles
calls Andrea and tells her that he has taken a position with a
large architectural firm in another state and cannot design
the house. Andrea decides to hire another architect that afternoon. Andrea can require restitution of $12,000 because
Myles has received an unjust benefit of $12,000. ●

---

[8] The rescission discussed here refers to *unilateral* rescission, in which
only one party wants to undo the contract. In *mutual* rescission, both
parties agree to undo the contract. Mutual rescission discharges the contract; unilateral rescission is generally available as a remedy for breach of
contract.

[9] *Restatement (Second) of Contracts,* Section 370.

Specific Performance

The equitable remedy of **specific performance** calls for the performance of the act promised in the contract. This remedy is often attractive to a nonbreaching party because it provides the exact bargain promised in the agreement. It also avoids some of the problems inherent in a suit for money damages. First, the nonbreaching party need not worry about collecting the judgment.[10] Second, the nonbreaching party need not look around for another contract. Third, the actual performance may be more valuable than the money damages. Although the equitable remedy of specific performance is often preferable to other remedies, normally it is not granted unless the party's legal remedy (money damages) is inadequate and the subject matter of the contract is unique.[11]

Contracts for the sale of goods that are readily available in the market, for instance, rarely qualify for specific performance. Money damages ordinarily are adequate in such situations because substantially identical goods can be bought or sold in the market. If the goods are unique, however, a court of equity will decree specific performance. For example, paintings, sculptures, and rare books and coins are often unique, and money damages will not enable a buyer to obtain substantially identical substitutes in the market. The same principle applies to contracts relating to sales of land or interests in land because each parcel of land is unique by legal description.

Courts refuse to grant specific performance of contracts for personal services. This is because to order a party to perform personal services against his or her will amounts to a type of involuntary servitude, which is contrary to the public policy expressed in the Thirteenth Amendment to the Constitution. Moreover, the courts do not want to monitor personal-services contracts. ● EXAMPLE #6 If you contract with a neurosurgeon to perform brain surgery on you and the surgeon refuses to perform, the court will not compel (and you certainly would not want) the surgeon to perform under these circumstances. There is no way the court can assure meaningful performance in such a situation.[12]●

Reformation

When the parties have imperfectly expressed their agreement in writing, the equitable remedy of *reformation* allows the contract to be rewritten to reflect the parties' true intentions. This remedy applies most often when fraud or mutual mistake has occurred. ● EXAMPLE #7 If Keshan contracts to buy a fork lift from Shelley but the written contract refers to a crane, a mutual mistake has occurred. Accordingly, a court could reform the contract so that the writing conforms to the parties' original intention regarding which piece of equipment is being sold.●

Two other examples deserve mention. The first involves two parties who have made a binding oral contract. They further agree to reduce the oral contract to a writing, but in doing so, they make an error in stating the terms. Universally, the courts allow into evidence the correct terms of the oral contract, thereby reforming the written contract.

The second example has to do with written covenants not to compete. As discussed in Chapter 9, if a covenant not to compete is for a valid and legitimate purpose (such as the sale of a business) but the area or time restraints of the covenant are unreasonable, some courts reform the restraints by making them reasonable and enforce the entire contract as reformed. Other courts throw the entire restrictive covenant out as illegal.

Recovery Based on Quasi Contract

Recall from Chapter 7 that a quasi contract is not a true contract but a fictional contract that is imposed on the parties to obtain justice and prevent unjust enrichment. Hence, a quasi contract becomes an equitable basis for relief. Generally, when one party confers a benefit on another, equity requires that the party receiving the benefit pay a reasonable value for it so as not to be unjustly enriched at the other party's expense.

Quasi-contractual recovery is useful when one party has partially performed under a contract that is unenforceable. It can be an alternative to suing for damages, and it allows the party to recover the reasonable value of the partial performance. For quasi-contractual recovery to occur, the party seeking recovery must show the following:

① A benefit was conferred on the other party.

② The party conferring the benefit did so with the expectation of being paid.

③ The party seeking recovery did not act as a volunteer in conferring the benefit.

④ Retaining the benefit without paying for it would result in an unjust enrichment of the party receiving the benefit.

---

[10] Courts dispose of cases, after trials, by entering judgments. A judgment may order the losing party to pay money damages to the winning party. Collecting a judgment, however, can pose problems—such as when the judgment debtor is insolvent (cannot pay his or her bills when they become due) or has only a small net worth, or when the debtor's assets cannot be seized, under exemption laws, by a creditor to satisfy a debt (see Chapter 21).

[11] *Restatement (Second) of Contracts,* Section 359.

[12] Similarly, courts often refuse to order specific performance of construction contracts because courts are not set up to operate as construction supervisors or engineers.

● **EXAMPLE #8** Ericson contracts to build two oil derricks for Petro Industries. The derricks are to be built over a period of three years, but the parties do not create a written contract. Enforcement of the contract will therefore be barred by the Statute of Frauds.[13] After Ericson completes one derrick, Petro Industries informs him that it will not pay for the derrick. Ericson can sue in quasi contract because all of the conditions just mentioned for quasi-contractual recovery have been fulfilled. Ericson should be able to recover the reasonable value of the oil derrick (under the theory of *quantum meruit*[14]—"as much as he deserves"). The reasonable value is ordinarily equal to the fair market value. ●

Provisions Limiting Remedies

A contract may include provisions stating that no damages can be recovered for certain types of breaches or that damages must be limited to a maximum amount. The contract may also provide that the only remedy for breach is replacement, repair, or refund of the purchase price. Provisions stating that no damages can be recovered are called *exculpatory clauses* (see Chapter 9). Provisions that affect the availability of certain remedies are called *limitation-of-liability clauses*.

Whether these contract provisions and clauses will be enforced depends on the type of breach that is excused by the provision. For example, a clause excluding liability for negligence may be enforced in some cases. When an exculpatory clause for negligence is contained in a contract made between parties who have roughly equal bargaining positions, the clause usually will be enforced. A provision excluding liability for fraudulent or intentional injury will not be enforced. Likewise, a clause excluding liability for illegal acts or violations of law will not be enforced.

---

[13] Contracts that by their terms cannot be performed within one year must be in writing to be enforceable. See Chapter 10.
[14] Pronounced *kwahn*-tuhm *mehr*-oo-wuht.

The UCC provides that in a contract for the sale of goods, remedies can be limited.[15] (See this chapter's *Business Law in the Online World* feature for a discussion of a limitation-of-liability clause in a licensing agreement accompanying the sale of a software program.) We will examine the UCC's provisions on limited remedies in more detail in Chapter 16.

Election of Remedies

In many cases, a nonbreaching party has several remedies available. Because the remedies may be inconsistent with one another, the common law of contracts requires the party to choose which remedy to pursue. This is called *election of remedies*. The purpose of the doctrine of election of remedies is to prevent double recovery. ● **EXAMPLE #9** Suppose that Jefferson agrees to sell his land to Adams. Then Jefferson changes his mind and repudiates the contract. Adams can sue for compensatory damages or for specific performance. If Adams receives damages as a result of the breach, she should not also be granted specific performance of the sales contract because that would mean she would unfairly end up with both the land and the money damages. The doctrine of election of remedies requires Adams to choose the remedy she wants, and it eliminates any possibility of double recovery. ●

In contrast, remedies under the UCC are cumulative. They include all of the remedies available under the UCC for breach of a sales or lease contract.[16]

In the following case, the frustrated sellers of a house were apparently attempting to avoid the doctrine of election of remedies in order to, as the old saying goes, "have their cake and eat it, too."

---

[15] UCC 2–719.
[16] See UCC 2–703 and 2–711.

CASE 12.3   **Palmer v. Hayes**

Court of Appeals of Utah, 1995.
892 P.2d 1059.

FACTS Kenneth and Rebecca Palmer wanted to sell their house. Edward and Stephanie Hayes signed a proposed contract of sale, under which they agreed to give the Palmers' real estate agent, Maple Hills Realty, $2,000 as a deposit on the house. The agreement provided that in the event of default, the

Palmers could either keep the deposit or sue to enforce their rights. The Palmers accepted the Hayeses' offer and signed the contract. Before the property changed hands, however, the Hayeses changed their minds and asked for the return of their deposit. The Palmers refused and filed a suit against the Hayeses in a Utah state court, seeking damages. The Hayeses filed a motion for summary judgment on the ground that, by not releasing the deposit, the Palmers had elected their remedy. The court ruled in favor of the Hayeses on this point, and the Palmers appealed.

CASE 12.3—Continued

ISSUE Did the Palmers' failure to release the deposit money before filing their suit for damages constitute an election of remedies?

DECISION Yes. The Court of Appeals of Utah, concluding that the Palmers had elected the remedy of retaining the deposit, affirmed the lower court's ruling.

REASON The state appellate court held that "a seller's failure to offer to return * * * deposits precludes the seller from

pursuing other remedies." The court explained that the Palmers "needed only to indicate to Maple Hills Realty, in writing, that they released the deposit money to the Hayeses. Then they could have proceeded with their suit for damages." The court concluded that "by failing to release the deposit money, the Palmers elected to retain it as liquidated damages."

FOR CRITICAL ANALYSIS—Economic Consideration
What are the reasons for applying the doctrine of election of remedies to preclude sellers who keep deposits from suing for damages?

BUSINESS LAW IN THE ONLINE WORLD
Limitation-of-Liability Clauses in Software Licenses

Businesses today rely to a significant extent on computer hardware and software to conduct their operations. While this technology simplifies and streamlines business operations, it also poses some hazards. For example, suppose that, due to a software glitch, a construction company's bid for a construction project is $2 million less than it should have been. Clearly, if the company is awarded the project due to the inaccurate bid, the firm stands to incur a significant loss. This was essentially the problem facing the M. A. Mortenson Company, a nationwide construction contractor, when a bug in a software program that it used to submit bids for construction work caused the bid to be significantly lower than it should have been.

THE PROBLEM FACING THE M. A. MORTENSON COMPANY
The M. A. Mortenson Company purchased software from Timberline Software Corporation. The software analyzed construction project requirements and bid information from subcontractors and found the lowest-cost combination of subcontractors to do the work. The software was distributed subject to a license set forth on the outside of each disk's pouch and on the inside cover of the instruction manuals. The first screen that appeared each time the program was used also referred to the license, which included a limitation on Timberline's liability arising from use of the software. After using the software to prepare a bid, Mortenson discovered that the bid was $1.95 million less than it should have been. The software clearly had a bug, and Timberline was aware of this problem. In fact,

Timberline had already provided a newer version of the software to some of its other customers.

WAS THE LIMITATION-OF-LIABILITY CLAUSE A PART OF THE CONTRACT?
Mortenson sued Timberline, alleging that the limitation on Timberline's liability was not a part of the parties' contract. Timberline filed a motion for summary judgment, which the court granted. Mortenson fared no better in its appeal—ultimately, to the Washington state supreme court. That court held that the terms of the license were part of the contract between Mortenson and Timberline, and that Mortenson's use of the software constituted its assent to the agreement, including the limitation-of-liability clause in the license. The court stated that "as the license was part of the contract between Mortenson and Timberline, its terms are enforceable."

The court noted that the parties had dealt with each other for years, and that the terms of the license, which were similar to those used throughout the software industry, were set forth in several locations. In other words, Mortenson had to accept that it had no legal recourse against Timberline because of the limitation-of-liability clause in the licensing agreement.[a]

FOR CRITICAL ANALYSIS
Is it fair to hold that a business firm is bound by an agreement to limit liability when the firm did not intend to be bound by such an agreement? Why or why not?

a. *M. A. Mortenson Co. v. Timberline Software Corp.*, 140 Wash.2d 568, 998 P.2d 305 (2000).

Terms and Concepts

consequential damages 234   nominal damages 234   restitution 236
liquidated damages 235   penalty 235   specific performance 237
mitigation of damages 234

Chapter Summary — Breach and Remedies

	COMMON REMEDIES AVAILABLE TO NONBREACHING PARTY
Damages (See pages 232–236.)	The legal remedy designed to compensate the nonbreaching party for the loss of the bargain. By awarding money damages, the court tries to place the parties in the positions that they would have occupied had the contract been fully performed. The nonbreaching party frequently has a duty to *mitigate* (lessen or reduce) the damages incurred as a result of the contract's breach. There are five broad categories of damages: 1. *Compensatory damages*—Damages that compensate the nonbreaching party for injuries actually sustained and proved to have arisen directly from the loss of the bargain resulting from the breach of contract. 2. *Consequential damages*—Damages resulting from special circumstances beyond the contract itself; the damages flow only from the consequences of a breach. For a party to recover consequential damages, the damages must be the foreseeable result of a breach of contract, and the breaching party must have known at the time the contract was formed that special circumstances existed that would cause the nonbreaching party to incur additional loss on breach of the contract. Also called *special damages.* 3. *Punitive damages*—Damages awarded to punish the breaching party. Usually not awarded in an action for breach of contract unless a tort is involved. 4. *Nominal damages*—Damages small in amount (such as one dollar) that are awarded when a breach has occurred but no actual damages have been suffered. Awarded only to establish that the defendant acted wrongfully. 5. *Liquidated damages*—Damages that may be specified in a contract as the amount to be paid to the nonbreaching party in the event the contract is breached in the future. Clauses providing for liquidated damages are enforced if the damages were difficult to estimate at the time the contract was formed and if the amount stipulated is reasonable. If construed to be a penalty, the clause will not be enforced.
Rescission and Restitution (See page 236.)	1. *Rescission*—A remedy whereby a contract is canceled and the parties are restored to the original positions that they occupied prior to the transaction. Available when fraud, a mistake, duress, or failure of consideration is present. The rescinding party must give prompt notice of the rescission to the breaching party. 2. *Restitution*—When a contract is rescinded, both parties must make restitution to each other by returning the goods, property, or funds previously conveyed. Restitution prevents the unjust enrichment of parties.
Specific Performance (See page 237.)	An equitable remedy calling for the performance of the act promised in the contract. This remedy is available only in special situations—such as those involving contracts for the sale of unique goods or land—and when monetary damages would be an inadequate remedy. Specific performance is not available as a remedy in breached contracts for personal services.
Reformation (See page 237.)	An equitable remedy allowing a contract to be "reformed," or rewritten, to reflect the parties' true intentions. Available when an agreement is imperfectly expressed in writing.

Chapter Summary	Breach and Remedies—Continued
Recovery Based on Quasi Contract (See pages 237–238.)	An equitable theory imposed by the courts to obtain justice and prevent unjust enrichment in a situation in which no enforceable contract exists. The party seeking recovery must show the following: 1. A benefit was conferred on the other party. 2. The party conferring the benefit did so with the expectation of being paid. 3. The benefit was not volunteered. 4. Retaining the benefit without paying for it would result in the unjust enrichment of the party receiving the benefit.
CONTRACT DOCTRINES RELATING TO REMEDIES	
Provisions Limiting Remedies (See page 238.)	A contract may provide that no damages (or only a limited amount of damages) can be recovered in the event the contract is breached. Clauses excluding liability for fraudulent or intentional injury or for illegal acts cannot be enforced. Clauses excluding liability for negligence may be enforced if both parties hold roughly equal bargaining power. Under the UCC, in contracts for the sale of goods, remedies may be limited.
Election of Remedies (See pages 238–239.)	A common law doctrine under which a nonbreaching party must choose one remedy from those available. This doctrine prevents double recovery. Under the UCC, in contracts for the sale of goods, remedies are cumulative.

For Review

① What is the difference between compensatory damages and consequential damages? What are nominal damages, and when might they be awarded by a court?

② What is the usual measure of damages on a breach of contract for a sale of goods?

③ Under what circumstances will the remedy of rescission and restitution be available?

④ When might specific performance be granted as a remedy?

⑤ What is the rationale underlying the doctrine of election of remedies?

Questions and Case Problems

12–1. Liquidated Damages. Carnack contracts to sell his house and lot to Willard for $100,000. The terms of the contract call for Willard to pay 10 percent of the purchase price as a deposit toward the purchase price, or as a down payment. The terms further stipulate that should the buyer breach the contract, the deposit will be retained by Carnack as liquidated damages. Willard pays the deposit, but because her expected financing of the $90,000 balance falls through, she breaches the contract. Two weeks later, Carnack sells the house and lot to Balkova for $105,000. Willard demands her $10,000 back, but Carnack refuses, claiming that Willard's breach and the contract terms entitle him to keep the deposit. Discuss who is correct.

12–2. Election of Remedies. Perez contracts to buy a new Oldsmobile from Central City Motors, paying $2,000 down and agreeing to make twenty-four monthly payments of $350 each. He takes the car home and, after making one payment, learns that his Oldsmobile has a Chevrolet engine in it rather than the famous Olds Super V-8 engine. Central City never informed Perez of this fact. Perez immediately notifies Central City of his dissatisfaction and returns the car to Central City. Central City accepts the car and returns to Perez the $2,000 down payment plus the one $350 payment. Two weeks later Perez, without a car and feeling angry, files a suit against Central City, seeking damages for breach of warranty and fraud. Discuss the effect of Perez's actions.

12–3. Specific Performance. In which of the following situations might a court grant specific performance as a remedy for the breach of the contract?

(a) Tarrington contracts to sell her house and lot to Rainier. Then, on finding another buyer willing to pay a higher purchase price, she refuses to deed the property to Rainier.

(b) Marita contracts to sing and dance in Horace's night-club for one month, beginning June 1. She then refuses to perform.

(c) Juan contracts to purchase a rare coin from Edmund, who is breaking up his coin collection. At the last minute, Edmund decides to keep his coin collection intact and refuses to deliver the coin to Juan.

(d) Astro Computer Corp. has three shareholders: Coase, who owns 48 percent of the stock; De Valle, who owns 48 percent; and Cary, who owns 4 percent. Cary contracts to sell his 4 percent to De Valle but later refuses to transfer the shares to him.

12–4. Measure of Damages. Johnson contracted to lease a house to Fox for $700 a month, beginning October 1. Fox stipulated in the contract that before he moved in, the interior of the house had to be completely repainted. On September 9, Johnson hired Keever to do the required painting for $1,000. He told Keever that the painting had to be finished by October 1 but did not explain why. On September 28, Keever quit without giving a reason, having completed approximately 80 percent of the work. Johnson then paid Sam $300 to finish the painting, but Sam did not finish until October 4. Fox, when the painting had not been completed as stipulated in his contract with Johnson, leased another home. Johnson found a new tenant who would lease the property at $700 a month, beginning October 15. Johnson then sued Keever for breach of contract, claiming damages of $650. This amount included the $300 Johnson paid Sam to finish the painting and $350 for rent for the first half of October, which Johnson had lost as a result of Keever's breach. Johnson had not yet paid Keever anything for Keever's work. Can Johnson collect the $650 from Keever? Explain.

12–5. Mitigation of Damages. Charles Kloss had worked for Honeywell, Inc., for over fifteen years when Honeywell decided to transfer the employees at its Ballard facility to its Harbour Pointe plant. Honeywell planned to hire a medical person at the Harbour Pointe facility and promised Kloss that if he completed a nursing program and became a registered nurse (RN), the company would hire him for the medical position. When Kloss graduated from his RN program, however, Honeywell did not assign him to a nursing or medical position. Instead, the firm gave Kloss a job in its maintenance department. Shortly thereafter, Kloss left the company and eventually sued Honeywell for damages (lost wages) resulting from Honeywell's breach of the employment contract. One of the issues facing the court was whether Kloss, by voluntarily leaving the maintenance job at Honeywell, had failed to mitigate his damages. How should the court rule on this issue? Discuss. [*Kloss v. Honeywell, Inc.,* 77 Wash.App. 294, 890 P.2d 480 (1995)]

12–6. Mitigation of Damages. Patricia Fair worked in a Red Lion restaurant. The employee manual provided that "[d]uring a medical leave of absence, every effort will be made to keep a position available for the employee's return." After sustaining an injury that was unrelated to her work, Fair was given a month's medical leave. On her return, she asked for, and was granted, additional time to submit a physician's release to return to work.

She provided the release within the extra time, but before she went back to work, she was terminated, effective as of her original return date. When she attempted to resolve the matter, Red Lion offered to reinstate her in her old job. Her response was to set several conditions for a return, including a different job. Red Lion said no, and Fair did not return. Fair filed a suit in a Colorado state court against Red Lion, alleging in part breach of contract. Red Lion argued that by rejecting its offer of reinstatement, Fair failed to mitigate her damages. Assuming that Red Lion was in breach of contract, did Fair fail to mitigate her damages? Explain. [*Fair v. Red Lion Inn, L.P.,* 943 P.2d 431 (Colo. 1997)]

12–7. Damages. In December 1992, Beys Specialty Contracting, Inc., contracted with New York City's Metropolitan Transportation Authority (MTA) for construction work. Beys subcontracted with Hudson Iron Works, Inc., to perform some of the work for $175,000. Under the terms of the subcontract, within seven days after the MTA approved Hudson's work and paid Beys, Beys would pay Hudson. The MTA had not yet approved any of Hudson's work when Beys submitted to the MTA invoices dated May 20 and June 21, 1993. Without proof that the MTA had paid Beys on those invoices, Hudson submitted to Beys an invoice dated September 10, claiming that the May 20 and June 21 invoices incorporated its work. Beys refused to pay, Hudson stopped working, and Beys paid another contractor $25,083 more to complete the job than if Hudson had fulfilled its subcontract. Hudson filed a suit in a New York state court to collect on its invoice. Beys filed a counterclaim for the additional money spent to finish Hudson's job. In whose favor should the court rule, and why? What might be the measure of damages, if any? [*Hudson Iron Works, Inc. v. Beys Specialty Contracting, Inc.,* 691 N.Y.S.2d 132 (N.Y.A.D., 2 Dept. 1999)]

CASE PROBLEM WITH SAMPLE ANSWER

12–8. Ms. Vuylsteke, a single mother with three children, lived in Portland, Oregon. Cynthia Broan also lived in Oregon until she moved to New York City to open and operate an art gallery. Broan contacted Vuylsteke to manage the gallery under a one-year contract for an annual salary of $72,000. To begin work, Vuylsteke relocated to New York. As part of the move, Vuylsteke transferred custody of her children to her husband, who lived in London, England. In accepting the job, Vuylsteke also forfeited her husband's alimony and child-support payments, including unpaid amounts of nearly $30,000. Before Vuylsteke started work, Broan repudiated the contract. Unable to find employment for more than an annual salary of $25,000, Vuylsteke moved to London to be near her children. Vuylsteke filed a suit in an Oregon state court against Broan, seeking damages for breach of contract. Should the court hold, as Broan argued, that Vuylsteke did not take reasonable steps to mitigate her damages? Why or why not? [*Vuylsteke v. Broan,* 172 Or.App. 74, 17 P.3d 1072 (2001)]

▶ To view a sample answer for this case problem, go to this book's Web site at **http://fundamentals.westbuslaw.com** and click on "Interactive Study Center."

12–9. Mitigation of Damages. William West, an engineer, worked for Bechtel Corp., an organization of about 150 engineering and construction companies, which is headquartered in San Francisco, California, and operates worldwide. Except for a two-month period in 1985, Bechtel employed West on long-term assignments or short-term projects for thirty years. In October 1997, West was offered a position on a project with Saudi Arabian Bechtel Co. (SABCO), which West understood would be for two years. In November, however, West was terminated for what he believed was his "age and lack of display of energy." After his return to California, West received numerous offers from Bechtel for work that suited his abilities and met his salary expectations, but he did not accept any of them and did not look for other work. Three months later, he filed a suit in a California state court against Bechtel, alleging in part breach of contract and seeking the salary he would have earned during two years with SABCO. Bechtel responded in part that, even if there had been a breach, West failed to mitigate his damages. Is Bechtel correct? Discuss. [*West v. Bechtel Corp.,* 96 Cal.App.4th 966, 117 Cal.Rptr.2d 647 (1 Dist. 2002)]

VIDEO QUESTION

12–10. Go to this text's Web site at **http://fundamentals.westbuslaw.com** and click on "Video Questions." Select "Chapter 12" and view the video titled *Breach and Remedies*. Then answer the following questions:

1. In the video, a carpenter is in the process of constructing shelves to display soda in a grocery store for a sale the next day. The carpenter says that he has an emergency and has to quit working on the project and leave. According to the chapter, what is the standard measure of damages for breaching this type of contract?
2. Can Oscar recover consequential damages for the carpenter's breach? Why or why not?
3. If Oscar did not attempt to find anyone else to complete the carpenter's work, would this affect the amount of damages to which Oscar is entitled? Why or why not?
4. List and describe any equitable remedies discussed in the chapter that would be available to Oscar in this scenario.

BREACH AND REMEDIES

For updated links to resources available on the Web, as well as other materials, visit this text's Web site at

http://fundamentals.westbuslaw.com

The following site offers information on contract law, including breach of contract and remedies:

http://www.nolo.com/lawcenter

Online Legal Research

Go to the *Fundamentals of Business Law* home page at **http://fundamentals.westbuslaw.com**. Select "Interactive Study Center" and then click on "Chapter 12." There you will find the following Internet research exercises that you can perform to learn more about topics covered in this chapter.

Activity 12–1: LEGAL PERSPECTIVE—Contract Damages and Contract Theory
Activity 12–2: MANAGEMENT PERSPECTIVE—The Duty to Mitigate

Before the Test

Go to the *Fundamentals of Business Law* home page at **http://fundamentals.westbuslaw.com**. Click on "Interactive Quizzes." You will find at least twenty interactive questions relating to this chapter.

Westlaw® Campus

If your textbook provided for a subscription to Westlaw® Campus, or if you have otherwise purchased access to the Westlaw Campus database, you can access any of the cases presented or cited in this chapter by using your Westlaw Campus account.

CHAPTER
13
E-Contracts

CHAPTER OBJECTIVES

After reading this chapter, you should be able to answer the following questions:

① What are some important clauses that offerors should include when making offers to form electronic contracts, or e-contracts?

② What are shrink-wrap agreements? What traditional laws have been applied to such agreements?

③ Do click-on acceptances in electronic contracts present problems that are not covered by traditional laws governing contracts, including the Uniform Commercial Code (UCC)?

④ What is an electronic signature? Are electronic signatures valid?

⑤ What is the Uniform Electronic Transactions Act (UETA)? What are some of its key provisions?

Many observers argue that the development of cyberspace is revolutionary. Therefore, new legal theories, and new laws, are needed to govern **e-contracts,** or contracts entered into electronically. To date, however, most courts have adapted traditional contract law principles and, when applicable, provisions of the Uniform Commercial Code (UCC) to cases involving e-contract disputes.

In the first part of this chapter, we look at how traditional laws are being applied to contracts formed online. We then examine some new laws that have been created to apply in situations in which traditional laws governing contracts have sometimes been thought inadequate. For example, traditional laws governing signature and writing requirements are not easily adapted to contracts formed in the online environment. Thus, new laws have been created to address these issues.

Forming Contracts Online

Today, numerous contracts are being formed online. Although the medium through which these contracts are generated has changed, the age-old problems attending contract formation have not. Disputes concerning contracts formed online continue to center around contract terms and whether the parties voluntarily assented to those terms.

244

Note that online contracts may be formed not only for the sale of goods and services but also for the purpose of *licensing*. For example, the "sale" of software generally involves a license, or a right to use the software, rather than the passage of title (ownership rights) from the seller to the buyer. As you read through the following pages, keep in mind that although we typically refer to the offeror and offeree as a *seller* and a *buyer*, in many transactions these parties would be more accurately described as a *licensor* and a *licensee*.

ONLINE OFFERS

Sellers doing business via the Internet can protect themselves against contract disputes and legal liability by creating offers that clearly spell out the terms that will govern their transactions if the offers are accepted. All important terms should be conspicuous and easily viewed by potential buyers.

An important rule for a seller to keep in mind is that the offeror controls the offer, and thus the resulting contract. Thus, the seller should anticipate the terms he or she wants to include in a contract and provide for them in the offer. In some instances, a standardized contract form may suffice. At a minimum, the following provisions should be included in an online offer:

- A provision specifying the remedies available to the buyer if the goods turn out to be defective or if the contract is otherwise breached, or broken. Any limitation of remedies should be clearly spelled out.
- A clause that clearly indicates what constitutes the buyer's agreement to the terms of the offer.
- A provision specifying how payment for the goods and of any applicable taxes must be made.
- A statement of the seller's refund and return policies.
- Disclaimers of liability for certain uses of the goods. For example, an online seller of business forms may add a disclaimer that the seller does not accept responsibility for the buyer's reliance on the forms rather than on an attorney's advice.
- How the information gathered about the buyer will be used by the seller.

Dispute-Settlement Provisions. In addition to the above provisions, many online offers include provisions relating to dispute settlement. For example, an arbitration clause might be included, specifying that any dispute arising under the contract will be arbitrated in a specified forum.

Many online contracts also contain a forum-selection clause (indicating the forum, or location, for the resolution of any dispute arising under the contract—see Chapter 1). As discussed in Chapter 2, significant jurisdictional issues may occur when parties are at a great distance, as they often are when they form contracts via the Internet. A forum-selection clause will help to avert future jurisdictional problems and also help to ensure that the seller will not be required to appear in court in a distant state. An online contract may also include a choice-of-law clause—see Chapter 1.

Displaying the Offer. The seller's Web site should include a hypertext link to a page containing the full contract so that potential buyers are made aware of the terms to which they are assenting. The contract generally must be displayed online in a readable format such as a twelve-point typeface. All provisions should be reasonably clear. ● **EXAMPLE #1** If a seller is offering certain goods priced according to a complex price schedule, that schedule must be fully provided and explained.●

Indicating How the Offer Can Be Accepted. An online offer should also include some mechanism by which the customer may accept the offer. Typically, online sellers include boxes containing the words "I agree" or "I accept the terms of the offer" that offerees can click on to indicate acceptance—thus creating a **click-on agreement**.

ONLINE ACCEPTANCES

In many ways, click-on agreements are the Internet equivalents of **shrink-wrap agreements** (or *shrink-wrap licenses,* as they are sometimes called). A *shrink-wrap agreement* is an agreement whose terms are expressed inside a box in which the goods are packaged. (The term *shrink-wrap* refers to the plastic that covers the box.) Usually, the party who opens the box is told that she or he agrees to the terms by keeping whatever is in the box. Similarly, when the purchaser opens a software package, he or she agrees to abide by the terms of the limited license agreement.

● **EXAMPLE #2** John orders a new computer from a national company, which ships the computer to John. Along with the computer, the box contains an agreement setting forth the terms of the sale, including what remedies are available. The document also states that John's retention of the computer for longer than thirty days will be construed as an acceptance of the terms.●

In most cases, a shrink-wrap agreement is not between a retailer and a buyer, but between the manufacturer of the hardware or software and the ultimate buyer-user of the product. The terms generally concern warranties, remedies, and other issues associated with the use of the product.

We look next at how the law has been applied to both shrink-wrap and click-on agreements.

Shrink-Wrap Agreements—Enforceable Contract Terms.
Section 2–204 of the Uniform Commercial Code (UCC), the law governing sales contracts, provides that any contract for the sale of goods "may be made in any manner sufficient to show agreement, including conduct by both parties which recognizes the existence of a contract." Thus, a buyer's failure to object to terms contained within a shrink-wrapped software package (or an online offer) may constitute an acceptance of the terms by conduct.[1]

_____

[1] For a leading case on this issue, see *ProCD, Inc. v. Zeidenberg,* 86 F.3d 1447 (7th Cir. 1996).

In many cases, the courts have enforced the terms of shrink-wrap agreements in the same way that they enforce the terms of other contracts. Some courts have reasoned that by including the terms with the product, the seller proposed a contract that the buyer could accept by using the product after having an opportunity to read the terms. Also, it seems practical from a business's point of view to enclose a full statement of the legal terms of a sale with the product rather than to read the statement over the phone, for example, when a buyer calls in an order for the product.

Even when a shrink-wrap agreement would be enforceable in principle, a court may refuse to enforce certain terms for any of the reasons that would render the terms of other contracts unenforceable. The following case illustrates this point.

CASE 13.1 People v. Network Associates, Inc.

New York Supreme Court, 2003.
195 Misc.2d 384,
758 N.Y.S.2d 466.

FACTS Network Associates, Inc., develops and sells software, including Gauntlet, a software firewall product, via the Internet and at retail locations. Network Associates included on the face of many of its disks, and on its download page on the Internet, a restrictive clause that provided:

> Installing this software constitutes acceptance of the terms and conditions of the license agreement in the box. Please read the license agreement before installation. Other rules and regulations of installing the software are: * * * The customer shall not disclose the result of any benchmark test to any third party without Network Associates' prior written approval. * * * The customer will not publish reviews of this product without prior consent from Network Associates.

In July 1999, *Network World Fusion,* an online magazine, published a comparative review of firewall software products, including Network Associates's Gauntlet, without the maker's permission. Network Associates protested. Eliot Spitzer, the attorney general of the state of New York, filed a suit in a New York state court on behalf of "The People of the State of New York" against Network Associates.

ISSUE Did the restrictive clause constitute fraud?

DECISION Yes. The court ordered Network Associates to stop including the restrictive clause on its software. The court

also directed the defendant to reveal "the number of instances in which software was sold on discs or through the Internet containing the above-mentioned language in order for the court to determine what, if any, penalties and costs should be ordered."

REASON The court reasoned that "[t]he language of the Restrictive Clause specifically directs consumers to read the license agreement. Because the license agreement * * * states that all of the rights and duties of the parties are contained within that agreement, and does not contain any of the restrictions on publishing reviews and result of benchmark testing, consumers may conclude that those restrictions are not contractual restrictions. Therefore, following respondent's instructions, after reading the license agreement and the Restrictive Clause, consumers may reasonably interpret that the rules and regulations enumerated in the Restrictive Clause exist independent of the license contract and are made and enforced by an entity other than the corporation itself. This language implies that limitations on the publication of reviews do not reflect the policy of Network Associates, but result from some binding law or other rules and regulations imposed by an entity other than Network Associates."

FOR CRITICAL ANALYSIS—Technological Consideration
Is there an important difference between reading a disputed clause as part of a shrink-wrap agreement and accessing it through a link as part of a click-on agreement?

Shrink-Wrap Agreements—Proposals for Additional Terms. Not all of the terms included in shrink-wrap agreements have been enforced. One important consideration is whether the parties form their contract before or after the seller communicates the terms of the shrink-wrap agreement to the buyer. If a court finds that the buyer learned of the shrink-wrap terms *after* the parties entered into a contract, the court may conclude that those terms were proposals for additional terms and were not part of the contract unless the buyer expressly agreed to them.

In the following case, the court was asked to decide, among other things, whether to enforce an arbitration clause that was part of a set of "Standard Terms and Conditions" included in the box of every computer the defendant sold.

CASE 13.2 Klocek v. Gateway, Inc.

United States District Court,
District of Kansas, 2000.
104 F.Supp.2d 1332.

FACTS Whenever it sells a computer, Gateway, Inc., includes a copy of its "Standard Terms and Conditions Agreement" in the box that contains the power cables and instruction manuals. At the top of the first page, in a printed box and in emphasized type, is the following: "NOTE TO THE CUSTOMER: * * * By keeping your Gateway 2000 computer system beyond five (5) days after the date of delivery, you accept these Terms and Conditions." This document is four pages long and contains sixteen numbered paragraphs. Paragraph 10 states, "DISPUTE RESOLUTION. Any dispute or controversy arising out of or relating to this Agreement or its interpretation shall be settled exclusively and finally by arbitration." William Klocek bought a Gateway computer. Dissatisfied when it proved to be incompatible with his other computer equipment, he filed a suit in a federal district court against Gateway and others, alleging in part breach of contract. Gateway filed a motion to dismiss, asserting that Klocek was required to submit his claims to arbitration under Gateway's "Standard Terms." Klocek argued that these terms were not part of the contract for the purchase of the computer.

ISSUE Is the arbitration clause, which was a part of the shrink-wrap license in the box with the computer, enforceable against Klocek?

DECISION No. The court denied Gateway's motion to dismiss. The court agreed with Klocek that the arbitration clause was not part of his contract with Gateway.[a]

REASON The court first pointed out that under UCC 2–207, an "expression of acceptance * * * operates as an acceptance even though it states terms additional to or different from those offered or agreed upon, unless acceptance is expressly made conditional on assent to the additional or different terms." Those "additional terms are to be construed as proposals for addition to the contract" if the contract is not between merchants. The court concluded that Gateway's "Standard Terms" constituted an acceptance. There was no evidence, however, that "the transaction was conditioned on plaintiff's acceptance of the Standard Terms." Because Klocek was not a merchant, the terms did not become part of the parties' agreement unless he expressly agreed to them. There was no evidence that he had agreed to the terms. "Gateway states only that it enclosed the Standard Terms inside the computer box for plaintiff to read afterwards."

FOR CRITICAL ANALYSIS—Technological Consideration
The court in this case applied UCC provisions to an electronic contract. Can you think of some unique aspects of electronic contracting that would not be covered by traditional laws, such as the UCC?

---

a. Klocek's complaint was later dismissed on the ground that his claim did not satisfy the court's amount-in-controversy requirement for diversity jurisdiction. See *Klocek v. Gateway, Inc.,* 104 F.Supp.2d 1332 (D.Kan. 2000).

Click-On Agreements. As noted earlier, a click-on agreement (also sometimes called a *click-on license* or *click-wrap agreement*) arises when a buyer, completing a transaction on a computer, indicates his or her assent to be bound by the terms of an offer by clicking on a button that says, for example, "I agree." The terms may be contained on a Web site through which the buyer is obtaining goods or services, or they may appear on a computer screen when software is loaded. Exhibit 13–1 on page 248 contains the language of a click-on agreement that accompanies a package of software made and marketed by Adobe Systems, Inc.

As noted, Article 2 of the UCC provides that acceptance can be shown by conduct. The *Restatement (Second) of Contracts,* a compilation of common law contract principles,

EXHIBIT 13–1   A CLICK-ON AGREEMENT

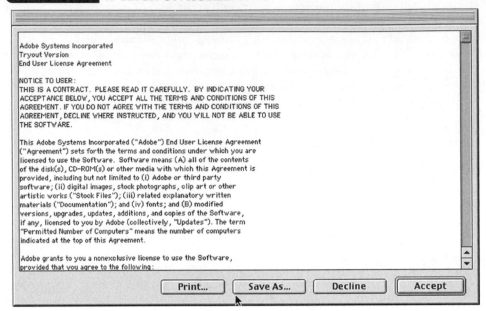

Adobe Systems Incorporated
Tryout Version
End User License Agreement

NOTICE TO USER:
THIS IS A CONTRACT. PLEASE READ IT CAREFULLY. BY INDICATING YOUR
ACCEPTANCE BELOW, YOU ACCEPT ALL THE TERMS AND CONDITIONS OF THIS
AGREEMENT. IF YOU DO NOT AGREE WITH THE TERMS AND CONDITIONS OF THIS
AGREEMENT, DECLINE WHERE INSTRUCTED, AND YOU WILL NOT BE ABLE TO USE
THE SOFTWARE.

This Adobe Systems Incorporated ("Adobe") End User License Agreement
("Agreement") sets forth the terms and conditions under which you are
licensed to use the Software. Software means (A) all of the contents
of the disk(s), CD-ROM(s) or other media with which this Agreement is
provided, including but not limited to (i) Adobe or third party
software; (ii) digital images, stock photographs, clip art or other
artistic works ("Stock Files"); (iii) related explanatory written
materials ("Documentation"); and (iv) fonts; and (B) modified
versions, upgrades, updates, additions, and copies of the Software,
if any, licensed to you by Adobe (collectively, "Updates"). The term
"Permitted Number of Computers" means the number of computers
indicated at the top of this Agreement.

Adobe grants to you a nonexclusive license to use the Software,
provided that you agree to the following:

[Print...]   [Save As...]   [Decline]   [Accept]

has a similar provision. It states that parties may agree to a contract "by written or spoken words or by other action or by failure to act."[2] The courts have used these provisions to conclude that a binding contract can be created by conduct, including actions accepting the terms of a shrink-wrap agreement or a click-on agreement.

---

[2] *Restatement (Second) of Contracts*, Section 19.

Generally, under the law governing contracts, including sales and lease contracts under the UCC, there is no requirement that all of the terms in a contract must actually have been read by all of the parties to be effective. For example, clicking on a button or box that states "I agree" to certain terms can be enough.

In the following case, the court considered the enforceability of a click-on (click-wrap) agreement under Article 2 of the UCC.

CASE 13.3   i.LAN Systems, Inc. v. NetScout Service Level Corp.

United States District Court,
District of Massachusetts, 2002.
183 F.Supp.2d 328.

FACTS NetScout Service Level Corp., formerly known as NextPoint Networks, Inc., designs software tools to troubleshoot network problems. A click-wrap provision in the NextPoint software states that the seller's liability is limited to the price paid for the software unless a different term is "specifically accepted by NextPoint in writing." In 1998, i.LAN Systems, Inc., and NextPoint signed an agreement under which i.LAN agreed to resell the software. In 1999, under a different purchase order, i.LAN bought what it thought was the unlimited right to rent, rather than sell, the software, com-

plete with perpetual upgrades and technical support. When NextPoint disputed this interpretation, i.LAN filed a suit in a federal district court, alleging, among other things, breach of contract. i.LAN sought specific performance (a remedy in which a court orders the breaching party to perform as specified in the contract—see Chapter 12) that included unlimited upgrades and support. The defendant argued that even if the allegation were true, the click-wrap provision limited its liability to the price paid for the software. Both parties filed motions for summary judgment.

ISSUE Was the click-wrap agreement enforceable?

DECISION Yes. The court denied the plaintiff's motion for summary judgment and instead issued a summary judgment in favor of the defendant (NextPoint).

CASE 13.3—Continued

REASON The court reasoned that the plaintiff agreed to the click-wrap terms when it clicked on the "I agree" box. Those terms effectively limited the defendant's liability. In the words of the court, "pursuant to UCC 2–204, the analysis is simple: i.LAN manifested assent to the clickwrap license agreement when it clicked on the box stating 'I agree,' so the agreement is enforceable."[a] The court reasoned that "'money

---

a. Under UCC 2–204, a contract "may be made in any manner sufficient to show agreement, including conduct by both parties which recognizes the existence of such a contract."

now, terms later' forms a contract * * * when the purchaser receives the box of software, sees the license agreement, and does not return the software. * * * 'Money now, terms later' is a practical way to form contracts, especially with purchasers of software. If [it is] correct to enforce a shrinkwrap license agreement, where any assent is implicit, then it must also be correct to enforce a clickwrap license agreement, where the assent is explicit."

FOR CRITICAL ANALYSIS—Economic Consideration
If click-wrap agreements were not enforceable, what effect would this have on the software industry?

Browse-Wrap Terms. Like the terms of a click-on agreement, **browse-wrap terms** can occur in a transaction conducted over the Internet. Unlike a click-on agreement, however, browse-wrap terms do not require an Internet user to assent to the terms before, say, downloading or using certain software. In other words, a person can install the software without clicking "I agree" to the terms of a license. Offerors of browse-wrap terms generally assert that the terms are binding without the users' active consent.

Critics contend that browse-wrap terms are not enforceable because they do not satisfy the basic elements of contract formation. It has been suggested that to form a valid contract online, a user must at least be presented with the

terms before indicating assent.[3] In the case of a browse-wrap term, this would require that a user navigate past it and agree to it before being able to obtain whatever is being granted to the user.

The following case involved the enforceability of a clause in an agreement that the court characterized as a browse-wrap license.

---

[3] American Bar Association Committee on the Law of Cyberspace, "Click-Through Agreements: Strategies for Avoiding Disputes on the Validity of Assent" (document presented at the annual American Bar Association meeting in August 2001).

CASE 13.4 **Specht v. Netscape Communications Corp.**

United States District Court,
Southern District of New York, 2001.
150 F.Supp.2d 585.

FACTS Netscape Communications Corporation's "SmartDownload" software makes it easier for users to download files from the Internet without losing progress if they pause to do some other task or their Internet connection is interrupted. Netscape offers SmartDownload free of charge on its Web site to those who indicate, by clicking the mouse in a designated box, that they wish to obtain it. John Gibson clicked in the box and downloaded the software. On the Web site's download page is a reference to a license agreement that is visible only by scrolling to the next screen. Affirmatively indicating assent to the agreement is not required to download the software. The agreement provides that any disputes arising from use of the software are to be submitted to arbitration in California. Believing that the use of SmartDownload

transmits private information about its users, Gibson and others filed a suit in a federal district court in New York against Netscape, alleging violations of federal law. Netscape asked the court to order the parties to arbitration in California, according to the license agreement.

ISSUE Was the arbitration clause in the license agreement enforceable?

DECISION No. The court denied the motion to compel arbitration.

REASON The court applied UCC Article 2 because, "[a]lthough in this case the product was provided free of charge, the roles are essentially the same as when an individual uses the Internet to purchase software from a company: here, the Plaintiff requested Defendant's product by clicking on an icon marked 'Download,' and Defendant then

(Continued)

CASE 13.4—Continued

tendered the product." The court emphasized that "[u]nless the Plaintiffs agreed to the License Agreement, they cannot be bound by the arbitration clause." The court discussed the forms of license agreements that accompany sales of software (shrink-wrap, click-on, and browse-wrap licenses) and their enforceability, and characterized Netscape's license in this case as a browse-wrap license. "Netscape's SmartDownload * * * allows a user to download and use the software without taking any action that plainly manifests assent to the terms of the associated license or indicates an understanding that a contract is being formed." The court pointed out that "the individual obtaining SmartDownload is not made aware that he is entering into a contract. * * * [T]he user need not view any license agreement terms or even any reference to a license agreement, and need not do anything to manifest assent." The court reasoned that "the user Plaintiffs did not assent to the license agreement," and thus "they are not subject to the arbitration clause."

FOR CRITICAL ANALYSIS—Social Consideration
What might be the result in other cases if the court in this case had held that the browse-wrap term was enforceable?

E-Signatures

In many instances, a contract cannot be enforced unless it is signed by the party against whom enforcement is sought. A significant issue in the context of e-commerce has to do with how electronic signatures, or **e-signatures**, can be created and verified on e-contracts.

In the days when many people could not write, they signed documents with an "X." Then handwritten signatures became common, followed by typed signatures, printed signatures, and, most recently, digital signatures that are transmitted electronically. Throughout the evolution of signature technology, the question of what constitutes a valid signature has arisen again and again, and with good reason—without some consensus on what constitutes a valid signature, little business or legal work could be accomplished. (Technology has also raised other questions relating to signature requirements—see, for example, the question discussed in this chapter's *Business Law in the Online World* feature.)

E-SIGNATURE TECHNOLOGIES

Today, numerous technologies allow electronic documents to be signed. These include digital signatures and alternative technologies.

Digital Signatures. The most prevalent e-signature technology is the *asymmetric cryptosystem*, which creates a digital signature using two different (asymmetric) cryptographic "keys." With this system, a person attaches a digital signature to a document using a private key, or code. The key has a publicly available counterpart. Anyone with the appropriate software can use the public key to verify that the digital signature was made using the private key. A **cybernotary**, or legally recognized certification authority, issues the key pair, identifies the owner of the keys, and certifies the validity of the public key. The cybernotary also serves as a repository for public keys. Cybernotaries already are available.

Signature Dynamics. With another type of signature technology, known as *signature dynamics,* a sender's signature is captured using a stylus and an electronic digitizer pad. A computer program takes the signature's measurements, the sender's identity, the time and date of the signature, and the identity of the hardware. This information is then placed in an encrypted *biometric token* attached to the document being transmitted. To verify the authenticity of the signature, the recipient of the document compares the measurements of the signature with the measurements in the token. When this type of e-signature is used, it is not necessary to have a third party verify the signatory's identity.

Other E-Signature Forms. Other forms of e-signatures have been—or are now being—developed as well. For example, some e-signatures use "smart cards." A smart card is a credit-card–size device that contains embedded code and other data. Like credit and debit cards, this smart card can be inserted into computers to transfer information. Unlike those other cards, however, a smart card could be used to establish a person's identity as validly as a signature on a piece of paper. In addition, technological innovations now under way will allow an e-signature to be evidenced by an image of a person's retina, fingerprint, or face that is scanned by a computer and then matched to a numeric code. The scanned image and the numeric code are registered with security companies that maintain files on an accessible server that can be used to authenticate a transaction.

STATE LAWS GOVERNING E-SIGNATURES

Most states have laws governing e-signatures. The problem is that the state e-signature laws are not uniform. Some

BUSINESS LAW IN THE ONLINE WORLD
E-Mailed Prescription Orders and Signature Requirements

"It is in the nature of things that statutes must at times be applied to situations unforeseen at the time of their enactment." So said a Wisconsin appellate court when trying to apply a state law governing the requirements of physicians' prescriptions to a program initiated by Walgreen Company. The program enabled physicians to transmit prescription orders to Walgreen pharmacies via e-mail.

The state statute defined a "prescription order" as simply "a written or oral order by a [physician] for a drug or device for a particular patient." If the prescription order was written, it had to be signed. If the order was transmitted to the pharmacist orally—by telephone, for example—it did not, of course, require a signature. The statute, however, said nothing about prescription orders transmitted electronically via e-mail, and therein lay the problem: If e-mailed prescription orders were considered to be "in writing," they violated the statutory requirement for written prescriptions because they were not signed. If such prescriptions were deemed to be oral transmissions, there was no violation.

THE PHARMACY BOARD'S POSITION ON THE ISSUE

The Wisconsin Pharmacy Examining Board had little trouble concluding that an e-mailed prescription order was analogous to a writing and that Walgreen's program violated the law. The board voiced a number of concerns to the court. One was that if e-mailed prescription orders were permitted, there would be less control over drugs. While pharmacists can recognize a caller's voice over the telephone and thus verify the caller's identity, a computerized communication is more anonymous, creating a danger that the prescription information "will fall into the wrong hands." The board argued that these security considerations should take priority and that the court should bar the use of e-mailed prescription orders.

THE COURT'S CONCLUSION The court was not convinced that it should defer to such security concerns. The court concluded that a computer-transmitted prescription was not analogous to a written prescription. Rather, it was more akin to an order transmitted orally by telephone. This, to the court, seemed to be "a more reasonable interpretation than the board's in light of the simple facts of computer transmission: The prescription is put into a computer as text and the message is then electronically transmitted to the pharmacy's terminal, much as a telephone call—or a facsimile—would be." Thus, concluded the court, the use of e-mailed prescription orders did not violate the statute.

The court justified its rather novel conclusion by perhaps equally novel reasoning. The court stated that when a statute must be applied to a situation unforeseen by its drafters, the court must try to determine the "manifest intent" of those lawmakers. The court must examine the "pictures actually drawn by the statutory text" and see if they are "sufficient to cover the new type of situation that the course of events has produced." If the legislature has supplied "sufficient specifications to provide a discernible frame of reference within which the situation now presented quite clearly fits, even though it represents in some degree a new condition of affairs unknown to the lawmakers," the statute may be interpreted accordingly.[a]

FOR CRITICAL ANALYSIS

Suppose that two parties form a contract through the exchange of e-mailed messages. Would this court classify the contract as an oral contract?

a. *Walgreen Co. v. Wisconsin Pharmacy Examining Board,* 217 Wis.2d 290, 577 N.W.2d 387 (Wis.App. 1998).

states—California is a notable example—provide that many types of documents cannot be signed with e-signatures, while other states are more permissive. Additionally, some states recognize only digital signatures as valid, while others permit other types of e-signatures.

In an attempt to create more uniformity among the states, the National Conference of Commissioners on Uniform State Laws and the American Law Institute promulgated the Uniform Electronic Transactions Act (UETA) in 1999. To date, the UETA has been adopted, at least in part, by more than forty states. The UETA states, among other things, that a signature may not be denied legal effect or enforceability solely because it is in electronic form. (Other aspects of the UETA will be discussed later in this chapter.)

FEDERAL LAW ON E-SIGNATURES AND E-DOCUMENTS

In 2000, Congress enacted the Electronic Signatures in Global and National Commerce Act (E-SIGN Act) to provide that no contract, record, or signature may be "denied legal effect" solely because it is in electronic form. In other words, under this law, an electronic signature is as valid as a signature on paper, and an electronic document can be as enforceable as a paper one.

For an electronic signature to be enforceable, the contracting parties must have agreed to use electronic signatures. For an electronic document to be valid, it must be in a form that can be retained and accurately reproduced.

The E-SIGN Act does not apply to all types of documents, however. Contracts and documents that are exempt include court papers, divorce decrees, evictions, foreclosures, health-insurance terminations, prenuptial agreements, and wills. Also, the only agreements governed by the Uniform Commercial Code (UCC) that fall under this law are those covered by Articles 2 and 2A and UCC 1–107 and 1–206.

Despite these limitations, the E-SIGN Act enormously expands the possibilities for contracting online. ● EXAMPLE #3 From a remote location, a businessperson can now open an account with a financial institution, obtain a mortgage or other loan, buy insurance, and purchase real estate via the Internet. Payments and transfers of funds can be done entirely online. Thus, using e-contracts can avoid the time and costs associated with producing, delivering, signing, and returning paper documents.●

Partnering Agreements

One way that online sellers and buyers can prevent disputes over signatures in their e-contracts, as well as over the terms and conditions of those contracts, is to form partnering agreements. In a **partnering agreement**, a seller and a buyer who frequently do business with each other agree in advance on the terms and conditions that will apply to all transactions subsequently conducted electronically. The partnering agreement can also establish special access and identification codes to be used by the parties when transacting business electronically.

A partnering agreement reduces the likelihood that disputes will arise under the contract because the buyer and the seller have agreed in advance to the terms and condi-

tions that will accompany each sale. Furthermore, if a dispute does arise, a court or arbitration forum will be able to refer to the partnering agreement when determining the parties' intent with respect to subsequent contracts. Of course, even with a partnering agreement fraud remains a possibility. If an unauthorized person uses a purchaser's designated access number and identification code, it may be some time before the problem is discovered.

The Uniform Electronic Transactions Act

As noted earlier, the National Conference of Commissioners on Uniform State Laws and the American Law Institute promulgated the Uniform Electronic Transactions Act (UETA) in 1999. The UETA represents one of the first comprehensive efforts to create uniformity and introduce certainty in state laws pertaining to e-commerce.

The primary purpose of the UETA is to remove barriers to e-commerce by giving the same legal effect to electronic records and signatures as is currently given to paper documents and signatures. As noted earlier, the UETA broadly defines an *e-signature* as "an electronic sound, symbol, or process attached to or logically associated with a record and executed or adopted by a person with the intent to sign the record."[4] An *e-signature* includes encrypted digital signatures, names (intended as signatures) at the ends of e-mail messages, and "clicks" on a Web page if the click includes the identification of the person. A **record** is "information that is inscribed on a tangible medium or that is stored in an electronic or other medium and is retrievable in perceivable [visual] form."[5]

THE SCOPE AND APPLICABILITY OF THE UETA

The UETA does not create new rules for electronic contracts but rather establishes that records, signatures, and contracts may not be denied enforceability solely due to their electronic form. The UETA does not apply to all writings and signatures but only to electronic records and electronic signatures *relating to a transaction*. A *transaction* is defined as an interaction between two or more people relating to business, commercial, or governmental activities.[6]

The act specifically does not apply to laws governing wills or testamentary trusts, the UCC (other than Articles 2 and 2A), or the Uniform Computer Information Transaction Act (discussed later in this chapter).[7] In addition, the provi-

---

[4] UETA 102(8).
[5] UETA 102(15).
[6] UETA 2(12) and 3.
[7] UETA 3(b).

sions of the UETA allow the states to exclude its application to other areas of law.

As described earlier, Congress passed the E-SIGN Act in 2000, a year after the UETA was presented to the states for adoption. Thus, a significant issue is whether and to what extent the federal E-SIGN Act preempts the UETA as adopted by the states.

THE FEDERAL E-SIGN ACT AND THE UETA

The E-SIGN Act refers explicitly to the UETA and provides that if a state has enacted the uniform version of the UETA, it is not preempted by the E-SIGN Act.[8] In other words, if the state has enacted the UETA without modification, state law will govern. The problem is that many states have enacted nonuniform (modified) versions of the UETA, largely for the purpose of excluding other areas of state law from the UETA's terms. The E-SIGN Act specifies that those exclusions will be preempted to the extent that they are inconsistent with the E-SIGN Act's provisions.

The E-SIGN Act, however, explicitly allows the states to enact alternative procedures or requirements for the use or acceptance of electronic records or electronic signatures, *if* certain conditions are met. Generally, the procedures or requirements must be consistent with the provisions of the E-SIGN Act, and the state must not give greater legal status or effect to one specific type of technology. Additionally, if a state has enacted alternative procedures or requirements *after* the E-SIGN Act was adopted, the state law must specifically refer to the E-SIGN Act.

Although the E-SIGN Act clearly contains some preemptive language, it is not yet clear exactly how the courts will interpret these provisions. If a state has enacted a modified version of the UETA, a court may find that only a certain provision of that modified version is preempted, or it may find that the entire modified version of the UETA is invalid. Generally, the relationship between the UETA and the E-SIGN Act remains to be clarified by the courts.

HIGHLIGHTS OF THE UETA

We look next at selected provisions of the UETA. Our discussion is, of course, based on the act's uniform provisions. Keep in mind that the states that have enacted the UETA may have adopted slightly different versions.

The Parties Must Agree to Conduct Transactions Electronically. The UETA will not apply to a transaction unless each of the parties has agreed to conduct transactions by electronic means. The agreement need not be explicit,

however, and it may be implied by the conduct of the parties and the surrounding circumstances.[9] In the comments that accompany the UETA, the drafters stated that it may be reasonable to infer that a person who gives out a business card with an e-mail address on it has consented to transact business electronically.[10] The party's agreement may also be inferred from a letter or other writing, as well as from some verbal communication. Nothing in the UETA requires that the agreement to conduct transactions electronically be made electronically.

A person who has previously agreed to an electronic transaction can also withdraw his or her consent and refuse to conduct further business electronically. Additionally, the act expressly gives parties the power to vary the UETA's provisions by contract. In other words, *parties can opt out of all or some of the terms of the UETA.* If the parties do not opt out of the terms of the UETA, however, the UETA will govern their electronic transactions.

Attribution. In the context of electronic transactions, the term *attribution* refers to the procedures that may be used to ensure that the person sending an electronic record is the same person whose e-signature accompanies the record. Under the UETA, if an electronic record or signature was the act of a particular person, the record or signature may be attributed to that person. If a person types her or his name at the bottom of an e-mail purchase order, that name would qualify as a "signature" and be attributed to the person whose name appeared. Just as in paper contracts, one may use any relevant evidence to prove that the record or signature is or is not the act of the person.[11]

Note that even if an individual's name does not appear on a record (such as in a voice-mail message), the UETA states that the effect of the record is to be determined from the context and surrounding circumstances. In other words, a record may have legal effect even if no one has signed it. For example, a fax that contains a letterhead identifying the sender may, depending on the circumstances, be attributed to that sender.

The UETA does not contain any express provisions about what constitutes fraud or whether an agent (a person who acts on behalf of another—see Chapter 22) is authorized to enter into a contract. Under the UETA, other state laws control if any issues relating to agency, authority, forgery, or contract formation arise.

Notarization. If a document is required to be notarized under existing state law, the UETA provides that this requirement is satisfied by the electronic signature of a

[8] 15 U.S.C. Section 7002(2)(A)(i).

[9] UETA 5(b).
[10] UETA 5, Comment 4B.
[11] UETA 9.

notary public or other person authorized to verify signatures. For example, if a person intends to accept an offer to purchase real estate via e-mail, the requirement is satisfied if a notary public is present to verify the person's identity and affix an electronic signature to the e-mail acceptance.

The Effect of Errors. The UETA encourages, but does not require, the use of security procedures (such as encryption) to verify changes to electronic documents and to correct errors. Section 10 of the UETA provides that if the parties have agreed to a security procedure and one party does not detect an error because he or she did not follow the procedure, the conforming party can legally avoid the effect of the change or error. If the parties have not agreed to use a security procedure, then other state laws (including contract law governing mistakes—see Chapter 10) will determine the effect of the error on the parties' agreement.

To avoid the effect of errors, a party must take certain steps. First, the party must promptly notify the other party of the mistake and of her or his intent not to be bound by it. Second, the party must take reasonable steps to return any benefit or consideration received. Parties cannot avoid a transaction from which they have benefited. For example, if as a result of the error a party received access to valuable information for which restitution cannot be made, the transaction may be unavoidable. In all other situations in which a change or error occurs in an electronic record (and the parties' agreement does not specifically address errors), the UETA states that the traditional law governing mistakes will govern.

Timing. Section 15 of the UETA sets forth provisions relating to the sending and receiving of electronic records. These provisions apply unless the parties agree to different terms. Under Section 15, an electronic record is considered *sent* when it is properly directed to the intended recipient in a form readable by the recipient's computer system. Once the electronic record leaves the control of the sender or comes under the control of the recipient, the UETA deems it to have been sent. An electronic record is considered *received* when it enters the recipient's processing system in a readable form— *even if no individual is aware of its receipt.*

Additionally, the UETA provides that, unless otherwise agreed, an electronic record is to be sent from or received at the party's principal place of business. If a party has no place of business, the provision then authorizes the place of sending or receipt to be the party's residence. If a party has multiple places of business, the record should be sent from or received at the location that has the closest relationship to the underlying transaction.

The Uniform Computer Information Transactions Act

The National Conference of Commissioners on Uniform State Laws (NCCUSL) promulgated the Uniform Computer Information Transactions Act (UCITA) in 1999. The primary purpose of the UCITA is to validate e-contracts to license or purchase software, or contracts that give access to—or allow the distribution of—computer information.[12] The UCITA is controversial, and only two states (Maryland and Virginia) have adopted it, while four states (Iowa, North Carolina, Vermont, and West Virginia) have passed anti–UCITA provisions. In 2003, the NCCUSL withdrew its support of the UCITA. Although the UCITA remains a legal resource, the NCCUSL will no longer seek its adoption by the states, which are thus unlikely to consider it further.

---

12 *Computer information* is "information in an electronic form obtained from or through use of a computer, or that is in digital or an equivalent form capable of being processed by a computer" [UCITA 102(10)].

Chapter Summary   **E-Contracts**

Online Offers (See page 245.)	Businesspersons who present contract offers via the Internet should keep in mind that the terms of the offer should be just as inclusive as the terms in an offer made in a written (paper) document. All possible contingencies should be anticipated and provided for in the offer. Because jurisdictional issues frequently arise with online transactions, it is particularly important to include dispute-settlement provisions in the offer, as well as a

Chapter Summary	E-Contracts—Continued
Online Offers— continued	forum-selection clause. The offer should be displayed in such a way as to be easily readable and clear. An online offer should also include some mechanism, such as providing an "I agree" or "I accept" box, by which the customer may accept the offer.
Online Acceptances (See pages 245–250.)	1. *Shrink-wrap agreement—* a. Definition—An agreement whose terms are expressed inside a box in which the goods are packaged. The party who opens the box is informed that by keeping the goods, he or she agrees to the terms of the shrink-wrap agreement. b. Enforceability—The courts have often enforced shrink-wrap agreements, even if the purchaser-user of the goods did not read the terms of the agreement. A court may deem a shrink-wrap agreement unenforceable, however, if the buyer learns of the shrink-wrap terms *after* the parties entered into the agreement. 2. *Click-on agreement—* a. Definition—An agreement created when a buyer, completing a transaction on a computer, is required to indicate his or her assent to be bound by the terms of an offer by clicking on a button that says, for example, "I agree." The terms of the agreement may appear on the Web site through which the buyer is obtaining goods or services, or they may appear on a computer screen when software is downloaded. b. Enforceability—The courts have enforced click-on agreements, holding that by clicking "I agree," the offeree has indicated acceptance by conduct. Browse-wrap terms, however (terms in a license that an Internet user does not have to read prior to downloading the product), may be unenforceable on the ground that the user is not made aware that he or she is entering into a contract.
E-Signatures (See pages 250–252.)	1. *Definition*—The Uniform Electronic Transactions Act (UETA) defines the term *e-signature* as an electronic sound, symbol, or process attached to or logically associated with a record and executed or adopted by a person with the intent to sign the record. 2. *E-signature technologies*—These include the *asymmetric cryptosystem* (which creates a digital signature using two different cryptographic "keys"); *signature dynamics* (which involves capturing a sender's signature using a stylus and an electronic digitizer pad); a *smart card* (a device the size of a credit card that contains embedded code and other data); and, probably in the near future, scanned images of retinas, fingerprints, or other physical characteristics linked to numeric codes. 3. *State laws governing e-signatures*—Although most states have laws governing e-signatures, these laws are not uniform. The UETA provides for the validity of e-signatures and may ultimately create more uniformity among the states in this respect. 4. *Federal law on e-signatures and e-documents*—The Electronic Signatures in Global and National Commerce Act (E-SIGN Act) of 2000 gave validity to e-signatures by providing that no contract, record, or signature may be "denied legal effect" solely because it is in an electronic form.
The Uniform Electronic Transactions Act (UETA) (See pages 252–254.)	1. *Definition*—A uniform act submitted to the states for adoption by the National Conference of Commissioners on Uniform State Laws and the American Legal Institute. The UETA has been adopted by more than forty states. 2. *Purpose*—To create rules to support the enforcement of e-contracts. Under the UETA, contracts entered into online, as well as other documents, are presumed valid. The UETA does not apply to transactions governed by the UCC or the UCITA, or to wills or testamentary trusts.

For Review

① What are some important clauses that offerors should include when making offers to form electronic contracts, or e-contracts?

② What are shrink-wrap agreements? What traditional laws have been applied to such agreements?

③ Do click-on acceptances in electronic contracts present problems that are not covered by traditional laws governing contracts, including the Uniform Commercial Code (UCC)?

④ What is an electronic signature? Are electronic signatures valid?

⑤ What is the Uniform Electronic Transactions Act (UETA)? What are some of its key provisions?

Questions and Case Problems

13–1. Click-On Agreements. Paul is a financial analyst for King Investments, Inc., a brokerage firm. He uses the Internet to investigate the background and activities of companies that might be good investments for King's customers. While visiting the Web site of Business Research, Inc., Paul sees on his screen a message that reads, "Welcome to businessresearch.com. By visiting our site, you have been entered as a subscriber to our e-publication, *Companies Unlimited.* This publication will be sent to you daily at a cost of $7.50 per week. An invoice will be included with *Companies Unlimited* every four weeks. You may cancel your subscription at any time." Has Paul entered into an enforceable contract to pay for *Companies Unlimited?* Why or why not?

13–2. Click-On Agreements. Anne is a reporter for *Daily Business Journal,* a print publication consulted by investors and other businesspersons. She often uses the Internet to perform research for the articles that she writes for the publication. While visiting the Web site of Cyberspace Investments Corp., Anne reads a pop-up window that states, "Our business newsletter, *E-Commerce Weekly,* is available at a one-year subscription rate of $5 per issue. To subscribe, enter your e-mail address below and click 'SUBSCRIBE.' By subscribing, you agree to the terms of the subscriber's agreement. To read this agreement, click 'AGREEMENT.'" Anne enters her e-mail address, but does not click on "AGREEMENT" to read the terms. Has Anne entered into an enforceable contract to pay for *E-Commerce Weekly?* Explain.

13–3. Online Acceptance. Bob, a sales representative for Central Computer Co., occasionally uses the Internet to obtain information about his customers and to look for new sales leads. While visiting the Web site of Marketing World, Inc., Bob is presented with an on-screen message that offers, "To improve your ability to make deals, read our monthly online magazine, *Sales Genius,* available at a subscription rate of $15 a month. To subscribe, fill in your name, company name, and e-mail address below, and click 'YES!' By clicking 'YES!' you agree to the terms of the subscription contract. To read this contract, click 'TERMS.'" Among those terms is a clause that allows Marketing World to charge interest for subscription bills not paid within a certain time. Bob subscribes without reading the terms. Marketing World later files a suit against Bob, based on his failure to pay for his subscription. Should the court hold that Bob is obligated to pay interest on the amount? Explain.

13–4. License Agreements. Management Computer Controls, Inc. (known as "MC 2"), is a Tennessee corporation in the business of selling software. Charles Perry Construction, Inc., a Florida corporation, entered into two contracts with MC 2 to buy software designed to perform estimating and accounting functions for construction firms. Each contract was printed on a standard order form containing a paragraph that referred to a license agreement. The license agreement included a choice-of-forum and choice-of-law provision: "Agreement is to be interpreted and construed according to the laws of the State of Tennessee. Any action, either by you or MC 2, arising out of this Agreement shall be initiated and prosecuted in the Court of Shelby County, Tennessee, and nowhere else." Each of the software packages arrived with the license agreement affixed to the outside of the box. Additionally, the boxes were sealed with an orange sticker bearing the following warning: "By opening this packet, you indicate your acceptance of the MC 2 license agreement." Alleging that the software was not suitable for use with Windows NT, Perry filed a suit against MC 2 in a Florida state court. MC 2 filed a motion to dismiss the complaint on the ground that the suit should be heard in Tennessee. How should the court rule? Why? [*Management Computer Controls, Inc. v. Charles Perry Construction, Inc.,* 743 So.2d 627 (Fla.App. 1 Dist. 1999)]

13–5. Browse-Wrap Terms. Ticketmaster Corp. operates a Web site that allows customers to buy tickets to concerts, ball games, and other events. On the site's home page are instructions and an index to internal pages (one page per event). Each event page provides basic information (a short description of the event, with the date, time, place, and price) and a description of how to order tickets over the Internet, by telephone, by mail, or in person. The home page contains—if a customer scrolls to the bottom—"terms and conditions" that proscribe, among other things, linking to Ticketmaster's internal pages. A customer need not view these terms to go to an event page. Tickets.Com, Inc., operates a Web site that also publicizes special events. Tickets.Com's site includes links to the internal events pages of Ticketmaster. These links bypass Ticketmaster's home page. Ticketmaster filed a suit in a federal district court against

Tickets.Com, alleging in part breach of contract on the ground that Tickets.Com's linking violated Ticketmaster's "terms and conditions." Tickets.Com filed a motion to dismiss. Should the court grant the motion? Why or why not? [*Ticketmaster Corp. v. Tickets.Com, Inc.,* 54 U.S.P.Q.2d 1344 (C.D.Cal. 2000)]

13–6. Shrink-Wrap/Click-On Agreements. 1-A Equipment Co. signed a sales order to lease Accware 10 User NT software, which is made and marketed by ICode, Inc. Just above the signature line, the order stated: "Thank you for your order. No returns or refunds will be issued for software license and/or services. All sales are final. Please read the End User License and Service Agreement." The software was delivered in a sealed envelope inside a box. On the outside of the envelope, an "End User Agreement" provided in part, "BY OPENING THIS PACKAGING, CLICKING YOUR ACCEPTANCE OF THE AGREEMENT DURING DOWNLOAD OR INSTALLATION OF THIS PRODUCT, OR BY USING ANY PART OF THIS PRODUCT, YOU AGREE TO BE LEGALLY BOUND BY THE TERMS OF THE AGREEMENT. . . . This agreement will be governed by the laws in force in the Commonwealth of Virginia . . . and exclusive venue for any litigation shall be in Virginia." Later, dissatisfied with the software, 1-A filed a suit in a Massachusetts state court against ICode, alleging breach of contract and misrepresentation. ICode asked the court to dismiss the case on the basis of the "End User Agreement." Is the agreement enforceable? Should the court dismiss the suit? Why or why not? [*1-A Equipment Co. v. ICode, Inc.,* 43 UCC Rep.Serv.2d 807 (Mass.Dist. 2000)]

CASE PROBLEM WITH SAMPLE ANSWER

13–7. Peerless Wall & Window Coverings, Inc., is a small business in Pennsylvania. To run the cash registers in its stores, manage inventory, and link the stores electronically, in 1994 Peerless installed Point of Sale V6.5 software produced by Synchronics, Inc., a small corporation in Tennessee that develops and markets business software. Point of Sale V6.5 was written with code that used only a two-digit year field—for example, 1999 was stored as "99." This meant that all dates were interpreted as falling within the twentieth century (2001, stored as "01," would be mistaken for 1901). In other words, Point of Sale V6.5 was not "Year 2000" (Y2K) compliant. The software was licensed under a shrink-wrap agreement printed on the envelopes containing the disks. The agreement included a clause that, among other things, limited remedies to replacement within ninety days if there was a defect in the disks. "The entire risk as to the quality and performance of the Software is with you." In 1995, Synchronics stopped selling and supporting Point of Sale V6.5. Two years later, Synchronics told Peerless that the software was not Y2K compliant and should be replaced. Peerless sued Synchronics in a federal district court, alleging, in part, breach of contract. Synchronics filed a motion for summary judgment. Who is most likely to bear the

cost of replacing the software? Why? [*Peerless Wall & Window Coverings, Inc. v. Synchronics, Inc.,* 85 F.Supp.2d 519 (W.D.Pa. 2000), *aff'd* 234 F.3d 1265 (3d Cir. 2000)]

▶ To view a sample answer for this case problem, go to this book's Web site at **http://fundamentals.westbuslaw.com** and click on "Interactive Study Center."

13–8. Click-On Agreements. America Online, Inc. (AOL), provided e-mail service to Walter Hughes and other members under a click-on agreement titled "Terms of Service." This agreement consisted of three parts: a "Member Agreement," "Community Guidelines," and a "Privacy Policy." The "Member Agreement" included a forum-selection clause that read, "You expressly agree that exclusive jurisdiction for any claim or dispute with AOL or relating in any way to your membership or your use of AOL resides in the courts of Virginia." When Officer Thomas McMenamon of the Methuen, Massachusetts, Police Department received threatening e-mail sent from an AOL account, he requested and obtained from AOL Hughes's name and other personal information. Hughes filed a suit in a federal district court against AOL, which filed a motion to dismiss on the basis of the forum-selection clause. Considering that the clause was a click-on provision, is it enforceable? Explain. [*Hughes v. McMenamon,* 204 F.Supp.2d 178 (D.Mass. 2002)]

VIDEO QUESTION

13–9. Go to this text's Web site at **http://fundamentals.westbuslaw.com** and click on "Video Questions." Select "Chapter 13" and view the video titled *E-Contracts: Agreeing Online.* Then answer the following questions:

1. According to the instructor in the video, what is the key factor in determining whether a particular term in an online agreement is enforceable?

2. Suppose that you click on "I accept" in order to download software from the Internet. You do not read the terms of the agreement before accepting it, even though you know that such agreements often contain forum-selection and arbitration clauses. The software later causes irreparable harm to your computer system, and you want to sue. When you go to the Web site and view the agreement, however, you discover that a choice-of-law clause in the contract specified that the law of Nigeria controls. Is this term enforceable? Is it a term that should be reasonably expected in an online contract?

3. Does it matter what the term actually says if it is a type of term that one could reasonably expect to be in the contract? What arguments can be made for and against enforcing a choice-of-law clause in an online contract?

E-CONTRACTS

For updated links to resources available on the Web, as well as other materials, visit this text's Web site at

http://fundamentals.westbuslaw.com

The law firm of Baker & McKenzie offers a summary of the scope and applicability of the E-SIGN Act of 2000 on its Web site. Go to

http://www.bmck.com/ecommerce/E-SIGN_Act.htm

The Web site of the National Conference of Commissioners on Uniform State Laws (NCCUSL) includes questions and answers about the UCC, UETA, and more. Go to

http://www.nccusl.org

Online Legal Research

Go to the *Fundamentals of Business Law* home page at **http://fundamentals.westbuslaw.com**. Select "Interactive Study Center" and then click on "Chapter 13." There you will find the following Internet research exercises that you can perform to learn more about topics covered in this chapter.

Activity 13–1: LEGAL PERSPECTIVE—E-Contract Formation
Activity 13–2: MANAGEMENT PERSPECTIVE—E-Signatures

Before the Test

Go to the *Fundamentals of Business Law* home page at **http://fundamentals.westbuslaw.com**. Click on "Interactive Quizzes." You will find at least twenty interactive questions relating to this chapter.

Westlaw® Campus

If your textbook provided for a subscription to Westlaw® Campus, or if you have otherwise purchased access to the Westlaw Campus database, you can access any of the cases presented or cited in this chapter by using your Westlaw Campus account.

Ford v. Trendwest Resorts, Inc.

INTRODUCTION

In Chapter 12, we outlined the remedies for a breach of contract. In this *Focus on Legal Reasoning,* we examine *Ford v. Trendwest Resorts, Inc.,*[1] a decision in which the court considered the appropriate measure for an award of damages for an employer's breach of an agreement to rehire a former employee.

CASE BACKGROUND

Trendwest Resorts, Inc., sells vacation time at a network of resorts in North America. Bobby Ford began working for Trendwest in 1991. By April 1997, Ford held a highly paid position in Trendwest's "Upgrades" department. On

---

1. 43 P.3d 1223 (Wash. 2002).

April 30, the department's assistant manager fired Ford for arriving at work a second time smelling of alcohol. The sales director, however, told Ford that if he completed an alcohol counseling program, the company would rehire him in "a position equal to that which [he] held." Ford agreed to participate in the program, and the parties signed an employee-assistance agreement.

After establishing a treatment schedule, Ford called Trendwest to arrange a new work schedule. The Upgrades department manager told Ford that he could not return to Upgrades, but that he could work in the "Discovery Program" as a telemarketer, a far less lucrative position than Ford had held. Ford declined. Trendwest terminated his employment.

Ford filed a suit in a Washington state court against Trendwest, alleging, among other things, breach of contract. A jury found that Trendwest had breached its promise to rehire Ford in a specific position and awarded him $235,000 in damages based on his anticipated lost earnings. A state intermediate appellate court affirmed the award, and Trendwest appealed to the Washington Supreme Court. The question was whether lost earnings are the measure of damages for a breach of an agreement to hire a person for employment at will.[2]

---

2. Under the employment-at-will doctrine, either party may terminate the relationship at any time for any reason, unless a contract or statute specifies otherwise—see Chapter 23.

MAJORITY OPINION

JOHNSON, J. [Justice]

* * * *

* * * To the extent possible, the law of contracts seeks to protect an injured party's reasonably expected benefit of the bargain * * *. Contract damages are ordinarily based on the injured party's expectation[s] * * * and are intended to give that party the benefit of the bargain by awarding him or her a sum of money that will, to the extent possible, put the injured party in as good a position as that party would have been in had the contract been performed. *The central objective behind the system of contract remedies is compensatory, not punitive. Punishment of a promisor for having broken his promise has no justification on either economic or other grounds* * * *. [Emphasis added.]

Employment contracts are governed by the same rules as other contracts. Thus, Ford argues, once the breach of contract was established, Ford's damages were limited only by their foreseeability.

But a contract confers no greater rights on a party than it bargains for. In other words, *a party to a contract has a contractual right only to that which it bargained for—its reasonable expectation.* The parties do not dispute Ford bargained for at-will employment, nor does Ford dispute Trendwest could have hired him as an at-will employee and then immediately fired him without fear of liability. An employee's expectations under an employment at-will contract are no different from the employment itself. Although Ford presents compelling facts that suggest he was treated unfairly by Trendwest, we are unwilling to abandon the long-standing distinction between at-will employment and for-cause employment [an employment contract providing that the employee can only be fired for cause]. Since we are dealing

with an at-will employment contract for hire and not a for-cause employment contract for hire, the question is whether we should treat the breach of one different from the breach of the other. The answer is yes, and the reason is because if we treat them the same (i.e., if the breach of either gives rise to expectation damages), there will be no difference between at-will or for-cause employment. [Emphasis added.]

When the parties contracted for at-will employment, Ford had no greater expectations than an at-will employee, and Trendwest had no fewer rights than an at-will employer. * * * Although Ford entered into a contract with Trendwest, neither party bargained for something other than employment at-will. Nothing in this contract changed the at-will employment relationship.

The Court of Appeals in *Bakotich v. Swanson,* 91 Wash.App. 311, 957 P.2d 275 (1998), reached the right result but for the wrong reasons. The court held that in a breach of an employment at-will contract case, anticipated lost earnings evidence is "highly speculative and [therefore] properly excluded by the trial court." But to simply characterize lost earnings as speculative does not fairly explain why they are [not] available to remedy * * * a breach of contract. We hold *lost earnings cannot measure damages for the breach of an employment at-will contract because the parties to such a contract do not bargain for future earnings.* By its very nature, at-will employment precludes an expectation of future earnings. Because Ford did not bargain for future earnings, he cannot claim they measure the harm he sustained by Trendwest's breach. * * * [Emphasis added.]

* * * *

(Continued)

* * * We reverse the Court of Appeals as to the damages award and remand this case for entry of nominal damages on Ford's breach of contract claim.

DISSENTING OPINION

CHAMBERS, J. (dissenting).

* * * *

* * * [I]f an employer, for whatever reason, creates an atmosphere of job security and fair treatment with promises of specific treatment in specific situations and an employee is induced thereby to remain on the job and not actively seek other employment, those promises are enforceable components of the employment relationship. * * *

* * * *

* * * Once breach of [an employment at-will] contract is established, the mere fact an employer could have fired the employee without liability the next day or under some other circumstance not amounting to breach of contract does not render the actual breach of contract null or render a claim for lost wages speculative.

* * * The majority cites only one Washington case for support, a Court of Appeals opinion, *Bakotich v. Swanson,* which the majority acknowledges was decided for the wrong reasons. The *Bakotich* court grounded its decision on the theory that lost wages, as an element of damages in an at-will employment relationship, is too speculative—an analysis that the majority concedes is simply wrong.

* * * I therefore propose a different analytical approach to Ford's claim against Trendwest. First, the [judge or jury] should determine whether a contract was created modifying the at-will employment relationship; second, if a contract was created, whether it was breached; and third, the measure of any damages. * * *

* * * *

* * * Bobby Ford pleaded and proved a violation of a contract. His damages should properly be entrusted to the jury to determine. Therefore, I would affirm the Court of Appeals.

LEGAL REASONING AND ANALYSIS

1 Legal Analysis. Find the *Bakotich v. Swanson* case (see the appendix to Chapter 1 for instructions on how to find state court opinions). Did the court's reasoning in the *Bakotich* case affect the majority's opinion or the dissent's opinion in this case? If so, how? If not, why was the case cited?

2 Legal Reasoning. What reasons do the majority and the dissent provide to support their conclusions?

3 Legal Application. According to the court in *Hadley v. Baxendale* (see Chapter 12), "damages recoverable for a breach of contract are those which may fairly and reasonably be considered either arising naturally, i.e., according to the usual course of things, from [the] breach of contract itself, or such as may reasonably be supposed to have been in the contemplation of both parties, at the time they made the contract, as the probable result of the breach of it." How does the majority apply this principle in this case? What is the dissent's position?

4 Implications for the Employer. Does the decision in this case indicate that damages are never recoverable for a breach of an agreement to hire for employment at will? Explain.

5 Case Briefing Assignment. Using the guidelines for briefing cases given in Appendix A of this text, brief the *Ford* case.

This text's Web site, at **http://fundamentals.westbuslaw.com**, offers links to West's Court Case Updates, as well as to other online research sources. You can also locate court cases at the Web sites listed in the *Accessing the Internet* section at the end of Chapter 2.

Additionally, you can find cases on contract law in the United States and around the world by going to the Hieros Gamos Web site at **http://www.hg.org**. On Hieros Gamos's home page, in the "Law Practice Center" section, click on "70 Areas of Practice." On the next page, in the "C" section, click on "Contract Law." HGE.org, Inc., in Houston, Texas, maintains this Web site.

UNIT 4

Sales and Lease Contracts

UNIT CONTENTS

CHAPTER
14
The Formation of Sales and Lease Contracts

CHAPTER OBJECTIVES

After reading this chapter, you should be able to answer the following questions:

① How do Article 2 and Article 2A of the UCC differ? What types of transactions does each article cover?

② What is a merchant's firm offer?

③ If an offeree includes additional or different terms in an acceptance, will a contract result? If so, what happens to these terms?

④ Article 2 and Article 2A of the UCC both define three exceptions to the writing requirements of the Statute of Frauds. What are these three exceptions?

⑤ What law governs contracts for the international sale of goods?

When we turn to contracts for the sale and lease of goods, we move away from common law principles and into the area of statutory law. State statutory law governing sales and lease transactions is based on the Uniform Commercial Code (UCC), which, as mentioned in Chapter 1, has been adopted as law by all of the states.[1]

We open this chapter with a discussion of the historical development of sales and lease law and the UCC's significance as a legal landmark. We then look at the scope of the UCC's Article 2 (on sales) and Article 2A (on leases) as a background to the topic of this chapter, which is the for-

mation of contracts for the sale and lease of goods. As you will read shortly, in 2003 the National Conference of Commissioners on Uniform State Laws (NCCUSL) and the American Law Institute (ALI) approved amendments to Article 2 and Article 2A. These amendments have now been submitted to the states for adoption. Appendix C at the back of this book includes both the version of Article 2 that is currently in effect in most states and selected provisions from the 2003 amendments to Article 2.

International sales transactions have become increasingly commonplace in the business world. Because of this, we conclude the chapter with an examination of the United Nations Convention on Contracts for the International Sale of Goods (CISG), which governs international sales contracts.

---

[1] Louisiana has not adopted Articles 2 and 2A, however.

The Uniform Commercial Code

In the early years of this nation, sales law varied from state to state, and this lack of uniformity complicated the formation of multistate sales contracts. The problems became especially troublesome in the late nineteenth century as multistate contracts became the norm. For this reason, numerous attempts were made to produce a uniform body of laws relating to commercial transactions. In the 1940s, the need to integrate the half dozen or so uniform acts covering commercial transactions into a single, comprehensive body of statutory law was recognized. The NCCUSL developed the Uniform Commercial Code (UCC) to serve that purpose. First issued in 1949, the UCC facilitates commercial transactions by making the laws governing sales and lease contracts clearer, simpler, and more readily applicable to the numerous difficulties that can arise during such transactions.

COMPREHENSIVE COVERAGE OF THE UCC

The UCC is the single most comprehensive codification of the broad spectrum of laws involved in a total commercial transaction. The UCC views the entire "commercial transaction for the sale of and payment for goods" as a single legal occurrence having numerous facets.

A Single, Integrated Framework for Commercial Transactions. An example will help to clarify how several articles of the UCC can be applied to a single commercial transaction. Suppose that a consumer—a person who purchases goods primarily for personal or household use—purchases a deluxe, side-by-side refrigerator with ice maker from an appliance store. The consumer agrees to pay for the refrigerator on an installment plan.

Because there is a contract for the sale of goods, Article 2 will apply. If the consumer gives a check as the down payment on the purchase price, it will be negotiated and ultimately passed through one or more banks for collection. This process is the subject matter of Article 3, Negotiable Instruments, and Article 4, Bank Deposits and Collections. If the appliance store extends credit to the consumer through the installment plan, and if it retains a lien on the refrigerator (the collateral), then Article 9, Secured Transactions, will be applicable.

Suppose, in addition, that the appliance company must obtain the refrigerator from the manufacturer's warehouse before shipping it by common carrier to the consumer. The storage and shipment of goods are the subject matter of Article 7, Documents of Title. To pay the manufacturer, which is located in another state, for the refrigerator supplied, the appliance company may use a letter of credit—the subject matter of Article 5. Thus, the UCC attempts to provide a consistent and integrated framework of rules to deal with all the phases *ordinarily arising* in a commercial sales transaction from start to finish.

Articles 6 and 8. Two articles of the UCC seem not to apply to an "ordinary" commercial sales transaction. Article 6, Bulk Transfers, involves merchants who sell off the major part of their inventory (sometimes leaving creditors unpaid). Because bulk sales ordinarily do not arise in a commercial sales transaction, most states have repealed Article 6 entirely, although some states have adopted the revised version of Article 6.

Article 8, Investment Securities, deals with transactions involving certain negotiable securities (stocks and bonds), transactions that do not involve a sale of (or payment for) *goods*. Nevertheless, the UCC's drafters considered the subject matter of Articles 6 and 8 to be related *sufficiently* to commercial transactions to warrant the inclusion of these articles in the UCC.

THE AMENDMENTS TO ARTICLES 2 AND 2A

In 2003, the NCCUSL and the ALI approved amendments to Articles 2 and 2A. For the most part, the 2003 amendments to Articles 2 and 2A mark an attempt by these organizations to update the UCC to accommodate electronic commerce. Among other things, the amendments include revised definitions of various terms to make the definitions consistent with those given in the Uniform Electronic Transactions Act and the federal Electronic Signatures in Global and National Commerce Act of 2000. (See Chapter 13 for a discussion of these acts.) Throughout the amendments, for example, the word *writing* has been replaced by *record*. The term *sign* has been amended to include electronic signatures. Provisions governing electronic contracts, including contracts formed by electronic agents, have also been added.

In addition, the amendments include a number of new protections for buyers, some of which apply only to buyers who are consumers. Other new or revised provisions relate to contract formation (offer and acceptance), the Statute of Frauds, the parol evidence rule, and other miscellaneous topics. Exhibit 14–1 on the following page summarizes the most significant changes made by the amendments. In this chapter and in those that follow, we will refer to the amendments in footnotes whenever the amendments significantly alter the existing law under Articles 2 and 2A.

EXHIBIT 14–1 THE 2003 UCC ARTICLE 2 AMENDMENTS: SELECTED PROVISIONS[a]

GENERAL CHANGES

- *Electronic contracting*—The amendments reflect the rise of electronic contracting (for example, the word *record* is substituted for the word *writing*) and the provisions of the federal law governing e-signatures (see Chapter 13).

- *Gender-neutral language has been incorporated throughout.*

- *New protections for buyers*—There are some new protections for buyers, and some provisions are applicable only to buyers who qualify as consumers. For example, the amendments make some changes in the language required to disclaim implied warranties and give consumers further protections with respect to rights and remedies (see Chapter 17).

- *Remedies*—The amendments in UCC 2–703 and UCC 2–711 give a complete list of the remedies available to buyers and sellers, respectively, on a breach of contract (see Chapter 16).

SOME IMPORTANT SPECIFIC CHANGES

- *Shipping and delivery terms*—Entirely eliminated are UCC Sections 2–319 through 2–324, which deal with shipping and delivery terms (F.O.B., C.I.F., and others listed in Chapter 15 in Exhibit 15–1). Additionally, risk of loss relating to goods to be delivered without movement now passes on the buyer's receipt of the goods regardless of the seller's status as a merchant or nonmerchant.

- *New sections on express warranties*—With respect to *new goods only,* two new sections extend express warranties made by a seller or lessor (such as a manufacturer) in an advertisement or in a record accompanying goods (such as a record enclosed in boxed goods) to remote purchasers (see Chapter 17).

- *Remedial promises*—Although not an express warranty, added to the sections on express warranties is a seller's obligation to honor a "remedial promise"—defined as a promise to repair, replace, or refund all or part of the price on the happening of a specified event (see Chapter 17).

- *The seller's right to cure*—This right has been extended (except in consumer contracts) to allow sellers, in some circumstances, to cure even after the time for performance has expired (see Chapter 16).

- *Contract formation*—Under the amendments, the terms of the contract, subject to the parol evidence rule, are (a) the terms that appear in the records of both parties, (b) the terms to which both parties agree, and (c) the terms supplied or incorporated under UCC Article 2.

MISCELLANEOUS CHANGES

- *Statute of Frauds*—The Statute of Frauds threshold amount increases from $500 to $5,000, and the one-year rule is repealed for contracts for the sale of goods [UCC 2–201].

- *Assignment and delegation*—Rules governing assignment and delegation [UCC 2–210] have been modified to conform to revised Article 9, which deals with secured transactions (see Chapter 20).

- *Buyer's acceptance of nonconforming goods*—When a buyer has accepted nonconforming goods [UCC 2–607(3)], the failure of the buyer to notify the seller of the breach no longer will operate as a bar to further recovery. Failure to give timely notice will bar a remedy "only to the extent that the seller is prejudiced by the failure" (see Chapters 16 and 17).

- *Consequential damages*—A seller can now recover consequential damages resulting from a buyer's breach under UCC 2–710. Under existing law, the seller is limited to incidental damages (see Chapter 16).

- *Statute of limitations*—The statute of limitations [UCC 2–725] has been modified to, among other things, clarify when a breach or cause of action accrues and to provide added protection for consumers (see Chapter 17).

a. This exhibit lists only selected changes made by the 2003 amendments. Although the National Conference of Commissioners on Uniform State Laws and the American Law Institute approved the amendments in 2003, as of this writing they have not yet been approved by any state.

The Scope of Article 2—Sales

Article 2 of the UCC governs **sales contracts**, or contracts for the sale of goods. To facilitate commercial transactions, Article 2 modifies some of the common law contract requirements that were summarized in Chapter 7 and discussed in detail in Chapters 8 through 12. To the extent that it has not been modified by the UCC, however, the common law of contracts also applies to sales contracts. In general, the rule is that when a UCC provision addresses a certain issue, the UCC governs; when the UCC is silent, the common law governs.

In regard to Article 2, you should keep in mind two things. First, Article 2 deals with the sale of *goods*; it does

EXHIBIT 14-2 LAW GOVERNING CONTRACTS

This exhibit graphically illustrates the relationship between general contract law and the law governing contracts for the sale of goods. Contracts for the sale of goods are not governed exclusively by Article 2 of the Uniform Commercial Code but are also governed by general contract law whenever it is relevant and has not been modified by the UCC.

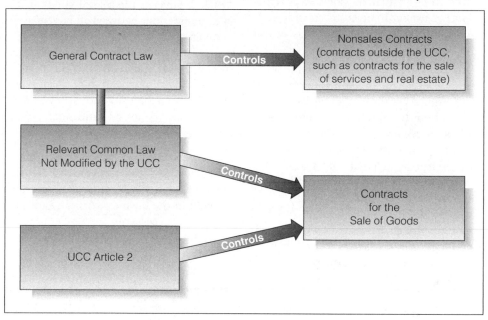

not deal with real property (real estate), services, or intangible property such as stocks and bonds. Thus, if the subject matter of a dispute is goods, the UCC governs. If it is real estate or services, the common law applies. The relationship between general contract law and the law governing sales of goods is illustrated in Exhibit 14–2 above. Second, in some cases, the rules may vary quite a bit, depending on whether the buyer or the seller is a merchant. We look now at how the UCC defines three important terms: *sale, goods,* and *merchant status.*

WHAT IS A SALE?

The UCC defines a **sale** as "the passing of title from the seller to the buyer for a price" [UCC 2–106(1)]. The price may be payable in money or in other goods, services, or realty (real estate).

WHAT ARE GOODS?

To be characterized as a *good,* the item of property must be *tangible,* and it must be *movable.* **Tangible property** has physical existence—it can be touched or seen. Intangible property—such as corporate stocks and bonds, patents and copyrights, and ordinary contract rights—has only concep-

tual existence and thus does not come under Article 2.[2] A movable item can be carried from place to place. Hence, real estate is excluded from Article 2.

Two areas of dispute arise in determining whether the object of a contract is goods and thus whether Article 2 is applicable. One problem has to do with *goods associated with real estate,* such as crops or timber, and the other concerns contracts involving a combination of *goods and services.*

Goods Associated with Real Estate. Goods associated with real estate often fall within the scope of Article 2. Section 2–107 provides the following rules:

① A contract for the sale of minerals or the like (including oil and gas) or a structure (such as a building) is a contract for the sale of goods if *severance,* or *separation,* is to

---

[2] Also specifically excluded under the 2003 amendments to Article 2 is "information" [Amended UCC 2–103(1)(k)]. The Comments explain that this article does not directly apply to electronic transfers of information, such as the transaction involved in *Specht v. Netscape,* 150 F.Supp.2d 585 (2001). (This case, which involved downloading software from the Internet, was presented in Chapter 13 as Case 13.4.) The comments further clarify that while the section does not apply to transactions involving information only, it *may* apply to transactions involving both goods and information. It is up to the courts to determine whether and to what extent the article should be applied to such transactions.

be made by the *seller*. If the *buyer* is to sever (separate) the minerals or structure from the land, the contract is considered to be a sale of real estate governed by the principles of real property law, not the UCC.

② A sale of growing crops[3] (such as potatoes, carrots, wheat, and the like) or timber to be cut is considered to be a contract for the sale of goods *regardless of who severs them.*

③ Other "things attached" to realty but capable of severance without material harm to the land are considered goods *regardless of who severs them.*[4] "Things attached" that are severable without harm to realty could include such items as a heater, a window air conditioner in a house, and stools in a restaurant. Thus, removal of one of these things would be considered a sale of goods. The test is whether removal will cause substantial harm to the real property to which the item is attached.

Goods and Services Combined. In cases in which goods and services are combined, courts disagree. For example, is the blood furnished to a patient during an operation a "sale of goods" or the "performance of a medical service"? Some courts say it is a good; others say it is a service. Similarly, contracts to sell and install software have posed the question of whether such contracts are primarily contracts for the sale of goods or contracts for the sale of services.[5] Because the UCC does not provide the answers to such questions, the courts try to determine which factor is predominant—the good or the service.

The UCC does stipulate, however, that serving food or drink to be consumed either on or off restaurant premises is a "sale of goods," at least for the purpose of an implied warranty of merchantability (to be explained in Chapter 17) [UCC 2–314(1)]. Other special transactions are also explicitly characterized as sales of goods by the UCC, including sales of unborn animals and rare coins. Whether the transaction in question involves the sale of goods or services is important because the majority of courts treat services as being excluded by the UCC. If the transaction is not covered by the UCC, then UCC provisions, including those relating to implied warranties, would not apply.

WHO IS A MERCHANT?

Article 2 governs the sale of goods in general. It applies to sales transactions between all buyers and sellers. In a limited number of instances, however, the UCC presumes that in certain phases of sales transactions involving merchants, special business standards ought to be imposed because of the merchants' relatively high degree of commercial expertise.[6] Such standards do not apply to the casual or inexperienced seller or buyer ("consumer"). Section 2–104 defines three ways in which merchant status can arise:

① A merchant is a person who *deals in goods of the kind* involved in the sales contract. Thus, a retailer, a wholesaler, or a manufacturer is a merchant of those goods sold in the business. A merchant for one type of goods is not necessarily a merchant for another type. For example, a sporting equipment retailer is a merchant when selling tennis equipment but not when selling a used computer.

② A merchant is a person who, by occupation, holds himself or herself out as having knowledge and skill unique to the practices or goods involved in the transaction. Note that this broad definition may include banks or universities as merchants.

③ A person who *employs a merchant as a broker, agent, or other intermediary* has the status of merchant in that transaction. Hence, if a "gentleman farmer" who ordinarily does not run the farm hires a broker to purchase or sell livestock, the farmer is considered a merchant in the transaction.

In summary, a person is a **merchant** when he or she, acting in a mercantile capacity, possesses or uses an expertise specifically related to the goods being sold. This basic distinction is not always clear-cut. For example, courts in most states have determined that farmers may be merchants if they sell products or livestock on a regular basis, but courts in other states have held that the drafters of the UCC did not intend to include farmers as merchants.

The court in the following case considered whether a trucking company, buying diesel fuel for its trucks, was a merchant under those circumstances for purposes of the UCC.

---

[3] Note that the 2003 amendments change this provision slightly so that growing crops are expressly included within the definition of *goods* in UCC 2–105. Contracts to sell timber, minerals, or structures to be removed from the land will continue to be controlled by UCC 2–107(1).

[4] The UCC avoids the term *fixtures* here because of the numerous definitions of the word. A fixture is anything so firmly or permanently attached to land or to a building as to become a part of it. Once personal property becomes a fixture, it is governed by real estate law. See Chapter 29.

[5] See, for example, *Richard Haney Ford v. Ford Dealer Computer Services*, 218 Ga.App. 315, 461 S.E.2d 282 (1995).

[6] The provisions that apply only to merchants deal principally with the Statute of Frauds, firm offers, confirmatory memoranda, warranties, and contract modification. These special rules reflect expedient business practices commonly known to merchants in the commercial setting. They will be discussed later in this chapter.

CASE 14.1 Ready Trucking, Inc. v. BP Exploration & Oil Co.

Georgia Court of Appeals, 2001.
248 Ga.App. 701,
548 S.E.2d 420.
http://www.ganet.org/appeals/opinions/
index.cgi[a]

FACTS Ready Trucking, Inc., is an interstate common carrier. At its terminal in Ellenwood, Georgia, Ready maintains two 10,000-gallon storage tanks for diesel fuel for its truck fleet. To facilitate regular purchases of the fuel, Ready opened an account with BP Exploration & Oil Company. Ready sent BP a Georgia state "ST-5 Sales and Use Tax Certificate," which provided that Ready was exempt from state taxes on the purchase of certain goods. Based on this certificate, BP mistakenly believed that Ready was exempt from state and local sales taxes on diesel fuel purchases. Consequently, on Ready's 149 separate purchases of fuel from BP, the seller did not collect these taxes, as was otherwise required by law. For each sale, BP sent Ready an invoice showing the price, the amount of fuel, and the unpaid taxes. The Georgia Department of Revenue discovered the error and billed Ready $37,801.46, including $25,560.55 in back taxes and $12,240.91 in penalties and interest. Ready filed a suit in a Georgia state court against BP, alleging breach of contract. BP responded that by accepting the fuel after seeing the invoices, Ready, as a merchant, had agreed that it would pay the taxes. The court granted BP's motion for summary judgment. Ready appealed to a state intermediate appellate court.

_____

a. Click on "Search Court of Appeals Opinions." In the resulting screen, set "Search Year" to "All" and type "Ready Trucking" into the keyword field. Then click on "search." This will lead you to a link to the case. This site is maintained by the state of Georgia.

ISSUE Was Ready a merchant for purposes of the UCC?

DECISION Yes. The state intermediate appellate court affirmed the decision of the lower court. Thus, BP's invoices governed the fuel sales, and there was no breach of contract. Ready alone was liable for the payment of the taxes.

REASON The court pointed out that between _merchants,_ under UCC 2–201(2), "if within a reasonable time a writing in confirmation of the contract and sufficient against the sender is received and the party receiving it has reason to know its contents, it [constitutes a writing enforceable] against such party unless written notice of objection to its contents is given within ten days after it is received." The writing then becomes the "final expression of their agreement." (This rule is discussed in detail later in this chapter.) A buyer may be considered a merchant when it is a "business professional as opposed to a casual or inexperienced seller or buyer, and the purchase involves a type of goods related and necessary to the business or occupation of the purchaser." Here "Ready is an interstate motor carrier and it made nearly 150 purchases from BP * * *. Ready was familiar with the purchase of diesel fuel and the taxation issues, and it had the knowledge necessary to discover BP's initial error. We therefore hold that Ready is a merchant for the purposes of [UCC 2–201(2)] when buying diesel fuel for its business." The invoices sent to Ready confirmed that BP was not withholding certain taxes, to which Ready did not object within ten days. Thus, the invoices constituted an agreement between the parties that the taxes would not be collected and remitted by BP.

FOR CRITICAL ANALYSIS—Social Consideration
How might these parties have avoided this situation?

The Scope of Article 2A—Leases

In the past few decades, leases of personal property (goods) have become increasingly common. Article 2A of the UCC was created to fill the need for uniform guidelines in this area. Article 2A covers any transaction that creates a lease of goods, as well as subleases of goods [UCC 2A–102, 2A–103(k)].[7] Except that it applies to leases of

goods, rather than sales of goods, Article 2A is essentially a repetition of Article 2 and varies only to reflect differences between sale and lease transactions. (Note that Article 2A is not concerned with leases of real property, such as land or buildings. The laws governing these types of transactions will be examined in Chapter 29.)

DEFINITION OF A LEASE

Article 2A defines a **lease agreement** as a lessor and lessee's bargain with respect to the lease of goods, as found in their language and as implied by other circumstances, including course of dealing and usage of trade or course of performance

_____

[7] The 2003 amendments to UCC Article 2A, like those to UCC Article 2, expressly exclude "information" from the definition of "goods" [Amended UCC 2A–103(1)(n) and (p)].

[UCC 2A–103(k)]. A **lessor** is one who sells the right to the possession and use of goods under a lease [UCC 2A–103(p)]. A **lessee** is one who acquires the right to the possession and use of goods under a lease [UCC 2A–103(n)]. Article 2A applies to all types of leases of goods, including commercial leases and consumer leases. Special rules apply to certain types of leases, however, including consumer leases and finance leases.

CONSUMER LEASES

A *consumer lease* involves three elements: (1) a lessor who regularly engages in the business of leasing or selling, (2) a lessee (except an organization) who leases the goods "primarily for a personal, family, or household purpose," and (3) total lease payments that are less than a dollar amount set by state statute [UCC 2A–103(1)(e)].[8] In the interest of providing special protection for consumers, certain provisions of Article 2A apply only to consumer leases. For example, one provision states that a consumer may recover attorneys' fees if a court finds that a term in a consumer lease contract is unconscionable [UCC 2A–108(4)(a)].

FINANCE LEASES

A *finance lease* involves a lessor, a lessee, and a supplier. The lessor buys or leases goods from a supplier and leases or subleases them to the lessee [UCC 2A–103(g)]. Typically, in a finance lease, the lessor is simply financing the transaction. ● **EXAMPLE #1** Suppose that Marlin Corporation wants to lease a crane for use in its construction business. Marlin's bank agrees to purchase the equipment from Jennco, Inc., and lease the equipment to Marlin. In this situation, the bank is the lessor-financer, Marlin is the lessee, and Jennco is the supplier.●

Article 2A, unlike ordinary contract law, makes the lessee's obligations under a commercial finance lease irrevocable and independent from the financer's obligations [UCC 2A–407]. That is, the lessee must perform whether or not the financer performs. The lessee also must look almost entirely to the supplier for warranties.

The Formation of Sales and Lease Contracts

In regard to the formation of sales and lease contracts, the UCC modifies the common law in several ways. We look here at how Article 2 and Article 2A of the UCC modify common law contract rules. Remember, though, that parties to sales contracts are free to establish whatever terms they wish. The UCC comes into play only when the parties have

failed to provide in their contract for a contingency that later gives rise to a dispute. The UCC makes this clear time and again by its use of such phrases as "unless the parties otherwise agree" or "absent a contrary agreement by the parties."

OFFER

In general contract law, the moment a definite offer is met by an unqualified acceptance, a binding contract is formed. In commercial sales transactions, the verbal exchanges, the correspondence, and the actions of the parties may not reveal exactly when a binding contractual obligation arises. The UCC states that an agreement sufficient to constitute a contract can exist even if the moment of its making is undetermined [UCC 2–204(2), 2A–204(2)].

Open Terms. Remember from Chapter 8 that under the common law of contracts, an offer must be definite enough for the parties (and the courts) to ascertain its essential terms when it is accepted. In contrast to the common law, the UCC states that a sales or lease contract will not fail for indefiniteness even if one or more terms are left open as long as (1) the parties intended to make a contract and (2) there is a reasonably certain basis for the court to grant an appropriate remedy [UCC 2–204(3), 2A–204(3)]. ● **EXAMPLE #2** Mike agrees to lease from CompuQuik a highly specialized computer workstation. Mike and one of CompuQuik's sales representatives sign a lease agreement that leaves some of the details blank, to be "worked out" the following week, when the leasing manager will be back from her vacation. In the meantime, CompuQuik obtains the necessary equipment from one of its suppliers and spends several days modifying the equipment to suit Mike's needs. When the leasing manager returns, she calls Mike and tells him that his workstation is ready. Mike says he is no longer interested in the workstation, as he has arranged to lease the same type of equipment for a lower price from another firm. CompuQuik sues Mike to recover its costs in obtaining and modifying the equipment, and one of the issues before the court is whether the parties had an enforceable contract. The court will likely hold that they did, based on their intent and conduct, despite the "blanks" in their written agreement.●

Although the UCC has radically lessened the requirement of definiteness of terms, keep in mind that the more terms left open, the less likely it is that a court will find that the parties intended to form a contract. (This is also true with respect to online contracts.)

Open Price Term. If the parties have not agreed on a price, the court will determine a "reasonable price at the time for delivery" [UCC 2–305(1)]. If either the buyer or the seller is to determine the price, the price is to be fixed (set) in good faith [UCC 2–305(2)].

---

[8] There is no dollar limit in the 2003 amendments to UCC Article 2A.

Sometimes the price fails to be fixed through the fault of one of the parties. In that situation, the other party can treat the contract as canceled or fix a reasonable price. ● **EXAMPLE #3** Johnson and Merrick enter into a contract for the sale of unfinished doors and agree that Johnson will determine the price. Johnson refuses to fix the price. Merrick can either treat the contract as canceled or set a reasonable price [UCC 2–305(3)]. ●

Open Payment Term. When parties do not specify payment terms, payment is due at the time and place at which the buyer is to receive the goods [UCC 2–310(a)]. The buyer can tender payment using any commercially normal or acceptable means, such as a check or credit card. If the seller demands payment in cash, however, the buyer must be given a reasonable time to obtain it [UCC 2–511(2)]. This is especially important when the contract states a definite and final time for performance.

Open Delivery Term. When no delivery terms are specified, the buyer normally takes delivery at the seller's place of business [UCC 2–308(a)]. If the seller has no place of business, the seller's residence is used. When goods are located in some other place and both parties know it, delivery is made there. If the time for shipment or delivery is not clearly specified in the sales contract, the court will infer a "reasonable" time for performance [UCC 2–309(1)].

Duration of an Ongoing Contract. A single contract might specify successive performances but not indicate how long the parties are required to deal with each other. Although either party may terminate the ongoing contractual relationship, principles of good faith and sound commercial practice call for reasonable notification before termination so as to give the other party reasonable time to seek a substitute arrangement [UCC 2–309(2), (3)].

Options and Cooperation Regarding Performance. When specific shipping arrangements have not been made but the contract contemplates shipment of the goods, the seller has the right to make these arrangements in good faith, using commercial reasonableness in the situation [UCC 2–311].

When terms relating to the assortment of goods are omitted from a sales contract, the *buyer* can specify the assortment. ● **EXAMPLE #4** Petry Drugs, Inc., agrees to purchase one thousand toothbrushes from Marconi's Dental Supply. The toothbrushes come in a variety of colors, but the contract does not specify color. Petry, the buyer, has the right to take six hundred blue toothbrushes and four hundred green ones if it wishes. Petry, however, must exercise good faith and commercial reasonableness in making its selection [UCC 2–311]. ●

Open Quantity Term. Normally, if the parties do not specify a quantity, a court will have no basis for determining a remedy. The UCC recognizes two exceptions in requirements and output contracts [UCC 2–306(1)]. In a **requirements contract**, the buyer agrees to purchase and the seller agrees to sell all or up to a stated amount of what the buyer *needs* or *requires*. ● **EXAMPLE #5** Southern State Cannery forms a contract with Al Cupp. The cannery agrees to purchase from Cupp, and Cupp agrees to sell to the cannery, all of the green beans that the cannery needs or requires during the summer of 2005. ● There is implicit consideration in a requirements contract, for the buyer (the cannery, in this situation) gives up a legal right—the right to buy green beans from any other seller.

Requirements contracts are common in the business world and are normally enforceable. If, however, the buyer promises to purchase only if the buyer *wishes* to do so, or if the buyer reserves the right to buy the goods from someone other than the seller, the promise is illusory (without consideration) and unenforceable by either party.

In an **output contract**, the seller agrees to sell and the buyer agrees to buy all or up to a stated amount of what the seller *produces*. ● **EXAMPLE #6** Al Cupp forms a contract with Southern State Cannery. Cupp agrees to sell to the cannery, and the cannery agrees to purchase from Cupp, all of the beans that Cupp produces on his farm during the summer of 2005. ● Again, because the seller essentially forfeits the right to sell goods to another buyer, there is implicit consideration in an output contract.

The UCC imposes a *good faith limitation* on requirements and output contracts. The quantity under such contracts is the amount of requirements or the amount of output that occurs during a *normal* production year. The actual quantity purchased or sold cannot be unreasonably disproportionate to normal or comparable prior requirements or output [UCC 2–306].

Merchant's Firm Offer. Under regular contract principles, an offer can be revoked at any time before acceptance. The major common law exception is an *option contract* (discussed in Chapter 8), in which the offeree pays consideration for the offeror's irrevocable promise to keep the offer open for a stated period. The UCC creates a second exception for firm offers made by a merchant to sell, buy, or lease goods. A **firm offer** arises when a merchant-offeror gives *assurances* in a *signed writing* that the offer will remain open. The merchant's firm offer is irrevocable without the necessity of consideration[9] for the stated period or, if no definite period is stated, a reasonable period (neither period to exceed three months) [UCC 2–205, 2A–205].

---

[9] If the offeree pays consideration, then an option contract (not a merchant's firm offer) is formed.

It is necessary that the offer be both *written* and *signed* by the offeror.[10] When a firm offer is contained in a form contract prepared by the offeree, the offeror must also sign a separate firm offer assurance. This requirement ensures that the offeror will be made aware of the offer. If the firm offer is buried amid copious language in one of the pages of the offeree's form contract, the offeror may inadvertently sign the contract without realizing that it contains a firm offer, thus defeating the purpose of the rule—which is to give effect to a merchant's deliberate intent to be bound to a firm offer.

ACCEPTANCE

The following sections examine the UCC's provisions governing acceptance. As you will see, acceptance of an offer to buy, sell, or lease goods generally may be made in any reasonable manner and by any reasonable means.

Methods of Acceptance. The general common law rule is that an offeror can specify, or authorize, a particular means of acceptance, making that means the only one effective for contract formation. As you read in Chapter 13, online sellers typically specify, or authorize, acceptance through "click-on" boxes. In other words, to accept an online offer, the offeree merely clicks on a box stating "I agree" or "I accept."

Even an unauthorized means of communication is effective, however, as long as the acceptance is received by the specified deadline. ● **EXAMPLE #7** Suppose that an offer states, "Answer by fax within five days." If the offeree sends a letter, and the offeror receives it within five days, a valid contract is still formed.●

Any Reasonable Means. When the offeror does not specify a means of acceptance, the UCC provides that acceptance can be made by any means of communication reasonable under the circumstances [UCC 2–206(1), 2A–206(1)]. This broadens the common law rules concerning authorized means of acceptance. (For a review of the requirements relating to mode and timeliness of acceptance, see Chapter 8.)
● **EXAMPLE #8** Anodyne Corporation writes Bethlehem Industries a letter offering to lease $1,000 worth of postage meters. The offer states that Anodyne will keep the offer open for only ten days from the date of the letter. Before the

ten days have lapsed, Bethlehem sends Anodyne an acceptance by fax. Is a valid contract formed? The answer is yes, because acceptance by fax is a commercially reasonable medium of acceptance under the circumstances. Acceptance would be effective on Bethlehem's transmission of the fax, which occurred before the offer lapsed.●

Promise to Ship or Prompt Shipment. The UCC permits a seller to accept an offer to buy goods for current or prompt shipment by either a prompt *promise* to ship the goods to the buyer or the *prompt shipment* of conforming goods (that is, goods that accord with the contract's terms) to the buyer [UCC 2–206(1)(b)]. The seller's prompt shipment of *nonconforming goods* in response to the offer constitutes both an acceptance (a contract) and a *breach* of that contract.

This rule does not apply if the seller **seasonably** (within a reasonable amount of time) notifies the buyer that the nonconforming shipment is offered only as an *accommodation,* or as a favor. The notice of accommodation must clearly indicate to the buyer that the shipment does not constitute an acceptance and that, therefore, no contract has been formed.
● **EXAMPLE #9** McFarrell Pharmacy orders five cases of Johnson & Johnson 3-by-5-inch gauze pads from Halderson Medical Supply, Inc. If Halderson ships five cases of Xeroform 3-by-5-inch gauze pads instead, the shipment acts as both an acceptance of McFarrell's offer and a *breach* of the resulting contract. McFarrell may sue Halderson for any appropriate damages. If, however, Halderson notifies McFarrell that the Xeroform gauze pads are being shipped *as an accommodation*—because Halderson has only Xeroform pads in stock—the shipment will constitute a counteroffer, not an acceptance. A contract will be formed only if McFarrell accepts the Xeroform gauze pads.●

Notice of Acceptance. As noted in Chapter 8, notice of acceptance is not an issue in *bilateral* contracts because such contracts are formed by an exchange of promises. In other words, a bilateral contract is formed when the promise is made. In contrast, unilateral contracts invite acceptance by performance. Under the common law, because acceptance (performance) of a unilateral contract was usually evident, the offeree normally was not required to notify the offeror of the acceptance. The UCC changes this common law rule. According to the UCC, when "the beginning of requested performance is a reasonable mode of acceptance[,] an offeror who is not notified of acceptance within a reasonable time may treat the offer as having lapsed before acceptance" [UCC 2–206(2), 2A–206(2)].

Additional Terms. Under the common law, if Alderman makes an offer to Beale, and Beale in turn accepts but in the acceptance makes some slight modification to the terms of

---

[10] "Signed" includes any symbol executed or adopted by a party with a present intention to authenticate a writing [UCC 1–201(39)]. A complete signature is not required. Therefore, initials, a thumbprint, a trade name, or any mark used in lieu of a written signature will suffice, regardless of its location on the document. Under the 2003 amendments to UCC Articles 2 and 2A, the definition of "sign" is broad enough to cover any record that contains an e-signature within the meaning of the Uniform Electronic Transactions Act.

the offer, there is no contract. The so-called *mirror image rule,* which requires that the terms of the acceptance exactly match those of the offer (see Chapter 8), makes Beale's action a rejection of—and a counteroffer to—Alderman's offer. This rule often results in the so-called *battle of the forms.*

• **EXAMPLE #10** A buyer negotiates with a seller over the phone to purchase DVD players. The parties agree to all of the specific terms of the sale—price, quantity, delivery date, and so on. The buyer then offers to buy the DVD players, using its standard purchase order form, and sends the form to the seller. At the same time, the seller accepts the offer, using its standard sales form. Because the parties presume that they have reached an agreement, discrepancies in the terms and conditions contained in their respective forms may go unnoticed. If a dispute arises, however, the discrepancies become significant, and a "battle of the forms" begins, in which each party claims that its form represents the true terms of the agreement.•

Under the common law, the courts tended to resolve this difficulty by holding that no contract was made, because the last form to be sent was not an acceptance but a counteroffer. To avoid the battle of the forms, the UCC dispenses with the mirror image rule. The UCC generally takes the position that if the offeree's response indicates a *definite* acceptance of the offer, a contract is formed even if the acceptance includes additional or different terms from those contained in the offer [UCC 2–207(1)]. What happens to these additional terms? The answer to this question depends, in part, on whether the parties are nonmerchants or merchants.[11]

One Party or Both Parties Are Nonmerchants. If one (or both) of the parties is a *nonmerchant,* the contract is formed according to the terms of the original offer submitted by the original offeror and not according to the additional terms of the acceptance [UCC 2–207(2)]. • **EXAMPLE #11** Tolsen offers in writing to sell his personal computer and color printer and scanner to Valdez for $1,500. Valdez faxes a reply to Tolsen in which Valdez states, "I accept your offer to purchase your computer, color printer, and scanner for $1,500. I *would like* two extra sets of color toner for the printer to be included in the purchase price." Valdez has given Tolsen a definite expression of acceptance

(creating a contract), even though the acceptance also suggests an added term for the offer. Because Tolsen is not a merchant, the additional term is merely a proposal (suggestion), and Tolsen is not legally obligated to comply with that term.•

Both Parties Are Merchants. In contracts *between merchants* (that is, when both parties to the contract are merchants), the additional terms automatically become part of the contract unless (1) the original offer expressly limits acceptance to the terms of the offer, (2) the new or changed terms *materially* alter the contract, or (3) the offeror objects to the new or changed terms within a reasonable period of time [UCC 2–207(2)].

What constitutes a material alteration is frequently a question of fact that only a court can decide. Generally, if the modification involves no unreasonable element of surprise or hardship for the offeror, the court will hold that the modification did not materially alter the contract.

Conditioned on Offeror's Assent. Regardless of merchant status, the UCC provides that the offeree's expression cannot be construed as an acceptance if additional or different terms in the acceptance are expressly conditioned on the offeror's assent to the additional or different terms [UCC 2–207(1)]. • **EXAMPLE #12** Philips offers to sell Hundert 650 pounds of turkey thighs at a specified price and with specified delivery terms. Hundert responds, "I accept your offer for 650 pounds of turkey thighs *on the condition that you give me ninety days to pay for them.*" Hundert's response will be construed not as an acceptance but as a counteroffer, which Philips may or may not accept.•

Additional Terms May Be Stricken. The UCC provides yet another option for dealing with conflicting terms in the parties' writings. Section 2–207(3) states that conduct by both parties that recognizes the existence of a contract is sufficient to establish a contract for the sale of goods even though the writings of the parties do not otherwise establish a contract. In this situation, "the terms of the particular contract will consist of those terms on which the writings of the parties agree, together with any supplementary terms incorporated under any other provisions of this Act." In a dispute over contract terms, this provision allows a court simply to strike from the contract those terms on which the parties do not agree. • **EXAMPLE #13** AAA Marketing Company orders goods over the phone from Big Sales, Inc., which ships the goods to AAA with an acknowledgment form. AAA accepts and pays for the goods. The parties' writings do not establish a contract, but there is no question that a contract exists. If a dispute arises over the terms—such as the extent of any warranties—UCC 2–207(3) provides the governing rule.•

---

[11] The 2003 amendments to UCC Article 2 do not distinguish between merchants and others in setting out rules for the effect of additional terms in contracts for sale, nor do they give a preference to the first or the last terms to be stated. Instead, a court is directed to determine whether (1) the terms appear in the records of both parties, (2) both parties agree to the terms even if they are not in a record, or (3) the terms are supplied or incorporated under another provision of Article 2 [Amended UCC 2–207]. The amendments give the courts more discretion to include or exclude certain terms.

CONSIDERATION

The common law rule that a contract requires consideration also applies to sales and lease contracts. Unlike the common law, however, the UCC does not require a contract modification to be supported by new consideration. An agreement modifying a contract for the sale or lease of goods "needs no consideration to be binding" [UCC 2–209(1), 2A–208(1)].

Modifications Must Be Made in Good Faith. Of course, contract modification must be sought in good faith [UCC 1–203]. ● **EXAMPLE #14** Allied, Inc., agrees to lease a new recreational vehicle (RV) to Louise for a stated monthly payment. Subsequently, a sudden shift in the market makes it difficult for Allied to lease the new RV to Louise at the contract price without suffering a loss. Allied tells Louise of the situation, and she agrees to pay an additional sum for the lease of the RV. Later Louise reconsiders and refuses to pay more than the original price. Under the UCC, Louise's promise to modify the contract needs no consideration to be binding. Hence, she is bound by the modified contract. ●

In this example, a shift in the market is a *good faith* reason for contract modification. What if there really was no shift in the market, however, and Allied knew that Louise needed to lease the new RV immediately but refused to deliver it unless she agreed to pay an additional sum of money? This attempt at extortion through modification without a legitimate commercial reason would be ineffective because it would violate the duty of good faith. Allied would not be permitted to enforce the higher price.

When Modification without Consideration Requires a Writing. In some situations, modification of a sales or lease contract without consideration must be in writing to be enforceable. If the contract itself prohibits any changes to the contract unless they are in a signed writing, for example, then only those changes agreed to in a signed writing are enforceable. If a consumer (nonmerchant buyer) is dealing with a merchant and the merchant supplies the form that contains a prohibition against oral modification, the consumer must sign a separate acknowledgment of such a clause [UCC 2–209(2), 2A–208(2)].

Additionally, any modification that brings a sales contract under the Statute of Frauds must usually be in writing to be enforceable. Thus, if an oral contract for the sale of goods priced at $400 is modified so that the contract goods are now priced at $600, the modification must be in writing to be enforceable [UCC 2–209(3)]. If, however, the buyer accepts delivery of the goods after the modification, he or she is bound to the $600 price [UCC 2–201(3)(c)]. (Unlike

Article 2, Article 2A does not say whether a lease as modified needs to satisfy the Statute of Frauds.)

STATUTE OF FRAUDS

The UCC contains Statute of Frauds provisions covering sales and lease contracts.[12] Under these provisions, sales contracts for goods priced at $500 or more and lease contracts requiring payments of $1,000 or more must be in writing to be enforceable [UCC 2–201(1), 2A–201(1)].[13]

Sufficiency of the Writing. The UCC has greatly relaxed the requirements for the sufficiency of a writing to satisfy the Statute of Frauds. A writing or a memorandum will be sufficient as long as it indicates that the parties intended to form a contract and as long as it is signed by the party (or agent of the party) against whom enforcement is sought. The contract normally will not be enforceable beyond the quantity of goods shown in the writing, however. All other terms can be proved in court by oral testimony. For leases, the writing must reasonably identify and describe the goods leased and the lease term.

(Note that other laws may require certain clauses in sales and lease contracts to be in writing. For an example of one such law as it applies to arbitration clauses, see this chapter's *Business Law in the Online World* feature.)

Written Confirmation between Merchants. Once again, the UCC provides a special rule for merchants. Merchants can satisfy the requirements of a writing for the Statute of Frauds if, after the parties have agreed orally, one of the merchants sends a signed written confirmation to the other merchant within a reasonable time after the oral agreement was reached. The communication must indicate the terms of the agreement, and the merchant receiving the confirmation must have reason to know of its contents. Unless the merchant who receives the confirmation gives written notice of objection to its contents within ten days after receipt, the writing is sufficient against the receiving merchant, even though he or she has not signed anything [UCC 2–201(2)].[14]

---

[12] Under the common law, a contract that by its own terms cannot be performed within one year from the day after the date of its formation must be in writing to be enforceable. The 2003 amendments to UCC Articles 2 and 2A provide that contracts for sales or leases of goods are not subject to this common law rule [Amended UCC 2–201(4), 2A–201(6)].

[13] Under the 2003 amendments to UCC 2–201(1), a contract for a sale of goods must be priced at $5,000 or more to be subject to the record (writing) requirement.

[14] According to the Comments accompanying UCC 2A–201 (Article 2A's Statute of Frauds), the "between merchants" provision was not included because the number of such transactions involving leases, as opposed to sales, was thought to be modest.

BUSINESS LAW IN THE ONLINE WORLD
Writing Requirements for Arbitration Clauses

As you learned in Chapter 2, parties frequently include arbitration clauses in their contracts. These clauses reflect the parties' agreement to submit any dispute that may arise under the contract to arbitration. Generally, public policy has long favored arbitration as a dispute-settlement method, as reflected in state statutes and the Federal Arbitration Act (FAA) of 1925, which provide for the enforcement of arbitration clauses. Yet the FAA also states that arbitration clauses must be in writing to be enforceable. Does that mean that arbitration clauses in electronic contracts are not enforceable? Does an electronic contract constitute a "writing" for FAA purposes?

THE CASE AGAINST REALNETWORKS, INC. This question came before a federal district court in 2000 in a case brought by a group of plaintiffs against RealNetworks, Inc. The plaintiffs complained that RealNetworks's software products secretly allowed RealNetworks to access and intercept users' electronic communications and stored information without their knowledge or consent and thus violated their privacy rights. RealNetworks asked the court to stay the proceedings and enforce the arbitration clause in the licensing agreement accepted by the plaintiffs when they downloaded the software. These agreements were "click-on" agreements (which were discussed in Chapter 13). Before the plaintiffs could install the software, they had to accept RealNetworks's licensing agreement, which appeared in a pop-up window on their computer screens. A provision at the end of the agreement stated that any disputes would be submitted to arbitration.

DOES AN ELECTRONIC CONTRACT CONSTITUTE A "WRITING" UNDER THE FAA? The question before the court was whether the click-on licensing agreement constituted a writing, as required by the FAA. The plaintiffs asserted that it did not, because the agreement could not be printed or saved. RealNetworks argued that it did and that it could indeed be printed and saved.

The court, after delving into a series of dictionary definitions to determine the plain meaning of the word *writing,* decided that the agreement did constitute a writing. Contrary to the plaintiffs' assertions, the agreement could be rather easily printed and automatically stored on the user's hard drive despite the absence of "print" and "save" buttons. In fact, noted the court, there was more than one way to print the agreement. While Congress did not specifically mention electronic communications when it enacted the FAA in 1925, it also did not specifically *exclude* electronic communications from the category of written communications. In short, the plaintiffs were bound by the "written" agreement, including its arbitration clause.[a]

FOR CRITICAL ANALYSIS

If an Internet user does not print out a document temporarily displayed on her or his computer screen, should that document still qualify as a "writing"?

a. *In re RealNetworks, Inc., Privacy Litigation,* 2000 WL 631341 (N.D.Ill. 2000).

● **EXAMPLE #15** Alfonso is a merchant buyer in Cleveland. He contracts over the telephone to purchase $4,000 worth of spare aircraft parts from Goldster, a New York City merchant seller. Two days later, Goldster sends a written confirmation detailing the terms of the oral contract, and Alfonso subsequently receives it. If Alfonso does not give Goldster written notice of objection to the contents of the written confirmation within ten days of receipt, Alfonso cannot raise the Statute of Frauds as a defense against the enforcement of the oral contract. ●

Exceptions. The UCC defines three exceptions to the writing requirements of the Statute of Frauds. An oral contract for the sale of goods priced at $500 or more or the lease of goods involving total payments of $1,000 or more will be enforceable despite the absence of a writing in the circumstances discussed in the following subsections [UCC 2–201(3), 2A–201(4)]. These exceptions and other ways in which sales law differs from general contract law are summarized in Exhibit 14–3 on the next page.

Specially Manufactured Goods. An oral contract is enforceable if it is for (1) goods that are specially manufactured for a particular buyer or specially manufactured or obtained for a particular lessee, (2) these goods are not suitable for resale or lease to others in the ordinary course of

EXHIBIT 14–3 MAJOR DIFFERENCES BETWEEN CONTRACT LAW AND SALES LAW

	CONTRACT LAW	SALES LAW
Contract terms	Contract must contain all material terms.	Open terms are acceptable if parties intended to form a contract, but contract not enforceable beyond quantity term.
Acceptance	Mirror image rule applies. If additional terms are added in acceptance, counteroffer is created.	Additional terms will not negate acceptance unless acceptance is made expressly conditional on assent to the additional terms.
Contract modification	Requires consideration.	Does not require consideration.
Irrevocable offers	Option contracts (with consideration).	Merchants' firm offers (without consideration).
Statute of Frauds requirements	All material terms must be included in the writing.	Writing required only in sale of goods priced at $500 or more but not enforceable beyond quantity specified. *Exceptions:* 1. Contracts for specially manufactured goods. 2. Contracts admitted to by party against whom enforcement is sought. 3. Contracts will be enforced to extent goods delivered or paid for. 4. A contract between merchants is enforceable if a merchant fails to object in writing to a confirming memorandum within ten days of its receipt.

the seller's or lessor's business, and (3) the seller or lessor has substantially started to manufacture the goods or has made commitments for the manufacture or procurement of the goods. In this situation, once the seller or lessor has taken action, the buyer or lessee cannot repudiate the agreement claiming the Statute of Frauds as a defense.

● **EXAMPLE #16** Womach orders custom-made draperies for her new boutique. The price is $1,000, and the contract is oral. When the merchant seller manufactures the draperies and tenders delivery to Womach, Womach refuses to accept them even though the quality of the work is satisfactory and the job has been completed on time. Womach claims that she is not liable because the contract was oral. Clearly, if the unique style and color of the draperies make it improbable that the seller can find another buyer, Womach is liable to the seller. Note that the seller must have made a substantial beginning in manufacturing the specialized item prior to the buyer's repudiation. (Here, the manufacture was completed.) Of course, the court must still be convinced by evidence of the terms of the oral contract.●

Admissions. An oral contract for the sale or lease of goods is enforceable if the party against whom enforcement of a contract is sought admits in pleadings, testimony, or other court proceedings that a contract for sale was made.[15] In this situation, the contract will be enforceable even though it was oral, but enforceability will be limited to the quantity of goods admitted.

● EXAMPLE #17 Lane and Pyron negotiate an agreement over the telephone. During the negotiations, Lane requests a delivery price for five hundred gallons of gasoline and a separate price for seven hundred gallons of gasoline. Pyron replies that the price would be the same, $1.10 per gallon. Lane orally orders five hundred gallons. Pyron honestly believes that Lane ordered seven hundred gallons and tenders that amount. Lane refuses the shipment of seven hundred gallons, and Pyron sues for breach. In his pleadings and testimony, Lane admits that an oral contract was made, but only for five hundred gallons. Because Lane admits the existence of the oral contract, Lane cannot plead the Statute of Frauds as a defense. The contract is enforceable, however, only to the extent of the quantity admitted (five hundred gallons). ●

Partial Performance. An oral contract for the sale or lease of goods is enforceable if payment has been made and accepted or goods have been received and accepted. This is the "partial performance" exception. The oral contract will be enforced at least to the extent that performance *actually* took place.

● EXAMPLE #18 Suppose that Jeffrey Allan orally contracts to lease to Opus Enterprises a thousand chairs at $2 each to be used during a one-day concert. Before delivery, Opus sends Allan a check for $1,000, which Allan cashes. Later, when Allan attempts to deliver the chairs, Opus refuses delivery, claiming the Statute of Frauds as a defense, and demands the return of its $1,000. Under the UCC's partial performance rule, Allan can enforce the oral contract by tender of delivery of five hundred chairs for the $1,000 accepted. Similarly, if Opus had made no payment but had accepted the delivery of five hundred chairs from Allan, the oral contract would have been enforceable against Opus for $1,000, the lease payment due for the five hundred chairs delivered. ●

PAROL EVIDENCE

If the parties to a contract set forth its terms in a confirmatory memorandum (a writing expressing offer and accep-

tance of the deal) or in a writing intended as their final expression, the terms of the contract cannot be contradicted by evidence of any prior agreements or contemporaneous oral agreements. The terms of the contract may, however, be explained or supplemented by *consistent additional terms* or by *course of dealing, usage of trade,* or *course of performance* [UCC 2–202, 2A–202].

Consistent Additional Terms. If the court finds an ambiguity in a writing that is supposed to be a complete and exclusive statement of the agreement between the parties, it may accept evidence of consistent additional terms to clarify or remove the ambiguity. The court will not, however, accept evidence of contradictory terms. This is the rule under both the UCC and the common law of contracts.

Course of Dealing and Usage of Trade. Under the UCC, the meaning of any agreement, evidenced by the language of the parties and by their actions, must be interpreted in light of commercial practices and other surrounding circumstances. In interpreting a commercial agreement, the court will assume that the course of prior dealing between the parties and the usage of trade were taken into account when the agreement was phrased.

A **course of dealing** is a sequence of previous actions and communications between the parties to a particular transaction that establishes a common basis for their understanding [UCC 1–205(1)]. A course of dealing is restricted to the sequence of actions and communications between the parties that has occurred prior to the agreement in question. The UCC states, "A course of dealing between the parties and any usage of trade in the vocation or trade in which they are engaged or of which they are or should be aware give particular meaning to [the terms of the agreement] and supplement or qualify the terms of [the] agreement" [UCC 1–205(3)].

Usage of trade is defined as any practice or method of dealing having such regularity of observance in a place, vocation, or trade as to justify an expectation that it will be observed with respect to the transaction in question [UCC 1–205(2)]. Further, the express terms of an agreement and an applicable course of dealing or usage of trade will be construed to be consistent with each other whenever reasonable. When such a construction is *unreasonable,* however, the express terms in the agreement will prevail [UCC 1–205(4)].

In the following case, the question was whether a clause in the seller's invoice was part of a contract between the parties, according to the usage of trade in their industry and the course of dealing between them.

---

[15] Any admission under oath, including one not made in a court, satisfies UCC 2–201(3)(b) and 2A–201(4)(b) under the 2003 amendments to Article 2 and 2A.

CASE 14.2 Puget Sound Financial, LLC v. Unisearch, Inc.

Supreme Court of Washington, 2002.
146 Wash.2d 428,
47 P.3d 940.
http://www.legalwa.org[a]

FACTS Puget Sound Financial, LLC, lends money to businesses.[b] In 1993, Puget hired Unisearch, Inc., to search the public records in the state of Washington to locate existing liens on potential borrowers' assets. Puget would request a search under a particular name. Unisearch would send a report and an invoice for $25 to Puget. Every invoice contained the statement "Liability Limited to Amount of Fee." In July 1996, Puget requested a search for "The Benefit Group, Inc." Unisearch reported that there were no liens. Puget loaned The Benefit Group $100,000, with payment guaranteed by the firm's assets. When The Benefit Group failed to pay, Puget discovered that another lender had priority to the assets under a previous lien filed in the public records under the name "The Benefits Group, Inc." Puget filed a suit in a Washington state court against Unisearch, alleging in part breach of contract. Unisearch argued that if it were liable, the amount of damages would be limited to $25 under the invoices' limitation-of-liability clause, which was part of its contract with Puget, according to the usage of trade in the

_____

a. Click on "Washington State Supreme and Appellate Court Opinions." In the "Search" box, type "Unisearch," select "Search case titles only," and click on "Search." Click on the case name in the "Results" list to access the opinion. Municipal Research and Services Center, which is funded by the state of Washington, maintains this Web site.

b. Before making a loan, a lender normally wants to know whether the property that will guarantee the potential borrower's payment of the loan is already being used to guarantee the payment of other debts of the borrower. If the borrower were to default on payment of the loan, the property's value might not be sufficient to pay all creditors. Loans guaranteed, or secured, by a debtor's personal property are known as secured transactions, which are discussed more fully in Chapter 20.

search industry and the course of dealing between the parties. The court ruled in favor of Unisearch on this issue. Puget appealed to a state intermediate appellate court, which reversed the judgment. Unisearch appealed to the Washington Supreme Court.

ISSUE Was Unisearch protected by the limitation-of-liability clause in its invoices?

DECISION Yes. The Washington Supreme Court reversed the appellate court's decision and affirmed the trial court's judgment limiting Unisearch's liability, if any, to the amount of its fee. The state supreme court held that the limitation-of-liability clause in Unisearch's invoices was part of the contract between Puget and Unisearch, according to the usage of trade in the industry and the parties' course of dealing.

REASON The court noted that, according to the _Restatement (Second) of Contracts,_ a "usage of trade is a usage having such regularity of observance in a place, vocation, or trade as to justify an expectation that it will be observed with respect to a particular agreement" and a "course of dealing is a sequence of previous conduct between the parties to an agreement which is fairly to be regarded as establishing a common basis of understanding for interpreting their expressions and other conduct." Unisearch provided "numerous examples of liability exclusions on invoices from other states as evidence of trade usage" and of search firms claiming "that they would reimburse the search fees paid, if they made a mistake." The court found this evidence "persuasive of trade usage." As for the course of dealing, the court decided that "after 48 transactions, a course of dealing was clearly established."

FOR CRITICAL ANALYSIS—Technological Consideration
How might search methods be modified to find most of the possible variations on a name?

_____

Course of Performance. A **course of performance** is the conduct that occurs under the terms of a particular agreement. Presumably, the parties themselves know best what they meant by their words, and the course of performance actually undertaken based on their agreement is the best indication of what they meant [UCC 2–208(1), 2A–207(1)].

● **EXAMPLE #19** Janson's Lumber Company contracts with Barrymore to sell Barrymore a specified number of "two-by-fours." The lumber in fact does not measure 2 inches by 4

inches but rather 1⅞ inches by 3¾ inches. Janson's agrees to deliver the lumber in five deliveries, and Barrymore, without objection, accepts the lumber in the first three deliveries. On the fourth delivery, however, Barrymore objects that the two-by-fours do not measure 2 inches by 4 inches. The course of performance in this transaction—that is, the fact that Barrymore accepted three deliveries without objection under the agreement—is relevant in determining that here the term "two-by-four" actually means "1⅞ by 3¾." Janson's can also prove that two-by-fours need not be exactly 2 inches by 4 inches by applying usage of trade, course of prior dealing, or both. Janson's can, for example, show that in previous transactions, Barrymore took 1⅞-by-3¾-inch lumber without objection. In addition, Janson's can show that in the lumber trade, two-by-fours are commonly 1⅞ inches by 3¾ inches. ●

Rules of Construction. The UCC provides *rules of construction* for interpreting contracts. Express terms, course of performance, course of dealing, and usage of trade are to be construed together when they do not contradict one another. When such a construction is unreasonable, however, the following order of priority controls: (1) express terms, (2) course of performance, (3) course of dealing, and (4) usage of trade [UCC 1–205(4), 2–208(2), 2A–207(2)].

Unconscionability

As discussed in Chapter 9, an unconscionable contract is one that is so unfair and one sided that it would be unreasonable to enforce it. The UCC allows the court to evaluate a contract or any clause in a contract, and if the court deems it to have been unconscionable at the time it was made, the court can (1) refuse to enforce the contract, (2) enforce the remainder of the contract without the unconscionable clause, or (3) limit the application of any unconscionable clauses to avoid an unconscionable result [UCC 2–302, 2A–108]. The following landmark case illustrates an early application of the UCC's unconscionability provisions.

Landmark and Classic Cases

CASE 14.3 Jones v. Star Credit Corp.

Supreme Court of New York, Nassau County, 1969.
59 Misc.2d 189,
298 N.Y.S.2d 264.

FACTS The Joneses, the plaintiffs, agreed to purchase a freezer for $900 as the result of a salesperson's visit to their home. Tax and financing charges raised the total price to $1,234.80. At trial, the freezer was found to have a maximum retail value of approximately $300. The plaintiffs, who had made payments totaling $619.88, brought a suit in a New York state court to have the purchase contract declared unconscionable under the UCC.

ISSUE Can this contract be denied enforcement on the ground of unconscionability?

DECISION Yes. The court held that the contract was not enforceable as it stood, and the contract was reformed so that no further payments were required.

REASON The court relied on UCC 2–302(1), which states that if "the court as a matter of law finds the contract or any clause of the contract to have been unconscionable at the time it was made the court may * * * so limit the application of any unconscionable clause as to avoid any unconscionable result." The court then examined the disparity between the $900 purchase price and the $300 retail value, as well as the fact that the credit charges alone exceeded the retail value. These excessive charges were exacted despite the seller's knowledge of the plaintiffs' limited resources. The court reformed the contract so that the plaintiffs' payments, amounting to more than $600, were regarded as payment in full.

COMMENT *In the sixth century, Roman civil law allowed the rescission of a contract when the court determined that the market value of the goods that were the subject of the contract equaled less than half the contract price. This same ratio has appeared over the last thirty years in many cases in which courts have found contract clauses to be unconscionable under UCC 2–302 on the ground that the price was excessive.*

Contracts for the International Sale of Goods

International sales contracts between firms or individuals located in different countries are governed by the 1980 United Nations Convention on Contracts for the International Sale of Goods (CISG)—if the countries of the parties to the contract have ratified the CISG (and if the parties have not agreed that some other law will govern their contract). As of 2003, sixty-two countries had ratified or acceded to the CISG, including the United States, Canada, Mexico, some Central and South American countries, and most European nations.

APPLICABILITY OF THE CISG

Essentially, the CISG is to international sales contracts what Article 2 of the UCC is to domestic sales contracts. As discussed in this chapter, in domestic transactions the UCC applies when the parties to a contract for a sale of goods have failed to specify in writing some important term concerning price, delivery, or the like. Similarly, whenever the parties subject to the CISG have failed to specify in writing the precise terms of a contract for the international sale of goods, the CISG will be applied. Although the UCC applies to consumer sales, the CISG does not, and neither the UCC nor the CISG applies to contracts for services.

Businesspersons must take special care when drafting international sales contracts to avoid problems caused by distance, including language differences and different national laws. The appendix just following this chapter, which shows an actual international sales contract used by Starbucks Coffee Company, illustrates many of the special terms and clauses that are typically contained in international contracts for the sale of goods. Annotations in the exhibit explain the meaning and significance of specific clauses in the contract.

A COMPARISON OF CISG AND UCC PROVISIONS

The provisions of the CISG, although similar for the most part to those of the UCC, differ from them in some respects. For example, the CISG does not include the requirements imposed by the UCC's Statute of Frauds. Rather, Article 11 of the CISG states that an international sales contract "need not be concluded in or evidenced by writing" and is not subject to any other requirements as to form.

With respect to contract formation, some other differences between the CISG and the UCC merit attention. First, under the UCC, if the price term is left open, the court will determine "a reasonable price at the time for delivery" [UCC 2–305(1)]. Under the CISG, however, the price term must be specified, or at least provisions for its specification must be included in the agreement; otherwise, normally no contract will exist.

Second, like UCC 2–207, the CISG provides that a contract can be formed even though the acceptance contains additional terms, unless the additional terms materially alter the contract. The definition of a "material alteration" under the CISG, however, involves virtually any differences in terms. In its effect, then, the CISG requires that the terms of the acceptance mirror those of the offer.

Third, under the UCC, an acceptance is effective on dispatch. Under the CISG, however, a contract is created not at the time the acceptance is transmitted but only on its receipt by the offeror. (The offer becomes irrevocable, however, when the acceptance is sent.) Additionally, in contrast to the UCC, the CISG provides that acceptance by performance does not require that the offeror be notified of the performance.

Terms and Concepts

Chapter Summary   The Formation of Sales and Lease Contracts

The Uniform Commercial Code (UCC) (See page 263.)	The UCC attempts to provide a consistent, uniform, and integrated framework of rules to deal with all phases *ordinarily arising* in a commercial sales or lease transaction, including contract formation, passage of title and risk of loss, performance, remedies, payment for goods, warehoused goods, and secured transactions. If there is a conflict between a common law rule and the UCC, the UCC controls.
The Scope of Article 2—Sales (See pages 264–267.)	Article 2 governs contracts for the sale of goods (tangible, movable personal property). The common law of contracts also applies to sales contracts to the extent that the common law has not been modified by the UCC.

Chapter Summary	The Formation of Sales and Lease Contracts—Continued
The Scope of Article 2A—Leases (See pages 267–268.)	Article 2A governs contracts for the lease of goods. Except that it applies to leases, instead of sales, of goods, Article 2A is essentially a repetition of Article 2, and varies only to reflect differences between sale and lease transactions.
Offer and Acceptance (See pages 268–271.)	1. *Offer—* a. Not all terms have to be included for a contract to be formed (only the subject matter and quantity term must be specified). b. The price need not be included for a contract to be formed. c. Particulars of performance can be left open. d. A written and signed offer by a *merchant,* covering a period of three months or less, is irrevocable without payment of consideration. 2. *Acceptance—* a. Acceptance may be made by any reasonable means of communication; it is effective when dispatched. b. The acceptance of a unilateral offer can be made by a promise to ship or by prompt shipment of conforming goods, or by prompt shipment of nonconforming goods if not accompanied by a notice of accommodation. c. Acceptance by performance requires notice within a reasonable time; otherwise, the offer can be treated as lapsed. d. A definite expression of acceptance creates a contract even if the terms of the acceptance vary from those of the offer unless the varied terms in the acceptance are expressly conditioned on the offeror's assent to the varied terms.
Consideration (See page 272.)	A modification of a contract for the sale of goods does not require consideration.
The Statute of Frauds (See pages 272–275.)	1. All contracts for the sale of goods priced at $500 or more must be in writing. A writing is sufficient as long as it indicates a contract between the parties and is signed by the party against whom enforcement is sought. A contract is not enforceable beyond the quantity shown in the writing. 2. When written confirmation of an oral contract *between merchants* is not objected to in writing by the receiver within ten days, the contract is enforceable. 3. Exceptions to the requirement of a writing exist in the following situations: a. When the oral contract is for specially manufactured goods not suitable for resale to others, and the seller has substantially started to manufacture the goods. b. When the defendant admits in pleadings, testimony, or other court proceedings that an oral contract for the sale of goods was made. In this case, the contract will be enforceable to the extent of the quantity of goods admitted. c. The oral agreement will be enforceable to the extent that payment has been received and accepted by the seller or to the extent that the goods have been received and accepted by the buyer.
Parol Evidence Rule (See pages 275–277.)	1. The terms of a clearly and completely worded written contract cannot be contradicted by evidence of prior agreements or contemporaneous oral agreements. 2. Evidence is admissible to clarify the terms of a writing in the following situations: a. If the contract terms are ambiguous. b. If evidence of course of dealing, usage of trade, or course of performance is necessary to learn or to clarify the intentions of the parties to the contract.

(Continued)

Chapter Summary	The Formation of Sales and Lease Contracts—Continued
Unconscionability (See page 277.)	An unconscionable contract is one that is so unfair and one sided that it would be unreasonable to enforce it. If the court deems a contract to have been unconscionable at the time it was made, the court can (1) refuse to enforce the contract, (2) refuse to enforce the unconscionable clause of the contract, or (3) limit the application of any unconscionable clauses to avoid an unconscionable result.
Contracts for the International Sale of Goods (See pages 277–278.)	International sales contracts are governed by the United Nations Convention on Contracts for the International Sale of Goods (CISG)—if the countries of the parties to the contract have ratified the CISG (and if the parties have not agreed that some other law will govern their contract). Essentially, the CISG is to international sales contracts what Article 2 of the UCC is to domestic sales contracts. Whenever parties who are subject to the CISG have failed to specify in writing the precise terms of a contract for the international sale of goods, the CISG will be applied.

For Review

① How do Article 2 and Article 2A of the UCC differ? What types of transactions does each article cover?

② What is a merchant's firm offer?

③ If an offeree includes additional or different terms in an acceptance, will a contract result? If so, what happens to these terms?

④ Article 2 and Article 2A of the UCC both define three exceptions to the writing requirements of the Statute of Frauds. What are these three exceptions?

⑤ What law governs contracts for the international sale of goods?

Questions and Case Problems

14–1. Terms of the Offer. The UCC changes the effect of the common law of contracts in several ways. For instance, at common law, an offer must be definite enough for the parties to ascertain its essential terms when it is accepted. What happens under the UCC if some of an offer's terms—the price term, for example—are left open? What if the quantity term is left open?

14–2. Statute of Frauds. Fresher Foods, Inc., orally agreed to purchase from Dale Vernon, a farmer, one thousand bushels of corn for $1.25 per bushel. Fresher Foods paid $125 down and agreed to pay the remainder of the purchase price on delivery, which was scheduled for one week later. When Fresher Foods tendered the balance of $1,125 on the scheduled day of delivery and requested the corn, Vernon refused to deliver it. Fresher Foods sued Vernon for damages, claiming that Vernon had breached their oral contract. Can Fresher Foods recover? If so, to what extent?

14–3. Merchant's Firm Offer. On September 1, Jennings, a used-car dealer, wrote a letter to Wheeler in which he stated, "I have a 1955 Thunderbird convertible in mint condition that I will sell you for $13,500 at any time before October 9. [signed] Robert Jennings." By September 15, having heard nothing from Wheeler, Jennings sold the Thunderbird to another party. On September 29, Wheeler accepted Jennings's offer and tendered the $13,500. When Jennings told Wheeler he had sold the car to another party, Wheeler claimed Jennings had breached their contract. Is Jennings in breach? Explain.

14–4. Accommodation Shipments. M. M. Salinger, Inc., a retailer of television sets, orders one hundred model Color-X sets from manufacturer Fulsom. The order specifies the price and that the television sets are to be shipped via Interamerican Freightways on or before October 30. Fulsom receives the order on October 5. On October 8, Fulsom writes Salinger a letter indicating that it has received the order and that it will ship the sets as directed, at the specified price. Salinger receives this letter on October 10. On October 28, Fulsom, in preparing the shipment, discovers it has only ninety Color-X sets in stock. Fulsom ships the ninety Color-X sets and ten television sets of a different model, stating clearly on the invoice that the ten sets are being shipped only as an accommodation. Salinger claims that Fulsom is in breach of contract. Fulsom claims that there was not an acceptance, and therefore no contract was formed. Explain who is correct, and why.

14–5. Goods and Services Combined. Jane Pittsley contracted with Donald Houser, who was doing business as the Hilton Contract Carpet Co., for the installation of carpet in her home. Following installation, Pittsley complained to Hilton that some seams were visible, gaps appeared, the carpet did not lie flat in all areas, and the carpet failed to reach the wall in certain locations. Although Hilton made various attempts to fix the installation by stretching the carpet and other methods, Pittsley was not satisfied with the work and eventually sued Hilton to recover the $3,500 she had paid toward the $4,319.50 contract price for the carpet and its installation. Hilton paid the installers $700 for the work done in laying Pittsley's carpet. One of the issues before the court was whether the contract was a contract for the sale of goods or a contract for the sale of services. How should the court decide this issue? Discuss fully. [*Pittsley v. Houser,* 125 Idaho 820, 875 P.2d 232 (1994)]

14–6. Statute of Frauds. GPL Treatment, Ltd., orally agreed to sell a large quantity of cedar shakes to Louisiana-Pacific Corp. (L-P). GPL sent L-P order confirmation forms that stated the prices and quantities of shakes ordered. Each form also contained a "sign and return" clause, asking L-P to sign and return one copy. L-P did not sign or return any of the forms, but it also did not object to any of the terms. When L-P accepted only about 15 percent of the orders, GPL filed a suit in an Oregon state court against the buyer for breach of contract. Do GPL's confirmation forms satisfy the requirement of a writing under the Statute of Frauds? Are they enforceable against L-P? Discuss fully. [*GPL Treatment, Ltd. v. Louisiana-Pacific Corp.,* 323 Or. 116, 914 P.2d 682 (1996)]

14–7. Statute of Frauds. SNK, Inc., makes video arcade games and sells them to distributors, including Entertainment Sales, Inc. (ESI). Most sales between SNK and ESI were phone orders. Over one four-month period, ESI phoned in several orders for "Samurai Showdown" games. SNK did not fill the orders. ESI filed a suit against SNK and others, alleging, among other things, breach of contract. There was no written contract covering the orders. ESI claimed that it had faxed purchase orders for the games to SNK but did not offer proof that the faxes had been sent or received. SNK filed a motion for summary judgment. In whose favor will the court rule, and why? [*Entertainment Sales Co. v. SNK, Inc.,* 232 Ga.App. 669, 502 S.E.2d 263 (1998)]

14–8. Goods and Services Combined. Dennis Dahlmann and Dahlmann Apartments, Ltd., entered into contracts with Sulchus Hospitality Technologies Corp. and Hospitality Management Systems, Inc. (HMS), to buy property management systems. The systems included computer hardware and software, as well as installation, training, and support services, for the Bell Tower Hotel and the Campus Inn in Ann Arbor, Michigan. The software controlled the central reservations systems at both hotels. When Dahlmann learned that the software was not Y2K compliant—that it could not be used to post reservations beyond December 31, 1999—he filed a suit against Sulchus and HMS, alleging in part breach of contract. The defendants filed a motion for summary judgment. One of the issues was whether the contracts were subject to Article 2 of the UCC. Are they? Why or why not? Explain fully. [*Dahlmann v. Sulchus Hospitality Technologies Corp.,* 63 F.Supp.2d 772 (E.D.Mich. 1999)]

CASE PROBLEM WITH SAMPLE ANSWER

14–9. In 1988, International Business Machines Corp. (IBM) and American Shizuki Corp. (ASC) signed an agreement for "future purchase by IBM" of plastic film capacitors made by ASC to be used in IBM computers. The agreement stated that IBM was not

obligated to buy from ASC and that future purchase orders "shall be [ASC]'s only authorization to manufacture Items." In February 1989, IBM wrote to ASC about "the possibility of IBM purchasing 15,000,000 Plastic Capacitors per two consecutive twelve (12) month periods. * * * This quantity is a forecast only, and represents no commitment by IBM to purchase these quantities during or after this time period." ASC said that it wanted greater assurances. In a second letter, IBM reexpressed its "intent to order" from ASC 30 million capacitors over a minimum period of two years, contingent on the condition "[t]hat IBM's requirements for these capacitors continue." ASC spent about $2.6 million on equipment to make the capacitors. By 1997, the need for plastic capacitors had dissipated with the advent of new technology, and IBM told ASC that it would no longer buy them. ASC filed a suit in a federal district court against IBM, seeking $8.5 million in damages. On what basis might the court rule in favor of IBM? Explain fully. [*American Shizuki Corp. v. International Business Machines Corp.,* 251 F.3d 1206 (8th Cir. 2001)]

▶ To view a sample answer for this case problem, go to this book's Web site at **http://fundamentals.westbuslaw.com** and click on "Interactive Study Center."

14–10. Goods Associated with Real Estate. Heatway Radiant Floors and Snowmelting Corp. sells parts for underground, radiant heating systems. These systems circulate warm fluid under indoor flooring as an alternative to conventional heating systems or under driveways and sidewalks to melt snow and ice. Goodyear Tire and Rubber Co. made and sold a hose, Entran II, that Heatway used in its radiant systems. Between 1989 and 1993, 25 million feet of Entran II was made by Goodyear and installed by Heatway. In 1992, homeowners began complaining about hardening of the hose and leaks in the systems. Linda Loughridge and other homeowners filed a suit in a federal district court against Goodyear and Heatway, alleging a variety of contract breaches under Colorado's version of the Uniform Commercial Code (UCC). Goodyear filed a motion for summary judgment, arguing in part that because Entran II was used in the construction of underground systems that were covered by flooring or cement, the hose was not a "good" and thus the UCC did not apply. Should the court agree with this interpretation of the scope of Article 2? Explain. [*Loughridge v. Goodyear Tire and Rubber Co.,* 192 F.Supp.2d 1175 (D.Colo. 2002)]

VIDEO QUESTION

14–11. Go to this text's Web site at **http://fundamentals.westbuslaw.com** and click on "Video Questions." Select "Chapter 14" and view the video titled *Sales and Lease Contracts: Price as a Term.* Then answer the following questions:

1. Is Anna correct in assuming that a contract can exist even though the sales price for the computer equipment was not specified? Explain.

2. According to the Uniform Commercial Code (UCC), what conditions must be satisfied in order for a contract to

be formed when certain terms are left open? What terms (in addition to price) can be left open?

3. Are the e-mail messages that Anna refers to sufficient proof of the contract? Would parol evidence be admissible?

4. How do the 2003 amendments to Article 2 of the UCC improve Anna's position?

THE FORMATION OF SALES AND LEASE CONTRACTS

For updated links to resources available on the Web, as well as other materials, visit this text's Web site at

http://fundamentals.westbuslaw.com

For information on proposed amendments to Articles 2 and 2A of the UCC, go to the Web site of the National Conference of Commissioners on Uniform State Laws (NCCUSL) at

http://www.nccusl.org

Cornell University provides an online version of the UCC (but without the official comments) at

Online Legal Research

Go to the *Fundamentals of Business Law* home page at **http://fundamentals. westbuslaw.com**. Select "Interactive Study Center" and then click on "Chapter 14." There you will find the following Internet research exercise that you can perform to learn more topics covered in this chapter.

Activity 14–1: LEGAL PERSPECTIVE—Is It a Contract?

Before the Test

Go to the *Fundamentals of Business Law* home page at **http://fundamentals. westbuslaw.com**. Click on "Interactive Quizzes." You will find at least twenty interactive questions relating to this chapter.

Westlaw® Campus

If your textbook provided for a subscription to Westlaw® Campus, or if you have otherwise purchased access to the Westlaw Campus database, you can access any of the cases presented or cited in this chapter by using your Westlaw Campus account.

Appendix to Chapter 14

An Example of a Contract for the International Sale of Coffee

① OVERLAND COFFEE IMPORT CONTRACT
OF THE
GREEN COFFEE ASSOCIATION
OF
② NEW YORK CITY, INC.*
Effective May 9, 1991

Contract Seller's No.: **504617**
Buyer's No.: **P9264**
Date: **9/11/05**

SOLD BY: **XYZ Co.**
TO: **Starbucks**

③ QUANTITY: **Five Hundred** (**500** (Bags) Tons of **Mexican** coffee
weighing about **152.117 lbs.** per bag.

PACKAGING: Coffee must be packed in clean sound bags of uniform size made of sisal, henequen, jute, burlap, or
similar woven material, without inner lining or outer covering of any material properly sewn by hand
④ and/or machine.
Bulk shipments are allowed if agreed by mutual consent of Buyer and Seller.

DESCRIPTION: **High grown Mexican Altura**
⑤

PRICE: At **Ten/$10.00 dollars** U. S. Currency, per **lb.** net, (U.S. Funds)
Upon delivery in Bonded Public Warehouse at **Laredo, TX**
(City and State)

PAYMENT: **Cash against warehouse receipts**
⑥

Bill and tender to DATE when all import requirements and governmental regulations have been satisfied,
and coffee delivered or discharged (as per contract terms). Seller is obliged to give the Buyer two (2)
calendar days free time in Bonded Public Warehouse following but not including date of tender.

⑦ ARRIVAL: During **December** via **truck**
(Period) (Method of Transportation)
from **Mexico** for arrival at **Laredo, TX**
(Country of Exportation) (Country of Importation)
Partial shipments permitted.

ADVICE OF
ARRIVAL: Advice of arrival with warehouse name and location, together with the quantity, description, marks and
place of entry, must be transmitted directly, or through Seller's Agent/Broker, to the Buyer or his Agent/
Broker. Advice will be given as soon as known but not later than the fifth business day following arrival
at the named warehouse. Such advice may be given verbally with written confirmation to be sent the
same day.

⑧ WEIGHTS: (1) DELIVERED WEIGHTS: Coffee covered by this contract is to be weighed at location named in
tender. Actual tare to be allowed.
(2) SHIPPING WEIGHTS: Coffee covered by this contract is sold on shipping weights. Any loss in
weight exceeding **1/2** percent at location named in tender is for account of Seller at contract price.
(3) Coffee is to be weighed within fifteen (15) calendar days after tender. Weighing expenses, if any, for
account of **Seller** (Seller or Buyer)

MARKINGS: Bags to be branded in English with the name of Country of Origin and otherwise to
comply with laws
and regulations of the Country of Importation, in effect at the time of entry, governing marking of import
merchandise. Any expense incurred by failure to comply with these regulations to be borne by
⑨ Exporter/Seller.

RULINGS: The "Rulings on Coffee Contracts" of the Green Coffee Association of New York City, Inc., in effect on
the date this contract is made, is incorporated for all purposes as a part of this agreement, and together
herewith, constitute the entire contract. No variation or addition hereto shall be valid unless signed by
the parties to the contract.
Seller guarantees that the terms printed on the reverse hereof, which by reference are made a part hereof,
are identical with the terms as printed in By-Laws and Rules of the Green Coffee Association of New
⑩ York City, Inc., heretofore adopted.
Exceptions to this guarantee are:

ACCEPTED: COMMISSION TO BE PAID BY:
XYZ Co. **seller**

Seller
BY
⑪ Agent
Starbucks

Buyer
BY **ABC Brokerage**
⑫ Agent Broker(s)
When this contract is executed by a person acting for another, such person hereby represents that he is
⑬ fully authorized to commit his principal.

(Continued)

❶ This is a contract for a sale of coffee to be *imported* internationally. If the parties have their principal places of business located in different countries, the contract may be subject to the United Nations Convention on Contracts for the International Sale of Goods (CISG). If the parties' principal places of business are located in the United States, the contract may be subject to the Uniform Commercial Code (UCC).

❷ Quantity is one of the most important terms to include in a contract. Without it, a court may not be able to enforce the contract.

❸ Weight per unit (bag) can be exactly stated or approximately stated. If it is not so stated, usage of trade in international contracts determines standards of weight.

❹ Packaging requirements can be conditions for acceptance and payment. Bulk shipments are not permitted without the consent of the buyer.

❺ A description of the coffee and the "Markings" constitute express warranties. Warranties in contracts for domestic sales of goods are discussed generally in Chapter 17. International contracts rely more heavily on descriptions and models or samples.

❻ Under the UCC, parties may enter into a valid contract even though the price is not set. Under the CISG, a contract must provide for an exact determination of the price.

❼ The terms of payment may take one of two forms: credit or cash. Credit terms can be complicated. A cash term can be simple, and payment may be by any means acceptable in the ordinary course of business (for example, a personal check or a letter of credit). If the seller insists on actual cash, the buyer must be given a reasonable time to get it. See Chapter 16.

❽ *Tender* means the seller has placed goods that conform to the contract at the buyer's disposition. What constitutes a valid tender is explained in Chapter 16. This contract requires that the coffee meet all import regulations and that it be ready for pickup by the buyer at a "Bonded Public Warehouse." (A *bonded warehouse* is a place in which goods can be stored without paying taxes until the goods are removed.)

❾ The delivery date is significant because, if it is not met, the buyer may hold the seller in breach of the contract. Under this contract, the seller can be given a "period" within which to deliver the goods, instead of a specific day, which could otherwise present problems. The seller is also given some time to rectify goods that do not pass inspection (see the "Guarantee" clause on page two of the contract). For a discussion of the remedies of the buyer and seller, see Chapter 16.

❿ As part of a proper tender, the seller (or its agent) must inform the buyer (or its agent) when the goods have arrived at their destination. The responsibilities of agents are set out in Chapter 22.

⓫ In some contracts, delivered and shipped weights can be important. During shipping, some loss can be attributed to the type of goods (spoilage of fresh produce, for example) or to the transportation itself. A seller and buyer can agree on the extent to which either of them will bear such losses.

⓬ Documents are often incorporated in a contract by reference, because including them word for word can make a contract difficult to read. If the document is later revised, the whole contract might have to be reworked. Documents that are typically incorporated by reference include detailed payment and delivery terms, special provisions, and sets of rules, codes, and standards.

⓭ In international sales transactions, and for domestic deals involving certain products, brokers are used to form the contracts. When so used, the brokers are entitled to a commission. See Chapter 22.

TERMS AND CONDITIONS

⑭ ARBITRATION: All controversies relating to, in connection with, or arising out of this contract, its modification, making or the authority or obligations of the signatories hereto, and whether involving the principals, agents, brokers, or others who actually subscribe hereto, shall be settled by arbitration in accordance with the "Rules of Arbitration" of the Green Coffee Association of New York City, Inc., as they exist at the time of the arbitration (including provisions as to payment of fees and expenses). Arbitration is the sole remedy hereunder, and it shall be held in accordance with the law of New York State, and judgment of any award may be entered in the courts of that State, or in any other court of competent jurisdiction. All notices or judicial service in reference to arbitration or enforcement shall be deemed given if transmitted as required by the aforesaid rules.

⑮ GUARANTEE: (a) If all or any of the coffee is refused admission into the country of importation by reason of any violation of governmental laws or acts, which violation existed at the time the coffee arrived at Bonded-Public Warehouse, seller is required, as to the amount not admitted and as soon as possible, to deliver replacement coffee in conformity to all terms and conditions of this contract, excepting only the Arrival terms, but not later than thirty (30) days after the date of the violation notice. Any payment made and expenses incurred for any coffee denied entry shall be refunded within ten (10) calendar days of denial of entry, and payment shall be made for the replacement delivery in accordance with the terms of this contract. Consequently, if Buyer removes the coffee from the Bonded Public Warehouse, Seller's responsibility as to such portion hereunder ceases.

⑯ (b) Contracts containing the overstamp "No Pass-No Sale" on the face of the contract shall be interpreted to mean: If any or all of the coffee is not admitted into the country of Importation in its original condition by reason of failure to meet requirements of the government's laws or Acts, the contract shall be deemed null and void as to that portion of the coffee which is not admitted in its original condition. Any payment made and expenses incurred for any coffee denied entry shall be refunded within ten (10) calendar days of denial of entry.

CONTINGENCY: This contract is not contingent upon any other contract.

CLAIMS: Coffee shall be considered accepted as to quality unless within *fifteen* (15) calendar days after delivery at Bonded Public Warehouse or within *fifteen* (15) calendar days after all Government clearances have been received, whichever is later, either:
(a) Claims are settled by the parties hereto, or,
(b) Arbitration proceedings have been filed by one of the parties in accordance with the provisions hereof.
⑰ (c) If neither (a) nor (b) has been done in the stated period or if any portion of the coffee has been removed from the Bonded Public Warehouse before representative sealed samples have been drawn by the Green Coffee Association of New York City, Inc., in accordance with its rules, Seller's responsibility for quality claims ceases for that portion so removed.
(d) Any question of quality submitted to arbitration shall be a matter of allowance only, unless otherwise provided in the contract.

⑱ DELIVERY: (a) No more than three (3) chops may be tendered for each lot of 250 bags.
(b) Each chop of coffee tendered is to be uniform in grade and appearance. All expense necessary to make coffee uniform shall be for account of seller.
(c) Notice of arrival and/or sampling order constitutes a tender, and must be given not later than the fifth business day following arrival at Bonded Public Warehouse stated on the contract.

INSURANCE: Seller is responsible for any loss or damage, or both, until Delivery and Discharge of coffee at the Bonded Public Warehouse in the Country of Importation.

All Insurance Risks, costs and responsibility are for Seller's Account until Delivery and Discharge of coffee at the Bonded Public Warehouse in the Country of Importation.

⑲ Buyer's insurance responsibility begins from the day of importation or from the day of tender, whichever is later.

⑳ FREIGHT: Seller to provide and pay for all transportation and related expenses to the Bonded Public Warehouse in the Country of Importation.

EXPORT DUTIES/TAXES: Exporter is to pay all Export taxes, duties or other fees or charges, if any, levied because of exportation.

㉑ IMPORT DUTIES/TAXES: Any Duty or Tax whatsoever, imposed by the government or any authority of the Country of Importation, shall be borne by the Importer/Buyer.

INSOLVENCY OR FINANCIAL FAILURE OF BUYER OR SELLER: If, at any time before the contract is fully executed, either party hereto shall meet with creditors because of inability generally to make payment of obligations when due, or shall suspend such payments, fail to meet his general trade obligations in the regular course of business, shall file a petition in bankruptcy or, for an arrangement, shall become insolvent, or commit an act of bankruptcy, then the other party may at his option, expressed in writing, declare the aforesaid to constitute a breach and default of this contract, and may, in addition to other remedies, decline to deliver further or make payment or may sell or purchase for the defaulter's account, and may collect damage for any injury or loss, or shall account for the profit, if any, occasioned by such sale or purchase.

㉒ This clause is subject to the provisions of (11 USC 365 (e) 1) if invoked.

㉓ BREACH OR DEFAULT OF CONTRACT: In the event either party hereto fails to perform, or breaches or repudiates this agreement, the other party shall subject to the specific provisions of this contract be entitled to the remedies and relief provided for by the Uniform Commercial Code of the State of New York. The computation and ascertainment of damages, or the determination of any other dispute as to relief, shall be made by the arbitrators in accordance with the Arbitration Clause herein.

Consequential damages shall not, however, be allowed.

(Continued)

⑭ Arbitration is the settling of a dispute by submitting it to a disinterested party (other than a court) that renders a decision. The procedures and costs can be provided for in an arbitration clause or incorporated through other documents. To enforce an award rendered in an arbitration, the winning party can "enter" (submit) the award in a court "of competent jurisdiction." For a general discussion of arbitration and other forms of dispute resolution (other than courts), see Chapter 2.

⑮ When goods are imported internationally, they must meet certain import requirements before being released to the buyer. Because of this, buyers frequently want a guaranty clause that covers the goods not admitted into the country and that either requires the seller to replace the goods within a stated time or allows the contract for those goods not admitted to be void.

⑯ In the "Claims" clause, the parties agree that the buyer has a certain time within which to reject the goods. The right to reject is a right by law and does not need to be stated in a contract. If the buyer does not exercise the right within the time specified in the contract, the goods will be considered accepted. See Chapter 16.

⑰ Many international contracts include definitions of terms so that the parties understand what they mean. Some terms are used in a particular industry in a specific way. Here, the word "chop" refers to a unit of like-grade coffee bean. The buyer has a right to inspect ("sample") the coffee. If the coffee does not conform to the contract, the seller must correct the nonconformity.

⑱ The "Delivery," "Insurance," and "Freight" clauses, with the "Arrival" clause on page one of the contract, indicate that this is a destination contract. The seller has the obligation to deliver the goods to the destination, not simply deliver them into the hands of a carrier. Under this contract, the destination is a "Bonded Public Warehouse" in a specific location. The seller bears the risk of loss until the goods are delivered at their destination. Typically, the seller will have bought insurance to cover the risk.

⑲ Delivery terms are commonly placed in all sales contracts. Such terms determine who pays freight and other costs, and, in the absence of an agreement specifying otherwise, who bears the risk of loss. International contracts may use these delivery terms or they may use INCOTERMS, which are published by the International Chamber of Commerce. For example, the INCOTERM "DDP" ("delivered duty paid") requires the seller to arrange shipment, obtain and pay for import or export permits, and get the goods through customs to a named destination.

⑳ Exported and imported goods are subject to duties, taxes, and other charges imposed by the governments of the countries involved. International contracts spell out who is responsible for these charges.

㉑ This clause protects a party if the other party should become financially unable to fulfill the obligations under the contract. Thus, if the seller cannot afford to deliver, or the buyer cannot afford to pay, for the stated reasons, the other party can consider the contract breached. This right is subject to "11 USC 365(e)(1)," which refers to a specific provision of the U.S. Bankruptcy Code dealing with executory contracts. Bankruptcy provisions are covered in Chapter 21.

㉒ In the "Breach or Default of Contract" clause, the parties agreed that the remedies under this contract are the remedies (except for consequential damages) provided by the UCC, as in effect in the state of New York. The amount and "ascertainment" of damages, as well as other disputes about relief, are to be determined by arbitration. Breach of contract and contractual remedies in general are explained in Chapter 16. Arbitration is discussed in Chapter 2.

㉓ Three clauses frequently included in international contracts are omitted here. There is no "Choice of Language" clause designating the official language to be used in interpreting the contract terms. There is no "Choice of Forum" clause designating the place in which disputes will be litigated, except for arbitration (law of New York State). Finally, there is no "*force majeure*" clause relieving the sellers or buyers from nonperformance due to events beyond their control.

CHAPTER OBJECTIVES

After reading this chapter, you should be able to answer the following questions:

① What is the significance of identifying goods to a contract?

② If the parties to a contract do not expressly agree on when title to goods passes, what determines when title passes?

③ Risk of loss does not necessarily pass with title. If the parties to a contract do not expressly agree when risk passes and the goods are to be delivered without movement by the seller, when does risk pass?

④ Under what circumstances will the seller's title to goods being sold be void? Under what circumstances will a seller have voidable title? What is the legal effect on a good faith purchaser of the goods of the seller's having a void title versus a voidable title?

⑤ At what point does the buyer acquire an insurable interest in goods subject to a sales contract? Can both the buyer and the seller have an insurable interest in the goods simultaneously?

A sale of goods transfers ownership rights in (title to) the goods from the seller to the buyer. Often, a sales contract is signed before the actual goods are available. For example, a sales contract for oranges might be signed in May, but the oranges may not be ready for picking and shipment until October. Any number of things can happen between the time the sales contract is signed and the time the goods are actually transferred into the buyer's possession. Fire, flood, or frost may destroy the orange groves, or the oranges may be lost or damaged in transit. The same problems may occur under a lease contract. Because of these possibilities, it is important to know the rights and liabilities of the parties between the time the contract is formed and the time the goods are actually received by the buyer or lessee.

Before the creation of the Uniform Commercial Code (UCC), *title*—the right of ownership—was the central concept in sales law, controlling all issues of rights and remedies of the parties to a sales contract. In some situations, title is still relevant under the UCC, and the UCC has special rules for determining who has title. These rules will be discussed in the sections that follow. In most situations, however, the UCC has replaced the concept of title with three other concepts: (1) identification, (2) risk of loss, and (3) insurable interest. By breaking down the transfer of ownership into these three components, the drafters of the UCC have created greater precision in the law governing sales.

In lease contracts, of course, title to the goods is retained by the lessor-owner of the goods. Hence, the UCC's provisions relating to passage of title do not apply to leased goods. Other concepts discussed in this chapter, though, including identification, risk of loss, and insurable interest, relate to lease contracts as well as to sales contracts.

Identification

Before any interest in specific goods can pass from the seller or lessor to the buyer or lessee, two conditions must prevail: (1) the goods must be in existence, and (2) they must be identified as the specific goods designated in the contract. **Identification** takes place when specific goods are designated as the subject matter of a sales or lease contract. Title and risk of loss cannot pass from seller to buyer unless the goods are identified to the contract. (As mentioned, title to leased goods remains with the lessor—or, if the owner is a third party, with that party. The lessee does not acquire title to leased goods.) Identification is significant because it gives the buyer or lessee the right to insure (or to have an insurable interest in) the goods and the right to recover from third parties who damage the goods.

In their contract, the parties can agree on when identification will take place, but identification is effective to pass title and risk of loss to the buyer only after the goods are considered to be in existence. If the parties do not so specify, however, the UCC provisions discussed here determine when identification takes place [UCC 2–501(1), 2A–217].

EXISTING GOODS

If the contract calls for the sale or lease of specific and ascertained goods that are already in existence, identification takes place at the time the contract is made. For example, you contract to purchase or lease a fleet of five cars by the serial numbers listed for the cars.

FUTURE GOODS

If a sale involves unborn animals to be born within twelve months after contracting, identification takes place when the animals are conceived. If a lease involves any unborn animals, identification occurs when the animals are conceived. If a sale involves crops that are to be harvested within twelve months (or the next harvest season occurring after contracting, whichever is longer), identification takes place when the crops are planted or begin to grow. In a sale or lease of any other future goods, identification occurs when the goods are shipped, marked, or otherwise designated by the seller or lessor as the goods to which the contract refers.

GOODS THAT ARE PART OF A LARGER MASS

As a general rule, goods that are part of a larger mass are identified when the goods are marked, shipped, or somehow designated by the seller or lessor as the particular goods to pass under the contract. ● **EXAMPLE #1** A buyer orders 1,000 cases of beans from a 10,000-case lot. Until the seller separates the 1,000 cases of beans from the 10,000-case lot, title and risk of loss remain with the seller. ●

A common exception to this rule involves fungible goods. **Fungible goods** are goods that are alike by physical nature, by agreement, or by trade usage. Typical examples are specific grades or types of wheat and oil, usually stored in large containers. If these goods are held or intended to be held by owners as tenants in common (owners having shares undivided from the entire mass), a seller-owner can pass title and risk of loss to the buyer without an actual separation. The buyer replaces the seller as an owner in common [UCC 2–105(4)].

● **EXAMPLE #2** Anselm, Braudel, and Carpenter are farmers. They deposit, respectively, 5,000 bushels, 3,000 bushels, and 2,000 bushels of grain of the same grade and quality in a bin. The three become owners in common, with Anselm owning 50 percent of the 10,000 bushels, Braudel 30 percent, and Carpenter 20 percent. Anselm contracts to sell her 5,000 bushels of grain to Tareyton; because the goods are fungible, she can pass title and risk of loss to Tareyton without physically separating the 5,000 bushels. Tareyton now becomes an owner in common with Braudel and Carpenter. ●

Passage of Title

Once goods exist and are identified, the provisions of UCC 2–401 apply to the passage of title. In virtually all subsections of UCC 2–401, the words "unless otherwise explicitly agreed" appear, meaning that any explicit understanding between the buyer and the seller determines when title passes. Unless an agreement is explicitly made, title passes to the buyer at the time and the place the seller performs the *physical* delivery of the goods [UCC 2–401(2)]. The following case illustrates the significance of this event.

CASE 15.1   In re Stewart

United States
Bankruptcy Court,
Western District of
Arkansas, 2002.
274 Bankr. 503.

FACTS In July 1997, Gary Stewart began to buy, and occasionally sell, cattle through Barry County Livestock Auction, Inc., in Exeter, Missouri. On January 29 and February 19, 2000, Stewart bought $46,749.55 worth of cattle through Barry County, but the checks he gave in payment were returned by the bank because his account did not have sufficient funds. By March 4, Stewart had given cashier's checks to Barry County to pay for the cattle.[a] Less than forty days later, on April 11, Stewart filed for bankruptcy in a federal bankruptcy court. Some payments made to creditors within ninety days of the filing of a petition in bankruptcy can be recovered so that their amounts can be distributed more equitably among a debtor's creditors.[b] Stewart asked the court to recover his payments to Barry County. Barry County claimed that the payments were "contemporaneous exchanges for new value," which cannot be recovered. The question on which this issue turned was whether the transfer of title to the cattle occurred on the day of the sale or on the day of the payment.

ISSUE Could Barry County keep the payments it received from Stewart on the ground that they were "contemporaneous exchanges"?

_____
a. A cashier's check is considered nearly the equivalent of cash because the bank assumes responsibility for paying it. See Chapter 19.
b. Bankruptcy law is discussed more fully in Chapter 21.

DECISION No. The court held that the transfer of title to the cattle occurred on the dates of the sales when the cattle were physically delivered. Thus, Stewart's payment with the cashier's checks was not part of a "contemporaneous exchange"—the payment occurred after the bank returned his personal checks for insufficient funds, more than two weeks after the transfer of title.

REASON The court noted that Barry County printed on each bill of sale: "ALL SALES ARE MADE, AND TITLE IS TRANSFERRED, SUBJECT TO FINAL PAYMENT * * * . IF ANY CHECK * * * TENDERED IN PAYMENT IS NOT PAID PROMPTLY ON PRESENTATION, THIS BILL OF SALE DOES NOT TRANSFER TITLE." The court stated that apparently "Barry County Livestock Auction was attempting to retain title to the cattle in the event the debtor's personal checks were not honored [paid]." The court explained, however, that "[a]ccording to the UCC, any attempt to retain title to the cattle pending the debtor's personal checks being honored by the bank is ineffective." Under UCC 2–401(2), "title passes to the buyer at the time and place at which the seller completes his performance with reference to the physical delivery of the goods." In other words, in this case, "under the UCC, title to the cattle passed upon delivery of the cattle on the day of the respective sales."

FOR CRITICAL ANALYSIS—Ethical Consideration
Often, by explicit agreement, the parties to a transaction can establish terms that differ from those provided by the UCC. In this case, why weren't the words on Barry County's bill of sale, "SUBJECT TO FINAL PAYMENT," effective in establishing the terms of the sale?

SHIPMENT AND DESTINATION CONTRACTS

Unless otherwise agreed, delivery arrangements can determine when title passes from the seller to the buyer. In a **shipment contract**, the seller is required or authorized to ship goods by carrier, such as a trucking company. Under a shipment contract, the seller is required only to deliver conforming goods into the hands of a carrier, and title passes to the buyer at the time and place of shipment [UCC 2–401(2)(a)]. Generally, _all contracts are assumed to be shipment contracts if nothing to the contrary is stated in the contract._

In a **destination contract**, the seller is required to deliver the goods to a particular destination, usually directly to the buyer, but sometimes the buyer designates that the goods should be delivered to another party. Title passes to the buyer when the goods are _tendered_ at that destination [UCC 2–401(2)(b)]. A tender of delivery is the seller's placing or holding of conforming goods at the buyer's disposition (with any necessary notice), enabling the buyer to take delivery [UCC 2–503(1)].

DELIVERY WITHOUT MOVEMENT OF THE GOODS

When the sales contract does not call for the seller to ship or deliver the goods (when the buyer is to pick up the goods), the passage of title depends on whether the seller must deliver a **document of title**, such as a bill of lading or a warehouse receipt, to the buyer. A *bill of lading* is a receipt for goods that is signed by a carrier and that serves as a contract for the transportation of the goods. A *warehouse receipt* is a receipt issued by a warehouser for goods stored in a warehouse.

When a document of title is required, title passes to the buyer *when and where the document is delivered.* Thus, if the goods are stored in a warehouse, title passes to the buyer when the appropriate documents are delivered to the buyer. The goods never move. In fact, the buyer can choose to leave the goods at the same warehouse for a period of time, and the buyer's title to those goods will be unaffected.

When no documents of title are required and delivery is made without moving the goods, title passes at the time and place the sales contract is made if the goods have already been identified. If the goods have not been identified, title does not pass until identification occurs. • **EXAMPLE #3** Rogers sells lumber to Bodan. They agree that Bodan will pick up the lumber at the lumberyard. If the lumber has been identified (segregated, marked, or in any other way distinguished from all other lumber), title passes to Bodan when the contract is signed. If the lumber is still in storage bins at the lumberyard, title does not pass to Bodan until the particular pieces of lumber to be sold under this contract are identified [UCC 2–401(3)]. •

SALES OR LEASES BY NONOWNERS

Problems occur when persons who acquire goods with imperfect titles attempt to sell or lease them. Sections 2–402 and 2–403 of the UCC deal with the rights of two parties who lay claim to the same goods, sold with imperfect titles. Generally, a buyer acquires at least whatever title the seller has to the goods sold.

The UCC also protects a person who leases such goods from the buyer. Of course, a lessee does not acquire whatever title the lessor has to the goods. A lessee acquires a right to possess and use the goods—that is, a *leasehold interest.* A lessee acquires whatever leasehold interest the lessor has or has the power to transfer, subject to the lease contract [UCC 2A–303, 2A–304, 2A–305].

Void Title. A buyer may unknowingly purchase goods from a seller who is not the owner of the goods. If the seller is a thief, the seller's title is *void*—legally, no title exists. Thus, the buyer acquires no title, and the real owner can reclaim the goods from the buyer. If the goods were only leased, the same result would occur because the lessor has no leasehold interest to transfer.

• **EXAMPLE #4** If Jim steals diamonds owned by Maren, Jim has a *void title* to those diamonds. If Jim sells the diamonds to Shannon, Maren can reclaim them from Shannon even though Shannon acted in good faith and honestly was not aware that the goods were stolen.• (Article 2A contains similar provisions for leases.)

Voidable Title. A seller has a *voidable title* if the goods that he or she is selling were obtained by fraud, paid for with a check that is later dishonored, purchased from a minor, or purchased on credit when the seller was insolvent. (Under the UCC, a person is **insolvent** when that person ceases to "pay his debts in the ordinary course of business or cannot pay his debts as they become due or is insolvent within the meaning of federal bankruptcy law" [UCC 1–201(23)].)

In contrast to a seller with *void title,* a seller with *voidable title* has the power to transfer a good title to a good faith purchaser for value. A **good faith purchaser** is one who buys without knowledge of circumstances that would make a person of ordinary prudence inquire about the validity of the seller's title to the goods. One who purchases *for value* gives legally sufficient consideration (value) for the goods purchased.

The real, or original, owner cannot recover goods from a good faith purchaser for value [UCC 2–403(1)].[1] If the buyer of the goods is not a good faith purchaser for value, then the actual owner of the goods can reclaim them from the buyer (or from the seller, if the goods are still in the seller's possession).

The same rules apply in circumstances involving leases. A lessor with voidable title has the power to transfer a valid leasehold interest to a good faith lessee for value. The real owner cannot recover the goods, except as permitted by the terms of the lease. The real owner can, however, receive all proceeds arising from the lease, as well as a transfer of all rights, title, and interest as lessor under the lease, including the lessor's interest in the return of the goods when the lease expires [UCC 2A–305(1)].

The question in the following case was whether a third party buyer was a good faith purchaser in the context of a sale of timber. The court emphasizes the elements that must be proved to establish the status of a good faith purchaser.

---

[1] The real owner could, of course, sue the person who initially obtained voidable title to the goods.

CASE 15.2 Memphis Hardwood Flooring Co. v. Daniel

Mississippi Supreme Court, 2000.
771 So.2d 924.
http://www.mslawyer.com/mssc/
handdown.html[a]

FACTS Jamie Swann Daniel, a retired teacher, owned approximately eight hundred acres of land in Union County, Mississippi. After an ice storm, Lucky Easley and William Heppler, officers of Northern Hardwood, Inc., convinced Daniel to allow some cutting of the storm-damaged timber on the land. Daniel contracted with Northern to cut from the southern half of the property the "disaster hardwood timber" that was twenty inches or more in diameter.[b] More than a year later, in a second contract, Daniel agreed to the cutting of the timber down to sixteen inches, for which Easley would pay her $150,000. The same day, Easley told Robert Luther, a timber buyer for Memphis Hardwood Flooring Company, that he had an agreement to cut all of the timber on all of Daniel's land. Luther and Easley agreed that Easley, acting for both Northern and Memphis, would buy Daniel's timber for Northern while concealing from Daniel that Northern was actually buying for Memphis. Luther agreed to pay $410,000 to Easley. At Easley's request, Luther had Memphis's lawyer draft the agreements ("timber deeds") between Daniel and Northern and between Northern and Memphis. When Memphis proceeded to cut the timber, Daniel filed a suit in a Mississippi state court against Memphis and the others, alleging fraud. Among other things, the court canceled the agree-

ment between Northern and Memphis.[c] Memphis appealed to the Mississippi Supreme Court, asserting that it was a good faith purchaser.

ISSUE Was Memphis a good faith purchaser?

DECISION No. The Mississippi Supreme Court affirmed the decision of the lower court.

REASON The state supreme court noted that to establish the status of a good faith purchaser, "[t]he elements the innocent purchaser must prove are a valuable consideration, the presence of good faith, and the absence of notice." In this case, "[t]he first element is established in favor of Memphis. The record reveals that Memphis paid $410,000 to Northern for the timber. * * * The second element, the presence of good faith, was not adequately shown by Memphis. * * * Easley made the deal with Daniel on behalf of both Northern and Memphis and * * * Memphis was a knowing participant in this scheme * * * . Such actions reveal the absence of good faith. Even the circumstances surrounding the drafting of the deeds indicate the joint nature of the scheme and Memphis' lack of good faith." As for the third element, "Memphis was not only on actual notice, it was a knowing and willing participant in the defrauding of Daniel. Thus, Memphis fails to establish the third element. The record supports the [lower court's] finding that Memphis was not" a good faith purchaser.

FOR CRITICAL ANALYSIS—Social Consideration
Would Memphis have been considered a participant in the fraud against Daniel if Memphis had not agreed specifically that Easley would act in its behalf?

a. Click on "2000 opinions." When the page opens, click on "November 22, 2000." The link to this case should be the second item on the resulting list. This site is maintained by LawNetCom, Inc.
b. For the sale of this timber, Northern received $498,905, of which Daniel's share under their contract was $299,343. Daniel was paid only $134,000, however. Ultimately, she reached a settlement with Northern, Easley, and Heppler as to their liability on this contract.

c. The court also awarded Daniel more than $800,000 in damages, including reforestation costs, and issued an injunction against Memphis's further cutting. In a separate case, Northern, Easley, and Heppler pleaded guilty to charges of embezzlement and agreed to make restitution to Daniel in the amount of $250,000.

The Entrustment Rule. According to Section 2–403(2), entrusting goods to a merchant *who deals in goods of that kind* gives the merchant the power to transfer all rights to *a buyer in the ordinary course of business.* Entrusting includes both turning over the goods to the merchant and leaving the purchased goods with the merchant for later delivery or pickup [UCC 2–403(3)]. A buyer in the ordinary course of business is a person who, in good faith and without knowl-

edge that the sale violates the ownership rights or security interest of a third party, buys in ordinary course from a person (other than a pawnbroker) in the business of selling goods of that kind [UCC 1–201(9)]. (A *security interest* is any interest in personal property that secures payment or the performance of an obligation—see Chapter 20.)

● **EXAMPLE #5** Jan leaves her watch with a jeweler to be repaired. The jeweler sells used watches. The jeweler sells

Jan's watch to Kim, a customer, who does not know that the jeweler has no right to sell it. Kim, as a good faith buyer, gets good title against Jan's claim of ownership.[2] Kim, however, obtains only those rights held by the person entrusting the goods (here, Jan). Suppose that in fact Jan had stolen the watch from Greg and then left it with the jeweler to be repaired. The jeweler then sells it to Kim. In this situation, Kim gets good title against Jan, who entrusted the watch to the jeweler, but not against Greg (the real owner), who neither entrusted the watch to Jan nor authorized Jan to entrust it.•

Risk of Loss

Under the UCC, risk of loss does not necessarily pass with title. When risk of loss passes from a seller or lessor to a buyer or lessee is generally determined by the contract between the parties. Sometimes, the contract states expressly when the risk of loss passes. At other times, it does not, and a court must interpret the performance and delivery terms of the contract to determine whether the risk has passed.

---

[2] Jan, of course, can sue the jeweler for the tort of trespass to personalty or conversion (see Chapter 4) for the equivalent money value of the watch.

DELIVERY WITH MOVEMENT OF THE GOODS—CARRIER CASES

When there is no specification in the agreement, the following rules apply to cases involving movement of the goods (carrier cases).

Shipment Contracts. In a shipment contract, if the seller or lessor is required or authorized to ship goods by carrier (but not required to deliver them to a particular final destination), risk of loss passes to the buyer or lessee when the goods are duly delivered to the carrier [UCC 2–319(1)(a), 2–509(1)(a), 2A–219(2)(a)].

•EXAMPLE #6 A seller in Texas sells five hundred cases of grapefruit to a buyer in New York, F.O.B. Houston (free on board in Houston—that is, the buyer pays the transportation charges from Houston). The contract authorizes shipment by carrier; it does not require that the seller tender the grapefruit in New York. Risk passes to the buyer when conforming goods are properly placed in the possession of the carrier. If the goods are damaged in transit, the loss is the buyer's. (Actually, buyers have recourse against carriers, subject to certain limitations, and buyers usually insure the goods from the time the goods leave the seller.)• The following case illustrates these principles.

CASE 15.3   Windows, Inc. v. Jordan Panel System Corp.

United States Court of Appeals,
Second Circuit, 1999.
177 F.3d 114.
http://csmail.law.pace.edu/lawlib/legal/
us-legal/judiciary/second-circuit.html[a]

FACTS Jordan Panel System Corporation, Inc., a construction subcontractor, contracted to install window wall panels at an air cargo facility at John F. Kennedy Airport in New York City. Jordan ordered custom-made windows from Windows, Inc., a fabricator and seller of windows based in South Dakota. The contract specified that the windows were to be shipped properly packaged for cross-country motor freight transit and "delivered to New York City." Windows built the windows and arranged to ship them to Jordan by Consolidated Freightways Corporation. During the shipment, much of the glass was bro-

ken, and many of the frames were gouged and twisted. Jordan employees disassembled the window frames to salvage as much of the shipment as possible. Jordan made a claim with Consolidated for the damages, including labor costs from the salvage efforts and other expenses arising from Jordan's inability to perform its contracts on schedule. Jordan also ordered a new shipment from Windows, which was delivered without incident. Jordan did not pay Windows for either shipment. As part of the ensuing litigation, a federal district court heard Jordan's claim against Windows for incidental and consequential damages resulting from the damaged shipment. The court granted Windows's motion for summary judgment, concluding that the contract was a shipment contract. Thus, when the seller (Windows) put conforming goods into the hands of the carrier (Consolidated), the risk of loss passed to the buyer (Jordan). Jordan appealed to the U.S. Court of Appeals for the Second Circuit.

ISSUE Was the contract in this case a shipment contract?

DECISION Yes. The U.S. Court of Appeals for the Second Circuit affirmed the lower court's decision.

---

a. This Web site is a joint project of Touro and Pace University School of Law with the cooperation of the U.S. Court of Appeals for the Second Circuit. In the "1999" column, click on "April." When that page opens, scroll down the list of cases to the case name and click on "Opinion" to access the case.

CASE 15.3—Continued

REASON The appellate court pointed out that "[w]here the terms of an agreement are ambiguous, there is a strong presumption under the U.C.C. favoring shipment contracts. Unless the parties 'expressly specify' that the contract requires the seller to deliver to a particular destination, the contract is generally construed as one for shipment." Thus, because the parties did not "expressly specify" that Windows was to deliver the goods to a particular destination, "the contract should be deemed a shipment contract. Under the terms of its contract,

Windows thus satisfied its obligations to Jordan when it put the goods, properly packaged, into the possession of the carrier for shipment." Therefore, in a shipment contract under UCC 2–509(1)(a), "the risk of loss passes to the buyer when the goods are duly delivered to the carrier."

FOR CRITICAL ANALYSIS—Ethical Consideration
Why do the courts assume that a contract is a shipment contract unless the contract expressly specifies that the goods are to be delivered to a particular destination? Is this fair? Why or why not?

Destination Contracts. In a destination contract, the risk of loss passes to the buyer or lessee when the goods are tendered to the buyer or lessee at the specified destination [UCC 2–319(1)(b), 2–509(1)(b), 2A–219(2)(b)]. In Example #6, if the contract had been F.O.B. New York, the risk of loss during transit to New York would have been the seller's.

Contract Terms. Specific terms in the contract help determine when risk of loss passes to the buyer. These terms, which are listed and defined in Exhibit 15–1 on the next page, relate generally to the determination of which party will bear the costs of delivery. Unless otherwise agreed, these terms also determine who has the risk of loss.

The 2003 amendments to UCC Article 2 omit these terms because they are "inconsistent with modern commercial practice." Until most states adopt the amended version of Article 2, however, these terms will remain in use.

DELIVERY WITHOUT MOVEMENT OF THE GOODS

The UCC also addresses situations in which the seller or lessor is required neither to ship nor to deliver the goods. Frequently, the buyer or lessee is to pick up the goods from the seller or lessor, or the goods are held by a bailee. Under the UCC, a **bailee** is a party who, by a bill of lading, warehouse receipt, or other document of title, acknowledges possession of goods and/or contracts to deliver them. A warehousing company, for example, or a trucking company that normally issues documents of title for the goods it receives is a bailee.[3]

Goods Held by the Seller. If the goods are held by the seller, a document of title is usually not used. If the seller is a merchant, risk of loss to goods held by the seller passes to the buyer when the buyer *actually takes physical possession of the goods* [UCC 2–509(3)]. If the seller is not a merchant,

the risk of loss to goods held by the seller passes to the buyer on *tender of delivery* [UCC 2–509(3)]. (As you will read in Chapter 16, tender of delivery occurs when the seller places conforming goods at the disposal of the buyer and gives the buyer whatever notification is reasonably necessary to enable the buyer to take possession.) With respect to leases, the risk of loss passes to the lessee on the lessee's receipt of the goods if the lessor—or supplier, in a finance lease (see Chapter 14)—is a merchant. Otherwise, the risk passes to the lessee on tender of delivery [UCC 2A–219(c)].[4]

Goods Held by a Bailee. When a bailee is holding goods for a person who has contracted to sell them and the goods are to be delivered without being moved, the goods are usually represented by a negotiable or nonnegotiable document of title (a bill of lading or a warehouse receipt). Risk of loss passes to the buyer when (1) the buyer receives a negotiable document of title for the goods, (2) the bailee acknowledges the buyer's right to possess the goods, or (3) the buyer receives a nonnegotiable document of title *and* has had a *reasonable time* to present the document to the bailee and demand the goods. Obviously, if the bailee refuses to honor the document, the risk of loss remains with the seller [UCC 2–503(4)(b), 2–509(2)].

In respect to leases, if goods held by a bailee are to be delivered without being moved, the risk of loss passes to the lessee on acknowledgment by the bailee of the lessee's right to possession of the goods [UCC 2A–219(2)(b)].

CONDITIONAL SALES

Buyers and sellers sometimes form sales contracts that are conditioned either on the buyer's approval of the goods or on the buyer's resale of the goods. Under such contracts, the

---

[3] Bailments will be discussed in detail in Chapter 28.

[4] Under the 2003 amendments to UCC 2–509(3) and 2A–219(c), the risk of loss passes to the buyer or the lessee on that party's receipt of the goods whether or not the seller or the lessor is a merchant.

EXHIBIT 15–1   CONTRACT TERMS—DEFINITIONS

F.O.B. (free on board)—Indicates that the selling price of goods includes transportation costs (and that the seller carries the risk of loss) to the specific F.O.B. place named in the contract. The place can be either the place of initial shipment (for example, the seller's city or place of business) or the place of destination (for example, the buyer's city or place of business) [UCC 2–319(1)].
F.A.S. (free alongside)—Requires that the seller, at his or her own expense and risk, deliver the goods "alongside the ship" before risk passes to the buyer [UCC 2–319(2)].
C.I.F. or **C.&F.** (cost, insurance, and freight, or just cost and freight)—Requires, among other things, that the seller "put the goods in possession of a carrier" before risk passes to the buyer [UCC 2–320(2)]. (These are basically pricing terms, and the contracts remain shipment contracts, not destination contracts.)
Delivery ex-ship (delivery from the carrying ship)—Means that risk of loss does not pass to the buyer until the goods leave the ship or are otherwise properly unloaded [UCC 2–322].

buyer is in possession of the goods. Sometimes, however, problems arise as to whether the buyer or seller should bear the loss if, for example, the goods are damaged or stolen while in the possession of the buyer.

Sale or Return. A sale or return (sometimes called a *sale and return*) is a type of contract by which the seller sells a quantity of goods to the buyer with the understanding that the buyer can set aside the sale by returning the goods or any portion of the goods. The buyer is required to pay for any goods *not* returned. When the buyer receives possession of the goods under a sale-or-return contract, the title and risk of loss pass to the buyer. Title and risk of loss remain with the buyer until the buyer returns the goods to the seller within the time period specified. If the buyer fails to return the goods within this time period, the sale is finalized. The return of the goods is made at the buyer's risk and expense. Goods held under a sale-or-return contract are subject to the claims of the buyer's creditors while they are in the buyer's possession (even if the buyer has not paid for the goods) [UCC 2–326, 2–327].

The UCC treats a **consignment** as a sale or return. Under a consignment, the owner of goods (the *consignor*) delivers them to another (the *consignee*) for the consignee to sell. If the consignee sells the goods, the consignee must pay the consignor for them. If the consignee does not sell the goods, they may simply be returned to the consignor. While the goods are in the possession of the consignee, the consignee holds title to them, and creditors of the consignee will prevail over the consignor in any action to repossess the goods [UCC 2–326(3)].[5]

---

[5] This provision is omitted from the 2003 amendments to UCC Article 2. Consignments are to be covered by UCC Article 9. See, for example, UCC 9–103(d), 9–109(a)(4), and 9–319.

Sale on Approval. When a seller offers to sell goods to a buyer and permits the buyer to take the goods on a trial basis, a **sale on approval** is usually made. The term *sale* here is a misnomer, as only an *offer* to sell has been made, along with a *bailment* created by the buyer's possession. (A bailment is a temporary delivery of personal property into the care of another—see Chapter 28.)

Therefore, title and risk of loss (from causes beyond the buyer's control) remain with the seller until the buyer accepts (approves) the offer. Acceptance can be made expressly, by any act inconsistent with the *trial* purpose or the seller's ownership, or by the buyer's election not to return the goods within the trial period. If the buyer does not wish to accept, the buyer may notify the seller of that fact within the trial period, and the return is made at the seller's expense and risk [UCC 2–327(1)]. Goods held on approval are not subject to the claims of the buyer's creditors until acceptance.

It is often difficult to determine what type of contract a particular transaction involves—a contract for a sale on approval, a contract for a sale or return, or a contract for sale. The UCC states that (unless otherwise agreed) "if the goods are delivered primarily for use," the transaction is a sale on approval; "if the goods are delivered primarily for resale," the transaction is a sale or return [UCC 2–326(1)].

RISK OF LOSS WHEN A SALES OR LEASE CONTRACT IS BREACHED

There are many ways to breach a sales or lease contract, and the transfer of risk operates differently depending on which party breaches. Generally, the party in breach bears the risk of loss.

When the Seller or Lessor Breaches. If the goods are so nonconforming that the buyer has the right to reject them, the risk of loss does not pass to the buyer until the defects are **cured** (that is, until the goods are repaired, replaced, or discounted in price by the seller) or until the buyer accepts the goods in spite of their defects (thus waiving the right to reject). ●EXAMPLE #7 A buyer orders ten white refrigerators from a seller, F.O.B. the seller's plant. The seller ships amber refrigerators instead. The amber refrigerators (nonconforming goods) are damaged in transit. The risk of loss falls on the seller. Had the seller shipped white refrigerators (conforming goods) instead, the risk would have fallen on the buyer [UCC 2–510(2)].●

If a buyer accepts a shipment of goods and later discovers a defect, acceptance can be revoked. Revocation allows the buyer to pass the risk of loss back to the seller, at least to the extent that the buyer's insurance does not cover the loss [UCC 2–510(2)].

In regard to leases, Article 2A states a similar rule. If the lessor or supplier tenders goods that are so nonconforming that the lessee has the right to reject them, the risk of loss remains with the lessor or the supplier until cure or acceptance [UCC 2A–220(1)(a)]. If the lessee, after acceptance, revokes his or her acceptance of nonconforming goods, the revocation passes the risk of loss back to the seller or supplier, to the extent that the lessee's insurance does not cover the loss [UCC 2A–220(1)(b)].

When the Buyer or Lessee Breaches. The general rule is that when a buyer or lessee breaches a contract, the risk of loss immediately shifts to the buyer or lessee. This rule has three important limitations:

① The seller or lessor must already have identified the contract goods.

② The buyer or lessee bears the risk for only a commercially reasonable time after the seller has learned of the breach.

③ The buyer or lessee is liable only to the extent of any deficiency in the seller's insurance coverage [UCC 2–510(3), 2A–220(2)].

Insurable Interest

Parties to sales and lease contracts often obtain insurance coverage to protect against damage, loss, or destruction of goods. Any party purchasing insurance, however, must have a sufficient interest in the insured item to obtain a valid policy. Insurance laws—not the UCC—determine sufficiency. The UCC is helpful, however, because it contains certain rules regarding insurable interests in goods.

INSURABLE INTEREST OF THE BUYER OR LESSEE

A buyer or lessee has an **insurable interest** in identified goods. The moment the contract goods are identified by the seller or lessor, the buyer or lessee has a special property interest that allows the buyer or lessee to obtain necessary insurance coverage for those goods even before the risk of loss has passed [UCC 2–501(1), 2A–218(1)].

The rule stated in UCC 2–501(1)(c) is that such buyers obtain an insurable interest in crops by identification, which occurs when the crops are planted or otherwise become growing crops, provided that the contract is for "the sale of crops to be harvested within twelve months or the next normal harvest season after contracting, whichever is longer." ●EXAMPLE #8 In March, a farmer sells a cotton crop he hopes to harvest in October. The buyer acquires an insurable interest in the crop when it is planted, because those goods (the cotton crop) are identified to the sales contract between the seller and the buyer.●

INSURABLE INTEREST OF THE SELLER OR LESSOR

A seller has an insurable interest in goods if she or he retains title to the goods. Even after title passes to a buyer, a seller who has a security interest in the goods (a right to secure payment—see Chapter 20) still has an insurable interest and can insure the goods [UCC 2–501(2)]. Hence, both a buyer and a seller can have an insurable interest in identical goods at the same time. Of course, the buyer or seller must sustain an actual loss to have the right to recover from an insurance company. In regard to leases, the lessor retains an insurable interest in leased goods until an option to buy has been exercised by the lessee and the risk of loss has passed to the lessee [UCC 2A–218(3)].

Bulk Transfers

Article 6 of the UCC covers bulk transfers. A *bulk transfer* is defined as any transfer of a major part of the transferor's material, supplies, merchandise, or other inventory *not made in the ordinary course of the transferor's business* [UCC 6–102(1)]. Article 6 was designed to prevent certain difficulties with such transfers—such as when a business sold a substantial part of its equipment and inventories to a buyer and then failed to pay its creditors. Today, changes in the business and legal contexts in which bulk sales are conducted have largely made their regulation unnecessary. For this reason, the majority of the states have repealed Article 6. Those states that have not repealed the article follow either the original version of Article 6 or an alternative version included in the UCC.

Terms and Concepts

Chapter Summary   **Title and Risk of Loss**

Shipment Contracts (See pages 289 and 292–293.)	In the absence of an agreement, title and risk pass on the seller's or lessor's delivery of conforming goods to the carrier [UCC 2–319(1)(a), 2–401(2)(a), 2–509(1)(a), 2A–219(2)(a)].
Destination Contracts (See pages 289 and 293.)	In the absence of an agreement, title and risk pass on the seller's or lessor's *tender* of delivery of conforming goods to the buyer or lessee at the point of destination [UCC 2–401(2)(b), 2–319(1)(b), 2–509(1)(b), 2A–219(2)(b)].

Delivery without Movement of the Goods (See pages 289–290 and 293.)	1. In the absence of an agreement, if the goods are not represented by a document of title:
	  a. Title passes on the formation of the contract [UCC 2–401(3)(b)].
	  b. Risk passes to the buyer or lessee, if the seller or lessor (or supplier, in a finance lease) is a merchant, on the buyer's or lessee's receipt of the goods or, if the seller or lessor is a nonmerchant, on the seller's or lessor's *tender* of delivery of the goods [UCC 2–509(3), 2A–219(c)].
	2. In the absence of an agreement, if the goods are represented by a document of title:
	  a. If the document is negotiable and the goods are held by a bailee, title and risk pass on the buyer's *receipt* of the document [UCC 2–401(3)(a), 2–509(2)(a)].
	  b. If the document is nonnegotiable and the goods are held by a bailee, title passes on the buyer's receipt of the document, but risk does *not* pass until the buyer, after receipt of the document, has had a reasonable time to present the document to demand the goods [UCC 2–401(3)(a), 2–509(2)(c), 2–503(4)(b)].
	3. In the absence of an agreement, if the goods are held by a bailee and no document of title is transferred, risk passes to the buyer when the bailee acknowledges the buyer's right to the possession of the goods [UCC 2–509(2)(b)].
	4. In respect to leases, if goods held by a bailee are to be delivered without being moved, the risk of loss passes to the lessee on acknowledgment by the bailee of the lessee's right to possession of the goods [UCC 2A–219(2)(b)].

Sales or Leases by Nonowners (See pages 290–292.)	Between the owner and a good faith purchaser or sublessee: 1. *Void title*—Owner prevails [UCC 2–403(1)]. 2. *Voidable title*—Buyer prevails [UCC 2–403(1)]. 3. *Entrusting to a merchant*—Buyer or sublessee prevails [UCC 2–403(2), (3); 2A–305(2)].
Sale-or-Return Contracts (See page 294.)	When the buyer receives possession of the goods, title and risk of loss pass to the buyer, with the buyer's option to return the goods to the seller. If the buyer returns the goods to the seller, title and risk of loss pass back to the seller [UCC 2–327(2)].
Sale-on-Approval Contracts (See page 294.)	Title and risk of loss (from causes beyond the buyer's control) remain with the seller until the buyer approves (accepts) the offer [UCC 2–327(1)].

Chapter Summary	Title and Risk of Loss—Continued
Risk of Loss When a Sales or Lease Contract Is Breached (See pages 294–295.)	1. If the seller or lessor breaches by tendering nonconforming goods that are rejected by the buyer or lessee, the risk of loss does not pass to the buyer or lessee until the defects are cured (unless the buyer or lessee accepts the goods in spite of their defects, thus waiving the right to reject) [UCC 2–510(1), 2A–220(1)]. 2. If the buyer or lessee breaches the contract, the risk of loss immediately shifts to the buyer or lessee. Limitations to this rule are as follows [UCC 2–510(3), 2A–220(2)]: a. The seller or lessor must already have identified the contract goods. b. The buyer or lessee bears the risk for only a commercially reasonable time after the seller or lessor has learned of the breach. c. The buyer or lessee is liable only to the extent of any deficiency in the seller's or lessor's insurance coverage.
Insurable Interest (See page 295.)	1. Buyers and lessees have an insurable interest in goods the moment the goods are identified to the contract by the seller or the lessor [UCC 2–501(1), 2A–218(1)]. 2. Sellers have an insurable interest in goods as long as they have (1) title to the goods or (2) a security interest in the goods [UCC 2–501(2)]. Lessors have an insurable interest in leased goods until an option to buy has been exercised by the lessee and the risk of loss has passed to the lessee [UCC 2A–218(3)].
Bulk Transfers (See page 295.)	A bulk transfer is defined as the transfer of a major part of the transferor's material, supplies, merchandise, or other inventory not made in the ordinary course of the transferor's business [UCC 6–102(1)]. Bulk transfers are governed by Article 6 of the UCC, which the majority of states have repealed.

For Review

① What is the significance of identifying goods to a contract?

② If the parties to a contract do not expressly agree on when title to goods passes, what determines when title passes?

③ Risk of loss does not necessarily pass with title. If the parties to a contract do not expressly agree when risk passes and the goods are to be delivered without movement by the seller, when does risk pass?

④ Under what circumstances will the seller's title to goods being sold be void? Under what circumstances will a seller have voidable title? What is the legal effect on a good faith purchaser of the goods of the seller's having a void title versus a voidable title?

⑤ At what point does the buyer acquire an insurable interest in goods subject to a sales contract? Can both the buyer and the seller have an insurable interest in the goods simultaneously?

Questions and Case Problems

15–1. Sales by Nonowners. In the following situations, two parties lay claim to the same goods sold. Discuss which party would prevail in each situation.

(a) Terry steals Dom's television set and sells the set to Blake, an innocent purchaser, for value. Dom learns that Blake has the set and demands its return.

(b) Karlin takes her television set for repair to Orken, a merchant who sells new and used television sets. By accident, one of Orken's employees sells the set to Grady, an innocent purchaser–customer, who takes possession. Karlin wants her set back from Grady.

15–2. Risk of Loss. When will risk of loss pass from the seller to the buyer under each of the following contracts, assuming the parties have not expressly agreed on when risk of loss would pass?

(a) A New York seller contracts with a San Francisco buyer to ship goods to the buyer F.O.B. San Francisco.

(b) A New York seller contracts with a San Francisco buyer to ship goods to the buyer in San Francisco. There is no indication as to whether the shipment will be F.O.B. New York or F.O.B. San Francisco.

(c) A seller contracts with a buyer to sell goods located on the seller's premises. The buyer pays for the goods and makes arrangements to pick them up the next week at the seller's place of business.

(d) A seller contracts with a buyer to sell goods located in a warehouse.

15–3. Sales by Nonowners. Julian Makepeace, who had been declared mentally incompetent by a court, sold his diamond ring to Golding for value. Golding later sold the ring to Carmichael for value. Neither Golding nor Carmichael knew that Makepeace had been adjudged mentally incompetent by a court. Farrel, who had been appointed as Makepeace's guardian, subsequently learned that the diamond ring was in Carmichael's possession and demanded its return from Carmichael. Who has legal ownership of the ring? Why?

15–4. Risk of Loss. Alberto's Food Stores contracts to purchase from Giant Food Distributors, Inc., one hundred cases of Golden Rod corn to be shipped F.O.B. seller's warehouse by Janson Truck Lines. Giant Food Distributors, by mistake, delivers one hundred cases of Gold Giant corn to Janson Truck Lines. While in transit, the Gold Giant corn is stolen. Between Alberto's and Giant Food Distributors, who suffers the loss? Explain.

15–5. Sale on Approval. Chi Moy, a student, contracts to buy a television set from Ted's Electronics. Under the terms of the contract, Moy is to try out the set for thirty days, and if he likes it, he is to pay for the set at the end of the thirty-day period. If he does not want to purchase the set after thirty days, he can return the TV to Ted's Electronics with no obligation. Ten days after Moy takes the set home, it is stolen from his apartment, although he was not negligent in his care of the set in any way. Ted's Electronics claims that Moy must pay for the stolen set. Moy argues that the risk of loss falls on Ted's Electronics. Which party will prevail?

15–6. Shipment and Destination Contracts. Roderick Cardwell owns Ticketworld, which sells tickets to entertainment and sporting events to be held at locations throughout the United States. Ticketworld's Massachusetts office sold tickets to an event in Connecticut to Mary Lou Lupovitch, a Connecticut resident, for $125 per ticket, although each ticket had a fixed price of $32.50. There was no agreement that Ticketworld would bear the risk of loss until the tickets were delivered to a specific location. Ticketworld gave the tickets to a carrier in Massachusetts, who delivered the tickets to Lupovitch in Connecticut. The state of Connecticut brought an action against Cardwell in a Connecticut state court, charging in part a violation of a state statute that prohibited the sale of a ticket for more than $3 over its fixed price. Cardwell contended that the statute did not apply because the sale to Lupovitch involved a shipment contract that was formed outside the state. Is Cardwell correct? How will the court rule? Why? [*State v. Cardwell*, 246 Conn. 721, 718 A.2d 954 (1998)]

15–7. Risk of Loss. Mark Olmstead sells trailers, doing business as World Cargo in St. Croix Falls, Wisconsin. In 1997, he also sold trailers from a site in Elk River, Minnesota. Gerald McKenzie ordered a custom-made trailer from Olmstead and mailed him a check for $3,620. McKenzie said that he would pick up the trailer at the Elk River site. After the trailer was made, Olmstead shipped it to Elk River and kept it in a locked,

fenced area. He told McKenzie that the trailer could be picked up any Tuesday or Thursday before 6:00 P.M. Over Olmstead's protest, McKenzie asked that the trailer be left outside the fenced area. Olmstead told McKenzie that the area was not secure and that the trailer could not be locked, except to chain the tires. McKenzie insisted, however, and Olmstead complied. When McKenzie arrived to pick up the trailer, it was gone—apparently stolen. McKenzie filed a suit in a Minnesota state court against Olmstead to recover the amount of the check. Who bore the risk of loss in these circumstances? Why? [*McKenzie v. Olmstead*, 587 N.W.2d 863 (Minn.App. 1999)]

CASE PROBLEM WITH SAMPLE ANSWER

15–8. Phillip and Genevieve Carboy owned and operated Gold Hill Service Station in Fairbanks, Alaska. Gold Hill maintained underground storage tanks on its property to hold gasoline. When Gold Hill needed more fuel, Phillip placed an order with Petroleum Sales, Inc., which delivered the gasoline by filling the tanks. Gold Hill and Petroleum Sales were separately owned companies. Petroleum Sales did not oversee or operate Gold Hill and did not construct, install, or maintain the station's tanks, and Gold Hill did not tell Petroleum Sales's personnel how to fill the tanks. Parks Hiway Enterprises, LLC, owned the land next to Gold Hill. The Alaska Department of Environmental Conservation determined that benzene had contaminated the groundwater under Parks Hiway's property and identified the gasoline in Gold Hill's tanks as the probable source. Gold Hill promptly removed the tanks, but because of the contamination, Parks Hiway stopped drawing drinking water from its well. Parks Hiway filed a suit in an Alaska state court against Petroleum Sales, among others. Should the court hold the defendant liable for the pollution? Who had title to the gasoline when it contaminated the water? Explain. [*Parks Hiway Enterprises, LLC v. CEM Leasing, Inc.*, 995 P.2d 657 (Alaska 2000)]

◗ To view a sample answer for this case problem, go to this book's Web site at **http://fundamentals.westbuslaw.com** and click on "Interactive Study Center."

15–9. Risk of Loss. H.S.A. II, Inc., made parts for motor vehicles. Under an agreement with Ford Motor Co., Ford provided steel to H.S.A. to make Ford parts. Ford's purchase orders for the parts contained the term "FOB Carrier Supplier's [Plant]." GMAC Business Credit, L.L.C., loaned money to H.S.A. under terms that guaranteed payment would be made, if the funds were not otherwise available, from H.S.A.'s inventory, raw materials, and finished goods. H.S.A. filed for bankruptcy on February 2, 2000, and ceased operations on June 20, when it had in its plant more than $1 million in finished goods for Ford. Ford sent six trucks to H.S.A. to pick up the goods. GMAC halted the removal. The parties asked the bankruptcy court to determine whose interest had priority. GMAC contended in part that Ford did not have an interest in the goods because there had not yet been a sale. Ford responded that under its purchase orders, title and risk of loss transferred on completion of the parts. In whose favor should the court rule, and why? [*In re H.S.A. II, Inc.,* 271 Bankr. 534 (E.D.Mich. 2002)]

A QUESTION OF ETHICS AND SOCIAL RESPONSIBILITY

15–10. Toby and Rita Kahr accidentally included a small bag containing their sterling silver in a bag of used clothing that they donated to Goodwill Industries, Inc. The silverware, which was valued at over $3,500, had been given to them twenty-seven years earlier by Rita's father as a wedding present and had great sentimental value for them. The Kahrs realized what had happened shortly after Toby returned from Goodwill, but when Toby called Goodwill, he was told that the silver had immediately been sold to a customer, Karon Markland, for $15. Although Goodwill called Markland and asked her to return the silver, Markland refused to return it. The Kahrs then brought an action against Markland to regain the silver, claiming that Markland did not have good title to it. In view of these circumstances, discuss the following issues. [*Kahr v. Markland,* 187 Ill.App.3d 603, 543 N.E.2d 579, 135 Ill.Dec. 196 (1989)]

1. Did Karon Markland act wrongfully in any way by not returning the silver to Goodwill Industries when requested to do so? What would you have done in her position?

2. Goodwill argued that the entrustment rule should apply. Why would Goodwill want the rule to be applied? How might Goodwill justify its argument from an ethical point of view?

VIDEO QUESTION

15–11. Go to this text's Web site at **http://fundamentals.westbuslaw.com** and click on "Video Questions." Select "Chapter 15" and view the video titled *Risk of Loss*. Then answer the following questions:

1. Does Oscar have a right to refuse the shipment because the lettuce is wilted? Why or why not? What type of contract is involved in this video?

2. Does Oscar have a right to refuse the shipment because the lettuce was not organic butter crunch lettuce? Why or why not?

3. Assume that you are in Oscar's position—that is, you are buying produce for a supermarket. What different approaches might you take to avoid having to pay for a delivery of wilted produce?

TITLE AND RISK OF LOSS

For updated links to resources available on the Web, as well as other materials, visit this text's Web site at

http://fundamentals.westbuslaw.com

Translation, Inc., provides a sample bill of lading at its Web site. Go to

http://www.showtrans.com/bl.htm

Online Legal Research

Go to the *Fundamentals of Business Law* home page at **http://fundamentals.westbuslaw.com**. Select "Interactive Study Center" and then click on "Chapter 15." There you will find the following Internet research exercises that you can perform to learn more about topics covered in this chapter.

Activity 15–1: LEGAL PERSPECTIVE—The Entrustment Rule
Activity 15–2: MANAGEMENT PERSPECTIVE—Passage of Title

Before the Test

Go to the *Fundamentals of Business Law* home page at **http://fundamentals.westbuslaw.com**. Click on "Interactive Quizzes." You will find at least twenty interactive questions relating to this chapter.

Westlaw® Campus

If your textbook provided for a subscription to Westlaw® Campus, or if you have otherwise purchased access to the Westlaw Campus database, you can access any of the cases presented or cited in this chapter by using your Westlaw Campus account.

16

Performance and Breach of Sales and Lease Contracts

CHAPTER OBJECTIVES

After reading this chapter, you should be able to answer the following questions:

① What are the respective obligations of the parties under a contract for the sale or lease of goods?

② What is the perfect tender rule? What are some important exceptions to this rule that apply to sales and lease contracts?

③ What options are available to the nonbreaching party when the other party to a sales or lease contract repudiates the contract prior to the time for performance?

④ What remedies are available to a seller or lessor when the buyer or lessee breaches the contract? What remedies are available to a buyer or lessee if the seller or lessor breaches the contract?

⑤ In contracts subject to the UCC, are parties free to limit the remedies available to the nonbreaching party on a breach of contract? If so, in what ways?

The performance that is required of the parties under a sales or lease contract consists of the duties and obligations each party has under the terms of the contract. Keep in mind that "duties and obligations" under the terms of the contract include those specified by the agreement, by custom, and by the Uniform Commercial Code (UCC). In this chapter, we examine the basic performance obligations of the parties under a sales or lease contract.

Sometimes, circumstances make it difficult for a person to carry out the promised performance, in which case the contract may be breached. When breach occurs, the aggrieved party looks for remedies—which we deal with in the second half of the chapter.

Performance Obligations

As discussed in previous chapters, the standards of good faith and commercial reasonableness are read into every contract. These standards provide a framework in which the parties can specify particulars of performance. Thus, when one party delays specifying particulars of performance for an unreasonable period of time or fails to cooperate with the other party, the innocent party is excused from any resulting delay in performance. The innocent party can proceed to perform in any reasonable manner, and the other party's failure to specify particulars or to cooperate can be treated as a breach of contract. Good faith is a question of fact for the jury. (For a further discussion of the importance of good faith and fair dealing in contracts subject to the UCC, see this chapter's *Management Perspective* feature on the following page.)

In the performance of a sales or lease contract, the basic obligation of the seller or lessor is to *transfer and deliver conforming goods.* The basic obligation of the buyer or lessee is to *accept and pay for conforming goods* in accordance with the contract [UCC 2–301, 2A–516(1)]. Overall performance of a sales or lease contract is controlled by the agreement between the parties. When the contract is unclear and disputes arise, the courts look to the UCC.

Obligations of the Seller or Lessor

The major obligation of the seller or lessor under a sales or lease contract is to tender conforming goods to the buyer or lessee.

TENDER OF DELIVERY

Tender of delivery requires that the seller or lessor have and hold *conforming goods* at the disposal of the buyer or lessee and give the buyer or lessee whatever notification is reasonably necessary to enable the buyer or lessee to take delivery [UCC 2–503(1), 2A–508(1)].

Tender must occur at a *reasonable hour* and in a *reasonable manner.* In other words, a seller cannot call the buyer at 2:00 A.M. and say, "The goods are ready. I'll give you twenty minutes to get them." Unless the parties have agreed otherwise, the goods must be tendered for delivery at a reasonable time and kept available for a reasonable period of time to enable the buyer to take possession of them [UCC 2–503(1)(a)].

All goods called for by a contract must be tendered in a single delivery unless the parties agree otherwise or the circumstances are such that either party can rightfully request delivery in lots [UCC 2–307, 2–612, 2A–510]. Hence, an order for one thousand shirts cannot be delivered two shirts at a time. If, however, the seller and the buyer contemplate that the shirts will be delivered in four orders of 250 each, as they are produced (for summer, fall, winter, and spring stock), and the price can be apportioned accordingly, it may be commercially reasonable to deliver the shirts in this way.

PLACE OF DELIVERY

The UCC provides for the place of delivery pursuant to a contract if the contract does not. Of course, the parties may agree on a particular destination, or their contract's terms or the circumstances may indicate the place of delivery.

Noncarrier Cases. If the contract does not designate the place of delivery for the goods, and the buyer is expected to pick them up, the place of delivery is the *seller's place of business* or, if the seller has none, the seller's residence [UCC 2–308]. If the contract involves the sale of *identified goods,* and the parties know when they enter into the contract that these goods are located somewhere other than at the seller's place of business (such as at a warehouse), then the *location of the goods* is the place for their delivery [UCC 2–308].

● **EXAMPLE #1** Rogers and Aguirre live in San Francisco. In San Francisco, Rogers contracts to sell Aguirre five used trucks, which both parties know are located in a Chicago warehouse. If nothing more is specified in the contract, the place of delivery for the trucks is Chicago.● The seller may tender delivery by either giving the buyer a *negotiable or nonnegotiable document of title* or obtaining the *bailee's (warehouser's) acknowledgment* that the buyer is entitled to possession.[1]

Carrier Cases. In many instances, attendant circumstances or delivery terms in the contract make it apparent that the parties intend that a carrier be used to move the goods. In carrier cases, a seller can complete performance of the obligation to deliver the goods in two ways—through a shipment contract and through a destination contract.

Shipment Contracts. Recall from Chapter 15 that a shipment contract requires or authorizes the seller to ship goods by a carrier. The contract does not require that the seller deliver the goods at a particular destination [UCC 2–319, 2–509]. Under a shipment contract, unless otherwise agreed, the seller must do the following:

① Put the goods into the hands of the carrier.

② Make a contract for their transportation that is reasonable according to the nature of the goods and their value. (For example, certain types of goods need refrigeration in transit.)

---

[1] If the seller delivers a nonnegotiable document of title or merely writes instructions to the bailee to release the goods to the buyer without the bailee's *acknowledgment* of the buyer's rights, this is also a sufficient tender, unless the buyer objects [UCC 2–503(4)]. Risk of loss, however, does not pass until the buyer has had a reasonable amount of time in which to present the document or to give the bailee instructions for delivery.

MANAGEMENT PERSPECTIVE
Good Faith and Fair Dealing

MANAGEMENT FACES A LEGAL ISSUE As discussed elsewhere, all contracts governed by the Uniform Commercial Code (UCC) must meet the requirements of good faith and fair dealing. Yet do these requirements supersede the written terms of a contract? In other words, if a party adheres strictly to the express, written terms of a contract, can the party nonetheless face liability for breaching the UCC's good faith requirements?

WHAT THE COURTS SAY Generally, the courts take the good faith provisions of the UCC very seriously. Consider, for example, a case brought by Sons of Thunder (Sons), a clam supplier, against Borden, Inc., a major food processing firm. Sons had contracted with Borden to supply a specified minimum number of clams to Borden every week for at least one year. The contract provided that either party could terminate the contract by giving advance notice of the termination, in writing, ninety days prior to the termination date.

Borden's performance of the contract left much to be desired. Among other things, Borden encouraged Sons to buy two large clamming boats, costing over $1 million; told the bank that gave credit to Sons that Borden expected to renew the contract for five years; failed to purchase the minimum number of clams; and finally, after Sons was facing financial difficulties for these and other reasons, refused to renew the contract after one year. In its suit against Borden, Sons alleged, among other things, that Borden had breached the implied covenant of good faith and fair dealing.

Ultimately, the New Jersey Supreme Court agreed and affirmed the jury's award of $412,000 to Sons for this breach of good faith. The court stated that "a party can violate the implied covenant of good faith and fair dealing without violating the express term of a contract." The issue of whether a party had breached an express provision of the contract was, in this court's opinion, separate and distinct from the issue of whether the implied

covenant of good faith had been breached. Thus, even though Borden's termination was consistent with the agreement, its "bad faith" during the performance of the contract, including the events surrounding the contract's termination, violated the UCC's good faith requirements.[a]

Although in this case the court emphasized the fact that Borden had superior bargaining power and preyed on Sons of Thunder's lack of sophistication and financial strength, other cases have held that good faith can be breached even when the parties have equal bargaining power. In one case, for example, the court held that although the plaintiffs were sophisticated businesspersons who had the assistance of highly competent counsel, they could still maintain an action for breach of good faith and fair dealing. The court reasoned that "the presence of bad faith is to be found in the eye of the beholder or, more to the point, in the eye of the trier of fact," indicating that it was up to a jury to determine whether the parties had performed in good faith.[b] In another case, the court held that a contract provision that gave a telephone company the right to reject potential cellular subscribers must be exercised in good faith and not selectively against the customers who were solicited by an electronics store.[c]

IMPLICATIONS FOR MANAGERS The message for business owners and managers involved in sales contracts is clear: compliance with the literal terms of a contract is not enough—the standards of good faith and fair dealing must also be met. While the specific standards of good faith performance are still evolving, the overriding principle is that the parties to a contract should do nothing to injure or destroy the rights of the other party to receive the fruits of the contract.

a. *Sons of Thunder, Inc. v. Borden, Inc.*, 148 N.J. 396, 690 A.2d 575 (1997).
b. *Seidenberg v. Summit Bank*, 2002 WL 276149 (N.J.Super. 2002).
c. *Electronics Store, Inc. v. Cellco Partnership*, 127 Md.App. 385, 732 A.2d 980 (1999).

③ Obtain and promptly deliver or tender to the buyer any documents necessary to enable the buyer to obtain possession of the goods from the carrier.

④ Promptly notify the buyer that shipment has been made [UCC 2–504].

If the seller fails to notify the buyer that shipment has been made or fails to make a proper contract for transportation, the buyer can treat the contract as breached and reject the goods, but only if a *material loss* of the goods or a significant *delay* results.

Destination Contracts. Under a *destination contract,* the seller agrees to see that conforming goods will be duly tendered to the buyer at a particular destination. The goods must be tendered at a reasonable hour and held at the buyer's disposal for a reasonable length of time. The seller must also give the buyer any appropriate notice that is necessary to enable the buyer to take delivery. In addition, the seller must provide the buyer with any documents of title necessary to enable the buyer to obtain delivery from the carrier [UCC 2–503].

THE PERFECT TENDER RULE

As previously noted, the seller or lessor has an obligation to ship or tender *conforming goods,* and the buyer or lessee is required to accept and pay for the goods according to the terms of the contract. Under the common law, the seller was obligated to deliver goods in conformity with the terms of the contract in every detail. This was called the *perfect tender* doctrine. The UCC preserves the perfect tender doctrine by stating that if goods or tender of delivery fail *in any respect* to conform to the contract, the buyer or lessee has the right to accept the goods, reject the entire shipment, or accept part and reject part [UCC 2–601, 2A–509].

● **EXAMPLE #2** A lessor contracts to lease fifty Vericlear monitors to be delivered at the lessee's place of business on or before October 1. On September 28, the lessor discovers that it has only thirty Vericlear monitors in inventory, but that it will have another forty Vericlear monitors within the next two weeks. The lessor tenders delivery of the thirty Vericlear monitors on October 1, with the promise that the other monitors will be delivered within three weeks. Because the lessor failed to make a perfect tender of fifty Vericlear monitors, the lessee has the right to reject the entire shipment and hold the lessor in breach. ●

EXCEPTIONS TO THE PERFECT TENDER RULE

Because of the rigidity of the perfect tender rule, several exceptions to the rule have been created, some of which are discussed here.

Agreement of the Parties. Exceptions to the perfect tender rule may be established by agreement. If the parties have agreed, for example, that defective goods or parts will not be rejected if the seller or lessor is able to repair or replace them within a reasonable period of time, the perfect tender rule does not apply.

Cure. The UCC does not specifically define the term *cure,* but it refers to the right of the seller or lessor to repair,

adjust, or replace defective or nonconforming goods [UCC 2–508, 2A–513]. When any tender of delivery is rejected because of nonconforming goods and the time for performance has not yet expired, the seller or lessor can notify the buyer or lessee promptly of the intention to cure and can then do so *within the contract time for performance* [UCC 2–508(1), 2A–513(1)]. Once the time for performance has expired, the seller or lessor can still, for a reasonable period, exercise the right to cure with respect to the rejected goods if he or she had, at the time of delivery, *reasonable grounds to believe that the nonconforming tender would be acceptable to the buyer or lessee* [UCC 2–508(2), 2A–513(2)].[2]

Sometimes, a seller or lessor will tender nonconforming goods with some type of price allowance. The allowance serves as the "reasonable grounds" for the seller or lessor to believe that the nonconforming tender will be acceptable to the buyer or lessee. Other reasons might also serve as the basis for the assumption that a buyer or lessee will accept a nonconforming tender. ● **EXAMPLE #3** Suppose that in the past a buyer, an office supply store, frequently accepted blue pens when the seller did not have black pens in stock. In this context, the seller has reasonable grounds to believe the store will again accept such a substitute. If the store rejects the substituted goods (blue pens) on a particular occasion, the seller nonetheless had reasonable grounds to believe that the blue pens would be acceptable. Therefore, the seller can cure within a reasonable period, even though the delivery of black pens will occur after the time limit for performance allowed under the contract. ●

The right to cure means that, in order to reject goods, the buyer or lessee must give notice to the seller or lessor of a particular defect. For example, if a lessee refuses a tender of goods as nonconforming but does not disclose the nature of the defect to the lessor, the lessee cannot later assert the defect as a defense if the defect is one that the lessor could have cured. Generally, buyers and lessees must act in good

---

[2] The 2003 amendments to UCC Articles 2 and 2A expressly exempt "consumer contracts" and "consumer leases" from these provisions [Amended UCC 2–508, 2A 508]. In other words, cure is not available as a matter of right after a justifiable revocation of acceptance under a consumer contract or lease. Also, the "reasonable grounds to believe" test has been abandoned in the new provisions, thus expanding the seller's right to cure after the time for performance has expired. Although this test has been abandoned, the requirement that the initial tender must have been made in good faith prevents a seller from deliberately tendering goods that the seller knows the buyer cannot use.

faith and state specific reasons for refusing to accept goods [UCC 2–605, 2A–514].[3]

Substitution of Carriers. When an agreed-on manner of delivery (such as which carrier will be used to transport the goods) becomes impracticable or unavailable through no fault of either party, but a commercially reasonable substitute is available, the seller must use this substitute performance, which is sufficient tender to the buyer [UCC 2–614(1)]. • EXAMPLE #4 A sales contract calls for the delivery of a large generator to be shipped by Roadway Trucking Corporation on or before June 1. The contract terms clearly state the importance of the delivery date. The employees of Roadway Trucking go on strike. The seller is required to make a reasonable substitute tender, perhaps by rail if one is available. Note that the seller here will normally be held responsible for any additional shipping costs, unless different arrangements have been made in the sales contract.•

Installment Contracts. An **installment contract** is a single contract that requires or authorizes delivery in two or more separate lots to be accepted and paid for separately. In an installment contract, a buyer or lessee can reject an installment *only if the nonconformity substantially impairs the value* of the installment and cannot be cured [UCC 2–612(2), 2–307, 2A–510(1)].[4]

Unless the contract provides otherwise, the entire installment contract is breached only when one or more nonconforming installments *substantially* impair the value of the *whole contract*. If the buyer or lessee subsequently accepts a nonconforming installment and fails to notify the seller or lessor of cancellation, however, the contract is reinstated [UCC 2–612(3), 2A–510(2)].

A major issue to be determined is what constitutes substantial impairment of the "value of the whole contract." • EXAMPLE #5 Consider an installment contract for the sale of twenty carloads of plywood. The first carload does not conform to the contract because 9 percent of the plywood deviates from the thickness specifications. The buyer cancels the contract, and immediately thereafter the second and third carloads of conforming plywood arrive at the buyer's place of business. If a lawsuit ensues, the court will have to grapple with the question of whether the 9 percent of nonconforming plywood substantially impaired the value of the whole.[5]•

The point to remember is that the UCC significantly alters the right of the buyer or lessee to reject the entire contract if the contract requires delivery to be made in several installments. The UCC strictly limits rejection to cases of *substantial* nonconformity.

Commercial Impracticability. As mentioned in Chapter 11, occurrences unforeseen by either party when a contract was made may make performance commercially impracticable. When this occurs, the rule of perfect tender no longer holds. According to UCC 2–615(a) and 2A–405(a), delay in delivery or nondelivery in whole or in part is not a breach when performance has been made impracticable "by the occurrence of a contingency the nonoccurrence of which was a basic assumption on which the contract was made." The seller or lessor must, however, notify the buyer or lessee as soon as practicable that there will be a delay or nondelivery.

Foreseeable versus Unforeseeable Contingencies. An increase in cost resulting from inflation does not in and of itself excuse performance, as this kind of risk is ordinarily assumed by a seller or lessor conducting business. The unforeseen contingency must be one that would have been impossible to contemplate in a given business situation. • EXAMPLE #6 A major oil company that receives its supplies from the Middle East has a contract to supply a buyer with 100,000 gallons of oil. Because of an oil embargo by the Organization of Petroleum Exporting Countries (OPEC), the seller is prevented from securing oil supplies to meet the terms of the contract. Because of the same embargo, the seller cannot secure oil from any other source. This situation comes fully under the commercial impracticability exception to the perfect tender doctrine.•

Can unanticipated increases in a seller's costs, which make performance "impracticable," constitute a valid defense to performance on the basis of commercial impracticability? The court dealt with this question in the following classic case.

---

[3] The 2003 amendments to UCC 2–605 and 2A–514 change this restriction in three ways. First, a buyer's or lessee's failure to disclose the nature of the defect affects only the right to reject or revoke acceptance, not the right to establish a breach. Second, the new sections expressly require that the seller or lessor must have had a right to cure, as well as the ability to cure. Finally, these sections extend to include not only rejection but also revocation of acceptance.

[4] The 2003 amendments make it clear that the buyer's or lessee's right to reject an installment depends on whether there has been a substantial impairment of the value of the installment to the buyer or lessee and not on the ability of the seller or lessor to cure [Amended UCC 2–612(2), 2A–510(2)].

[5] *Continental Forest Products, Inc. v. White Lumber Sales, Inc.,* 256 Or. 466, 474 P.2d 1 (1970). The court held that the deviation did not substantially impair the value of the whole contract. Additionally, the court stated that the nonconformity could be cured by an adjustment in the price.

Landmark and Classic Cases

CASE 16.1 **Maple Farms, Inc. v. City School District of Elmira**

Supreme Court of New York, 1974.
76 Misc.2d 1080,
352 N.Y.S.2d 784.

FACTS On June 15, 1973, Maple Farms, Inc., formed an agreement with the city school district of Elmira, New York, to supply the school district with milk for the 1973–1974 school year. The agreement was in the form of a requirements contract, under which Maple Farms would sell to the school district all the milk the district required at a fixed price—which was the June market price of milk. By December 1973, the price of raw milk had increased by 23 percent over the price specified in the contract. This meant that if the terms of the contract were fulfilled, Maple Farms would lose $7,350. Because it had similar contracts with other school districts, Maple Farms stood to lose a great deal if it was held to the price stated in the contracts. When the school district would not agree to release Maple Farms from its contract, Maple Farms brought an action in a New York state court for a declaratory judgment (a determination of the parties' rights under a contract). Maple Farms contended that the substantial increase in the price of raw milk was an event not contemplated by the parties when the contract was formed and that, given the increased price, performance of the contract was commercially impracticable.

ISSUE Can Maple Farms be released from the contract on the ground of commercial impracticability?

DECISION No. the court ruled that performance in this case was not impracticable.

REASON The court reasoned that commercial impracticability arises when an event occurs that is totally unexpected and unforeseeable by the parties. The increased price of raw milk was not totally unexpected, given that in the previous year the price of milk had risen 10 percent and that the price of milk had traditionally varied. Additionally, the general inflation of prices in the United States should have been anticipated. Maple Farms had reason to know these facts and could have included a clause in its contract with the school district to protect itself from its present situation. The court also noted that the primary purpose of the contract, on the part of the school district, was to protect itself (for budgeting purposes) against price fluctuations.

COMMENT *This case is a classic illustration of the UCC's commercial impracticability doctrine. Under this doctrine, parties who freely enter into contracts normally will not be excused from their contractual obligations simply because changed circumstances make performance difficult or very costly. Rather, to be excused from performance, a party must show that the changed circumstances were impossible to foresee at the time the contract was formed. This principle continues to be applied today.*

Partial Performance. Sometimes, an unforeseen event only *partially* affects the capacity of the seller or lessor to perform, and the seller or lessor is thus able to fulfill the contract *partially* but cannot tender total performance. In this event, the seller or lessor is required to allocate in a fair and reasonable manner any remaining production and deliveries among those to whom it is contractually obligated to deliver the goods, and this allocation may take into account its regular customers [UCC 2–615(b), 2A–405(b)]. The buyer or lessee must receive notice of the allocation and has the right to accept or reject the allocation [UCC 2–615(c), 2A–405(c)].

● **EXAMPLE #7** A Florida orange grower, Best Citrus, Inc., contracts to sell this season's production to a number of customers, including Martin's grocery chain. Martin's contracts to purchase two thousand crates of oranges. Best Citrus has sprayed some of its orange groves with a chemical called Karmoxin. The Department of Agriculture discovers that persons who eat products sprayed with Karmoxin may develop cancer. The department issues an order prohibiting the sale of these products. Best Citrus picks all of the oranges not sprayed with Karmoxin, but the quantity does not fully meet all the contracted-for deliveries. In this situation, Best Citrus is required to allocate its production, and it notifies Martin's that it cannot deliver the full quantity agreed on in the contract and specifies the amount it will be able to deliver under the circumstances. Martin's can either accept or reject the allocation, but Best Citrus has no further contractual liability.●

Destruction of Identified Goods. The UCC provides that when an unexpected event, such as a fire, totally destroys *goods identified at the time the contract is formed* through no fault of either party and *before risk passes to the buyer or lessee,* the parties are excused from performance [UCC 2–613, 2A–221]. If the goods are only partially destroyed, however, the buyer or lessee can inspect them and either treat the contract as void or accept the goods with a reduction of the contract price.

● EXAMPLE #8 Atlas Sporting Equipment agrees to lease to River Bicycles sixty bicycles of a particular model that has been discontinued. No other bicycles of that model are available. River specifies that it needs the bicycles to rent to tourists. Before Atlas can deliver the bikes, they are destroyed by a fire. In this situation, Atlas is not liable to River for failing to deliver the bikes. The goods were destroyed through no fault of either party, before the risk of loss passed to the lessee. The loss was total, so the contract is avoided. Clearly, Atlas has no obligation to tender the bicycles, and River has no obligation to pay for them.●

Assurance and Cooperation. Two other exceptions to the perfect tender doctrine apply equally to parties to sales and lease contracts: the right of assurance and the duty of cooperation.

The Right of Assurance. The UCC provides that if one of the parties to a contract has "reasonable grounds" to believe that the other party will not perform as contracted, he or she may *in writing* "demand adequate assurance of due performance" from the other party. Until such assurance is received, he or she may "suspend" further performance (such as payments due under the contract) without liability. What constitutes "reasonable grounds" is determined by commercial standards. If such assurances are not forthcoming within a reasonable time (not to exceed thirty days), the failure to respond may be treated as a *repudiation* of the contract [UCC 2–609, 2A–401]. The following case provides an example.

CASE 16.2   **Koch Materials Co. v. Shore Slurry Seal, Inc.**

United States District Court,
District of New Jersey, 2002.
205 F.Supp.2d 324.
http://lawlibrary.rutgers.edu/fed/search.html[a]

FACTS Koch Materials Company is a manufacturer of road surfacing materials. In February 1998, Koch agreed to pay $5 million, payable in three installments, to Shore Slurry Seal, Inc., for an asphalt plant in New Jersey and the rights to license a specialty road surfacing substance known as Novachip. Shore also agreed that for seven years following the sale, it would buy all of its asphalt requirements from Koch, or at least 2 million gallons of asphalt per year (the Exclusive Supply Agreement). Shore promised to use at least 2.5 million square yards of Novachip annually and to pay royalties to Koch accordingly (the Sublicense Agreement). Midway through the term of the contract, Shore told Koch that it planned to sell its assets to Asphalt Paving Systems,

Inc. Koch sought assurances that Asphalt Paving would continue the original deal. Shore refused to provide any more information. Koch filed a suit in a federal district court against Shore, asking in part for the right to treat Shore's failure to give assurances as a repudiation of their contract. Koch filed a motion for summary judgment on this issue.

ISSUE Did Shore in effect repudiate the contract?

DECISION Yes. The court issued a summary judgment in Koch's favor. The court concluded that Shore's failure to provide assurances to Koch constituted a repudiation of its contract, authorizing Koch to terminate the contract and seek damages.

REASON The court concluded that Koch had a commercially reasonable basis for demanding assurances. Shore planned to sell all of its assets, but retain the licensing agreement. The court stated that "any reasonable person would wonder how Shore planned to sell anything with no telephones, no computers, and no office furniture." As for leasing these items, a party might also ask, "Would Shore have had the financial capacity to obtain leases and hire a sales staff?" As for the requirements supply contract, the court pointed out that "[s]tart-up construction businesses * * * begin

---

a. In the "Find Decisions by Docket Number" section, select "Civil Case," type "01-2059" in the "Enter Docket Number" box, and click on "Submit Form." From the results, click on "ca01-2059-1.html" to access the opinion. Rutgers University School of Law in Camden, New Jersey, maintains this Web site.

CASE 16.2—Continued

unbonded, unable to win any bid for their first year and unable to secure sufficient bonding for large construction bids for several years.[b] Koch had no way of knowing whether Asphalt was already a going business, and, if not, whether it would be able to win sufficient sub-contracting bids even to

---

b. In this context, a *bond* is a guaranty to complete or to pay the cost of a construction contract if the contractor defaults.

---

meet the minimum requirements, let alone approach the potential upside of an established enterprise like Shore."

FOR CRITICAL ANALYSIS—Economic Consideration *In this case, the Exclusive Supply Agreement had an antiassignment clause (see Chapter 11). Could Koch have argued that Shore had repudiated the contract on the basis of that clause?*

The Duty of Cooperation. Sometimes, the performance of one party depends on the cooperation of the other. The UCC provides that when such cooperation is not forthcoming, the other party can suspend her or his own performance without liability and hold the uncooperative party in breach or proceed to perform the contract in any reasonable manner [UCC 2–311(3)(b)].

Obligations of the Buyer or Lessee

Once the seller or lessor has adequately tendered delivery, the buyer or lessee is obligated to accept the goods and pay for them according to the terms of the contract. In the absence of any specific agreements, the buyer or lessee must make payment at the time and place the buyer or lessee receives the goods [UCC 2–310(a), 2A–516(1)].

PAYMENT

When a sale is made on credit, the buyer is obliged to pay according to the specified credit terms (for example, 60, 90, or 120 days), not when the goods are received. The credit period usually begins on the *date of shipment* [UCC 2–310(d)]. Under a lease contract, a lessee must pay the lease payment that was specified in the contract [UCC 2A–516(1)].

Payment can be made by any means agreed on by the parties—cash or any other method generally acceptable in the commercial world. If the seller demands cash when the buyer offers a check, credit card, or the like, the seller must permit the buyer reasonable time to obtain legal tender [UCC 2–511].

RIGHT OF INSPECTION

Unless otherwise agreed, or for C.O.D. (collect on delivery) transactions, the buyer or lessee has an absolute right to inspect the goods. This right allows the buyer or lessee to verify, before making payment, that the goods tendered or delivered are what were contracted for or ordered. If the

goods are not what were ordered, the buyer or lessee has no duty to pay. *An opportunity for inspection is therefore a condition precedent to the right of the seller or lessor to enforce payment* [UCC 2–513(1), 2A–515(1)].

Unless otherwise agreed, inspection can take place at any reasonable place and time and in any reasonable manner. Generally, what is reasonable is determined by custom of the trade, past practices of the parties, and the like. Costs of inspecting conforming goods are borne by the buyer unless otherwise agreed [UCC 2–513(2)].

C.O.D. Shipments. If a seller ships goods to a buyer C.O.D. (or under similar terms) and the buyer has not agreed to a C.O.D. shipment in the contract, the buyer can rightfully *reject* the goods. This is because a C.O.D. shipment does not permit inspection before payment, which is a denial of the buyer's right of inspection. When the buyer has agreed to a C.O.D. shipment in the contract, however, or has agreed to pay for the goods on the presentation of a bill of lading, no right of inspection exists because it was negated by the agreement [UCC 2–513(3)].[6]

Payment Due—Documents of Title. Under certain contracts, payment is due on the receipt of the required documents of title even though the goods themselves may not have arrived at their destination. With C.I.F. and C.&F. contracts (see Exhibit 15–1 in Chapter 15), payment is required on receipt of the documents unless the parties have agreed otherwise. Thus, payment may be required prior to inspection, and payment must be made unless the buyer knows that the goods are nonconforming [UCC 2–310(b), 2–513(3)].

---

[6] References to "C.O.D." and similar terms that represent commercial shorthand have been deleted in the 2003 amendments to UCC Article 2 [see, for example, Amended UCC 2–513(3)(a)].

ACCEPTANCE

A buyer or lessee can manifest assent to the delivered goods in the following ways, each of which constitutes acceptance:

①　The buyer or lessee can expressly accept the shipment by words or conduct. For example, there is an acceptance if the buyer or lessee, after having had a reasonable opportunity to inspect the goods, signifies agreement to the seller or lessor that the goods are either conforming or are acceptable despite their nonconformity [UCC 2–606(1)(a), 2A–515(1)(a)].

②　Acceptance is presumed if the buyer or lessee has had a reasonable opportunity to inspect the goods and has failed to reject them within a reasonable period of time [UCC 2–606(1)(b), 2–602(1), 2A–515(1)(b)].

Additionally, in sales contracts, the buyer will be deemed to have accepted the goods if he or she performs any act that would indicate that the seller no longer owns the goods. For example, any use or resale of the goods generally constitutes an acceptance. Limited use for the sole purpose of testing or inspecting the goods is not an acceptance, however [UCC 2–606(1)(c)].

If some of the goods delivered do not conform to the contract and the seller or lessor has failed to cure, the buyer or lessee can make a *partial* acceptance [UCC 2–601(c), 2A–509(1)]. The same is true if the nonconformity was not reasonably discoverable before acceptance. (In the latter situation, the buyer or lessee may be able to revoke the acceptance, as will be discussed later in this chapter.) A buyer or lessee cannot accept less than a single commercial unit, however. A *commercial unit* is defined by the UCC as a unit of goods that, by commercial usage, is viewed as a "single whole" for purposes of sale, division of which would materially impair the character of the unit, its market value, or its use [UCC 2–105(6), 2A–103(1)(c)]. A commercial unit can be a single article (such as a machine), a set of articles (such as a suite of furniture or an assortment of sizes), a quantity (such as a bale, a gross, or a carload), or any other unit treated in the trade as a single whole.

Anticipatory Repudiation

What if, before the time for contract performance, one party clearly communicates to the other the intention not to perform? As discussed in Chapter 11, such an action is a breach of the contract by anticipatory repudiation.[7]

When anticipatory repudiation occurs, the nonbreaching party has a choice of two responses: (1) treat the repudiation as a final breach by pursuing a remedy or (2) wait to see if the repudiating party will decide to honor the obligations required by the contract despite the avowed intention to renege [UCC 2–610, 2A–402]. In either situation, the nonbreaching party may suspend performance.

Should the latter course be pursued, the UCC permits the breaching party (subject to some limitations) to "retract" her or his repudiation. This can be done by any method that clearly indicates an intent to perform. Once retraction is made, the rights of the repudiating party under the contract are reinstated [UCC 2–611, 2A–403].

Remedies of the Seller or Lessor

When the buyer or lessee is in breach, the seller or lessor has numerous remedies available under the UCC. Generally, the remedies available to the seller or lessor depend on the circumstances existing at the time of the breach, such as which party has possession of the goods, whether the goods are in transit, and whether the buyer or lessee has rejected or accepted the goods.

WHEN THE GOODS ARE IN THE POSSESSION OF THE SELLER OR LESSOR

Under the UCC, if the buyer or lessee breaches the contract before the goods have been delivered to the buyer or lessee, the seller or lessor has the right to pursue the remedies discussed here.

The Right to Cancel the Contract. One of the options available to a seller or lessor when the buyer or lessee breaches the contract is simply to cancel (rescind) the contract [UCC 2–703(f), 2A–523(1)(a)]. The seller must notify the buyer or lessee of the cancellation, and at that point all remaining obligations of the seller or lessor are discharged. The buyer or lessee is not discharged from all remaining obligations, however; he or she is in breach, and the seller or lessor can pursue remedies available under the UCC for breach.

The Right to Withhold Delivery. In general, sellers and lessors can withhold or discontinue performance of their obligations under sales or lease contracts when the buyers or lessees are in breach. If a buyer or lessee has wrongfully rejected or revoked acceptance of contract goods (rejection and revocation of acceptance will be discussed later), failed to make proper and timely payment, or repudiated a part of the contract, the seller or lessor can withhold delivery of

---

[7] This doctrine was first enunciated in an English case decided in 1853, *Hochster v. De La Tour,* 2 Ellis and Blackburn Reports 678 (1853).

the goods in question [UCC 2–703(a), 2A–523(1)(c)]. If the breach results from the buyer's or the lessee's insolvency (inability to pay debts as they become due), the seller or lessor can refuse to deliver the goods unless the buyer or lessee pays in cash [UCC 2–702(1), 2A–525(1)].

The Right to Resell or Dispose of the Goods. When a buyer or lessee breaches or repudiates a sales contract while the seller or lessor is still in possession of the goods, the seller or lessor can resell or dispose of the goods. The seller can retain any profits made as a result of the sale and can hold the buyer or lessee liable for any loss [UCC 2–703(d), 2–706(1), 2A–523(1)(e), 2A–527(1)].[8]

When the goods contracted for are unfinished at the time of breach, the seller or lessor can do one of two things: (1) cease manufacturing the goods and resell them for scrap or salvage value or (2) complete the manufacture and resell or dispose of them, holding the buyer or lessee liable for any deficiency. In choosing between these two alternatives, the seller or lessor must exercise reasonable commercial judgment to mitigate the loss and obtain maximum value from the unfinished goods [UCC 2–704(2), 2A–524(2)]. Any resale of the goods must be made in good faith and in a commercially reasonable manner.

In sales transactions, the seller can recover any deficiency between the resale price and the contract price, along with **incidental damages**, defined as those costs to the seller resulting from the breach [UCC 2–706(1), 2–710]. The resale can be private or public, and the goods can be sold as a unit or in parcels. The seller must give the original buyer reasonable notice of the resale, unless the goods are perishable or will rapidly decline in value [UCC 2–706(2), (3)]. A good faith purchaser in a resale takes the goods free of any of the rights of the original buyer, even if the seller fails to comply with these requirements of the UCC [UCC 2–706(5)].

In lease transactions, the lessor may lease the goods to another party and recover from the original lessee, as damages, any unpaid lease payments up to the beginning date of the lease term under the new lease. The lessor can also recover any deficiency between the lease payments due

under the original lease contract and under the new lease contract, along with incidental damages [UCC 2A–527(2)].

The Right to Recover the Purchase Price or the Lease Payments Due. Under the UCC, an unpaid seller or lessor can bring an action to recover the purchase price or payments due under the lease contract, plus incidental damages, if the seller or lessor is unable to resell or dispose of the goods [UCC 2–709(1), 2A–529(1)].

● **EXAMPLE #9** Suppose that Southern Realty contracts with Gem Point, Inc., to purchase one thousand pens with Southern Realty's name inscribed on them. Gem Point tenders delivery of the one thousand pens, but Southern Realty wrongfully refuses to accept them. In this situation, Gem Point has, as a proper remedy, an action for the purchase price. Gem Point tendered delivery of conforming goods, and Southern Realty, by failing to accept the goods, is in breach. Gem Point obviously cannot sell to anyone else the pens inscribed with the buyer's business name, so this situation falls under UCC 2–709. ●

If a seller or lessor is unable to resell or dispose of goods and sues for the contract price or lease payments due, the goods must be held for the buyer or lessee. The seller or lessor can resell or dispose of the goods at any time prior to collection (of the judgment) from the buyer or lessee, but the net proceeds from the sale must be credited to the buyer or lessee. This is an example of the duty to mitigate damages.

The Right to Recover Damages. If a buyer or lessee repudiates a contract or wrongfully refuses to accept the goods, a seller or lessor can maintain an action to recover the damages that were sustained. Ordinarily, the amount of damages equals the difference between the contract price or lease payments and the market price or lease payments (at the time and place of tender of the goods), plus incidental damages [UCC 2–708(1), 2A–528(1)]. The time and place of tender are frequently given by such terms as F.O.B., F.A.S., C.I.F., and the like, which determine whether there is a shipment or destination contract (see Chapter 15).

WHEN THE GOODS ARE IN TRANSIT

If the seller or lessor has delivered the goods to a carrier or a bailee but the buyer or lessee has not as yet received them, the goods are said to be in transit. If, while the goods are in transit, the seller or lessor learns that the buyer or lessee is insolvent, the seller or lessor can stop the carrier or bailee from delivering the goods, regardless of the quantity of goods shipped.

● **EXAMPLE #10** Suppose that Alvin Johnson orders a truckload of lumber from Timber Products, Inc., to be

---

[8] Under the 2003 amendments to UCC Articles 2 and 2A, this loss includes consequential damages, except that a seller or lessor cannot recover consequential damages from a consumer under a consumer contract or lease [Amended UCC 2–706(1), 2–710, 2A–527(2), 2A–530]. Consequential damages may also be recovered, except from a consumer under a consumer contract or lease, when a seller or lessor has a right to recover the purchase price or lease payments due or to recover other damages [Amended UCC 2–708(1), 2–709(1), 2–710, 2A–528(1), 2A–529(1), 2A–530]. Subtracted from these amounts, of course, would be any expenses saved as a consequence of the buyer's or lessee's breach.

shipped to Johnson six weeks later. Johnson, who owes Timber Products for a past shipment, promises to pay the debt immediately and to pay for the current shipment as soon as it is received. After the lumber has been shipped to Johnson, Timber Products learns that Johnson has filed a petition in bankruptcy and listed Timber Products as one of his creditors (see Chapter 21). If the goods are still in transit, Timber Products can stop the carrier from delivering the lumber to Johnson.● If the buyer or lessee is in breach but is not insolvent, the seller or lessor can stop the goods in transit only if the quantity shipped is at least a carload, a truckload, a planeload, or a larger shipment [UCC 2–705(1), 2A–526(1)].[9]

To stop delivery, the seller or lessor must *timely notify* the carrier or other bailee that the goods are to be returned or held for the seller or lessor. If the carrier has sufficient time to stop delivery, the goods must be held and delivered according to the instructions of the seller or lessor, who is liable to the carrier for any additional costs incurred [UCC 2–705(3), 2A–526(3)].

UCC 2–705(2) and 2A–526(2) provide that the right of the seller or lessor to stop delivery of goods in transit is lost when any of the following events occur:

①　The buyer or lessee obtains possession of the goods.

②　The carrier acknowledges the rights of the buyer or lessee by reshipping or storing the goods for the buyer or lessee.

③　A bailee of the goods other than a carrier acknowledges that he or she is holding the goods for the buyer or lessee.

Additionally, in sales transactions, the seller loses the right to stop delivery of goods in transit when a negotiable document of title covering the goods has been negotiated (properly transferred, giving the buyer ownership rights in the goods) to the buyer [UCC 2–705(2)].

Once the seller or lessor reclaims the goods in transit, she or he can pursue the remedies allowed to sellers and lessors when the goods are in their possession. In other words, the seller or lessor who has reclaimed goods may do the following:

①　Cancel (rescind) the contract.

②　Resell the goods and recover any deficiency.

③　Sue for any deficiency between the contract price (or lease payments due) and the market price (or market lease payments), plus incidental damages.

④　Sue to recover the purchase price or lease payments due if the goods cannot be resold, plus incidental damages.

⑤　Sue to recover damages.

WHEN THE GOODS ARE IN THE POSSESSION OF THE BUYER OR LESSEE

When the buyer or lessee breaches a sales or lease contract and the goods are in the buyer's or lessee's possession, the UCC gives the seller or lessor the following limited remedies.

The Right to Recover the Purchase Price or Payments Due under the Lease Contract. If the buyer or lessee has accepted the goods but refuses to pay for them, the seller or lessor can sue for the purchase price of the goods or for the lease payments due, plus incidental damages [UCC 2–709(1), 2A–529(1)].

The Right to Reclaim the Goods. In regard to sales contracts, if a seller discovers that the buyer has received goods on credit and is insolvent, the seller can demand return of the goods, if the demand is made within ten days of the buyer's receipt of the goods. The seller can demand and reclaim the goods at any time if the buyer misrepresented his or her solvency in writing within three months prior to the delivery of the goods [UCC 2–702(2)].[10] The seller's right to reclaim the goods, however, is subject to the rights of a good faith purchaser or other subsequent buyer in the ordinary course of business who purchases the goods from the buyer before the seller reclaims.

Under the UCC, a seller seeking to exercise the right to reclaim goods receives preferential treatment over the buyer's other creditors—the seller need only demand the return of the goods within ten days after the buyer has received them.[11] Because of this preferential treatment, the UCC provides that reclamation *bars* the seller from pursuing any other remedy as to these goods [UCC 2–702(3)].

In regard to lease contracts, if the lessee is in default (fails to make payments that are due, for example), the lessor may reclaim the leased goods that are in the possession of the lessee [UCC 2A–525(2)].

Remedies of the Buyer or Lessee

Under the UCC, numerous remedies are available to the buyer or lessee when the seller or lessor breaches the con-

---

[9] The 2003 amendments to UCC Articles 2 and 2A omit the restriction that prohibited the stoppage of less than "a carload, truckload, planeload, or larger shipments" because carriers can now identify a shipment as small as a single package [Amended UCC 2–705(1), 2A–526(1)].

[10] One of the 2003 amendments to UCC Article 2 omits the ten-day limitation and the three-month exception to the ten-day limitation, referring instead to "a reasonable time" [Amended UCC 2–702(2)].

[11] A seller who has delivered goods to an insolvent buyer also receives preferential treatment if the buyer enters into bankruptcy proceedings (discussed in Chapter 21).

tract. As with the remedies available to sellers and lessors, the remedies of buyers and lessees depend on the circumstances existing at the time of the breach.

WHEN THE SELLER OR LESSOR REFUSES TO DELIVER THE GOODS

If the seller or lessor refuses to deliver the goods or the buyer or lessee has rejected the goods, the remedies available to the buyer or lessee include those discussed here.

The Right to Cancel the Contract. When a seller or lessor fails to make proper delivery or repudiates the contract, the buyer or lessee can cancel, or rescind, the contract. On notice of cancellation, the buyer or lessee is relieved of any further obligations under the contract but retains all rights to other remedies against the seller [UCC 2–711(1), 2A–508(1)(a)].

The Right to Recover the Goods. If a buyer or lessee has made a partial or full payment for goods that remain in the possession of the seller or lessor, the buyer or lessee can recover the goods if the seller or lessor is insolvent or becomes insolvent within ten days after receiving the first payment and if the goods are identified to the contract. To exercise this right, the buyer or lessee must tender to the seller any unpaid balance of the purchase price [UCC 2–502, 2A–522].[12]

The Right to Obtain Specific Performance. A buyer or lessee can obtain specific performance when the goods are unique and the remedy at law is inadequate [UCC 2–716(1), 2A–521(1)]. Ordinarily, a successful suit for money damages is sufficient to place a buyer or lessee in the position he or she would have occupied if the seller or lessor had fully performed. When the contract is for the purchase of a particular work of art or a similarly unique item, however, money damages may not be sufficient. Under these circumstances, equity will require that the seller or lessor perform exactly by delivering the particular goods identified to the contract (the remedy of specific performance).

The Right of Cover. In certain situations, buyers and lessees can protect themselves by obtaining **cover**—that is, by purchasing other goods to substitute for those that were due under the sales contract. This option is available when the seller or lessor repudiates the contract or fails to deliver

the goods, or when a buyer or lessee has rightfully rejected goods or revoked acceptance.

In obtaining cover, the buyer or lessee must act in good faith and without unreasonable delay [UCC 2–712, 2A–518]. After purchasing or leasing substitute goods, the buyer or lessee can recover from the seller or lessor the difference between the cost of cover and the contract price (or lease payments), plus incidental and consequential damages, less the expenses (such as delivery costs) that were saved as a result of the breach [UCC 2–712, 2–715, 2A–518]. Consequential damages are any losses suffered by the buyer or lessee that the seller or lessor could have foreseen (had reason to know about) at the time of contract formation and any injury to the buyer's or lessee's person or property proximately resulting from the contract's breach [UCC 2–715(2), 2A–520(2)].

Buyers and lessees are not required to cover, and failure to do so will not bar them from using any other remedies available under the UCC. A buyer or lessee who fails to cover, however, may *not* be able to collect consequential damages that could have been avoided had he or she purchased or leased substitute goods.

The Right to Replevy Goods. Buyers and lessees also have the right to replevy goods. **Replevin**[13] is an action to recover specific goods in the hands of a party who is wrongfully withholding them from the other party. Outside the UCC, the term *replevin* refers to a *prejudgment process* (a proceeding that takes place prior to a court's judgment) that permits the seizure of specific personal property in which a party claims a right or an interest. Under the UCC, the buyer or lessee can replevy goods subject to the contract if the seller or lessor has repudiated or breached the contract. To maintain an action to replevy goods, usually buyers and lessees must show that they are unable to cover for the goods after a reasonable effort [UCC 2–716(3), 2A–521(3)].

The Right to Recover Damages. If a seller or lessor repudiates the sales contract or fails to deliver the goods, or the buyer or lessee has rightfully rejected or revoked acceptance of the goods, the buyer or lessee can sue for damages. The measure of recovery is the difference between the contract price (or lease payments) and the market price of (or lease payments that could be obtained for) the goods at the time the buyer (or lessee) *learned* of the breach.[14] The

---

[12] The 2003 amendments to UCC Articles 2 and 2A create a new right to recover goods identified to a contract when a consumer buyer or lessee makes a down payment and the seller or lessor then repudiates the contract or lease or fails to deliver the goods [Amended UCC 2–502(1)(a), 2A–522].

[13] Pronounced ruh-*pleh*-vun.

[14] One of the 2003 amendments to UCC Article 2 changes the rule that the time for measuring damages is the time that the buyer learned of the breach. In a case not involving repudiation, the buyer's damages are to be based on the market price at the time for tender [Amended UCC 2–713(1)(a)].

market price or market lease payments are determined at the place where the seller or lessor was supposed to deliver the goods. The buyer or lessee can also recover incidental and consequential damages, less the expenses that were saved as a result of the breach [UCC 2–713, 2A–519].

● **EXAMPLE #11** Schilling orders ten thousand bushels of wheat from Valdone for $5 a bushel, with delivery due on June 14 and payment due on June 20. Valdone does not deliver on June 14. On June 14, the market price of wheat is $5.50 per bushel. Schilling chooses to do without the wheat. He sues Valdone for damages for nondelivery. Schilling can recover $0.50 × 10,000, or $5,000, plus any expenses the breach may have caused him. The measure of damages is the market price less the contract price on the day Schilling was to have received delivery. (Any expenses Schilling saved by the breach would be deducted from the damages.) ●

WHEN THE SELLER OR LESSOR DELIVERS NONCONFORMING GOODS

When the seller or lessor delivers nonconforming goods, the buyer or lessee has several remedies available under the UCC.

The Right to Reject the Goods. If either the goods or the tender of the goods by the seller or lessor fails to conform to the contract *in any respect*, the buyer or lessee can reject the goods. If some of the goods conform to the contract, the buyer or lessee can keep the conforming goods and reject the rest [UCC 2–601, 2A–509]. If the buyer or lessee rejects the goods, she or he may then obtain cover, cancel the contract, or sue for damages for breach of contract, just as if the seller or lessor had refused to deliver the goods (see the earlier discussion of these remedies).

Whether a buyer's actions constituted a rejection of the goods was at issue in the following case.

CASE 16.3   **China National Metal Products Import/Export Co. v. Apex Digital, Inc.**

United States District Court,
Central District of California, 2001.
141 F.Supp.2d 1013.
http://cisgw3.law.pace.edu[a]

FACTS Apex Digital, Inc., imports consumer electronic goods and distributes them under the "Apex Digital" brand name to national retailers, such as Circuit City Stores, Inc., Best Buy Company, and Kmart Corporation. Apex is based in California. China National Metal Products Import/Export Company is a corporation based in Beijing, China. China National facilitates the import and export of goods between Chinese and foreign companies. Between July and December 2000, Apex imported more than 300,000 DVD players under several contracts with Chinese companies through China National. Soon after selling the first shipment of players in July and August, Apex began receiving customer complaints about the quality, and a flood of returned players began to fill Apex's warehouse. Apex continued to order the players through China National and sell them to retail outlet chains, but Apex refused to pay for them. The parties submitted their dispute to arbitration. Meanwhile, China National filed a suit in a California state court against Apex to obtain a writ of attachment (an order to seize Apex's property to secure payment for the DVD players). Apex claimed in part

that it was not liable under the contracts because it had rejected the goods by withholding payment for them.

ISSUE Did Apex's withholding of payment for the DVD players constitute rejection of the goods, as allowed under the UCC?

DECISION No. The court granted China National's request for a writ of attachment in an amount of more than $18 million.[b]

REASON The court acknowledged that if Apex had rejected the DVD players, "Apex would have been relieved of its duty to pay for the goods." The court noted that "[t]here can be little doubt in this case that China National failed to deliver conforming goods. Whether it was loader doors falling off or the failure to play DVD movies or the pause function self-activating, many of the DVD players delivered by China National were more useful as doorstops, or as one creative consumer noted, as boat anchors, than as players of multimedia disks and files. These defects provided Apex with the option to reject the contract or contracts affected by the nonconformities or to reject the particular units containing those defects." The court added, however, that buyers can accept nonconforming goods. "Indeed, if the buyer does nothing after receiving goods it learns are nonconforming, the law deems him to have accepted those goods. * * * Once the nonconforming goods are accepted, the buyer is under a duty to pay for them." In this case, "despite knowing of [the

---

a. Under "Cases on the CISG," click on "Search form for cases of interest." Type "Apex" into one of the "Term" fields and click on "Submit Query." The resulting page contains a link to the case, plus commentary. This site is maintained by the Institute of International Commercial Law at the Pace Law School.

b. This total represented the amount of the outstanding invoices under the contracts for the delivered DVD players, minus the contract value of the players that Apex returned.

CASE 16.3—Continued

players'] defects Apex continued and, in fact, accelerated the number of DVD players it ordered from China National and then sold to its retail distributors."

FOR CRITICAL ANALYSIS—Social Consideration
Can a buyer successfully argue that, by continuing to order and sell goods pursuant to a contract, it was only trying to mitigate damages and that it refused to pay for the goods only when selling them proved unsuccessful?

Timeliness and Reason for Rejection Required. The buyer or lessee must reject the goods within a reasonable amount of time, and the seller or lessor must be notified seasonably—that is, in a timely fashion or at the proper time [UCC 2–602(1), 2A–509(2)]. If the buyer or lessee fails to reject the goods within a reasonable amount of time, acceptance will be presumed. Furthermore, the buyer or lessee must designate defects that would have been apparent to the seller or lessor on reasonable inspection. Failure to do so precludes the buyer or lessee from using such defects to justify rejection or to establish breach when the seller could have cured the defects if they had been stated seasonably [UCC 2–605, 2A–514].[15]

Duties of Merchant Buyers and Lessees When Goods Are Rejected. If a merchant buyer or lessee rightfully rejects goods, and the seller or lessor has no agent or business at the place of rejection, the buyer or lessee is required to follow any reasonable instructions received from the seller or lessor with respect to the goods controlled by the buyer or lessee. The buyer or lessee is entitled to reimbursement for the care and cost entailed in following the instructions [UCC 2–603, 2A–511]. The same requirements hold if the buyer or lessee rightfully revokes his or her acceptance of the goods at some later time [UCC 2–608(3), 2A–517(5)]. (Revocation of acceptance will be discussed shortly.)

If no instructions are forthcoming and the goods are perishable or threaten to decline in value quickly, the buyer can resell the goods in good faith, taking the appropriate reimbursement from the proceeds. In addition, the buyer is entitled to a selling commission (not to exceed 10 percent of the gross proceeds) [UCC 2–603(1), (2); 2A–511(1)]. If the goods are not perishable, the buyer or lessee may store them for the seller or lessor or reship them to the seller or lessor [UCC 2–604, 2A–512].[16]

Buyers who rightfully reject goods that remain in their possession or control have a *security interest* in the goods (basically, a legal claim to the goods to the extent necessary to recover expenses, costs, and the like—see Chapter 20). The security interest encompasses any payments the buyer has made for the goods, as well as any expenses incurred with regard to inspection, receipt, transportation, care, and custody of the goods [UCC 2–711(3)]. A buyer with a security interest in the goods is a "person in the position of a seller." This gives the buyer the same rights as an unpaid seller. Thus, the buyer can resell, withhold delivery of, or stop delivery of the goods. A buyer who chooses to resell must account to the seller for any amounts received in excess of the security interest [UCC 2–706(6), 2–711].

Revocation of Acceptance. Acceptance of the goods precludes the buyer or lessee from exercising the right of rejection, but it does not necessarily preclude the buyer or lessee from pursuing other remedies. In certain circumstances, a buyer or lessee is permitted to *revoke* his or her acceptance of the goods. Acceptance of a lot or a commercial unit can be revoked if the nonconformity *substantially* impairs the value of the lot or unit and if one of the following factors is present:

① If acceptance was predicated on the reasonable assumption that the nonconformity would be cured, and it has not been cured within a reasonable period of time [UCC 2–608(1)(a), 2A–517(1)(a)].[17]

② If the buyer or lessee did not discover the nonconformity before acceptance, either because it was difficult to discover before acceptance or because assurances made by the seller or lessor that the goods were conforming kept the buyer or lessee from inspecting the goods [UCC 2–608(1)(b), 2A–517(1)(b)].

Revocation of acceptance is not effective until notice is given to the seller or lessor, which must occur within a reasonable time after the buyer or lessee either discovers or *should have discovered* the grounds for revocation. Additionally, revocation must occur before the goods have undergone any substantial change (such as spoilage) not caused by their own defects [UCC 2–608(2), 2A–517(4)].

---

[15] As noted earlier in this chapter, amendments to UCC 2–605 and 2A–514 change this restriction. Under the 2003 amendments, a buyer's or lessee's failure to disclose the nature of the defect affects only the right to reject or revoke acceptance, not the right to establish a breach. The new sections expressly require that the seller or lessor have had a right to cure, as well as the ability to cure. Also, those sections extend to include not only rejection but revocation of acceptance.

[16] Under the 2003 amendments to UCC 2–608(4) and 2A–517(6), use of the goods by the buyer or lessee following rejection or revocation of acceptance is not wrongful if the use is reasonable in the circumstances, as it would be, for example, in an attempt to mitigate damages. Of course, the buyer or lessee must compensate the seller or lessor for the value of the use.

[17] Under the 2003 amendments to UCC 2–508 and 2A–513, cure after a justifiable revocation of acceptance is not available as a matter of right in a consumer contract or lease.

The Right to Recover Damages for Accepted Goods. A buyer or lessee who has accepted nonconforming goods may also keep the goods and recover damages caused by the breach. The buyer or lessee, however, must notify the seller or lessor of the breach within a reasonable time after the defect was or should have been discovered. Failure to give notice of the defects (breach) to the seller or lessor bars the buyer or lessee from pursuing any remedy [UCC 2–607(3), 2A–516(3)].[18] In addition, the parties to a sales or lease contract can insert a provision requiring that the buyer or lessee give notice of any defects in the goods within a prescribed period.

When the goods delivered and accepted are not as promised, the measure of damages equals the difference between the value of the goods as accepted and their value if they had been delivered as promised [UCC 2–714(2), 2A–519(4)]. For this and other types of breaches in which the buyer or lessee has accepted the goods, the buyer or lessee is entitled to recover for any loss "resulting in the ordinary course of events . . . as determined in any manner which is reasonable" [UCC 2–714(1), 2A–519(3)]. The UCC also permits the buyer or lessee, with proper notice to the seller or lessor, to deduct all or any part of the damages from the price or lease payments still due and payable to the seller or lessor [UCC 2–717, 2A–516(1)].

Who qualifies as a "buyer" under these provisions? Is a party who does not actually purchase a product but who is injured by its alleged defects required to give notice of those defects within a reasonable time in order to recover for those injuries? This was an important question in the following case.

---

[18] Under the 2003 amendments to UCC Articles 2 and 2A, failure to give timely notice bars the buyer or lessee from recovery for the breach only to the extent that the seller or lessor is prejudiced by the failure. For example, a buyer or lessee will be barred from the recovery of damages if the failure to notify was material and implementing the bar will not be disproportionate to the harm [Amended UCC 2–607(3)(a), 2A–516(3)(a)].

CASE 16.4 **Yates v. Pitman Manufacturing, Inc.**

Supreme Court of Virginia, 1999.
257 Va. 601,
514 S.E.2d 605.
http://www.courts.state.va.us/opin.htm[a]

FACTS In 1982, Pitman Manufacturing, Inc., made and sold a construction crane to Shelton Witt Equipment, a distributor. At the time, Pitman certified that the outrigger on the crane could be seen from its "actuating location"—that is, it could be seen by anyone activating the outrigger. In 1991, Koch Carbon owned the crane and was using it to deliver equipment to Baldwin Coal Corporation. Ira Stiltner, a Koch employee, activated the outrigger from the front of the truck. At the time, he could not see the outrigger or Eddie Yates, a Baldwin employee, who was simultaneously releasing restraining chains from the crane truck's bed. Without warning, the outrigger dropped onto Yates's foot. Yates filed a suit in a Virginia state court against Pitman, seeking $3 million in damages for his injuries on the basis of breach of warranty (see Chapter 17). One of the issues was whether Yates had provided reasonable notice, under UCC 2–607(3), to Pitman of its breach of warranty. Yates argued in part that he did not

have to give the notice because he was not the purchaser of the crane. The court entered a judgment in Pitman's favor. Yates appealed to the Virginia Supreme Court.

ISSUE Was Yates required to give notice under UCC 2–607(3) to recover for his injuries?

DECISION No. The Virginia Supreme Court reversed the judgment of the lower court and remanded the case for further proceedings consistent with this decision.

REASON The state supreme court held that "only buyers * * * must give notice of breach of warranty to the seller as a prerequisite to recovery" under UCC 2–607(3). Thus, Yates, because he was not a "buyer," did not have to give the notice to recover for his injuries. The court explained, "It is firmly established that, when a statute is clear and unambiguous, a court must accept its plain meaning and not resort to extrinsic evidence or rules of construction." The statute in this case "is unambiguous and clearly states that 'the buyer must * * * notify the seller of [the] breach.' Thus, accepting the statute's plain meaning, it is apparent that the notice of breach is required from the 'buyer' of the goods. In the present case, Yates was not the buyer of the crane unit."

FOR CRITICAL ANALYSIS—Social Consideration
Suppose that the court had held that Yates was required to give notice to recover for his injuries. Would such a ruling have left Yates entirely without legal recourse? Explain.

---

a. In the "Supreme Court of Virginia" section, click on the version in which you want to read this opinion. To view the opinion in text format, click on "Opinions in Text Format." On that page, scroll down the list of cases to the *Yates* case and click on the docket number ("981474") to access the opinion.

Limitation of Remedies

The parties to a sales or lease contract can vary their respective rights and obligations by contractual agreement. For example, a seller and buyer can expressly provide for remedies in addition to those furnished in the UCC. They can also provide for remedies in lieu of those provided in the UCC, or they can change the measure of damages. The seller can provide that the buyer's only remedy on breach of warranty will be repair or replacement of the item, or the seller can limit the buyer's remedy to return of the goods and refund of the purchase price. In sales and lease contracts, an agreed-on remedy is in addition to those provided in the UCC unless the parties expressly agree that the remedy is exclusive of all others [UCC 2–719(1), 2A–503(1)].

If the parties state that a remedy is exclusive, then it is the sole remedy. When circumstances cause an exclusive remedy to fail in its essential purpose, however, it is no longer exclusive [UCC 2–719(2), 2A–503(2)]. For example, a sales contract that limits the buyer's remedy to repair or replacement fails in its essential purpose if the item cannot be repaired and no replacements are available.

A contract can limit or exclude consequential damages, provided the limitation is not unconscionable. When the buyer or lessee is a consumer, the limitation of consequential damages for personal injuries resulting from nonconforming goods is *prima facie* (on its face) unconscionable. The limitation of consequential damages is not necessarily unconscionable, however, when the loss is commercial in nature—for example, if the loss consists of lost profits and property damage [UCC 2–719(3), 2A–503(3)].

Statute of Limitations

An action for breach of contract under the UCC must be commenced *within four years after the cause of action accrues*—that is, within four years after the breach occurs. In addition to filing suit within the four-year period, an aggrieved party who has accepted nonconforming goods usually must notify the breaching party of the breach within a reasonable time, or the buyer or lessee is barred from pursuing any remedy [UCC 2–607(3)(a), 2A–516(3)]. By agreement in the contract, the parties can reduce this period to not less than one year but cannot extend it beyond four years [UCC 2–725(1), 2A–506(1)]. A cause of action accrues for breach of warranty when the seller or lessor tenders delivery. This is the rule even if the aggrieved party is unaware that the cause of action has accrued [UCC 2–725(2), 2A–506(2)].

Terms and Concepts

cover 311	installment contract 304	replevin 311
incidental damages 309		

Chapter Summary   Performance and Breach of Sales and Lease Contracts

REQUIREMENTS OF PERFORMANCE	
Obligations of the Seller or Lessor (See pages 301–307.)	1. The seller or lessor must tender *conforming* goods to the buyer. Tender must take place at a *reasonable hour* and in a *reasonable manner.* Under the perfect tender doctrine, the seller or lessor must tender goods that conform exactly to the terms of the contract [UCC 2–503(1), 2A–508(1)].
	2. If the seller or lessor tenders nonconforming goods prior to the performance date and the buyer or lessee rejects them, the seller or lessor may *cure* (repair or replace the goods) within the contract time for performance [UCC 2–508(1), 2A–513(1)]. If the seller or lessor has reasonable grounds to believe the buyer or lessee would accept the tendered goods, on the buyer's or lessee's rejection the seller or lessor has a reasonable time to substitute conforming goods without liability [UCC 2–508(2), 2A–513(2)].
	3. If the agreed-on means of delivery becomes impracticable or unavailable, the seller must substitute an alternative means (such as a different carrier) if one is available [UCC 2–614(1)].

(Continued)

Chapter Summary	**Performance and Breach of Sales and Lease Contracts—Continued**
Obligations of the Seller or Lessor—continued	4. If a seller or lessor tenders nonconforming goods in any one installment under an installment contract, the buyer or lessee may reject the installment only if its value is substantially impaired and cannot be cured. The entire installment contract is breached when one or more nonconforming installments *substantially* impair the value of the *whole* contract [UCC 2–612, 2A–510].
	5. When performance becomes commercially impracticable owing to circumstances unforeseen when the contract was formed, the perfect tender rule no longer holds [UCC 2–615, 2A–405].
Obligations of the Buyer or Lessee (See pages 307–308.)	1. On tender of delivery by the seller or lessor, the buyer or lessee must pay for the goods at the time and place the buyer or lessee *receives* the goods, even if the place of shipment is the place of delivery, unless the sale is made on credit. Payment may be made by any method generally acceptable in the commercial world unless the seller demands cash [UCC 2–310, 2–511]. In lease contracts, the lessee must make lease payments in accordance with the contract [UCC 2A–516(1)].
	2. Unless otherwise agreed, the buyer or lessee has an absolute right to inspect the goods before acceptance [UCC 2–513(1), 2A–515(1)].
	3. The buyer or lessee can manifest acceptance of delivered goods expressly in words or by conduct or by failing to reject the goods after a reasonable period of time following inspection or after having had a reasonable opportunity to inspect them [UCC 2–606(1), 2A–515(1)]. A buyer will be deemed to have accepted goods if he or she performs any act inconsistent with the seller's ownership [UCC 2–606(1)(c)].
	4. Following the acceptance of delivered goods, the buyer or lessee may revoke acceptance only if the nonconformity *substantially* impairs the value of the unit or lot and if one of the following factors is present:
	a. Acceptance was predicated on the reasonable assumption that the nonconformity would be cured and it was not cured within a reasonable time [UCC 2–608(1)(a), 2A–517(1)(a)].
	b. The buyer or lessee did not discover the nonconformity before acceptance, either because it was difficult to discover before acceptance or because the seller's or lessor's assurance that the goods were conforming kept the buyer or lessee from inspecting the goods [UCC 2–608(1)(b), 2A–517(1)(b)].
Anticipatory Repudiation (See page 308.)	If, before the time for performance, either party clearly indicates to the other an intention not to perform, under UCC 2–610 and 2A–402 the aggrieved party may do the following:
	1. Await performance by the repudiating party for a commercially reasonable time.
	2. Resort to any remedy for breach.
	3. In either situation, suspend performance.
REMEDIES FOR BREACH OF CONTRACT	
Remedies of the Seller or Lessor (See pages 308–310.)	1. *When the goods are in the possession of the seller or lessor*—The seller or lessor may do the following:
	a. Cancel the contract [UCC 2–703(f), 2A–523(1)(a)].
	b. Withhold delivery [UCC 2–703(a), 2A–523(1)(c)].
	c. Resell or dispose of the goods [UCC 2–703(d), 2–706(1), 2A–523(1)(e), 2A–527(1)].
	d. Sue to recover the purchase price or lease payments due [UCC 2–709(1), 2A–529(1)].
	e. Sue to recover damages [UCC 2–708, 2A–528].

Chapter Summary	Performance and Breach of Sales and Lease Contracts—Continued

Remedies of the Seller or Lessor—continued	2. *When the goods are in transit*—The seller may stop the carrier or bailee from delivering the goods [UCC 2–705, 2A–526].
	
	3. *When the goods are in the possession of the buyer or lessee*—The seller may do the following:
	
	  a. Sue to recover the purchase price or lease payments due [UCC 2–709(1), 2A–529(1)].
	
	  b. Reclaim the goods. A seller may reclaim goods received by an insolvent buyer if the demand is made within ten days of receipt (reclaiming goods excludes all other remedies) [UCC 2–702]; a lessor may repossess goods if the lessee is in default [UCC 2A–525(2)].

Remedies of the Buyer or Lessee
(See pages 310–314.)
	1. *When the seller or lessor refuses to deliver the goods*—The buyer or lessee may do the following:
	
	  a. Cancel the contract [UCC 2–711(1), 2A–508(1)(a)].
	
	  b. Recover the goods if the seller or lessor becomes insolvent within ten days after receiving the first payment and the goods are identified to the contract [UCC 2–502, 2A–522].
	
	  c. Obtain specific performance (when the goods are unique and when the remedy at law is inadequate) [UCC 2–716(1), 2A–521(1)].
	
	  d. Obtain cover [UCC 2–712, 2A–518].
	
	  e. Replevy the goods (if cover is unavailable) [UCC 2–716(3), 2A–521(3)].
	
	  f. Sue to recover damages [UCC 2–713, 2A–519].
	
	2. *When the seller or lessor delivers or tenders delivery of nonconforming goods*—The buyer or lessee may do the following:
	
	  a. Reject the goods [UCC 2–601, 2A–509].
	
	  b. Revoke acceptance (in certain circumstances) [UCC 2–608, 2A–517].
	
	  c. Accept the goods and recover damages [UCC 2–607, 2–714, 2–717, 2A–519].

Limitation of Remedies (See page 315.)	Remedies may be limited in sales or lease contracts by agreement of the parties. If the contract states that a remedy is exclusive, then that is the sole remedy—unless the remedy fails in its essential purpose. Sellers and lessors can also limit the rights of buyers and lessees to consequential damages—unless the limitation is unconscionable [UCC 2–719, 2A–503].
Statute of Limitations (See page 315.)	The UCC has a four-year statute of limitations for actions involving breach of contract. By agreement, the parties to a sales or lease contract can reduce this period to not less than one year, but they cannot extend it beyond four years [UCC 2–725(1), 2A–506(1)].

For Review

① What are the respective obligations of the parties under a contract for the sale or lease of goods?

② What is the perfect tender rule? What are some important exceptions to this rule that apply to sales and lease contracts?

③ What options are available to the nonbreaching party when the other party to a sales or lease contract repudiates the contract prior to the time for performance?

④ What remedies are available to a seller or lessor when the buyer or lessee breaches the contract? What remedies are available to a buyer or lessee if the seller or lessor breaches the contract?

⑤ In contracts subject to the UCC, are parties free to limit the remedies available to the nonbreaching party on a breach of contract? If so, in what ways?

Questions and Case Problems

16–1. Revocation of Acceptance. What events or circumstances must occur before a buyer can rightfully revoke his or her acceptance of a sales contract?

16–2. Remedies. Genix, Inc., has contracted to sell Larson five hundred washing machines of a certain model at list price. Genix is to ship the goods on or before December 1. Genix produces one thousand washing machines of this model but has not yet prepared Larson's shipment. On November 1, Larson repudiates the contract. Discuss the remedies available to Genix in this situation.

16–3. Right of Inspection. Cummings ordered two model X Super Fidelity speakers from Jamestown Wholesale Electronics, Inc. Jamestown shipped the speakers via United Parcel Service, C.O.D. (collect on delivery), although Cummings had not requested or agreed to a C.O.D. shipment of the goods. When the speakers were delivered, Cummings refused to accept them because he would not be able to inspect them before payment. Jamestown claimed that it had shipped conforming goods and that Cummings had breached their contract. Had Cummings breached the contract? Explain.

16–4. Anticipatory Repudiation. Moore contracted in writing to sell her 1996 Ford Taurus to Hammer for $8,500. Moore agreed to deliver the car on Wednesday, and Hammer promised to pay the $8,500 on the following Friday. On Tuesday, Hammer informed Moore that he would not be buying the car after all. By Friday, Hammer had changed his mind again and tendered $8,500 to Moore. Moore, although she had not sold the car to another party, refused the tender and refused to deliver. Hammer claimed that Moore had breached their contract. Moore contended that Hammer's repudiation released her from her duty to perform under the contract. Who is correct, and why?

16–5. Remedies. Rodriguez is an antique car collector. He contracts to purchase spare parts for a 1938 engine from Gerrard. These parts are not made anymore and are scarce. To get the contract with Gerrard, Rodriguez has to pay 50 percent of the purchase price in advance. On May 1, Rodriguez sends the required payment, which is received on May 2. On May 3, Gerrard, having found another buyer willing to pay substantially more for the parts, informs Rodriguez that he will not deliver as contracted. That same day, Rodriguez learns that Gerrard is insolvent. Gerrard has the parts, and Rodriguez wants them. Discuss fully any remedies available to Rodriguez.

16–6. Commercial Impracticability. E+E (US), Inc., Manley-Regan Chemicals Division, agreed to sell to Rockland Industries, Inc., three containers of antimony oxide for $1.80 per pound. At the time, both parties knew that there was a global shortage of the chemical, that prices were rising, and that Manley-Regan would obtain its supply from GFI Chemicals, Inc. When GFI could not deliver, Manley-Regan told Rockland that it could not fulfill the contract. Rockland bought an equivalent amount of the chemical elsewhere at an increased price and filed a suit in a federal district court against Manley-Regan to recover the difference between the cost of the cover and the contract price.

Manley-Regan argued that the failure of GFI, its sole source for the oxide, excused its failure to perform on the ground of commercial impracticability. Will the court agree? Why or why not? [*Rockland Industries, Inc. v. E+E (US), Inc., Manley-Regan Chemicals Division,* 991 F.Supp. 468 (D.Md. 1998)]

16–7. Acceptance. OSHI Global Co. designs and sells novelty items, including a small children's plastic toy referred to as the "Number 89 Frog," a realistic replica of a frog that squeaks when it is squeezed. At a trade show in Chicago, Michael Osaraprasop, the owner of OSHI, sold a quantity of the frogs to Jay Gilbert, the president of S.A.M. Electronics, Inc. Gilbert asked Osaraprasop to design, make, and sell to S.A.M. a larger version of the frog with a motion sensor that would activate a "ribbit" sound. Osaraprasop agreed. OSHI delivered fourteen containers of the frogs, a number of which S.A.M. resold to its customers. When some of the buyers complained that the frogs were defective, S.A.M. had them repaired. S.A.M. refused to pay OSHI for any of the frogs and wrote a letter claiming to revoke acceptance of them. S.A.M. filed a suit in a federal district court against OSHI and others, alleging in part breach of contract; OSHI responded with a similar claim against S.A.M. OSHI argued that by reselling some of the frogs from the fourteen containers, S.A.M. had accepted all of them and must pay. In whose favor will the court rule? Discuss fully. [*S.A.M. Electronics, Inc. v. Osaraprasop,* 39 F.Supp.2d 1074 (N.D.Ill. 1999)]

16–8. Limitation of Remedies. Destileria Serralles, Inc., a distributor of rum and other products, operates a rum bottling plant in Puerto Rico. Figgie International, Inc., contracted with Serralles to provide bottle-labeling equipment capable of placing a clear label on a clear bottle of "Cristal" rum within a raised glass oval. The contract stated that Serralles's remedy, in case of a breach of contract, was limited to repair, replacement, or refund. When the equipment was installed in the Serralles plant, problems arose immediately. Figgie attempted to repair the equipment, but when it still did not work properly several months later, Figgie refunded the purchase price and Serralles returned the equipment. Serralles asked Figgie to pay for Serralles's losses caused by the failure of the equipment and by the delay in obtaining alternative machinery. Figgie filed a suit in a federal district court, asserting that it owed nothing to Serralles because the remedy for breach was limited to repair, replacement, or refund. Serralles responded that the limitation had failed in its essential purpose. In whose favor will the court resolve this dispute? Why? [*Figgie International, Inc. v. Destileria Serralles, Inc.,* 190 F.3d 252 (4th Cir. 1999)]

CASE PROBLEM WITH SAMPLE ANSWER

16–9. Metro-North Commuter Railroad Co. decided to install a fall-protection system for elevated walkways, roof areas, and interior catwalks in Grand Central Terminal, in New York City. The system was needed to ensure the safety of Metro-North employees when they worked at great heights on the interior and exterior of the terminal. Sinco, Inc., proposed a system called "Sayfglida," which involved a harness worn by the worker, a network of cables, and metal clips or sleeves called "Sayflinks" that connected the harness to the cables. Metro-North agreed to pay $197,325 for the installation of this system by June 26, 1999. Because the system's reliability was crucial, the contract required certain quality control processes. During a training session for Metro-North employees on June 29, the Sayflink sleeves fell apart. Within two days, Sinco manufactured and delivered two different types of replacement clips without subjecting them to the contract's quality control process, but Metro-North rejected them. Sinco suggested other possible solutions, which Metro-North did not accept. In September, Metro-North terminated its contract with Sinco and awarded the work to Surety, Inc., at a price of about $348,000. Sinco filed a suit in a federal district court, alleging breach of contract. Metro-North counterclaimed for its cost of cover. In whose favor should the court rule, and why? [*Sinco, Inc. v. Metro-North Commuter Railroad Co.*, 133 F.Supp.2d 308 (S.D.N.Y. 2001)]

▶ To view a sample answer for this case problem, go to this book's Web site at **http://fundamentals.westbuslaw.com** and click on "Interactive Study Center."

16–10. Acceptance. In April 1996, Excalibur Oil Group, Inc., applied for credit and opened an account with Standard Distributors, Inc., to obtain snack foods and other items for Excalibur's convenience stores. For three months, Standard delivered the goods and Excalibur paid the invoices. In July, Standard was dissolved and its assets were distributed to J. F. Walker Co. Walker continued to deliver the goods to Excalibur, which continued to pay the invoices until November, when the firm began to experience financial difficulties. By January 1997, Excalibur owed Walker $54,241.77. Walker then dealt with Excalibur only on a collect-on-delivery basis until Excalibur's stores closed in 1998. Walker filed a suit in a Pennsylvania state court against Excalibur and its owner to recover amounts due on unpaid invoices. To successfully plead its case, Walker had to show that there was a contract between the parties. One question was whether Excalibur had manifested acceptance of the goods delivered by Walker. How does a buyer manifest acceptance? Was there an acceptance in this case? In whose favor should the court rule, and why? [*J. F. Walker Co. v. Excalibur Oil Group, Inc.*, 792 A.2d 1269 (Pa.Super. 2002)]

PERFORMANCE AND BREACH OF SALES AND LEASE CONTRACTS

For updated links to resources available on the Web, as well as other materials, visit this text's Web site at

http://fundamentals.westbuslaw.com

For an example of a warranty providing for an exclusive remedy, see the "Warranty and Limited Remedy" of 3M Company, which is online at

http://www.mmm.com/promote/warranty.htm

Online Legal Research

Go to the *Fundamentals of Business Law* home page at **http://fundamentals.westbuslaw. com**. Select "Interactive Study Center" and then click on "Chapter 16." There you will find the following Internet research exercises that you can perform to learn more about topics covered in this chapter.

Activity 16–1: LEGAL PERSPECTIVE—Good Faith and Fair Dealing
Activity 16–2: MANAGEMENT PERSPECTIVE—The Right to Reject Goods

Before the Test

Go to the *Fundamentals of Business Law* Web site at **http://fundamentals. westbuslaw.com**. Click on "Interactive Quizzes." You will find at least twenty interactive questions relating to this chapter.

Westlaw® Campus

If your textbook provided for a subscription to Westlaw® Campus, or if you have otherwise purchased access to the Westlaw Campus database, you can access any of the cases presented or cited in this chapter by using your Westlaw Campus account.

17 Warranties and Product Liability

CHAPTER OBJECTIVES

After reading this chapter, you should be able to answer the following questions:

① What factors determine whether a seller's or lessor's statement constitutes an express warranty or merely "puffing"?

② What implied warranties arise under the UCC?

③ Can a manufacturer be held liable to any person who suffers an injury proximately caused by the manufacturer's negligently made product?

④ What are the elements of a cause of action in strict product liability?

⑤ What defenses to liability can be raised in a product liability lawsuit?

Warranty is an age-old concept. In sales and lease law, a warranty is an assurance by one party of the existence of a fact on which the other party can rely. Sellers and lessors warrant to those who purchase or lease their goods that the goods are as represented or will be as promised.

The Uniform Commercial Code (UCC) has numerous rules governing the concept of product warranty as it occurs in sales and lease contracts. That will be the subject matter of the first part of this chapter. A natural addition to the discussion is *product liability:* Who is liable to consumers, users, and bystanders for physical harm and property damage caused by a particular good or the use thereof? Product liability encompasses the contract theory of war-

ranty, as well as the tort theories of negligence and strict liability (discussed in Chapter 4).

Warranties

Article 2 (on sales) and Article 2A (on leases) of the UCC designate several types of warranties that can arise in a sales or lease contract, including warranties of title, express warranties, and implied warranties.

WARRANTIES OF TITLE

Title warranty arises automatically in most sales contracts. The UCC imposes three types of warranties of title.

Good Title. In most cases, sellers warrant that they have good and valid title to the goods sold and that transfer of the title is rightful [UCC 2–312(1)(a)].[1] ● EXAMPLE #1 Sharon steals goods from Miguel and sells them to Carrie, who does not know that the goods are stolen. If Miguel reclaims the goods from Carrie, which he has a right to do, Carrie can then sue Sharon for breach of warranty. When Sharon sold Carrie the goods, Sharon *automatically* warranted to her that the title conveyed was valid and that its transfer was rightful. Because this was not in fact the case, Sharon breached the warranty of title imposed by UCC 2–312(1)(a) and became liable to the buyer for the appropriate damages. ●

No Liens. A second warranty of title provided by the UCC protects buyers who are *unaware* of any encumbrances (claims, charges, or liabilities—usually called **liens**[2]) against goods at the time the contract is made [UCC 2–312(1)(b)]. This warranty protects buyers who, for example, unknowingly purchase goods that are subject to a creditor's security interest (see Chapter 20). If a creditor legally repossesses the goods from a buyer *who had no actual knowledge of the security interest,* the buyer can recover from the seller for breach of warranty.

Article 2A affords similar protection for lessees. Section 2A–211(1) provides that during the term of the lease, no claim of any third party will interfere with the lessee's enjoyment of the leasehold interest.

No Infringements. A merchant seller is also deemed to warrant that the goods delivered are free from any copyright, trademark, or patent claims of a third person[3] [UCC 2–312(3), 2A–211(2)]. If this warranty is breached and the buyer is sued by the party holding copyright, trademark, or patent rights in the goods, the buyer must notify the seller of the litigation within a reasonable time to enable the seller to decide whether to defend the lawsuit. If the seller states in writing that she or he has decided to defend and agrees to bear all expenses, including that of an adverse judgment, then the buyer must let the seller undertake litigation; otherwise, the

buyer loses all rights against the seller if any infringement liability is established [UCC 2–607(3)(b), 2–607(5)(b)].

Article 2A provides for the same notice of litigation in situations that involve leases rather than sales [UCC 2A–516(3)(b), 2A–516(4)(b)]. There is an exception for leases to individual consumers for personal, family, or household purposes. A consumer who fails to notify the lessor within a reasonable time does not lose his or her remedy against the lessor for any liability established in the litigation [UCC 2A–516(3)(b)].

Disclaimer of Title Warranty. In an ordinary sales transaction, the title warranty can be disclaimed or modified only by *specific language* in the contract [UCC 2–312(2)]. For example, sellers can assert that they are transferring only such rights, title, and interest as they have in the goods. In a lease transaction, the disclaimer must "be specific, be by a writing, and be conspicuous" [UCC 2A–214(4)].

EXPRESS WARRANTIES

A seller or lessor can create an **express warranty** by making representations concerning the quality, condition, description, or performance potential of the goods. Under UCC 2–313 and 2A–210, express warranties arise when a seller or lessor indicates any of the following:

① That the goods conform to any affirmation (declaration that something is true) or promise of fact that the seller or lessor makes to the buyer or lessee about the goods. Such affirmations or promises are usually made during the bargaining process. Statements such as "these drill bits will penetrate stainless steel—and without dulling" are express warranties.[4]

② That the goods conform to any description of them. For example, a label that reads "Crate contains one 150-horse-power diesel engine" or a contract that calls for the delivery of a "camel's-hair coat" creates an express warranty.

③ That the goods conform to any sample or model of the goods shown to the buyer or lessee.

To succeed in a suit against a manufacturer for a breach of express warranty, does a plaintiff have to prove that a specific defect caused the breach? That was the question in the following case.

---

[1] One of the 2003 amendments to UCC Article 2 expressly provides protection for a buyer when the title is subject to an apparently plausible claim that affects the value of the goods [Amended UCC 2–312(1)(a)]. This section recognizes that a buyer is entitled not only to a good title, but to a marketable title, which a buyer may not have until all reasonable claims are resolved. Amendments to UCC Article 2A also provide for the doctrine of marketable title in the context of leases [Amended UCC 2A–211(1), (2)].

[2] Pronounced *leens.*

[3] Recall from Chapter 14 that a *merchant* is defined in UCC 2–104(1) as a person who deals in goods of the kind involved in the sales contract or who, by occupation, presents himself or herself as having knowledge or skill peculiar to the goods involved in the transaction.

[4] The 2003 amendments to UCC Article 2 introduce the term *remedial promise,* which is "a promise by the seller to repair or replace the goods or to refund all or part of the price on the happening of a specified event" [Amended UCC 2–103(1)(n), 2–313(4)]. A remedial promise is not an express warranty, so a right of action for its breach accrues not at the time of tender, as with warranties, but if the promise is not performed when due [Amended UCC 2–725(2)(c)].

CASE 17.1   Genetti v. Caterpillar, Inc.

Nebraska Supreme Court, 2001.
261 Neb. 98,
621 N.W.2d 529.
**http://www.findlaw.com/11stategov/ne/
neca.html**[a]

FACTS Robert and Sherrie Genetti are in the business of delivering furniture nationwide. In 1996, they bought a new General Motors Corporation (GMC) truck and trailer for $97,043 from Omaha Truck Center, Inc. The truck was equipped with a model 3116 medium-duty diesel engine manufactured by Caterpillar, Inc. GMC and Caterpillar expressly warranted the truck for three years or 150,000 miles. Over the next seven months, the truck broke down four times. Each time, the Genettis lost the use of the truck, costing them time and money, including a fourth repair bill of $12,000. They had the truck repaired through GMC and Caterpillar dealerships, whose mechanics stated that the cause of the breakdowns was "engine failure." When GMC and Caterpillar refused to replace the vehicle or refund the price, the Genettis filed a suit in a Nebraska state court against the manufacturers, alleging, in part, breach of express warranty. The court entered separate judgments against GMC and Caterpillar in favor of the Genettis on this claim. The manufacturers appealed to the state supreme court, arguing, in part, that the plaintiffs could not recover for a breach of express warranty simply by asserting "engine failure."

a. Under "2001," click on "January." Scroll down to the name of the case, and use one of the provided links to access either the HTML or PDF versions of the case. This site is provided by FindLaw, a part of West Group.

ISSUE To recover for a breach of express warranty, do plaintiffs have to prove that a specific defect caused the breach?

DECISION No. The court affirmed this part of the lower court's judgment and remanded the case for a new trial on other grounds.

REASON The state supreme court reasoned that "a precise or specific defect does not need to be proved" in order to find a product defective under the UCC. The court explained that under many warranties, "a consumer requiring warranty service on a vehicle may take the damaged vehicle only to a service department at an authorized dealer. * * * Placing the burden on the consumer to prove a precise defect is unfair and unconscionable since the dealer and manufacturer could tamper (whether intentionally or inadvertently) with the evidence. * * * To impose an unreasonably heavy burden on consumers is to deny them a meaningful remedy." In this case, the Genettis presented evidence that the actions of their employees were proper. This eliminated abuse or misuse as the cause of the breakdown. "Looking at the evidence," said the court, "a jury using common sense and experience could reasonably arrive at the conclusion that the * * * breakdown[s] [were] caused by a defect in the engine and should have been covered by the warranty."

FOR CRITICAL ANALYSIS—Economic Consideration
In a suit for breach of warranty involving more than one defendant and resulting in a verdict in the plaintiff's favor, how should the damages be apportioned?

Basis of the Bargain. To create an express warranty, a seller or lessor does not have to use formal words such as *warrant* or *guarantee* [UCC 2–313(2), 2A–210(2)]. The UCC requires that for an express warranty to be created, the affirmation, promise, description, or sample must become part of the "basis of the bargain" [UCC 2–313(1), 2A–210(1)]. Just what constitutes the basis of the bargain is hard to say. The UCC does not define the concept, and it is a question of fact in each case whether a representation was made at such a time and in such a way that it induced the buyer or lessee to enter into the contract.

Statements of Opinion. Statements of fact create express warranties. If the seller or lessor merely makes a statement that relates to the supposed value or worth of the goods, or makes a statement of opinion or recommendation about the goods, however, the seller or lessor is not creating an express warranty [UCC 2–313(2), 2A–210(2)].

● **EXAMPLE #2** A seller claims that "this is the best used car to come along in years; it has four new tires and a 250-horsepower engine just rebuilt this year." The seller has made several *affirmations of fact* that can create a warranty: the automobile has an engine; it has a 250-horsepower engine; it was rebuilt this year; there are four tires on the automobile; and the tires are new. The seller's *opinion* that the vehicle is "the best used car to come along in years," however, is known as "puffing" and creates no warranty. (*Puffing* is the expression of opinion by a seller or lessor that is not made as a representation of fact.)●

A statement relating to the value of the goods, such as "it's worth a fortune" or "anywhere else you'd pay $10,000 for it," usually does not create a warranty. If the seller or lessor is an expert and gives an opinion as an expert to a layperson, though, a warranty may be created.

It is not always easy to determine what constitutes an express warranty and what constitutes puffing. The reasonableness of the buyer's or lessee's reliance appears to be the controlling criterion in many cases. For example, a salesperson's statements that a ladder "will never break" and will "last a lifetime" are so clearly improbable that no reasonable buyer should rely on them. Additionally, the context in which a statement is made might be relevant in determining the reasonableness of the buyer's or lessee's reliance. For example, a reasonable person is more likely to rely on a written statement made in an advertisement than on a statement made orally by a salesperson.

IMPLIED WARRANTIES

An **implied warranty** is one that *the law derives* by implication or inference from the nature of the transaction or the relative situation or circumstances of the parties. In an action based on breach of implied warranty, it is necessary to show that an implied warranty existed and that the breach of the warranty proximately caused[5] the damage sustained. We look here at some of the implied warranties that arise under the UCC.

Implied Warranty of Merchantability. Every sale or lease of goods made *by a merchant* who deals in goods of the kind sold or leased automatically gives rise to an **implied warranty of merchantability** [UCC 2–314, 2A–212]. Thus, a merchant who is in the business of selling ski equipment makes an implied warranty of merchantability every time the merchant sells a pair of skis, but a neighbor selling his or her skis at a garage sale does not.

Merchantable Goods. Goods that are *merchantable* are "reasonably fit for the ordinary purposes for which such goods are used." They must be of at least average, fair, or medium-grade quality. The quality must be comparable to a level that will pass without objection in the trade or market for goods of the same description. To be merchantable, the goods must also be adequately packaged and labeled as provided by the agreement, and they must conform to the promises or affirmations of fact made on the container or label, if any.

It makes no difference whether the merchant knew of or could have discovered that a product was defective (not merchantable). Of course, merchants are not absolute insurers against all accidents arising in connection with the goods. For example, a bar of soap is not unmerchantable merely because a user could slip and fall by stepping on it.

Merchantable Food. The UCC recognizes the serving of food or drink to be consumed on or off the premises as a sale of goods subject to the implied warranty of merchantability [UCC 2–314(1)]. "Merchantable" food means food that is fit to eat. Courts generally determine whether food is fit to eat on the basis of consumer expectations. For example, the courts assume that consumers should reasonably expect to find on occasion bones in fish fillets, cherry pits in cherry pie, a nutshell in a package of shelled nuts, and so on—because such substances are natural incidents of the food. In contrast, consumers would not reasonably expect to find an inchworm in a can of peas or a piece of glass in a soft drink—because these substances are not natural to the food product.[6] In the following classic case, the court had to determine whether a fish bone was a substance that one should reasonably expect to find in fish chowder.

---

[5] Proximate cause, or legal cause, exists when the connection between an act and an injury is strong enough to justify imposing liability—see Chapter 4.

[6] See, for example, *Mexicali Rose v. Superior Court*, 1 Cal.4th 617, 822 P.2d 1292, 4 Cal.Rptr.2d 145 (1992).

Landmark and Classic Cases

CASE 17.2 **Webster v. Blue Ship Tea Room, Inc.**

Supreme Judicial Court of Massachusetts, 1964.
347 Mass. 421,
198 N.E.2d 309.

FACTS Blue Ship Tea Room, Inc., was located in Boston in an old building overlooking the ocean. Webster, who had been born and raised in New England, went to the restaurant and ordered fish chowder. The chowder was milky in color. After three or four spoonfuls, she felt something lodged in her throat. As a result, she underwent two esophagoscopies; in the second esophagoscopy, a fish bone was found and removed. Webster filed suit against the restaurant in a Massachusetts state court for breach of the implied warranty of merchantability. The jury rendered a verdict for Webster, and the restaurant appealed to the state's highest court.

(Continued)

CASE 17.2—Continued

ISSUE Does serving fish chowder that contains a bone constitute the breach of an implied warranty of merchantability on the part of the restaurant?

DECISION No. The Supreme Judicial Court of Massachusetts held that Webster could not recover against Blue Ship Tea Room because no breach of warranty had occurred.

REASON The court, citing UCC Section 2–314, stated that "a warranty that goods shall be merchantable is implied in a contract for their sale if the seller is a merchant with respect to goods of that kind. Under this section the serving for value of food or drink to be consumed either on the premises or elsewhere is a sale. * * * Goods to be merchantable must at least be * * * fit for the ordinary purposes for which such goods are used." The question here is whether a fish

bone made the chowder unfit for eating. In the judge's opinion, "the joys of life in New England include the ready availability of fresh fish chowder. We should be prepared to cope with the hazards of fish bones, the occasional presence of which in chowders is, it seems to us, to be anticipated, and which, in the light of a hallowed tradition, do not impair their fitness or merchantability."

COMMENT *This classic case, phrased in memorable language, was an early application of the UCC's implied warranty of merchantability to food products. The case established the rule that consumers should expect to find, on occasion, elements of food products that are natural to the product (such as fish bones in fish chowder). In such cases, the food preparers or packagers will not be liable. This rule continues to be applied today in cases involving similar issues.*

Implied Warranty of Fitness for a Particular Purpose. The **implied warranty of fitness for a particular purpose** arises when any seller or lessor (merchant or nonmerchant) knows the particular purpose for which a buyer or lessee will use the goods and knows that the buyer or lessee is relying on the skill and judgment of the seller or lessor to select suitable goods [UCC 2–315, 2A–213].

A "particular purpose" of the buyer or lessee differs from the "ordinary purpose for which goods are used" (merchantability). Goods can be merchantable but unfit for a particular purpose. ● **EXAMPLE #3** Suppose that you need a gallon of paint to match the color of your living room walls—a light shade somewhere between coral and peach. You take a sample to your local hardware store and request a gallon of paint of that color. Instead, you are given a gallon of bright blue paint. Here, the salesperson has not breached any warranty of implied merchantability—the bright blue paint is of high quality and suitable for interior walls—but he or she has breached an implied warranty of fitness for a particular purpose. ●

A seller or lessor does not need to have actual knowledge of the buyer's or lessee's particular purpose. It is sufficient if a seller or lessor "has reason to know" the purpose. The buyer or lessee, however, must have *relied* on the skill or judgment of the seller or lessor in selecting or furnishing suitable goods for an implied warranty to be created.

● **EXAMPLE #4** Bloomberg leases a computer from Future Tech, a lessor of technical business equipment. Bloomberg

tells the clerk that she wants a computer that will run a complicated new engineering graphics program at a realistic speed. Future Tech leases Bloomberg an Architex One computer with a CPU speed of only 550 megahertz, even though a speed of at least 1,200 megahertz would be required to run Bloomberg's graphics program at a "realistic speed." Bloomberg, after discovering that it takes forever to run her program, wants her money back. Here, because Future Tech has breached the implied warranty of fitness for a particular purpose, Bloomberg normally will be able to recover. The clerk knew specifically that Bloomberg wanted a computer with enough speed to run certain software. Furthermore, Bloomberg relied on the clerk to furnish a computer that would fulfill this purpose. Because Future Tech did not do so, the warranty was breached. ●

Other Implied Warranties. Implied warranties can also arise (or be excluded or modified) as a result of course of dealing or usage of trade [UCC 2–314(3), 2A–212(3)]. In the absence of evidence to the contrary, when both parties to a sales or lease contract have knowledge of a well-recognized trade custom, the courts will infer that both parties intended for that trade custom to apply to their contract. For example, if an industry-wide custom is to lubricate a new car before it is delivered and a dealer fails to do so, the dealer can be held liable to a buyer for damages resulting from the breach of an implied warranty. This, of course, would also be negligence on the part of the dealer.

OVERLAPPING WARRANTIES

Sometimes, two or more warranties are made in a single transaction. An implied warranty of merchantability, an implied warranty of fitness for a particular purpose, or both can exist in addition to an express warranty. For example, when a sales contract for a new car states that "this car engine is warranted to be free from defects for 36,000 miles or thirty-six months, whichever occurs first," there is an express warranty against all defects and an implied warranty that the car will be fit for normal use.

The rule under the UCC is that express and implied warranties are construed as *cumulative* if they are consistent with one another [UCC 2–317, 2A–215]. If the warranties are inconsistent, the courts usually hold as follows:

① *Express* warranties displace inconsistent *implied* warranties, except for implied warranties of fitness for a particular purpose.

② Samples take precedence over inconsistent general descriptions.

③ Technical specifications displace inconsistent samples or general descriptions.

In the example presented earlier, suppose that when Bloomberg leases the computer from Future Tech, the contract contains an express warranty concerning the speed of the CPU and the application programs that the computer is capable of running. Bloomberg does not realize that the speed expressly warranted in the contract is insufficient for her needs. Bloomberg later claims that Future Tech has breached the implied warranty of fitness for a particular purpose. Here, although the express warranty would take precedence over any implied warranty of merchantability, it normally would not take precedence over an implied warranty of fitness for a particular purpose. Bloomberg therefore has a good claim for the breach of implied warranty of fitness for a particular purpose, because she made it clear that she was leasing the computer to perform certain tasks.

THIRD PARTY BENEFICIARIES OF WARRANTIES

One of the general principles of contract law is that unless you are one of the parties to a contract, you have no rights under the contract. In other words, *privity of contract* must exist between a plaintiff and a defendant before any action based on a contract can be maintained. Two notable exceptions to the rule of privity are assignments and third party beneficiary contracts (these topics were discussed in Chapter 11). Another exception is made under warranty laws so that third parties can recover for harms suffered as a result of breached warranties.

There has been sharp disagreement among state courts as to how far warranty liability should extend, however. In view of this disagreement, the UCC offers three alternatives for liability to third parties [UCC 2–318, 2A–216].[7] All three alternatives are intended to eliminate the privity requirement with respect to certain enumerated types of injuries (personal versus property) for certain beneficiaries (for example, household members or bystanders).

WARRANTY DISCLAIMERS

Because each type of warranty is created in a special way, the manner in which warranties can be disclaimed or qualified by a seller or lessor varies depending on the type of warranty.

Express Warranties. As already stated, any affirmation of fact or promise, description of the goods, or use of samples or models by a seller or lessor creates an express warranty. Obviously, then, express warranties can be excluded if the seller or lessor carefully refrains from making any promise or affirmation of fact relating to the goods, describing the goods, or using a sample or model.

The UCC does permit express warranties to be negated or limited by specific and unambiguous language, provided that this is done in a manner that protects the buyer or lessee from surprise. Therefore, a written disclaimer in language that is clear and conspicuous, and called to a buyer's or lessee's attention, could negate all oral express warranties not included in the written sales contract [UCC 2–316(1), 2A–214(1)]. This allows the seller or lessor to avoid false allegations that oral warranties were made, and it ensures that only representations made by properly authorized individuals are included in the bargain.

Note, however, that a buyer or lessee must be made aware of any warranty disclaimers or modifications *at the time the contract is formed*. In other words, any oral or written warranties—or disclaimers—made during the bargaining process as part of a contract's formation cannot be modified at a later time by the seller or lessor.

Implied Warranties. Generally speaking, unless circumstances indicate otherwise, the implied warranties of merchantability and fitness are disclaimed by the expressions "as is," "with all faults," and other similar expressions that in common understanding call the buyer's or lessee's

---

[7] Under the 2003 amendments to the UCC, each alternative is expanded to cover remedial promises, as well as obligations to immediate buyers and remote purchasers [see Amended UCC 2–313, 2–313A, 2–313B, and 2–318].

attention to the fact that there are no implied warranties [UCC 2–316(3)(a), 2A–214(3)(a)].

The UCC also permits a seller or lessor to specifically disclaim an implied warranty either of fitness or of merchantability [UCC 2–316(2), 2A–214(2)]. To disclaim an implied warranty of fitness for a particular purpose, the disclaimer *must* be in writing and be conspicuous. The word *fitness* does not have to be mentioned in the writing; it is sufficient if, for example, the disclaimer states, "THERE ARE NO WARRANTIES THAT EXTEND BEYOND THE DESCRIPTION ON THE FACE HEREOF." A merchantability disclaimer must be more specific; it must mention the word *merchantability*. It need not be written, but if it is, the writing must be conspicuous [UCC 2–316(2), 2A–214(4)].[8] According to UCC 1–201(10),

> [a] term or clause is conspicuous when it is so written that a reasonable person against whom it is to operate ought to have noticed it. A printed heading in capitals . . . is conspicuous. Language in the body of a form is conspicuous if it is in larger or other contrasting type or color.[9]

---

[8] Under the 2003 amendments to UCC Articles 2 and 2A, if a consumer contract or lease is set forth in a record (writing), the implied warranty of merchantability can be disclaimed only by language also set forth conspicuously in the record [Amended UCC 2–316(3) and 2A–214(3)].

[9] The 2003 amendments to UCC Articles 2 and 2A expand the concept to include terms in electronic records [Amended UCC 2–103(1)(b), 2A–103(1)(e)]. These sections also add a special rule for the situation in which a sender of an e-record intends to evoke a response from an e-agent.

● **EXAMPLE #5** Forbes, a merchant, sells Maves a particular lawn mower selected by Forbes with the characteristics clearly requested by Maves. At the time of the sale, Forbes orally tells Maves that he does not warrant the merchantability of the mower, as it is last year's model and has been used extensively as a demonstrator. If the mower proves to be defective and does not work, Maves can hold Forbes liable for breach of the warranty of fitness for a particular purpose but not for breach of the warranty of merchantability. Forbes's oral disclaimer mentioning the word *merchantability* is a proper disclaimer. For Forbes to have disclaimed the implied warranty of fitness for a particular purpose, however, a conspicuous writing would have been required. Because he made no written disclaimer, Forbes can still be held liable.●

Disclaimers of warranties, both express and implied, are frequently contained in contracts formed online. For a discussion of one such warranty disclaimer, see this chapter's *Business Law in the Online World* feature on page 328.

At the center of the dispute in the following case was a disclaimer, in a lease, of all warranties. In defense against a suit for amounts due under the lease, the lessee contended that the leased goods were defective when delivered and not fit for the purpose intended and that, for this reason, the consideration for the contract failed. What was the effect of the disclaimer in this situation?

CASE 17.3 **International Turbine Services, Inc. v. VASP Brazilian Airlines**

United States Court of Appeals,
Fifth Circuit, 2002.
278 F.3d 494.
**http://www.ca5.uscourts.gov/Opinions/
OpinHome.cfm**[a]

FACTS On October 1, 1997, International Turbine Services, Inc. (ITS), leased an aircraft turbine engine to VASP Brazilian Airlines. The lease required ITS to deliver the engine with a Federal Aviation Administration (FAA) approved service tag. VASP otherwise leased the engine in "'AS IS, WHERE IS' condition and with all faults." VASP bore "the risk of loss and damage to the Engine and all component parts from any and every cause whatsoever" with one exception: ITS agreed to

overhaul and repair "time controlled" and "on-condition" parts.[b] At the end of the term—which the parties extended through August 18, 1998—VASP was to return the engine in operable condition to ITS's facility in Dallas. On June 15, the pilot of a VASP plane on which the engine was mounted aborted takeoff due to strong vibrations in the engine. VASP discovered that a high-pressure turbine (HPT) blade had failed, causing severe damage to the engine. VASP disputed responsibility for the repair cost and stopped making payments under the lease. ITS filed a suit against VASP, alleging breach of contract. A federal district court awarded ITS $8,825,000 in damages, including the cost to repair the engine and the past-due lease payments. On appeal to the U.S. Court of Appeals for the Fifth Circuit, VASP argued, in part, that it had not bargained for a defective engine.

---

a. In the "Search Start Date" box, type "01," "04," and "2002," respectively. Next, select "Published" and click on "submit." In the results, scroll to the name of the case, and click on the docket number to access the opinion. The Clerk's Office of the U.S. Court of Appeals for the Fifth Circuit maintains this Web site.

b. A time-controlled part must be replaced or repaired after a specified number of hours or cycles. An on-condition part must be replaced or repaired whenever, on inspection, it does not comply with relevant FAA specifications.

CASE 17.3—Continued

ISSUE Did VASP receive bargained-for consideration when it accepted the engine?

DECISION Yes. The U.S. Court of Appeals for the Fifth Circuit affirmed the judgment of the lower court. The appellate court held that VASP could not successfully assert the defense of a failure of consideration, because "[t]he Lease validly excludes all warranties with the exception of title and requires only delivery of an engine with an FAA approved return to service tag." This exclusion meant that VASP could not legitimately complain about the condition of the leased goods.

REASON According to the court, VASP "acknowledged that the engine arrived with the appropriate FAA tag" but argued that the tag constituted "an implied representation that all applicable maintenance regulations and manufacturers' recom-

mendations have been followed, including the manufacturer's recommendations regarding HPT blades." The court reiterated that "this is precisely the type of implied representation or warranty the Lease expressly excludes." The court added, "VASP representatives signed an Equipment Delivery Receipt acknowledging the engine's compliance with the terms and conditions of the Lease. VASP also was sufficiently satisfied with the engine's performance to execute a series of extensions and amendments to the original two-month lease term."

FOR CRITICAL ANALYSIS—Social Consideration
Suppose the lease in this case had not contained a disclaimer and that the HPT blade had been defective on the engine's receipt. The defect would have been discovered on a reasonable inspection, but VASP declined to examine the engine. In this situation, would the outcome of the case have been different?

Buyer's or Lessee's Refusal to Inspect. If a buyer or lessee actually examines the goods (or a sample or model) as fully as desired before entering into a contract, or if the buyer or lessee refuses to examine the goods on the seller's or lessor's demand that he or she do so, *there is no implied warranty with respect to defects that a reasonable examination would reveal or defects that are actually found* [UCC 2–316(3)(b), 2A–214(2)(b)].

• **EXAMPLE #6** Suppose that Joplin buys an ax at Gershwin's Hardware Store. No express warranties are made. Joplin, even after Gershwin requests that she inspect the ax, refuses to inspect it before buying it. Had she done so, she would have noticed that the handle of the ax was obviously cracked. If Joplin is later injured by the defective ax, she normally will not be able to hold Gershwin liable for breach of the warranty of merchantability, because she would have spotted the defect during an inspection.•

Warranty Disclaimers and Unconscionability. The UCC sections dealing with warranty disclaimers do not refer specifically to unconscionability as a factor. Ultimately, however, the courts will test warranty disclaimers with reference to the UCC's unconscionability standards [UCC 2–302, 2A–108]. Such things as lack of bargaining position, "take-it-or-leave-it" choices, and a buyer's or lessee's failure to understand or know of a warranty disclaimer will become relevant to the issue of unconscionability.

MAGNUSON-MOSS WARRANTY ACT

The Magnuson-Moss Warranty Act of 1975[10] was designed to prevent deception in warranties by making them easier

to understand. The act is mainly enforced by the Federal Trade Commission (FTC). Additionally, the attorney general or a consumer who has been injured can enforce the act if informal procedures for settling disputes prove to be ineffective. The act modifies UCC warranty rules to some extent when consumer transactions are involved. The UCC, however, remains the primary codification of warranty rules for industrial and commercial transactions.

Under the Magnuson-Moss Act, no seller or lessor is required to give an express written warranty for consumer goods sold. If a seller or lessor chooses to make an express written warranty, however, and the cost of the consumer goods is more than $10, the warranty must be labeled as "full" or "limited." In addition, if the cost of the goods is more than $15, by FTC regulation, the warrantor must make certain disclosures fully and conspicuously in a single document in "readily understood language." This disclosure must state the names and addresses of the warrantor(s), what specifically is warranted, procedures for enforcement of the warranty, any limitations on warranty relief, and that the buyer has legal rights.

Full Warranty. Although a *full warranty* may not cover every aspect of the consumer product sold, what it covers ensures some type of consumer satisfaction in case the product is defective. A full warranty requires free repair or replacement of any defective part; if the product cannot be repaired within a reasonable time, the consumer has the choice of a refund or a replacement without charge. The full warranty frequently does not have a time limit on it. Any limitation on consequential damages must be *conspicuously* stated. Additionally, the warrantor need not perform

---

[10] 15 U.S.C. Sections 2301–2312.

BUSINESS LAW IN THE ONLINE WORLD
Online Warranty Disclaimers

All too often, purchasers of goods or services fail to read the "fine print" of contracts. This is a problem not only with respect to traditional (paper) contracts but also with contracts formed online. Indeed, parties may be more likely to overlook contract provisions when the terms of the contract appear on a computer screen. Consider a case that came before a New York court in 2001.

WEB SITE REPRESENTATIONS The plaintiffs in the case were a group of subscribers to a DSL (digital subscriber line) service offered by Bell Atlantic Corporation. The subscribers claimed that Bell Atlantic had misrepresented the quality of its DSL service in statements made on its Web site. The representations at issue stated that subscribers would have "high-speed Internet access service up to 126 times faster than your 56K modem" and that the service was dedicated—"You're always connected—no dialing in and no busy signals, ever!" When the subscribers became dissatisfied with the actual connection speed and the fact that they sometimes had difficulty accessing Web sites, they sued Bell Atlantic for, among other things, breach of warranty. Bell Atlantic moved to dismiss the case on the ground that it had disclaimed all warranties in its online "Terms and Conditions" agreement.

IT'S ALL IN THE CONTRACT—INCLUDING THE WARRANTY DISCLAIMER The court had little difficulty in granting Bell Atlantic's motion to dismiss the

case. For one thing, stated the court, the plaintiffs had misunderstood the representations made by Bell Atlantic on its Web site. The representation as to high-speed service set forth a maximum possible speed, not the standard speed at which the service would operate. The representation regarding the dedicated connection referred to the fact that the connection need not be dialed up, not that the connection was infallible and would never be interrupted for any reason. The court also noted that the subscribers were given thirty days to try out the service and, if they were dissatisfied, to cancel it and receive a full refund.

Finally, Bell Atlantic's online "Terms and Conditions" agreement stated, in boldface, large capital letters, that the service was provided on an "as is" or "as available" basis and that "any and all warranties for the services, whether express or implied, including but not limited to the implied warranties of merchantability and fitness for a particular purpose," were disclaimed. In response to the plaintiffs' argument that it was possible to use the service without having read the "Terms and Conditions," the court simply stated that this "does not impair the enforcement of the agreement."[a]

FOR CRITICAL ANALYSIS

If Bell Atlantic had promised on its Web site that DSL subscribers would have maximum-speed Internet access, would the subscribers have had a cause of action for breach of warranty? Why or why not?

a. *Scott v. Bell Atlantic Corp.*, 726 N.Y.S.2d 60 (N.Y.A.D. 1st Dept. 2001).

---

warranty services if the problem with the product was caused by the consumer's unreasonable use of the product.

Limited Warranty. A *limited warranty* arises when the written warranty fails to meet one of the minimum requirements of a full warranty. The fact that only a limited warranty is being given must be conspicuously designated. If the only distinction between a limited warranty and a full warranty is a time limitation, the Magnuson-Moss Warranty Act allows the warrantor to identify the warranty as a full warranty by such language as "full twelve-month warranty."

Implied Warranties. Implied warranties do not arise under the Magnuson-Moss Warranty Act; they continue to be created according to UCC provisions. Implied warranties may not be disclaimed under the Magnuson-Moss Warranty Act, however. Although a warrantor can impose a time limit on the duration of an implied warranty, it must correspond to the duration of the express warranty.[11]

---

[11] The time limit on an implied warranty occurring by virtue of the warrantor's express warranty must, of course, be reasonable, conscionable, and set forth in clear and conspicuous language on the face of the warranty.

Lemon Laws

Some purchasers of defective automobiles—called "lemons"—found that the remedies provided by the UCC were inadequate due to limitations imposed by the seller. In response to the frustrations of these buyers, all of the states have enacted *lemon laws*. Basically, lemon laws provide that if an automobile under warranty possesses a defect that significantly affects the vehicle's value or use, and the seller fails to remedy the defect within a specified number of opportunities (usually four), the buyer is entitled to a new car, replacement of defective parts, or return of all consideration paid.

In most states, lemon laws require an aggrieved new-car owner to notify the dealer or manufacturer of the problem and to provide the dealer or manufacturer with an opportunity to solve it. If the problem remains, the owner must then submit complaints to the arbitration program specified in the manufacturer's warranty before taking the case to court. Decisions by arbitration panels are binding on the manufacturer (that is, cannot be appealed by the manufacturer to the courts) but usually are not binding on the purchaser.

Most major automobile companies use their own arbitration panels. Some companies, however, subscribe to independent arbitration services, such as those provided by the Better Business Bureau. Although arbitration boards must meet state and/or federal standards of impartiality, industry-sponsored arbitration boards have been criticized for not being truly impartial. In response to this criticism, some states have established mandatory, government-sponsored arbitration programs for lemon-law disputes.

Product Liability

Manufacturers, sellers, and lessors of goods can be held liable to consumers, users, and bystanders for physical harm or property damage that is caused by the goods. This is called **product liability**. Product liability may be based on the warranty theories just discussed, as well as on the theories of negligence, misrepresentation, and strict liability. In this section, we look at product liability based on negligence and misrepresentation.

NEGLIGENCE

Chapter 4 defined *negligence* as the failure to exercise the degree of care that a reasonable, prudent person would have exercised under the circumstances. If a manufacturer fails to exercise "due care" to make a product safe, a person who is injured by the product may sue the manufacturer for negligence.

Due Care Must Be Exercised. Due care must be exercised in designing the product, selecting the materials, using the appropriate production process, assembling the product, and placing adequate warnings on the label informing the user of dangers of which an ordinary person might not be aware. The duty of care also extends to the inspection and testing of any purchased products that are used in the final product sold by the manufacturer.

Privity of Contract Not Required. A product liability action based on negligence does not require privity of contract between the injured plaintiff and the negligent defendant manufacturer. Section 395 of the *Restatement (Second) of Torts* states as follows:

> A manufacturer who fails to exercise reasonable care in the manufacture of a chattel [movable good] which, unless carefully made, he should recognize as involving an unreasonable risk of causing physical harm to those who lawfully use it for a purpose for which the manufacturer should expect it to be used and to those whom he should expect to be endangered by its probable use, is subject to liability for physical harm caused to them by its lawful use in a manner and for a purpose for which it is supplied.

In other words, a manufacturer is liable for its failure to exercise due care to any person who sustained an injury proximately caused by a negligently made (defective) product, regardless of whether the injured person is in privity of contract with the negligent defendant manufacturer or lessor.[12]

MISREPRESENTATION

When a fraudulent misrepresentation has been made to a user or consumer, and that misrepresentation ultimately results in an injury, the basis of liability may be the tort of fraud. For example, the intentional mislabeling of packaged cosmetics and the intentional concealment of a product's defects would constitute fraudulent misrepresentation.

Strict Product Liability

Under the doctrine of strict liability (discussed in Chapter 4), people may be liable for the results of their acts regardless of their intentions or their exercise of reasonable care. Under this doctrine, liability does not depend on privity of contract. The injured party does not have to be the buyer or a third party beneficiary, as required under contract warranty theory. Indeed, this type of liability in law is not governed by the

---

[12] A landmark case in which the court abandoned the privity requirement is *MacPherson v. Buick Motor Co.*, 217 N.Y. 382, 111 N.E. 1050 (1916).

provisions of the UCC because it is a tort doctrine, not a principle of the law relating to sales contracts.

STRICT PRODUCT LIABILITY AND PUBLIC POLICY

Strict product liability is imposed by law as a matter of public policy—the general principle of the law that prohibits actions that tend to be injurious to the public. With respect to strict liability, the policy rests on the threefold assumption that (1) consumers should be protected against unsafe products; (2) manufacturers and distributors should not escape liability for faulty products simply because they are not in privity of contract with the ultimate user of those products; and (3) manufacturers, sellers, and lessors of products are generally in a better position than consumers to bear the costs associated with injuries caused by their products—costs that they can ultimately pass on to all consumers in the form of higher prices.

California was the first state to impose strict product liability in tort on manufacturers. In the landmark case that follows, the California Supreme Court set out the reason for applying tort law rather than contract law in cases involving consumers injured by defective products.

Landmark and Classic Cases

CASE 17.4   Greenman v. Yuba Power Products, Inc.

Supreme Court of California, 1962.
59 Cal.2d 57,
377 P.2d 897,
27 Cal.Rptr. 697.

FACTS The plaintiff, Greenman, wanted a Shopsmith—a combination power tool that could be used as a saw, drill, and wood lathe—after seeing a Shopsmith demonstrated by a retailer and studying a brochure prepared by the manufacturer. The plaintiff's wife bought and gave him one for Christmas. More than a year later, a piece of wood flew out of the lathe attachment of the Shopsmith while the plaintiff was using it, inflicting serious injuries on him. About ten and a half months later, the plaintiff filed a suit in a California state court against both the retailer and the manufacturer for breach of warranties and negligence. The trial court jury found for the plaintiff. The case was ultimately appealed to the Supreme Court of California.

ISSUE Can the manufacturer and retailer be held liable for the plaintiff's injuries?

DECISION Yes. The Supreme Court of California upheld the verdict for the plaintiff.

REASON The plaintiff had successfully proved that the design and construction of the Shopsmith were defective, that statements in the manufacturer's brochure constituted express warranties and were untrue, and that the plaintiff's injuries were caused by the breach of these express war-

ranties. The manufacturer argued that the plaintiff had waited too long to give notice of the breach of warranty, but the court, in imposing strict liability on the manufacturer, held that it was not necessary for the plaintiff to establish an express warranty or a breach of warranty. The court stated that "a manufacturer is strictly liable in tort when an article he places on the market, knowing that it is to be used without inspection for defects, proves to have a defect that causes injury to a human being." The court stated that the "purpose of such liability is to [e]nsure that the costs of injuries resulting from defective products are borne by the manufacturers * * * rather than by the injured persons who are powerless to protect themselves."

COMMENT *From the earliest days of the common law, English courts applied a doctrine of strict liability. Often, persons whose conduct resulted in injuries to others were held liable for damages, even if they had not intended to injure anyone and had exercised reasonable care. This approach was abandoned around 1800 in favor of a fault-based approach, in which an action was considered tortious only if it was wrongful or blameworthy in some respect. Strict liability began to be reapplied to manufactured goods in several landmark cases in the 1960s, a decade when many traditional assumptions were being challenged. The case just presented is considered a landmark in U.S. law not only because it resuscitated the doctrine of strict liability for defective products but also because it enunciated a compelling reason for doing so—protecting "injured persons who are powerless to protect themselves."*

REQUIREMENTS FOR STRICT LIABILITY

Section 402A of the *Restatement (Second) of Torts* indicates how the drafters envisioned that the doctrine of strict liability should be applied. It was issued in 1964, and during the next decade, it became a widely accepted statement of the liabilities of sellers of goods (including manufacturers, processors, assemblers, packagers, bottlers, wholesalers, distributors, retailers, and lessors). Section 402A states as follows:

(1) One who sells any product in a defective condition unreasonably dangerous to the user or consumer or to his property is subject to liability for physical harm thereby caused to the ultimate user or consumer or to his property, if

    (a) the seller is engaged in the business of selling such a product, and

    (b) it is expected to and does reach the user or consumer without substantial change in the condition in which it is sold.

(2) The rule stated in Subsection (1) applies although

    (a) the seller has exercised all possible care in the preparation and sale of his product, and

    (b) the user or consumer has not bought the product from or entered into any contractual relation with the seller.

The Six Requirements for Strict Liability. The bases for an action in strict liability as set forth in Section 402A of the *Restatement (Second) of Torts,* and as the doctrine came to be commonly applied, can be summarized as a series of six requirements, which are listed here. Depending on the jurisdiction, if these requirements are met, a manufacturer's liability to an injured party can be virtually unlimited.

① The product must be in a defective condition when the defendant sells it.

② The defendant must normally be engaged in the business of selling (or otherwise distributing) that product.

③ The product must be unreasonably dangerous to the user or consumer because of its defective condition (in most states).

④ The plaintiff must incur physical harm to self or property by use or consumption of the product.

⑤ The defective condition must be the proximate cause of the injury or damage.

⑥ The goods must not have been substantially changed from the time the product was sold to the time the injury was sustained.

Unreasonably Dangerous Products. Under the requirements just listed, in any action against a manufacturer, seller, or lessor, the plaintiff does not have to show why or in what manner the product became defective. To recover damages, however, the plaintiff must show that the product was so "defective" as to be "unreasonably dangerous"; that the product caused the plaintiff's injury; and that at the time the injury was sustained, the product was in essentially the same condition as when it left the hands of the defendant manufacturer, seller, or lessor.

A court may consider a product so defective as to be an **unreasonably dangerous product** if either (1) the product is dangerous beyond the expectation of the ordinary consumer or (2) a less dangerous alternative was economically feasible for the manufacturer, but the manufacturer failed to produce it. As will be discussed in the next section, a product may be unreasonably dangerous due to a flaw in the manufacturing process, a design defect, or an inadequate warning.

Statutes of Repose. As discussed in Chapter 1, *statutes of limitations* restrict the time within which an action may be brought. A typical statute of limitations provides that an action must be brought within a specified period of time after the cause of action accrues. Generally, a cause of action is held to accrue when some damage occurs. Sometimes, the running of the prescribed period is *tolled* (that is, suspended) until the party suffering an injury has discovered it or should have discovered it.

Many states have passed laws, called **statutes of repose**, placing outer time limits on some claims so that the defendant will not be left vulnerable to lawsuits indefinitely. These statutes may limit the time within which a plaintiff can file a product liability suit. Typically, a statute of repose begins to run at an earlier date and runs for a longer time than a statute of limitations. For example, a statute of repose may require that claims must be brought within twelve years from the date of sale or manufacture of the defective product. It is immaterial that the product is defective or causes an injury if the injury occurs *after* this statutory period has lapsed. In addition, some of these legislative enactments have limited the application of the doctrine of strict liability only to new goods.

MARKET-SHARE LIABILITY

Generally, in all cases involving product liability, a plaintiff must prove that the defective product that caused her or his injury was the product of a specific defendant. In the last decade or so, however, some courts have dropped this requirement when plaintiffs could not prove which of many distributors of a harmful product supplied the particular product that caused the injuries.

This has occurred in several cases involving DES (diethylstilbestrol), a drug administered in the past to prevent miscarriages. DES's harmful character was not realized until, a generation later, daughters of the women who had taken DES developed health problems, including vaginal carcinoma, that were linked to the drug. Partly because of the passage of time, a plaintiff daughter often could not prove which pharmaceutical company—out of as many as three hundred—had marketed the DES her mother had ingested. In these cases, some courts applied market-share liability, holding that all firms that manufactured and distributed DES during the period in question were liable for the plaintiffs' injuries in proportion to the firms' respective shares of the market.[13]

Market-share liability has also been applied in other situations. ● **EXAMPLE #7** In one case, a plaintiff who was a hemophiliac received injections of a blood protein known as antihemophiliac factor (AHF) concentrate. The plaintiff later tested positive for the AIDS (acquired immune deficiency syndrome) virus. Because it was not known which manufacturer was responsible for the particular AHF received by the plaintiff, the court held that all of the manufacturers of AHF could be held liable under a market-share theory of liability.[14] ●

OTHER APPLICATIONS OF STRICT LIABILITY

Although the drafters of the *Restatement (Second) of Torts,* Section 402A, did not take a position on bystanders, all courts extend the strict liability of manufacturers and other sellers to injured bystanders. ● **EXAMPLE #8** In one case, an automobile manufacturer was held liable for injuries caused by the explosion of a car's motor. A cloud of steam that resulted from the explosion caused multiple collisions because other drivers could not see well.[15] ●

The rule of strict liability is also applicable to suppliers of component parts. ● **EXAMPLE #9** General Motors buys brake pads from a subcontractor and puts them in Chevrolets without changing their composition. If those pads are defective, both the supplier of the brake pads and General Motors will be held strictly liable for the damages caused by the defects. ●

Restatement (Third) of Torts: Products Liability

Because Section 402A of the *Restatement (Second) of Torts* did not clearly define such terms as "defective" and "unrea-

sonably dangerous," these terms have been subject to different interpretations by different courts. In 1997, to address these concerns, the American Law Institute (ALI) issued the *Restatement (Third) of Torts: Products Liability.* The *Restatement* defines the three types of product defects that have traditionally been recognized in product liability law—manufacturing defects, design defects, and warning defects.

MANUFACTURING DEFECTS

According to Section 2(a) of the latest *Restatement,* a product "contains a manufacturing defect when the product departs from its intended design even though all possible care was exercised in the preparation and marketing of the product." This statement imposes liability on the manufacturer (and on the wholesaler and retailer) whether or not the manufacturer acted "reasonably." This is strict liability, or liability without fault.

DESIGN DEFECTS

A determination that a product has a design defect (or a warning defect, as will be discussed shortly) can affect all of the units of a product. A product "is defective in design when the foreseeable risks of harm posed by the product could have been reduced or avoided by the adoption of a reasonable alternative design by the seller or other distributor, or a predecessor in the commercial chain of distribution, and the omission of the alternative design renders the product not reasonably safe."[16]

Different states have applied different tests to determine whether a product has a design defect under the *Restatement (Second) of Torts,* Section 402A. There has been much controversy about the various tests, particularly over one that focused on the "consumer expectations" concerning a product. The test prescribed by the *Restatement (Third) of Torts: Products Liability* focuses on a product's actual design and the reasonableness of that design.

To succeed in a product liability suit alleging a design defect, a plaintiff has to show that there is a reasonable alternative design. In other words, a manufacturer or other defendant is liable only when the harm was reasonably preventable. According to the Official Comments accompanying the latest *Restatement,* factors that a court may consider on this point include

the magnitude and probability of the foreseeable risks of harm, the instructions and warnings accompanying the product, and the nature and strength of consumer expectations regarding the product, including expectations arising from product portrayal and marketing. The relative advan-

---

[13] See, for example, *Martin v. Abbott Laboratories,* 102 Wash.2d 581, 689 P.2d 368 (1984).

[14] *Smith v. Cutter Biological, Inc.,* 72 Haw. 416, 823 P.2d 717 (1991).

[15] *Giberson v. Ford Motor Co.,* 504 S.W.2d 8 (Mo. 1974).

---

[16] *Restatement (Third) of Torts: Products Liability,* Section 2(b).

tages and disadvantages of the product as designed and as it alternatively could have been designed may also be considered. Thus, the likely effects of the alternative design on production costs; the effects of the alternative design on product longevity, maintenance, repair, and esthetics; and the range of consumer choice among products are factors that may be taken into account.

WARNING DEFECTS

Product warnings and instructions alert consumers to the risks of using a product. A "reasonableness" test applies to this material. A product "is defective because of inadequate instructions or warnings when the foreseeable risks of harm posed by the product could have been reduced or avoided by the provision of reasonable instructions or warnings by the seller or other distributor, or a predecessor in the commercial chain of distribution, and the omission of the instructions or warnings renders the product not reasonably safe."[17] Generally, a seller must warn those who purchase its product of the harm that can result from the *foreseeable misuse* of the product as well.

Important factors for a court to consider under the *Restatement (Third) of Torts: Products Liability* include the risks of a product, the "content and comprehensibility" and "intensity of expression" of warnings and instructions, and the "characteristics of expected user groups."[18] For example, children would likely respond more readily to bright, bold, simple warning labels, while educated adults might need more detailed information.

There is no duty to warn about risks that are obvious or commonly known. Warnings about such risks do not add to the safety of a product and could even detract from it by making other warnings seem less significant. The obviousness of a risk and a user's decision to proceed in the face of that risk may be a defense in a product liability suit based on a warning defect. (Defenses in product liability suits are discussed next.)

Defenses to Product Liability

Manufacturers, sellers, or lessors can raise several defenses to avoid liability for harms caused by their products. We look at some of these defenses in the following subsections.

ASSUMPTION OF RISK

Assumption of risk can sometimes be used as a defense in a product liability action. For example, if a buyer fails to heed

a product recall by the seller, a court might conclude that the buyer assumed the risk caused by the defect that led to the recall. To establish such a defense, the defendant must show that (1) the plaintiff knew and appreciated the risk created by the product defect and (2) the plaintiff voluntarily assumed the risk, even though it was unreasonable to do so. (See Chapter 4 for a more detailed discussion of assumption of risk.)

PRODUCT MISUSE

Similar to the defense of voluntary assumption of risk is that of misuse of the product. Here, the injured party *does not know that the product is dangerous for a particular use* (contrast this with assumption of risk), but the use is not the one for which the product was designed. The courts have severely limited this defense, however. Even if the injured party does not know about the inherent danger of using the product in a wrong way, if the misuse is foreseeable, the seller must take measures to guard against it.

COMPARATIVE NEGLIGENCE

Developments in the area of comparative negligence (discussed in Chapter 4) have even affected the doctrine of strict liability—the most extreme theory of product liability. Whereas previously the plaintiff's conduct was not a defense to strict liability, today many jurisdictions, when apportioning liability and damages, consider the negligent or intentional actions of both the plaintiff and the defendant. This means that even if the plaintiff misused the product, she or he may nonetheless be able to recover at least some damages for injuries caused by the defendant's defective product.

COMMONLY KNOWN DANGERS

The dangers associated with certain products (such as sharp knives and guns) are so commonly known that manufacturers need not warn users of those dangers. If a defendant succeeds in convincing the court that a plaintiff's injury resulted from a *commonly known danger,* the defendant normally will not be liable.

● **EXAMPLE #10** A classic case on this issue involved a plaintiff who was injured when an elastic exercise rope that she had purchased slipped off her foot and struck her in the eye, causing a detachment of the retina. The plaintiff claimed that the manufacturer should be liable because it had failed to warn users that the exerciser might slip off a foot in such a manner. The court stated that to hold the manufacturer liable in these circumstances "would go beyond the reasonable dictates of justice in fixing the liabilities of manufacturers." After all, stated the court,

---

[17] *Restatement (Third) of Torts: Products Liability,* Section 2(c).
[18] *Restatement (Third) of Torts: Products Liability,* Section 2, Comment h.

"[a]lmost every physical object can be inherently dangerous or potentially dangerous in a sense. . . . A manufacturer cannot manufacture a knife that will not cut or a hammer that will not mash a thumb or a stove that will not burn a finger. The law does not require [manufacturers] to warn of such common dangers."[19] ●

A related defense is the *knowledgeable user* defense. If a particular danger (such as electrical shock) is or should be

commonly known by particular users of the product (such as electricians), the manufacturer of electrical equipment need not warn these users of the danger.

The following case was the first of its kind. As the defendants argued, and the court acknowledged, the outcome of the case "could spawn thousands of similar 'McLawsuits' against restaurants. Even if limited to that ilk of fare dubbed 'fast food,' the potential for lawsuits is great."

---

[19] *Jamieson v. Woodward & Lothrop*, 247 F.2d 23, 101 D.C.App. 32 (1957).

CASE 17.5 **Pelman v. McDonald's Corp.**

United States District Court,
Southern District of New York, 2003.
237 F.Supp.2d 512.

FACTS McDonald's, with about 13,000 restaurants in the United States, has a 43 percent share of the U.S. fast-food market. Ashley Pelman, a New York resident, and other teenagers who often ate at McDonald's outlets, became overweight and developed adverse health effects. Their parents filed a suit in a New York state court against McDonald's and others, alleging that, among other things, the defendants failed to warn of the quantities, qualities, and levels of cholesterol, fat, salt, sugar, and other ingredients in their products, and that a diet high in fat, salt, sugar, and cholesterol could lead to obesity and health problems. The suit was transferred to a federal district court. The defendants filed a motion to dismiss the complaint.

ISSUE Were the products consumed by the plaintiffs dangerous in any way that was not open and obvious to a reasonable consumer?

DECISION No. The court dismissed the plaintiffs' complaint.

REASON The plaintiffs asserted in part that McDonald's failed to include nutritional labeling on its products. The court

pointed out that "McDonalds has made its nutritional information available online and * * * upon request. Unless McDonalds has specifically promised to provide nutritional information on all its products * * *, plaintiffs do not state a claim." The court added that the plaintiffs might have alleged "the attributes of McDonalds products are so extraordinarily unhealthy that they are outside the reasonable contemplation of the consuming public," but they "merely allege[d] that the foods contain high levels of cholesterol, fat, salt and sugar, and that the foods are therefore unhealthy. It is well-known that * * * McDonalds' products * * * contain high levels of cholesterol, fat, salt, and sugar, and that such attributes are bad for one." The court concluded, "If a person knows or should know that eating copious orders of supersized McDonalds' products is [not healthful] and may result in weight gain (and its [attending] problems) because of the high levels of cholesterol, fat, salt and sugar, it is not the place of the law to protect them from their own excesses. Nobody is forced to eat at McDonalds."

FOR CRITICAL ANALYSIS—Social Consideration
Where should the line be drawn between an individual's responsibility to take care of himself or herself and society's responsibility to protect that individual?

OTHER DEFENSES

A defendant can also defend against product liability by showing that there is no basis for the plaintiff's claim. Suppose that a plaintiff alleges that a seller breached an implied warranty. If the seller can prove that he or she effectively disclaimed all implied warranties, the plaintiff cannot recover. Similarly, in a product liability case based on negli-

gence, a defendant who can show that the plaintiff has not met the requirements (such as causation or the breach of a duty of care) for an action in negligence will not be liable. In regard to strict product liability, a defendant could claim that the plaintiff failed to meet one of the requirements for an action in strict liability. If, for example, the defendant establishes that the goods were subsequently altered after they were sold, the defendant will not be held liable.

Terms and Concepts

Chapter Summary Warranties and Product Liability

WARRANTIES	
Warranties of Title (See pages 320–321.)	The UCC provides for the following warranties of title [UCC 2–312, 2A–211]: 1. *Good title*—A seller warrants that he or she has the right to pass good and rightful title to the goods. 2. *No liens*—A seller warrants that the goods sold are free of any encumbrances (claims, charges, or liabilities—usually called *liens*). A lessor warrants that the lessee will not be disturbed in his or her possession of the goods by the claims of a third party. 3. *No infringements*—A merchant seller warrants that the goods are free of infringement claims (claims that a patent, trademark, or copyright has been infringed) by third parties. Lessors make similar warranties.
Express Warranties (See pages 321–323 and 327–328.)	1. *Under the UCC*—An express warranty arises under the UCC when a seller or lessor indicates, as part of the basis of the bargain, any of the following: a. An affirmation or promise of fact. b. A description of the goods. c. A sample shown as conforming to the contract goods [UCC 2–313, 2A–210]. 2. *Under the Magnuson-Moss Warranty Act*—Express written warranties covering consumer goods priced at more than $10, *if made,* must be labeled as one of the following: a. Full warranty—Free repair or replacement of defective parts; refund or replacement for goods if they cannot be repaired in a reasonable time. b. Limited warranty—When less than a full warranty is being offered.
Implied Warranty of Merchantability (See pages 323–324.)	When a seller or lessor is a merchant who deals in goods of the kind sold or leased, the seller or lessor warrants that the goods sold or leased are properly packaged and labeled, are of proper quality, and are reasonably fit for the ordinary purposes for which such goods are used [UCC 2–314, 2A–212].
Implied Warranty of Fitness for a Particular Purpose (See page 324.)	Arises when the buyer's or lessee's purpose or use is expressly or impliedly known by the seller or lessor, and the buyer or lessee purchases or leases the goods in reliance on the seller's or lessor's selection [UCC 2–315, 2A–213].
Other Implied Warranties (See page 324.)	Other implied warranties can arise as a result of course of dealing or usage of trade [UCC 2–314(3), 2A–212(3)].

(Continued)

| Chapter Summary | **Warranties and Product Liability—Continued** |

PRODUCT LIABILITY	
Liability Based on Negligence (See page 329.)	1. Due care must be used by the manufacturer in designing the product, selecting materials, using the appropriate production process, assembling and testing the product, and placing adequate warnings on the label or product.
	2. Privity of contract is not required. A manufacturer is liable for failure to exercise due care to any person who sustains an injury proximately caused by a negligently made (defective) product.
Liability Based on Misrepresentation (See page 329.)	Fraudulent misrepresentation of a product may result in product liability based on the tort of fraud.
Strict Liability—Requirements (See page 331.)	1. The defendant must sell the product in a defective condition.
	2. The defendant must normally be engaged in the business of selling that product.
	3. The product must be unreasonably dangerous to the user or consumer because of its defective condition (in most states).
	4. The plaintiff must incur physical harm to self or property by use or consumption of the product. (Courts will also extend strict liability to include injured bystanders.)
	5. The defective condition must be the proximate cause of the injury or damage.
	6. The goods must not have been substantially changed from the time the product was sold to the time the injury was sustained.
Market-Share Liability (See pages 331–332.)	In cases in which plaintiffs cannot prove which of many distributors of a defective product supplied the particular product that caused the plaintiffs' injuries, some courts apply market-share liability. All firms that manufactured and distributed the harmful product during the period in question are then held liable for the plaintiffs' injuries in proportion to the firms' respective shares of the market, as directed by the court.
Other Applications of Strict Liability (See page 332.)	1. Manufacturers and other sellers are liable for harms suffered by bystanders as a result of defective products.
	2. Suppliers of component parts are strictly liable for defective parts that, when incorporated into a product, cause injuries to users.
Strict Liability—Product Defects (See pages 332–333.)	A product may be defective in three basic ways:
	1. In its manufacture.
	2. In its design.
	3. In the instructions or warnings that come with it.
Defenses to Product Liability (See pages 333–334.)	1. *Assumption of risk*—The user or consumer knew of the risk of harm and voluntarily assumed it.
	2. *Product misuse*—The user or consumer misused the product in a way that was unforeseeable by the manufacturer.
	3. *Comparative negligence and liability*—Liability may be distributed between the plaintiff and the defendant under the doctrine of comparative negligence if the plaintiff's misuse of the product contributed to the risk of injury.
	4. *Commonly known dangers*—If a defendant succeeds in convincing the court that a plaintiff's injury resulted from a commonly known danger, such as the danger associated with using a sharp knife, the defendant will not be liable.
	5. *Other defenses*—A defendant can also defend against a strict liability claim by showing that there is no basis for the plaintiff's claim (that the plaintiff has not met the requirements for an action in negligence or strict liability, for example).

For Review

① What factors determine whether a seller's or lessor's statement constitutes an express warranty or merely "puffing"?

② What implied warranties arise under the UCC?

③ Can a manufacturer be held liable to any person who suffers an injury proximately caused by the manufacturer's negligently made product?

④ What are the elements of a cause of action in strict product liability?

⑤ What defenses to liability can be raised in a product liability lawsuit?

Questions and Case Problems

17–1. Product Liability. Under what contract theory can a seller be held liable to a consumer for physical harm or property damage that is caused by the goods sold? Under what tort theories can the seller be held liable?

17–2. Product Liability. Carmen buys a television set manufactured by AKI Electronics. She is going on vacation, so she takes the set to her mother's house for her mother to use. Because the set is defective, it explodes, causing considerable damage to her mother's house. Carmen's mother sues AKI for the damages to her house. Discuss the theories under which Carmen's mother can recover from AKI.

17–3. Warranty Disclaimers. Tandy purchased a washing machine from Marshall Appliances. The sales contract included a provision explicitly disclaiming all express or implied warranties, including the implied warranty of merchantability. The disclaimer was printed in the same size and color as the rest of the contract. The machine turned out to be a "lemon" and never functioned properly. Tandy sought a refund of the purchase price, claiming that Marshall had breached the implied warranty of merchantability. Can Tandy recover her money, notwithstanding the warranty disclaimer in the contract? Explain.

17–4. Implied Warranties. Sam, a farmer, needs to install a two-thousand-pound piece of equipment in his barn. The equipment must be lifted thirty feet into a hayloft. Sam goes to Durham Hardware and tells Durham that he needs some heavy-duty rope to be used on his farm. Durham recommends a one-inch-thick nylon rope, and Sam purchases two hundred feet of it. Sam ties the rope around the piece of equipment, puts the rope through a pulley, and with the aid of a tractor lifts the equipment off the ground. Suddenly, the rope breaks. The equipment crashes to the ground and is extensively damaged. Sam files suit against Durham for breach of the implied warranty of fitness for a particular purpose. Discuss how successful Sam will be with his suit.

17–5. Failure to Warn. When Mary Bresnahan drove her Chrysler LeBaron, she sat very close to the steering wheel—less than a foot away from the steering-wheel enclosure of the driver's side air bag. At the time, Chrysler did not provide any warning that a driver should not sit close to the air bag. In an accident with another car, Bresnahan's air bag deployed. The bag caused her elbow to strike the windshield pillar and fracture in three places, resulting in repeated surgery and physical therapy.

Bresnahan filed a suit in a California state court against Chrysler to recover for her injuries, alleging in part that they were caused by Chrysler's failure to warn consumers about sitting near the air bag. At the trial, an expert testified that the air bag was not intended to prevent arm injuries, which were "a predictable, incidental consequence" of the bag's deploying. Should Chrysler pay for Bresnahan's injuries? Why or why not? [*Bresnahan v. Chrysler Corp.*, 76 Cal.Rptr.2d 804, 65 Cal.App.4th 1149 (1998)]

17–6. Product Liability. Among the equipment that Ingersoll-Rand Co. makes is a milling machine. The maintenance manual that accompanies the machine contains warnings that users should stay ten feet away from the rear of the machine when it is operating, verify that the back-up alarm is working, and check the area for the presence of others. There is also a sign on the machine that tells users to stay ten feet away. While using the machine to strip asphalt from a road being repaved, Terrill Wilson backed up. The alarm did not sound, and Cosandra Rogers, who was standing with her back to the machine, was run over and maimed. Rogers filed a suit in a federal district court against Ingersoll-Rand, alleging in part strict liability on the basis of a design defect. The jury awarded Rogers $10.2 million in compensatory damages and $6.5 million in punitive damages. Ingersoll-Rand appealed, emphasizing the adequacy of its warnings. Can an adequate warning immunize a manufacturer from any liability caused by a defectively designed product? Discuss fully. [*Rogers v. Ingersoll-Rand Co.*, 144 F.3d 841 (D.C. Cir. 1998)]

17–7. Express Warranties. Ronald Anderson, Jr., a self-employed construction contractor, went to a Home Depot store to buy lumber for a construction project. It was raining, so Anderson bought a tarp to cover the bed of his pickup truck. To secure the tarp, Anderson bought a bag of cords made by Bungee International Manufacturing Corp. The printed material on the Bungee bag included the words "Made in the U.S.A." and "Premium Quality." To secure the tarp at the rear of the passenger's side, Anderson put one hook into the eyelet of the tarp, stretched the cord over the utility box, and hooked the other end in the drainage hole in the bottom of the box. As Anderson stood up, the upper hook dislodged and hit him in the left eye. Anderson filed a suit in a federal district court against Bungee and others, alleging in part breach of express warranty. Anderson alleged that the labeling on the bag of cords was an express warranty that "played some role in [his] decision to purchase this product." Bungee argued that, in regard to the cords' quality, the statements were puffery. Bungee filed a motion for summary judgment on this issue. Will the court grant the motion? Why or why not? [*Anderson v. Bungee International Manufacturing Corp.*, 44 F.Supp.2d 534 (S.D.N.Y. 1999)]

17–8. Product Liability. New England Ecological Development, Inc. (NEED), a recycling station in Rhode Island, required a conveyor belt system and gave the specifications to Colmar Belting Co. Colmar did not design or make belts but merely distributed the component parts. For this system, Emerson Power Transmission Corp. (EPT) manufactured the wing pulley, a component of the nip point (the point at which a belt moves over the stationary part of the system). Kenneth Butler, a welder, assembled the system with assistance from Colmar. Neither Colmar nor EPT recommended the use of a protective shield to guard the nip point, and as finally built, NEED's system did not have a shield. Later, as Americo Buonanno, a NEED employee, was clearing debris from the belt, his arm was pulled into the nip point. The arm was severely crushed and later amputated at the elbow. Buonanno filed a suit in a Rhode Island state court against Colmar and EPT, alleging in part strict liability. The defendants filed a motion for summary judgment, arguing that as sellers of component parts, they had no duty to ensure the proper design of the final product. On what grounds might the court deny the motion? [*Buonanno v. Colmar Belting Co.*, 733 A.2d 712 (R.I. 1999)]

CASE PROBLEM WITH SAMPLE ANSWER

17–9. In May 1995, Ms. McCathern and her daughter, together with McCathern's cousin, Ms. Sanders, and her daughter, were riding in Sanders's 1994 Toyota 4Runner. Sanders was driving, McCathern was in the front passenger seat, and the children were in the back seat. Everyone was wearing a seat belt. While the group was traveling south on Oregon State Highway 395 at a speed of approximately 50 miles per hour, an oncoming vehicle veered into Sanders's lane of travel. When Sanders tried to steer clear, the 4Runner rolled over and landed upright on its four wheels. During the rollover, the roof over the front passenger seat collapsed, and as a result, McCathern sustained serious, permanent injuries. McCathern filed a suit in an Oregon state court against Toyota Motor Corp. and others, alleging in part that the 1994 4Runner "was dangerously defective and unreasonably dangerous in that the vehicle, as designed and sold, was unstable and prone to rollover." What is the test for product liability based on a design defect? What would McCathern have to prove to succeed under that test? [*McCathern v. Toyota Motor Corp.*, 332 Or. 59, 23 P.3d 320 (2001)]

◆ To view a sample answer for this case problem, go to this book's Web site at **http://fundamentals.westbuslaw.com** and click on "Interactive Study Center."

17–10. Liability to Third Parties. Lee Stegemoller was a union member who insulated large machinery between 1947 and 1988. During his career, he worked for a number of different companies. Stegemoller primarily worked with asbestos insulation, which was used on industrial boilers, engines, furnaces, and turbines. After he left a work site, some of the asbestos dust always remained on his clothing. His wife, Ramona, who laundered his work clothes, was also exposed to the dust on a daily basis. Allegedly, as a result of this contact, she was diagnosed with colon cancer, pulmonary fibrosis, and pleural thickening in April 1998. The Stegemollers filed a suit in an Indiana state court against ACandS, Inc., and thirty-three others, contending among other things that the asbestos originated from products attributable to some of the defendants and from the premises of other defendants. Several defendants filed a motion to dismiss the complaint, asserting that Ramona was not a "user or consumer" of asbestos because she was not in the vicinity of the product when it was used. Should the court dismiss the suit on this basis? Explain. [*Stegemoller v. ACandS, Inc.*, 767 N.E.2d 974 (Ind. 2002)]

17–11. Implied Warranties. Shalom Malul contracted with Capital Cabinets, Inc., in August 1999 for new kitchen cabinets made by Holiday Kitchens. The price was $10,900. On Capital's recommendation, Malul hired Barry Burger to install the cabinets for $1,600. Burger finished the job in March 2000, and Malul contracted for more cabinets at a price of $2,300, which Burger installed in April. Within a couple of weeks, the doors on several of the cabinets began to "melt"—the laminate (surface covering) began to pull away from the substrate (the material underneath the surface). Capital replaced several of the doors, but the problem occurred again, to a total of six of thirty doors. A Holiday Kitchens representative inspected the cabinets and concluded that the melting was due to excessive heat, the result of the doors being placed too close to the stove. Malul filed a suit in a New York state court against Capital, alleging, among other things, a breach of the implied warranty of merchantability. Were these goods "merchantable"? Why or why not? [*Malul v. Capital Cabinets, Inc.*, 191 Misc.2d 399, 740 N.Y.S.2d 828 (N.Y.City Civ.Ct. 2002)]

VIDEO QUESTION

17–12. Go to this text's Web site at **http://fundamentals.westbuslaw.com** and click on "Video Questions." Select "Chapter 17" and view the video titled *Warranties*. Then answer the following questions:

1. Discuss whether the grocery store's label of a "Party Platter for Twenty" creates an express warranty under the UCC that the platter will actually serve twenty people.
2. List and describe any implied warranties discussed in the chapter that apply to this scenario.
3. How would a court determine whether Oscar had breached any express or implied warranties concerning the quantity of food on the platter?

WARRANTIES AND PRODUCT LIABILITY

For updated links to resources available on the Web, as well as other materials, visit this text's Web site at

http://fundamentals.westbuslaw.com

For a discussion of "Lemon Law Basics," go to Car Talk's Web site at

http://www.cartalk.com/Got-A-Car/Lemon/lemon_general.html

You can find an article on implied warranties in the "Guard Duty" section of the contents.

The law firm of Grimes & Reese, P.L.L.C., sponsors a Web site providing information on warranties at

http://www.mlmlaw.com/library/guides/ftc/warranties/toc.htm

For information on product liability suits against tobacco companies and recent settlements, go to the Web site of the Tobacco Control Archives at the University of California, San Francisco, at

http://www.library.ucsf.edu/tobacco/litigation

Online Legal Research

Go to the *Fundamentals of Business Law* home page at **http://fundamentals.westbuslaw. com**. Select "Interactive Study Center" and then click on "Chapter 17." There you will find the following Internet research exercises that you can perform to learn more about topics covered in this chapter.

Activity 17–1: LEGAL PERSPECTIVE—Product Liability Litigation
Activity 17–2: ECONOMIC PERSPECTIVE—Lemon Laws
Activity 17–3: MANAGEMENT PERSPECTIVE—Warranties

Before the Test

Go to the *Fundamentals of Business Law* Web site at **http://fundamentals. westbuslaw.com**. Click on "Interactive Quizzes." You will find at least twenty interactive questions relating to this chapter.

Westlaw® Campus

If your textbook provided for a subscription to Westlaw® Campus, or if you have otherwise purchased access to the Westlaw Campus database, you can access any of the cases presented or cited in this chapter by using your Westlaw Campus account.

Parker Tractor & Implement Co. v. Johnson

INTRODUCTION

We discussed, in Chapter 17, the warranties that apply to sales contracts. In this *Focus on Legal Reasoning,* we look at *Parker Tractor & Implement Co. v. Johnson,*[1] a decision in which the court considered the sufficiency of the proof for an award of damages on a seller's breach of warranty.

CASE BACKGROUND

In August 1994, Edward Johnson, Jr., went to Parker Tractor & Implement Company in Tunica, Mississippi, to buy a

---

1. 819 So.2d 1234 (Miss. 2002).

rice combine. Johnson told Parker's salesperson Walter Gray that he planned to use the combine to work on his own farm and to do custom cutting for other farmers.

Gray showed Johnson a model made by John Deere & Company that had a one-year warranty under which either the manufacturer or the dealer would take care of any problem that arose. Gray represented that the combine's average speed was 4.5 to 5.0 miles per hour. Johnson bought the model with a first payment of $30,634.36 and agreed to pay $32,510.75 annually for five years.

Before the new combine was delivered, however, it needed repair, and for several months after delivery Johnson complained

about problems. Most significantly, the combine would travel only 1.7 to 1.9 miles per hour. The slow speed more than doubled his harvest time.

In 1994, 1995, and 1996, Johnson cut about half as many acres of beans and rice as he later claimed he could have cut if the combine had been in good repair and had operated at the speed that Gray represented.

Johnson filed a suit in a Mississippi state court against Parker, alleging, among other things, breach of warranty. The court awarded him damages of $90,000. Parker appealed to the Mississippi Supreme Court, arguing in part that Johnson's proof of damages was too "speculative and unsubstantiated."

MAJORITY OPINION

McRAE, P.J. [Presiding Justice], for the court
* * * *

[Mississippi Code Annotated Section 75-2-715(2)(a)—Mississippi's version of UCC 2–715(2)(a)] allows a buyer suing for breach of warranty to recover consequential damages for "any loss resulting from general or particular requirements and needs of which the seller at the time of the contracting had reason to know and which could not reasonably be prevented by cover or otherwise * * * ." *This authorizes the recovery of lost profits if the seller had reason to know at the time of contracting that if he breached the buyer would lose, the loss of such profits is foreseeable, the lost profits are readily ascertainable, and the losses could not have been reasonably prevented.* In this case, Parker's representative knew that Johnson intended on using the combine to custom harvest * * * . It was reasonably foreseeable that any problems with the combine, including a reduced speed, would cause Johnson to lose anticipated profits. [Emphasis added.]

* * * *

* * * [W]hen the cause of the damages is reasonably certain, recovery is not to be denied because the data in proof does not furnish a perfect measure * * * . [I]t is enough that sufficient facts are given from which the [court] may safely make at least a minimum estimate.

Additionally, damages are speculative only when the cause is uncertain, not when the amount is uncertain.

* * * [A]ll existing records which could have shown pertinent losses were introduced, including a summary of loss calculations and Johnson's tax reports. Additionally, the acreage was calculated at the previous speed of an older combine compared with the slower speed with the lemon. This is sufficient to show

the loss of profits. In addition, since the contracts that Johnson had to break with other farmers were not in writing,[2] the best evidence possible was Johnson's testimony. He listed those farmers who he had contracts with, the amount of losses suffered and the amount he paid his father for help in cutting. We * * * held [in *Puckett Machine Co. v. Edwards,* 641 So.2d 29 (Miss.1994)] that lost profits in a business can be allowed if the data of estimation are so definite and certain that they can be ascertained reasonably by calculation.

Johnson is an expert in his own right. He is a 44-year-old man who has spent most of his childhood and his entire adult life farming. He was the one in charge of running his business, and he would have firsthand knowledge of profits and losses. In addition to his testimony, Johnson called an accountant with experience in custom harvesting to calculate the damages using testimony regarding contracts and the usual rate charged for custom harvesting.

* * * In this case, the testimony of Johnson and his accountant was the best evidence available.

It is totally reasonable to find that a defective combine would reduce the amount of farm work that the owner of the combine can perform and that the owner of the combine would surely, as a result, suffer a loss of profits. The combine was a lemon, and Johnson was forced out of business for some time. Johnson put on evidence of his losses, and the burden was shifted to Parker to negate any damages. Parker failed to do so and is bound by the award.

---

2. Written contracts are not customary in the custom-harvesting business.

DISSENTING OPINION

SMITH, * * * J., Dissenting:

* * * *

* * * In order to recover on a claim for lost profits, the profit lost must be proven to a reasonable certainty, and the lost profits must not be based on speculation. In my view, Johnson failed to carry his burden of proving lost profits to a reasonable certainty. Johnson testified that his losses for 1994, 1995, and 1996 were the result of the defective combine. For 1996 specifically, Johnson's proof consisted only of his statement that his lost profits totaled $26,000. While Johnson's testimony is certainly relevant to his losses, his testimony alone is simply too speculative to support an award for lost profits in this case. Johnson produced no other evidence in the form of contracts, witness testimony, or financial records to establish his claims of lost acreage. Nor did he establish that, time and weather permitting, he would have been able to cut the additional acreage.

As in [this] case * * * , the only support offered by the plaintiff in *Puckett Machine Co. v. Edwards,* 641 So.2d 29 (Miss.1994), was oral testimony. In that case, Edwards contended his Caterpillar 518 tree shearer's slower-than-expected output required him to hire additional sawmen. While Edwards testified his out-of-pocket cost was $100 per day, no * * * evidence such as truck tickets, payroll receipts, tax records, or banking records was offered in support of his claim. In holding that Edwards' testimony was insufficient to prove his claim for consequential damages, this Court * * * cited the rule on the recovery of profits lost through breach of contract: losses of profits in a business cannot be allowed, unless the data of estimation are so definite and certain that they can be ascertained reasonably by calculation.

* * * *

* * * [T]his Court should reverse and remand for a new trial.

LEGAL REASONING AND ANALYSIS

❶ Legal Analysis. Find the *Puckett Machine Co. v. Edwards* case (see the appendix to Chapter 1 for instructions on how to find state court opinions). How do the facts and result in the *Puckett* case compare with the circumstances and outcome in the *Parker* case? For what principle did the majority and dissent cite this case?

❷ Legal Reasoning. What is the basis for the disagreement between the majority and the dissent over the decision in this case?

❸ Legal Analysis. What arguments did the majority make to support its conclusion that the lower court's judgment was correct? What arguments did the dissent make to justify its position?

❹ Implications for Sellers and Buyers. How is the holding in this case of interest to businesses that buy or sell goods subject to warranties?

❺ Case Briefing Assignment. Using the guidelines for briefing cases given in Appendix A of this text, brief the *Parker* case.

This text's Web site, at **http://fundamentals.westbuslaw.com**, offers links to West's Court Case Updates, as well as to other online research sources. You can also locate court cases at the Web sites listed in the *Accessing the Internet* section at the end of Chapter 2.

The Legal Information Institute, at **http://www.law.cornell.edu/uniform/ucc.html**, provides links to state statutes that correspond to UCC articles, including Article 2 and Article 2A. The page includes links to an index of state cases and other materials on sales and other legal topics. Cornell Law School in Ithaca, New York, maintains this Web site.

UNIT 5

Negotiable Instruments

343

CHAPTER OBJECTIVES

After reading this chapter, you should be able to answer the following questions:

① What requirements must an instrument meet to be negotiable?

② What are the requirements for attaining the status of a holder in due course (HDC)?

③ What is the key to liability on a negotiable instrument? What is the difference between signature liability and warranty liability?

④ Certain defenses are valid against all holders, including HDCs. What are these defenses called? Name four defenses that fall within this category.

⑤ Certain defenses can be used to avoid payment to an ordinary holder of a negotiable instrument but are not effective against an HDC. What are these defenses called? Name four defenses that fall within this category.

The vast number of commercial transactions that occur daily in today's business world would be inconceivable without negotiable instruments. A **negotiable instrument** can be defined as a signed writing that contains an unconditional promise or order to pay an exact sum of money on demand or at a specified future time to a specific person or order, or to bearer. The checks you write to pay for groceries and other items are negotiable instruments.

A negotiable instrument can function in two ways—as a substitute for money or as an extension of credit. When a buyer writes a check to pay for goods, the check serves as a substitute for money. When a buyer gives a seller a promissory note in which the buyer promises to pay the seller the purchase price within sixty days, the seller has essentially extended credit to the buyer for a sixty-day period. For a negotiable instrument to operate *practically* as either a substitute for money or a credit device, or both, it is essential that the instrument be easily transferable without danger of being uncollectible. Each rule described in the following pages can be examined in light of this essential function of negotiable instruments.

Article 3 of the UCC

Negotiable instruments must meet special requirements relating to form and content. These requirements, which are imposed by Article 3 of the Uniform Commercial Code

(UCC), will be discussed at length in this chapter. When an instrument is negotiable, its transfer from one person to another is also governed by Article 3. Indeed, UCC 3–104(b) defines *instrument* as a "negotiable instrument." For that reason, whenever the term *instrument* is used in this book, it refers to a negotiable instrument.

THE 1990 REVISION OF ARTICLE 3

In 1990, a revised version of Article 3 was issued for adoption by the states. Many of the changes to Article 3 simply clarified old sections, but some significantly altered the former provisions. Because almost all of the states have adopted the revised article, references to Article 3 in this chapter and in the following chapter are to the revised Article 3. When the revised Article 3 has made important changes in the law, however, we discuss the previous law in footnotes.

Article 4 of the UCC, which governs bank deposits and collections (discussed in Chapter 19), was also revised in 1990. In part, these changes were necessary to reflect changes in Article 3 that affect Article 4 provisions. The revised Articles 3 and 4 are included in their entirety in Appendix C.

THE 2002 AMENDMENTS TO ARTICLES 3 AND 4

In 2002, the National Conference of Commissioners on Uniform State Laws and the American Law Institute approved a number of amendments to Articles 3 and 4 of the UCC. One of the purposes of the amendments was to update the law with respect to e-commerce. For example, the amended versions of the articles implement the policy of the Uniform Electronic Transactions Act (see Chapter 13) by removing unnecessary obstacles to electronic communications. Additionally, the word *writing* has been replaced with the term *record* throughout the articles. Other amendments relate to such topics as telephone-generated checks and the payment and discharge of negotiable instruments. In this chapter and in the chapter that follows, we will indicate in footnotes whenever the amendments significantly alter existing law.

Types of Instruments

The UCC specifies four types of negotiable instruments: *drafts, checks, promissory notes,* and *certificates of deposit* (*CDs*). These instruments are frequently divided into the two classifications that we will discuss in the following subsections: *orders to pay* (drafts and checks) and *promises to pay* (promissory notes and CDs).

Negotiable instruments may also be classified as either demand instruments or time instruments. A *demand instrument* is payable on demand; that is, it is payable immediately after it is issued and thereafter for a reasonable period of time. All checks are demand instruments because, by definition, they must be payable on demand. A *time instrument* is payable at a future date.

DRAFTS AND CHECKS (ORDERS TO PAY)

A **draft** (bill of exchange) is an unconditional written order that involves three parties. The party creating the draft (the **drawer**) orders another party (the **drawee**) to pay money, usually to a third party (the **payee**). A *time draft* is payable at a definite future time. A *sight draft* (or demand draft) is payable on sight—that is, when it is presented for payment. A draft can be both a time and a sight draft; such a draft is payable at a stated time after sight.

Exhibit 18–1 on the next page shows a typical time draft. For the drawee to be obligated to honor the order, the drawee must be obligated to the drawer either by agreement or through a debtor-creditor relationship. ● **EXAMPLE #1** On November 16, the Bank of Ourtown orders $1,000 worth of office supplies from Eastman Supply Company, with payment due January 16. On December 16, Eastman borrows $1,000 from the First National Bank of Whiteacre, with payment also due January 16. The First National Bank of Whiteacre will usually accept a draft drawn by Eastman on the Bank of Ourtown as payment for the loan. ●

A **trade acceptance** is a type of draft that is frequently used in the sale of goods. The seller is both the drawer and the payee on this draft. Essentially, the draft orders the buyer to pay a specified sum of money to the seller, usually at a stated time in the future. (If the draft orders the buyer's bank to pay, it is called a *banker's acceptance*.) ● **EXAMPLE #2** Jackson River Fabrics sells fabric priced at $50,000 to Comfort Creations, Inc., each year on terms requiring payment to be made in ninety days. One year Jackson River needs cash, so it draws a *trade acceptance* (see Exhibit 18–2 on the next page) that orders Comfort Creations to pay $50,000 to the order of Jackson River Fabrics ninety days hence. Jackson River presents the paper to Comfort Creations. Comfort Creations *accepts* the draft, by signing the face of the draft, and returns it to Jackson River Fabrics. The acceptance by Comfort Creations gives rise to an enforceable obligation to pay the draft when it comes due in ninety days. Jackson River can then immediately sell the trade acceptance in the commercial money market for cash. ●

The most commonly used type of draft is a **check**. The writer of the check is the drawer, the bank on which the check is drawn is the drawee, and the person to whom

EXHIBIT 18–1 A TYPICAL TIME DRAFT

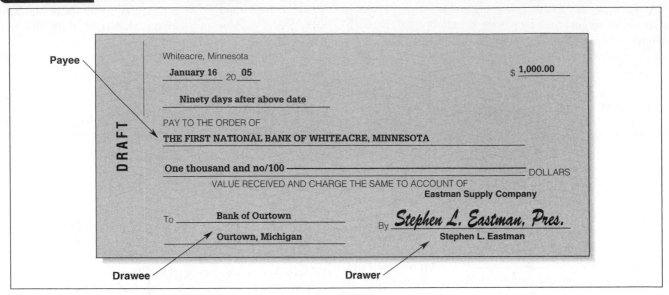

the check is payable is the payee. As mentioned earlier, checks, because they are payable on demand, are demand instruments.

Checks will be discussed more fully in Chapter 19, but it should be noted here that with certain types of checks, such as *cashier's checks,* the bank is both the drawer and the drawee. The bank customer purchases a cashier's check from the bank—that is, pays the bank the amount of the check—and indicates to whom the check should be made payable. The bank, not the customer, is the drawer of the check—as well as the drawee. The following case illustrates what this means to the payee of a cashier's check.

EXHIBIT 18–2 A TYPICAL TRADE ACCEPTANCE

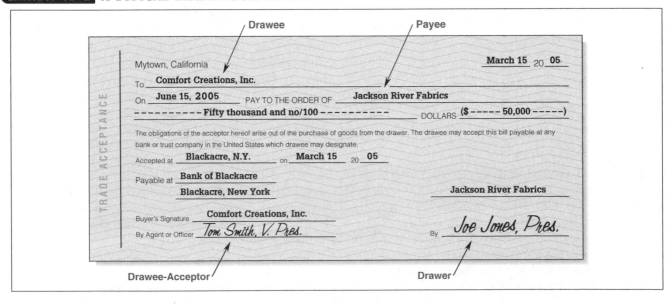

CASE 18.1 Flatiron Linen, Inc. v. First American State Bank

Colorado Supreme Court, 2001.
23 P.3d 1209.

FACTS Fluffy Reed Foundation, Inc., and one of its officers, Bilgen Reed, promised to secure a $2 million loan for Flatiron Linen, Inc., for which Flatiron paid a fee. Flatiron later accused Fluffy and Reed of fraud in the deal. As a partial refund of the fee, Fluffy issued a check to Flatiron for $4,100, drawn on an account at First American State Bank. When Flatiron attempted to deposit the check, First American returned it due to insufficient funds in the account. Five months later, when the account had sufficient funds, Flatiron took the check to First American and exchanged it for a cashier's check in the amount of $4,100. In the meantime, however, Fluffy had asked First American not to pay the check. When the bank discovered its mistake, it refused to pay the cashier's check. Flatiron filed a suit in a Colorado state court against a number of parties, including First American, from which Flatiron sought to recover the amount of the cashier's check. The court granted a summary judgment in favor of First American. The state intermediate appellate court affirmed this judgment, and Flatiron appealed to the Colorado Supreme Court.

ISSUE Should Flatiron be allowed to recover the amount of the cashier's check?

DECISION Yes. The Colorado Supreme Court reversed this part of the lower court's judgment and remanded the

case for proceedings consistent with this opinion. Once a cashier's check has been issued, a bank may not legitimately refuse to pay it.

REASON The state supreme court pointed out that it agreed with the majority of courts, which "hold that a cashier's check is the equivalent of cash, accepted when issued." The court explained that UCC 3–104(g) "defines a cashier's check as 'a draft with respect to which the drawer and drawee are the same bank or branches of the same bank.' Because the bank serves as both the drawer and the drawee of the cashier's check, the check becomes a promise by the bank to draw the amount of the check from its own resources and to pay the check upon demand. * * * Once the bank issues and delivers the cashier's check to the payee, the transaction is complete as far as the payee is concerned." The court also noted that "[t]he commercial world treats cashier's checks as the equivalent of cash. People accept cashier's checks as a substitute for cash because the bank, not an individual, stands behind it." To allow a bank not to pay a cashier's check "would be inconsistent with the representation it makes in issuing the check. Such a rule would undermine the public confidence in the bank and its checks and thereby deprive the cashier's check of the essential incident which makes it useful."

FOR CRITICAL ANALYSIS—Economic Consideration
What advantages might cashier's checks have over cash?

PROMISSORY NOTES AND CERTIFICATES OF DEPOSIT (PROMISES TO PAY)

A **promissory note** is a written promise made by one person (the **maker** of the promise to pay) to another (the payee, or the one to whom the promise is made). A promissory note, which is often referred to simply as a *note,* can be made payable at a definite time or on demand. It can name a specific payee or merely be payable to bearer (bearer instruments are discussed later in this chapter). ● **EXAMPLE #3** On April 30, Laurence and Margaret Roberts sign a writing unconditionally promising to pay "to the order of" the First National Bank of Whiteacre $3,000 (with 8 percent interest) on or before June 29. This writing is a promissory note.● A typical promissory note is shown in Exhibit 18–3 on the following page.

Notes are used in a variety of credit transactions and often carry the name of the transaction involved. For example, a note that is secured by personal property, such as an automobile, is called a *collateral note,* because the property pledged as security for the satisfaction of the debt is called collateral (see Chapter 20). A note payable in installments, such as for payment for a suite of furniture over a twelve-month period, is called an *installment note.*

A **certificate of deposit (CD)** is a type of note. A CD is issued when a party deposits funds with a bank that the bank promises to repay, with interest, on a certain date [UCC 3–104(j)]. The bank is the maker of the note, and the depositor is the payee. ● **EXAMPLE #4** On February 15, Sara Levin deposits $5,000 with the First National Bank of Whiteacre. The bank issues a CD, in which it promises to repay the $5,000, plus 5 percent interest, on August 15.●

EXHIBIT 18–3 A TYPICAL PROMISSORY NOTE

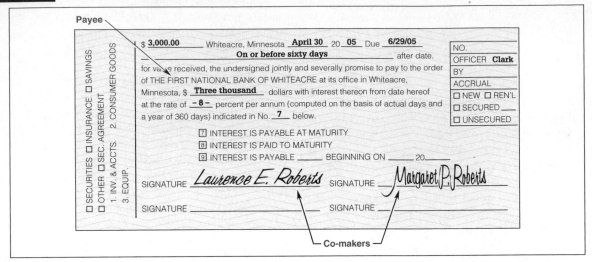

Certificates of deposit in small denominations (for amounts up to $100,000) are often sold by savings and loan associations, savings banks, and commercial banks. Certificates of deposit for amounts over $100,000 are called large (or jumbo) CDs. Exhibit 18–4 shows a typical small CD.

Requirements for Negotiability

For an instrument to be negotiable, it must meet the following requirements:

① Be in writing.

② Be signed by the maker or the drawer.

③ Be an unconditional promise or order to pay.

④ State a fixed amount of money.

⑤ Be payable on demand or at a definite time.

⑥ Be payable to order or to bearer, unless it is a check.

SIGNATURES

The UCC grants extreme latitude in regard to what constitutes a signature. UCC 1–201(39) provides that a **signature** may include "any symbol executed or adopted by a party with a present intention to authenticate a writing." UCC 3–401(b) expands on this by stating that a "signature may be

EXHIBIT 18–4 A TYPICAL SMALL CD

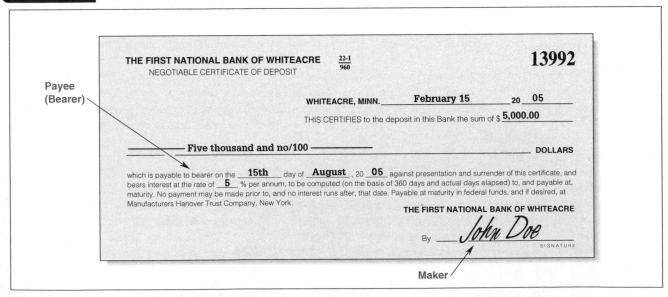

made (i) manually or by means of a device or machine, and (ii) by the use of any name, including a trade or assumed name, or by a word, mark, or symbol executed or adopted by a person with present intention to authenticate a writing." Thus, initials, an X (if the writing is signed by a witness), or a thumbprint will normally suffice as a signature. A trade name or an assumed name is also sufficient. Signatures that are placed onto instruments by means of rubber stamps are permitted and frequently used in the business world.

UNCONDITIONAL PROMISE OR ORDER TO PAY

For an instrument to be negotiable, it must contain an express order or promise to pay. A mere acknowledgment of the debt, which might logically *imply* a promise, is not sufficient under the UCC, because the promise must be an affirmative (express) undertaking [UCC 3–103(a)(9)]. The traditional I.O.U. (short for "I owe you") is only an acknowledgment of indebtedness. Although the I.O.U. might logically imply a promise, it is not a negotiable instrument because it does not contain an express promise to repay the debt.

A promise or order is conditional (and *not* negotiable) if it states (1) an express condition to payment, (2) that the promise or order is subject to or governed by another writing, or (3) that the rights or obligations with respect to the promise or order are stated in another writing. A reference to another writing, however, does not of itself make the promise or order conditional [UCC 3–106(a)]. For example, the words "As per contract" or "This debt arises from the sale of goods X and Y" do not render an instrument nonnegotiable.

A FIXED AMOUNT OF MONEY

The term *fixed amount* means an amount that is ascertainable from the face of the instrument. A demand note payable with 8 percent interest meets the requirement of a fixed amount[1] because its amount can be determined at the time it is payable or at any time thereafter [UCC 3–104(a)]. The rate of interest may also be determined with reference to information that is not contained in the instrument but that is readily ascertainable by reference to a formula or a source described in the instrument [UCC 3–112(b)].[2] For example,

when an instrument is payable at the *legal rate of interest* (a rate of interest fixed by statute), the instrument is negotiable. Mortgage notes tied to a variable rate of interest (a rate that fluctuates as a result of market conditions) can also be negotiable. The requirement that to be negotiable a writing must contain a promise or order to pay a fixed amount applies only to the principal [UCC 3–104(a)].

PAYABLE TO ORDER OR TO BEARER

An **order instrument** is an instrument that is payable (1) "to the order of an identified person" or (2) "to an identified person or order" [UCC 3–109(b)]. An identified person is the person "to whom the instrument is initially payable" as determined by the intent of the maker or drawer [UCC 3–110(a)]. The identified person, in turn, may transfer the instrument to whomever he or she wishes. Thus, the maker or drawer is agreeing to pay either the person specified on the instrument or whomever that person might designate. In this way, the instrument retains its transferability. ● **EXAMPLE #5** Suppose that an instrument states, "Payable to the order of Rocky Reed" or "Pay to Rocky Reed or order." Clearly, the maker or drawer has indicated that a payment will be made to Reed or to whomever Reed designates. The instrument is negotiable.●

A **bearer instrument** is an instrument that does not designate a specific payee [UCC 3–109(a)]. The term **bearer** refers to a person in the possession of an instrument that is payable to bearer or indorsed in blank (with a signature only, as will be discussed shortly) [UCC 1–201(5); 3–109(a), (c)]. This means that the maker or drawer agrees to pay anyone who presents the instrument for payment.

Transfer of Instruments

Once issued, a negotiable instrument can be transferred by *assignment* or by *negotiation*.

TRANSFER BY ASSIGNMENT

Recall from Chapter 11 that an assignment is a transfer of rights under a contract. Under general contract principles, a transfer by assignment to an assignee gives the assignee only those rights that the assignor possessed. Any defenses that can be raised against an assignor can normally be raised against the assignee. This same principle applies when an instrument, such as a promissory note, is transferred by assignment. The transferee is then an *assignee* rather than a *holder*. Sometimes, a transfer fails to qualify as a negotiation because it fails to meet one or more of the requirements of a negotiable instrument. When this occurs, the transfer becomes an assignment.

---

[1] Under Section 3–104(1)(b) of the unrevised Article 3, the amount to be paid was called a *sum certain*.

[2] This was not possible under the unrevised Article 3, which required that an amount or rate of interest could be determined only from the instrument without reference to any outside source [UCC 3–106].

TRANSFER BY NEGOTIATION

Negotiation is the transfer of an instrument in such form that the transferee (the person to whom the instrument is transferred) becomes a *holder* [UCC 3–201(a)]. The Uniform Commercial Code (UCC) defines a **holder** as a person in the possession of an instrument drawn, issued, or indorsed to him or her, to his or her order, to bearer, or in blank [UCC 1–201(20)]. Under UCC principles, a transfer by negotiation creates a holder who, at the very least, receives the rights of the previous possessor [UCC 3–203(b)]. Unlike an assignment, a transfer by negotiation can make it possible for a holder to receive more rights in the instrument than the prior possessor had [UCC 3–202(b), 3–305, 3–306]. A holder who receives greater rights is known as a *holder in due course,* a concept we discuss later in this chapter.

There are two methods of negotiating an instrument so that the receiver becomes a holder. The method used depends on whether the instrument is order paper or bearer paper.

Negotiating Order Instruments. An order instrument contains the name of a payee capable of indorsing it, as in "Pay to the order of Lloyd Sorenson." If the instrument is an order instrument, it is negotiated by delivery with any necessary indorsements. An **indorsement** is a signature placed on an instrument, such as on the back of a check, for the purpose of transferring one's ownership rights in the instrument. An *indorsement in blank* specifies no particular indorsement and can consist of a mere signature. ● **EXAMPLE #6** National Express Corporation issues a payroll check "to the order of Lloyd Sorenson." Sorenson takes the check to the supermarket, signs his name on the back (an indorsement), gives it to the cashier (a delivery), and receives cash. Sorenson has *negotiated* the check to the supermarket [UCC 3–201(b)].● Types of indorsements and their effects are listed in Exhibit 18–5.

Negotiating Bearer Instruments. If an instrument is payable to bearer, it is negotiated by delivery—that is, by transfer into another person's possession. Indorsement is not necessary [UCC 3–201(b)]. The use of bearer instruments thus involves more risk through loss or theft than the use of order instruments.

● **EXAMPLE #7** Assume that Richard Kray writes a check "payable to cash" and hands it to Jessie Arnold (a delivery). Kray has issued the check (a bearer instrument) to Arnold. Arnold places the check in her wallet, which is subsequently stolen. The thief has possession of the check. At this point, the thief has no rights to the check. If the thief "delivers" the check to an innocent third person, however, negotiation has occurred. All rights to the check will be passed absolutely to that third person, and Arnold will lose all rights to recover the proceeds of the check from him or her [UCC 3–306]. Of course, Arnold could attempt to recover the money from the thief if the thief can be found.●

Holder in Due Course (HDC)

An ordinary holder obtains only those rights that the transferor had in the instrument. In this respect, a holder has the same status as an assignee (see Chapter 11). Like an assignee, a holder normally is subject to the same defenses that could be asserted against the transferor.

In contrast, a **holder in due course (HDC)** is a holder who, by meeting certain acquisition requirements (to be discussed shortly), takes the instrument *free* of most of the defenses and claims that could be asserted against the transferor. Stated another way, an HDC can normally acquire a higher level of immunity than can an ordinary holder in regard to defenses against payment on the instrument or ownership claims to the instrument by other parties.

● **EXAMPLE #8** Marcia Cambry signs a $1,000 note payable to Alex Jerrod in payment for some ancient Roman coins. Jerrod negotiates the note to Alicia Larson, who promises to pay Jerrod for it in thirty days. During the next month, Larson learns that Jerrod has breached his contract with Cambry by delivering coins that were not from the Roman era, as promised, and that for this reason Cambry will not honor the $1,000 note. Whether Larson can hold Cambry liable on the note depends on whether Larson has met the requirements for HDC status. If Larson has met these requirements and thus has HDC status, Larson is entitled to payment on the note. If Larson has not met these requirements, she has the status of an ordinary holder, and Cambry's defense of breach of contract against payment to Jerrod will also be effective against Larson.●

Requirements for HDC Status

The basic requirements for attaining HDC status are set forth in UCC 3–302. A holder of a negotiable instrument is an HDC if she or he takes the instrument (1) for value; (2) in good faith; and (3) without notice that it is overdue, that it has been dishonored, that any person has a defense against it or a claim to it, or that the instrument contains unauthorized signatures, contains alterations, or is so irregular or incomplete as to call into question its authenticity. We now examine each of these requirements.

TAKING FOR VALUE

An HDC must have given *value* for the instrument [UCC 3–302(a)(2)(i)]. A person who receives an instrument as a gift or inherits it has not met the requirement of value. In

EXHIBIT 18–5 TYPES OF INDORSEMENTS AND THEIR CONSEQUENCES

WORDS CONSTITUTING THE INDORSEMENT	TYPE OF INDORSEMENT	INDORSER'S SIGNATURE LIABILITY[a]
"Rosemary White"	Blank	Unqualified signature liability on proper presentment and notice of dishonor.[b]
"Pay to Sam Wilson, Rosemary White"	Special	Unqualified signature liability on proper presentment and notice of dishonor.
"Without recourse, Rosemary White"	Qualified (blank for further negotiation)	No signature liability. Transfer warranty liability if breach occurs.[c]
"Pay to Sam Wilson, without recourse, Rosemary White"	Qualified (special for further negotiation)	No signature liability. Transfer warranty liability if breach occurs.
"Pay to Sam Wilson on condition he completes painting my house at 23 Elm Street by 9/1/05, Rosemary White"	Restrictive—conditional (special for further negotiation)	Signature liability only if condition is met. If condition is met, signature liability on proper presentment and notice of dishonor.
"Pay to Sam Wilson only, Rosemary White"	Restrictive—prohibitive (special for further negotiation)	Signature liability only on Sam Wilson's receiving payment. If Wilson receives payment, signature liability on proper presentment and notice of dishonor.
"For deposit, Rosemary White"	Restrictive—for deposit (blank for further negotiation)	Signature liability only on White having amount deposited in her account. If deposit is made, signature liability on proper presentment and notice of dishonor.
"Pay to Ann South in trust for John North, Rosemary White"	Restrictive—trust (special for further negotiation)	Signature liability only on payment to Ann South for John North's benefit. If restriction is met, signature liability on proper presentment and notice of dishonor.

a. *Signature liability* refers to the liability of a party who signs an instrument, as will be discussed later in this chapter. The basic questions include whether there is any liability and, if so, whether it is unqualified or restricted.

b. When an instrument is dishonored—that is, when, for example, a drawer's bank refuses to cash the drawer's check on proper presentment—an indorser of the check may be liable on it if he or she is given proper *notice of dishonor.*

c. The transferor of an instrument makes certain warranties to the transferee and subsequent holders, and thus, even if the transferor's signature does not render him or her liable on the instrument, he or she may be liable for breach of a transfer warranty. Transfer warranties are discussed later in this chapter.

these situations, the person becomes an ordinary holder and does not possess the rights of an HDC.

The concept of value in the law of negotiable instruments is not the same as the concept of *consideration* in the law of contracts. A promise to give value in the future is clearly sufficient consideration to support a contract [UCC 1–201(44)]. A promise to give value in the future, however, normally does not constitute value sufficient to make one an HDC. A holder takes an instrument for value only to the extent that the promise has been performed [UCC 3–303(a)(1)]. Therefore, if the holder plans to pay for the instrument later or plans to perform the required services at some future date, the holder has not yet given value. In that situation, the holder is not yet an HDC.

In the Larson-Cambry example presented earlier, Larson is not an HDC because she did not take the instrument

(Cambry's note) for value—she had not yet paid Jerrod for the note. Thus, Cambry's defense of breach of contract is valid not only against Jerrod but also against Larson. If Larson had paid Jerrod for the note at the time of transfer (which would mean she had given value for the instrument), she would be an HDC. As an HDC, she could hold Cambry liable on the note even though Cambry has a valid defense against Jerrod on the basis of breach of contract. Exhibit 18–6 on the next page illustrates these concepts.

Under UCC 3–303(a), a holder can take an instrument for value in one of five ways:

① By performing the promise for which the instrument was issued or transferred.

② By acquiring a security interest or other lien in the instrument, excluding a lien obtained by a judicial

EXHIBIT 18–6 **TAKING FOR VALUE**

By exchanging defective goods for the note, Jerrod breached his contract with Cambry. Cambry could assert this defense if Jerrod presented the note to her for payment. Jerrod exchanged the note for Larson's promise to pay in thirty days, however. Because Larson did not take the note for value, she is not a holder in due course. Thus, Cambry can assert against Larson the defense of Jerrod's breach when Larson submits the note to Cambry for payment. If Larson had taken the note for value, Cambry could not assert that defense and would be liable to pay the note.

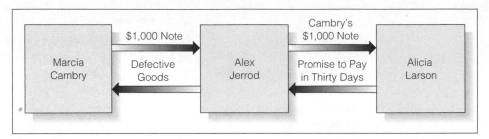

proceeding. (Security interests and liens are discussed in Chapters 20 and 21.)

③ By taking an instrument in payment of (or as security for) a preexisting debt.

④ By giving a negotiable instrument as payment.

⑤ By giving an irrevocable commitment as payment.

TAKING IN GOOD FAITH

The second requirement for HDC status is that the holder take the instrument in *good faith* [UCC 3–302(a)(2)(ii)]. This means that the holder must have acted honestly in the process of acquiring the instrument. UCC 3–103(a)(4) defines *good faith* as "honesty in fact and the observance of reasonable commercial standards of fair dealing." The good faith requirement applies only to the *holder*. It is immaterial whether the transferor acted in good faith. Thus, even a person who takes a negotiable instrument from a thief may become an HDC if the person acquires the instrument in good faith.

Because of the good faith requirement, one must ask whether the purchaser, when acquiring the instrument, honestly believed that the instrument was not defective. If a person purchases a $10,000 note for $300 from a stranger on a street corner, the issue of good faith can be raised on the grounds of both the suspicious circumstances and the grossly inadequate consideration (value). In the following case, the court considered whether a credit union fulfilled the good faith requirement to qualify as an HDC.

CASE 18.2   **Maine Family Federal Credit Union v. Sun Life Assurance Co. of Canada**

Supreme Judicial Court of Maine, 1999.
727 A.2d 335.
**http://www.courts.state.me.us/
opinions/supreme**[a]

FACTS On the death of Elden Guerrette, Sun Life Assurance Company of Canada issued three checks, each in the amount of $40,759.35, to each of Elden's three children. The checks were drawn on Sun Life's account at Chase Manhattan Bank in Syracuse, New York, and given to Steven Hall, a Sun Life

agent, to give to the Guerrettes. Hall and an associate, Paul Richard, fraudulently induced the Guerrettes to indorse the checks in blank and transfer them to Hall and Richard, purportedly to be invested in "HER, Inc.," a corporation formed by Hall and Richard. Richard deposited the checks in his account at the Maine Family Federal Credit Union, which immediately made the funds available. The next day, the Guerrettes contacted Sun Life, which ordered Chase Manhattan to stop payment on the checks. When the checks were presented for payment, the bank refused to pay them, and they were returned to the credit union. By that time, however, Richard had withdrawn from his account all of the funds represented by the checks. The credit union recovered almost $80,000 from Richard, but an unpaid balance of $42,366.56 remained. The credit union filed a suit in a Maine state court

---

a. Enter "Sun Life" into the "Opinions & Orders Search" field and click on "Go." The link to this case should be the first of a long list of matches.

CASE 18.2—Continued

against the Guerrettes and others. When the court entered a judgment against the credit union, it appealed to the Supreme Judicial Court of Maine, the state's highest court.

ISSUE Did the credit union act in good faith?

DECISION No. The Supreme Judicial Court of Maine, the state's highest court, affirmed the judgment of the lower court, as it related to the Guerrettes. The appellate court held that in relation to the Guerrettes, the credit union was not a holder in due course.

REASON The court explained that on the facts in this case, "the jury could rationally have concluded that the reasonable

commercial standard of fair dealing would require the placing of a hold on the uncollected funds for a reasonable period of time and that, in giving value under these circumstances, the credit union did not act according to commercial standards that were reasonably structured to result in fair dealing." Because of this, the credit union had not acted in good faith and could not claim the status of a holder in due course. The court vacated the portion of the judgment entered in favor of Sun Life and against the credit union on other grounds, however, and remanded that part of the case for further proceedings.

FOR CRITICAL ANALYSIS—Ethical Consideration
Why is good faith required to attain HDC status?

TAKING WITHOUT NOTICE

The final requirement for HDC status involves *notice* [UCC 3–302]. A person will not be afforded HDC protection if he or she acquires an instrument and is *on notice* (knows or has reason to know) that it is defective in any one of the following ways [UCC 3–302(a)]:

① It is overdue.

② It has been previously dishonored.

③ There is an uncured (uncorrected) default with respect to another instrument issued as part of the same series.

④ The instrument contains an unauthorized signature or has been altered.

⑤ There is a defense against the instrument or a claim to the instrument.

⑥ The instrument is so irregular or incomplete as to call into question its authenticity.

What Constitutes Notice? Notice of a defective instrument is given whenever the holder (1) has actual knowledge of the defect; (2) has received a notice of the defect (such as a bank's receipt of a letter listing the serial numbers of stolen bearer instruments); or (3) has reason to know that a defect exists, given all the facts and circumstances known at the time in question [UCC 1–201(25)]. The holder must also have received the notice "at a time and in a manner that gives a reasonable opportunity to act on it" [UCC 3–302(f)]. A purchaser's knowledge of certain facts, such as insolvency proceedings against the maker or drawer of the instrument, does not constitute notice that the instrument is defective [UCC 3–302(b)].

The following case raised questions concerning the potential liability of a party that accepted a check for deposit, despite arguably visible evidence that the check was irregular.

CASE 18.3 Travelers Casualty and Surety Co. of America v. Wells Fargo Bank, N.A.[a]

United States District Court,
Northern District
of Illinois, 2002.
205 F.Supp.2d 920.

FACTS Allianz Life Insurance of North America opened a checking account with Wells Fargo Bank, N.A., in the name of the Allianz Employees' Medical Plan to reimburse its employees

for medical expenses. First Health Strategies, Inc., managed the account. Two First Health employees, Mary Anne Carpenter and Jerry Seiler, were the only authorized signatories. Travelers Casualty and Surety Company of America insured Allianz against losses resulting from forged checks drawn on the account. On July 18, 2000, James Carden opened an account with Charles Schwab & Company, using a counterfeit check drawn on the Allianz account in the amount of $287,651.23. On the check were Carpenter's and Seiler's forged signatures.

---

a. The initials *N.A.* stand for *National Association.*

(Continued)

CASE 18.3—Continued

Schwab presented the check to Wells Fargo, which paid it and debited Allianz's account. Carden withdrew $271,238.22. When Wells Fargo and Schwab learned that the check was unauthorized, Schwab returned the balance in the Carden account—$16,413.01—to Wells Fargo, which credited Allianz's account. Allianz recovered the rest of the money from Travelers, which filed a suit in a federal district court against Wells Fargo and Schwab to recover that amount. Schwab filed a motion to dismiss the complaint against it. Schwab argued that when it accepted the forged check without notice of the fraud, it took the instrument as an HDC and was therefore not liable for the loss. In the court's opinion, the court refers to the action brought by Travelers against Schwab only and not the action against Wells Fargo.

ISSUE Was Schwab's claim to HDC status strong enough to support a motion to dismiss Travelers's suit against Schwab?

DECISION No. The court denied Schwab's motion to dismiss.

REASON The court held that Schwab could be disqualified from HDC status and held liable for the loss on the check,

because Schwab had notice of the invalidity of the check, which did not contain the "usual and customary magnetic ink containing check-processing information" and "usual and customary anti-forgery and anti-copying measures, including but not limited to an imbedded artificial watermark." Also, Schwab may have owed Allianz a common law duty, under which "a payee bank owes to the drawer of a check made payable to the bank a duty of care beyond that owed by an ordinary payee." In that case, Schwab's notice of a claim to the check could be presumed. The court explained, "When a drawer owes nothing to a bank but writes a check payable to the bank's order, the drawer places that check in the bank's custody, with the expectation that the bank will negotiate the check according to the drawer's wishes; the bank may not, therefore, treat the check as bearer paper and blindly disburse the proceeds according to the instructions of any individual who happens to present the check to the bank."

FOR CRITICAL ANALYSIS—Social Consideration
Charles Schwab is primarily a securities brokerage firm. In what circumstances can it be appropriate to consider a brokerage firm to be a bank?

Overdue Instruments. What constitutes notice that an instrument is overdue depends on whether it is a demand instrument (payable on demand) or a time instrument (payable at a definite time). For example, a purchaser has notice that a *demand instrument* is overdue if he or she takes the instrument an unreasonable length of time after its issue. A "reasonable time" for the taking of a check is ninety days, but for other demand instruments, what will be considered a reasonable time depends on the circumstances [UCC 3–304(a)].[3]

A holder of a *time instrument* who takes the instrument at any time after its expressed due date is on notice that it is overdue [UCC 3–304(b)(2)]. Nonpayment by the due date should indicate to any purchaser that the instrument may be defective. Thus, a promissory note due on May 15 must be acquired before midnight on May 15. If it is purchased on May 16, the purchaser will be an ordinary holder, not an HDC.

Sometimes, an instrument reads, "Payable in thirty days." A promissory note dated December 1 that is payable in thirty days is due by midnight on December 31. If the payment date

falls on a Sunday or a holiday, the instrument is payable on the next business day. If a debt is to be paid in installments or through a series of notes, the maker's default on any installment of principal (not interest) or on any one note of the series will constitute notice to the purchaser that the instrument is overdue [UCC 3–304(b)(1)].

Holder through an HDC

A person who does not qualify as an HDC but who derives his or her title through an HDC can acquire the rights and privileges of an HDC. According to UCC 3–203(b),

> Transfer of an instrument, whether or not the transfer is a negotiation, vests in the transferee any right of the transferor to enforce the instrument, including any right as a holder in due course, but the transferee cannot acquire rights of a holder in due course by a transfer, directly or indirectly, from a holder in due course if the transferee engaged in fraud or illegality affecting the instrument.

Under this rule, which is sometimes called the **shelter principle**, anyone—no matter how far removed from an HDC—who can trace his or her title ultimately back to an HDC may acquire the rights of an HDC.

---

[3] Under the unrevised Article 3, a reasonable time for the taking of a domestic check was *presumed* to be thirty days [UCC 3–304(3)(c)].

There are some limitations on the shelter principle, however. Certain persons who formerly held instruments cannot improve their positions by later reacquiring the instruments from HDCs [UCC 3–203(b)]. Thus, if a holder was a party to fraud or illegality affecting the instrument or if, as a prior holder, she or he had notice of a claim or defense against an instrument, that holder is not allowed to improve her or his status by repurchasing from a later HDC.

Signature Liability

The key to liability on a negotiable instrument is a *signature*. The general rule is as follows: Every party, except a qualified indorser,[4] who signs a negotiable instrument is either primarily or secondarily liable for payment of that instrument when it comes due. The following subsections discuss these two types of liability, as well as the conditions that must be met before liability can arise.

PRIMARY LIABILITY

A person who is primarily liable on a negotiable instrument is absolutely required to pay the instrument—unless, of course, he or she has a valid defense to payment [UCC 3–305]. Only *makers* and *acceptors* of instruments are primarily liable.

The maker of a promissory note promises to pay the note. It is the maker's promise to pay that makes the note a negotiable instrument. The words "I promise to pay" embody the maker's obligation to pay the instrument according to the terms as written at the time of the signing. If the instrument is incomplete when the maker signs it, then the maker's obligation is to pay it to an HDC according to the terms written when it is completed [UCC 3–115, 3–407(a), 3–412].

A drawee that promises to pay an instrument when it is presented later for payment is called an **acceptor**. A drawee's acceptance of a draft, which is made by signing the draft, guarantees that the drawee will pay the draft when it is presented in the future for payment [UCC 3–409(a)]. A drawee that refuses to accept a draft that *requires* the drawee's acceptance (such as a trade acceptance or a draft payable thirty days after acceptance) has dishonored the instrument. Acceptance of a check is called *certification* (discussed in Chapter 19). Certification is not necessary on checks, and a bank is under no obligation to certify checks. On certifica-

tion, however, the drawee bank occupies the position of an acceptor and is primarily liable on the check to any holder [UCC 3–409(d)].

SECONDARY LIABILITY

Drawers and indorsers are secondarily liable. Secondary liability on a negotiable instrument is similar to the liability of a guarantor in a simple contract (described in Chapter 11) in the sense that it is *contingent liability*. In other words, a drawer or an indorser will be liable only if the party that is primarily liable on the instrument dishonors it by nonpayment or, in regard to drafts and checks, the drawee fails to pay or to accept the instrument, whichever is required [UCC 3–412, 3–415].

Dishonor of an instrument thus triggers the liability of parties who are secondarily liable on the instrument—that is, the drawer and *unqualified* indorsers. For example, Nina Lee writes a check on her account at Universal Bank payable to the order of Stephen Miller. Universal Bank refuses to pay the check when Miller presents it for payment, thus dishonoring the check. In this situation, Lee will be liable to Miller on the basis of her secondary liability. Drawers are secondarily liable on drafts unless they disclaim their liability by drawing the instruments "without recourse" (if the draft is a check, however, a drawer cannot disclaim liability) [UCC 3–414(e)].

Parties that are secondarily liable on a negotiable instrument promise to pay on that instrument only if the following events occur:[5]

① The instrument is properly and timely presented.

② The instrument is dishonored.

③ Timely notice of dishonor is given to the secondarily liable party.

Proper and Timely Presentment. The UCC requires that presentment by a holder must be made to the proper person, must be made in a proper manner, and must be timely [UCC 3–414(f), 3–415(e), 3–501]. The party to whom the instrument must be presented depends on what type of instrument is involved. A note or certificate of deposit (CD) must be presented to the maker for payment. A draft is presented by the holder to the drawee for acceptance, payment, or both, whichever is required. A check is presented to the drawee for payment [UCC 3–501(a), 3–502(b)].

---

[4] A qualified indorser—one who indorses "without recourse"—undertakes no contractual obligation to pay. A qualified indorser merely assumes warranty liability, which is discussed later in this chapter.

[5] These requirements are necessary for a secondarily liable party to have signature liability on a negotiable instrument, but they are not necessary for a secondarily liable party to have warranty liability (to be discussed later in the chapter).

EXHIBIT 18–7   TIME FOR PROPER PRESENTMENT

TYPE OF INSTRUMENT	FOR ACCEPTANCE	FOR PAYMENT
Time	On or before due date.	On due date.
Demand	Within a reasonable time (after date or issue or after secondary party becomes liable on the instrument).	
Check	Not applicable.	Within ninety days of its date, to hold drawer secondarily liable. Within thirty days of indorsement, to hold indorser secondarily liable.[a]

a.   Under the unrevised Article 3, these periods are *presumed* to be thirty days to hold the drawer secondarily liable, and seven days to hold the indorser secondarily liable.

Presentment can be properly made in any of the following ways, depending on the type of instrument involved [UCC 3–501(b)]:

1. By any commercially reasonable means, including oral, written, or electronic communication (but presentment is not effective until the demand for payment or acceptance is received).

2. Through a clearinghouse procedure used by banks, such as for deposited checks (see Chapter 19).

3. At the place specified in the instrument for acceptance or payment.

One of the most crucial criteria for proper presentment is timeliness [UCC 3–414(f), 3–415(e), 3–501(b)(4)]. Failure to present on time is the most common reason for improper presentment and results in the complete discharge of unqualified indorsers from secondary liability. For checks, failure to properly present a check discharges the drawer's secondary liability only to the extent that the drawee is deprived of the funds required to pay the check. The time for proper presentment for different types of instruments is shown in Exhibit 18–7 above.

Dishonor. An instrument is dishonored when the required acceptance or payment is refused or cannot be obtained within the prescribed time, or when required presentment is excused (as it would be, for example, if the maker had died) and the instrument is not properly accepted or paid [UCC 3–502(e), 3–504].

Payment can be postponed without dishonoring the instrument if presentment is made after an established cutoff hour (not earlier than 2:00 P.M.), but payment cannot be postponed beyond the close of the next business day after the day of presentment [UCC 3-501(b)(4)]. In addition, the party to whom presentment is made may refuse payment without dishonoring the instrument if the holder refuses to exhibit the instrument, to give reasonable identification and/or authority to receive payment, or to sign on the instrument as a receipt for any payment made [UCC 3–501(b)(2)].

Some banks require a check holder who does not have an account at the bank to provide a thumbprint before the bank will honor the check. The issue in the following case was whether this practice is lawful.

CASE 18.4   Messing v. Bank of America, N.A.

Maryland Court of Special Appeals, 2002.
143 Md.App. 1,
792 A.2d 312.

FACTS On August 3, 2000, Jeff Messing attempted to cash a check payable to his order for $976 at a branch office of Bank of America, N.A., in Baltimore City, Maryland. The check was drawn on a checking account of one of the bank's customers. A teller confirmed the availability of funds in the

account and asked Messing if he was a bank customer. When he said "no," the teller asked Messing to place his "thumbprint signature" on the check in accord with the bank's policy for "non-account holders."[a] Messing refused, and the teller refused to cash the check. Messing demanded to speak with

---

a. Messing was asked to create a thumbprint signature by applying his right thumb to an inkless fingerprinting device, which leaves no ink stain or residue, and then placing his thumb on the face of the check between the memo and signature lines. Similar procedures are used at other banks.

CASE 18.4—Continued

the branch manager, who also refused to cash the check. Messing filed a suit against the bank in a Maryland state court, asking the court to declare, among other things, that requiring a thumbprint was not "reasonable identification" under Maryland Code Section 3–501(b)(2) of the state's Commercial Law Article, which is Maryland's version of UCC 3–501(b)(2). The bank filed a motion for summary judgment, which the court granted. Messing appealed to a state intermediate appellate court.

ISSUE Is it reasonable for a bank to require a thumbprint as a form of identification?

DECISION Yes. The state intermediate appellate court upheld the lower court's judgment in favor of the bank. The appellate court held that requiring thumbprint signatures for check holders without accounts is lawful under the UCC, in part as "a reasonable and necessary answer to the growing incidence of check fraud."

REASON The court pointed out that a "thumbprint signature has been accepted by the drafters of the Maryland UCC as an effective, reliable, and accurate way to authenticate a writing on a negotiable instrument," that "the process that a non-account holder goes through to provide a thumbprint signature is not unreasonably inconvenient," and that providing a thumbprint signature "assist[s] in the identification of the check holder should the check later prove to be bad. It therefore serves as a powerful deterrent to those who might otherwise attempt to pass a bad check." The court also noted that thumbprint signatures "have been endorsed by the American Bankers Association and more than thirty (30) state bankers associations."

FOR CRITICAL ANALYSIS—Social Consideration
Why might a customer be reluctant to provide a thumbprint to a bank, even if he or she is presenting a valid check?

Proper Notice. Once an instrument has been dishonored, proper notice must be given to secondary parties for them to be held contractually liable. Notice may be given in any reasonable manner. This includes oral notice, written notice (including notice by fax, e-mail, and the like), and notice written or stamped on the instrument itself. Any necessary notice must be given by a bank before its midnight deadline (midnight of the next banking day after receipt). Notice by any party other than a bank must be given within thirty days following the day of dishonor or the day on which the person who is secondarily liable receives notice of dishonor [UCC 3–503].[6]

UNAUTHORIZED SIGNATURES

People normally are not liable to pay on negotiable instruments unless their signatures appear on the instruments. As already stated, the general rule is that an unauthorized signature is wholly inoperative and will not bind the person whose name is forged. ● **EXAMPLE #9** Parra finds Dolby's checkbook lying in the street, writes out a check to himself, and forges Dolby's signature. If a bank fails to ascertain that Dolby's signature is not genuine (which banks normally have a duty to do) and cashes the check for Parra, the bank will generally be liable to Dolby for the amount. ● (The lia-

bility of banks for paying checks with forged signatures is discussed further in Chapter 19.) There are two exceptions to this general rule:

① Any unauthorized signature will bind the person whose name is forged if the person whose name is signed ratifies (affirms) it [UCC 3–403(a)]. For example, a mother may ratify her daughter's forgery of the mother's name so that her daughter will not be prosecuted for forgery.

② A person may be precluded from denying the effectiveness of an unauthorized signature if the person's negligence led to the forgery [UCC 3–115, 3–406, 4–401(d)(2)]. ● **EXAMPLE #10** Suppose that Jonathan leaves a blank check in a public place. If someone else finds the check, fills it out, and forges Jonathan's signature, Jonathan can be estopped (prevented), on the basis of negligence, from denying liability for payment of the check. ●

An unauthorized signature operates as the signature of the unauthorized signer in favor of an HDC. A person who forges a check, for example, can be held personally liable for payment by an HDC [UCC 3–403(a)].

SPECIAL RULES FOR UNAUTHORIZED INDORSEMENTS

Generally, when an indorsement is forged or unauthorized, the burden of loss falls on the first party to take the instrument with the forged or unauthorized indorsement. If the

---

[6] Under the unrevised Article 3, notice by a person other than a bank has to be given "before midnight of the third business day after dishonor or receipt of notice of dishonor" [UCC 3–508(2)].

indorsement was made by an imposter or by a fictitious payee, however, the loss falls on the maker or drawer. We look at these two situations here.

Imposters. An **imposter** is one who, by use of the mails, telephone, or personal appearance, induces a maker or drawer to issue an instrument in the name of an impersonated payee. If the maker or drawer believes the imposter to be the named payee at the time of issue, the indorsement by the imposter is not treated as unauthorized when the instrument is transferred to an innocent party. This is because the maker or drawer intended the imposter to receive the instrument. In this situation, under the UCC's *imposter rule,* the imposter's indorsement will be effective— that is, not considered a forgery—insofar as the drawer or maker is concerned [UCC 3–404(a)]. ● **EXAMPLE #11** Carol impersonates Donna and induces Edward to write a check payable to the order of Donna. Carol, continuing to impersonate Donna, negotiates the check to First National Bank. As the drawer of the check, Edward is liable for its amount to First National.●

Fictitious Payees. An unauthorized indorsement will also be effective when a person causes an instrument to be issued to a payee who will have *no interest* in the instrument [UCC 3–404(b), 3–405]. In this situation, the payee is referred to as a **fictitious payee.** Situations involving fictitious payees most often arise when (1) a dishonest employee deceives the employer into signing an instrument payable to a party with no right to receive payment on the instrument or (2) a dishonest employee or agent has the authority to issue an instrument on behalf of the employer. Under the UCC's *fictitious payee rule,* the payee's indorsement is not treated as a forgery, and the employer can be held liable on the instrument by an innocent holder or a party (such as a bank) that pays the instrument in good faith.

● **EXAMPLE #12** Flair Industries, Inc., gives its bookkeeper, Axel Ford, general authority to issue checks in the company name drawn on First State Bank so that Ford can pay employees' wages and other corporate bills. Ford decides to cheat Flair Industries out of $10,000 by issuing a check payable to Erica Nied, an old acquaintance. Neither Flair nor Ford intends Nied to receive any of the money, and Nied is not an employee or creditor of the company. Ford indorses the check in Nied's name, naming himself as indorsee. He then cashes the check at a local bank, which collects payment from the drawee bank, First State Bank. First State Bank charges the Flair Industries account $10,000. Flair Industries discovers the fraud and demands that the account be recredited.

Who bears the loss? UCC 3–404(b)(2) provides the answer. Neither the local bank that first accepted the check nor First State Bank is liable. Because Ford's indorsement in the name of a payee with no interest in the instrument is "effective," there is no "forgery." Hence, the collecting bank is protected in paying on the check, and the drawee bank is protected in charging Flair's account. It is the employer-drawer, Flair Industries, that bears the loss. Of course, Flair Industries has recourse against Axel Ford.●

Regardless of whether a dishonest employee actually signs the check or merely supplies the employer with names of fictitious creditors (or with true names of creditors having fictitious debts), the UCC makes no distinction in result. ● **EXAMPLE #13** Nathan Holtz draws up the payroll list from which employees' salary checks are written. He fraudulently adds the name Sally Slight (a fictitious person) to the payroll, and the employer signs checks to be issued to her. Again, it is the employer-drawer who bears the loss.●

Warranty Liability

In addition to the signature liability discussed in the preceding pages, transferors make certain implied warranties regarding the instruments that they are negotiating. Liability under these warranties is not subject to the conditions of proper presentment, dishonor, or notice of dishonor. These warranties arise even when a transferor does not indorse the instrument (as in the delivery of a bearer instrument) [UCC 3–416, 3–417].

Warranties fall into two categories: those that arise on the *transfer* of a negotiable instrument and those that arise on *presentment.* Both transfer and presentment warranties attempt to shift liability back to a wrongdoer or to the person who dealt face to face with the wrongdoer and thus was in the best position to prevent the wrongdoing.

TRANSFER WARRANTIES

The UCC describes five **transfer warranties** [UCC 3–416]. These warranties provide that any person who transfers an instrument *for consideration* makes the following warranties to all subsequent transferees and holders who take the instrument in good faith (with some exceptions, as will be noted shortly):

① The transferor is entitled to enforce the instrument.

② All signatures are authentic and authorized.

③ The instrument has not been altered.

④ The instrument is not subject to a defense or claim of any party that can be asserted against the transferor.[7]

⑤ The transferor has no knowledge of any insolvency proceedings against the maker, the acceptor, or the drawer of the instrument.[8]

The manner of transfer and the negotiation that is used determine how far and to whom a transfer warranty will run. Transfer of order paper, for consideration, by indorsement and delivery extends warranty liability to any subsequent holder who takes the instrument in good faith. The warranties of a person who transfers *without indorsement* (by the delivery of a bearer instrument), however, will extend the transferor's warranties solely to the immediate transferee [UCC 3–416(a)].

● **EXAMPLE #14** Abraham forges Peter's name as a maker of a promissory note. The note is made payable to Abraham. Abraham indorses the note in blank, negotiates it to Carla, and then leaves the country. Carla, without indorsement, delivers the note to Frank for consideration. Frank, in turn, without indorsement, delivers the note to Ricardo for consideration. On Ricardo's presentment of the note to Peter, the forgery is discovered. Ricardo can hold Frank (the immediate transferor) liable for breach of the transfer warranty that all signatures are genuine. Ricardo cannot hold Carla liable because the transfer warranties made by Carla, who negotiated the bearer instrument by delivery only, extend solely to Frank, the immediate transferee.●

Note that if Abraham had added a special indorsement ("Payable to Carla") instead of a blank indorsement, the instrument would have remained an order instrument. In that situation, to negotiate the instrument to Frank, Carla would have had to indorse the instrument, and her transfer warranties would extend to all subsequent holders, including Ricardo. This example shows the importance of the distinction between a transfer by indorsement and delivery (of an order instrument) and a transfer by delivery only, without indorsement (of a bearer instrument).

PRESENTMENT WARRANTIES

Any person who presents an instrument for payment or acceptance makes the following **presentment warranties** to any other person who in good faith pays or accepts the instrument [UCC 3–417(a), (d)]:

① The person obtaining payment or acceptance is entitled to enforce the instrument or is authorized to obtain payment or acceptance on behalf of a person who is entitled to enforce the instrument. (This is, in effect, a warranty that there are no missing or unauthorized indorsements.)

② The instrument has not been altered.

③ The person obtaining payment or acceptance has no knowledge that the signature of the issuer of the instrument is unauthorized.[9]

These warranties are referred to as presentment warranties because they protect the person to whom the instrument is presented. The second and third warranties do not apply to makers, acceptors, and drawers. It is assumed, for example, that a drawer or a maker will recognize his or her own signature and that a maker or an acceptor will recognize whether an instrument has been materially altered.

Defenses to Liability

Persons who would otherwise be liable on negotiable instruments may be able to avoid liability by raising certain defenses. There are two general categories of defenses—*universal defenses* and *personal defenses*.

UNIVERSAL DEFENSES

Universal defenses (also called *real defenses*) are valid against *all* holders, including HDCs and holders who take through an HDC. Universal defenses include those described here.

Forgery. Forgery of a maker's or drawer's signature cannot bind the person whose name is used unless that person ratifies (approves or validates) the signature or is precluded from denying it (because the forgery was made possible by the maker's or drawer's negligence, for example) [UCC 3–403(a)]. Thus, when a person forges an instrument, the

---

[7] Under the unrevised Article 3, a qualified indorser who indorses an instrument "without recourse" limits this warranty to a warranty that he or she has "no knowledge" of such a defense (rather than that there is no defense). This limitation does not apply under the revised Article 3.

[8] A 2002 amendment to UCC 3–416(a) adds a sixth warranty: "with respect to a remotely created consumer item, that the person on whose account the item is drawn authorized the issuance of the item in the amount for which the item is drawn." For example, a telemarketer submits an instrument to a bank for payment, claiming that the consumer on whose account the instrument purports to be drawn authorized it over the phone. Under this amendment, a bank that accepts and pays the instrument warrants to the next bank in the collection chain that the consumer authorized the item in that amount.

[9] The warranty added by a 2002 amendment to UCC 3–416(a), "with respect to a remotely created consumer item," referred to in footnote 8, is also added as a fourth warranty by a proposed amendment to UCC 3–417(a).

person whose name is forged normally has no liability to pay any holder or any HDC the value of the forged instrument.

Fraud in the Execution. If a person is deceived into signing a negotiable instrument, believing that she or he is signing something other than a negotiable instrument (such as a receipt), *fraud in the execution,* or fraud in the inception, is committed against the signer [UCC 3–305(a)(1)]. ● EXAMPLE #15 A salesperson asks a customer to sign a paper, which the salesperson says is a receipt for the delivery of goods that the customer is picking up from the store. In fact, the paper is a promissory note, but the customer, who is unfamiliar with the English language, does not realize this. In this situation, even if the note is negotiated to an HDC, the customer has a valid defense against payment.●

The defense of fraud in the execution cannot be raised, however, if a reasonable inquiry would have revealed the nature and terms of the instrument.[10] Thus, the signer's age, experience, and intelligence are relevant because they frequently determine whether the signer should have understood the nature of the transaction before signing.

Material Alteration. An alteration is material if it changes the contract terms between any two parties in any way. Examples of material alterations include completing an incomplete instrument, adding words or numbers to an instrument, or making any other change to an instrument in an unauthorized manner that affects the obligation of a party to the instrument [UCC 3–407(a)].

Thus, cutting off part of the paper of a negotiable instrument; adding clauses; or making any change in the amount, the date, or the rate of interest—even if the change is only one penny, one day, or 1 percent—is material. It is not a material alteration, however, to correct the maker's address, for example, or to change the figures on a check so that they agree with the written amount (words outweigh figures if there is a conflict between the written amount and the amount given in figures). If the alteration is not material, any holder is entitled to enforce the instrument according to its terms.

Material alteration is a *complete defense* against an ordinary holder. An ordinary holder can recover nothing on an instrument if it has been materially altered [UCC 3–407(b)]. Material alteration, however, may be only a *partial defense* against an HDC. When the holder is an HDC, if an original term, such as the monetary amount payable, has been

altered, the HDC can enforce the instrument against the maker or drawer according to the original terms but not for the altered amount. If the instrument was originally incomplete and was later completed in an unauthorized manner, however, alteration no longer can be claimed as a defense against an HDC, and the HDC can enforce the instrument as completed [UCC 3–407(b)]. This is because the drawer or maker of the instrument, by issuing an incomplete instrument, will normally be held responsible for the alteration, which could have been avoided by the exercise of greater care. If the alteration is readily apparent, then obviously the holder has notice of some defect or defense and therefore cannot be an HDC [UCC 3–302(a)(1)].

Discharge in Bankruptcy. Discharge in bankruptcy is an absolute defense on any instrument, regardless of the status of the holder, because the purpose of bankruptcy is to settle finally all of the insolvent party's debts [UCC 3–305(a)(1)].

Minority. Minority, or infancy, is a universal defense only to the extent that state law recognizes it as a defense to a simple contract (see Chapter 9). Because state laws on minority vary, so do determinations of whether minority is a universal defense against an HDC [UCC 3–305(a)(1)(i)].

Illegality. Certain types of illegality constitute universal defenses. Other types constitute personal defenses—that is, defenses that are effective against ordinary holders but not against HDCs. The difference lies in the state statutes or ordinances that make the transactions illegal. If a statute provides that an illegal transaction is void, the defense is universal—that is, absolute against both an ordinary holder and an HDC. If the law merely makes the instrument voidable, the illegality is still a defense against an ordinary holder but not against an HDC [UCC 3–305(a)(1)(ii)].

Mental Incapacity. If a person is adjudged mentally incompetent by state proceedings, any instrument issued thereafter by that person is void. The instrument is void *ab initio* (from the beginning) and unenforceable by any holder or HDC [UCC 3–305(a)(1)(ii)]. Mental incapacity in these circumstances is thus a universal defense. If a person has not been adjudged mentally incompetent by state proceedings, mental incapacity operates as a defense against an ordinary holder but not against an HDC.

Extreme Duress. When a person signs and issues a negotiable instrument under such extreme duress as an immediate threat of force or violence (for example, at gunpoint), the instrument is void and unenforceable by any holder or HDC [UCC 3–305(a)(1)(ii)]. Ordinary duress is a defense against ordinary holders but not against HDCs.

---

[10] *Burchett v. Allied Concord Financial Corp.,* 74 N.M. 575, 396 P.2d 186 (1964).

PERSONAL DEFENSES

Personal defenses (sometimes called *limited defenses*), such as those described here, can be used to avoid payment to an ordinary holder of a negotiable instrument, but not to an HDC or a holder with the rights of an HDC.

Breach of Contract or Breach of Warranty. When there is a breach of the underlying contract for which the negotiable instrument was issued, the maker of a note can refuse to pay it, or the drawer of a check can order his or her bank to stop payment on the check. Breach of warranty can also be claimed as a defense to liability on the instrument.
● EXAMPLE #16 Rhodes agrees to purchase several sets of imported china from Livingston. The china is to be delivered in four weeks. Rhodes gives Livingston a promissory note for $2,000, which is the price of the china. The china arrives, but many of the pieces are broken, and several others are chipped or cracked. Rhodes refuses to pay the note on the basis of breach of contract and breach of warranty. (Under sales law, a seller impliedly promises that the goods are at least merchantable—see Chapter 17.) Livingston cannot enforce payment on the note because of the breach of contract and breach of warranty. If Livingston has negotiated the note to a third party, however, and the third party is an HDC, Rhodes will not be able to use breach of contract or warranty as a defense against liability on the note. ●

Lack or Failure of Consideration. The absence of consideration (value) may be a successful personal defense in some instances [UCC 3–303(b), 3–305(a)(2)]. ● EXAMPLE #17 Tara gives Clem, as a gift, a note that states, "I promise to pay you $100,000." Clem accepts the note. Because there is no consideration for Tara's promise, a court will not enforce the promise. ●

Fraud in the Inducement (Ordinary Fraud). A person who issues a negotiable instrument based on false statements by the other party will be able to avoid payment on that instrument, unless the holder is an HDC. ● EXAMPLE #18 Jerry agrees to purchase Howard's used tractor for $24,500. Howard, knowing his statements to be false, tells Jerry that the tractor is in good working order, that it has been used for only one harvest, and that he owns the tractor free and clear of all claims. Jerry pays Howard $4,500 in cash and issues a negotiable promissory note for the balance. As it turns out, Howard still owes the original seller $10,000 on the purchase of the tractor. In addition, the tractor is three years old and has been used in three harvests. Jerry can refuse to pay the note if it is held by an ordinary holder. If Howard has negotiated the note to an HDC, however, Jerry must pay the HDC. (Of course, Jerry can then sue Howard to recover the money.) ● This chapter's *Business Law in the Online World* fea-

ture on the next page looks at a case involving promissory notes and charges of fraud.

Illegality. As mentioned, if a statute provides that an illegal transaction is void, a universal defense exists. If, however, the statute provides that an illegal transaction is voidable, the defense is personal.

Mental Incapacity. As mentioned, if a maker or drawer has been declared by a court to be mentally incompetent, any instrument issued by the maker or drawer is void. Hence, mental incapacity can serve as a universal defense [UCC 3–305(a)(1)(ii)]. If a maker or drawer issues a negotiable instrument while mentally incompetent but before a formal court hearing has declared him or her to be so, however, the instrument is voidable. In this situation, mental incapacity can serve only as a personal defense.

Other Personal Defenses. Other personal defenses can be used to avoid payment to an ordinary holder of a negotiable instrument, including the following:

① Discharge by payment or cancellation [UCC 3–601(b), 3–602(a), 3–603, 3–604].

② Unauthorized completion of an incomplete instrument [UCC 3–115, 3–302, 3–407, 4–401(d)(2)].

③ Nondelivery of the instrument [UCC 1–201(14), 3–105(b), 3–305(a)(2)].

④ Ordinary duress or undue influence rendering the contract voidable [UCC 3–305(a)(1)(ii)].

Discharge from Liability

Discharge from liability on an instrument can occur in several ways. The liability of all parties to an instrument is discharged when the party primarily liable on it pays to the holder the amount due in full [UCC 3–602, 3–603]. Payment by any other party discharges only the liability of that party and subsequent parties.

Intentional cancellation of an instrument discharges the liability of all parties [UCC 3–604]. Intentionally writing "Paid" across the face of an instrument cancels it. Intentionally tearing up an instrument cancels it. If a holder intentionally crosses out a party's signature, that party's liability and the liability of subsequent indorsers who have already indorsed the instrument are discharged. Materially altering an instrument may discharge the liability of any party affected by the alteration, as previously discussed [UCC 3–407(b)]. (An HDC may be able to enforce a materially altered instrument against its maker or drawer according to the instrument's original terms, however.)

BUSINESS LAW IN THE ONLINE WORLD
From Start-Up to Finish

When a new business—based on a new idea in a new industry—starts up, the potential for profit may appear unlimited. When the founders of the business include students of computer science and physics, as well as a former vice president of a well-known investment management firm, this expectation may even seem reasonable.

Dreams of wealth can be undercut by reality, however. Day-to-day business operations can be expensive. For this reason, whoever oversees the financial development of a business is as important to the firm as the scientist behind the firm's product or service.

If capital is not forthcoming at the rate that the firm needs it, the founders may resort to desperate measures to keep the business from failing. In the end, the firm may be sold, and relations among the founders may become less than cordial, with each blaming the other. This set of circumstances is not new, but it has been much in the public eye in the twenty-first century with the collapse of many businesses in the online world.

THE PROMISSORY NOTES The founders of the Worldwide Broadcasting Network (WBN) intended to make television programming available over the Internet through customized video channels. Dariush Gholizadeh and Ali Kazeroonian had the technological expertise. Ali Malihi had the financial background, having worked for fourteen years for Paine Webber, where he managed over $100 million in assets.

In January 1996, Malihi agreed to obtain $5 million in financing for WBN by June. In March, however, Malihi lowered the amount to $2 million and extended the date to October. Meanwhile, he used his own money to fund WBN, including $40,910 for which he asked Gholizadeh to sign promissory notes. At Gholizadeh's insistence, each note provided that repayment depended on his

WBN salary, which in turn depended on Malihi's obtaining financing.

By March 1997, Malihi had not met the $2 million goal, and WBN faced a financial crisis. Gholizadeh found an investor willing to help in exchange for WBN stock. When WBN fired Malihi as an employee and discharged him as a director, he filed a suit in a Massachusetts state court against Gholizadeh, seeking payment on the notes.

FRAUD IN THE INDUCEMENT? Gholizadeh argued that he should not be held liable on the notes because "Malihi fraudulently misrepresented that his departure from Paine Webber was voluntary." According to Gholizadeh, Malihi's "statement that he left Paine Webber because WBN offered a great start-up opportunity constituted a half truth because he failed to disclose Paine Webber had terminated him."

The court acknowledged that Malihi "may have been less than totally forthcoming about the details of his departure from Paine Webber" but added that he was never asked whether he left voluntarily. Besides, to avoid liability on a negotiable instrument, the alleged fraud must be material to the issuing of the instrument. As the court explained, Gholizadeh and Kazeroonian "brought plaintiff into WBN because of his obvious financial and marketing expertise. There is no credible evidence that plaintiff's involuntary departure from Paine Webber related in any way to his undisputed fund-raising abilities." The court held that Gholizadeh was obligated to repay the notes.[a]

FOR CRITICAL ANALYSIS
In cases involving negotiable instruments issued to support emerging and start-up ventures, should the courts take into special consideration the firms' need for money?

a. *Malihi v. Gholizadeh*, 11 Mass.L.Rptr. 659 (Mass.Super. 2000).

Discharge of liability can also occur when a party's right of recourse is impaired [UCC 3–605]. A *right of recourse* is a right to seek reimbursement. Ordinarily, when a holder collects the amount of an instrument from an indorser, the indorser has a right of recourse against prior indorsers, the maker or drawer, and accommodation parties. If the holder has adversely affected the indorser's right to seek reimbursement from these other parties, however, the indorser is not liable on the instrument. This occurs when, for example, the holder releases or agrees not to sue a party against whom the indorser has a right of recourse.

Terms and Concepts

Chapter Summary — Negotiability, Transferability, and Liability

Types of Instruments (See pages 345–348.)	The UCC specifies four types of negotiable instruments: drafts, checks, promissory notes, and certificates of deposit (CDs). Two basic classification systems are used to describe negotiable instruments:
	1. *Demand instruments versus time instruments*—A demand instrument is payable on demand (when the holder presents it to the maker or drawer). A time instrument is payable at a future date.
	2. *Orders to pay versus promises to pay*—Checks and drafts are *orders* to pay. Promissory notes and certificates of deposit (CDs) are *promises* to pay.
Requirements for Negotiability (See pages 348–349.)	To be negotiable, an instrument must meet the following requirements:
	1. Be in writing.
	2. Be signed by the maker or drawer.
	3. Be an unconditional promise or order to pay.
	4. State a fixed amount of money.
	5. Be payable on demand or at a definite time.
	6. Be payable to order or bearer (unless it is a check).
Transfer of Instruments (See pages 349–350.)	1. *Transfer by assignment*—A transfer by assignment to an assignee gives the assignee only those rights that the assignor possessed. Any defenses against payment that can be raised against an assignor can normally be raised against the assignee.
	2. *Transfer by negotiation*—An order instrument is negotiated by indorsement and delivery; a bearer instrument is negotiated by delivery only.
Holder in Due Course (HDC) (See page 350.)	1. *Holder*—A person in the possession of an instrument drawn, issued, or indorsed to him or her, to his or her order, or to bearer or in blank. A holder obtains only those rights that the transferor had in the instrument.
	2. *Holder in due course (HDC)*—A holder who, by meeting certain acquisition requirements (summarized next), takes the instrument free of most defenses and claims to which the transferor was subject.
Requirements for HDC Status (See pages 350–354.)	To be an HDC, a holder must take the instrument:
	1. *For value*—A holder can take an instrument for value in one of five ways [UCC 3–303]:
	a. By performing the promise for which the instrument was issued or transferred.

(Continued)

Chapter Summary	Negotiability, Transferability, and Liability—Continued

Requirements for HDC Status—continued	b. By acquiring a security interest or other lien in the instrument, excluding a lien obtained by a judicial proceeding.
	
	c. By taking an instrument in payment of (or as security for) a preexisting debt.
	
	d. By giving a negotiable instrument as payment.
	
	e. By giving an irrevocable commitment as payment.
	
	2. *In good faith*—Good faith is defined as "honesty in fact and the observance of reasonable commercial standards of fair dealing" [UCC 3–103(a)(4)].
	
	3. *Without notice*—To be an HDC, a holder must not be on notice that the instrument is defective in any of the following ways [UCC 3–302, 3–304]:
	
	  a. It is overdue.
	
	  b. It has been dishonored.
	
	  c. There is an uncured (uncorrected) default with respect to another instrument issued as part of the same series.
	
	  d. The instrument contains an unauthorized signature or has been altered.
	
	  e. There is a defense against the instrument or a claim to the instrument.
	
	  f. The instrument is so irregular or incomplete as to call into question its authenticity.

Holder through an HDC (See pages 354–355.)	A holder who cannot qualify as an HDC has the *rights* of an HDC if he or she derives title through an HDC unless the holder engaged in fraud or illegality affecting the instrument [UCC 3–203(b)].

Signature Liability
(See pages 355–358.)
	Every party (except a qualified indorser) who signs a negotiable instrument is either primarily or secondarily liable for payment of the instrument when it comes due.
	
	1. *Primary liability*—Makers and acceptors are primarily liable (an acceptor is a drawee that promises in writing to pay an instrument when it is presented for payment at a later time) [UCC 3–115, 3–407, 3–409, 3–412].
	
	2. *Secondary liability*—Drawers and indorsers are secondarily liable [UCC 3–412, 3–414, 3–415, 3–501, 3–502, 3–503]. Parties who are secondarily liable on an instrument promise to pay on that instrument if the following events occur:
	
	  a. The instrument is properly and timely presented.
	
	  b. The instrument is dishonored.
	
	  c. Timely notice of dishonor is given to the secondarily liable party.
	
	3. *Unauthorized signatures*—An unauthorized signature is wholly inoperative unless:
	
	  a. The person whose name is signed ratifies (affirms) it or is precluded from denying it [UCC 3–115, 3–401, 3–403, 3–406].
	
	  b. The instrument has been negotiated to an HDC [UCC 3–403].
	
	4 *Special rules for unauthorized indorsements*—An unauthorized indorsement will not bind the maker or drawer except in the following circumstances:
	
	  a. When an imposter induces the maker or drawer of an instrument to issue it to the imposter (imposter rule) [UCC 3–404(a)].
	
	  b. When a person signs as or on behalf of a maker or drawer, intending that the payee will have no interest in the instrument, or when an agent or employee of the maker or drawer has supplied him or her with the name of the payee, also intending the payee to have no such interest (fictitious payee rule) [UCC 3–404(b), 3–405].

Chapter Summary	Negotiability, Transferability, and Liability—Continued

Warranty Liability
(See pages 358–359.)
	1. *Transfer warranties*—Any person who transfers an instrument for consideration makes the following warranties to all subsequent transferees and holders who take the instrument in good faith (but when a bearer instrument is transferred by delivery only, the transferor's warranties extend only to the immediate transferee) [UCC 3–416]:
	
	   a. The transferor is entitled to enforce the instrument.
	
	   b. All signatures are authentic and authorized.
	
	   c. The instrument has not been altered.
	
	   d. The instrument is not subject to a defense or claim of any party that can be asserted against the transferor.
	
	   e. The transferor has no knowledge of any insolvency proceedings against the maker, the acceptor, or the drawer of the instrument.
	
	2. *Presentment warranties*—Any person who presents an instrument for payment or acceptance makes the following warranties to any other person who in good faith pays or accepts the instrument [UCC 3–417(a), (d)]:
	
	   a. The person obtaining payment or acceptance is entitled to enforce the instrument or is authorized to obtain payment or acceptance on behalf of a person who is entitled to enforce the instrument. (This is, in effect, a warranty that there are no missing or unauthorized indorsements.)
	
	   b. The instrument has not been altered.
	
	   c. The person obtaining payment or acceptance has no knowledge that the signature of the drawer of the instrument is unauthorized.

Defenses to Liability
(See pages 359–361.)
	1. *Universal (real) defenses*—The following defenses are valid against all holders, including HDCs and holders with the rights of HDCs [UCC 3–305, 3–401, 3–403, 3–407]:
	
	   a. Forgery.
	
	   b. Fraud in the execution.
	
	   c. Material alteration.
	
	   d. Discharge in bankruptcy.
	
	   e. Minority—if the contract is voidable under state law.
	
	   f. Illegality, mental incapacity, or extreme duress—if the contract is void under state law.
	
	2. *Personal (limited) defenses*—The following defenses are valid against ordinary holders but not against HDCs or holders with the rights of HDCs [UCC 3–105, 3–115, 3–302, 3–305, 3–306, 3–407, 3–601, 3–602, 3–603, 3–604, 4–401]:
	
	   a. Breach of contract or breach of warranty.
	
	   b. Lack or failure of consideration (value).
	
	   c. Fraud in the inducement.
	
	   d. Illegality and mental incapacity—if the contract is voidable.
	
	   e. Previous payment or cancellation of the instrument.
	
	   f. Unauthorized completion of the instrument.
	
	   g. Nondelivery of the instrument.
	
	   h. Ordinary duress or undue influence that renders the contract voidable.

(Continued)

Chapter Summary	Negotiability, Transferability, and Liability—Continued
Discharge from Liability (See pages 361–363.)	All parties to a negotiable instrument will be discharged when the party primarily liable on it pays to a holder the amount due in full. Discharge can also occur in other circumstances (if the instrument has been canceled or materially altered, for example) [UCC 3–601 through 3–606].

For Review

① What requirements must an instrument meet to be negotiable?

② What are the requirements for attaining the status of a holder in due course (HDC)?

③ What is the key to liability on a negotiable instrument? What is the difference between signature liability and warranty liability?

④ Certain defenses are valid against all holders, including HDCs. What are these defenses called? Name four defenses that fall within this category.

⑤ Certain defenses can be used to avoid payment to an ordinary holder of a negotiable instrument but are not effective against an HDC. What are these defenses called? Name four defenses that fall within this category.

Questions and Case Problems

18–1. Parties to Negotiable Instruments. A note has two original parties. What are these parties called? A check has three original parties. What are these parties called?

18–2. Requirements for Negotiability. The following note is written by Muriel Evans on the back of an envelope: "I, Muriel Evans, promise to pay Karen Marvin or bearer $100 on demand." Is this a negotiable instrument? Discuss fully.

18–3. Unauthorized Indorsements. What are the exceptions to the rule that a bank will be liable for paying a check over an unauthorized indorsement?

18–4. Defenses. Jules sold Alfred a small motorboat for $1,500; Jules maintained to Alfred that the boat was in excellent condition. Alfred gave Jules a check for $1,500, which Jules indorsed and gave to Sherry for value. When Alfred took the boat for a trial run, he discovered that the boat leaked, needed to be painted, and needed a new motor. Alfred stopped payment on his check, which had not yet been cashed. Jules has disappeared. Can Sherry recover from Alfred as a holder in due course? Discuss.

18–5. Defenses. Fox purchased a used car from Emerson for $1,000. Fox paid for the car with a check, written in pencil, payable to Emerson for $1,000. Emerson, through careful erasures and alterations, changed the amount on the check to read $10,000 and negotiated the check to Sanderson. Sanderson took the check for value, in good faith, and without notice of the alteration and thus met the UCC requirements for HDC status. Can Fox successfully raise the universal defense of material alteration to avoid payment on the check? Explain.

18–6. Signature Liability. Marion makes a promissory note payable to the order of Perry. Perry indorses the note by writing "without recourse, Perry" and transfers the note for value to Steven. Steven, in need of cash, negotiates the note to Harriet by indorsing it with the words "Pay to Harriet, [signed] Steven." On the due date, Harriet presents the note to Marion for payment, only to learn that Marion has filed for bankruptcy and will have all debts (including the note) discharged in bankruptcy. Discuss fully whether Harriet can hold Marion, Perry, or Steven liable on the note.

18–7. Requirements for Negotiability. The following instrument was written on a sheet of paper by Jeff Nolan: "I, the undersigned, do hereby acknowledge that I owe Stephanie Craig one thousand dollars, with interest, payable out of the proceeds of the sale of my horse, Swiftfoot, next month. Payment is to be made on or before six months from date." Discuss specifically why this instrument is not negotiable.

18–8. Requirements for Negotiability. Walter Peffer loaned $125,000 to the Pefferoni Pizza Co. The note included a clause that allowed the maker (Pefferoni Pizza) to renegotiate the terms of repayment at any time and then extend the time for repayment by up to eighty-four months. Later, Peffer borrowed money from Northern Bank, using the Pefferoni Pizza note as collateral. When Peffer failed to repay his loan, the bank tried to collect on the collateral note, but the pizza company failed to pay. The bank filed a suit in a Nebraska state court against Pefferoni Pizza to recover on the collateral note. Pefferoni Pizza argued in part that its note was not a negotiable instrument because under the renegotiation clause, it was not payable at a definite time. Was the note a negotiable instrument? Explain. [*Northern Bank v. Pefferoni Pizza Co.,* 5 Neb.App. 50, 555 N.W.2d 338 (1996)]

CASE PROBLEM WITH SAMPLE ANSWER

18–9. In October 1998, Somerset Valley Bank notified Alfred Hauser, president of Hauser Co., that the bank had begun to receive what appeared to be Hauser Co. payroll checks. None of the payees were Hauser Co. employees, however, and Hauser had not written the checks or authorized anyone to sign them on his behalf. Automatic Data Processing, Inc., provided payroll services for Hauser Co. and used a facsimile signature on all its payroll checks. Hauser told the bank not to cash the checks. In early 1999, Robert Triffin, who deals in negotiable instruments, bought eighteen of the checks, totaling more than $8,800, from various check-cashing agencies. The agencies stated that they had cashed the checks expecting the bank to pay them. Each check was payable to a bearer for a fixed amount, on demand, and did not state any undertaking by the person promising payment other than the payment of money. Each check bore a facsimile drawer's signature stamp identical to Hauser Co.'s authorized stamp. Each check had been returned to an agency marked "stolen check" and stamped "do not present again." When the bank refused to cash the checks, Triffin filed a suit in a New Jersey state court against Hauser Co. Were the checks negotiable instruments? Why or why not? [*Triffin v. Somerset Valley Bank,* 777 A.2d 993 (N.J.Super.App.Div. 2001)]

◆ To view a sample answer for this case problem, go to this book's Web site at **http://fundamentals.westbuslaw.com** and click on "Interactive Study Center."

18–10. Requirements for HDC Status. In February 2001, New York Linen Co., a party rental company, agreed to buy 550 chairs from Elite Products. On delivery of the chairs, New York Linen issued a check (dated February 27) for $13,300 to Elite. Elite's owner, Meir Shmeltzer, transferred the check to General Credit Corp., a company in the business of buying instruments from payees for cash. Meanwhile, after recounting the chairs, New York Linen discovered that delivery was not complete and stopped payment of the check. The next day, New York Linen drafted a second check, reflecting an adjusted payment of $11,275, and delivered it to Elite. A notation on the second check indicated that it was a replacement for the first check. When the first check was dishonored, General Credit filed a suit in a New York state court against New York Linen to recover the amount. New York Linen argued in part that General Credit was not a holder in due course because of the notation on the second check. In whose favor should the court rule? Why? [*General Credit Corp. v. New York Linen Co.,* ___ Misc.2d ___ (N.Y.City Civ.Ct. 2002)]

18–11. Defenses. On September 13, 1979, Barbara Shearer and Barbara Couvion signed a note for $22,500, with interest at 11 percent, payable in monthly installments of $232.25 to

Edgar House and Paul Cook. House and Cook assigned the note to Southside Bank in Kansas City, Missouri. In 1997, the note was assigned to Midstates Resources Corp., which assigned the note to The Cadle Co. in 2000. According to the payment history that Midstates gave to Cadle, the interest rate on the note was 12 percent. A Cadle employee noticed the discrepancy and recalculated the payments at 11 percent. When Shearer and Couvion refused to make further payments on the note, Cadle filed a suit in a Missouri state court against them to collect. Couvion and Shearer responded that they had made timely payments on the note, that Cadle and the previous holders had failed to accurately apply the payments to the reduction of principal and interest, and that the note "is either paid in full and satisfied or very close to being paid in full and satisfied." Is the makers' answer sufficient to support a verdict in their favor? If so, on what ground? If not, why not? [*The Cadle Co. v. Shearer,* 69 S.W.3d 122 (Mo.App. W.D. 2002)]

A QUESTION OF ETHICS AND SOCIAL RESPONSIBILITY

18–12. Richard Caliendo, an accountant, prepared tax returns for various clients. To satisfy their tax liabilities, the clients issued checks payable to various state taxing entities and gave them to Caliendo. Between 1977 and 1979, Caliendo forged indorsements on these checks, deposited them in his own bank account, and subsequently withdrew the proceeds. In 1983, after learning of these events and after Caliendo's death, the state brought an action against Barclays Bank of New York, N.A., the successor to Caliendo's bank, to recover the amount of the checks. Barclays moved for dismissal on the ground that because the checks had never been delivered to the state, the state never acquired the status of holder and therefore never acquired any rights in the instruments. The trial court held for the state, but the appellate court reversed. The state then appealed the case to the state's highest court. That court ruled that the state could not recover the amount of the checks from the bank because, although the state was the named payee on the checks, the checks had never been delivered to the payee. [*State v. Barclays Bank of New York, N.A.,* 561 N.Y.2d 533, 563 N.E.2d 11, 561 N.Y.S.2d 697 (1990)]

1. If you were deciding this case, would you make an exception to the rule and let the state collect the funds from Barclays Bank? Why or why not? What ethical policies must be balanced in this situation?
2. Under agency law, which will be discussed in Chapter 22, delivery to the agent of a given individual or entity constitutes delivery to that person or entity. The court deemed that Caliendo was not an agent of the state but an agent of the taxpayers. Does it matter that the taxpayers may not have known this principle of agency law and might have thought that, by delivering their checks to Caliendo, they were delivering them to the state?

VIDEO QUESTION

18–13. Go to this text's Web site at **http://fundamentals.westbuslaw.com** and click on "Video Questions." Select "Chapter 18" and view the video titled *Negotiable Instruments*. Then answer the following questions:

1. Who is the maker of the promissory note discussed in the video?

2. Is the note in the video payable on demand or at a definite time?

3. Does the note contain an unconditional promise or order to pay?

4. If the note does not meet the requirements of negotiability, can Onyx assign the note (assignment was discussed in Chapter 11) to the bank in exchange for cash?

NEGOTIABILITY, TRANSFERABILITY, AND LIABILITY

For updated links to resources available on the Web, as well as a variety of other materials, visit this text's Web site at

http://fundamentals.westbuslaw.com

The National Conference of Commissioners on Uniform State Laws, in association with the University of Pennsylvania Law School, now offers an official site for final drafts of uniform and model acts. For an index of final acts, including UCC Articles 3 and 4, go to

http://www.law.upenn.edu/bll/ulc/ulc_final.htm

Cornell University's Legal Information Institute offers online access to the UCC, as well as to UCC articles as enacted by particular states and proposed revisions to articles, at

http://www.law.cornell.edu/ucc/ucc.table.html

Online Legal Research

Go to the *Fundamentals of Business Law* home page at **http://fundamentals.westbuslaw.com**. Select "Interactive Study Center" and then click on "Chapter 18." There you will find the following Internet research exercises that you can perform to learn more about topics covered in this chapter.

Activity 18–1: ECONOMIC PERSPECTIVE—Overview of Negotiable Instruments
Activity 18–2: LEGAL PERSPECTIVE—Fictitious Payees
Activity 18–3: MANAGEMENT PERSPECTIVE—Check Fraud

Before the Test

Go to the *Fundamentals of Business Law* home page at **http://fundamentals.westbuslaw.com**. Click on "Interactive Quizzes." There you will find at least twenty interactive questions relating to this chapter.

Westlaw® Campus

If your textbook provided for a subscription to Westlaw® Campus, or if you have otherwise purchased access to the Westlaw Campus database, you can access any of the cases presented or cited in this chapter by using your Westlaw Campus account.

CHAPTER OBJECTIVES

After reading this chapter, you should be able to answer the following questions:

① Checks are usually three-party instruments. On what type of check, however, does a bank serve as both the drawer and the drawee? What type of check does a bank agree in advance to accept when the check is presented for payment?

② When may a bank properly dishonor a customer's check without liability to the customer?

③ In what circumstances might a bank not be liable for payment of a check containing an unauthorized signature of the drawer?

④ Under the Electronic Fund Transfer Act, under what conditions will a bank be liable for an unauthorized fund transfer? When will the consumer be liable?

⑤ What is e-money? How is e-money stored and used? What are the provisions of the Uniform Money Services Act?

Checks are the most common type of negotiable instruments regulated by the Uniform Commercial Code (UCC). It is estimated that over sixty-five billion personal and commercial checks are written each year in the United States. Checks are more than a daily convenience; they are an integral part of the American economic system.

Issues relating to checks are governed by Article 3 and Article 4 of the UCC. Recall from Chapter 18 that Article 3 establishes the requirements that all negotiable instruments, including checks, must meet. Article 3 also sets forth the rights and liabilities of parties to negotiable instruments. Article 4 of the UCC governs the relationships of banks with one another as they process checks for payment, and it establishes a framework for deposit and checking agreements between a bank and its customers. A check therefore may fall within the scope of Article 3 and yet be subject to the provisions of Article 4 while in the course of collection. If a conflict between Article 3 and Article 4 arises, Article 4 controls [UCC 4–102(a)].

In this chapter, we first identify the legal characteristics of checks and the legal duties and liabilities that arise when a check is issued. Then we examine the collection process—that is, the actual procedure by which the checks deposited into bank accounts move through banking channels, causing the

369

underlying funds to be shifted from one bank account to another. Increasingly, credit cards, debit cards, and other devices and methods to transfer funds electronically are being used to pay for goods and services. In the latter part of this chapter, we look at the law governing electronic fund transfers.

Checks

A **check** is a special type of draft that is drawn on a bank, ordering the bank to pay a fixed amount of money on demand [UCC 3–104(f)]. Article 4 defines a bank as "a person engaged in the business of banking, including a savings bank, savings and loan association, credit union or trust company" [UCC 4–105(1)]. If any other institution (such as a brokerage firm) handles a check for payment or for collection, the check is not covered by Article 4.

Recall from the discussion of negotiable instruments in Chapter 18 that a person who writes a check is called the drawer. The drawer is a depositor in the bank on which the check is drawn. The person to whom the check is payable is the payee. The bank or financial institution on which the check is drawn is the *drawee*. If Anita Cruzak writes a check from her checking account to pay her college tuition, she is the drawer, her bank is the drawee, and her college is the payee. We now look at some special types of checks.

CASHIER'S CHECKS

Checks are usually three-party instruments, but on certain types of checks, the bank can serve as both the drawer and the drawee. For example, when a bank draws a check on

itself, the check is called a **cashier's check** and is a negotiable instrument on issue (see Exhibit 19–1) [UCC 3–104(g)]. Normally, a cashier's check indicates a specific payee. In effect, with a cashier's check, the bank assumes responsibility for paying the check, thus making the check more readily acceptable as a substitute for cash.

● **EXAMPLE #1** Kramer needs to pay a moving company $8,000 for moving his household goods to a new home in another state. The moving company requests payment in the form of a cashier's check. Kramer goes to a bank (he need not have an account at the bank) and purchases a cashier's check, payable to the moving company, in the amount of $8,000. Kramer has to pay the bank the $8,000 for the check, plus a small service fee. He then gives the check to the moving company.●

Cashier's checks are sometimes used in the business community as nearly the equivalent of cash. Except in very limited circumstances, the issuing bank must honor its cashier's checks when they are presented for payment. If a bank wrongfully dishonors a cashier's check, a holder can recover from the bank all expenses incurred, interest, and consequential damages [UCC 3–411]. This same rule applies if a bank wrongfully dishonors a certified check (to be discussed shortly) or a teller's check. (A *teller's check* is a check drawn by a bank on another bank or, when drawn on a nonbank, payable at or through a bank [UCC 3–104(h)].)

TRAVELER'S CHECKS

A **traveler's check** has the characteristics of a teller's check. It is an instrument that is payable on demand, drawn on or

EXHIBIT 19–1 **A CASHIER'S CHECK**

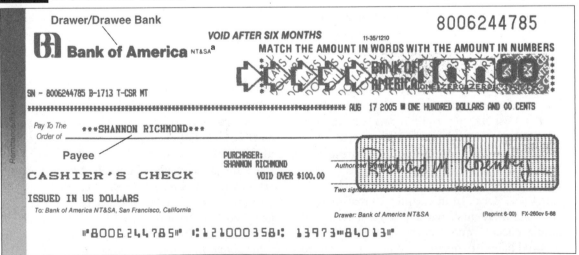

a. The letters *NT&SA* stand for *National Trust and Savings Association*.

payable at or through a financial institution (such as a bank), and designated as a traveler's check. The institution is directly obligated to accept and pay its traveler's check according to the check's terms. The purchaser is required to sign the check at the time it is bought and again at the time it is used [UCC 3–104(i)]. Exhibit 19–2 shows an example of a traveler's check.

CERTIFIED CHECKS

A **certified check** is a check that has been *accepted* in writing by the bank on which it is drawn [UCC 3–409(d)]. When a drawee bank *certifies* (accepts) a check, it immediately charges the drawer's account with the amount of the check and transfers those funds to its own certified-check account. In effect, the bank is agreeing in advance to accept that check when it is presented for payment and to make payment from those funds reserved in the certified-check account. Essentially, certification prevents the bank from denying liability. It is a promise that sufficient funds are on deposit *and have been set aside* to cover the check.

A drawee bank is not obligated to certify a check, and failure to do so is not a dishonor of the check [UCC 3–409(d)]. If a bank does certify a check, however, the bank should write on the check the amount that it will pay. If the certification does not state an amount, and the amount is later increased and the instrument negotiated to a holder in due course (HDC), the obligation of the certifying bank is the amount of the instrument when it was taken by the HDC [UCC 3–413(b)].

Certification may be requested by a holder (to ensure that the check will not be dishonored for insufficient funds) or by the drawer. In either circumstance, on certification the drawer and any prior indorsers are completely discharged from liability on the instrument [UCC 3–414(c), 3–415(d)].[1]

The Bank-Customer Relationship

The bank-customer relationship begins when the customer opens a checking account and deposits funds that the bank will use to pay for checks written by the customer. The rights and duties of the bank and the customer are contractual and depend on the nature of the transaction.

A creditor-debtor relationship is created between a customer and a bank when, for example, the customer makes cash deposits into a checking account. When a customer makes a deposit, the customer becomes a creditor, and the bank a debtor, for the amount deposited.

An agency relationship also arises between the customer and the bank when the customer writes a check on his or her account. In effect, the customer is ordering the bank to pay the amount specified on the check to the holder when the holder presents the check to the bank for payment. In this situation, the bank becomes the customer's agent and is obligated to honor the customer's request. Similarly, if the customer deposits a check into her or his account, the bank, as the customer's agent, is obligated to collect payment on the check from the bank on which the check was

---

[1] Under Section 3–411 of the unrevised Article 3, the legal liability of a drawer varies according to whether certification is requested by the drawer or a holder. The drawer who obtains certification remains *secondarily liable* on the instrument if the certifying bank does not honor the check when it is presented for payment. If the check is certified at the request of a holder, the drawer and anyone who indorses the check before certification are completely discharged.

EXHIBIT 19–2 **A TRAVELER'S CHECK**

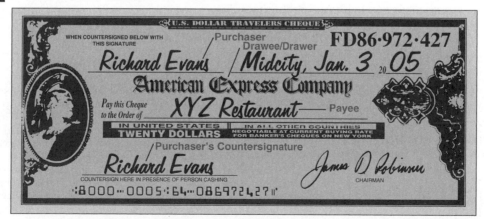

drawn. To transfer checkbook funds among different banks, each bank acts as the agent of collection for its customer [UCC 4–201(a)].

Whenever a bank-customer relationship is established, certain contractual rights and duties arise. The respective rights and duties of banks and their customers are discussed in detail in the following pages.

Bank's Duty to Honor Checks

When a commercial bank provides checking services, it agrees to honor the checks written by its customers with the usual stipulation that there be sufficient funds available in the account to pay each check [UCC 4–401(a)]. The customer is generally obligated to keep sufficient funds on deposit to cover all checks written. The customer is liable to the payee or to the holder of a check in a civil suit if a check is dishonored for insufficient funds. If intent to defraud can be proved, the customer can also be subject to criminal prosecution for writing a bad check.

When the bank properly dishonors a check for insufficient funds, it has no liability to the customer. When a drawee bank *wrongfully* fails to honor a customer's check, however, it is liable to its customer for damages resulting from its refusal to pay [UCC 4–402].

Clearly, the bank's duty to honor its customers' checks is not absolute. As noted, the bank is under no duty to honor a check when there are insufficient funds in the customer's account. In other circumstances, the bank may rightfully make payment or refuse payment on a customer's check. We look here at the rights and duties of both the bank and its customers in relation to specific situations.

OVERDRAFTS

When the bank receives an item properly payable from its customer's checking account but the account contains insufficient funds to cover the amount of the check, the bank has two options. It can either (1) dishonor the item or (2) pay the item and charge the customer's account, thus creating an **overdraft**, providing that the customer has authorized the payment and the payment does not violate any bank-customer agreement [UCC 4–401(a)].[2] The bank can subtract the difference (plus a service charge) from the customer's next deposit or eventually from other deposits made by the customer, because the check carries with it an enforceable implied promise to reimburse the bank.

A bank can expressly agree with a customer to accept overdrafts through what is sometimes called an "overdraft protection agreement." If such an agreement is formed, any failure of the bank to honor a check because it would create an overdraft breaches this agreement and is treated as wrongful dishonor [UCC 4–402(a)].

When a check "bounces," a holder can resubmit the check, hoping that at a later date sufficient funds will be available to pay it. The holder must notify any indorsers on the check of the first dishonor, however; otherwise, they will be discharged from their signature liability.

POSTDATED CHECKS

A bank may also charge a postdated check against a customer's account, unless the customer notifies the bank, in a timely manner, not to pay the check until the stated date. The notice of postdating must be given in time to allow the bank to act on the notice before commiting itself to pay on the check. The UCC states that the bank should treat a notice of postdating the same as a stop-payment order (to be discussed shortly). Generally, if the bank receives timely notice from the customer and nonetheless charges the customer's account before the date on the postdated check, the bank may be liable for any damages incurred by the customer as a result [UCC 4–401(c)].[3]

STALE CHECKS

Commercial banking practice regards a check that is presented for payment more than six months from its date as a **stale check**. A bank is not obligated to pay an uncertified check presented more than six months from its date [UCC 4–404]. When receiving a stale check for payment, the bank has the option of paying or not paying the check. The bank may consult the customer before paying the check. If a bank pays a stale check in good faith without consulting the customer, however, the bank has the right to charge the customer's account for the amount of the check.

---

[2] If there is a joint account, the bank cannot hold any joint-account customer liable for payment of an overdraft unless the customer has signed the check or has benefited from the proceeds of the check [UCC 4–401(b)].

[3] Under the UCC, postdating does not affect the negotiability of a check. In the past, instead of treating postdated checks as checks payable on demand, some courts treated them as time drafts. Thus, regardless of whether the customer notified the bank of the postdating, a bank could not charge a customer's account for a postdated check without facing potential liability for the payment of later checks. Under the automated check-collection system currently in use, however, a check is usually paid without respect to its date. Thus, today the bank can ignore the postdate on the check (treat it as a demand instrument) unless it has received notice of the postdate.

EXHIBIT 19–3 A STOP-PAYMENT ORDER

Bank of America

Checking Account
Stop Payment Order

To: Bank of America NT&SA
I want to stop payment on the following check(s).

ACCOUNT NUMBER: ☐☐☐☐☐–☐☐☐☐☐

SPECIFIC STOP

*ENTER DOLLAR AMOUNT: ☐ *CHECK NUMBER: ☐

THE CHECK WAS SIGNED BY: ____

THE CHECK IS PAYABLE TO: ____

THE REASON FOR THIS STOP PAYMENT IS: ____

STOP RANGE (Use for lost or stolen check(s) only.)

DOLLAR AMOUNT: 000

*ENTER STARTING CHECK NUMBER: ☐ *END CHECK NUMBER: ☐

THE REASON FOR THIS STOP PAYMENT IS: ____

BANK USE ONLY

TRANCODE:

☐ 21—ENTER STOP PAYMENT (SEE OTHER SIDE TO REMOVE)

NON READS: ____
UNPROC. STMT HIST: ____
PRIOR STMT CYCLE: ____
HOLDS ON COOLS: ____
REJECTED CHKS: ____
LARGE ITEMS: ____
FEE COLLECTED: ____
DATE ACCEPTED: ____
TIME ACCEPTED: ____

I agree that this order (1) is effective only if the above check(s) has (have) not yet been cashed or paid against my account, (2) will end six months from the date it is delivered to you unless I renew it in writing, and (3) is not valid if the check(s) was (were) accepted on the strength of my Bank of America courtesy-check guarantee card by a merchant participating in that program. I also agree (1) to notify you immediately to cancel this order if the reason for the stop payment no longer exists or (2) that closing the account on which the check(s) is (are) drawn automatically cancels this order.

IF ANOTHER BRANCH OF THIS BANK OR ANOTHER PERSON OR ENTITY BECOMES A "HOLDER IN DUE COURSE" OF THE ABOVE CHECK, I UNDERSTAND THAT PAYMENT MAY BE ENFORCED AGINST THE CHECK'S MAKER (SIGNER).

*I CERTIFY THE AMOUNT AND CHECK NUMBER(S) ABOVE ARE CORRECT.

☐ I have written a replacement check (number and date of check).

____

(Optional—please circle one: Mr., Ms., Mrs., Miss) CUSTOMER'S SIGNATURE **X** ____ DATE ____

STOP-PAYMENT ORDERS

A **stop-payment order** is an order by a customer to his or her bank not to pay or certify a certain check. Only a customer or a person authorized to draw on the account can order the bank not to pay the check when it is presented for payment [UCC 4–403(a)]. For a deceased customer, any person claiming a legitimate interest in the account may issue a stop-payment order [UCC 4–405]. A customer has no right to stop payment on a check that has been certified or accepted by a bank, however. Also, a stop-payment order must be received within a reasonable time and in a reasonable manner to permit the bank to act on it [UCC 4–403(a)]. Although a stop-payment order can be given orally, usually by phone, it is binding on the bank for only fourteen calendar days unless confirmed in writing.[4] A written stop-payment order (see Exhibit 19–3) or an oral order confirmed in writing is effective for six months, at which time it must be renewed in writing [UCC 4–403(b)].

If the bank pays the check over the customer's properly instituted stop-payment order, the bank will be obligated to recredit the customer's account—but only for the amount of the actual loss suffered by the drawer because of the wrongful payment [UCC 4–403(c)]. • EXAMPLE #2 Arlene Drury orders six bamboo palms from a local nursery at $50 each and gives the nursery a check for $300. Later that day, the nursery tells Drury that it will not deliver the palms as arranged. Drury immediately calls her bank and stops payment on the check. If the bank nonetheless honors the check, the bank will be liable to Drury for the full $300. The result would be different, however, if the nursery had delivered five palms. In that situation, Drury would owe the nursery $250 for the delivered palms, and her actual losses would be only $50. Consequently, the bank would be liable to Drury for only $50. •

A stop-payment order has its risks for a customer. The customer-drawer must have a *valid legal ground* for issuing such an order; otherwise, the holder can sue the drawer for payment. Moreover, defenses sufficient to refuse payment against a payee may not be valid grounds to prevent payment against a subsequent holder in due course [UCC 3–305, 3–306]. A person who wrongfully stops payment on a check not only will be liable to the payee for the amount of the check but also may be liable for consequential damages incurred by the payee as a result of the wrongful stop-payment order.

DEATH OR INCOMPETENCE OF A CUSTOMER

A customer's death or incompetence does not affect the bank's authority to honor a check until the bank knows of the situation and has had a reasonable period of time to act on the information. Article 4 provides that if, at the time a check is issued or its collection has been undertaken, a bank does not know of an adjudication of incompetence or

4. Some states do not recognize oral stop-payment orders; they must be in writing.

of the death of its customer, an item can be paid, and the bank will not incur liability.

Even when a bank knows of the death of its customer, for ten days after the *date of death*, it can pay or certify checks drawn on or before the date of death—unless a person claiming an interest in that account, such as an heir, orders the bank to stop payment [UCC 4–405]. Without this provision, banks would constantly be required to verify the continued life and competence of their drawers.

FORGED DRAWERS' SIGNATURES

When a bank pays a check on which the drawer's signature is forged, generally the bank is liable. A bank, however, may be able to recover at least some of the loss from the customer (if the customer's negligence contributed to the making of the forgery), from the forger of the check (if he or she can be found), or from the holder who presented the check for payment (if the holder knew that the signature was forged).

The General Rule. A forged signature on a check has no legal effect as the signature of a drawer [UCC 3–403(a)]. For this reason, banks require signature cards from each customer who opens a checking account. Signature cards allow the bank to verify whether the signatures on their customers' checks are genuine. The general rule is that the bank must recredit the customer's account when it pays a check with a forged signature.

Customer Negligence. When the customer's negligence substantially contributes to the forgery, the bank normally will not be obligated to recredit the customer's account for the amount of the check [UCC 3–406]. The customer's liability may be reduced, however, by the amount of loss caused by negligence on the part of the bank (or other "person") paying the instrument or taking it for value if the negligence substantially contributed to the loss [UCC 3–406(b)].[5]

● **EXAMPLE #3** Gemco Corporation uses special check-writing equipment to write its payroll and business checks. Gemco discovers that one of its employees used the equipment to write himself a check for $10,000 and that the bank subsequently honored it. Gemco requests the bank to recredit $10,000 to its account for improperly paying the forged check. If the bank can show that Gemco failed to take reasonable care in controlling access to the check-writing equipment, the bank will not be required to recredit Gemco's account for the amount of the forged check. If Gemco can show that negligence on the part of the bank (or another person) contributed substantially to the loss, however, then Gemco's liability may be reduced proportionately.●

Timely Examination of Bank Statements Required. Banks typically send their customers monthly statements detailing activity in their checking accounts. Banks are not obligated to include the canceled checks themselves with the statement sent to the customer. If the bank does not send the canceled checks (or photocopies of the canceled checks), however, it must provide the customer with information (check number, amount, and date of payment) on the statement that will allow the customer to reasonably identify the checks that the bank has paid [UCC 4–406(a), (b)]. If the bank retains the canceled checks, it must keep the checks—or legible copies of the checks—for a period of seven years [UCC 4–406(b)]. The customer may obtain a check (or a copy of the check) during this period of time.

The customer has a duty to examine bank statements (and canceled checks or photocopies, if they are included with the statements) promptly and with reasonable care, and to report any alterations or forged signatures promptly [UCC 4–406(c)]. This includes forged signatures of indorsers, to be discussed later. If the customer fails to fulfill this duty and the bank suffers a loss as a result, the customer will be liable for the loss [UCC 4–406(d)]. Even if the customer can prove that she or he took reasonable care against forgeries, the UCC provides that the customer must discover the forgeries and notify the bank within a specific time frame in order to require the bank to recredit her or his account.

Consequences of Failing to Detect Forgeries. When a series of forgeries by the same wrongdoer has taken place, the UCC provides that the customer, to recover for all the forged items, must have discovered and reported the first forged check to the bank within thirty calendar days of the receipt of the bank statement (and canceled checks or copies, if they are included) [UCC 4–406(d)(2)].[6] Failure to notify the bank within this period of time discharges the bank's liability for all forged checks that it pays prior to notification. ● **EXAMPLE #4** Alan forges Beth's signature as the drawer on three checks. Alan presents the first forged check to the bank, and Beth's bank honors the first check on March 15, debits Beth's account, and includes the canceled check with Beth's statement, which Beth receives on April 1 but does not review until May 7. Meanwhile, Alan cashes the second check at Beth's bank on April 10. Beth notifies the bank of the first forgery on May 8. On May 10, Alan cashes the third check. In this situation, the bank is liable only for the amount of the third check, for which it must recredit Beth's account.●

In the following case, the court was asked to apply this time-limit rule.

---

[5] The unrevised Article 4 does not include a similar provision.

[6] The unrevised Article 4 limits the period for examining and reporting to *fourteen* days [UCC 4–406(2)(b)].

CASE 19.1 **Espresso Roma Corp. v. Bank of America, N.A.**

Court of Appeal of California,
First District, Division 1, 2002.
100 Cal.App.4th 525,
124 Cal.Rptr.2d 549.

FACTS David Boyd is the president of Espresso Roma Corporation and also runs Hillside Residence Hall on the Berkeley campus of the University of California. Espresso Roma and the other businesses had checking accounts with Bank of America, N.A. All of the businesses employed Joseph Montanez, whose duties included bookkeeping. As an employee, Montanez learned how to generate company checks on the computer and had access to blank company checks. In October 1997, Montanez began to steal blank checks and, using stolen company computer programs, printed company checks on his home computer. He forged the checks in amounts totaling more than $330,000. When the bank statements containing the forged checks arrived in the mail, Montanez sorted through the statements and removed the checks. Boyd discovered the forgeries and reported them to the bank in May 1999. Boyd and the businesses filed a suit in a California state court against the bank, alleging, among other things, unauthorized payment of the checks. The bank filed a motion for summary judgment in its favor, in part on the ground that UCC 4–406(d) precluded the claims. The court granted the motion, and the plaintiffs appealed to a state intermediate appellate court.

ISSUE Was the bank liable for payment of the checks?

DECISION No. The state intermediate appellate court affirmed the judgment of the lower court. Because the bank's customers did not report the first forged check to the bank within the thirty-day period required under UCC 4–406(d), the bank's liability for payment of the checks was discharged.

REASON The court emphasized that a customer must notify "the bank no more than 30 days after the *first* forged item was included in the monthly statement or canceled checks and should have been discovered." The court explained that here "the forged checks were presented for payment between October 1997, and May 1999, but appellants [Boyd and the businesses] did not discover, or report them until on, or about, May 15, 1999," although they had received statements on a monthly basis, and the statements included canceled checks. "[T]he first monthly statement that would have reflected the forgery by Montanez would have been in November 1997. Yet, despite having the means to discover the forgeries, more than a year and a half elapsed before appellants discovered and reported any of them."

FOR CRITICAL ANALYSIS—Management Consideration
What steps can a small business take to protect itself against embezzlement by a key employee?

When the Bank Is Also Negligent. In one situation, a bank customer can escape liability, at least in part, for failing to notify the bank of forged or altered checks promptly or within the required thirty-day period. If the customer can prove that the bank was also negligent—that is, that the bank failed to exercise ordinary care—then the bank will also be liable, and the loss will be allocated between the bank and the customer on the basis of comparative negligence [UCC 4–406(e)].[7]

In other words, even though a customer may have been negligent, the bank may still have to recredit the customer's account for a portion of the loss if the bank failed to exercise ordinary care.

Regardless of the degree of care exercised by the customer or the bank, the UCC places an absolute time limit on the liability of a bank for paying a check with a forged customer signature. A customer who fails to report a forged signature within one year from the date that the statement was made available for inspection loses the legal right to have the bank recredit his or her account [UCC 4–406(f)]. The court in the following case was asked to apply this rule.

---

[7] Under the unrevised Article 4, if both parties are negligent, then the bank is wholly liable [UCC 4–406(3)].

CASE 19.2 **Halifax Corp. v. First Union National Bank**

Supreme Court of Virginia, 2001.
262 Va. 91,
546 S.E.2d 696.

FACTS Between August 1995 and March 1999, Mary Adams served as Halifax Corporation's comptroller. Between

August 1995 and January 1997, she wrote at least eighty-eight checks on Halifax's account at First Union National Bank. Adams used facsimile signatures on the checks, made them payable to herself or cash, and deposited them in her personal account at Wachovia Bank. First Union paid the

(Continued)

CASE 19.2—Continued

checks and debited Halifax's account. Most of the checks were drawn in amounts exceeding $10,000, and about twenty were drawn in amounts of between $50,000 and $100,000 each. First Union knew Adams was an employee of Halifax. In January 1999, Halifax discovered accounting irregularities and, during an investigation, learned that Adams had embezzled more than $15 million from its checking account. Halifax filed a suit in a Virginia state court against First Union and others, seeking recovery on the ground of negligence under, in part, UCC 4–406. First Union filed a motion for summary judgment. The court granted the motion. Halifax appealed to the Virginia state supreme court.

ISSUE Were Halifax's claims against First Union barred by the one-year limit of UCC 4–406(f)?

DECISION Yes. The state supreme court affirmed the lower court's judgment.

REASON The state supreme court explained that UCC 4–406(f) "bars a customer, who received a statement or item from a bank but failed to discover or report the customer's unauthorized signature or alteration on the item to the bank within one year after the statement or item is made available to the customer, from asserting a claim against the bank for the unauthorized signature or alteration." UCC 4–406(f) "is devoid of any language which limits the customer's duty to discover and report unauthorized signatures and alterations to items paid in good faith by the bank." The court noted that the UCC includes the phrase "good faith" in other subsections of UCC 4–406. The court concluded that "the exclusion of the good faith requirement in [UCC 4–406(f)] was intentional, and the General Assembly [the Virginia state legislature] did not intend to impose that requirement upon a bank."

FOR CRITICAL ANALYSIS—Ethical Consideration
Why should a customer have to report a forged or unauthorized signature on a paid check within a certain time to recover the amount of the payment?

FORGED INDORSEMENTS

A bank that pays a customer's check bearing a forged indorsement must recredit the customer's account or be liable to the customer-drawer for breach of contract. ● **EXAMPLE #5** Suppose that Brian issues a $50 check "to the order of Antonio." Jimmy steals the check, forges Antonio's indorsement, and cashes the check. When the check reaches Brian's bank, the bank pays it and debits Brian's account. The bank must recredit the $50 to Brian's account because it failed to carry out Brian's order to pay "to the order of Antonio" [UCC 4–401(a)]. Of course, Brian's bank can in turn recover—for breach of warranty (see Chapter 18)—from the bank that paid the check when Jimmy presented it [UCC 4–207(a)(2)].●

Eventually, the loss usually falls on the first party to take the instrument bearing the forged indorsement because, as discussed in Chapter 18, a forged indorsement does not transfer title. Thus, whoever takes an instrument with a forged indorsement cannot become a holder.

In any event, the customer has a duty to examine the returned checks (or copies of the checks) and statements received from the bank and to report forged indorsements promptly. A customer's failure to report forged indorsements within a three-year period after the forged items have been made available to the customer relieves the bank of liability [UCC 4–111].

ALTERED CHECKS

The customer's instruction to the bank is to pay the exact amount on the face of the check to the holder. The bank has a duty to examine each check before making final payment. If it fails to detect an alteration, it is liable to its customer for the loss because it did not pay as the customer ordered. The loss is the difference between the original amount of the check and the amount actually paid [UCC 4–401(d)(1)]. ● **EXAMPLE #6** Suppose that a check written for $11 is raised to $111. The customer's account will be charged $11 (the amount the customer ordered the bank to pay). The bank will normally be responsible for the $100.●

The bank is entitled to recover the amount of loss from the transferor, who, by presenting the check for payment, warrants that the check has not been materially altered. If the bank is the drawer (as it is on a cashier's check and a teller's check), however, it cannot recover on this ground from the presenting party if the party is an HDC acting in good faith [UCC 3–417(a)(2), 4–208(a)(2)]. The reason is that an instrument's drawer is in a better position than an HDC to know whether the instrument has been altered.

Similarly, an HDC, acting in good faith in presenting a certified check for payment, will not be held liable under warranty principles if the check was altered before the HDC acquired it [UCC 3–417(a)(2), 4–207(a)(2)]. ● **EXAMPLE #7** Jordan draws a check for $500 payable to Deffen. Deffen

EXHIBIT 19–4 A POORLY FILLED-OUT CHECK

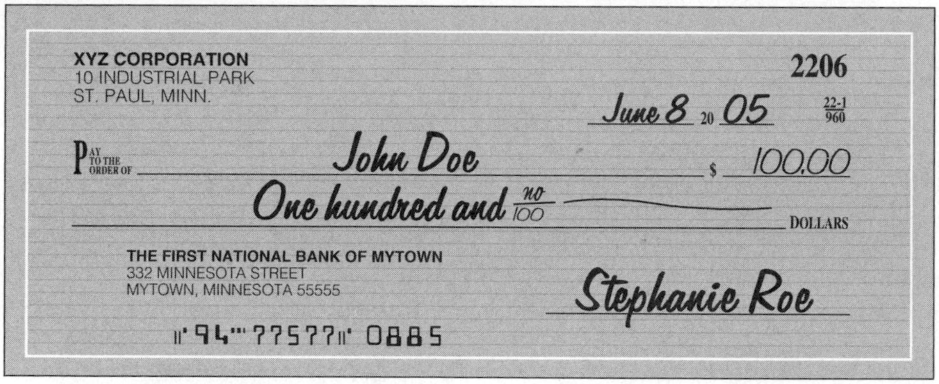

alters the amount to $5,000. The First National Bank of Whiteacre, the drawee bank, certifies the check for $5,000. Deffen negotiates the check to Evans, an HDC. The drawee bank pays Evans $5,000. On discovering the mistake, the bank cannot recover from Evans the $4,500 paid in error, even though the bank was not in a superior position to detect the alteration. This is in accord with the purpose of certification, which is to obtain the definite obligation of a bank to honor a definite instrument.●

As in a situation involving a forged drawer's signature, when payment is made on an altered check, a customer's negligence can shift the loss (unless the bank was also negligent). A common example occurs when a person carelessly writes a check and leaves large gaps around the numbers and words where additional numbers and words can be inserted (see Exhibit 19–4). Similarly, a person who signs a check and leaves the dollar amount for someone else to fill in is barred from protesting when the bank unknowingly and in good faith pays whatever amount is shown [UCC 4–401(d)(2)]. Finally, if the bank can trace its loss on successive altered checks to the customer's failure to discover the initial alteration, the bank can reduce its liability for reimbursing the customer's account [UCC 4–406]. The law governing the customer's duty to examine monthly statements and canceled checks (or copies), and to discover and report unauthorized signatures to the drawee bank, applies to altered instruments as well as forgeries.

Bank's Duty to Accept Deposits

A bank has a duty to its customer to accept the customer's deposits of cash and checks. When checks are deposited, the bank must make the funds represented by those checks available within certain time frames. A bank also has a duty to collect payment on any checks payable or indorsed to its customers and deposited by them into their accounts. Cash deposits made in U.S. currency are received into customers' accounts without being subject to further collection procedures. (For a discussion of deposits made via night depositories, see this chapter's *Management Perspective* on page 378.)

AVAILABILITY SCHEDULE FOR DEPOSITED CHECKS

The Expedited Funds Availability Act of 1987[8] and Regulation CC,[9] which was issued by the Federal Reserve Board of Governors (the Federal Reserve System will be discussed shortly) to implement the act, require that any local check deposited must be available for withdrawal by check or as cash within one business day from the date of deposit. A check is classified as a local check if the first bank to receive the check for payment and the bank on which the check is drawn are located in the same check-processing region (check-processing regions are designated by the Federal Reserve Board of Governors). For nonlocal checks, the funds must be available for withdrawal within not more than five business days.

In addition, the act requires the following:

① That funds be available on the next business day for cash deposits and wire transfers, government checks, the first $100 of a day's check deposits, cashier's checks, certified checks, and checks for which the depositary and payor banks are branches of the same institution.

② That the first $100 of any deposit be available for cash withdrawal on the opening of the next business day after deposit. If a local check is deposited, the next $400 is to be available for withdrawal by no later than 5:00 P.M. the next business day. If, for example, you deposit a

---

8 12 U.S.C. Sections 4001–4010.
9 12 C.F.R. Sections 229.1–229.42.

MANAGEMENT PERSPECTIVE
Night Depositories

MANAGEMENT FACES A LEGAL ISSUE Most banks provide night depositories for their customers—secured facilities into which customers can drop their deposits while the bank is closed. As a business owner or manager, you may find it convenient to use, or have your employees use, a night depository so that you can make deposits without having to spend time during the workday traveling to and from the bank. What happens, though, if you deposit some checks in the night depository and the bank claims that it never received them? Is there anything you can do?

WHAT THE COURTS SAY If the checks were lost due to the bank's negligence, certainly a court would hold that the bank would be liable to you for any damages resulting from the loss. For example, if the bank later found the checks, it would be clear that the (temporary) loss was due to the bank's negligence. Suppose, though, that the checks never turn up and it is evident that the bank exercised due care in handling all deposits dropped into its night depository. Will you have to assume the loss?

This question came before a New York court in *Epic Security Corp. v. Banco Popular (New York).*[a] The case arose after Lane Bryant, a customer of Banco Popular, claimed that the bank had not credited to its account deposits contained in a night depository bag. Lane Bryant's agent, Epic Security Corporation, stated that it had deposited the bag in the night depository chute at one of the bank's branch locations. The bank claimed that it had not received the deposits. Furthermore, the bank provided documentary evidence and affidavits to the court that bank personnel at that branch had followed all of the proper procedures governing night deposits on the night in question.

The fact was, there was simply no evidence to support Epic Security's assertion that it had delivered the bag to the bank. The court thus granted summary judgment in favor of the bank. "To hold otherwise," said the court, "would be sheer folly and permit unrestrained and unlimited suits against banks simply on the bare assertion of an individual that he made a deposit."

IMPLICATIONS FOR MANAGERS Businesspersons (and others) should be wary of using night depositories unless they can produce evidence, such as affidavits from witnesses, that such deposits were actually made. Although night depositories may be convenient, they are not totally risk free.

a. 1997 WL 823591 (N.Y.Civ.Ct. 1997).

---

local check for $500 on Monday, you can withdraw $100 in cash at the opening of the business day on Tuesday, and an additional $400 must be available for withdrawal by no later than 5:00 P.M. on Wednesday.

A different availability schedule applies to deposits made at nonproprietary automated teller machines (ATMs). These are ATMs that are not owned or operated by the depository institution. Basically, a five-day hold is permitted on all deposits, including cash deposits, made at nonproprietary ATMs.

Other exceptions also exist. A depository institution has eight days to make funds available in new accounts (those open less than thirty days). It has an extra four days on deposits over $5,000 (except deposits of government and cashier's checks), on accounts with repeated overdrafts, and on checks of questionable collectibility (if the institution tells the depositor it suspects fraud or insolvency).

THE COLLECTION PROCESS

Usually, deposited checks involve parties who do business at different banks, but sometimes checks are written between customers of the same bank. Either situation brings into play the bank collection process as it operates within the statutory framework of Article 4 of the UCC.

Designations of Banks Involved in the Collection Process. The first bank to receive a check for payment is the **depositary bank**.[10] For example, when a person deposits an IRS tax-refund check into a personal checking account at

---

[10] All definitions in this section are found in UCC 4–105. The terms *depositary* and *depository* have different meanings in the banking context. A depository bank refers to a *physical place* (a bank or other institution) in which deposits or funds are held or stored.

EXHIBIT 19–5 THE CHECK-COLLECTION PROCESS

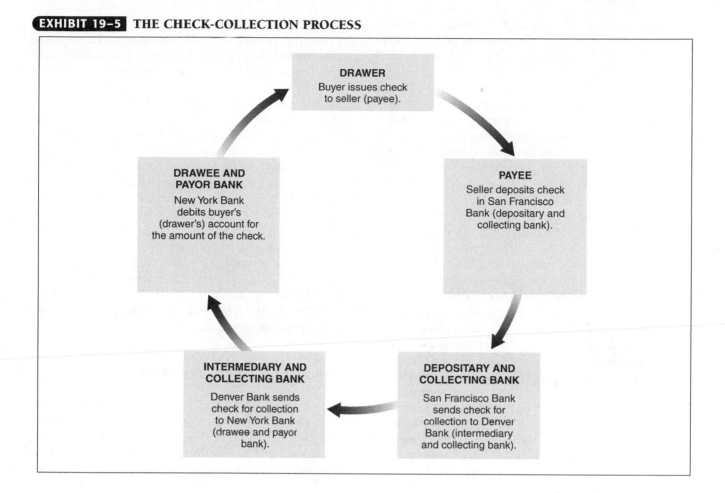

the local bank, that bank is the depositary bank. The bank on which a check is drawn (the drawee bank) is called the **payor bank**. Any bank except the payor bank that handles a check during some phase of the collection process is a **collecting bank**. Any bank except the payor bank or the depositary bank to which an item is transferred in the course of this collection process is called an **intermediary bank**.

During the collection process, any bank can take on one or more of the various roles of depositary, payor, collecting, and intermediary bank. ● **EXAMPLE #8** A buyer in New York writes a check on her New York bank and sends it to a seller in San Francisco. The seller deposits the check in her San Francisco bank account. The seller's bank is both a *depositary bank* and a *collecting bank*. The buyer's bank in New York is the *payor bank*. As the check travels from San Francisco to New York, any collecting bank handling the item in the collection process (other than the ones acting as a depositary bank and a payor bank) is also called an *intermediary bank*. Exhibit 19–5 illustrates how various

banks function in the collection process in the context of this example. ●

Check Collection between Customers of the Same Bank. An item that is payable by the depositary bank (also the payor bank) that receives it is called an "on-us item." If the bank does not dishonor the check by the opening of the second banking day following its receipt, the check is considered paid [UCC 4–215(e)(2)]. ● **EXAMPLE #9** Williams and Merkowitz both have checking accounts at State Bank. On Monday morning, Merkowitz deposits into his own checking account a $300 check drawn by Williams. That same day, State Bank issues Merkowitz a "provisional credit" for $300. When the bank opens on Wednesday, Williams's check is considered honored, and Merkowitz's provisional credit becomes a final payment. ●

Check Collection between Customers of Different Banks. Once a depositary bank receives a check, it must arrange to present it either directly or through intermediary banks to the appropriate payor bank. Each bank in the collection chain must pass the check on before midnight of the next banking day following its receipt [UCC 4–202(b)].[11] A "banking day" is any part of a day that the bank is open to carry on substantially all of its banking functions. Thus, if a bank has only its drive-through facilities open, a check deposited on Saturday would not trigger a bank's midnight deadline until the following Monday. When the check reaches the payor bank, unless the payor bank dishonors the check or returns it by midnight on the next banking day following receipt, the payor bank is accountable for the face amount of the check [UCC 4–302].[12]

Because of this deadline and because banks need to maintain an even work flow in the many items they handle daily, the UCC permits what is called *deferred posting*. According to UCC 4–108, "a bank may fix an afternoon hour of 2:00 P.M. or later as a cutoff hour for the handling of money and items and the making of entries on its books." Any checks received after that hour "may be treated as being received at the opening of the next banking day." Thus, if a bank's "cutoff hour" is 3:00 P.M., a check received by a payor bank at 4:00 P.M. on Monday would be deferred for posting until Tuesday. In this situation, the payor bank's deadline would be midnight Wednesday.

How the Federal Reserve System Clears Checks. The **Federal Reserve System** is our nation's central bank. It consists of twelve district banks and related branches located around the country and is headed by the Federal Reserve Board of Governors. Most banks in the United States have Federal Reserve accounts. The Federal Reserve System has greatly simplified the check-collection process by acting as a **clearinghouse**—a system or a place where banks exchange checks and drafts drawn on each other and settle daily balances.

● **EXAMPLE #10** Suppose that Pamela Moy of Philadelphia writes a check to Jeanne Sutton in San Francisco. When Sutton receives the check in the mail, she deposits it in her bank. Her bank then deposits the check in the Federal Reserve Bank of San Francisco, which transfers it to the Federal Reserve Bank of Philadelphia. That Federal Reserve bank then sends the check to Moy's bank, which deducts the amount of the check from Moy's account. Exhibit 19–6 illustrates this process.●

---

[11] A bank may take a "reasonably longer time," such as when the bank's computer system is down due to a power failure, but the bank must show that its action is still timely [UCC 4–202(b)].

[12] Most checks are cleared by a computerized process, and communication and computer facilities may fail because of weather, equipment malfunction, or other conditions. If such conditions arise and a bank fails to meet its midnight deadline, the bank is "excused" from liability if the bank has exercised "such diligence as the circumstances require" [UCC 4–109(d)].

Most electronic payment (e-payment) processing services also use the Federal Reserve's **automated clearinghouse (ACH)**. Under ACH rules, a debit from a customer's bank account is reversible for up to forty-eight hours.

Electronic Check Presentment. In the past, most checks were processed manually—the employees of each bank in the collection chain would physically handle each check that passed through the bank for collection or payment. Today, however, most checks are processed electronically. In contrast to manual check processing, which can take days, *electronic check presentment* can be done on the day of the deposit. With electronic check presentment, items may be encoded with information (such as the amount of the check) that is read and processed by other banks' computers. In some situations, a check may be retained at its place of deposit, and only its image or description is presented for payment under a Federal Reserve agreement, clearinghouse rule, or truncation agreement [UCC 4–110]. The term *truncation* refers to presentment by notice rather than by delivery.

Electronic Fund Transfers

The application of computer technology to banking, in the form of electronic fund transfer systems, helped to relieve banking institutions of the burden of having to move mountains of paperwork to process fund transfers. An **electronic fund transfer (EFT)** is a transfer of funds through the use of an electronic terminal, a telephone, a computer, or magnetic tape.

The benefits of electronic banking are obvious. Automatic payments, direct deposits, and other fund transfers are now made electronically; no physical transfers of cash, checks, or other negotiable instruments are involved. Not surprisingly, though, electronic banking also poses difficulties on occasion, including the following:

① It is difficult to issue stop-payment orders.

② Fewer records are available to prove or disprove that a transaction took place.

③ The possibilities for tampering (with a resulting decrease in privacy) are increased.

④ The time between the writing of a check and its deduction from an account (float time) is lost.

TYPES OF EFT SYSTEMS

Most banks today offer EFT services to their customers. The four most common types of EFT systems used by bank customers are (1) automated teller machines, (2) point-of-sale systems, (3) systems handling direct deposits and with-

EXHIBIT 19–6 **HOW A CHECK IS CLEARED**

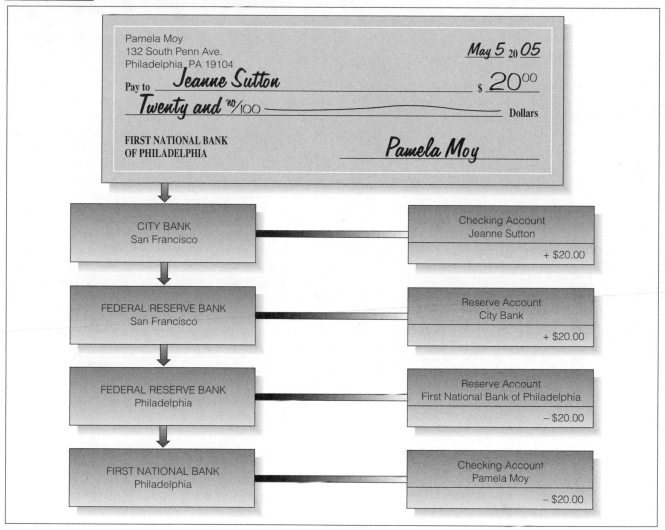

drawals, and (4) pay-by-telephone systems. We look here at each of these types of EFT systems. Not surprisingly, technology has led to new forms of electronic payment systems. We will look at some emerging forms of online fund transfers later in this chapter. In terms of dollar volume, the most significant fund transfers are those between financial institutions. These commercial transfers of funds will also be discussed later in the chapter.

Automated Teller Machines. Automated teller machines (ATMs) are located either on the bank's premises or at convenient locations such as supermarkets, drugstores and other stores, airports, and shopping centers. Automated teller machines receive deposits, dispense funds from checking or savings accounts, make credit-card advances, and receive

payments. The devices are connected online to the bank's computers. To access an account through an ATM, the bank customer uses a plastic card (debit card or access card), issued to him or her by the bank, plus a secret *personal identification number (PIN)*. The PIN prevents someone else from using a customer's lost or stolen access card.

Point-of-Sale Systems. Point-of-sale systems allow consumers to transfer funds to merchants to pay for purchases. Online terminals are located in, for example, grocery stores. When a purchase is made, the customer's **debit card** (issued by the bank to the customer) is inserted into the terminal, which reads the data encoded on it. The computer at the customer's bank verifies that the card and identification code are valid and that there are enough funds in the customer's account to cover the purchase. After the purchase is made, the customer's account is debited for the amount of the purchase.

Direct Deposits and Withdrawals. A direct deposit may be made to a customer's account through an electronic terminal when the customer has authorized the deposit in advance. The federal government often uses this type of EFT to deposit Social Security payments directly into beneficiaries' accounts. Similarly, an employer may agree to make payroll and pension payments directly into an employee's account at specified intervals.

A customer may also authorize the bank (or other financial institution at which the customer's funds are on deposit) to make automatic payments at regular, recurrent intervals to a third party. For example, insurance premiums, utility bills, and automobile installment loan payments may often be made automatically.

Pay-by-Telephone Systems. When it is undesirable to arrange in advance for an automatic payment—as, for example, when the amount of a regular payment varies—some financial institutions permit customers to pay bills through a pay-by-telephone system. This allows the customer to access the institution's computer system by telephone and direct a transfer of funds. Customers frequently pay utility bills directly using pay-by-telephone systems. Customers may also be permitted to transfer funds between accounts—for example, to withdraw funds from a savings account and deposit them in a checking account—in this way.

CONSUMER FUND TRANSFERS

Consumer fund transfers are governed by the Electronic Fund Transfer Act (EFTA) of 1978.[13] This act provides a basic framework for the rights, liabilities, and responsibilities of users of EFT systems. Additionally, the act gave the Federal Reserve Board authority to issue rules and regulations to help implement the act's provisions. The Federal Reserve Board's implemental regulation is called Regulation E.

The EFTA governs financial institutions that offer electronic fund transfers involving consumer accounts. The types of accounts covered include checking accounts, savings accounts, and any other asset accounts established for personal, family, or household purposes. Note that telephone transfers are covered by the EFTA only if they are made in accordance with a prearranged plan under which periodic or recurring transfers are contemplated.[14]

Major Rules under the EFTA. Congress passed the EFTA "to provide a basic framework establishing the rights, liabilities, and responsibilities of participants in electronic fund transfers." The EFTA is designed to protect consumers. It is not concerned with commercial electronic fund transfers—transfers between businesses or between businesses and financial institutions. (Commercial fund transfers are governed by Article 4A of the UCC.)

The EFTA is essentially a disclosure law benefiting consumers. The act requires financial institutions to inform consumers of their rights and responsibilities, including those listed here, with respect to EFT systems.

① If a customer's debit card is lost or stolen and used without his or her permission, the customer may be required to pay no more than $50. The customer, however, must notify the bank of the loss or theft within two days of learning about it. Otherwise, the liability increases to $500. The customer may be liable for more than $500 if he or she does not report the unauthorized use within sixty days after it appears on the customer's statement. (Even the $50 limit does not apply if the customer gives his or her card to someone who uses it improperly or if fraud is committed.)

② The customer must discover any error on the monthly statement within sixty days, and he or she must notify the bank. The bank then has ten days to investigate and must report its conclusions to the customer in writing. If the bank takes longer than ten days, it must return the disputed amount of money to the customer's account until it finds the error. If there is no error, the customer has to return the money to the bank.

③ The bank must furnish receipts for transactions made through computer terminals, but it is not obligated to do so for telephone transfers.

④ The bank must make a monthly statement for every month in which there is an electronic transfer of funds. Otherwise, the bank must make statements every quarter. The statement must show the amount and date of the transfer, the names of the retailers or other third parties involved, the location or identification of the terminal, and the fees. Additionally, the statement must give an address and a phone number for inquiries and error notices.

---

[13] 15 U.S.C. Sections 1693 *et seq.* The EFTA amended Title IX of the Consumer Credit Protection Act.

[14] *Kashanchi v. Texas Commerce Medical Bank, N.A.,* 703 F.2d 936 (5th Cir. 1983).

⑤ Any authorized prepayment for utility bills and insurance premiums can be stopped three days before the scheduled transfer.

Unauthorized Electronic Fund Transfers. Unauthorized electronic fund transfers are one of the hazards of electronic banking. A paper check leaves visible evidence of a transaction, and a customer can easily detect a forgery or an alteration on a check with ordinary vigilance. Evidence of an electronic transfer, however, is often only an entry in a computer printout of the various debits and credits made to a particular account during a specified time period.

Because of the vulnerability of EFT systems to fraudulent activities, the EFTA of 1978 clearly defined what constitutes an unauthorized transfer. Under the act, a transfer is unauthorized if (1) it is initiated by a person other than the consumer who has no actual authority to initiate the transfer; (2) the consumer receives no benefit from it; and (3) the consumer did not furnish the person "with the card, code, or other means of access" to her or his account.

Error Resolution and Damages. Banks must strictly follow the error-resolution procedures prescribed by the EFTA. If a bank fails to investigate an error and report its conclusion promptly to the customer, in the specific manner designated by the EFTA, it will be in violation of the act and subject to civil liability. Its liability extends to any actual damages sustained by a customer and to all the costs of a successful action brought against the bank by a customer, including attorneys' fees. In addition, the bank may be liable for punitive damages ranging from $100 to $1,000 for each individual action. Failure to investigate an error in good faith makes the bank liable for treble damages. Even when a customer has sustained no actual damage, the bank may be liable for legal costs and punitive damages if it fails to follow the proper procedures outlined by the EFTA in regard to error resolution.

COMMERCIAL TRANSFERS

The transfer of funds "by wire" between commercial parties is another way in which funds are transferred electronically. In fact, the dollar volume of payments by wire transfer is more than $1 trillion a day—an amount that far exceeds the dollar volume of payments made by other means. The two major wire payment systems are the Federal Reserve wire transfer network (Fedwire) and the New York Clearing House Interbank Payments Systems (CHIPS).

Unauthorized wire transfers are obviously possible and, indeed, have become a problem. If an imposter, for example, succeeds in having funds wired from another's account, the other party will bear the loss (unless he or she can recover from the imposter). In the past, any disputes arising as a result of unauthorized or incorrectly made transfers were settled by the courts under the common law principles of tort law or contract law. To clarify the rights and liabilities of parties involved in fund transfers not subject to the EFTA or other federal or state statutes, Article 4A of the UCC was promulgated in 1989. Almost all of the states have adopted this article.

The type of fund transfer covered by Article 4A is illustrated in the following example. ● **EXAMPLE #11** Jellux, Inc., owes $5 million to Perot Corporation. Instead of sending Perot a check or some other instrument that would enable Perot to obtain payment, Jellux tells its bank, East Bank, to credit $5 million to Perot's account in West Bank. East Bank debits Jellux's account by $5 million, and through a wire message, instructs West Bank to credit $5 million to Perot's account. In more complex transactions, additional banks would be involved.●

In these and similar circumstances, ordinarily a financial institution's instruction is transmitted electronically. Any means may be used, however, including first-class mail. To reflect this fact, Article 4A uses the term *funds transfer* rather than wire transfer to describe the overall payment transaction. The full text of Article 4A is included in Appendix C, following Article 4 of the Uniform Commercial Code.

E-Money

New forms of electronic payments (e-payments) have the potential to replace *physical* cash—coins and paper currency—with *virtual* cash in the form of electronic impulses. This is the unique promise of **digital cash**, or **e-money**, which consists of funds stored on microchips and other computer devices.

SMART CARDS

Plastic cards containing minute computer microchips that can hold far more information than a magnetic stripe (used in a *stored-value card*, the simplest kind of e-money system) are called **smart cards**. Because of microchip technology, a smart card can do much more than maintain a running cash balance in its memory or authorize the transfer of funds.

A smart card carries and processes security programming. This capability gives smart cards a technical advantage over stored-value cards. The microprocessors on smart cards can also authenticate the validity of transactions. Retailers can program electronic cash registers to confirm the authenticity of a smart card by examining a unique digital signature stored on its microchip.

Deposit Insurance for Smart-Card Balances. Normally, all depository institutions—including commercial banks and savings and loan associations—offer $100,000 of federally backed insurance for deposits. The Federal Deposit Insurance Corporation (FDIC) offers this insurance.

The FDIC has said that most forms of e-money do not qualify as deposits and thus are not covered by deposit insurance. If a bank becomes insolvent, an e-money holder would then be in the position of a general creditor. This means that he or she would be entitled to reimbursement only after nearly everyone else who is owed money is paid. At that point, there may not be any funds left.

Legal Protection for Smart Cards. Some laws extend to e-money and e-money transactions. The Federal Trade Commission Act of 1914[15] prohibits unfair or deceptive practices in, or affecting, commerce. Under this law, e-money issuers who misrepresent the value of their products or make other misrepresentations on which e-money consumers rely to their detriment may be liable for engaging in deceptive practices. General common law principles also apply. For example, the rights and liabilities of e-money issuers and consumers are subject to the common law of contracts.

PRIVACY PROTECTION

Currently, it is not clear which, if any, laws apply to the security of e-money payment information and e-money issuers' financial records. This is partly because it is not clear whether e-money issuers fit within the traditional definition of a financial institution.

E-Money Payment Information. The Federal Reserve has decided not to impose **Regulation E**, which governs certain electronic fund transfers, on e-money transactions. Federal laws prohibiting unauthorized access to electronic communications might apply, however. For example, the Electronic Communications Privacy Act of 1986[16] prohibits any person from knowingly divulging to any other person the contents of an electronic communication while that communication is in transmission or in electronic storage.

E-Money Issuers' Financial Records. Under the Right to Financial Privacy Act of 1978,[17] before a financial institution may give financial information about you to a federal agency, you must explicitly consent. If you do not, a federal agency wishing to obtain your financial records must obtain a warrant. A digital cash issuer may be subject to this act if that issuer is deemed to be (1) a bank by virtue of its holding customer funds or (2) any entity that issues a physical card similar to a credit or debit card.

Consumer Financial Data. In 1999, Congress passed the Financial Services Modernization Act,[18] also known as the Gramm-Leach-Bliley Act, in an attempt to delineate how financial institutions should treat customer data. In general, the act and its rules[19] place restrictions and obligations on financial institutions to protect consumer data and privacy. All financial institutions must provide their customers with information on their privacy policies and practices. No financial institution can disclose nonpublic personal information about a consumer to an unaffiliated third party unless the act's disclosure and opt-out requirements are met.

Online Banking

Banks have an interest in seeing the widespread use of online banking because of its significant potential for profit. As in other areas of cyberspace, however, it is unclear which laws apply to online banking activities.

Most online bank customers use three kinds of services. One of the most popular is bill consolidation and payment. Another is transferring funds among accounts. These online services are now offered via the Internet as well as by phone. The third is applying for loans, which many banks permit customers to do over the Internet. Customers typically have to appear in person to finalize the terms of a loan.

Two important banking activities generally are not yet available online: depositing and withdrawing funds. With smart cards, people could transfer funds on the Internet, thereby effectively transforming their personal computers into ATMs. Many observers believe that online banking is the way to introduce people to e-money and smart cards.

Since the late 1990s, several banks, such as Bank of Internet (http://www.bofi.com), have operated exclusively on the Internet. These "virtual banks" have no physical branch offices. Because few people are equipped to send funds to virtual banks via smart-card technology, the virtual banks have accepted deposits through physical delivery systems, such as the U.S. Postal Service or FedEx.

---

15. 15 U.S.C. Sections 41–58.
16. 18 U.S.C. Sections 2510–2521.
17. 12 U.S.C. Sections 3401 *et seq.*

---

18. 12 U.S.C. Sections 24a, 248b, 1820a, 1828b, 1831v–1831y, 1848a, 2908, 4809; 15 U.S.C. Sections 80b-10a, 6701, 6711–6717, 6731–6735, 6751–6766, 6781, 6801–6809, 6821–6827, 6901–6910; and others.
19. 12 C.F.R. Part 40.

The Uniform Money Services Act

Over the past few years, many states have enacted various regulations that apply to money services in a rather haphazard fashion. At the same time, e-money services that operate on the Internet—which, of course, cuts across jurisdictional lines—have been asking that these regulations be made more predictable.

In 2001, the National Conference of Commissioners on Uniform State Laws recommended to state legislatures a new law that would subject traditional money services, as well as online and e-money services, to the same regulations that apply to other, traditional financial service businesses. This law is known as the Uniform Money Services Act (UMSA).[20]

TRADITIONAL MONEY SERVICES

Before the UMSA, traditional money service businesses were not subject to all of the same regulations that cover other traditional financial services. Unlike banks, money service businesses do not accept deposits. Money service businesses do, however, issue money orders, traveler's checks, and stored-value cards; exchange foreign currency; and cash checks. Immigrants often use these businesses to send money to their relatives in other countries. Because these businesses often do not have continuing relationships with their customers, these customers have sometimes evaded federal law with respect to large currency transactions or used the services to launder money (see Chapter 6). This has been particularly true with respect to financing terrorist activities.

The UMSA covers persons engaged in money transmission, check cashing, or currency exchange. The new law requires a money service business involved in these activities to obtain a license from a state, to be examined by state officials, to report on its activities to the state, and to comply with certain record-keeping requirements [UMSA 1–104]. Each of these subjects has its provisions and exceptions.

Under the UMSA, money service businesses would also be covered by rules that govern investments, including restrictions on the types of investments. They would be required to follow what are known as "safety and soundness rules," which concern both the posting of bonds as a guaranty of their financial soundness and the annual auditing of their books [see, for example, UMSA 2–204].

INTERNET-BASED MONEY SERVICES

Under the UMSA, Internet-based money services, and other types of e-money services, would be treated the same as other money services.[21] The drafters of the UMSA ensured that it would cover these services by referring to *monetary value* instead of simply *money* [UMSA 1–102(c)(11)].

Internet-based monetary value systems subject to the new law may include:

① *E-money and Internet payment mechanisms*—Money, or its substitute, that is stored as data on a chip or a personal computer so that it can be transferred over the Internet or an intranet.

② *Internet scrip*—Monetary value that may be exchanged over the Internet but can also be redeemed for cash.

③ *Stored-value products*—Smart cards, prepaid cards, or value-added cards [UMSA 1–102(c)(21)].

---

[20] For a draft of the UMSA, go to the Web site of the National Conference of Commissioners on Uniform State Laws at **http://www.law.upenn.edu/bll/ulc/ulc_frame.htm** and click on the appropriate links.

[21] The UMSA does not apply to state governments, the federal government, securities dealers, banks, businesses that incidentally transport currency and instruments in the normal course of business, payday loan businesses, and others [UMSA 1–103].

Terms and Concepts

automated
   clearinghouse (ACH) 380
cashier's check 370
certified check 371
check 370
clearinghouse 380
collecting bank 379

debit card 381
depositary bank 378
digital cash 383
electronic fund transfer (EFT) 380
e-money 383
Federal Reserve System 380
intermediary bank 379

overdraft 372
payor bank 379
Regulation E 384
smart card 383
stale check 372
stop-payment order 373
traveler's check 370

Chapter Summary	Checks, the Banking System, and E-Money
Checks (See pages 370–371.)	1. *Cashier's check*—A check drawn by a bank on itself (the bank is both the drawer and the drawee) and purchased by a customer. In effect, the bank lends its credit to the purchaser of the check, thus making the funds available for immediate use in banking circles. 2. *Traveler's check*—An instrument on which a financial institution is both the drawer and the drawee. The purchaser must provide his or her signature as a countersignature for a traveler's check to become a negotiable instrument. 3. *Certified check*—A check for which the drawee bank certifies in writing that it will set aside funds in the drawer's account to ensure payment of the check on presentation. On certification, the drawer and all prior indorsers are completely discharged from liability on the check.
The Bank-Customer Relationship (See pages 371–372.)	1. *Contractual relationship*—The bank's relationship with its customer is contractual; both the bank and the customer assume certain contractual duties when a customer opens a bank account. 2. *Creditor-debtor relationship*—The relationship is also a creditor-debtor relationship (the bank is the debtor because it holds the customer's funds on deposit). 3. *Agency relationship*—Because a bank must act in accordance with the customer's orders in regard to the customer's deposited money, an agency relationship also arises—the bank is the agent for the customer, who is the principal.
Bank's Duty to Honor Checks (See pages 372–377.)	Generally, a bank has a duty to honor its customers' checks, provided that the customers have sufficient funds on deposit to cover the checks [UCC 4–401(a)]. The bank is liable to its customers for actual damages proved to be due to wrongful dishonor. The bank's duty to honor its customers' checks is not absolute. The following list summarizes the rights and liabilities of the bank and the customer in various situations. 1. *Overdrafts*—The bank has the right to charge a customer's account for any item properly payable, even if the charge results in an overdraft [UCC 4–401(a)]. 2. *Postdated checks*—A bank may charge a postdated check against a customer's account as a demand instrument, unless the customer notifies the bank of the postdating in time to allow the bank to act on the notice before the bank commits itself to pay on the check [UCC 4–401(c)]. 3. *Stale checks*—The bank is not obligated to pay an uncertified check presented more than six months after its date, but it may do so in good faith without liability [UCC 4–404]. 4. *Stop-payment orders*—The customer must make a stop-payment order in time for the bank to have a reasonable opportunity to act. Oral orders are binding for only fourteen days unless they are confirmed in writing. Written orders are effective for only six months unless renewed in writing. The bank is liable for wrongful payment over a timely stop-payment order, but only to the extent of the loss suffered by the drawer-customer [UCC 4–403]. 5. *Death or incompetence of a customer*—So long as the bank does not know of the death or incompetence of a customer, the bank can pay an item without liability to the customer's estate. Even with knowledge of a customer's death, a bank can honor or certify checks (in the absence of a stop-payment order) for ten days after the date of the customer's death [UCC 4–405]. 6. *Forged drawers' signatures, forged indorsements, and altered checks*—The customer has a duty to examine account statements with reasonable care on receipt and to

Chapter Summary	**Checks, the Banking System, and E-Money—Continued**
Bank's Duty to Honor Checks—continued	notify the bank promptly of any forged signatures, forged or unauthorized indorsements, or alterations. On a series of unauthorized signatures or alterations by the same wrongdoer, examination and report must occur within thirty calendar days of receipt of the statement. Failure to notify the bank releases the bank from any liability unless the bank failed to exercise ordinary care. Regardless of care or lack of care, the customer is estopped from holding the bank liable after one year for unauthorized customer signatures or alterations and after three years for unauthorized indorsements [UCC 3–403, 4–111, 4–401(a), 4–406].
Bank's Duty to Accept Deposits (See pages 377–380.)	A bank has a duty to accept deposits made by its customers into their accounts. Funds represented by checks deposited must be made available to customers according to a schedule mandated by the Expedited Funds Availability Act of 1987 and Regulation CC. A bank also has a duty to collect payment on any checks deposited by its customers. When checks deposited by customers are drawn on other banks, as they often are, the check-collection process comes into play (summarized next). 1. *Definitions of banks*—UCC 4–105 provides the following definitions of banks involved in the collection process: 　a. Depositary bank—The first bank to accept a check for payment. 　b. Payor bank—The bank on which a check is drawn. 　c. Collecting bank—Any bank except the payor bank that handles a check during the collection process. 　d. Intermediary bank—Any bank except the payor bank or the depositary bank to which an item is transferred in the course of the collection process. 2. *Check collection between customers of the same bank*—A check payable by the depositary bank that receives it is an "on-us item"; if the bank does not dishonor the check by the opening of the second banking day following its receipt, the check is considered paid [UCC 4–215(e)(2)]. 3. *Check collection between customers of different banks*—Each bank in the collection process must pass the check on to the next appropriate bank before midnight of the next banking day following its receipt [UCC 4–108, 4–202(b), 4–302]. 4. *How the Federal Reserve System clears checks*—The Federal Reserve System facilitates the check-clearing process by serving as a clearinghouse for checks. 5. *Electronic check presentment*—When checks are presented electronically, items may be encoded with information (such as the amount of the check) that is read and processed by other banks' computers. In some situations, a check may be retained at its place of deposit, and only its image or information describing it is presented for payment under a Federal Reserve agreement, clearinghouse rule, or other agreement [UCC 4–110].
Electronic Fund Transfers (See pages 380–383.)	1. *Types of electronic fund transfer (EFT) systems*— 　a. Automated teller machines (ATMs). 　b. Point-of-sale systems. 　c. Direct deposits and withdrawals. 　d. Pay-by-telephone systems. 2. *Consumer fund transfers*—Consumer fund transfers are governed by the Electronic Fund Transfer Act (EFTA) of 1978. The EFTA is basically a disclosure law that sets forth the rights and duties of the bank and the customer in respect to electronic fund transfer systems. Banks must comply strictly with EFTA requirements.

(Continued)

Chapter Summary	Checks, the Banking System, and E-Money—Continued
Electronic Fund Transfers—continued	3. *Commercial transfers*—Disputes arising as a result of unauthorized or incorrectly made fund transfers between financial institutions are not covered under the EFTA. Article 4A of the UCC, which has been adopted by almost all of the states, governs fund transfers not subject to the EFTA or other federal or state statutes.
E-Money (See pages 383–384.)	1. *New forms of e-payments*—These include stored-value cards and smart cards. 2. *Deposit insurance*—Most forms of e-money do not qualify as deposits and thus are not covered by federally guaranteed deposit insurance. 3. *Legal protection*—Statutes such as the Federal Trade Commission Act may cover e-money and e-payment transactions. General common law principles also apply. 4. *Privacy protection*—It is not entirely clear which, if any, laws apply to e-payment information and records. The Financial Services Modernization Act (the Gramm-Leach-Bliley Act), however, outlines the way financial institutions should treat consumer data and privacy in general.
Online Banking (See page 384.)	*Current online banking services*— 1. Bill consolidation and payment. 2. Transferring funds among accounts. 3. Applying for loans.
The Uniform Money Services Act (See page 385.)	In August 2001, the National Conference of Commissioners on Uniform State Laws recommended to state legislatures the Uniform Money Services Act. The purpose of the act is to subject online and e-money services to the same regulations that apply to traditional financial service businesses.

For Review

① Checks are usually three-party instruments. On what type of check, however, does a bank serve as both the drawer and the drawee? What type of check does a bank agree in advance to accept when the check is presented for payment?

② When may a bank properly dishonor a customer's check without liability to the customer?

③ In what circumstances might a bank not be liable for payment of a check containing an unauthorized signature of the drawer?

④ Under the Electronic Fund Transfer Act, under what conditions will a bank be liable for an unauthorized fund transfer? When will the consumer be liable?

⑤ What is e-money? How is e-money stored and used? What are the provisions of the Uniform Money Services Act?

Questions and Case Problems

19–1. Error Resolution. Sheridan has a checking account at Gulf Bank. She frequently uses her access card to obtain money from the automated teller machines. She always withdraws $50 when she makes a withdrawal, but she never withdraws more than $50 in any one day. When she received the April statement on her account, she noticed that on April 13 two with-drawals for $50 each had been made from the account. Believing this to be a mistake, she went to her bank on May 10 to inform the bank of the error. A bank officer told her that the bank would investigate and inform her of the result. On May 26, the bank officer called her and said that bank personnel were having trouble locating the error but would continue to try to find it. On June 20, the bank sent her a full written report advising her that no error had been made. Sheridan, unhappy with the bank's explanation, filed a suit against the bank, alleging that it had violated the Electronic Fund Transfer Act. What was the outcome of the suit? Would it matter if the bank could show that on the day in question it had deducted $50 from Sheridan's account to cover a check that Sheridan had written to a local department store and that had cleared the bank on that day?

19–2. Forged Signatures. Gary goes grocery shopping and carelessly leaves his checkbook in his shopping cart. Dolores steals his checkbook, which has two blank checks remaining. On May 5, Dolores forges Gary's name on a check for $100 and cashes the check at Gary's bank, Citizens Bank of Middletown. Gary has not reported the theft of his blank checks to his bank. On June 1, Gary receives his monthly bank statement and canceled checks from Citizens Bank, including the forged check, but he does not examine the canceled checks. On June 20, Dolores forges Gary's last check. This check is for $1,000 and is cashed at Eastern City Bank, a bank with which Dolores has previously done business. Eastern City Bank puts the check through the collection process, and Citizens Bank honors it. On July 1, Gary receives his bank statement and canceled checks. On July 4, Gary discovers both forgeries and immediately notifies Citizens Bank. Dolores cannot be found. Gary claims that Citizens Bank must recredit his account for both checks, as his signature was forged. Discuss fully Gary's claim.

19–3. Article 3 versus Article 4. Gary Morgan Chevrolet and Oldsmobile, Inc., issued four checks payable to General Motors Acceptance Corp. (GMAC) on Morgan's account with the Bank of Richmondville. There were insufficient funds in Morgan's account, and the bank gave GMAC oral notice of dishonor. The bank returned the checks two days later. GMAC filed a suit against the bank in a New York state court, claiming that the bank failed to dishonor the checks before its midnight deadline, because notice of dishonor must be in writing under Article 4. The bank countered that notice of dishonor may be made orally under Article 3. Which article controls when there is such a conflict? [*General Motors Acceptance Corp. v. Bank of Richmondville*, 203 A.D.2d 851, 611 N.Y.S.2d 338 (1994)]

19–4. Forged Checks. Roy Supply, Inc., and R.M.R. Drywall, Inc., had checking accounts at Wells Fargo Bank. Both accounts required all checks to carry two signatures—that of Edward Roy and that of Twila June Moore, both of whom were executive officers of both companies. Between January 1989 and March 1991, the bank honored hundreds of checks on which Roy's signature was forged by Moore. On January 31, 1992, Roy and the two corporations notified the bank of the forgeries and then filed a suit in a California state court against the bank, alleging negligence. Who is liable for the amounts of the forged checks? Why? [*Roy Supply, Inc. v. Wells Fargo Bank, N.A.*, 39 Cal.App.4th 1051, 46 Cal.Rptr.2d 309 (1995)]

19–5. Customer Negligence. Clem Macke Bindery hired Vincent Jones without investigating his background. At Clem Macke, blank checks were kept in a safe that was unlocked during working hours. Jones surreptitiously obtained two checks on which he forged Clem Macke's signature. The checks were made payable to a fictitious "Larry Pope," whose name Jones signed on the back. Jones cashed the checks at The Provident Bank, which did not ask for identification. Clem Macke assigned its claim against the bank for the amount of the checks to Atlantic Mutual Insurance Co., which filed a suit in an Ohio state court against the bank, alleging negligence. The bank responded that the employer had been negligent in hiring and failing to monitor Jones. If the court finds that both parties in this case were negligent, which party will bear the loss? Would the result be the same if the unrevised Article 3 were applied? Explain. [*Atlantic Mutual Insurance Co. v. The Provident Bank*, 79 Ohio Misc.2d 5, 669 N.E.2d 90 (1996)]

19–6. Stale Checks. On July 15, 1986, IBP, Inc., issued to Meyer Land & Cattle Co. a check for $135,234.18 payable to both Meyer and Sylvan State Bank for the purchase of cattle. IBP wrote the check on its account at Mercantile Bank of Topeka. Someone at the Meyer firm misplaced the check. In the fall of 1995, Meyer's president, Tim Meyer, found the check behind a desk drawer. Jana Huse, Meyer's office manager, presented the check for deposit at Sylvan, which accepted it. After Mercantile received the instrument and its computers noted the absence of any stop-payment order, it paid the check with funds from IBP's checking account. IBP insisted that Mercantile recredit IBP's account. Mercantile refused. IBP filed a suit in a federal district court against Mercantile and others, claiming, among other things, that Mercantile had not acted in good faith because it had processed the check by automated means without examining it manually. Mercantile responded that its check-processing procedures adhered to its own policies, as well as reasonable commercial standards of fair dealing in the banking industry. Mercantile filed a motion for summary judgment. Should the court grant the motion? Why or why not? [*IBP, Inc. v. Mercantile Bank of Topeka*, 6 F.Supp.2d 1258 (D.Kan. 1999)]

19–7. Debit Cards. On April 20, 1999, while visiting her daughter and son-in-law Michael Dowdell, Carol Farrow asked Dowdell to fix her car. She gave him her car keys, attached to which was a small wallet containing her debit card. Dowdell repaired her car and returned the keys. Two days later, Farrow noticed that her debit card was missing and contacted Auburn Bank, which had issued the card. Farrow reviewed her automated teller machine (ATM) transaction record and noticed that a large amount of cash had been withdrawn from her checking account on April 22 and April 23. When Farrow reviewed the photos taken by the ATM cameras at the time of the withdrawals, she recognized Dowdell as the person using her debit card. Dowdell was convicted in an Alabama state court of the crime of fraudulent use of a debit card. What procedures are involved in a debit-card transaction? What problems with debit-card transactions are apparent from the facts of this case? How might these problems be prevented? [*Dowdell v. State*, 790 So.2d 359 (Ala.Crim.App. 2000)]

CASE PROBLEM WITH SAMPLE ANSWER

19–8. Robert Santoro was the manager of City Check Cashing, Inc., a check-cashing service in New Jersey, and Peggyann Slansky was the clerk. On July 14, Misir Koci presented Santoro with a $290,000 check signed by Melvin Green and drawn on Manufacturers Hanover Trust Co. (a bank). The check was stamped with a Manufacturers certification stamp. The date on the check had clearly been changed from August 8 to July 7. Slansky called the bank to verify the check and was told that the serial number "did not sound like one belonging to the bank." Slansky faxed the check to the bank with a query about the date, but received no reply. Slansky also called Green, who stated that the date on the check was altered before it was certified. City Check Cashing cashed and deposited the check within two hours. The drawee bank found the check to be invalid and timely returned it unpaid. City Check Cashing filed a suit in a New Jersey state court against Manufacturers and others, asserting that the bank should have responded to the fax before the midnight deadline under UCC 4–302. Did the bank violate the midnight-deadline rule? Explain. [*City Check Cashing, Inc. v. Manufacturers Hanover Trust Co.*, 166 N.J. 49, 764 A.2d 411 (2001)]

◗ To view a sample answer for this case problem, go to this book's Web site at http://fundamentals.westbuslaw.com and click on "Interactive Study Center."

19–9. Forged Signatures. Visiting Nurses Association of Telfair County, Inc. (VNA), maintained a checking account at Security State Bank in Valdosta, Georgia. Wanda Williamson, a VNA clerk, was responsible for making VNA bank deposits, but she was not a signatory on the association's account. Over a four-year period, Williamson embezzled more than $250,000 from VNA by forging its indorsement on checks, cashing them at the bank, and keeping a portion of the proceeds. Williamson was arrested, convicted, sentenced to a prison term, and ordered to pay restitution. VNA filed a suit in a Georgia state court against the bank, alleging, among other things, negligence. The bank filed a motion for summary judgment on the ground that VNA was precluded by UCC 4–406(f) from recovering on checks with forged indorsements. Should the court grant the motion? Explain. [*Security State Bank v. Visiting Nurses Association of Telfair County, Inc.*, 568 S.E.2d 491 (Ga.App. 2002)]

CHECKS, THE BANKING SYSTEM, AND E-MONEY

For updated links to resources available on the Web, as well as other materials, visit this text's Web site at

http://fundamentals.westbuslaw.com

You can obtain information about banking regulation from the Federal Deposit Insurance Corporation (FDIC) at

http://www.fdic.gov

You can get additional information on banking from the Federal Reserve System at

http://woodrow.mpls.frb.fed.us/info

The American Bankers Association is the largest banking trade association in the United States. To learn more about the banking industry, go to

http://www.aba.com

You can find the Uniform Money Services Act by going to the following site and clicking on "Uniform Money Services Business Act" (the act's original name):

http://www.law.upenn.edu/bll/ulc/ulc_frame.htm

Online Legal Research

Go to the *Fundamentals of Business Law* home page at **http://fundamentals. westbuslaw.com**. Select "Interactive Study Center" and then click on "Chapter 19."

There you will find the following Internet research exercises that you can perform to learn more about topics covered in this chapter.

Activity 19–1: LEGAL PERSPECTIVE—Smart Cards
Activity 19–2: MANAGEMENT PERSPECTIVE—Check Fraud

Before the Test

Go to the *Fundamentals of Business Law* home page at **http://fundamentals. westbuslaw.com**. Click on "Interactive Quizzes." You will find at least twenty interactive questions relating to this chapter.

Westlaw® Campus

If your textbook provided for a subscription to Westlaw® Campus, or if you have otherwise purchased access to the Westlaw Campus database, you can access any of the cases presented or cited in this chapter by using your Westlaw Campus account.

Scalise v. American Employers Insurance Co.

INTRODUCTION

In Chapter 19, we discussed time periods within which bank customers must act to avoid a discharge of the bank's liability for paying forged checks. In this *Focus on Legal Reasoning,* we look at *Scalise v. American Employers Insurance Co.,*[1] a decision in which the court considered, in the context of a time period within which a party must act, when "payment" occurs if a check is taken as payment.

CASE BACKGROUND

American Employers Insurance Company issued an automobile insur-

_____

1. 67 Conn.App. 753, 789 A.2d 1066 (2002).

ance policy to Anthony Scalise in Stamford, Connecticut. Under the policy, if Scalise and American disagreed about a claim, either party could demand arbitration.

On April 1, 1989, Scalise was in an automobile accident caused by another driver, who was insured with USAA General Indemnity Company. Scalise filed a claim with General Indemnity. He also filed a claim with American to cover the cost of his personal injuries and property damage that exceeded the limits of the other driver's policy. General Indemnity offered to settle for $20,000, its policy limits. Scalise accepted the offer and signed a release. General Indemnity issued a check to

Scalise, whose attorney deposited it on Scalise's behalf on April 26, 1991.

Six years and three days later, Scalise demanded arbitration of his still-pending American claim. American refused. Scalise filed a suit in a Connecticut state court against American, asking the court to compel the insurer to arbitrate. American asserted that Scalise's claim had expired under a state statute requiring a cause of action to be brought within six years after the right to bring it accrues. All parties agreed that the right accrued on General Indemnity's payment, but they disagreed as to when that payment occurred. The court ruled in American's favor. Scalise appealed to a state intermediate appellate court.

MAJORITY OPINION

FOTI, P.J. [Presiding Judge]

* * * *

"[T]he giving of a draft by a debtor to his creditor does not discharge the debt itself until the draft is paid, it being a means adopted to enable the creditor to obtain payment of the debt and remaining, until honored or paid, but evidence of the indebtedness * * *." *Huybrechts v. Huybrechts,* 4 Conn.App. 319, 494 A.2d 593 (1985). In that light, * * * the delivery of a note or an uncertified check suspends an obligation to pay until dishonor of the note or uncertified check or until either is paid.

It is well settled, however, that a debtor's delivery of an uncertified check as payment for an obligation not only suspends his obligation to pay until such check is, upon its presentment, either honored or dishonored, but that *once the check is honored, the obligation to pay no longer exists.* Our legislature codified that principle in General Statutes Section 42a-3-310(b) [Connecticut's version of UCC 3–310(b)] which provides in relevant part: "[I]f a note or an uncertified check is taken for an obligation, the obligation is suspended to the same extent the obligation would be discharged if an amount of money equal to the amount of the instrument were taken, and * * * [i]n the case of an uncertified check, suspension of the obligation continues until dishonor of the check or until it is paid or certified. Payment or certification of the check results in discharge of the obligation to the extent of the amount of the check * * *." [Emphasis added.]

It is not disputed that General Indemnity was free to satisfy its settlement by paying the plaintiff with a check, a customary practice. We also recognize that payment by check is ordinarily understood to constitute payment for an obligation as of the

moment of delivery of the check, provided that the check is honored upon its presentment. *Where a check delivered to a creditor * * * is in fact paid in due course, the debt is discharged [to the extent of the amount of the check], as of the time at which the check was received * * *.* A check is * * * often referred to as conditional payment, the condition being its collectability from the bank on which it is drawn. On fulfillment of the condition by payment of the check on presentation, the payment, which was previously conditional, becomes absolute. [Emphasis added.]

* * * [T]hat rule recognizes the realities of modern day commerce and yields a sensible result, for if the check is dishonored on presentment to the drawee, no timely payment has been made. * * * [I]f a party's act of delivering a check as payment for an obligation is not the sending of money in discharge of the debt it is hard to figure out what a payment can be. * * * Accordingly, we hold that *if an uncertified check is honored and paid on presentment, its conditional nature ends and it becomes absolute payment at that time. The date of the payment for the underlying obligation relates back to the date of the delivery of the check.* We believe that this "conditional payment" rule is fair and that it reflects the common understanding of the practice of paying by check. * * * [Emphasis added.]

Having reached that point in our analysis, we conclude that General Indemnity exhausted by payment its settlement with the plaintiff [satisfied the plaintiff's claim] on April 26, 1991. * * * The six-year statute of limitations * * * permitted the plaintiff to bring a claim against the defendant, if he so desired, within six years. The plaintiff did not do so. Instead, he filed his written demand for arbitration on April 29, 1997. Accordingly, the plaintiff's application for an order to compel the defendant to proceed with arbitration is barred.

DISSENTING OPINION

FLYNN, J., dissenting.

I respectfully dissent from the opinion of the majority. * * *
* * * *

* * * [T]he giving of a check by a debtor to his creditor does not discharge the debt until the check is paid. * * * If the delivery of an uncertified check is a means for later obtaining payment, I do not understand how we arrive at the legal conclusion that payment has already been made upon its mere delivery. * * *

A check is a form of written instruction to pay a sum of money to a payee. If it is honored, it constitutes payment. Under most circumstances, a check also evidences a promise to pay a sum of money, in the event that the check is dishonored. * * *

If an insurer agrees to a settlement of a third party claim and issues its check for the amount agreed upon, but the check is not honored, then payment of the claim has not been made.

* * * *

The majority treats the delivery of an uncertified check by the * * * insurer as the commencement date of the statute of limitations period, or not, depending on future events unknown at the time of the check's delivery. Under this rule, if the uncertified check is in fact paid in due course at a later date, then the earlier delivery is treated as the beginning of the statute of limitations period. Conversely, if the check is later dishonored on presentment, the majority states that delivery is then deemed not to have triggered the limitations period after all. Where does this leave the plaintiff when he takes delivery of the check? Under this rule, the plaintiff's time to exercise his rights * * * begins to run before he even has any such rights. * * *

LEGAL REASONING AND ANALYSIS

1 Legal Analysis. Find the *Huybrechts v. Huybrechts* case (see the appendix to Chapter 1 for instructions on how to find state court opinions). For what purpose did the majority refer to the *Huybrechts* case? Compare the facts and issues of the *Huybrechts* and *Scalise* cases. How are they similar? How important are their differences?

2 Legal Reasoning. What reasons did the majority and the dissent provide to justify their respective positions?

3 Commercial Application. How might the result in this case have been different if the plaintiff's claim had been paid with a certified check, instead of an uncertified check, or if payment had been through an electronic fund transfer?

4 Implications for Businesspersons. What does the decision in this case indicate for those who accept uncertified checks in payment of obligations?

5 Case Briefing Assignment. Using the guidelines for briefing cases given in Appendix A of this text, brief the *Scalise* case.

This text's Web site, at **http://fundamentals.westbuslaw.com**, offers links to West's Court Case Updates, as well as to other online research sources. You can also locate court cases at the Web sites listed in the *Accessing the Internet* section at the end of Chapter 2.

News and recent decisions of the courts on laws affecting negotiable instruments and other subjects can be found at **http://www.law.com/jsp/nylj/index.jsp**. The *National Law Journal*, an information service of American Lawyer Media, maintains this Web site.

UNIT 6

Debtor-Creditor Relationships

20 Secured Transactions

CHAPTER OBJECTIVES

After reading this chapter, you should be able to answer the following questions:

① What is a security interest? Who is a secured party? What is a security agreement? What is a financing statement?

② What three requirements must be met to create an enforceable security interest?

③ What is the most common method of perfecting a security interest under Article 9?

④ If two secured parties have perfected security interests in the collateral of the debtor, which party has priority to the collateral on the debtor's default?

⑤ What rights does a secured creditor have on the debtor's default?

Whenever the payment of a debt is guaranteed, or secured, by personal property owned by the debtor or in which the debtor has a legal interest, the transaction becomes known as a **secured transaction**. The concept of the secured transaction is as basic to modern business practice as the concept of credit. Logically, sellers and lenders do not want to risk nonpayment, so they usually will not sell goods or lend funds unless the promise of payment is somehow guaranteed. Indeed, business as we know it could not exist without laws permitting and governing secured transactions. Article 9 of the Uniform Commercial Code (UCC) governs secured transactions. Debtor-creditor transactions that are not covered under Article 9 are discussed in the next chapter.

In 1999, the National Conference of Commissioners on Uniform State Laws (NCCUSL) promulgated a revised version of Article 9. Because the revised version, which was later amended, has now been adopted by all of the states, we base this chapter's discussion of secured transactions entirely on the provisions of the revised version.

The Terminology of Secured Transactions

The UCC's terminology is now uniformly adopted in all documents used in situations involving secured transactions. A brief summary of the UCC's definitions of terms relating to secured transactions follows.

① A **secured party** is any creditor who has a *security interest in the debtor's collateral*. This creditor can be a seller, a lender, a cosigner, and even a buyer of accounts or chattel paper [UCC 9–102(a)(72)].

② A **debtor** is the "person" who *owes payment* or other performance of a secured obligation [UCC 9–102(a)(28)].

③ A **security interest** is the *interest* in the collateral (personal property, fixtures, and so on) that *secures payment or performance of an obligation* [UCC 1–201(37)].

④ A **security agreement** is an *agreement* that *creates* or provides for a *security interest* [UCC 9–102(a)(73)].

⑤ **Collateral** is the *subject* of the *security interest* [UCC 9–102(a)(12)].

⑥ A **financing statement**—referred to as the UCC-1 form—is the *instrument normally filed to give public notice to third parties of the secured party's security interest* [UCC 9–102(a)(39)].

These basic definitions form the concept under which a debtor-creditor relationship becomes a secured transaction relationship (see Exhibit 20–1).

Creating and Perfecting a Security Interest

A creditor has two main concerns if the debtor **defaults** (fails to pay the debt as promised): (1) satisfaction of the debt through the possession and (usually) sale of the collateral and (2) priority over any other creditors or buyers who may have rights in the same collateral. We look here at how these two concerns are met through the creation and perfection of a security interest.

CREATING A SECURITY INTEREST

To become a secured party, the creditor must obtain a security interest in the collateral of the debtor. Three requirements must be met for a creditor to have an enforceable security interest:

① Either (a) the collateral must be in the possession of the secured party in accordance with an agreement, or (b) there must be a written or authenticated security agreement describing the collateral subject to the security interest and signed or authenticated by the debtor.

② The secured party must give to the debtor something of value.

③ The debtor must have "rights" in the collateral.

Once these requirements have been met, the creditor's rights are said to attach to the collateral. **Attachment** gives the creditor an enforceable security interest in the collateral [UCC 9–203].[1]

Written or Authenticated Security Agreement. When the collateral is not in the possession of the secured party, the security agreement must be either written or authenticated, and it must describe the collateral. Note here that *authentication* includes any agreement or signature inscribed on a tangible medium or stored in an electronic or other medium (called a record) that is retrievable [UCC 9–102(a)(7)(69)]. If the security agreement is in writing or authenticated, only the debtor's signature or authentication is required to create the security interest. The reason that

---

[1] Note that in the context of judicial liens, discussed in Chapter 21, the term *attachment* has a different meaning. In that context, it refers to a court-ordered seizure and taking into custody of property prior to the securing of a court judgment for a past-due debt.

EXHIBIT 20–1 SECURED TRANSACTIONS—CONCEPT AND TERMINOLOGY

In a security agreement, a debtor and a creditor agree that the creditor will have a security interest in collateral in which the debtor has rights. In essence, the collateral secures the loan and ensures the creditor of payment should the debtor default.

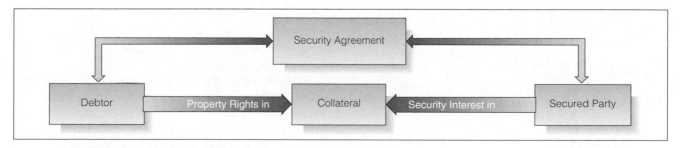

EXHIBIT 20-2   **AN EXAMPLE OF A SIMPLE SECURITY AGREEMENT**

_____
Date

_____
Name   No. and Street   City   County   State

(hereinafter called "Debtor") hereby grants to _____
                                                        Name

_____
No. and Street   City   County   State

(hereinafter called "Secured Party") a security interest in the following property (hereinafter called the "Collateral"): _____

_____

_____

to secure payment and performance of obligations identified or set out as follows (hereinafter called the "Obligations"): _____

_____

_____

   Default in payment or-performance of any of the Obligations or default under any
agreement evidencing any of the Obligations is a default under this agreement. Upon
such default Secured Party may declare all Obligations immediately due and payable
and shall have the remedies of a secured party under the _____ Uniform Commercial Code.
   Signed in (duplicate) triplicate.

_____ | _____
Debtor | Secured Party
By _____ | By _____

---

authentication is acceptable is to provide for electronic filing (the filing process will be discussed later).

A security agreement must contain a description of the
collateral that reasonably identifies it. Generally, such
words as "all the debtor's personal property" or "all the
debtor's assets" would not constitute a sufficient descrip-

tion [UCC 9–108(c)]. See Exhibit 20–2 for a sample security agreement.

At issue in the following case was whether two documents, when read together, created an enforceable security
interest. The debtor signed one of the documents, but the
description of the collateral was in the other.

CASE 20.1   **In re Cantu**

United States Bankruptcy Appellate Panel,[a]
Eighth Circuit, 1999.
238 Bankr. 796.

FACTS Under the Hormel Employees Credit Union's loan
program, an employee who fills out and signs a general loan
agreement is eligible to draw funds. The agreement grants a
security interest to the credit union but does not describe the
property that is to serve as collateral. Instead, the agreement
refers to a second document called a "funds advance
voucher." This document includes a detailed description of
the collateral. The debtor is not required to sign the funds

---

a. A _bankruptcy appellate panel,_ with the consent of the parties,
hears appeals from final judgments, orders, and decrees of bankruptcy judges.

CASE 20.1—Continued

advance voucher. Jesus Cantu bought a truck with financing provided through this program. Cantu signed a loan agreement, and the credit union issued the funds advance voucher, fully describing the collateral by make, model, year, and vehicle identification number. The voucher also provided that all of its terms were incorporated into the loan agreement. Cantu later filed a petition in a federal bankruptcy court to declare bankruptcy. One of the issues was whether the credit union had an enforceable security interest in the truck. Cantu argued that the credit union did not have such an interest because no single document contained his signature, language granting a security interest, and a description of the collateral. The court issued a summary judgment in favor of the credit union. Cantu appealed to the U.S. Bankruptcy Appellate Panel for the Eighth Circuit.

ISSUE Did the general loan agreement and the funds advance voucher, when read together, create an enforceable security interest?

DECISION Yes. The U.S. Bankruptcy Appellate Panel for the Eighth Circuit affirmed the lower court's judgment. The

appellate court held that the requirements of UCC 9–203 were satisfied.[b]

REASON The court explained, "The loan agreement grants the Credit Union a security interest in property and expressly states that such property will be described in a separate funds advance voucher. The funds advance voucher, when issued thereafter, contains a full description of the collateral and provides that its terms are made part of the loan agreement. By cross-reference, the description of the collateral in the funds advance voucher is made part and parcel of the loan agreement bearing the debtor's signature." The court added, "The course of conduct of the parties and the purpose of the open-end loan program also support the conclusion that the loan agreement and funds advance voucher are to be read together as comprising the security agreement."

FOR CRITICAL ANALYSIS—Ethical Consideration
Should the court have considered whether the debtor had actually read the loan agreement?

---

b. This case was decided before the effective date of the revised version of Article 9, but the result would likely have been the same under the revised version.

Secured Party Must Give Value. The secured party must give to the debtor something of value. Some examples would be a binding commitment to extend credit, as security for the satisfaction of a preexisting debt, or consideration to support a simple contract [UCC 1–201(44)]. Normally, the value given by a secured party is in the form of a direct loan, or it involves a commitment to sell goods on credit.

Debtor Must Have Rights in the Collateral. The debtor must have rights in the collateral; that is, the debtor must have some ownership interest or right to obtain possession of that collateral. The debtor's rights can represent either a current or a future legal interest in the collateral. For example, a retail seller-debtor can give a secured party a security interest not only in existing inventory owned by the retailer but also in *future* inventory to be acquired by the retailer.

One common misconception about having rights in the collateral is that the debtor must have title. This is not a requirement. A beneficial interest in a trust, when title to the trust property is held by the trustee, may be made the subject of a security interest for a loan made to the beneficiary by a secured party (a creditor).

CLASSIFICATIONS AND DEFINITIONS OF COLLATERAL

Where or how to perfect a security interest (perfection will be discussed shortly) sometimes depends on the classification or definition of the collateral. Collateral is generally divided into two classifications: *tangible collateral* (collateral that can be seen, felt, touched, and so on) and *intangible collateral* (collateral that consists of or generates rights).

Exhibit 20–3 on the next two pages summarizes the various classifications of collateral and the methods of perfecting a security interest in collateral falling within each of those classifications.[2]

PERFECTING A SECURITY INTEREST

Perfection represents the legal process by which secured parties protect themselves against the claims of third parties who may wish to have their debts satisfied out of the same collateral. Usually, perfection is accomplished by the filing of a financing statement with the office of the appropriate

---

[2] There are additional classifications, such as agricultural liens, investment property, and commercial tort claims. For definitions of these types of collateral, see UCC 9–102(a)(5), (a)(13), and (a)(49).

EXHIBIT 20-3 TYPES OF COLLATERAL AND METHODS OF PERFECTION

TANGIBLE	All things that are movable at the time the security interest attaches (such as livestock) or that are attached to the land, including timber to be cut and growing crops.	
1. Consumer goods [UCC 9–301, 9–303, 9–309(1), 9–310(a), 9–313(a)]	Goods used or bought primarily for personal, family, or household purposes—for example, household furniture [UCC 9–102(a)(23)].	For purchase-money security interest, attachment (that is, the creation of a security interest) is sufficient; for boats, motor vehicles, and trailers, filing or compliance with a certificate-of-title statute is required; for other consumer goods, general rules of filing or possession apply.
2. Equipment [UCC 9–301, 9–310(a), 9–313(a)]	Goods bought for or used primarily in business (and not part of inventory or farm products)—for example, a delivery truck [UCC 9–102(a)(33)].	Filing or (rarely) possession by secured party.
3. Farm products [UCC 9–301, 9–310(a), 9–313(a)]	Crops (including aquatic goods), livestock, or supplies produced in a farming operation—for example, ginned cotton, milk, eggs, and maple syrup [UCC 9–102(a)(34)].	Filing or (rarely) possession by secured party.
4. Inventory [UCC 9–301, 9–310(a), 9–313(a)]	Goods held by a person for sale or under a contract of service or lease; raw materials held for production and work in progress [UCC 9–102(a)(48)].	Filing or (rarely) possession by secured party.
5. Accessions [UCC 9–301, 9–310(a), 9–313(a)]	Personal property that is so attached, installed, or fixed to other personal property (goods) that it becomes a part of these goods—for example, a compact disc player installed in an automobile [UCC 9–102(a)(1)].	Filing or (rarely) possession by secured party (same as personal property being attached).
INTANGIBLE	Nonphysical property that exists only in connection with something else.	
1. Chattel paper [UCC 9–301, 9–310(a), 9–312(a), 9–313(a), 9–314(a)]	A writing or writings (records) that evidence both a monetary obligation and a security interest in goods and software used in goods—for example, a security agreement or a security agreement and promissory note. Note: If the record or records consist of information stored in an electronic medium, the collateral is called electronic chattel paper. If the information is inscribed on a tangible medium, it is called tangible chattel paper [UCC 9–102(a)(11), (a)(31), and (a)(78)].	Filing or possession or control by secured party.
2. Instruments [UCC 9–301, 9–309(4), 9–310(a), 9–312(a) and (e), 9–313(a)]	A negotiable instrument, such as a check, note, certificate of deposit, or draft, or other writing that evidences a right to the payment of money and is not a security agreement or lease but rather a type that can ordinarily be transferred (after indorsement, if necessary) by delivery [UCC 9–102(a)(47)].	Except for temporary perfected status, filing or possession. For the sale of promissory notes, perfection can be by attachment (automatically on the creation of the security interest).

EXHIBIT 20–3 TYPES OF COLLATERAL AND METHODS OF PERFECTION—CONTINUED

3. Accounts [UCC 9–301, 9–309(2) and (5), 9–310(a)]	Any right to receive payment for the following: (a) any property, real or personal, sold, leased, licensed, assigned, or otherwise disposed of, including intellectual licensed property; (b) services rendered or to be rendered, such as contract rights; (c) policies of insurance; (d) secondary obligations incurred; (e) use of a credit card; (f) winnings of a government-sponsored or government-authorized lottery or other game of chance; and (g) health-care insurance receivables, defined as an interest or claim under a policy of insurance to payment for health-care goods or services provided [UCC 9–102(a)(2) and (a)(46)].	Filing required except for certain assignments that can be perfected by attachment (automatically on the creation of the security interest).
4. Deposit accounts [UCC 9–104, 9–304, 9–312(b), 9–314(a)]	Any demand, time, savings, passbook, or similar account maintained with a bank [UCC 9–102(a)(29)].	Perfection by control, such as when the secured party is the bank in which the account is maintained or when the parties have agreed that the secured party can direct the disposition of funds in a particular account.
5. General intangibles [UCC 9–301, 9–309(3), 9–310(a) and (b)(8)]	Any personal property (or debtor's obligation to pay money on such) other than that defined above [UCC 9–102(a)(42)], including software that is independent from a computer or a good [UCC 9–102(a)(44), (a)(61), and (a)(75)].	Filing only (for copyrights, with the U.S. Copyright Office), except a sale of a payment intangible by attachment (automatically on the creation of the security interest).

government official. In some circumstances, however, a security interest becomes perfected without the filing of a financing statement.

Perfection by Filing. As mentioned, the most common means of perfection is by filing a *financing statement*—a document that gives public notice to third parties of the secured party's security interest—with the office of the appropriate government official. The security agreement itself can also be filed to perfect the security interest. The financing statement must provide the names of the debtor and the secured party and indicate the collateral covered by the financing statement. There is now a uniform financing statement form to be used in all states [see UCC 9–521]. The uniform financing statement is shown in Exhibit 20–4 on the next page.

Communication of the financing statement to the appropriate filing office, together with the correct filing fee, or the acceptance of the financing statement by the filing officer constitutes a filing [UCC 9–516(a)]. The word *communication* means that the filing can be accomplished electronically [UCC 9–102(a)(18)]. Once completed, filings are indexed in the name of the debtor so that they can be located by subse-

quent searchers. A financing statement may be filed even before a security agreement is made or a security interest attaches [UCC 9–502(d)].

The Debtor's Name. The UCC requires that a financing statement be filed under the name of the debtor [UCC 9–502(a)(1)]. Because of the use of electronic filing systems in most states, UCC 9–503 sets out some detailed rules for determining when the debtor's name as it appears on a financing statement is sufficient. For corporations, which are part of "registered organizations," the debtor's name on the financing statement must be "the name of the debtor indicated on the public record of the debtor's jurisdiction of organization" [UCC 9–503(a)(1)]. Slight variations in names normally will not be considered misleading if a search of the filing office's records, using a standard computer search engine routinely used by that office, would disclose the filings [UCC 9–506(c)]. Note that if the debtor is identified by the correct name at the time of the filing of a financing statement, the secured party's interest retains its priority even if the debtor later changes his or her name.

If the debtor is a trust, or a trustee with respect to property held in trust, this information must be disclosed on the

EXHIBIT 20-4 THE UNIFORM FINANCING STATEMENT

UCC FINANCING STATEMENT
FOLLOW INSTRUCTIONS (front and back) CAREFULLY

A. NAME & PHONE OF CONTACT AT FILER (optional)

B. SEND ACKNOWLEDGEMENT TO: (Name and Address)

THE ABOVE SPACE IS FOR FILING OFFICE USE ONLY

1. DEBTOR'S EXACT FULL LEGAL NAME - Insert only one debtor name (1a or 1b) - do not abbreviate or combine names

1a. ORGANIZATION'S NAME			

OR

1b. INDIVIDUAL'S LAST NAME	FIRST NAME	MIDDLE NAME	SUFFIX
1c. MAILING ADDRESS	CITY	STATE	POSTAL CODE	COUNTRY

| 1d. TAX ID# SSN OR EIN | ADDL INFO RE ORGANIZATION DEBTOR | 1e. TYPE OF ORGANIZATION | 1f. JURISDICTION OR ORGANIZATION | 1g. ORGANIZATIONAL ID #, if any □NONE |

2. ADDITIONAL DEBTOR'S EXACT FULL LEGAL NAME - Insert only one debtor name (2a or 2b) - do not abbreviate or combine names

2a. ORGANIZATION'S NAME			

OR

2b. INDIVIDUAL'S LAST NAME	FIRST NAME	MIDDLE NAME	SUFFIX
2c. MAILING ADDRESS	CITY	STATE	POSTAL CODE	COUNTRY

| 2d. TAX ID# SSN OR EIN | ADDL INFO RE ORGANIZATION DEBTOR | 1e. TYPE OF ORGANIZATION | 1f. JURISDICTION OR ORGANIZATION | 1g. ORGANIZATIONAL ID #, if any □NONE |

3. SECURED PARTY'S NAME - (or NAME of TOTAL ASSIGNOR S/P) Insert only one secured party name (3a or 3b)

3a. ORGANIZATION'S NAME			

OR

3b. INDIVIDUAL'S LAST NAME	FIRST NAME	MIDDLE NAME	SUFFIX
3c. MAILING ADDRESS	CITY	STATE	POSTAL CODE	COUNTRY

4. This FINANCING STATEMENT covers the following collateral:

5. ALTERNATIVE DESIGNATION (if applicable) □ LESSEE/LESSOR □ CONSIGNEE/CONSIGNOR □ BAILEE/BAILOR □ SELLER/BUYER □ AG. LIEN □ NON-UCC FILING

6. □ This FINANCING STATEMENT is to be filed [for record] (or recorded) in the REAL ESTATE RECORDS. Attach Addendum (if applicable)   7. Check to REQUEST SEARCH REPORT(S) on Debtor(s) (ADDITIONAL FEE) (optional)   □ All Debtors □ Debtor 1 □ Debtor 2

OPTIONAL FILER REFERENCE DATA

NATIONAL UCC FINANCING STATEMENT (FORM UCC1) REV. 07/29/98

filed financing statement, and it must provide the trust name as specified in its official documents [UCC 9–503(a)(3)]. In other cases, the filed financing statement must disclose "the individual or organizational name of the debtor" [UCC 9–503(a)(4)(A)]. As used here, the word *organization* includes unincorporated associations, such as clubs and some churches, as well as joint ventures and general partnerships, even when these organizations are created without obtaining any formal certificate of formation.

In general, providing only the debtor's trade name (or a fictitious name) in a financing statement is not sufficient for perfection [UCC 9–503(c)]. The reason for this rule is that a sole proprietorship is not a legal entity distinct from the person who owns it. The rule also furthers an important goal of Article 9: to ensure that the debtor's name on a financing statement is one that prospective lenders can locate and recognize in future searches.

Changes in the Debtor's Name. A problem arises when the debtor subject to a filed perfected security interest changes his or her (or its) name. What happens if a subsequent creditor extends credit to the debtor and perfects its security interest under the debtor's new name? Obviously, a search by this subsequent creditor for filed security interests under the debtor's changed name may not disclose the previously filed security interest.

The UCC's revised Article 9 attempts to prevent potential conflicts caused by changes in the debtor's name if the

debtor goes into default. First, UCC 9–503 states specifically what constitutes the "sufficiency" of the debtor's name in a financing statement. Second, if the debtor's name is insufficient, the filing is seriously misleading unless a search of records using the debtor's correct name by the filing officer's search engine would disclose the security interest [UCC 9–506(b) and (c)]. Third, even if the change of name renders the financing statement misleading, the financing statement is effective as a perfection of a security interest in collateral acquired by the debtor before or within four months after the name change. Unless an amendment is filed within this four-month period, collateral acquired by the debtor after the four-month period is unperfected [UCC 9–507(b) and (c)].

CASE 20.2 **Cabool State Bank v. Radio Shack, Inc.**

Missouri Court of Appeals,
Southern District, Division One, 2002.
65 S.W.3d 613.
http://www.osca.state.mo.us[a]

ISSUE Did the bank's security interest take priority over Radio Shack's claim?

DECISION Yes. The state intermediate appellate court affirmed the lower court's judgment in the bank's favor.

FACTS In June 1995, Michael and Debra Boudreaux, doing business as D & J Enterprises, Inc., bought from Van Pamperien a retail electronics store operated under a franchise from Radio Shack. To pay for the business, the Boudreauxes borrowed money from Cabool State Bank in Springfield, Missouri. The loan documents included a financing statement. On the statement's signature lines, the only capacity identified for the Boudreauxes' signatures was that of "Debtors." Elsewhere on the form, the bank listed "D & J Enterprises, Inc., Radio Shack, Dealer, Debra K. Boudreaux, Michael C. Boudreaux" as "Debtors." The statement covered, in part, the store inventory. Before the end of the year, the Boudreauxes changed the name of their business to Tri-B Enterprises, Inc. In January 1998, the store closed. The next month, Radio Shack terminated the franchise and, despite the lack of a security interest, took possession of the inventory, claiming the Boudreauxes and Tri-B owed Radio Shack $6,394.73. The bank filed a suit in a Missouri state court against Radio Shack, claiming a perfected security interest in the inventory with priority over Radio Shack's claim. The court entered a judgment for $15,529.43 in the bank's favor. Radio Shack appealed to a state intermediate appellate court.

REASON Contrary to Radio Shack's assertion that "the so-called change of name was seriously misleading," Radio Shack was not misled by the debtors' change of their business name, because the bank's financing statement was filed under the "true name" of at least one of the debtors with whom Radio Shack admitted doing business. Radio Shack also had actual knowledge of the bank loan. The appellate court noted that "(1) Boudreauxes bought the original inventory in their individual names, (2) Boudreauxes gave Bank a security interest in the original inventory and 'all inventory purchased or replaced,' (3) Bank perfected its security interest in existing and future inventory owned by Boudreauxes by filing * * * financing statements that listed Boudreauxes and D & J Enterprises, Inc., as 'Debtors,' (4) Radio Shack had actual knowledge of the loan transaction between Bank and Boudreauxes, and (5) the subject inventory was sold to both the Boudreauxes and Tri-B." The court emphasized that "[f]rom the outset, Bank listed Boudreauxes (who admittedly had an ownership interest in the inventory) as 'Debtors' on the [UCC] filings."

FOR CRITICAL ANALYSIS—Social Consideration
If the bank had not listed the Boudreauxes as debtors on the financing statement, would Radio Shack have prevailed in this case?

---

a. In the "Court of Appeals" pull-down menu, select "Southern District" and click on "Go!" On that page, click on "Opinions and Orders." Scroll to "01/30/2002" and click on the name of the case to access the opinion. The Missouri judiciary maintains this Web site.

Description of the Collateral. The UCC requires that both the security agreement and the financing statement contain a description of the collateral in which the secured party has a security interest. The security agreement must include a description of the collateral because no security interest in goods can exist unless the parties agree on which goods are subject to the security interest. The financing statement must include a description of the collateral because the purpose of filing the statement is to give public notice of the fact that certain goods of the debtor are subject to a security interest. Other parties who might later wish to lend money to the debtor or buy the collateral can thus learn of the security interest by checking with the state or local office in which a financing statement for that type of collateral would be filed. For land-related security interests, a legal description of the realty is also required [UCC 9–502(b)].

Sometimes, the descriptions in the two documents vary, with the description in the security agreement being more precise than the description in the financing statement, which is allowed to be more general. ● EXAMPLE #1 A security agreement for a commercial loan to a manufacturer may list all of the manufacturer's equipment subject to the loan by serial number, whereas the financing statement may simply state "all equipment owned or hereafter acquired." ● The UCC permits broad, general descriptions in the financing statement, such as "all assets" or "all personal property." Generally, therefore, whenever the description in a financing statement accurately describes the agreement between the secured party and the debtor, the description is sufficient [UCC 9–504].

Where to File. In most states, a financing statement must be filed centrally in the appropriate state office, such as the office of the secretary of state, in the state where the debtor is located. County filings, where the collateral is located, are required only when the collateral consists of timber to be cut, fixtures, and collateral to be extracted—such as oil, coal, gas, and minerals [UCC 9–301(3) and (4), 9–502(b)].

The state office in which a financing statement should be filed depends on the *debtor's location,* not the location of the collateral (as was required under the unrevised Article 9) [UCC 9–301]. The debtor's location is determined as follows [UCC 9–307]:

① For *individual debtors,* it is the state of the debtor's principal residence.

② For a chartered entity created by a filing (such as a corporation), it is in the state of charter or filing. For example, if a debtor is incorporated in Maryland, with its chief executive office in New York, a secured party would file the financing statement in Maryland, which is the state of the debtor's organizational formation.

③ For all other entities, it is the state where the business is located or, if more than one, the state where the chief executive office is located.

Consequences of an Improper Filing. Any improper filing renders the secured party unperfected and reduces a secured party's claim in bankruptcy to that of an unsecured creditor. For example, if the debtor's name on the financing statement is inaccurate or if the collateral is not sufficiently described on the filing statement, the filing may not be effective.

Perfection without Filing. In two types of situations, security interests can be perfected without filing a financing statement. First, when the collateral is transferred into the possession of the secured party, the secured party's security interest in the collateral is perfected. Second, there are thirteen different types of security interests that can be perfected on attachment without a filing and without having to possess the goods [UCC 9–309]. The phrase *perfected on attachment* means that these security interests are automatically perfected at the time of their creation. Two of the most common security interests that are perfected on attachment are a *purchase-money security interest* in consumer goods (defined and explained below) and an assignment of a beneficial interest in a decedent's estate [UCC 9–309(1) and (13)].

Perfection by Possession. Under the common law, one of the most prevalent means of obtaining financing was to **pledge** certain collateral as security for the debt and transfer the collateral into the creditor's possession. When the debt was paid, the collateral was returned to the debtor. Usually, the transfer of collateral was accompanied by a written security agreement, but the agreement did not have to be in writing. In other words, an oral security agreement was effective as long as the secured party possessed the collateral. Article 9 of the UCC retained the common law pledge and the principle that the security agreement need not be in writing to be enforceable if the collateral is transferred to the secured party [UCC 9–310, 9–312(b), and 9–313].

For most collateral, possession by the secured party is impractical because it denies the debtor the right to use or derive income from the property to pay off the debt. ● EXAMPLE #2 Suppose that a farmer takes out a loan to finance the purchase of a piece of heavy farm equipment needed to harvest crops and uses the equipment as collateral. Clearly, the purpose of the purchase would be defeated if the farmer transferred the collateral into the creditor's possession. ● Certain items, however, such as stocks, bonds, instruments, and jewelry, are commonly transferred into the creditor's possession when they are used as collateral for loans.

Purchase-Money Security Interest. Often, sellers of consumer goods (defined as goods bought or used by the debtor primarily for personal, family, or household purposes [UCC 9–102(a)(23)]) agree to extend credit for part or all of the purchase price of those goods. Additionally, financial institutions that are not in the business of selling such goods often agree to lend consumers much of the purchase price for the goods. The security interest that the seller or the lender obtains when such a transaction occurs is called a **purchase-money security interest (PMSI)** because the lender or seller has essentially provided a buyer with the "purchase money" to buy goods [UCC 9–103(a)(2)].

●EXAMPLE #3 Suppose that Jamie wants to purchase a new large-screen TV from ABC Television, Inc. The purchase price is $2,500. Not being able to pay the entire amount in cash, Jamie signs a purchase agreement to pay $1,000 down and $100 per month until the balance plus interest is fully paid. ABC is to retain a security interest in the purchased goods until full payment has been made. Because the security interest was created as part of the purchase agreement, it is a PMSI.●

A PMSI in consumer goods is perfected automatically at the time of a credit sale—that is, at the time that the PMSI is created. The seller in this situation need do nothing more to perfect her or his interest.

A PMSI may also exist with respect to goods sold to businesses or entities that are not considered "consumers" for Article 9 purposes. (See Example #9 later in this chapter for an example of this type of PMSI.)

Effective Time Duration of Perfection. A financing statement is effective for five years from the date of filing [UCC 9–515]. If a **continuation statement** is filed within six months *prior* to the expiration date, the effectiveness of the original statement is continued for another five years, starting with the expiration date of the first five-year period [UCC 9–515(d) and (e)]. The effectiveness of the statement can be continued in the same manner indefinitely. Any attempt to file a continuation statement outside the six-month window will render the continuation ineffective, and the perfection will lapse at the end of the five-year period.

If a financing statement lapses, the security interest that had been perfected by the filing now becomes unperfected. It is as if it had never been perfected as against a purchaser for value [UCC 9–515(c)].

The Scope of a Security Interest

In addition to covering collateral already in the debtor's possession, a security agreement can cover various other types of property, including the proceeds of the sale of collateral, after-acquired property, and future advances.

PROCEEDS

Proceeds are defined as whatever is received when collateral is sold or disposed of in some other way [UCC 9–102(a)(64)]. A secured party's security interest in the collateral includes a security interest in the proceeds of the sale of that collateral. ●EXAMPLE #4 Suppose that a bank has a perfected security interest in the inventory of a retail seller of heavy farm machinery. The retailer sells a tractor out of this inventory to a farmer, who is by definition a buyer in the ordinary course of business. The farmer agrees, in a security agreement, to make monthly payments to the retailer for a period of twenty-four months. If the retailer should go into default on the loan from the bank, the bank is entitled to the remaining payments the farmer owes to the retailer as proceeds.●

A security interest in proceeds perfects automatically on the *perfection* of the secured party's security interest in the original collateral and remains perfected for twenty days after receipt of the proceeds by the debtor. One way to extend the twenty-day automatic perfection period is to provide for such extended coverage in the original security agreement [UCC 9–315(c) and (d)]. This is typically done when the collateral is the type that is likely to be sold, such as a retailer's inventory—for example, of computers or DVD players. The UCC also permits a security interest in identifiable cash proceeds to remain perfected after twenty days [UCC 9–315(d)(2)].

AFTER-ACQUIRED PROPERTY

After-acquired property of the debtor is property that the debtor acquired after the execution of the security agreement. The security agreement may provide for a security interest in after-acquired property [UCC 9–204(1)]. This is particularly useful for inventory financing arrangements, because a secured party whose security interest is in existing inventory knows that the debtor will sell that inventory, thereby reducing the collateral subject to the security interest.

Generally, the debtor will purchase new inventory to replace the inventory sold. The secured party wants this newly acquired inventory to be subject to the original security interest. Thus, the after-acquired property clause continues the secured party's claim to any inventory acquired thereafter. This is not to say that the original security interest will be superior to the rights of all other creditors with regard to this after-acquired inventory, as will be discussed later.

●EXAMPLE #5 Amato buys factory equipment from Bronson on credit, giving as security an interest in all of her equipment—both what she is buying and what she already owns. The security interest with Bronson contains an after-acquired property clause. Six months later, Amato pays cash to another seller of factory equipment for more equipment. Six months after that, Amato goes out of business before she has paid off her debt to Bronson. Bronson has a security interest in all of Amato's equipment, even the equipment bought from the other seller. ●

FUTURE ADVANCES

Often, a debtor will arrange with a bank to have a *continuing line of credit* under which the debtor can borrow funds intermittently. Advances against lines of credit can be subject to a properly perfected security interest in certain collateral. The security agreement may provide that any future advances made against that line of credit are also subject to the security interest in the same collateral [UCC 9–204(c)]. Future advances do not have to be of the same type or otherwise related to the original advance to benefit from this type of cross-collateralization.[3]

● **EXAMPLE #6** Stroh is the owner of a small manufacturing plant with equipment valued at $1 million. He has an immediate need for $50,000 of working capital, so he obtains a loan from Midwestern Bank and signs a security agreement, putting up all of his equipment as security. The bank properly perfects its security interest. The security agreement provides that Stroh can borrow up to $500,000 in the future, using the same equipment as collateral for any future advances. In this situation, Midwestern Bank does not have to execute a new security agreement and perfect a security interest in the collateral each time an advance is made up to a cumulative total of $500,000. For priority purposes, each advance is perfected as of the date of the original perfection. ●

THE FLOATING-LIEN CONCEPT

A security agreement that provides for a security interest in proceeds, in after-acquired property, or in collateral subject to future advances by the secured party (or in all three) is often characterized as a **floating lien.** This type of security interest continues in the collateral or proceeds even if the collateral is sold, exchanged, or disposed of in some other way. Floating liens commonly arise in the financing of inventories. A creditor is not interested in specific pieces of inventory, which are constantly changing, so the lien "floats" from one item to another, as the inventory changes.

● **EXAMPLE #7** Suppose that Cascade Sports, Inc., a corporation chartered in Oregon that operates as a cross-country ski dealer, has a line of credit with Portland First Bank to finance an inventory of cross-country skis. Cascade and Portland First enter into a security agreement that provides for coverage of proceeds, after-acquired inventory, present inventory, and future advances. This security interest in inventory is perfected by filing centrally (with the office of the secretary of state in Oregon). One day, Cascade sells a new pair of the latest cross-country skis and receives a used pair in trade. That same day, Cascade purchases two new pairs of cross-country skis from a local manufacturer for cash. Later that day, Cascade borrows $2,000 from Portland First Bank under the security agreement to meet its payroll. Portland First gets a perfected security interest in the used pair of skis under the proceeds clause, has a perfected security interest in the two new pairs of skis purchased from the local manufacturer under the after-acquired property clause, and has the new amount of funds advanced to Cascade secured on all of the above collateral by the future-advances clause. All of this is accomplished under the original perfected security interest. The various items in the inventory have changed, but Portland First still has a perfected security interest in Cascade's inventory. Hence, it has a floating lien on the inventory. ●

The concept of the floating lien can also apply to a shifting stock of goods. The lien can start with raw materials; follow them as they become finished goods and inventories; and continue as the goods are sold and are turned into accounts receivable, chattel paper, or cash.

Priorities

The importance of being perfected as a secured party cannot be overemphasized, particularly when another party is claiming an interest in the same collateral as covered by the perfected secured party's security interest.

THE GENERAL RULE

The general rule is that a perfected secured party's interest has priority over the interests of the following parties [UCC 9–317, 9–322]:

① An unsecured creditor.

② An unperfected secured party.

③ A subsequent lien creditor, such as a judgment creditor who acquires a lien on the collateral by execution and levy—a process discussed later in this chapter.

④ A trustee in bankruptcy (see Chapter 21)—at least, the perfected secured party has priority to the proceeds from the sale of the collateral by the trustee.

⑤ Most buyers who *do not* purchase the collateral in the ordinary course of a seller's business.

---

[3] See official Comment 5 to UCC 9–204.

In addition, whether a secured party's security interest is perfected or unperfected may have serious consequences for the secured party if the debtor defaults on the debt or files for bankruptcy. For example, what if the debtor has borrowed money from two different creditors, using the same property as collateral for both loans? If the debtor defaults on both loans, which of the two creditors has first rights to the collateral? In this situation, the creditor with a perfected security interest will prevail.

BUYERS OF THE COLLATERAL

Sometimes, the conflict is between a perfected secured party and a buyer of the collateral. The question then arises as to which party has priority to the collateral.

The UCC recognizes that there are five types of buyers whose interest in purchased goods could conflict with those of a perfected secured party on the debtor's default. These five types are as follows:

① Buyers in the ordinary course of business—this type of buyer will be discussed in detail shortly.

② Buyers *not* in the ordinary course of business of consumer goods (see Exhibit 20–5 on page 408 for details).

③ Buyers of chattel paper [UCC 9–330].

④ Buyers of instruments, documents, or securities [UCC 9–330(d), 9–331(a)].

⑤ Buyers of farm products.[4]

Because buyers should not be required to find out if there is an outstanding security interest in, for example, a merchant's inventory, the UCC also provides that a person who buys "in the ordinary course of business" will take the goods free from any security interest created by the seller in the purchased collateral. This is so even if the security interest is perfected and *even if the buyer knows of its existence* [UCC 9–320(a)].[5] The UCC defines a *buyer in the ordinary course of business* as any person who in good faith, and without knowledge that the sale is in violation of the ownership rights or security interest of a third party in the goods, buys in ordinary course from a person in the business of selling goods of that kind [UCC 1–201(9)].

• **EXAMPLE #8** On August 1, West Bank has a perfected security interest in all of ABC Television's existing inventory and any inventory thereafter acquired. On September 1, Carla, a student at Central University, purchases one of the TVs in ABC's inventory. If on December 1, ABC goes into default, can West Bank repossess the TV set sold to Carla? The answer is no, because Carla is a buyer in the ordinary course of business (ABC is in the business of selling goods of that kind) and obtained the TV free and clear of West Bank's perfected security interest. •

CREDITORS OR SECURED PARTIES

Generally, the following UCC rules apply when more than one creditor claims rights in the same collateral:

① *Conflicting perfected security interests.* When two or more secured parties have perfected security interests in the same collateral, generally the first to perfect (file or take possession of the collateral) has priority, unless the state's statute provides otherwise [UCC 9–322(a)(1)].

② *Conflicting unperfected security interests.* When two conflicting security interests are unperfected, the first to attach has priority [UCC 9–322(a)(3)].

③ *Conflicting perfected security interests in commingled or processed goods.* When goods to which two or more perfected security interests attach are so manufactured or commingled that they lose their identities into a product or mass, the perfected parties' security interests attach to the new product or mass "according to the ratio that the cost of goods to which each interest originally attached bears to the cost of the total product or mass" [UCC 9–336].

Under some circumstances, on the debtor's default, the perfection of a security interest will not protect a secured party against certain other third parties having claims to the collateral. For example, the UCC provides that in some instances a PMSI, properly perfected,[6] will prevail over another security interest in after-acquired collateral, even though the other was perfected first (see Exhibit 20–5 on page 408).

An important exception to the first-in-time rule deals with certain types of collateral, such as equipment, in which one of the perfected security parties has a PMSI [UCC 9–324(a)]. • **EXAMPLE #9** Suppose that Smith borrows funds from West Bank, signing a security agreement in which she puts up all of her present and after-acquired equipment as security. On May 1, West Bank perfects this

---

[4] Under the Food Security Act of 1985, buyers in the ordinary course of business include buyers of farm products from a farmer. Under this act, these buyers are protected from prior perfected security interests unless the secured parties perfected centrally by a special form called an *effective financing statement (EFS)* or the buyers received proper notice of the secured party's security interest.

[5] Remember that, generally, there are three methods of perfection: by filing, by possession, and by attachment.

[6] Recall that, with some exceptions (such as motor vehicles), a PMSI in consumer goods is automatically perfected—no filing is necessary.

EXHIBIT 20–5 PRIORITY OF CLAIMS TO A DEBTOR'S COLLATERAL

PARTIES	PRIORITY
Unperfected secured party	An unperfected secured party prevails over unsecured creditors and creditors who have obtained judgments against the debtor but who have not begun the legal process to collect on those judgments [UCC 9–201(a)].
Purchaser of debtor's collateral	1. *Goods purchased in the ordinary course of the seller's business*—Buyer prevails over a secured party's security interest, even if perfected and even if the buyer knows of the security interest [UCC 9–320(a)]. 2. *Consumer goods purchased outside the ordinary course of business*—Buyer prevails over a secured party's interest, even if perfected by attachment, providing buyer purchased as follows: a. For value. b. Without actual knowledge of the security interest. c. For use as a consumer good. d. Prior to secured party's perfection by *filing* [UCC 9–320(b)]. 3. *Buyers of chattel paper*—Buyer prevails if the buyer: a. Gave new value in making the purchase. b. Took possession in the ordinary course of the buyer's business. c. Took without knowledge of the security interest [UCC 9–330]. 4. *Buyers of instruments, documents, or securities*—Buyers who are holders in due course, holders to whom negotiable documents have been duly negotiated, or bona fide purchasers of securities have priority over a previously perfected security interest [UCC 9–330(d), 9–331(a)]. 5. *Buyers of farm products*—Buyers from a farmer take free and clear of perfected security interests unless, where permitted, a secured party files centrally an effective financing statement (EFS) or the buyer receives proper notice of the security interest before the sale.
Perfected secured parties to the same collateral	1. *The general rule*—Between two perfected secured parties in the same collateral, the general rule is that first in time of perfection is first in right to the collateral [UCC 9–322(a)(1)]. 2. *Exception: purchase-money security interest (PMSI)*—A PMSI, even if second in time of perfection, has priority providing that the following conditions are met: a. Inventory—PMSI is perfected, and proper written or authenticated notice is given to the other security-interest holder *on* or *before* the time that debtor takes possession [UCC 9–324(b)]. b. Other collateral—PMSI has priority, providing it is perfected within twenty days after debtor receives possession [UCC 9–324(a)]. c. Software—Applies to a PMSI in software only if used in goods subject to a PMSI. Priority is determined the same as if the goods are inventory (if the goods are, in fact, inventory), or if not, as if the goods are other than inventory [UCC 9–103(c) and 9–324(f)].

security interest (which is not a PMSI). On July 1, Smith purchases a new piece of equipment from XYZ Company on credit, signing a security agreement. XYZ Company thus has a (nonconsumer) PSMI in the new equipment. The delivery date for the new piece of equipment is August 1. If Smith defaults on her payments to both West Bank and XYZ, which party—West Bank or XYZ—has priority to the new piece of equipment? Generally, West Bank would have priority because its interest was perfected first in time. In this situation, however, XYZ has a PMSI, and if it perfects its interest by filing before Smith takes possession on August 1, or within twenty days after that date, XYZ has priority. If XYZ had a PMSI in inventory instead of equipment, XYZ would have priority only if it both perfected *and* gave notice of its security interest to West Bank on or before August 1.●

Another important exception to the first-in-time rule has to do with security interests in inventory [UCC 9–324(b)]. ● **EXAMPLE #10** On May 1, ABC borrows funds from West Bank. ABC signs a security agreement, putting up all of its present inventory and any thereafter acquired as collateral. West Bank perfects its non–PMSI on that date. On June 10, ABC buys new inventory from Martin, Inc., a manufacturer, to use for its Fourth of July sale. ABC makes a down payment for the new inventory and signs a security agreement giving Martin a PMSI in the new inventory as collateral for the remaining debt. Martin delivers the inventory to ABC on June 28. Due to a hurricane in the area, ABC's Fourth of July sale is a disaster, and most of ABC's inventory remains unsold. In August, ABC defaults on its payments to both West Bank and Martin. As between West Bank and Martin, who has priority to the new inventory delivered on June 28? If Martin has not perfected its security interest by June 28, West Bank's after-acquired collateral clause has priority because it was the first to be perfected. If, however, Martin has perfected and gives proper notice of its security interest to West Bank before ABC takes possession of the goods on June 28, Martin has priority.●

Rights and Duties of Debtors and Creditors

The security agreement itself determines most of the rights and duties of the debtor and the secured party. The UCC, however, imposes some rights and duties that are applicable in the absence of a valid security agreement that states the contrary.

INFORMATION REQUESTS

Under UCC 9–523(a), a secured party has the option, when making the filing, of furnishing a *copy* of the financing statement being filed to the filing officer and requesting that the filing officer make a note of the file number, the date, and the hour of the original filing on the copy. The filing officer must send this copy to the person designated by the secured party or to the debtor, if the debtor makes the request. Under UCC 9–523(c) and (d), a filing officer must also give information to a person who is contemplating obtaining a security interest from a prospective debtor. The filing officer must issue a certificate that provides information on possible perfected financing statements with respect to the named debtor. The filing officer will charge a fee for the certification and for any information copies provided [UCC 9–525(d)].

RELEASE, ASSIGNMENT, AND AMENDMENT

A secured party can release all or part of any collateral described in the filing, thereby terminating its security interest in that collateral. The release is recorded by filing a uniform amendment form [UCC 9–512 and 9–521(b)]. A secured party can assign all or part of the security interest to a third party (the assignee). The assignee can become the secured party of record if the assignment is filed by use of a uniform amendment form [UCC 9–514 and 9–521(a)].

If the debtor and secured parties so agree, the filing can be amended—by adding new collateral if authorized by the debtor, for example—by filing a uniform amendment form that indicates by file number the initial financing statement [UCC 9–512(a)]. The amendment does not extend the time period of perfection. If, however, the amendment adds collateral, the perfection date (for priority purposes) for the new collateral begins only on the date of the filing of the amendment [UCC 9–512(b) and (c)].

CONFIRMATION OR ACCOUNTING REQUEST BY DEBTOR

The debtor may believe that the unpaid debt amount or the listing of the collateral subject to the security interest is inaccurate. The debtor has the right to request a confirmation of his or her view of the unpaid debt or listing of collateral. The secured party must either approve or correct this confirmation request [UCC 9–210].

The secured party must comply with the debtor's confirmation request by authenticating and sending to the debtor an accounting within fourteen days after the request is received. Otherwise, the secured party will be held liable for any loss suffered by the debtor, plus $500 [UCC 9–210 and 9–625(f)].

The debtor is entitled to one request without charge every six months. For any additional requests, the secured party is entitled to the payment of a statutory fee of up to $25 per request [UCC 9–210(f)].

TERMINATION STATEMENT

When the debtor has fully paid the debt, if the secured party perfected the collateral by filing, the debtor is entitled to have a termination statement filed. Such a statement demonstrates to the public that the filed perfected security interest has been terminated [UCC 9–513].

Whenever consumer goods are involved, the secured party must file a termination statement (or, in the alternative, a release) within one month of the final payment or within twenty days of receipt of the debtor's authenticated demand, whichever is earlier [UCC 9–513(b)].

When the collateral is other than consumer goods, on an authenticated demand by the debtor, the secured party must either send a termination statement to the debtor or file such a statement within twenty days [UCC 9–513(c)]. Otherwise, when the collateral is other than consumer goods, the secured party is not required to file or send a termination statement. Whenever a secured party fails to file or, as required, to send the termination statement as requested, the debtor can recover $500 plus any additional loss suffered [UCC 9–625(e)(4) and (f)].

Default

Article 9 defines the rights, duties, and remedies of the secured party and of the debtor on the debtor's default. Should the secured party fail to comply with his or her duties, the debtor is afforded particular rights and remedies.

The topic of default is one of great concern to secured lenders and to the lawyers who draft security agreements. What constitutes *default* is not always clear. In fact, Article 9 does not define the term. Consequently, parties are encouraged in practice—and by the UCC—to include in their security agreements certain standards to be applied in determining when default has actually occurred. In so doing, parties can stipulate the conditions that will constitute a default [UCC 9–601 and 9–603]. Often, these critical terms are shaped by the creditor in an attempt to provide the maximum protection possible. The ultimate terms, however, are not allowed to go beyond the limitations imposed by the good faith requirement and the unconscionability provisions of the UCC. Article 9's definition of good faith includes "honesty in fact and the observance of reasonable commercial standards of fair dealing" [UCC 9–102(a)(43)].

Although any breach of the terms of the security agreement can constitute default, default occurs most commonly when the debtor fails to meet the scheduled payments that the parties have agreed on or when the debtor becomes bankrupt.

BASIC REMEDIES

A secured party's remedies can be divided into two basic categories:

① A secured party can take peaceful or judicial possession of the collateral covered by the security agreement [UCC 9–609(b)]. On taking possession, the secured party may either want to retain the collateral for satis-

faction of the debt [UCC 9–620] or resell the goods and apply the proceeds toward the debt [UCC 9–610].

② A secured party can relinquish a security interest and use any judicial remedy available, such as proceeding to judgment on the underlying debt, followed by execution and levy. (**Execution** is the implementation of a court's decree or judgment. **Levy** is the obtaining of funds by legal process through the seizure and sale of noncollateralized property, usually done after a writ of execution has been issued.) Execution and levy are rarely undertaken unless the collateral is no longer in existence or has declined so much in value that it is worth substantially less than the amount of the debt and the debtor has other assets available that may be legally seized to satisfy the debt [UCC 9–601(a)].[7]

The rights and remedies under UCC 9–601(a) are *cumulative* [UCC 9–601(c)]. Therefore, if a creditor is unsuccessful in enforcing rights by one method, he or she can pursue another method.[8]

When a security agreement covers both real and personal property, the secured party can proceed against the personal property in accordance with the remedies of Article 9. Alternatively, the secured party can proceed against the entire collateral under procedures set down by local real estate law, in which case the UCC does not apply [UCC 9–604(a)]. Determining whether particular collateral is personal or real property at times can prove difficult, especially when dealing with fixtures—things affixed to real property. Under certain circumstances, the UCC allows the removal of fixtures on default; such removal, however, is subject to the provisions of Article 9 [UCC 9–604(c)].

It is clear that a creditor can retain collateral in full satisfaction of a debt. The issue in the following case was whether a creditor could retain the collateral in *partial* satisfaction of the debt.

---

[7] Some assets are exempt from creditors' claims—see Chapter 21.
[8] See James J. White and Robert S. Summers, *Uniform Commercial Code*, 4th ed. (St. Paul: West Publishing Co., 1995), pp. 908–909.

CASE 20.3 **Banks Brothers Corp. v. Donovan Floors, Inc.**

Wisconsin Court of Appeals, 2000.
2000 WI App 253,
239 Wis.2d 381,
620 N.W.2d 631.
http://www.wisbar.org/WisCtApp/index.html[a]

FACTS Donovan Floors, Inc., and Breakfall, Inc., two companies controlled by James and Jo-Ann Donovan, borrowed $245,000 from Bank One, Milwaukee, N.A.[b] The companies gave Bank One security interests in their assets, and the Donovans gave the lender a mortgage on their home. When Donovan Floors and Breakfall defaulted on the debt in 1991, Bank One filed a suit in a Wisconsin state court against the debtors. The Donovans agreed to surrender to Bank One some

---

a. In the "Court of Appeals Archive" section, click on "Index of 2000 Published Opinions." On that page, scroll to the "November, 2000" section and the name of the case, and click on the docket number to access the opinion. The State Bar of Wisconsin maintains this Web site.

b. The initials *N.A.* stand for *National Association.*

CASE 20.3—Continued

of the firms' assets and agreed to a foreclosure[c] on the home. Bank One promised not to act on the agreement immediately to give the Donovans a chance to revitalize their business. In 1993, Bank One assigned the debt and its security interest to Banks Brothers Corporation. Banks, the Donovans, and the Donovans' firms (Donovan Floors and Breakfall) signed an agreement under which, among other things, Banks was given some of the firms' assets (three cars, a truck, and a van), and Breakfall was released from the debt while the others remained liable. A payment schedule was set up, but none of the payments were made. Six years later, Banks scheduled a sale of the house. The Donovans and Donovan Floors filed a suit in a Wisconsin state court against Banks, arguing that the creditor's retention of assets and release of Breakfall operated as a full satisfaction of the debt. The court denied the request, and the debtors appealed to a state intermediate appellate court.

ISSUE Can a creditor retain collateral that secures a debt in less than full satisfaction of the debt?

_____

c. A *foreclosure* is a proceeding in which a lender takes title to or sells the borrower's property in satisfaction of a debt.

DECISION Yes. The state intermediate appellate court affirmed the order of the lower court.

REASON The appellate court acknowledged that "[u]nderstandably, the Donovans and Donovan Floors would love to have their cake (the chance to save their business given to them by Banks's agreement to hold off on its right to claim the assets pledged for the debt) and eat it also (keep those assets). But that is not the way [Article 9] works. Banks had a right * * * to immediate strict foreclosure of all the pledged assets. It gave up that right in consideration for a partial payment on the debt and the concomitant [accompanying] partial satisfaction. The Donovans and Donovan Floors have no legal or moral ground to complain; they agreed to that arrangement, and did so in a statement signed after default." The court noted that although this case involved a provision in effect before the revision of Article 9, under the revised article's UCC 9–620, the result would have been the same.

FOR CRITICAL ANALYSIS—Economic Consideration
What might be the effect on a lender's willingness to loan money if the law allowed the lender to retain collateral only in full satisfaction of the debt?

REPOSSESSION OF COLLATERAL— THE SELF-HELP REMEDY

On the debtor's default, the secured party is entitled to take peaceful possession of the collateral without the use of judicial process [UCC 9–609(b)]. The UCC does not define *peaceful possession,* however. The general rule is that the collateral has been taken peacefully if the secured party can take possession without committing (1) trespass onto realty, (2) assault and/or battery, or (3) breaking and entering.

The "self-help" provision of Article 9 has generated substantial controversy because of its potential adverse consequences for both creditors and debtors. If a repossession attempt results in a "breach of the peace," the creditor may be barred from recovering the remainder of the debt from the debtor, and the breach may result in tort liability as well. A breach of the peace can, in turn, be emotionally distressful for the debtor. For example, suppose that a creditor (or someone hired by the creditor) appears on the debtor's property in the middle of the night to repossess collateral. A debtor in this situation may logically assume that someone is trying to steal his or her property; thus, violence and a "breach of the peace" may ensue. Finally, the "self-help" provision implicitly gives debtors a motive for resorting to violence and forcing a confrontation when collateral is being repossessed—because if the creditor breaches the

peace, the creditor may be barred from recovering the rest of the debt.

DISPOSITION OF COLLATERAL

Once default has occurred and the secured party has obtained possession of the collateral, the secured party may attempt to retain the collateral in full satisfaction of the debt or may sell, lease, or otherwise dispose of the collateral in any commercially reasonable manner [UCC 9–602(7), 9–603, 9–610(a), and 9–620]. Any sale is always subject to procedures established by state law.

Retention of Collateral by the Secured Party. The UCC acknowledges that parties are sometimes better off if they do not sell the collateral. Therefore, a secured party may retain the collateral unless it consists of consumer goods subject to a PMSI and the debtor has paid 60 percent or more of the purchase price or debt—as will be discussed shortly [UCC 9–620(e)].

This general right, however, is subject to several conditions. The secured party must send notice of the proposal to the debtor if the debtor has not signed a statement renouncing or modifying her or his rights *after default* [UCC 9–620(a) and 9–621]. If the collateral is consumer goods, the secured party does not need to give any other notice. In all other situations, the secured party must also send notice to any other secured party from whom the secured party has received written or authenticated notice of a claim of interest in the collateral in question and any other junior lien claimant (one holding a lien that is subordinate to a prior lien) who has filed a statutory lien (such as a mechanic's lien—see Chapter 21) or a security interest in the collateral ten days before the debtor consented to the retention [UCC 9–621].

If, within twenty days after the notice is sent, the secured party receives an objection sent by a person entitled to receive notification, the secured party must sell or otherwise dispose of the collateral in accordance with the provisions of UCC 9–602, 9–603, 9–610, and 9–613 (disposition procedures will be discussed shortly). If no such written objection is forthcoming, the secured party may retain the collateral in full or partial satisfaction of the debtor's obligation [UCC 9–620(a), 9–621].

Consumer Goods. When the collateral is consumer goods with a PMSI and the debtor has paid 60 percent or more of the debt or the purchase price, the secured party must sell or otherwise dispose of the repossessed collateral within ninety days [UCC 9–620(e), (f)]. Failure to comply opens the secured party to an action for conversion or other liability under UCC 9–625(b), (c) unless the consumer-debtor signed a written statement *after default* renouncing or modifying the right to demand the sale of the goods [UCC 9–624].

Disposition Procedures. A secured party who does not choose to retain the collateral or who is required to sell it must resort to the disposition procedures prescribed under UCC 9–602(7), 9–603, 9–610(a), and 9–613. The UCC allows a great deal of flexibility with regard to disposition. UCC 9–610(a) states that after default, a secured party may sell, lease, license, or otherwise dispose of any or all of the collateral in its present condition or following any commercially reasonable preparation or processing. While the secured party may purchase the collateral at a public sale, it may not do so at a private sale—unless the collateral is of a kind customarily sold on a recognized market or is the subject of widely distributed standard price quotations [UCC 9–610(c)].

One of the major limitations with respect to the disposition of collateral is that it must be accomplished in a commercially reasonable manner. UCC 9–610(b) states as follows:

> Every aspect of a disposition of collateral, including the method, manner, time, place, and other terms, must be commercially reasonable. If commercially reasonable, a secured party may dispose of collateral by public or private proceedings, by one or more contracts, as a unit or in parcels, and at any time and place and on any terms.

Unless the collateral is perishable or will decline rapidly in value or is a type customarily sold on a recognized market, a secured party must send to the debtor and other identified persons "a reasonable authenticated notification of disposition" [UCC 9–611(b), (c)]. The debtor may waive the right to receive this notice, but only after default [UCC 9–624(a)].

Proceeds from Disposition. Proceeds from the disposition of collateral after default on the underlying debt are distributed in the following order:

① Expenses incurred by the secured party in repossessing, storing, and reselling the collateral.

② Balance of the debt owed to the secured party.

③ Junior lienholders who have made written or authenticated demands.

④ Unless the collateral consists of accounts, payment intangibles, promissory notes, or chattel paper, any surplus goes to the debtor [UCC 9–608(a), 9–615(a) and (e)].

Noncash Proceeds. Whenever the secured party receives noncash proceeds from the disposition of collateral after default, the secured party must make a value determination and apply this value in a commercially reasonable manner [UCC 9–608(a)(3) and 9–615(c)].

Deficiency Judgment. Often, after proper disposition of the collateral, the secured party has not collected all that the debtor still owes. Unless otherwise agreed, the debtor is liable for any deficiency, and the creditor can obtain a **deficiency judgment** from a court to collect the deficiency. Note, however, that if the underlying transaction was, for example, a sale of accounts or of chattel paper, the debtor is entitled to any surplus or is liable for any deficiency only if the security agreement so provides [UCC 9–615(d) and (e)].

Whenever the secured party fails to conduct a disposition in a commercially reasonable manner or to give proper notice, the deficiency of the debtor is reduced to the extent that such failure affected the price received at the disposition [UCC 9–626(a)(3)].

Redemption Rights. At any time before the secured party disposes of the collateral or enters into a contract for its disposition, or before the debtor's obligation has been discharged through the secured party's retention of the collateral, the debtor or any other secured party can exercise the right of *redemption* of the collateral. The debtor or other secured party can do this by tendering performance of all obligations secured by the collateral and by paying the expenses reasonably incurred by the secured party in retaking and maintaining the collateral [UCC 9–623].

Terms and Concepts

after-acquired property   405
attachment   397
collateral   397
continuation statement   405
debtor   397
default   397
deficiency judgment   412

execution   410
financing statement   397
floating lien   406
levy   410
perfection   399
pledge   404
proceeds   405

purchase-money security
   interest (PMSI)   405
secured party   397
secured transaction   396
security agreement   397
security interest   397

Chapter Summary — Secured Transactions

Creating a Security Interest (See pages 397–399.)	1. Unless the creditor has possession of the collateral, there must be a written or authenticated security agreement signed or authenticated by the debtor describing the collateral subject to the security interest.
	2. The secured party must give value to the debtor.
	3. The debtor must have rights in the collateral—some ownership interest or right to obtain possession of the specified collateral.
Perfecting a Security Interest (See pages 399–405.)	1. *Perfection by filing*—The most common method of perfection is by filing a financing statement containing the names of the secured party and the debtor and indicating the collateral covered by the financing statement.
	a. Communication of the financing statement to the appropriate filing office, together with the correct filing fee, constitutes a filing.
	b. The financing statement must be filed under the name of the debtor; fictitious (trade) names normally are not accepted.
	c. The classification of collateral determines whether filing is necessary and where to file (see Exhibit 20–3).
	2. *Perfection without filing*—
	a. By transfer of collateral—The debtor can transfer possession of the collateral to the secured party. For example, a *pledge* is this type of transfer.
	b. By attachment, such as the attachment of a purchase-money security interest (PMSI) in consumer goods—If the secured party has a PMSI in consumer goods (goods bought or used by the debtor for personal, family, or household purposes), the secured party's security interest is perfected automatically. In all, thirteen types of security interests can be perfected by attachment.
The Scope of a Security Interest (See pages 405–406.)	A security agreement can cover the following types of property:
	1. *Collateral in the present possession or control of the debtor.*
	2. *Proceeds from a sale, exchange, or disposition of secured collateral.*
	3. *After-acquired property*—A security agreement may provide that property acquired after the execution of the security agreement will also be secured by the agreement. This provision often accompanies security agreements covering a debtor's inventory.
	4. *Future advances*—A security agreement may provide that any future advances made against a line of credit will be subject to the initial security interest in the same collateral.

(Continued)

Chapter Summary   **Secured Transactions—Continued**

Priority of Claims to a Debtor's Collateral (See page 408.)	See Exhibit 20–5.
Rights and Duties of Debtors and Creditors (See pages 409–410.)	1. *Information request*—On request by any person, the filing officer must send a statement listing the file number, the date, and the hour of the filing of financing statements and other documents covering collateral of a particular debtor; a fee is charged.
	2. *Release, assignment, and amendment*—A secured party may (a) release part or all of the collateral described in a filed financing statement, thus ending the creditor's security interest; (b) assign part or all of the security interest to another party; and (c) amend a filed financing statement.
	3. *Confirmation or accounting request by debtor*—If a debtor believes that the unpaid debt amount or the listing of the collateral subject to the security interest is inaccurate, the debtor has the right to request a confirmation of his or her view of the unpaid debt or listing of collateral. The secured party must authenticate and send to the debtor an accounting within fourteen days after the request is received. Only one request without charge is permitted per six-month period.
	4. *Termination statement*—When a debt is paid, the secured party generally must send a termination statement to the debtor or file such a statement with the filing officer to whom the original financing statement was given. Failure to comply results in the secured party's liability to the debtor for $500 plus any loss suffered by the debtor. a. If the financing statement covers consumer goods, the termination statement must be filed by the secured party within one month after the debt is paid, or if the debtor makes an authenticated demand, it must be filed within twenty days of the demand or one month after the debt is paid—whichever is earlier. b. In all other cases, the termination statement must be filed or furnished to the debtor within twenty days after an authenticated demand is made by the debtor.
Default (See pages 410–412.)	On the debtor's default, the secured party may do either of the following: 1. Take possession (peacefully or by court order) of the collateral covered by the security agreement and then pursue one of two alternatives: a. Retain the collateral (unless the secured party has a PMSI in consumer goods and the debtor has paid 60 percent or more of the selling price or loan), in which case the secured party must— (1) Give notice to the debtor if the debtor has not signed a statement renouncing or modifying his or her rights after default. With consumer goods, no other notice is necessary. (2) Send notice to any other secured party who has given written or authenticated notice of a claim to the same collateral or who has filed a security interest or a statutory lien ten days before the debtor consented to the retention. If an objection is received from the debtor or any other secured party given notice within twenty days, the creditor must dispose of the collateral according to the requirements of UCC 9–602, 9–603, 9–610, and 9–613. Otherwise, the creditor may retain the collateral in full or partial satisfaction of the debt. b. Dispose of the collateral in accordance with the requirements of UCC 9–602(7), 9–603, 9–610(a), and 9–613, in which case the secured party must—

Chapter Summary	Secured Transactions—Continued

Default—continued	(1) Dispose of (sell, lease, or license) the goods in a commercially reasonable manner.
	
	 (2) Notify the debtor and (except in sales of consumer goods) other identified persons, including those who have given notice of claims to the collateral to be sold (unless the collateral is perishable or will decline rapidly in value).
	
	 (3) Apply the proceeds in the following order:
	
	    (a) Expenses incurred by the secured party in repossessing, storing, and reselling the collateral.
	
	    (b) The balance of the debt owed to the secured party.
	
	    (c) Junior lienholders who have made written or authenticated demands.
	
	    (d) Surplus to the debtor (unless the collateral consists of accounts, payment intangibles, promissory notes, or chattel paper).
	
	 2. Relinquish the security interest and proceed with any judicial remedy available, such as to reduce the claim to judgment on the underlying debt, followed by execution and levy on the nonexempt assets of the debtor.

For Review

① What is a security interest? Who is a secured party? What is a security agreement? What is a financing statement?

② What three requirements must be met to create an enforceable security interest?

③ What is the most common method of perfecting a security interest under Article 9?

④ If two secured parties have perfected security interests in the collateral of the debtor, which party has priority to the collateral on the debtor's default?

⑤ What rights does a secured creditor have on the debtor's default?

Questions and Case Problems

20–1. Priority Disputes. Redford is a seller of electric generators. He purchases a large quantity of generators from a manufacturer, Mallon Corp., by making a down payment and signing an agreement to make the balance of payments over a period of time. The agreement gives Mallon Corp. a security interest in the generators and the proceeds. Mallon Corp. properly files a financing statement on its security interest. Redford receives the generators and immediately sells one of them to Garfield on an installment contract, with payment to be made in twelve equal installments. At the time of sale, Garfield knows of Mallon's security interest. Two months later Redford goes into default on his payments to Mallon. Discuss Mallon's rights against purchaser Garfield in this situation.

20–2. Oral Security Agreements. Marsh has a prize horse named Arabian Knight. Marsh is in need of working capital. She borrows $5,000 from Mendez, who takes possession of Arabian Knight as security for the loan. No written agreement is signed. Discuss whether, in the absence of a written agreement, Mendez has a security interest in Arabian Knight. If Mendez does have a security interest, is it a perfected security interest?

20–3. Default. Delgado is a retail seller of television sets. He sells a color television set to Cummings for $600. Cummings cannot pay cash, so she signs a security agreement, paying $100 down and agreeing to pay the balance, plus interest, in twelve equal installments of $50 each. The security agreement gives Delgado a security interest in the television set sold. Cummings makes six payments on time; then she goes into default because of unexpected financial problems. Delgado repossesses the set and wants to keep it in full satisfaction of the debt. Discuss Delgado's rights and duties in this matter.

20–4. The Scope of a Security Interest. Edward owned a retail sporting goods shop. A new ski resort was being created in his area, and to take advantage of the potential business, Edward decided to expand his operations. He borrowed a large sum of money from his bank, which took a security interest in his present inventory and any after-acquired inventory as collateral for the loan. The bank properly perfected the security interest by filing a financing statement. Edward's business was profitable, so he doubled his inventory. A year later, just a few months after the ski resort had opened, an avalanche destroyed the ski slope and lodge. Edward's business consequently took a turn for the worse, and he defaulted on his debt to the bank. The bank then sought possession of his entire inventory, even though the inventory was now twice as large as it had been when the loan was made. Edward claimed that the bank only had rights to half of his inventory. Is Edward correct? Explain.

20–5. Debtor's Name. Cambria Fuel Oil Co. sold its business to 306 Fuel Oil Corp. As part of the deal, Cambria Fuel took a security interest in 306 Fuel's assets and filed a financing statement that identified 306 Fuel as the debtor. Six weeks later, 306 Fuel changed its name to Cambria Petroleum Co. Cambria Fuel did not file a new financing statement. Fleet Factors Corp. loaned money to Cambria Petroleum and took a security interest in the same assets as those subject to Cambria Fuel's security interest. When Cambria Petroleum failed to repay the loan, Fleet Factors filed a suit in a New York state court to foreclose its security interest. Cambria Fuel claimed that its interest had priority. Whose security interest has priority? Why? [*Fleet Factors Corp. v. Bandolene Industries Corp.,* 86 N.Y.2d 519, 658 N.E.2d 202, 634 N.Y.S.2d 425 (1995)]

20–6. Repossession. Leroy Headspeth bought a car under an installment sales contract that expressly permitted the creditor to repossess the car if the debtor defaulted on the payments. The seller assigned the contract to Mercedes-Benz Credit Corp. (MBCC). When Headspeth defaulted on the payments, an agent of Laurel Adjustment Bureau, Inc. (LAB), went onto Headspeth's property and repossessed the car on MBCC's behalf. Headspeth filed a suit against MBCC and LAB, contending in part that LAB trespassed onto his property to retake the car and that therefore the repossession was wrongful. Headspeth admitted that the repossession occurred without confrontation. Can a secured creditor legally retake possession of collateral, on the debtor's default, by entering onto the debtor's land, or would that be an illegal breach of the peace? How will the court rule? Explain. [*Headspeth v. Mercedes-Benz Credit Corp.,* 709 A.2d 717 (D.C.App. 1998)]

20–7. Financing Statement. In 1994, SouthTrust Bank, N.A., loaned money to Environmental Aspecs, Inc. (EAI), and its subsidiary, EAI of NC. SouthTrust perfected its security interest by filing financing statements that listed only EAI as the debtor, described only EAI's assets as collateral, and was signed only on EAI's behalf. SouthTrust believed that both companies were operating as a single business represented by EAI. In 1996, EAI of NC borrowed almost $300,000 from Advanced Analytics Laboratories, Inc. (AAL). AAL filed financing statements that listed the assets of EAI of NC as collateral but identified the debtor as EAI. The statements referred, however, to attached copies of the security agreements, which were signed by the president of EAI of NC and identified the debtor as EAI of NC. One year later, EAI and EAI of NC renegotiated their loan with SouthTrust, and the bank filed financing statements listing both companies as debtors. In 1998, EAI and EAI of NC filed for bankruptcy. One of the issues was the priority of the security interests of SouthTrust and AAL. AAL contended that its failure to identify, on its financing statements, EAI of NC as the debtor did not give SouthTrust priority. Is AAL correct? Why or why not? [*In re Environmental Aspecs, Inc.,* 235 Bankr. 378 (E.D.N.C., Raleigh Div. 1999)]

CASE PROBLEM WITH SAMPLE ANSWER

20–8. When a customer opens a credit-card account with Sears, Roebuck & Co., the customer fills out an application and sends it to Sears for review; if the application is approved, the customer receives a Sears card. The application contains a security agreement, a copy of which is also sent with the card. When a customer buys an item using the card, the customer signs a sales receipt that describes the merchandise and contains language granting Sears a purchase-money security interest (PMSI) in the merchandise. Dayna Conry bought a variety of consumer goods from Sears on her card. When she did not make payments on her account, Sears filed a suit against her in an Illinois state court to repossess the goods. Conry filed for bankruptcy and was granted a discharge. Sears then filed a suit against her to obtain possession of the goods through its PMSI, but it could not find Conry's credit-card application to offer into evidence. Is a signed Sears sales receipt sufficient proof of its security interest? In whose favor should the court rule? Explain. [*Sears, Roebuck & Co. v. Conry,* 321 Ill.App.3d 997, 748 N.E.2d 1248, 255 Ill.Dec. 178 (3 Dist. 2001)]

◗ To view a sample answer for this case problem, go to this book's Web site at **http://fundamentals.westbuslaw.com** and click on "Interactive Study Center."

20–9. Pledge. On April 14, 1992, David and Myrna Grossman borrowed $10,000 from Brookfield Bank in Brookfield, Connecticut, and signed a note to repay the principal with interest. As collateral, the Grossmans gave the bank possession of stock certificates representing 123 shares in General Electric Co. The note was nonnegotiable and thus was not subject to UCC Article 3. On May 8, the bank closed its doors. The Grossmans did not make any payments on the note and refused to permit the sale of the stock to apply against the debt. The Grossmans' note and collateral were assigned to Premier Capital, Inc., which filed a suit in a Connecticut state court against them, seeking to collect the principal and interest due. The Grossmans responded in part that they were entitled to credit for the value of the stock that secured the note. By the time of the trial, the stock certificates had been lost. What should be the duty of a creditor toward collateral that is transferred into the creditor's possession as security for a loan? What should the court rule, and why? [*Premier Capital, Inc. v. Grossman*, 68 Conn.App. 51, 789 A.2d 565 (2002)]

VIDEO QUESTION

20–10. Go to this text's Web site at **http://fundamentals.westbuslaw.com** and click on "Video Questions." Select "Chapter 20" and view the video titled *Secured Transactions*. Then answer the following questions:

1. This chapter lists three requirements for creating a security interest. In the video, which requirement does Laura assert has not been met?

2. What, if anything, must the bank have done to perfect its interest in the editing equipment?

3. If the bank exercises its self-help remedy to repossess Onyx's editing equipment, does Laura have any chance of getting it back? Explain.

4. Assume that the bank had a perfected security interest and repossessed the editing equipment. Also assume that the purchase price (and the loan amount) for the equipment was $100,000, of which Onyx has paid $65,000. Discuss the rights and duties of the bank with regard to the collateral in this situation.

SECURED TRANSACTIONS

For updated links to resources available on the Web, as well as other materials, visit this text's Web site at

http://fundamentals.westbuslaw.com

To find Article 9 of the UCC as modified by a particular state on adoption, go to

http://www.law.cornell.edu/ucc/ucc.table.html

For an overview of secured transactions law and links to UCC provisions and case law on this topic, go to

http://www.law.cornell.edu/topics/secured_transactions.html

Online Legal Research

Go to the *Fundamentals of Business Law* home page at **http://fundamentals.westbuslaw.com**. Select "Interactive Study Center" and then click on "Chapter 20." There you will find the following Internet research exercises that you can perform to learn more about topics covered in this chapter.

Activity 20–1: LEGAL PERSPECTIVE—Debtor-Creditor Relations
Activity 20–2: ETHICAL PERSPECTIVE—Repossession

Before the Test

Go to the *Fundamentals of Business Law* home page at **http://fundamentals.westbuslaw.com**. Click on "Interactive Quizzes." You will find at least twenty interactive questions relating to this chapter.

Westlaw® Campus

If your textbook provided for a subscription to Westlaw® Campus, or if you have otherwise purchased access to the Westlaw Campus database, you can access any of the cases presented or cited in this chapter by using your Westlaw Campus account.

21

Creditors' Rights and Bankruptcy

CHAPTER OBJECTIVES

After reading this chapter, you should be able to answer the following questions:

① What is a prejudgment attachment? What is a writ of execution? How does a creditor use these remedies?

② What is garnishment? When might a creditor undertake a garnishment proceeding?

③ In a bankruptcy proceeding, what constitutes the debtor's estate in property? What property is exempt from the estate under federal bankruptcy law?

④ What is the difference between an exception to discharge and an objection to discharge?

⑤ In a Chapter 11 reorganization, what is the role of the debtor in possession?

Historically, debtors and their families have been subjected to punishment, including involuntary servitude and imprisonment, for their inability to pay debts. The modern legal system, however, has moved away from a punishment philosophy in dealing with debtors. In fact, many observers say that it has moved too far in the other direction, to the detriment of creditors.

Normally, creditors have no problem collecting the debts owed to them. When disputes arise over the amount owed, however, or when the debtor simply cannot or will not pay, what happens? What remedies are available to creditors when debtors default? We have already discussed, in Chapter 20, the remedies available to secured creditors

under Article 9 of the Uniform Commercial Code (UCC). In the first part of this chapter, we focus on other laws that assist the debtor and creditor in resolving their disputes without the debtor's having to resort to bankruptcy. The second part of this chapter discusses bankruptcy as a last resort in resolving debtor-creditor problems.

Laws Assisting Creditors

Both the common law and statutory laws other than Article 9 of the UCC create various rights and remedies for creditors. We discuss here some of these rights and remedies.

LIENS

As discussed in Chapter 17, a *lien* is an encumbrance on (claim against) property to satisfy a debt or protect a claim for the payment of a debt. Creditors' liens include mechanic's, artisan's, innkeeper's, and judicial liens.

Mechanic's Lien. When a person contracts for labor, services, or materials to be furnished for the purpose of making improvements on real property (land and things attached to the land, such as buildings and trees—see Chapter 29) but does not immediately pay for the improvements, the creditor can file a **mechanic's lien** on the property. This creates a special type of debtor-creditor relationship in which the real estate itself becomes security for the debt.

● **EXAMPLE #1** A painter agrees to paint a house for a homeowner for a specified price to cover labor and materials. If the homeowner refuses to pay for the work or pays only a portion of the charges, a mechanic's lien against the property can be created. The painter is the lienholder, and the real property is encumbered (burdened) with a mechanic's lien for the amount owed. If the homeowner does not pay the lien, the property can be sold to satisfy the debt. Notice of the foreclosure (the process by which the creditor deprives the debtor of his or her property) and sale must be given to the debtor in advance, however. ●

Note that state law governs mechanic's liens. The time period within which a mechanic's lien must be filed is usually 60 to 120 days from the last date labor or materials were provided.

The following case concerned the amount owed under a lien filed by an unpaid subcontractor against a property owner after the primary contractor, whom the owner had paid in advance of the work, went out of business.

CASE 21.1 **AEG Holdings, L.L.C. v. Tri-Gem's Builders, Inc.**

Superior Court of New Jersey,
Appellate Division, 2002.
347 N.J.Super. 511,
790 A.2d 954.
http://lawlibrary.rutgers.edu/search.shtml[a]

FACTS L & N Enterprises–Hammonton, L.L.C., contracted with Tri-Gem's Builders, Inc., to construct an addition to L & N's commercial building in New Jersey for $198,200. Tri-Gem's hired AEG Holdings, L.L.C., as a subcontractor for some of the work. During the project, L & N paid Tri-Gem's a total of $129,604. Tri-Gem's went out of business, however, without finishing the job and without paying anything to its subcontractor. AEG filed a lien against L & N for $126,717, which was the amount owed to AEG for the work it had performed. AEG then filed a suit in a New Jersey state court for a judgment on the lien. The court awarded AEG the difference between the price of the contract between L & N and Tri-Gem's and the amount that L & N paid to Tri-Gem's ($198,200 minus $129,604, which equals $68,596). L & N appealed to a state intermediate appellate court, arguing that Tri-Gem's left the job without completing much work, which meant that L & N would have to hire others to finish the job at a cost exceeding the total original contract price.

ISSUE Is AEG entitled to the amount awarded it by the trial court?

DECISION Yes. The state intermediate appellate court affirmed the judgment in favor of AEG.

REASON According to the appellate court, "[l]ien statutes are remedial and are designed to guarantee effective security to those who furnish labor or materials used to enhance the value of the property of others. * * * While it is true * * * that a property owner should not be made to pay twice, what is meant by that is that the property owner is never subject to liens in an amount greater than the amount unpaid by the owner to its prime contractor at the time the lien claim is filed by one claiming a lien through that prime contractor." The court recognized that the result in this case "may not be fair to L & N, but leaving an innocent subcontractor without any payment is too high a price for correcting the inequity placed upon the property owner." The state lien statute "suggests that when choosing between two innocent persons in these circumstances, it is the lien holder who prevails."

FOR CRITICAL ANALYSIS—Economic Consideration
What might L & N have done to avoid the financial loss it faced when Tri-Gem's abandoned the job before completing much work on the project?

---

a. In the "Find Case by Citation" section, enter "347" in the "Volume" box and "511" in the "Page" box, and select "N.J.Super." as the "Reporter." Click on "Submit Form" to access the opinion. Rutgers University School of Law in Camden, New Jersey, maintains this Web site.

Artisan's Lien. An **artisan's lien** is a security device created at common law through which a creditor can recover payment from a debtor for labor and materials furnished in the repair or improvement of personal property. ●**EXAMPLE #2** Cindy leaves her diamond ring at the jeweler's to be repaired and to have her initials engraved on the band. In the absence of an agreement, the jeweler can keep the ring until Cindy pays for the services. Should Cindy fail to pay, the jeweler has a lien on Cindy's ring for the amount of the bill and normally can sell the ring in satisfaction of the lien.●

In contrast to a mechanic's lien, an artisan's lien is *possessory.* The lienholder ordinarily must have retained possession of the property and have expressly or impliedly agreed to provide the services on a cash, not a credit, basis. Usually, the lienholder retains possession of the property. When this occurs, the lien remains in existence as long as the lienholder maintains possession, and the lien is terminated once possession is voluntarily surrendered—unless the surrender is only temporary. If it is a temporary surrender, there must be an agreement that the property will be returned to the lienholder. Even with such an agreement, if a third party obtains rights in that property while it is out of the possession of the lienholder, the lien is lost. The only way that a lienholder can protect a lien and surrender possession at the same time is to record notice of the lien (if state law so permits) in accordance with state lien and recording statutes.

Modern statutes permit the holder of an artisan's lien to foreclose and sell the property subject to the lien to satisfy payment of the debt. As with the mechanic's lien, the holder of an artisan's lien is required to give notice to the owner of the property prior to foreclosure and sale. The sale proceeds are used to pay the debt and the costs of the legal proceedings, and the surplus, if any, is paid to the former owner.

Innkeeper's Lien. An **innkeeper's lien** is another security device created at common law. An innkeeper's lien is placed on the baggage of guests for the agreed-on hotel charges that remain unpaid. If no express agreement has been made concerning the amount of those charges, then the lien will be for the reasonable value of the accommodations furnished. The innkeeper's lien is terminated either by the guest's payment of the hotel charges or by the innkeeper's surrender of the baggage to the guest, unless the surrender is temporary. Additionally, the lien is terminated by the innkeeper's foreclosure and sale of the property.

Judicial Liens. When a debt is past due, a creditor can bring a legal action against the debtor to collect the debt. If the creditor is successful in the action, the court awards the creditor a judgment against the debtor (usually for the amount of the debt plus any interest and legal costs incurred in obtaining the judgment). Frequently, however, the creditor is unable to collect the awarded amount.

To ensure that a judgment in the creditor's favor will be collectible, creditors are permitted to request that certain nonexempt property of the debtor be seized to satisfy the debt. (As will be discussed later in this chapter, under state or federal statutes, certain property is exempt from attachment by creditors.) If the court orders the debtor's property to be seized prior to a judgment in the creditor's favor, the court's order is referred to as a *writ of attachment.* If the court orders the debtor's property to be seized following a judgment in the creditor's favor, the court's order is referred to as a *writ of execution.*

Attachment. Recall from Chapter 20 that *attachment,* in the context of secured transactions, refers to the process through which a security interest in a debtor's collateral becomes enforceable. In the context of judicial liens, this word has another meaning: **attachment** is a court-ordered seizure and taking into custody of property prior to the securing of a judgment for a past-due debt. Attachment rights are created by state statutes. Attachment is a *prejudgment* remedy because it occurs either at the time of or immediately after the commencement of a lawsuit and before the entry of a final judgment. By statute, to attach before judgment, a creditor must comply with specific restrictions and requirements. The due process clause of the Fourteenth Amendment to the U.S. Constitution limits the courts' power to authorize seizure of a debtor's property without notice to the debtor or a hearing on the facts.

To use attachment as a remedy, the creditor must have an enforceable right to payment of the debt under law and must follow certain procedures. Otherwise, the creditor can be liable for damages for wrongful attachment. She or he must file with the court an *affidavit* (a written or printed statement, made under oath or sworn to) declaring that the debtor is in default and outlining the statutory grounds under which attachment is sought. The creditor must also post a bond to cover at least court costs, the value of the loss of use of the good suffered by the debtor, and the value of the property attached. When the court is satisfied that all the requirements have been met, it issues a **writ of attachment,** which directs the sheriff or other public officer to seize nonexempt property. If the creditor prevails at trial, the seized property can be sold to satisfy the judgment.

Writ of Execution. If the debtor will not or cannot pay the judgment, the creditor is entitled to go back to the court and obtain a court order directing the sheriff to seize (levy) and sell any of the debtor's nonexempt real or personal property that is within the court's geographic jurisdiction (usually the county in which the courthouse is located). This order is called a **writ of execution**. The proceeds of the sale are used to pay off the judgment, accrued interest, and the costs of the sale. Any excess is paid to the debtor. The debtor can pay the judgment and redeem the nonexempt property any time before the sale takes place. (Because of exemption laws and bankruptcy laws, however, many judgments are virtually uncollectible.)

GARNISHMENT

Garnishment occurs when a creditor is permitted to collect a debt by seizing property of the debtor that is being held by a third party. Typically, a garnishment judgment is served on a debtor's employer so that part of the debtor's usual paycheck will be paid to the creditor. As a result of a garnishment proceeding, the court orders the debtor's employer to turn over a portion of the debtor's wages to pay the debt.

The legal proceeding for a garnishment action is governed by state law, and garnishment operates differently from state to state. According to the laws in some states, the creditor needs to obtain only one order of garnishment, which will then continuously apply to the debtor's weekly wages until the entire debt is paid. In other states, the creditor must go back to court for a separate order of garnishment for each pay period. Garnishment is usually a postjudgment remedy, but it can be a prejudgment remedy with a proper hearing by a court.

Both federal laws and state laws limit the amount of money that can be garnished from a debtor's weekly take-home pay.[1] Federal law provides a framework to protect debtors from suffering unduly when paying judgment debts.[2] State laws also provide dollar exemptions, and these amounts are often larger than those provided by federal law. Under federal law, garnishment of an employee's wages for any one indebtedness cannot be a ground for dismissal of an employee.

CREDITORS' COMPOSITION AGREEMENTS

Creditors may contract with the debtor for discharge of the debtor's liquidated debts (debts that are definite, or fixed, in amount) on payment of a sum less than that owed. These agreements are called **creditors' composition agreements**, or simply *composition agreements,* and are usually held to be enforceable.

MORTGAGE FORECLOSURE

Mortgage holders have the right to foreclose on mortgaged property in the event of a debtor's default. The usual method of foreclosure is by judicial sale of the property, although the statutory methods of foreclosure vary from state to state. If the proceeds of the foreclosure sale are sufficient to cover both the costs of the foreclosure and the mortgaged debt, the debtor receives any surplus. If the sale proceeds are insufficient to cover the foreclosure costs and the mortgaged debt, however, the **mortgagee** (the creditor-lender) can seek to recover the difference from the **mortgagor** (the debtor) by obtaining a deficiency judgment representing the difference between the mortgaged debt and the amount actually received from the proceeds of the foreclosure sale.

The mortgagee obtains a deficiency judgment in a separate legal action pursued subsequent to the foreclosure action. The deficiency judgment entitles the mortgagee to recover the amount of the deficiency from other property owned by the debtor.

SURETYSHIP AND GUARANTY

When a third person promises to pay a debt owed by another in the event the debtor does not pay, either a *suretyship* or a *guaranty* relationship is created. Suretyship and guaranty have a long history under the common law and provide creditors with the right to seek payment from the third party if the primary debtor defaults on his or her obligations. Exhibit 21–1 on the next page illustrates the relationship between a suretyship or guaranty party and the creditor.

Surety. A contract of strict **suretyship** is a promise made by a third person to be responsible for the debtor's obligation. It is an express contract between the **surety** (the third party) and the creditor. The surety in the strictest sense is primarily liable for the debt of the principal. The creditor need not exhaust all legal remedies against the principal debtor before holding the surety responsible for payment. The creditor can demand payment from the surety from the moment the debt is due.

• **EXAMPLE #3** Robert Delmar wants to borrow money from the bank to buy a used car. Because Robert is still in college, the bank will not lend him the money unless his father, Joseph Delmar, who has dealt with the bank before, will cosign the note (add his signature to the note, thereby becoming a surety and thus jointly liable for payment of the debt). When Joseph Delmar cosigns the note, he becomes

---

[1] Some states (for example, Texas) do not permit garnishment of wages by private parties except under a child-support order.

[2] For example, the federal Consumer Credit Protection Act of 1968, 15 U.S.C. Sections 1601–1693r, provides that a debtor can retain either 75 percent of his or her disposable earnings per week or the sum equivalent to thirty hours of work paid at federal minimum-wage rates, whichever is greater.

EXHIBIT 21–1 SURETYSHIP AND GUARANTY PARTIES

In a suretyship or guaranty arrangement, a third party promises to be responsible for a debtor's obligations. A third party who agrees to be *primarily* liable for the debt (that is, liable even if the principal debtor does not default) is known as a surety; a third party who agrees to be *secondarily* liable for the debt (that is, liable only if the principal debtor defaults) is known as a guarantor. As noted in Chapter 10, normally a promise of guaranty (a collateral, or secondary, promise) must be in writing to be enforceable.

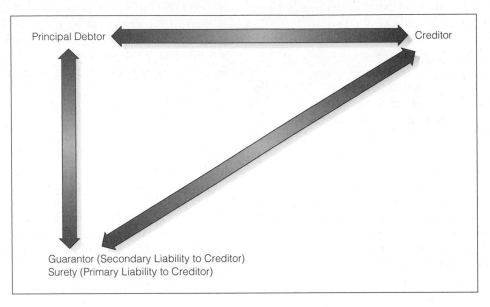

Principal Debtor

Creditor

Guarantor (Secondary Liability to Creditor)
Surety (Primary Liability to Creditor)

primarily liable to the bank. On the note's due date, the bank has the option of seeking payment from either Robert or Joseph Delmar, or both jointly.●

Guaranty. A guaranty contract is similar to a suretyship contract in that it includes a promise to answer for the debt or default of another. With a guaranty arrangement, the **guarantor**—the third person making the guaranty—is *secondarily* liable. The guarantor can be required to pay the obligation *only after the principal debtor defaults,* and default usually takes place only after the creditor has made an attempt to collect from the debtor.

●**EXAMPLE #4** A small corporation, BX Enterprises, needs to borrow money to meet its payroll. The bank is skeptical about the creditworthiness of BX and requires Dawson, its president, who is a wealthy businessperson and the owner of 70 percent of BX Enterprises, to sign an agreement making himself personally liable for payment if BX does not pay off the loan. As a guarantor of the loan, Dawson cannot be held liable until BX Enterprises is in default.●

The Statute of Frauds requires that a guaranty contract between the guarantor and the creditor must be in writing to be enforceable unless the *main purpose* exception applies. As discussed in Chapter 10, this exception provides that if the main purpose of the guaranty agreement is to benefit

the guarantor, then the contract need not be in writing to be enforceable.

Defenses of the Surety and the Guarantor. The defenses of the surety and the guarantor are basically the same. Therefore, the following discussion applies to both, although it refers only to the surety.

Certain actions will release the surety from the obligation. For example, any binding material modification in the terms of the original contract made between the principal debtor and the creditor—including a binding agreement to extend the time for making payment—without first obtaining the consent of the surety will discharge a gratuitous surety completely and a compensated surety to the extent that the surety suffers a loss. (An example of a gratuitous surety is a father who agrees to assume responsibility for his daughter's obligation; an example of a compensated surety is a venture capitalist who will profit from a loan made to the principal debtor.)

Naturally, if the principal obligation is paid by the debtor or by another person on behalf of the debtor, the surety is discharged from the obligation. Similarly, if valid tender of payment is made, and the creditor rejects it with knowledge of the surety's existence, the surety is released from any obligation on the debt.

Generally, the surety can use any defenses available to a principal debtor to avoid liability on the obligation to the creditor. Defenses available to the principal debtor that the surety *cannot* use include the principal debtor's incapacity or bankruptcy and the statute of limitations. The ability of the surety to assert any defenses the debtor may have against the creditor is the most important concept in suretyship, because a majority of the defenses available to the surety are also those of the debtor.

Obviously, a surety may also have his or her own defenses—for example, incapacity or bankruptcy. If the creditor fraudulently induced the surety to guarantee the debt of the debtor, the surety can assert fraud as a defense. In most states, the creditor has a legal duty to inform the surety, prior to the formation of the suretyship contract, of material facts known by the creditor that would substantially increase the surety's risk. Failure to do so is fraud and makes the suretyship obligation voidable. In addition, if a creditor surrenders the collateral to the debtor or impairs the collateral while knowing of the surety and without the surety's consent, the surety is released to the extent of any loss suffered from the creditor's actions. The primary reason for this requirement is to protect the surety who agreed to become obligated only because the debtor's collateral was in the possession of the creditor.

Rights of the Surety and the Guarantor. The rights of the surety and the guarantor are basically the same. Therefore, again, the following discussion applies to both.

When the surety pays the debt owed to the creditor, the surety is entitled to certain rights. First, the surety has the legal **right of subrogation.** Simply stated, this means that any right the creditor had against the debtor now becomes the right of the surety. Included are creditor rights in bankruptcy, rights to collateral possessed by the creditor, and rights to judgments secured by the creditor. In short, the surety now stands in the shoes of the creditor and may pursue any remedies that were available to the creditor against the debtor.

Second, the surety has the **right of reimbursement** from the debtor. Basically, the surety is entitled to receive from the debtor all outlays made on behalf of the suretyship arrangement. Such outlays can include expenses incurred as well as the actual amount of the debt paid to the creditor.

Third, in the case of **co-sureties** (two or more sureties on the same obligation owed by the debtor), a surety who pays more than her or his proportionate share on a debtor's default is entitled to recover from the co-sureties the amount paid above the surety's obligation. This is the **right of contribution.** Generally, a co-surety's liability either is determined by agreement or, in the absence of agreement

between the co-sureties, can be specified in the suretyship contract itself.

● **EXAMPLE #5** Assume that two co-sureties are obligated under a suretyship contract to guarantee the debt of a debtor. Together, the sureties' maximum liability is $25,000. As specified in the suretyship contract, surety A's maximum liability is $15,000, and surety B's is $10,000. The debtor owes $10,000 and is in default. Surety A pays the creditor the entire $10,000. In the absence of any agreement between the two co-sureties, surety A can recover $4,000 from surety B ($10,000/$25,000 × $10,000 = $4,000).●

Laws Assisting Debtors

The law protects debtors as well as creditors. Certain property of the debtor, for example, is exempt from creditors' actions. Probably the most familiar of these exemptions is the **homestead exemption.** Each state permits the debtor to retain the family home, either in its entirety or up to a specified dollar amount, free from the claims of unsecured creditors or trustees in bankruptcy. The purpose of the homestead exemption is to ensure that the debtor will retain some form of shelter.

● **EXAMPLE #6** Suppose that Van Cleave owes Acosta $40,000. The debt is the subject of a lawsuit, and the court awards Acosta a judgment of $40,000 against Van Cleave. Van Cleave's home is valued at $50,000, and the state exemption on homesteads is $25,000. There are no outstanding mortgages or other liens. To satisfy the judgment debt, Van Cleave's family home is sold at public auction for $45,000. The proceeds of the sale are distributed as follows:

① Van Cleave is given $25,000 as his homestead exemption.

② Acosta is paid $20,000 toward the judgment debt, leaving a $20,000 deficiency judgment that can be satisfied from any other nonexempt property (personal or real) that Van Cleave may have, if allowed by state law.●

State exemption statutes usually include both real and personal property. Personal property that is most often exempt from satisfaction of judgment debts includes the following:

① Household furniture up to a specified dollar amount.

② Clothing and certain personal possessions, such as family pictures or a Bible.

③ A vehicle (or vehicles) for transportation (at least up to a specified dollar amount).

④ Certain classified animals, usually livestock but including pets.

⑤ Equipment that the debtor uses in a business or trade, such as tools or professional instruments, up to a specified dollar amount.

Consumer protection statutes also protect debtors' rights. Of course, bankruptcy laws, which are discussed in the next section, are designed specifically to assist debtors in need of relief from their debts.

Bankruptcy and Reorganization

At one time, debtors who could not pay their debts as they came due faced harsh consequences, including imprisonment and involuntary servitude. Today, in contrast, debtors have numerous rights. Some of these rights have already been mentioned. We now look at another significant right of debtors: the right to petition for bankruptcy relief under federal law.

Bankruptcy law in the United States has two goals—to protect a debtor by giving him or her a fresh start, free from creditors' claims, and to ensure equitable treatment to creditors who are competing for a debtor's assets. Bankruptcy law is federal law, but state laws on secured transactions, liens, judgments, and exemptions also play a role in federal bankruptcy proceedings.

Current bankruptcy law is based on the Bankruptcy Reform Act of 1978, as amended. In this chapter, we refer to this act, as amended, as the Bankruptcy Code (or, more simply, the Code). The 1978 act represented a major overhaul of U.S. bankruptcy law. If proposed bankruptcy reform legislation currently before Congress is enacted, as it may be by the time this book is in print, the Bankruptcy Code will undergo further significant changes.

BANKRUPTCY COURTS

Bankruptcy proceedings are held in federal bankruptcy courts. A bankruptcy court's primary function is to hold *core proceedings*[3] dealing with the procedures required to administer the estate of the debtor in bankruptcy. Bankruptcy courts are under the authority of U.S. district courts (see the chart showing the federal court system in Exhibit 2–2 in Chapter 2), and rulings from bankruptcy courts can be appealed to the district courts. Fundamentally, a bankruptcy court fulfills the role of an administrative court for the district court concerning matters in bankruptcy. A bankruptcy court can conduct a jury trial if the appropriate district court has authorized it and if the parties to the bankruptcy consent to a jury trial.

TYPES OF BANKRUPTCY RELIEF

The Bankruptcy Code, which is contained in Title 11 of the U.S. Code (U.S.C.), is divided into a series of "chapters." Chapters 1, 3, and 5 of the Code include general definitional provisions and provisions governing case administration and procedures, creditors, the debtor, and the estate. These three chapters of the Code apply generally to all types of bankruptcies. The next five chapters set forth the different types of relief that debtors may seek. Chapter 7 provides for **liquidation** proceedings (the selling of all nonexempt assets and the distribution of the proceeds to the debtor's creditors). Chapter 9 governs the adjustment of the debts of municipalities. Chapter 11 governs reorganizations. Chapter 12 (for family farmers) and Chapter 13 (for individuals) provide for adjustment of the debts of parties with regular income.[4]

In the following pages, we deal first with liquidation proceedings under Chapter 7 of the Code. We then examine the procedures required for Chapter 11 reorganizations and for Chapter 12 and Chapter 13 plans.

Chapter 7—Liquidation

Liquidation is the most familiar type of bankruptcy proceeding and is often referred to as an *ordinary,* or *straight, bankruptcy.* Put simply, debtors in straight bankruptcies state their debts and turn their assets over to trustees. The trustees sell the assets and distribute the proceeds to creditors. With certain exceptions, the remaining debts are then **discharged** (extinguished), and the debtors are relieved of the obligation to pay the debts.

Any "person"—defined as including individuals, partnerships, and corporations—may be a debtor under Chapter 7. Railroads, insurance companies, banks, savings and loan associations, investment companies licensed by the Small Business Administration, and credit unions *cannot* be Chapter 7 debtors, however. Other chapters of the Code or other federal or state statutes apply to them. A husband and wife may file jointly for bankruptcy under a single petition.

---

[3] *Core proceedings* are procedural functions, such as allowance of claims, decisions on preferences, automatic-stay proceedings, confirmation of bankruptcy plans, discharge of debts, and so on. These terms and procedures are defined and discussed in the following sections of this chapter.

[4] There are no Chapters 2, 4, 6, 8, or 10 in Title 11. Such "gaps" are not uncommon in the U.S.C. This is because, when a statute is enacted, chapter numbers (or other subdivisional unit numbers) are sometimes reserved for future use. (A gap may also appear if a law has been repealed.)

FILING THE PETITION

A straight bankruptcy may be commenced by the filing of either a voluntary or an involuntary **petition in bankruptcy**—the document that is filed with a bankruptcy court to initiate bankruptcy proceedings.

Voluntary Bankruptcy. A voluntary petition is brought by the debtor, who files official forms designated for that purpose in the bankruptcy court. A **consumer-debtor** (defined as an individual whose debts are primarily consumer debts) who has selected Chapter 7 must state in the petition, at the time of filing, that he or she understands the relief available under other chapters and has chosen to proceed under Chapter 7. If the consumer-debtor is represented by an attorney, the attorney must file an affidavit stating that she or he has informed the debtor of the relief available under each chapter. Any debtor who is liable on a claim held by a creditor can file a voluntary petition. The debtor does not even have to be insolvent to do so.[5] The voluntary petition contains the following schedules:

① A list of both secured and unsecured creditors, their addresses, and the amount of debt owed to each.

② A statement of the financial affairs of the debtor.

③ A list of all property owned by the debtor, including property claimed by the debtor to be exempt.

④ A listing of current income and expenses.

The official forms must be completed accurately, sworn to under oath, and signed by the debtor. To conceal assets or knowingly supply false information on these schedules is a crime under the bankruptcy laws. If the voluntary petition for bankruptcy is found to be proper, the filing of the petition will itself constitute an order for relief. An **order for relief** relieves the debtor of the immediate obligation to pay the debts listed in the petition. Once a consumer-debtor's voluntary petition has been filed, the clerk of the court (or person directed) must give the trustee and creditors mailed notice of the order for relief not more than twenty days after the entry of the order.

As mentioned previously, debtors do not have to be insolvent to file for voluntary bankruptcy. Debtors do not have unfettered access to Chapter 7 bankruptcy proceedings, however. Section 707(b) of the Bankruptcy Code allows a bankruptcy court to dismiss a petition for relief under Chapter 7 if the granting of relief would constitute "substantial abuse" of Chapter 7.

● **EXAMPLE #7** Howard Rock, a consumer-debtor, petitions for Chapter 7 relief. The court might determine, after evaluating Rock's schedule listing current income and expenses, that he would be able to pay his creditors a reasonable amount from future income. In this situation, the court might conclude that it would be a substantial abuse of Chapter 7 to allow Rock to have his debts completely discharged. The court might dismiss Rock's Chapter 7 petition after a hearing and encourage him to file a repayment plan under Chapter 13 of the Code, if that would substantially increase the likelihood that the creditors would receive payment.●

Involuntary Bankruptcy. An involuntary bankruptcy occurs when the debtor's creditors force the debtor into bankruptcy proceedings. An involuntary case cannot be commenced against a farmer[6] or a charitable institution (or those entities not eligible for Chapter 7 relief—mentioned earlier), however. For an involuntary action to be filed against other debtors, the following requirements must be met: If the debtor has twelve or more creditors, three or more of those creditors having unsecured claims totaling at least $11,625 must join in the petition. If a debtor has fewer than twelve creditors, one or more creditors having a claim of $11,625 may file.

If the debtor challenges the involuntary petition, a hearing will be held, and the debtor's challenge will fail if the bankruptcy court finds either of the following:

① That the debtor is generally not paying debts as they become due.

② That a general receiver, custodian, or assignee took possession of, or was appointed to take charge of, substantially all of the debtor's property within 120 days before the filing of the petition.

If the court allows the bankruptcy to proceed, the debtor will be required to supply the same information in the bankruptcy schedules as in a voluntary bankruptcy.

An involuntary petition should not be used as an everyday debt-collection device, and the Code provides penalties for the filing of frivolous (unjustified) petitions against debtors. Judgment may be granted against the petitioning

---

[5] The inability to pay debts as they become due is known as *equitable* insolvency. A *balance-sheet* insolvency, which exists when a debtor's liabilities exceed his or her assets, is not the test. Thus, it is possible for debtors to petition voluntarily for bankruptcy even though their assets far exceed their liabilities. This situation may occur when a debtor's cash flow problems become severe.

[6] *Farmers* are defined as persons who receive more than 80 percent of their gross income from farming operations, such as tilling the soil; dairy farming; ranching; or the production or raising of crops, poultry, or livestock. Corporations and partnerships, as well as individuals, can be farmers.

creditors for the costs and attorneys' fees incurred by the debtor in defending against an involuntary petition that is dismissed by the court. If the petition is filed in bad faith, damages can be awarded for injury to the debtor's reputation. Punitive damages may also be awarded.

AUTOMATIC STAY

The filing of a petition, either voluntary or involuntary, operates as an **automatic stay** on (suspension of) virtually all litigation and other action by creditors against the debtor or the debtor's property. In other words, once a petition is filed, creditors cannot commence or continue most legal actions against the debtor to recover claims or to repossess property in the hands of the debtor. A secured creditor, however, may petition the bankruptcy court for relief from the automatic stay in certain circumstances. Additionally, the automatic stay does not apply to paternity, alimony, or family maintenance and support debts.

A creditor's failure to abide by an automatic stay imposed by the filing of a petition can be costly. If a creditor *knowingly* violates the automatic-stay provision (a willful violation), any party injured is entitled to recover actual damages, costs, and attorneys' fees and may also be entitled to recover punitive damages.

CREDITORS' MEETING AND CLAIMS

Within a reasonable time after the order of relief is granted (not less than ten days or more than thirty days), the bankruptcy court must call a meeting of the creditors listed in the schedules filed by the debtor. The bankruptcy judge does not attend this meeting. The debtor must attend this meeting (unless excused by the court) and submit to an examination under oath. Failure to appear or the making of false statements under oath may result in the debtor's being denied a discharge of bankruptcy. At the meeting, the trustee ensures that the debtor is advised of the potential consequences of bankruptcy and of his or her ability to file under a different chapter.

In a bankruptcy case in which the debtor has no assets (called a "no-asset" case), creditors are notified of the debtor's petition for bankruptcy but are instructed not to file a claim. In such a situation, the creditors will receive no payment, and most, if not all, of the debtor's debts will be discharged.

If there are sufficient assets to be distributed to creditors, however, each creditor must normally file a *proof of claim* with the bankruptcy court clerk within ninety days of the creditors' meeting to be entitled to receive a portion of the debtor's estate. The proof of claim lists the creditor's name and address, as well as the amount that the creditor asserts

is owed to the creditor by the debtor. If a creditor fails to file a proof of claim, the bankruptcy court or trustee may file the proof of claim on the creditor's behalf but is not obligated to do so. If a claim is for a disputed amount, the bankruptcy court will set the value of the claim.

Creditors' claims are automatically allowed unless contested by the trustee, the debtor, or another creditor. The Code, however, does not allow claims for breach of employment contracts or real estate leases for terms longer than one year. These claims are limited to one year's wages or rent, despite the remaining length of either contract in breach.

PROPERTY OF THE ESTATE

On the commencement of a liquidation proceeding under Chapter 7, an **estate in property** is created. The estate consists of all the debtor's legal and equitable interests in property currently held, wherever located, together with certain jointly owned property, property transferred in transactions voidable by the trustee, proceeds and profits from the property of the estate, and certain after-acquired property. Interests in certain property—such as gifts, inheritances, property settlements (resulting from divorce), or life insurance death proceeds—to which the debtor becomes *entitled within 180 days after filing* may also become part of the estate. Thus, the filing of a bankruptcy petition generally fixes a dividing line: property acquired prior to the filing becomes property of the estate, and property acquired after the filing, except as just noted, remains the debtor's.

EXEMPTED PROPERTY

Any individual debtor is entitled to exempt certain property from the property of the estate. The Bankruptcy Code establishes a federal exemption scheme under which the following property is exempt:[7]

① Up to $17,425 in equity in the debtor's residence and burial plot (the homestead exemption).

② Interest in a motor vehicle up to $2,775.

③ Interest in household goods and furnishings, wearing apparel, appliances, books, animals, crops, and musical instruments up to $450 in a particular item but limited to $9,300 in total.

④ Interest in jewelry up to $1,150.

---

[7] The dollar amounts stated in the Bankruptcy Code were adjusted automatically on April 1, 1998, and will be adjusted every three years thereafter based on changes in the Consumer Price Index. The amounts stated in this chapter are in accordance with those computed on April 1, 2001.

⑤ Any other property worth up to $925, plus any unused part of the $17,425 homestead exemption up to an amount of $8,725.

⑥ Interest in any tools of the debtor's trade, up to $1,750.

⑦ Certain life insurance contracts owned by the debtor.

⑧ Certain interests in accrued dividends or interests under life insurance contracts owned by the debtor.

⑨ Professionally prescribed health aids.

⑩ The right to receive Social Security and certain welfare benefits, alimony and support payments, and certain pension benefits.

⑪ The right to receive certain personal-injury and other awards, up to $17,425.

Individual states have the power to pass legislation precluding debtors in their states from using the federal exemptions. At least thirty-five states have done this. In those states, debtors may use only state (not federal) exemptions. In the rest of the states, an individual debtor (or husband and wife who file jointly) may choose between the exemptions provided under state law and the federal exemptions. State laws may provide significantly greater protection for debtors than federal law. For example, Florida and Texas traditionally have provided for generous exemptions for homeowners. State laws may also define the property coming within an exemption differently than does the federal law.

THE TRUSTEE'S ROLE

Promptly after the order for relief has been entered, an interim, or provisional, trustee is appointed by the U.S. **trustee** (a government official who performs certain administrative tasks that a bankruptcy judge would otherwise have to perform). The interim trustee administers the debtor's estate until the first meeting of creditors, at which time either a permanent trustee is elected or the interim trustee becomes the permanent trustee. Trustees are entitled to compensation for services rendered, plus reimbursement for expenses.

The basic duty of the trustee is to collect the debtor's available estate and reduce it to money for distribution, preserving the interests of both the debtor and unsecured creditors. In other words, the trustee is accountable for administering the debtor's estate. To enable the trustee to accomplish this duty, the Code gives her or him certain powers, stated in both general and specific terms.

Trustee's Powers. The trustee has the power to require persons holding the debtor's property at the time the peti-

tion is filed to deliver the property to the trustee. To enable the trustee to implement this power, the Code provides that the trustee occupies a position equivalent in rights to that of certain other parties. For example, in some situations, the trustee has the same rights as creditors and can obtain a judicial lien or levy execution on the debtor's property. This means that a trustee has priority over an unperfected secured party (see Chapter 20) to the debtor's property. The trustee also has rights equivalent to those of the debtor.

In addition, the trustee has the power to avoid (cancel) certain types of transactions, including those transactions that the debtor could rightfully avoid, *preferences,* certain statutory liens, and *fraudulent transfers* by the debtor. Avoidance powers must be exercised within two years of the order for relief (the period runs even if a trustee has not been appointed). These powers of the trustee are discussed in more detail in the following subsections.

Voidable Rights. A trustee steps into the shoes of the debtor. Thus, any reason that a debtor can use to obtain the return of his or her property can be used by the trustee as well. These grounds for recovery include fraud, duress, incapacity, and mutual mistake.

●**EXAMPLE #8** Rob sells his boat to Inga. Inga gives Rob a check, knowing that there are insufficient funds in her bank account to cover the check. Inga has committed fraud. Rob has the right to avoid that transfer and recover the boat from Inga. Thus, if Rob petitions for bankruptcy and the court enters an order for relief, the trustee can exercise the same right to recover the boat from Inga.● If the trustee does not take action to enforce one of his or her rights, the debtor in a Chapter 7 bankruptcy will nevertheless be able to enforce that right.[8]

Preferences. A debtor is not permitted to transfer property or to make a payment that favors—or gives a **preference** to—one creditor over others. The trustee is allowed to recover payments made both voluntarily and involuntarily to one creditor in preference over another.

To have made a preferential payment that can be recovered, an *insolvent* debtor generally must have transferred property, for a *preexisting* debt, during the *ninety days* prior to the filing of the petition in bankruptcy. The transfer must give the creditor more than the creditor would have received as a result of the bankruptcy proceedings. The

---

[8] In a Chapter 11 reorganization (to be discussed later), for which generally no trustee exists, the debtor has the same avoidance powers as a trustee in a Chapter 7 liquidation. In repayment plans under Chapters 12 and 13 (also to be discussed later), a trustee must be appointed.

trustee does not have to prove insolvency, as the Code provides that the debtor is presumed to be insolvent during this ninety-day period.

Sometimes, the creditor receiving the preference is an insider—an individual, a partner, a partnership, or an officer or a director of a corporation (or a relative of one of these) who has a close relationship with the debtor. In this situation, the avoidance power of the trustee is extended to transfers made within *one year* before filing; however, the *presumption* of insolvency is confined to the ninety-day period. Therefore, the trustee must prove that the debtor was insolvent at the time of an earlier transfer.

Not all transfers are preferences. To be a preference, the transfer must be made for something other than current consideration. Therefore, most courts generally assume that payment for services rendered within ten to fifteen days prior to the payment of the current consideration is not a preference. If a creditor receives payment in the ordinary course of business, such as payment of last month's telephone bill, the payment cannot be recovered by the trustee in bankruptcy. To be recoverable, a preference must be a transfer for an antecedent (preexisting) debt, such as a year-old printing bill. In addition, the Code permits a consumer-debtor to transfer any property to a creditor up to a total value of $600 without the transfer's constituting a preference. Also, certain other debts, including alimony and child support, are not preferences.

If a preferred creditor has sold the property to an innocent third party, the trustee cannot recover the property from the innocent party. The creditor, however, generally can be held accountable for the value of the property.

Liens on Debtor's Property. The trustee is permitted to avoid the fixing of certain statutory liens, such as a mechanic's lien, on property of the debtor. Liens that first became effective at the time the bankruptcy petition was filed or the debtor became insolvent are voidable by the trustee. Liens that are not perfected or enforceable against a good faith purchaser on the date of the petition are also voidable.

Fraudulent Transfers. The trustee may avoid fraudulent transfers or obligations if they were made within one year of the filing of the petition or if they were made with actual intent to hinder, delay, or defraud a creditor. Transfers made for less than reasonably equivalent consideration are also vulnerable if the debtor thereby became insolvent, was left engaged in business with an unreasonably small amount of capital, or intended to incur debts that would be beyond his or her ability to pay. When a fraudulent transfer is made outside the Code's one-year limit, creditors may seek alternative relief under state laws. State laws often allow creditors to recover for transfers made up to three years prior to the filing of a petition.

PROPERTY DISTRIBUTION

Creditors are either secured or unsecured. As discussed in Chapter 20, a *secured* creditor has a security interest in collateral that secures the debt. An unsecured creditor does not have any security interest.

Secured Creditors. The Code provides that a consumer-debtor, within thirty days of the filing of a Chapter 7 petition or before the date of the first meeting of the creditors (whichever is first), must file with the clerk a statement of intention with respect to the secured collateral. The statement must indicate whether the debtor will retain the collateral or surrender it to the secured party. Additionally, if applicable, the debtor must specify whether the collateral will be claimed as exempt property and whether the debtor intends to redeem the property or reaffirm the debt secured by the collateral. The trustee is obligated to enforce the debtor's statement within forty-five days after the statement is filed.

If the collateral is surrendered to the perfected secured party, the secured creditor can enforce the security interest either by accepting the property in full satisfaction of the debt or by foreclosing on the collateral and using the proceeds to pay off the debt. Thus, the secured party has priority over unsecured parties to the proceeds from the disposition of the secured collateral. Indeed, the Code provides that if the value of the secured collateral exceeds the secured party's claim, the secured party also has priority to the proceeds in an amount that will cover reasonable fees (including attorneys' fees, if provided for in the security agreement) and costs incurred because of the debtor's default. Any excess over this amount is used by the trustee to satisfy the claims of unsecured creditors. Should the secured collateral be insufficient to cover the secured debt owed, the secured creditor becomes an unsecured creditor for the remainder of the debt.

Unsecured Creditors. Bankruptcy law establishes an order or priority for classes of debts owed to *unsecured* creditors, and they are paid in the order of their priority. Each class of debt must be fully paid before the next class is entitled to any of the proceeds—if there are sufficient funds to pay the entire class. If not, the proceeds are distributed *proportionately* to each creditor in the class, and all classes lower in priority on the list receive nothing. The order of priority among classes of unsecured creditors is as follows:

① Administrative expenses—including court costs, trustee fees, and bankruptcy attorneys' fees.

② In an involuntary bankruptcy, expenses incurred by the debtor in the ordinary course of business from the date of the filing of the petition up to the appointment of the trustee or the issuance by the court of an order for relief.

③ Unpaid wages, salaries, and commissions earned within ninety days of the filing of the petition, limited to $4,650 per claimant. Any claim in excess of $4,650 is treated as a claim of a general creditor (listed as number 9 below).

④ Unsecured claims for contributions to be made to employee benefit plans, limited to services performed during 180 days prior to the filing of the bankruptcy petition and $4,650 per employee.

⑤ Claims by farmers and fishers, up to $4,650, against debtor-operators of grain storage or fish storage or processing facilities.

⑥ Consumer deposits of up to $2,100 given to the debtor before the petition was filed in connection with the purchase, lease, or rental of property or the purchase of services that were not received or provided. Any claim in excess of $2,100 is treated as a claim of a general creditor (listed as number 9 below).

⑦ Paternity, alimony, maintenance, and support debts.

⑧ Certain taxes and penalties due to government units, such as income and property taxes.

⑨ Claims of general creditors.

⑩ Commitments to the Federal Deposit Insurance Corporation, and other organizations, to maintain the capital of an insured depository institution.

If any amount remains after the priority classes of creditors have been satisfied, it is turned over to the debtor.

DISCHARGE

From the debtor's point of view, the purpose of a liquidation proceeding is to obtain a fresh start through the discharge of debts.[9] Certain debts, however, are not dischargeable in a liquidation proceeding. Also, some debtors may not qualify—because of their conduct—to have all debts discharged in bankruptcy.

Exceptions to Discharge. Claims that are not dischargeable under Chapter 7 include the following:

① Claims for back taxes accruing within three years prior to bankruptcy.

② Claims for amounts borrowed by the debtor to pay federal taxes.

③ Claims against property or money obtained by the debtor under false pretenses or by false representations.

④ Claims by creditors who were not notified of the bankruptcy; these claims did not appear on the schedules the debtor was required to file.

⑤ Claims based on fraud or misuse of funds by the debtor while she or he was acting in a fiduciary capacity or claims involving the debtor's embezzlement or larceny.

⑥ Alimony, child support, and (with certain exceptions) property settlements.

⑦ Claims based on willful or malicious conduct by the debtor toward another or the property of another.

⑧ Certain government fines and penalties.

⑨ Certain student loans, unless payment of the loans imposes an undue hardship on the debtor and the debtor's dependents.

⑩ Consumer debts of more than $1,150 for luxury goods or services owed to a single creditor incurred within sixty days of the order for relief. This denial of discharge is a rebuttable presumption (that is, the denial may be challenged by the debtor), however, and any debts reasonably incurred to support the debtor or dependents are not classified as luxuries.

⑪ Cash advances totaling more than $1,150 that are extensions of open-end consumer credit obtained by the debtor within sixty days of the order for relief. A denial of discharge of these debts is also a rebuttable presumption.

⑫ Judgments or consent decrees against a debtor as a result of the debtor's operation of a motor vehicle while intoxicated.

One of the questions that has come before bankruptcy courts has to do with whether debtors who run up credit-card bills, knowing that they cannot pay them, are engaged in fraud. For a discussion of this issue, see this chapter's *Management Perspective* on page 431.

In the following case, an employer sought to have a debt to an ex-employee for unpaid commissions discharged in bankruptcy. The question before the court was whether the debt arose from "willful and malicious injury" caused by the debtor's tortious conduct, which would mean that it was not dischargeable.

---

[9] Discharges are granted under Chapter 7 only to *individuals*, not to corporations or partnerships. The latter may use Chapter 11, or they may terminate their existence under state law.

CASE 21.2 In re Jercich

United States Court of Appeals,
Ninth Circuit, 2001.
238 F.3d 1202.

FACTS In June 1981, James Petralia began to work for George Jercich, Inc., a mortgage company wholly owned and operated by George Jercich. Petralia's primary duty was to obtain investors to fund the home loans. Jercich agreed to pay Petralia a salary plus monthly commissions for loans that were funded through his efforts. When Jercich failed to pay the commissions, Petralia quit and filed a suit in a California state court against Jercich. The court found that Jercich had not paid Petralia; that Jercich had the clear ability to make the payments to Petralia, but chose not to do so; that instead of paying Petralia and other employees, Jercich used the money for personal investments, including a horse ranch; and that Jercich's behavior was willful and deliberate and constituted "substantial oppression." The court ruled in Petralia's favor. Jercich appealed this ruling to a state intermediate appellate court and filed for bankruptcy in a federal bankruptcy court. The state court affirmed the judgment against Jercich, but the bankruptcy court held that the debt was dischargeable. A bankruptcy appellate panel affirmed this holding.[a] Petralia appealed to the U.S. Court of Appeals for the Ninth Circuit.

ISSUE Did Jercich's debt to Petralia arise from "willful and malicious injury" caused by the debtor's tortious (wrongful) conduct?

―――――――――――
a. A bankruptcy appellate panel, with the consent of the parties, has jurisdiction to hear appeals from final judgments, orders, and decrees of bankruptcy judges.

DECISION Yes. The U.S. Court of Appeals for the Ninth Circuit reversed the decision of the bankruptcy appellate panel, holding that Jercich's debt to Petralia was not dischargeable.

REASON The U.S. Court of Appeals for the Ninth Circuit recognized that "an intentional breach of contract *generally* will not give rise to a nondischargeable debt." The court held, however, that "where an intentional breach of contract is accompanied by tortious conduct which results in willful and malicious injury, the resulting debt is excepted from discharge." Based on the state court's findings, "Jercich's nonpayment of wages * * * constituted tortious conduct." Furthermore, "the injury to Petralia was willful. As the state court found, Jercich knew he owed the wages to Petralia and that injury to Petralia was substantially certain to occur if the wages were not paid; and Jercich had the clear ability to pay Petralia his wages, yet chose not to pay and instead used the money for his own personal benefit. He therefore inflicted willful injury on Petralia. * * * Jercich's deliberate and willful failure to pay was found by the state trial court to constitute substantial oppression, which by definition is 'despicable conduct that subjects a person to cruel and unjust hardship in conscious disregard of that person's rights.' We hold that these * * * findings are sufficient to show that the injury inflicted by Jercich was malicious."

FOR CRITICAL ANALYSIS—Social Consideration
A fundamental policy of bankruptcy law is to give a "fresh start" only to the "honest but unfortunate debtor." What corollary to this policy is the basis for some of the exceptions to discharge listed previously?

―――

Objections to Discharge. In addition to the exceptions to discharge previously listed, the following circumstances (relating to the debtor's conduct and not the debt) will cause a discharge to be denied:

① The debtor's concealment or destruction of property with the intent to hinder, delay, or defraud a creditor.

② The debtor's fraudulent concealment or destruction of financial records.

③ The granting of a discharge to the debtor within six years of the filing of the petition.[10]

―――――――――――
[10] A discharge under Chapter 13 of the Code within six years of the filing of the petition does not bar a subsequent Chapter 7 discharge when a good faith Chapter 13 plan paid at least 70 percent of all allowed unsecured claims and was the debtor's "best effort."

When a discharge is denied under these circumstances, the assets of the debtor are still distributed to the creditors, but the debtor remains liable for the unpaid portions of all claims.

Effect of Discharge. The primary effect of a discharge is to void, or set aside, any judgment on a discharged debt and prohibit any action to collect a discharged debt. A discharge does not affect the liability of a co-debtor.

Revocation of Discharge. The Code provides that a debtor's discharge may be revoked. On petition by the trustee or a creditor, the bankruptcy court may, within one year, revoke the discharge decree if it is discovered that the debtor was dishonest or committed fraud during the bankruptcy pro-

MANAGEMENT PERSPECTIVE
Credit-Card Fraud—The Intent Factor

MANAGEMENT FACES A LEGAL ISSUE At issue in a number of bankruptcy cases is the following question: When debtors run up credit-card bills, knowing that they lack the ability to pay them, have they engaged in fraud? How the courts answer this question is important for both creditors and debtors. If you are in the credit-card business, for example, it would be in your interest to have the court deem that such actions amount to fraud—because if it does, the debt will not be dischargeable in bankruptcy. Naturally, the debtor would want the court to reach the opposite conclusion.

WHAT THE COURTS SAY Fraud, of course, requires intent. So a central question in bankruptcy cases dealing with this issue is whether a debtor's knowledge of his or her inability to pay a debt, at the time the debt is incurred, equates to intent to defraud. In the past, many lower courts dealing with this issue held that it did. This assumption seems to be changing, however.

Consider a case that came before the Sixth Circuit Court of Appeals. The case involved a woman who had taken $11,600 in cash advances on her credit cards to finance her gambling habit. During bankruptcy proceedings, she testified that she had hoped to repay the debt out of her gambling winnings, even though she realized that there was no reasonable expectation of being able to

do this. The court, concluding that there was no fraud because the debtor had *intended* to repay the debt, allowed the debt to be discharged in bankruptcy. According to the court, "To measure a debtor's intention to repay by her ability to do so, without more, would be contrary to one of the main reasons consumers use credit cards: because they often lack the ability to pay in full at the time they desire credit."[a] In an earlier case, another federal appellate court had held similarly, concluding that the "hopeless state of a debtor's financial condition should never become a substitute for an actual finding of bad faith."[b]

IMPLICATIONS FOR MANAGERS These rulings, while they may be good news for debtors, are not so for creditors. According to attorney Robert Markoff of Chicago, "Creditors are faced with a real uphill battle. If the debtor says she intended to pay, you're pretty much stuck."[c] (A provision in a bankruptcy reform bill currently pending in Congress addresses this problem by stating that any debt incurred by the use of a credit card within ninety days before a bankruptcy petition is filed would be nondischargeable.)

a. *In re Rembert*, 141 F.3d 277 (6th Cir. 1998).
b. *In re Anastas*, 94 F.3d 1280 (9th Cir. 1996).
c. As quoted in Jake Halpern, "Credit Cards Easier to Discharge," *Lawyers Weekly USA*, May 4, 1998, p. 19.

---

ceedings. The revocation renders the discharge void, allowing creditors not satisfied by the distribution of the debtor's estate to proceed with their claims against the debtor.

Reaffirmation of Debt. A debtor may voluntarily agree to pay off a debt—for example, a debt owed to a family member, close friend, or some other party—even though the debt could be discharged in bankruptcy. An agreement to pay a debt dischargeable in bankruptcy is referred to as a *reaffirmation agreement.*

To be enforceable, reaffirmation agreements must be made before a debtor is granted a discharge, and they must be filed with the court. If the debtor is represented by an attorney, court approval is not required if the attorney files a declaration or affidavit stating that (1) the debtor has been

fully informed of the consequences of the agreement (and a default under the agreement), (2) the agreement is made voluntarily, and (3) the agreement does not impose undue hardship on the debtor or the debtor's family. If the debtor is not represented by an attorney, court approval is required, and the agreement will be upheld only if the court finds that the agreement will result in no undue hardship to the debtor and is in his or her best interest.

The agreement must contain a clear and conspicuous statement advising the debtor that reaffirmation is not required. The debtor can rescind, or cancel, the agreement at any time prior to discharge or within sixty days of filing the agreement, whichever is later. This rescission period must be stated *clearly* and *conspicuously* in the reaffirmation agreement.

Chapter 11—Reorganization

The type of bankruptcy proceeding used most commonly by a corporate debtor is the Chapter 11 *reorganization*. In a reorganization, the creditors and the debtor formulate a plan under which the debtor pays a portion of his or her debts and the rest of the debts are discharged. The debtor is allowed to continue in business. Although this type of bankruptcy is commonly a corporate reorganization, any debtor (except a stockbroker or a commodities broker) who is eligible for Chapter 7 relief is eligible for relief under Chapter 11.[11] Railroads are also eligible.

The same principles that govern the filing of a liquidation petition apply to reorganization proceedings. The case may be brought either voluntarily or involuntarily. The same principles govern the entry of the order for relief. The automatic-stay provision is also applicable in reorganizations. This chapter's *Business Law in the Online World* feature looks at circumstances involving a failed online business that was petitioned into involuntary bankruptcy under Chapter 11.

In some instances, creditors may prefer private, negotiated debt-adjustment agreements, also known as **workouts**, to bankruptcy proceedings. Often, these out-of-court workouts are much more flexible and thus more conducive to a speedy settlement. Speed is critical because delay is one of the most costly elements in any bankruptcy proceeding. Another advantage of workouts is that they avoid the various administrative costs of bankruptcy proceedings.

A bankruptcy court, after notice and a hearing, may dismiss or suspend all proceedings in a case at any time if dismissal or suspension would better serve the interests of the creditors. The Code also allows a court, after notice and a hearing, to dismiss a case under reorganization "for cause." Cause includes the absence of a reasonable likelihood of rehabilitation, the inability to effect a plan, and an unreasonable delay by the debtor that is prejudicial to (may harm the interests of) creditors.[12] A debtor need not be insolvent to be entitled to Chapter 11 protection.[13]

Debtor in Possession

On entry of the order for relief, the debtor generally continues to operate her or his business as a **debtor in possession (DIP)**. The court, however, may appoint a trustee (often referred to as a *receiver*) to operate the debtor's business if gross mismanagement of the business is shown or if appointing a trustee is in the best interests of the estate.

The DIP's role is similar to that of a trustee in a liquidation. The DIP is entitled to avoid preferential payments made to creditors and fraudulent transfers of assets that occurred prior to the filing of the Chapter 11 petition. The DIP has the power to decide whether to cancel or assume obligations under executory contracts (contracts that have not yet been performed) that were made prior to the petition.

Creditors' Committees

As soon as practicable after the entry of the order for relief, a creditors' committee of unsecured creditors is appointed. The committee may consult with the trustee or the DIP concerning the administration of the case or the formulation of the reorganization plan. Additional creditors' committees may be appointed to represent special interest creditors. Orders affecting the estate generally will not be made without either the consent of the committee or a hearing in which the judge hears the position of the committee.

Certain small businesses that do not own or manage real estate can avoid creditors' committees. In these cases, bankruptcy judges may enter orders without a committee's consent.

The Reorganization Plan

A reorganization plan to rehabilitate the debtor is a plan to conserve and administer the debtor's assets in the hope of an eventual return to successful operation and solvency. The plan must be fair and equitable and must do the following:

① Designate classes of claims and interests.

② Specify the treatment to be afforded the classes. (The plan must provide the same treatment for each claim in a particular class.)

③ Provide an adequate means for execution.

Filing the Plan. Only the debtor may file a plan within the first 120 days after the date of the bankruptcy court's order for relief. If the debtor does not meet the 120-day deadline, however, or if the debtor fails to obtain the required creditor consent (see below) within 180 days, any party may propose a plan. The plan need not provide for full repayment to unsecured creditors. Instead, unsecured creditors receive a percentage of each dollar owed to them by the debtor. If a small-business debtor chooses to avoid creditors' committees, the time for the debtor's filing is shortened to 100 days, and any other party's plan must be filed within 160 days.

[11] *Toibb v. Radloff,* 501 U.S. 157, 111 S.Ct. 2197, 115 L.Ed.2d 145 (1991).
[12] See 11 U.S.C. Section 1112(b).
[13] *In re Johns-Manville Corp.,* 36 Bankr. 727 (S.D.N.Y. 1984).

BUSINESS LAW IN THE ONLINE WORLD
Personal Data on the Auction Block

Businesses on the verge of failure, and businesses that have failed, often find themselves in bankruptcy court. In the spring and summer of 2000, with the sudden drop of investors' interest in online businesses, many of those firms filed for bankruptcy.

One problem facing a failed online business is what to do with its customer list. Offline companies (firms not based on the Web) have commonly bought and sold customer lists, which can attract high prices because they include information about customer buying habits, as well as addresses and other personal data. E-commerce companies, however, generally promise not to sell this information to third parties.

WHAT AM I BID? Toysmart.com, LLC, had this policy. Toysmart.com was also a failing dot.com. In June 2000, the company's creditors filed a petition for the firm's involuntary bankruptcy under Chapter 11. As part of the process, Toysmart.com filed a motion seeking court approval for the sale of its assets, including its customer list and customer-profile information. The court put off making a judgment on the propriety of the sale until a prospective purchaser appeared. Toysmart.com then placed an ad in the *Wall Street Journal,* offering to sell its customer data to the highest bidder.

TRUSTe, a nonprofit privacy organization that awards seals of approval to Web sites with strict privacy policies, asked the Federal Trade Commission (FTC) about the legality of this auction. The FTC filed a suit in a federal district court against Toysmart.com, alleging violations of the FTC Act and the Children's Online Privacy Protection Act. The controversy swelled because the personal information had been provided, in some instances, by children using the Toysmart.com Web site. More than forty state attorneys general joined the battle against the auction.[a]

GOING, GOING, GONE Toysmart.com reached a settlement with the FTC, agreeing, in the event of a sale of substantially all of its assets, to transfer the data to a family-friendly company that would agree to comply with Toysmart.com's privacy policy. When the creditors objected to this proposal, the judge refused to consent to it. Eventually, the creditors agreed to a deal in which Walt Disney Company, one of the owners of Toysmart.com, paid $50,000 to have the data destroyed.

Response to Toysmart.com's case was dramatic. Since the summer of 2000, fewer bankrupt online businesses have tried to sell their customer information. Others have changed their privacy policies to allow for such sales. In 2001, TRUSTe issued guidelines on the use of personal information in bankruptcies and other major fundamental changes that occur to Web-based businesses. The guidelines ask that the firms notify customers and offer them the choice to keep their personal data out of a deal (see http://www.truste.com for more information).

Finally, one version of the bankruptcy reform bill being considered by the U.S. Congress would prohibit the sale of customer information if that sale would violate a privacy policy.

FOR CRITICAL ANALYSIS
What effect might the privacy policy amendment in the bankruptcy reform bill before Congress have on bankrupt online businesses?

a. For the court's response to a request by the state of Texas regarding the case, see *Federal Trade Commission v. Toysmart.com, LLC,* 2000 WL 1523287 (D.Mass. 2000).

Acceptance and Confirmation of the Plan. Once the plan has been developed, it is submitted to each class of creditors for acceptance. Each class must accept the plan unless the class is not adversely affected by the plan. A class has accepted the plan when a majority of the creditors, representing two-thirds of the amount of the total claim, vote to approve it. Even when all classes of claims accept the plan, the court may refuse to confirm it if it is not "in the best interests of the cred-

itors." A spouse or child of the debtor can block the plan if it does not provide for payment of his or her claims in cash.

Even if only one class of claims has accepted the plan, the court may still confirm the plan under the Code's so-called **cram-down provision.** In other words, the court may confirm the plan over the objections of a class of creditors. Before the court can exercise this right of cram-down confirmation, it must be demonstrated that the plan "does not discriminate unfairly" against any creditors and that the plan is "fair and equitable."

The plan is binding on confirmation. The debtor is given a reorganization discharge from all claims not protected under the plan. This discharge does not apply to any claims that would be denied discharge under liquidation.

Debtors are allowed considerable freedom under Chapter 11 to do business. But this freedom is not as unlimited as it is outside the bankruptcy process, as the following case illustrates.

CASE 21.3 **In re Beyond.com Corp.**

United States Bankruptcy Court,
Northern District of California, 2003.
289 Bankr. 138.

FACTS Beyond.com Corporation principally built, hosted, managed, and marketed online stores from its base in Santa Clara, California. In 2002, Beyond.com filed a Chapter 11 petition and a reorganization plan in a federal bankruptcy court. The company also filed a disclosure statement, which set out the details underlying the plan. Among other things, the plan envisioned that the reorganized debtor would "retain all of the rights, powers, and duties of a trustee under the Bankruptcy Code." The plan appointed the debtor's former chief operating officer, John Barratt, "Liquidation Manager." In this capacity, Barratt could dispose of the debtor's property, enter into agreements on the debtor's behalf, file suits against unidentified defendants, and retain and pay advisers and other "professionals." Under most circumstances, none of these actions would be subject to court supervision or limitation. The plan also limited Barratt's personal liability for acts performed in this capacity. The debtor asked the court to approve the disclosure statement, as required before a plan is submitted to creditors.

ISSUE Did the plan comply with the notice requirements and court supervision provisions of the Bankruptcy Code?

DECISION No. The court refused to confirm Beyond.com's disclosure statement and reorganization plan.

REASON The court stated, "Conceptually, Beyond.com's plan and disclosure statement is as freewheeling with the Bankruptcy Code * * * as Enron's accountants were with the tax laws in the 1990s." The court found that "Beyond.com's proposed plan contains numerous provisions that modify the requirements of the Bankruptcy Code," including "provisions that dramatically reduce notice to creditors of matters that the drafters of the Bankruptcy Code * * * considered fundamental." These "modifications to the applicable provisions of [the Code] are not minor, ministerial or simply pragmatic. In effect, the plan affords the reorganized debtor the prerogative to comply selectively with the provisions of the Bankruptcy Code * * * without judicial supervision." The court concluded, "These defects cannot be cured."

FOR CRITICAL ANALYSIS—Social Consideration
How much information should be revealed in a disclosure statement accompanying a reorganization plan?

Chapter 13—Repayment Plan

Chapter 13 of the Bankruptcy Code provides for the "Adjustment of Debts of an Individual with Regular Income." Individuals (not partnerships or corporations) with regular income who owe fixed unsecured debts of less than $290,525 or fixed secured debts of less than $871,550 may take advantage of bankruptcy repayment plans. This includes salaried employees; individual proprietors; and individuals who live on welfare, Social Security, fixed pensions, or investment income. Many small-business debtors have a choice of filing under either Chapter 11 or Chapter 13. Repayment plans offer several advantages. One advan-

tage is that they are less expensive and less complicated than reorganization or liquidation proceedings.

A Chapter 13 repayment plan can be initiated only by the filing of a voluntary petition by the debtor. Certain liquidation and reorganization cases may be converted to Chapter 13 with the consent of the debtor. A Chapter 13 repayment plan may be converted to a Chapter 7 liquidation at the request of either the debtor or, under certain circumstances, a creditor. A Chapter 13 repayment plan may also be converted to a Chapter 11 reorganization after a hearing. On the filing of a petition under Chapter 13, a trustee must be appointed. The automatic stay previously discussed also takes effect. Although the stay applies to all or part of a consumer debt, it does not apply to any business debt incurred by the debtor.

THE REPAYMENT PLAN

Shortly after the petition is filed, the debtor must file a repayment plan. This plan may provide either for payment of all obligations in full or for payment of a lesser amount. A plan of rehabilitation by repayment provides for the debtor's future earnings or income to be turned over to the trustee as necessary for execution of the plan. The time for payment under the plan may not exceed three years unless the court approves an extension. The term, with extension, may not exceed five years.

The Code requires the debtor to make "timely" payments, and the trustee is required to ensure that the debtor commences these payments. The debtor must begin making payments under the proposed plan within thirty days after the plan has been filed with the court. If the plan has not been confirmed, the trustee is instructed to retain the payments until the plan is confirmed and then distribute them accordingly. If the plan is denied, the trustee will return the payments to the debtor less any costs. If the debtor fails to make timely payments or to begin payments within the thirty-day period, the court may convert the repayment plan to a liquidation bankruptcy or dismiss the petition.

Confirmation of the Plan. After the plan is filed, the court holds a confirmation hearing, at which interested parties may object to the plan. The court will confirm a plan with respect to each claim of a secured creditor under any of the following circumstances:

①　The secured creditors have accepted the plan.

②　The plan provides that creditors retain their claims against the debtor's property, and the value of the property to be distributed to the creditors under the plan is not less than the secured portion of their claims.

③　The debtor surrenders the property securing the claim to the creditors.

Objection to the Plan. Unsecured creditors do not have a vote to confirm a repayment plan, but they can object to it. The court can approve a plan over the objection of the trustee or any unsecured creditor only in either of the following situations:

①　The value of the property to be distributed under the plan is at least equal to the amount of the claims.

②　All the debtor's projected disposable income to be received during the three-year plan period will be applied to making payments. Disposable income is all income received less amounts needed to support the debtor and dependents and/or amounts needed to meet ordinary expenses to continue the operation of a business.

As emphasized by the decision in the following case, the timing of creditors' objections to a Chapter 13 plan is critical.

CASE 21.4　In re Andersen

United States Bankruptcy Appellate Panel,
Tenth Circuit, 1998.
215 Bankr. 792.

FACTS　Resolving disputes as to the dischargeability of student loans has been a thorny issue for the courts. The Bankruptcy Code appears to require an all-or-nothing finding—that is, the entire amount of a student loan is either dischargeable or not. Doreen Andersen had student loan obligations to a number of educational loan guaranty agencies and lending banks. She filed a Chapter 13 plan that contained the following information:

All timely filed and allowed unsecured claims, including the claims of Higher Education Assistance Foundation [HEAF] and [other] government guaranteed education loans, shall be paid ten percent (10%) of each claim, and the balance of each claim shall be discharged. *　*　* [E]xcepting

the aforementioned education loans from discharge will impose an undue hardship on the debtor and the debtor's dependents. Confirmation of debtor's plan shall constitute a finding to that effect and that said debt is dischargeable.

The lenders filed an objection to the treatment of their claims. Because the objection was untimely, however, the court denied it and confirmed the plan. Three years later, after Andersen fulfilled the plan, the court entered a discharge. When the lenders attempted to collect the balance of the loans, Andersen filed a suit in a bankruptcy court against them. The court held that the debts had not been discharged. Andersen appealed.

ISSUE　Did the confirmation of the plan constitute a binding determination that payment of the student loans (beyond what was provided in the plan) would be an undue hardship, making the loans dischargeable?

(Continued)

CASE 21.4—Continued

DECISION Yes. The bankruptcy appellate panel reversed the decision of the lower court and remanded the case for further proceedings, including the entry of a judgment that the unpaid student loans were discharged.

REASON The appellate panel explained that a bankruptcy plan is agreed to "through a bargaining process." There are few requirements, and the Bankruptcy Code allows much flexibility in devising a plan. The court pointed out that "[a] plan that is filed and served is simply an offer to the creditors, one that may be deemed to have been accepted if the creditor does not object." In this case, the lenders received notice of the plan and had an opportunity to object, but failed to object in time. The plan was then confirmed and, once confirmed, "resolved a potential controversy about whether payment of the student [loans] would result in an undue hardship to the debtor." The confirmation rendered the loans dischargeable, and the final order of discharge discharged them.

FOR CRITICAL ANALYSIS—Economic Consideration
How might the lenders have avoided the outcome in this case?

Modification of the Plan. Prior to the completion of payments, the plan may be modified at the request of the debtor, the trustee, or an unsecured creditor. If any interested party has an objection to the modification, the court must hold a hearing to determine approval or disapproval of the modified plan.

DISCHARGE

After the completion of all payments, the court grants a discharge of all debts provided for by the repayment plan. Except for allowed claims not provided for by the plan, certain long-term debts provided for by the plan, and claims for alimony and child support, all other debts are dischargeable. A discharge of debts under a Chapter 13 repayment plan is sometimes referred to as a "superdischarge." One of the reasons for this is that the law allows a Chapter 13 discharge to include fraudulently incurred debt and claims resulting from malicious or willful injury. Therefore, a discharge under Chapter 13 may be much more beneficial to some debtors than a liquidation discharge under Chapter 7 might be.

Even if the debtor does not complete the plan, a hardship discharge may be granted if failure to complete the plan was due to circumstances beyond the debtor's control and if the value of the property distributed under the plan was greater than creditors would have received in a liquidation proceeding. A discharge can be revoked within one year if it was obtained by fraud.

Chapter 12—Family-Farmer Plan

The Bankruptcy Code defines a *family farmer*[14] as one whose gross income is at least 50 percent farm dependent and whose debts are at least 80 percent farm related. The total debt must not exceed $1.5 million. A partnership or closely held corporation that is at least 50 percent owned by the farm family can also take advantage of Chapter 12.

The procedure for filing a family-farmer bankruptcy plan is very similar to the procedure for filing a repayment plan under Chapter 13. The farmer-debtor must file a plan not later than ninety days after the order for relief. The filing of the petition acts as an automatic stay against creditors' actions against the estate.

The content of a family-farmer plan is basically the same as that of a Chapter 13 repayment plan. The plan can be modified by the farmer-debtor but, except for cause, must be confirmed or denied within forty-five days of the filing of the plan.

Court confirmation of the plan is the same as for a repayment plan. In summary, the plan must provide for payment of secured debts at the value of the collateral. If the secured debt exceeds the value of the collateral, the remaining debt is unsecured. For unsecured debtors, the plan must be confirmed if either the value of the property to be distributed under the plan equals the amount of the claim or the plan provides that all of the farmer-debtor's disposable income to be received in a three-year period (or longer, by court approval) will be applied to making payments. Completion of payments under the plan discharges all debts provided for by the plan.

A farmer who has already filed a reorganization or repayment plan may convert the plan to a family-farmer plan. The farmer-debtor may also convert a family-farmer plan to a liquidation plan.

---

[14] Contrast this definition with the definition of a *farmer* given in footnote 6.

Terms and Concepts

Chapter Summary — Creditors' Rights and Bankruptcy

REMEDIES AVAILABLE TO CREDITORS	

Liens (See pages 419–421.)	1. *Mechanic's lien*—A nonpossessory, filed lien on an owner's real estate for labor, services, or materials furnished to or made on the realty.
	
	2. *Artisan's lien*—A possessory lien on an owner's personal property for labor performed or value added.
	
	3. *Innkeeper's lien*—A possessory lien on a hotel guest's baggage for hotel charges that remain unpaid.
	
	4. *Judicial liens*—
	
	   a. *Attachment*—A court-ordered seizure of property prior to a court's final determination of the creditor's rights to the property. Attachment is available only on the creditor's posting of a bond and strict compliance with the applicable state statutes.
	
	   b. *Writ of execution*—A court order directing the sheriff to seize (levy) and sell a debtor's nonexempt real or personal property to satisfy a court's judgment in the creditor's favor.

Garnishment (See page 421.)	A collection remedy that allows the creditor to attach a debtor's money (such as wages owed or bank accounts) and property that are held by a third person.
Creditors' Composition Agreement (See page 421.)	A contract between a debtor and his or her creditors by which the debtor's debts are discharged by payment of a sum less than the sum that is actually owed.
Mortgage Foreclosure (See page 421.)	On the debtor's default, the entire mortgage debt is due and payable, allowing the creditor to foreclose on the realty by selling it to satisfy the debt.
Suretyship or Guaranty (See pages 421–423.)	Under contract, a third person agrees to be primarily or secondarily liable for the debt owed by the principal debtor. A creditor can turn to this third person for satisfaction of the debt.
LAWS ASSISTING DEBTORS	
Exemptions (See pages 423–424.)	Numerous laws, including consumer protection statutes, assist debtors. Additionally, state laws exempt certain types of real and personal property from levy of execution or attachment.

(Continued)

Chapter Summary — Creditors' Rights and Bankruptcy—Continued

Exemptions—continued	1. *Real property*—Each state permits a debtor to retain the family home, either in its entirety or up to a specified dollar amount, free from the claims of unsecured creditors or trustees in bankruptcy (homestead exemption).
	2. *Personal property*—Personal property that is most often exempt from satisfaction of judgment debts includes the following:
	a. Household furniture up to a specified dollar amount.
	b. Clothing and certain personal possessions.
	c. Transportation vehicles up to a specified dollar amount.
	d. Certain classified animals, such as livestock and pets.
	e. Equipment used in a business or trade up to a specified dollar amount.

BANKRUPTCY—A COMPARISON OF CHAPTERS 7, 11, 12, AND 13

Issue	Chapter 7	Chapter 11	Chapters 12 and 13
Purpose	Liquidation.	Reorganization.	Adjustment.
Who Can Petition	Debtor (voluntary) or creditors (involuntary).	Debtor (voluntary) or creditors (involuntary).	Debtor (voluntary) only.
Who Can Be a Debtor	Any "person" (including partnerships and corporations) except railroads, insurance companies, banks, savings and loan institutions, investment companies licensed by the Small Business Administration, and credit unions. Farmers and charitable institutions cannot be involuntarily petitioned.	Any debtor eligible for Chapter 7 relief; railroads are also eligible.	*Chapter 12*—Any family farmer (one whose gross income is at least 50 percent farm dependent and whose debts are at least 80 percent farm related) or any partnership or closely held corporation at least 50 percent owned by a farm family, when total debt does not exceed $1.5 million. *Chapter 13*—Any individual (not partnerships or corporations) with regular income who owes fixed unsecured debts of less than $290,525 or fixed secured debts of less than $871,550.
Procedure Leading to Discharge	Nonexempt property is sold with proceeds to be distributed (in order) to priority groups. Dischargeable debts are terminated.	Plan is submitted; if it is approved and followed, debts are discharged.	Plan is submitted and must be approved if the debtor turns over disposable income for a three-year period; if the plan is followed, debts are discharged.
Advantages	On liquidation and distribution, most debts are discharged, and the debtor has an opportunity for a fresh start.	Debtor continues in business. Creditors can either accept the plan, or it can be "crammed down" on them. The plan allows for the reorganization and liquidation of debts over the plan period.	Debtor continues in business or possession of assets. If the plan is approved, most debts are discharged after a three-year period.

For Review

① What is a prejudgment attachment? What is a writ of execution? How does a creditor use these remedies?

② What is garnishment? When might a creditor undertake a garnishment proceeding?

③ In a bankruptcy proceeding, what constitutes the debtor's estate in property? What property is exempt from the estate under federal bankruptcy law?

④ What is the difference between an exception to discharge and an objection to discharge?

⑤ In a Chapter 11 reorganization, what is the role of the debtor in possession?

Questions and Case Problems

21–1. Creditors' Remedies. In what circumstances would a creditor resort to each of the following remedies when trying to collect on a debt?

    (a) Mechanic's lien.
    (b) Artisan's lien.
    (c) Innkeeper's lien.
    (d) Writ of attachment.
    (e) Writ of execution.
    (f) Garnishment.

21–2. Rights of the Surety. Meredith, a farmer, borrowed $5,000 from Farmer's Bank and gave the bank $4,000 in bearer bonds to hold as collateral for the loan. Meredith's neighbor, Peterson, who had known Meredith for years, signed as a surety on the note. Because of a drought, Meredith's harvest that year was only a fraction of what it normally was, and he was forced to default on his payments to Farmer's Bank. The bank did not immediately sell the bonds but instead requested $5,000 from Peterson. Peterson paid the $5,000 and then demanded that the bank give him the $4,000 in securities. Can Peterson enforce this demand? Explain.

21–3. Rights of the Guarantor. Sabrina is a student at Sunnyside University. In need of funds to pay for tuition and books, she attempts to secure a short-term loan from University Bank. The bank agrees to make a loan if Sabrina will have someone financially responsible guarantee the loan payments. Abigail, a well-known businessperson and a friend of Sabrina's family, calls the bank and agrees to pay the loan if Sabrina cannot. Because of Abigail's reputation, the bank makes the loan. Sabrina makes several payments on the loan, but because of illness she is not able to work for one month. She requests that University Bank extend the loan for three months. The bank agrees and raises the interest rate for the extended period. Abigail has not been notified of the extension (and therefore has not consented to it). One month later, Sabrina drops out of school. All attempts to collect from Sabrina have failed. University Bank wants to hold Abigail liable. Will the bank succeed? Explain.

21–4. Distribution of Property. Runyan voluntarily petitions for bankruptcy. He has three major claims against his estate. One is by Calvin, a friend who holds Runyan's nego-

tiable promissory note for $2,500; one is by Kohak, an employee who is owed three months' back wages of $4,500; and one is by the First Bank of Sunny Acres on an unsecured loan of $5,000. In addition, Martinez, an accountant retained by the trustee, is owed $500, and property taxes of $1,000 are owed to Micanopa County. Runyan's nonexempt property has been liquidated, with the proceeds totaling $5,000. Discuss fully what amount each party will receive, and why.

21–5. Creditors' Remedies. Orkin owns a relatively old home valued at $45,000. He notices that the bathtubs and fixtures in both bathrooms are leaking and need to be replaced. He contracts with Pike to replace the bathtubs and fixtures. Pike replaces them and submits her bill of $4,000 to Orkin. Because of financial difficulties, Orkin does not pay the bill. Orkin's only asset is his home, which under state law is exempt up to $40,000 as a homestead. Discuss fully Pike's remedies in this situation.

21–6. Guaranty. In 1988, Jamieson-Chippewa Investment Co. entered into a five-year commercial lease with TDM Pharmacy, Inc., for certain premises in Ellisville, Missouri, on which TDM intended to operate a small drugstore. Dennis and Tereasa McClintock ran the pharmacy business. The lease granted TDM three additional five-year options to renew. The lease was signed by TDM and by the McClintocks individually as guarantors. The lease did not state that the guaranty was continuing. In fact, there were no words of guaranty in the lease other than the single word "Guarantors" on the signature page. In 1993, Dennis McClintock, acting as the president of TDM, exercised TDM's option to renew the lease for one term. Three years later, when the pharmacy failed, TDM defaulted on the lease. Jamieson-Chippewa filed a suit in a Missouri state court against the McClintocks for the rent for the rest of the term, based on their guaranty. The McClintocks filed a motion for summary judgment, contending that they had not guaranteed any rent payments beyond the initial five-year term. How should the court rule? Why? [*Jamieson-Chippewa Investment Co. v. McClintock,* 996 S.W.2d 84 (Mo.App.E.D. 1999)]

21–7. Voidable Preference. The Securities and Exchange Commission (SEC) filed a suit in a federal district court against First Jersey Securities, Inc., and others, alleging fraud in First Jersey's sale of securities (stock). The court ordered the defendants to turn over to the SEC $75 million in illegal profits. This order made the SEC the largest unsecured creditor of First Jersey. First Jersey filed a voluntary petition in a federal bankruptcy court to declare bankruptcy under Chapter 11. On the same day, the debtor transferred 200,001 shares of stock to its law firm, Robinson, St. John, & Wayne (RSW), in payment for services in the SEC suit and the bankruptcy petition. The stock represented essentially all of the debtor's assets. RSW did not find a buyer for the stock for more than two months. The SEC objected to the transfer, contending that it was a voidable preference, and asked that RSW be disqualified from representing the debtor. RSW responded that the transfer was made in the ordinary course of business. Also, asserted RSW, the transfer was not in payment of an "antecedent debt," because the firm had not presented First Jersey with a bill for its services and therefore the debt was not yet past due. Was the stock transfer a voidable preference? Should the court disqualify RSW? Why or why not? [*In re First Jersey Securities, Inc.,* 180 F.3d 504 (3d Cir. 1999)]

CASE PROBLEM WITH SAMPLE ANSWER

21–8. Mr. Mallinckrodt received an undergraduate degree from the University of Miami and, in 1995, a graduate degree from Barry University in mental health counseling. To finance this education, Mallinckrodt borrowed from The Education Resources Institute, Inc., and others. Unable to find a job as a counselor, Mallinckrodt worked as a tennis instructor and coach. (At one time, he had played professional tennis and was ranked among the top eight hundred players in the world.) In 1996, he ruptured his Achilles tendon and was unable to work. After a lengthy rehabilitation, he was hired on a part-time, hourly basis at Horizon Psychological Services, but the work was intermittent and low paying. He continued to work as a tennis instructor and was also a licensed real estate broker, but had little income in either field. With monthly income of about $549 after taxes, and expenses of $544, Mallinckrodt filed a bankruptcy petition to discharge his student loan debt, which with interest totaled nearly $73,000. Is this debt dischargeable? Discuss. [*In re Mallinckrodt,* 260 Bankr. 892 (S.D.Fla. 2001)]

◆ To view a sample answer for this case problem, go to this book's Web site at **http://fundamentals.westbuslaw.com** and click on "Interactive Study Center."

21–9. Guaranty. In 1981, in Troy, Ohio, Willis and Mary Jane Ward leased a commercial building to Buckeye Pizza Corp. to operate a pizza parlor. Two years later, Buckeye assigned its interest in the building to Ohio, Ltd. In 1985, Ohio sold its pizza business, including its lease of the Wards' building, to NR Dayton Mall, Inc., an Indiana corporation and a subsidiary of Noble Roman's, Inc. As part of the deal, Noble Roman's agreed that it "unconditionally guarantees the performance by N.R. DAYTON MALL, INC., of all its obligations under the Assumption Undertaking." In the "Assumption Undertaking," NR agreed to accept assignment of the Ward lease and to pay Buckeye's and Ohio's expenses if they were sued under it. A

dozen years later, NR defaulted on the lease and abandoned the premises. The Wards filed a suit in an Indiana state court against Noble Roman's and others, contending that the firm was liable for NR's default. Noble Roman's argued that it had guaranteed only to indemnify Buckeye and Ohio. The Wards filed a motion for summary judgment. Should the court grant the motion? Explain. [*Noble Roman's, Inc. v. Ward,* 760 N.E.2d 1132 (Ind.App. 2002)]

21–10. Discharge in Bankruptcy. Jon Goulet attended the University of Wisconsin in Eau Claire and Regis University in Denver, Colorado, from which, in 1972, he earned a bachelor's degree in history. Over the next ten years, he worked as a bartender and restaurant manager. In 1984, he became a life insurance agent, and his income ranged from $20,000 to $30,000. In 1989, however, his agent's license was revoked for insurance fraud, and he was arrested for cocaine possession. From 1991 to 1995, Goulet was again at the University of Wisconsin, working toward, but failing to obtain, a master's degree in psychology. To pay for his studies, he took out student loans totaling $76,000. Goulet then returned to bartending and restaurant management and tried real estate sales. His income for the year 2000 was $1,490, and his expenses, excluding a child-support obligation, were $5,904. When the student loans came due, Goulet filed a petition for bankruptcy. On what ground might the loans be dischargeable? Should the court grant a discharge on this ground? Why or why not? [*Goulet v. Educational Credit Management Corp.,* 284 F.3d 773 (7th Cir. 2002)]

A QUESTION OF ETHICS AND SOCIAL RESPONSIBILITY

21–11. In September 1986, Edward and Debora Davenport pleaded guilty in a Pennsylvania court to welfare fraud and were sentenced to probation for one year. As a condition of their probation, the Davenports were ordered to make monthly restitution payments to the county probation department, which would forward the payments to the Pennsylvania Department of Public Welfare, the victim of the Davenports' fraud. In May 1987, the Davenports filed a petition for Chapter 13 relief and listed the restitution payments among their debts. The bankruptcy court held that the restitution obligation was a dischargeable debt. Ultimately, the United States Supreme Court reviewed the case. The Court noted that under the Bankruptcy Code, a debt is defined as a liability on a claim, and a claim is defined as a right to payment. Because the restitution obligations clearly constituted a right to payment, the Court held that the obligations were dischargeable in bankruptcy. [*Pennsylvania Department of Public Welfare v. Davenport,* 495 U.S. 552, 110 S.Ct. 2126, 109 L.Ed.2d 588 (1990)]

1. Critics of this decision contend that the Court adhered to the letter, but not the spirit, of bankruptcy law in arriving at its conclusion. In what way, if any, did the Court not abide by the "spirit" of bankruptcy law?

2. Do you think that Chapter 13 plans, which allow nearly all types of debts to be discharged, tip the scales of justice too far in favor of debtors?

CREDITORS' RIGHTS AND BANKRUPTCY

For updated links to resources available on the Web, as well as other materials, visit this text's Web site at

http://fundamentals.westbuslaw.com

The Legal Information Institute at Cornell University offers a collection of law materials concerning debtor-creditor relationships, including federal statutes and recent Supreme Court decisions on this topic, at

http://www.law.cornell.edu/topics/debtor_creditor.html

The U.S. Department of Labor's Web site contains a page on garnishment and employees' rights in relation to garnishment proceedings at

http://www.dol.gov/dol/topic/wages/garnishments.htm

The U.S. Bankruptcy Code is online at

http://www4.law.cornell.edu/uscode/11

Another good resource for bankruptcy information is the American Bankruptcy Institute (ABI) at

http://www.abiworld.org

Online Legal Research

Go to the *Fundamentals of Business Law* home page at **http://fundamentals.westbuslaw.com**. Select "Interactive Study Center" and then click on "Chapter 21." There you will find the following Internet research exercises that you can perform to learn more about topics covered in this chapter.

Activity 21–1: LEGAL PERSPECTIVE—**Mechanic's Liens**
Activity 21–2: MANAGEMENT PERSPECTIVE—**Bankruptcy Alternatives**

Before the Test

Go to the *Fundamentals of Business Law* home page at **http://fundamentals.westbuslaw.com**. Click on "Interactive Quizzes." You will find at least twenty interactive questions relating to this chapter.

Westlaw® Campus

If your textbook provided for a subscription to Westlaw® Campus, or if you have otherwise purchased access to the Westlaw Campus database, you can access any of the cases presented or cited in this chapter by using your Westlaw Campus account.

In re Stanton

INTRODUCTION

From studying the chapters in this unit, it should be clear that a court can enforce a lien. In this *Focus on Legal Reasoning*, we look at *In re Stanton*,[1] a decision in which the court considered the priority of a creditor's lien on the debtors' house. The house had been used to secure loans to the debtors' business, and the debtors—but not the business—had filed for bankruptcy.

CASE BACKGROUND

Kevin and Maryann Stanton owned Fleet Manufacturing Corporation. In

1994, International Factors, Inc., took a security interest in Fleet's property under several continuing financing arrangements. In April, the Stantons also signed a personal guaranty of Fleet's obligations to International Factors.

In July, Fleet received a big order from Kmart Corporation and needed additional money to fill the order. International Factors agreed to increase its advances to Fleet in exchange for a second mortgage[2] on the Stantons'

house. Despite efforts to maintain the business and their personal finances, in September the Stantons filed a petition for personal bankruptcy. International Factors continued to advance funds to Fleet under the lien on the house.

The bankruptcy trustee sold the house, and International Factors sought to attach the proceeds of the sale, based on its lien. The trustee filed a suit in the bankruptcy court against International Factors, seeking to avoid the lien. The court granted a summary judgment in the trustee's favor. A bankruptcy appellate panel reversed this judgment. The trustee appealed to the U.S. Court of Appeals for the Ninth Circuit.

---

1. 285 F.3d 888 (9th Cir. 2002).

2. A second mortgage ranks in priority immediately after a first mortgage on the same property in terms of payment out of the proceeds from a sale of the property.

MAJORITY OPINION

KLEINFELD, Circuit Judge.

* * * *

The trustee argues that the [Bankruptcy Code's] automatic stay provision [which suspends all creditors' actions against the debtor] applied and prohibited [International Factors'] advances to Fleet. Violation of the automatic stay is a serious business, exposing the violator in some circumstances to punitive damages and [other] sanctions * * *. Banks and other lenders may well tremble at the notion that they and possibly their officers could face such severe sanctions if they lend money to a corporation one of whose shareholders has gone bankrupt. Many close corporations [corporations owned by relatively few persons], such as small manufacturers and professional practices, secure debt with shareholders' property as well as corporate property. Shareholders sometimes go bankrupt while the corporation continues as a financially healthy business.

[The automatic stay provision] does not apply. That subsection stays [suspends] any "act to create, perfect or enforce any lien against property of the estate." A loan of money to a debtor not in bankruptcy does none of those things * * *. *A business relationship of stock ownership does not * * * extend the automatic stay to non-bankrupts.* The lien against the Stantons' house was created when they gave [International Factors] a second mortgage, prior to the bankruptcy filing. * * * The subsequent advances merely affected how much money the lien secured. [Emphasis added.]

[The automatic stay provision] is therefore beside the point. * * * The reason this is beside the point is that the Stantons' house was encumbered [burdened by a lien] *before* the bankruptcy, and International Factors did not lend any money to the Stantons. * * * International Factors * * * loaned

the money to a going, non-bankrupt corporation in which the Stantons owned stock. Fleet did not need court approval to incur debt because Fleet was not in bankruptcy. The Stantons would have needed court approval to incur additional secured debt, but they did not incur any additional secured debt. * * *

* * * *

This does not mean that International Factors necessarily wins all the marbles. Under *John M. Keltch, Inc. v. Don Hoyt, Inc.,* 4 Wash.App. 580, 483 P.2d 135 (1971), and under *National Bank of Washington v. Equity Investors, Inc.,* 81 Wash.2d 886, 506 P.2d 20 (1973), it matters that [International Factors] had discretion whether to make the subsequent advances to Fleet, and was not obligated to do so. * * * [W]here the advances of promised loan moneys are, under an agreement to lend money, largely optional * * * liens attaching prior to an optional advance would thus be superior to it. * * * Thus, the bankruptcy trustee was senior to [International Factors'] lien for advances [the lender] made after the Stantons filed for bankruptcy. * * *

[International Factors'] lien preexisted the bankruptcy. No one violated the automatic stay provision. Neither [International Factors] nor Fleet Manufacturing needed court permission for the * * * advance [of] additional money to Fleet. To hold otherwise would allow the bankruptcy of a corporation's shareholder to clog the going business of the corporation and its creditors. What did happen to [International Factors'] security because of the bankruptcy is that its *priority* as to the proceeds from sale of the Stantons' house (rather than its lien) became limited to the extent of its advances prior to the bankruptcy, because subsequent advances were optional.

* * * *

AFFIRMED.

DISSENTING OPINION

GOULD, Circuit Judge, dissenting:

* * * *

I [believe that the automatic stay provision] barred the debtors' attempt to use their house as collateral without prior court approval because, in continuing to use their house as collateral for Fleet's debts on post-petition advances, the debtors "incurr[ed] debt" within the meaning of [the automatic stay provision]. The bankruptcy code defines "debt" as "liability on a claim" and defines "claim" as either a "right to payment" or to "[a] remedy for breach of performance if such breach gives rise to a right to payment." It is difficult, if not impossible, to dispute that the debtors' continued use of their house as collateral for Fleet's debts on new advances resulted in their incurring new and increased liability on creditor's lien claim * * * against debtors as guarantors, for breach of performance by Fleet on its obligations arising after the petition was filed. To increase the amount of the liens was to increase liability on a claim, and, as such, creditor's actions increasing debtors' liability required prior court approval, which was not obtained.

Those who file for bankruptcy receive considerable advantages, namely the discharge of their debts. In exchange, the debtor's estate after filing is protected against encumbrance except as provided in the bankruptcy laws. The fact that debtors' estate was encumbered on behalf of or with aim to benefit another entity, i.e., their * * * corporation, rather than on their own behalf, does not change the fact that it was incorrect further to encumber the estate of the bankrupt without court approval in violation of the bankruptcy laws. * * *

* * * *

Under Washington law, liens based on optional advances take effect at the time of each advance. See *National Bank of Washington v. Equity Investors, Inc.; cf. John M. Keltch, Inc. v. Don Hoyt, Inc.* * * * The new liens on the debtors' estate to secure new advances to Fleet after the bankruptcy proceeding was commenced required approval by the bankruptcy court.

LEGAL REASONING AND ANALYSIS

❶ **Legal Reasoning.** Contrast the conclusions of the majority and the dissent. What reasons did each provide to justify its position?

❷ **Legal Interpretation.** Find the *National Bank of Washington v. Equity Investors, Inc.,* and *John M. Keltch, Inc. v. Don Hoyt, Inc.,* cases (see the appendix to Chapter 1 for instructions on finding state court opinions). What do the holdings in these cases, and the different references to them by the majority and dissent in the *Stanton* case, indicate about the U.S. judicial system?

❸ **Legal Application.** How might the result in this case have been different if the court had concluded that Fleet and its owners were not separate entities?

❹ **Implications for Creditors.** What does the decision in this case indicate to those who lend money to businesses secured by the owners' personal property?

❺ **Case Briefing Assignment.** Using the guidelines for briefing cases given in Appendix A of this text, brief the *Stanton* case.

This text's Web site, at **http://fundamentals.westbuslaw.com**, offers links to West's Court Case Updates, as well as to other online research sources. You can also locate court cases at the Web sites listed in the *Accessing the Internet* section at the end of Chapter 2.

The American Bankruptcy Institute (ABI) provides links to decisions in select bankruptcy cases, as well as to other resources, at **http://www.abiworld.org**. The ABI's members include accountants, attorneys, professors, and other bankruptcy professionals.

UNIT 7

Employment Relations

CHAPTER
22 Agency Relationships

CHAPTER OBJECTIVES

After reading this chapter, you should be able to answer the following questions:

① What is the difference between an employee and an independent contractor?

② How do agency relationships arise?

③ What duties do agents and principals owe to each other?

④ When is a principal liable for the agent's actions with respect to third parties? When is the agent liable?

⑤ What are some of the ways in which an agency relationship can be terminated?

One of the most common, important, and pervasive legal relationships is that of **agency**. As discussed in Chapter 18, in an agency relationship between two parties, one of the parties, called the *agent,* agrees to represent or act for the other, called the *principal.* The principal has the right to control the agent's conduct in matters entrusted to the agent, and the agent must exercise his or her powers for the benefit of the principal only. By using agents, a principal can conduct multiple business operations simultaneously in various locations. Thus, for example, contracts that bind the principal can be made at different places with different persons at the same time.

Agency relationships permeate the business world. Indeed, agency law is essential to the existence and operation of a corporate entity, because only through its agents can a corporation function and enter into contracts. A familiar example of an agent is a corporate officer who serves in a representative capacity for the owners of the corporation. In this capacity, the officer has the authority to bind the principal (the corporation) to a contract.

Agency Relationships

Section 1(1) of the *Restatement (Second) of Agency*[1] defines agency as "the fiduciary relation which results from the manifestation of consent by one person to another that the other

---

[1] The *Restatement (Second) of Agency* is an authoritative summary of the law of agency and is often referred to by jurists in their decisions and opinions.

shall act in his behalf and subject to his control, and consent by the other so to act." In other words, in a principal-agent relationship, the parties have agreed that the agent will act *on behalf and instead of* the principal in negotiating and transacting business with third persons.

The term **fiduciary** is at the heart of agency law. The term can be used both as a noun and as an adjective. When used as a noun, it refers to a person having a duty created by her or his undertaking to act primarily for another's benefit in matters connected with the undertaking. When used as an adjective, as in "fiduciary relationship," it means that the relationship involves trust and confidence.

Agency relationships commonly exist between employers and employees. Agency relationships may sometimes also exist between employers and independent contractors who are hired to perform special tasks or services.

EMPLOYER-EMPLOYEE RELATIONSHIPS

Normally, all employees who deal with third parties are deemed to be agents. A salesperson in a department store, for example, is an agent of the store's owner (the principal) and acts on the owner's behalf. Any sale of goods made by the salesperson to a customer is binding on the principal. Similarly, most representations of fact made by the salesperson with respect to the goods sold are binding on the principal.

Because employees who deal with third parties are normally deemed to be agents of their employers, agency law and employment law overlap considerably. Agency relationships, though, as will become apparent, can exist outside an employer-employee relationship and thus have a broader reach than employment laws do. Additionally, bear in mind that agency law is based on the common law. In the employment realm, many common law doctrines have been displaced by statutory law and government regulations governing employment relationships.

Employment laws (state and federal) apply only to the employer-employee relationship. Statutes governing Social Security, withholding taxes, workers' compensation, unemployment compensation, workplace safety, employment discrimination, and the like (see Chapter 23) are applicable only if there is employer-employee status. *These laws do not apply to the independent contractor.*

EMPLOYER–INDEPENDENT CONTRACTOR RELATIONSHIPS

Independent contractors are not employees because, by definition, those who hire them have no control over the details of their physical performance. Section 2 of the *Restatement (Second) of Agency* defines an independent contractor as follows:

> [An independent contractor is] a person who contracts with another to do something for him, but who is not controlled by the other nor subject to the other's right to control with respect to his physical conduct in the performance of the undertaking. *He may or may not be an agent.* [Emphasis added.]

Building contractors and subcontractors are independent contractors, and a property owner does not control the acts of either of these professionals. Truck drivers who own their equipment and hire themselves out on a per-job basis are independent contractors, but truck drivers who drive company trucks on a regular basis are usually employees.

The relationship between a person or firm and an independent contractor may or may not involve an agency relationship. An owner of real estate who hires a real estate broker to negotiate a sale of his or her property not only has contracted with an independent contractor (the real estate broker) but also has established an agency relationship for the specific purpose of assisting in the sale of the property. Similarly, an insurance agent is both an independent contractor and an agent of the insurance company for which he or she sells policies. (Note that an insurance broker, in contrast to an insurance agent, normally is an agent of the person obtaining insurance and not of the insurance company.) Typically, in deciding whether an independent contractor is also an agent, the courts look at several factors, including those discussed in this chapter's *Business Law in the Online World* feature on the following page.

DETERMINING EMPLOYEE STATUS

A question the courts frequently face in determining liability under agency law is whether a person hired by another to do a job is an employee or an independent contractor. Because employers are normally held liable as principals for the actions taken by their employee-agents within the scope of employment (as will be discussed later in this chapter), the court's decision as to employee versus independent-contractor status can be significant for the parties.

Criteria Used by the Courts. In determining whether a worker has the status of an employee or an independent contractor, the courts often consider the following questions:

1. How much control can the employer exercise over the details of the work? (If an employer can exercise considerable control over the details of the work, this would indicate employee status.)
2. Is the worker engaged in an occupation or business distinct from that of the employer? (If not, this would indicate employee status.)

BUSINESS LAW IN THE ONLINE WORLD
Agent or Independent Contractor?

Independent contractors may or may not be agents. That said, how is it determined whether an independent contractor is or is not an agent? This question often comes before the courts, as it did in a case involving a company hired to distribute ads via bulk e-mail.

AN UNFORESEEN CONSEQUENCE When Modern Computing agreed to advertise online mortgages made available through Greentree Mortgage Company, it had no idea of the problems its advertising would cause for Matthew Seidl. Modern had contracted with Greentree to advertise Greentree's mortgages by bulk e-mail advertising (spamming). The ad contained Greentree's 800 telephone number and its e-mail address. Modern's ad also contained, in its return path fields, the address "nobody@localhost.com." Messages that were sent to incorrect addresses or that were otherwise undelivered would be returned to this address.

Unbeknownst to Modern, Seidl, a graduate student in computer science at a Colorado university, had registered localhost.com as one of his domain names. As a result of Modern's advertising campaign, Seidl received over 7,000 bounced-back ads. He sued Greentree Mortgage, claiming that the messages tied up his computer for three days. He also claimed that because some ads were bounced back by people angry about spamming, his reputation in the Internet community was injured. Greentree countered that Modern was an independent contractor, not an agent, and thus Greentree could not be held liable for Modern's actions.

CAN GREENTREE BE HELD LIABLE? Seidl asserted that Greentree should be held liable for the damage he suffered because Modern was Greentree's agent. After all, argued Seidl, Modern acted "for or in place of" Greentree when doing the mailing. The court, however, pointed out that an independent contractor ordinarily performs services for others. The court stated, "If this court were to adopt plaintiff's position that such actions make an independent contractor an agent because he or she 'acts for' the other, it would eliminate the distinction between [an] independent contractor and an agent."

The court emphasized that "an agent is one who represents (and may bind) the principal contractually." There was no evidence in this case to show that Modern had the ability to bind Greentree contractually. "This fact alone," stated the court, was enough to show that Modern was an independent contractor and not an agent. Additionally, Greentree exercised no control over the details of Modern's distribution of the spam. Thus, concluded the court, the "undisputed facts" show that Modern was an independent contractor and that Greentree was not responsible for Modern's errors in transmitting the spam.[a]

FOR CRITICAL ANALYSIS

Suppose that Greentree and Modern had formed a written contract in which Modern was designated an independent contractor. Would this contractual designation alone be sufficient evidence for the court to conclude that Modern was an independent contractor?

a. *Seidl v. Greentree Mortgage Co.*, 30 F.Supp.2d 1292 (D.Colo. 1998).

③ Is the work usually done under the employer's direction or by a specialist without supervision? (If the work is usually done under the employer's direction, this would indicate employee status.)

④ Does the employer supply the tools at the place of work? (If so, this would indicate employee status.)

⑤ For how long is the person employed? (If the person is employed for a long period of time, this would indicate employee status.)

⑥ What is the method of payment—by time period or at the completion of the job? (Payment by time period,

such as once every two weeks or once a month, would indicate employee status.)

⑦ What degree of skill is required of the worker? (If little skill is required, this may indicate employee status.)

Sometimes, it is advantageous to have employee status—to take advantage of laws protecting employees, for example. At other times, it may be beneficial to have independent-contractor status—for tax purposes, for example, as you will read shortly.

Criteria Used by the IRS. Often, the criteria for determining employee status are established by a statute or an administrative agency. Businesspersons should be aware that the Internal Revenue Service (IRS) has established its own criteria for determining whether a worker is an independent contractor or an employee. Until 1996 the IRS considered twenty factors in determining a worker's status, but these criteria were abolished in favor of rules that essentially encourage IRS examiners to focus on just one factor—the degree of control the business exercises over the worker.

The IRS tends to scrutinize closely a firm's classification of a worker as an independent contractor rather than an employee because independent contractors can avoid certain tax liabilities by taking advantage of business organizational forms available to small businesses. Even though a firm classifies a worker as an independent contractor, if the IRS decides that the worker should be classified as an employee, the employer will be responsible for paying any applicable Social Security, withholding, and unemployment taxes.

Employee Status and "Works for Hire." Under the Copyright Act of 1976, any copyrighted work created by an employee within the scope of her or his employment at the request of the employer is a "work for hire," and the employer owns the copyright to the work. When an employer hires an independent contractor—a freelance artist, writer, or computer programmer, for example—the independent contractor owns the copyright unless the parties agree in writing that the work is a "work for hire" and the work falls into one of nine specific categories, including audiovisual and other works.

The following case involved a dispute over ownership rights in a computer program. The outcome of the case hinged on whether the creator of the program, at the time it was created, was an employee or an independent contractor.

CASE 22.1 Graham v. James

United States Court of Appeals,
Second Circuit, 1998.
144 F.3d 229.
**http://www.findlaw.com/casecode/courts/
2nd.html**[a]

FACTS Richard Graham marketed CD-ROM discs containing compilations of shareware, freeware, and public-domain software.[b] With five to ten thousand programs per disc, Graham needed a file-retrieval program to allow users to access the software on the discs. Larry James agreed to create the program in exchange for, among other things, credit on the final product. James built into the final version of the program a notice attributing authorship and copyright to himself. Graham removed the notice, claiming that the program was a work for hire and the copyright was his. Graham used the program on several subsequent releases. When James sold the program to another CD-ROM publisher, Graham

filed a suit in a federal district court against James, alleging, among other things, copyright infringement. The court ruled that James was an independent contractor and that he owned the copyright. Graham appealed the ruling.

ISSUE Is a skilled person who controls the manner and method of his work, who is paid no employee benefits and has no payroll taxes withheld, and who is engaged on a project-by-project basis an independent contractor?

DECISION Yes. The U.S. Court of Appeals for the Second Circuit affirmed the lower court's judgment on this issue. The court agreed that James owned the copyright because he was an independent contractor when he developed the program.

REASON The court acknowledged that under the Copyright Act, work done by an employee is work for hire for which the employer owns the copyright. In determining whether a hired party is an employee, the court stated that the important factors are "(i) the hiring party's right to control the manner and means of creation; (ii) the skill required; (iii) the provision of employee benefits; (iv) the tax treatment of the hired party; and (v) whether the hiring party had the right to assign additional projects to the hired party." The court concluded that in this case, these factors favored James.

FOR CRITICAL ANALYSIS—Economic Consideration
What are some other advantages of being an independent contractor? What might be some disadvantages?

---

a. This is a page with links to some of the opinions of the U.S. Court of Appeals for the Second Circuit. In the "Party Name Search" Section, key in "Graham" and then click on "Search." When that page opens, scroll down the list of cases to the *Graham* case and click on the link to access it. This is part of the FindLaw (now a part of West Group) Web site.

b. *Shareware* is software released to the public to sample, with the understanding that anyone using it will register with the author and pay a fee. *Freeware* is software available for free use. *Public-domain software* is software unprotected by copyright.

Agency Formation

Agency relationships normally are consensual; that is, they come about by voluntary consent and agreement between the parties. Generally, the agreement need not be in writing,[2] and consideration is not required.

A principal must have contractual capacity. A person who cannot legally enter into contracts directly should not be allowed to do so indirectly through an agent. Because an agent derives the authority to enter into contracts from the principal and because a contract made by an agent is legally viewed as a contract of the principal, it is immaterial whether the agent personally has the legal capacity to make that contract. Thus, a minor can be an agent but in some states cannot be a principal appointing an agent.[3] (When a minor is permitted to be a principal, however, any resulting contracts will be voidable by the minor principal but not by the adult third party.) In sum, any person can be an agent, regardless of whether he or she has the capacity to contract. Even a person who is legally incompetent can be appointed an agent.

An agency relationship can be created for any legal purpose. An agency relationship that is created for an illegal purpose or that is contrary to public policy is unenforceable. ●**EXAMPLE #1** Suppose that Sharp (as principal) contracts with Blesh (as agent) to sell illegal narcotics. This agency relationship is unenforceable because selling illegal narcotics is a felony and is contrary to public policy.● It is also illegal for medical doctors and other licensed professionals to employ unlicensed agents to perform professional actions.

Generally, an agency relationship can arise in four ways: by agreement of the parties, by ratification, by estoppel, and by operation of law. We look here at each of these possibilities.

AGENCY BY AGREEMENT

Because an agency relationship is, by definition, consensual, normally it must be based on an express or implied agreement that the agent will act for the principal and that the principal agrees to have the agent so act. An agency agreement can take the form of an express written contract. ●**EXAMPLE #2** Renato enters into a written agreement with Troy, a real estate agent, to sell Renato's house. An agency relationship exists between Renato and Troy for the sale of the house and is detailed in a document that both parties sign.●

Many express agency agreements are oral. ●**EXAMPLE #3** Suppose that Renato asks Cary, a gardener, to contract with others for the care of his lawn on a regular basis. Cary agrees. In this situation, an agency relationship exists between Renato and Cary for the lawn care.●

An agency agreement can also be implied by conduct. ●**EXAMPLE #4** A hotel expressly allows only Boris Koontz to park cars, but Boris has no employment contract there. The hotel's manager tells Boris when to work, as well as where and how to park the cars. The hotel's conduct amounts to a manifestation of its willingness to have Boris park its customers' cars, and Boris can infer from the hotel's conduct that he has authority to act as a parking valet. It can be inferred that Boris is an agent-employee for the hotel, his purpose being to provide valet parking services for hotel guests.●

AGENCY BY RATIFICATION

On occasion, a person who is in fact not an agent (or who is an agent acting outside the scope of his or her authority) may make a contract on behalf of another (a principal). If the principal approves or affirms that contract by word or by action, an agency relationship is created by **ratification**. Ratification is a question of intent, and intent can be expressed by either words or conduct. The basic requirements for ratification are discussed later in this chapter.

AGENCY BY ESTOPPEL

When a principal causes a third person to believe that another person is his or her agent, and the third person deals with the supposed agent, the principal is "estopped to deny" the agency relationship. In such a situation, the principal's actions create the appearance of an agency that does not in fact exist.

●**EXAMPLE #5** Suppose that Andrew accompanies Charles, a seed sales representative, to call on a customer, Steve, the proprietor of the General Seed Store. Andrew has done independent sales work but has never signed an employment agreement with Charles. Charles boasts to Steve that he wishes he had three more assistants "just like Andrew." Steve has reason to believe from Charles's statements that Andrew is an agent for Charles. Steve then places seed orders with Andrew. If Charles does not correct the impression that Andrew is an agent, Charles will be

---

[2] There are two main exceptions to the statement that agency agreements need not be in writing: (1) Whenever agency authority empowers the agent to enter into a contract that the Statute of Frauds requires to be in writing, the agent's authority from the principal must likewise be in writing (this is called the *equal dignity rule*, to be discussed later in this chapter). (2) A power of attorney, which confers authority to an agent, must be in writing.

[3] Some courts have granted exceptions to allow a minor to appoint an agent for the limited purpose of contracting for the minor's necessities of life. See *Casey v. Kastel*, 237 N.Y. 305, 142 N.E. 671 (1924).

bound to fill the orders just as if Andrew were really Charles's agent. Charles's representation to Steve created the impression that Andrew was Charles's agent and had authority to solicit orders.●

The acts or declarations of a purported *agent* in and of themselves do not create an agency by estoppel. Rather, it is the deeds or statements of the principal that create an agency by estoppel. ● **EXAMPLE #6** Suppose that Olivia walks into Dru's Dress Boutique and claims to be a sales agent for an exclusive Paris dress designer, Pierre Clinet. Dru has never had business relations with Pierre Clinet. Based on Olivia's claim, however, Dru gives Olivia an order and prepays 15 percent of the sales price. Olivia is not an agent, and the dresses are never delivered. Dru cannot hold Pierre Clinet liable. Olivia's acts and declarations alone do not create an agency by estoppel.●

In addition, to assert the creation of an agency by estoppel, the third person must prove that she or he *reasonably* believed that an agency relationship existed and that the agent had authority. Facts and circumstances must show that an ordinary, prudent person familiar with business practice and custom would have been justified in concluding that the agent had authority.

AGENCY BY OPERATION OF LAW

In certain other situations, the courts will also find an agency relationship in the absence of a formal agreement. This may occur in family relationships. For example, suppose one spouse purchases certain basic necessaries and charges them to the other spouse's charge account. The courts will often rule that the latter is liable for payment for the necessaries, either because of a social policy of promoting the general welfare of the spouse or because of a legal duty to supply necessaries to family members.

Agency by operation of law may also occur in emergency situations, when the agent's failure to act outside the scope of his or her authority would cause the principal substantial loss. If the agent is unable to contact the principal, the courts will often grant this emergency power. For example, a railroad engineer may contract on behalf of her or his employer for medical care for an injured motorist hit by the train.

Duties of Agents and Principals

The principal-agent relationship gives rise to duties that govern both parties' conduct. As discussed previously, an agency relationship is *fiduciary*—one of trust. In a fiduciary relationship, each party owes the other the duty to act with the utmost good faith.

We now examine the various duties of agents and principals. In general, for every duty of the principal, the agent has a corresponding right, and vice versa. When one party to the agency relationship violates his or her duty to the other party, the remedies available to the nonbreaching party arise out of contract and tort law. These remedies include monetary damages, termination of the agency relationship, injunction, and required accountings.

AGENT'S DUTIES TO THE PRINCIPAL

Generally, the agent owes the principal five duties—performance, notification, loyalty, obedience, and accounting.

Performance. An implied condition in every agency contract is the agent's agreement to use reasonable diligence and skill in performing the work. When an agent fails to perform her or his duties entirely, liability for breach of contract normally will result. The degree of skill or care required of an agent is usually that expected of a reasonable person under similar circumstances. Generally, this is interpreted to mean ordinary care. An agent may, however, have represented himself or herself as possessing special skills (such as those that an accountant or attorney possesses). In these situations, the agent is expected to exercise the skill or skills claimed. Failure to do so constitutes a breach of the agent's duty.

Not all agency relationships are based on contract. In some situations, an agent acts gratuitously—that is, not for money. A gratuitous agent cannot be liable for breach of contract, as there is no contract; he or she is subject only to tort liability. Once a gratuitous agent has begun to act in an agency capacity, he or she has the duty to continue to perform in that capacity in an acceptable manner and is subject to the same standards of care and duty to perform as other agents.

Notification. According to a maxim in agency law, notice to the agent is notice to the principal. An agent is thus required to notify the principal of all matters that come to her or his attention concerning the subject matter of the agency. This is the duty of notification. The law assumes that the principal knows of any information acquired by the agent that is relevant to the agency—regardless of whether the agent actually passes on this information to the principal.

Loyalty. Loyalty is one of the most fundamental duties in a fiduciary relationship. Basically, the agent has the duty to act solely for the benefit of his or her principal and not in the interest of the agent or a third party. For example, an agent cannot represent two principals in the same transaction unless both know of the dual capacity and consent to it. The duty of loyalty also means that any information or knowledge acquired through the agency relationship is considered confidential. It would be a breach of loyalty to disclose such information either during the agency relationship or after its termination. Typical examples of confidential information are trade secrets and customer lists compiled by the principal.

In short, the agent's loyalty must be undivided. The agent's actions must be strictly for the benefit of the principal and must not result in any secret profit for the agent. ●**EXAMPLE #7** Suppose that Ryder contracts with Alton, a

real estate agent, to sell Ryder's property. Alton knows that he can find a buyer who will pay substantially more for the property than Ryder is asking. If Alton were to secretly purchase Ryder's property, however, and then sell it at a profit to another buyer, Alton would breach his duty of loyalty as Ryder's agent. Alton has a duty to act in Ryder's best interests and can only become the purchaser in this situation with Ryder's knowledge and approval.●

Does an agent breach the duty of loyalty if, while working for a principal, the agent solicits the principal's customers for a new competing business? That was an issue in the following case.

CASE 22.2 ▸ **American Express Financial Advisors, Inc. v. Topel**

United States District Court,
District of Colorado, 1999.
38 F.Supp.2d 1233.

ISSUE Had Topel breached his fiduciary duty of loyalty?

DECISION Yes. The court granted AMEX's motion for summary judgment in its favor with respect to this claim.

REASON The court held that Topel breached his duty of loyalty when, while working for his principal, he solicited his principal's customers for his new competing business. The court cited the rule that an agent has a duty to act solely for the benefit of the principal in all matters connected with an agency. "While an agent is entitled to make some preparations to compete with his principal after the termination of their relationship," the court acknowledged, "an agent violates his duty of loyalty if he engages in pre-termination solicitation of customers for a new competing business." That Topel did not solicit Benavidez's business until after Topel left AMEX "does not negate the testimony of other customers that he solicited their business for Multi-Financial while he was still affiliated with AMEX." As for the letter that Topel sent to all of his clients before resigning, "many customers had already signed new account forms with Multi-Financial by the time this neutral letter was purportedly sent."

FACTS Stephen Topel worked as a financial planner for American Express Financial Advisors, Inc. (AMEX), beginning in April 1992. More than four years later, Topel decided to resign to work for Multi-Financial Securities Corporation, an AMEX competitor. Before resigning, Topel encouraged his customers to liquidate their AMEX holdings and sent them new account forms for Multi-Financial. He ignored the request of customers James and Nancy Hemming to keep their investments with AMEX. In a letter on AMEX letterhead, Topel told Chris and Teresa Mammel to liquidate their AMEX holdings and invest in Multi-Financial's products. Another couple, Mr. and Ms. Rogers, changed their investments on Topel's advice. Before leaving AMEX, Topel sent a letter to all of his clients telling them that he was ending his relationship with AMEX and that their accounts would be assigned to another AMEX adviser. After Topel resigned in May 1997, he solicited the business of Theodore Benavidez, another AMEX customer. AMEX filed a suit in a federal district court against Topel, alleging, among other things, breach of fiduciary duty (duty of loyalty) and seeking damages. AMEX filed a motion for summary judgment on this issue.

FOR CRITICAL ANALYSIS—Ethical Consideration
Can you think of any situations in which the duty of loyalty to one's employer could come into conflict with other duties? Explain.

Obedience. When acting on behalf of a principal, an agent has a duty to follow all lawful and clearly stated instructions of the principal. Any deviation from such instructions is a violation of this duty. During emergency situations, however, when the principal cannot be con-

sulted, the agent may deviate from the instructions without violating this duty. Whenever instructions are not clearly stated, the agent can fulfill the duty of obedience by acting in good faith and in a manner reasonable under the circumstances.

Accounting. Unless an agent and a principal agree otherwise, the agent has the duty to keep and make available to the principal an account of all property and money received and paid out on behalf of the principal. This includes gifts from third persons in connection with the agency. For example, a gift from a customer to a salesperson for prompt deliveries made by the salesperson's firm, in the absence of a company policy to the contrary, belongs to the firm. The agent has a duty to maintain separate accounts for the principal's funds and for the agent's personal funds, and no intermingling of these accounts is allowed.

PRINCIPAL'S DUTIES TO THE AGENT

The principal also owes certain duties to the agent. These duties relate to compensation, reimbursement and indemnification, cooperation, and safe working conditions.

Compensation. In general, when a principal requests certain services from an agent, the agent reasonably expects payment. The principal therefore has a duty to pay the agent for services rendered. For example, when an accountant or an attorney is asked to act as an agent, an agreement to compensate the agent for such service is implied. The principal also has a duty to pay that compensation in a timely manner. Except in a gratuitous agency relationship, in which an agent does not act for money, the principal must pay the agreed-on value for an agent's services. If no amount has been expressly agreed on, the principal owes the agent the customary compensation for such services.

Reimbursement and Indemnification. Whenever an agent disburses sums of money to fulfill the request of the principal or to pay for necessary expenses in the course of a reasonable performance of his or her agency duties, the principal has the duty to reimburse the agent for these payments. Agents cannot recover for expenses incurred by their own misconduct or negligence, however.

Subject to the terms of the agency agreement, the principal has the duty to compensate, or *indemnify,* an agent for liabilities incurred because of authorized and lawful acts and transactions. For example, if the principal fails to perform a contract formed by the agent with a third party and the third party then sues the agent, the principal is obligated to compensate the agent for any costs incurred in defending against the lawsuit.

Additionally, the principal must indemnify (pay) the agent for the value of benefits that the agent confers on the principal. The amount of indemnification is usually specified in the agency contract. If it is not, the courts will look to the nature of the business and the type of loss to determine the amount.

Cooperation. A principal has a duty to cooperate with the agent and to assist the agent in performing his or her duties. The principal must do nothing to prevent such performance.

● **EXAMPLE #8** Suppose that Akers (the principal) grants Johnson (the agent) an exclusive territory within which Johnson may sell Akers's products, thus creating an exclusive agency. In this situation, Akers cannot compete with Johnson within that territory—or appoint or allow another agent to so compete—because this would violate the exclusive agency. If Akers did so, he would be exposed to liability for Johnson's lost sales or profits.●

Safe Working Conditions. The common law requires the principal to provide safe working premises, equipment, and conditions for all agents and employees. The principal has a duty to inspect the working conditions and to warn agents and employees about any unsafe areas. When the agency is one of employment, the employer's liability and the safety standards with which the employer must comply normally are covered by federal and state statutes and regulations (see Chapter 23).

Agent's Authority

An agent's authority to act can be either *actual* (express or implied) or *apparent.* If an agent contracts outside the scope of his or her authority, the principal may still become liable by ratifying the contract.

ACTUAL AUTHORITY

As indicated, an agent's actual authority can be express or implied. We look here at both of these forms of actual authority.

Express Authority. *Express authority* is authority declared in clear, direct, and definite terms. Express authority can be given orally or in writing. In most states, the **equal dignity rule** requires that if the contract being executed is or must be in writing, then the agent's authority must also be in writing.[4] Failure to comply with the equal dignity rule can make a contract voidable *at the option of the principal.* The law regards the contract at that point as a mere offer. If the principal decides to accept the offer, acceptance must be in writing.

---

[4] An exception to the equal dignity rule exists in modern business practice. An executive officer of a corporation, when acting for the corporation in an ordinary business situation, is not required to obtain written authority from the corporation.

● **EXAMPLE #9** Klee (the principal) orally asks Parkinson (the agent) to sell a ranch that Klee owns. Parkinson finds a buyer and signs a sales contract (a contract for an interest in realty must be in writing) on behalf of Klee to sell the ranch. The buyer cannot enforce the contract unless Klee subsequently ratifies Parkinson's agency status *in writing.* Once Parkinson's agency status is ratified, either party can enforce rights under the contract.●

The equal dignity rule does not apply when an agent acts in the presence of a principal or when the agent's act of signing is merely perfunctory. Thus, if Dickens (the principal) negotiates a contract but is called out of town the day it is to be signed and orally authorizes Santini to sign the contract, the oral authorization is sufficient.

Giving an agent a **power of attorney** confers express authority.[5] The power of attorney normally is a written document and is usually notarized. (A document is notarized when a **notary public**—a public official authorized to attest to the authenticity of signatures—signs and dates the document and imprints it with his or her seal of authority.) A power of attorney can be special (permitting the agent to do specified acts only), or it can be general (permitting the agent to transact all business for the principal). An agent holding a power of attorney for a client is authorized to act *only* on the principal's behalf when exercising that power. An ordinary power of attorney terminates on the incapacity or death of the person giving the power.[6] Exhibit 22–1 shows a sample power of attorney.

Implied Authority. *Implied authority* can be (1) conferred by custom, (2) inferred from the position the agent occupies, or (3) inferred as being reasonably necessary to carry out express authority. ● **EXAMPLE #10** Mueller is employed by Al's Supermarket to manage one of its stores. Al's has not expressly stated that Mueller has authority to contract with third persons. In this situation, however, authority to manage a business implies authority to do what is reasonably required (as is customary or can be inferred from a manager's position) to operate the business. Reasonably required actions include creating contracts to hire employees, to buy merchandise and equipment, and to arrange for advertising the products sold in the store.●

---

[5] An agent who holds the power of attorney is called an *attorney-in-fact* for the principal. The holder does not have to be an attorney-at-law (and often is not).

[6] A *durable* power of attorney, however, provides an agent with very broad powers to act and make decisions for the principal and specifies that it is not affected by the principal's incapacity. An elderly person, for example, might grant a durable power of attorney to provide for the handling of property and investments should she or he become incompetent.

APPARENT AUTHORITY

Actual authority arises from what the principal manifests *to the agent.* Apparent authority exists when the principal, by either words or actions, causes a *third party* reasonably to believe that an agent has authority to act, even though the agent has no express or implied authority. If the third party changes his or her position in reliance on the principal's representations, the principal may be *estopped* from denying that the agent had authority. Note that here, in contrast to agency formation by estoppel, the issue has to do with the apparent authority of an *agent,* not the apparent authority of a person who is in fact not an agent.

● **EXAMPLE #11** Suppose that a traveling salesperson, Anderson (the agent), is authorized to take customers' orders. Anderson, however, does not deliver the ordered goods and is not authorized to collect payments for the goods. A customer, Byron, pays Anderson for a solicited order. Anderson then takes the payment to the principal's accounting department, and an accountant accepts the payment and sends Byron a receipt. This procedure is thereafter followed for other orders solicited from and paid for by Byron. Later, Anderson solicits an order, and Byron pays her as before. This time, however, Anderson absconds with the money. Can Byron claim that the payment to the agent was authorized and was thus, in effect, a payment to the principal?

The answer is normally yes, because the principal's repeated acts of accepting Byron's payment led Byron reasonably to expect that Anderson had authority to receive payments for goods solicited. Although Anderson did not have express or implied authority, the principal's conduct gave Anderson apparent authority to collect. In this situation, the principal would be estopped from denying that Anderson had authority to collect payments.●

RATIFICATION

As already mentioned, *ratification* is the affirmation of a previously unauthorized contract. Ratification can be either express or implied. If the principal does not ratify, there is no contract binding on the principal, and the third party's agreement with the agent is viewed merely as an unaccepted offer. The third party can revoke the offer at any time prior to the principal's ratification without liability. Death or incapacity of the third party before ratification will void an unauthorized contract.

The requirements for ratification can be summarized as follows:

① The purported agent must have acted on behalf of a principal who subsequently ratifies the action.

② The principal must know of all material facts involved in the transaction.

EXHIBIT 22–1   A SAMPLE POWER OF ATTORNEY

POWER OF ATTORNEY
GENERAL

Know All Men by These Presents: That I, _____

_____

the undersigned (jointly and severally, if more than one) hereby make, constitute and appoint _____

_____

as a true and lawful Attorney for me and in my name, place and stead and for my use and benefit:

(a) To ask, demand, sue for, recover, collect and receive each and every sum of money, debt, account, legacy, bequest, interest, dividend, annuity and demand (which now is or hereafter shall become due, owing or payable) belonging to or claimed by me, and to use and take any lawful means for the recovery thereof by legal process or otherwise, and to execute and deliver a satisfaction or release therefore, together with the right and power to compromise or compound any claim or demand;

(b) To exercise any or all of the following powers as to real property, any interest therein and/or any building thereon: To contract for, purchase, receive and take possession thereof and or evidence of title thereto; to lease the same for any term or purpose, including leases for business, residence, and oil and/or mineral development; to sell, exchange, grant or convey the same with or without warranty; and to mortgage, transfer in trust, or otherwise encumber or hypothecate the same to secure payment of a negotiable or non-negotiable note or performance of any obligation or agreement;

(c) To exercise any or all of the following powers as to all kinds of personal property and goods, wares and merchandise, choses in action and other property in possession or in action: To contract for, buy, sell, exchange, transfer and in any legal manner deal in and with the same; and to mortgage, transfer in trust, or otherwise encumber or hypothecate the same to secure payment of a negotiable or non-negotiable note or performance of any obligation or agreement;

(d) To borrow money and to execute and deliver negotiable or non-negotiable notes therefore with or without security; and to loan money and receive negotiable or non-negotiable notes therefore with such security as he shall deem proper;

(e) To create, amend, supplement and terminate any trust and to instruct and advise the trustee of any trust wherein I am or may be trustor or beneficiary; to represent and vote stock, exercise stock rights, accept and deal with any dividend, distribution or bonus, join in any corporate financing, reorganization, merger, liquidation, consolidation or other action and the extension, compromise, conversion, adjustment, enforcement or foreclosure, singly or in conjunction with others, of any corporate stock, bond, note, debenture or other security; to compound, compromise, adjust, settle and satisfy any obligation, secured or unsecured, owing by or to me and to give or accept any property and/or money whether or not equal to or less in value than the amount owing in payment, settlement or satisfaction thereof;

(f) To transact business of any kind or class and as my act and deed to sign, execute, acknowledge and deliver any deed, lease, assignment of lease, covenant, indenture, indemnity, agreement, mortgage, deed of trust, assignment of mortgage or of the beneficial interest under deed of trust, extension or renewal of any obligation, subordination or waiver of priority, hypothecation, bottomry, charter-party, bill of lading, bill of sale, bill, bond, note, whether negotiable or non-negotiable, receipt, evidence of debt, full or partial release or satisfaction of mortgage, judgment and other debt, request for partial or full reconveyance of deed of trust and such other instruments in writing of any kind or class as may be necessary or proper in the premises.

Giving and Granting unto my said Attorney full power and authority to do so and perform all and every act and thing whatsoever requisite, necessary or appropriate to be done in and about the premises as fully to all intents and purposes as I might or could do if personally present, hereby ratifying all that my said Attorney shall lawfully do or cause to be done by virtue of these presents. The powers and authority hereby conferred upon my said Attorney shall be applicable to all real and personal property or interests therein now owned or hereafter acquired by me and wherever situated.

My said Attorney is empowered hereby to determine in his sole discretion the time when, purpose for and manner in which any power herein conferred upon him shall be exercised, and the conditions, provisions and covenants of any instrument or document which may be executed by him pursuant hereto; and in the acquisition or disposition of real or personal property, my said Attorney shall have exclusive power to fix the terms thereof for cash, credit and/or property, and if on credit with or without security.

The undersigned, if a married woman, hereby further authorizes and empowers my said Attorney, as my duly authorized agent, to join in my behalf, in the execution of any instrument by which any community real property or any interest therein, now owned or hereafter acquired by my spouse and myself, or either of us, is sold, leased, encumbered, or conveyed.

When the context so requires, the masculine gender includes the feminine and/or neuter, and the singular number includes the plural.

WITNESS my hand this _____ day of _____ , 20 ____

_____   _____

_____   _____

State of California
   County of _____ } SS.

On _____ , before me, the undersigned, a Notary Public in and for said
State, personally appeared _____

_____

known to me to be the person _____ whose name _____ subscribed
to the within instrument and acknowledged that _____ executed the same.

Witness my hand and official seal.   (Seal) _____

                                                      Notary Public in and for said State.

③ The agent's act must be affirmed in its entirety by the principal.

④ The principal must have the legal capacity to authorize the transaction at the time the agent engages in the act and at the time the principal ratifies.

⑤ The principal's affirmance must occur prior to the withdrawal of the third party from the transaction.

⑥ The principal must observe the same formalities when approving the act purportedly done by the agent on the principal's behalf as would have been required to authorize it initially.

Liability in Agency Relationships

Frequently, the issue arises as to which party, the principal or the agent, should be held liable for the contracts formed by the agent or for the torts or crimes committed by the agent. We look here at these aspects of agency law.

LIABILITY FOR CONTRACTS

An important consideration in determining liability for a contract formed by an agent is whether the third party knew the identity of the principal at the time the contract was made. The *Restatement (Second) of Agency*, Section 4, classifies principals as disclosed, partially disclosed, or undisclosed.

Disclosed or Partially Disclosed Principal. A principal whose identity is known to the third party at the time the agent makes the contract is a **disclosed principal**. ● EXAMPLE #12 Martha Evans, president of Comquant Computing, Inc., purchases ten new copiers for the business from ABC Copiers. She signs the purchase order, "Comquant Computing, Inc., by Martha Evans, President." In this situation, the principal (Comquant Computing, Inc.) is clearly disclosed to the third party (ABC Copiers). ●

The identity of a **partially disclosed principal** is not known by the third party, but the third party knows that the agent is or may be acting for a principal at the time the contract is made. ● EXAMPLE #13 Sarah has contracted with a real estate agent to sell certain property. She wishes to keep her identity a secret, but the agent can make it perfectly clear to a purchaser of the real estate that the agent is acting in an agency capacity for a principal. In this situation, Sarah is a partially disclosed principal. ●

A disclosed or partially disclosed principal is liable to a third party for a contract made by an agent who is acting within the scope of her or his authority. Ordinarily, if the principal is disclosed or partially disclosed, the agent has no contractual liability if the principal or the third party does not perform the contract. If the agent exceeds the scope of her or his authority and the principal fails to ratify the contract, however, the third party cannot hold the principal liable for nonperformance. In such situations, the agent is generally liable unless the third party knew of the agent's lack of authority. The following case illustrates the rules that apply to contracts signed by agents on behalf of fully disclosed principals.

CASE 22.3 McBride v. Taxman Corp.

Appellate Court of Illinois,
First District, 2002.
327 Ill.App.3d 992,
765 N.E.2d 51,
262 Ill.Dec. 225.
http://state.il.us/court/default.htm[a]

FACTS Walgreens Company entered into a lease with Taxman Corporation to operate a drugstore in Kedzie Plaza, a shopping center in Chicago, Illinois, owned by Kedzie Plaza Associates; Taxman was the center's property manager. The lease required the "Landlord" to promptly remove snow and ice from the center's sidewalks. Taxman also signed, on behalf of Kedzie Associates, an agreement with Arctic Snow and Ice Control, Inc., to remove ice and snow from the sidewalks surrounding the Walgreens store. On January 27, 1996, Grace McBride, a Walgreens employee, slipped and fell on snow and ice outside the entrance to the store. McBride filed a suit in an Illinois state court against Taxman and others, alleging, among other things, that Taxman had negligently failed to remove the accumulation of ice and snow.[b] Taxman

---

a. On this page, click on "Appellate Court of Illinois." On the next page, in the "Appellate Court Documents" section, click on "Appellate Court Opinions." In the result, in the "Appellate Court" section, click on "2002." On the next page, in the "First District" section, click on "January." Finally, scroll to the bottom of the chart and click on the case name to access the opinion. The state of Illinois maintains this Web site.

b. McBride included in her suit complaints against Walgreens and Kedzie Associates but settled these complaints before trial.

CASE 22.3—Continued

filed a motion for summary judgment in its favor, which the court granted. McBride appealed to a state intermediate appellate court.

ISSUE Could Taxman be held liable for McBride's injuries?

DECISION No. The state intermediate appellate court affirmed the judgment of the lower court. The appellate court held that Taxman entered into the snow removal contracts only as the agent of the owner, whose identity was fully disclosed.

REASON The court reasoned that as the agent for a disclosed principal, Taxman had no liability for the nonperformance of the principal or the third party to the contract. The court pointed out that "the Arctic proposal and contract was

signed 'Kedzie Associates by the Taxman.' The Taxman-drafted portion of the contract contained a line above the signature of Taxman's director or property management stating 'The Taxman Corporation, agent for per contracts attached.' The latter document specifically stated that the contract was not an obligation of Taxman and that all liabilities were those of the owner and not Taxman. We conclude that Taxman was the management company for the property owner and entered into the two contracts for snow and ice removal only as the owner's agent. Taxman did not assume a contractual obligation to remove snow and ice; it merely retained Arctic as a contractor on behalf of the owner."

FOR CRITICAL ANALYSIS—Economic Consideration
Suppose that the Arctic contract had not identified Kedzie as the principal. Would the court's decision in this case have been different?

Undisclosed Principal. The identity of an **undisclosed principal** is totally unknown to the third party. Furthermore, the third party has no knowledge that the agent is acting in an agency capacity at the time the contract is made.

When neither the fact of agency nor the identity of the principal is disclosed, a third party is deemed to be dealing with the agent personally, and the agent is liable as a party to the contract. If an agent has acted within the scope of his or her authority, the undisclosed principal is also liable as a party to the contract, just as if the principal had been fully disclosed at the time the contract was made. Conversely, the undisclosed principal can hold the third party to the contract, unless (1) the undisclosed principal was expressly excluded as a party in the contract, (2) the contract is a negotiable instrument signed by the agent with no indication of signing in a representative capacity, or (3) the performance of the agent is personal to the contract, allowing the third party to refuse the principal's performance.

LIABILITY FOR TORTS AND CRIMES

Obviously, any person, including an agent, is liable for her or his own torts and crimes. Whether a principal can also be held liable for an agent's torts and crimes depends on several factors, which we examine here. In some situations, a principal may be held liable not only for the torts of an agent but also for the torts committed by an independent contractor.

Liability for Agent's Torts. As mentioned, an agent is liable for her or his own torts. A principal may also be liable for an agent's torts under the doctrine of *respondeat*

superior,[7] a Latin term meaning "let the master respond." This doctrine is similar to the theory of strict liability discussed in Chapter 17. The doctrine imposes vicarious (indirect) liability on the employer without regard to the personal fault of the employer for torts committed by an employee in the course or scope of employment.

Scope of Employment. The key to determining whether a principal may be liable for the torts of an agent under the doctrine of *respondeat superior* is whether the torts are committed within the scope of the agency or employment. The *Restatement (Second) of Agency*, Section 229, indicates the factors that today's courts will consider in determining whether a particular act occurred within the course and scope of employment. These factors are as follows:

1. Whether the act was authorized by the employer.
2. The time, place, and purpose of the act.
3. Whether the act was one commonly performed by employees on behalf of their employers.
4. The extent to which the employer's interest was advanced by the act.
5. The extent to which the private interests of the employee were involved.
6. Whether the employer furnished the means or instrumentality (for example, a truck or a machine) by which the injury was inflicted.

---

[7] Pronounced ree-*spahn*-dee-uht soo-*peer*-ee-your.

⑦ Whether the employer had reason to know that the employee would perform the act in question and whether the employee had ever done it before.

⑧ Whether the act involved the commission of a serious crime.

A useful insight into the "scope of employment" concept may be gained from Baron Parke's classic distinction between a "detour" and a "frolic" in the case of *Joel v. Morison* (1834).[8] In this case, the English court held that if a servant merely took a detour from his master's business, the master will be responsible. If, however, the servant was on a "frolic of his own" and not in any way "on his master's business," the master will not be liable.

Misrepresentation. A principal is exposed to tort liability whenever a third person sustains a loss due to the agent's misrepresentation. The principal's liability depends on whether the agent was actually or apparently authorized to make representations and whether such representations were made within the scope of the agency. The principal is always directly responsible for an agent's misrepresentation made within the scope of the agent's authority, whether the misrepresentation was made fraudulently or simply by the agent's mistake or oversight.

Liability for Independent Contractor's Torts. Generally, the principal is not liable for physical harm caused to a third person by the negligent act of an independent contractor in the performance of the contract. This is because the employer does not have *the right to control* the details of an independent contractor's performance. Exceptions to this rule are made in certain situations, however, as when particularly hazardous activities are involved. Examples of such activities include blasting operations, the transportation of highly volatile chemicals, and the use of poisonous gases. In these situations, a principal cannot be shielded from liability merely by using an independent contractor. Strict liability is imposed on the principal as a matter of law and, in some states, by statute.

Liability for Agent's Crimes. An agent is liable for his or her own crimes. A principal or employer is not liable for an agent's crime even if the crime was committed within the scope of authority or employment—unless the principal participated by conspiracy or other action. In some jurisdictions, under specific statutes, a principal may be liable for an agent's violation, in the course and scope of employment, of regulations, such as those governing sanitation, prices, weights, and the sale of liquor.

---

[8] 6 Car. & P. 501, 172 Eng. Reprint 1338 (1834).

Agency Termination

Agency law is similar to contract law in that both an agency and a contract can be terminated by an act of the parties or by operation of law. Once the relationship between the principal and the agent has ended, the agent no longer has the right to bind the principal. For an agent's apparent authority to be terminated, however, third persons may also need to be notified when the agency has been terminated.

TERMINATION BY ACT OF THE PARTIES

An agency may be terminated by act of the parties in several ways, including those discussed here.

Lapse of Time. An agency agreement may specify the time period during which the agency relationship will exist. If so, the agency ends when that time period expires. For example, if the parties agree that the agency will begin on January 1, 2004, and end on December 31, 2005, the agency is automatically terminated on December 31, 2005. If no definite time is stated, the agency continues for a reasonable time and can be terminated at will by either party. What constitutes a "reasonable time" depends, of course, on the circumstances and the nature of the agency relationship.

Purpose Achieved. An agent can be employed to accomplish a particular objective, such as the purchase of stock for a cattle rancher. In that situation, the agency automatically ends after the cattle have been purchased. If more than one agent is employed to accomplish the same purpose, such as the sale of real estate, the first agent to complete the sale automatically terminates the agency relationship for all the others.

Occurrence of a Specific Event. An agency can be created to terminate on the happening of a certain event. If Posner appoints Rubik to handle his business affairs while he is away, the agency automatically terminates when Posner returns.

Mutual Agreement. Recall from the chapters on contract law that parties can cancel (rescind) a contract by mutually agreeing to terminate the contractual relationship. The same holds true under agency law regardless of whether the agency contract is in writing or whether it is for a specific duration.

Termination by One Party. As a general rule, either party can terminate the agency relationship. The agent's act is called a *renunciation of authority*. The principal's act is referred to as a *revocation of authority*. Although both parties have the power to terminate the agency, they may not possess the right to do so.

Wrongful termination can subject the canceling party to a suit for damages. ●**EXAMPLE #14** Rawlins has a one-year employment contract with Munro to act as an agent in return for $35,000. Munro can discharge Rawlins before the contract period expires (Munro has the power to breach the contract); however, Munro will be liable to Rawlins for money damages because Munro has no right to breach the contract.●

A special rule applies in an agency coupled with an interest. This type of agency is not an agency in the usual sense because it is created for the agent's benefit instead of for the principal's benefit. ●**EXAMPLE #15** Suppose that Julie borrows $5,000 from Rob, giving Rob some of her jewelry and signing a letter giving Rob the power to sell the jewelry as her agent if she fails to repay the loan. After receiving the $5,000 from Rob, Julie attempts to revoke Rob's authority to sell the jewelry as her agent. Julie would not succeed in this attempt because a principal cannot revoke an agency created for the agent's benefit.●

Notice of Termination. If the parties themselves have terminated the agency, it is the principal's duty to inform any third parties who know of the existence of the agency that it has been terminated (although notice of the termination may be given by others).

An agent's authority continues until the agent receives some notice of termination. Notice to third parties follows the general rule that an agent's *apparent* authority continues until the third party receives notice (from any source of information) that such authority has been terminated. The principal is expected to notify directly any third person who the principal knows has dealt with the agent. For third persons who have heard about the agency but have not yet dealt with the agent, *constructive notice* is sufficient.[9]

No particular form is required for notice of agency termination to be effective. The principal can actually notify the agent, or the agent can learn of the termination through some other means. ●**EXAMPLE #16** Manning bids on a shipment of steel, and Stone is hired as an agent to arrange transportation of the shipment. When Stone learns that Manning has lost the bid, Stone's authority to make the transportation arrangement terminates.●

If the agent's authority is written, it must be revoked in writing, and the writing must be shown to all people who saw the original writing that established the agency relationship. Sometimes, a written authorization (such as a power of attorney) contains an expiration date. The passage of the expiration date is sufficient notice of termination for third parties.

TERMINATION BY OPERATION OF LAW

Termination of an agency by operation of law occurs in the circumstances discussed here. Note that when an agency terminates by operation of law, there is no duty to notify third persons.

Death or Insanity. The general rule is that the death or mental incompetence of either the principal or the agent automatically and immediately terminates the ordinary agency relationship. Knowledge of the death is not required. ●**EXAMPLE #17** Suppose that Geer sends Pyron to China to purchase a rare painting. Before Pyron makes the purchase, Geer dies. Pyron's agent status is terminated at the moment of Geer's death, even though Pyron does not know that Geer has died.● Some states, however, have changed this common law rule by statute, and death does not terminate an agency coupled with an interest.

An agent's transactions that occur after the death of the principal are not binding on the principal's estate.[10] ●**EXAMPLE #18** Assume that Carson is hired by Perry to collect a debt from Thomas (a third party). Perry dies, but Carson, not knowing of Perry's death, still collects the money from Thomas. Thomas's payment to Carson is no longer legally sufficient to discharge Thomas's debt to Perry because Carson's authority to collect the money ended on Perry's death. If Carson absconds with the money, Thomas is still liable for the debt to Perry's estate.●

Impossibility. When the specific subject matter of an agency is destroyed or lost, the agency terminates. ●**EXAMPLE #19** Bullard employs Gonzalez to sell Bullard's house. Prior to the sale, the premises are destroyed by fire. In this situation, Gonzalez's agency and authority to sell Bullard's house terminate.● The agency also terminates when it is impossible for the agent to lawfully perform the agency.

---

[9] *Constructive notice* is information or knowledge of a fact imputed by law to a person if he or she could have discovered the fact by proper diligence. Constructive notice is often accomplished by newspaper publication.

[10] There is an exception to this rule in banking under which the bank, as the agent of the customer, can continue to exercise specific types of authority even after the customer has died or become mentally incompetent unless it has knowledge of the death or incompetence [UCC 4–405]. As noted in Chapter 19, even with knowledge of the customer's death, the bank has authority for ten days following the customer's death to honor checks in the absence of a stop-payment order.

Changed Circumstances. When an event occurs that has such an unusual effect on the subject matter of the agency that the agent can reasonably infer that the principal will not want the agency to continue, the agency terminates. ● EXAMPLE #20 Roberts hires Mullen to sell a tract of land for $20,000. Subsequently, Mullen learns that there is oil under the land and that the land is worth $1 million. The agency and Mullen's authority to sell the land for $20,000 are terminated. ●

Bankruptcy and War. Bankruptcy of the principal or the agent usually terminates the agency relationship. When the principal's country and the agent's country are at war with each other, the agency is terminated, or at least suspended.

Terms and Concepts

Chapter Summary   Agency Relationships

Agency Relationships (See pages 446–449.)	In a principal-agent relationship, an agent acts on behalf of and instead of the principal in dealing with third parties. An employee who deals with third parties is normally an agent. An independent contractor is not an employee, and the employer has no control over the details of physical performance. The independent contractor may or may not be an agent.
Agency Formation (See pages 450–451.)	1. *By agreement*—An agency relationship may be formed through express consent (oral or written) or implied by conduct.
	2. *By ratification*—The principal, either by act or agreement, ratifies the conduct of an agent who acted outside the scope of authority or the conduct of a person who is in fact not an agent.
	3. *By estoppel*—When the principal causes a third person to believe that another person is his or her agent, and the third person deals with the supposed agent in reasonable reliance on the agency's existence, the principal is "estopped to deny" the agency relationship.
	4. *By operation of law*—An agency relationship may arise based on a social duty (such as the need to support family members) or be created in emergency situations when the agent is unable to contact the principal.
Duties of Agents and Principals (See pages 451–453.)	1. *Duties of the agent*—
	a. Performance—The agent must use reasonable diligence and skill in performing her or his duties or use the special skills that the agent has represented to the principal that the agent possesses.
	b. Notification—The agent is required to notify the principal of all matters that come to his or her attention concerning the subject matter of the agency.
	c. Loyalty—The agent has a duty to act solely for the benefit of his or her principal and not in the interest of the agent or a third party.
	d. Obedience—The agent must follow all lawful and clearly stated instructions of the principal.

Chapter Summary — Agency Relationships—Continued

Duties of Agents and Principals—continued	e. Accounting—The agent has a duty to make available to the principal records of all property and money received and paid out on behalf of the principal. 2. *Duties of the principal*— a. Compensation—Except in a gratuitous agency relationship, the principal must pay the agreed-on value (or reasonable value) for an agent's services. b. Reimbursement and indemnification—The principal must reimburse the agent for all sums of money disbursed at the request of the principal and for all sums of money the agent disburses for necessary expenses in the course of reasonable performance of his or her agency duties. c. Cooperation—A principal must cooperate with and assist an agent in performing his or her duties. d. Safe working conditions—A principal must provide safe working conditions for the agent-employee.
Agent's Authority (See pages 453–456.)	1. *Express authority*—Can be oral or in writing. Authorization must be in writing if the agent is to execute a contract that must be in writing. 2. *Implied authority*—Authority customarily associated with the position of the agent or authority that is deemed necessary for the agent to carry out expressly authorized tasks. 3. *Apparent authority*—Exists when the principal, by word or action, causes a third party reasonably to believe that an agent has authority to act, even though the agent has no express or implied authority. 4. *Ratification*—The affirmation by the principal of an agent's unauthorized action or promise. For the ratification to be effective, the principal must be aware of all material facts.
Liability in Agency Relationships (See pages 456–458.)	1. *Liability for contracts*—If the principal's identity is disclosed or partially disclosed at the time the agent forms a contract with a third party, the principal is liable to the third party under the contract if the agent acted within the scope of his or her authority. If the principal's identity is undisclosed at the time of contract formation, the agent is personally liable to the third party, but if the agent acted within the scope of authority, the principal is also bound by the contract. 2. *Liability for agent's torts*—Under the doctrine of *respondeat superior,* the principal is liable for any harm caused to another through the agent's torts if the agent was acting within the scope of his or her employment at the time the harmful act occurred. The principal is also liable for an agent's misrepresentation, whether made knowingly or by mistake. 3. *Liability for independent contractor's torts*—A principal is not liable for harm caused by an independent contractor's negligence, unless hazardous activities are involved (in which situation the principal is strictly liable for any resulting harm) or other exceptions apply. 4. *Liability for agent's crimes*—An agent is responsible for his or her own crimes, even if the crimes were committed while the agent was acting within the scope of authority or employment. A principal will be liable for an agent's crime only if the principal participated by conspiracy or other action or (in some jurisdictions) if the agent violated certain government regulations in the course of employment.

(Continued)

Chapter Summary	Agency Relationships—Continued

| **Agency Termination**
(See pages 458–460.) | 1. *By act of the parties—*
   a. Lapse of time (when a definite time for the duration of the agency was agreed on when the agency was established).
   b. Purpose achieved.
   c. Occurrence of a specific event.
   d. Mutual rescission (requires mutual consent of principal and agent).
   e. Termination by act of either the principal (revocation) or the agent (renunciation). (A principal cannot revoke an agency coupled with an interest.)
   f. When an agency is terminated by act of the parties, all third persons who have previously dealt with the agency must be directly notified; constructive notice will suffice for all other third parties.
2. *By operation of law—*
   a. Death or mental incompetence of either the principal or the agent (except in an agency coupled with an interest).
   b. Impossibility (when the purpose of the agency cannot be achieved because of an event beyond the parties' control).
   c. Changed circumstances (in which it would be inequitable to require that the agency be continued).
   d. Bankruptcy of the principal or the agent, or war between the principal's and agent's countries.
   e. When an agency is terminated by operation of law, no notice to third parties is required. |

For Review

① What is the difference between an employee and an independent contractor?

② How do agency relationships arise?

③ What duties do agents and principals owe to each other?

④ When is a principal liable for the agent's actions with respect to third parties? When is the agent liable?

⑤ What are some of the ways in which an agency relationship can be terminated?

Questions and Case Problems

22–1. Agency Formation. Pete Gaffrey is a well-known, wealthy financier living in the city of Takima. Alan Winter, Gaffrey's friend, tells Til Borge that he (Winter) is Gaffrey's agent for the purchase of rare coins. Winter even shows Borge a local newspaper clipping mentioning Gaffrey's interest in coin collecting. Borge, knowing of Winter's friendship with Gaffrey, contracts with Winter to sell to Gaffrey a rare coin valued at $25,000. Winter takes the coin and disappears with it. On the date of contract payment, Borge seeks to collect from Gaffrey, claiming that Winter's agency made Gaffrey liable. Gaffrey does not deny that Winter was a friend, but he claims that Winter was never his agent. Discuss fully whether an agency was in existence at the time the contract for the rare coin was made.

22–2. Ratification by Principal. Springer was a political candidate running for congressional office. He was operating on a tight budget and instructed his campaign staff not to purchase any campaign materials without his explicit authoriza-

CHAPTER 22 • AGENCY RELATIONSHIPS

tion. In spite of these instructions, one of his campaign workers ordered Dubychek Printing Co. to print some promotional materials for Springer's campaign. When the printed materials were received, Springer did not return them but instead used them during his campaign. When Dubychek failed to obtain payment from Springer for the materials, he sued for recovery of the price. Springer contended that he was not liable on the sales contract because he had not authorized his agent to purchase the printing services. Dubychek argued that the campaign worker was Springer's agent and that the worker had authority to make the printing contract. Additionally, Dubychek claimed that even if the purchase was unauthorized, Springer's use of the materials constituted ratification of his agent's unauthorized purchase. Is Dubychek correct? Explain.

22–3. Agent's Duties to Principal. Iliana is a traveling sales agent. Iliana not only solicits orders but also delivers the goods and collects payments from her customers. Iliana places all payments in her private checking account and at the end of each month draws sufficient cash from her bank to cover the payments made. Giberson Corp., Iliana's employer, is totally unaware of this procedure. Because of a slowdown in the economy, Giberson tells all its sales personnel to offer 20 percent discounts on orders. Iliana solicits orders, but she offers only 15 percent discounts, pocketing the extra 5 percent paid by customers. Iliana has not lost any orders by this practice, and she is rated as one of Giberson's top salespersons. Giberson now learns of Iliana's actions. Discuss fully Giberson's rights in this matter.

22–4. Liability for Agent's Contracts. Michael Mosely works as a purchasing agent for Suharto Coal Supply, a partnership. Mosely has authority to purchase the coal needed by Suharto to satisfy the needs of its customers. While Mosely is leaving a coal mine from which he has just purchased a large quantity of coal, his car breaks down. He walks into a small roadside grocery store for help. While there, he runs into Wiley, who owns 360 acres back in the mountains with all mineral rights. Wiley, in need of money, offers to sell Mosely the property at $1,500 per acre. On inspection, Mosely concludes that the subsurface may contain valuable coal deposits. Mosely contracts to purchase the property for Suharto, signing the contract, "Suharto Coal Supply, Michael Mosely, agent." The closing date is set for August 1. Mosely takes the contract to the partnership. The managing partner is furious, as Suharto is not in the property business. Later, just before August 1, both Wiley and the partnership learn that the value of the land is at least $15,000 per acre. Discuss the rights of Suharto and Wiley concerning the land contract.

22–5. Liability for Employee's Acts. Federated Financial Reserve Corp. leases consumer and business equipment. As part of its credit approval and debt-collection practices, Federated hires credit collectors, whom it authorizes to obtain credit reports on its customers. Janice Caylor, a Federated collector, used this authority to obtain a report on Karen Jones, who was not a Federated customer but who was the ex-wife of Caylor's

roommate, Randy Lind. When Jones discovered that Lind had her address and how he had obtained it, she filed a suit in a federal district court against Federated and others. Jones claimed in part that they had violated the Fair Credit Reporting Act, the goal of which is to protect consumers from the improper use of credit reports. Under what theory might an employer be held liable for an agent-employee's violation of a statute? Does that theory apply in this case? Explain. [*Jones v. Federated Financial Reserve Corp.*, 144 F.3d 961 (6th Cir. 1998)]

22–6. Implied Authority. Juanita Miller filed a complaint in an Indiana state court against Red Arrow Ventures, Ltd., Thomas Hayes, and Claudia Langman, alleging that they had breached their promise to make payments on a promissory note issued to Miller. The defendants denied this allegation and asserted a counterclaim against Miller. After a trial, the judge announced that, although he would be ruling against the defendants, he had not yet determined what amount of damages would be awarded to Miller. Over the next three days, the parties' attorneys talked and agreed that the defendants would pay Miller $21,000. The attorneys exchanged correspondence acknowledging this settlement. When the defendants balked at paying this amount, the trial judge issued an order to enforce the settlement agreement. The defendants appealed to a state intermediate appellate court, arguing that they had not consented to the settlement agreement. What is the rule regarding the authority of an agent—in this case, the defendants' attorney—to agree to a settlement? How should the court apply the rule in this case? Why? [*Red Arrow Ventures, Ltd. v. Miller*, 692 N.E.2d 939 (Ind.App. 1998)]

22–7. Agent's Duties to Principal. Ana Barreto and Flavia Gugliuzzi asked Ruth Bennett, a real estate salesperson who worked for Smith Bell Real Estate, to list for sale their house in the Pleasant Valley area of Underhill, Vermont. Diana Carter, a California resident, visited the house as a potential buyer. Bennett worked under the supervision of David Crane, an officer of Smith Bell. Crane knew, but did not disclose to Bennett or Carter, that the house was subject to frequent and severe winds, that a window had blown in years earlier, and that other houses in the area had suffered wind damage. Crane knew of this because he lived in the Pleasant Valley area, had sold a number of nearby properties, and had been Underhill's zoning officer. Many valley residents, including Crane, had wind gauges on their homes to measure and compare wind speeds with their neighbors. Carter bought the house, and several months later, high winds blew in a number of windows and otherwise damaged the property. Carter filed a suit in a Vermont state court against Smith Bell and others, alleging fraud. She argued in part that Crane's knowledge of the winds was imputable to Smith Bell. Smith Bell responded that Crane's knowledge was obtained outside the scope of employment. What is the rule regarding how much of an agent's knowledge a principal is assumed to know? How should the court rule in this case? Why? [*Carter v. Gugliuzzi*, 716 A.2d 17 (Vt. 1998)]

CASE PROBLEM WITH SAMPLE ANSWER

22–8. Ford Motor Credit Co. is a subsidiary of Ford Motor Co. with its own offices, officers, and directors. Ford Credit buys contracts and leases of automobiles entered into by dealers and consumers. Ford Credit also provides inventory financing for dealers' purchases of Ford and non-Ford vehicles and makes loans to Ford and non-Ford dealers. Dealers and consumers are not required to finance their purchases or leases of Ford vehicles through Ford Credit. Ford Motor is not a party to the agreements between Ford Credit and its customers and does not directly receive any payments under those agreements. Also, Ford Credit is not subject to any agreement with Ford Motor "restricting or conditioning" its ability to finance the dealers' inventories or the consumers' purchases or leases of vehicles. A number of plaintiffs filed a product liability suit in a Missouri state court against Ford Motor. Ford Motor claimed that the court did not have venue. The plaintiffs asserted that Ford Credit, which had an office in the jurisdiction, acted as Ford's "agent for the transaction of its usual and customary business" there. Is Ford Credit an agent of Ford Motor? Discuss. [*State ex rel. Ford Motor Co. v. Bacon*, 63 S.W.3d 641 (Mo. 2002)]

▶ To view a sample answer for this case problem, go to this book's Web site at **http://fundamentals.westbuslaw.com** and click on "Interactive Study Center."

22–9. Liability for Independent Contractor's Torts. Greif Brothers Corp., a steel drum manufacturer, owned and operated a manufacturing plant in Youngstown, Ohio. In 1987, Lowell Wilson, the plant superintendent, hired Youngstown Security Patrol, Inc. (YSP), a security company, to guard Greif property and "deter thieves and vandals." Some YSP security guards, as Wilson knew, carried firearms. Eric Bator, a YSP security guard, was not certified as an armed guard but nevertheless took his gun, in a briefcase, to work. While working at the Greif plant on August 12, 1991, Bator fired his gun at Derrell Pusey, in the belief that Pusey was an intruder. The bullet struck and killed Pusey. Pusey's mother filed a suit in an Ohio state court against Greif and others, alleging in part that her son's death was the result of YSP's negligence, for which Greif was responsible. Greif filed a motion for a directed verdict. What is the plaintiff's best argument that Greif is responsible for YSP's actions? What is Greif's best defense? Explain. [*Pusey v. Bator*, 94 Ohio St.3d 275, 762 N.E.2d 968 (2002)]

A QUESTION OF ETHICS AND SOCIAL RESPONSIBILITY

22–10. In 1990, the Internal Revenue Service (IRS) determined that a number of independent contractors working for Microsoft Corp. were actually employees of the company for tax purposes. The IRS arrived at this conclusion based on the significant control that Microsoft exercised over the independent contractors' work performance. As a result of the IRS's findings, Microsoft was ordered to pay back payroll taxes for hundreds of independent contractors who should have been classified as employees. Rather than contest the ruling, Microsoft required most of the workers in question, as well as a number of its other independent contractors, to become associated with employment agencies and work for Microsoft as temporary workers ("temps") or lose the opportunity to work for Microsoft. Workers who refused to register with employment agencies, as well as some who did register, sued Microsoft. The workers alleged that they were actually employees of the company and, as such, entitled to participate in Microsoft's stock option plan for employees. Microsoft countered that it need not provide such benefits because each of the workers had signed an independent-contractor agreement specifically stating that the worker was responsible for his or her own benefits. In view of these facts, consider the following questions. [*Vizcaino v. U.S. District Court for the Western District of Washington*, 173 F.3d 713 (9th Cir. 1999)]

1. If the decision were up to you, how would you rule in this case? Why?
2. Normally, when a company hires temporary workers from an employment agency, the agency—not the employer—is responsible for paying Social Security taxes and other withholding taxes. Yet the U.S. Court of Appeals for the Ninth Circuit held that being an employee of a temporary employment agency did not preclude the employee from having the status of a common law employee of Microsoft at the same time. Is this fair to the employer? Why or why not?
3. Generally, do you believe that Microsoft was trying to "skirt the law"—and its ethical responsibilities—by requiring its employees to sign up as "temps"?
4. Each of the employees involved in this case had signed an independent-contractor agreement. In view of this fact, is this decision fair to Microsoft? Why or why not?

AGENCY RELATIONSHIPS

For updated links to resources available on the Web, as well as other materials, visit this text's Web site at

http://fundamentals.westbuslaw.com

The Legal Information Institute at Cornell University is an excellent source for information on agency law, including court cases involving agency concepts. Go to

http://www.law.cornell.edu/topics/agency.html

The 'Lectric Law Library's Lawcopedia contains a summary of agency laws at

http://www.lectlaw.com/d-a.htm

Scroll down through the A's and select the link to "Agent" for useful information on this area of the law.

Online Legal Research

Go to the *Fundamentals of Business Law* home page at **http://fundamentals. westbuslaw.com**. Select "Interactive Study Center" and then click on "Chapter 22." There you will find the following Internet research exercises that you can perform to learn more about topics covered in this chapter.

Activity 22–1: LEGAL PERSPECTIVE—Liability in Agency Relationships
Activity 22–2: MANAGEMENT PERSPECTIVE—Employees or Independent Contractors?

Before the Test

Go to the *Fundamentals of Business Law* home page at **http://fundamentals. westbuslaw.com**. Click on "Interactive Quizzes." You will find at least twenty interactive questions relating to this chapter.

Westlaw® Campus

If your textbook provided for a subscription to Westlaw® Campus, or if you have otherwise purchased access to the Westlaw Campus database, you can access any of the cases presented or cited in this chapter by using your Westlaw Campus account.

CHAPTER
23
Employment Law

CHAPTER OBJECTIVES

After reading this chapter, you should be able to answer the following questions:

① What is the employment-at-will doctrine? When and why are exceptions to this doctrine made?

② What federal statute governs working hours and wages? What federal statutes govern labor unions and collective bargaining?

③ What federal act was enacted to protect the health and safety of employees? What are workers' compensation laws?

④ Generally, what kind of conduct is prohibited by Title VII of the Civil Rights Act of 1964, as amended?

⑤ What remedies are available under Title VII of the 1964 Civil Rights Act, as amended?

Until the early 1900s, most employer-employee relationships were governed by the common law. Under the common law doctrine of **employment at will**, either party may terminate the employment relationship at any time and for any reason—provided, of course, that the employment termination does not violate the provisions of an employment contract or a statute. Other common law concepts governing employment relationships include contract, agency, and tort law. Today, the workplace is extensively regulated by statutes and administrative agency regulations, thus narrowing the applicability of common law doctrines to employment relationships.

In the 1930s, during the Great Depression, both state and federal governments began to regulate employment relationships. Legislation during the 1930s and subsequent decades established the right of employees to form labor unions. At the heart of labor rights is the right to unionize and bargain with management for improved working conditions, salaries, and benefits. The ultimate weapon of labor is, of course, the strike. The labor leader Samuel Gompers concluded that without the right to strike, there could be no liberty. A succession of other laws during and since the 1930s provided further protection for employees. Today's employers must comply with a myriad of laws and regulations to ensure that employee rights are protected.

In this chapter, we look first at the most significant laws regulating employment relationships. We then conclude the chapter with a discussion of other important laws regulating the workplace—those that prohibit employment discrimination.

Wage-Hour Laws

In the 1930s, Congress enacted several laws regulating the wages and working hours of employees. In 1931, Congress passed the Davis-Bacon Act,[1] which requires contractors and subcontractors working on government construction projects to pay "prevailing wages" to their employees. In 1936, the Walsh-Healey Act[2] was passed. This act requires that employees of manufacturers or suppliers entering into contracts with agencies of the federal government be paid a minimum wage, as well as overtime pay of time and a half. In 1938, Congress passed the Fair Labor Standards Act[3] (FLSA). This act extended wage-hour requirements to cover all employers engaged in interstate commerce or engaged in the production of goods for interstate commerce, plus selected types of businesses.

CHILD LABOR

The FLSA prohibits oppressive child labor. Children under fourteen years of age are allowed to do certain types of jobs, such as deliver newspapers, work for their parents, and work in the entertainment and (with some exceptions) agricultural areas. Children who are fourteen or fifteen years of age are allowed to be employed, but not in hazardous occupations. Most states require persons under sixteen years of age to obtain work permits. There are also numerous restrictions on how many hours per day and per week they can work. ● **EXAMPLE #1** Children under the age of sixteen cannot work during school hours, for more than three hours on a school day (or eight hours on a nonschool day), for more than eighteen hours during a school week (or forty hours during a nonschool week), or before 7 A.M. or after 7 P.M. (9 P.M. during the summer).● Persons between the ages of sixteen and eighteen do not face such restrictions on working times and hours, but they cannot be employed in hazardous jobs or in jobs detrimental to their health and well-being. Persons over the age of eighteen are not affected by any of these restrictions.

HOURS AND WAGES

Under the FLSA, any employee who agrees to work more than forty hours per week must be paid no less than one and a half times his or her regular pay for all hours over forty. Certain employees are exempt from the overtime provisions of the act. Exempt employees fall into four categories: executives, administrative employees such as supervisors, professional employees, and outside salespersons.

The FLSA provides that a **minimum wage** of a specified amount (currently, $5.15 per hour) must be paid to employees in covered industries. Congress periodically revises this minimum wage.[4] Under the FLSA, the term *wages* includes the reasonable cost to the employer of furnishing employees with board, lodging, and other facilities if they are customarily furnished by that employer.

Do the FLSA's provisions apply to "telecommuters" and others in the work force who do not perform their jobs in the employer's workplace? For a discussion of this issue and others relating to the "virtual workplace," see this chapter's *Business Law in the Online World* feature on page 468.

Labor Unions

In the 1930s, in addition to wage-hour laws, the government also enacted the first of several labor laws. These laws protect employees' rights to join labor unions, to bargain with management over the terms and conditions of employment, and to conduct strikes. Subsequent legislation placed some restraints on unions and granted rights to employers. We look here at four major federal statutes regulating union-employer relations.

NORRIS-LAGUARDIA ACT

In 1932, Congress protected peaceful strikes, picketing, and boycotts in the Norris-LaGuardia Act.[5] The statute restricted the power of federal courts to issue injunctions against unions engaged in peaceful strikes. In effect, this act established a national policy permitting employees to organize.

---

[1] 40 U.S.C. Sections 276a–276a-5.
[2] 41 U.S.C. Sections 35–45.
[3] 29 U.S.C. Sections 201–260.

[4] Note that many state and local governments also have minimum-wage laws; these laws provide for higher minimum-wage rates than that required by the federal government.
[5] 29 U.S.C. Sections 101–110, 113–115.

BUSINESS LAW IN THE ONLINE WORLD
Employment Issues in the Virtual Workplace

Over thirty million workers in the United States telecommute, up from fewer than twenty million at the end of the last decade. Between eight and ten million U.S. workers now telecommute full-time—never laying eyes on, or feet in, a physical office building. As often happens, though, a spurt in technology—mainly due to the growth in Internet use—has caused real-world conditions to leap ahead of the law. After all, virtually all state and federal statutes governing employment were drafted when the only workplace was the traditional workplace.

OVERTIME AND MINIMUM-WAGE LAWS Not until the early 1990s did the U.S. Department of Labor issue regulations defining exemptions to the overtime-pay requirements for employees in computer-related occupations. Under the regulations, these employees can qualify as "professionals" and thus be exempt from the overtime-pay requirements. When an employee falls within this (or any other) exemption to the overtime-pay requirements of the Fair Labor Standards Act, the employee is not entitled to be paid time and a half for overtime hours.

The professional exemption does not apply to trainees or to entry-level employees in computer specialties, such as programming and analysis. Individuals operating computers or manufacturing, repairing, or maintaining computer hardware are also not included in the professional exemption for overtime pay. Under most circumstances, junior programmers, programmer trainees, keypunch operators, and computer operators are considered not to

have sufficient discretion and independence to qualify as administrative employees. They are, consequently, subject to federal overtime regulations.

REGULATING THE SAFETY OF AT-HOME WORK SITES
The Occupational Safety and Health Administration (OSHA), which will be discussed later in this chapter, did not issue a formal directive on home-office safety until 2000. At that time, OSHA stated that it would not conduct home-office inspections and would not hold employers liable for their employees' home offices. It also stated that it did not expect employers to inspect the home offices of their telecommuting employees.

Nonetheless, OSHA holds employers responsible for any situation in which hazardous materials or work processes are provided or required to be used in an employee's home office. Additionally, employers are required to keep OSHA injury and illness records for any work-related injuries and illnesses that occur in home work environments (these records will be discussed further later in this chapter). In contrast, OSHA has not applied these record-keeping requirements to virtual workers working out of their cars, hotel rooms, and airports, for example. At some point in the future, however, OSHA may audit remote work sites and increase record-keeping requirements.

FOR CRITICAL ANALYSIS
Why might telecommuting employees sometimes accept being wrongly classified (and not being paid overtime)?

NATIONAL LABOR RELATIONS ACT

One of the foremost statutes regulating labor is the National Labor Relations Act (NLRA) of 1935.[6] This act established the rights of employees to engage in collective bargaining and to strike. The act also specifically defined a number of employer practices as unfair to labor:

① Interference with the efforts of employees to form, join, or assist labor organizations or interference with the

efforts of employees to engage in concerted activities for their mutual aid or protection.

② An employer's domination of a labor organization or contribution of financial or other support to it.

③ Discrimination based on union affiliation in the hiring or awarding of tenure to employees.

④ Discrimination against employees for filing charges under the act or giving testimony under the act.

⑤ Refusal to bargain collectively with the duly designated representative of the employees.

---

[6] 20 U.S.C. Section 151.

The act also created the National Labor Relations Board (NLRB) to oversee union elections and to prevent employers from engaging in unfair and illegal union activities and unfair labor practices. The NLRB has the authority to investigate employees' charges of unfair labor practices and to serve complaints against employers in response to these charges. The NLRB may also issue cease-and-desist orders—orders compelling employers to cease engaging in the unfair practices—when violations are found. Cease-and-desist orders can be enforced by a circuit court of appeals if necessary. Arguments over alleged unfair labor practices are first decided by the NLRB and may then be appealed to a federal court.

To be protected under the NLRA, an individual must be an "employee," as that term is defined in the statute. Courts have long held that job applicants fall within this definition (otherwise, the NLRA's ban on discrimination in hiring would mean nothing).

LABOR-MANAGEMENT RELATIONS ACT

The Labor-Management Relations Act (LMRA) of 1947, commonly known as the Taft-Hartley Act,[7] was passed to proscribe certain union practices, such as the *closed shop*. A **closed shop** requires union membership by its workers as a condition of employment. Although the act made the closed shop illegal, it preserved the legality of the union shop. A **union shop** does not require membership as a prerequisite for employment but can, and usually does, require that workers join the union after a specified amount of time on the job.

The LMRA also prohibited unions from refusing to bargain with employers, engaging in certain types of picketing, and *featherbedding*—causing employers to hire more employees than necessary. The act also allowed individual states to pass their own **right-to-work laws**—laws making it illegal for union membership to be required for *continued* employment in any establishment. Thus, union shops are technically illegal in states with right-to-work laws.

LABOR-MANAGEMENT REPORTING AND DISCLOSURE ACT

In 1959, Congress enacted the Labor-Management Reporting and Disclosure Act (LMRDA).[8] The act established an employee bill of rights and reporting requirements for union activities. The act strictly regulates unions' internal business procedures. Union elections, for example, are regulated by the LMRDA, which requires that regularly scheduled elections of officers be held and that secret ballots be used. Persons who have been convicted of certain felonies are prohibited from holding union office. Moreover, union officials are accountable for union property and funds. Members have the right to attend and to participate in union meetings, to nominate officers, and to vote in most union proceedings.

Under the NLRA, employers and unions have a duty to bargain in good faith. Certain subjects are mandatory, and a party's refusal to bargain over these subjects is an unfair labor practice. The question in the following case was whether an employer's use of hidden surveillance cameras could be bargained over.

---

[7] 29 U.S.C. Sections 141 *et seq.*

[8] 29 U.S.C. Sections 401 *et seq.*

CASE 23.1   National Steel Corp. v. NLRB

United States Court of Appeals,
Seventh Circuit, 2003.
324 F.3d 928.
http://laws.findlaw.com/7th/952521.html[a]

FACTS National Steel Corporation operates a plant in Granite City, Illinois, where it employs approximately 3,000 employees, who are represented by ten different unions and covered by seven different collective bargaining agreements. National Steel maintains over a hundred video cameras, which are in plain view, to monitor various areas of the plant, and periodically uses hidden cameras to investigate suspected misconduct. In February 1999, National Steel installed a hidden camera to discover who was accessing a manager's office when the manager was not at work. The camera revealed a union member using the office to make long-distance phone calls. When National Steel discharged the employee, the union asked the company about other hidden cameras and indicated that it wanted to bargain over their use. National Steel refused to supply the information. The union filed a charge with the NLRB, which ordered National Steel to provide the information and bargain over the use of

---

a. This is a page within the Web site maintained by FindLaw (now a part of West Group).

(Continued)

CASE 23.1—Continued

the cameras. National Steel appealed to the U.S. Court of Appeals for the Seventh Circuit.

ISSUE Can an employer be required to bargain over the use of hidden cameras in the workplace?

DECISION Yes. The U.S. Court of Appeals for the Seventh Circuit upheld the NLRB's order to National Steel to bargain over the use of hidden surveillance cameras in the workplace. The court emphasized that this order did not prohibit their use, but only made that use a subject of collective bargaining.

REASON The court repeated the NLRB's conclusion that "the use of hidden surveillance cameras is a mandatory subject of collective bargaining because * * * the installation and use of such cameras [is] analogous to physical examinations, drug/alcohol testing requirements, and polygraph testing, all of which the Board has found to be mandatory

subjects." The court noted that "hidden cameras are focused primarily on the 'working environment' that employees experience on a daily basis and are used to expose misconduct or violations of the law by employees or others." Such "changes in an employer's methods have serious implications for its employees' job security" and "the use of such devices is not entrepreneurial in character [and] is not fundamental to the basic direction of the enterprise." The court also explained that the order "only requires National Steel to negotiate with the unions over the company's installation and use of hidden surveillance cameras and * * * does not dictate how the legitimate interests of the parties are to be accommodated in the process. * * * [I]t simply directs National Steel to initiate an accommodation process, and to provide assertedly confidential information in accord with whatever accommodation the parties agree upon."

FOR CRITICAL ANALYSIS—Social Consideration
Can an employer's confidentiality interests ever justify the nondisclosure of certain information?

The act also made all **secondary boycotts** illegal. In a secondary boycott, a union refuses to work for, purchase from, or handle the products of a secondary employer, with whom the union has no dispute, in an attempt to force that employer to stop doing business with the primary employer, with whom the union does have a labor dispute. The act also outlawed **hot-cargo agreements**, in which employers voluntarily agree with unions not to handle, use, or deal in other employers' goods that were not produced by union employees.

Worker Health and Safety

Numerous state and federal statutes protect employees and their families from the risk of accidental injury, death, or disease resulting from their employment. This section discusses the primary federal statute governing health and safety in the workplace, along with state workers' compensation acts.

THE OCCUPATIONAL SAFETY AND HEALTH ACT

At the federal level, the primary legislation for employee health and safety protection is the Occupational Safety and Health Act of 1970.[9] Congress passed this act in an attempt to ensure safe and healthful working conditions for practically every employee in the country. The act provides for specific standards that employers must meet, plus a general duty to keep workplaces safe.

Enforcement Agencies. Three federal agencies develop and enforce the standards set by the Occupational Safety and Health Act. The Occupational Safety and Health Administration (OSHA) is part of the Department of Labor and has the authority to promulgate standards, make inspections, and enforce the act. OSHA has developed safety standards governing many workplace details, such as the structural stability of ladders and the requirements for railings. OSHA also establishes standards that protect employees against exposure to substances that may be harmful to their health.

The National Institute for Occupational Safety and Health is part of the Department of Health and Human Services. Its main duty is to conduct research on safety and health problems and to recommend standards for OSHA to adopt. Finally, the Occupational Safety and Health Review Commission is an independent agency set up to handle appeals from actions taken by OSHA administrators.

Procedures and Violations. OSHA compliance officers may enter and inspect facilities of any establishment covered by the Occupational Safety and Health Act.[10] Employees may also file complaints of violations. Under the act, an employer cannot discharge an employee who files a

---

[9] 29 U.S.C. Sections 553, 651–678.

[10] In the past, warrantless inspections were conducted. In 1978, however, the United States Supreme Court held that warrantless inspections violated the warrant clause of the Fourth Amendment to the Constitution. See *Marshall v. Barlow's, Inc.*, 436 U.S. 307, 98 S.Ct. 1816, 56 L.Ed.2d 305 (1978).

complaint or who, in good faith, refuses to work in a high-risk area if bodily harm or death might result.

Employers with eleven or more employees are required to keep occupational injury and illness records for each employee. Each record must be made available for inspection when requested by an OSHA inspector. Whenever a work-related injury or disease occurs, employers must make reports directly to OSHA. Whenever an employee is killed in a work-related accident or when five or more employees are hospitalized in one accident, the employer must notify the Department of Labor within forty-eight hours. If the company fails to do so, it will be fined. Following the accident, a complete inspection of the premises is mandatory.

Criminal penalties for willful violation of the Occupational Safety and Health Act are limited. Employers may be prosecuted under state laws, however. In other words, the act does not preempt state and local criminal laws.[11]

WORKERS' COMPENSATION

State **workers' compensation laws** establish an administrative procedure for compensating workers injured on the job. Instead of suing, an injured worker files a claim with the administrative agency or board that administers local workers' compensation claims.

Most workers' compensation statutes are similar. No state covers all employees. Typically excluded are domestic workers, agricultural workers, temporary employees, and employees of common carriers (companies that provide transportation services to the public). Typically, the statutes cover minors. Usually, the statutes allow employers to purchase insurance from a private insurer or a state fund to pay workers' compensation benefits in the event of a claim. Most states also allow employers to be self-insured—that is, employers who show an ability to pay claims do not need to buy insurance.

In general, the right to recover benefits is predicated wholly on the existence of an employment relationship and the fact that the injury was *accidental* and *occurred on the job or in the course of employment,* regardless of fault. Intentionally inflicted self-injury, for example, would not be considered accidental and hence would not be covered. If an injury occurred while an employee was commuting to or from work, it usually would not be considered to have occurred on the job or in the course of employment and hence would not be covered.

An employee must notify her or his employer promptly (usually within thirty days) of an injury. Generally, an employee must also file a workers' compensation claim with the appropriate state agency or board within a certain period (sixty days to two years) from the time the injury is first noticed, rather than from the time of the accident.

An employee's acceptance of workers' compensation benefits bars the employee from suing for injuries caused by the employer's negligence. By barring lawsuits for negligence, workers' compensation laws also bar employers from raising common law defenses to negligence, such as contributory negligence, assumption of risk, or injury caused by a "fellow servant" (another employee). A worker may sue an employer who *intentionally* injures the worker, however.

Income Security

Federal and state governments participate in insurance programs designed to protect employees and their families by covering the financial impact of retirement, disability, death, hospitalization, and unemployment. The key federal law on this subject is the Social Security Act of 1935.[12]

SOCIAL SECURITY AND MEDICARE

The Social Security Act provides for old-age (retirement), survivors, and disability insurance. The act is therefore often referred to as OASDI. Both employers and employees must "contribute" under the Federal Insurance Contributions Act (FICA)[13] to help pay for the employees' loss of income on retirement. The basis for the employee's and the employer's contribution is the employee's annual wage base—the maximum amount of the employee's wages that are subject to the tax. The employer withholds the employee's FICA contribution from the employee's wages and then matches this contribution.

Medicare, a health-insurance program, is administered by the Social Security Administration for people sixty-five years of age and older and for some under the age of sixty-five who are disabled. It has two parts, one pertaining to hospital costs and the other to nonhospital medical costs, such as visits to doctors' offices. People who have Medicare hospital insurance can also obtain additional federal medical insurance if they pay small monthly premiums, which increase as the cost of medical care increases. As with Social Security contributions, both the employer and the employee contribute to Medicare.

One issue that has arisen under FICA and the Federal Unemployment Tax Act (FUTA) (discussed later in this chapter) is whether wages should be taxed according to the rates in effect when the wages are owed or the rates in effect when the wages are actually paid. The amounts in dispute can be large, as the following case illustrates.

---

[11] *Pedraza v. Shell Oil Co.,* 942 F.2d 48 (1st Cir. 1991); *cert.* denied, *Shell Oil Co. v. Pedraza,* 502 U.S. 1082, 112 S.Ct. 993, 117 L.Ed.2d 154 (1992).

[12] 42 U.S.C. Sections 301–1397e.

[13] 26 U.S.C. Sections 3101–3125.

CASE 23.2   **United States v. Cleveland Indians Baseball Co.**

Supreme Court of the United States, 2001.
532 U.S. 200,
121 S.Ct. 1433,
149 L.Ed.2d 401.
**http://supct.law.cornell.edu/supct/cases/
historic.htm[a]**

FACTS   In 1994, the Major League Baseball Players
Association settled a grievance with twenty-six major league
baseball teams for conspiring to stop the steep escalation of
salaries for free agent players. Several teams agreed to pay a
total of $280 million to the players. Under the agreement,
the Cleveland Indians Baseball Company owed eight players
a total of $610,000 in salary for 1986, and fourteen players
a total of $1,457,848 for 1987. The company paid the
amounts in 1994. The company also paid taxes on the
amounts according to the 1994 rates and ceilings and then
applied for a refund of more than $100,000, claiming that
the taxes should have been computed according to the 1986
and 1987 rates and ceilings.[b] The Internal Revenue Service
(IRS) denied the claim, and the company filed a suit in a federal district court against the federal government. The court

---

a. In the "Search" box, type "Cleveland Indians" and click on
"submit." In the result, scroll to the name of the case and click on it
to access the opinion. The Legal Information Institute of Cornell Law
School in Ithaca, New York, maintains this Web site.
b. All but one of the players had collected wages from the company
exceeding the ceilings in 1986 and 1987. Because those players,
and the company, paid the maximum amount of employment taxes
in 1986 and 1987, allocating the 1994 payments back to those
years would mean that they would not owe taxes on the amounts.
Treating the back wages as taxable in 1994, however, would incur
significant tax liability, partly because the company did not pay any
of the players any other wages in 1994.

ordered a refund of the FICA and FUTA taxes. The government appealed to the U.S. Court of Appeals for the Sixth
Circuit, which affirmed the lower court's order. The government appealed to the United States Supreme Court.

ISSUE   Should wages be taxed by reference to the year that
they are actually paid?

DECISION   Yes. The United States Supreme Court held
that taxes on wages should be computed using the rates and
ceilings that apply in the year when the wages are actually
paid, not those in effect in the year when the wages should
have been paid. The Court reversed the decision of the lower
court.

REASON   The United States Supreme Court deferred to the
IRS's long-standing, "steady" interpretation of the FICA and
FUTA tax provisions and the IRS's own regulations. The regulations specify that the applicable employer tax is determined
at the time the wages are paid by the employer, not when
they were earned. In other words, the tax "is computed by
applying to the wages paid by the employer the rate in effect
at the time such wages are paid." The regulations do not
specifically mention back wages, but the Court pointed out
that the IRS "has consistently interpreted them to require taxation of back wages according to the year the wages are
actually paid, regardless of when those wages were earned or
should have been paid."

FOR CRITICAL ANALYSIS—Political Consideration
*In this case the rule applied by the Court disadvantaged the
taxpayer; in other cases, it has disadvantaged the government. With that in mind, what was Congress's likely intent
regarding the FICA and FUTA tax provisions?*

PRIVATE PENSION PLANS

Significant legislation has been enacted to regulate
employee retirement plans set up by employers to supplement Social Security benefits. The major federal act covering these retirement plans is the Employee Retirement
Income Security Act (ERISA) of 1974.[14] This act empowers
the Labor Management Services Administration of the
Department of Labor to enforce its provisions governing
employers who have private pension funds for their
employees. ERISA does not require an employer to establish

a pension plan. When a plan exists, however, ERISA establishes standards for its management.

UNEMPLOYMENT INSURANCE

The United States has a system of unemployment insurance
in which employers pay into a fund, the proceeds of which
are paid out to qualified unemployed workers. The Federal
Unemployment Tax Act (FUTA) of 1935[15] created a state-
administered system that provides unemployment compensation to eligible individuals. The FUTA and state laws

---

14. 29 U.S.C. Sections 1001 *et seq.*

15. 26 U.S.C. Sections 3301–3310.

require employers that fall under the provisions of the act to pay unemployment taxes at regular intervals.

COBRA

Federal legislation also addresses the issue of health insurance for workers whose jobs have been terminated—and who are thus no longer eligible for group health-insurance plans. The Consolidated Omnibus Budget Reconciliation Act (COBRA) of 1985[16] prohibits the elimination of a worker's medical, optical, or dental insurance coverage on the voluntary or involuntary termination of the worker's employment. Employers, with some exceptions, must comply with COBRA if they employ twenty or more workers and provide a benefit plan to those workers. An employer must inform employees of COBRA's provisions when a group health plan is established and must also inform a worker of the provisions if he or she faces termination or a reduction of hours that would affect his or her eligibility for coverage under the plan. The worker does not receive a free ride, however. To receive continued benefits, she or he may be required to pay all of the premium, as well as a 2 percent administrative charge.

Family and Medical Leave

In 1993, Congress passed the Family and Medical Leave Act (FMLA)[17] to allow employees to take time off work for fam-

[16] 29 U.S.C. Sections 1161–1169.
[17] 29 U.S.C. Sections 2601, 2611–2619, 2651–2654.

ily or medical reasons. A majority of the states also have legislation allowing for a leave from employment for family or medical reasons, and many employers maintain private family-leave plans for their workers.

The FMLA requires employers who have fifty or more employees to provide employees with up to twelve weeks of unpaid family or medical leave during any twelve-month period. During the employee's leave, the employer must continue the worker's health-care coverage and guarantee employment in the same position or a comparable position when the employee returns to work. An important exception to the FMLA, however, allows the employer to avoid reinstating a *key employee*—defined as an employee whose pay falls within the top 10 percent of the firm's work force. Additionally, the act does not apply to employees who have worked less than one year or less than twenty-five hours a week during the previous twelve months.

The FMLA expressly covers private and public (government) employees. Some states argued, and some courts agreed, however, that public employees could not sue their state employers in federal courts to enforce their FMLA rights unless the states consented to be sued.[18] This argument was before the United States Supreme Court in the following case.

[18] Under the Eleventh Amendment to the U.S. Constitution, a state is immune from suit in a federal court unless the state agrees to be sued.

CASE 23.3 **Nevada Department of Human Resources v. Hibbs**

Supreme Court of the United States, 2003.
__ U.S. __,
123 S.Ct. 1972,
155 L.Ed.2d 953.
http://supct.law.cornell.edu/supct/cases/ historic.htm[a]

FACTS William Hibbs worked for the Nevada Department of Human Resources. In April 1997, Hibbs asked for time off under the FMLA to care for his sick wife, who was recovering from a car accident and neck surgery. The department granted Hibbs's request, allowing him to use the leave intermittently, as needed, beginning in May. Hibbs did this until August 5, after which he did not return to work. In October, the department told Hibbs that he had exhausted his FMLA leave, that

a. In the "Search" box, type "Nevada Department of Human Resources" and click on "submit." Scroll to the name of the case and click on it to access the opinion.

no further leave would be granted, and that he must return to work by November 12. When he did not return, he was discharged. Hibbs filed a suit in a federal district court against the department. The court held that the Eleventh Amendment to the U.S. Constitution barred the suit. On Hibbs's appeal, the U.S. Court of Appeals for the Ninth Circuit reversed this holding. The Department of Human Resources appealed to the United States Supreme Court.

ISSUE Can the FMLA, which expressly covers public employees, serve as the basis for a suit against a state employer whether or not the state consents to the suit?

DECISION Yes. The United States Supreme Court affirmed the lower court's decision, concluding that the FMLA is

(Continued)

CASE 23.3—Continued

"congruent and proportional" to the discrimination that Congress intended the FMLA to address.

REASON The Court pointed out that when Congress enacted the FMLA, parental leave for fathers was rare. Even "[w]here child-care leave policies do exist, men, both in the public and private sectors, receive notoriously discriminatory treatment in their requests for such leave." For example, "[f]ifteen States provided women up to one year of extended maternity leave, while only four provided men with the same. This and other differential leave policies were not attributable to any differential physical needs of men and women, but

rather to the pervasive sex-role stereotype that caring for family members is women's work. * * * By setting a minimum standard of family leave for all eligible employees, irrespective of gender, the FMLA attacks the formerly state-sanctioned stereotype that only women are responsible for family caregiving, thereby reducing employers' incentives to engage in discrimination by basing hiring and promotion decisions on stereotypes."

FOR CRITICAL ANALYSIS—Cultural Consideration
Can a law foster discrimination even when the law is not obviously discriminatory?

Wrongful Discharge

Whenever an employer discharges an employee in violation of the law, the employee may bring an action for **wrongful discharge**. An employee who is protected by a statute, such as one prohibiting employment discrimination (discussed later in this chapter), may bring a cause of action under that statute. If an employer's actions do not violate any statute, then the question is whether the employer has violated an employment contract or a common law doctrine.

As mentioned, under the employment-at-will doctrine, an employer may hire and fire employees at will (regardless of the employees' performance) without liability, unless the decision violates the terms of an employment contract or statutory law. Because of the harsh effects of the employment-at-will doctrine for employees, courts have carved out various exceptions to the doctrine. These exceptions are based on contract theory, tort theory, and public policy.

EXCEPTIONS BASED ON CONTRACT THEORY

Some courts have held that an implied employment contract exists between an employer and an employee. If an employee is fired outside the terms of the implied contract, he or she may succeed in an action for breach of contract even though no written employment contract exists. ● EXAMPLE #2 An employer's manual or personnel bulletin may state that, as a matter of policy, workers will be dismissed only for good cause. If the employee is aware of this policy and continues to work for the employer, a court may find that there is an implied contract based on the terms stated in the manual or bulletin.[19]●

Promises that an employer makes to employees regarding discharge policy may also be considered part of an implied contract. If the employer fires a worker in a way that is contrary to the manner promised, a court may hold that the employer has violated the implied contract and is liable for damages. A few states have gone further and held that all employment contracts contain an implied covenant of good faith. This means that both sides promise to abide by the contract in good faith. If an employer fires an employee for an arbitrary or unjustified reason, the employee can claim that the covenant of good faith was breached and the contract violated.

Generally, the key consideration in determining whether an employment manual creates an implied contractual obligation is the employee's reasonable expectations.[20] For this reason, today's employers often include disclaimers in their employment manuals. Such disclaimers usually state, clearly and conspicuously, that the manual does not modify the employer's employment-at-will policy in any way and does not provide the employee with any kind of contractual rights.

EXCEPTIONS BASED ON TORT THEORY

In a few cases, the discharge of an employee may give rise to an action for wrongful discharge under tort theories. Abusive discharge procedures may result in intentional infliction of emotional distress or defamation. ● EXAMPLE #3 Suppose that an employer induces a prospective employee to leave a lucrative job and move to another state by offering "a long-term job with a thriving business." In fact, however, the employer is having significant financial problems.

---

[19] See, for example, *Pepe v. Rival Co.*, 85 F.Supp.2d 349 (D.N.J. 1999).

[20] See, for example, *Doll v. Port Authority Trans-Hudson Corp.*, 92 F.Supp.2d 416 (D.N.J. 2000).

Furthermore, the employer is planning a merger that will result in the elimination of the position offered to the prospective employee. If the employee takes the job in reliance on the employer's representations and is fired shortly thereafter, the employee may be able to bring an action against the employer for fraud.●

EXCEPTIONS BASED ON PUBLIC POLICY

The most widespread common law exception to the employment-at-will doctrine is an exception made on the basis of public policy. Courts may apply this exception when an employer fires a worker for reasons that violate a fundamental public policy of the jurisdiction. For example, a court may prevent an employer from firing a worker who serves on a jury and therefore cannot work during her or his normally scheduled working hours.

Sometimes, an employer will direct an employee to do something that violates the law. If the employee refuses to perform the illegal act, the employer might decide to fire the worker. Similarly, employees who "blow the whistle" on the wrongdoing of their employers often find themselves disciplined or even out of a job. **Whistleblowing** occurs when an employee tells a government official, upper-management authorities, or the press that his or her employer is engaged in some unsafe or illegal activity. Whistleblowers on occasion have been protected from wrongful discharge for reasons of public policy. For example, a bank was held to have wrongfully discharged an employee who pressured the employer to comply with state and federal consumer credit laws.[21]

Whistleblower Statutes

To encourage workers to report employer wrongdoing, such as fraud, most states have enacted so-called whistleblower statutes. These statutes protect whistleblowers from subsequent retaliation on the part of employers. On the federal level, the Whistleblower Protection Act of 1989[22] protects federal employees who blow the whistle on their employers from their employers' retaliatory actions. Whistleblower statutes may also provide an incentive to disclose information by providing the whistleblower with a monetary reward. For example, the federal False Claims Reform Act of 1986[23] requires that a whistleblower who has disclosed information relating to a fraud perpetrated against the U.S.

government receive between 15 and 25 percent of the proceeds if the government brings suit against the wrongdoer.

Employment Discrimination

During the early 1960s we, as a nation, focused our attention on the civil rights of all Americans, including our rights under the Fourteenth Amendment to the equal protection of the laws. Out of this movement grew a body of law protecting workers against discrimination on the basis of race, color, religion, national origin, gender, age, or disability. A class of persons defined by one or more of these criteria is known as a **protected class**.

Several federal statutes prohibit discrimination in the employment context against members of protected classes. The most important statute is Title VII of the Civil Rights Act of 1964.[24] Title VII prohibits discrimination on the basis of race, color, religion, national origin, and gender at any stage of employment. The Age Discrimination in Employment Act of 1967[25] and the Americans with Disabilities Act of 1990[26] prohibit discrimination on the basis of age and disability, respectively.

The focus here is on the kinds of discrimination prohibited by these federal statutes. Note, however, that discrimination against employees on the basis of any of these criteria may also violate state human rights statutes or other state laws or public policies prohibiting discrimination.

TITLE VII OF THE CIVIL RIGHTS ACT OF 1964

Title VII of the Civil Rights Act of 1964 and its amendments prohibit **employment discrimination** against employees, job applicants, and union members on the basis of race, color, national origin, religion, and gender at any stage of employment. Title VII applies to employers with fifteen or more employees, labor unions with fifteen or more members, labor unions that operate hiring halls (to which members go regularly to be rationed jobs as they become available), employment agencies, and state and local governing units or agencies. A special section of the act prohibits discrimination in most federal government employment.

Compliance with Title VII is monitored by the Equal Employment Opportunity Commission (EEOC). A victim of alleged discrimination, before bringing a suit against the employer, must first file a claim with the EEOC. The EEOC may investigate the dispute and attempt to obtain the parties' voluntary consent to an out-of-court settlement. If

---

[21] *Harless v. First National Bank in Fairmont*, 162 W.Va. 116, 246 S.E.2d 270 (1978).
[22] 5 U.S.C. Section 1201.
[23] 31 U.S.C. Sections 3729–3733. This act amended the False Claims Act of 1863.

[24] 42 U.S.C. Sections 2000e–2000e-17.
[25] 29 U.S.C. Sections 621–634.
[26] 42 U.S.C. Sections 12102–12118.

voluntary agreement cannot be reached, the EEOC may then file a suit against the employer on the employee's behalf. If the EEOC decides not to investigate the claim, the victim may bring her or his own lawsuit against the employer.

Types of Discrimination. Title VII prohibits both intentional and unintentional discrimination. Intentional discrimination by an employer against an employee is known as **disparate-treatment discrimination.** Because intent may sometimes be difficult to prove, courts have established certain procedures for resolving disparate-treatment cases. Suppose that a woman applies for employment with a construction firm and is rejected. If she sues on the basis of disparate-treatment discrimination in hiring, she must show that (1) she is a member of a protected class, (2) she applied and was qualified for the job in question, (3) she was rejected by the employer, and (4) the employer continued to seek applicants for the position or filled the position with a person not in a protected class.

If the woman can meet these relatively easy requirements, she makes out a *prima facie* case of illegal discrimination. Making out a *prima facie* case of discrimination means that the plaintiff has met her initial burden of proof and will win in the absence of a legally acceptable employer defense (defenses to claims of employment discrimination will be discussed later in this chapter). The burden then shifts to the employer-defendant, who must articulate a legal reason for not hiring the plaintiff. To prevail, the plaintiff must then show that the employer's reason is a *pretext* (not the true reason) and that discriminatory intent actually motivated the employer's decision.

Employers often find it necessary to use interviews and testing procedures to choose from among a large number of applicants for job openings. Minimum educational requirements are also common. Employer practices, such as those involving educational requirements, may have an unintended discriminatory impact on a protected class. **Disparate-impact discrimination** occurs when, as a result of educational or other job requirements or hiring procedures, an employer's work force does not reflect the percentage of nonwhites, women, or members of other protected classes that characterizes qualified individuals in the local labor market. If a person challenging an employment practice having a discriminatory effect can show a connection between the practice and the disparity, he or she makes out a *prima facie* case, and no evidence of discriminatory intent needs to be shown. Disparate-impact discrimination can also occur when an educational or other job requirement or hiring procedure excludes members of a protected class from an employer's work force at a substantially higher rate than nonmembers, regardless of the racial balance in the employer's work force.

Discrimination Based on Race, Color, and National Origin. If a company's standards or policies for selecting or promoting employees have the effect of discriminating against employees or job applicants on the basis of race, color, or national origin, they are illegal—unless (except for race) they have a substantial, demonstrable relationship to realistic qualifications for the job in question. Discrimination against these protected classes in regard to employment conditions and benefits is also illegal.

● **EXAMPLE #4** In one case, Cynthia McCullough, an African American woman with a college degree, worked at a deli in a grocery store. More than a year later, the owner of the store promoted a white woman as "deli manager." The white woman had worked in the deli for just three months, had only a sixth-grade education, and could not calculate prices or read recipes. Although the owner gave various reasons for promoting the white woman instead of McCullough, a federal appellate court held that these reasons were likely just excuses and that the real reason was discriminatory intent.[27] ●

Discrimination Based on Religion. Title VII of the Civil Rights Act of 1964 also prohibits government employers, private employers, and unions from discriminating against persons because of their religion. An employer must "reasonably accommodate" the religious practices of its employees, unless to do so would cause undue hardship to the employer's business. For example, if an employee's religion prohibits him or her from working on a certain day of the week or at a particular type of job, the employer must make a reasonable attempt to accommodate these religious requirements. Employers must reasonably accommodate an employee's religious belief even if the belief is not based on the tenets or dogma of a particular church, sect, or denomination. The only requirement is that the belief be sincerely held by the employee.[28]

Discrimination Based on Gender. Under Title VII, as well as other federal acts, employers are forbidden to discriminate against employees on the basis of gender. Employers are prohibited from classifying jobs as male or female and from advertising in help-wanted columns that are designated male or female unless the employer can prove that the gender of the applicant is essential to the job. Furthermore, employers cannot have separate male and female seniority lists.

[27] *McCullough v. Real Foods, Inc.*, 140 F.3d 1123 (8th Cir. 1998). The federal district court had granted summary judgment for the employer in this case. The Eighth Circuit Court of Appeals reversed the district court's decision and remanded the case for trial.
[28] *Frazee v. Illinois Department of Employment Security*, 489 U.S. 829, 109 S.Ct. 1514, 103 L.Ed.2d 914 (1989).

Generally, to succeed in a suit for gender discrimination, a plaintiff must demonstrate that gender was a determining factor in the employer's decision to hire, fire, or promote her or him. Typically, this involves looking at all of the surrounding circumstances.

The Pregnancy Discrimination Act of 1978,[29] which amended Title VII, expanded the definition of gender discrimination to include discrimination based on pregnancy. Women affected by pregnancy, childbirth, or related medical conditions must be treated—for all employment-related purposes, including the receipt of benefits under employee benefit programs—the same as other persons not so affected but similar in ability to work.

Sexual Harassment. Title VII also protects employees against **sexual harassment** in the workplace. Sexual harassment has often been classified as either *quid pro quo* harassment or hostile-environment harassment. *Quid pro quo* is a Latin phrase that is often translated to mean "something in exchange for something else." *Quid pro quo* harassment occurs when job opportunities, promotions, salary increases, and so on are given in return for sexual favors. According to the United States Supreme Court, hostile-environment harassment occurs when "the workplace is permeated with discriminatory intimidation, ridicule, and insult, that is sufficiently severe or pervasive to alter the conditions of the victim's employment and create an abusive working environment."[30]

Generally, the courts apply this Supreme Court guideline on a case-by-case basis. Some courts have held that just one incident of sexually offensive conduct—such as a sexist remark by a co-worker or a photo on an employer's desk of his bikini-clad wife—can create a hostile environment.[31] At least one court has held that a worker may recover damages under Title VII because *other* persons were sexually harassed in the workplace.[32] According to some employment specialists, employers should assume that hostile-environment harassment has occurred if an employee claims that it has. For either type of harassment to be *sexual* harassment, it must involve gender-based discrimination.

Harassment by Supervisors. What if an employee is harassed by a manager or supervisor of a large firm, and the firm itself (the "employer") is not aware of the harassment? Should the employer be held liable for the harassment

nonetheless? For some time, the courts were in disagreement on this issue. Typically, employers were held liable for Title VII violations by the firm's managerial or supervisory personnel in *quid pro quo* harassment cases regardless of whether the employer knew about the harassment. In hostile-environment cases, the majority of courts tended to hold employers liable only if the employer knew or should have known of the harassment and failed to take prompt remedial action.

In 1998, in two separate cases, the United States Supreme Court issued some significant guidelines relating to the liability of employers for their supervisors' harassment of employees in the workplace. In *Faragher v. City of Boca Raton*,[33] the Court held that an employer (a city) could be held liable for a supervisor's harassment of employees even though the employer was unaware of the behavior. The Court reached this conclusion primarily because, although the city had a written policy against sexual harassment, the policy had not been distributed to city employees. Additionally, the city had not established any procedures that could be followed by employees who felt that they were victims of sexual harassment. In *Burlington Industries, Inc. v. Ellerth*,[34] the Court ruled that a company could be held liable for the harassment of an employee by one of its vice presidents even though the employee suffered no adverse job consequences.

The guidelines set forth in these two cases have been helpful to employers and employees alike. On the one hand, employees benefit by the ruling that employers may be held liable for their supervisors' harassment even though the employers were unaware of the actions and even though the employees suffered no adverse job consequences. On the other hand, the Court made it clear in both decisions that employers have an affirmative defense against liability for their supervisors' harassment of employees if the employers can show that (1) they have taken "reasonable care to prevent and correct promptly any sexually harassing behavior" (by establishing effective harassment policies and complaint procedures, for example), and (2) the employees suing for harassment failed to follow these policies and procedures.

Harassment by Co-Workers and Nonemployees. Often, employees alleging harassment complain that the actions of co-workers, not supervisors, are responsible for creating a hostile working environment. In such cases, the employee still has a cause of action against the employer. Normally, though, the employer will be held liable only if it knew, or should have known, about the harassment and failed to take immediate remedial action.

---

[29] 42 U.S.C. Section 2000e(k).

[30] *Harris v. Forklift Systems*, 510 U.S. 17, 114 S.Ct. 367, 126 L.Ed.2d 295 (1993).

[31] For other examples, see *Radtke v. Everett*, 442 Mich. 368, 501 N.W.2d 155 (1993); and *Nadeau v. Rainbow Rugs, Inc.*, 675 A.2d 973 (Me. 1996).

[32] *Leibovitz v. New York City Transit Authority*, 4 F.Supp.2d 144 (E.D.N.Y. 1998).

[33] 524 U.S. 775, 118 S.Ct. 2275, 141 L.Ed.2d 662 (1998).

[34] 524 U.S. 742, 118 S.Ct. 2257, 141 L.Ed.2d 633 (1998).

Employers may also be liable for harassment by *nonemployees* in certain circumstances. • EXAMPLE #5 If a restaurant owner or manager knows that a certain customer repeatedly harasses a waitress and permits the harassment to continue, the restaurant owner may be liable under Title VII even though the customer is not an employee of the restaurant. The issue turns on the control that the employer exerts over a nonemployee. In one case, an owner of a Pizza Hut franchise was held liable for the harassment of a waitress by two male customers because no steps were taken to prevent the harassment.[35]•

Same-Gender Harassment. The courts have also had to address the issue of whether men who are harassed by other men, or women who are harassed by other women, are also protected by laws that prohibit gender-based discrimination in the workplace. For example, what if the male president of a firm demands sexual favors from a male employee? Does this action qualify as sexual harassment? For some time, the courts were widely split on this issue. In 1998, in *Oncale v. Sundowner Offshore Services, Inc.,*[36] the Supreme Court resolved the issue by holding that Title VII protection extends to situations in which individuals are harassed by members of the same gender.

Remedies under Title VII. Employer liability under Title VII may be extensive. If the plaintiff successfully proves that unlawful discrimination occurred, he or she may be awarded reinstatement, back pay, retroactive promotions, and damages. Compensatory damages are available only in cases of intentional discrimination. Punitive damages may be recovered against a private employer only if the employer acted with malice or reckless indifference to an individual's rights. The sum of the amount of compensatory and punitive damages is limited by the statute to specific amounts against specific employers—ranging from $50,000 against employers with one hundred or fewer employees to $300,000 against employers with more than five hundred employees.

DISCRIMINATION BASED ON AGE

Age discrimination is potentially the most widespread form of discrimination, because anyone—regardless of race, color, national origin, or gender—could be a victim at some point in life. The Age Discrimination in Employment Act (ADEA) of 1967, as amended, prohibits employment discrimination on the basis of age against individuals forty years of age or older. An amendment to the act prohibits mandatory retirement for nonmanagerial workers. For the act to apply, an employer must have twenty or more employees, and the employer's business activities must affect interstate commerce.

Procedures under the ADEA. The burden-shifting procedure under the ADEA is similar to that under Title VII. If a plaintiff can establish that she or he (1) was a member of the protected age group, (2) was qualified for the position from which she or he was discharged, and (3) was discharged under circumstances that give rise to an inference of discrimination, the plaintiff has established a *prima facie* case of unlawful age discrimination. The burden then shifts to the employer, who must articulate a legitimate reason for the discrimination. If the plaintiff can prove that the employer's reason is only a pretext and that the plaintiff's age was a determining factor in the employer's decision, the employer will be held liable under the ADEA.

Numerous cases of alleged age discrimination have been brought against employers who, to cut costs, replaced older, higher-salaried employees with younger, lower-salaried workers. Whether a firing is discriminatory or simply part of a rational business decision to prune the company's ranks is not always clear. Companies generally defend a decision to discharge a worker by asserting that the worker could no longer perform his or her duties or that the worker's skills were no longer needed. The employee must prove that the discharge was motivated, at least in part, by age bias. Proof that qualified older employees are generally discharged before younger employees or that co-workers continually made unflattering age-related comments about the discharged worker may be enough. The plaintiff need not prove that he or she was replaced by a person outside the protected class—that is, by a person under the age of forty years.[37] Rather, the issue in all ADEA cases turns on whether age discrimination has, in fact, occurred, regardless of the age of the replacement worker.

State Employees and the ADEA. As mentioned earlier in this chapter, under the Eleventh Amendment to the Constitution, as that amendment has generally been interpreted by the United States Supreme Court, states are immune from lawsuits brought by private individuals in federal court, unless a state consents to the suit. In a number of cases brought in the late 1990s, state agencies that were sued by state employees for age discrimination sought to have the suits dismissed on this ground.

---

[35] *Lockard v. Pizza Hut, Inc.,* 162 F.3d 1062 (10th Cir. 1998).
[36] 523 U.S. 75, 118 S.Ct. 998, 140 L.Ed.2d 207 (1998).

[37] *O'Connor v. Consolidated Coin Caterers Corp.,* 517 U.S. 308, 116 S.Ct. 1307, 134 L.Ed.2d 433 (1996).

● EXAMPLE #6 In two Florida cases, professors and librarians contended that their employers—two Florida state universities—denied them salary increases and other benefits because they were getting old and their successors could be hired at lower cost. The universities claimed that as agencies of a sovereign state, they could not be sued in federal court without the state's consent. Because the courts were rendering conflicting opinions in these cases, the United States Supreme Court agreed to address the issue. In *Kimel v. Florida Board of Regents,*[38] decided in early 2000, the Court held that the sovereign immunity granted the states by the Eleventh Amendment precluded suits against them by private parties alleging violations of the ADEA. According to the Court, Congress had exceeded its constitutional authority when it included in the ADEA a provision stating that "all employers," including state employers, were subject to the act.●

DISCRIMINATION BASED ON DISABILITY

The Americans with Disabilities Act (ADA) of 1990 is designed to eliminate discriminatory employment practices that prevent otherwise qualified workers with disabilities from fully participating in the national labor force. Basically, the ADA requires that employers "reasonably accommodate" the needs of persons with disabilities unless to do so would cause the employer to suffer an "undue hardship." The ADA extends federal protection against disability-based discrimination to all workplaces with fifteen or more workers. Note, though, that the United States Supreme Court has held, as it did with respect to the ADEA, that lawsuits under the ADA cannot be brought against state government employers.[39]

To prevail on a claim under the ADA, a plaintiff must show that he or she (1) has a disability, (2) is otherwise qualified for the employment in question, and (3) was excluded from the employment solely because of the disability. As in Title VII cases, a claim alleging violation of the ADA may be commenced only after the plaintiff has pursued the claim through the EEOC. Plaintiffs may sue for many of the same remedies available under Title VII. They may seek reinstatement, back pay, a limited amount of compensatory and punitive damages (for intentional discrimination), and certain other forms of relief. Repeat violators may be ordered to pay fines of up to $100,000.

The ADA does not apply to very small businesses. Under the ADA, an "employer" is not covered unless its work force includes "15 or more employees for each working day in each of 20 or more calendar weeks in the current or preceding calendar year." The question in the following case was whether certain individuals should be counted as "employees" of the corporation.

---

[38] 528 U.S. 62, 120 S.Ct. 631, 145 L.Ed.2d 522 (2000).

[39] *Board of Trustees of the University of Alabama v. Garrett,* 531 U.S. 356, 121 S.Ct. 955, 148 L.Ed.2d 866 (2001).

CASE 23.4 **Clackamas Gastroenterology Associates, P.C.ª v. Wells**

Supreme Court of the United States, 2003.
__ U.S. __,
123 S.Ct. 1673,
155 L.Ed.2d 615.
http://supct.law.cornell.edu/supct/search/search.htmlb

FACTS Clackamas Gastroenterology Associates, P.C., a medical clinic in Oregon, employed Deborah Anne Wells as a bookkeeper from 1986 until 1997. After the clinic terminated Wells's employment, she filed a suit in a federal district court against the clinic, alleging discrimination on the basis of disability in violation of the ADA. The clinic asserted that the ADA did not cover it because it did not employ fifteen workers, and filed a motion for summary judgment. The court granted the motion, and Wells appealed to the U.S. Court of

Appeals for the Ninth Circuit, which reversed the judgment. The clinic appealed to the United States Supreme Court. The question was whether the four physician-shareholders who owned the corporation and constituted its board of directors counted as employees.

ISSUE Can shareholders and directors of a corporation qualify as "employees" of the corporation for purposes of the ADA?

DECISION Yes. The United States Supreme Court reversed the lower court's decision and remanded the case to that court to determine whether the four director-shareholder physicians were employees of the clinic.

REASON The Court reasoned that because the definition of "employee" in the ADA "simply states that an 'employee'

---

a. *P.C.* is an abbreviation for *professional corporation,* a form of business organization. See Chapter 25.

b. Scroll to the name of the case and click on it to access the opinion.

(Continued)

CASE 23.4—Continued

is 'an individual employed by an employer,' * * * the common-law element of control is the principal guidepost that should be followed in this case." The Court cited the view of the Equal Employment Opportunity Commission that "[i]f the shareholder-directors operate independently and manage the business, they are proprietors and not employees; if they are subject to the firm's control, they are employees." Under this standard, "an employer is the person, or group of persons, who owns and manages the enterprise. The employer can hire and fire employees, can assign tasks to employees and supervise their performance, and can decide how the profits and losses of the business are to be

distributed. The mere fact that a person has a particular title—such as partner, director, or vice president—should not necessarily be used to determine whether he or she is an employee or a proprietor. Nor should the mere existence of a document styled 'employment agreement.'" Instead, "the answer to whether a shareholder-director is an employee depends on all of the incidents of the relationship * * * with no one factor being decisive."

FOR CRITICAL ANALYSIS—Social Consideration
What factors might be relevant to determining whether an individual controls a business organization or is controlled by it?

What Is a Disability? The ADA is broadly drafted to define persons with disabilities as persons with a physical or mental impairment that "substantially limits" their everyday activities. More specifically, the ADA defines *disability* as "(1) a physical or mental impairment that substantially limits one or more of the major life activities of such individuals; (2) a record of such impairment; or (3) being regarded as having such an impairment."

Health conditions that have been considered disabilities under federal law include blindness, alcoholism, heart disease, cancer, muscular dystrophy, cerebral palsy, paraplegia, diabetes, acquired immune deficiency syndrome (AIDS) and the human immunodeficiency virus (HIV), and morbid obesity (defined as existing when an individual's weight is two times that of the normal person).[40] The ADA excludes

from coverage certain conditions, such as kleptomania. For some time, the courts were divided on the issue of whether carpal tunnel syndrome (or other repetitive-stress injury) constituted a disability under the ADA. In 2002, in a case involving this issue, the Supreme Court unanimously held that it did not. Although an employee with carpal tunnel syndrome could not perform the manual tasks associated with her job, the injury did not "substantially limit the major life activity of performing manual tasks."[41]

A question that frequently arises in ADA cases is whether a person whose disability is controlled by medication or a corrective device still qualifies for protection under the ADA. That issue arose in the following case.

---

[40] *Cook v. Rhode Island Department of Mental Health,* 10 F.3d 17 (1st Cir. 1993).

[41] *Toyota Motor Manufacturing, Kentucky, Inc. v. Williams,* 534 U.S. 184, 122 S.Ct. 681, 151 L.Ed.2d 615 (2002).

CASE 23.5 **Sutton v. United Airlines, Inc.**

Supreme Court of the United States, 1999.
527 U.S. 471,
119 S.Ct. 2139,
144 L.Ed.2d 450.

FACTS Karen and Kimberly Sutton are twin sisters, both of whom have severe myopia. Each woman's uncorrected visual acuity is 20/200 or worse in her right eye and 20/400 or worse in her left eye, but with the use of corrective lenses, such as glasses or contact lenses, each has vision that is 20/20 or better. In other words, without corrective lenses, neither individual can see well enough to do such things as drive a vehicle, watch television, or shop, but with corrective

measures, each functions identically to individuals without a similar impairment. In 1992, the Suttons applied to United Airlines, Inc. (UA), for employment as commercial airline pilots. They met UA's age, education, experience, and Federal Aviation Administration certification qualifications and were invited to flight simulator tests and interviews. Because the Suttons did not meet UA's minimum vision requirement, which was uncorrected visual acuity of 20/100 or better, the interviews were terminated, and neither pilot was offered a position. The Suttons filed a suit in a federal district court against UA, alleging discrimination under the Americans with Disabilities Act (ADA). The Suttons asserted in part that due to their severe myopia, they have a substantially limiting

CASE 23.5—Continued

impairment and are thus disabled. The court disagreed and dismissed their complaint, and the U.S. Court of Appeals for the Tenth Circuit affirmed this judgment. The Suttons appealed to the United States Supreme Court.

ISSUE Is a condition that can be corrected with medication or a corrective device considered a disability for purposes of the ADA?

DECISION No. The United States Supreme Court affirmed the decision of the lower court.

REASON The Supreme Court held that a person is not disabled (substantially limited in any major life activity) under the ADA if he or she has a condition that can be rectified with medication or one, such as poor vision, that can be

rectified with corrective devices, such as glasses. The Court stated, "A 'disability' exists only where an impairment 'substantially limits' a major life activity, not where it 'might,' 'could,' or 'would' be substantially limiting if mitigating measures were not taken. * * * To be sure, a person whose physical or mental impairment is corrected by mitigating measures still has an impairment, but if the impairment is corrected it does not 'substantially limi[t]' a major life activity."

FOR CRITICAL ANALYSIS—Political Consideration
Some claim that the courts have, in effect, "written" the ADA to some extent because it has been left to the courts to decide a number of questions that the act left open—such as the question addressed in this case. Should Congress pay more attention to details when it drafts legislation? Is it appropriate for the courts to assume such "lawmaking" responsibilities?

Reasonable Accommodation. The ADA does not require that *unqualified* applicants with disabilities be hired or retained. Therefore, employers are not obligated to accommodate the needs of job applicants or employees with disabilities who are not otherwise qualified for the work. If a job applicant or an employee with a disability, with reasonable accommodation, can perform essential job functions, however, the employer must make the accommodation. Required modifications may include installing ramps for a wheelchair, establishing flexible working hours, creating or modifying job assignments, and creating or improving training materials and procedures.

Employers who do not accommodate the needs of persons with disabilities must demonstrate that the accommodations will cause "undue hardship." Generally, the law offers no uniform standards for identifying what is an undue hardship other than the imposition of a "significant difficulty or expense" on the employer.

Usually, the courts decide whether an accommodation constitutes an undue hardship on a case-by-case basis. In one case, the court decided that paying for a parking space near the office for an employee with a disability was not an undue hardship.[42] In another case, the court held that accommodating the request of an employee with diabetes for indefinite leave until his disease was under control would create an undue hardship for the employer because the employer would not know when the employee was returning to work. The court stated that reasonable accommodation under the ADA means accommodation so that the employee can perform the job now or "in the immediate future" rather than at some unspecified distant time.[43]

Defenses to Employment Discrimination

The first line of defense for an employer charged with employment discrimination is, of course, to assert that the plaintiff has failed to meet his or her initial burden of proving that discrimination in fact occurred. As noted, plaintiffs bringing cases under the ADA sometimes find it difficult to meet this initial burden because they must prove that their alleged disabilities are disabilities covered by the ADA. Furthermore, plaintiffs in ADA cases must prove that they were otherwise qualified for the job and that their disabilities were the sole reason they were not hired or were fired.

Once a plaintiff succeeds in proving that discrimination occurred, the burden shifts to the employer to justify the discriminatory practice. Often, employers attempt to justify the discrimination by claiming that it was a result of a business necessity, a bona fide occupational qualification, or a seniority system. In some cases, as noted earlier, an effective antiharassment policy and prompt remedial action when harassment occurs may shield employers from liability under Title VII for sexual harassment.

---

[42] See *Lyons v. Legal Aid Society,* 68 F.3d 1512 (2d Cir. 1995).

[43] *Myers v. Hase,* 50 F.3d 278 (4th Cir. 1995).

BUSINESS NECESSITY

An employer may defend against a claim of disparate-impact discrimination by asserting that a practice that has a discriminatory effect is a **business necessity**. ● EXAMPLE #7 If requiring a high school diploma is shown to have a discriminatory effect, an employer might argue that a high school education is necessary for workers to perform the job at a required level of competence. If the employer can demonstrate to the court's satisfaction that there is a definite connection between a high school education and job performance, the employer will succeed in this business necessity defense.●

BONA FIDE OCCUPATIONAL QUALIFICATION

Another defense applies when discrimination against a protected class is essential to a job—that is, when a particular trait is a **bona fide occupational qualification (BFOQ)**. For example, a men's fashion magazine might legitimately hire only male models. Similarly, the Federal Aviation Administration can legitimately impose age limits for airline pilots. Race, however, can never be a BFOQ. Generally, courts have restricted the BFOQ defense to instances in which the employee's gender is essential to the job. In 1991, the United States Supreme Court held that even a fetal protection policy that was adopted to protect the unborn children of female employees from the harmful effects of exposure to lead was an unacceptable BFOQ.[44]

SENIORITY SYSTEMS

An employer with a history of discrimination may have no members of protected classes in upper-level positions. Even if the employer now seeks to be unbiased, it may face a lawsuit in which the plaintiff asks a court to order that minorities be promoted ahead of schedule to compensate for past discrimination. If no present intent to discriminate is shown, and promotions or other job benefits are distributed according to a fair **seniority system** (in which workers with more years of service are promoted first, or laid off last), however, the employer has a good defense against the suit.

Affirmative Action

Federal statutes and regulations providing for equal opportunity in the workplace were designed to reduce or eliminate discriminatory practices with respect to hiring,

retaining, and promoting employees. **Affirmative action** programs go a step further and attempt to "make up" for past patterns of discrimination by giving members of protected classes preferential treatment in hiring or promotion.

Affirmative action policies were first mandated by an executive order issued by President Lyndon Johnson in 1965. All government agencies, including those of state and local governments, were required to implement such policies. Affirmative action requirements were also imposed on companies that contract to do business with the federal government and on institutions that receive federal funds. Because a significant percentage of the nation's employees work for government agencies or for firms that do business with the government, this presidential executive order has had a profound impact on the American workplace.

Title VII of the Civil Rights Act of 1964 neither requires nor prohibits affirmative action, and thus private companies and organizations that do not do business with the government or receive federal funds have not been required to implement such policies—although many have done so voluntarily. Note, though, that the courts and the Equal Employment Opportunity Commission have sometimes ordered private companies to undertake affirmative action when they found evidence of past discrimination. Labor unions that have been found to discriminate against women or minorities in the past have also been required to establish and follow affirmative action plans.

CHALLENGES TO AFFIRMATIVE ACTION

Affirmative action programs have caused much controversy, particularly when they result in what is frequently called "reverse discrimination"—discrimination against "majority" workers, such as white males (or discrimination against other minority groups that are not given preferential treatment under a particular affirmative action program). At issue is whether affirmative action programs, because of their inherently discriminatory nature, violate employee rights or the equal protection clause of the Fourteenth Amendment to the U.S. Constitution.

When an affirmative action plan undertaken by a private employer (one that does not do business with the government) is challenged on the basis of reverse discrimination, the court decides the issue under Title VII. Generally, the courts have held that an affirmative action plan is valid if the employer can show that minorities and women have been notably underrepresented in the workplace in the past and that the plan does not unnecessarily restrict the rights of male or nonminority employees. More controversial today is the issue of whether affirmative action plans required by the government (that is, plans undertaken by

---

[44] *United Auto Workers v. Johnson Controls, Inc.,* 113 U.S. 158, 111 S.Ct. 1196, 113 L.Ed.2d 158 (1991).

employers that receive government funds or that do business with the government) violate the equal protection clause of the Fourteenth Amendment to the Constitution.

The *Bakke* Case. An early nonemployment-related case addressing this issue, *Regents of the University of California v. Bakke,*[45] involved an affirmative action program implemented by the University of California at Davis. Allan Bakke, who had been turned down for medical school at the Davis campus, sued the university for reverse discrimination after he discovered that his academic record was better than the records of some of the minority applicants who had been admitted to the program.

The United States Supreme Court held that affirmative action programs were subject to intermediate scrutiny. Any law or action evaluated under a standard of intermediate scrutiny, to be constitutionally valid, must be substantially related to important government objectives. Applying this standard, the Court held that the university could give favorable weight to minority applicants as part of a plan to increase minority enrollment so as to achieve a more culturally diverse student body. The Court stated, however, that the use of a quota system, in which a certain number of places are explicitly reserved for minority applicants, violated the equal protection clause of the Fourteenth Amendment.

The *Adarand* Case. Although the *Bakke* case and later court decisions alleviated the harshness of the quota system, today's courts are going even further in questioning the constitutional validity of affirmative action programs. In 1995, in its landmark decision in *Adarand Constructors, Inc. v. Peña,*[46] the United States Supreme Court held that any federal, state, or local affirmative action program that uses racial or ethnic classifications as the basis for making decisions is subject to strict scrutiny by the courts.

In effect, the Court's ruling in *Adarand* means that an affirmative action program is constitutional only if it attempts to remedy past discrimination and does not make use of quotas or preferences. Furthermore, once such a program has succeeded in the goal of remedying past discrimination, it must be changed or dropped.

Subsequent Court Decisions. In 1996, in *Hopwood v. State of Texas,*[47] the Court of Appeals for the Fifth Circuit went beyond the Supreme Court's *Adarand* decision. In the *Hopwood* case, two white law school applicants sued the University of Texas School of Law in Austin, alleging that they were denied admission because of the school's affirma-

tive action program. The program allowed admitting officials to take racial and other factors into consideration when determining which students would be admitted. The court held that the program violated the equal protection clause because it discriminated in favor of minority applicants. In its decision, the court directly challenged the *Bakke* decision by stating that the use of race even as a means of achieving diversity on college campuses "undercuts the Fourteenth Amendment."

In 2003, the United States Supreme Court reviewed two cases involving issues similar to that in the *Hopwood* case. Both cases involved admissions programs at the University of Michigan. In *Gratz v. Bollinger,*[48] two white applicants who were denied undergraduate admission to the university alleged reverse discrimination. The school's policy gave each applicant a score based on a number of factors, including grade point average, standardized test results, and personal achievements. The system automatically awarded every "underrepresented" minority (African American, Hispanic, and Native American) applicant twenty points—one-fifth of the points needed to guarantee admission. The Court held that this policy violated the equal protection clause.

In contrast, in *Grutter v. Bollinger,*[49] the Court held that the University of Michigan Law School's admission policy was constitutional. In that case, the Court concluded that "[u]niversities can, however, consider race or ethnicity more flexibly as a 'plus' factor in the context of individualized consideration of each and every applicant." The significant difference between the two admissions policies, in the Court's view, was that the law school's approach did not apply a mechanical formula giving "diversity bonuses" based on race or ethnicity.

STATE ACTIONS

In the meantime, some state governments have been taking action. California and Washington, by voter initiatives in 1996 and 1998, respectively, ended state-government-sponsored affirmative action in those states. Similar movements are currently under way in other state and local areas as well. Additionally, a number of universities have modified their admissions policies.

State Statutes

In addition to the federal legislation discussed in this chapter, most states also have statutes that prohibit employment discrimination. Generally, the kinds of discrimination

---

[45] 438 U.S. 265, 98 S.Ct. 2733, 57 L.Ed.2d 750 (1978).
[46] 515 U.S. 200, 115 S.Ct. 2097, 132 L.Ed.2d 158 (1995).
[47] 84 F.3d 720 (5th Cir. 1996).

[48] __U.S. __, 123 S.Ct. 2411, 156 L.Ed.2d 257 (2003).
[49] __U.S. __, 123 S.Ct. 2325, 156 L.Ed.2d 304 (2003).

MANAGEMENT PERSPECTIVE
Employment Discrimination and Public Policy

MANAGEMENT FACES A LEGAL ISSUE Employees of small businesses are often precluded from seeking protection under federal or state laws prohibiting employment discrimination. This is because, as already mentioned, these statutes typically restrict their coverage to employers that have a specified number of workers. Does this mean that if a company you own or manage has less than that specified number, you can avoid liability for discriminatory actions in your workplace?

WHAT THE COURTS SAY Not necessarily, say the courts. According to a number of courts, employees in small firms who are victims of employment discrimination do have recourse against their employers despite the fact that federal or state statutory remedies are not available.

For example, in one case a woman was fired from a veterinary clinic that had a small number of employees (fewer than eight), allegedly because she became pregnant. She sued the employer for wrongful discharge on the ground that her employer's action violated the public policy against discrimination. The court held that her case could go forward because, even though the state

statute prohibiting gender discrimination applied only to firms with eight or more employees, it reflected a broad public policy against gender discrimination.[a] In another case, a woman who was fired because she refused to have sex with her supervisor sued her employer for wrongful discharge in violation of the state's public policy against prostitution. The Maryland Court of Appeals allowed her suit to go forward.[b] Increasingly, the courts are allowing employees in similar situations to recover damages for discrimination on the basis of public policy.

IMPLICATIONS FOR MANAGERS Owners and managers of firms with only a few employees should realize that, even though they may not be subject to statutory laws prohibiting employment discrimination, common law concepts, such as wrongful discharge, may apply. Indeed, even when employers are subject to federal or state discrimination statutes, a plaintiff may find it preferable to sue the employer for wrongful discharge for various reasons—for example, to avoid the cap on damages imposed by the major federal law prohibiting discrimination.

a. *Roberts v. Dudley,* 92 Wash.App. 652, 966 P.2d 377 (1998).
b. *Insignia Residential Corp. v. Ashton,* 359 Md. 560, 755 A.2d 1080 (2000).

prohibited under federal legislation are also prohibited by state laws. In addition, state statutes often provide protection for certain individuals who are not covered under federal laws. For example, a New Jersey appellate court has held that anyone over the age of eighteen is entitled to sue for age discrimination under the state law, which specifies no threshold age limit.[50] State laws may also provide addi-

tional damages, such as damages for emotional distress, that are not provided for under federal statutes.

Furthermore, as discussed in this chapter's *Management Perspective* feature above, some courts have held small firms liable for employment discrimination on the basis of public policy.

---

[50] *Bergen Commercial Bank v. Sisler,* 307 N.J.Super. 333, 704 A.2d 1017 (1998).

Terms and Concepts

Chapter Summary	Employment Law
Wage-Hour Laws (See page 467.)	1. *Davis-Bacon Act (1931)*—Requires contractors and subcontractors working on federal government construction projects to pay their employees "prevailing wages." 2. *Walsh-Healey Act (1936)*—Requires that employees of firms that contract with federal agencies be paid a minimum wage and overtime pay. 3. *Fair Labor Standards Act (1938)*—Extended wage-hour requirements to cover all employers whose activities affect interstate commerce plus certain businesses. The act has specific requirements in regard to child labor, maximum hours, and minimum wages.
Labor Unions (See pages 467–470.)	1. *Norris-LaGuardia Act (1932)*—Protects peaceful strikes, picketing, and primary boycotts. 2. *National Labor Relations Act (1935)*—Established the rights of employees to engage in collective bargaining and to strike; also defined specific employer practices as unfair to labor. The National Labor Relations Board (NLRB) was created to administer and enforce the act. 3. *Labor-Management Relations Act (Taft-Hartley Act, 1947)*—Proscribes certain union practices, such as the closed shop. 4. *Labor-Management Reporting and Disclosure Act (1959)*—Established an employee bill of rights and reporting requirements for union activities.
Worker Health and Safety (See pages 470–471.)	1. The Occupational Safety and Health Act of 1970 requires employers to meet specific safety and health standards that are established and enforced by the Occupational Safety and Health Administration (OSHA). 2. State workers' compensation laws establish an administrative procedure for compensating workers who are injured in accidents that occur on the job, regardless of fault.
Income Security (See pages 471–473.)	1. *Social Security and Medicare*—The Social Security Act of 1935 provides for old-age (retirement), survivors, and disability insurance. Both employers and employees must make contributions under the Federal Insurance Contributions Act (FICA) to help pay for the employees' loss of income on retirement. The Social Security Administration administers Medicare, a health-insurance program for older or disabled persons. 2. *Private pension plans*—The federal Employee Retirement Income Security Act (ERISA) of 1974 establishes standards for the management of employer-provided pension plans. 3. *Unemployment insurance*—The Federal Unemployment Tax Act (FUTA) of 1935 created a system that provides unemployment compensation to eligible individuals. Covered employers are taxed to help defray the costs of unemployment compensation.
COBRA (See page 473.)	The Consolidated Omnibus Budget Reconciliation Act (COBRA) of 1985 requires employers to give employees, on termination of employment, the option of continuing their medical, optical, or dental insurance coverage for a certain period.

(Continued)

Chapter Summary	**Employment Law—Continued**
Family and Medical Leave (See pages 473–474.)	The Family and Medical Leave Act (FMLA) of 1993 requires employers with fifty or more employees to provide their employees (except for key employees) with up to twelve weeks of unpaid family or medical leave during any twelve-month period.
Wrongful Discharge (See pages 474–475.)	Wrongful discharge occurs whenever an employer discharges an employee in violation of the law or of an employment contract. To protect employees from some of the harsh results of the common law employment-at-will doctrine (under which employers may hire or fire employees "at will" unless a contract indicates to the contrary), courts have made exceptions to the doctrine on the basis of contract theory, tort theory, and public policy.
Whistleblower Statutes (See page 475.)	Most states have passed whistleblower statutes specifically to protect employees who "blow the whistle" on their employers from subsequent retaliation by those employers. The federal Whistleblower Protection Act of 1989 protects federal employees who report their employers' wrongdoing. The federal False Claims Reform Act of 1986 provides monetary rewards for whistleblowers who disclose information relating to fraud perpetrated against the U.S. government.
Title VII of the Civil Rights Act of 1964 (See pages 475–478.)	Title VII prohibits employment discrimination based on race, color, national origin, religion, or gender. 1. *Procedures*—Employees must file a claim with the Equal Employment Opportunity Commission (EEOC). The EEOC may sue the employer on the employee's behalf; if not, the employee may sue the employer directly. 2. *Types of discrimination*—Title VII prohibits both intentional (disparate-treatment) and unintentional (disparate-impact) discrimination. Disparate-impact discrimination occurs when an employer's practice, such as hiring only persons with a certain level of education, has the effect of discriminating against a class of persons protected by Title VII. 3. *Sexual harassment*—Title VII also protects employees against sexual harassment. *Quid pro quo* harassment takes place when job opportunities, promotions, or raises are given in return for sexual favors. Hostile-environment harassment takes place when discrimination alters the conditions of the victim's employment and creates an abusive environment. 4. *Remedies for discrimination under Title VII*—If a plaintiff proves that unlawful discrimination occurred, he or she may be awarded reinstatement, back pay, and retroactive promotions. Damages (both compensatory and punitive) may be awarded for intentional discrimination.
Discrimination Based on Age (See pages 478–479.)	The Age Discrimination in Employment Act (ADEA) of 1967 prohibits employment discrimination on the basis of age against individuals forty years of age or older. Procedures for bringing a case under the ADEA are similar to those for bringing a case under Title VII.
Discrimination Based on Disability (See pages 479–481.)	The Americans with Disabilities Act (ADA) of 1990 prohibits employment discrimination against persons with disabilities who are otherwise qualified to perform the essential functions of the jobs for which they apply. 1. *Procedures and remedies*—To prevail on a claim under the ADA, the plaintiff must show that she or he has a disability, is otherwise qualified for the employment in question, and was excluded from the employment solely because of the disability. Procedures under the ADA are similar to those required in Title VII cases; remedies are also similar to those under Title VII.

Chapter Summary	Employment Law—Continued
Discrimination Based on Disability—continued	2. *Definition of disability*—The ADA defines the term *disability* as a physical or mental impairment that substantially limits one or more major life activities; a record of such impairment; or being regarded as having such an impairment. 3. *Reasonable accommodation*—Employers are required to reasonably accommodate the needs of persons with disabilities. Reasonable accommodations may include altering job-application procedures, modifying the physical work environment, and permitting more flexible work schedules. Employers are not required to accommodate the needs of all workers with disabilities.
Defenses to Employment Discrimination (See pages 481–482.)	If a plaintiff proves that employment discrimination occurred, employers may avoid liability by successfully asserting certain defenses. Employers may assert that the discrimination was required for reasons of business necessity, to meet a bona fide occupational qualification, or to maintain a legitimate seniority system.
Affirmative Action (See pages 482–483.)	Affirmative action programs attempt to "make up" for past patterns of discrimination by giving members of protected classes preferential treatment in hiring or promotion. Increasingly, such programs are being strictly scrutinized by the courts, and state-sponsored affirmative action has been banned in California and Washington.
State Statutes (See pages 483–484.)	Generally, the kinds of discrimination prohibited by federal statutes are also prohibited by state laws. State laws may provide for more extensive protection and remedies than federal laws.

For Review

① What is the employment-at-will doctrine? When and why are exceptions to this doctrine made?

② What federal statute governs working hours and wages? What federal statutes govern labor unions and collective bargaining?

③ What federal act was enacted to protect the health and safety of employees? What are workers' compensation laws?

④ Generally, what kind of conduct is prohibited by Title VII of the Civil Rights Act of 1964, as amended?

⑤ What remedies are available under Title VII of the 1964 Civil Rights Act, as amended?

Questions and Case Problems

23–1. Health and Safety Regulations. Denton and Carlo were employed at an appliance plant. Their job required them to do occasional maintenance work while standing on a wire mesh twenty feet above the plant floor. Other employees had fallen through the mesh, one of whom was killed by the fall. When Denton and Carlo were asked by their supervisor to do work that would likely require them to walk on the mesh, they refused due to their fear of bodily harm or death. Because of their refusal to do the requested work, the two employees were fired from their jobs. Was their discharge wrongful? If so, under what federal employment law? To what federal agency or department should they turn for assistance?

23–2. Unfair Labor Practices. Suppose that Consolidated Stores is undergoing a unionization campaign. Prior to the union election, management says that the union is unnecessary to protect workers. Management also provides bonuses and wage increases to the workers during this period. The employees reject the union. Union organizers protest that the wage increases during the election campaign unfairly prejudiced the vote. Should these wage increases be regarded as an unfair labor practice? Discuss.

23–3. Workers' Compensation. Galvin Strang worked for a tractor company in one of its factories. Near his work station was a conveyor belt that ran through a large industrial oven. Sometimes, the workers would use the oven to heat their meals. Thirty-inch-high flasks containing molds were fixed at regular intervals on the conveyor and were transported into the oven. Strang had to walk between the flasks to get to his work station. One day, the conveyor was not moving, and Strang used the oven to cook a frozen pot pie. As he was removing the pot pie from the oven, the conveyor came on. One of the flasks struck Strang and seriously injured him. Strang sought recovery under the state workers' compensation law. Should he recover? Why or why not?

23–4. Title VII Violations. Discuss fully whether any of the following actions would constitute a violation of Title VII of the 1964 Civil Rights Act, as amended:

(a) Tennington, Inc., is a consulting firm and has ten employees. These employees travel on consulting jobs in seven states. Tennington has an employment record of hiring only white males.

(b) Novo Films, Inc., is making a film about Africa and needs to employ approximately one hundred extras for this picture. Novo advertises in all major newspapers in southern California for the hiring of these extras. The ad states that only African Americans need apply.

23–5. Discrimination Based on Age. Tavo Jones had worked since 1974 for Westshore Resort, where he maintained golf carts. During the first decade, he received positive job evaluations and numerous merit pay raises. He was promoted to the position of supervisor of golf-cart maintenance at three courses. Then a new employee, Ben Olery, was placed in charge of the golf courses. He demoted Jones, who was over the age of forty, to running only one of the three cart facilities, and he froze Jones's salary indefinitely. Olery also demoted five other men over the age of forty. Another cart facility was placed under the supervision of Blake Blair. Later, the cart facilities for the three courses were again consolidated, but Blair—not Jones—was put in charge. At the time, Jones was still in his forties, and Blair was in his twenties. Jones overheard Blair say that "we are going to have to do away with these . . . old and senile" men. Jones quit and sued Westshore for employment discrimination. Should he prevail? Explain.

23–6. Discrimination Based on Disability. Vaughn Murphy was first diagnosed with hypertension (high blood pressure) when he was ten years old. Unmedicated, his blood pressure is approximately 250/160. With medication, however, he can function normally and engage in the same activities as anyone else. In 1994, United Parcel Service, Inc. (UPS), hired Murphy to be a mechanic, a position that required him to drive commercial motor vehicles. To get the job, Murphy had to meet a U.S. Department of Transportation (DOT) regulation that a driver have "no current clinical diagnosis of high blood pressure likely to interfere with his/her ability to operate a commercial vehicle safely." At the time, Murphy's blood pressure was measured at 186/124, but he was erroneously certified and started work. Within a month, the error was discovered and he was fired. Murphy obtained another mechanic's job—one that

did not require DOT certification—and filed a suit in a federal district court against UPS, claiming discrimination under the Americans with Disabilities Act. UPS filed a motion for summary judgment. Should the court grant UPS's motion? Explain. [*Murphy v. United Parcel Service, Inc.,* 527 U.S. 516, 119 S.Ct. 2133, 144 L.Ed.2d 484 (1999)]

23–7. Hours and Wages. Richard Ackerman was an advance sales representative and account manager for Coca-Cola Enterprises, Inc. His primary responsibility was to sell Coca-Cola products to grocery stores, convenience stores, and other sales outlets. Coca-Cola also employed merchandisers, who did not sell Coca-Cola products but performed tasks associated with their distribution and promotion, including restocking shelves, filling vending machines, and setting up displays. The account managers, who serviced the smaller accounts themselves, regularly worked between fifty-five and seventy-two hours each week. Coca-Cola paid them a salary, bonuses, and commissions, but it did not pay them—unlike the merchandisers—additional compensation for the overtime. Ackerman and the other account managers filed a suit in a federal district court against Coca-Cola, alleging that they were entitled to overtime compensation. Coca-Cola responded that because of an exemption under the Fair Labor Standards Act, it was not required to pay them overtime. Is Coca-Cola correct? Explain. [*Ackerman v. Coca-Cola Enterprises, Inc.,* 179 F.3d 1260 (10th Cir. 1999)]

CASE PROBLEM WITH SAMPLE ANSWER

23–8. PGA Tour, Inc., sponsors professional golf tournaments. A player may enter in several ways, but the most common method is to successfully compete in a three-stage qualifying tournament known as the "Q-School." Anyone may enter the Q-School by submitting two letters of recommendation and paying $3,000 to cover greens fees and the cost of a golf cart, which is permitted during the first two stages, but is prohibited during the third stage. The rules governing the events include the "Rules of Golf," which apply at all levels of amateur and professional golf and do not prohibit the use of golf carts, and the "hard card," which applies specifically to the PGA tour and requires the players to walk the course during most of a tournament. Casey Martin is a talented golfer with a degenerative circulatory disorder that prevents him from walking golf courses. Martin entered the Q-School and asked for permission to use a cart during the third stage. PGA refused. Martin filed a suit in a federal district court against PGA, alleging a violation of the Americans with Disabilities Act. Is a golf cart in these circumstances a "reasonable accommodation" under the ADA? Why or why not? [*PGA Tour, Inc. v. Martin,* 532 U.S. 661, 121 S.Ct. 1879, 149 L.Ed.2d 904 (2001)]

🢒 To view a sample answer for this case problem, go to this book's Web site at **http://fundamentals.westbuslaw.com** and click on "Interactive Study Center."

23–9. Unfair Labor Practice. The New York Department of Education's e-mail policy prohibits the use of the e-mail system for unofficial purposes, except that officials of the New York Public Employees Federation (PEF), the union representing state employees, can use the system for some limited communications, including the scheduling of union meetings and activities. In 1998, Michael Darcy, an elected PEF official, began sending mass, union-related e-mails to employees, including a summary of a union delegates' convention, a union newsletter, a criticism of proposed state legislation, and a criticism of the state governor and the Governor's Office of Employee Relations. Richard Cate, the department's chief operating officer, met with Darcy and reiterated the department's e-mail policy. When Darcy refused to stop his use of the e-mail system, Cate terminated his access to it. Darcy filed a complaint with the New York Public Employment Relations Board, alleging an unfair labor practice. Do the circumstances support Cate's action? Why or why not? [*Benson v. Cuevas*, 293 A.D.2d 927, 741 N.Y.S.2d 310 (3 Dept. 2002)]

23–10. Discrimination Based on Race. The hiring policy of Phillips Community College of the University of Arkansas (PCCUA) is to conduct an internal search for qualified applicants before advertising outside the college. Steven Jones, the university's chancellor, can determine the application and appointment process for vacant positions, however, and is the ultimate authority in hiring decisions. Howard Lockridge, an African American, was the chair of PCCUA's Technical and Industrial Department. Between 1988 and 1998, Lockridge applied for several different positions, some of which were unadvertised, some of which were unfilled for years, and some of which were filled with less qualified persons from outside the college. In 1998, when Jones advertised an opening for the position of Dean of Industrial Technology and Workforce Development, Lockridge did not apply for the job. Jones hired Tracy McGraw, a white male. Lockridge filed a suit in a federal district court against the university under Title VII. The university filed a motion for summary judgment in its favor. What are the elements of a *prima facie* case of disparate-treatment discrimination? Can Lockridge pass this test, or should the court issue a judgment in the university's favor? Explain. [*Lockridge v. Board of Trustees of the University of Arkansas*, 294 F.3d 1010 (8th Cir. 2002)]

VIDEO QUESTION

23–11. Go to this text's Web site at **http://fundamentals.westbuslaw.com** and click on "Video Questions." Select "Chapter 23" and view the video titled *Employment at Will*. Then answer the following questions:

1. In the video, Laura asserts that she can fire Ray "For any reason. For no reason." Is this true? Explain your answer.
2. What are the exceptions listed in the chapter to the employment-at-will doctrine? Does Ray's situation fit into any of these exceptions?
3. Would Ray be protected from wrongful discharge under whistleblowing statutes? Why or why not?
4. Assume that you are the employer in this scenario. What arguments can you make that Ray should not be able to sue for wrongful discharge in this situation?

EMPLOYMENT LAW

For updated links to resources available on the Web, as well as other materials, visit this text's Web site at

http://fundamentals.westbuslaw.com

An excellent Web site for information on employee benefits, including the full text of the FMLA, COBRA, other relevant statutes and case law, and current articles, is BenefitsLink. Go to

http://www.benefitslink.com

The American Federation of Labor–Congress of Industrial Organizations (AFL–CIO) provides links to a variety of labor-related resources at

http://www.aflcio.org

The Occupational Safety and Health Administration (OSHA) offers information related to workplace health and safety at

http://www.osha.gov

The National Labor Relations Board is online at the following URL:

http://www.nlrb.gov

The Job Accommodation Network of the U.S. Department of Labor provides extensive information on the Americans with Disabilities Act of 1990 at

http://www.jan.wvu.edu/links/adalinks.htm

Online Legal Research

Go to the *Fundamentals of Business Law Today* home page at **http://fundamentals. westbuslaw.com**. Select "Interactive Study Center" and then click on "Chapter 23." There you will find the following Internet research exercises that you can perform to learn more about topics covered in this chapter:

Activity 23–1: LEGAL PERSPECTIVE—Workers' Compensation
Activity 23–2: MANAGEMENT PERSPECTIVE—Equal Employment Opportunity
Activity 23–3: SOCIAL PERSPECTIVE—Americans with Disabilities

Before the Test

Go to the *Fundamentals of Business Law Today* home page at **http://fundamentals. westbuslaw.com**. Click on "Interactive Quizzes." You will find at least twenty interactive questions relating to this chapter.

Westlaw® Campus

If your textbook provided for a subscription to Westlaw® Campus, or if you have otherwise purchased access to the Westlaw Campus database, you can access any of the cases presented or cited in this chapter by using your Westlaw Campus account.

Redi-Floors, Inc. v. Sonenberg Co.

INTRODUCTION

In Chapter 22, we outlined the liability of principals and agents for contracts formed by agents. In this *Focus on Legal Reasoning,* we look at *Redi-Floors, Inc. v. Sonenberg Co.,*[1] a decision in which the court set out these principles.

CASE BACKGROUND

Sonenberg Company managed Westchester Manor Apartments in Atlanta, Georgia. Manor Associates Limited Partnership owned the complex.[2] Manor's partners included

---

1. 254 Ga.App. 615, 563 S.E.2d 505 (2002).
2. A *limited partnership* is a form of business organization discussed in Chapter 24.

Westchester Manor, Limited. The entry sign to the property disclosed only that Sonenberg managed it.

Sonenberg's on-site property manager contacted Redi-Floors, Inc., and requested a proposal for installing carpet in several apartments. In preparing the proposal, Redi-Floors confirmed that Sonenberg was the managing company. The property manager ordered, and Redi-Floors installed, the carpet as per the proposal. Redi-Floors sent invoices to the complex and received checks from "Westchester Manor Apartments." Believing that Sonenberg owned the complex, Redi-Floors did not learn the true owner's identity until a dispute arose concerning payment for some of the invoices.

To recover on the outstanding invoices, Redi-Floors filed a suit in a Georgia state court against Sonenberg, Manor Associates, and Westchester Manor. The court granted Sonenberg's motion for a directed verdict[3] on the ground that Redi-Floors knew Sonenberg was only an agent. Against the other parties, Redi-Floors obtained a verdict exceeding $20,000. Unable to collect on this judgment, Redi-Floors appealed to a state intermediate appellate court.

---

3. Recall from Chapter 2 that a *motion for a directed verdict* is a motion for the judge to take the decision out of the hands of the jury and direct a verdict for the party who filed the motion on the ground that the other party has not produced sufficient evidence to support his or her claim.

MAJORITY OPINION

BLACKBURN, Chief Judge.

* * * *

An agent who makes a contract without identifying his principal becomes personally liable on the contract. *If the agent wishes to avoid personal liability, the duty is on him to disclose his agency, and not on the party with whom he deals to discover it.* The agent's disclosure of a trade name and the plaintiff's awareness of that name are not necessarily sufficient so as to protect the agent from liability. *The disclosure of an agency is not complete for the purpose of relieving the agent from personal liability unless it embraces the name of the principal.* [Emphasis added.]

Based on these principles, *Reed v. Burns International Security Services,* 215 Ga.App. 60, 449 S.E.2d 888 (1994), upheld a judgment in favor of a security company and against the apartment management company that contracted for security services at the apartment complex but failed to identify to the security company the name of the limited partnership owning the complex. * * * Here, at least some evidence showed that Sonenberg never disclosed the name of Manor Associates Limited Partnership to Redi-Floors. Accordingly, the trial court erred in entering a directed verdict in favor of Sonenberg.

* * * *

With respect to an undisclosed principal, the rule in Georgia is that if the buyer is in fact merely an agent and acts with the authority of an undisclosed principal, either he or such principal may be held liable at the election of the opposite party; but the contractual liability of such agent and principal is not joint, and, after an election to proceed against one, the other cannot be held. Thus, if an agent buys in his own name, without disclosing his principal, and the seller subsequently discovers that the purchase

was, in fact, made for another, he may, at his choice, look for payment either to the agent or the principal * * *. On the other hand, if, at the time of the sale, the seller knows not only the person, who is nominally dealing with him, is not principal, but agent, and also knows who the principal really is, and notwithstanding all the knowledge, chooses to make the agent his debtor—dealing with him and him alone—the seller must be taken to have abandoned his recourse against the principal, and cannot afterwards, upon the failure of the agent, turn round and charge the principal, having once made his election at the time when he had the power of choosing between the one and the other. An election deliberately made, with knowledge of facts and absence of fraud, is conclusive; and the party who has once elected, can claim no right to make a second choice. Thus, while it is true that a judgment against both the agent and the principal cannot stand, it is the plaintiff who is entitled to elect against which of the defendants, principal or agent, to take the judgment. * * *

* * * In the present case the trial court's erroneous granting of a directed verdict deprived the plaintiff of its right to elect which defendant it would proceed against. * * *

* * * *

This case must be remanded to the trial court with instructions to allow Redi-Floors to make an election as to which defendant it wishes to proceed against, thus restoring to Redi-Floors the right to make such election. Should Redi-Floors elect to hold Manor Associates liable, nothing further is required as the existing judgment would stand against this defendant. On the other hand, should Redi-Floors seek to proceed against Sonenberg, the existing judgment is vacated and a new trial will be necessary.

DISSENTING OPINION

MILLER, Judge, * * * dissenting * * * .

* * * I dissent * * * because I believe that Redi-Floors's decision to obtain a judgment against Manor Associates Limited Partnership has rendered the error harmless. Redi-Floors had the right, as do all plaintiffs, to pursue mutually exclusive remedies prior to the verdict; but once Redi-Floors procured a judgment order which was reduced to writing against Manor Associates, that constituted an election of alternative remedies that precluded plaintiff from pursuing the excluded remedy against Sonenberg.

A corollary to the principle that a nondisclosing agent is personally liable is that the contract liability of a principal and his agent is not joint, and after election to proceed against one, the other cannot be held. As the plaintiff may not obtain judgment against both, he must make an election *prior to judgment* as to whether he wants a judgment against the agent or against the principal. If the plaintiff does not expressly announce an election, his taking a judgment against the principal constitutes an election and precludes any further action against the agent. Here, after the court entered a directed verdict in favor of Sonenberg, Redi-Floors (1) had every opportunity to reevaluate its case and to obtain court permission to dismiss its case * * * against Manor Associates instead of proceeding further or (2) could have had the court withhold entry of judgment (once the verdict against Manor Associates was obtained) until an appeal of the directed verdict was decided. In either case, Redi-Floors could have then brought this issue here as an appeal from the directed verdict *without* electing to obtain a judgment against Manor Associates. Redi-Floor's decision to obtain a judgment against the principal, however, was an election and precludes it from pursuing Sonenberg further.

LEGAL REASONING AND ANALYSIS

❶ Legal Analysis. The majority cites, in its opinion, *Reed v. Burns International Security Services,* 215 Ga.App. 60, 449 S.E.2d 888 (1994) (see the appendix to Chapter 1 for instructions on how to access state court opinions). How do the facts, issues, and holdings of the *Redi-Floors* and *Reed* cases compare? Why does the majority in the *Redi-Floors* case cite the *Reed* case?

❷ Legal Reasoning. What reasons does the majority provide to justify its conclusion? How do those reasons contrast with the dissent's reasoning? With whom do you agree? Why?

❸ Commercial Application. Do agents owe to those with whom they deal on behalf of their principals any obligations besides a public duty to obey the law? If so, what is the nature of those obligations?

❹ Implications for Creditors. What does the outcome in this case indicate to those who do business with others' agents on a credit basis?

❺ Case Briefing Assignment. Using the guidelines for briefing cases given in Appendix A of this text, brief the *Redi-Floors* case.

This text's Web site, at **http://fundamentals.westbuslaw.com**, offers links to West's Court Case Updates, as well as to other online research sources. You can also locate court cases at the Web sites listed in the *Accessing the Internet* section at the end of Chapter 2.

The Legal Information Institute (LII) offers links to state court decisions on agency principles at **http://www.law.cornell.edu/topics/agency.html**, a page within the LII Web site. LII is affiliated with Cornell Law School in Ithaca, New York.

UNIT 8

Business Organizations

24

Sole Proprietorships, Partnerships, and Limited Liability Companies

CHAPTER OBJECTIVES

After reading this chapter, you should be able to answer the following questions:

① Which form of business organization is the simplest? Which form arises from an agreement between two or more persons to carry on a business for profit?

② What are the three essential elements of a partnership?

③ What is meant by joint and several liability? Why is this often considered to be a disadvantage of the partnership form of business?

④ What is a limited liability company? What are some of the advantages and disadvantages of this business form?

⑤ Why do professional groups organize as a limited liability partnership? How does this form differ from a general partnership?

An entrepreneur's primary motive for undertaking a business enterprise is to make profits. An *entrepreneur* is by definition one who initiates and *assumes the financial risks* of a new enterprise and undertakes to provide or control its management.

One of the questions faced by any entrepreneur who wishes to start up a business is what form of business organization should be chosen for the business endeavor. In making this determination, a number of factors need to be considered. Four important factors are (1) ease of creation, (2) the liability of the owners, (3) tax considerations, and (4) the need for capital. In studying this unit on business organizations, keep these factors in mind as you read about the various business organizational forms available to entre-

preneurs. You might also find it helpful to refer to Exhibit 26–2 in Chapter 26, on pages 558 and 559, for a comparison of the major business forms in use today with respect to formation, liability of owners, taxation, and other factors.

Traditionally, entrepreneurs have used three major forms to structure their business enterprises—the sole proprietorship, the partnership, and the corporation. In this chapter, we examine the first two of these forms. The third major traditional form—the corporation—is discussed in detail in Chapters 25 through 27. Two relatively new forms of business enterprise—limited liability companies (LLCs) and limited liability partnerships (LLPs)—offer special advantages to businesspersons, particularly with respect to taxation and liability. We look at these business forms later in this chapter.

Sole Proprietorships

The simplest form of business is a **sole proprietorship**. In this form, the owner is the business; thus, anyone who does business without creating a separate business organization has a sole proprietorship.[1] Over two-thirds of all American businesses are sole proprietorships. They are usually small enterprises—about 99 percent of the sole proprietorships existing in the United States have revenues of less than $1 million per year. Sole proprietors can own and manage any type of business, ranging from an informal, home-office undertaking to a large restaurant or construction firm. Today, a number of online businesses that sell goods and services on a nationwide basis are organized as sole proprietorships—see, for example, the enterprise discussed in this chapter's *Business Law in the Online World* feature on page 496.

A major advantage of the sole proprietorship is that the proprietor receives all of the profits (because he or she assumes all of the risk). In addition, it is often easier and less costly to start a sole proprietorship than to start any other kind of business, as few legal forms are involved. This type of business organization also entails more flexibility than does a partnership or a corporation. The sole proprietor is free to make any decision she or he wishes concerning the business—whom to hire, when to take a vacation, what kind of business to pursue, and so on. A sole proprietor pays only personal income taxes on profits, which are reported as personal income on the proprietor's personal income tax return. Sole proprietors are also allowed to establish tax-exempt retirement accounts in the form of Keogh plans.[2]

The major disadvantage of the sole proprietorship is that, as sole owner, the proprietor alone bears the burden of any losses or liabilities incurred by the business enterprise. In other words, the sole proprietor has unlimited liability, or legal responsibility, for all obligations incurred in doing business. This unlimited liability is a major factor to be considered in choosing a business form. The sole proprietorship also has the disadvantage of lacking continuity on the death of the proprietor. When the owner dies, so does the business—it is automatically dissolved. If the business is transferred to family members or other heirs, a new proprietorship is created.

Another disadvantage is that the proprietor's opportunity to raise capital is limited to personal funds and the funds of those who are willing to make loans. If the owner wishes to expand the business significantly, one way to raise more capital to finance the expansion is to join forces with another entrepreneur and establish a partnership or form a corporation.

The Law Governing Partnerships

When two or more persons agree to do business as partners, they enter into a special relationship with one another. To an extent, their relationship is similar to an agency relationship because each partner is deemed to be the agent of the other partners and of the partnership. The common law agency concepts outlined in Chapter 22 thus apply—specifically, the imputation of knowledge of, and responsibility for, acts done within the scope of the partnership relationship. In their relations with one another, partners, like agents, are bound by fiduciary ties.

In one important way, however, partnership law is distinct from agency law. A partnership is based on a voluntary contract between two or more competent persons who agree to place financial capital, labor, and skill in a business with the understanding that profits and losses will be shared. In a nonpartnership agency relationship, the agent usually does not have an ownership interest in the business, nor is he or she obliged to bear a portion of the ordinary business losses.

Partnerships are also governed by statutory law. The Uniform Partnership Act (UPA) governs the operation of partnerships *in the absence of express agreement* and has done much to reduce controversies in the law relating to partnerships. Except for Louisiana, all of the states, as well as the District of Columbia, have adopted the UPA. A revised version of the UPA, known as the Revised Uniform Partnership Act (RUPA), was formally adopted by the National Conference of Commissioners on Uniform State Laws in 1992 and has been adopted in several states. The RUPA significantly changes some of the rules governing partnerships. If the RUPA has significantly changed particular UPA provisions, we indicate these changes in footnotes.

DEFINITION OF A PARTNERSHIP

Conflicts commonly arise over whether a business enterprise is legally a partnership, especially in the absence of a formal, written partnership agreement. The UPA defines a **partnership** as "an association of two or more persons to carry on as

---

[1] Although starting up a sole proprietorship involves relatively few legal formalities compared to other business organizational forms, even small sole proprietorships may need to comply with certain zoning requirements, obtain appropriate licenses, and the like.

[2] A *Keogh plan* is a retirement program designed for self-employed persons. The person can contribute a certain percentage of income to the plan, and interest earnings are not taxed until funds are withdrawn from the plan.

BUSINESS LAW IN THE ONLINE WORLD
Online Sole Proprietorships and Venue Requirements

The Internet has expanded the ability of sole proprietorships to market their products nationwide without greatly increasing their costs. As a result, many small sole proprietorships market their goods online on a national basis. Does this mean that sole proprietorships, like unincorporated associations, should now be considered the equivalent of corporations for certain purposes, such as venue requirements?[a] In 2000, a federal district court faced this question in a case brought by a corporation against a competitor that operated as a sole proprietorship.

BACKGROUND TO THE VENUE QUESTION The case involved competing sellers of exercise machines. One of the sellers was Hsin Ten Enterprise USA, Inc., a corporation with its principal place of business in Farmingdale, New York. Hsin Ten manufactured and distributed an aerobic exercise product called "The Chi Machine." Hsin Ten also made and sold other products under the "Chi" trademark, which it owned. The other seller was Clark Enterprises, a sole proprietorship owned and operated by Clifford Clark in Salina, Kansas. Clark sold its exercise machines through representatives, trade shows, and its Web sites. One of Clark's Web sites used the name "Chi Exerciser 2000" to promote its exercise machine, and the term *Chi* was frequently used on the Web sites to refer to the product.

Hsin Ten filed a suit in a federal district court in New York against Clark, alleging, among other things, that Clark had infringed on its trademark. Clark filed a motion to dismiss the trademark claim, arguing in part that because it was a sole proprietorship, the court did not have venue under 28 U.S.C. Section 1391(c), the applicable statute. That section provides, "For purposes of venue

. . . , a defendant that is a corporation shall be deemed to reside in any judicial district in which it is subject to personal jurisdiction." Hsin Ten asserted that although Clark is an unincorporated sole proprietorship with its principal offices in Kansas, it should be deemed a "corporation" for venue purposes. After all, argued Hsin Ten, Clark is unlike other sole proprietorships because it does business in forty-seven states and resembles a national corporation in all respects except its choice of legal structure.

THE COURT SAYS NO—A SOLE PROPRIETORSHIP IS NOT A CORPORATION FOR VENUE PURPOSES The court noted that although the United States Supreme Court has held that Section 1391(c) extends to unincorporated associations, the courts have been *unwilling* to further extend the definition of "corporation" to include sole proprietorships. First, stated the court, a broad geographic distribution, in itself, does not convert a small sole proprietorship into the functional equivalent of a corporation. Second, continued the court, "Venue is primarily a question of convenience for litigants and witnesses, and venue provisions should be treated in practical terms. In practical terms, expanding the definition of 'corporation' to include sole proprietorships would be overly burdensome and inconvenient to sole proprietors, most of whom would be unable to afford the expense of litigating in distant states."[b] Thus, the court did not have venue under 28 U.S.C. Section 1391(c).

FOR CRITICAL ANALYSIS

If courts could "hear" disputes online, as may occur in the future, how might that have affected the court's reasoning in this case?

---

a. As explained in Chapter 2, venue concerns the most appropriate location for a trial. Venue requirements are often established by statute.

b. *Hsin Ten Enterprise USA, Inc. v. Clark Enterprises*, 138 F.Supp.2d 449 (S.D.N.Y. 2000).

---

co-owners a business for profit" [UPA 6(1)]. The intent to associate is a key element of a partnership, and one cannot join a partnership unless all other partners consent [UPA 18(g)].

Partnership Status. In resolving disputes over whether partnership status exists, courts will usually look for the

following three essential elements, which are implicit in the UPA's definition of a partnership:

① A sharing of profits and losses.

② A joint ownership of the business.

③ An equal right in the management of the business.

If the evidence in a particular case is insufficient to establish all three factors, the UPA provides a set of guidelines to be used. For example, the sharing of profits and losses from a business is considered *prima facie* ("on the face of it") evidence that a partnership has been created. No such inference is made, however, if the profits were received as payment of any of the following [UPA 7(4)]:

① A debt by installments or interest on a loan.

② Wages of an employee.

③ Rent to a landlord.

④ An annuity to a surviving spouse or representative of a deceased partner.

⑤ A sale of goodwill of a business or property.

Joint ownership of property, obviously, does not in and of itself create a partnership. Therefore, if persons own real property as joint tenants or as tenants in common (forms of joint ownership, to be discussed in Chapter 28), this does not mean that they are partners in a partnership. In fact, the sharing of gross returns and even profits from such ownership is usually not enough to create a partnership [UPA 7(2) and (3)].

● **EXAMPLE #1** Suppose that Ablat and Burke jointly own a piece of rural property. They lease the land to a farmer, with the understanding that they will receive a share of the profits from the farming operation conducted by the farmer in lieu of set rental payments. This arrangement normally would not make Ablat, Burke, and the farmer partners. Note, though, that although the sharing of profits does not prove the existence of a partnership, sharing *both profits and losses* usually does. ●

Entity versus Aggregate. A partnership is sometimes called a *firm* or a *company,* terms that connote an entity separate and apart from its aggregate members. Sometimes, the law of partnership recognizes a partnership as an independent entity, but for most other purposes, the law treats it as an *aggregate of the individual partners.*

At common law, a partnership was never treated as a separate legal entity. Thus, at common law a suit could never be brought by or against the firm in its own name; each individual partner had to sue or be sued. Today, most states provide specifically that the partnership can be treated as an entity for certain purposes. For example, a partnership usually can sue or be sued, collect judgments, and have all accounting procedures in the name of the partnership entity. In addition, the UPA recognizes that partnership property may be held in the name of the partnership rather than in the names of the individual partners. Finally, federal procedural laws frequently permit the partnership to be treated as an entity in such matters as suits in federal courts, bankruptcy proceedings, and informational federal tax returns.

When the partnership is not regarded as a separate legal entity, it is treated as an aggregate of the individual partners. For example, for federal income tax purposes, a partnership is not a tax-paying entity. The income and losses it incurs are passed through the partnership framework and attributed to the partners on their individual tax returns.

PARTNERSHIP FORMATION

A partnership is ordinarily formed by an explicit agreement among the parties. The law does recognize another form of partnership, however, called *partnership by estoppel,* which arises when persons who are not partners represent themselves as partners when dealing with third parties. This section will describe the requirements for the creation of a partnership, including references to liability with respect to *alleged* partners.

The Partnership Agreement. Agreements to form a partnership can be oral, written, or implied by conduct. Some partnership agreements, however, must be in writing to be legally enforceable within the Statute of Frauds (discussed in Chapter 10). For example, a partnership agreement that, by its terms, is to continue for more than one year must be evidenced by a sufficient writing.

A partnership agreement, called **articles of partnership,** usually specifies the name and location of the business, the duration of the partnership, the purpose of the business, each partner's share of the profits, how the partnership will be managed, how assets will be distributed on dissolution, and other provisions.[3] (Notice that the sample partnership agreement shown in Exhibit 24–1 on the next two pages includes an arbitration clause at the end of the agreement.) As mentioned, the UPA applies only in the absence of the parties' agreement on a particular issue. The partnership agreement is thus binding on the parties, even if certain provisions, such as the distribution of profits, seem to be unfair.

Partnership Duration. The partnership agreement can specify the duration of the partnership in terms of a date or the completion of a particular project. A partnership that is specifically limited in duration is called a *partnership for a*

---

[3] The RUPA provides for the voluntary filing of a partnership statement, containing such information as the agency authority of the partners, with the secretary of state. The statement must be executed by at least two partners, a copy must be sent to all of the partners, and a certified copy must be filed in the office for recording transfers of real property (in most states, in the county in which the property is located).

EXHIBIT 24-1 A SAMPLE PARTNERSHIP AGREEMENT

PARTNERSHIP AGREEMENT

This agreement, made and entered into as of the _____, by and among _____
_____ (hereinafter collectively sometimes referred to as "Partners").

WITNESSETH:

Whereas, the Parties hereto desire to form a General Partnership (hereinafter referred to as the "Partnership"), for the term and upon the conditions hereinafter set forth;

Now, therefore, in consideration of the mutual covenants hereinafter contained, it is agreed by and among the Parties hereto as follows:

Article I
BASIC STRUCTURE

Form. The Parties hereby form a General Partnership pursuant to the Laws of _____ _____.

Name. The business of the Partnership shall be conducted under the name of _____ _____.

Place of Business. The principal office and place of business of the Partnership shall be located at _____ , or such other place as the Partners may from time to time designate.

Term. The Partnership shall commence on _____, and shall continue for _____ years, unless earlier terminated in the following manner: (a) By the completion of the purpose intended, or (b) Pursuant to this Agreement, or (c) By applicable _____ law, or (d) By death, insanity, bankruptcy, retirement, withdrawal, resignation, expulsion, or disability of all of the then Partners.

Purpose—General. The purpose for which the Partnership is organized is _____
_____

Article II
FINANCIAL ARRANGEMENTS

Each Partner has contributed to the initial capital of the Partnership property in the amount and form indicated on Schedule A attached hereto and made a part hereof. Capital contributions to the Partnership shall not earn interest. An individual capital account shall be maintained for each Partner. If at any time during the existence of the Partnership it shall become necessary to increase the capital with which the said Partnership is doing business, then (upon the vote of the Managing Partner[s]): each party to this Agreement shall contribute to the capital of this Partnership within ___ days notice of such need in an amount according to his then Percentage Share of Capital as called for by the Managing Partner(s).

The Percentage Share of Profits and Capital of each Partner shall be (unless otherwise modified by the terms of this Agreement) as follows:

Names	Initial Percentage Share of Profits and Capital
_____	_____
_____	_____
_____	_____

No interest shall be paid on any contribution to the capital of the Partnership. No Partner shall have the right to demand the return of his capital contributions except as herein provided. The individual Partners shall have no right to any priority over each other as to the return of capital contributions except as herein provided.

Distributions to the Partners of net operating profits of the Partnership, as hereinafter defined, shall be made at _____. Such distributions shall be made to the Partners simultaneously.

For the purpose of this Agreement, net operating profit for any accounting period shall mean the gross receipts of the Partnership for such period, less the sum of all cash expenses of operation of the Partnership, and such sums as may be necessary to establish a reserve for operating expenses. In determining net operating profit, deductions for depreciation, amortization, or other similar charges not requiring actual current expenditures of cash shall *not* be taken into account in accordance with generally accepted accounting principles.

EXHIBIT 24–1 A SAMPLE PARTNERSHIP AGREEMENT—CONTINUED

No partner shall be entitled to receive any compensation from the Partnership, nor shall any Partner receive any drawing account from the Partnership.

Article III
MANAGEMENT

The Managing Partner(s) shall be _____ .

The Managing Partner(s) shall have the right to vote as to the management and conduct of the business of the Partnership as follows:

Names	**Vote**
_____	_____
_____	_____
_____	_____

Article IV
DISSOLUTION

In the event that the Partnership shall hereafter be dissolved for any reason whatsoever, a full and general account of its assets, liabilities, and transactions shall at once be taken. Such assets may be sold and turned into cash as soon as possible and all debts and other amounts due the Partnership collected. The proceeds thereof shall thereupon be applied as follows:

(a) To discharge the debts and liabilities of the Partnership and the expenses of liquidation.

(b) To pay each Partner or his or her legal representative any unpaid salary, drawing account, interest or profits to which he or she shall then be entitled and in addition, to repay to any Partner his capital contributions in excess of his or her original capital contribution.

(c) To divide the surplus, if any, among the Partners or their representatives as follows:

(1) First (to the extent of each Partner's then capital account) in proportion to their then capital accounts. (2) Then according to each Partner's then Percentage Share of [*Capital/Income*].

No Partner shall have the right to demand and receive property in kind for his distribution.

Article V
MISCELLANEOUS

The Partnership's fiscal year shall commence on January 1st of each year and shall end on December 31st of each year. Full and accurate books of account shall be kept at such place as the Managing Partner(s) may from time to time designate, showing the condition of the business and finances of the Partnership; and each Partner shall have access to such books of account and shall be entitled to examine them at any time during ordinary business hours. At the end of each year, the Managing Partner(s) shall cause the Partnership's accountant to prepare a balance sheet setting forth the financial position of the Partnership as of the end of that year and a statement of operations (income and expenses) for that year. A copy of the balance sheet and statement of operations shall be delivered to each Partner as soon as it is available.

Each Partner shall be deemed to have waived all objections to any transaction or other facts about the operation of the Partnership disclosed in such balance sheet and/or statement of operations unless he or she shall have notified the Managing Partner(s) in writing of his or her objectives within thirty (30) days of the date on which such statement is mailed.

The Partnership shall maintain a bank account or bank accounts in the Partnership's name in a national or state bank in the State of _____ . Checks and drafts shall be drawn on the Partnership's bank account for Partnership purposes only and shall be signed by the Managing Partner(s) or their designated agent.

Any controversy or claim arising out of or relating to this Agreement shall only be settled by arbitration in accordance with the rules of the American Arbitration Association, one Arbitrator, and shall be enforceable in any court having competent jurisdiction.

Witnesses	**Partners**
_____	_____
_____	_____

Date: _____

term. A dissolution without the consent of all the partners prior to the expiration of the partnership term constitutes a breach of the agreement, and the responsible partner can be liable for any losses resulting from it. If no fixed duration is specified, the partnership is a *partnership at will.* This type of partnership can be dissolved at any time by any partner without violating the agreement and without incurring liability for losses to other partners resulting from the termination.

The Corporation as Partner. General partners are personally liable for the debts incurred by the partnership. If one of the general partners is a corporation, however, what does *personal liability* mean? Basically, the capacity of corporations to contract is a question of corporation law. Many states have restrictions on corporations becoming partners, although such restrictions have become less common over the years. The Revised Model Business Corporation Act (discussed in Chapter 25), however, generally allows corporations to make contracts and incur liabilities, and the UPA specifically permits a corporation to be a partner. By definition, "a partnership is an association of two or more persons," and the UPA defines *person* as including corporations [UPA 2].

Partnership by Estoppel. Parties who are not partners sometimes represent themselves as such and cause third persons to rely on their representations. The law of partnership does not confer any partnership rights on these persons, but it may impose liability on them. This is also true when a partner represents, expressly or impliedly, that a nonpartner is a member of the firm. Whenever a third person has reasonably and detrimentally relied on the representation that a nonpartner was part of the partnership, partnership by estoppel is deemed to exist. When this occurs, the nonpartner is regarded as an agent whose acts are binding on the partnership.

RIGHTS AMONG PARTNERS

The rights and duties of partners are governed largely by the specific terms of their partnership agreement. In the absence of provisions to the contrary in the partnership agreement, the law imposes the rights and duties discussed here. The character and nature of the partnership business generally influence the application of these rights and duties.

Interest in the Partnership. A partner's interest in the partnership is a personal asset consisting of a proportionate share of the profits earned [UPA 26] and a return of capital after the partnership is terminated. Each partner is entitled to the proportion of business profits and losses designated in the partnership agreement.

Profits and Losses. If the agreement does not apportion profits or losses, the UPA provides that *profits shall be shared equally and losses shall be shared in the same ratio as profits* [UPA 18(a)]. ● **EXAMPLE #2** The partnership agreement for Ponce and Brent provides for capital contributions of $6,000 from Ponce and $4,000 from Brent, but it is silent as to how Ponce and Brent will share profits or losses. In this situation, Ponce and Brent will share both profits and losses equally. If the partnership agreement provided for profits to be shared in the same ratio as capital contributions, however, 60 percent of the profits would go to Ponce, and 40 percent of the profits would go to Brent. If their partnership agreement was silent as to losses, losses would be shared in the same ratio as profits (60 percent to 40 percent). ●

Assignment of Partnership Interest. A partner may assign (transfer) her or his interest in the partnership to another party. When a partner's interest is assigned, the assignee (the person to whom the interest was transferred) has the right to receive the partner's share of the profits and, on the partnership's termination, the partner's capital contribution. The assignee, however, does not become a partner in the partnership and thus has no say in the management or administration of the partnership affairs and no right to inspect the partnership books. Rather, the partner who assigned her or his interest remains a partner with the full rights of a partner with respect to those rights that cannot be assigned.

Creditor's Lien on Partnership Interest. A partner's interest is also subject to a judgment creditor's lien (described in Chapter 21). A judgment creditor can attach a partner's interest by petitioning the court that entered the judgment to grant the creditor a **charging order.** This order entitles the creditor to the profits of the partner and to any assets available to the partner on the firm's dissolution [UPA 28].

Management Rights. Under the UPA, all partners have equal rights in managing the partnership [UPA 18(e)]. Each partner has one vote in management matters *regardless of the proportional size of his or her interest in the firm.* Often, in a large partnership, partners will agree to delegate daily management responsibilities to a management committee made up of one or more of the partners.

The majority rule controls decisions in ordinary matters connected with partnership business, unless otherwise specified in the agreement. Decisions that significantly affect the nature of the partnership, however, require the *unanimous* consent of the partners [UPA 9(3), 18(g), and 18(h)]. Unanimous consent is required for a decision to undertake any of the following actions:

① To alter the essential nature of the firm's business as expressed in the partnership agreement or to alter the capital structure of the partnership.

② To admit new partners or to enter a wholly new business.

③ To assign partnership property into a trust for the benefit of creditors.

④ To dispose of the partnership's goodwill.

⑤ To confess judgment against the partnership or to submit partnership claims to arbitration. (A **confession of judgment** is the act of a debtor in permitting a judgment to be entered against him or her by a creditor, for an agreed sum, without the institution of legal proceedings.)

⑥ To undertake any act that would make further conduct of partnership business impossible.

⑦ To amend the articles of the partnership agreement.

Compensation. A partner has a duty to expend time, skill, and energy on behalf of the partnership business, and such services are generally not compensable in the form of a salary. Rather, as mentioned, a partner's income from the partnership takes the form of a distribution of profits according to the partner's share in the business. Partners can, however, agree otherwise. For example, partners in a law firm often agree that the managing partner of the firm should receive a salary in addition to her or his share of profits for performing special administrative duties in office and personnel management. When a partnership must be terminated because a partner dies, a surviving partner is entitled to reasonable compensation for services relating to the final settlement (winding up) of partnership affairs (and reimbursement for expenses incurred in the process) above and apart from his or her share in the partnership profits [UPA 18(f)].

Each partner impliedly promises to subordinate his or her interests to those of the partnership. ● EXAMPLE #3 Assume that Hall, Banks, and Porter enter into a partnership. Porter undertakes independent consulting, in the same area in which the partnership specializes, for an outside firm without the consent of Hall and Banks. Porter's compensation from the outside firm is considered partnership income [UPA 21]. ● A partner cannot engage in any independent business that involves the partnership's time unless the partnership expressly agrees.

Inspection of Books. Partnership books and records must be kept accessible to all partners. Each partner has the right to receive (and each partner has the corresponding duty to produce) full and complete information concerning the conduct of all aspects of partnership business [UPA 20]. Each firm keeps books for recording and preserving such information. Partners contribute the information, and a bookkeeper or an accountant typically has the duty to preserve it. The books must be kept at the firm's principal business office and cannot be removed without the consent of all of the partners [UPA 19]. Every partner, whether active or inactive, is entitled to inspect all books and records on demand and can make copies of the materials. The personal representative of a deceased partner's estate has the same right of access to partnership books and records that the decedent would have had.

Accounting of Assets. An accounting of partnership assets or profits is required to determine the value of each partner's share in the partnership. An accounting can be performed voluntarily, or it can be compelled by a court. Under UPA 22, a partner has the right to a formal accounting in the following situations:

① When the partnership agreement provides for a formal accounting.

② When a partner is wrongfully excluded from the business or from the possession of its property, from access to the books, or both.

③ When any partner is withholding profits or benefits belonging to the partnership in breach of his or her fiduciary duty.

④ When circumstances "render it just and reasonable."

A formal accounting also occurs by right in connection with *dissolution* proceedings (discussed later in this chapter). Generally, the principal remedy of a partner against co-partners is a suit for dissolution, an accounting, or both. With minor exceptions, a partner cannot maintain an action against other firm members for damages until partnership affairs are settled and an accounting is done. This rule is necessary because legal disputes between partners invariably involve conflicting claims to shares in the partnership. Logically, the value of each partner's share must first be determined by an accounting.

Property Rights. One of the property rights of partners—the right to a share of the profits made by the partnership—has already been discussed. A partner also has ownership rights in any real or personal property owned by the partnership. Property owned by the partnership, or *partnership property,* is defined by the UPA as "all property originally brought into the partnership's stock or subsequently acquired, by purchase or otherwise, on account of the partnership" [UPA 8(1)].

For example, in the formation of a partnership, a partner may bring into the partnership any property that he or she owns as a part of his or her capital contribution. This property becomes partnership property even though title to it may still be in the name of the contributing partner. The intention that certain assets are to be partnership assets is the heart of the phrase "on account of the partnership." Thus, the more closely an asset is associated with the business operations of the partnership, the more likely it is to be a partnership asset.[4]

UPA 25(1) states that partners are tenants in partnership. This means that every partner is a co-owner with all other partners of specific partnership property, such as office equipment, paper supplies, and vehicles. Each partner has equal rights to possess partnership property for business purposes or in satisfaction of firm debts, but not for any other purpose without the consent of all the other partners. Tenancy in partnership has several important effects. If a partner dies, the surviving partners, not the heirs of the deceased partner, have the right of survivorship to the specific property. Although surviving partners are entitled to possession, they have a duty to account to the decedent's estate for the value of the deceased partner's interest in the property [UPA 25(2)(d), (e)].

A partner has no right to sell, assign, or in any way deal with a particular item of partnership property as an exclusive owner [UPA 25(2)(a) and (b)]. Therefore, creditors cannot use partnership property to satisfy the personal debts of a partner. Partnership property is available only to satisfy partnership debts, to enhance the firm's credit, or to achieve other business purposes of the partnership.

DUTIES AND LIABILITIES OF PARTNERS

The duties and liabilities of partners are basically derived from agency law. Each partner is an agent of every other partner and acts as both a principal and an agent in any business transaction within the scope of the partnership agreement. Each partner is also a general agent of the partnership in carrying out the usual business of the firm.[5] Thus, every act of a partner concerning partnership busi-

ness and every contract signed in the partnership's name bind the firm [UPA 9(1)]. The UPA affirms general principles of agency law that pertain to the authority of a partner to bind a partnership in contract or tort.

We examine here the fiduciary duties of partners, the authority of partners, the joint and several liability that characterizes partnerships, and the limitations imposed on the liability of incoming partners for preexisting partnership debts.

Fiduciary Duties. Partners stand in a fiduciary relationship to one another just as principals and agents do. As indicated in Chapter 22, a fiduciary relationship is one of extraordinary trust and loyalty. Each partner has a fiduciary duty to act in good faith and for the benefit of the partnership. Each partner must also subordinate her or his personal interests to those of the partnership if a conflict of interests arises.[6]

This fiduciary duty underlies the entire body of law pertaining to partnership and agency. From it, certain other duties are commonly implied. Thus, a partner must account to the partnership for personal profits or benefits derived from any partnership transaction that is undertaken without the consent of all of the partners.[7]

Authority of Partners. Agency concepts relating to actual (express and implied) authority, apparent authority, and ratification are also applicable to partnerships. In an ordinary partnership, firm members can exercise all implied powers reasonably necessary and customary to carry on that particular business. Some customarily implied powers include the authority to make warranties on goods in the sales business, the power to convey real property in the firm's name when such conveyances are part of the ordinary course of partnership business, the power to enter into contracts consistent with the firm's regular course of business, and the power to make admissions and representations concerning partnership affairs [UPA 11].

When a partner acts within the scope of authority, the partnership is bound to third parties by these acts. For example, a partner's authority to sell partnership products carries with it the implied authority to transfer title and to make the usual warranties. Hence, in a partnership that operates a retail tire store, any partner negotiating a contract with a customer for the sale of a set of tires can war-

---

[4] Under the RUPA, property that is not acquired in the name of the partnership is nonetheless partnership property if the instrument transferring title (1) refers to the person taking title as a partner or (2) indicates the existence of the partnership [RUPA 204(a)(2)]. Also, the property is still presumed to be partnership property if it is acquired with partnership funds [RUPA 204(c)]. If none of the above occurs, the property is presumed to be the property of individual partners, even if it is used in the partnership business [RUPA 204(d)].
[5] The RUPA adds "or business of the kind carried on by the partnership" [RUPA 301(1)]. Basically, this addition gives added protection to third persons who deal with an unfamiliar partnership.

[6] The RUPA states that partners may pursue their own interests without automatically violating their fiduciary duties [RUPA 404(e)].
[7] In this sense, to account to the partnership means not only to divulge the information but also to determine the value of any benefits or profits derived and to hold that money or property in trust on behalf of the partnership.

rant that "each tire will be warranted for normal wear for 40,000 miles."

This same partner, however, does not have the authority to sell office equipment, fixtures, or the partnership office building without the consent of all of the other partners. In addition, because partnerships are formed to create profits, a partner generally does not have the authority to make charitable contributions without the consent of the other partners. Such actions are not binding on the partnership unless they are ratified by all of the other partners.

As in the law of agency, the law of partnership imputes one partner's knowledge to all other partners because members of a partnership stand in a fiduciary relationship to one another. This relationship implies that each partner will fully disclose to every other partner all information pertaining to the business of the partnership [UPA 12].

The court in the following case was asked to consider whether one partner was liable for another partner's creation of overdrafts in one of the partnership's bank accounts "in the ordinary course of the partnership business."

CASE 24.1   Helpinstill v. Regions Bank

Texas Court of Appeals—Texarkana, 2000.
33 S.W.3d 401.

FACTS Bobby Helpinstill and Mike Brown were partners in MBO Computers. They opened a partnership bank account at Longview National Bank in Longview, Texas, each agreeing in writing that he would be individually liable for any overdrafts created on the account. Brown, who was actively managing the business, regularly wrote overdrafts on the account and covered them later with deposits. In January 1997, to pay creditors of the partnership, Brown began shuffling funds between MBO accounts at the Longview bank and two other banks in a check-kiting scheme.[a] Brown was convicted and sentenced to a term in federal prison. Regions Bank (which had acquired Longview) filed a suit in a Texas state court against Helpinstill to recover $381,011.15, the amount of the overdrafts. When the court ruled in favor of the bank, Helpinstill appealed to a state intermediate appellate court,

arguing in part that he was not liable because Brown's check kiting was not within the ordinary course of partnership business.

ISSUE Is Helpinstill liable to the bank for the amount of the overdrafts?

DECISION Yes. The state intermediate appellate court affirmed the judgment of the lower court, concluding that Helpinstill's liability to the bank was established as a matter of law.

REASON The appellate court explained that "Helpinstill's liability was established by virtue of the fact that the partnership was indebted to the bank for the overdrafts that Brown created in the ordinary course of the partnership's business, and Helpinstill, as a general partner, is responsible for such partnership debts." The court reasoned that "[t]he kiting scheme, rather than creating the overdrafts, was being used to disguise them; and, while not in itself in the ordinary course of the partnership's business, the kiting scheme did not change the fact that the creation of overdrafts was in the ordinary course of the partnership's business."

FOR CRITICAL ANALYSIS—Social Consideration
What is meant by the phrase "in the ordinary course of business"?

---

a. *Check kiting* refers to the practice of moving funds between bank accounts for the purpose of covering account deficiencies. For example, a check drawn on an account in bank A is written to cover a deficiency in an account in bank B. Then a check drawn on an account in bank B is written to cover the deficiency in bank A—and so on.

Joint Liability. In most states, partners are subject to joint liability on partnership debts and contracts [UPA 15(b)]. **Joint liability** means that if a third party sues a partner on, for example, a partnership debt, the partner has the right to insist that the other partners be sued with him or her. If the third party does not sue all of the partners, the partner sued cannot be required to pay a judgment, and the assets of the partnership cannot be used to satisfy the judgment.

(Similarly, a release of one partner releases all partners.) In other words, to bring a successful claim against the partnership on a debt or contract, a plaintiff must name all the partners as defendants.

To simplify this rule, some states, such as California, have enacted statutes providing that a partnership may be sued in its own name and that a judgment will bind the partnership's and the individual partners' property even though not all the partners are named in the complaint. If the third party is successful, she or he may collect on the judgment against the assets of one or more of the partners. In other words, each partner is liable and may be required to pay the entire amount of the judgment. When one partner pays the entire amount, the partnership is required to indemnify that partner [UPA 18(b)]. If the partnership cannot do so, the obligation falls on the other partners.

Joint and Several Liability. In some states, partners are both jointly liable and severally, or individually, liable for partnership debts and contracts. In all states, partners are jointly and severally liable for torts and breaches of trust [UPA 15(a)].[8] **Joint and several**[9] **liability** means that a third party may sue any one or more of the partners without suing all of them or the partnership itself. In other words, a third party may sue one or more of the partners separately (severally) or all of the partners together (jointly), at his or her option. This is true even if the partner did not participate in, ratify, or know about whatever it was that gave rise to the cause of action.[10]

A judgment against one partner on her or his several liability does not extinguish the others' liability. (Similarly, a release of one partner discharges the partners' joint but not several liability.) Thus, those not sued in the first action may be sued subsequently. The first action, however, may have been conclusive on the question of liability. If, for example, in an action against one partner, the court held that the partnership was in no way liable, the third party cannot bring an action against another partner and succeed on the issue of the partnership's liability.

If the third party is successful in a suit against a partner or partners, he or she may collect on the judgment only against the assets of those partners named as defendants. The partner who committed the tort is required to indemnify the partnership for any damages it pays.

Liability of Incoming Partner. A newly admitted partner to an existing partnership normally has limited liability for whatever debts and obligations the partnership incurred prior to the new partner's admission. The new partner's liability can be satisfied only from partnership assets [UPA 17]. This means that the new partner usually has no personal liability for these debts and obligations, but any capital contribution made by him or her to the partnership is subject to these debts.

PARTNERSHIP TERMINATION

Any change in the relations of the partners that demonstrates unwillingness or inability to carry on partnership business dissolves the partnership, resulting in termination [UPA 29]. If one of the partners wishes to continue the business, she or he is free to reorganize into a new partnership with the remaining members.

The termination of a partnership has two stages, both of which must take place before termination is complete. The first stage, **dissolution**, occurs when any partner (or partners) indicates an intention to disassociate from the partnership. The second stage, **winding up**,[11] is the actual process of collecting and distributing the partnership assets.

Dissolution. Dissolution of a partnership can be brought about by the acts of the partners, by the operation of law, and by judicial decree. Each of these events will be discussed here.

Dissolution by Acts of the Partners. Dissolution of a partnership may come about through the acts of the partners in several ways. First, the partnership can be dissolved by the partners' agreement. For example, when a partnership agreement expresses a fixed term or a particular business objective to be accomplished, the passing of the date or the accomplishment of the objective dissolves the partnership.

Second, because a partnership is a voluntary association, a partner has the power to disassociate himself or herself from the partnership at any time and thus dissolve the partnership. Any change in the partnership, whether by the withdrawal of a partner or by the admission of a new partner, results in dissolution.[12] In practice, this is modified by the provision that the remaining or new partners may continue in the firm's business. Nonetheless, a new partnership arises. Creditors of the prior partnership become creditors of the new partnership [UPA 41].

Finally, the UPA provides that neither a voluntary assignment of a partner's interest nor an involuntary sale of a

---

[8] Under the RUPA, partners' liability is joint and several for all debts [RUPA 306].

[9] The term *several* stems from the medieval English term *severall,* which meant "separately," or "severed from" one another. As used here, *several* liability means separate liability, or individual liability.

[10] The RUPA prevents creditors from bringing an action to collect debts from the partners of a nonbankrupt partnership without first attempting unsuccessfully to collect from the partnership (or convincing a court that the attempt would be unsuccessful) [RUPA 307(d)].

[11] Although "winding down" would seem to describe more accurately the process of settling accounts and liquidating the assets of a partnership, "winding up" has been traditionally used in English and U.S. statutory and case law to denote this final stage of a partnership's existence.

[12] The RUPA distinguishes the withdrawal of a partner that causes a breakup of a partnership from a withdrawal that causes only the end of a partner's participation in the business (and results in a buyout of that partner's interest) [RUPA 601, 701, 801]. Dissolution results only if the partnership must be liquidated [RUPA 801].

partner's interest for the benefit of creditors [UPA 27 and 28] by itself dissolves the partnership. Either occurrence, however, can ultimately lead to judicial dissolution of the partnership. (Judicial dissolution will be discussed shortly.)

Dissolution by Operation of Law. If one of the partners dies, the partnership is dissolved by operation of law, even if the partnership agreement provides for carrying on the business with the executor of the decedent's estate.[13] The bankruptcy of a partner will also dissolve a partnership, and naturally, the bankruptcy of the partnership itself will result in dissolution [UPA 31(4) and (5)].

Additionally, any event that makes it unlawful for the partnership to continue its business or for any partner to carry on in the partnership will result in dissolution [UPA 31(3)]. Note, however, that if the illegality of the partnership business is a cause for dissolution, the partners can decide to change the nature of their business and continue in the partnership. When the illegality applies to an individual partner, dissolution is mandatory. ● **EXAMPLE #4** Suppose that a state legislature passes a law making it illegal for judges in that state to engage in the practice of law. If Gerald Fowler, an attorney in a law firm, is appointed or elected to a judgeship, then Fowler must leave the law firm, and the partnership must be dissolved.●

Dissolution by Judicial Decree. For dissolution of a partnership by judicial decree to occur, an application or petition must be made in an appropriate court. The court then either denies the petition or grants a decree of dissolution. UPA 32 cites situations in which a court can dissolve a partnership. One situation occurs when a partner is adjudicated mentally incompetent or is shown to be of unsound mind. Another situation arises when a partner appears incapable of performing his or her duties under the partnership agreement. If the incapacity is likely to be permanent and to have substantial effect on the partner's ability to discharge his or her duties to the firm, a court will dissolve the partnership by decree.

A court may also order dissolution when it becomes obviously impractical for the firm to continue—for example, if the business can only be operated at a loss. Additionally, a partner's impropriety involving partnership business (for example, fraud perpetrated on the other partners) or improper behavior reflecting unfavorably on the firm may provide grounds for a judicial decree of dissolution. Finally, if dissension between partners becomes so persistent and harmful as to undermine the confidence and cooperation necessary to carry on the firm's business, dissolution may also be granted.

Notice of Dissolution. The intent to dissolve or to withdraw from a firm must be communicated clearly to each partner. A partner can express this notice of intent by either actions or words. All partners will share liability for the acts of any partner who continues conducting business for the firm without knowing that the partnership has been dissolved.

Dissolution of a partnership by the act of a partner requires notice to all affected third persons as well. Any third person who has extended credit to the firm must receive actual notice (notice given to the party directly and personally). For all others, constructive notice (a newspaper announcement or similar public notice) is sufficient [UPA 35]. Dissolution resulting from the operation of law generally requires no notice to third parties.[14]

Winding Up. Once dissolution occurs and the partners have been notified, the partners cannot create new obligations on behalf of the partnership. Their only authority is to complete transactions begun but not finished at the time of dissolution and to wind up the business of the partnership [UPA 33 and 37]. *Winding up* includes collecting and preserving partnership assets, discharging liabilities (paying debts), and accounting to each partner for the value of her or his interest in the partnership.

Both creditors of the partnership and creditors of the individual partners can make claims on the partnership's assets. In general, creditors of the partnership have priority over creditors of individual partners in the distribution of partnership assets; the converse priority is usually followed in the distribution of individual partner assets, except under bankruptcy law. A partnership's assets are distributed according to the following priorities [UPA 40]:[15]

① Payment of third party debts.

② Refund of advances (loans) made to or for the firm by a partner.

③ Return of capital contribution to a partner.

④ Distribution of the balance, if any, to partners in accordance with their respective shares in the profits.

If the partnership's liabilities are greater than its assets, the partners bear the losses—in the absence of a contrary agreement—in the same proportion in which they shared

---

[13] Under the RUPA, the death of a partner represents that partner's "dissociation" from the partnership, but it is not an automatic ground for the partnership's dissolution [RUPA 601].

[14] *Childers v. United States*, 442 F.2d 1299 (5th Cir. 1971).

[15] Under the RUPA, partner creditors are included among creditors who take first priority [RUPA 808]. Capital contributions and profits or losses are then calculated together to determine the amounts that the partners receive or the amounts that they must pay.

the profits (rather than, for example, in proportion to their contributions to the partnership's capital). Partners continue in their fiduciary relationship until the winding-up process is completed.

Does winding up require that all of the assets of a partnership be liquidated? Or is it enough if, on the death of a partner, the surviving partners take an inventory, provide an accounting to the dead partner's estate for the value of the business as of the date of dissolution, and pay the estate its proportionate share of the value of the partnership? Can the surviving partners then continue in business as a new partnership? Those were the questions in the following case.

CASE 24.2 Creel v. Lilly

Court of Appeals of Maryland, 1999.
354 Md. 77,
725 A.2d 385.

FACTS Joseph Creel, Arnold Lilly, and Roy Altizer formed a general partnership called "Joe's Racing" to sell NASCAR racing memorabilia. Their written agreement stated, in paragraph 7(a), that "at the termination of this partnership a full and accurate inventory shall be prepared, and the assets, liabilities, and income * * * shall be ascertained." Paragraph 7(d) added, "Upon the death or illness of a partner, his share will go to his estate. If his estate wishes to sell his interest, they must offer it to the remaining partners first." Nine months later, Creel died, and Joe's Racing dissolved. Creel's spouse, Anne Creel, was appointed personal representative of his estate.[a] Lilly and Altizer asked Mrs. Creel to release funds in a partnership account to which only Creel had had access. When she refused, Lilly and Altizer filed a suit in a Maryland state court against her. Meanwhile, Lilly and Altizer took an inventory of the merchandise, had an accountant compute the value of the business, and offered Mrs. Creel payment for Creel's share. Lilly and Altizer then ceased doing business as Joe's Racing and used the assets to begin doing business as "Good Ole Boys Racing." The court held, among other things, that Lilly and Altizer did not breach any fiduciary duty to Creel's estate. Mrs. Creel appealed, arguing in part that they should have liquidated the assets of Joe's Racing.

_____

a. A *personal representative* administers a deceased person's estate. This administration includes taking an inventory of the deceased's assets and managing them to preserve their value.

The state intermediate appellate court affirmed the lower court's judgment. Mrs. Creel appealed to the Maryland Court of Appeals, the state's highest court.

ISSUE Does winding up require that all partnership assets be liquidated (sold) to determine the value of the business?

DECISION No. The Maryland Court of Appeals affirmed the decision of the lower court. Winding up does not require a forced sale of all partnership assets to determine the value of the business.

REASON The court stated that on the death of a partner, it is acceptable to pay the deceased partner's estate its proportionate share of the value of the partnership, derived from an accurate accounting, without having to fully liquidate the business. The court said, "Paragraph 7(a) requires that the assets, liabilities, and income be 'ascertained,' but it in no way mandates that this must be accomplished by a forced sale of the partnership assets. * * * [A] sale of all partnership assets is not required under either UPA or RUPA * * * . We find it is sound public policy to permit a partnership to continue either under the same name or as a successor partnership without all of the assets being liquidated. Liquidation * * * is often unnecessary to determining the true value of the partnership."

FOR CRITICAL ANALYSIS—Economic Consideration
At one point in its opinion, the court stated, "Liquidation can be a harmful and destructive measure, especially to a small business like Joe's Racing." Would the forced liquidation of partnership assets be equally "harmful and destructive" to a large business? Why or why not?

Limited Liability Companies

A relatively new form of business organization, the **limited liability company** (LLC), is a hybrid that offers the limited liability of a corporation (see Chapter 25) and the tax advantages of a partnership. Increasingly, LLCs are becoming an organizational form of choice among businesspersons, a trend encouraged by state statutes permitting their use.

LLCs are governed by state LLC statutes. These laws vary, of course, from state to state. In an attempt to create more uniformity among the states in this respect, in 1995 the National Conference of Commissioners on Uniform State Laws issued the Uniform Limited Liability Company Act (ULLCA). To date, less than one-fourth of the states have adopted the ULLCA, and thus the law governing LLCs remains far from uniform. Some provisions are common to most state statutes, however.

Like corporations, LLCs are legal entities apart from their owners, who are called **members**. As a legal person, the LLC can sue or be sued, enter into contracts, and hold title to property [ULLCA 201]. Similar to shareholders in a corporation, members of an LLC enjoy limited liability [ULLCA 303]. To form an LLC, **articles of organization** must be filed with a central state agency—usually the secretary of state's office [ULLCA 202]. Typically, the articles are required to include such information as the name of the business, its principal address, the name and address of a registered agent, the names of the members, and informa-

tion on how the LLC will be managed [ULLCA 203]. The business's name must include the words "Limited Liability Company" or the initials "LLC" [ULLCA 105(a)].

As you will read in Chapter 25, on occasion the courts will disregard the corporate entity ("pierce the corporate veil") and hold a shareholder personally liable for corporate obligations. At issue in the following case was whether this same principle should be extended to an LLC. Could the managing member of an LLC be held personally liable for property damage caused by the LLC?

CASE 24.3   Kaycee Land and Livestock v. Flahive

Wyoming Supreme Court, 2002.
2002 WY 73,
46 P.3d 323.

FACTS Roger Flahive is the managing member of Flahive Oil & Gas, LLC. To exercise mineral rights beneath certain real property, Flahive Oil & Gas entered into a contract with Kaycee Land and Livestock in Johnson County, Wyoming, allowing Flahive Oil & Gas to use the surface of Kaycee's land. Later, alleging environmental contamination to its property, Kaycee filed a suit in a Wyoming state court against Flahive and his LLC. On discovering that Flahive Oil & Gas had no assets as of the time of the suit, Kaycee asked the court to disregard the LLC entity and hold Flahive personally liable for the contamination. Before issuing a judgment in the case, the court submitted this question to the Wyoming Supreme Court: "[I]s a claim to pierce the Limited Liability entity veil or disregard the Limited Liability Company entity in the same manner as a court would pierce a corporate veil or disregard a corporate shield, an available remedy" against an LLC? Unlike some states' statutes, Wyoming's LLC provisions do not address this issue.

ISSUE May a court "pierce the veil" of an LLC and hold a member personally liable?

DECISION Yes. The Wyoming Supreme Court held that an LLC entity could be pierced. The court remanded the case for

a determination as to whether piercing the veil was appropriate under the circumstances.

REASON The court pointed out that "[e]very state that has enacted LLC piercing legislation has chosen to follow corporate law standards and not develop a separate LLC standard. Statutes which create corporations and LLCs have the same basic purpose—to limit the liability of individual investors with a corresponding benefit to economic development. Statutes created the legal fiction of the corporation being a completely separate entity which could act independently from individual persons. * * * [W]hen corporations fail to follow the statutorily mandated formalities, co-mingle funds, or ignore the restrictions in their articles of incorporation regarding separate treatment of corporate property, the courts deem it appropriate to disregard the separate identity and do not permit shareholders to be sheltered from liability to third parties for damages caused by the corporations' acts." The court concluded, "If the members and officers of an LLC fail to treat it as a separate entity as contemplated by statute, they should not enjoy immunity from individual liability for the LLC's acts that cause damage to third parties."

FOR CRITICAL ANALYSIS—Ethical Consideration
Suppose that Flahive had scrupulously followed all statutorily mandated formalities, had not commingled personal and LLC funds, and had always treated LLC property as separate and distinct from his personal property. Would the decision in this case likely have been different?

One of the significant differences between LLCs and corporations has to do with federal jurisdictional requirements. The federal jurisdiction statute provides that a corporation is deemed to be a citizen of the state where it is incorporated and maintains its principal place of business. The statute does not mention the citizenship of partnerships, LLCs, and other unincorporated associations, but the

courts have tended to regard these entities as citizens of every state in which their members are citizens.

ADVANTAGES AND DISADVANTAGES OF THE LLC

A key advantage of the LLC is that the liability of members is limited to the amount of their investments. Another advantage is that an LLC with two or more members can choose to be taxed either as a partnership or as a corporation. An LLC that wants to distribute profits to the members may prefer to be taxed as a partnership to avoid the "double taxation" characteristic of the corporate entity. (A corporation as an entity pays income taxes on its profits, and the shareholders pay personal income taxes on profits distributed as dividends.) Unless an LLC indicates that it wishes to be taxed as a corporation, it is automatically taxed as a partnership by the IRS. This means that the LLC as an entity pays no taxes; rather, as in a partnership, profits are "passed through" the LLC to the members who then personally pay taxes on the profits.

If LLC members want to reinvest profits in the business, however, rather than distribute the profits to members, they may prefer to be taxed as a corporation if corporate income tax rates are lower than personal tax rates. Part of the attractiveness of the LLC is this flexibility with respect to taxation. For federal income tax purposes, one-member LLCs are automatically taxed as sole proprietorships unless they indicate that they wish to be taxed as corporations. With respect to state taxes, most states follow the IRS rules. Still another advantage of the LLC for businesspersons is the flexibility it offers in terms of business operations and management—as will be discussed shortly.

The disadvantages of the LLC are relatively few. Although initially there was uncertainty over how LLCs would be taxed, that disadvantage no longer exists. One remaining disadvantage is that state LCC statutes are not yet uniform. Until all of the states have adopted the ULLCA, an LLC in one state will have to check the rules in the other states in which the firm does business to ensure that it retains its limited liability. Generally, though, most— if not all—states apply to a foreign LLC (an LLC formed in

another state) the law of the state where the LLC was formed. Still another disadvantage is the lack of case law dealing with LLCs. How the courts interpret statutes provides important guidelines for businesses. Given the relative newness of the LLC as a business form in the United States, there is not, as yet, a substantial body of case law to provide this kind of guidance.

THE LLC OPERATING AGREEMENT

In an LCC, the members themselves can decide how to operate the various aspects of the business by forming an **operating agreement** [ULLCA 103(a)]. Operating agreements typically contain provisions relating to management, how profits will be divided, the transfer of membership interests, whether the LLC will be dissolved on the death or departure of a member, and other important issues.

An operating agreement need not be in writing and indeed need not even be formed for an LLC to exist. Generally, though, LLC members should protect their interests by forming a written operating agreement. As with any business arrangement, disputes may arise over any number of issues. If there is no agreement covering the topic under dispute, such as how profits will be divided, the state LLC statute will govern the outcome. For example, most LLC statutes provide that if the members have not specified how profits will be divided, they will be divided equally among the members.

Generally, when an issue is not covered by an operating agreement or by an LLC statute, the principles of partnership law are applied. At issue in the following case was whether partnership law should apply to a dispute between LLC members as to how business receipts were to be divided on the firm's dissolution.

CASE 24.4 Hurwitz v. Padden

Court of Appeals of Minnesota, 1998.
581 N.W.2d 359.
http://www.lawlibrary.state.mn.us/archive/ capgi.html[a]

FACTS Thomas Hurwitz and Michael Padden formed a two-person law firm as a partnership without a written agreement. They shared all proceeds on a fifty-fifty basis and reported all income as partnership income. Less than eighteen months

later, Hurwitz filed articles of organization with the state of Minnesota to establish the firm as an LLC. More than three years later, Padden told Hurwitz that he wanted to dissolve their professional relationship. They resolved all business issues between them, except for a division of fees from several of the firm's cases. Hurwitz filed a suit in a Minnesota state court against Padden, seeking, among other things, a distribution of the fees on a fifty-fifty basis. The court applied the principles of partnership law, ruled that the fees should be divided equally, and entered a judgment in favor of Hurwitz for $101,750. Padden appealed, arguing in part that these principles of partnership law should not apply to an LLC.

ISSUE Do partnership principles apply to the dissolution, the winding up, and the distribution of business receipts of an LLC?

---

a. This page includes a partial list of Minnesota Court of Appeals opinions available in the Minnesota State Law Library online database. The last name of the parties in these cases begins with the letter G, H, or I. Scroll down the list to the *Hurwitz* name and click on the link to read the case.

CASE 24.4—Continued

DECISION Yes. The state intermediate appellate court affirmed the decision of the lower court. The appellate court concluded that the disputed fees should be divided equally, as the receipts were divided before the dissolution.

REASON The court pointed out that the state LLC act specifically incorporated the definition and use of the term *dissolution* from the Uniform Partnership Act (UPA). Under both statutes, a business entity is not terminated on dissolu-

tion but continues until all business is taken care of. The court noted in particular that the firm had no written agreement regarding the division of receipts before or on dissolution, that the disputed fees related to work acquired before the dissolution, and that before the dissolution the firm divided receipts equally between the parties.

FOR CRITICAL ANALYSIS—Social Consideration
Should the principles of partnership law apply to other forms of business entities?

MANAGEMENT OF AN LLC

Basically, there are two options for managing an LLC. The members may decide in their operating agreement to be either a "member-managed" LLC or a "manager-managed" LLC. Most LLC statutes and the ULLCA provide that unless the articles of organization specify otherwise, an LLC is assumed to be member managed [ULLCA 203(a)(6)]. In a *member-managed* LLC, all of the members participate in management, and decisions are made by majority vote [ULLCA 404(a)]. In a *manager-managed* LLC, the members designate a group of persons to manage the firm. The management group may consist of only members, both members and nonmembers, or only nonmembers. Managers in a manager-managed LLC owe fiduciary duties to the LLC and its members, including the duty of loyalty and the duty of care [ULLCA 409(a) and 409(h)].

The members of an LLC can also set forth in their operating agreement provisions governing decision-making procedures. For example, the agreement can include procedures for choosing or removing managers, an issue on which most LLC statutes are silent, although the ULLCA provides that members may choose and remove managers by majority vote [ULLCA 404(b)(3)]. The members are also free to include in the agreement provisions designating when and for what purposes formal members' meetings will be held. In contrast to state laws governing corporations, most state LLC statutes have no provisions regarding members' meetings. Members may also specify in their agreement how voting rights will be apportioned. If they do not, LLC statutes in most states provide that voting rights are apportioned according to each member's capital contributions. Some states provide that, in the absence of an agreement to the contrary, each member has one vote.

Limited Liability Partnerships

The **limited liability partnership (LLP)** is similar to the LLC but is designed more for professionals who normally do business as partners in a partnership. The major advan-

tage of the LLP is that it allows a partnership to continue as a pass-through entity for tax purposes but limits the personal liability of the partners.

In 1991, Texas became the first state to enact an LLP statute. Other states quickly followed suit, and by 1997, virtually all of the states had enacted LLP statutes. Like LLCs, LLPs must be formed and operated in compliance with state statutes. The appropriate form must be filed with a central state agency, usually the secretary of state's office, and the business's name must include either "Limited Liability Partnership" or "LLP."

In most states, it is relatively easy to convert a traditional partnership into an LLP because the firm's basic organizational structure remains the same. Additionally, all of the statutory and common law rules governing partnerships still apply (apart from those modified by the LLP statute). Normally, LLP statutes are simply amendments to a state's already existing partnership law.

The LLP is especially attractive for two categories of businesses: professional services and family businesses. Professional service firms include law firms and accounting firms. Family limited liability partnerships are basically business organizations in which all of the partners are related.

LIABILITY IN AN LLP

Many professionals, such as attorneys and accountants, work together using the business form of the partnership. A major disadvantage of the partnership is the unlimited personal liability of its owner-partners. Partners are also subject to joint and several (individual) liability for partnership obligations. ● **EXAMPLE #5** A group of lawyers is operating as a partnership. A client sues one of the attorneys for malpractice and wins a large judgment, and the firm's malpractice insurance is insufficient to cover the obligation. When the attorney's personal assets are exhausted, the personal assets of the other, innocent partners can be used to satisfy the judgment.●

The LLP allows professionals to avoid personal liability for the malpractice of other partners. Although LLP statutes vary from state to state, generally each state statute limits the liability of partners in some way. For example, Delaware law protects each innocent partner from the "debts and obligations of the partnership arising from negligence, wrongful acts, or misconduct." In North Carolina, Texas, and Washington, D.C., the statutes protect innocent partners from obligations arising from "errors, omissions, negligence, incompetence, or malfeasance." Although the language of these statutes may seem to apply specifically to attorneys, virtually any group of professionals can use the LLP.

Questions remain, however, concerning the exact limits of this exemption from liability. One question is whether limits on liability apply outside the state in which the LLP was formed. Another question involves whether liability should be imposed to some extent on a negligent partner's supervising partner.

FAMILY LIMITED LIABILITY PARTNERSHIPS

A **family limited liability partnership (FLLP)** is a limited liability partnership in which the majority of the partners are persons related to each other, essentially as spouses, parents, grandparents, siblings, cousins, nephews, or nieces. A person acting in a fiduciary capacity for persons so related can also be a partner. All of the partners must be natural persons or persons acting in a fiduciary capacity for the benefit of natural persons.

Probably the most significant use of the FLLP form of business organization is in agriculture. Family-owned farms sometimes find this form to their benefit. The FLLP offers the same advantages as other LLPs with some additional advantages, such as, in Iowa, an exemption from real estate transfer taxes when partnership real estate is transferred among partners.[16]

Limited Partnerships

We have been discussing relatively new forms of limited liability business organizations. We now look at an older business organizational form that limits the liability of some of its owners—the **limited partnership**. In many ways, limited partnerships are like general partnerships, but they differ from general partnerships in several ways. Because of this, they are sometimes referred to as *special partnerships*.

A limited partnership consists of at least one **general partner** and one or more **limited partners**. A general partner assumes management responsibility for the partnership and so has full responsibility for the partnership and for all

debts of the partnership. A limited partner contributes cash or other property and owns an interest in the firm but does not undertake any management responsibilities and is not personally liable for partnership debts beyond the amount of his or her investment. A limited partner can forfeit limited liability by taking part in the management of the business. Exhibit 24–2 compares characteristics of general and limited partnerships.[17]

Until 1976, the law governing limited partnerships in all states except Louisiana was the Uniform Limited Partnership Act (ULPA). Since 1976, most states and the District of Columbia have adopted the revised version of the ULPA, known as the Revised Uniform Limited Partnership Act (RULPA). Because the RULPA is the dominant law governing limited partnerships in the United States, we will refer to the RULPA in the following discussion of limited partnerships.

FORMATION OF THE LIMITED PARTNERSHIP

In contrast to the informal, private, and voluntary agreement that usually suffices for a general partnership, the formation of a limited partnership is a public and formal proceeding that must follow statutory requirements. A limited partnership must have at least one general partner and one limited partner, as mentioned previously. Additionally, the partners must sign a **certificate of limited partnership**, which requires information similar to that found in a corporate charter (see Chapter 25). The certificate must be filed with the designated state official—under the RULPA, the secretary of state. The certificate is usually open to public inspection.

RIGHTS AND LIABILITIES OF PARTNERS

General partners, unlike limited partners, are personally liable to the partnership's creditors; thus, at least one general partner is necessary in a limited partnership so that someone has personal liability. This policy can be circumvented in states that allow a corporation to be the general partner in a partnership. Because the corporation has limited liability by virtue of corporate laws, if a corporation is the general partner, no one in the limited partnership has personal liability.

Rights of Limited Partners. Subject to the limitations that will be discussed here, limited partners have essentially the

---

[16] Iowa Statutes Section 428A.2.

[17] Under the RUPA, a general partnership can be converted into a limited partnership and vice versa [RUPA 902, 903]. The RUPA also provides for the merger of a general partnership with one or more general or limited partnerships under rules that are similar to those governing corporate mergers [RUPA 905].

EXHIBIT 24–2 A COMPARISON OF GENERAL PARTNERSHIPS AND LIMITED PARTNERSHIPS

CHARACTERISTIC	GENERAL PARTNERSHIP (UPA)	LIMITED PARTNERSHIP (RULPA)
Creation	By agreement of two or more persons to carry on a business as co-owners for profit.	By agreement of two or more persons to carry on a business as co-owners for profit. Must include one or more general partners and one or more limited partners. Filing of a certificate with the secretary of state is required.
Sharing of Profits and Losses	By agreement; or, in the absence of agreement, profits are shared equally by the partners, and losses are shared in the same ratio as profits.	Profits are shared as required in the certificate agreement, and losses are shared likewise, up to the amount of the limited partners' capital contributions. In the absence of a provision in the certificate agreement, profits and losses are shared on the basis of percentages of capital contributions.
Liability	Unlimited personal liability of all partners.	Unlimited personal liability of all general partners; limited partners liable only to the extent of their capital contributions.
Capital Contribution	No minimum or mandatory amount; set by agreement.	Set by agreement.
Management	By agreement, or in the absence of agreement, all partners have an equal voice.	General partners by agreement, or else each has an equal voice. Limited partners have no voice or else are subject to liability as general partners (but *only* if a third party has reason to believe that the limited partner is a general partner). A limited partner may act as an agent or employee of the partnership and vote on amending the certificate or on the sale or dissolution of the partnership.
Duration	By agreement, or can be dissolved by action of the partners (withdrawal), operation of law (death or bankruptcy), or court decree.	By agreement in the certificate or by withdrawal, death, or mental incompetence of a general partner in the absence of the right of the other general partners to continue the partnership. Death of a limited partner, unless he or she is the only remaining limited partner, does not terminate the partnership.
Distribution of Assets on Liquidation— Order of Priorities	1. Outside creditors. 2. Partner creditors. 3. Partners, according to capital contributions. 4. Partners, according to profits.	1. Outside creditors and partner creditors. 2. Partners and former partners entitled to distributions before withdrawal under the agreement or the RULPA. 3. Partners, according to capital contributions. 4. Partners, according to profits.

same rights as general partners, including the right of access to partnership books and the right to other information regarding partnership business. On dissolution, limited partners are entitled to a return of their contributions in accordance with the partnership certificate [RULPA 201(a)(10)]. They can also assign their interests subject to the certificate [RULPA 702, 704].

The RULPA provides a limited partner with the right to sue an outside party on behalf of the firm if the general partners with authority to do so have refused to file suit

[RULPA 1001]. In addition, investor protection legislation, such as securities laws (discussed in Chapter 27), may give some protection to limited partners.

Liabilities of Limited Partners. In contrast to the personal liability of general partners, the liability of a limited partner is limited to the capital that she or he contributes or agrees to contribute to the partnership [RULPA 502].

A limited partnership is formed by good faith compliance with the requirements for signing and filing the certificate, even if it is incomplete or defective. When a limited partner discovers a defect in the formation of the limited partnership, she or he can avoid future liability by causing an appropriate amendment or certificate to be filed or by renouncing an interest in the profits of the partnership [RULPA 304]. If the limited partner takes neither of these actions on discovering the defect, however, the partner can be held personally liable by the firm's creditors. Liability for false statements in a partnership certificate runs in favor of persons relying on the false statements and against members who know of the falsity but still sign the certificate [RULPA 207].

Limited Partners and Management. Limited partners enjoy limited liability so long as they do not participate in management [RULPA 303]. A limited partner who participates in management will be just as liable as a general partner to any creditor who transacts business with the limited partnership and believes, based on a limited partner's conduct, that the limited partner is a general partner [RULPA 303]. How much actual review and advisement a limited partner can engage in before being exposed to liability is an unsettled question.[18] A limited partner who knowingly permits his or her name to be used in the name of the limited partnership is liable to creditors who extend credit to the limited partnership without knowledge that the limited partner is not a general partner [RULPA 102, 303(d)].

Although limited partners cannot participate in management, this does not mean that the general partners are totally free of restrictions in running the business. The general partners in a limited partnership have fiduciary obligations to the partnership and to the limited partners, as the following case illustrates.

---

[18] It is an unsettled question partly because different states have different laws. Factors to be considered are listed in RULPA 303(b), (c).

CASE 24.5 BT-I v. Equitable Life Assurance Society of the United States

California Court of Appeal,
Fourth District, 1999.
75 Cal.App.4th 1406,
89 Cal.Rptr.2d 811.

FACTS BT-I, a general partnership, entered into a general partnership with Equitable Life Assurance Society of the United States to develop and operate an office building and retail complex in California. Banque Paribas lent the firm $62.5 million for the project. Six years later, BT-I and Equitable dissolved their general partnership and entered into a limited partnership, with Equitable as general partner and BT-I as limited partner. Equitable was given title to the retail complex and the sole right to manage the partnership. Paragraph 5.1(c) of the limited partnership agreement gave Equitable broad powers, "provided, however, * * * that in no event shall the General Partner be required to take any action * * * to prevent Banque Paribas or any other lender from exercising any remedies in connection with any loan made to the Partnership." Later, when Banque Paribas solicited bids to "sell" its loan, Equitable (in its capacity as a corporate entity) bought it for $38.5 million. On the due date, Equitable demanded full payment from the partnership,

but none was made. A month later, Equitable offered to sell the loan to the partnership, but the offer was not accepted. Equitable scheduled a foreclosure sale. Three days before the sale, BT-I offered $39 million for the project, but Equitable turned it down. At the sale, Equitable bought the partnership's office building. BT-I filed a suit in a California state court against Equitable, alleging in part breach of fiduciary duty. Equitable argued that the partnership agreement allowed it to buy the loans and foreclose the same as any other lender. The court entered a judgment in Equitable's favor. BT-I appealed to a state intermediate appellate court.

ISSUE Did Equitable breach a fiduciary duty to BT-I?

DECISION Yes. The state intermediate appellate court reversed the judgment of the lower court.

REASON The appellate court held that "[a] general partner of a limited partnership is subject to the same restrictions, and has the same liabilities to the partnership and other partners, as in a general partnership." As for Equitable's argument concerning the partnership agreement, the court stated that "[e]ven if the language were broad enough to justify such an

CASE 24.5—Continued

interpretation, we hold a partnership agreement cannot relieve a general partner of its fiduciary duties to a limited partner and the partnership where the purchase and foreclosure of partnership debt is involved." According to the court, Equitable's conduct in buying and foreclosing the loans went "far beyond" what was permitted under the partnership agreement. Also, "the fact that the [Revised Uniform Limited

Partnership Act] allows the parties to structure many aspects of their relationship is not a license to freely engage in self-dealing * * *. Equitable was still a fiduciary, and its conduct must be measured by fiduciary standards."

FOR CRITICAL ANALYSIS—Ethical Consideration
Generally, why does the law impose fiduciary obligations on general partners?

DISSOLUTION

A limited partnership is dissolved in much the same way as an ordinary partnership. The retirement, death, or mental incompetence of a general partner can dissolve the partnership, but not if the business can be continued by one or more of the other general partners in accordance with their certificate or by the consent of all of the members [RULPA 801]. The death or assignment of interest of a limited partner does not dissolve the limited partnership [RULPA 702, 704, 705]. A limited partnership can be dissolved by court decree [RULPA 802].

Bankruptcy or the withdrawal of a general partner dissolves a limited partnership. Bankruptcy of a limited partner, however, does not dissolve the partnership unless it causes the bankruptcy of the limited partnership. The retirement of a general partner causes a dissolution unless the members consent to a continuation by the remaining general partners or unless this contingency is provided for in the certificate.

On dissolution, creditors' rights, including those of partners who are creditors, take first priority. Then partners and former partners receive unpaid distributions of partnership assets and, except as otherwise agreed, amounts representing returns on their contributions and amounts proportionate to their shares of the distributions [RULPA 804].

LIMITED LIABILITY LIMITED PARTNERSHIPS

A **limited liability limited partnership (LLLP)** is a type of limited partnership. An LLLP differs from a limited partnership in that a general partner in an LLLP has the same liability as a limited partner; that is, the liability of all partners is limited to the amount of their investments in the firm.

A few states provide expressly for LLLPs.[19] In states that do not provide for LLLPs but do allow for limited partner-

ships and limited liability partnerships, a limited partnership should probably still be able to register with the state as an LLLP.

Special Business Forms

In addition to the major business organizational forms, several special forms exist. For the most part, however, they are hybrid organizations—that is, they have characteristics similar to those of partnerships or corporations or they combine features of both.

JOINT VENTURES, SYNDICATES, AND JOINT STOCK COMPANIES

A *joint venture* is treated much like a partnership, but it differs in that its creation is in contemplation of a limited activity or a single transaction. The form of a *syndicate* or an *investment group* can vary considerably. They may exist as corporations or as general or limited partnerships. In some cases, the members merely own property jointly and have no legally recognized business arrangement. The *joint stock company* is a true hybrid of a partnership and a corporation. It is similar to a corporation in that it is a shareholder organization; because of the personal liability of its members and other characteristics, however, it is usually treated like a partnership.

BUSINESS TRUSTS AND COOPERATIVES

The *business trust*, a popular form of business organization in nineteenth-century America, is somewhat similar to the corporation (see Chapter 25). Although legal ownership and management of the property of the business stay with one or more of the trustees, the beneficiaries—who receive profits from the enterprise—are not personally responsible for the debts or obligations of the business trust, and in some states business trusts must pay corporate taxes. The *cooperative* is a nonprofit organization formed to provide an

---

[19] See, for example, Colorado Revised Statutes Annotated Section 7-62-109. Other states that provide expressly for limited liability limited partnerships include Delaware, Florida, Missouri, Pennsylvania, Texas, and Virginia.

economic service to its members. Unincorporated cooperatives are often treated like partnerships; incorporated cooperatives, as with all corporations, are subject to state corporate law.

FRANCHISES

One can also venture into business by purchasing a franchise. About 25 percent of all retail sales and an increasing part of the gross national product of the United States are generated by private franchises. A **franchise** is any arrangement in which the owner of a trademark, a trade name, or a copyright has licensed others to use the trademark, trade name, or copyright in selling goods or services. As a **franchisee** (a purchaser of a franchise), you are generally legally independent of, but economically dependent on, the integrated business system of the **franchisor** (the seller of the franchise). In other words, you can operate as an independent businessperson but still obtain the advantages of a regional or national organization. Well-known franchises include Hilton Hotels, McDonald's, and Burger King. Franchising is not so much a *form* of business organization as a way of doing business. Sole proprietorships, partnerships, and corporations can all buy and sell franchises.

Terms and Concepts

Chapter Summary — Sole Proprietorships, Partnerships, and Limited Liability Companies

Sole Proprietorship (See page 495.)	The simplest form of business; used by anyone who does business without creating an organization. The owner is the business. The owner pays personal income taxes on all profits and is personally liable for all business debts.
Partnership (See pages 495–506.)	1. Created by agreement of the parties. 2. Not treated as an entity except for limited purposes. 3. Partners have unlimited liability for partnership debts. 4. Each partner has an equal voice in management unless otherwise provided for in the partnership agreement. 5. In the absence of an agreement, partners share profits equally and share losses in the same ratio as they share profits. 6. The capital contribution of each partner is determined by agreement. 7. Each partner pays a proportionate share of income taxes on the net profits of the partnership, whether or not they are distributed; the partnership files only an information return with the Internal Revenue Service. 8. Terminated by agreement or can be dissolved by action of the partners (withdrawal), operation of law (death or bankruptcy), or court decree.

Chapter Summary	Sole Proprietorships, Partnerships, and Limited Liability Companies—Continued
Limited Liability Company (LLC) (See pages 506–509.)	The limited liability company (LLC) is a hybrid form of business organization that offers the limited liability feature of corporations but the tax benefits of partnerships. Unlike limited partners, LLC members participate in management. Members of LLCs may be corporations or partnerships and are not restricted in number.
Limited Liability Partnership (LLP) (See pages 509–510.)	1. Must be formed in compliance with statutory requirements. 2. Most state statutes make it relatively easy to establish an LLP, particularly if a firm is already doing business as a partnership. 3. Statutes vary from state to state, but generally, each state statute limits in some way the personal liability of innocent partners for the wrongful acts of other partners.
Limited Partnership (See pages 510–513.)	1. Must be formed in compliance with statutory requirements. 2. Consists of one or more general partners and one or more limited partners. 3. Only general partners can participate in management. Limited partners have no voice in management; if they do participate in management activities, they risk having general-partner liability. 4. General partners have unlimited liability for partnership losses; limited partners are liable only to the extent of their contributions.
Limited Liability Limited Partnership (LLLP) (See page 513.)	A special type of limited partnership in which the liability of all partners, including general partners, is limited to the amount of their investments.
Special Business Forms (See pages 513–514.)	A number of special business forms exist. Typically, they are hybrid organizations having characteristics similar to partnerships or corporations, or combining features of both. Special business forms include joint ventures, syndicates or investment groups, joint stock companies, business trusts, and cooperatives. A widely used way of conducting business is the franchise.

For Review

① Which form of business organization is the simplest? Which form arises from an agreement between two or more persons to carry on a business for profit?

② What are the three essential elements of a partnership?

③ What is meant by joint and several liability? Why is this often considered to be a disadvantage of the partnership form of business?

④ What is a limited liability company? What are some of the advantages and disadvantages of this business form?

⑤ Why do professional groups organize as a limited liability partnership? How does this form differ from a general partnership?

Questions and Case Problems

24–1. Distribution of Partnership Assets. Shawna and David formed a partnership. At the time of the partnership's formation, Shawna's capital contribution was $10,000, and David's was $15,000. Later, Shawna made a $10,000 loan to the partnership when it needed working capital. The partnership agreement provided that profits were to be shared, with 40 percent for Shawna and 60 percent for David. The partnership was dis-

solved by David's death. At the end of the dissolution and the winding up of the partnership, the partnership's assets were $50,000, and the partnership's debts were $8,000. Discuss fully how the assets should be distributed.

24–2. Partnership Property. Schwartz and Zenov were partners in an accounting firm. Because business was booming and profits were better than ever, they decided to invest some of the firm's profits in Munificent Corp. stock. The investment turned out to be a good one, as the stock continued to increase in value. On Schwartz's death several years later, Zenov assumed full ownership of the business, including the Munificent Corp. stock, a partnership asset. Schwartz's daughter Rosalie, however, claimed a 50 percent ownership interest in the Munificent Corp. stock as Schwartz's sole heir. Can Rosalie enforce her claim? Explain.

24–3. Partner's Property Rights. Maruta, Samms, and Ortega were partners in a business firm. The firm's business equipment included several expensive computers. One day, Maruta borrowed one of the computers for use in his home and never bothered to return it. When the other partners asked him about it, Maruta claimed he had a right to keep the computer because it represented less than one-third of the computers owned by the partnership and he owned one-third of the business. Was he right? Explain.

24–4. Limited Liability Companies. John, Lesa, and Trevor form an LLC. John contributes 60 percent of the capital, and Lesa and Trevor each contribute 20 percent. Nothing is decided about how profits will be divided. John assumes that he will be entitled to 60 percent of the profits, in accordance with his contribution. Lesa and Trevor, however, assume that the profits will be divided equally. A dispute over the profits arises, and ultimately a court has to decide the issue. What law will the court apply? In most states, what will result? How could this dispute have been avoided in the first place? Discuss fully.

24–5. Liability of Limited Partners. Asher and Breem form a limited partnership with Asher as the general partner and Breem as the limited partner. Breem puts up $15,000, and Asher contributes some office equipment that he owns. A certificate of limited partnership is properly filed, and business is begun. One month later, Asher becomes ill. Instead of hiring someone to manage the business, Breem takes over complete management himself. While Breem is in control, he makes a contract with Thaler involving a large sum of money. Asher returns to work. Because of other commitments, Asher and Breem breach the Thaler contract. Thaler contends that Asher and Breem will be personally liable for damages caused by the breach if the damages cannot be satisfied out of the assets of the limited partnership. Discuss this contention.

24–6. Limited Partners. Caton Avenue Associates was a limited partnership that owned rental property. Caton paid Theodore Dalmazio, one of the general partners, a management fee to manage the property. Dalmazio paid his employees with Caton's money. Dalmazio billed Caton for services that are normally performed by property management firms at no cost and also billed Caton at an hourly rate for work that is normally billed per rental unit. Alfred Friedman and the other limited partners filed a suit on Caton's behalf in a New York state court against Dalmazio and the other general partner to recover damages. On what basis might the court rule in favor of the limited partners? Explain. [*Friedman v. Dalmazio,* 644 N.Y.S.2d 548 (App.Div. 1996)]

24–7. Liability of Partners. Frank Kolk was the manager of Triples American Grill, a sports bar and restaurant. Kolk and John Baines opened bank accounts in the name of the bar, each

signing the account signature cards as "owner." Baines was often at the bar and had free access to its office. Baines told others that he was "an owner" and "a partner." Kolk told Steve Mager, the president of Cheesecake Factory, Inc., that Baines was a member of a partnership that owned Triples. On this basis, Cheesecake delivered its goods to Triples on credit. In fact, the bar was owned by a corporation. When the unpaid account totaled more than $20,000, Cheesecake filed a suit in a New Mexico state court against Baines to collect. On what basis might Baines be liable to Cheesecake? What does Cheesecake have to show to win its case? [*Cheesecake Factory, Inc. v. Baines,* 964 P.2d 183 (N.M.App. 1998)]

24–8. Indications of Partnership. Sandra Lerner was one of the original founders of Cisco Systems. When she sold her interest in Cisco, she received a substantial amount of money, which she invested, and she became extremely wealthy. Patricia Holmes met Lerner at Holmes's horse-training facility, and they became friends. One evening in Lerner's mansion, while applying nail polish, Holmes layered a raspberry color over black to produce a new color, which Lerner liked. Later, the two created other colors with names like "Bruise," "Smog," and "Oil Slick" and titled their concept "Urban Decay." Lerner and Holmes started a firm to produce and market the polishes but never discussed the sharing of profits and losses. They agreed to build the business and then sell it. Together, they did market research, experimented with colors, worked on a logo and advertising, obtained capital from an investment firm, and hired employees. Then Lerner began working to edge Holmes out of the firm. Several months later, when Holmes was told not to attend meetings of the firm's officers, she filed a suit in a California state court against Lerner, claiming, among other things, a breach of their partnership agreement. Lerner responded in part that there was no partnership agreement because there was no agreement to divide profits. Was Lerner right? Why or why not? How should the court rule? [*Holmes v. Lerner,* 74 Cal.App.4th 442, 88 Cal.Rptr.2d 130 (1 Dist. 1999)]

CASE PROBLEM WITH SAMPLE ANSWER

24–9. Walter Matjasich and Cary Hanson organized Capital Care, LLC, in Utah. Capital Care operated, and Matjasich and Hanson managed, Heartland Care Center in Topeka, Kansas. LTC Properties, Inc., held a mortgage on the Heartland facilities. When Heartland failed as a business, its residents were transferred to other facilities. Heartland employees who provided care to the residents for five days during the transfers were not paid wages. The employees filed claims with the Kansas Department of Human Resources for the unpaid wages. Kansas state law provides that a *corporate* officer or manager may be liable for a firm's unpaid wages, but protects LLC members from personal liability generally and states that an LLC cannot be construed as a corporation. Under Utah state law, the members of an LLC can be personally liable for wages due the LLC's employees. Should Matjasich and Hanson be held personally liable for the unpaid wages? Explain. [*Matjasich v. State, Department of Human Resources,* 21 P.3d 985 (Kan. 2001)]

▶ To view a sample answer for this case problem, go to this book's Web site at **http://fundamentals.westbuslaw.com** and click on "Interactive Study Center."

24–10. Limited Liability Companies. Michael Collins entered into a three-year employment contract with E-Magine, LLC. In business for only a brief time, E-Magine lost a considerable sum of money. In terminating operations, which ceased before the term of the contract with Collins expired, E-Magine also terminated Collins's services. Collins signed a "final payment agreement," which purported to be a settlement of any claims that he might have against E-Magine in exchange for a payment of $24,240. Collins filed a suit in a New York state court against E-Magine, its members and managers, and others, alleging, among other things, breach of his employment contract. Collins claimed that signing the "final payment agreement" was the only means for him to obtain what he was owed for past sales commissions and asked the court to impose personal liability on the members and managers of E-Magine for breach of contract. Should the court grant this request? Why or why not? [*Collins v. E-Magine, LLC,* 291 A.D.2d 350, 739 N.Y.S.2d 15 (1 Dept. 2002)]

SOLE PRORIETORSHIPS, PARTNERSHIPS, AND LIMITED LIABILITY COMPANIES

For updated links to resources available on the Web, as well as other materials, visit this text's Web site at

http://fundamentals.westbuslaw.com

To learn how the U.S. Small Business Administration (SBA) assists in forming, financing, and operating businesses, go to

http://www.sbaonline.sba.gov

Nolo Press provides a chapter of information on major business forms. Go to

http://www.nolo.com/chapter/RUNS/RUNS_toc.html

Then scroll down to "Read sample chapter" and click on that link.

Online Legal Research

Go to the *Fundamentals of Business Law* home page at **http://fundamentals. westbuslaw.com**. Select "Interactive Study Center" and then click on "Chapter 24." There you will find the following Internet research exercises that you can perform to learn more about topics covered in this chapter.

Activity 24–1: LEGAL PERSPECTIVE—Limited Liability Companies
Activity 24–2: MANAGEMENT PERSPECTIVE—Partnerships

Before the Test

Go to the *Fundamentals of Business Law* home page at **http://fundamentals. westbuslaw.com**. Click on "Interactive Quizzes." You will find at least twenty interactive questions relating to this chapter.

Westlaw® Campus

If your textbook provided for a subscription to Westlaw® Campus, or if you have otherwise purchased access to the Westlaw Campus database, you can access any of the cases presented or cited in this chapter by using your Westlaw Campus account.

25

Corporate Formation, Financing, and Termination

After reading this chapter, you should be able to answer the following questions:

① What are the steps for bringing a corporation into existence? Who is liable for preincorporation contracts?

② What is the difference between a *de jure* corporation and a *de facto* corporation?

③ In what circumstances might a court disregard the corporate entity ("pierce the corporate veil") and hold the shareholders personally liable?

④ What are the four steps of the merger or consolidation procedure?

⑤ What are the two ways in which a corporation can be voluntarily dissolved? Under what circumstances might a corporation be involuntarily dissolved by state action?

The corporation is a creature of statute. Its existence generally depends on state law, although some corporations, especially public organizations, can be created under state or federal law.

Each state has its own body of corporate law, and these laws are not entirely uniform. The Model Business Corporation Act (MBCA) is a codification of modern corporation law that has been influential in the drafting and revision of state corporation statutes. Today, the majority of state statutes are guided by the revised version of the MBCA, which is often referred to as the Revised Model Business Corporation Act (RMBCA). You should keep in mind, however, that there is considerable variation among the statutes of the states that have used the MBCA or the RMBCA as a

basis for their statutes, and several states do not follow either act. Consequently, individual state corporation laws should be relied on rather than the MBCA or RMBCA.

The Nature of the Corporation

A **corporation** is a legal entity created and recognized by state law. It can consist of one or more *natural* persons (as opposed to the artificial "person" of the corporation) identified under a common name. A corporation can be owned by a single person, or it can have hundreds, thousands, or even millions of owners (shareholders). The corporation substitutes itself for its shareholders in conducting corporate business and in incurring liability, yet its authority to act and the liability for its actions are separate and apart from the individuals who own it.

In a corporation, the responsibility for the overall management of the firm is entrusted to a *board of directors,* which is elected by the shareholders. The board of directors hires *corporate officers* and other employees to run the daily business operations of the corporation. When an individual purchases a share of stock in a corporation, that person becomes a *shareholder* and an owner of the corporation. Unlike the members of a partnership, the body of shareholders can change constantly without affecting the continued existence of the corporation. A shareholder can sue the corporation, and the corporation can sue a shareholder. Also, under certain circumstances, a shareholder can sue on behalf of a corporation. The rights and duties of corporate personnel will be examined in detail in Chapter 26.

The shareholder form of business organization emerged in Europe at the end of the seventeenth century. Called *joint stock companies,* these organizations frequently collapsed because their organizers absconded with the funds or proved to be incompetent. Because of this history of fraud and collapse, organizations resembling corporations were regarded with suspicion in the United States during its early years. Although several business corporations were formed after the Revolutionary War, it was not until the nineteenth century that the corporation came into common use for private business. Today, the corporation is one of the most important forms of business organization in the United States.

THE CONSTITUTIONAL RIGHTS OF CORPORATIONS

A corporation is recognized under state and federal law as a "person," and it enjoys many of the same rights and privileges that U.S. citizens enjoy. The Bill of Rights guarantees a person, as a citizen, certain protections, and corporations are considered persons in most instances. Accordingly, a corporation has the same right as a natural person to equal protection of the laws under the Fourteenth Amendment. It has the right of access to the courts as an entity that can sue or be sued. It also has the right of due process before denial of life, liberty, or property, as well as freedom from unreasonable searches and seizures (see Chapter 6 for a discussion of searches and seizures in the business context) and from double jeopardy.

Under the First Amendment, corporations are entitled to freedom of speech. As we pointed out in Chapter 1, however, commercial speech (such as advertising) and political speech (such as contributions to political causes or candidates) receive significantly less protection than noncommercial speech.

Only the corporation's individual officers and employees possess the Fifth Amendment right against self-incrimination.[1] Additionally, the privileges and immunities clause of the Constitution (Article IV, Section 2) does not protect corporations, nor does it protect an unincorporated association.[2] This clause requires each state to treat citizens of other states equally with respect to access to courts, travel rights, and so forth.

THE LIMITED LIABILITY OF SHAREHOLDERS

One of the key advantages of the corporate form is the limited liability of its owners (shareholders). Corporate shareholders normally are not personally liable for the obligations of the corporation beyond the extent of their investments. In certain limited situations, however, the "corporate veil" can be pierced and liability for the corporation's obligations extended to shareholders—a concept that will be explained later in this chapter.

CORPORATE TAXATION

Corporate profits are taxed by state and federal governments. Corporations can do one of two things with corporate profits—retain them or pass them on to shareholders in the form of **dividends**. The corporation receives no tax deduction for dividends distributed to shareholders. Dividends are again taxable (except when they represent distributions of capital) as ordinary income to the shareholder receiving them. This double-taxation feature of the corporation is one of its major disadvantages.

Profits that are not distributed are retained by the corporation. These **retained earnings**, if invested properly, will yield higher corporate profits in the future and thus cause the price of the company's stock to rise. Individual shareholders can then reap the benefits of these retained earnings in the capital gains they receive when they sell their shares.

The consequences of a failure to pay corporate taxes can be severe. As will be discussed later in this chapter, the state may dissolve a corporation for this reason. Alternatively, corporate status may be suspended until the taxes are paid.

In the following case, the state had revoked a corporation's **corporate charter** (the document issued by a state agency or authority—usually the secretary of state—that grants a corporation legal existence and the right to function) because of the corporation's failure to pay certain taxes. The issue before the court was whether a shareholder who had assumed an obligation of the corporation could be held personally liable for the unsatisfactory performance of the contract.

---

[1] *In re Grand Jury No. 86-3 (Will Roberts Corp.),* 816 F.2d 569 (11th Cir. 1987).
[2] *W. C. M. Window Co. v. Bernardi,* 730 F.2d 486 (7th Cir. 1984).

CASE 25.1   Bullington v. Palangio

Arkansas Supreme Court, 2001.
345 Ark. 320,
45 S.W.3d 834.
**http://courts.state.ar.us/opinions/
opinions.html**[a]

FACTS Jerry Bullington, doing business as Bullington Builders, Inc. (BBI), entered into a contract with Helen Palangio for the construction of a new house in Damascus, Arkansas. Bullington signed the contract "Jerry Bullington, d/b/a Bullington Builders, Inc.," but did not indicate any official capacity as a corporate officer. BBI had been incorporated in 1993. Its only shareholders were Bullington, who managed the business, and his wife. About one and a half months before Palangio's house was completed, BBI's charter was revoked for failure to pay Arkansas franchise taxes,[b] and it was not reinstated. Bullington finished the house, but Palangio was not satisfied with the work or with Bullington's attempts to address her complaints. More than a year later, Palangio hired another builder to remedy the alleged defects. Palangio then filed a suit in an Arkansas state court against Bullington, alleging, in part, breach of contract and asserting that the corporate entity did not shield him from personal liability. The court held that Bullington was liable to Palangio for $19,000. Bullington appealed to the Arkansas Supreme Court.

a. In the "Search Cases by Party Name" box, enter "Bullington" and click on the "Search" icon. The case will be the first one on the resulting list. Click on the case name to access the opinion. The Arkansas judiciary maintains this Web site.
b. A *franchise tax* is an annual tax imposed for the privilege of doing business in a state.

ISSUE Is a corporate officer who assumes the firm's obligation after its charter has been revoked personally liable for the performance of the obligation?

DECISION Yes. The Arkansas Supreme Court affirmed the lower court's judgment, holding Bullington personally liable for the unsatisfactory performance of the contract with Palangio.

REASON The court stated that "to exempt any association of persons from personal liability for the debts of a proposed corporation, they must comply fully with the [law] under which the corporation is created and that partial compliance with the [law] is not sufficient." The court noted that Arkansas state law required the payment of franchise taxes and provided for the revocation of the charter of a corporation that did not pay them, which occurred in this case. Also, the court explained that "the reasoning behind cases holding officers and stockholders individually liable for obligations that arise during the operation of a corporation when the corporate charter has been revoked for nonpayment of franchise taxes is that they ought not be allowed to avoid personal liability because of their nonfeasance [nonperformance of a duty or a responsibility]."

FOR CRITICAL ANALYSIS—Social Consideration
Would it have made a difference in the outcome of this case if Bullington had not known about the revocation of the corporate charter?

TORTS AND CRIMINAL ACTS

A corporation is liable for the torts committed by its agents or officers within the course and scope of their employment. This principle applies to a corporation exactly as it applies to the ordinary agency relationships discussed in Chapter 22. It follows the doctrine of *respondeat superior.*

Under modern criminal law, a corporation may be held liable for the criminal acts of its agents and employees, provided the punishment is one that can be applied to the corporation. Although corporations cannot be imprisoned, they can be fined. Of course, corporate directors and officers can be imprisoned, and in recent years, many have faced criminal penalties for their own actions or for the actions of employees under their supervision.

Recall from Chapter 6 that the U.S. Sentencing Commission, which was established by the Sentencing Reform Act of 1984, created standardized sentencing guidelines for federal crimes. These guidelines went into effect in 1987. The commission subsequently created specific sentencing guidelines for crimes committed by corporate employees (white-collar crimes). The net effect of the guidelines has been an increase in criminal penalties for crimes committed by corporate personnel.

Corporate Powers

When a corporation is created, the express and implied powers necessary to achieve its purpose also come into existence. The express powers of a corporation are found in its **articles of incorporation** (a document containing information about the corporation, including its organization and functions), in the law of the state of incorporation, and in the state and federal constitutions. Corporate **bylaws** (rules of management adopted by the corporation at its first organizational meeting) and the resolutions of the corporation's board of directors also grant or restrict certain powers. The following order of priority is used when conflicts arise among documents involving corporations:

① The U.S. Constitution.

② State constitutions.

③ State statutes.

④ The articles of incorporation.

⑤ Bylaws.

⑥ Resolutions of the board of directors.

Certain implied powers attach when a corporation is created. Barring express constitutional, statutory, or other prohibitions, the corporation has the implied power to perform all acts reasonably appropriate and necessary to accomplish its corporate purposes. For this reason, a corporation has the implied power to borrow funds within certain limits, to lend funds or to extend credit to those with whom it has a legal or contractual relationship, and to make charitable contributions.[3] To borrow money, the corporation acts through its board of directors to authorize the loan. Most often, the president or chief executive officer of the corporation will execute the necessary papers on behalf of the corporation. In so doing, corporate officers have the implied power to bind the corporation in matters directly connected with the *ordinary* business affairs of the enterprise.

The term *ultra vires* means "beyond the powers." In corporate law, acts of a corporation that are beyond its express and implied powers are *ultra vires* acts. Under Section 3.04 of the RMBCA, the following remedies are available for *ultra vires* acts:

① The shareholders may sue on behalf of the corporation to obtain an injunction (to prohibit the corporation from engaging in the *ultra vires* transactions) or to obtain damages for the harm caused by the transactions.

② The corporation itself can sue the officers and directors who were responsible for the *ultra vires* transactions to recover damages.

③ The attorney general of the state may institute a proceeding to obtain an injunction against the *ultra vires* transactions or to institute dissolution proceedings against the corporation for *ultra vires* acts.

---

[3] Early law held that a corporation had no implied authority to make charitable contributions because charitable activities were contrary to the primary purpose of the corporation to make a profit. Modern law, by statutes and court decisions, holds that a corporation has such implied authority.

Classification of Corporations

The classification of a corporation depends on its purpose, ownership characteristics, and location.

DOMESTIC, FOREIGN, AND ALIEN CORPORATIONS

A corporation is referred to as a **domestic corporation** by its home state (the state in which it incorporates). A corporation formed in one state but doing business in another is referred to in that other state as a **foreign corporation**. A corporation formed in another country—say, Mexico—but doing business in the United States is referred to in the United States as an **alien corporation**.

A corporation does not have an automatic right to do business in a state other than its state of incorporation. In some instances, it must obtain a *certificate of authority* in any state in which it plans to do business. Once the certificate has been issued, the powers conferred on a corporation by its home state generally can be exercised in the other state.

PUBLIC AND PRIVATE CORPORATIONS

A public corporation is one formed by the government to meet some political or governmental purpose. Cities and towns that incorporate are common examples. In addition, many federal government organizations, such as the U.S. Postal Service, the Tennessee Valley Authority, and AMTRAK, are public corporations. Note that a public corporation is not the same as a *publicly held* corporation. A publicly held corporation is any corporation whose shares are publicly traded in securities markets, such as the New York Stock Exchange or the over-the-counter market.

In contrast to public corporations, private corporations are created either wholly or in part for private benefit. Most corporations are private. Although they may serve a public purpose, as a public electric or gas utility does, they are owned by private persons rather than by the government.

NONPROFIT CORPORATIONS

Corporations formed without a profit-making purpose are called *nonprofit* or *not-for-profit* corporations. Private hospitals, educational institutions, charities, and religious organizations, for example, are frequently organized as nonprofit corporations. The nonprofit corporation is a convenient form of organization that allows various groups to own property and to form contracts without the individual members' being personally exposed to liability.

CLOSE CORPORATIONS

Most corporate enterprises in the United States fall into the category of close corporations. A **close corporation** is one whose shares are held by members of a family or by relatively few persons. Close corporations are also referred to as *closely held, family,* or *privately held* corporations. Usually, the members of the small group constituting a close corporation are personally known to each other. Because the number of shareholders is so small, there is no trading market for the shares.

Some states have enacted special statutory provisions that apply to close corporations. These provisions expressly permit close corporations to depart significantly from certain formalities required by traditional corporation law.[4] Additionally, Section 7.32 of the RMBCA, a provision added to the RMBCA in 1991 and adopted in several states, gives close corporations a substantial amount of flexibility in determining the rules by which they will operate. Under Section 7.32, if all of the shareholders of a corporation agree in writing, the corporation can operate without directors, bylaws, annual or special shareholders' or directors' meetings, stock certificates, or formal records of shareholders' or directors' decisions.[5]

Management of Close Corporations. The close corporation has a single shareholder or a closely knit group of shareholders, who usually hold the positions of directors and officers. Management of a close corporation resembles that of a sole proprietorship or a partnership.

To prevent a majority shareholder from dominating a close corporation, the corporation may require that more than a simple majority of the directors approve any action taken by the board. Typically, this would not apply to ordinary business decisions but only to extraordinary actions, such as changing the amount of dividends or dismissing an employee-shareholder.

Transfer of Shares in Close Corporations. Because, by definition, a close corporation has a small number of shareholders, the transfer of one shareholder's shares to someone else can cause serious management problems. The other shareholders may find themselves required to share control with someone they do not know or like.

● **EXAMPLE #1** Three brothers, Terry, Damon, and Henry Johnson, are the only shareholders of Johnson's Car Wash, Inc. Terry and Damon do not want Henry to sell his shares

---

[4] For example, in some states (such as Maryland), the close corporation need not have a board of directors.

[5] Shareholders cannot agree, however, to eliminate certain rights of shareholders, such as the right to inspect corporate books and records or the right to bring derivative actions (lawsuits on behalf of the corporation—see Chapter 26).

to an unknown third person. To avoid this situation, the articles of incorporation could restrict the transferability of shares to outside persons by stipulating that shareholders offer their shares to the corporation or the other shareholders before selling them to an outside purchaser. In fact, a few states have statutes that prohibit the transfer of close corporation shares unless certain persons—including shareholders, family members, and the corporation—are first given the opportunity to purchase the shares for the same price.●

Another way that control of a close corporation can be stabilized is through the use of a shareholder agreement. A shareholder agreement can provide that when one of the original shareholders dies, her or his shares of stock in the corporation will be divided in such a way that the proportionate holdings of the survivors, and thus their proportionate control, will be maintained. Courts are generally reluctant to interfere with private agreements, including shareholder agreements.

S CORPORATIONS

A close corporation that meets the qualifying requirements specified in Subchapter S of the Internal Revenue Code can operate as an **S corporation**. If a corporation has S corporation status, it can avoid the imposition of income taxes at the corporate level while retaining many of the advantages of a corporation, particularly limited liability.

Qualification Requirements for S Corporations. Among the numerous requirements for S corporation status, the following are the most important:

① The corporation must be a domestic corporation.

② The corporation must not be a member of an affiliated group of corporations.

③ The shareholders of the corporation must be individuals, estates, or certain trusts. Partnerships and nonqualifying trusts cannot be shareholders. Corporations can be shareholders under certain circumstances.

④ The corporation must have seventy-five or fewer shareholders.

⑤ The corporation must have only one class of stock, although not all shareholders need have the same voting rights.

⑥ No shareholder of the corporation may be a nonresident alien.

Benefits of S Corporations. At times, it is beneficial for a regular corporation to elect S corporation status. Benefits include the following:

① When the corporation has losses, the S election allows the shareholders to use the losses to offset other income.

② When the stockholder's tax bracket is lower than the corporation's tax bracket, the S election causes the corporation's pass-through net income to be taxed in the stockholder's bracket (because it is taxed as personal income). This is particularly attractive when the corporation wants to accumulate earnings for some future business purpose.

Because of these tax benefits, many close corporations have opted for S corporation status. Today, however, the S corporation is losing some of its significance—because the limited liability company and the limited liability partnership (discussed in Chapter 24) offer similar advantages plus additional benefits, including more flexibility in forming and operating the business.

PROFESSIONAL CORPORATIONS

Professional persons such as physicians, lawyers, dentists, and accountants can incorporate. Professional corporations are typically identified by the letters *S.C.* (service corporation), *P.C.* (professional corporation), or *P.A.* (professional association). In general, the laws governing professional corporations are similar to those governing ordinary business corporations, but three basic areas of liability deserve special attention.

First, some courts might, for liability purposes, regard the professional corporation as a partnership in which each partner can be held liable for any malpractice liability incurred by the others within the scope of the partnership. Second, a shareholder in a professional corporation is protected from the liability imposed because of any torts (unrelated to malpractice) committed by other members. Third, many professional corporation statutes retain personal liability of professional persons for their acts and the professional acts performed under their supervision.

Corporate Formation

Up to this point, we have discussed some of the general characteristics of corporations. We now examine the process in which corporations come into existence. Generally, this process involves two steps: (1) preliminary organizational and promotional undertakings, particularly obtaining capital for the future corporation; and (2) the legal process of incorporation.

Note that one of the most common reasons for changing from a sole proprietorship or a partnership to a corporation is the need for additional capital to finance expansion. A sole proprietor can seek partners who will bring capital with them. The partnership might be able to secure more funds from potential lenders than could the sole proprietor. When a firm wants to expand greatly, however, simply increasing

the number of partners can result in so many partners that it becomes difficult for the firm to operate effectively. Therefore, incorporation might be the best choice for an expanding business organization because a corporation can obtain more capital by issuing shares of stock.

PROMOTIONAL ACTIVITIES

Before a corporation becomes a reality, **promoters**—those who, for themselves or others, take the preliminary steps in organizing a corporation—frequently make contracts with investors and others on behalf of the future corporation. One of the tasks of the promoter is to issue a prospectus. A **prospectus** is a document required by federal or state securities laws (discussed in Chapter 27) that describes the financial operations of the corporation, thus allowing investors to make informed decisions. The promoter also secures the corporate charter.

In addition, a promoter may purchase or lease property with a view to selling or transferring it to the corporation when the corporation is formed. A promoter may also enter into contracts with attorneys, accountants, architects, or other professionals whose services will be needed in planning for the proposed corporation. Finally, a promoter induces people to purchase stock in the corporation.

Promoter's Liability. As a general rule, a promoter is held personally liable on preincorporation contracts. Courts simply hold that promoters are not agents when a corporation has yet to come into existence. If, however, the promoter secures the contracting party's agreement to hold only the corporation (and not the promoter) liable on the contract, the promoter will not be liable in the event of any breach of contract. Basically, the personal liability of the promoter continues even after incorporation unless the third party releases the promoter. In most states, this rule is applied whether or not the promoter made the agreement in the name of, or with reference to, the proposed corporation.

Once the corporation is formed (the charter issued), the promoter remains personally liable until the corporation assumes the preincorporation contract by *novation* (discussed in Chapter 11). Novation releases the promoter and makes the corporation liable for performing the contractual obligations. In some situations, the corporation *adopts* the promoter's contract by undertaking to perform it. Most courts hold that adoption in and of itself does not discharge the promoter from contractual liability. Normally, a corporation cannot *ratify* a preincorporation contract, as no principal was in existence at the time the contract was made.

Subscribers and Subscriptions. Prior to the actual formation of the corporation, the promoter can contact potential individual investors, and they can agree to purchase capital stock in the future corporation. This agreement is often called a *subscription agreement,* and the potential investor is called a *subscriber.* Depending on state law, subscribers become shareholders as soon as the corporation is formed or as soon as the corporation accepts the agreement.

Most courts view preincorporation subscriptions as continuing offers to purchase corporate stock. On or after its formation, the corporation can choose to accept the offer to purchase stock. Many courts also treat a subscription offer as irrevocable except with the consent of all of the subscribers. A subscription is irrevocable for a period of six months unless the subscription agreement provides otherwise or unless all the subscribers agree to the revocation of the subscription [RMBCA 6.20]. In some courts and jurisdictions, the preincorporation subscriber can revoke the offer to purchase before acceptance without liability, however.

INCORPORATION PROCEDURES

Exact procedures for incorporation differ among states, but the basic requirements are similar.

State Chartering. The first step in the incorporation procedure is to select a state in which to incorporate. Because state incorporation laws differ, individuals may look for the states that offer the most advantageous tax or incorporation provisions. Delaware has historically had the least restrictive laws. Consequently, many corporations, including a number of the largest, have incorporated there. Delaware's statutes permit firms to incorporate in that state and conduct business and locate their operating headquarters elsewhere. Most other states now permit this as well. Note, though, that closely held corporations, particularly those of a professional nature, generally incorporate in the state where their principal shareholders live and work.

Articles of Incorporation. The primary document needed to begin the incorporation process is called the *articles of incorporation* (see Exhibit 25–1). The articles include basic information about the corporation and serve as a primary source of authority for its future organization and business functions. The person or persons who execute the articles are called *incorporators.* Generally, the articles of incorporation should include the elements discussed in the following subsections.

Corporate Name. The choice of a corporate name is subject to state approval to ensure against duplication or deception. State statutes usually require that the secretary of state run a check on the proposed name in the state of incorporation. Some states require that the incorporators, at their own expense, run a check on the proposed name for the newly formed corporation. Once cleared, a name can be reserved for a short time, for a fee, pending the completion of the articles of incorporation. All corporate statutes require the corporation name to include the word *Corporation, Incorporated, Company,* or *Limited,* or abbreviations of these terms.

A corporate name cannot be the same as (or deceptively similar to) the name of an existing corporation doing business within the state. ● **EXAMPLE #2** Suppose that there is an existing corporation named General Dynamics, Inc. The state will not allow another corporation to be called General Dynamic, Inc., because that name is deceptively similar to the first and impliedly transfers a part of the goodwill established by the first corporate user to the second corporation.● Note that if a future firm contemplates doing business in other states, the incorporators also need to check on existing corporate names in those states as well. Otherwise, if the firm does business under a name that is the same as or deceptively similar to an existing company's name, it may be liable for trade name infringement.

Duration. A corporation has perpetual existence unless stated otherwise in the articles. The owners may want to prescribe a maximum duration, however, after which the corporation must formally renew its existence.

Nature and Purpose. The articles must specify the intended business activities of the corporation, and naturally, these activities must be lawful. A general statement of corporate purpose is usually sufficient to give rise to all of the powers necessary to carry out the purpose of the organization. The articles of incorporation can state, for example, that the corporation is organized "to engage in the production and sale of agricultural products." There is a trend toward allowing corporate articles to state that the corporation is organized for "any legal business," with no mention of specifics, to avoid the need for future amendments to the corporate articles.

Capital Structure. The articles generally set forth the capital structure of the corporation. A few state statutes require a relatively small capital investment (for example, $1,000) for ordinary business corporations but a larger capital investment for those engaged in insurance or banking. The articles must outline the number of shares of stock authorized for issuance; their valuation; the various types or classes of stock authorized for issuance; and other relevant information concerning equity, capital, and credit.

EXHIBIT 25-1 ARTICLES OF INCORPORATION

ARTICLE ONE

The name of the corporation is _____ .

ARTICLE TWO

The period of its duration is _____ (may be a number of years or until a certain date).

ARTICLE THREE

The purpose (or purposes) for which the corporation is organized is (are) _____
_____ .

ARTICLE FOUR

The aggregate number of shares that the corporation shall have authority to issue is _____ of the par value of
_____ dollar(s) each (or without par value).

ARTICLE FIVE

The corporation will not commence business until it has received for the issuance of its shares consideration of the value of $1,000 (can be any sum not less than $1,000).

ARTICLE SIX

The address of the corporation's registered office is _____ ,
and the name of its registered agent at such address is _____
_____ .

(Use the street or building or rural address of the registered office, not a post office box number.)

ARTICLE SEVEN

The number of initial directors is _____ , and the names and addresses of the directors are
_____
_____ .

ARTICLE EIGHT

The name and address of the incorporator is _____
_____ .

(signed) _____
Incorporator

Sworn to on _____ by the above-named incorporator.
(date)

_____
Notary Public _____ County

(Notary Seal)

Internal Organization. The articles should describe the internal management structure of the corporation, although this can be included in bylaws adopted after the corporation is formed. The articles of incorporation commence the corporation; the bylaws are formed after commencement by the board of directors. Bylaws cannot conflict with the incorporation statute or the corporation's charter [RMBCA 2.06].

Under the RMBCA, shareholders may amend or repeal bylaws. The board of directors may also amend or repeal bylaws unless the articles of incorporation or provisions of the incorporation statute reserve this power to shareholders exclusively [RMBCA 10.20]. Typical bylaw provisions describe such things as voting requirements for shareholders, the election of the board of directors, the methods of replacing directors, and the manner and time of scheduling shareholders' and board meetings (these corporate activities will be discussed in Chapter 26).

Registered Office and Agent. The corporation must indicate the location and address of its registered office within the state. Usually, the registered office is also the principal office of the corporation. The corporation must give the name and address of a specific person who has been designated as an agent and who can receive legal documents (such as orders to appear in court) on behalf of the corporation.

Incorporators. Each incorporator must be listed by name and must indicate an address. An incorporator is a person—often, the corporate promoter—who applies to the state on behalf of the corporation to obtain its corporate charter. The incorporator need not be a subscriber and need not have any interest at all in the corporation. Many states do not impose residency or age requirements for incorporators. States vary on the required number of incorporators; it can be as few as one or as many as three. Incorporators are required to sign the articles of incorporation when they are submitted to the state; often, this is their only duty. In some states, they participate at the first organizational meeting of the corporation.

Certificate of Incorporation. Once the articles of incorporation have been prepared, signed, and authenticated by the incorporators, they are sent to the appropriate state official, usually the secretary of state, along with the required filing fee. In many states, the secretary of state then issues a **certificate of incorporation** representing the state's authorization for the corporation to conduct business. (This may be called the *corporate charter.*) The certificate and a copy of the articles are returned to the incorporators.

First Organizational Meeting. The first organizational meeting is provided for in the articles of incorporation but is held after the charter has actually been granted. At this meeting, the incorporators elect the first board of directors and complete the routine business of incorporation (pass bylaws and issue stock, for example). Sometimes, the meeting is held after the election of the board, and the business transacted depends on the requirements of the state's incorporation statute, the nature of the business, the provisions made in the articles, and the desires of the promoters. Adoption of bylaws—the internal rules of management for the corporation—is probably the most important function of the meeting. The shareholders, directors, and officers must abide by the bylaws in conducting corporate business.

Corporate Status

The procedures for incorporation are very specific. If they are not followed precisely, others may be able to challenge the existence of the corporation. Errors in the incorporation procedures can become important when, for example, a third person who is attempting to enforce a contract or bring suit for a tort injury learns of them. On the basis of improper incorporation, the plaintiff could seek to make the would-be shareholders personally liable. Additionally, when the corporation seeks to enforce a contract against a defaulting party, that party may be able to avoid liability on the ground of a defect in the incorporation procedure.

To prevent injustice, courts will sometimes attribute corporate status to an improperly formed corporation by holding it to be a *de jure* corporation or a *de facto* corporation. Occasionally, a corporation may be held to exist by estoppel. Additionally, in certain circumstances involving abuse of the corporate form, a court may disregard the corporate entity and hold the shareholders personally liable.

DE JURE AND DE FACTO CORPORATIONS

In the event of substantial compliance with all conditions precedent to incorporation, the corporation is said to have *de jure* (rightful and lawful) existence. In most states and under the RMBCA, the certificate of incorporation is viewed as evidence that all mandatory statutory provisions have been met. This means that the corporation is properly formed, and neither the state nor a third party can attack its existence. If, for example, an incorporator's address was incorrectly listed, this would technically mean that the corporation was improperly formed; but the law does not regard such inconsequential procedural defects as detracting from substantial compliance, and courts will uphold the *de jure* status of the corporate entity.

Sometimes, there is a defect in complying with statutory mandates—for example, the corporation's charter may have expired. Under these circumstances, the corporation may have *de facto* (actual) status, meaning that the corporation in fact exists, even if not rightfully or lawfully. A corporation with *de facto* status cannot be challenged by third persons (except for the state). The following elements are required for *de facto* status:

① There must be a state statute under which the corporation can be validly incorporated.

② The parties must have made a good faith attempt to comply with the statute.

③ The enterprise must already have undertaken to do business as a corporation.

CORPORATION BY ESTOPPEL

If an association that is neither an actual corporation nor a *de facto* or *de jure* corporation holds itself out as being a corporation, it normally will be estopped from denying corporate status in a lawsuit by a third party. This usually occurs when a third party contracts with an association that claims to be a corporation but does not hold a certificate of incorporation. When the third party brings suit naming the so-called corporation as the defendant, the association may not escape liability on the ground that no corporation exists. When justice requires, the courts treat an alleged corporation as if it were an actual corporation for the purpose of determining the rights and liabilities involved in a particular situation. Corporation by estoppel is thus determined by the situation. It does not extend recognition of corporate status beyond the resolution of the problem at hand.

DISREGARDING THE CORPORATE ENTITY

Occasionally, the owners use a corporate entity to perpetrate a fraud, circumvent the law, or in some other way accomplish an illegitimate objective. In these situations, the court will ignore the corporate structure by **piercing the corporate veil** and exposing the shareholders to personal liability. Generally, when the corporate privilege is abused for personal benefit or when the corporate business is treated in such a careless manner that the corporation and the shareholder in control are no longer separate entities, the court will require an owner to assume personal liability to creditors for the corporation's debts.

In short, when the facts show that great injustice would result from the use of a corporation to avoid individual responsibility, a court of equity will look behind the corporate structure to the individual stockholder. The following

are some of the factors that frequently cause the courts to pierce the corporate veil:

① A party is tricked or misled into dealing with the corporation rather than the individual.

② The corporation is set up never to make a profit or always to be insolvent, or it is too "thinly" capitalized—that is, it has insufficient capital at the time of formation to meet its prospective debts or potential liabilities.

③ Statutory corporate formalities, such as holding required corporation meetings, are not followed.

④ Personal and corporate interests are **commingled** (mixed together) to the extent that the corporation has no separate identity.

To elaborate on the fourth factor in the preceding list, consider a close corporation that is formed according to law by a single person or by a few family members. In such a situation, the separate status of the corporate entity and the sole stockholder (or family-member stockholders) must be carefully preserved. Certain practices invite trouble for the one-person or family-owned corporation: the commingling of corporate and personal funds, the failure to hold and record minutes of board of directors' meetings, or the shareholders' continuous personal use of corporate property (for example, vehicles).

Corporation laws usually do not specifically prohibit a stockholder from lawfully lending money to her or his corporation. When an officer or director lends the corporation money and takes back security in the form of corporate assets, however, the courts will scrutinize the transaction closely. Any such transaction must be made in good faith and for fair value.

In the following case, in response to a creditor's motion before a court to "pierce the corporate veil," the plaintiffs argued that "this is not a fraud, this is a family business."

CASE 25.2 **Dimmitt & Owens Financial, Inc. v. Superior Sports Products, Inc.**

United States District Court,
Northern District of Illinois, 2002.
196 F.Supp.2d 731.

FACTS To import sport-fishing products for wholesale distribution in North America, Donald Park incorporated Superior Sports Products, Inc. (SSP), in September 1996. Park's mother, Chong Hyok Park, was SSP's president at its incorporation, but she did not participate in its operations. Donald Park handled most of its activities out of his apartment in Schaumburg, Illinois, drawing funds from SSP when he

needed to pay personal expenses. There were no employees. To engage in the same business, Superior Sports International, Inc. (SSII), was formed in February 1997, and Superior Source, Inc. (SSI), in October. Chong was the president and sole shareholder of SSII, which had no employees and operated out of Chong's home in Ontario, Canada. SSI was formed with Chong's friends, but it conducted only one sale as a wholesaler and was dissolved. None of the corporations issued stock or paid dividends, maintained corporate records, or followed other corporate formalities. All of the

(Continued)

CASE 25.2—Continued

corporations, none of which made a profit, were financed by occasional loans by Park or his parents. This capital proved to be inadequate. In January 1998, Donald Park—representing himself as president of SSP, vice president of SSII, and manager of SSI, when actually he was none of these—applied for, and obtained, loans from Dimmitt & Owens Financial, Inc. (Dimmitt). When the loans were not paid, Dimmitt filed a suit in a federal district court against SSP, SSII, SSI, and Donald Park, seeking, in part, a summary judgment to impose personal liability on Donald Park.

ISSUE Should the court "pierce the corporate veil" and impose personal liability on Donald Park?

DECISION Yes. The court granted Dimmitt's motion and issued a summary judgment in the creditor's favor, holding that piercing the corporate veil was justified.

REASON The court noted that "Illinois courts apply a two-prong test to determine whether to pierce the corporate veil: (1) there must be such unity of interest and ownership that the separate personalities of the corporation and the individ-

ual or other corporation no longer exist; and (2) circumstances must be that such an adherence to the fiction of separate corporate existence would sanction a fraud or promote injustice." The commingling of personal and corporate funds, among other misconduct, demonstrated to the court that Donald Park would be unjustly enriched, to Dimmitt's detriment, if he were shielded from personal liability by SSP. The court reasoned that "Park exercised great personal control over the existing corporations thereby creating the sufficient unity of interest and ownership between Park and the corporations to warrant piercing the corporate veil." Also, Park's "misrepresentations equal something akin to fraud or deception. Additionally, we find that there is a compelling public interest that individuals should not execute contracts while misrepresenting themselves and escape personal liability when monies, advanced on the basis of such contracts, disappear without a proper accounting for their disappearance."

FOR CRITICAL ANALYSIS—Social Consideration
If Park had not made the misrepresentations regarding his positions with the corporations, would the "other misconduct" noted by the court have been enough to justify piercing the corporate veil in this case?

Corporate Financing

Part of the process of corporate formation involves corporate financing. Corporations are financed by the issuance and sale of corporate securities. **Securities** (stocks and bonds) evidence the obligation to pay money or the right to participate in earnings and the distribution of corporate property.

Stocks, or *equity securities,* represent the purchase of ownership in the business firm. **Bonds** (debentures), or *debt securities,* represent the borrowing of money by firms (and governments). Of course, not all debt is in the form of debt securities. For example, some debt is in the form of accounts payable and notes payable. Accounts and notes payable are typically short-term debts. Bonds are simply a way for the corporation to split up its long-term debt so that it can market it more easily.

BONDS

Bonds are issued by business firms and by governments at all levels as evidence of the funds they are borrowing from investors. Bonds normally have a designated *maturity date*—the date when the principal, or face, amount of the bond is returned to the investor. They are sometimes

referred to as *fixed-income securities* because their owners (that is, the creditors) receive fixed-dollar interest payments, usually semiannually, during the period of time prior to maturity.

Because debt financing represents a legal obligation on the part of the corporation, various features and terms of a particular bond issue are specified in a lending agreement called a **bond indenture.** A corporate trustee, often a commercial bank trust department, represents the collective well-being of all bondholders in ensuring that the corporation meets the terms of the bond issue. The bond indenture specifies the maturity date of the bond and the pattern of interest payments until maturity. The different types of corporate bonds are described in Exhibit 25–2.

STOCKS

Issuing stocks is another way that corporations can obtain financing. The ways in which stocks differ from bonds are summarized in Exhibit 25–3. Basically, as mentioned, stocks represent ownership in a business firm, whereas bonds represent borrowing by the firm.

Exhibit 25–4 on page 530 summarizes the types of stocks issued by corporations. We look now at the two major types of stock—*common stock* and *preferred stock.*

EXHIBIT 25–2 TYPES OF CORPORATE BONDS

Debenture Bonds	Bonds for which no specific assets of the corporation are pledged as backing. Rather, they are backed by the general credit rating of the corporation, plus any assets that can be seized if the corporation allows the debentures to go into default.
Mortgage Bonds	Bonds that pledge specific property. If the corporation defaults on the bonds, the bondholders can take the property.
Convertible Bonds	Bonds that can be exchanged for a specified number of shares of common stock under certain conditions.
Callable Bonds	Bonds that may be called in and the principal repaid at specified times or under conditions specified in the bond when it is issued.

Common Stock. The true ownership of a corporation is represented by **common stock**. Common stock provides a proportionate interest in the corporation with regard to (1) control, (2) earnings, and (3) net assets. A shareholder's interest is generally in proportion to the number of shares he or she owns out of the total number of shares issued.

Voting rights in a corporation apply to the election of the firm's board of directors and to any proposed changes in the ownership structure of the firm. For example, a holder of common stock generally has the right to vote in a decision on a proposed merger, as mergers can change the proportion of ownership. State corporation law specifies the types of actions for which shareholder approval must be obtained.

Firms are not obligated to return a principal amount per share to each holder of common stock because no firm can ensure that the market price per share of its common stock will not decline over time. The issuing firm also does not have to guarantee a dividend; indeed, some corporations never pay dividends.

Holders of common stock are a group of investors who assume a *residual* position in the overall financial structure of a business. In terms of receiving payment for their investments, they are last in line. They are entitled to the

EXHIBIT 25–3 HOW DO STOCKS AND BONDS DIFFER?

STOCKS	BONDS
1. Stocks represent ownership.	1. Bonds represent debt.
2. Stocks (common) do not have a fixed dividend rate.	2. Interest on bonds must always be paid, whether or not any profit is earned.
3. Stockholders can elect a board of directors, which controls the corporation.	3. Bondholders usually have no voice in, or control over, management of the corporation.
4. Stocks do not have a maturity date; the corporation usually does not repay the stockholder.	4. Bonds have a maturity date, when the corporation is to repay the bondholder the face value of the bond.
5. All corporations issue or offer to sell stocks. This is the usual definition of a corporation.	5. Corporations do not necessarily issue bonds.
6. Stockholders have a claim against the property and income of a corporation after all creditors' claims have been met.	6. Bondholders have a claim against the property and income of a corporation that must be met before the claims of stockholders.

EXHIBIT 25-4   **TYPES OF STOCKS**

Common Stock	Voting shares that represent ownership interest in a corporation. Common stock has the lowest priority with respect to payment of dividends and distribution of assets on the corporation's dissolution.
Preferred Stock	Shares of stock that have priority over common-stock shares as to payment of dividends and distribution of assets on dissolution. Dividend payments are usually a fixed percentage of the face value of the share.
Cumulative Preferred Stock	Required dividends not paid in a given year must be paid in a subsequent year before any common-stock dividends are paid.
Participating Preferred Stock	Stock entitling the owner to receive the preferred-stock dividend and additional dividends if the corporation has paid dividends on common stock.
Convertible Preferred Stock	Stock entitling the owners to convert their shares into a specified number of common shares either in the issuing corporation or, sometimes, in another corporation.
Redeemable, or Callable, Preferred Stock	Preferred shares issued with the express condition that the issuing corporation has the right to repurchase the shares as specified.

earnings that are left after preferred stockholders, bondholders, suppliers, employees, and other groups have been paid. Once those groups are paid, however, the owners of common stock may be entitled to *all* the remaining earnings as dividends. (The board of directors normally is not under any duty to declare the remaining earnings as dividends, however.)

Preferred Stock. Preferred stock is stock with *preferences*. Usually, this means that holders of preferred stock have priority over holders of common stock as to dividends and as to payment on dissolution of the corporation. Holders of preferred stock may or may not have the right to vote.

Preferred stock is not included among the liabilities of a business because it is equity. Like other equity securities, preferred shares have no fixed maturity date on which the firm must pay them off. Although firms occasionally buy back preferred stock, they are not legally obligated to do so. A sample cumulative convertible preferred-stock certificate is shown in Exhibit 25–5.

Holders of preferred stock are investors who have assumed a rather cautious position in their relationship to the corporation. They have a stronger position than common shareholders with respect to dividends and claims on assets, but as a result, they will not share in the full prosperity of the firm if it grows successfully over time. This is because the value of preferred shares will not rise as rapidly

as that of common shares during a period of financial success. Preferred stockholders do receive fixed dividends periodically, however, and they may benefit to some extent from changes in the market price of the shares.

The return and the risk for preferred stock lie somewhere between those for bonds and those for common stock. Preferred stock is more similar to bonds than to common stock, even though preferred stock appears in the ownership section of the firm's balance sheet. As a result, preferred stock is often categorized with corporate bonds as a fixed-income security, even though the legal status is not the same.

Merger and Consolidation

Often, a corporation will extend its operations through a merger or consolidation. The terms *merger* and *consolidation* often are used interchangeably, but they refer to two legally distinct proceedings. The rights and liabilities of the corporation, its shareholders, and its creditors are the same for both, however.

MERGER

A **merger** involves the legal combination of two or more corporations in such a way that only one of the corporations continues to exist. ● **EXAMPLE #3** Corporation A and

EXHIBIT 25–5 CUMULATIVE CONVERTIBLE PREFERRED-STOCK CERTIFICATE

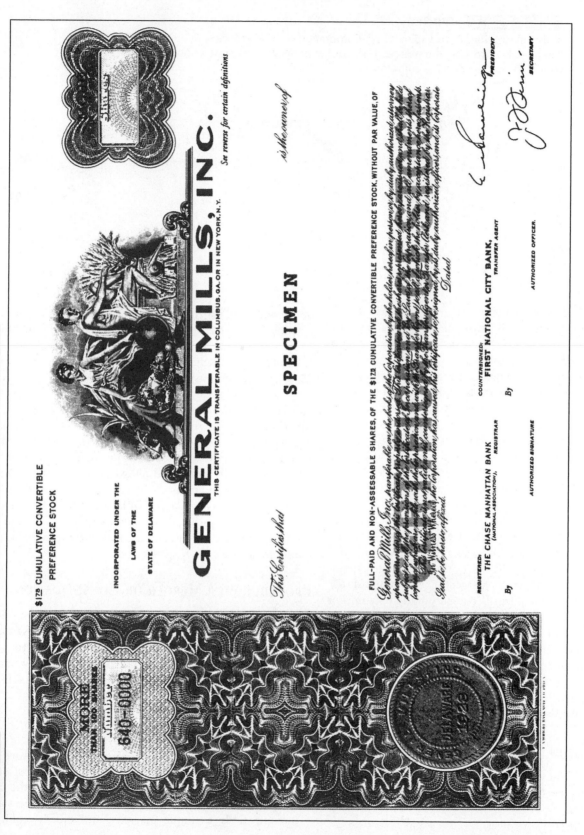

EXHIBIT 25–6 MERGER

In this illustration, Corporation A and Corporation B decide to merge. They agree that A will absorb B, so after the merger, B no longer exists as a separate entity, and A continues as the surviving corporation.

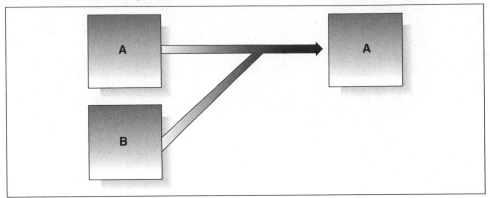

Corporation B decide to merge. It is agreed that A will absorb B, so on merging, B ceases to exist as a separate entity, and A continues as the *surviving corporation.*● Exhibit 25–6 graphically illustrates this process.

After the merger, A is recognized as a single corporation, possessing all the rights, privileges, and powers of itself and B. It automatically acquires all of B's property and assets without the necessity of formal transfer. Additionally, A becomes liable for all of B's debts and obligations. Finally, A's articles of incorporation are deemed amended to include any changes that are stated in the *articles of merger* (a document setting forth the terms and conditions of the merger that is filed with the secretary of state).

In a merger, the surviving corporation inherits the disappearing corporation's preexisting legal rights and obligations. For example, if the disappearing corporation had a right of action against a third party, the surviving corporation can bring suit after the merger to recover the disappearing corporation's damages. The corporation statutes of many states provide that a successor (surviving) corporation inherits a **chose**[6] **in action** (a right to sue for a debt or sum of money) from a merging corporation as a matter of law. The common law similarly recognizes that, following a merger, a chose in action to enforce a property right will vest with the successor (surviving) corporation, and no right of action will remain with the disappearing corporation.

CONSOLIDATION

In a **consolidation,** two or more corporations combine in such a way that each corporation ceases to exist and a new

---

[6] The word *chose* is French for "thing."

one emerges. ● **EXAMPLE #4** Corporation A and Corporation B consolidate to form an entirely new organization, Corporation C. In the process, A and B both terminate, and C comes into existence as an entirely new entity.● Exhibit 25–7 graphically illustrates this process.

As a result of the consolidation, C is recognized as a new corporation and a single entity; A and B cease to exist. C inherits all of the rights, privileges, and powers that A and B previously held. Title to any property and assets owned by A and B passes to C without formal transfer. C assumes liability for all of the debts and obligations owed by A and B. The terms and conditions of the consolidation are set forth in the *articles of consolidation,* which are filed with the secretary of state. These articles *take the place of* A's and B's original corporate articles and are thereafter regarded as C's corporate articles.

PROCEDURE FOR MERGER OR CONSOLIDATION

All states have statutes authorizing mergers and consolidations for domestic (in-state) corporations, and most states allow the combination of domestic and foreign (out-of-state) corporations. Although the procedures vary somewhat among jurisdictions, the basic requirements for a merger or a consolidation are as follows:

① The board of directors of each corporation involved must approve a merger or consolidation plan.

② The shareholders of each corporation must approve the plan, by vote, at a shareholders' meeting. Most state statutes require the approval of two-thirds of the outstanding shares of voting stock, although some states require only a simple majority, and others require a

EXHIBIT 25–7 CONSOLIDATION

In this illustration, Corporation A and Corporation B consolidate to form an entirely new organization, Corporation C. In the process, A and B terminate, and C comes into existence as an entirely new entity.

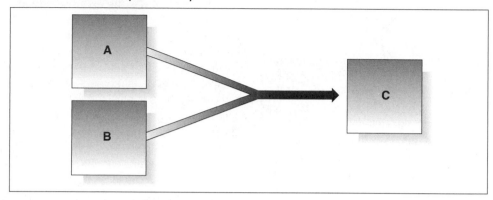

four-fifths vote. Frequently, statutes require that each class of stock approve the merger; thus, the holders of nonvoting stock must also approve. A corporation's bylaws can provide for a stricter requirement.

③ Once approved by all of the directors and shareholders, the plan (articles of merger or consolidation) is filed, usually with the secretary of state.

④ When state formalities are satisfied, the state issues a certificate of merger to the surviving corporation or a certificate of consolidation to the newly consolidated corporation.

Section 11.04 of the Revised Model Business Corporation Act (RMBCA) provides for a simplified procedure for the merger of a substantially owned subsidiary corporation into its parent corporation. Under these provisions, a **short-form merger** can be accomplished *without the approval of the shareholders* of either corporation. The short-form merger can be used only when the parent corporation owns at least 90 percent of the outstanding shares of each class of stock of the subsidiary corporation. The simplified procedure requires that a plan for the merger be approved by the board of directors of the parent corporation before it is filed with the state. A copy of the merger plan must be sent to each shareholder of record of the subsidiary corporation.

SHAREHOLDER APPROVAL

Shareholders invest in a corporate enterprise with the expectation that the board of directors will manage the enterprise and will approve ordinary business matters. Actions taken on extraordinary matters must be authorized by the board of directors and the shareholders. Often, mod-

ern statutes require that the shareholders approve certain types of extraordinary matters—such as the sale, lease, or exchange of all or substantially all corporate assets outside of the corporation's regular course of business. Other examples of matters requiring shareholder approval include amendments to the articles of incorporation, transactions concerning merger or consolidation, and dissolution.

APPRAISAL RIGHTS

What if a shareholder disapproves of a merger or a consolidation but is outvoted by the other shareholders? The law recognizes that a dissenting shareholder should not be forced to become an unwilling shareholder in a corporation that is new or different from the one in which the shareholder originally invested. The shareholder has the right to dissent and may be entitled to be paid the fair value for the number of shares held on the date of the merger or consolidation. This right is referred to as the shareholder's **appraisal right.**

Appraisal rights are available only when a state statute specifically provides for them. Appraisal rights normally extend to regular mergers, consolidations, short-form mergers, and sales of substantially all of the corporate assets not in the ordinary course of business. Shareholders may lose their appraisal rights if they do not follow precisely the elaborate statutory procedures. Whenever they lose the right to an appraisal, dissenting shareholders must go along with the transaction despite their objections.

In a short-form merger, is the exercise of an appraisal right a minority shareholder's only remedy when he or she dissents from the merger? That was the question in the following case.

CASE 25.3 Glassman v. Unocal Exploration Corp.

Delaware Supreme Court, 2001.
777 A.2d 242.

FACTS Unocal Corporation is an earth resources company primarily engaged in the exploration for, and production of, crude oil and natural gas. Unocal owned approximately 96 percent of the stock of Unocal Exploration Corporation (UXC), an oil and gas company operating in the Gulf of Mexico. In 1991, low natural gas prices caused a drop in both companies' revenues and earnings. Unocal decided that by merging with UXC, it could reduce expenses and save money. The boards of directors of the two firms appointed special committees to consider a short-form merger. The UXC committee agreed to a merger exchange ratio of about half a share of Unocal stock for each UXC share. Glassman and other UXC minority shareholders filed a suit in a Delaware state court against Unocal, alleging in part that the firm had breached its fiduciary duty of "entire fairness and full disclosure." The court held that the only remedy in connection with this short-form merger was the minority's appraisal right. The plaintiffs appealed to the Delaware Supreme Court.

ISSUE Is exercising appraisal rights the only recourse for a minority stockholder who is dissatisfied with a short-form merger?

DECISION Yes. The Delaware Supreme Court affirmed the decision of the lower court, holding that in these circumstances appraisal was the exclusive remedy.

REASON The Delaware Supreme Court noted first that the state's short-form merger statute specifically provides for appraisal rights. The court then explained, "In a short-form merger, there is no agreement of merger negotiated by two companies; there is only a unilateral act—a decision by the parent company that its 90% owned subsidiary shall no longer exist as a separate entity. The minority stockholders receive no advance notice of the merger; their directors do not consider or approve it; and there is no vote. Those who object are given the right to obtain fair value for their shares through appraisal. * * * If * * * the corporate fiduciary sets up negotiating committees, hires independent financial and legal experts, etc., then it will have lost the very benefit provided by the statute—a simple, fast and inexpensive process for accomplishing a merger."

FOR CRITICAL ANALYSIS—Ethical Consideration
Does the court's holding in this case mean that a parent corporation does not have a duty of full disclosure in a short-form merger? Explain why or why not.

Purchase of Assets

When a corporation acquires all or substantially all of the assets of another corporation by direct purchase, the purchasing, or *acquiring*, corporation simply extends its ownership and control over more physical assets. Because no change in the legal entity occurs, the acquiring corporation is not required to obtain shareholder approval for the purchase.[7] The U.S. Department of Justice and the Federal Trade Commission, however, significantly constrain and often prohibit mergers that could result from a purchase of assets, including takeover bids.

Note that the corporation that is selling all its assets is substantially changing its business position and perhaps its ability to carry out its corporate purposes. For that reason, the corporation whose assets are being sold must obtain the approval of both the board of directors and the shareholders. In most states and under RMBCA 13.02, a dissenting shareholder of the selling corporation can demand appraisal rights. (Occasionally, disputes arise over whether particular property or property rights were included in "all of the assets" being sold. For an example of one such dispute, see this chapter's *Business Law in the Online World* feature.)

Generally, a corporation that purchases the assets of another corporation is not responsible for the liabilities of the selling corporation. Exceptions to this rule are made in certain circumstances, however. In any of the situations listed below, the acquiring corporation will be held to have assumed *both* the assets and the liabilities of the selling corporation.

① When the purchasing corporation impliedly or expressly assumes the seller's liabilities.

② When the sale amounts to what is in fact a merger or consolidation.

---

[7] If the acquiring corporation plans to pay for the assets with its own corporate stock and not enough authorized unissued shares are available, the shareholders must vote to approve the issuance of additional shares by amendment of the corporate articles. Additionally, acquiring corporations whose stock is traded in a national stock exchange can be required to obtain their own shareholders' approval if they plan to issue a significant number of shares, such as a number equal to 20 percent or more of the outstanding shares.

BUSINESS LAW IN THE ONLINE WORLD
Who Owns the Web Site?

Most contracts to purchase the assets of another corporation are performed with little difficulty. At times, however, a dispute may arise over some matter connected with the transaction. In one case, for example, the dispute had to do with ownership rights in a Web site. The case arose after 1-800-Postcards, Inc. (1-800), purchased the assets of Popsmear, Inc., which owned and operated a Web site postcard-advertising business. The Web address for Popsmear's business was http://www.1800Postcards.com. According to the purchase agreement, Popsmear's trademark rights were included in "all of the assets" being sold by Popsmear to 1-800.

THE PROBLEM WITH THE WEB SITE Problems arose when the sole owner and shareholder of Popsmear, James Morel, changed the password to the Web site. This meant that 1-800 was unable to make any administrative changes to the Web site or to create and change its e-mail boxes. When 1-800 objected to Morel's action, Morel contended that he personally, and not Popsmear, was the registered owner of the domain name and, as such, had a right to change the password. 1-800 then sued Morel for fraud and breach of contract and asked the court for a preliminary injunction against Morel's

changing of the password. After all, argued 1-800, by making it impossible for 1-800 to control the Web site, Morel, in effect, had been "selling nothing" when Popsmear sold 1-800 its "trademark rights."

DID THE ASSETS BEING SOLD INCLUDE THE DOMAIN NAME RIGHTS? In determining whether to grant the preliminary injunction, the court had to decide whether the sale of assets included the domain name rights. The question was complicated by the fact that Morel was the registered owner of the domain name. The court, however, held that this "nuance" was of little significance because both Morel and Popsmear were parties to the purchase agreement. The court also emphasized that the parties "quite likely understood that the domain name registration for the Web site was among the 'assets of the business' irrespective of whether record title was in [Popsmear] or its sole shareholder, Morel." Concluding that 1-800 would likely succeed in its case against Morel and Popsmear, the court granted 1-800's request for a preliminary injunction.[a]

FOR CRITICAL ANALYSIS
Would the court have reached the same conclusion if Morel had not been a party to the purchase agreement? Why or why not?

a. *1-800-Postcards, Inc. v. Morel*, 153 F.Supp.2d 359 (S.D.N.Y. 2001).

③ When the purchaser continues the seller's business and retains the same personnel (same shareholders, directors, and officers).

④ When the sale is fraudulently executed to escape liability.

In the following case, the court was asked to determine to what extent a corporation that bought the assets of another firm was responsible for the liability of the seller.

CASE 25.4 **Lee-Thomas, Inc. v. Hallmark Cards, Inc.**

United States Court of Appeals, Eighth Circuit, 2002.
275 F.3d 702.
http://www.findlaw.com/casecode/courts/8th.html[a]

a. In the "Party Name Search" box, type "Lee-Thomas" and click on "search." In the result, click on the name of the case to access the opinion.

FACTS In the 1970s, Lee-Thomas, Inc., bought the assets of Patty Woodard, a manufacturer of women's clothing. Hallmark Cards, Inc., through its subsidiary Halls Merchandising, Inc., operates Halls, a department store in Kansas City, Missouri, that sells clothing and other merchandise. Deborah Reithmeyer bought a vintage Patty Woodard blouse from the store. Alleging that the blouse was defective,

(Continued)

CASE 25.4—Continued

Reithmeyer filed a suit in a Missouri state court against Hallmark, on a theory of product liability (see Chapter 17). Hallmark contended that Lee-Thomas was obligated to defend or pay the expenses of defending against the suit. When Lee-Thomas refused, Hallmark settled the suit for $50,000 and filed a suit in a federal district court against Lee-Thomas, seeking the amount of the settlement, fees, and other costs. The court issued a summary judgment in Hallmark's favor. Lee-Thomas appealed to the U.S. Court of Appeals for the Eighth Circuit.

ISSUE Had Lee-Thomas assumed the liabilities, as well as the assets, of Patty Woodard?

DECISION Yes. The U.S. Court of Appeals for the Eighth Circuit affirmed the lower court's judgment, holding that Lee-Thomas had assumed the liabilities of Patty Woodard.

REASON Under the asset-purchase agreement between Patty Woodard and Lee-Thomas, the buyer agreed to

"*assume all the liabilities of the seller* existing on the date of the closing, *and liabilities arising solely out of the business conducted by seller prior to the closing* and shall indemnify seller from the same and from all costs or expenses associated therewith." The appellate court found that this "assumption of liability provision unambiguously requires Appellant to assume Patty Woodard's liabilities with respect to the products liability suit." The court reiterated that under the agreement, "[a]ppellant agreed to indemnify Patty Woodard for all 'liabilities arising solely out of the business conducted by the seller prior to the closing.' Liabilities based on the sale of defective products sold by Patty Woodard prior to closing clearly fall within this category."

FOR CRITICAL ANALYSIS—Economic Consideration
Why would a company, when purchasing the assets of another firm, ever agree to assume the liabilities of that firm as well?

Purchase of Stock

An alternative to the purchase of another corporation's assets is the purchase of a substantial number of the voting shares of its stock. This enables the acquiring corporation to control the **target corporation** (the corporation being acquired). The acquiring corporation deals directly with the target company's shareholders in seeking to purchase the shares they hold. It does this by making a *tender offer* to all of the shareholders of the target corporation. The tender offer is publicly advertised and addressed to all shareholders of the target company. The price of the stock in the tender offer is generally higher than the market price of the target stock prior to the announcement of the tender offer. The higher price induces shareholders to tender their shares to the acquiring firm.

Termination

The termination of a corporation's existence has two phases. **Dissolution** is the legal death of the artificial "person" of the corporation. **Liquidation** is the process by which corporate assets are converted into cash and distributed among creditors and shareholders according to specific rules of preference.

DISSOLUTION

Dissolution of a corporation can be brought about in any of the following ways:

① An act of a legislature in the state of incorporation.

② Expiration of the time provided in the certificate of incorporation.

③ Voluntary approval of the shareholders and the board of directors.

④ Unanimous action by all shareholders.[8]

⑤ A court decree brought about by the attorney general of the state of incorporation for any of the following reasons: (a) the failure to comply with administrative requirements (for example, failure to pay annual franchise taxes, to submit an annual report, or to have a designated registered agent), (b) the procurement of a corporate charter through fraud or misrepresentation on the state, (c) the abuse of corporate powers (*ultra vires* acts), (d) the violation of the state criminal code after the demand to discontinue has been made by the secretary of state, (e) the failure to commence business operations, or (f) the abandonment of operations before starting up [RMBCA 14.20].

---

8 This is permitted under Delaware law—see Delaware Code Section 275(c)—but not under the RMBCA.

Sometimes a shareholder or a group of shareholders petitions a court for corporate dissolution. For example, the board of directors may be deadlocked. Courts hesitate to order involuntary dissolution in such circumstances unless there is specific statutory authorization to do so. If the shareholders cannot resolve the deadlock and if it will irreparably injure the corporation, however, the court will proceed with an involuntary dissolution. Courts can also dissolve a corporation in other circumstances, such as when the controlling shareholders or directors are committing fraudulent or oppressive acts or when management is misapplying or wasting corporate assets [RMBCA 14.30].

LIQUIDATION

When dissolution takes place by voluntary action, the members of the board of directors act as trustees of the corporate assets. As trustees, they are responsible for winding up the affairs of the corporation for the benefit of corporate creditors and shareholders. This makes the board members personally liable for any breach of their fiduciary trustee duties.

Liquidation can be accomplished without court supervision unless the members of the board do not wish to act as trustees of the corporate assets, or unless shareholders or creditors can show cause to the court why the board should not be permitted to assume the trustee function. In either situation, the court will appoint a receiver to wind up the corporate affairs and liquidate corporate assets. A receiver is always appointed by the court if the dissolution is involuntary.

Terms and Concepts

alien corporation   521
appraisal right   533
articles of incorporation   520
bond   528
bond indenture   528
bylaws   521
certificate of incorporation   526
chose in action   532
close corporation   522
commingle   527
common stock   529

consolidation   532
corporate charter   519
corporation   518
dissolution   536
dividend   519
domestic corporation   521
foreign corporation   521
liquidation   536
merger   530
piercing the corporate veil   527
preferred stock   530

promoter   523
prospectus   523
retained earnings   519
S corporation   522
securities   528
short-form merger   533
stock   528
target corporation   536
ultra vires   521

Chapter Summary Corporate Formation, Financing, and Termination

The Nature of the Corporation (See pages 518–520.)	A corporation is a legal entity distinct from its owners. Formal statutory requirements, which vary somewhat from state to state, must be followed in forming a corporation. The corporation can have perpetual existence or be chartered for a specific period of time. 1. *Corporate parties*—The shareholders own the corporation. They elect a board of directors to govern the corporation. The board of directors hires corporate officers and other employees to run the daily business of the firm. 2. *Corporate taxation*—The corporation pays income tax on net profits; shareholders pay income tax on the disbursed dividends that they receive from the corporation (double-taxation feature).

(Continued)

Chapter Summary	**Corporate Formation, Financing, and Termination—Continued**
The Nature of the Corporation—continued	3. *Torts and criminal acts*—The corporation is liable for the torts committed by its agents or officers within the course and scope of their employment (under the doctrine of *respondeat superior*). In some circumstances, a corporation can be held liable (and be fined) for the criminal acts of its agents and employees. In certain situations, corporate officers may be held personally liable for corporate crimes.
Corporate Powers (See pages 520–521.)	1. *Express powers*—The express powers of a corporation are granted by the following laws and documents (listed according to their priority): federal constitution, state constitutions, state statutes, articles of incorporation, bylaws, and resolutions of the board of directors. 2. *Implied powers*—Barring express constitutional, statutory, or other prohibitions, the corporation has the implied power to do all acts reasonably appropriate and necessary to accomplish its corporate purposes. 3. *Ultra vires doctrine*—Any act of a corporation that is beyond its express or implied powers to undertake is an *ultra vires* act. 　a. *Ultra vires* contracts may or may not be enforced by the courts, depending on the circumstances. 　b. The corporation (or shareholders on behalf of the corporation) may sue to enjoin or recover damages for *ultra vires* acts of corporate officers or directors. In addition, the state attorney general may bring an action either to institute an injunction against the transaction or to institute dissolution proceedings against the corporation for *ultra vires* acts.
Classification of Corporations (See pages 521–523.)	1. *Domestic, foreign, and alien corporations*—A corporation is referred to as a *domestic corporation* within its home state (the state in which it incorporates). A corporation is referred to as a *foreign corporation* by any state that is not its home state. A corporation is referred to as an *alien corporation* if it originates in another country but does business in the United States. 2. *Public and private corporations*—A public corporation is one formed by government (for example, cities, towns, and public projects). A private corporation is one formed wholly or in part for private benefit. Most corporations are private corporations. 3. *Nonprofit corporations*—Corporations formed without a profit-making purpose (for example, charitable, educational, and religious organizations and hospitals). 4. *Close corporations*—Corporations owned by a family or a relatively small number of individuals; transfer of shares is usually restricted, and the corporation does not make a public offering of its securities. 5. *S corporations*—Small domestic corporations (must have seventy-five or fewer shareholders as members) that, under Subchapter S of the Internal Revenue Code, are given special tax treatment. These corporations allow shareholders to enjoy the limited legal liability of the corporate form but avoid its double-taxation feature (taxes are paid by shareholders as personal income, and the S corporation is not taxed separately). 6. *Professional corporations*—Corporations formed by professionals (for example, doctors and lawyers) to obtain the benefits of incorporation (such as tax benefits and limited liability). In most situations, the professional corporation is treated as other corporations, but sometimes the courts will disregard the corporate form and treat the shareholders as partners.

Chapter Summary	Corporate Formation, Financing, and Termination—Continued

Corporate Formation (See pages 523–526.)	1. *Promotional activities*—A corporate promoter is one who takes the preliminary steps in organizing a corporation (issues prospectus, secures charter, interests investors in the purchase of corporate stock, forms subscription agreements, makes contracts with third parties so that the corporation can immediately begin doing business on its formation, and so on).
	
	 2. *Incorporation procedures*—
	
	   a. A state in which to incorporate is selected.
	
	   b. The articles of incorporation are prepared and filed. The articles generally should include the corporate name, duration, nature and purpose, capital structure, internal organization, registered office and agent, and incorporators.
	
	   c. The certificate of incorporation (or charter), which authorizes the corporation to conduct business, is received from the appropriate state office (usually the secretary of state) after the articles of incorporation have been filed.
	
	   d. The first organizational meeting is held after the charter is granted. The board of directors is elected and other business completed (bylaws passed, stock issued, and so on).

Corporate Status (See pages 526–528.)	1. *De jure or de facto corporation*—If a corporation has been improperly incorporated, courts will sometimes impute corporate status to the firm by holding that the firm is a *de jure* corporation (cannot be challenged by the state or third persons) or a *de facto* corporation (can be challenged by the state but not by third persons). 2. *Corporation by estoppel*—If a firm is neither a *de jure* nor a *de facto* corporation but represents itself to be a corporation and is sued as such by a third party, it may be held to be a corporation by estoppel. 3. *Disregarding the corporate entity*—To avoid injustice, courts may "pierce the corporate veil" and hold a shareholder or shareholders personally liable for a judgment against the corporation. This usually occurs only when the corporation was established to circumvent the law, when the corporate form is used for an illegitimate or fraudulent purpose, or when the controlling shareholder commingles his or her own interests with those of the corporation to such an extent that the corporation no longer has a separate identity.
Corporate Financing—Bonds (See page 528.)	Corporate bonds are securities representing *corporate debt*—money borrowed by a corporation. See Exhibit 25–2 for a list describing the various types of corporate bonds.

Corporate Financing—Stocks (See pages 528–530.)	Stocks are equity securities issued by a corporation that represent the purchase of ownership in the business firm.
	
	 1. *Important characteristics of stockholders*—
	
	   a. They need not be paid back.
	
	   b. The stockholder receives dividends only when so voted by the directors.
	
	   c. Stockholders are the last investors to be paid on dissolution.
	
	   d. Stockholders vote for management and on major issues.
	
	 2. *Types of stock (see Exhibit 25–4 for details)*—
	
	   a. Common stock—Represents the true ownership of the firm. Holders of common stock share in the control, earning capacity, and net assets of the corporation. Common stockholders carry more risk than preferred stockholders but, if the corporation is successful, are compensated for this risk by greater returns on their investments.

(Continued)

Chapter Summary	**Corporate Formation, Financing, and Termination—Continued**
Corporate Financing—Stocks—continued	b. Preferred stock—Stock whose holders have a preferred status. Preferred stockholders have a stronger position than common shareholders with respect to dividends and claims on assets, but as a result, they will not share in the full prosperity of the firm if it grows successfully over time. The return and risk for preferred stock lie somewhere between those for bonds and those for common stock.
Merger and Consolidation (See pages 530–534.)	1. *Merger*—The legal combination of two or more corporations, the result of which is that the surviving corporation acquires all the assets and obligations of the other corporation, which then ceases to exist.
	2. *Consolidation*—The legal combination of two or more corporations, the result of which is that each corporation ceases to exist and a new one emerges. The new corporation assumes all the assets and obligations of the former corporations.
	3. *Procedure*—Determined by state statutes. Basic requirements are the following:
	a. The board of directors of each corporation involved must approve the merger or consolidation plan.
	b. The shareholders of each corporation must approve the merger or consolidation plan at a shareholders' meeting.
	c. Articles of merger or consolidation (the plan) must be filed, usually with the secretary of state.
	d. The state issues a certificate of merger (or consolidation) to the surviving (or newly consolidated) corporation.
	4. *Short-form merger (parent-subsidiary merger)*—Possible when the parent corporation owns at least 90 percent of the outstanding shares of each class of stock of the subsidiary corporation.
	a. Shareholder approval is not required.
	b. The merger must be approved only by the board of directors of the parent corporation.
	c. A copy of the merger plan must be sent to each shareholder of record.
	d. The merger plan must be filed with the state.
	5. *Appraisal rights*—Rights of dissenting shareholders (given by state statute) to receive the *fair value* for their shares when a merger or consolidation takes place. If the shareholder and the corporation do not agree on the fair value, a court will determine it.
Purchase of Assets (See pages 534–536.)	A purchase of assets occurs when one corporation acquires all or substantially all of the assets of another corporation. The acquiring (purchasing) corporation is not required to obtain shareholder approval; the corporation is merely increasing its assets, and no fundamental business change occurs. The acquired (purchased) corporation is required to obtain the approval of both its directors and its shareholders for the sale of its assets, because this creates a substantial change in the corporation's business position.
Purchase of Stock (See page 536.)	A purchase of stock occurs when one corporation acquires a substantial number of the voting shares of the stock of another (target) corporation.
Termination (See pages 536–537.)	The termination of a corporation involves the following two phases:
	1. *Dissolution*—The legal death of the artificial "person" of the corporation. Dissolution can be brought about in any of the following ways:
	a. An act of a legislature in the state of incorporation.
	b. Expiration of the time provided in the corporate charter.

Chapter Summary	Corporate Formation, Financing, and Termination—Continued
Termination— continued	c. Voluntary approval of the shareholders and the board of directors. d. Unanimous action by all shareholders. e. Court decree. 2. *Liquidation*—The process by which corporate assets are converted into cash and distributed to creditors and shareholders according to specified rules of preference. May be supervised by members of the board of directors (when dissolution is voluntary) or by a receiver appointed by the court to wind up corporate affairs.

For Review

① What are the steps for bringing a corporation into existence? Who is liable for preincorporation contracts?

② What is the difference between a *de jure* corporation and a *de facto* corporation?

③ In what circumstances might a court disregard the corporate entity ("pierce the corporate veil") and hold the shareholders personally liable?

④ What are the four steps of the merger or consolidation procedure?

⑤ What are the two ways in which a corporation can be voluntarily dissolved? Under what circumstances might a corporation be involuntarily dissolved by state action?

Questions and Case Problems

25–1. Corporate Status. Three brothers inherited a small paper-supply business from their father, who had operated the business as a sole proprietorship. The brothers decided to incorporate under the name of Gomez Corp. and retained an attorney to draw up the necessary documents. The attorney drew up the papers and had the brothers sign them but neglected to send the application for a corporate charter to the secretary of state's office. The brothers assumed that all necessary legal work had been taken care of, and they proceeded to do business as Gomez Corp. One day, a Gomez Corp. employee, while making a delivery to one of Gomez's customers, negligently ran a red light and caused a car accident. Baxter, the driver of the other vehicle, was injured as a result and sued Gomez Corp. for damages. Baxter then learned that no state charter had ever been issued to Gomez Corp., so he sued each of the brothers personally for damages. Can the brothers avoid personal liability for the tort of their employee? Explain.

25–2. Liability for Preincorporation Contracts. Christy, Briggs, and Dobbs are recent college graduates who want to form a corporation to manufacture and sell personal computers. Perez tells them that he will set in motion the formation of their corporation. Perez first makes a contract with Oliver for the purchase of a parcel of land for $25,000. Oliver does not know of the prospective corporate formation at the time the contract is signed. Perez then makes a contract with Kovac to build a small plant on the property being purchased. Kovac's contract is conditional on the corporation's formation. Perez secures all neces-

sary subscription agreements and capitalization, and he files the articles of incorporation. A charter is issued.

(a) Discuss whether the newly formed corporation or Perez (or both) is liable on the contracts with Oliver and Kovac.

(b) Discuss whether the corporation, on coming into legal existence, is automatically liable to Kovac.

25–3. Corporate Powers. Kora Nayenga and two business associates formed a corporation called Nayenga Corp. for the purpose of selling computer services. Kora, who owned 50 percent of the corporate shares, served as the corporation's president. Kora wished to obtain a personal loan from his bank for $250,000, but the bank required the note to be cosigned by a third party. Kora cosigned the note in the name of the corporation. Later, Kora defaulted on the note, and the bank sued the corporation for payment. The corporation asserted, as a defense, that Kora had exceeded his authority when he cosigned the note. Had he? Explain.

25–4. Consolidations. Determine which of the following situations describes a consolidation:

(a) Arkon Corp. purchases all of the assets of Botrek Co.

(b) Arkon Corp. and Botrek Co. combine their firms, with Arkon Corp. as the surviving corporation.

(c) Arkon Corp. and Botrek Co. agree to combine their assets, dissolve their old corporations, and form a new corporation under a new name.

(d) Arkon Corp. agrees to sell all its accounts receivable to Botrek Co.

25–5. Mergers. Tally Ho Co. was merged into Perfecto Corp., with Perfecto being the surviving corporation in the merger. Hanjo, a creditor of Tally Ho, brought suit against Perfecto Corp. for payment of the debt. The directors of Perfecto refused to pay, stating that Tally Ho no longer existed and that Perfecto had never agreed to assume any of Tally Ho's liabilities. Discuss fully whether Hanjo will be able to recover from Perfecto.

25–6. Dissolution. In 1988, Farad Mohammed and Syed Parveen formed Hina Pharmacy, Health & Beauty Aids, Inc., to operate a pharmacy in New York. Syed, an experienced pharmacist, contributed his expertise and $7,000. Farad contributed $120,000. Each took 50 percent of the Hina stock. Farad assigned his shares to his brother Azam, and Syed assigned his to his wife, Aisha. A dispute soon arose over the disparity in capital contributions. The parties held only one shareholders' meeting, and they never attempted to elect directors. Syed later claimed that Azam, who exercised sole control over the daily management of Hina, kept 80 percent of the profits. Azam argued that Syed had agreed to work for 20 percent of the profits plus a salary. Syed stopped working at the pharmacy in 1994. Aisha filed a petition in a New York state court to dissolve Hina. Should the court grant the petition? If so, on what basis? If not, why not? [*In re Parveen,* 259 A.D.2d 389, 687 N.Y.S.2d 90 (1 Dept. 1999)]

25–7. Successor Liability. In 1996, Robert McClellan, a licensed contractor doing business as McClellan Design and Construction, entered into a contract with Peppertree North Condominium Association, Inc., to do earthquake repair work on Peppertree's seventy-six–unit condominium complex in Northridge, California. McClellan completed the work, but Peppertree failed to pay. In an arbitration proceeding against Peppertree to collect the amount due, McClellan was awarded $141,000, plus 10 percent interest, attorneys' fees, and costs. McClellan filed a suit in a California state court against Peppertree to confirm the award. Meanwhile, the Peppertree board of directors filed articles of incorporation for Northridge Park Townhome Owners Association, Inc., and immediately transferred Peppertree's authority, responsibilities, and assets to the new association. Two weeks later, the court issued a judgment against Peppertree. When McClellan learned about the new association, he filed a motion asking the court to add Northridge as a debtor to the judgment. Should the court grant the motion? Why or why not? [*McClellan v. Northridge Park Townhome Owners Association, Inc.,* 89 Cal.App.4th 746, 107 Cal.Rptr.2d 702 (2 Dist. 2001)]

CASE PROBLEM WITH SAMPLE ANSWER

25–8. William Soerries was the sole shareholder of Chickasaw Club, Inc., which operated a popular nightclub of the same name in Columbus, Georgia. Soerries maintained corporate checking accounts, but he paid his employees, suppliers, and entertainers in cash out of the club's proceeds. He owned the property on which the club was located and rented it to the club, but made the mortgage payments out of the club's proceeds. Soerries often paid corporate expenses out of his personal funds. At 11:45 P.M. on July 31, 1996, eighteen-year-old Aubrey Lynn Pursley, who was already intoxicated, entered the Chickasaw Club. A city ordinance prohibited individuals under the age of twenty-one from entering nightclubs, but Chickasaw employees did not check Pursley's identification. Pursley drank more alcohol and was visibly intoxicated when she left the club at 3:00 A.M. with a beer in her hand. Shortly afterward, Pursley was killed when she lost control of her car and struck a tree. Joseph Dancause, Pursley's stepfather, filed a suit in a Georgia state court against Chickasaw Club, Inc., and Soerries for damages. Can Soerries be held personally liable? If so, on what basis? Explain. [*Soerries v. Dancause,* 546 S.E.2d 356 (Ga.App. 2001)]

◆ To view a sample answer for this case problem, go to this book's Web site at **http://fundamentals.westbuslaw.com** and click on "Interactive Study Center."

25–9. Corporate Dissolution. Trans System, Inc. (TSI), is an interstate trucking business. In 1994, to provide a source of well-trained drivers, TSI formed Northwestern Career Institute, Inc., a school for persons interested in obtaining a commercial driver's license. Tim Scott, who had worked for TSI since 1987, was named chief administrative officer and director, with responsibility for day-to-day operations, which included recruiting new students, personnel matters, record keeping, and debt collecting. Scott, a Northwestern shareholder, disagreed with James Williams, the majority shareholder of both TSI and Northwestern, over four equipment leases between the two firms under which the sum of the payments exceeded the value of the equipment. Scott also disputed TSI's use, for purposes unrelated to the driving school, of $125,000 borrowed by Northwestern. Scott was terminated in 1998. He filed a suit in a Washington state court against TSI, seeking, among other things, the dissolution of Northwestern on the ground that the directors of the two firms had acted in an oppressive manner and misapplied corporate assets. Should the court grant this relief? Discuss. [*Scott v. Trans System, Inc.,* 110 Wash.App. 44, 38 P.3d 379 (Div. 3 2002)]

25–10. Torts and Criminal Acts. Greg Allen is an employee, shareholder, director, and the president of Greg Allen Construction Co. In 1996, Daniel and Sondra Estelle hired Allen's firm to renovate a home they owned in Ladoga, Indiana. To finance the cost, they obtained a line of credit from Banc One, Indiana, which required periodic inspections to disburse funds. Allen was on the job every day and supervised all of the work. He designed all of the structural changes, including a floor system for the bedroom over the living room, the floor system of the living room, and the stairway to the second floor. He did all of the electrical, plumbing, and carpentry work and installed all of the windows. He did most of the drywall taping and finishing and most of the painting. The Estelles found much of this work to be unacceptable, and the bank's inspector agreed that it was of poor quality. When Allen failed to act on the Estelles' complaints, they filed a suit in an Indiana state court against Allen Construction and Allen personally, alleging in part that his individual work on the project was negligent. Can both Allen and his corporation be held liable for this tort? Explain. [*Greg Allen Construction Co. v. Estelle,* 762 N.E.2d 760 (Ind.App. 2002)]

A QUESTION OF ETHICS AND SOCIAL RESPONSIBILITY

25–11. In a corporate merger, Diamond Shamrock retained its corporate identity, and Natomas Corp. was absorbed into Diamond's corporate hierarchy. Five inside directors (directors who are also officers of the corporation) of Natomas had "golden parachutes," which were incorporated into the merger agreement. (*Golden parachutes* are special benefits provided to a corporation's top managers in the event that the company is taken over and they are forced to leave.) The terms of the parachute agreements provided that each of the five individuals would receive a payment equal to three years' compensation in the event that they left their positions at Natomas at any time for any reason other than termination for just cause. Three of the five voluntarily left their positions after three years. Under the terms of their parachute agreements, they collected over $10 million. A suit challenging the golden parachutes was brought by Gaillard, a Natomas shareholder. A trial court granted the defendants' motion for summary judgment; the court sustained the golden parachutes on the ground that the directors were protected by the business judgment rule (a rule under which a corporate officer or director may avoid liability to the corporation or its shareholders for poor business judgments—see Chapter 26) in effecting the agreement. The appellate court held that the business judgment rule does not apply in a review of the conduct of inside directors and remanded the case for trial. [*Gaillard v. Natomas,* 208 Cal.App.3d 1250, 256 Cal.Rptr. 702 (1989)]

1. Regardless of the legal issues, are golden parachutes ethical in a general sense? Discuss.
2. What practical considerations would lead a corporation to grant its top management such seemingly one-sided agreements?
3. In the *Gaillard* case, how would your views be affected by evidence showing that the golden parachutes had been developed and presented to the board by the very individuals who were the beneficiaries of the agreements—that is, by the five inside directors?

CORPORATE FORMATION, FINANCING, AND TERMINATION

For updated links to resources available on the Web, as well as other materials, visit this text's Web site at

http://fundamentals.westbuslaw.com

Cornell University's Legal Information Institute has links to state corporation (and other) statutes at

http://www.law.cornell.edu/topics/state_statutes.html

Garage Technology Ventures offers services that help high-tech companies locate potential investors. To learn more, and to read articles of interest to investors and entrepreneurs, go to

http://www.garage.com

For information on incorporation, including a list of frequently asked questions on the topic, go to

http://www.bizfilings.com

The court opinions of Delaware's Court of Chancery, widely considered to be the nation's premier trial court for corporate law, are made available on the Web by the Delaware Corporate Law Clearinghouse, a project of the Widener University School of Law. Go to

http://corporate-law.widener.edu

Ballard, Spahr, Andrews & Ingersoll, LLP, a law firm in Philadelphia, offers a guide on how to uncover company information that may be of interest to shareholders and others. Go to

http://www.virtualchase.com/coinfo

Online Legal Research

Go to the *Fundamentals of Business Law* home page at **http://fundamentals. westbuslaw.com**. Select "Interactive Study Center" and then click on "Chapter 25." There you will find the following Internet research exercises that you can perform to learn more about topics covered in this chapter.

Activity 25-1: LEGAL PERSPECTIVE—Corporate Law
Activity 25-2: MANAGEMENT PERSPECTIVE—Mergers
Activity 25-3: ECONOMIC PERSPECTIVE—Financing a Business

Before the Test

Go to the *Fundamentals of Business Law* home page at **http://fundamentals. westbuslaw.com**. Click on "Interactive Quizzes." You will find at least twenty interactive questions relating to this chapter.

Westlaw® Campus

If your textbook provided for a subscription to Westlaw® Campus, or if you have otherwise purchased access to the Westlaw Campus database, you can access any of the cases presented or cited in this chapter by using your Westlaw Campus account.

26

Corporate Directors, Officiers, and Shareholders

CHAPTER OBJECTIVES

After reading this chapter, you should be able to answer the following questions:

① What are the duties of corporate directors and officers?

② Directors are expected to use their best judgment in managing the corporation. What must directors do to avoid liability for honest mistakes of judgment and poor business decisions?

③ What is a voting proxy? What is cumulative voting?

④ If a group of shareholders perceives that the corporation has suffered a wrong and the directors refuse to take action, can the shareholders compel the directors to act? If so, how?

⑤ From what sources may dividends be paid legally? In what circumstances is a dividend illegal? What happens if a dividend is illegally paid?

A corporation is not a "natural" person but a legal fiction. No one individual shareholder or director bears sole responsibility for the corporation and its actions. Rather, a corporation joins the efforts and resources of a large number of individuals for the purpose of producing returns greater than the returns those persons could have obtained individually.

Sometimes, actions that benefit the corporation as a whole do not coincide with the separate interests of the individuals making up the corporation. In such situations, it is important to know the rights and duties of all participants in the corporate enterprise. This chapter focuses on the rights and duties of directors, officers, and shareholders and the ways in which conflicts among them are resolved.

Role of Directors

A corporation typically is governed by a board of directors. A director occupies a position of responsibility unlike that of other corporate personnel. Directors are sometimes inappropriately characterized as *agents* because they act on behalf of the corporation. No *individual* director, however, can act as an agent to bind the corporation; and as a group,

545

directors collectively control the corporation in a way that no agent is able to control a principal. Directors are often incorrectly characterized as *trustees* because they occupy positions of trust and control over the corporation. Unlike trustees, however, they do not own or hold title to property for the use and benefit of others.

ELECTION OF DIRECTORS

Subject to statutory limitations, the number of directors is set forth in the corporation's articles or bylaws. Historically, the minimum number of directors has been three, but today many states permit fewer. Indeed, the Revised Model Business Corporation Act (RMBCA), in Section 8.01, permits corporations with fewer than fifty shareholders to eliminate the board of directors.

The initial board of directors is normally appointed by the incorporators on the creation of the corporation, or directors are named by the corporation itself in the articles. The first board serves until the first annual shareholders' meeting. Subsequent directors are elected by a majority vote of the shareholders. The term of office for a director is usually one year—from annual meeting to annual meeting. Longer and staggered terms are permissible under most state statutes. A common practice is to elect one-third of the board members each year for a three-year term. In this way, there is greater management continuity.

A director can be removed *for cause* (that is, for failing to perform a required duty), either as specified in the articles or bylaws or by shareholder action. Even the board of directors itself may be given power to remove a director for cause, subject to shareholder review. In most states, a director cannot be removed without cause unless the shareholders have reserved that right at the time of election. Vacancies can occur on the board of directors because of death or resignation, or when a new position is created through amendment of the articles or bylaws. In these situations, either the shareholders or the board itself can fill the position, depending on state law or on the provisions of the bylaws.

More than 50 percent of the publicly traded companies in the United States are incorporated under Delaware law. Consequently, decisions of the Delaware courts on questions of corporate law have a wide impact. In the following case, a board increased the number of its members to diminish the effect that subsequently elected directors would have on the board's decisions. This may have been "acceptable" under the firm's bylaws, but was it legal according to Delaware law?

CASE 26.1 **MM Companies, Inc. v. Liquid Audio, Inc.**

Delaware Supreme Court, 2003.
813 A.2d 1118.

FACTS Liquid Audio, Inc., a Delaware corporation with its principal place of business in Redwood City, California, provides software and services for the delivery of music over the Internet. MM Companies, Inc., a Delaware corporation with its principal place of business in New York City, owned 7 percent of Liquid Audio's stock. In October 2001, MM sent a letter to Liquid Audio's board of directors offering to buy all of the company's stock for about $3 per share. The board rejected the offer. Liquid Audio's bylaws provide for a board of five directors divided into three classes. One class is elected each year. The next election, at which two directors would be chosen, was set for September 2002. By mid-August, it appeared that MM's nominees, Seymour Holtzman and James Mitarotonda, would win the election. The board amended the bylaws to increase the number of directors to seven, and appointed Judith Frank and James Somes to fill the new positions. In September, MM's nominees were elected to the board, but their influence was diminished because there were now seven directors. MM filed a suit in a Delaware state court against Liquid Audio and others, challenging the board's actions. The court ruled in favor of the defendants. MM appealed to the Delaware Supreme Court.

ISSUE Was the board's action to amend the bylaws to increase the number of directors and fill the new positions with appointments valid?

DECISION No. The Delaware Supreme Court reversed the judgment of the lower court and remanded the case for further proceedings. The state supreme court concluded that the board acted primarily to impede the shareholders' right to vote in an impending election for successor directors.

REASON The court reasoned that "[m]aintaining a proper balance in the allocation of power between the stockholders' right to elect directors and the board of directors' right to manage the corporation is dependent upon the stockholders' unimpeded right to vote effectively in an election of directors." The court determined that "[w]hen the *primary purpose* of a board of directors' [action] is to interfere with or impede the effective exercise of the shareholder franchise in a con-

CASE 26.1—Continued

tested election for directors, the board must * * * demonstrate a compelling justification for such action." In this case, the directors' action, which had "the primary purpose of diminishing the influence of MM's two nominees[,] * * * compromised the essential role of corporate democracy in maintaining the proper allocation of power between the shareholders and the Board, because that action was taken in the context of a contested election for successor directors. Since the * * * Defendants did not demonstrate a compelling justification * * * , the bylaw amendment that expanded the size of the Liquid Audio board, and permitted the appointment of two new members on the eve of a contested election, should have been invalidated."

FOR CRITICAL ANALYSIS—Political Consideration
How could MM's newly elected nominees, or any two directors, affect the decisions of a five-member board?

DIRECTORS' QUALIFICATIONS AND COMPENSATION

Few legal requirements exist concerning directors' qualifications. Only a handful of states impose minimum age and residency requirements. A director is sometimes a shareholder, but this is not a necessary qualification—unless, of course, statutory provisions or corporate articles or bylaws require ownership.

Compensation for directors is ordinarily specified in the corporate articles or bylaws. Because directors have a fiduciary relationship to the shareholders and to the corporation, an express agreement or provision for compensation often is necessary for them to receive money income from the funds that they control and for which they have responsibilities.

BOARD OF DIRECTORS' MEETINGS

The board of directors conducts business by holding formal meetings with recorded minutes. The date on which regular meetings are held is usually established in the articles or bylaws or by board resolution, and no further notice is customarily required. Special meetings can be called, with notice sent to all directors.

Quorum requirements can vary among jurisdictions. (A **quorum** is the minimum number of members of a body of officials or other group that must be present in order for business to be validly transacted.) Many states leave the decision as to quorum requirements to the corporate articles or bylaws. In the absence of specific state statutes, most states provide that a quorum is a majority of the number of directors authorized in the articles or bylaws. Voting is done in person (unlike voting at shareholders' meetings, which can be done by proxy, as discussed later in this chapter).[1] The rule is one vote per director. Ordinary matters gener-

ally require a simple majority vote; certain extraordinary issues may require a greater-than-majority vote.

RIGHTS OF DIRECTORS

A director of a corporation has a number of rights, including the rights of participation, inspection, compensation, and indemnification.

Participation and Inspection. A corporate director must have certain rights to function properly in that position. The main right is one of participation—meaning that the director must be notified of board of directors' meetings so he or she can participate in them. As pointed out earlier in this chapter, regular board meetings are usually established by the bylaws or by board resolution, and no notice of these meetings is required. If special meetings are called, however, notice is required unless waived by the director.

A director must have access to all of the corporate books and records to make decisions and to exercise the necessary supervision over corporate officers and employees. This right of inspection is virtually absolute and cannot be restricted.

Compensation and Indemnification. Historically, directors have had no inherent right to compensation for their services as directors. Nominal sums are often paid as honorariums to directors, however. In many corporations, directors are also chief corporate officers (president or chief executive officer, for example) and receive compensation in their managerial positions. Most directors, however, gain through indirect benefits, such as business contacts, prestige, and other rewards, such as stock options. There is a trend toward providing more than nominal compensation for directors, especially in large corporations where the time, work, effort, and risk involved can impose enormous burdens. Many states permit the corporate articles or bylaws to authorize compensation for directors, and in

---

[1] Except in Louisiana, which allows a director to vote by proxy under certain circumstances.

some cases the board can set its own compensation unless the articles or bylaws provide otherwise.

Corporate directors may become involved in lawsuits by virtue of their positions and their actions as directors. Most states (and RMBCA 8.51) permit a corporation to indemnify (guarantee reimbursement to) a director for legal costs, fees, and judgments involved in defending corporation-related suits. Many states specifically permit a corporation to purchase liability insurance for the directors and officers to cover indemnification. When the statutes are silent on this matter, the authority to purchase such insurance is usually considered to be part of the corporation's implied power.

MANAGEMENT RESPONSIBILITIES

Directors have responsibility for all policymaking decisions necessary to the management of corporate affairs. Just as shareholders cannot act individually to bind the corporation, the directors must act as a body in carrying out routine corporate business. The general areas of responsibility of the board of directors include the following:

① The declaration and payment of corporate dividends to shareholders.

② The authorization for major corporate policy decisions—for example, the initiation of proceedings for the sale or lease of corporate assets outside the regular course of business, the determination of new product lines, and the overseeing of major contract negotiations and significant management-labor negotiations.

③ The appointment, supervision, and removal of corporate officers and other managerial employees and the determination of their compensation.

④ Financial decisions, such as the decision to issue authorized shares and bonds.

The board of directors can delegate some of its functions to an executive committee or to corporate officers. In doing so, the board is not relieved of its overall responsibility for directing the affairs of the corporation, but corporate officers and managerial personnel are empowered to make decisions relating to ordinary, daily corporate affairs within well-defined guidelines.

Role of Corporate Officers and Executives

The officers and other executive employees are hired by the board of directors or, in rare instances, by the shareholders. In addition to carrying out the duties articulated in the bylaws, corporate and managerial officers act as agents of the corporation, and the ordinary rules of agency (dis-

cussed in Chapter 22) normally apply to their employment. The qualifications required of officers and executive employees are determined at the discretion of the corporation and are included in the articles or bylaws. In most states, a person can hold more than one office and can be both an officer and a director of the corporation.

The rights of corporate officers and other high-level managers are defined by employment contracts because these persons are employees of the company. Corporate officers normally can be removed by the board of directors at any time with or without cause and regardless of the terms of the employment contracts—although in so doing, the corporation may be liable for breach of contract. The duties of corporate officers are the same as those of directors because both groups are involved in decision making and are in similar positions of control. Hence, officers are viewed as having the same fiduciary duties of care and loyalty in their conduct of corporate affairs as directors have, a subject to which we now turn.

Duties of Directors and Officers

Directors and officers are deemed *fiduciaries* of the corporation because their relationship with the corporation and its shareholders is one of trust and confidence. The fiduciary duties of the directors and officers include the duty of care and the duty of loyalty.

DUTY OF CARE

Directors and officers must exercise due care in performing their duties. The standard of *due care* has been variously described in judicial decisions and codified in many corporation codes. Generally, a director or officer is expected to act in good faith, to exercise the care that an ordinarily prudent person would exercise in similar circumstances, and to act in what he or she considers to be the best interests of the corporation.[2] Directors and officers who have not exercised the required duty of care can be held liable for the harms suffered by the corporation as a result of their negligence.

Duty to Make Informed and Reasonable Decisions. Directors and officers are expected to be informed on corporate matters. To be informed, the director or officer must do what is necessary to become informed: attend presentations, ask for information from those who have it, read reports, review other written materials such as contracts—in other words, carefully study a situation and its alternatives. Depending on the nature of the business, directors and officers are often expected to act in accordance with their own

---

[2] RMBCA 8.30.

knowledge and training. Most states (and Section 8.30 of the RMBCA), however, allow a director to make decisions in reliance on information furnished by competent officers or employees, professionals such as attorneys and accountants, or even an executive committee of the board without being accused of acting in bad faith or failing to exercise due care if such information turns out to be faulty.

Directors are also expected to make reasonable decisions. For example, a director should not accept a **tender offer** (an offer to purchase shares in the company that is made by another company directly to the shareholders, sometimes referred to as a "takeover bid") with only a moment's consideration based solely on the price per share offered by the group making the tender offer.

Duty to Exercise Reasonable Supervision. Directors are also expected to exercise a reasonable amount of supervision when they delegate work to corporate officers and employees. ● **EXAMPLE #1** Suppose that a corporate bank director fails to attend any board of directors' meetings for five years, never inspects any of the corporate books or records, and generally fails to supervise the efforts of the bank president and the loan committee. Meanwhile, a corporate officer, the bank president, makes various improper loans and permits large overdrafts. In this situation, the corporate director may be held liable to the corporation for losses resulting from the unsupervised actions of the bank president and the loan committee.●

Dissenting Directors. Directors are expected to attend board of directors' meetings, and their votes should be entered into the minutes of corporate meetings. Unless a dissent is entered, the director is presumed to have assented. Directors who dissent are rarely held individually liable for mismanagement of the corporation. For this reason, a director who is absent from a given meeting sometimes registers with the secretary of the board a dissent to actions taken at the meeting.

DUTY OF LOYALTY

Loyalty can be defined as faithfulness to one's obligations and duties. In the corporate context, the duty of loyalty requires directors and officers to subordinate their personal interests to the welfare of the corporation. This means, among other things, that directors may not use corporate funds or confidential corporate information for personal advantage. Similarly, they must refrain from self-dealing. For example, a director should not oppose a tender offer that is in the corporation's best interest simply because its acceptance may cost the director her or his position. Cases dealing with fiduciary duty typically involve one or more of the following:

① Competing with the corporation.

② Usurping (taking advantage of) a corporate opportunity.

③ Having an interest that conflicts with the interest of the corporation.

④ Engaging in insider trading (using information that is not public to make a profit trading securities, as discussed in Chapter 27).

⑤ Authorizing a corporate transaction that is detrimental to minority shareholders.

⑥ Using corporate facilities for personal business.

An officer or director usurps a corporate opportunity when he or she, for personal gain, takes advantage of a business opportunity that is financially within the corporation's reach, is in line with the firm's business, is to the firm's practical advantage, and is one in which the corporation has an interest.

The availability of cash to repay a corporation's debts can represent a "corporate opportunity." Does the use of that cash to repay a loan to a director constitute a "usurping" of that opportunity? That was the question in the following case.

CASE 26.2 **In re Cumberland Farms, Inc.**

United States Court of Appeals,
First Circuit, 2002.
284 F.3d 216.
**http://www.ca1.uscourts.gov/opinions/
main.php[a]**

FACTS In 1938, Vasilios and Aphrodite Haseotes bought a dairy farm in Cumberland, Rhode Island. Demetrios Haseotes became Cumberland's chief executive officer and chairman of its board of directors in 1960. In the 1970s, to ensure Cumberland greater security in its gas supply, Haseotes acquired a refinery in Newfoundland, Canada. Because some states prohibit a company that operates a refinery from selling petroleum products retail, Haseotes chose to own the refinery through his own businesses, including Cumberland

---

a. In the left column, click on "Search." In the "Opinion Number" box, type "01-1344.01A," and click on "Submit Query." In the result, click on the "Opinion" number to access the opinion. The U.S. Court of Appeals for the First Circuit maintains this Web site.

(Continued)

CASE 26.2—Continued

Crude Processing, Inc. (CCP). To operate the refinery, CCP borrowed more than $70 million from Cumberland, under an agreement that required the payment of that loan first. Haseotes also loaned money to CCP. When cash was available, Haseotes had CCP repay $5.75 million to him, without telling the Cumberland board. CCP defaulted on its debt to Cumberland, which filed a bankruptcy petition in 1992. Haseotes filed a claim for $3 million against the firm, which asserted a claim for $5.75 million against him. Cumberland argued that Haseotes breached his duty of loyalty when he had CCP pay its debt to him while ignoring its debt to Cumberland. The court disallowed Haseotes's claim. On appeal, a federal district court affirmed this ruling. Haseotes appealed to the U.S. Court of Appeals for the First Circuit.

ISSUE Had Haseotes breached his duty of loyalty to Cumberland by having CCP pay its debt to him while ignoring its debt to Cumberland?

DECISION Yes. the U.S. Court of Appeals for the First Circuit affirmed the lower court's judgment. The appellate court held that Haseotes breached his duty of loyalty to Cumberland when, without informing Cumberland's board that money had become available in CCP, he had CCP apply the money toward its debt to himself rather than to its debt to Cumberland.

REASON The court explained, "As a member of Cumberland's board of directors, Haseotes owed the corporation a fiduciary duty of loyalty and fair dealing. * * * [D]irectors must act with absolute fidelity to the corporation and must place their duties to the corporation above every other financial or business obligation. The fiduciary duty is especially exacting where the corporation is closely held." Thus, "[w]hen a corporate director learns of an opportunity that could benefit the corporation, she must inform the disinterested shareholders of all the material details of the opportunity so that they may decide whether the corporation can and should take advantage of it. It is inherently unfair for the director to deny the corporation that choice and instead take the opportunity for herself." Here, "any funds that became available in CCP provided an opportunity to pay down CCP's * * * debt to Cumberland[,]" and the loan agreement "explicitly required Haseotes to apply any available money toward Cumberland's loan before paying down CCP's debt to himself." In these circumstances, "Haseotes was obligated to seek approval from Cumberland's board before acting."

FOR CRITICAL ANALYSIS—Ethical Consideration
The court noted that the fiduciary duty of loyalty "is especially exacting where the corporation is closely held." Why is this?

CONFLICTS OF INTEREST

The duty of loyalty also requires officers and directors to disclose fully to the board of directors any possible conflict of interest that might occur in conducting corporate transactions. The various state statutes contain different standards, but a contract will generally *not* be voidable if it was fair and reasonable to the corporation at the time it was made, if there was a full disclosure of the interest of the officers or directors involved in the transaction, and if the contract was approved by a majority of the disinterested directors or shareholders.

● **EXAMPLE #2** Southwood Corporation needs office space. Lambert Alden, one of its five directors, owns the building adjoining the corporation's main office building. He negotiates a lease with Southwood for the space, making a full disclosure to Southwood and the other four board directors. The lease arrangement is fair and reasonable, and it is unanimously approved by the corporation's board of directors. In this situation, Alden has not breached his duty of loyalty to the corporation, and the contract is thus valid. If it were otherwise, directors would be prevented from ever giving financial assistance to the corporations they serve.●

Liability of Directors and Officers

Directors and officers are exposed to liability on many fronts. Corporate directors and officers may be held liable for the crimes and torts committed by themselves or by corporate employees under their supervision, as discussed in Chapter 6 and Chapter 22, respectively. Additionally, shareholders may perceive that the corporate directors are not acting in the best interests of the corporation and may sue the directors, in what is called a *shareholder's derivative suit*, on behalf of the corporation. (This type of action is discussed later in this chapter, in the context of shareholders' rights.) Here, we examine the **business judgment rule**, under which a corporate director or officer may be able to avoid liability to the corporation or to its shareholders for poor business judgments.

Directors and officers are expected to exercise due care and to use their best judgment in guiding corporate management, but they are not insurers of business success. Honest mistakes of judgment and poor business decisions on their part do not make them liable to the corporation for resulting damages. The business judgment rule generally immunizes directors and officers from liability for the consequences of a decision that is within managerial authority, as long as the decision complies with management's fiduciary duties and as long as acting on the decision is within the powers of the corporation. Consequently, if there is a reasonable basis for a business decision, it is unlikely that the court will interfere with that decision, even if the corporation suffers as a result.

To benefit from the rule, directors and officers must act in good faith, in what they consider to be the best interests of the corporation, and with the care that an ordinarily prudent person in a similar position would exercise in similar circumstances. This requires an informed decision, with a rational basis, and with no conflict between the decision maker's personal interest and the interest of the corporation.

Role of Shareholders

The acquisition of a share of stock makes a person an owner and shareholder in a corporation. Shareholders thus own the corporation. Although they have no legal title to corporate property, such as buildings and equipment, they do have an equitable (ownership) interest in the firm.

As a general rule, shareholders have no responsibility for the daily management of the corporation, although they are ultimately responsible for choosing the board of directors, which does have such control. Ordinarily, corporate officers and other employees owe no direct duty to individual shareholders. Their duty is to the corporation as a whole. A director, however, is in a fiduciary relationship to the corporation and therefore serves the interests of the shareholders. Generally, there is no legal relationship between shareholders and creditors of the corporation. Shareholders can, in fact, be creditors of the corporation and thus have the same rights of recovery against the corporation as any other creditor.

In this section, we look at the powers and voting rights of shareholders, which are generally established in the articles of incorporation and under the state's general incorporation law.

SHAREHOLDERS' POWERS

The shareholders' approval is needed before any fundamental corporate changes can be effected. Hence, shareholders are empowered to amend the articles of incorporation (charter) and bylaws, approve a merger or the dissolution of the corporation, and approve the sale of all or substantially all of the corporation's assets. Some of these powers are subject to prior board approval.

Directors are elected to (and removed from) the board of directors by a vote of the shareholders. The first board of directors is either named in the articles of incorporation or chosen by the incorporators to serve until the first shareholders' meeting. From that time on, the selection and retention of directors are exclusively shareholder functions.

Directors usually serve their full terms; if they are unsatisfactory, they are simply not reelected. Shareholders have the inherent power, however, to remove a director from office *for cause* (breach of duty or misconduct) by a majority vote.[3] Some state statutes (and some corporate charters) even permit removal of directors without cause by the vote of a majority of the holders of outstanding shares entitled to vote.

SHAREHOLDERS' MEETINGS

Shareholders' meetings must occur at least annually, and additional, special meetings can be called as needed to take care of urgent matters.

Notice of Meetings. Each shareholder must receive written notice of the date, time, and place of a shareholders' meeting.[4] The notice must be received within a reasonable length of time prior to the date of the meeting. Notice of a special meeting must include a statement of the purpose of the meeting, and business transacted at the meeting is limited to that purpose.

Proxies and Proxy Materials. Because it is usually not practical for owners of only a few shares of stock of publicly traded corporations to attend shareholders' meetings, such shareholders normally give third parties written authorization to vote their shares at the meeting. This authorization is called a **proxy** (from the Latin *procurare,* "to manage, take care of"). Proxies are often solicited by management, but any person can solicit proxies to concentrate voting power. Proxies have been used by a group of shareholders as a device for taking over a corporation (corporate takeovers were discussed in Chapter 25). Proxies are normally revocable (that is, they can be withdrawn), unless they are specifically designated as irrevocable. Under RMBCA 7.22(c), proxies last for eleven months, unless the proxy agreement provides for a longer period.

When shareholders want to change a company policy, they can put their idea up for a shareholder vote. They can

---

[3] A director can often demand court review of removal for cause.

[4] The shareholder can waive the requirement of written notice by signing a waiver form. In some states, a shareholder who does not receive written notice, but who learns of the meeting and attends without protesting the lack of notice, is said to have waived notice by such conduct. State statutes and corporate bylaws typically set forth the time within which notice must be sent, what methods can be used, and what the notice must contain.

do this by submitting a shareholder proposal to the board of directors and asking the board to include the proposal in the proxy materials that are sent to all shareholders before meetings.

The Securities and Exchange Commission (SEC), which regulates the purchase and sale of securities (see Chapter 27), has established special provisions relating to proxies and shareholder proposals. SEC Rule 14a-8 requires that when a company sends proxy materials to its shareholders, the company must also include whatever proposals will be considered at the meeting and provide shareholders with the opportunity to vote on the proposals by marking and returning their proxy cards. SEC Rule 14a-8 provides that all shareholders who own stock worth at least $1,000 are eligible to submit proposals for inclusion in corporate proxy material. Only those proposals that relate to significant policy considerations must be included, however. A corporation is not required to include in proxy materials proposals that relate to "ordinary business operations."

SHAREHOLDER VOTING

Shareholders exercise ownership control through the power of their votes. Each shareholder is entitled to one vote per share, although the voting techniques that will be discussed shortly all enhance the power of the shareholder's vote. The articles of incorporation can exclude or limit voting rights, particularly for certain classes of shares. For example, owners of preferred shares are usually denied the right to vote.

Quorum Requirements. For shareholders to act during a meeting, a quorum must be present. Generally, a quorum exists when shareholders holding more than 50 percent of the outstanding shares are present. Corporate business matters are presented in the form of *resolutions,* which shareholders vote to approve or disapprove. Some state statutes have set forth specific voting requirements, and corporations' articles or bylaws must abide by these statutory requirements. Some states provide that the unanimous written consent of shareholders is a permissible alternative to holding a shareholders' meeting. Once a quorum is present, a majority vote of the shares represented at the meeting is usually required to pass resolutions.

● EXAMPLE #3 Assume that Novo Pictures, Inc., has 10,000 outstanding shares of voting stock. Its articles of incorporation set the quorum at 50 percent of outstanding shares and provide that a majority vote of the shares present is necessary to pass resolutions concerning ordinary matters. Therefore, for this firm, a quorum of shareholders representing 5,000 outstanding shares must be present at a shareholders' meeting to conduct business. If exactly 5,000

shares are represented at the meeting, a vote of at least 2,501 of those shares is needed to pass a resolution. If 6,000 shares are represented, a vote of 3,001 will be required, and so on. ●

At times, a greater-than-majority vote will be required either by a state statute or by the corporate charter. Extraordinary corporate matters, such as a merger, consolidation, or dissolution of the corporation (see Chapter 25), require a higher percentage of the representatives of all corporate shares entitled to vote, not just a majority of those present at that particular meeting.

Voting Lists. The corporation prepares voting lists prior to each meeting of the shareholders. Persons whose names appear on the corporation's shareholder records as owners are the ones ordinarily entitled to vote.[5] The voting list contains the name and address of each shareholder as shown on the corporate records on a given cutoff date, or record date. (Under RMBCA 7.07, the record date may be as much as seventy days before the meeting.) The voting list also includes the number of voting shares held by each owner. The list is usually kept at the corporate headquarters and is available for shareholder inspection.

Cumulative Voting. Most states permit or even require shareholders to elect directors by *cumulative voting,* a method of voting designed to allow minority shareholders representation on the board of directors.[6] When cumulative voting is allowed or required, the number of members of the board to be elected is multiplied by the number of voting shares a shareholder owns. The result equals the number of votes the shareholder has, and this total can be cast for one or more nominees for director. All nominees stand for election at the same time. When cumulative voting is not required either by statute or under the articles, the entire board can be elected by a simple majority of shares at a shareholders' meeting.

Cumulative voting can best be understood by an example. ● EXAMPLE #4 Suppose that a corporation has 10,000 shares issued and outstanding. One group of shareholders (the minority shareholders) holds only 3,000 shares, and the other group of shareholders (the majority shareholders) holds the other 7,000 shares. Three members of the board are to be elected. The majority shareholders' nominees are

---

[5] When the legal owner is deceased, bankrupt, incompetent, or in some other way under a legal disability, his or her vote can be cast by a person designated by law to control and manage the owner's property.

[6] See, for example, California Corporate Code Section 708. Under RMBCA 7.28, however, no cumulative voting rights exist unless the articles of incorporation so provide.

Acevedo, Barkley, and Craycik. The minority shareholders' nominee is Drake. Can Drake be elected by the minority shareholders?

If cumulative voting is allowed, the answer is yes. The minority shareholders have 9,000 votes among them (the number of directors to be elected times the number of shares held by the minority shareholders equals 3 times 3,000, which equals 9,000 votes). All of these votes can be cast to elect Drake. The majority shareholders have 21,000 votes (3 times 7,000 equals 21,000 votes), but these votes have to be distributed among their three nominees. Under the principle of cumulative voting, no matter how the majority shareholders cast their 21,000 votes, they will not be able to elect all three directors if the minority shareholders cast all of their 9,000 votes for Drake, as illustrated in Exhibit 26–1.●

Other Voting Techniques. Before a shareholders' meeting, a group of shareholders can agree in writing, in a *shareholder voting agreement,* to vote their shares together in a specified manner. Such agreements usually are held to be valid and enforceable. A shareholder can also appoint a voting agent and vote by proxy. As mentioned, a proxy is a written authorization to cast the shareholder's vote, and a person can solicit proxies from a number of shareholders in an attempt to concentrate voting power.

Another technique is for shareholders to enter into a **voting trust,** which is an agreement (a trust contract) under which legal title (record ownership on the corporate books) is transferred to a trustee who is responsible for voting the shares. The agreement can specify how the trustee is to vote, or it can allow the trustee to use his or her discretion. The trustee takes physical possession of the stock certificate and in return gives the shareholder a voting trust certificate. The shareholder retains all of the rights of ownership (for example, the right to receive dividend payments) except for the power to vote the shares.

Rights of Shareholders

Shareholders possess numerous rights. A significant right—the right to vote their shares—has already been discussed. We now look at some additional rights of shareholders.

STOCK CERTIFICATES

A **stock certificate** is a certificate issued by a corporation that evidences ownership of a specified number of shares in the corporation. In jurisdictions that require the issuance of stock certificates, shareholders have the right to demand that the corporation issue certificates. In most states and under RMBCA 6.26, boards of directors may provide that shares of stock be uncertificated—that is, that physical stock certificates need not be issued. In that circumstance, the corporation may be required to send the holders of uncertificated shares letters or some other form of notice containing the same information as that included on stock certificates.

Stock is intangible personal property, and the ownership right exists independently of the certificate itself. A stock certificate may be lost or destroyed, but ownership is not destroyed with it. A new certificate can be issued to replace one that has been lost or destroyed.[7] Notice of shareholders' meetings, dividends, and operational and financial reports are all distributed according to the recorded ownership listed in the corporation's books, not on the basis of possession of the certificate.

---

[7] For a lost or destroyed certificate to be reissued, a shareholder normally must furnish an indemnity bond to protect the corporation against potential loss should the original certificate reappear at some future time in the hands of a bona fide purchaser [UCC 8–302, 8–405(2)].

EXHIBIT 26–1 **RESULTS OF CUMULATIVE VOTING**

This exhibit illustrates how cumulative voting gives minority shareholders a greater chance of electing a director of their choice. By casting all of their 9,000 votes for one candidate (Drake), the minority shareholders will succeed in electing Drake to the board of directors.

BALLOT	MAJORITY SHAREHOLDERS' VOTES			MINORITY SHAREHOLDERS' VOTES	DIRECTORS ELECTED
	Acevedo	Barkley	Craycik	Drake	
1	10,000	10,000	1,000	9,000	Acevedo/Barkley/Drake
2	9,001	9,000	2,999	9,000	Acevedo/Barkley/Drake
3	6,000	7,000	8,000	9,000	Barkley/Craycik/Drake

PREEMPTIVE RIGHTS

A **preemptive right** is a common law concept under which a preference is given to shareholders over all other purchasers to subscribe to or purchase shares of a new issue of stock in proportion to the percentage of total shares they already hold. This allows each shareholder to maintain her or his portion of control, voting power, or financial interest in the corporation. Most statutes either (1) grant preemptive rights but allow them to be negated in the corporation's articles or (2) deny preemptive rights except to the extent that they are granted in the articles. The result is that the articles of incorporation determine the existence and scope of preemptive rights. Generally, preemptive rights apply only to additional, newly issued stock sold for cash, and the preemptive rights must be exercised within a specified time period, which is usually thirty days.

● **EXAMPLE #5** Detering Corporation authorizes and issues 1,000 shares of stock. Lebow purchases 100 shares, making her the owner of 10 percent of the company's stock. Subsequently, Detering, by vote of the shareholders, authorizes the issuance of another 1,000 shares (by amending the articles of incorporation). This increases its capital stock to a total of 2,000 shares. If preemptive rights have been provided, Lebow can purchase one additional share of the new stock being issued for each share she currently owns—or 100 additional shares. Thus, she can own 200 of the 2,000 shares outstanding, and she will maintain her relative position as a shareholder. If preemptive rights are not allowed, her proportionate control and voting power may be diluted from that of a 10 percent shareholder to that of a 5 percent shareholder because of the issuance of the additional 1,000 shares.●

Preemptive rights can be very important for shareholders in close corporations because each shareholder owns a relatively small number of shares but controls a substantial interest in the corporation. Without preemptive rights, it would be possible for a shareholder to lose his or her proportionate control over the firm.

STOCK WARRANTS

Usually, when preemptive rights exist and a corporation is issuing additional shares, each shareholder is given **stock warrants**, which are transferable options to acquire a given number of shares from the corporation at a stated price. Warrants are often publicly traded on securities exchanges. When the option to purchase is in effect for a short period of time, the stock warrants are usually referred to as *rights*.

DIVIDENDS

As mentioned in Chapter 25, a *dividend* is a distribution of corporate profits or income *ordered by the directors* and paid

to the shareholders in proportion to their respective shares in the corporation. Dividends can be paid in cash, property, stock of the corporation that is paying the dividends, or stock of other corporations.[8]

State laws vary, but each state determines the general circumstances and legal requirements under which dividends are paid. State laws also control the sources of revenue to be used; only certain funds are legally available for paying dividends. Depending on state law, dividends may be paid from the following sources:

① *Retained earnings.* All state statutes allow dividends to be paid from the undistributed net profits earned by the corporation, including capital gains from the sale of fixed assets. The undistributed net profits are called retained earnings.

② *Net profits.* A few state statutes allow dividends to be issued from current net profits without regard to deficits in prior years.

③ *Surplus.* A number of statutes allow dividends to be paid out of any surplus.

Illegal Dividends. A dividend paid while the corporation is insolvent is automatically an illegal dividend, and shareholders may be liable for returning the payment to the corporation or its creditors. Furthermore, as just discussed, dividends are generally required by statute to be distributed only from certain authorized corporate accounts. Sometimes, dividends are improperly paid from an unauthorized account, or their payment causes the corporation to become insolvent. Generally, in such cases, shareholders must return illegal dividends only if they knew that the dividends were illegal when they received them. Whenever dividends are illegal or improper, the board of directors can be held personally liable for the amount of the payment. When directors can show that a shareholder knew that a dividend was illegal when it was received, however, the directors are entitled to reimbursement from the shareholder.

Directors' Failure to Declare a Dividend. When directors fail to declare a dividend, shareholders can ask a court to compel the directors to meet and to declare a dividend. For the shareholders to succeed, they must show that the directors have acted so unreasonably in withholding the dividend that the directors' conduct is an abuse of their discretion.

---

[8] Technically, dividends paid in stock are not dividends. They maintain each shareholder's proportional interest in the corporation. On one occasion, a distillery declared and paid a "dividend" in bonded whiskey.

Often, large money reserves are accumulated for a bona fide purpose, such as expansion, research, or other legitimate corporate goals. The mere fact that sufficient corporate earnings or surplus is available to pay a dividend is not enough to compel directors to distribute funds that, in the board's opinion, should not be paid. The courts are reluctant to interfere with corporate operations and will not compel directors to declare dividends unless abuse of discretion is clearly shown.

INSPECTION RIGHTS

Shareholders in a corporation enjoy both common law and statutory inspection rights.[9] The shareholder's right of inspection is limited, however, to the inspection and copying of corporate books and records for a *proper purpose,* provided the request is made in advance. The shareholder can inspect in person, or an attorney, agent, accountant, or other type of assistant can do so. The RMBCA requires the corporation to maintain an alphabetical voting list of shareholders with addresses and number of shares owned; this list must be kept open at the annual meeting for inspection by any shareholder of record [RMBCA 7.20].

The power of inspection is fraught with potential abuses, and the corporation is allowed to protect itself from them. For example, a shareholder can properly be denied access to corporate records to prevent harassment or to protect trade secrets or other confidential corporate information. Some states require that a shareholder must have held his or her shares for a minimum period of time immediately preceding the demand to inspect or must hold a minimum number of outstanding shares. The RMBCA provides, however, that every shareholder is entitled to examine specified corporate records [RMBCA 16.02].

TRANSFER OF SHARES

Stock certificates generally are negotiable and freely transferable by indorsement and delivery. Transfer of stock in closely held corporations, however, usually is restricted by the bylaws, by a restriction stamped on the stock certificate, or by a shareholder agreement (see Chapter 25). The existence of any restrictions on transferability must always be noted on the face of the stock certificate, and these restrictions must be reasonable.

Sometimes, corporations or their shareholders restrict transferability by reserving the option to purchase any shares offered for resale by a shareholder. This **right of first refusal** remains with the corporation or the shareholders

for only a specified time or a reasonable time. Variations on the purchase option are possible. For example, a shareholder might be required to offer the shares to other shareholders first or to the corporation first.

When shares are transferred, a new entry is made in the corporate stock book to indicate the new owner. Until the corporation is notified and the entry is complete, the current owner of record has the right to be notified of (and attend) shareholders' meetings, the right to vote the shares, the right to receive dividends, and all other shareholder rights.

CORPORATE DISSOLUTION

When a corporation is dissolved and its outstanding debts and the claims of its creditors have been satisfied, the remaining assets are distributed to the shareholders in proportion to the percentage of shares owned by each shareholder. Certain classes of preferred stock can be given priority. If no preferences to distribution of assets on liquidation are given to any class of stock, the shareholders are entitled to the remaining assets.

In some circumstances, shareholders may petition a court to have the corporation dissolved. Suppose, for example, that the minority shareholders know that the board of directors is mishandling corporate assets. The minority shareholders are not powerless to intervene. They can petition a court to appoint a **receiver,** who will wind up corporate affairs and liquidate the business assets of the corporation.

The RMBCA permits any shareholder to initiate such an action in any of the following circumstances [RMBCA 14.30]:

① The directors are deadlocked in the management of corporate affairs. The shareholders are unable to break that deadlock, and irreparable injury to the corporation is being suffered or threatened.

② The acts of the directors or those in control of the corporation are illegal, oppressive, or fraudulent.

③ Corporate assets are being misapplied or wasted.

④ The shareholders are deadlocked in voting power and have failed, for a specified period (usually two annual meetings), to elect successors to directors whose terms have expired or would have expired with the election of successors.

THE SHAREHOLDER'S DERIVATIVE SUIT

When those in control of a corporation—the corporate directors—fail to sue in the corporate name to redress a wrong suffered by the corporation, shareholders are permitted to do so "derivatively" in what is known as a **shareholder's derivative suit.** Some wrong must have been done to the

---

9 See, for example, *Schwartzman v. Schwartzman Packing Co.,* 99 N.M. 436, 659 P.2d 888 (1983).

corporation, and before a derivative suit can be brought, the shareholders must first state their complaint to the board of directors. Only if the directors fail to solve the problem or to take appropriate action can the derivative suit go forward.

The right of shareholders to bring a derivative action is especially important when the wrong suffered by the corporation results from the actions of corporate directors or officers. This is because the directors and officers would probably want to prevent any action against themselves.

The shareholder's derivative suit is unusual in that those suing are not pursuing rights or benefits for themselves personally but are acting as guardians of the corporate entity. Therefore, any damages recovered by the suit normally go into the corporation's treasury, not to the shareholders personally. This is true even if the company is a small, closely held corporation. ● **EXAMPLE #6** Suppose that a corporation is owned by two shareholders, each holding 50 percent of the corporate shares. If one of the shareholders wants to sue the other for, say, misusing corporate assets or usurping corporate opportunities, the plaintiff-shareholder would have to bring a shareholder's derivative suit (not a suit in his or her own name) because the harm complained of was suffered by the corporation, not the plaintiff personally. Thus, any damages awarded would go to the corporation, not to the plaintiff-shareholder. While this may seem unfair, there are other interests to consider—including the corporation's creditors, whose claims might not be paid if the damages were awarded to the plaintiff-shareholder and not the corporation. ●

Liability of Shareholders

One of the hallmarks of the corporate organization is that shareholders are not personally liable for the debts of the corporation. If the corporation fails, shareholders can lose their investments, but that is generally the limit of their liability. As discussed in Chapter 25, in certain instances of fraud, undercapitalization, or careless observance of corporate formalities, a court will pierce the corporate veil (disregard the corporate entity) and hold the shareholders individually liable. These situations are the exception, however, not the rule. A shareholder can also be personally liable in certain other rare instances. One relates to illegal dividends, which were discussed previously. Two others relate to stock subscriptions and watered stock, which we discuss here.

Sometimes stock-subscription agreements—written contracts by which one agrees to buy capital stock of a corporation—exist prior to incorporation. Normally, these agreements are treated as continuing offers and are irrevocable (for up to six months under RMBCA 6.20). Once the corporation has been formed, it can sell shares to shareholder investors. In either situation, once the subscription

agreement or stock offer is accepted, a binding contract is formed. Any refusal to pay constitutes a breach resulting in the personal liability of the shareholder.

Shares of stock can be paid for by property or by services rendered instead of cash. They cannot be purchased with promissory notes, however. The general rule is that for **par-value shares** (shares that have a specific face value, or formal cash-in value, written on them, such as one penny or one dollar), the corporation must receive a value at least equal to the par-value amount. For **no-par shares** (shares that have no face value—no specific amount printed on their face), the corporation must receive the value of the shares as determined by the board or the shareholders when the stock was issued. When the corporation issues shares for less than these stated values, the shares are referred to as **watered stock**.[10] Usually, the shareholder who receives watered stock must pay the difference to the corporation (the shareholder is personally liable). In some states, the shareholder who receives watered stock may be liable to creditors of the corporation for unpaid corporate debts.

● **EXAMPLE #7** Suppose that during the formation of a corporation, Gomez, one of the incorporators, transfers his property, Sunset Beach, to the corporation for 10,000 shares of stock. The stock has a par value of $100 per share, and thus the total price of the 10,000 shares is $1 million. After the property is transferred and the shares are issued, Sunset Beach is carried on the corporate books at a value of $1 million. On appraisal, it is discovered that the market value of the property at the time of transfer was only $500,000. The shares issued to Gomez are therefore watered stock, and he is liable to the corporation for the difference. ●

Duties of Majority Shareholders

In some cases, a majority shareholder is regarded as having a fiduciary duty to the corporation and to the minority shareholders. This occurs when a single shareholder (or a few shareholders acting in concert) owns a sufficient number of shares to exercise *de facto* control over the corporation. In these situations, when the majority shareholder sells her or his shares, the shareholder owes a fiduciary duty to the minority shareholders because such a sale is, in fact, a transfer of control of the corporation.

A breach of fiduciary duty also occurs when the majority shareholders of a closely held corporation use their control to their own advantage and exclude the minority from the benefits of participating in the firm unless, of course, there

---

[10] The phrase *watered stock* was originally used to describe cattle that—kept thirsty during a long drive—were allowed to drink large quantities of water just prior to their sale. The increased weight of the "watered stock" allowed the seller to reap a higher profit.

is a genuine business purpose for the exercise of control. Such a breach of fiduciary duties by those who control a closely held corporation normally constitutes what is known as *oppressive conduct*. The court in the following case was asked to examine a pattern of conduct by those in control and determine whether that conduct was oppressive.

CASE 26.3 **Hayes v. Olmsted & Associates, Inc.**

Oregon Court of Appeals, 2001.
173 Or.App. 259,
21 P.3d 178.
**http://www.publications.ojd.state.or.us/
appeals.htm**[a]

FACTS Olmsted & Associates, Inc. (O&A), was a food-brokerage firm in Oregon. Under O&A's bylaws, the board of directors and the shareholders were to hold annual meetings at which the price of O&A stock was to be set. The bylaws also stated that terminated employees were to sell their stock to the firm. The voting shareholders, including David Arbanas, Arthur Olmsted, and Dan Hayes, were also the firm's officers and managers. In 1991, management of the firm was shifted to a "team," which consisted of the voting shareholders and the directors. In 1995, the team implemented a bonus compensation plan. Arbanas took his bonus in cash. During a corporate restructuring, an "Executive Committee," consisting of Arbanas, Olmsted, and two nonshareholders, assumed the functions of the board. The board and the shareholders stopped meeting. Arbanas exchanged his bonus for additional voting shares, and voting control shifted to Olmsted and Arbanas. In 1996, the members of the Executive Committee secretly voted to pay themselves bonuses of more than $100,000 each. Hayes asked about the bonuses, but was denied the information. When he complained, he was fired. O&A offered to buy his stock for $67 per share. Hayes claimed that the price per share was too low. When he was removed from the board, Hayes filed a suit in an Oregon state court against Olmsted, Arbanas, and O&A, alleging, among other things, breach of fiduciary duty and asking that the court determine whether he should have been offered a higher price for his shares. The court declared the price to be $67 per share. Hayes appealed to a state intermediate appellate court, asserting that the price should be higher, in part because Olmsted and Arbanas had engaged in oppressive conduct.

ISSUE Did the majority shareholders act oppressively toward Hayes?

DECISION Yes. The state intermediate appellate court reversed part of the lower court's judgment and remanded the case for the entry of a modified judgment to reflect a higher price for Hayes's stock.

REASON The appellate court concluded that "minority shareholders were not given the formal and required opportunities to participate in or comment upon major changes in direction of O&A." The court explained that "Olmsted and Arbanas assumed control of O&A by creating a *de facto* Executive Committee in violation of the bylaws. From 1995 to 1997, when plaintiff was fired, the Executive Committee did not observe corporate formalities and failed to hold regular meetings of the corporation's Board of Directors and shareholders. Executive Committee members paid themselves bonuses that were not authorized by or reported to the Board of Directors, also in violation of the bylaws. They kept their bonuses secret from the other shareholders and board members, despite plaintiff's requests for the bonus information, again in violation of the bylaws. . . . When plaintiff complained about his exclusion from corporate decisions and information, the Executive Committee fired him."

FOR CRITICAL ANALYSIS—Economic Consideration
What should be the basis for a "fair and reasonable" price for minority shareholders' stock in a case involving oppressive conduct by majority shareholders?

---

a. Click on "Cases decided in 2001." In the result, in the "03/28/01" section, click on the name of the case to access the opinion. The Oregon Judicial Department maintains this Web site.

Major Business Forms Compared

As mentioned in Chapter 24, when deciding which form of business organization would be most appropriate, businesspersons normally consider several factors, including ease of creation, the liability of the owners, tax ramifications, and the need for capital. Each major form of business organization offers distinct advantages and disadvantages with respect to these and other factors. Exhibit 26–2 on pages 558 and 559 summarizes the essential advantages and disadvantages of each of the forms of business organization discussed in Chapters 24 and 25, as well as in this chapter.

EXHIBIT 26–2 MAJOR FORMS OF BUSINESS COMPARED

CHARACTERISTIC	SOLE PROPRIETORSHIP	PARTNERSHIP	CORPORATION
Method of Creation	Created at will by owner.	Created by agreement of the parties.	Charter issued by state—created by statutory authorization.
Legal Position	Not a separate entity; owner is the business.	Not a separate legal entity in many states.	Always a legal entity separate and distinct from its owners—a legal fiction for the purposes of owning property and being a party to litigation.
Liability	Unlimited liability.	Unlimited liability.	Limited liability of shareholders—shareholders are not liable for the debts of the corporation.
Duration	Determined by owner; automatically dissolved on owner's death.	Terminated by agreement of the partners, by the death of one or more of the partners, by withdrawal of a partner, by bankruptcy, and so on.	Can have perpetual existence.
Transferability of Interest	Interest can be transferred, but individual's proprietorship then ends.	Although partnership interest can be assigned, assignee does not have full rights of a partner.	Shares of stock can be transferred.
Management	Completely at owner's discretion.	Each general partner has a direct and equal voice in management unless expressly agreed otherwise in the partnership agreement.	Shareholders elect directors, who set policy and appoint officers.
Taxation	Owner pays personal taxes on business income.	Each partner pays pro rata share of income taxes on net profits, whether or not they are distributed.	Double taxation—corporation pays income tax on net profits, with no deduction for dividends, and shareholders pay income tax on disbursed dividends they receive.
Organizational Fees, Annual License Fees, and Annual Reports	None.	None.	All required.
Transaction of Business in Other States	Generally no limitation.	Generally no limitation.[a]	Normally must qualify to do business and obtain certificate of authority.

a. A few states have enacted statutes requiring that foreign partnerships must register to do business there.

EXHIBIT 26–2 MAJOR FORMS OF BUSINESS COMPARED—CONTINUED

CHARACTERISTIC	LIMITED PARTNERSHIP	LIMITED LIABILITY COMPANY	LIMITED LIABILITY PARTNERSHIP
Method of Creation	Created by agreement to carry on a business for profit. At least one party must be a general partner and the other(s) limited partner(s). Certificate of limited partnership is filed. Charter must be issued by the state.	Created by an agreement of the owner-members of the company. Articles of organization are filed. Charter must be issued by the state.	Created by agreement of the partners. Certificate of a limited liability partnership is filed. Charter must be issued by state.
Legal Position	Treated as a legal entity.	Treated as a legal entity.	Generally, treated same as a general partnership.
Liability	Unlimited liability of all general partners; limited partners are liable only to the extent of capital contributions.	Member-owners' liability is limited to the amount of capital contributions or investment.	Varies from state to state, but liability of a partner for certain acts committed by other partners is usually limited.
Duration	By agreement in certificate, or by termination of the last general partner (withdrawal, death, and so on) or last limited partner.	Unless a single-member LLC, can have perpetual existence (same as a corporation).	Terminated by agreement of partners, by death or withdrawal of a partner, or by law (such as bankruptcy).
Transferability of Interest	Interest can be assigned (same as general partnership), but if assignee becomes a member with consent of other partners, certificate must be amended.	Member interests are freely transferable.	Interest can be assigned same as in a general partnership.
Management	General partners have equal voice or by agreement. Limited partners may not retain limited liability if they actively participate in management.	Member-owners can fully participate in management, or management is selected by owner-members who manage on behalf of the members.	Same as a general partnership.
Taxation	Generally taxed as a partnership.	LLC is not taxed, and members are taxed personally on profits "passed through" the LCC.	Same as a general partnership.
Organizational Fees, Annual License Fees, and Annual Reports	Organizational fee required; usually not others.	Organizational fee required; others vary with states.	Organizational fee required (such as a set amount per partner); usually not others.
Transaction of Business in Other States	Generally, no limitations.	Generally, no limitation, but may vary depending on state.	Generally, no limitation, but state laws vary as to formation and limitation of liability.

Terms and Concepts

business judgment rule   550
no-par share   556
par-value share   556
preemptive right   554
proxy   551

quorum   547
receiver   555
right of first refusal   555
shareholder's derivative suit   555
stock certificate   553

stock warrant   554
tender offer   549
voting trust   553
watered stock   556

Chapter Summary — Corporate Directors, Officers, and Shareholders

Role of Directors (See pages 545–548.)	1. *Election of directors*—The first board of directors is usually appointed by the incorporators; thereafter, directors are elected by the shareholders. Directors usually serve a one-year term, although the term can be longer, and staggered terms are permitted under most state statutes. 2. *Directors' qualifications and compensation*—Few qualifications are required; a director can be a shareholder but is not required to be. Compensation is usually specified in the corporate articles or bylaws. 3. *Board of directors' meetings*—The board of directors conducts business by holding formal meetings with recorded minutes. The date of regular meetings is usually established in the corporate articles or bylaws; special meetings can be called, with notice sent to all directors. Quorum requirements vary from state to state; usually, a quorum is a majority of the corporate directors. Voting must usually be done in person, and in ordinary matters only a majority vote is required. 4. *Rights of directors*—Directors' rights include the rights of participation, inspection, compensation, and indemnification. 5. *Directors' management responsibilities*—Directors are responsible for declaring and paying corporate dividends to shareholders; authorizing major corporate decisions; appointing, supervising, and removing corporate officers and other managerial employees; determining employees' compensation; making financial decisions necessary to the management of corporate affairs; and issuing authorized shares and bonds. Directors may delegate some of their responsibilities to executive committees and corporate officers and executives.
Role of Corporate Officers and Executives (See page 548.)	Corporate officers and other executive employees are normally hired by the board of directors. In most states, a person can hold more than one office and can be both an officer and a director of a corporation. The rights of corporate officers and executives are defined by employment contracts. The duties of corporate officers are the same as those of directors.
Duties of Directors and Officers (See pages 548–550.)	1. *Duty of care*—Directors are obligated to act in good faith, to use prudent business judgment in the conduct of corporate affairs, and to act in the corporation's best interests. If a director fails to exercise this duty of care, he or she can be answerable to the corporation and to the shareholders for breaching the duty. 2. *Duty of loyalty*—Directors have a fiduciary duty to subordinate their own interests to those of the corporation in matters relating to the corporation. 3. *Conflicts of interest*—To fulfill their duty of loyalty, directors and officers must make a full disclosure of any potential conflicts of interest between their personal interests and those of the corporation.

Chapter Summary	**Corporate Directors, Officers, and Shareholders—Continued**
Liability of Directors and Officers (See pages 550–551.)	Corporate directors and officers are personally liable for their own torts and crimes; additionally, they may be held personally liable for the torts and crimes committed by corporate personnel under their direct supervision (see Chapters 6 and 22). The *business judgment rule* immunizes a director from liability for a corporate decision as long as the decision was within the power of the corporation and the authority of the director to make, and the decision was informed, reasonable, and loyal.

Role of Shareholders (See pages 551–553.)	1. *Shareholders' powers*—Shareholders' powers include the approval of all fundamental changes affecting the corporation and the election of the board of directors.
	
	 2. *Shareholders' meetings*—Shareholders' meetings must occur at least annually; special meetings can be called when necessary. Notice of the date, time, and place of the meeting (and its purpose, if it is specially called) must be sent to shareholders. Shareholders may vote by proxy (authorizing someone else to vote their shares) and may submit proposals to be included in the company's proxy materials sent to shareholders before meetings.
	
	 3. *Shareholder voting*—Shareholder voting requirements and procedures are as follows:
	
	    a. A minimum number of shareholders (a quorum—generally, more than 50 percent of shares held) must be present at a meeting for business to be conducted; resolutions are passed (usually) by simple majority vote.
	
	    b. The corporation must prepare voting lists of shareholders on record prior to each shareholders' meeting.
	
	    c. Cumulative voting may or may not be required or permitted. Cumulative voting gives minority shareholders a better chance to be represented on the board of directors.
	
	    d. A shareholder voting agreement (an agreement of shareholders to vote their shares together) is usually held to be valid and enforceable.
	
	    e. A shareholder may appoint a proxy (substitute) to vote her or his shares.
	
	    f. A shareholder may enter into a voting trust agreement by which title (record ownership) of his or her shares is given to a trustee, and the trustee votes the shares in accordance with the trust agreement.

Rights of Shareholders (See page 553–556.)	Shareholders have numerous rights, which may include the following: 1. The right to a stock certificate, preemptive rights, and the right to stock warrants (depending on the corporate charter). 2. The right to obtain a dividend (at the discretion of the directors). 3. Voting rights. 4. The right to inspect the corporate records. 5. The right to transfer shares (this right may be restricted in close corporations). 6. The right to a share of corporate assets when the corporation is dissolved. 7. The right to sue on behalf of the corporation (bring a shareholder's derivative suit) when the directors fail to do so.
Liability of Shareholders (See page 556.)	Shareholders may be liable for the retention of illegal dividends, for breach of a stock-subscription agreement, and for the value of watered stock.
Duties of Majority Shareholders (See pages 556–557.)	In certain situations, majority shareholders may be regarded as having a fiduciary duty to minority shareholders and will be liable if that duty is breached.

For Review

① What are the duties of corporate directors and officers?

② Directors are expected to use their best judgment in managing the corporation. What must directors do to avoid liability for honest mistakes of judgment and poor business decisions?

③ What is a voting proxy? What is cumulative voting?

④ If a group of shareholders perceives that the corporation has suffered a wrong and the directors refuse to take action, can the shareholders compel the directors to act? If so, how?

⑤ From what sources may dividends be paid legally? In what circumstances is a dividend illegal? What happens if a dividend is illegally paid?

Questions and Case Problems

26–1. Rights of Shareholders. Dmitri has acquired one share of common stock of a multimillion-dollar corporation with over 500,000 shareholders. Dmitri's ownership is so small that he is questioning what his rights are as a shareholder. For example, he wants to know whether this one share entitles him to attend and vote at shareholders' meetings, inspect the corporate books, and receive periodic dividends. Discuss Dmitri's rights in these matters.

26–2. Voting Techniques. Algonquin Corp. has issued and has outstanding 100,000 shares of common stock. Four stockholders own 60,000 of these shares, and for the past six years they have nominated a slate of people for membership on the board, all of whom have been elected. Sergio and twenty other shareholders, owning 20,000 shares, are dissatisfied with corporate management and want a representative on the board who shares their views. Explain under what circumstances Sergio and the minority shareholders can elect their representative to the board.

26–3. Duties of Directors. Starboard, Inc., has a board of directors consisting of three members (Ellsworth, Green, and Morino) and approximately five hundred shareholders. At a regular meeting of the board, the board selects Tyson as president of the corporation by a two-to-one vote, with Ellsworth dissenting. The minutes of the meeting do not register Ellsworth's dissenting vote. Later, during an audit, it is discovered that Tyson is a former convict and has openly embezzled $500,000 from Starboard. This loss is not covered by insurance. The corporation wants to hold directors Ellsworth, Green, and Morino liable. Ellsworth claims no liability. Discuss the personal liability of the directors to the corporation.

26–4. Liability of Shareholders. Mallard has made a preincorporation subscription agreement to purchase 500 shares of a newly formed corporation. The shares have a par value of $100 per share. The corporation is formed, and it accepts Mallard's subscription. Mallard transfers a piece of land he owns to the corporation as payment for 250 of the shares, and the corporation issues 250 shares for it. Mallard pays for the other 250 shares with cash. One year later, with the corporation in serious financial difficulty, the board declares and pays a $5-per-share dividend. It is now learned that the land transferred by Mallard had a market value of $18,000. Discuss any liability that shareholder Mallard has to the corporation or to the creditors of the corporation.

26–5. Duties of Directors. Overland Corp. is negotiating with Wharton Construction Co. for the renovation of Overland's corporate headquarters. Wharton, the owner of Wharton Construction, is also one of the five members of the board of directors of Overland. The contract terms are standard for this type of contract. Wharton has previously informed two of the other Overland directors of his interest in the construction company. Overland's board approves the contract on a three-to-two vote, with Wharton voting with the majority. Discuss whether this contract is binding on the corporation.

26–6. Duty of Loyalty. Mackinac Cellular Corp. offered to sell Robert Broz a license to operate a cellular phone system in Michigan. Broz was a director of Cellular Information Systems, Inc. (CIS). CIS, as a result of bankruptcy proceedings, was in the process of selling its cellular holdings. Broz did not formally present the opportunity to the CIS board, but he told some of the firm's officers and directors, who replied that CIS was not interested. At the time, PriCellular, Inc., a firm that was interested in the Michigan license, was attempting to buy CIS. Without telling PriCellular, Broz bought the license himself. After PriCellular took over CIS, the company filed a suit in a Delaware state court against Broz, alleging that he had usurped a corporate opportunity. For what reasons might a court decide that Broz had done nothing wrong? Discuss. [*Broz v. Cellular Information Systems, Inc.*, 673 A.2d 148 (Del. 1996)]

26–7. Business Judgment Rule. The board of directors of Baltimore Gas and Electric Company (BGE) recommended a merger with Potomac Electric Power Company (PEPCO). After full disclosure, the BGE shareholders approved the merger. On the ground that each BGE director stood a chance of being named to the new company's board, Janice Wittman, a BGE shareholder, filed a suit in a Maryland state court against the directors, alleging, among other things, that they were prohibited from deciding whether to recommend the merger. Did the directors breach their duty of care by voting in favor of the merger? How should the court rule? Discuss. [*Wittman v. Crooke,* 120 Md.App. 369, 707 A.2d 422 (1998)]

26–8. Business Judgment Rule. Charles Pace and Maria Fuentez were shareholders of Houston Industries, Inc. (HII), and employees of Houston Lighting & Power, a subsidiary of HII, when they lost their jobs because of a company-wide reduction in its work force. Pace, as a shareholder, three times wrote to HII, demanding that the board of directors terminate certain HII directors and officers and file a suit to recover damages for breach of fiduciary duty. Three times, the directors referred the charges to board committees and an outside law firm, which found that the facts did not support the charges. The board also received input from federal regulatory authorities about the facts behind some of the charges. The board notified Pace that it was refusing his demands. In response, Pace and Fuentez filed a shareholder's derivative suit in a Texas state court against Don Jordan and the other HII directors, contending that the board's investigation was inadequate. The defendants filed a motion for summary judgment, arguing that the suit was barred by the business judgment rule. Are the defendants right? How should the court rule? Why? [*Pace v. Jordan,* 999 S.W.2d 615 (Tex.App.—Houston [1 Dist.] 1999)]

CASE PROBLEM WITH SAMPLE ANSWER

26–9. Atlas Food Systems & Services, Inc., based in South Carolina, was a food vending service that provided refreshments to factories and other businesses. Atlas was a closely held corporation. John Kiriakides was a minority shareholder of Atlas. Alex Kiriakides was the majority shareholder. Throughout most of Atlas's history, Alex was the chairman of the board, which included John as a director. In 1995, while John was the president of the firm, the board and shareholders decided to convert Atlas to an S corporation. A few months later, however, Alex, without calling a vote, decided that the firm would not convert. In 1996, a dispute arose over Atlas's contract to buy certain property. John and others decided not to buy it. Without consulting anyone, Alex elected to go through with the sale. Within a few days, Alex refused to allow John to stay on as president. Two months later, Atlas offered to buy John's interest in the firm for almost $2 million. John refused, believing the offer was too low. John filed a suit in a South Carolina state court against Atlas and Alex, seeking, among other things, to force a buyout of John's shares. On what basis might the court grant John's request? Discuss. [*Kiriakides v. Atlas Food Systems & Services, Inc.,* 541 S.E.2d 257 (S.C. 2001)]

◗ To view a sample answer for this case problem, go to this book's Web site at **http://fundamentals.westbuslaw.com** and click on "Interactive Study Center."

26–10. Inspection Rights. Craig Johnson founded Distributed Solutions, Inc. (DSI), in 1991 to make software and provide consulting services, including payroll services for small companies. Johnson was the sole officer and director and the majority shareholder. Jeffrey Hagen was a minority shareholder. In 1993, Johnson sold DSI's payroll services to himself and a few others and set up Distributed Payroll Solutions, Inc. (DPSI). In 1996, DSI had revenues of $739,034 and assets of $541,168. DSI's revenues in 1997 were $934,532. Within a year, however, all of DSI's assets were sold, and Johnson told Hagen that he was dissolving the firm because, in part, it conducted no business and had no prospects for future clients. Hagen asked for corporate records to determine the value of DSI's stock, DSI's financial condition, and "whether unauthorized and oppressive acts had occurred in connection with the operation of the corporation which impacted the value of" the stock. When there was no response, Hagen filed a suit in an Illinois state court against DSI and Johnson, seeking an order to compel the inspection. The defendants filed a motion to dismiss, arguing that Hagen had failed to plead a proper purpose. Should the court grant Hagen's request? Discuss. [*Hagen v. Distributed Solutions, Inc.,* 328 Ill.App.3d 132, 764 N.E.2d 1141, 262 Ill.Dec. 24 (1 Dist. 2002)]

VIDEO QUESTION

26–11. Go to this text's Web site at **http://fundamentals.westbuslaw.com** and click on "Video Questions." Select "Chapter 26" and view the video titled *Corporation or LLC: Which Is Better?* Then answer the following questions:

1. Compare the liability that Anna and Caleb would be exposed to as shareholders/owners in a coporation versus as members in a limited liability company (LLC).

2. How are corporations taxed differently than LLCs?

3. Given that Anna and Caleb conduct their business (Wizard Internet) over the Internet, can you think of any drawbacks to becoming an LLC?

4. Suppose that you were in the position of Anna and Caleb. Would you choose to create a corporation or an LLC? Why?

CORPORATE DIRECTORS, OFFICERS, AND SHAREHOLDERS

For updated links to resources available on the Web, as well as other materials, visit this text's Web site at

http://fundamentals.westbuslaw.com

One of the best sources on the Web for information on corporations, including their directors, is the EDGAR database of the Securities and Exchange Commission at

http://www.sec.gov/edgar.shtml

In a review of major cases to come before the New York Court of Appeals, Stewart E. Sterk discusses a leading case on the duties owed by majority shareholders to minority shareholders. Go to

http://www6.law.com/ny/links/150sterk.html

You can find definitions of terms used in corporate law, as well as court decisions and articles on corporate law, at

http://www.law.com

Online Legal Research

Go to the *Fundamentals of Business Law* home page at **http://fundamentals. westbuslaw.com**. Select "Interactive Study Center" and then click on "Chapter 26." There you will find the following Internet research exercises that you can perform to learn more about topics covered in this chapter.

Activity 26–1: Legal Perspective—Liability of Directors and Officers
Activity 26–2: Management Perspective—D&O Insurance

Before the Test

Go to the *Fundamentsls of Business Law* home page at **http://fundamentals. westbuslaw.com**. Click on "Interactive Quizzes." You will find at least twenty interactive questions relating to this chapter.

Westlaw® Campus

If your textbook provided for a subscription to Westlaw® Campus, or if you have otherwise purchased access to the Westlaw Campus database, you can access any of the cases presented or cited in this chapter by using your Westlaw Campus account.

27

Investor Protection and Online Securities Offerings

CHAPTER OBJECTIVES

After reading this chapter, you should be able to answer the following questions:

① What is meant by the term *securities*?

② What are the two major statutes regulating the securities industry? When was the Securities and Exchange Commission created, and what are its major purposes and functions?

③ What is insider trading? Why is it prohibited?

④ What are some of the features of state securities laws?

⑤ How are securities laws being applied in the online environment?

The stock market crash of October 29, 1929, and the ensuing economic depression caused the public to focus on the importance of securities markets for the economic well-being of the nation. Congress was pressured to regulate securities trading, and the result was the Securities Act of 1933[1] and the Securities Exchange Act of 1934.[2] Both acts were designed to provide investors with more information to help them make buying and selling decisions about securities—generally defined as any documents evidencing corporate ownership (stock) or debts (bonds)—and to prohibit deceptive, unfair, and manipulative practices in the purchase and sale of securities. Today, the sale and transfer of securities are heavily regulated by federal and state statutes and by government agencies.

This chapter discusses the nature of federal securities regulation and its effect on the business world. We begin by looking at the federal administrative agency that regulates securities transactions, the Securities and Exchange Commission. Next, we discuss the Sarbanes-Oxley Act, which was passed by Congress in 2002 and which will have a significant impact on certain types of securities transactions. We then examine the major traditional laws governing securities offerings and trading. The online world has brought some dramatic changes to securities offerings and regulation. In the concluding pages of this chapter, we look at how securities laws are being adapted to the online environment.

---

[1] 15 U.S.C. Sections 77a–77aa.
[2] 15 U.S.C. Sections 78a–78mm.

The Securities and Exchange Commission

The 1934 act created the Securities and Exchange Commission (SEC) as an independent regulatory agency whose function was to administer the 1933 and 1934 acts. The SEC plays a key role in interpreting the provisions of these acts (and their amendments) and in creating regulations governing the purchase and sale of securities.

THE BASIC FUNCTIONS OF THE SEC

The SEC regulates the securities industry by undertaking the following activities:

① Requiring disclosure of facts concerning offerings of securities listed on national securities exchanges and offerings of certain securities traded over the counter (OTC).

② Regulating the trade in securities on the national and regional securities exchanges and in the OTC markets.

③ Investigating securities fraud.

④ Requiring the registration of securities brokers, dealers, and investment advisers and regulating their activities.

⑤ Supervising activities conducted by mutual funds companies.

⑥ Recommending administrative sanctions, injunctive remedies, and criminal prosecution in cases involving violations of securities laws. (The Fraud Section of the Criminal Division of the U.S. Department of Justice prosecutes violations of federal securities laws.)

THE EXPANDING REGULATORY POWERS OF THE SEC

Since its creation, the SEC's regulatory functions have gradually been increased by legislation granting it authority in different areas. A number of amendments during the 1990s significantly enlarged the regulatory powers of the SEC. In the 2002 legislation mentioned earlier, Congress again expanded the regulatory scope of the SEC. Since the early 1990s, Congress has passed five acts that have significantly expanded the SEC's powers:

① *The Penny Stock Reform Act of 1990.*[3] This act amended existing securities laws to allow SEC administrative law judges to hear many more types of securities violation cases and to greatly expand the SEC's enforcement options. The act also provides that courts can prevent persons who have engaged in securities fraud from serving as officers and directors of publicly held corporations. (Note that the Sarbanes-Oxley Act of 2002 also has provisions to this effect.)

② *The Securities Acts Amendments of 1990.*[4] These amendments authorized the SEC to seek sanctions against those who violate foreign securities laws.

③ *The Market Reform Act of 1990.*[5] Under this act, the SEC can suspend trading in securities in the event that prices rise and fall excessively in a short period of time.

④ *The National Securities Markets Improvement Act of 1996.*[6] This act expanded the power of the SEC to exempt persons, securities, and transactions from the requirements of the securities laws. (This part of the act is also known as the Capital Markets Efficiency Act.) The act also limited the authority of the states to regulate certain securities transactions, as well as particular investment advisory firms.[7]

⑤ *The Sarbanes-Oxley Act of 2002.*[8] As will be discussed shortly, this act represents a sweeping revision of federal securities laws. Among other things, this act further expanded the authority of the SEC by directing the agency to issue new rules relating to corporate disclosure requirements and by creating an SEC oversight board.

STREAMLINING THE REGULATORY PROCESS

For years, Congress and the SEC have been attempting to streamline the regulatory process generally. The goal is to make the process more efficient and more relevant to today's securities trading practices, including those occurring in the online environment. Another goal is to create more oversight over securities transactions and accounting practices. Additionally, as the number and types of online securities frauds increase, the SEC is trying to keep pace by expanding its online fraud division.

The Sarbanes-Oxley Act of 2002

In 2002, following a series of corporate scandals, Congress passed the Sarbanes-Oxley Act, which some regard as one of the most significant modifications of securities regulation since the 1930s. Generally, the act attempts to increase corporate accountability by imposing stricter disclosure requirements and harsher penalties for violations of securities laws. Among other things, the act requires chief corporate executives to take responsibility for the accuracy of financial statements and reports that are filed with the SEC. Chief executive

---

[3] 15 U.S.C. Section 77g.

[4] 15 U.S.C. Section 78a.
[5] 15 U.S.C. Section 78i(h).
[6] 15 U.S.C. Sections 77z-3, 78mm.
[7] 15 U.S.C. Section 80b-3a.
[8] H.R. 3762. This act was signed by President George W. Bush on July 30, 2002, and became effective on August 29, 2002.

officers and chief financial officers personally must certify that the statements and reports are accurate and complete.

Additionally, the new rules require that certain financial and stock-transaction reports must be filed with the SEC earlier than was required under the previous rules. The act also mandates SEC oversight over a new entity, called the Public Company Accounting Oversight Board, that will reg-ulate and oversee public accounting firms. Other provisions of the act create new private civil actions and expand the SEC's remedies in administrative and civil actions.

Because of the importance of this act for corporate lead-ers and for those dealing with securities transactions, we present some of the act's key provisions relating to corpo-rate accountability in Exhibit 27–1. Provisions of the act

---

EXHIBIT 27–1 **SOME KEY PROVISIONS OF THE SARBANES-OXLEY ACT OF 2002 RELATING TO CORPORATE ACCOUNTABILITY**

Certification Requirements—Under Section 906 of the Sarbanes-Oxley Act, the chief executive officers (CEOs) and chief financial officers (CFOs) of most major companies listed on public stock exchanges must now certify financial statements that are filed with the SEC. For virtually all filed financial reports, CEOs and CFOs have to certify that such reports "fully comply" with SEC requirements and that all of the information reported "fairly represents in all material respects, the financial conditions and results of operations of the issuer." Under Section 302 of the act, CEOs and CFOs of reporting companies are required to certify, for each quarterly and annual filing with the SEC, the following:

- That a signing officer reviewed the report.
- That to the best of the signing officer's knowledge, the report contains no untrue statements of material fact and does not omit statements of material fact.
- That the signing officer or officers have established an internal control system designed to ensure discovery of material information that should be in the report.
- That the signing officer disclosed to the auditors any significant deficiencies in the internal control system.

Loans to Directors and Officers—To prevent companies from making loans to corporate officers and later forgiving those loans (to the detriment of shareholders), the Sarbanes-Oxley Act included a provision targeting this practice. Section 402 of the act prohibits any reporting company, as well as any private company that is filing an initial public offering, from extending, renewing, arranging, or maintaining personal loans to directors and executive officers. There are some exceptions under the act for certain consumer and housing loans.

Protection for Whistleblowers—The Sarbanes-Oxley Act also offers protection for "whistleblowers"—those employees who report ("blow the whistle" on) wrongdoing by their employers. Section 806 of the act prohibits publicly traded companies from discharging, demoting, suspending, threatening, harassing, or otherwise discriminating against an employee who provides information to the government or assists in any government investigation regarding conduct that the employee reasonably believes constitutes a violation of securities laws.

Blackout Periods—Rules established under Section 306 of the act prohibit certain types of securities transactions during "blackout periods"—periods during which the issuer's ability to purchase, sell, or otherwise transfer funds in individual account plans (such as pension funds) is suspended.

Enhanced Penalties—
- *Violations of Section 906 Certification Requirements*—A CEO or CFO who certifies a financial report or statement to be filed with the SEC knowing that the report or statement does not fulfill all of the requirements of Section 906 will be subject to criminal penalties up to $1 million in fines, up to ten years in prison, or both. Moreover, if a CEO or CFO "willfully" certifies a report knowing that it does not comport with all of the requirements of Section 906, the penalty can extend to up to $5 million in fines, twenty years in prison, or both.
- *Violations of the Securities Exchange Act of 1934*—Penalties for securities fraud under the Securities Exchange Act of 1934 were also increased (see the discussion of these penalties later in this chapter).
- *Destruction or Alteration of Documents*—The act provides that anyone who alters, destroys, or conceals documents or other-wise obstructs or impedes any official proceeding will be subject to fines, imprisonment for up to twenty years, or both.
- *Other Forms of White-Collar Crime*—The act also stiffened the criminal penalties for violations of federal mail and wire fraud laws (see Chapter 6) and the Employment Retirement Income Security Act of 1974 (see Chapter 23). The act orders the U.S. Sentencing Commission (discussed in Chapter 6) to revise the sentencing guidelines for white-collar crimes to conform with the provisions of the Sarbanes-Oxley Act.

Statute of Limitations for Securities Fraud—Section 804 of the act provides that a private right of action for securities fraud may be brought no later than two years after the discovery of the violation or five years after the violation, whichever is earlier.

that relate to public accounting firms and accounting practices will be discussed in Chapter 31, in the context of the liability of accountants.

Securities Act of 1933

The Securities Act of 1933[9] was designed to prohibit various forms of fraud and to stabilize the securities industry by requiring that all relevant information concerning the issuance of securities be made available to the investing public. Essentially, the purpose of this act is to require disclosure.

WHAT IS A SECURITY?

Section 2(1) of the Securities Act states that securities include the following:

> [A]ny note, stock, treasury stock, bond, debenture, evidence of indebtedness, certificate of interest or participation in any profit-sharing agreement, collateral-trust certificate, preorganization certificate or subscription, transferable share, investment contract, voting-trust certificate, certificate of deposit for a security, fractional undivided interest in oil, gas, or other mineral rights, or, in general, any interest or instrument commonly known as a "security," or any certificate of interest or participation in, temporary or interim certificate for, receipt

---

[9] 15 U.S.C. Sections 77–77aa.

for, guarantee of, or warrant or right to subscribe to or purchase, any of the foregoing.[10]

Generally, the courts have interpreted the Securities Act's definition of what constitutes a security[11] to include investment contracts. An investment contract is any transaction in which a person (1) invests (2) in a common enterprise (3) reasonably expecting profits (4) derived *primarily* or *substantially* from others' managerial or entrepreneurial efforts.[12]

For our purposes, it is probably convenient to think of securities in their most common forms—stocks and bonds issued by corporations. Bear in mind, however, that securities can take many forms and have been held to include whiskey, cosmetics, worms, beavers, boats, vacuum cleaners, muskrats, and cemetery lots, as well as investment contracts in condominiums, franchises, limited partnerships, oil or gas or other mineral rights, and farm animals accompanied by care agreements. (Whether ownership interests in limited liability companies are securities is a question explored in this chapter's *Management Perspective* on page 570.)

In the following case, the question was whether sales of pay phones and agreements to service the phones constituted sales of securities.

---

[10] 15 U.S.C. Section 77b(1). Amendments in 1982 added stock options.
[11] See 15 U.S.C. Section 77b(a)(1).
[12] *SEC v. W. J. Howey Co.*, 328 U.S. 293, 66 S.Ct. 1100, 90 L.Ed. 1244 (1946).

CASE 27.1 **SEC v. Alpha Telcom, Inc.**

United States District Court,
District of Oregon, 2002.
187 F.Supp.2d 1250.

FACTS Paul Rubera started Alpha Telcom, Inc., in 1986 to sell, install, and maintain phones and business systems in Grants Pass, Oregon. In 1997, Alpha began to sell pay phones to buyers, most of whom also entered into service agreements with Alpha. Most of these buyers selected a "Level Four Service Agreement," which required Alpha to select a location for a phone, install it, obtain all licenses, maintain and clean the phone, pay the bills, and collect the revenue. Buyers were guaranteed—and were paid—a 14 percent return on the amount of their purchase. The pay-phone program was presented and promoted through American Telecommunications Company (ATC), Alpha's marketing subsidiary. From July 1998 through June 2001, Alpha's expenses for the program were $21,798,000, while revenues were

$21,698,000. Despite the loss, Alpha paid investors approximately $17.9 million. To make these payments, Alpha borrowed money from ATC. Alpha filed for bankruptcy in August 2001. The Securities and Exchange Commission (SEC) filed a suit in a federal district court against Alpha and Rubera, alleging violations of the Securities Act of 1933. The defendants argued that the pay-phone program did not involve sales of securities.

ISSUE Was the pay-phone program a security?

DECISION Yes. The court concluded that the pay-phone program was a security because it involved an investment contract, which is a contract that is "(1) an investment of money; (2) in a common enterprise; (3) with the expectation of profits to be derived from the efforts of others." The court issued an injunction to prohibit further violations of the Securities Act of 1933 and ordered Rubera to disgorge profits of more than $3.7 million, plus interest.

CASE 27.1—Continued

REASON Regarding the individual elements of the definition of "an investment contract," the court reasoned that "[t]he investors make cash investments with the expectation of receiving profits. * * * Investors relied on the expertise of Alpha," as a common enterprise, to do all of the work, including making all of the business decisions with regard to the phones. Also, "ATC's only source of revenue was money from new investors. As a result, new investor money was being used to pay returns to existing investors," and "[i]nvestors would receive their 14 percent return * * *

regardless of whether their particular phone actually generated that much money." Finally, "Alpha was ultimately responsible for those essential managerial efforts [that] affect the failure or success of the enterprise, and the investors retained no control over the business."

FOR CRITICAL ANALYSIS—Social Consideration
The court also noted that 90 percent of the investors chose Alpha as their service provider. Does this fact have any bearing on the question of whether the pay-phone program was an investment contract?

REGISTRATION STATEMENT

Section 5 of the Securities Act of 1933 broadly provides that if a security does not qualify for an exemption, that security must be *registered* before it is offered to the public either through the mails or through any facility of interstate commerce, including securities exchanges. Issuing corporations must file a *registration statement* with the SEC. Investors must be provided with a prospectus that describes the security being sold, the issuing corporation, and the investment or risk attaching to the security. In principle, the registration statement and the prospectus supply sufficient information to enable unsophisticated investors to evaluate the financial risk involved.

Contents of the Registration Statement. The registration statement must include the following:

① A description of the significant provisions of the security offered for sale, including the relationship between that security and the other capital securities of the registrant. Also, the corporation must disclose how it intends to use the proceeds of the sale.

② A description of the registrant's properties and business.

③ A description of the management of the registrant and its security holdings; remuneration; and other benefits, including pensions and stock options. Any interests of directors or officers in any material transactions with the corporation must be disclosed.

④ A financial statement certified by an independent public accounting firm.

⑤ A description of pending lawsuits.

Those who register securities offerings with the SEC should realize that as of 1998, the SEC requires certain documents, or portions of documents, to be written in "plain English."

Other Requirements. Before filing the registration statement and the prospectus with the SEC, the corporation is allowed to obtain an *underwriter*—a company that agrees to purchase the new issue of securities for resale to the public. There is a twenty-day waiting period (which can be accelerated by the SEC) after registration before the securities can be sold. During this period, oral offers between interested investors and the issuing corporation concerning the purchase and sale of the proposed securities may take place, and very limited written advertising is allowed. At this time, the so-called **red herring** prospectus may be distributed. It gets its name from the red legend printed across it stating that the registration has been filed but has not become effective.

After the waiting period, the registered securities can be legally bought and sold. Written advertising is allowed in the form of a **tombstone ad,** so named because historically the format resembled a tombstone. Such ads simply tell the investor where and how to obtain a prospectus. Normally, any other type of advertising is prohibited.

EXEMPT SECURITIES

A number of specific securities are exempt from the registration requirements of the Securities Act of 1933. These securities—which can also generally be resold without being registered—include the following:[13]

① All bank securities sold prior to July 27, 1933.

② Commercial paper (such as negotiable instruments), if the maturity date does not exceed nine months.

③ Securities of charitable organizations.

④ Securities resulting from a corporate reorganization issued for exchange with the issuer's existing security

---

[13] 15 U.S.C. Section 77c.

MANAGEMENT PERSPECTIVE
LLC Memberships and Securities Law

MANAGEMENT FACES A LEGAL ISSUE Although securities most commonly take the form of stocks and bonds issued by corporations, they can take many other forms as well. Under the Securities Act of 1933, as interpreted by the courts, securities include investment contracts. An investment contract is one in which a person (1) invests (2) in a common enterprise (3) reasonably expecting profits (4) derived *primarily* or *substantially* from others' managerial or entrepreneurial efforts. Those who contemplate organizing a business as a limited liability company (LLC—see Chapter 24) should consider the following question: Are ownership interests in LLCs considered securities and thus subject to the securities laws?

WHAT THE COURTS SAY To date, the courts have tended to hold that interests in an LLC that is managed by all of its members are not securities. If an LLC is managed by just some of the members, by nonmembers, or by some of the members along with nonmembers, however, an ownership interest in the firm may meet the definition of a security. In other words, if a person becomes a member of (invests in) an LLC, does not participate in the firm's management, and reasonably expects to make profits derived primarily from the efforts of the LLC's management group, it is very possible that the member's interest in the LLC will qualify as a security.

For example, in one case Albert Koenigsberg and others organized several LLCs, each of which was part of an elaborate telecommunications network. As a result of extensive marketing efforts, Koenigsberg and the others were able to collect over $10.4 million from over nine hundred investors. Not only were the investor-members deprived of any opportunity to decide on how the firms would be managed, but most of them lacked the technical expertise that would have allowed them to participate in managerial decision making. Because the investors expected to make a profit primarily derived from the managerial efforts of others, particularly Koenigsberg, the LLC membership interests were deemed securities.[a]

IMPLICATIONS FOR MANAGERS Clearly, an important factor in determining whether LLC ownership interests constitute securities is how the LLC is managed. Ownership interests in a manager-managed LLC may qualify as securities, depending on the circumstances—such as whether the nonmanaging members rely on the managers' expertise to make a profit. In contrast, ownership interests in member-managed LLCs are not securities, because the members have not invested in an enterprise in the hope of making profits derived substantially from others' managerial or entrepreneurial efforts.

a. *Nutek Information Systems, Inc. v. Arizona Corporation Commission,* 194 Ariz. 104, 977 P.2d 826 (Ct.App. 1998), *cert. denied sub nom* (under a different case name). See also *Ak's Daks Communications, Inc. v. Securities Div.,* 138 Md.App. 314, 771 A.2d 487 (2001).

---

holders and certificates issued by trustees, receivers, or debtors in possession under the bankruptcy laws (bankruptcy laws were discussed in Chapter 21).

5. Securities issued exclusively for exchange with the issuer's existing security holders, provided no commission is paid (for example, stock dividends and stock splits).

6. Securities issued to finance the acquisition of railroad equipment.

7. Any insurance, endowment, or annuity contract issued by a state-regulated insurance company.

8. Government-issued securities.

9. Securities issued by banks, savings and loan associations, farmers' cooperatives, and similar institutions subject to supervision by governmental authorities.

10. In consideration of the "small amount involved,"[14] an issuer's offer of up to $5 million in securities in any twelve-month period.

For the last exemption, under Regulation A,[15] the issuer must file with the SEC a notice of the issue and an offering circular, which must also be provided to investors before the sale. This is a much simpler and less expensive process than the procedures associated with full registration. Companies are allowed to "test the waters" for potential interest before preparing the offering circular. To *test the waters* means to determine potential interest without actually selling any securities or requiring any commitment on

[14] 15 U.S.C. Section 77c(b).
[15] 17 C.F.R. Sections 230.251–230.263.

the part of those who are interested. Small-business issuers (companies with less than $25 million in annual revenues and less than $25 million in outstanding voting stock) can also use an integrated registration and reporting system that uses simpler forms than the full registration system.

Exhibit 27–2 summarizes the securities and transactions (discussed next) that are exempt from the registration requirements under the Securities Act of 1933 and SEC regulations.

EXEMPT TRANSACTIONS

An issuer of securities that are not exempt under one of the ten categories listed in the previous subsection can avoid the high cost and complicated procedures associated with registration by taking advantage of certain transaction exemptions. An offering may qualify for more than one exemption. These exemptions are very broad, and thus many sales occur without registration. Because there is some overlap in the coverage of the exemptions, an offering may qualify for more than one.

Small Offerings—Regulation D. The SEC's Regulation D contains four separate exemptions from registration requirements for limited offers (offers that either involve a small amount of money or are made in a limited manner). Regulation D provides that any of these offerings made during any twelve-month period are exempt from the registration requirements.

Rule 504. Noninvestment company offerings up to $1 million in any one year are exempt. In contrast to investment companies (discussed later in this chapter), noninvestment companies are firms that are not engaged primarily in the business of investing or trading in securities.

Rule 504a. Offerings up to $500,000 in any one year by so-called blank-check companies—companies with no specific business plans except to locate and acquire currently unknown businesses or opportunities—are exempt if no general solicitation or advertising is used; the SEC is notified of the sales; and precaution is taken against nonexempt,

EXHIBIT 27–2 **EXEMPTIONS UNDER THE 1933 SECURITIES ACT**

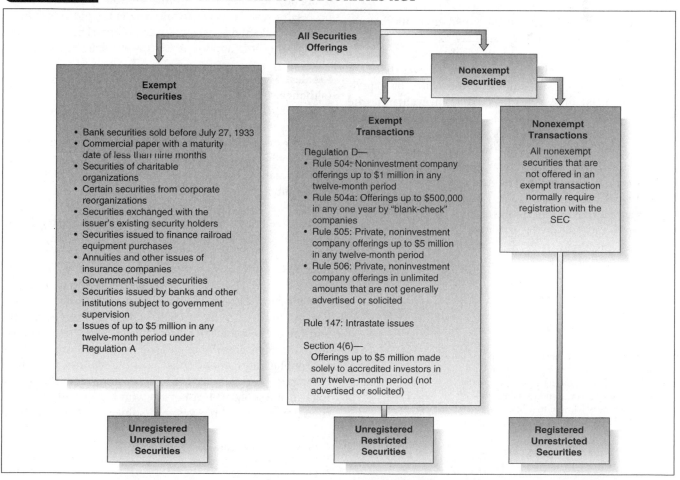

unregistered resales.[16] The limits on advertising and unregistered resales do not apply if the offering is made solely in states that provide for registration and disclosure and the securities are sold in compliance with those provisions.[17]

Rule 505. Private, noninvestment company offerings up to $5 million in any twelve-month period are exempt, regardless of the number of **accredited investors** (banks, insurance companies, investment companies, the issuer's executive officers and directors, and persons whose income or net worth exceeds certain limits), so long as there are no more than thirty-five unaccredited investors; no general solicitation or advertising is used; the SEC is notified of the sales; and precaution is taken against nonexempt, unregistered resales. If the sale involves *any* unaccredited investors, *all* investors must be given material information about the offering company, its business, and the securities before the sale. Unlike Rule 506 (discussed next), Rule 505 includes no requirement that the issuer believe each unaccredited investor "has such knowledge and experience in financial and business matters that he is capable of evaluating the merits and the risks of the prospective investment."[18]

Rule 506. Private offerings in unlimited amounts that are not generally solicited or advertised are exempt if the SEC is notified of the sales; precaution is taken against nonexempt, unregistered resales; and the issuer believes that each unaccredited investor has sufficient knowledge or experience in financial matters to be capable of evaluating the investment's merits and risks. There may be no more than thirty-five unaccredited investors, although there may be an unlimited number of accredited investors. If there are any unaccredited investors, the issuer must provide to all purchasers material information about itself, its business, and the securities before the sale.[19]

This exemption is perhaps most important to those firms that want to raise funds through the sale of securities without registering them. It is often referred to as the *private placement* exemption because it exempts "transactions not involving any public offering."[20] This provision applies to private offerings to a limited number of persons who are sufficiently sophisticated and in a sufficiently strong bargaining position to be able to assume the risk of the investment (and who thus have no need for federal registration protection), as well as to private offerings to similarly situated institutional investors.

Small Offerings—Section 4(6). Under Section 4(6) of the Securities Act of 1933, an offer made solely to accredited investors is exempt if its amount is not more than $5 million. Any number of accredited investors may participate, but no unaccredited investors may do so. No general solicitation or advertising may be used; the SEC must be notified of all sales; and precaution must be taken against nonexempt, unregistered resales. Precaution is necessary because these are *restricted* securities and may be resold only by registration or in an exempt transaction.[21] (The securities purchased and sold by most people who deal in stock are called, in contrast, *unrestricted* securities.)

Intrastate Issues—Rule 147. Also exempt are intrastate transactions involving purely local offerings.[22] This exemption applies to most offerings that are restricted to residents of the state in which the issuing company is organized and doing business. For nine months after the last sale, virtually no resales may be made to nonresidents, and precautions must be taken against this possibility. These offerings remain subject to applicable laws in the state of issue.

Resales. Most securities can be resold without registration (although some resales may be subject to restrictions, as discussed above in connection with specific exemptions). The Securities Act of 1933 provides exemptions for resales by most persons other than issuers or underwriters. The average investor who sells shares of stock does not have to file a registration statement with the SEC. Resales of restricted securities acquired under Rule 504a, Rule 505, Rule 506, or Section 4(6), however, trigger the registration requirements unless the party selling them complies with Rule 144 or Rule 144A. These rules are sometimes referred to as "safe harbors."

Rule 144. Rule 144 exempts restricted securities from registration on resale if there is adequate current public information about the issuer, the person selling the securities has owned them for at least one year, they are sold in certain limited amounts in unsolicited brokers' transactions, and the SEC is given notice of the resale.[23] "Adequate current public information" consists of the reports that certain companies are required to file under the Securities Exchange Act of 1934. A person who has owned the securities for at least three years is subject to none of these

---

[16] Precautions to be taken against nonexempt, unregistered resales include asking the investor whether he or she is buying the securities for others; before the sale, disclosing to each purchaser in writing that the securities are unregistered and thus cannot be resold, except in an exempt transaction, without first being registered; and indicating on the certificates that the securities are unregistered and restricted.

[17] 17 C.F.R. Section 230.504a.

[18] 17 C.F.R. Section 230.505.

[19] 17 C.F.R. Section 230.506.

[20] 15 U.S.C. Section 77d(2).

[21] 15 U.S.C. Section 77d(6).

[22] 15 U.S.C. Section 77c(a)(11); 17 C.F.R. Section 230.147.

[23] 17 C.F.R. Section 230.144.

requirements, unless the person is an affiliate. An *affiliate* is one who controls, is controlled by, or is in common control with the issuer. Sales of *nonrestricted* securities by an affiliate are also subject to the requirements for an exemption under Rule 144 (except that the affiliate need not have owned the securities for at least two years).

Rule 144A. Securities that at the time of issue are not of the same class as securities listed on a national securities exchange or quoted in a U.S. automated interdealer quotation system may be resold under Rule 144A.[24] They may be sold only to a qualified institutional buyer (an institution, such as an insurance company, an investment company, or a bank, that owns and invests at least $100 million in securities). The seller must take reasonable steps to ensure that the buyer knows that the seller is relying on the exemption under Rule 144A. A sample restricted stock certificate is shown in Exhibit 27–3.

---

[24] 17 C.F.R. Section 230.144A.

VIOLATIONS OF THE 1933 ACT

As mentioned, the SEC has the power to investigate and bring civil enforcement actions against companies that violate federal securities laws, including the Securities Act of 1933. Criminal violations are prosecuted by the Department of Justice. Violators may be penalized by fines up to $10,000, imprisonment for up to five years, or both. Private parties may also bring suits against those who violate federal securities laws. Those who purchase securities and suffer harm as a result of false or omitted statements, or other violations, may bring a suit in a federal court to recover their losses and other damages.

Securities Exchange Act of 1934

The Securities Exchange Act of 1934 provides for the regulation and registration of securities exchanges; brokers; dealers; and national securities associations, such as the National Association of Securities Dealers (NASD). The SEC regulates

---

EXHIBIT 27–3 **A SAMPLE RESTRICTED STOCK CERTIFICATE**

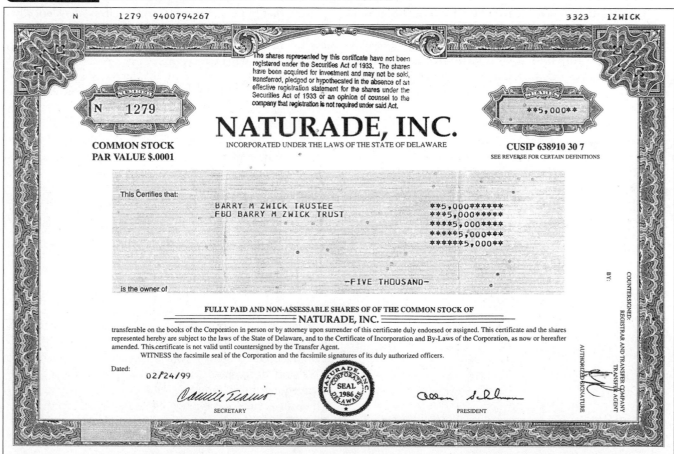

the markets in which securities are traded by maintaining a continuous disclosure system for all corporations with securities on the securities exchanges and for those companies that have assets in excess of $10 million and five hundred or more shareholders. These corporations are referred to as Section 12 companies because they are required to register their securities under Section 12 of the 1934 act.

The act regulates proxy solicitation for voting (discussed in Chapter 26) and allows the SEC to engage in market surveillance to regulate undesirable market practices such as fraud, market manipulation, and misrepresentation.

Section 10(b), SEC Rule 10b-5, and Insider Trading

Section 10(b) is one of the most important sections of the Securities Exchange Act of 1934. This section proscribes the use of "any manipulative or deceptive device or contrivance in contravention of such rules and regulations as the [SEC] may prescribe." Among the rules that the SEC has promulgated pursuant to the 1934 act is **SEC Rule 10b-5**, which prohibits the commission of fraud in connection with the purchase or sale of any security.

One of the major goals of Section 10(b) and SEC Rule 10b-5 is to prevent so-called **insider trading**. Because of their positions, corporate directors and officers often obtain advance inside information that can affect the future market value of the corporate stock. Obviously, their positions give them a trading advantage over the general public and shareholders. The 1934 Securities Exchange Act defines inside information and extends liability to officers and directors for taking advantage of such information in their personal transactions when they know that it is unavailable to the persons with whom they are dealing.

Section 10(b) of the 1934 act and SEC Rule 10b-5 cover not only corporate officers, directors, and majority shareholders but also any persons having access to or receiving information of a nonpublic nature on which trading is based.

Disclosure Requirements under SEC Rule 10b-5. Any material omission or misrepresentation of material facts in connection with the purchase or sale of a security may violate not only Section 11 of the Securities Act of 1933 but also the antifraud provisions of Section 10(b) and SEC Rule 10b-5 of the 1934 act. The key to liability (which can be civil or criminal) under Section 10(b) and SEC Rule 10b-5 is whether the insider's information is *material*.

Examples of Material Facts Calling for Disclosure. The following are some examples of material facts calling for a disclosure under the rule:

① Fraudulent trading in the company stock by a broker-dealer.

② A dividend change (whether up or down).

③ A contract for the sale of corporate assets.

④ A new discovery (process or product).

⑤ A significant change in the firm's financial condition.

⑥ Potential litigation against the company.

Note that none of these facts, in itself, is *automatically* a material fact. Rather, it will be regarded as a material fact if it is significant enough that it will likely affect an investor's decision about whether to purchase or sell certain securities.

The following is one of the landmark cases interpreting SEC Rule 10b-5. The SEC sued Texas Gulf Sulphur Company for issuing a misleading press release. The release underestimated the magnitude and the value of a mineral discovery. The SEC also sued several of Texas Gulf Sulphur's directors, officers, and employees under SEC Rule 10b-5 for purchasing large amounts of the corporate stock prior to the announcement of the corporation's rich ore discovery.

Landmark and Classic Cases

CASE 27.2   **SEC v. Texas Gulf Sulphur Co.**

United States Court of Appeals,
Second Circuit, 1968.
401 F.2d 833.

FACTS The Texas Gulf Sulphur Company (TGS) drilled a hole on November 12, 1963, near Timmins, Ontario, that

appeared to yield a core with an exceedingly high mineral content. TGS kept secret the results of the core sample. Officers and employees of the company made substantial purchases of TGS's stock or accepted stock options after learning of the ore discovery, even though further drilling was necessary to establish whether there was enough ore to be mined commercially. On April 11, 1964, an unauthorized report of the mineral find appeared in the newspapers. On the following day, April 12,

CASE 27.2—Continued

TGS issued a press release that downplayed the discovery and stated that it was too early to tell whether the ore finding would be a significant one. Later on, TGS announced a strike of at least twenty-five million tons of ore, substantially driving up the price of TGS stock. The SEC brought suit in a federal district court against the officers and employees of TGS for violating the insider-trading prohibition of SEC Rule 10b-5. The officers and employees argued that the prohibition did not apply. They reasoned that the information on which they had traded was not material, as the mine had not been commercially proved. The court held that most of the defendants had not violated SEC Rule 10b-5, and the SEC appealed.

ISSUE Had the officers and employees of TGS violated SEC Rule 10b-5 by purchasing the stock, even though they did not know the full extent and profit potential of the mine at the time they purchased the stock?

DECISION Yes. The federal appellate court reversed the lower court's decision and remanded the case to the trial court, holding that the employees and officers violated SEC Rule 10b-5's prohibition against insider trading.

REASON For SEC Rule 10b-5 purposes, the test of materiality is whether the information would affect the judgment of reasonable investors. Reasonable investors include speculative as well as conservative investors. "[A] major factor in determining whether the * * * discovery [of the ore] was a material fact is the importance attached to the drilling results by those who knew about it. * * * [T]he timing by those who knew of it of their stock purchases and their purchases of short-term calls [rights to buy shares at a specified price within a specified time period]—purchases in some cases by individuals who had never before purchased calls or even TGS stock—virtually compels the inference that the insiders were influenced by the drilling results. * * * We hold, therefore, that all transactions in TGS stock or calls by individuals apprised of the drilling results * * * were made in violation of Rule 10b-5."

COMMENT *This landmark case affirmed the principle that the test of whether information is "material," for SEC Rule 10b-5 purposes, is whether it would affect the judgment of reasonable investors. The corporate insiders' purchases of stock and stock options (rights to purchase stock) indicated that they were influenced by the drilling results and that the information about the drilling results was material. The courts continue to cite this case when applying SEC Rule 10b-5 to cases of alleged insider trading.*

The Private Securities Litigation Reform Act of 1995. Ironically, one of the effects of SEC Rule 10b-5 was to deter disclosure of forward-looking information. ● **EXAMPLE #1** A company announces that its projected earnings in a certain time period will be X amount. It turns out that the forecast is wrong. The earnings are in fact much lower, and the price of the company's stock is affected—negatively. The shareholders then bring a class-action suit against the company, alleging that the directors violated SEC Rule 10b-5 by disclosing misleading financial information. ●

In an attempt to rectify this problem and promote disclosure, Congress passed the Private Securities Litigation Reform Act of 1995. Among other things, the act provides a "safe harbor" for publicly held companies that make forward-looking statements, such as financial forecasts. Those who make such statements are protected against federal liability for securities fraud as long as the statements are accompanied by "meaningful cautionary statements identifying important factors that could cause actual results to differ materially from those in the forward-looking statement."[25]

After the 1995 act was passed, a number of securities class-action suits were filed in state courts to skirt the requirements of the 1995 federal act. In response to this problem, Congress passed the Securities Litigation Uniform Standards Act of 1998. The act placed stringent limits on the ability of plaintiffs to bring class-action suits in state courts against firms whose securities are traded on national stock exchanges. Exceptions were made to preserve certain suits brought under state law affecting the conduct of corporate officers with respect to particular corporate actions, including tender offers.

Applicability of SEC Rule 10b-5. SEC Rule 10b-5 applies in virtually all cases concerning the trading of securities, whether on organized exchanges, in over-the-counter markets, or in private transactions. The rule covers, among other things, notes, bonds, agreements to form a corporation, and joint-venture agreements. Generally, it covers just about any form of security. It is immaterial whether a firm has securities registered under the 1933 act for the 1934 act to apply.

Although SEC Rule 10b-5 is applicable only when the requisites of federal jurisdiction—such as the use of the

---

[25] 15 U.S.C. Sections 77z-2, 78u-5.

mails, of stock exchange facilities, or of any instrumentality of interstate commerce—are present, virtually no commercial transaction can be completed without such contact. In addition, the states have corporate securities laws, many of which include provisions similar to SEC Rule 10b-5.

Outsiders and SEC Rule 10b-5. The traditional insider-trading case involves true insiders—corporate officers, directors, and majority shareholders who have access to (and trade on) inside information. Increasingly, liability under Section 10(b) of the 1934 act and SEC Rule 10b-5 has been extended to include certain "outsiders"—those persons who trade on inside information acquired indirectly. Two theories have been developed under which outsiders may be held liable for insider trading: the *tipper/tippee theory* and the *misappropriation theory*.

Tipper/Tippee Theory. Anyone who acquires inside information as a result of a corporate insider's breach of his or her fiduciary duty can be liable under SEC Rule 10b-5. This liability extends to **tippees** (those who receive "tips" from insiders) and even remote tippees (tippees of tippees).

The key to liability under this theory is that the inside information must be obtained as a result of someone's breach of a fiduciary duty to the corporation whose shares are involved in the trading. Unless there was a breach of a duty not to disclose inside information, the disclosure was in exchange for personal benefit, and the tippee knew of this breach (or should have known of it) and benefited from it, there is no liability under this theory.[26]

Misappropriation Theory. Liability for insider trading may also be established under the misappropriation theory. This theory holds that if an individual wrongfully obtains (misappropriates) inside information and trades on it for her or his personal gain, then the individual should be held liable because, in essence, the individual stole information rightfully belonging to another.

The misappropriation theory has been controversial because it significantly extends the reach of SEC Rule 10b-5 to outsiders who would not ordinarily be deemed fiduciaries of the corporations in whose stock they trade. The United States Supreme Court, however, has held that liability under SEC Rule 10b-5 can be based on the misappropriation theory.[27]

INSIDER REPORTING AND TRADING—SECTION 16(b)

Officers, directors, and certain large stockholders[28] of Section 12 corporations (corporations that are required to register their securities under Section 12 of the 1934 act) must file reports with the SEC concerning their ownership and trading of the corporations' securities.[29] To discourage such insiders from using nonpublic information about their companies for their personal benefit in the stock market, Section 16(b) of the 1934 act provides for the recapture by the corporation of all profits realized by an insider on any purchase and sale or sale and purchase of the corporation's stock within any six-month period.[30] It is irrelevant whether the insider actually uses inside information; all such short-swing profits must be returned to the corporation.

Section 16(b) applies not only to stock but to warrants, options, and securities convertible into stock. In addition, the courts have fashioned complex rules for determining profits. Corporate insiders are wise to seek specialized counsel prior to trading in the corporation's stock. Exhibit 27–4 compares the effects of SEC Rule 10b-5 and Section 16(b).

PROXY STATEMENTS

Section 14(a) of the Securities Exchange Act of 1934 regulates the solicitation of proxies from shareholders of Section 12 companies. The SEC regulates the content of proxy statements. As discussed in Chapter 26, a *proxy statement* is a statement that is sent to shareholders by corporate officials who are requesting authority to vote on behalf of the shareholders in a particular election on specified issues. Whoever solicits a proxy must fully and accurately disclose in the proxy statement all of the facts that are pertinent to the matter on which the shareholders are to vote. SEC Rule 14a-9 is similar to the antifraud provisions of SEC Rule 10b-5. Remedies for violations are extensive; they range from injunctions that prevent a vote from being taken to monetary damages.

VIOLATIONS OF THE 1934 ACT

Violations of Section 10(b) of the Securities Exchange Act of 1934 and SEC Rule 10b-5 include insider trading. This is a criminal offense, with criminal penalties. Violators of these laws may also be subject to civil liability. For any

---

[26] See, for example, *Chiarella v. United States,* 445 U.S. 222, 100 S.Ct. 1108, 63 L.Ed.2d 348 (1980); and *Dirks v. SEC,* 463 U.S. 646, 103 S.Ct. 3255, 77 L.Ed.2d 911 (1983).
[27] *United States v. O'Hagan,* 521 U.S. 642, 117 S.Ct. 2199, 138 L.Ed.2d 724 (1997).

[28] Those stockholders owning 10 percent of the class of equity securities registered under Section 12 of the 1934 act.
[29] 15 U.S.C. Section 78l.
[30] When a decline is predicted in the market for a particular stock, one can realize profits by "selling short"—selling at a high price and repurchasing later at a lower price to cover the "short sale."

EXHIBIT 27–4 COMPARISON OF COVERAGE, APPLICATION, AND LIABILITIES UNDER SEC RULE 10b-5 AND SECTION 16(b)

AREA OF COMPARISON	SEC RULE 10b-5	SECTION 16(b)
What is the subject matter of the transaction?	Any security (does not have to be registered).	Any security (does not have to be registered).
What transactions are covered?	Purchase or sale.	Short-swing purchase and sale or short-swing sale and purchase.
Who is subject to liability?	Virtually anyone with inside information under a duty to disclose—including officers, directors, controlling stockholders, and tippees.	Officers, directors, and certain 10 percent stockholders.
Is omission or misrepresentation necessary for liability?	Yes.	No.
Are there any exempt transactions?	No.	Yes, there are a variety of exemptions.
Is direct dealing with the party necessary?	No.	No.
Who may bring an action?	A person transacting with an insider, the SEC, or a purchaser or seller damaged by a wrongful act.	A corporation or a shareholder by derivative action.

sanctions to be imposed, however, there must be *scienter*—the violator must have had an intent to defraud or knowledge of his or her misconduct (see Chapter 10). *Scienter* can be proved by showing that a defendant made false statements or wrongfully failed to disclose material facts.

Violations of Section 16(b) include the sale by insiders of stock acquired less than six months before the sale. These violations are subject to civil sanctions. Liability under Section 16(b) is strict liability. *Scienter* is not required.

In the following case, investors charged a corporation with violating Section 10(b) and SEC Rule 10b-5. The question before the court was whether the investors alleged sufficient facts to indicate *scienter*.

CASE 27.3 In re MCI Worldcom, Inc., Securities Litigation

United States District Court,
Eastern District of New York, 2000.
93 F.Supp.2d 276.

FACTS In early 1999, MCI Worldcom, Inc., began negotiating to buy SkyTel Communications, Inc., then a leading provider of wireless messaging services. When investors heard rumors of the deal, the price of SkyTel stock rose 12 percent. On the morning of May 25, an Internet news service, the Company Sleuth, reported that MCI had registered "skytelworldcom.com" as an Internet domain name.[a] SkyTel's stock price rose 16 percent before noon. At noon, Barbara Gibson, an MCI spokesperson and senior manager of corporate communication, told the media that the name registration was done by an employee acting alone and "is not an indication of official company intention." Immediately following Gibson's statement, SkyTel's stock price fell to less than the previous day's price. On May 28, MCI announced that it would buy all of SkyTel's stock for $1.3 billion. Paul Curnin and other investors who sold the stock between May 25 and 28 filed a suit in a federal district court against MCI, alleging violations of Section 10(b) and SEC Rule 10b-5. MCI filed a motion to dismiss.

---

a. It is common for business firms to register domain names before their actual use to protect them from cybersquatters—see Chapter 5.

(Continued)

CASE 27.3—Continued

ISSUE Did the shareholders properly allege *scienter*?

DECISION Yes. The court denied the motion to dismiss. The investors successfully alleged *scienter* through motive and opportunity, as well as facts from which an inference of conscious misbehavior or recklessness could be drawn.

REASON The court explained that a plaintiff can plead *scienter* in one of two ways: "(1) by identifying circumstances indicating conscious or reckless behavior by the defendant, or (2) by alleging facts showing a motive to commit fraud and a clear opportunity to do so." Here, the plaintiffs "assert that MCI was motivated to artificially deflate the price of SkyTel stock in order to help ensure that the acquisition price would not have to be increased. * * * [B]eing able to acquire a

company for a significantly reduced price is a sufficient economic benefit to satisfy the motive requirement for *scienter*." The court added, "Plaintiffs have also alleged facts that constitute strong circumstantial evidence of conscious misbehavior or recklessness by MCI." This included MCI's denial of the domain name registration. "The [investors] understood the denial to mean there would be no takeover, as evidenced by the drop in SkyTel's price," but it "was MCI itself that registered the domain name, and not, as Ms. Gibson suggested, an MCI employee acting alone."

FOR CRITICAL ANALYSIS—Technological Consideration
What effect has the Internet had on the opportunity to commit violations of the securities laws, as well as to avoid such violations?

Criminal Penalties. For violations of Section 10(b) and Rule 10b-5, an individual may be fined up to $5 million, imprisoned for up to twenty years, or both.[31] A partnership or a corporation may be fined up to $25 million. Under Section 807 of the Sarbanes-Oxley Act of 2002, for a willful violation of the 1934 act the violator may, in addition to being subject to a fine, be imprisoned for up to twenty-five years.

Civil Sanctions. The Insider Trading Sanctions Act of 1984 permits the SEC to bring suit in a federal district court against anyone violating or aiding in a violation of the 1934 act or SEC rules by purchasing or selling a security while in the possession of material nonpublic information.[32] The violation must occur on or through the facilities of a national securities exchange or from or through a broker or dealer. Transactions pursuant to a public offering by an issuer of securities are excepted. The court may assess as a penalty as much as triple the profits gained or the loss avoided by the guilty party. Profit or loss is defined as "the difference between the purchase or sale price of the security and the value of that security as measured by the trading price of the security at a reasonable period of time after public dissemination of the nonpublic information."[33]

The Insider Trading and Securities Fraud Enforcement Act of 1988 enlarged the class of persons who may be subject to civil liability for insider-trading violations. This act also gave the SEC authority to award **bounty payments**

(rewards given by government officials for acts beneficial to the state) to persons providing information leading to the prosecution of insider-trading violations.[34]

Private parties may also sue violators of Section 10(b) and Rule 10b-5. A private party may obtain rescission of a contract to buy securities or damages to the extent of the violator's illegal profits. Those found liable have a right to seek contribution from those who share responsibility for the violations, including accountants, attorneys, and corporations.[35] For violations of Section 16(b), a corporation can bring an action to recover the short-swing profits.

The Regulation of Investment Companies

Investment companies, and mutual funds in particular, grew rapidly after World War II. **Investment companies** act on behalf of many smaller shareholders/owners by buying a large portfolio of securities and managing that portfolio professionally. A **mutual fund** is a specific type of investment company that continually buys or sells to investors shares of ownership in a portfolio. Such companies are regulated by the Investment Company Act of 1940,[36] which

---

[31] These numbers reflect the increased penalties imposed by the Sarbanes-Oxley Act of 2002.

[32] 15 U.S.C. Section 78u(d)(2)(A).

[33] 15 U.S.C. Section 78u(d)(2)(C).

[34] 15 U.S.C. Section 78u-1.

[35] Note that a private cause of action under Section 10(b) and SEC Rule 10b-5 cannot be brought against accountants, attorneys, and others who "aid and abet" violations of the act. Only the SEC can bring actions against so-called aiders and abettors. See *SEC v. Fehn,* 97 F.3d 1276 (9th Cir. 1996).

[36] 15 U.S.C. Sections 80a-1 to 80a-64.

provides for SEC regulation of their activities. The 1940 act was expanded by the Investment Company Act Amendments of 1970. Further minor changes were made in the Securities Acts Amendments of 1975. The National Securities Markets Improvement Act of 1996 increased the SEC's authority to regulate investment companies by limiting virtually all of the authority of the states to regulate these enterprises.

DEFINITION OF AN INVESTMENT COMPANY

For the purposes of the act, an *investment company* is defined as any entity that (1) "is . . . engaged primarily . . . in the business of investing, reinvesting, or trading in securities" or (2) is engaged in such business and more than 40 percent of the company's assets consist of investment securities. Excluded from coverage by the act are banks, insurance companies, savings and loan associations, finance companies, oil and gas drilling firms, charitable foundations, tax-exempt pension funds, and other special types of institutions, such as closely held corporations.

REGISTRATION AND REPORTING REQUIREMENTS

The 1940 act requires that every investment company register with the SEC by filing a notification of registration. Each year, registered investment companies must file reports with the SEC. To safeguard company assets, all securities must be held in the custody of a bank or stock exchange member, and that bank or stock exchange member must follow strict procedures established by the SEC.

RESTRICTIONS ON INVESTMENT COMPANIES

The 1940 act also imposes restrictions on the activities of investment companies and persons connected with them. For example, investment companies are not allowed to purchase securities on the margin (pay only part of the total price, borrowing the rest), sell short (sell shares not yet owned), or participate in joint trading accounts. Additionally, no dividends may be paid from any source other than accumulated, undistributed net income.

State Securities Laws

Today, all states have their own corporate securities laws, or *blue sky laws,* that regulate the offer and sale of securities within individual state borders. (As mentioned in Chapter 9, the phrase *blue sky laws* dates to a 1917 United States Supreme Court decision in which the Court declared that the purpose of such laws was to prevent "speculative schemes which have no more basis than so many feet of 'blue sky.'"[37]) Article 8 of the Uniform Commercial Code, which has been adopted by all of the states, also imposes various requirements relating to the purchase and sale of securities.

REQUIREMENTS UNDER STATE SECURITIES LAWS

Despite some differences in philosophy, all state blue sky laws have certain common features. Typically, state laws have disclosure requirements and antifraud provisions, many of which are patterned after Section 10(b) of the Securities Exchange Act of 1934 and SEC Rule 10b-5. State laws also provide for the registration or qualification of securities offered or issued for sale within the state and impose disclosure requirements. Unless an exemption from registration is applicable, issuers must register or qualify their stock with the appropriate state official, often called a *corporations commissioner.* Additionally, most state securities laws regulate securities brokers and dealers. The Uniform Securities Act, which has been adopted in part by several states, was drafted to be acceptable to states with differing regulatory philosophies.

CONCURRENT REGULATION

State securities laws apply mainly to intrastate transactions. Since the adoption of the 1933 and 1934 federal securities acts, the state and federal governments have regulated securities concurrently. Issuers must comply with both federal and state securities laws, and exemptions from federal law are not necessarily exemptions from state laws.

The dual federal and state system has not always worked well, particularly during the early 1990s, when there was considerable expansion of the securities markets. The National Securities Markets Improvement Act of 1996 eliminated some of the duplicate regulations. While the states still regulate local and regional matters, the SEC exclusively regulates most national securities activities.

Online Securities Offerings and Disclosures

The Spring Street Brewing Company, headquartered in New York, made history when it became the first company to attempt to sell securities via the Internet. Through its online *initial public offering (IPO),* which ended in early 1996, Spring Street raised about $1.6 million—without

---

[37] *Hall v. Geiger-Jones Co.,* 242 U.S. 539, 37 S.Ct. 217, 61 L.Ed. 480 (1917).

having to pay any commissions to brokers or underwriters. The offering was made pursuant to Regulation A, which, as mentioned earlier in this chapter, allows small-business issuers to use a simplified registration procedure.

Such online IPOs are particularly attractive to small companies and start-up ventures that may find it difficult to raise capital from institutional investors or through underwriters. By making the offering online under Regulation A, the company can avoid both commissions and the costly and time-consuming filings required for a traditional IPO under federal and state law.

Clearly, technological advances have affected the securities industry—and securities law—just as they have affected other areas of the law. Corporations are now using the Internet to communicate information to the SEC, shareholders, potential investors, and others. Indeed, as you will read shortly, the SEC has changed or modified a number of its rules to encourage online filings of securities documents, including prospectuses.

Investors, in turn, can now use the Internet to access information that can help them make informed decisions. The SEC's EDGAR (Electronic Data Gathering, Analysis, and Retrieval) database includes IPOs, proxy statements, annual corporate reports, registration statements, and other documents that have been filed with the commission. These and other developments have brought about what one scholar calls a "near-revolution" in the way securities are issued and traded.[38]

REGULATIONS GOVERNING ONLINE SECURITIES OFFERINGS

One of the early questions posed by online offerings was whether the delivery of securities *information* via the Internet met the requirements of the 1933 Securities Act, which traditionally were applied to the delivery of paper documents. In an interpretative release issued in 1995, the SEC stated that "[t]he use of electronic media should be at least an equal alternative to the use of paper-based media" and that anything that can be delivered in paper form under the current securities laws might also be delivered in electronic form.[39] For example, a prospectus in downloadable form will meet SEC requirements.

Basically, there has been no change in the substantive law of disclosure; only the delivery vehicle has changed. When the Internet is used for delivery of a prospectus, the same rules apply as for the delivery of a paper prospectus. These rules are as follows:

① *Timely and adequate notice of the delivery of information is required.* Hosting a prospectus on a Web site does not constitute adequate notice, but separate e-mails or even postcards will satisfy the SEC's notice requirements.

② *The online communication system must be easily accessible.* This is very simple to accomplish today because virtually anyone interested in purchasing securities has access to the Web.

③ *Some evidence of delivery must be created.* This requirement is relatively easy to satisfy. Those making online offerings can require an e-mail return receipt verification of any materials sent electronically.

Once these three requirements have been satisfied, the prospectus has been successfully delivered.

POTENTIAL LIABILITY CREATED BY ONLINE OFFERING MATERIALS

All printed prospectuses indicate that only the information given in the prospectuses can be used in making an investment decision about the securities offered. The same wording, of course, appears on Web-based offerings. Those who create such Web-based offerings may be tempted, however, to go one step further. They may include hyperlinks to other sites that have analyzed the future prospects of the company, the products and services sold by the company, or the offering itself. To avoid potential liability, however, online offerors (the entities making the offerings) need to exercise caution when including such hyperlinks.

● **EXAMPLE #2** Suppose that a hyperlink goes to an analyst's Web page on which the company making the offering is heavily touted. Further suppose that after the IPO, the stock price falls. By including the hyperlink on its Web site, the offering company is impliedly supporting the information presented on the linked page. In such a situation, the company may be liable under federal securities laws.[40] ●

Potential problems may also occur with some Regulation D offerings, if the offeror places the offering circular on its Web site for general consumption by anybody on the

---

[38] Robert A. Prentice, "The Future of Corporate Disclosure: The Internet, Securities Fraud, and Rule 10b-5," 47 *Emory Law Journal* 1 (Winter 1998).

[39] "Use of Electronic Media for Delivery Purposes," Securities Act Release No. 33-7233 (October 6, 1995). The rules governing the use of electronic transmissions for delivery purposes were subsequently confirmed in Securities Act Release No. 33-7289 (May 9, 1996) and expanded in Securities Act Release No. 33-7856 (April 28, 2000).

---

[40] See, for example, *In re Syntex Corp. Securities Litigation*, 95 F.3d. 922 (9th Cir. 1996).

Internet. Because Regulation D offerings are private placements, general solicitation is restricted. If anyone can have access to the offering circular on the Web, the Regulation D exemption may be disqualified.

ONLINE SECURITIES OFFERINGS BY FOREIGN COMPANIES

Online securities offerings by foreign companies may also present problems. Traditionally, foreign companies have not been able to offer new shares to the U.S. public without first registering them with the SEC. Today, however, anybody in the world can offer shares of stock worldwide via the Web.

The SEC asks that foreign issuers on the Internet implement measures to warn U.S. investors. For example, a foreign company offering shares of stock on the Internet must include a disclaimer on its Web site stating that it has not gone through the registration procedure in the United States. If the SEC believes that a Web site's offering of foreign securities has been targeted at U.S. residents, it will pursue that company in an attempt to require it to register in the United States.[41]

Online Securities Fraud

The Internet, of course, has also been used to commit fraud. A major problem facing the SEC today is how to enforce the antifraud provisions of the securities laws in the online environment. In 1999, in the first cases involving illegal online securities offerings, the SEC filed suit against three individuals for illegally offering securities on an Internet auction site.[42] In essence, all three indicated that their companies would go public soon and attempted to sell unregistered securities via the Web auction site. All of these actions were in violation of Sections 5, 17(a)(1), and 17(a)(3) of the 1933 Securities Act. Since then, the SEC has brought a variety of Internet-related fraud cases, including cases involving investment scams and the manipulation of stock prices in Internet chat rooms.

INVESTMENT SCAMS

An ongoing problem for the SEC is how to curb investment scams. One fraudulent investment scheme involved twenty thousand investors, who lost, in all, more than $3 million. Some cases have involved false claims about the earnings potential of home-business programs, such as the claim that one could "earn $4,000 or more each month." Others have concerned claims of "guaranteed credit repair."

USING CHAT ROOMS TO MANIPULATE STOCK PRICES

"Pumping and dumping" occurs when a person who has purchased a particular stock heavily promotes ("pumps up") that stock—thereby creating a great demand for it and driving up its price—and then sells ("dumps") it. The practice of pumping up a stock and then dumping it is quite old. In the online world, however, the process can occur much more quickly and efficiently.

● **EXAMPLE #3** The most famous case in this area involved Jonathan Lebed, a fifteen-year-old stock trader and Internet user from New Jersey. Lebed was the first minor ever charged with securities fraud by the SEC, but he is unlikely to be the last. The SEC charged that Lebed bought thinly traded stocks. After purchasing a stock, he would flood stock-related chat rooms, particularly at Yahoo!'s finance boards, with messages touting the stock's virtues. He used numerous false names so that no one would know that a single person was posting the messages. He would say that the stock was the most "undervalued stock in history" and that its price would jump by 1,000 percent "very soon." When other investors would buy the stock, the price would go up quickly, and Lebed would sell out. The SEC forced the teenager to repay almost $300,000 in gains plus interest. He was allowed, however, to keep about $500,000 of the profits he made trading small-company stocks that he also touted on the Internet.●

The SEC has been bringing an increasing number of cases against those who manipulate stock prices in this way. Consider that in 1995, such fraud resulted in only six SEC cases. By 2003, the SEC had brought an estimated two hundred actions against online perpetrators of fraudulent stock-price manipulation. (Stock prices may also be affected by negative statements about a company and its officers—see, for example, the case discussed in this chapter's *Business Law in the Online World* feature on page 582.)

---

[41] International Series Release No. 1125 (March 23, 1998).
[42] *In re Davis*, SEC Administrative File No. 3-10080 (October 20, 1999); *In re Haas*, SEC Administrative File No. 3-10081 (October 20, 1999); *In re Sitaras*, SEC Administrative File No. 3-10082 (October 20, 1999).

BUSINESS LAW IN THE ONLINE WORLD
Fact versus Opinion

The SEC typically claims that fraud occurs when a false statement of fact is made. Many statements about stock, however, such as "this stock is headed for $20," are simply opinions. Opinions can never be labeled true or false at the time they are made; otherwise, they would not be opinions. As long as a person has a "genuine belief" that such an opinion is true, then, presumably, no fraud is involved. Thus, a defense that is often raised in cases involving allegedly untrue statements made via the Internet is that the statements were simply statements of opinion, not statements of fact.

In determining whether a statement is one of fact or opinion, a court will normally consider a number of factors. By way of illustration, consider a case brought by Global Telemedia International, Inc. (GTMI), against a number of "John Does" who had posted messages in online chat rooms.

THE PROBLEM FACING GTMI In March 2000, GTMI's stock was trading at $4.70 per share. That month, persons using various aliases began to post messages in the GTMI chat room on the Raging Bull Web site. (Raging Bull is a financial service Web site that organizes chat rooms dedicated to publicly traded companies.) The messages were critical of GTMI and its officers. Over the next six months, GTMI's stock price decreased significantly—by October, the stock was closing at $0.25 a share. GTMI and its officers sued those who posted the messages, most of whom were listed as "John Does" in the suit. In the suit, GTMI alleged, among other things, defamation (see Chapter 4).

DISTINGUISHING BETWEEN FACT AND OPINION
The court noted that defamation of a publicly traded company requires a "false statement of fact made with malice that caused damage." The defendants (those who posted the messages) asserted that their online statements were not actionable because they were statements of opinion, not statements of fact. Ultimately, the court agreed with the defendants. In making its decision, the court looked at the "totality of the circumstances," including the context and format of the statements, as well as the expectations of the audience in that particular situation.

Here, said the court, the context and format strongly suggested that the postings constituted opinion, not fact. "The statements were posted anonymously in the general cacophony of an Internet chat room in which about 1,000 messages a week are posted about GTMI. . . . They were part of an ongoing, freewheeling and highly animated exchange about GTMI and its turbulent history. At least several participants in addition to Defendants were repeat posters, indicating that the posters were just random individual investors interested in exchanging their views with other investors." The court went on to stress that the postings were "full of hyperbole, invective, shorthand phrases and language not generally found in fact-based documents, such as corporate press releases or SEC filings." In sum, concluded the court, the statements were not statements of fact, but statements of opinion. As such, they were not defamatory.[a]

FOR CRITICAL ANALYSIS
Why didn't GTMI sue the Web site operator, Raging Bull, instead of—or in addition to—the "John Does"?

a. *Global Telemedia International, Inc. v. Does,* 132 F.Supp.2d 1261 (C.D.Cal. 2001).

Terms and Concepts

Chapter Summary	Investor Protection and Online Securities Offerings
Securities Act of 1933 (See pages 568–573.)	Prohibits fraud and stabilizes the securities industry by requiring disclosure of all essential information relating to the issuance of stocks to the investing public. 1. *Registration requirements*—Securities, unless exempt, must be registered with the SEC before being offered to the public through the mails or any facility of interstate commerce (including securities exchanges). The *registration statement* must include detailed financial information about the issuing corporation; the intended use of the proceeds of the securities being issued; and certain disclosures, such as interests of directors or officers and pending lawsuits. 2. *Prospectus*—A prospectus must be provided to investors, describing the security being sold, the issuing corporation, and the risk attaching to the security. 3. *Exemptions*—The SEC has exempted certain offerings from the requirements of the Securities Act of 1933. Exemptions may be determined on the basis of the size of the issue, whether the offering is private or public, and whether advertising is involved. These exemptions are summarized in Exhibit 27–2.

Securities Exchange Act of 1934
(See pages 573–578.)
	Provides for the regulation and registration of securities exchanges, brokers, dealers, and national securities associations (such as the NASD). Maintains a continuous disclosure system for all corporations with securities on the securities exchanges and for those companies that have assets in excess of $5 million and five hundred or more shareholders (Section 12 companies).
	
	1. *SEC Rule 10b-5 [under Section 10(b) of the 1934 act]*—
	   a. Applies to insider trading by corporate officers, directors, majority shareholders, and any persons receiving information not available to the public who base their trading on this information.
	   b. Liability for violation can be civil or criminal.
	   c. May be violated by failing to disclose "material facts" that must be disclosed under this rule.
	   d. Applies in virtually all cases concerning the trading of securities—a firm does not have to have its securities registered under the 1933 act for the 1934 act to apply.
	   e. Liability may be based on the tipper/tippee or the misappropriation theory.
	   f. Applies only when the requisites of federal jurisdiction (such as use of the mails, stock exchange facilities, or any facility of interstate commerce) are present.
	
	2. *Insider trading [under Section 16(b) of the 1934 act]*—To prevent corporate officers and directors from taking advantage of inside information (information not available to the investing public), the 1934 act requires officers, directors, and shareholders owning 10 percent or more of the issued stock of a corporation to turn over to the corporation all short-term profits (called *short-swing profits*) realized from the purchase and sale or sale and purchase of corporate stock within any six-month period.
	
	3. *Proxies [under Section 14(a) of the 1934 act]*—The SEC regulates the content of proxy statements sent to shareholders by corporate managers of Section 12 companies who are requesting authority to vote on behalf of the shareholders in a particular election on specified issues. Section 14(a) is essentially a disclosure law, with provisions similar to the antifraud provisions of SEC Rule 10b-5.

The Regulation of Investment Companies (See pages 578–579.)	The Investment Company Act of 1940 provides for SEC regulation of investment company activities. It was altered and expanded by the amendments of 1970 and 1975.

(Continued)

Chapter Summary	Investor Protection and Online Securities Offerings—Continued
State Securities Laws (See page 579.)	All states have corporate securities laws *(blue sky laws)* that regulate the offer and sale of securities within state borders; these laws are designed to prevent "speculative schemes which have no more basis than so many feet of 'blue sky.'" States regulate securities concurrently with the federal government.
Online Securities Offerings and Disclosures (See pages 579–581.)	In 1995, the SEC announced that anything that can be delivered in paper form under current securities laws may also be delivered in electronic form. Generally, when the Internet is used for the delivery of a prospectus, the same rules apply as for the delivery of a paper prospectus. When securities offerings are made online, the offerors should be careful that any hyperlinked materials do not mislead investors. Caution should also be used when making Regulation D offerings (private placements), because general solicitation is restricted with these offerings.
Online Securities Fraud (See pages 581–582.)	A major problem facing the SEC today is how to enforce the antifraud provisions of the securities laws in the online environment. Internet-related forms of securities fraud include the manipulation of stock prices in online chat rooms and illegal securities offerings.

For Review

① What is meant by the term *securities?*

② What are the two major statutes regulating the securities industry? When was the Securities and Exchange Commission created, and what are its major purposes and functions?

③ What is insider trading? Why is it prohibited?

④ What are some of the features of state securities laws?

⑤ How are securities laws being applied in the online environment?

Questions and Case Problems

27–1. Registration Requirements. Langley Brothers, Inc., a corporation incorporated and doing business in Kansas, decides to sell no-par common stock worth $1 million to the public. The stock will be sold only within the state of Kansas. Joseph Langley, the chairman of the board, says the offering need not be registered with the Securities and Exchange Commission. His brother, Harry, disagrees. Who is right? Explain.

27–2. Registration Requirements. Huron Corp. has 300,000 common shares outstanding. The owners of these outstanding shares live in several different states. Huron decides to split the 300,000 shares two for one. Will Huron Corp. have to file a registration statement and prospectus on the 300,000 new shares to be issued as a result of the split? Explain.

27–3. SEC Rule 10b-5. Louis Ferraro was the chairman and president of Anacomp, Inc. In June 1988, Ferraro told his good friend Michael Maio that Anacomp was negotiating a tender offer for stock in Xidex Corp. Maio passed on the information to Patricia Ladavac, a friend of both Ferraro and Maio. Maio and Ladavac immediately purchased shares in Xidex stock. On the day that the tender offer was announced—an announcement that caused the price of Xidex shares to increase—Maio and Ladavac sold their Xidex stock and made substantial prof-

its (Maio made $211,000 from the transactions, and Ladavac gained $78,750). The Securities and Exchange Commission (SEC) brought an action against the three individuals, alleging that they had violated, among other laws, SEC Rule 10b-5. Maio and Ladavac claimed that they had done nothing illegal. They argued that they had no fiduciary duty either to Anacomp or to Xidex, and therefore they had no duty to disclose or abstain from trading in the stock of those corporations. Had Maio and Ladavac violated SEC Rule 10b-5? Discuss fully. [*SEC v. Maio,* 51 F.3d 623 (7th Cir. 1995)]

27–4. Definition of a Security. Life Partners, Inc. (LPI), facilitates the sale of life insurance policies that are owned by persons suffering from AIDS (acquired immune deficiency syndrome) to investors at a discount. The investors pay LPI, and LPI pays the policyholder. Typically, the policyholder, in turn, assigns the policy to LPI, which also obtains the right to make LPI's president the beneficiary of the policy. On the policyholder's death, LPI receives the proceeds of the policy and pays the investor. In this way, the terminally ill sellers secure much-needed income in the final years of life, when employment is unlikely and medical bills are often staggering. The Securities and Exchange Commission (SEC) sought to enjoin (prevent) LPI from engaging in further transactions on the ground that the investment contracts were securities, which LPI had failed to register with the SEC in violation of securities laws. Do the investment contracts meet the definition of a security discussed in this chapter? Discuss fully. [*SEC v. Life Partners, Inc.,* 87 F.3d 536 (D.C.Cir. 1996)]

27–5. Section 10(b). Joseph Jett worked for Kidder, Peabody & Co., a financial services firm owned by General Electric Co. (GE). Over a three-year period, Jett allegedly engaged in a scheme to generate false profits at Kidder, Peabody to increase his performance-based bonuses. When the scheme was discovered, Daniel Chill and other GE shareholders who had bought stock in the previous year filed a suit in a federal district court against GE. The shareholders alleged that GE had engaged in securities fraud in violation of Section 10(b). They claimed that GE's interest in justifying its investment in Kidder, Peabody gave GE "a motive to willfully blind itself to facts casting doubt on Kidder's purported profitability." On what basis might the court dismiss the shareholders' complaint? Discuss fully. [*Chill v. General Electric Co.,* 101 F.3d 263 (2d Cir. 1996)]

27–6. SEC Rule 10b-5. Grand Metropolitan PLC (Grand Met) planned to make a tender offer as part of an attempted takeover of the Pillsbury Co. Grand Met hired Robert Falbo, an independent contractor, to complete electrical work as part of security renovations to its offices to prevent leaks of information concerning the planned tender offer. Falbo was given a master key to access the executive offices. When an executive secretary told Falbo that a takeover was brewing, he used his key to access the offices and eavesdrop on conversations; in this way, he learned that Pillsbury was the target. Falbo bought thousands of shares of Pillsbury stock for less than $40 per share. Within two months, Grand Met made an offer for all outstanding Pillsbury stock at $60 per share and ultimately paid up to $66 per share. Falbo made over $165,000 in profit. The Securities and Exchange Commission (SEC) filed a suit in a federal district court against Falbo and others for alleged violations of, among other things, SEC Rule 10b-5. Under what theory might Falbo be liable? Do the circumstances of this case meet all of the requirements for liability under that theory? Explain. [*SEC v. Falbo,* 14 F.Supp.2d 508 (S.D.N.Y. 1998)]

27–7. Definition of a Security. In 1997, Scott and Sabrina Levine formed Friendly Power Co. (FPC) and Friendly Power Franchise Co. (FPC-Franchise). FPC obtained a license to operate as a utility company in California. FPC granted FPC-Franchise the right to pay commissions to "operators" who converted residential customers to FPC. Each operator paid for a "franchise"—a geographic area, determined by such factors as the number of households and competition from other utilities. In exchange for 50 percent of FPC's net profits on sales to residential customers in its territory, each franchise was required to maintain a 5 percent market share of power customers in that territory. Franchises were sold to telemarketing firms, which solicited customers. The telemarketers sold interests in each franchise to between fifty and ninety-four "partners," each of whom invested money. FPC began supplying electricity to its customers in May 1998. Less than three

months later, the Securities and Exchange Commission (SEC) filed a suit in a federal district court against the Levines and others, alleging that the "franchises" were unregistered securities offered for sale to the public in violation of the Securities Act of 1933. What is the definition of a *security*? Should the court rule in favor of the SEC? Why or why not? [*SEC v. Friendly Power Co., LLC,* 49 F.Supp.2d 1363 (S.D.Fla. 1999)]

CASE PROBLEM WITH SAMPLE ANSWER

27–8. 2TheMart.com, Inc., was conceived in January 1999 to launch an auction Web site to compete with eBay, Inc. On January 19, 2TheMart announced that its Web site was in its "final development" stages and expected to be active by the end of July as a "preeminent" auction site, and that the company had "retained the services of leading Web site design and architecture consultants to design and construct" the site. Based on the announcement, investors rushed to buy 2TheMart's stock, causing a rapid increase in the price. On February 3, 2TheMart entered into an agreement with IBM to take preliminary steps to plan the site. Three weeks later, 2TheMart announced that the site was "currently in final development." On June 1, 2TheMart signed a contract with IBM to design, build, and test the site, with a target delivery date of October 8. When 2TheMart's site did not debut as announced, Mary Harrington and others who had bought the stock filed a suit in a federal district court against the firm's officers, alleging violations of the Securities Exchange Act of 1934. The defendants responded, in part, that any alleged misrepresentations were not material and asked the court to dismiss the suit. How should the court rule, and why? [*In re 2TheMart.com, Inc. Securities Litigation,* 114 F.Supp.2d 955 (C.D.Cal. 2000)]

▶ To view a sample answer for this case problem, go to this book's Web site at **http://fundamentals.westbuslaw.com** and click on "Interactive Study Center."

27–9. Insider Reporting and Trading. Ronald Bleakney, an officer at Natural Microsystems Corp. (NMC), a Section 12 corporation, directed NMC sales in North America, South America, and Europe. In November 1998, Bleakney sold more than 7,500 shares of NMC stock. The following March, Bleakney resigned from the firm, and the next month, he bought more than 20,000 shares of its stock. NMC provided some guidance to employees concerning the rules of insider trading, and with regard to Bleakney's transactions, the corporation said nothing about potential liability. Richard Morales, an NMC shareholder, filed a suit against NMC and Bleakney to compel recovery, under Section 16(b) of the Securities Exchange Act of 1934, of Bleakney's profits from the purchase and sale of his shares. (When Morales died, his executor Deborah Donoghue became the plaintiff.) Bleakney argued that he should not be liable because he relied on NMC's advice. Should the court order Bleakney to disgorge his profits? Explain. [*Donoghue v. Natural Microsystems Corp.,* 198 F.Supp.2d 487 (S.D.N.Y. 2002)]

VIDEO QUESTION

27–10. Go to this text's Web site at **http://fundamentals.westbuslaw.com** and click on "Video Questions." Select "Chapter 27" and view the video titled *Mergers and Acquisitions*. Then answer the following questions:

1. Analyze whether the purchase of Onyx Advertising is a material fact that the Quigley Company had a duty to disclose under SEC Rule 10b-5.

2. Does it matter whether Quigley personally knew about or authorized the company spokesperson's statements? Why or why not?

3. Which case discussed in the chapter presented issues that are very similar to those presented in the video? Under the holding of that case, would Onyx Advertising be able to maintain a suit against the Quigley Company for violation of SEC Rule 10b-5?

4. Who else might be able to bring a suit against Quigley Company for insider trading under SEC Rule 10b-5?

INVESTOR PROTECTION AND ONLINE SECURITIES OFFERINGS

For updated links to resources available on the Web, as well as other materials, visit this text's Web site at

http://fundamentals.westbuslaw.com

To access the EDGAR database of the Securities and Exchange Commission (SEC), go to

http://www.sec.gov/edgar.shtml

The Center for Corporate Law of the University of Cincinnati College of Law maintains the *Securities Lawyer's Deskbook* online. The *Deskbook* contains the basic federal securities laws and regulations and links to the principal SEC forms under those laws and regulations. Go to

http://www.law.uc.edu/CCL

For information on investor protection and securities fraud, including answers to frequently asked questions about securities fraud, go to

http://www.securitieslaw.com

Online Legal Research

Go to the *Fundamentals of Business Law* home page at **http://fundamentals.westbuslaw.com**. Select "Interactive Study Center" and then click on "Chapter 27." There you will find the following Internet research exercises that you can perform to learn more about topics covered in this chapter.

Activity 27-1: LEGAL PERSPECTIVE—Electronic Delivery
Activity 27-2: MANAGEMENT PERSPECTIVE—The SEC's Role

Before the Test

Go to the *Fundamentals of Business Law* home page at **http://fundamentals.westbuslaw.com**. Click on "Interactive Quizzes." You will find at least twenty interactive questions relating to this chapter.

Westlaw® Campus

If your textbook provided for a subscription to Westlaw® Campus, or if you have otherwise purchased access to the Westlaw Campus database, you can access any of the cases presented or cited in this chapter by using your Westlaw Campus account.

In re Miller

INTRODUCTION

Section 10(b) of the Securities Exchange Act of 1934 and Rule 10b-5 issued by the Securities and Exchange Commission pursuant to the act are discussed in Chapter 27. In this *Focus on Legal Reasoning,* we look at *In re Miller,*[1] a decision in which the court considered whether a broker's violation of those laws could be imputed to his superiors under Section 20 of the 1934 act, which is known as the "control person" provision.[2]

---

1. 276 F.3d 424 (8th Cir. 2002).
2. Section 20—15 U.S.C. Section 78t(a)—provides that "[e]very person who, directly or indirectly, controls any person liable under any provision of this [portion of the act] or of any rule or regulation thereunder shall also be liable jointly and severally with and to the same extent as such controlled person."

CASE BACKGROUND

When Ronald Owens, Nicola Angelicola, and Ernest Waterman retired from their work at a steel mill in Utica, New York, they received large lump-sum distributions from the mill's retirement plan. All of them wanted secure, income-producing investments to supplement their retirement income. They took their money to Gary Bohling, a vice president of Andover Securities, Inc.

Ignoring the retirees' desires, Bohling invested their funds in speculative, high-risk investments, including private placement offerings of a catfish farm, a medical office complex, and a credit company. Bohling told them that the investments were safe ("even better than Social Security") and falsified various documents. Ultimately, the investments failed.

At the time, Kent Miller was chairman of Andover, and Terry McGavern was president. Miller, who was responsible for reviewing Bohling's documents, later admitted that he "missed some inconsistencies and red flags." McGavern further admitted that "he may have conveyed the impression to his brokers that it was permissible to sell unaccredited investors 'a little bit' of the higher risk investments." Bohling quit Andover in 1993 and filed for bankruptcy.

The retirees settled their claims with Bohling for $12,000 and filed a complaint with the National Association of Securities Dealers (NASD) against Andover, Miller, and McGavern. NASD arbitrators found Andover and the officers jointly and severally liable for $226,000, plus interest. A federal district court affirmed the award. Miller and McGavern filed for bankruptcy, seeking to discharge this liability. When the court ruled against them, Miller and McGavern appealed to the U.S. Court of Appeals for the Eighth Circuit.

MAJORITY OPINION

WOLLMAN, Chief Judge.

* * * *

* * * [The bankruptcy court] concluded * * * that Bohling's conduct violated [Section] 10b of the Securities Exchange Act of 1934 and Rule 10b-5 * * * [and] that pursuant to [Section] 20 of the Act, Miller and McGavern, as controlling persons, were jointly and severally liable for Bohling's fraud to the same extent that Bohling was liable * * * . In short, the bankruptcy court concluded that [Section] 20(a) created an "agency-like relationship" sufficient to impute Bohling's fraud to Miller and McGavern and therefore concluded that the debt in question was nondischargeable under [the Bankruptcy Code].

* * * *

The United States Supreme Court has recognized that a debt may be nondischargeable when the debtor personally commits fraud or when actual fraud is imputed to the debtor under agency principles. *Strang v. Bradner,* 114 U.S. 555, 5 S.Ct. 1038, 29 L.Ed. 248 (1885). *Strang* specifically relied on the common law of agency and partnership to impute the fraud of an innocent debtor's business partner to that debtor and so render his debt nondischargeable. The bankruptcy court determined that, like common law agency principles, [Section] 20(a) of the Securities Exchange Act of 1934 renders an innocent person's debt nondischargeable when a person over whom the innocent person exercised control committed actual fraud.

* * * *

We see nothing in the Bankruptcy Code or the securities laws indicating that these two separate provisions of law should be combined in the manner the bankruptcy court did. * * * *[T]he Bankruptcy Code prevents persons from committing actual fraud and then wiping away their resulting debt. It also provides other specific exceptions to discharge, which do not include an exception for liability under the securities laws.* Section 20(a) of the Securities Exchange Act of 1934, on the other hand, is designed to ensure that securities brokers act properly and supervise their employees, and, therefore, it imposes liability in those cases in which the supervisor did not directly participate in the bad acts. Section 20(a) extends liability well beyond traditional doctrines, providing expansive remedies in a highly regulated industry. * * * *[T]he Bankruptcy Code addresses actual, traditional fraud, and we are not persuaded that it should be read in such a way as to encompass the nontraditional liability imposed under [Section] 20(a). * * * [Emphasis added.]*

The judgment is reversed, and the case is remanded to the district court for further proceedings not inconsistent with this opinion.

(Continued)

DISSENTING OPINION

BEAM, Circuit Judge, dissenting.

* * * *

I conclude that the bankruptcy court did not err by imputing Bohling's fraud to Miller and McGavern by way of [Section] 20(a) of the Securities Exchange Act. The court's determination that Bohling's conduct constituted fraud within the meaning of both [the Bankruptcy Code] and Rule 10b-5 is well supported. Thus, there is no question but that Bohling's individual debt to the appellees would be nondischargeable. The bankruptcy court also correctly held that Miller and McGavern were "control persons" and therefore, pursuant to [Section] 20(a), were jointly and severally liable to the same extent as Bohling. Accordingly, the bankruptcy court did not err in concluding that the debts in question are nondischargeable * * * .

* * * Miller and McGavern * * * argue that an agency-principal relationship is necessary to impute fraud for the purposes of dischargeability.

* * * The fact that Miller and McGavern cannot be liable under common law agency principles does not necessarily mean that they may not be liable under [Section] 20(a). The bankruptcy court applied [Section] 20(a) to supplement common law agency principles * * * . Thus, I respectfully disagree with the [majority] * * * because [their opinion does] not take [Section] 20(a) on its own terms, independent of agency law. *Strang*, decided nearly a half-century before the enactment of the Securities Exchange Act, should not be read to control the reach of the Act. * * * The statute's language is straightforward: control persons are liable to the same extent as the persons they control. Here, an aspect of Bohling's liability is that his debt to the appellees would be nondischargeable. Section 20(a) extends that aspect of Bohling's liability to Miller and McGavern as control persons, along with all other features of his liability.

LEGAL REASONING AND ANALYSIS

1 Legal Analysis. The majority cites, in its opinion, *Strang v. Bradner,* 114 U.S. 555, 5 S.Ct. 1038, 29 L.Ed. 248 (1885) (see the *Accessing the Internet* feature at the end of Chapter 2 for instructions on how to access federal court opinions). How do the facts and issues in that case compare with the facts and issues of the *Miller* case? How do the applicable legal principles and holdings compare? Is the majority correct in applying the *Strang* case in the *Miller* case, or is the dissent correct in asserting that *Strang* "should not be read to control"?

2 Legal Reasoning. What reasons does the majority provide to justify its conclusion? Do you agree? Why or why not?

3 Ethical Considerations. What ethical obligations do officers in the positions of Miller and McGavern have to their subordinates and to their subordinates' clients?

4 Implications for Investors. What are the implications of the decision in this case for those who invest through brokers?

5 Case Briefing Assignment. Using the guidelines for briefing cases given in Appendix A of this text, brief the *Miller* case.

This text's Web site, at **http://fundamentals.westbuslaw.com**, offers links to West's Court Case Updates, as well as to other online research sources. You can also locate court cases at the Web sites listed in the *Accessing the Internet* section at the end of Chapter 2.

Sec Law.com, a Web site at **http://www.seclaw.com/Welcome.shtml**, is "an online guide to securities law." The site provides links to a variety of securities law resources, including its own monthly "Securities Law Letter," which covers recent developments in securities law. New York securities attorney Mark Astarita maintains this Web site.

UNIT 9

Property and Its Protection

589

28
Personal Property and Bailments

CHAPTER OBJECTIVES

After reading this chapter, you should be able to answer the following questions:

① What is real property? What is personal property?

② What does it mean to own property in fee simple? What is the difference between a joint tenancy and a tenancy in common?

③ What are the three elements necessary for an effective gift? How else can property be acquired?

④ What are the three elements of a bailment?

⑤ What are the basic rights and duties of the bailee? What are the rights and duties of the bailor?

Property consists of the legally protected rights and interests a person has in anything with an ascertainable value that is subject to ownership. Property would have little value (and the word would have little meaning) if the law did not define the right to use it, to sell or dispose of it, and to prevent trespass on it.

Property is divided into real property and personal property. **Real property** (sometimes called *realty* or *real estate*) means the land and everything permanently attached to it. Everything else is **personal property**, or *personalty*. Attorneys sometimes refer to personal property as **chattel**, a term used under the common law to denote all forms of personal property. Personal property can be tangible or intangible. *Tangible* personal property, such as a TV set or a

car, has physical substance. *Intangible* personal property represents some set of rights and interests but has no real physical existence. Stocks and bonds, patents, and copyrights are examples of intangible personal property.

In the first part of this chapter, we look at the ways in which title to property is held; the methods of acquiring ownership of personal property; and issues relating to mislaid, lost, and abandoned personal property. In the second part of the chapter, we examine bailment relationships. A *bailment* is created when personal property is temporarily delivered into the care of another without a transfer of title. This is the distinguishing characteristic of a bailment compared with a sale or a gift—there is no passage of title and no intent to transfer title.

Property Ownership

Property ownership[1] can be viewed as a bundle of rights, including the right to possess property and to dispose of it—by sale, gift, lease, or other means.

FEE SIMPLE

A person who holds the entire bundle of rights to property is said to be the owner in **fee simple**. The owner in fee simple is entitled to use, possess, or dispose of the property as he or she chooses during his or her lifetime, and on this owner's death, the interests in the property descend to his or her heirs. We will return to this form of property ownership in Chapter 29, in the context of ownership rights in real property. (Whether a domain name is property that can be garnished to satisfy a debt is a question explored in this chapter's *Business Law in the Online World* feature on page 592.)

CONCURRENT OWNERSHIP

Persons who share ownership rights simultaneously in a particular piece of property are said to be *concurrent* owners. There are two principal types of concurrent ownership: tenancy in common and joint tenancy. Other types of concurrent ownership include tenancy by the entirety and community property.

Tenancy in Common. The term **tenancy in common** refers to a form of co-ownership in which each of two or more persons owns an *undivided* interest in the property. The interest is undivided because each tenant has rights in the *whole* property. ● **EXAMPLE #1** Rosa and Chad together own a collection of rare stamps as tenants in common. This does not mean that Rosa owns some particular stamps and Chad others. Rather, it means that Rosa and Chad each have rights in the *entire* collection. (If Rosa owned some of the stamps and Chad owned others, then the interest would be *divided*.)●

On the death of a tenant in common, that tenant's interest in the property passes to her or his heirs. ● **EXAMPLE #2** Should Rosa die before Chad, a one-half interest in the stamp collection would become the property of Rosa's heirs. If Rosa sold her interest to Fred before she died, Fred and Chad would be co-owners as tenants in common. If Fred died, his interest in the personal property would pass to his heirs, and they in turn would own the property with Chad as tenants in common.●

---

[1] The principles discussed in this section apply equally to real property ownership, which will be discussed in Chapter 29.

Joint Tenancy. In a **joint tenancy**, each of two or more persons owns an undivided interest in the property, and a deceased joint tenant's interest passes to the surviving joint tenant or tenants. The rights of a surviving joint tenant to inherit a deceased joint tenant's ownership interest, which are referred to as *survivorship rights,* distinguish the joint tenancy from the tenancy in common. A joint tenancy can be terminated before a joint tenant's death by gift or by sale; in this situation, the person who receives the property as a gift or who purchases the property becomes a tenant in common, not a joint tenant.

● **EXAMPLE #3** If, in the preceding example, Rosa and Chad held their stamp collection in a joint tenancy and if Rosa died before Chad, the entire collection would become the property of Chad; Rosa's heirs would receive absolutely no interest in the collection. If Rosa, while living, sold her interest to Fred, however, the sale would terminate the joint tenancy, and Fred and Chad would become co-owners as tenants in common.●

Tenancy by the Entirety. Concurrent ownership of property can also take the form of a **tenancy by the entirety**—a form of co-ownership between a husband and wife that is similar to a joint tenancy, except that a spouse cannot transfer his or her interest during his or her lifetime without the consent of the other spouse.

Community Property. When property is held as **community property**, each spouse technically owns an undivided one-half interest in property acquired during the marriage. The community property form of ownership occurs in only ten states and Puerto Rico.

Acquiring Ownership of Personal Property

The most common way of acquiring personal property is by purchasing it. We have already discussed the purchase and sale of personal property (goods) in Chapters 14 through 17. Often, property is acquired by will or inheritance, a topic we cover in Chapter 30. Here we look at additional ways in which ownership of personal property can be acquired, including acquisition by possession, production, gift, accession, and confusion.

POSSESSION

One example of acquiring ownership by possession is the capture of wild animals. Wild animals belong to no one in their natural state, and the first person to take possession of

BUSINESS LAW IN THE ONLINE WORLD
Is a Domain Name Property?

Recall from Chapter 21 that garnishment occurs when a creditor is permitted, by court order, to collect a debt by seizing property of the debtor that is being held by a third party. Typically, garnishment involves obtaining from the debtor's employer a portion of the debtor's wages or obtaining from the debtor's bank the funds in the debtor's bank account. In this context, consider a question that recently came before a Virginia state court: Can a debtor's domain names be garnished and sold to the highest bidder to collect a court judgment? Are domain names "property" subject to garnishment?

The question arose after a federal district court had awarded Umbro International, Inc., nearly $24,000 to cover its attorneys' fees and expenses in a lawsuit concerning a dispute over rights to the domain name *umbro.com*. Because the defendants in the suit, James Tombas and his Canadian corporation, had no assets in the United States to satisfy the judgment, Umbro instituted a garnishment proceeding in a Virginia state court against Network Solutions, Inc. (NSI), with which Tombas had registered more than twenty other domain names. Umbro sought to force a judicial sale of those names. NSI objected to the garnishment summons, arguing that domain names cannot function on the Internet in the absence of the services provided by a domain name registrar such as NSI. Thus, domain name registration agreements are essentially contracts for services, which are not subject to garnishment.

A CASE OF FIRST IMPRESSION—THE TRIAL COURT'S DECISION In this case of first impression (a case involving an issue never before decided by Virginia courts), the Virginia trial court determined that the judgment debtor's (Tombas's) domain name registrations were a new and "valuable form of intangible property subject to garnishment." In return for registering the names and paying the appropriate fees, the debtor obtained the exclusive right to use the names for a specified period of time. The court

thus held that the debtor had a "possessory interest"—a form of property interest—in the domain names registered with NSI and that this property interest was subject to garnishment. Accordingly, the court ordered NSI to deposit control over all of the judgment debtor's Internet domain name registrations into the registry of the court for sale by the sheriff's office to the highest bidders.

THE VIRGINIA SUPREME COURT REVERSES NSI appealed the case to the Virginia Supreme Court, which reversed the trial court's decision and entered a judgment in NSI's favor. NSI argued that although a domain name registrant acquires the contractual right to the exclusive use of a unique domain name for a specified time period, that right is inextricably bound to the domain name services that NSI provides. The court agreed, stating that "whatever contractual rights the judgment debtor has in the domain names at issue in this appeal, those rights do not exist separate and apart from NSI's services that make the domain names operational Internet addresses."

The court pointed out that in garnishment cases, usually the question is whether the garnishee is liable to the judgment debtor and, if so, the amount due. In this case, said the court, "the only liability on the part of NSI is the provision of its Internet domain name services to the judgment debtor. Although, as Umbro points out, domain names are being bought and sold in today's marketplace, we are not willing to sanction the garnishment of NSI's services under the terms of our present garnishment statutes. Even though the Internet is a 'new avenue of commerce,' we cannot extend established legal principles beyond their statutory parameters."[a]

FOR CRITICAL ANALYSIS
Analyze the reasoning of the lower court and the state supreme court, respectively. Which argument do you find more convincing? Explain.

a. *Network Solutions, Inc. v. Umbro International, Inc.*, 259 Va. 759, 529 S.E.2d 80 (2000).

---

a wild animal normally owns it. The killing of a wild animal amounts to assuming ownership of it. Merely being in hot pursuit does not give title, however. There are two exceptions to this basic rule. First, any wild animals captured by a trespasser are the property of the landowner, not the tres-

passer. Second, if wild animals are captured or killed in violation of wild-game statutes, the capturer does not obtain title to the animals; rather, the state does.

Those who find lost or abandoned property also can acquire ownership rights through mere possession of the property, as will be discussed later in the chapter. (Ownership rights in real property can also be acquired through possession, such as adverse possession—see Chapter 29.)

PRODUCTION

Production—the fruits of labor—is another means of acquiring ownership of personal property. For example, writers, inventors, and manufacturers all produce personal property and thereby acquire title to it. (In some situations, though, as when a researcher is hired to invent a new product or technique, the researcher-producer may not own what is produced—see Chapter 22.)

GIFTS

A **gift** is another fairly common means of acquiring and transferring ownership of real and personal property. A gift is essentially a voluntary transfer of property ownership for which no consideration is given. As discussed in Chapter 8, the presence of consideration is what distinguishes a contract from a gift. Certain conditions must exist, however, before a gift will be deemed effective in the eyes of the law. The donor (the one making the gift) must intend to make the gift, the gift must be delivered to the donee (the recipient of the gift), and the donee must accept the gift. We examine each of these requirements here, as well as the requirements of a gift made in contemplation of imminent death.

Donative Intent. When a gift is challenged in court, the court will determine whether donative intent exists by looking at the surrounding circumstances. ● EXAMPLE #4 A court may look at the relationship between the parties and the size of the gift in relation to the donor's other assets. A gift to a mortal enemy is viewed with suspicion. Similarly, when a gift represents a large portion of a person's assets,

the court will scrutinize the transaction closely to determine the mental capacity of the donor and ascertain whether any element of fraud or duress is present.●

Delivery. The gift must be delivered to the donee. An effective delivery requires giving up complete control and **dominion** (ownership rights) over the subject matter of the gift. When a gift cannot be physically delivered, a symbolic, or *constructive*, delivery will be sufficient. **Constructive delivery** is an act that the law holds to be equivalent to an act of actual delivery. ● EXAMPLE #5 Suppose that you want to make a gift of various old rare coins that you have stored in a safe-deposit box. You certainly cannot deliver the box itself to the donee, and you do not want to take the coins out of the bank. In this situation, the delivery of the key to the safe-deposit box (along with appropriate instructions to the bank) constitutes a constructive delivery of the contents of the box.●

The delivery of intangible property—such as stocks, bonds, insurance policies, contracts, and so on—is always accomplished by symbolic, or constructive, delivery. This is because the documents represent rights and are not, in themselves, the true property.

Delivery may be accomplished by means of a third party. If the third party is the agent of the donor, the delivery is effective when the agent delivers the gift to the donee. If the third party is the agent of the donee, the gift is effectively delivered when the donor delivers the property to the donee's agent.[2] Naturally, no delivery is necessary if the gift is already in the hands of the donee.

In the following classic case, the court focused on the requirement that a donor must give up complete control and dominion over property given to the donee before a gift can be effectively delivered.

---

[2] *Bickford v. Mattocks*, 95 Me. 547, 50 A. 894 (1901).

Landmark and Classic Cases

CASE 28.1 In re Estate of Piper

Missouri Court of Appeals, 1984.
676 S.W.2d 897.

FACTS Gladys Piper died intestate (without a will) in 1982. At her death, she owned miscellaneous personal property worth $5,000 and had in her purse $200 in cash and two

diamond rings, known as the Andy Piper rings. The contents of her purse were taken by her niece Wanda Brown, allegedly to preserve them for the estate. Clara Kaufmann, a friend of Piper's, filed a claim against the estate for $4,800. From October 1974 until Piper's death, Kaufmann had taken Piper to the doctor, beauty shop, and grocery store; had written her checks to pay her bills; and had helped her care for her

(Continued)

CASE 28.1—Continued

home. Kaufmann maintained that Piper had promised to pay her for these services and had given her the diamond rings as a gift. A Missouri state trial court denied her request for payment; the court found that her services had been voluntary. Kaufmann then filed a petition for delivery of personal property, the rings, which was granted by the trial court. Brown, other heirs, and the administrator of Piper's estate appealed.

ISSUE Had Gladys Piper made an effective gift of the rings to Clara Kaufmann?

DECISION No. The state appellate court reversed the judgment of the trial court on the ground that Piper had never delivered the rings to Kaufmann.

REASON Kaufmann claimed that the rings belonged to her by reason of a "consummated gift long prior to the death of Gladys Piper." Two witnesses testified for Kaufmann at the trial that Piper had told them the rings belonged to Kaufmann but that she was going to wear them until she died. The appellate court found "no evidence of any actual delivery." The court held that the essentials of a gift are (1) a

present intention to make a gift on the part of the donor, (2) a delivery of the property by the donor to the donee, and (3) an acceptance by the donee. The evidence in the case showed only an intent to make a gift. Because there was no delivery—either actual or constructive—a valid gift was not made. For Piper to have made a gift, her intention would have to have been executed by the complete and unconditional delivery of the property or the delivery of a proper written instrument evidencing the gift. As this did not occur, the court found that there had been no gift.

COMMENT *Although this case is relatively recent in the long span of the law governing gifts, we present it here as a classic case because it so clearly illustrates the delivery requirement when making a gift. Assuming that Piper did, indeed, intend for Kaufmann to have the rings, it was unfortunate that Kaufmann had no right to receive them after Piper's death. Yet the alternative could lead to perhaps even more unfairness. The policy behind the delivery requirement is to protect alleged donors and their heirs from fraudulent claims based solely on parol evidence. If not for this policy, an alleged donee could easily claim that a gift was made when, in fact, it was not.*

Acceptance. The final requirement of a valid gift is acceptance by the donee. This rarely presents any problem, as most donees readily accept their gifts. The courts generally assume acceptance unless shown otherwise.

Gifts *Causa Mortis*. A gift made during one's lifetime is termed a **gift *inter vivos*.** **Gifts *causa mortis*** (so-called *deathbed gifts*), in contrast, are made in contemplation of imminent death. A gift *causa mortis* does not become absolute until the donor dies from the contemplated illness, and it is automatically revoked if the donor recovers from the illness. Moreover, the donee must survive to take the gift. To be effective, a gift *causa mortis* must also meet the three requirements discussed earlier—donative intent, delivery, and acceptance by the donee.

● **EXAMPLE #6** Suppose that Young is to be operated on for a cancerous tumor. Before the operation, he delivers an envelope to a close business associate. The envelope contains a letter saying, "I realize my days are numbered, and I want to give you this check for $1 million in the event of my death from this operation." The business associate cashes the check. The surgeon performs the operation to remove the tumor. Young recovers fully. Several months later, Young dies from a heart attack that is totally unrelated to the operation. If Young's personal representative (the

party charged with administering Young's estate) tries to recover the $1 million, normally she will succeed. The gift *causa mortis* is automatically revoked if the donor recovers. The *specific event* that was contemplated in making the gift was death from a particular operation. Because Young's death was not the result of this event, the gift is revoked, and the $1 million passes to Young's estate. ●

ACCESSION

Accession, which means "adding on" to something, occurs when someone adds value to an item of personal property by either labor or materials. When accession is accomplished with the permission of the owner, generally there is no dispute about who owns the property after the accession occurred. When accession occurs without the permission of the owner, the courts will tend to favor the owner over the improver—the one who improves the property—provided that the accession was wrongful and undertaken in bad faith. In addition, many courts will deny the improver any compensation for the value added; for example, a car thief who puts new tires on the stolen car will obviously not be compensated for the value of the new tires when the rightful owner recovers the car.

If the accession is performed in good faith, however, even without the owner's consent, ownership of the improved item most often depends on whether the accession has increased the value of the property or changed its identity. The greater the increase in value, the more likely it is that ownership will pass to the improver. If ownership so passes, the improver obviously must compensate the original owner for the value of the property prior to the accession. If the increase in value is not sufficient for ownership to pass to the improver, most courts will require the owner to compensate the improver for the value added.

CONFUSION

Confusion is defined as the commingling (mixing together) of goods so that one person's personal property cannot be distinguished from another's. Confusion frequently occurs when the goods are *fungible,* meaning that each particle is identical to every other particle, as with grain and oil, and the goods are owned by two or more parties as tenants in common. For example, if two farmers put their Number 2–grade winter wheat into the same storage bin, confusion would occur.

If confusion of goods is caused by a person who wrongfully and willfully mixes the goods for the purpose of rendering them indistinguishable, the innocent party acquires title to the whole. If confusion occurs as a result of agreement, an honest mistake, or the act of some third party, the owners share ownership as tenants in common and will share any loss in proportion to their shares of ownership of the property.

Mislaid, Lost, and Abandoned Property

As already mentioned, one of the methods of acquiring ownership of property is to possess it. Simply finding something and holding on to it, however, does not necessarily give the finder any legal rights in the property. Different rules apply, depending on whether the property was mislaid, lost, or abandoned.

MISLAID PROPERTY

Property that has been placed somewhere by the owner voluntarily and then inadvertently forgotten is **mislaid property.** ● EXAMPLE #7 Suppose that you go to the theater. You leave your gloves on the concession stand and then forget about them. The gloves are mislaid property, and the theater owner is entrusted with the duty of reasonable care for them.● When mislaid property is found, the finder does not obtain title to the goods. Instead, the owner of the place

where the property was mislaid becomes the caretaker of the property, because it is highly likely that the true owner will return.[3]

LOST PROPERTY

Property that is involuntarily left and forgotten is **lost property.** A finder of the property can claim title to the property against the whole world, *except the true owner.*[4] If the true owner demands that the lost property be returned, the finder must return it. If a third party takes possession of lost property from a finder, however, the third party cannot assert a better title than the finder. When a finder knows who the true owner of the property is and fails to return it to that person, the finder is guilty of the tort of *conversion* (the wrongful taking of another's property—see Chapter 4). Finally, many states require the finder to make a reasonably diligent search to locate the true owner of lost property.

● EXAMPLE #8 Suppose that Kormian works in a large library at night. In the courtyard on her way home, she finds a piece of gold jewelry set with stones that look like precious stones to her. She takes it to a jeweler to have it appraised. While pretending to weigh the jewelry, an employee of the jeweler removes several of the stones. If Kormian brings an action to recover the stones from the jeweler, she normally will win because she found lost property and holds valid title against everyone *except the true owner.* Because the property was lost, rather than mislaid, the finder is not the caretaker of the jewelry. Instead, the finder acquires title good against the whole world (except the true owner).●

Many states have laws that encourage and facilitate the return of property to its true owner and then reward a finder for honesty if the property remains unclaimed. These laws, called **estray statutes,** provide an incentive for finders to report their discoveries by making it possible for them, after the passage of a specified period of time, to acquire legal title to the property they have found. The statute usually requires the county clerk to advertise the property in an attempt to enhance the opportunity of the owner to recover what has been lost. Some preliminary questions must always be resolved before the estray statute can be employed. The item must be lost property, not merely mislaid property. When the circumstances indicate that the property was probably lost and not mislaid or abandoned, loss is presumed as a matter of public policy, and the estray statute applies.

---

[3] The finder of mislaid property is an involuntary bailee (to be discussed later in this chapter).

[4] See *Armory v. Delamirie,* 93 Eng.Rep. 664 (K.B. [King's Bench] 1722).

The law that finders of lost property may obtain good title to the property has a long history. Under the doctrine of *relativity of title*, if two contestants are before the court, neither of whom can claim absolute title to the property, the one who can claim prior possession will likely have established sufficient rights to the property to win the case.

ABANDONED PROPERTY

Property that has been discarded by the true owner, who has no intention of reclaiming title to it, is **abandoned property.**

Someone who finds abandoned property acquires title to it, and such title is good against the whole world, *including the original owner.* The owner of lost property who eventually gives up any further attempt to find it is frequently held to have abandoned the property. If a person finds abandoned property while trespassing on the property of another, title vests not in the finder but in the owner of the land.

The following case involved a find of sunken vessels embedded in the "submerged lands" off the coast of Virginia.

CASE 28.2   **Sea Hunt, Inc. v. Unidentified Shipwrecked Vessel or Vessels**

United States Court of Appeals,
Fourth Circuit, 2000.
221 F.3d 634.
http://www.law.emory.edu/4circuit[a]

FACTS Under the 1902 Treaty of Friendship and General Relations between the United States and Spain, Spanish vessels, like those belonging to the United States, may only be abandoned by express acts. Sailing from Cuba to Spain at the end of August 1750, *La Galga* ("The Greyhound"), a fifty-gun frigate in the Spanish Navy, sank in a hurricane off the coast of Virginia. *Juno,* a thirty-four-gun frigate, bound from Mexico for Spain, sank in a storm off the Virginia coast in January 1802. The Virginia Marine Resources Commission granted Sea Hunt, Inc., a maritime salvage company, permits to explore for shipwrecks off the Virginia coast and conduct salvage operations. Sea Hunt found the remains of *La Galga* and *Juno.* Virginia asserted ownership over the ships under the Abandoned Shipwreck Act of 1987 (ASA).[b] Sea Hunt filed a suit in a federal district court, seeking payment for salvaging the vessels or a declaratory judgment that Virginia owned them (which would mean that items salvaged by Sea Hunt would belong to Sea Hunt under its permit). Spain opposed Sea Hunt's request, arguing that the ships belonged to Spain. The court held that Spain had abandoned *La Galga,* but had not abandoned *Juno,* and denied the salvage award. Sea Hunt and Spain appealed to the U.S. Court of Appeals for the Fourth Circuit.

ISSUE Is a nation required to expressly abandon its shipwrecks before another party can acquire title to them?

DECISION Yes. The U.S. Court of Appeals for the Fourth Circuit reversed the judgment of the lower court with regard to *La Galga* and affirmed the judgment concerning *Juno* and the denial of the salvage award.

REASON The U.S. Court of Appeals for the Fourth Circuit acknowledged that the wrecks were embedded within Virginia's submerged lands. "That, however, is not enough." The court explained that "for Virginia to acquire title to the shipwrecks and to issue salvage permits to Sea Hunt, these vessels must have been abandoned by Spain. * * * Because Spain has asserted an ownership claim to the shipwrecks, * * * express abandonment is the governing standard. To adopt a lesser standard would not only go beyond what the ASA requires. It would also abrogate America's obligations to Spain under the 1902 Treaty of Friendship and General Relations." The ASA states that "abandoned shipwrecks" are those "to which the owner has relinquished ownership rights with no retention." The court pointed out that "[w]hen an owner comes before the court to assert his rights, relinquishment would be hard, if not impossible, to show. Requiring express abandonment where an owner makes a claim thus accords with the statutory text." The court added that abandonment may be implied, "as by an owner never asserting any control over or otherwise indicating his claim of possession." The court concluded, however, that "[a]n owner who comes forward has definitely indicated his claim of possession, and in such a case abandonment cannot be implied."

FOR CRITICAL ANALYSIS—Political Consideration
Considering the decision in the Sea Hunt *case, what might the salvage industry do to further its interest in the commercial recovery of sunken ships?*

---

a. Under "2000," click on "July." In the result, click on the case name to access the opinion. Emory University School of Law in Atlanta maintains this Web site for the U.S. Court of Appeals for the Fourth Circuit.
b. 43 U.S.C. Sections 2101–2106. The ASA gives a state such as Virginia title to shipwrecks that are abandoned and embedded in the state's submerged lands.

Bailments

A **bailment** is formed by the delivery of personal property, without transfer of title, by one person, called a **bailor**, to another, called a **bailee**, usually under an agreement for a particular purpose (for example, for storage, repair, or transportation). On completion of the purpose, the bailee is obligated to return the bailed property to the bailor or to a third person or to dispose of it as directed.

Bailments usually are created by agreement but not necessarily by contract, because in many bailments not all of the elements of a contract (such as mutual assent and consideration) are present. For example, if you lend your bicycle to a friend, a bailment is created, but not by contract, because there is no consideration. Many commercial bailments, such as the delivery of clothing to the cleaner's for dry cleaning, are based on contract, however.

Virtually every individual or business is affected by the law of bailments at one time or another (and sometimes even on a daily basis). When individuals deal with bailments, whether they realize it or not, they are subject to the obligations and duties that arise from the bailment relationship. The number, scope, and importance of bailments created daily in the business community and in everyday life make it desirable for every person to understand the elements necessary for the creation of a bailment and to know what rights, duties, and liabilities flow from bailments.

ELEMENTS OF A BAILMENT

Not all transactions involving the delivery of property from one person to another create a bailment. For such a transfer to become a bailment, three conditions must be met. We look here at each of these conditions.

Personal Property. Bailment involves only personal property; there can be no bailment of persons. Although a bailment of your luggage is created when it is transported by an airline, as a passenger you are not the subject of a bailment. Additionally, you cannot bail realty; thus, leasing your house to a tenant does not create a bailment.

Delivery of Possession. In a voluntary bailment, possession of the property must be transferred to the bailee in such a way that (1) the bailee is given exclusive possession and control over the property and (2) the bailee *knowingly* accepts the personal property. If either of these conditions for effective delivery of possession is lacking, there is no bailment relationship. ● EXAMPLE #9 Suppose that you take a friend out to dinner at an expensive restaurant. When you enter the restaurant, your friend checks her coat. In the pocket of the coat is a $20,000 diamond necklace. The bailee, by accepting the coat, does not knowingly also accept the necklace; thus, a bailment of the coat exists—because the restaurant has exclusive possession and control over the coat and knowingly accepted it—but a bailment of the necklace does not exist.●

Two types of delivery—*physical* and *constructive*—will result in the bailee's exclusive possession of and control over the property. As discussed earlier, in the context of gifts, constructive delivery is a substitute, or symbolic, delivery. What is delivered to the bailee is not the actual property bailed (such as a car) but something so related to the property (such as the car keys) that the requirement of delivery is satisfied.

In certain unique situations, a bailment is found despite the apparent lack of the requisite elements of control and knowledge. In particular, the rental of a safe-deposit box is usually held to create a bailor-bailee relationship between the customer and the bank, despite the bank's lack of knowledge of the contents and its inability to have exclusive control of the property.[5] Another example of such a situation occurs when the bailee acquires the property accidentally or by mistake—as in finding someone else's lost or mislaid property. A bailment is created even though the bailor did not voluntarily deliver the property to the bailee. Such bailments are called *constructive* or *involuntary* bailments.

Bailment Agreement. A bailment agreement, or contract, can be express or implied. Although a written agreement is not required for bailments of less than one year (that is, the Statute of Frauds does not apply—see Chapter 10), it is a good idea to have one, especially when valuable property is involved.

The bailment agreement expressly or impliedly provides for the return of the bailed property to the bailor or to a third person, or it provides for disposal by the bailee. The agreement presupposes that the bailee will return the identical goods originally given by the bailor. In certain types of bailments, however, such as bailments of fungible goods, the property returned need only be equivalent property. ● EXAMPLE #10 If Holman stores his grain (fungible goods) in Joe's Warehouse, a bailment is created. At the end of the storage period, however, the warehouse is not obligated to return to Holman exactly the same grain that he stored. As long as the warehouse returns goods of the same *type, grade,* and *quantity,* the warehouse—the bailee—has performed its obligation.●

---

[5] By statute or by express contract, the rental of a safe-deposit box may be regarded as a lease of space or a license (a revocable right to use the space, for a fee—see Chapter 29) instead of a bailment.

ORDINARY BAILMENTS

Bailments are either *ordinary* or *special (extraordinary)*. There are three types of ordinary bailments. The distinguishing feature among them is *which party receives a benefit from the bailment*. Ultimately, the courts may use this factor to determine the standard of care required of the bailee in possession of the personal property, and this factor will dictate the rights and liabilities of the parties. The three types of ordinary bailments are as follows:

① *Bailment for the sole benefit of the bailor.* This is a gratuitous bailment (a bailment without consideration) for the convenience and benefit of the bailor. For example, if Allen asks his friend, Sumi, to store Allen's car in her garage, and Sumi agrees to do so, the bailment of the car is for the sole benefit of the bailor (Allen).

② *Bailment for the sole benefit of the bailee.* This type of bailment typically occurs when one person lends an item to another person (the bailee) solely for the bailee's convenience and benefit. For example, Allen asks to borrow his friend Sumi's boat so that Allen can go sailing over the weekend. The bailment of the boat is for Allen's (the bailee's) sole benefit.

③ *Bailment for the mutual benefit of the bailee and the bailor.* This is the most common kind of bailment and involves some form of compensation for storing items or holding property while it is being serviced. It is a contractual bailment and is often referred to as a bailment for hire. For example, leaving your car at a service station for an oil change is a mutual-benefit bailment.

Rights of the Bailee. Certain rights are implicit in the bailment agreement. A hallmark of the bailment agreement is that the bailee acquires the *right to control and possess the property temporarily*. The bailee's right of possession permits the bailee to recover damages from any third person for damage or loss of the property. If the property is stolen, the bailee has a legal right to regain possession of it or to obtain damages from any third person who has wrongfully interfered with the bailee's possessory rights. The bailee's right to regain possession of the property or to obtain damages is important because, as you will read shortly, a bailee is liable to the bailor for any loss or damage to bailed property resulting from the bailee's negligence.

Depending on the type of bailment and the terms of the bailment agreement, a bailee may also have a *right to use the bailed property.* ● **EXAMPLE #11** If you borrow a friend's car to drive to the airport, you, as the bailee, would obviously be expected to use the car. In a bailment involving the long-term storage of a car, however, the bailee is not expected to use the car because the ordinary purpose of a storage bailment does not include use of the property.●

Except in a gratuitous bailment, a bailee has a *right to be compensated* as provided for in the bailment agreement, a right to be reimbursed for costs and services rendered in the keeping of the bailed property, or both. Even in a gratuitous bailment, a bailee has a right to be reimbursed or compensated for costs incurred in the keeping of the bailed property. ● **EXAMPLE #12** Margo loses her pet dog, and Judith finds it. Judith takes the dog to her home and feeds it. Even though she takes good care of the dog, it becomes ill, and she calls a veterinarian. Judith pays the bill for the veterinarian's services and the medicine. Judith normally will be entitled to be reimbursed by Margo for all reasonable costs incurred in the keeping of Margo's dog.●

To enforce the right of compensation, the bailee has a right to place a *possessory lien* (which entitles a creditor to retain possession of the debtor's goods until a debt is paid) on the specific bailed property until he or she has been fully compensated. This type of lien, sometimes referred to as an artisan's lien or a *bailee's lien,* was discussed in Chapter 21.

Ordinary bailees have the *right to limit their liability* as long as the limitations are called to the attention of the bailor and are not against public policy. It is essential that the bailor in some way know of the limitation. Even if the bailor has notice, certain types of disclaimers of liability have been considered to be against public policy and therefore illegal. For example, certain exculpatory clauses limiting a person's liability for her or his own wrongful acts are often scrutinized by the courts and, in the case of bailments, are routinely held to be illegal. This is particularly true in bailments for the mutual benefit of the bailor and the bailee.

Duties of the Bailee. The bailee has two basic responsibilities: (1) to take proper care of the property and (2) to surrender the property to the bailor or dispose of it in accordance with the bailor's instructions at the end of the bailment. The bailee must exercise reasonable care in preserving the bailed property. What constitutes reasonable care in a bailment situation normally depends on the nature and specific circumstances of the bailment. Traditionally, courts have determined the appropriate standard of care on the basis of the type of bailment involved. In a bailment for the sole benefit of the bailor, for example, the bailee need exercise only a slight degree of care. In a bailment for the sole benefit of the bailee, however, the bailee must exercise great care. In a mutual-benefit bailment, courts normally impose a reasonable standard of care—that is, the bailee must exercise the degree of care that a reasonable and prudent person would exercise in the same circumstances. Exhibit 28–1 illustrates these concepts.

EXHIBIT 28–1 DEGREE OF CARE REQUIRED OF A BAILEE

Bailment for the Sole Benefit of the Bailor	Mutual-Benefit Bailment	Bailment for the Sole Benefit of the Bailee
	DEGREE OF CARE →	
SLIGHT	REASONABLE	GREAT

A bailee's failure to exercise appropriate care in handling the bailor's property results in tort liability. The duty to relinquish the property at the end of the bailment is grounded in both contract and tort law principles. Failure to return the property constitutes a breach of contract or the tort of conversion, and with one exception, the bailee is liable for damages. The exception is when the obligation is excused because the goods or chattels have been destroyed, lost, or stolen through no fault of the bailee (or claimed by a third party with a superior claim).

Under the law of bailments, a bailor's proof that damage or loss to the property has occurred will, in and of itself, raise a presumption that the bailee is guilty of negligence or conversion. In other words, whenever a bailee fails to return bailed property, the bailee's negligence will be presumed by the court.

The following case involved the bailment, or lease, of a construction crane. The question was whether the bailee, or lessee, was liable under the lease for not returning the crane.

CASE 28.3 **Sunbelt Cranes Construction and Hauling, Inc. v. Gulf Coast Erectors, Inc.**

United States District Court,
Middle District of Florida, 2002.
189 F.Supp.2d 1341.

FACTS In April 2000, Sunbelt Cranes Construction and Hauling, Inc., leased a construction crane to Gulf Coast Erectors, Inc., in Tampa, Florida. Clause twelve of the parties' "Operated and Maintained Equipment Lease" agreement provided as follows:

> Lessee agrees that Lessee has accepted the entire risk of loss of, loss of use of, and damage to, the Equipment. Lessee agrees to pay Lessor for any and all loss of, loss of use of, and/or damage to, the Equipment, due to any reason or cause * * * until the Equipment has been returned to and accepted by Lessor, even though the reason or cause may be due to accident or act of God * * *.

Gulf used the crane in a residential construction project in Tampa's Ybor City neighborhood. On May 19, an accident at the construction site caused a fire that engulfed many city blocks and destroyed much property, including the crane. Sunbelt filed a suit in a federal district court against Gulf, alleging breach of contract, to recover the cost of the crane, plus interest and attorneys' fees. Sunbelt filed a motion for summary judgment in its favor.

ISSUE Was Gulf liable for the failure to return the crane?

DECISION Yes. The court granted Sunbelt's motion for summary judgment. Gulf was liable for the failure to return the crane, because Gulf assumed the risk of the crane's loss under the parties' lease.

REASON The court explained, "A lease is a contract. Ordinary rules of contract construction apply and the unambiguous terms of the lease must be construed based upon its plain language. Absent agreement or negligence, the lessor is not responsible for destruction, injury or loss of the leased property. However, the lessor may properly agree to greater responsibility than the law requires." In this case, "Sunbelt and Gulf entered into an agreement where Gulf would bear the risk of loss under any circumstance. The clause held Gulf liable for any negligence of its own, for a third party or for any acts of God. The language is clear and unambiguous on its face. Gulf chose to accept the risk of loss. The parties were equipped with the knowledge of contractual agreements and chose to model their agreement in such a manner. As such, Gulf is liable to Sunbelt according to the contract."

FOR CRITICAL ANALYSIS—Economic Consideration
What might Gulf have done to protect itself from the loss it incurred when the crane was destroyed?

Duties of the Bailor. It goes without saying that the rights of a bailor are essentially the same as the duties of a bailee. The major duty of the bailor is to provide the bailee with goods or chattels that are free from known defects that could cause injury to the bailee. In the case of a mutual-benefit bailment, the bailor must also notify the bailee of any hidden defects that the bailor could have discovered with reasonable diligence and proper inspection.

The bailor's duty to reveal defects is based on a negligence theory of tort law. A bailor who fails to give the appropriate notice is liable to the bailee and to any other person who might reasonably be expected to come into contact with the defective article. For example, if an equipment rental firm leases equipment with a *discoverable* defect, and the lessee (bailee) is not notified of such a defect and is harmed because of it, the rental firm is liable for negligence under tort law.

An exception to this rule exists if the bailment is created for the sole benefit of the bailee. Thus, if you lend your car to a friend as a favor to your friend and not for any direct return benefit to yourself, you are required to notify your friend of any *known* defect of the automobile that could cause injury but not of a defect of which you are unaware (even if it is a *discoverable* defect). If your friend is injured in an accident as a result of a defect unknown to you, you normally will not be liable.

A bailor can also incur *warranty liability* based on contract law (see Chapter 17) for injuries resulting from the bailment of defective articles. Property leased by a bailor must be *fit for the intended purpose of the bailment*. Warranties of fitness arise by law in sales contracts and leases and by judicial interpretation in the case of bailments for hire. Article 2A of the Uniform Commercial Code (UCC) extends implied warranties of merchantability and fitness for a particular purpose to bailments whenever the bailments include rights to use the bailed goods.[6]

SPECIAL TYPES OF BAILMENTS

Up to this point, our discussion of bailments has been concerned with ordinary bailments—bailments in which bailees are expected to exercise ordinary care in the handling of bailed property. Some bailment transactions warrant special consideration, however. These include bailments in which the bailee's duty of care is *extraordinary*—that is, the bailee's liability for loss or damage to the property is absolute—as is generally true in cases involving common carriers and innkeepers. Warehouse companies have the same duty of care as ordinary bailees; but, like carriers, they are subject to

extensive regulation under federal and state laws, including Article 7 of the UCC.

Common Carriers. Transportation providers that are publicly licensed to provide transportation services to the general public are referred to as **common carriers**. Common carriers are distinguished from private carriers, which operate transportation facilities for a select clientele. Whereas a private carrier is not bound to provide service to every person or company making a request, a common carrier must arrange carriage for all who apply, within certain limitations.[7]

The delivery of goods to a common carrier creates a bailment relationship between the shipper (bailor) and the common carrier (bailee). Unlike ordinary bailees, the common carrier is held to a standard of care based on *strict liability*, rather than reasonable care, in protecting the bailed personal property. This means that the common carrier is absolutely liable, regardless of due care, for all loss or damage to goods except damage caused by one of the following common law exceptions: (1) an act of God, (2) an act of a public enemy, (3) an order of a public authority, (4) an act of the shipper, or (5) the inherent nature of the goods.

Common carriers cannot contract away their liability for damaged goods. Subject to government regulations, however, they are permitted to limit their dollar liability to an amount stated on the shipment contract or rate filing.[8]

Warehouse Companies. *Warehousing* is the business of providing storage of property for compensation.[9] A warehouse company is a professional bailee whose responsibility differs from an ordinary bailee's in two important aspects. First, a warehouse company is empowered to issue documents of title—in particular, warehouse receipts.[10] Second, warehouse companies are subject to an extraordinary network of state and federal statutes, including Article 7 of the UCC.

---

[6] UCC 2A–212, 2A–213.

[7] A common carrier is not required to take any and all property anywhere in all instances. Public regulatory agencies govern common carriers, and carriers can be restricted to geographic areas. They can also be limited to carrying certain kinds of goods or to providing only special types of transportation equipment.

[8] Federal laws require common carriers to offer shippers the opportunity to obtain higher dollar limits for loss by paying a higher fee for the transport.

[9] UCC 7–102(h) defines the person engaged in the storing of goods for hire as a *warehouseman*.

[10] A *document of title* is defined in UCC 1–201(15) as any "document which in the regular course of business or financing is treated as adequately evidencing that the person in possession of it is entitled to receive, hold, and dispose of the document and the goods it covers. To be a document of title, a document must purport to be issued by or addressed to a bailee and purport to cover goods in the bailee's possession."

A warehouse company accepts goods for storage and issues a warehouse receipt describing the property and the terms of the bailment contract. The warehouse receipt can be negotiable or nonnegotiable, depending on how it is written. It is negotiable if its terms provide that the warehouse company will deliver the goods "to the bearer" of the receipt or "to the order of" a person named on the receipt.[11]

The warehouse receipt serves multiple functions. It is a receipt for the goods stored; it is a contract of bailment; and it also represents the goods (that is, it indicates title) and hence has value and utility in financing commercial transactions. ● **EXAMPLE #13** Ossip, a processor and canner of corn, delivers 6,500 cases of corn to Shaneyfelt, the owner of a warehouse. Shaneyfelt issues a negotiable warehouse receipt payable "to bearer" and gives it to Ossip. Ossip sells and delivers the warehouse receipt to a large supermarket chain, Better Foods, Inc. Better Foods is now the owner of the corn and has the right to obtain the cases from Shaneyfelt. It will present the warehouse receipt to Shaneyfelt, who in return will release the cases of corn to the grocery chain.●

Like ordinary bailees, a warehouse company is liable for loss or damage to property resulting from *negligence* (and therefore does not have the same liability as a common carrier). As a professional bailee, however, it is expected to exercise a high degree of care to protect and preserve the goods. A warehouse company can limit the dollar amount of its liability, but the bailor must be given the option of paying an increased storage rate for an increase in the liability limit.

Innkeepers. At common law, innkeepers, hotel owners, and similar operators were held to the same strict liability as common carriers with respect to property brought into the rooms by guests. Today, only those who provide lodging

---

[11] UCC 7–104.

to the public for compensation as a *regular* business are covered under this rule of strict liability. Moreover, the rule applies only to those who are guests, as opposed to lodgers. A lodger is a permanent resident of the hotel or inn, whereas a guest is a transient traveler.

In many states, innkeepers can avoid strict liability for loss of guests' valuables and funds by providing a safe in which to keep them. Each guest must be clearly notified of the availability of such a safe. Statutes often limit the liability of innkeepers with regard to articles that are not kept in the safe or are of such a nature that they normally are not kept in a safe. These statutes may limit the amount of monetary damages or even provide for no liability in the absence of innkeeper negligence.

● **EXAMPLE #14** Suppose that Joyce stays for a night at the Harbor Hotel. When she returns from eating breakfast in the hotel restaurant, she discovers that the people in the room next door have forced the lock on the door between the two rooms and stolen her suitcase. Joyce claims that the hotel is liable for her loss. The hotel maintains that because it was not negligent, it is not liable. At common law, the hotel would have been liable because innkeepers were actually insurers of the property of their guests. Today, however, state statutes limit strict liability by limiting the amount of monetary damages for which the innkeeper is liable or providing that the innkeeper has no liability in the absence of negligence. Most statutes require these limitations to be posted or the guest to be notified. Such postings, or notices, are frequently found on the doors of the rooms in the motel or hotel.●

Normally, the innkeeper (a motel keeper, for example) assumes no responsibility for the safety of a guest's automobile because the guest usually retains possession and control over it. If, however, the innkeeper provides parking facilities and the guest's car is entrusted to the innkeeper or to an employee, the innkeeper will be liable under the rules that pertain to parking-lot bailments (which are ordinary bailments).

Terms and Concepts

Chapter Summary	**Personal Property and Bailments**

PERSONAL PROPERTY	
Definition of Personal Property (See page 590.)	Personal property (personalty) is considered to include all property not classified as real property (realty). Personal property can be tangible (such as a TV set or a car) or intangible (such as stocks or bonds). Personal property may be referred to legally as *chattel*—a term used under the common law to denote all forms of personal property.
Property Ownership (See page 591.)	1. *Fee simple*—Exists when individuals have the right to use, possess, or dispose of the property as they choose during their lifetimes and to pass on the property to their heirs at death. 2. *Concurrent ownership*— a. Tenancy in common—Co-ownership in which two or more persons own an undivided interest in the property; on one tenant's death, the property interest passes to his or her heirs. b. Joint tenancy—Exists when two or more persons own an undivided interest in property; on the death of a joint tenant, the property interest transfers to the remaining tenant(s), not to the heirs of the deceased. c. Tenancy by the entirety—A form of co-ownership between a husband and wife that is similar to a joint tenancy, except that a spouse cannot transfer separately his or her interest during his or her lifetime without the consent of the other spouse. d. Community property—A form of co-ownership in which each spouse technically owns an undivided one-half interest in property acquired during the marriage. This type of ownership occurs in only a few states.
Acquiring Ownership of Personal Property (See pages 591–595.)	The most common means of acquiring ownership in personal property is by purchasing it (see Chapters 14 through 17). Another way in which personal property is often acquired is by will or inheritance (see Chapter 30). The following are additional methods of acquiring personal property: 1. *Possession*—Ownership may be acquired by possession if no other person has ownership title (for example, capturing wild animals or finding abandoned property). 2. *Production*—Any product or item produced by an individual (with minor exceptions) becomes the property of that individual. 3. *Gift*—An effective gift exists when the following conditions exist: a. There is evidence of *intent* to make a gift of the property in question. b. The gift is *delivered* (physically or constructively) to the donee or the donee's agent. c. The gift is *accepted* by the donee or the donee's agent. 4. *Accession*—When someone adds value to an item of personal property by labor or materials, the added value generally becomes the property of the owner of the original property (includes accessions made in bad faith or wrongfully). Good faith accessions that substantially increase the property's value or change the identity of the property may cause title to pass to the improver. 5. *Confusion*—In the case of fungible goods, if a person wrongfully and willfully commingles goods with those of another in order to render them indistinguishable, the innocent party acquires title to the whole. Otherwise, the owners become tenants in common of the commingled goods.

Chapter Summary	Personal Property and Bailments—Continued
Mislaid, Lost, and Abandoned Property (See pages 595–596.)	1. *Mislaid property*—Property that is placed somewhere voluntarily by the owner and then inadvertently forgotten. A finder of mislaid property will not acquire title to the goods, and the owner of the place where the property was mislaid becomes a caretaker of the mislaid property.
	2. *Lost property*—Property that is involuntarily left and forgotten. A finder of lost property can claim title to the property against the whole world *except the true owner*.
	3. *Abandoned property*—Property that has been discarded by the true owner, who has no intention of claiming title to the property in the future. A finder of abandoned property can claim title to it against the whole world, *including the original owner*.
BAILMENTS	
Elements of a Bailment (See page 597.)	1. *Personal property*—Bailments involve only personal property.
	2. *Delivery of possession*—For an effective bailment to exist, the bailee (the one receiving the property) must be given exclusive possession and control over the property, and in a voluntary bailment, the bailee must knowingly accept the personal property.
	3. *The bailment agreement*—Expressly or impliedly provides for the return of the bailed property to the bailor or a third party, or for the disposal of the bailed property by the bailee.
Ordinary Bailments (See pages 598–600.)	1. *Types of bailments*—
	a. Bailment for the sole benefit of the bailor—A gratuitous bailment undertaken for the sole benefit of the bailor (for example, as a favor to the bailor).
	b. Bailment for the sole benefit of the bailee—A gratuitous loan of an article to a person (the bailee) solely for the bailee's benefit.
	c. Mutual-benefit (contractual) bailment—The most common kind of bailment; involves compensation between the bailee and bailor for the service provided.
	2. *Rights of a bailee (duties of a bailor)*—
	a. The right of possession—Allows actions against third persons who damage or convert the bailed property and allows actions against the bailor for wrongful breach of the bailment.
	b. The right to be compensated and reimbursed for expenses—In the event of nonpayment, the bailee has the right to place a possessory (bailee's) lien on the bailed property.
	c. The right to limit liability—An ordinary bailee can limit his or her liability for loss or damage, provided proper notice is given and the limitation is not against public policy. In special bailments, limitations on liability for negligence or on types of losses usually are not allowed, but limitations on the monetary amount of liability are permitted.
	3. *Duties of a bailee (rights of a bailor)*—
	a. A bailee must exercise appropriate care over property entrusted to her or him. What constitutes appropriate care normally depends on the nature and circumstances of the bailment.
	b. Bailed goods in a bailee's possession must be either returned to the bailor or disposed of according to the bailor's directions. A bailee's failure to return the bailed property creates a presumption of negligence and constitutes a breach of contract or the tort of conversion of goods.

(Continued)

Chapter Summary	**Personal Property and Bailments—Continued**
Special Types of Bailments (See pages 600–601.)	1. *Common carriers*—Carriers that are publicly licensed to provide transportation services to the general public. The common carrier is held to a standard of care based on *strict liability* unless the bailed property is lost or destroyed due to (a) an act of God, (b) an act of a public enemy, (c) an order of a public authority, (d) an act of the shipper, or (e) the inherent nature of the goods. 2. *Warehouse companies*—Professional bailees that differ from ordinary bailees because they (a) can issue documents of title (warehouse receipts) and (b) are subject to state and federal statutes, including Article 7 of the UCC (as are common carriers). They must exercise a high degree of care over the bailed property and are liable for loss of or damage to property if they fail to do so. 3. *Innkeepers (hotel operators)*—Those who provide lodging to the public for compensation as a *regular* business. The common law strict liability standard to which innkeepers were once held is limited today by state statutes, which vary from state to state.

For Review

① What is real property? What is personal property?

② What does it mean to own property in fee simple? What is the difference between a joint tenancy and a tenancy in common?

③ What are the three elements necessary for an effective gift? How else can property be acquired?

④ What are the three elements of a bailment?

⑤ What are the basic rights and duties of the bailee? What are the rights and duties of the bailor?

Questions and Case Problems

28–1. Duties of the Bailee. Discuss the standard of care traditionally required of the bailee for the bailed property in each of the following situations, and determine whether the bailee breached that duty.

(a) Ricardo borrows Steve's lawn mower to mow his front yard. To mow the back yard, he needs to move some hoses, and he leaves the mower in front of his house while doing so. When he returns to the front yard, he discovers that the mower has been stolen.

(b) Alicia owns a valuable speedboat. She is going on vacation and asks her neighbor, Maureen, to store the boat in one stall of Maureen's double garage. Maureen consents, and the boat is moved into the garage. Maureen needs some grocery items for dinner and drives to the store. She leaves the garage door open while she is gone, as is her custom, and the speedboat is stolen during that time.

28–2. Gifts. Reineken, very old and ill, wanted to make a gift to his nephew, Gerald. He had a friend obtain $2,500 in cash for him from his bank account, placed this cash in an envelope,

and wrote on the envelope, "This is for my nephew, Gerald." Reineken then placed the envelope in his dresser drawer. When Reineken died a month later, his family found the envelope, and Gerald got word of the intended gift. Gerald then demanded that Reineken's daughter, the executor of Reineken's estate (the person who was appointed by Reineken to handle his affairs after his death), turn over the gift to him. The daughter refused to do so. Discuss fully whether Gerald can successfully claim ownership rights to the $2,500.

28–3. Gifts. In 1968, Armando was about to be shipped to Vietnam for active duty with the U.S. Marines. Shortly before he left, he gave an expensive stereo set and other personal belongings to his girlfriend, Sara, saying, "I'll probably not return from this war, so I'm giving these to you." Armando returned eighteen months later and requested that Sara return the property. Sara said that because Armando had given her these items to keep, she was not required to return them. Was a gift made in this instance, and can Armando recover his property? Discuss fully.

28–4. Requirements of a Bailment. Calvin is an executive on a business trip to the West Coast. He has driven his car on this trip and checks into the Hotel Ritz. The hotel has a guarded underground parking lot. Calvin gives his car keys to the parking-lot attendant but fails to notify the attendant that his wife's $10,000 diamond necklace is in a box in the trunk. The next day, on checking out, he discovers that his car has been stolen. Calvin wants to hold the hotel liable for both the car and the necklace. Discuss the probable success of his claim.

28–5. Gifts. William Yee and S. Hing Woo had been lovers for nearly twenty years. They held themselves out as husband and wife, and Woo wore a wedding band. Two days before his death, Yee told Woo that he felt "terribly bad" and believed he would die. He gave Woo three checks, for $42,700, $80,000, and $1,900, and told her that if he died, he wanted her "to be taken care of." After Yee's death, Woo cashed the $42,700 check and the $1,900 check. She never cashed the $80,000 check. The administrator of Yee's estate petitioned a Virginia state court to declare that Woo was not entitled to the funds represented by the checks. What will the court decide, and why? [*Woo v. Smart,* 247 Va. 365, 442 S.E.2d 690 (1994)]

28–6. Gratuitous Bailments. Raul Covarrubias, David Haro, and Javier Aguirre immigrated to the United States from Colima, Mexico, to find jobs and help their families. When they learned that Francisco Alcaraz-Garcia planned to travel to Colima, they asked him to deliver various sums, totaling more than $25,000, to their families. During customs inspections at the border, Alcaraz told officers of the U.S. Customs Service that he was not carrying more than $10,000. In fact, he carried more than $35,000. He was charged with—and convicted of—criminal currency and customs violations, and the government seized most of the cash. Covarrubias, Haro, and Aguirre filed a petition for the return of their money, arguing that Alcaraz was a gratuitous bailee and that they still had title to the money. Are they right? Explain fully. [*United States v. Alcaraz-Garcia,* 79 F.3d 769 (9th Cir. 1996)]

28–7. Gifts. Hugh Chalmers issued a promissory note to his father in the amount of $50,000, plus interest. The note was secured by a deed of trust on certain real estate and was payable on demand or within sixty days of the father's death. More than seventeen years later, the father assigned the deed of trust to his wife, Nina. The existence of the note was mentioned in the assignment, which was recorded in the appropriate state office with the deed of trust. After the father died, Nina found the note in a safe-deposit box. On the back of the note, the father had indorsed the note to Nina. When Chalmers refused to pay the amount due, Nina filed a lawsuit in an Arkansas state court against him. Chalmers argued that the note had not been effectively delivered. What should the court hold? Discuss. [*Chalmers v. Chalmers,* 937 S.W.2d 171 (Ark. 1997)]

28–8. Gift *Inter Vivos*. Thomas Stafford owned four promissory notes. Payments on the notes were deposited into a bank account in the names of Stafford and his daughter, June Zink, "as joint tenants with right of survivorship." Stafford kept control of the notes and would not allow Zink to spend any of the proceeds. He also kept the interest on the account. On one note, Stafford indorsed "Pay to the order of Thomas J. Stafford or June S. Zink, or the survivor." The payee on each of the other notes was "Thomas J. Stafford and June S. Zink, or the survivor." When Stafford died, Zink took possession of the notes, claiming that she had been a joint tenant of the notes with her father. Stafford's son, also Thomas, filed a suit in a Virginia state court against Zink, claiming that the notes were partly his. The son argued that their father had not made a valid gift *inter vivos* of the notes to Zink. In whose favor will the court rule? Why? [*Zink v. Stafford,* 509 S.E.2d 833 (Va. 1999)]

28–9. A. D. Lock owned Lock Hospitality, Inc., which in turn owned the Best Western motel in Conway, Arkansas. Joe Terry and David Stocks were preparing the motel for renovation. As they were removing the ceiling tiles in room 118, with Lock present in the room, a dusty cardboard box was noticed near the heating and air-supply vent where it had apparently been concealed. Terry climbed a ladder to reach the box, opened it, and handed it to Stocks. The box was filled with more than $38,000 in old currency. Lock took possession of the box and its contents. Terry and Stocks filed a suit in an Arkansas state court against Lock and his corporation to obtain the money. Should the money be characterized as lost, mislaid, or abandoned property? To whom should the court award it? Explain. [*Terry v. Lock,* 37 S.W.3d 202 (Ark. 2001)]

▶ **To view a sample answer for this case problem, go to this book's Web site at http://fundamentals.westbuslaw.com and click on "Interactive Study Center."**

VIDEO QUESTION

28–10. Go to this text's Web site at **http://fundamentals.westbuslaw.com** and click on "Video Questions." Select "Chapter 28" and view the video titled *Personal Property and Bailments*. Then answer the following questions:

1. What type of bailment is discussed in the video?
2. What were Vinny's duties with respect to the rug-cleaning machine?
3. Did Vinny exercise the appropriate degree of care? Why or why not? How would a court decide this issue?

PERSONAL PROPERTY AND BAILMENTS

For updated links to resources available on the Web, as well as other materials, visit this text's Web site at

http://fundamentals.westbuslaw.com

To learn whether a married person has ownership rights in a gift received by his or her spouse, go to the Web page of the Scott Law Firm at

http://www.scottlawfirm.com/property.htm

Some states and government agencies now post lists of unclaimed property online. For examples of various types of unclaimed property, go to the following Web page maintained by the state of Delaware:

http://www.state.de.us/revenue/escheat/escheat.htm

For a discussion of the origins of the term *bailment* and how bailment relationships have been defined, go to

http://www.lectlaw.com/def/b005.htm

Online Legal Research

Go to the *Fundamentals of Business Law* home page at **http://fundamentals.westbuslaw.com**. Select "Interactive Study Center" and then click on "Chapter 28." There you will find the following Internet research exercises that you can perform to learn more about topics covered in this chapter.

Activity 28–1: LEGAL PERSPECTIVE—**Lost Property**
Activity 28–2: MANAGEMENT PERSPECTIVE—**Bailments**

Before the Test

Go to the *Fundamentals of Business Law* home page at **http://fundamentals.westbuslaw.com**. Click on "Interactive Quizzes." You will find at least twenty interactive questions relating to this chapter.

Westlaw® Campus

If your textbook provided for a subscription to Westlaw® Campus, or if you have otherwise purchased access to the Westlaw Campus database, you can access any of the cases presented or cited in this chapter by using your Westlaw Campus account.

After reading this chapter, you should be able to answer the following questions:

① What can a person who holds property in fee simple absolute do with the property? Can a person who holds property as a life estate do the same?

② What are the requirements for acquiring property by adverse possession?

③ What limitations may be imposed on the rights of property owners?

④ What is a leasehold estate? What types of leasehold estates, or tenancies, can be created when real property is leased?

⑤ What are the respective duties of the landlord and tenant concerning the use and maintenance of leased property? Is the tenant responsible for all damages that he or she causes?

From earliest times, property has provided a means for survival. Primitive peoples lived off the fruits of the land, eating the vegetation and wildlife. Later, as the wildlife was domesticated and the vegetation cultivated, property provided pasturage and farmland. In the twelfth and thirteenth centuries in Europe, the power of feudal lords was determined by the amount of land that they held; the more land they held, the more powerful they were. After the age of feudalism passed, property continued to be an indicator of family wealth and social position. In the Western world, the protection of an individual's right to his or her property has become one of the most important rights of citizenship.

In this chapter, we first examine closely the nature of real property. We then look at the various ways in which real property can be owned and at how ownership rights in real property are transferred from one person to another. We conclude the chapter with a discussion of leased property and landlord-tenant relationships.

The Nature of Real Property

Real property consists of land and the buildings, plants, and trees that it contains. Real property also includes subsurface and air rights, as well as personal property that has become

607

permanently attached to real property. Whereas personal property is movable, real property—also called *real estate* or *realty*—is immovable.

LAND

Land includes the soil on the surface of the earth and the natural or artificial structures that are attached to it. It further includes all the waters contained on or under the surface and much, but not necessarily all, of the airspace above it. The exterior boundaries of land extend down to the center of the earth and up to the farthest reaches of the atmosphere (subject to certain qualifications).

AIR AND SUBSURFACE RIGHTS

The owner of real property has rights to the airspace above the land, as well as to the soil and minerals underneath it.

Air Rights. Early cases involving air rights dealt with such matters as the right to run a telephone wire across a person's property when the wire did not touch any of the property[1] and whether a bullet shot over a person's land constituted trespass.[2] Today, disputes concerning air rights may involve the right of commercial and private planes to fly over property and the right of individuals and governments to seed clouds and produce rain artificially. Flights over private land normally do not violate the property owners' rights unless the flights are low and frequent enough to cause a direct interference with the enjoyment and use of the land.[3] Leaning walls or buildings and projecting eave spouts or roofs may also violate the air rights of an adjoining property owner.

Subsurface Rights. In many states, the owner of the surface of a piece of land is not the owner of the subsurface, and hence the land ownership may be separated. Subsurface rights can be extremely valuable, as these rights include the ownership of minerals and, in most states, oil and natural gas. Water rights are also extremely valuable, especially in the West. When the ownership is separated into surface and subsurface rights, each owner can pass title to what she or he owns without the consent of the other owner. Each owner has the right to use the land owned, and sometimes a conflict arises between a surface owner's use and the subsurface owner's need to extract minerals, oil, or

natural gas. When this occurs, one party's interest may become subservient to the other party's interest, either by statute or case decision.

Significant limitations on either air rights or subsurface rights normally must be indicated on the deed transferring title at the time of purchase. (Deeds and the types of warranties they contain are discussed later in this chapter.)

PLANT LIFE AND VEGETATION

Plant life, both natural and cultivated, is also considered to be real property. In many instances, the natural vegetation, such as trees, adds greatly to the value of the realty. When a parcel of land is sold and the land has growing crops on it, the sale includes the crops, unless otherwise specified in the sales contract. When crops are sold by themselves, however, they are considered to be personal property or goods. Consequently, the sale of crops is a sale of goods, and therefore it is governed by the Uniform Commercial Code rather than by real property law.[4]

FIXTURES

Certain personal property can become so closely associated with the real property to which it is attached that the law views it as real property. Such property is known as a **fixture**—a thing *affixed* to realty, meaning it is attached to the real property by roots; embedded in it; permanently situated on it; or permanently attached by means of cement, plaster, bolts, nails, or screws. The fixture can be physically attached to real property, be attached to another fixture, or even be without any actual physical attachment to the land (such as a statue). As long as the owner intends the property to be a fixture, normally it will be a fixture.

Fixtures are included in the sale of land if the sales contract does not provide otherwise. The sale of a house includes the land and the house and the garage on the land, as well as the cabinets, plumbing, and windows. Because these are permanently affixed to the property, they are considered to be a part of it. Unless otherwise agreed, however, the curtains and throw rugs are not included. Items such as drapes and window-unit air conditioners are difficult to classify. Thus, a contract for the sale of a house or commercial realty should indicate which items of this sort are included in the sale.

At issue in the following case was whether an agricultural irrigation system qualified as a fixture.

---

[1] *Butler v. Frontier Telephone Co.*, 186 N.Y. 486, 79 N.E. 716 (1906).
[2] *Herrin v. Sutherland*, 74 Mont. 587, 241 P. 328 (1925). Shooting over a person's land constitutes trespass.
[3] *United States v. Causby*, 328 U.S. 256, 66 S.Ct. 1062, 90 L.Ed. 1206 (1946).

[4] See UCC 2–107(2).

CASE 29.1 In re Sand & Sage Farm & Ranch, Inc.

United States Bankruptcy Court,
District of Kansas, 2001.
266 Bankr. 507.

FACTS In 1988, Randolf and Sandra Ardery bought an eighty-acre tract in Edwards County, Kansas. On the land was an eight-tower center-pivot irrigation system. The system consisted of an underground well and pump connected to a pipe that ran to the pivot, where the water line was attached to a further system of pipes and sprinklers suspended from the towers, extending over the land in a circular fashion. The system's engine and gearhead were bolted to a concrete slab above the pump and well and were attached to the pipe. To secure a loan to buy the land, the Arderys granted to Farmers State Bank a mortgage that covered "all buildings, improvements, and fixtures." In 1996, the Arderys, and their firm Sand & Sage Farm & Ranch, Inc., granted Ag Services of America a security interest in the farm's "equipment." Nothing in the security agreement or financing statement referred to fixtures.[a] In 2000, the Arderys and Sand & Sage filed for bankruptcy in a federal bankruptcy court and asked for permission to sell the land, with the irrigation system, to Bohn Enterprises, Limited Partnership. Ag Services claimed that it had priority to the proceeds covering the value of the irrigation system. The bank responded that it had priority because the system was a "fixture."

---

a. Security agreements and financing statements were discussed in Chapter 20.

ISSUE Was this irrigation system a "fixture"?

DECISION Yes. The court concluded that the system was a fixture. The bank was entitled to the proceeds from its sale.

REASON The court explained that whether personal property attached to land is a fixture depends on "(i) how firmly the goods are attached or the ease of their removal (annexation); (ii) the relationship of the parties involved (intent); and (iii) how operation of the goods is related to the use of the land (adaptation). Of the three factors, intent is the controlling factor and is deduced largely from the property-owner's acts and the surrounding circumstances." Here, the irrigation system "is firmly attached to the realty. * * * [D]isassembly and removal * * * would be time-consuming and * * * expensive." As for intent, in each transaction all of the parties—except Ag Services, whose security agreement and financing statement did not refer to the irrigation system— "share[d] the intent that the system in question should pass with the land." Furthermore, the system "is suitably adapted to the land. There can be little dispute concerning the need for pivot irrigation in the semi-arid conditions of southwestern Kansas. * * * This alone demonstrates the relation between the operation of the goods and use of the land."

FOR CRITICAL ANALYSIS—Social Consideration
How can a court objectively determine whether someone did, or did not, intend an item to be a fixture?

Ownership of Real Property

Ownership of property is an abstract concept that cannot exist independently of the legal system. No one can actually possess or *hold* a piece of land, the air above it, the earth below it, and all the water contained on it. The legal system therefore recognizes certain rights and duties that constitute ownership interests in real property.

Recall from Chapter 28 that property ownership is often viewed as a bundle of rights. One who possesses the entire bundle of rights is said to hold the property in *fee simple,* which is the most complete form of ownership. When only some of the rights in the bundle are transferred to another person, the effect is to limit the ownership rights of both the transferor of the rights and the recipient.

OWNERSHIP IN FEE SIMPLE

The most common type of property ownership today is the fee simple. Generally, the term *fee simple* is used to designate a **fee simple absolute,** in which the owner has the greatest possible aggregation of rights, privileges, and power. The fee simple is limited absolutely to a person and his or her heirs and is assigned forever without limitation or condition. Furthermore, the owner has the rights of *exclusive* possession and use of the property. A fee simple is potentially infinite in duration and can be disposed of by deed or by will (by selling or giving away). When there is no will, the fee simple passes to the owner's legal heirs.

The rights that accompany a fee simple include the right to use the land for whatever purpose the owner sees fit. Of course, certain uses of the property may be prohibited by applicable laws, including zoning laws, environmental regulations, and laws that prevent the owner from unreasonably interfering with another person's land. Another limitation on the absolute rights of owners in fee simple is the government's power of eminent domain, as you will read later in this chapter.

Ownership in fee simple may also become limited whenever a **conveyance**, or transfer of real property, is made to another party *conditionally*. When this occurs, the fee simple is known as a **fee simple defeasible** (the word *defeasible* means capable of being terminated or annulled). ● EXAMPLE #1 A conveyance "to A and his heirs as long as the land is used for charitable purposes" creates a fee simple defeasible because ownership of the property is conditioned on the land's being used for charitable purposes. The original owner retains a *partial* ownership interest because if the specified condition does not occur (if the land ceases to be used for charitable purposes), the land reverts, or returns, to the original owner. If the original owner is not living at the time, the land passes to her or his heirs.●

LIFE ESTATES

A **life estate** is an estate that lasts for the life of some specified individual. A conveyance "to A for his life" creates a life estate.[5] In a life estate, the life tenant has fewer rights of ownership than the holder of a fee simple defeasible because the rights necessarily cease to exist on the life tenant's death.

The life tenant has the right to use the land, provided that he or she commits no waste (injury to the land). In other words, the life tenant cannot injure the land in a manner that would adversely affect its value. The life tenant can use the land to harvest crops or, if mines and oil wells are already on the land, can extract minerals and oil from it, but the life tenant cannot exploit the land by creating new wells or mines. The life tenant is entitled to any rents or royalties generated by the realty and has the right to mortgage the life estate and create liens, easements, and leases; but none can extend beyond the life of the tenant. In addition, with few exceptions, the owner of a life estate has an exclusive right to possession during his or her life.

Along with these rights, the life tenant also has some duties—to keep the property in repair and to pay property taxes. In short, the owner of the life estate has the same rights as a fee simple owner except that the life tenant must

maintain the value of the property during her or his tenancy, less the decrease in value resulting from the normal use of the property allowed by the life tenancy.

FUTURE INTERESTS

When an owner in fee simple absolute conveys the estate conditionally to another (such as with a fee simple defeasible) or for a limited period of time (such as with a life estate), the original owner still retains an interest in the land. The owner retains the right to repossess ownership of the land if the conditions of the fee simple defeasible are not met or when the life of the life-estate holder ends. The interest in the property that the owner retains (or transfers to another) is called a **future interest** because if it arises, it will only arise in the future.

If the owner retains ownership of the future interest, the future interest is described as a **reversionary interest** because the property will revert to the original owner if the condition specified in a fee simple defeasible fails or when a life tenant dies. If, however, the owner of the future interest transfers ownership rights in that future interest to another, the future interest is described as a **remainder.** For example, a conveyance "to A for life, then to B" creates a life estate for A and a remainder (future interest) for B. An **executory interest** is a type of future interest very similar to a remainder, the difference being that an executory interest does not take effect immediately on the expiration of another interest, such as a life estate. For example, a conveyance "to A and his heirs, as long as the premises are used for charitable purposes, and if not so used for charitable purposes, then to B" creates an executory interest in the property for B.

NONPOSSESSORY INTERESTS

In contrast to the types of property interests just described, some interests in land do not include any rights to possess the property. These interests are thus known as *nonpossessory interests.* Three forms of nonpossessory interests are easements, profits, and licenses.

Easements and Profits. An **easement** is the right of a person to make limited use of another person's real property without taking anything from the property. An easement, for example, can be the right to travel over another's property. In contrast, a **profit**[6] is the right to go onto land in possession of another and take away some part of the land itself or some product of the land. ● EXAMPLE #2 If Akmed, the

---

[5] A less common type of life estate is created by the conveyance "to A for the life of B." This is known as an estate *pur autre vie,* or an estate for the duration of the life of another.

[6] The term *profit,* as used here, does not refer to the "profits" made by a business firm. Rather, it means a gain or an advantage.

owner of Sandy View, gives Carmen the right to go there and remove all the sand and gravel that she needs for her cement business, Carmen has a profit.● Easements and profits can be classified as either *appurtenant* or *in gross.* Because easements and profits are similar and the same rules apply to both, they are discussed together.

Easement or Profit Appurtenant. An easement or profit appurtenant arises when the owner of one piece of land has a right to go onto (or to remove things from) an *adjacent* piece of land owned by another. ● **EXAMPLE #3** Suppose that Acosta, the owner of Juniper Hills, has a right to drive his car across Green's land, Greenacres, which is adjacent to Juniper Hills. This right-of-way over Green's property is an easement appurtenant to Juniper Hills and can be used only by the owner of Juniper Hills. Acosta can convey the easement when he conveys Juniper Hills. Now suppose that the highway is on the other side of Bancroft's property, which is on the other side of Green's property. To reach the highway, Acosta has easements across both Green's and Bancroft's properties. Juniper Hills and Bancroft's property are not adjacent, but Green's and Bancroft's properties are, so Acosta has an easement appurtenant.●

Easement or Profit in Gross. An easement or profit in gross exists when one's right to use or take things from another's land does not depend on one's owning an adjacent tract of land. ● **EXAMPLE #4** Suppose that Avery owns a parcel of land with a marble quarry. Avery conveys to XYZ Corporation, which owns no land, the right to come onto his land and remove up to five hundred pounds of marble per day. XYZ Corporation owns a profit in gross.● When a utility company is granted an easement to run its power lines across another's property, it obtains an easement in gross.

Effect of a Sale of Property. When a parcel of land that is *benefited* by an easement or profit appurtenant is sold, the property carries the easement or profit along with it. Thus, in Example #3, if Acosta sells Juniper Hills to Thomas and includes the appurtenant right-of-way across Green's property in the deed to Thomas, Thomas will own both the property and the easement that benefits it.

When a parcel of land that has the *burden* of an easement or profit appurtenant is sold, the new owner must recognize its existence only if he or she knew or should have known of it or if it was recorded in the appropriate office of the county. Thus, if Acosta records his easement across Green's property in the appropriate county office before Green conveys the land, the new owner of Green's property will have to allow Acosta, or any subsequent owner of Juniper Hills, to continue to use the path across Green's property.

Creation of an Easement or Profit. Easements and profits can be created by deed; by will; or by implication, necessity, or prescription. Two parties can create a contract in which they agree that one party has the right to an easement or profit on a portion of the other party's land. Creation by *deed* or *will* simply involves the delivery of a deed or a disposition in a will by the owner of an easement stating that the grantee (the person receiving the easement or profit) is granted the owner's rights in the easement or profit.

An easement or profit may be created by *implication* when the circumstances surrounding the division of a parcel of property imply its creation. If Barrow divides a parcel of land that has only one well for drinking water and conveys the half without a well to Jarad, a profit by implication arises because Jarad needs drinking water.

An easement may also be created by *necessity.* An easement by necessity does not require division of property for its existence. A person who rents an apartment, for example, has an easement by necessity in the private road leading up to it.

Easements and profits by *prescription* are created in much the same way as title to property is obtained by *adverse possession* (discussed later in this chapter). An easement arises by prescription when one person exercises an easement, such as a right-of-way, on another person's land without the landowner's consent, and the use is apparent and continues for a period of time equal to the applicable statute of limitations.

Termination of an Easement or Profit. An easement or profit can be terminated or extinguished in several ways. The simplest way is to deed it back to the owner of the land that is burdened by it. Another way is to abandon it and create evidence of intent to relinquish the right to use it. Mere nonuse will not extinguish an easement or profit *unless the nonuse is accompanied by an intent to abandon.* If the easement or profit is created merely by contract, the termination of the contract terminates the easement or profit. Finally, when the owner of an easement or profit becomes the owner of the property burdened by it, it is merged into the property.

Licenses. A **license** is the revocable right of a person to come onto another person's land. It is a personal privilege that arises from the consent of the owner of the land and that can be revoked by the owner. A ticket to attend a movie at a theater is an example of a license. ● **EXAMPLE #5** Assume that a Broadway theater owner issues to Carla a ticket to see a play. If Carla is refused entry into the theater because she is improperly dressed, she has no right to force her way into the theater. The ticket is only a revocable license, not a conveyance of an interest in property.●

Transfer of Ownership

Ownership of real property can pass from one person to another in a number of ways. Commonly, ownership interests in land are transferred by sale, and the terms of the transfer are specified in a real estate sales contract. When real property is sold or transferred as a gift, title to the property is conveyed by means of a **deed**—the instrument of conveyance of real property. We look here at transfers of real property by deed, as well as some other ways in which ownership rights in real property can be transferred.

DEEDS

A valid deed must contain the following elements:

① The names of the buyer (grantee) and seller (grantor).

② Words evidencing an intent to convey the property (for example, "I hereby bargain, sell, grant, or give").

③ A legally sufficient description of the land.

④ The grantor's (and, sometimes, the spouse's) signature.

Additionally, to be valid, a deed must be delivered to the person to whom the property is being conveyed or to his or her agent.

Warranty Deeds. Different types of deeds provide different degrees of protection against defects of title. A **warranty deed** warrants the greatest number of things and thus provides the greatest protection for the buyer, or grantee. In most states, special language is required to make a deed a general warranty deed; normally, the deed must include a written promise to protect the buyer against all claims of ownership of the property. A sample warranty deed is shown in Exhibit 29–1. Warranty deeds commonly include a number of *covenants,* or promises, that the grantor makes to the grantee.

A *covenant of seisin*[7] and a *covenant of the right to convey* warrant that the seller has title to the estate that the deed describes and the power to convey the estate, respectively. The covenant of seisin specifically assures the buyer that the grantor has the property in the purported quantity and quality.

A *covenant against encumbrances* is a covenant that the property being sold or conveyed is not subject to any outstanding rights or interests that will diminish the value of the land, except as explicitly stated. Examples of common encumbrances include mortgages, liens, profits, easements, and private deed restrictions on the use of the land.

A *covenant of quiet enjoyment* guarantees that the buyer will not be disturbed in her or his possession of the land by the seller or any third persons. ● **EXAMPLE #6** Assume that Julio sells a two-acre lot and office building by warranty deed. Subsequently, a third person shows better title than Julio had and proceeds to evict the buyer. Here, the covenant of quiet enjoyment has been breached, and the buyer can sue to recover the purchase price of the land plus any other damages incurred as a result of the eviction.●

Quitclaim Deeds. A **quitclaim deed** offers the least amount of protection against defects in the title. Basically, a quitclaim deed conveys to the grantee whatever interest the grantor had; so if the grantor had no interest, then the grantee receives no interest. Quitclaim deeds are often used when the seller, or grantor, is uncertain as to the extent of his or her rights in the property.

Recording Statutes. Every jurisdiction has **recording statutes**, which allow deeds to be recorded. Recording a deed gives notice to the public that a certain person is now the owner of a particular parcel of real estate. Thus, prospective buyers can check the public records to see whether there have been earlier transactions creating interests or rights in specific parcels of real property. Placing everyone on notice as to the identity of the true owner is intended to prevent the previous owners from fraudulently conveying the land to other purchasers. Deeds are recorded in the county where the property is located. Many state statutes require that the grantor sign the deed in the presence of two witnesses before it can be recorded.

WILL OR INHERITANCE

Property that is transferred on an owner's death is passed either by will or by state inheritance laws. If the owner of land dies with a will, the land passes in accordance with the terms of the will. If the owner dies without a will, state inheritance statutes prescribe how and to whom the property will pass. Transfers of property by will or inheritance will be examined in detail in Chapter 30.

ADVERSE POSSESSION

Adverse possession is a means of obtaining title to land without delivery of a deed. Essentially, when one person possesses the property of another for a certain statutory period of time (three to thirty years, with ten years being most common), that person, called the *adverse possessor,* acquires title to the land and cannot be removed from it by the original owner. The adverse possessor is vested with a perfect title just as if there had been a conveyance by deed.

---

[7] Pronounced *see*-zuhn.

EXHIBIT 29-1 **A SAMPLE WARRANTY DEED**

Date: May 31, 2005

Grantor: GAYLORD A. JENTZ AND WIFE, JOANN H. JENTZ

Grantor's Mailing Address (including county):
4106 North Loop Drive
Austin, Travis County, Texas

Grantee: DAVID F. FRIEND AND WIFE, JOAN E. FRIEND AS JOINT TENANTS
WITH RIGHT OF SURVIVORSHIP

Grantee's Mailing Address (including county):
5929 Fuller Drive
Austin, Travis County, Texas

Consideration:
For and in consideration of the sum of Ten and No/100 Dollars ($10.00) and other valuable consideration to the undersigned paid by the grantees herein named, the receipt of which is hereby acknowledged, and for which no lien is retained, either express or implied.

Property (including any improvements):
Lot 23, Block "A", Northwest Hills, Green Acres Addition, Phase 4, Travis County, Texas, according to the map or plat of record in volume 22, pages 331-336 of the Plat Records of Travis County, Texas.

Reservations from and Exceptions to Conveyance and Warranty:

This conveyance with its warranty is expressly made subject to the following:

Easements and restrictions of record in Volume 7863, Page 53, Volume 8430, Page 35, Volume 8133, Page 152 of the Real Property Record of Travis County, Texas; Volume 22, Pages 335-339, of the Plat Records of Travis County, Texas; and to any other restrictions and easements affecting said property which are of record in Travis County, Texas.

Grantor, for the consideration and subject to the reservations from and exceptions to conveyance and warranty, grants, sells, and conveys to Grantee the property, together with all and singular the rights and appurtenances thereto in any wise belonging, to have and hold it to Grantee, Grantee's heirs, executors, administrators, successors, or assigns forever. Grantor binds Grantor and Grantor's heirs, executors, administrators, and successors to warrant and forever defend all and singular the property to Grantee and Grantee's heirs, executors, administrators, successors, and assigns against every person whomsoever lawfully claiming or to claim the same or any part thereof, except as to the reservations from and exceptions to conveyance and warranty.

When the context requires, singular nouns and pronouns include the plural.

BY: _____
Gaylord A. Jentz

BY: _____
JoAnn H. Jentz

(Acknowledgment)

STATE OF TEXAS
COUNTY OF TRAVIS

This instrument was acknowledged before me on the 31st day of May, 2005
by Gaylord A. and JoAnn H. Jentz

_____
Notary Public, State of Texas
Notary's name (printed): Rosemary Potter

Notary Seal

Notary's commission expires: 1/31/2008

For property to be held adversely, four elements must be satisfied:

① Possession must be actual and exclusive; that is, the possessor must take sole physical occupancy of the property.

② The possession must be open, visible, and notorious, not secret or clandestine. The possessor must occupy the land for all the world to see.

③ Possession must be continuous and peaceable for the required period of time. This requirement means that the possessor must not be interrupted in the occupancy by the true owner or by the courts.

④ Possession must be hostile and adverse. In other words, the possessor must claim the property as against the whole world. He or she cannot be living on the property with the permission of the owner.

Limitations on the Rights of Property Owners

No ownership rights in real property can ever really be absolute. That is, an owner of real property cannot always do whatever she or he wishes on or with the property. Nuisance and environmental laws, for example, restrict certain types of activities. Holding the property is also conditional on the payment of property taxes. If these taxes are not paid, ownership of the property will be forfeited to the state. In addition, if a property owner fails to pay debts, the property may be seized to satisfy judgment creditors. In short, the rights of every property owner are subject to certain conditions and limitations. In this section of this chapter, we look at some of the important ways in which owners' rights in real property can be limited.

EMINENT DOMAIN

Even if ownership in real property is in fee simple absolute, there is still a superior ownership that limits the fee simple absolute. Just as in medieval England, the king was the ultimate landowner, so in the United States, the government has ultimate ownership rights in all land. This right is called **eminent domain**, and it allows the government to take land, from a small parcel of property to a large tract of land, for public use. Eminent domain gives the government the right to acquire possession of real property in the manner directed by the U.S. Constitution and the laws of the state whenever the public interest requires it. Property may be taken only for public use, not for private benefit.

For example, when a new public highway is to be built, the government decides where to build it and how much land to condemn. The power of eminent domain is generally invoked through **condemnation** proceedings—thus, the power of eminent domain is sometimes referred to as the *condemnation power* of government. After the government determines that a particular parcel of land is needed for public use, it brings a judicial proceeding to obtain title to the land. Then, in another proceeding, the court determines the fair value of the land, which is usually approximately equal to its market value.

When the government takes land owned by a private party for public use, it is referred to as a **taking,** and the government must compensate the private party. Under the so-called *takings clause* of the Fifth Amendment to the U.S. Constitution, the government may not take private property for public use without "just compensation." State constitutions contain similar provisions.

ZONING

The state's power to control the use of land through legislation is derived from two sources: eminent domain and police power. Through eminent domain, the government can take land for public use, but it must pay just compensation. Consequently, eminent domain is an expensive method of land-use control. Under its police power, however, the state can pass laws aimed at protecting public health, safety, morals, and general welfare. These laws include *zoning laws,* by which the state can regulate uses of land without having to compensate the landowner.

There are some limits on a state's power to control the use of land. If a state law restricts a landowner's property rights too significantly, the state's regulation will be deemed a *confiscation,* or a taking, and may be subject to the eminent domain requirement that just compensation be paid.

The state's power to regulate the use of land is limited in two other ways, both of which arise from the Fourteenth Amendment. First, the state cannot regulate the use of land arbitrarily or unreasonably because this would be taking property without due process. There must be a *rational basis* for the classifications that the state imposes on property. Any act that is reasonably related to the health or general welfare of the public is deemed to have a rational basis. Second, a state's regulation of land use cannot be discriminatory. A zoning ordinance is considered discriminatory if it affects one parcel of land differently from surrounding parcels and there is no rational basis for the difference.

ENVIRONMENTAL TAKINGS

A question subject to ongoing debate is whether landowners should be compensated when restrictions are placed on the use of their property in the interests of protecting the environment. In some cases, the courts have sided with the state or local regulators on this issue. (See, for example, the case discussed in the *Focus on Legal Reasoning* feature following Chapter 30.)

In other cases, however, courts have held for the property owners in these situations. ● **EXAMPLE #7** In one case, an owner of ocean-front property in Monterey, California, had applied to the city of Monterey on several occasions for a permit to build a residential development. Each time, the city denied the use of a greater portion of the property until none of it remained available for any use at all. In effect, the entire property had to be left in its natural state. The city claimed that it was seeking to protect various forms of wildlife that inhabit the coastal sand dunes, particularly the endangered Smith's blue butterfly. Eventually, the property owner sold the property to the city and then sued the city, claiming that the restrictions on use amounted to an unconstitutional taking without just compensation. The jury agreed and awarded the owner nearly $1.45 million in damages. The award was affirmed on appeal and, ultimately, by the United States Supreme Court.[8]●

TAKINGS FOR PRIVATE DEVELOPMENTS

For some time, state and local governments have been using the power of eminent domain to transfer property to private developers. Government officials claim that this use of eminent domain helps bring in private developers and businesses that provide jobs and increase tax revenues, thus revitalizing communities. Eminent domain is also being commonly employed to encourage redevelopment—in blighted areas of a city, for example. When eminent domain is used in this way, essentially one group of private owners is replaced by another group of private owners.

Takings for private development or redevelopment have sometimes been challenged on the ground that the property is not being taken for "public" use, as required by the U.S. Constitution. In these cases, the courts have generally focused on whether the proposed use of the land is genuinely in the public interest or is mainly to further private gain. By and large, the courts have supported the government agencies in these situations, although a series of cases in recent years indicates that this pattern may be changing. ● **EXAMPLE #8** A case decided by the Illinois Supreme Court in 2002 involved an Illinois state agency that had issued bonds and lent the proceeds of the bonds to Gateway International Motorsports Corporation. The purpose of the loan was to finance the development of a sports facility (a racetrack) in the region. The racetrack flourished, and soon Gateway needed more parking space. The state agency then condemned a parcel of property adjacent to the racetrack for Gateway to use for additional parking. The owner of the adjacent property challenged the taking, contending that it was for private, not public, use. Ultimately, the Illinois Supreme Court sided with the property owner. According to the court, the power of eminent domain is to be "exercised with restraint, not abandon," and it was "a violation of the constitutional public use limitation for a government agency to take unoffending property in order to convey it for the expansion of parking of another private business."[9]● Other courts in the early 2000s have reached similar conclusions in cases involving takings for purposes not clearly in the public interest.[10]

Leasehold Estates

Often, real property is used by those who do not own it. A **lease** is a contract by which the owner of real property (the landlord, or lessor) grants to a person (the tenant, or lessee) an exclusive right to use and possess the property, usually for a specified period of time, in return for rent or some other form of payment. Property in the possession of a tenant is referred to as a **leasehold estate**.

The respective rights and duties of the landlord and tenant that arise under a lease agreement will be discussed shortly. Here we look at the types of leasehold estates, or tenancies, that can be created when real property is leased.

TENANCY FOR YEARS

A **tenancy for years** is created by an express contract by which property is leased for a specified period of time, such as a day, a month, a year, or a period of years. For example, signing a one-year lease to occupy an apartment creates a tenancy for years. At the end of the period specified in the lease, the lease ends (without notice), and possession of the apartment returns to the lessor. If the tenant dies during the period of the lease, the lease interest passes to the tenant's heirs as personal property. Often, leases include renewal or extension provisions.

PERIODIC TENANCY

A **periodic tenancy** is created by a lease that does not specify how long it is to last but does specify that rent is to be

---

[8] *Del Monte Dunes at Monterey, Ltd. v. City of Monterey,* 95 F.3d 1422 (9th Cir. 1996). As mentioned, this case was appealed to the United States Supreme Court, which reviewed the question of whether it was up to a judge, not a jury, to decide the issue of whether a taking had occurred. The Court held that this was a predominantly factual question and thus one for the jury to decide. See *City of Monterey v. Del Monte Dunes at Monterey, Ltd.,* 526 U.S. 687, 119 S.Ct. 1624, 143 L.Ed.2d 882 (1999).

[9] *Southwestern Illinois Development Authority v. National City Environmental, L.L.C.,* 199 Ill.2d 225, 768 N.E.2d 1, 263 Ill.Dec. 241 (2002).

[10] See, for example, *99 Cents Only Stores v. Lancaster Redevelopment Agency,* 237 F.Supp.2d 1123 (C.D.Cal. 2001).

paid at certain intervals. This type of tenancy is automatically renewed for another rental period unless properly terminated. For example, a periodic tenancy is created by a lease that states, "Rent is due on the tenth day of every month." This provision creates a tenancy from month to month. This type of tenancy can also extend from week to week or from year to year.

Under the common law, to terminate a periodic tenancy, the landlord or tenant must give at least one period's notice to the other party. If the tenancy extends from month to month, for example, one month's notice must be given prior to the last month's rent payment. State statutes may require a different period for notice of termination in a periodic tenancy, however.

TENANCY AT WILL

Suppose that a landlord rents an apartment to a tenant "for as long as both agree." In such a situation, the tenant receives a leasehold estate known as a **tenancy at will.** Under the common law, either party can terminate the tenancy without notice (that is, "at will"). This type of estate usually arises when a tenant who has been under a tenancy for years retains possession after the termination date of that tenancy with the landlord's consent. Before the tenancy has been converted into a periodic tenancy (by the periodic payment of rent), it is a tenancy at will, terminable by either party without notice. Once the tenancy is treated as a periodic tenancy, termination notice must conform to the one already discussed for that type of tenancy. The death of either party or the voluntary commission of waste by the tenant will terminate a tenancy at will.

TENANCY AT SUFFERANCE

The mere possession of land without right is called a **tenancy at sufferance.** It is not a true tenancy. A tenancy at sufferance is not an estate because it is created when a tenant *wrongfully* retains possession of property. Whenever a tenancy for years, periodic tenancy, or tenancy at will ends and the tenant continues to retain possession of the premises without the owner's permission, a tenancy at sufferance is created. When a tenancy at sufferance arises, the owner can immediately evict the tenant.

Landlord-Tenant Relationships

In the past several decades, landlord-tenant relationships have become much more complex, as has the law governing them. Generally, the law has come to apply contract doctrines, such as those providing for implied warranties and unconscionability, to the landlord-tenant relationship. Increasingly, landlord-tenant relationships have become subject to specific state and local statutes and ordinances as well. In 1972, in an effort to create more uniformity in the law governing landlord-tenant relationships, the National Conference of Commissioners on Uniform State Laws issued the Uniform Residential Landlord and Tenant Act (URLTA). We look now at how a landlord-tenant relationship is created and at the respective rights and duties of landlords and tenants.

CREATING THE LANDLORD-TENANT RELATIONSHIP

A landlord-tenant relationship is established by a lease contract. As mentioned, a lease contract arises when a property owner (landlord) agrees to give another party (the tenant) the exclusive right to possess the property—usually for a price and for a specified term.

Form of the Lease. A lease contract may be oral or written. Under the common law, an oral lease is valid. As with most oral contracts, however, a party who seeks to enforce an oral lease may have difficulty proving its existence. In most states, statutes mandate that leases be in writing for some tenancies (such as those exceeding one year). To ensure the validity of a lease agreement, it should therefore be in writing and do the following:

① Express an intent to establish the relationship.

② Provide for the transfer of the property's possession to the tenant at the beginning of the term.

③ Provide for the landlord's reversionary interest, which entitles the property owner to retake possession at the end of the term.

④ Describe the property—for example, give its street address.

⑤ Indicate the length of the term, the amount of the rent, and how and when it is to be paid.

Legal Requirements. State or local law often dictates permissible lease terms. For example, a statute or ordinance might prohibit the leasing of a structure that is in a certain physical condition or is not in compliance with local building codes. Similarly, a statute may prohibit the leasing of property for a particular purpose. For instance, a state law might prohibit gambling houses. Thus, if a landlord and tenant intend that the leased premises be used only to house an illegal betting operation, their lease is unenforceable.

A property owner cannot legally discriminate against prospective tenants on the basis of race, color, national origin, religion, gender, or disability. Similarly, a tenant cannot legally promise to do something counter to laws prohibiting discrimination. A tenant, for example, cannot legally promise to do business only with members of a particular race.

The public policy underlying these prohibitions is to treat all people equally. In the following case, a rental housing applicant claimed that her rental application had been denied because of her live-in boyfriend's race.

CASE 29.2 Osborn v. Kellogg

Court of Appeals of Nebraska, 1996.
4 Neb.App. 594,
547 N.W.2d 504.

FACTS Kristi Kellogg, her daughter Mindy, and her boyfriend James Greene attempted to lease half of a house. The house was owned by Keith Osborn and Pam Lyman, and managed, as rental property, by Keith's mother, Barbara Osborn. Kellogg was white. Greene was African American. The owners refused to rent to them, claiming, among other things, that three people were too many, Greene's income was too low, and Greene had not provided credit references. They later rented half of the house to the Li family, which had five members, and the other half to the Suggett family, which numbered three. Both the Li family and the Suggett family had less income than Kellogg and Greene. Kellogg had provided extensive credit references, but the Lis and the Suggetts had provided none. Kellogg filed a complaint with the Nebraska Equal Opportunity Commission (NEOC) against the Osborns and Lyman. The NEOC concluded that the defendants had discriminated against Kellogg in violation of state fair housing laws. A Nebraska state trial court adopted the NEOC's conclusion. The defendants appealed to an intermediate state appellate court.

ISSUE Had the defendants discriminated against Kellogg in violation of state fair housing laws?

DECISION Yes. The intermediate state appellate court affirmed the judgment of the lower court.

REASON The appellate court reasoned that "[w]hile Kellogg is not a member of a racial minority [but Greene was], we note that she qualifies as * * * a person who claims to have been injured by a discriminatory housing practice." The court stated, "The NEOC hearing examiner found that Kellogg proved by a preponderance of the evidence that the Osborns' seemingly legitimate reasons for rejecting Kellogg were, in fact, a pretext for intentional discrimination. * * * [W]e conclude that competent evidence supports the NEOC hearing examiner's factual findings."

FOR CRITICAL ANALYSIS—Ethical Consideration
What if the Osborns and Lyman discriminated against Kellogg not because her boyfriend was African American but because they disapproved of cohabitation by unmarried couples? Should this form of discrimination be permissible?

RIGHTS AND DUTIES

The rights and duties of landlords and tenants generally pertain to four broad areas of concern—the possession, use, and maintenance of leased property and, of course, rent.

Possession. Possession involves both the obligation of the landlord to deliver possession to the tenant at the beginning of the lease term and the right of the tenant to obtain possession and retain it until the lease expires.

The covenant of quiet enjoyment mentioned previously also applies to leased premises. Under this covenant, the landlord promises that during the lease term, neither the landlord nor anyone having a superior title to the property will disturb the tenant's use and enjoyment of the property. This covenant forms the essence of the landlord-tenant

relationship, and if it is breached, the tenant can terminate the lease and sue for damages.

If the landlord deprives the tenant of possession of the leased property or interferes with the tenant's use or enjoyment of it, an **eviction** occurs. An eviction occurs, for example, when the landlord changes the lock and refuses to give the tenant a new key. A **constructive eviction** occurs when the landlord wrongfully performs or fails to perform any of the undertakings the lease requires, thereby making the tenant's further use and enjoyment of the property exceedingly difficult or impossible. Examples of constructive eviction include a landlord's failure to provide heat in the winter, light, or other essential utilities.

Use and Maintenance of the Premises. If the parties do not limit by agreement the uses to which the property may be put, the tenant may make any use of it, as long as the use is legal and reasonably relates to the purpose for which the property is adapted or ordinarily used and does not injure the landlord's interest.

The tenant is responsible for any damages to the premises that he or she causes, intentionally or negligently, and the tenant may be held liable for the cost of returning the property to the physical condition it was in at the lease's inception. Unless the parties have agreed otherwise, the tenant is not responsible for ordinary wear and tear and the property's consequent depreciation in value.

Usually, the landlord must comply with state statutes and city ordinances that delineate specific standards for the construction and maintenance of buildings. Typically, these codes contain structural requirements common to the construction, wiring, and plumbing of residential and commercial buildings. In some jurisdictions, landlords of residential property are required by statute to maintain the premises in good repair.

Implied Warranty of Habitability. The **implied warranty of habitability** requires a landlord who leases residential property to deliver the premises to the tenant in a habitable condition—that is, in a condition that is safe and suitable for people to live in—at the beginning of a lease term and to maintain them in that condition for the lease's duration. Some state legislatures have enacted this warranty into law. In other jurisdictions, courts have based the warranty on the existence of a landlord's statutory duty to keep leased premises in good repair, or they have simply applied it as a matter of public policy.

Generally, this warranty applies to major, or substantial, physical defects that the landlord knows or should know about and has had a reasonable time to repair—for example, a large hole in the roof. An unattractive or annoying feature, such as a crack in the wall, may be unpleasant, but unless the crack is a structural defect or affects the residence's heating capabilities, it is probably not sufficiently substantial to make the place uninhabitable.

At issue in the following case was whether the lack of a smoke detector constituted a violation of a statutory requirement that rental property be "in reasonable repair and fit for human habitation."

CASE 29.3 **Schiernbeck v. Davis**

United States Court of Appeals, Eighth Circuit, 1998.
143 F.3d 434.
http://laws.findlaw.com/8th[a]

FACTS Linda Schiernbeck rented a house from Clark and Rosa Davis in South Dakota. A month after moving into the house, Schiernbeck noticed a discolored circular area where, she determined, a smoke detector had previously been attached to the wall. Schiernbeck later claimed that she told Clark Davis about the missing detector. Davis did not remember the conversation. He admitted, however, that he gave Schiernbeck a detector, which she denied. At any rate, when a fire in the house severely injured Schiernbeck, she filed a suit in a federal district court against the Davises, alleging negligence and breach of contract for failing to provide a detector. The Davises filed a motion for summary judgment, arguing that they had no duty to install a detector in a rental house. The court ruled in the Davises' favor, and Schiernbeck appealed to the U.S. Court of Appeals for the Eighth Circuit.

ISSUE Does a landlord's statutory duty to keep rental premises "in reasonable repair and fit for human habitation" include installing a smoke detector?

DECISION No. The U.S. Court of Appeals for the Eighth Circuit affirmed the lower court's judgment.

REASON The U.S. Court of Appeals for the Eighth Circuit recognized that South Dakota Codified Laws, Section 43-32-8, requires a landlord to maintain leased premises "in reasonable repair and fit for human habitation." The question was whether the installation of a smoke detector fell within the language of the statute. Schiernbeck cited part of a dictionary definition of "repair" ("to supply * * * that which is lost or destroyed") and argued that this included replacing a missing smoke detector. The court disagreed, concluding that "when reading the entire definition, the term 'repair' does not encompass replacing a missing smoke detector." As for the "fit for human habitation" requirement, the court stated that a lack of running water, heat, or electricity made a place unfit, while a lack of smoke detectors, fire extinguishers, and so on, did not.

FOR CRITICAL ANALYSIS—Ethical Consideration *What is a landlord's ethical duty with respect to keeping rental premises "fit for human habitation"?*

---

a. This page provides access to some of the opinions of the U.S. Court of Appeals for the Eighth Circuit. In the "Search" box, type "97-3431" and click on "Search" to access a link to the *Schiernbeck* opinion. This Web site is maintained by FindLaw (now a part of West Group).

Rent. *Rent* is the tenant's payment to the landlord for the tenant's occupancy or use of the landlord's real property. Generally, the tenant must pay the rent even if she or he refuses to occupy the property or moves out, as long as the refusal or the move is unjustifiable and the lease is in force.

Under the common law, destruction by fire or flood of a building leased by a tenant did not relieve the tenant of the obligation to pay rent and did not permit the termination of the lease. Today, however, state statutes have altered the common law rule. If the building burns down, apartment dwellers in most states are not continuously liable to the landlord for the payment of rent.

In some situations, such as when a landlord breaches the implied warranty of habitability, a tenant is allowed to withhold rent as a remedy. When rent withholding is authorized under a statute (sometimes referred to as a "rent-strike" statute), the tenant must usually put the amount withheld into an *escrow account*. This account is held in the name of the depositor (in this case, the tenant) and an *escrow agent* (in this case, usually the court or a government agency), and the funds are returnable to the depositor if the third person (in this case, the landlord) fails to fulfill the escrow condition. Generally, the tenant may withhold an amount equal to the amount by which the defect rendering the premises unlivable reduces the property's rental value. How much that is may be determined in different ways, and the tenant who withholds more than is legally permissible is liable to the landlord for the excessive amount withheld.

TRANSFERRING RIGHTS TO LEASED PROPERTY

Either the landlord or the tenant may wish to transfer her or his rights to the leased property during the term of the lease.

Transferring the Landlord's Interest. Just as any other real property owner can sell, give away, or otherwise trans-fer her or his property, so can a landlord—who is, of course, the leased property's owner. If complete title to the leased property is transferred, the tenant becomes the tenant of the new owner. The new owner may collect subsequent rent but must abide by the terms of the existing lease agreement.

Transferring the Tenant's Interest. The tenant's transfer of his or her entire interest in the leased property to a third person is an *assignment of the lease*. A lease assignment is an agreement to transfer all rights, title, and interest in the lease to the assignee. It is a complete transfer. Many leases require that the assignment have the landlord's written consent, and an assignment that lacks consent can be avoided (nullified) by the landlord. A landlord who knowingly accepts rent from the assignee, however, will be held to have waived the requirement. An assignment does not terminate a tenant's liabilities under a lease agreement, however, because the tenant may assign rights but not duties. Thus, even though the assignee of the lease is required to pay rent, the original tenant is not released from the contractual obligation to pay the rent if the assignee fails to do so.

The tenant's transfer of all or part of the premises for a period shorter than the lease term is a **sublease**. The same restrictions that apply to an assignment of the tenant's interest in leased property apply to a sublease. ● EXAMPLE #9 Derek, a student, leases an apartment for a two-year period. Although Derek had planned on attending summer school, he is offered a job in Europe for the summer months and accepts. Because he does not wish to pay three months' rent for an unoccupied apartment, Derek subleases the apartment to Singleton, who becomes a sublessee. (Derek may have to obtain his landlord's consent for this sublease if the lease requires it.) Singleton is bound by the same terms of the lease as Derek, but as in a lease assignment, Derek remains liable for the obligations under the lease if Singleton fails to fulfill them.●

Terms and Concepts

Chapter Summary	Real Property
The Nature of Real Property (See pages 607–609.)	Real property (also called real estate or realty) is immovable. It includes land, subsurface and air rights, plant life and vegetation, and fixtures.
Ownership of Real Property (See pages 609–611.)	1. *Fee simple absolute*—The most complete form of ownership. 2. *Fee simple defeasible*—Ownership in fee simple that can end if a specified event or condition occurs. 3. *Life estate*—An estate that lasts for the life of a specified individual, during which time the individual is entitled to possess, use, and benefit from the estate; ownership rights in a life estate are subject to the rights of the future-interest holder. 4. *Future interest*—A residuary interest not granted by the grantor in conveying an estate to another for life, for a specified period of time, or on the condition that a specific event does or does not occur. The grantor may retain the residuary interest (which is then called a *reversionary interest*) or transfer ownership rights in the future interest to another (the interest is then referred to as a *remainder*). 5. *Nonpossessory interest*—An interest that involves the right to use real property but not to possess it. Easements, profits, and licenses are nonpossessory interests.
Transfer of Ownership (See pages 612–614.)	1. *By deed*—When real property is sold or transferred as a gift, title to the property is conveyed by means of a deed. A deed must meet specific legal requirements. A *warranty deed* warrants the most extensive protection against defects of title. A *quitclaim deed* conveys to the grantee only whatever interest the grantor had in the property. A deed may be recorded in the manner prescribed by *recording statutes* in the appropriate jurisdiction to give third parties notice of the owner's interest. 2. *By will or inheritance*—If the owner dies after having made a valid will, the land passes as specified in the will. If the owner dies without having made a will, the heirs inherit according to state inheritance statutes. 3. *By adverse possession*—When a person possesses the property of another for a statutory period of time (three to thirty years, with ten years being the most common), that person acquires title to the property, provided the possession is actual and exclusive, open and visible, continuous and peaceable, and hostile and adverse (without the permission of the owner).
Limitations on the Rights of Property Owners (See pages 614–615.)	1. *Eminent domain*—The government can take land for public use, with just compensation, when the public interest requires the taking. 2. *Zoning*—Through its eminent domain and police powers, state and local governments may limit what an owner can do with a piece of land. Limits must not be confiscatory, must have a rational basis, and cannot be discriminatory. 3. *Environmental takings*—Whether restrictions on the uses of private property in the interests of protecting the environment constitute a taking is a controversial issue. If a court deems the restrictions a taking, the private property owner must be compensated. 4. *Takings for private developments*—Whether taking private property for the purpose of turning it over to another private entity (for development or redevelopment) meets the requirement of "public use" is a question that has often come before the courts.
Leasehold Estates (See pages 615–616.)	A leasehold estate is an interest in real property that is held for only a limited period of time, as specified in the lease agreement. Types of tenancies relating to leased property include the following: 1. *Tenancy for years*—Tenancy for a period of time stated by express contract.

Chapter Summary	Real Property—Continued
Leasehold Estates— continued	2. *Periodic tenancy*—Tenancy for a period determined by the frequency of rent payments; automatically renewed unless proper notice is given.
	3. *Tenancy at will*—Tenancy for as long as both parties agree; no notice of termination is required.
	4. *Tenancy at sufferance*—Possession of land without legal right.
Landlord-Tenant Relationships (See pages 616–619.)	1. *Lease agreement*—The landlord-tenant relationship is created by a lease agreement. State or local laws may dictate whether the lease must be in writing and what lease terms are permissible.
	2. *Rights and duties*—The rights and duties that arise under a lease agreement generally pertain to the following areas:
	a. Possession—The tenant has an exclusive right to possess the leased premises, which must be available to the tenant at the agreed-on time. Under the covenant of quiet enjoyment, the landlord promises that during the lease term neither the landlord nor anyone having superior title to the property will disturb the tenant's use and enjoyment of the property.
	b. Use and maintenance of the premises—Unless the parties agree otherwise, the tenant may make any legal use of the property. The tenant is responsible for any damage that he or she causes. The landlord must comply with laws that set specific standards for the maintenance of real property. The implied warranty of habitability requires that a landlord furnish and maintain residential premises in a habitable condition (that is, in a condition safe and suitable for human life).
	c. Rent—The tenant must pay the rent as long as the lease is in force, unless the tenant justifiably refuses to occupy the property or withholds the rent because of the landlord's failure to maintain the premises properly.
	3. *Transferring rights to leased property*—
	a. If the landlord transfers complete title to the leased property, the tenant becomes the tenant of the new owner. The new owner may then collect the rent but must abide by the existing lease.
	b. Generally, in the absence of an agreement to the contrary, tenants may assign their rights (but not their duties) under a lease contract to a third person. Tenants may also sublease leased property to a third person, but the original tenant is not relieved of any obligations to the landlord under the lease. In either case, the landlord's consent may be required.

For Review

① What can a person who holds property in fee simple absolute do with the property? Can a person who holds property as a life estate do the same?

② What are the requirements for acquiring property by adverse possession?

③ What limitations may be imposed on the rights of property owners?

④ What is a leasehold estate? What types of leasehold estates, or tenancies, can be created when real property is leased?

⑤ What are the respective duties of the landlord and tenant concerning the use and maintenance of leased property? Is the tenant responsible for all damages that he or she causes?

Questions and Case Problems

29–1. Tenant's Rights and Responsibilities. You are a student in college and plan to attend classes for nine months. You sign a twelve-month lease for an apartment. Discuss fully each of the following situations:

(a) You have a summer job in another town and wish to assign the balance of your lease (three months) to a fellow student who will be attending summer school. Can you do so?

(b) You are graduating in May. The lease will have three months remaining. Can you terminate the lease without liability by giving thirty days' notice to the landlord?

29–2. Property Ownership. Antonio is the owner of a lakeside house and lot. He deeds the house and lot "to my wife, Angela, for life, then to my son, Charles." Given these facts, answer the following questions:

(a) Does Antonio have any ownership interest in the lakeside house after making these transfers? Explain.

(b) What is Angela's interest called? Is there any limitation on her rights to use the property as she wishes?

(c) What is Charles's interest called? Why?

29–3. Property Ownership. Lorenz was a wanderer twenty-two years ago. At that time, he decided to settle down on an unoccupied, three-acre parcel of land that he did not own. People in the area indicated to him that they had no idea who owned the property. Lorenz built a house on the land, got married, and raised three children while living there. He fenced in the land, installed a gate with a sign above it that read "Lorenz's Homestead," and had trespassers removed. Lorenz is now confronted by Joe Reese, who has a deed in his name as owner of the property. Reese, claiming ownership of the land, orders Lorenz and his family off the property. Discuss who has the better "title" to the property.

29–4. Deeds. Wiley and Gemma are neighbors. Wiley's lot is extremely large, and his present and future use of it will not involve the entire area. Gemma wants to build a single-car garage and driveway along the present lot boundary. Because of ordinances requiring buildings to be set back fifteen feet from an adjoining property line, and because of the placement of her existing structures, Gemma cannot build the garage. Gemma contracts to purchase ten feet of Wiley's property along their boundary line for $3,000. Wiley is willing to sell but will give Gemma only a quitclaim deed, whereas Gemma wants a warranty deed. Discuss the differences between these deeds as they would affect the rights of the parties if the title to this ten feet of land later proved to be defective.

29–5. Warranty of Habitability. James and Bernadine Winn rented a house from Rick and Cynthia McGeehan. Each month, the rent was either late or underpaid. When the McGeehans told the Winns that no further late payments would be accepted, the Winns complained of a number of habitability problems. The McGeehans made repairs. The Winns again failed to pay the rent on time. The McGeehans filed a suit in an Oregon state court to

regain possession of the house. While the suit was pending, the Winns paid the rent to the court. The court held that the McGeehans were entitled to possession. The Winns appealed, claiming that they were entitled to possession. Who should have possession of the house, and why? [*Winn v. McGeehan,* 142 Or.App. 390, 921 P.2d 1337 (1996)]

29–6. Taking. Richard and Jaquelyn Jackson owned property in a residential subdivision near an airport operated by the Metropolitan Knoxville Airport Authority in Blount County, Tennessee. The Airport Authority considered extending a runway near the subdivision and undertook a study that found that the noise, vibration, and pollution from aircraft using the extension would render the Jacksons' property incompatible with residential use. The airport built the extension, bringing about the predicted results, and the Jacksons filed a suit against the Airport Authority, alleging a taking of their property. The Airport Authority responded that there was no taking because there were no direct flights over the Jacksons' property. In whose favor will the court rule, and why? [*Jackson v. Metropolitan Knoxville Airport Authority,* 922 S.W.2d 860 (Tenn. 1996)]

29–7. Warranty of Habitability. Three-year-old Nkenge Lynch fell from the window of her third-floor apartment and suffered serious and permanent injuries. There were no window stops or guards on the window. The use of window stops, even if installed, is optional with the tenant. Stanley James owned the apartment building. Zsa Zsa Kinsey, Nkenge's mother, filed a suit on Nkenge's behalf in a Massachusetts state court against James, alleging in part a breach of an implied warranty of habitability. The plaintiff did not argue that the absence of stops or guards made the apartment unfit for human habitation but that their absence "endangered and materially impaired her health and safety," and therefore the failure to install them was a breach of warranty. Should the court rule that the absence of window stops breached a warranty of habitability? Should the court mandate that landlords provide window guards? Why or why not? [*Lynch v. James,* 44 Mass.App.Ct. 448, 692 N.E.2d 81 (1998)]

29–8. Adverse Possession. In 1972, Ted Pafundi bought a quarry in West Pawlet, Vermont, from his neighbor, Marguerite Scott. The deed vaguely described the eastern boundary of the quarry as "the westerly boundary of the lands of" the neighboring property owners. Pafundi quarried green slate from the west wall until his death in 1979, when his son Gary began to work the east wall until his death in 1989. Gary's daughter Connie then took over operations. All of the Pafundis used the floor of the quarry as their base of operations. In 1992, N.A.S. Holdings, Inc., bought the neighboring property. A survey revealed that virtually the entire quarry was within the boundaries of N.A.S.'s property and that twenty years earlier, Ted had actually bought only a small strip of land on the west side. When N.A.S. attempted to begin quarrying, Connie blocked the access. N.A.S. filed a suit in a Vermont state court against Connie, seeking to establish title. Connie argued that she had title to the quarry through adverse possession under a state statute with a possessory period of fifteen years. What are the elements to acquire title by adverse possession? Are they satisfied in this case? In whose favor should the court rule, and why? [*N.A.S. Holdings, Inc. v. Pafundi,* 736 A.2d 280 (Vt. 1999)]

CASE PROBLEM WITH SAMPLE ANSWER

29–9. Jennifer Tribble leased an apartment from Spring Isle II, a limited partnership. The written lease agreement provided that if Tribble was forced to move because of a job transfer or because she accepted a new job, she could vacate on sixty days' notice and owe only an extra two months' rent plus no more than a $650 rerenting fee. The initial term was for one year, and the parties renewed the lease for a second one-year term. The security deposit was $900. State law allowed a landlord to withhold a security deposit for the nonpayment of rent but required timely notice stating valid reasons for the withholding or the tenant would be entitled to twice the amount of the deposit as damages. One month into the second term, Tribble notified Spring Isle in writing that she had accepted a new job and would move out within a week. She paid the extra rent required by the lease, but not the rerental fee, and vacated the apartment. Spring Isle wrote her a letter, stating that it was keeping the entire security deposit until the apartment was rerented or the lease term ended, whichever came first. Spring Isle later filed a suit in a Wisconsin state court against Tribble, claiming that she owed, among other things, the rest of the rent until the apartment had been rerented and the costs of rerenting. Tribble responded that withholding the security deposit was improper, and she was entitled to "any penalties." Does Tribble owe Spring Isle anything? Does Spring Isle owe Tribble anything? Explain. [*Spring Isle II v. Tribble,* 610 N.W.2d 229 (Wis.App. 2000)]

◆ To view a sample answer for this case problem, go to this book's Web site at **http://fundamentals.westbuslaw.com** and click on "Interactive Study Center."

29–10. Commercial Lease Terms. Metropolitan Life Insurance Co. leased space in its Trail Plaza Shopping Center in Florida to Winn-Dixie Stores, Inc., to operate a supermarket. Under the lease, the landlord agreed not to permit "any [other] property located within the shopping center to be used for or occupied by any business dealing in or which shall keep in

stock or sell for off-premises consumption any staple or fancy groceries" in more than "500 square feet of sales area." In 1999, Metropolitan leased 22,000 square feet of space in Trail Plaza to 99 Cent Stuff-Trail Plaza, LLC, under a lease that prohibited it from selling "groceries" in more than 500 square feet of "sales area." Shortly after 99 Cent Stuff opened, it began selling food and other products, including soap, matches, and paper napkins. Alleging that these sales violated the parties' leases, Winn-Dixie filed a suit in a Florida state court against 99 Cent Stuff and others. The defendants argued in part that the groceries provision covered only food and the 500-square-foot restriction included only shelf space, not store aisles. How should these lease terms be interpreted? Should the court grant an injunction in Winn-Dixie's favor? Explain. [*Winn-Dixie Stores, Inc. v. 99 Cent Stuff-Trail Plaza, LLC,* 811 So.2d 719 (Fla.App. 3 Dist. 2002)]

A QUESTION OF ETHICS AND SOCIAL RESPONSIBILITY

29–11. John and Terry Hoffius own property in Jackson, Michigan, which they rent. Kristal McCready and Keith Kerr responded to the Hoffiuses' ad about the property. The Hoffiuses refused to rent to McCready and Kerr, however, when they learned that the two were single and intended to live together. John Hoffius told all prospective tenants that unmarried cohabitation violated his religious beliefs. McCready and others filed a suit in a Michigan state court against the Hoffiuses. They alleged in part that the Hoffiuses' actions violated the plaintiffs' civil rights under a state law that prohibits discrimination on the basis of "marital status." The Hoffiuses responded in part that forcing them to rent to unmarried couples in violation of the Hoffiuses' religious beliefs would be unconstitutional. [*McCready v. Hoffius,* 586 N.W.2d 723 (Mich. 1998)]

1. Did the defendants violate the plaintiffs' civil rights? Explain.

2. Should a court, in the interest of preventing discrimination in housing, compel a landlord to violate his or her conscience? In other words, whose rights should prevail in this case? Why?

3. Is there an objective rule that determines when civil rights or religious freedom, or any two similarly important principles, should prevail? If so, what is it? If not, should there be?

ACCESSING THE INTERNET

REAL PROPERTY

For updated links to resources available on the Web, as well as other materials, visit this text's Web site at

http://fundamentals.westbuslaw.com

For a variety of links to real property resources, go to

http://findlaw.com/01topics/33property

For information on condemnation procedures and rules under California law, go to

http://www.eminentdomainlaw.net/propertyguide.html

The Web site of the U.S. Department of Housing and Urban Development (HUD) has information of interest to both consumers and businesses. Go to

http://www.hud.gov

For information on Veterans Administration home loans, go to

http://www.homeloans.va.gov

To find the Uniform Residential Landlord and Tenant Act, go to

http://www.law.upenn.edu/bll/ulc/ulc_frame.htm

and click on "Final Acts" in the left-hand frame. Then scroll down to find the link to the act.

Tenant Net is an advocacy Web site focusing on New York City and the state of New York. To view this site, go to

http://www.tenant.net

Online Legal Research

Go to the *Fundamentals of Business Law* home page at **http://fundamentals. westbuslaw.com**. Select "Interactive Study Center" and then click on "Chapter 29." There you will find the following Internet research exercises that you can perform to learn more about topics covered in this chapter.

Activity 29-1: LEGAL PERSPECTIVE—**Eminent Domain**
Activity 29-2: MANAGEMENT PERSPECTIVE—**The Rights of Tenants**
Activity 29-3: SOCIAL PERSPECTIVE—**Fair Housing**

Before the Test

Go to the *Fundamentals of Business Law* home page at **http://fundamentals. westbuslaw.com**. Click on "Interactive Quizzes." You will find at least twenty interactive questions relating to this chapter.

Westlaw® Campus

If your textbook provided for a subscription to Westlaw® Campus, or if you have otherwise purchased access to the Westlaw Campus database, you can access any of the cases presented or cited in this chapter by using your Westlaw Campus account.

CHAPTER OBJECTIVES

After reading this chapter, you should be able to answer the following questions:

① What is an insurable interest? When must an insurable interest exist—at the time the insurance policy is obtained, at the time the loss occurs, or both?

② Is an insurance broker the agent of the insurance applicant or the agent of the insurer?

③ What are the basic requirements for executing a will? How may a will be revoked?

④ What is the difference between a *per stirpes* and a *per capita* distribution of an estate to the grandchildren of the deceased?

⑤ What are the four essential elements of a trust? What is the difference between an express trust and an implied trust?

Most individuals insure both real and personal property (as well as their lives). By insuring our property, we protect ourselves against damage and loss. The first part of this chapter focuses on insurance, which is a foremost concern of all property owners. We then examine how property is transferred on the death of its owner. Certainly, the laws of succession of property are a necessary corollary to the concept of private ownership of property. Our laws require that on death, title to the property of a decedent (one who has recently died) must be delivered in full somewhere. In this chapter, we see that this can be done by will, through trusts, or through state laws prescribing distribution of property among heirs or next of kin.

Insurance

Insurance is a contract by which the insurance company (the insurer) promises to pay a sum of money or give something of value to another (either the insured or the beneficiary) in the event that the insured is injured, dies, or sustains damage to her or his property as a result of particular, stated contingencies. Basically, insurance is an arrangement for *transferring and allocating risk.* In many cases, **risk** can be described as a prediction concerning potential loss based on known and unknown factors. Insurance, however, involves much more than a game of chance.

Many precautions may be taken to protect against the hazards of life. For example, an individual may wear a seat belt to protect against injuries from automobile accidents or install smoke detectors to guard against injury from fire. Of course, no one can predict whether an accident or a fire will ever occur, but individuals and businesses must establish plans to protect their personal and financial interests should some event threaten to undermine their security. This concept is known as **risk management**. The most common method of risk management is the transfer of certain risks from the individual to the insurance company.

Risk is transferred to an insurance company by a contractual agreement. The insurance contract and its provisions will be examined shortly. First, however, we look at the different types of insurance that can be obtained, insurance terminology, and the concept of insurable interest.

CLASSIFICATIONS OF INSURANCE

Insurance is classified according to the nature of the risk involved. For example, fire insurance, casualty insurance, life insurance, and title insurance apply to different types of risk. Furthermore, policies of these types differ in the persons and interests that they protect. This is reasonable because the types of losses that are expected and the types that are foreseeable or unforeseeable vary with the nature of the activity. Exhibit 30–1 presents a list of insurance classifications. (For a discussion of insurance and losses caused by computer "downtime," see this chapter's *Management Perspective* on page 628.)

INSURANCE TERMINOLOGY

An insurance contract is called a **policy**; the consideration paid to the insurer is called a **premium**; and the insurance company is sometimes called an **underwriter**.

The parties to an insurance policy are the *insurer* (the insurance company) and the *insured* (the person covered by

EXHIBIT 30–1   INSURANCE CLASSIFICATIONS

TYPE OF INSURANCE	COVERAGE
Accident	Covers expenses, losses, and suffering incurred by the insured because of accidents causing physical injury and any consequent disability; sometimes includes a specified payment to heirs of the insured if death results from an accident.
All-risk	Covers all losses that the insured may incur except those resulting from fraud on the part of the insured.
Automobile	May cover damage to automobiles resulting from specified hazards or occurrences (such as fire, vandalism, theft, or collision); normally provides protection against liability for personal injuries and property damage resulting from the operation of the vehicle.
Casualty	Protects against losses that may be incurred by the insured as a result of being held liable for personal injuries or property damage sustained by others.
Credit	Pays to a creditor the balance of a debt on the disability, death, insolvency, or bankruptcy of the debtor; often offered by lending institutions.
Decreasing-term life	Provides life insurance; requires uniform payments over the life (term) of the policy, but with a decreasing face value (amount of coverage).
Employer's liability	Insures employers against liability for injuries or losses sustained by employees during the course of their employment; covers claims not covered under workers' compensation insurance.
Fidelity or guaranty	Provides indemnity against losses in trade or losses caused by the dishonesty of employees, the insolvency of debtors, or breaches of contract.
Fire	Covers losses incurred by the insured as a result of fire.
Floater	Covers movable property, as long as the property is within the territorial boundaries specified in the contract.
Group	Provides individual life, medical, or disability insurance coverage but is obtainable through a group of persons, usually employees; the policy premium is paid either entirely by the employer or partially by the employer and partially by the employee.

the insurer's provisions or the holder of the policy). Insurance contracts are usually obtained through an *agent,* who ordinarily works for the insurance company, or through a *broker,* who is ordinarily an *independent contractor.* When a broker deals with an applicant for insurance, the broker is, in effect, the applicant's agent. In contrast, an insurance agent is an agent of the insurance company, not of the applicant. As a general rule, the insurance company is bound by the acts of its agents when they act within the agency relationship (discussed in Chapter 22). A broker, however, normally has no relationship with the insurance company and is an agent of the insurance applicant. In most situations, state law determines the status of all parties writing or obtaining insurance.

INSURABLE INTEREST

A person can insure anything in which he or she has an **insurable interest.** Without this insurable interest, there is no enforceable contract, and a transaction to insure would have to be treated as a wager. In regard to real and personal property, an insurable interest exists when the insured derives a pecuniary benefit (a benefit consisting of or relating to money) from the preservation and continued existence of the property. Put another way, one has an insurable interest in property when one would sustain a pecuniary loss from its destruction. In regard to life insurance, a person must have a reasonable expectation of benefit from the continued life of another in order to have an insurable interest in that person's life. The benefit may be pecuniary (as with so-called *key-person insurance,* which insures the lives of important employees, usually in small companies), or it may be founded on the relationship between the parties (by blood or affinity).

For property insurance, the insurable interest must exist at the time the loss occurs but need not exist when the policy is purchased. In contrast, for life insurance, the insurable interest must exist at the time the policy is obtained. The existence of an insurable interest is a primary concern in determining liability under an insurance policy.

EXHIBIT 30–1	**INSURANCE CLASSIFICATIONS—CONTINUED**

TYPE OF INSURANCE	COVERAGE
Health	Covers expenses incurred by the insured resulting from physical injury or illness and other expenses relating to health and life maintenance.
Homeowners'	Protects homeowners against some or all risks of loss to their residences and the residences' contents or liability arising from the use of the property.
Key-person	Protects a business in the event of the death or disability of a key employee.
Liability	Protects against liability resulting from injuries to the person or property of another.
Life	Covers the death of the policyholder. On the death of the insured, an amount specified in the policy is paid by the insurer to the insured's beneficiary.
Major medical	Protects the insured against major hospital, medical, or surgical expenses.
Malpractice	Protects professionals (doctors, lawyers, and others) against malpractice claims brought against them by their patients or clients; a form of liability insurance.
Marine	Covers movable property (including ships, freight, and cargo) against certain perils or navigation risks during a specific voyage or time period.
Mortgage	Covers a mortgage loan; the insurer pays the balance of the mortgage to the creditor on the death or disability of the debtor.
No-fault auto	Covers personal injury and (sometimes) property damage resulting from automobile accidents. The insured submits his or her claims to his or her own insurance company, regardless of who was at fault. A person may sue the party at fault or that party's insurer only in cases involving serious medical injury and consequent high medical costs. Governed by state "no-fault" statutes.
Term life	Provides life insurance for a specified period of time (term) with no cash surrender value; usually renewable.
Title	Protects against any defects in title to real property and any losses incurred as a result of existing claims against or liens on the property at the time of purchase.

MANAGEMENT PERSPECTIVE
Insurance Coverage and Cyber Losses

MANAGEMENT FACES A LEGAL ISSUE Traditionally, owners and managers of businesses have been unable to obtain insurance policies that specifically covered the risks associated with computer "downtime" or "cyber losses." In today's economy, however, when a business's computer system fails, the damage is often extensive. Customer service may come to a standstill, and data may disappear. If so, it may take hours or even days to put the data back into the computer and get the system up and running again. Will all-risk commercial property insurance cover the losses associated with computer downtime? Although the exact language varies among policies, such policies generally cover "direct physical loss of or damage to covered property."

WHAT THE COURTS SAY In the past, courts have been hesitant to find that computer failures amounted to a business interruption covered by commercial property insurance. This may be changing, however. Consider, for example, a case involving Ingram Micro, Inc. (Ingram), a wholesale distributor of microcomputer products that operated a worldwide computer network to track its customers, products, and daily transactions. A half-hour power outage caused Ingram's computers to lose all of their programming information. Employees had to reload the data and configuration settings into the mainframes, and the computer network was not restored to full operation for nearly eight hours. Ingram had an insurance policy with American Guarantee & Liability Insurance Company that covered "property, business income, and operations." When Ingram submitted a claim to the insurer for the costs associated with the downtime, however, the insurer refused to pay.

The insurer argued that the computer system was not "physically damaged" by the power outage because it "did not adversely affect the equipment's inherent ability to accept and process data" once the information was reentered into the computer system. Ingram contended that despite the fact that the computers retained the ability to accept the data and eventually operate as before, they did undergo physical damage as covered by the policy. According to Ingram, physical damage included loss of use and functionality.

The question before the federal district court was whether the term *physical damage* in the insurance policy included the kinds of problems encountered by Ingram after the power outage. The court held that it did. Specifically, the court found that physical damage was "not restricted to the physical destruction or harm of computer circuitry but includes loss of access, loss of use, and loss of functionality." The court reasoned that "[l]awmakers around the country have determined that when a computer's data is unavailable, there is damage; when a computer's services are interrupted, there is damage; and when a computer's software or network is altered, there is damage."[a] At least one other federal district court has cited the *Ingram* court's decision with approval.[b]

IMPLICATIONS FOR MANAGERS The law pertaining to insurance coverage for computer downtime is far from settled. Although the court in the case just discussed concluded that physical damage includes computer downtime, that does not mean all courts will follow suit. In the meantime, business owners and managers should carefully scrutinize the terms of insurance contracts in order to find a policy that will cover the broadest possible range of losses.

a. *American Guarantee & Liability Insurance Co. v. Ingram Micro, Inc.,* ___ F.Supp.2d ___ (D.Ariz. 2000).
b. *America Online, Inc. v. National Health Care Discount, Inc.,* 121 F.Supp.2d 1255 (N.D. Iowa 2000).

THE INSURANCE CONTRACT

An insurance contract is governed by the general principles of contract law, although the insurance industry is heavily regulated by each state. Several aspects of the insurance contract will be treated here, including the application for insurance, when the contract takes effect, important contract provisions, cancellation of the policy, and defenses that can be raised by insurance companies against payment on a policy.

Application. The filled-in application form for insurance is usually attached to the policy and made a part of the insurance contract. Thus, an insurance applicant is bound by any false statements that appear in the application (subject to certain exceptions). Because the insurance company evaluates the risk factors based on the information included in the insurance application, misstatements or misrepresentations can void a policy, especially if the insurance company can show that it would not have extended insurance if it had known the true facts.

Effective Date. The effective date of an insurance contract is important. In some instances, the insurance applicant is not protected until a formal written policy is issued. In other situations, the applicant is protected between the time the application is received and the time the insurance company either accepts or rejects it. Four facts should be kept in mind:

① A broker is merely the agent of an applicant. Therefore, until the broker obtains a policy, the applicant normally is not insured.

② A person who seeks insurance from an insurance company's agent will usually be protected from the moment the application is made, provided that some form of premium has been paid. Between the time the application is received and either rejected or accepted, the applicant is covered (possibly subject to medical examination). Usually, the agent will write a memorandum, or **binder**, indicating that a policy is pending and stating its essential terms.

③ If the parties agree that the policy will be issued and delivered at a later time, the contract is not effective until the policy is issued and delivered or sent to the applicant, depending on the agreement. Thus, any loss sustained between the time of application and the delivery of the policy is not covered.

④ Parties may agree that a life insurance policy will be binding at the time the insured pays the first premium, or the policy may be expressly contingent on the applicant's passing a physical examination. In the latter situation, if the applicant pays the premium and passes the examination, the policy coverage is in effect. If the applicant pays the premium but dies before having the physical examination, then to collect, the applicant's estate must show that the applicant *would have passed* the examination had he or she not died.

Coinsurance Clauses. Often, when taking out fire insurance policies, property owners insure their property for less than full value. Part of the reason for this is that most fires do not result in a total loss. To encourage owners to insure their property for an amount as close to full value as possible, fire insurance policies commonly include a coinsurance clause. Typically, a *coinsurance clause* provides that if the owner insures the property up to a specified percentage—usually 80 percent—of its value, she or he will recover any loss up to the face amount of the policy. If the insurance is for less than the fixed percentage, the owner is responsible for a proportionate share of the loss.

Coinsurance applies only in instances of partial loss. ● EXAMPLE #1 If the owner of property valued at $100,000 takes out a policy in the amount of $40,000 and suffers a loss of $30,000, the recovery will be $15,000. The formula for calculating the recovery amount is as follows:

$$\frac{\text{amount of insurance (\$40,000)}}{\text{coinsurance percentage (80\%)} \times \text{property value (\$100,000)}} = \frac{\text{recovery percentage}}{(50\%)}$$

recovery percentage (50%) × amount of loss ($30,000) = recovery amount ($15,000)

If the owner had taken out a policy in the amount of $80,000, then, according to the same formula, the full loss would have been recovered up to the face value of the policy. ●

Other Provisions and Clauses. Some other important provisions and clauses contained in insurance contracts are listed in Exhibit 30–2 on page 630. The courts are aware that most people do not have the special training necessary to understand the intricate terminology used in insurance policies. Thus, the words used in an insurance contract have their ordinary meanings. They are interpreted by the courts in light of the nature of the coverage involved.

When there is an ambiguity in the policy, the provision generally is interpreted against the insurance company. When the written policy has not been delivered and it is unclear whether an insurance contract actually exists, the uncertainty normally will be resolved against the insurance company. The court will presume that the policy is in effect unless the company can show otherwise. Similarly, an insurer must make certain that the insured is adequately notified of any change in coverage under an existing policy.

EXHIBIT 30-2 INSURANCE CONTRACT PROVISIONS AND CLAUSES

Incontestability clause	An incontestability clause provides that after a policy has been in force for a specified length of time—usually two or three years—the insurer cannot contest statements made in the application.
Appraisal clause	Insurance policies frequently provide that if the parties cannot agree on the amount of a loss covered under the policy or the value of the property lost, an appraisal, or estimate, by an impartial and qualified third party can be demanded.
Arbitration clause	Many insurance policies include clauses that call for arbitration of disputes that may arise between the insurer and the insured concerning the settlement of claims.
Antilapse clause	An antilapse clause provides that the policy will not automatically lapse if no payment is made on the date due. Ordinarily, under such a provision, the insured has a *grace period* of thirty or thirty-one days within which to pay an overdue premium before the policy is canceled.
Cancellation	An insurance policy can be canceled for various reasons, depending on the type of insurance. When an insurance company can cancel its insurance contract, the policy or a state statute usually requires that the insurer give advance written notice of the cancellation. An insurer cannot cancel—or refuse to renew—a policy because of the national origin or race of an applicant or because the insured has appeared as a witness in a case against the company.

Cancellation. The insured can cancel a policy at any time, and the insurer can cancel under certain circumstances. When an insurance company can cancel its insurance contract, the policy or a state statute usually requires that the insurer give advance written notice of the cancellation to the insured.

The insurer may cancel an insurance policy for various reasons, depending on the type of insurance. For example, automobile insurance can be canceled for nonpayment of premiums or suspension of the insured's driver's license. Property insurance can be canceled for nonpayment of premiums or for other reasons, including the insured's fraud or misrepresentation, conviction for a crime that increases the hazard insured against, or gross negligence that increases the hazard insured against. Life and health policies can be canceled because of false statements made by the insured in the application. An insurer cannot cancel—or refuse to renew—a policy for discriminatory reasons or other reasons that violate public policy, or because the insured has appeared as a witness in a case against the company.

State laws normally require that an insured be notified in writing of an insurance policy cancellation.[1] The same requirement applies when only part of a policy is canceled.

Basic Duties and Rights. Essentially, the parties to an insurance contract are responsible for the obligations the contract imposes. These include the basic contractual duties discussed in Chapters 7 through 13 of this text, which cover contract law.

In applying for insurance, for example, the obligation to act in good faith means that a party must reveal everything necessary for the insurer to evaluate the risk. In other words, the applicant must disclose all material facts. These include all facts that an insurer would consider in determining whether to charge a higher premium or to refuse to issue a policy altogether.

Once the insurer has accepted the risk, and on the occurrence of an event giving rise to a claim, the insurer has a duty to investigate to determine the facts. When a policy provides insurance against third party claims, the insurer is obligated to make reasonable efforts to settle such a claim. If a settlement cannot be reached, then regardless of the claim's merit, the insurer must defend any suit against the insured. Usually, a policy provides that in this situation the insured must cooperate. A policy provision may expressly require the insured to attend hearings and trials, to help in obtaining evidence and witnesses, and to assist in reaching a settlement.

The question in the following case was whether the insurer acted in bad faith in investigating and paying an insured's claim.

---

[1] At issue in one case was whether a notification of cancellation included on a diskette sent to the insured constituted "written notice" of cancellation. The court held that the computerized document, which could be printed out as "hard copy," constituted written notice. See *Clyburn v. Allstate Insurance Co.*, 826 F.Supp. 955 (D.S.C. 1993).

CASE 30.1 Columbia National Insurance Co. v. Freeman

Supreme Court
of Arkansas, 2002.
347 Ark. 423,
64 S.W.3d 720.
http://courts.state.ar.us/opinions/opinions.html[a]

FACTS Gary and Peggy Freeman owned and operated Circle F Trading Company, a western wear and general store, in Arkansas. The Freemans were insured against losses to the building and its contents, continuing business expenses, and other risks under a policy with Columbia National Insurance Company. In October 1997, a fire damaged Circle F's building and destroyed its inventory. The Freemans filed a claim with Columbia, providing an appraisal of the lost merchandise at $107,905.13 and a list of their continuing business expenses. Columbia obtained a second appraisal of $71,231.69 and attempted to find Circle F a building to serve as a temporary office. In December, Columbia paid the Freemans $77,892.28 for inventory, supplies, and lost income. No payment was made for continuing business expenses, and no office was provided. The parties agreed on an amount of $32,725 to cover the cost of the damage to the building, but Columbia offered to pay only 80 percent of this amount. Circle F never reopened. The Freemans filed a suit in an Arkansas state court against Columbia, alleging, among other things, bad faith. A jury returned a verdict for the Freemans, awarding $170,000 in compensatory damages and $200,000 in punitive damages. Columbia filed a motion for a directed verdict, which the court denied. Columbia appealed to the Arkansas Supreme Court.

---

a. In the "Search Cases by Party Name" section, enter "Freeman" in the "Party Name" box and select "Search by Date Range." For the date range, choose "From January 2002" and "To February 2002," and click on "Search." From the list of results, click on the name of the case to access the opinion. The Arkansas judiciary maintains this Web site.

ISSUE Had Columbia acted in bad faith in investigating and paying the Freemans' claim?

DECISION Yes. The Arkansas Supreme Court affirmed the lower court's judgment. The state supreme court concluded that there was substantial evidence to support the jury's verdict that Columbia's actions constituted oppressive conduct carried out with a state of mind characterized by ill will.

REASON The court stated that "[a]n insurance company commits the tort of bad faith when it affirmatively engages in dishonest, malicious, or oppressive conduct in order to avoid a just obligation to its insured. We have defined 'bad faith' as dishonest, malicious, or oppressive conduct carried out with a state of mind characterized by hatred, ill will, or a spirit of revenge. Mere negligence or bad judgment is insufficient." In this case, the court noted there was sufficient evidence "to support a finding that failure to cover appellees' ongoing business expenses, to which they were entitled, was an act of bad faith." The court also found sufficient evidence to support the jury's findings that the "appellant acted in bad faith when it failed to provide appellees with a temporary location for their business," when it agreed to pay "$32,725 for the cost of repairing the building but * * * tendered only eighty percent of the amount agreed on," and "when it requested that two appraisals be performed on appellees' inventory and chose to pay appellees based on the lower of the two appraisals."

FOR CRITICAL ANALYSIS—Social Consideration
Suppose that after an investigation, Columbia had simply refused to pay the Freemans' claim. Would the result in this case have been the same?

Defenses against Payment. In attempting to avoid payment on a policy claim, an insurance company can raise any of the defenses that would be valid in any ordinary action on a contract, as well as some defenses that do not apply in routine contract actions. If the insurance company can show that the policy was procured by fraud, misrepresentation, or violation of warranties, it may have a valid defense for not paying on a claim. Improper actions, such as those that are against public policy or that are otherwise illegal, can also give the insurance company a defense against the payment of a claim or allow it to rescind the contract.

An insurance company can be prevented from asserting some defenses that are normally available, however. For example, if a company tells an insured that information requested on a form is optional, and the insured provides it anyway, the company cannot use the information to avoid its contractual obligation under the insurance contract. Similarly, incorrect statements as to the age of the insured normally do not allow the insurer to avoid payment on the death of the insured.

In the following case, an insurance company attempted to avoid payment under a policy for life and disability insurance by claiming that the policy owner did not have an insurable interest, thus rendering the policy void from the outset.

CASE 30.2   Paul Revere Life Insurance Co. v. Fima

United States Court of Appeals,
Ninth Circuit, 1997.
105 F.3d 490.
http://www.ca9.uscourts.gov[a]

FACTS Disability insurance can replace part of the income that an individual loses after suffering a disabling accident or illness. Raoul Fima applied to Paul Revere Life Insurance Company for a disability policy. On the application, Fima stated his income as $105,000 for the previous year and $85,000 for the current year. His actual income for those years was $21,603 and $6,320, respectively. The policy included the following incontestability clause: "After your policy has been in force for two years, * * * we cannot contest the statements in the application." Three years later, when Fima filed a claim under the policy, Revere discovered

the truth regarding his income. Revere filed a suit in a federal district court against Fima, seeking to have the policy declared void *ab initio* (from the beginning) on the ground that he lacked an insurable interest. The court denied the request. Revere appealed.

ISSUE Did Fima have an insurable interest at the time he obtained the insurance policy?

DECISION Yes. The U.S. Court of Appeals for the Ninth Circuit affirmed the judgment of the lower court.

REASON The appellate court reasoned that "[e]very person has an insurable interest in his or her own life and health." Therefore, the policy was not void *ab initio*. Also, the court pointed out that "because the period for contesting the policy has passed under the incontestability clause, Revere may not now challenge the terms of the policy or the extent of Fima's insurable interest."

FOR CRITICAL ANALYSIS—Ethical Consideration
What is the underlying rationale for including incontestability clauses in insurance contracts?

---

a. This page lists decisions of the U.S. Court of Appeals for the Ninth Circuit. In the left-hand column, select "Opinions." Locate the "1997" link, and click on it. Then select "January." Scroll down the list to the *Fima* case and click on the link to access the opinion.

Wills

Private ownership of property leads logically to both the protection of that property by insurance coverage while the owner is alive and the transfer of that property on the death of the owner to those designated in the owner's will. A **will** is the final declaration of how a person desires to have his or her property disposed of after death. A will, because it is a person's "last will and testament," is referred to as a *testamentary disposition* of property. It is a formal instrument that must follow exactly the requirements of state law to be effective. The reasoning behind such a strict requirement is obvious. A will becomes effective only after death. No attempts to modify it after the death of the maker are allowed because the court cannot ask the maker to confirm the attempted modifications. (Sometimes, however, the wording of the will must be "interpreted" by the courts.)

A will can serve other purposes besides the distribution of property. It can appoint a guardian for minor children or incapacitated adults. It can also appoint a personal representative to settle the affairs of the deceased. Exhibit 30–3 presents a copy of John Lennon's will. Lennon was a member of the Beatles, the 1960s rock music group. He was murdered in December 1980.

A person who dies without having created a valid will is said to have died **intestate.** In this situation, state **intestacy laws** prescribe the distribution of the property among heirs or next of kin. If no heirs or kin can be found, title to the property will be transferred to the state.

TERMINOLOGY OF WILLS

A person who makes out a will is known as a **testator** (from the Latin *testari,* "to make a will"). The court responsible for administering any legal problems surrounding a will is called a *probate court,* as mentioned in Chapter 2. When a person dies, a personal representative administers the estate and settles finally all of the decedent's (deceased person's) affairs. An **executor** is a personal representative named in the will; an **administrator** is a personal representative appointed by the court for a decedent who dies without a will, who fails to name an executor in the will, who names an executor lacking the capacity to serve, or who writes a will that the court refuses to admit to probate.

A gift of real estate by will is generally called a **devise,** and a gift of personal property by will is called a **bequest,** or **legacy.** The recipient of a gift by will is a **devisee** or **legatee,** depending on whether the gift was a devise or a legacy.

EXHIBIT 30–3 A SAMPLE WILL

LAST WILL AND TESTAMENT
OF
JOHN WINSTON ONO LENNON

I, JOHN WINSTON ONO LENNON, a resident of the County of New York, State of New York, which I declare to be my domicile do hereby make, publish and declare this to be my Last Will and Testament, hereby revoking all other Wills, Codicils and Testamentary dispositions by me at any time heretofore made.

FIRST: The expenses of my funeral and the administration of my estate, and all inheritance, estate or successions taxes, including interest and penalties, payable by reason of my death shall be paid out of and charged generally against the principal of my residuary estate without apportionment or proration. My Executor shall not seek contribution or reimbursement for any such payments.

SECOND: Should my wife survive me, I give, devise and bequeath to her absolutely, an amount equal to that portion of my residuary estate, the numerator and denominator of which shall be determined as follows:

1. The numerator shall be an amount equal to one-half (½) of my adjusted gross estate less the value of all other property included in my gross estate for Federal Estate Tax purposes and which pass or shall have passed to my wife either under any other provision of this Will or in any manner outside of this Will in such manner as to qualify for and be allowed as a marital deduction. The words "pass," "have passed," "marital deduction" and "adjusted gross estate" shall have the same meaning as said words have under those provisions of the United States Internal Revenue Code applicable to my estate.

2. The denominator shall be an amount representing the value of my residuary estate.

THIRD: I give, devise and bequeath all the rest, residue and remainder of my estate, wheresoever situate, to the Trustees under a Trust Agreement dated November 12, 1979, which I signed with my wife YOKO ONO, and ELI GARBER as Trustees, to be added to the trust property and held and distributed in accordance with the terms of that agreement and any amendments made pursuant to its terms before my death.

FOURTH: In the event that my wife and I die under such circumstances that there is not sufficient evidence to determine which of us has predeceased the other, I hereby declare it to be my will that it shall be deemed that I shall have predeceased her and that this, my Will, and any and all of its provisions shall be construed based upon that assumption.

FIFTH: I hereby nominate, constitute and appoint my beloved wife, YOKO ONO, to act as the Executor of this my Last Will and Testament. In the event that my beloved wife YOKO ONO shall predecease me or chooses not to act for any reason, I nominate and appoint ELI GARBER, DAVID WARMFLASH and CHARLES PETTIT, in the order named, to act in her place and stead.

SIXTH: I nominate, constitute and appoint my wife YOKO ONO, as the Guardian of the person and property of any children of the marriage who may survive me. In the event that she predeceases me, or for any reason she chooses not to act in that capacity, I nominate, constitute and appoint SAM GREEN to act in her place and stead.

SEVENTH: No person named herein to serve in any fiduciary capacity shall be required to file or post any bond for the faithful performance of his or her duties, in that capacity in this or in any other jurisdiction, any law to the contrary notwithstanding.

EIGHTH: If any legatee or beneficiary under this will or the trust agreement between myself as Grantor and YOKO ONO LENNON and ELI GARBER as Trustees, dated November 12, 1979 shall interpose objections to the probate of this Will, or institute or prosecute or be in any way interested or instrumental in the institution or prosecution of any action or proceeding for the purpose of setting aside or invalidating this Will, then and in each such case, I direct that such legatee or beneficiary shall receive nothing whatsoever under this Will or the aforementioned Trust.

IN WITNESS WHEREOF, I have subscribed and sealed and do publish and declare these presents as and for my Last Will and Testament, this 12th day of November, 1979.

/s/

John Winston Ono Lennon

THE FOREGOING INSTRUMENT consisting of four (4) typewritten pages, including this page, was on the 12th day of November, 1979, signed, sealed, published and declared by JOHN WINSTON ONO LENNON, the Testator therein named as and for his Last Will and Testament, in the presence of us, who at his request, and in his presence, and in the presence of each other, have hereunto set our names as witnesses.

[The names of the three witnesses are illegible.]

TYPES OF GIFTS

Gifts by will can be specific, general, or residuary. A *specific* devise or bequest (legacy) describes particular property (such as "Eastwood Estate" or "my gold pocket watch") that can be distinguished from all the rest of the testator's property. A *general* devise or bequest (legacy) uses less restrictive terminology. For example, "I devise all my lands" is a general devise. A general bequest often specifies a sum of money instead of a particular item of property, such as a watch or an automobile. For example, "I give to my nephew, Carleton, $30,000" is a general bequest.

If the assets of an estate are insufficient to pay in full all general bequests provided for in the will, an *abatement,* by which the legatees receive reduced benefits, takes place. If a legatee dies prior to the death of the testator or before the legacy is payable, a *lapsed legacy* results. At common law, the legacy failed. Today, the legacy may not lapse if the legatee is in a certain blood relationship to the testator (such as a child, grandchild, brother, or sister) and has left a child or other surviving descendant.

Sometimes, a will provides that the *residuum*—any assets remaining after the estate's debts have been paid and specific gifts have been made—is to be distributed through a *residuary clause.* A residuary clause is used when the exact amount to be distributed cannot be determined until all of the other gifts and payouts have been made. A residuary clause can pose problems, however, when the will does not specifically name the beneficiaries to receive the residuum. In such a situation, if the court cannot determine the testator's intent, the residuum passes according to state laws of intestacy.

PROBATE PROCEDURES

Laws governing wills come into play when a will is probated. To *probate* a will means to establish its validity and to carry the administration of the estate through a court process. Probate laws vary from state to state. In 1969, however, the American Bar Association and the National Conference of Commissioners on Uniform State Laws approved the Uniform Probate Code (UPC). The UPC codifies general principles and procedures for the resolution of conflicts in settling estates and relaxes some of the requirements for a valid will contained in earlier state laws. Nearly all of the states have adopted some part of the UPC. Because succession and inheritance laws vary widely among states, one should always check the particular laws of the state involved.[2] Typically, probate procedures vary, depending on the size of the decedent's estate.

Informal Probate. For smaller estates, most state statutes provide for the distribution of assets without formal probate proceedings. Faster and less expensive methods are then used. For example, property can be transferred by affidavit (a written statement taken before a person who has authority to affirm it), and problems or questions can be handled during an administrative hearing. In addition, some state statutes provide that title to cars, savings and checking accounts, and certain other property can be passed merely by filling out forms.

A majority of states also provide for *family settlement agreements,* which are private agreements among the beneficiaries. Once a will is admitted to probate, the family members can agree to settle among themselves the distribution of the decedent's assets. Although a family settlement agreement speeds the settlement process, a court order is still needed to protect the estate from future creditors and to clear title to the assets involved. The use of these and other types of summary procedures in estate administration can save time and dollars.

Formal Probate. For larger estates, formal probate proceedings normally are undertaken, and the probate court supervises every aspect of the settlement of the decedent's estate. Additionally, in some situations—such as when a guardian for minor children or for an incompetent person must be appointed, and a trust has been created to protect the minor or the incompetent person—more formal probate procedures cannot be avoided. Formal probate proceedings may take several months to complete, and as a result, a sizable portion of the decedent's assets (up to perhaps 10 percent or more) may go toward payment of court costs and fees charged by attorneys and personal representatives.

Property Transfers outside the Probate Process. In the ordinary situation, a person can employ various will substitutes to avoid the cost of probate—for example, *inter vivos* trusts (discussed later in this chapter), life insurance policies or Individual Retirement Accounts (IRAs) with named beneficiaries, or joint-tenancy arrangements. Not all methods are suitable for every estate, but there are alternatives to complete probate administration.

REQUIREMENTS FOR A VALID WILL

A will must comply with statutory formalities designed to ensure that the testator understood his or her actions at the time the will was made. These formalities are intended to help prevent fraud. Unless they are followed, the will is declared void, and the decedent's property is distributed according to the laws of intestacy of that state. The requirements are not uniform among the jurisdictions. Most states, however, uphold certain basic requirements for executing a will. We now look at these requirements.

---

[2] For example, California law differs substantially from the UPC.

Testamentary Capacity and Intent. For a will to be valid, the testator must have testamentary capacity—that is, the testator must be of legal age and sound mind *at the time the will is made*. The legal age for executing a will varies, but in most states and under the UPC, the minimum age is eighteen years [UPC 2–501]. Thus, the will of a twenty-one-year-old decedent written when the person was sixteen is invalid if, under state law, the legal age for executing a will is eighteen.

The concept of "being of sound mind" refers to the testator's ability to formulate and to comprehend a personal plan for the disposition of property. Generally, a testator must (1) intend the document to be his or her last will and testament, (2) comprehend the kind and character of the property being distributed, and (3) comprehend and remember the "natural objects of his or her bounty" (usually, family members and persons for whom the testator has affection).

A valid will is one that represents the maker's intention to transfer and distribute her or his property. When it can be shown that the decedent's plan of distribution was the result of fraud or of undue influence, the will is declared invalid. Undue influence may be inferred by the court if the testator ignored blood relatives and named as beneficiary a nonrelative who was in constant close contact with the testator and in a position to influence the making of the will. For example, if a nurse or friend caring for the testator at the time of death was named as beneficiary to the exclusion of all family members, the validity of the will might well be challenged on the basis of undue influence.

In the following case, the issue before the court was whether the testator intended his estate to be distributed to his relatives and friends in sixteen equal shares or in fourteen equal shares. The court looked first at the words used by the testator in his will to determine his intent.

CASE 30.3 Estate of Klauzer

Supreme Court of South Dakota, 2000.
604 N.W.2d 474.
http://www.sdbar.org/opinions/default.htm[a]

FACTS John Klauzer executed a will in 1990 and passed away in 1996. His estate was valued at $1.4 million. The will appointed his brother Frank as personal representative of the estate. The will disposed of the majority of his estate in a residuary clause:

> I hereby give, devise and bequeath unto my brother, Thomas Klauzer, my sister, Agnes Blake, my sister, Anna Malenovsky Baker, my brother, Raymond Klauzer, my niece, Jenny Culver, my niece, Judy Klauzer, my niece, Bernice Cunningham, my nephew, Wade Klauzer, my nephew, Jim Klauzer, my niece, Debra Klauzer, friends, Douglas Olson and Fern Olson, and my friends, William Hollister and Shirley Hollister, my brother, Frank Klauzer, and my sister-in-law, Patricia Klauzer, all of my property of every kind and character and wheresoever situated, in equal shares, share and share alike. That should any of the individuals above named predecease me, then their share of my estate shall go to their [descendants] surviving.

Klauzer's nephew Wade asked a South Dakota state court to supervise the administration of the estate. The court ordered in part that, under the residuary clause, the estate should be dis-

tributed in sixteen equal shares. Frank objected and appealed to the South Dakota Supreme Court. Frank argued that the twelve Klauzer relatives named in the clause should take one share each while friends, Doug and Fern Olson and William and Shirley Hollister, should receive one share per couple, resulting in a division of the estate into fourteen equal shares.

ISSUE Should the property be divided into sixteen equal shares or fourteen equal shares?

DECISION Sixteen equal shares. The South Dakota Supreme Court affirmed the decision of the lower court. The language of the will evidenced the testator's intent that his property be distributed in sixteen equal shares.

REASON The court pointed out that "[a]ll the words and provisions appearing in a will must be given effect as far as possible, and none should be cast aside as meaningless." In the will in this case, the court reasoned, "First, John refers to his friends as individuals. Second, he requests that they receive his property 'in equal shares, share and share alike.' Third, he states that if one individual predeceases him, his or her share 'shall go to their [descendants] surviving.' * * * We determine that the testator's intent is clearly expressed within the four corners of the document. We are bound by the unambiguous language of the will."

FOR CRITICAL ANALYSIS—Social Consideration
What if the court had found that the terms of the will were ambiguous? How would the estate have been distributed in that situation?

---

a. This Web site is maintained by the State Bar of South Dakota. In the left column, click on "SD Index." On the page that opens, in the left column, click on "2000 Opinions." On that page, scroll down under the "January 2000" section to the case name and click on it to access the opinion.

Writing Requirements. Generally, a will must be in writing. The writing itself can be informal as long as it substantially complies with the statutory requirements. In some states, a will can be handwritten in crayon or ink. It can be written on a sheet or scrap of paper, on a paper bag, or on a piece of cloth. A will that is completely in the handwriting of the testator is called a **holographic will** (sometimes referred to as an *olographic will*). In some—but not all—states, a holographic will does not have to be witnessed.

In certain cases, oral wills are found valid. A **nuncupative will** is an oral will made before witnesses. Nuncupative wills are not permitted in most states. Where authorized by statute, such wills are generally valid only if made during the last illness of the testator and are therefore sometimes referred to as *deathbed wills*. Normally, only personal property can be transferred by a nuncupative will. Statutes frequently permit soldiers and sailors to make nuncupative wills when on active duty.

Signature Requirements. It is a fundamental requirement that the testator's signature appear, generally at the end of the will. Each jurisdiction dictates by statute and court decision what constitutes a signature. Initials, an X or other mark, and words such as "Mom" have all been upheld as valid when it was shown that the testators *intended* them to be signatures.

Witness Requirements. Unless a will is a holographic will, it must be attested (sworn to) by two, and sometimes three, witnesses. The number of witnesses, their qualifications, and the manner in which the witnessing must be done are generally set out in a statute. A witness can be required to be disinterested—that is, not a beneficiary under the will. The UPC, however, provides that a will is valid even if it is attested by an interested witness [UPC 2–505]. There are no age requirements for witnesses, but they must be mentally competent.

The purpose of witnesses is to verify that the testator actually executed (signed) the will and had the requisite intent and capacity at the time. A witness does not have to read the contents of the will. Usually, the testator and all witnesses must sign in the sight or the presence of one another, but the UPC deems it sufficient if the testator acknowledges her or his signature to the witnesses [UPC 2–502]. The UPC does not require all parties to sign in the presence of one another.

Publication Requirements. A will is *published* by an oral declaration by the maker to the witnesses that the document they are about to sign is his or her "last will and testament." Publication is becoming an unnecessary formality in most states, and it is not required under the UPC.

REVOCATION OF WILLS

An executed will is revocable by the maker at any time during the maker's lifetime. The maker may revoke a will by a physical act, such as tearing up the will, or by a subsequent writing. Wills can also be revoked by operation of law. Revocation can be partial or complete, and it must follow certain strict formalities.

Revocation by a Physical Act of the Maker. A testator may revoke a will by intentionally burning, tearing, canceling, obliterating, or otherwise destroying it, or by having someone else do so in the presence of the maker and at the maker's direction.[3] In some states, partial revocation by physical act of the maker is recognized. Thus, those portions of a will lined out or torn away are dropped, and the remaining parts of the will are valid. In no circumstances, however, can a provision be crossed out and an additional or substitute provision written in. Such altered portions require reexecution (re-signing) and reattestation (rewitnessing).

To revoke a will by physical act, it is necessary to follow the mandates of a state statute exactly. When a state statute prescribes the specific methods for revoking a will by physical act, those are the only methods that will revoke the will.

Revocation by a Subsequent Writing. A will may also be wholly or partially revoked by a **codicil**, a written instrument separate from the will that amends or revokes provisions in the will. A codicil eliminates the necessity of redrafting an entire will merely to add to it or amend it. A codicil can also be used to revoke an entire will. The codicil must be executed with the same formalities required for a will, and it must refer expressly to the will. In effect, it updates a will because the will is "incorporated by reference" into the codicil.

A new will (second will) can be executed that may or may not revoke the first or a prior will, depending on the language used. To revoke a prior will, the second will must use language specifically revoking other wills, such as, "This will hereby revokes all prior wills." If the second will is otherwise valid and properly executed, it will revoke all prior wills. If the express *declaration of revocation* is missing, then both wills are read together. If any of the dispositions made in the second will are inconsistent with the prior will, the second will controls.

---

[3] The destruction cannot be inadvertent. The maker's intent to revoke must be shown. Consequently, when a will has been burned or torn accidentally, it is normally recommended that the maker have a new document created so that it will not falsely appear that the maker intended to revoke the will.

Revocation by Operation of Law. Revocation by *operation of law* occurs when marriage, divorce or annulment, or the birth of a child takes place after a will has been executed. In most states, when a testator marries after executing a will that does not include the new spouse, on the testator's death the spouse can still receive the amount he or she would have taken had the testator died intestate (how an intestate's property is distributed under state laws will be discussed shortly). In effect, the will is revoked to the point of providing the spouse with an intestate share. The rest of the estate is passed under the will [UPC 2–301, 2–508]. If, however, the new spouse is otherwise provided for in the will (or by transfer of property outside the will), the new spouse will not be given an intestate amount.

At common law and under the UPC, divorce does not necessarily revoke the entire will. A divorce or an annulment occurring after a will has been executed will revoke those dispositions of property made under the will to the former spouse [UPC 2–508].

If a child is born after a will has been executed and if it appears that the deceased parent would have made a provision for the child, the child is entitled to receive whatever portion of the estate she or he is allowed under state laws providing for the distribution of an intestate's property. Most state laws allow a child to receive some portion of a parent's estate if no provision is made in the parent's will, unless it appears from the terms of the will that the testator intended to disinherit the child. Under the UPC, the rule is the same.

INTESTACY LAWS

As mentioned, state intestacy laws determine how property will be distributed when a person dies intestate (without a valid will). These statutes are more formally known as *statutes of descent and distribution.* Intestacy laws attempt to carry out the likely intent and wishes of the decedent. These laws assume that deceased persons would have intended that their natural heirs (spouses, children, grandchildren, or other family members) inherit their property. Therefore, intestacy statutes set out rules and priorities under which these heirs inherit the property. If no heirs exist, the state will assume ownership of the property. The rules of descent vary widely from state to state.

Surviving Spouse and Children. Usually, state statutes provide that first the debts of the decedent must be satisfied out of the estate; then the remaining assets pass to the surviving spouse and to the children. A surviving spouse usually receives only a share of the estate—one-half if there is also a surviving child and one-third if there are two or more

children. Only if no children or grandchildren survive the decedent will a surviving spouse succeed to the entire estate.

● **EXAMPLE #2** Assume that Allen dies intestate and is survived by his wife, Della, and his children, Duane and Tara. Allen's property passes according to intestacy laws. After Allen's outstanding debts are paid, Della will receive the homestead (either in fee simple or as a life estate) and ordinarily a one-third interest in all other property. The remaining real and personal property will pass to Duane and Tara in equal portions.● Under most state intestacy laws and under the UPC, in-laws do not share in an estate. If a child dies before his or her parents, the child's spouse will not receive an inheritance on the parents' death. For example, if Duane died before his father (Allen), Duane's spouse would not inherit Duane's share of Allen's estate.

When there is no surviving spouse or child, the order of inheritance is grandchildren, then brothers and sisters, and, in some states, parents of the decedent. These relatives are usually called *lineal descendants.* If there are no lineal descendants, then *collateral heirs*—nieces, nephews, aunts, and uncles of the decedent—make up the next group to share. If there are no survivors in any of these groups, most statutes provide for the property to be distributed among the next of kin of the collateral heirs.

Stepchildren, Adopted Children, and Illegitimate Children. Under intestacy laws, stepchildren are not considered kin. Legally adopted children, however, are recognized as lawful heirs of their adoptive parents. Statutes vary from state to state in regard to the inheritance rights of illegitimate children. Generally, an illegitimate child is treated as the child of the mother and can inherit from her and her relatives. The child is usually not regarded as the legal child of the father with the right of inheritance unless paternity is established through some legal proceeding prior to the father's death.

Distribution to Grandchildren. When an intestate is survived by descendants of deceased children, a question arises as to what share these descendants (that is, grandchildren of the intestate) will receive. One method of dividing an intestate's estate is *per stirpes.* Under this method, within a class or group of distributees (for example, grandchildren), the children of any one descendant take the share that their deceased parent *would have been* entitled to inherit.

● **EXAMPLE #3** Assume that Michael, a widower, has two children, Scott and Jonathan. Scott has two children (Becky and Holly), and Jonathan has one child (Paul). Scott and Jonathan die before their father, and then Michael dies. If Michael's estate is distributed *per stirpes,* Becky and Holly

EXHIBIT 30-4 *PER STIRPES* DISTRIBUTION

Under this method of distribution, an heir takes the share that his or her deceased parent would have been entitled to inherit, had the parent lived. This may mean that a class of distributees—the grandchildren in this example—will not inherit in equal portions. Note that Becky and Holly receive only one-fourth of Michael's estate while Paul inherits one-half.

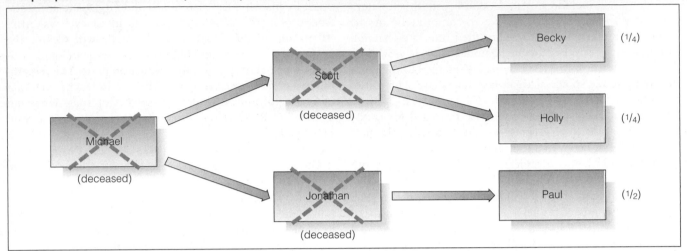

will each receive one-fourth of the estate (dividing Scott's one-half share). Paul will receive one-half of the estate (taking Jonathan's one-half share). Exhibit 30–4 illustrates the *per stirpes* method of distribution.●

An estate may also be distributed on a *per capita* basis, which means that each person in a class or group takes an equal share of the estate. If Michael's estate is distributed *per capita*, Becky, Holly, and Paul will each receive a one-third share. Exhibit 30–5 illustrates the *per capita* method of distribution.

Trusts

A **trust** is any arrangement through which property is transferred from one person to a trustee to be administered for the transferor's or another party's benefit. It can also be

EXHIBIT 30-5 *PER CAPITA* DISTRIBUTION

Under this method of distribution, all heirs in a certain class—in this case, the grandchildren—inherit equally. Note that Becky and Holly in this situation each inherit one-third, as does Paul.

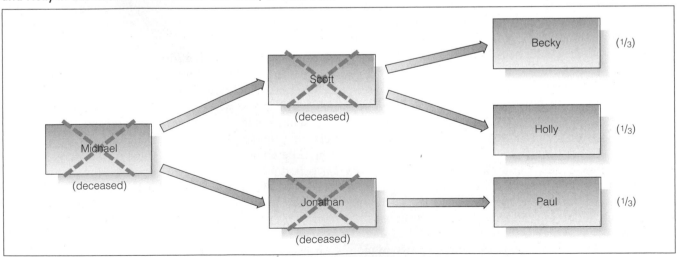

defined as a right of property, real or personal, held by one party for the benefit of another. A trust can be created for any purpose that is not illegal or against public policy. Its essential elements are as follows:

① A designated beneficiary.

② A designated trustee.

③ A fund sufficiently identified to enable title to pass to the trustee.

④ Actual delivery by the settlor or grantor (the person creating the trust) to the trustee with the intention of passing title.

● **EXAMPLE #4** If James conveys his farm to the First Bank of Minnesota to be held for the benefit of his daughters, he has created a trust. James is the settlor, the First Bank of Minnesota is the trustee, and James's daughters are the beneficiaries. This arrangement is illustrated in Exhibit 30–6.● Numerous types of trusts can be established. In this section, we look at some of the major types of trusts and their characteristics.

EXPRESS TRUSTS

An *express trust* is one created or declared in explicit terms, usually in writing. Express trusts fall into two categories: *inter vivos* (living) trusts and testamentary trusts (trusts provided for in a last will and testament).

An *inter vivos* **trust** is a trust executed by a grantor during her or his lifetime. The grantor (settlor) executes a *trust deed*, and legal title to the trust property passes to the named trustee. The trustee has a duty to administer the property as directed by the grantor for the benefit and in the interest of the beneficiaries. The trustee must preserve the trust property, make it productive, and, if required by the terms of the trust agreement, pay income to the beneficiaries, all in accordance with the terms of the trust. Once the *inter vivos* trust is created, the grantor has, in effect, given over the property for the benefit of the beneficiaries. Often, setting up this type of trust offers tax-related benefits.

A **testamentary trust** is a trust created by a will to come into existence on the settlor's death. Although a testamentary trust has a trustee who maintains legal title to the trust property, the trustee's actions are subject to judicial approval. This trustee can be named in the will or be appointed by the court. Thus, a testamentary trust does not fail because a trustee has not been named in the will. The legal responsibilities of the trustee are the same as in an *inter vivos* trust. If the will setting up a testamentary trust is invalid, the trust will also be invalid. The property that was supposed to be in the trust will then pass according to intestacy laws, not according to the terms of the trust.

IMPLIED TRUSTS

Sometimes, a trust will be imposed (implied) by law, even in the absence of an express trust. Implied trusts include resulting trusts and constructive trusts.

A **resulting trust** arises from the conduct of the parties. Here, the trust results, or is created, when circumstances raise an inference that the party holding legal title to the property does so for the benefit of another. ● **EXAMPLE #5** Suppose that Garrison wants to put one acre of land she owns on the market for sale. Because she is going out of the

---

EXHIBIT 30–6 **TRUST ARRANGEMENT**

In a trust, there is a separation of interests in the trust property. The trustee takes *legal* title, which is the complete ownership and possession but which does not include the right to receive any benefits from the property. The beneficiary takes *equitable* title, which is the right to receive benefits from the property.

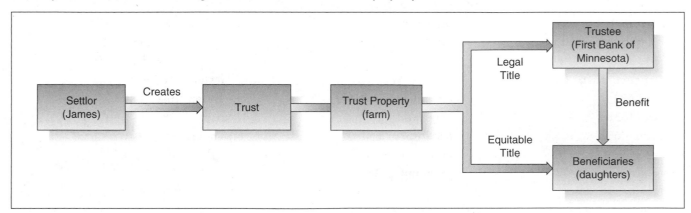

country for two years and would not be able to deed the property to a buyer during that period, Garrison conveys the property to her good friend Oswald. Oswald will attempt to sell the property while Garrison is gone. Because the intent of the transaction in which Garrison conveyed the property to Oswald is neither a sale nor a gift, the property will be held in trust (a resulting trust) by Oswald for the benefit of Garrison. Therefore, on Garrison's return, Oswald will be required either to deed back the property to Garrison or, if the property has been sold, to turn over the proceeds (held in trust) to her. Here, the trust arises (*results*) from the *apparent intention* of the parties. ●

A **constructive trust** is an equitable trust imposed in the interests of fairness and justice. If someone wrongfully holds legal title to property—for example, if the property was obtained through fraud or in breach of a legal duty—a court may require that owner to hold the property in trust for the person or persons who rightfully should own the property. ● **EXAMPLE #6** Suppose that Kraft is a partner in a partnership that purchases and develops real estate. Kraft learns in a partners' meeting that the partnership is considering the purchase of a vacant lot that will soon come on the market. Kraft secretly purchases the property in his own name, thus violating his fiduciary duty of loyalty to the partnership. If the partnership discovers what Kraft has done and brings a legal action against him, a court may impose a constructive trust, thus requiring Kraft to hold the property in trust for the partnership. ●

SPECIAL TYPES OF TRUSTS

Certain trusts are created for special purposes. Three of these trusts that warrant discussion are charitable, spendthrift, and Totten trusts. A **charitable trust** is designed for the benefit of a segment of the public or of the public in general. Usually, to be deemed a charitable trust, a trust must be created for charitable, educational, religious, or scientific purposes.

A **spendthrift trust** is created to provide for the maintenance of a beneficiary by preventing his or her improvidence with the bestowed funds. Essentially, the beneficiary is permitted to draw only a certain portion of the total amount to which he or she is entitled at any one time. The majority of states allow spendthrift trust provisions that prohibit creditors from attaching such trusts.

A **Totten trust**[4] is created when one person deposits funds in her or his own name as a trustee for another. This trust is tentative in that it is revocable at will until the depositor dies or completes the gift in her or his lifetime by some unequivocal act or declaration (for example, delivery of the funds to the intended beneficiary). If the depositor should die before the beneficiary dies and if the depositor has not revoked the trust expressly or impliedly, the beneficiary obtains property rights to the balance on hand.

---

[4] This type of trust derives its unusual name from *In re Totten*, 179 N.Y. 112, 71 N.E. 748 (1904).

Terms and Concepts

administrator 632	insurance 625	resulting trust 639
bequest 632	*inter vivos* trust 639	risk 626
binder 629	intestacy laws 632	risk management 626
charitable trust 640	intestate 632	spendthrift trust 640
codicil 636	legacy 632	testamentary trust 639
constructive trust 640	legatee 632	testator 632
devise 632	nuncupative will 636	Totten trust 640
devisee 632	*per capita* 638	trust 638
executor 632	*per stirpes* 637	underwriter 626
holographic will 636	policy 626	will 632
insurable interest 627	premium 626	

Chapter Summary	Insurance, Wills, and Trusts

INSURANCE	
Classifications (See pages 626–627.)	See Exhibit 30–1.
Terminology (See pages 626–627.)	1. *Policy*—The insurance contract. 2. *Premium*—The consideration paid to the insurer for a policy. 3. *Underwriter*—The insurance company. 4. *Parties*—Include the insurer (the insurance company), the insured (the person covered by insurance), an agent (a representative of the insurance company) or a broker (ordinarily an independent contractor), and a beneficiary (a person to receive proceeds under the policy).
Insurable Interest (See page 627.)	An insurable interest exists whenever an individual or entity benefits from the preservation of the health or life of the insured or the property to be insured. For life insurance, an insurable interest must exist at the time the policy is issued. For property insurance, an insurable interest must exist at the time of the loss.
The Insurance Contract (See pages 629–632.)	1. *Laws governing*—The general principles of contract law are applied; the insurance industry is also heavily regulated by the states. 2. *Application*—An insurance applicant is bound by any false statements that appear in the application (subject to certain exceptions), which is part of the insurance contract. Misstatements or misrepresentations may be grounds for voiding the policy. 3. *Effective date*—Coverage on an insurance policy can begin when the *binder* (a written memorandum indicating that a formal policy is pending and stating its essential terms) is written; when the policy is issued; at the time of contract formation; or, depending on the terms of the contract, when certain conditions are met. 4. *Provisions and clauses*—See Exhibit 30–2. Words will be given their ordinary meanings, and any ambiguity in the policy will be interpreted against the insurance company. When the written policy has not been delivered and it is unclear whether an insurance contract actually exists, the uncertainty will be determined against the insurance company. The court will presume that the policy is in effect unless the company can show otherwise. 5. *Defenses against payment to the insured*—Defenses include misrepresentation, fraud, or violation of warranties by the applicant.
WILLS	
Terminology (See page 632.)	1. *Intestate*—One who dies without a valid will. 2. *Testator*—A person who makes out a will. 3. *Personal representative*—A person appointed in a will or by a court to settle the affairs of a decedent. A personal representative named in the will is an *executor;* a personal representative appointed by the court for an intestate decedent is an *administrator.* 4. *Devise*—A gift of real estate by will; may be general or specific. The recipient of a devise is a devisee. 5. *Bequest, or legacy*—A gift of personal property by will; may be general or specific. The recipient of a bequest (legacy) is a *legatee.*

(Continued)

Chapter Summary	**Insurance, Wills, and Trusts—Continued**
Probate Procedures (See page 634.)	To probate a will means to establish its validity and to carry the administration of the estate through a court process. Probate laws vary from state to state. Probate procedures may be informal or formal, depending on the size of the estate and other factors, such as whether a guardian for minor children must be appointed.
Requirements for a Valid Will (See pages 634–636.)	1. The testator must have testamentary capacity (be of legal age and sound mind at the time the will is made). 2. A will must be in writing (except for nuncupative wills). A holographic will is completely in the handwriting of the testator. 3. A will must be signed by the testator; what constitutes a signature varies from jurisdiction to jurisdiction. 4. A nonholographic will (an attested will) must be witnessed in the manner prescribed by state statute. 5. A will may have to be *published*—that is, the testator may be required to announce to witnesses that this is his or her "last will and testament"; not required under the UPC.

Revocation of Wills
(See pages 636–637.)
	1. *By physical act of the maker*—Tearing up, canceling, obliterating, or deliberately destroying part or all of a will.
	2. *By subsequent writing*—
	  a. Codicil—A formal, separate document to amend or revoke an existing will.
	  b. Second will or new will—A new, properly executed will expressly revoking the existing will.
	3. *By operation of law*—
	  a. Marriage—Generally revokes part of a will written before the marriage.
	  b. Divorce or annulment—Revokes dispositions of property made under a will to a former spouse.
	  c. Subsequently born child—It is *implied* that the child is entitled to receive the portion of the estate granted under intestacy distribution laws.

Intestacy Laws (See pages 637–638.)	1. Intestacy laws vary widely from state to state. Usually, the law provides that the surviving spouse and children inherit the property of the decedent (after the decedent's debts are paid). The spouse usually will inherit the entire estate if there are no children, one-half of the estate if there is one child, and one-third of the estate if there are two or more children. 2. If there is no surviving spouse or child, then, in order, lineal descendants (grandchildren, brothers and sisters, and—in some states—parents of the decedent) inherit. If there are no lineal descendants, then collateral heirs (nieces, nephews, aunts, and uncles of the decedent) inherit.
	TRUSTS
Definition (See pages 638–639.)	A trust is any arrangement through which property is transferred from one person to a trustee to be administered for another party's benefit. The essential elements of a trust are (1) a designated beneficiary, (2) a designated trustee, (3) a fund sufficiently identified to enable title to pass to the trustee, and (4) actual delivery to the trustee with the intention of passing title.

Chapter Summary	Insurance, Wills, and Trusts—Continued
Express Trusts (See page 639.)	Express trusts are created by expressed terms, usually in writing, and fall into two categories: 1. *Inter vivos trust*—A trust executed by a grantor during his or her lifetime. 2. *Testamentary trust*—A trust created by will and coming into existence on the death of the grantor.
Implied Trusts (See pages 639–640.)	Implied trusts, which are imposed by law in the interests of fairness and justice, include the following: 1. *Resulting trust*—Arises from the conduct of the parties when an *apparent intention* to create a trust is present. 2. *Constructive trust*—Arises by operation of law whenever a transaction takes place in which the person who takes title to property is in equity not entitled to enjoy the beneficial interest therein.
Special Types of Trusts (See page 640.)	1. *Charitable trust*—A trust designed for the benefit of a public group or the public in general. 2. *Spendthrift trust*—A trust created to provide for the maintenance of a beneficiary by allowing only a certain portion of the total amount to be received by the beneficiary at any one time. 3. *Totten trust*—A trust created when one person deposits funds in his or her own name as a trustee for another.

For Review

① What is an insurable interest? When must an insurable interest exist—at the time the insurance policy is obtained, at the time the loss occurs, or both?

② Is an insurance broker the agent of the insurance applicant or the agent of the insurer?

③ What are the basic requirements for executing a will? How may a will be revoked?

④ What is the difference between a *per stirpes* and a *per capita* distribution of an estate to the grandchildren of the deceased?

⑤ What are the four essential elements of a trust? What is the difference between an express trust and an implied trust?

Questions and Case Problems

30–1. Timing of Insurance Coverage. On October 10, Joleen Vora applied for a $50,000 life insurance policy with Magnum Life Insurance Co.; she named her husband, Jay, as the beneficiary. Joleen paid the insurance company the first year's policy premium on making the application. Two days later, before she had a chance to take the physical examination required by the insurance company and before the policy was issued, Joleen was killed in an automobile accident. Jay submitted a claim to the insurance company for the $50,000. Can Jay collect? Explain.

30–2. Validity of Wills. Merlin Winters had three sons. Merlin and his youngest son, Abraham, had a falling out in 1998 and never spoke to each other again. Merlin made a formal will in 2000, leaving all his property to the two older sons and deliberately excluding Abraham. Merlin's health began to deteriorate, and by 2001 he was under the full-time care of a nurse, Julia. In 2002, he made a new will expressly revoking the 2000 will and leaving all his property to Julia. On Merlin's death, the two older sons contested the 2002 will, claiming that Julia had exercised undue influence over their father.

Abraham claimed that both wills were invalid. He contended that the first one had been revoked by the second will and that the second will was invalid on the ground of undue influence. Is Abraham's contention correct? Explain.

30–3. Wills. Gary Mendel drew up a will in which he left his favorite car, a 1966 red Ferrari, to his daughter, Roberta. A year prior to his death, Mendel sold the 1966 Ferrari and purchased a 1969 Ferrari. Discuss whether Roberta will inherit the 1969 Ferrari under the terms of her father's will.

30–4. Estate Distribution. Benjamin is a widower who has two married children, Edward and Patricia. Patricia has two children, Perry and Paul. Edward has no children. Benjamin dies, and his typewritten will leaves all his property equally to his children, Edward and Patricia, and provides that should a child predecease him, the grandchildren are to take *per stirpes*. The will was witnessed by Patricia and by Benjamin's lawyer and was signed by Benjamin in their presence. Patricia has predeceased Benjamin. Edward claims the will is invalid.

  (a) Discuss whether the will is valid.

  (b) Discuss the distribution of Benjamin's estate if the will is invalid.

  (c) Discuss the distribution of Benjamin's estate if the will is valid.

30–5. Interpretation of an Insurance Contract's Terms. RLI Insurance Co. issued an insurance policy to Richard Brown to cover his aircraft. One provision of the policy excluded coverage for a "resident spouse." A different provision included coverage for "any passenger." Richard was piloting the aircraft with his wife, Janet, as a passenger when the aircraft crashed. Richard was killed, and Janet was injured. At the time, Janet and Richard had been living together. Janet filed a suit in a federal district court to collect under the policy for her injuries. RLI claimed that the policy clearly excluded Janet. Janet argued that the policy was ambiguous. What will the court decide? Why? [*RLI Insurance Co. v. Drollinger,* 97 F.3d 230 (8th Cir. 1996)]

30–6. Revocation. William Laneer urged his son, also William, to join the family business. The son, who was made partner, became suspicious about the way the business's finances were being handled. He filed a suit against the business and reported it to the Internal Revenue Service. The elder Laneer then executed a will that disinherited his son, giving him one dollar and leaving the balance of the estate equally to his four daughters, including Bellinda Barrera. Until his death more than twenty years later, Laneer harbored ill feelings toward his son. After Laneer's death, his original copy of the will could not be found. A photocopy was found in his safe-deposit box, however, and his lawyer's original copy was entered for probate in an Arkansas state court. Barrera, who wanted her brother William to share an equal portion of the inheritance, filed a petition to contest the will. Barrera claimed, among other things, that Laneer had revoked the will, and that was why his original copy of the will could not be found. Was the will revoked? If so, to whom would the estate be distributed? [*Barrera v. Vanpelt,* 332 Ark. 482, 965 S.W.2d 780 (1998)]

30–7. Insurer's Defenses. The City of Worcester, Massachusetts, adopted an ordinance in 1990 that required rooming houses to be equipped with automatic sprinkler systems no later than September 25, 1995. In Worcester, James and Mark Duffy owned a forty-eight–room lodging house with two retail stores on the first floor. In 1994, the Duffys applied with General Star Indemnity Co. for an insurance policy to cover the premises. The application indicated that the premises had a sprinkler system. General issued a policy that required, among other safety features, a sprinkler system. Within a month, the premises were inspected on behalf of General. On the inspection form forwarded to the insurer, in the list of safety systems, next to the word *sprinkler* the inspector had inserted only a hyphen. In July 1995, when the premises sustained over $100,000 in fire damage, General learned that there was no sprinkler system. The insurer filed a suit in a federal district court against the Duffys to rescind the policy, alleging misrepresentation in their insurance application about the presence of sprinklers. How should the court rule, and why? [*General Star Indemnity Co. v. Duffy,* 191 F.3d 55 (1st Cir. 1999)]

CASE PROBLEM WITH SAMPLE ANSWER

30–8. Valley Furniture & Interiors, Inc., bought an insurance policy from Transportation Insurance Co. (TIC). The policy provided coverage of $50,000 for each occurrence of property loss caused by employee dishonesty. An "occurrence" was defined as "a single act or series of related acts." Valley allowed its employees to take pay advances and to buy discounted merchandise, with the advances and the cost of the merchandise deducted from their paychecks. The payroll manager was to notify the payroll company to make the deductions. Over a period of six years, without notifying the payroll company, the payroll manager issued advances to other employees and herself and bought merchandise for herself, in amounts totaling more than $200,000. Valley filed claims with TIC for three "occurrences" of employee theft. TIC considered the acts a "series of related acts" and paid only $50,000. Valley filed a suit in a Washington state court against TIC, alleging, in part, breach of contract. What is the standard for interpreting an insurance clause? How should this court define "series of related acts"? Why? [*Valley Furniture & Interiors, Inc. v. Transportation Insurance Co.,* 107 Wash.App. 104, 26 P.3d 952 (Div. 1 2001)]

▶ To view a sample answer for this case problem, go to this book's Web site at **http://fundamentals.westbuslaw.com** and click on "Interactive Study Center."

30–9. Insurable Interest. Scott Mayo worked for Camelot Music, Inc., in the 1980s and 1990s. Camelot secretly bought insurance policies on the life of Mayo and the lives of other employees—none of whom were key persons—through Hartford Life Insurance Co. and other insurers. The policies listed Camelot as the sole beneficiary. Camelot borrowed money from Hartford to pay the premiums and claimed the interest on the loans as tax deductions. Camelot earned nontaxable interest through the policies and, on the death of an employee, used the death benefit to repay the premium loans. Mayo and other Camelot employees, as well as the employees of other firms that secretly insured their workers' lives, filed a suit in a federal district court against the employers, seeking to be paid the policies' benefits. The plaintiffs argued that the policies were illegal because the defendants did not have insurable interests in the employees' lives. What are the requirements for an insurable interest in a life? Are those requirements satisfied in this case? Why or why not? [*Mayo v. Hartford Life Insurance Co.*, 193 F.Supp.2d 927 (S.D.Tex. 2002)]

30–10. Intestacy Laws. In January 1993, three and a half years after Lauren and Warren Woodward were married, they were informed that Warren had leukemia. At the time, the couple had no children, and the doctors told the Woodwards that the leukemia treatment might leave Mr. Woodward sterile. The couple arranged for Mr. Woodward's sperm to be collected and placed in a sperm bank for later use. In October 1993, Warren

Woodward died. Two years later, Lauren Woodward gave birth to twin girls who had been conceived through artificial insemination using Mr. Woodward's sperm. The following year, Mrs. Woodward applied for Social Security survivor benefits for the two children. The Social Security Administration (SSA) rejected her application, on the ground that she had not established that the twins were the husband's children within the meaning of the Social Security Act of 1935. Mrs. Woodward then filed a paternity action in Massachusetts, and the probate court determined that Warren Woodward was the twins' father. Mrs. Woodward resubmitted her application to the SSA but was again refused survivor benefits for the twins. She then filed an action in a federal district court to determine the inheritance rights, under Massachusetts intestacy law, of children conceived from the sperm of a deceased individual and his surviving spouse. How should the court resolve this case? Should children conceived after a parent's death (by means of artificial insemination or *in vitro* fertilization) still inherit under intestate succession laws? Why or why not? [*Woodward v. Commissioner of Social Security*, 435 Mass. 536, 760 N.E.2d 257 (2002)]

INSURANCE, WILLS, AND TRUSTS

For updated links to resources available on the Web, as well as other materials, visit this text's Web site at

http://fundamentals.westbuslaw.com

For a summary of the law governing insurance contracts in the United States, including rules of interpretation, go to

http://www.consumerlawpage.com/article/insureds.shtml

The law firm of Anderson Kill & Olick usually includes a number of articles on insurance at its Web site. Go to

http://www.andersonkill.com/Whats_New

You can find the Uniform Probate Code, as well as links to various state probate statutes, at Cornell University's Legal Information Institute. Go to

http://www.law.cornell.edu/uniform/probate.html

Online Legal Research

Go to the *Fundamentals of Business Law* home page at **http://fundamentals.westbuslaw.com**. Select "Interactive Study Center" and then click on "Chapter 30." There you will find the following Internet research exercises that you can perform to learn more about topics covered in this chapter.

Activity 30-1: LEGAL PERSPECTIVE—**Disappearing Decisions**
Activity 30-2: MANAGEMENT PERSPECTIVE—**Wills and Trusts**
Activity 30-3: SOCIAL PERSPECTIVE—**Elder Law**

Before the Test

Go to the *Fundamentals of Business Law* home page at **http://fundamentals. westbuslaw.com**. Click on "Interactive Quizzes." You will find at least twenty interactive questions relating to this chapter.

Westlaw® Campus

If your textbook provided for a subscription to Westlaw® Campus, or if you have otherwise purchased access to the Westlaw Campus database, you can access any of the cases presented or cited in this chapter by using your Westlaw Campus account.

Tahoe-Sierra Preservation Council, Inc. v. Tahoe Regional Planning Agency

INTRODUCTION

The power of a state to regulate the use of land was discussed in Chapter 29. In this *Focus on Legal Reasoning,* we look at *Tahoe-Sierra Preservation Council, Inc. v. Tahoe Regional Planning Agency,*[1] a decision in which the United States Supreme Court considered whether a moratorium, or suspension, on development imposed during the process of devising a comprehensive land-use plan constituted a taking of property requiring the payment of just compensation.

_____

1. 535 U.S. 302, 122 S.Ct. 1465, 152 L.Ed.2d 517 (2002).

CASE BACKGROUND

Lake Tahoe, near Reno, Nevada, was long noted for its water's exceptional clarity, attributed to the absence of the algae that obscure the water of most other lakes. Over the last forty years, however, increased development in the Lake Tahoe Basin decreased this clarity. Run-off from asphalt, concrete, buildings, and packed dirt increased the amounts of nitrogen and phosphorus in the lake, which experienced a consequent increase in algae.

In the 1960s, California and Nevada created the Tahoe Regional Planning Agency (TRPA) to coordinate and regulate development in the Basin and to conserve its natural resources. In 1981, while drafting and adopting a revised regional plan, the TRPA ordered two separate halts to the development of new subdivisions, condominiums, and apartment buildings in the Basin. The halts lasted a total of thirty-two months.

Tahoe-Sierra Preservation Council, Inc., an association of two thousand landowners affected by the moratoria, and others filed a suit in a federal district court against the TRPA, claiming in part that its actions constituted a taking of property without just compensation. The court concluded that there was a taking, but on appeal to the U.S. Court of Appeals for the Ninth Circuit, the TRPA successfully challenged this determination. The plaintiffs appealed to the United States Supreme Court.

MAJORITY OPINION

Justice STEVENS delivered the opinion of the Court.

* * * *

When the government physically takes possession of an interest in property for some public purpose, it has a categorical duty to compensate the former owner * * *. Thus, *compensation is mandated when a leasehold is taken and the government occupies the property for its own purposes, even though that use is temporary.* * * * But a government regulation that merely prohibits landlords from evicting tenants unwilling to pay a higher rent, that bans certain private uses of a portion of an owner's property, or that forbids the private use of certain airspace, *Penn Central Transportation Co. v. New York City,* 438 U.S. 104, 98 S.Ct. 2646, 57 L.Ed.2d 631 (1978), does not constitute a categorical taking. The first category of cases requires courts to apply a clear rule; the second necessarily entails complex factual assessments of the purposes and economic effects of government actions. * * * This case does not present the classic taking in which the government directly appropriates private property for its own use; instead the interference with property rights arises from some public program adjusting the benefits and burdens of economic life to promote the common good. [Emphasis added.]

* * * *

* * * Petitioners * * * [argue] that we can effectively sever a 32-month segment from the remainder of each landowner's fee simple estate, and then ask whether that segment has been taken in its entirety by the moratoria. Of course, defining the property interest taken in terms of the very regulation being challenged is circular. With property so divided, every delay would become a total ban; the moratorium and the normal permit process alike would constitute categorical takings. * * *

An interest in real property is defined by the metes and bounds [boundary lines] that describe its geographic dimensions and the term of years that describes the temporal aspect of the owner's interest. Both dimensions must be considered if the interest is to be viewed in its entirety. Hence, a permanent deprivation of the owner's use of the entire area is a taking of the parcel as a whole, whereas a temporary restriction that merely causes a diminution in value is not. Logically, a fee simple estate cannot be rendered valueless by a temporary prohibition on economic use, because the property will recover value as soon as the prohibition is lifted.

* * * *

* * * [M]oratoria * * * are used widely among land-use planners to preserve the status quo while formulating a more permanent development strategy. In fact, the consensus in the planning community appears to be that moratoria, or "interim development controls" as they are often called, are an essential tool of successful development. Yet even the weak version of petitioners' categorical rule would treat these interim measures as takings regardless of the good faith of the planners, the reasonable expectations of the landowners, or the actual impact of the moratorium on property values.

The interest in facilitating informed decision making by regulatory agencies counsels against adopting a [categorical] rule that would impose such severe costs on their deliberations.

Otherwise, the financial constraints of compensating property owners during a moratorium may force officials to rush through the planning process or to abandon the practice altogether. To the extent that communities are forced to abandon using moratoria, landowners will have incentives to develop their property quickly before a comprehensive plan can be enacted, thereby fostering inefficient and ill-conceived growth. *   *   *

*   *   *   *

*   *   * [T]he judgment of the Court of Appeals is affirmed.

DISSENTING OPINION

Chief Justice REHNQUIST, *   *   * dissenting.

*   *   *   *

*   *   * [W]hen the owner of real property has been called upon to sacrifice *all* economically beneficial uses in the name of the common good, that is, to leave his property economically idle, he has suffered a taking. *   *   * The Court does not dispute that petitioners were forced to leave their land economically idle during [the moratoria]. But the Court refuses to [award compensation] on the ground that the deprivation was "temporary."

Neither the Takings Clause nor our case law supports such a distinction. For one thing, a distinction between "temporary" and "permanent" prohibitions is tenuous. *   *   * Land-use regulations are not irrevocable. And the government can even abandon condemned land. Under the Court's decision today, the takings question turns entirely on the initial label given a regulation, a label that is often without much meaning. There is every incentive for government to simply label any prohibition on development "temporary," or to fix a set number of years. *   *   * [T]his initial designation does not preclude the government from repeatedly extending the "temporary" prohibition into a long-term ban on all development. The Court now holds that such a designation by the government is conclusive *   *   *.

*   *   *   *

*   *   * From petitioners' standpoint, what happened in this case is no different than if the government had taken a 6-year lease of their property. The Court ignores this practical equivalence between respondent's deprivation and the deprivation resulting from a leasehold. In so doing, the Court allows the government to do by regulation what it cannot do through eminent domain—i.e., take private property without paying for it.

LEGAL REASONING AND ANALYSIS

❶ Legal Reasoning. On what points do the majority and the dissent disagree in the *Tahoe* case? What conclusions do they reach, and what arguments do they use to support their conclusions? With whom do you agree, and why?

❷ Legal Analysis. The majority cites, in its opinion, *Penn Central Transportation Co. v. New York City,* 438 U.S. 104, 98 S.Ct. 2646, 57 L.Ed.2d 631 (1978) (see the *Accessing the Internet* feature at the end of Chapter 2 for instructions on how to access federal court opinions). How do the law and the reasoning of the *Penn Central* case relate to the position of the majority in the *Tahoe* case?

❸ Political Considerations. According to the majority in the *Tahoe* case, for what purpose does a local government use a moratorium on development? What might be the consequences of such use if the majority in the *Tahoe* case had adopted "the petitioners' categorical rule"?

❹ Implications for Property Owners. How is the holding in this case of interest to property owners who are restricted by local governments in the use of their property?

❺ Case Briefing Assignment. Using the guidelines for briefing cases given in Appendix A of this text, brief the *Tahoe* case.

This text's Web site, at **http://fundamentals.westbuslaw.com**, offers links to West's Court Case Updates, as well as to other online research sources. You can also locate court cases at the Web sites listed in the *Accessing the Internet* section at the end of Chapter 2.

The Web site for the Center on Environmental and Land Use Law at **http://www.nyu.edu/pages/elc** contains a "Program on Land Use Law." Here you can find links to United States Supreme Court decisions on takings, state takings legislation, and other resources.

UNIT 10

Special Topics

Professional Liability

CHAPTER OBJECTIVES

After reading this chapter, you should be able to answer the following questions:

① Under what common law theories may professionals be liable to clients?

② What are the rules concerning an auditor's liability to third parties?

③ How might an accountant violate federal securities laws?

④ What crimes might an accountant commit under the Internal Revenue Code?

⑤ What constrains professionals to keep communications with their clients confidential?

Accountants, attorneys, physicians, and other professionals have found themselves increasingly subject to liability in the past decade or so. This more extensive liability has resulted in large part from a greater public awareness of the fact that professionals are required to deliver competent services and are obligated to adhere to standards of performance commonly accepted within their professions.

Certainly, the dizzying collapse of Enron Corporation and the failure of other major companies, including WorldCom, Inc., in the early 2000s called attention to the importance of abiding by professional accounting standards. Arthur Andersen, LLP, one of the world's leading public accounting firms, ended up being indicted on criminal charges in 2002 for its role in thwarting the government's investigation into Enron's accounting practices. As a result, that company will probably never recover. Moreover, under the Sarbanes-Oxley Act of 2002 (discussed in Chapter 27), which Congress passed in response to these events, public accounting firms throughout the nation will feel the effects for years to come. Among other things, the act imposed stricter regulation and oversight on the public accounting industry.

Considering the many potential sources of legal liability that may be imposed on them, accountants, attorneys, and other professionals should be well aware of their legal obligations. In the first part of this chapter, we look at the potential common law liability of professionals and then examine the potential liability of accountants under securities laws and the Internal Revenue Code. The chapter concludes with a brief examination of the relationship of professionals, particularly accountants and attorneys, with their clients and a discussion of limits on the liability of professionals.

Potential Common Law Liability to Clients

Under the common law, professionals may be liable to clients for breach of contract, negligence, or fraud.

LIABILITY FOR BREACH OF CONTRACT

Accountants and other professionals face liability for any breach of contract under the common law. A professional owes a duty to his or her client to honor the terms of the contract and to perform the contract within the stated time period. If the professional fails to perform as agreed in the contract, then he or she has breached the contract, and the client has the right to recover damages from the professional. A professional may be held liable for expenses incurred by his or her client in securing another professional to provide the contracted-for services, for penalties imposed on the client for failure to meet time deadlines, and for any other reasonable and foreseeable monetary losses that arise from the professional's breach.

LIABILITY FOR NEGLIGENCE

Accountants and other professionals may also be held liable under the common law for negligence in the performance of their services. The elements that must be proved to establish negligence on the part of a professional are as follows:

① A duty of care existed.

② That duty of care was breached.

③ The plaintiff suffered an injury.

④ The injury was proximately caused by the defendant's breach of the duty of care.

All professionals are subject to standards of conduct established by codes of professional ethics, by state statutes, and by judicial decisions. They are also governed by the contracts they enter into with their clients. In their performance of contracts, professionals must exercise the established standard of care, knowledge, and judgment generally accepted by members of their professional group. We look below at the duty of care owed by two groups of professionals that frequently perform services for business firms: accountants and attorneys.

Accountant's Duty of Care. Accountants play a major role in a business's financial system. Accountants have the necessary expertise and experience in establishing and maintaining accurate financial records to design, control, and audit record-keeping systems; to prepare reliable statements that reflect an individual's or a business's financial status; and to give tax advice and prepare tax returns.

GAAP and GAAS. In the performance of their services, accountants must comply with **generally accepted accounting principles (GAAP)** and **generally accepted auditing standards (GAAS)**. The Financial Accounting Standards Board (FASB, usually pronounced "faz-bee") determines what accounting conventions, rules, and procedures constitute GAAP at a given point in time. GAAS are standards concerning an auditor's professional qualities and the judgment that he or she exercises in performing an audit and report. GAAS are established by the American Institute of Certified Public Accountants. As long as an accountant conforms to generally accepted accounting principles and acts in good faith, he or she normally will not be held liable to the client for incorrect judgment.

As a general rule, an accountant is not required to discover every impropriety, **defalcation** (embezzlement), or fraud in his or her client's books.[1] If, however, the impropriety, defalcation, or fraud has gone undiscovered because of an accountant's negligence or failure to perform an express or implied duty, the accountant will be liable for any resulting losses suffered by his or her client. Therefore, an accountant who uncovers suspicious financial transactions and fails to investigate the matter fully or to inform his or her client of the discovery can be held liable to the client for the resulting loss.

A violation of GAAP and GAAS will be considered *prima facie* evidence of negligence on the part of the accountant. Compliance with GAAP and GAAS, however, does not necessarily relieve an accountant from potential legal liability. An accountant may be held to a higher standard of conduct established by state statute and by judicial decisions.

Defenses to Negligence. If an accountant is deemed guilty of negligence, the client can collect damages for losses that arose from the accountant's negligence. An accountant, however, is not without possible defenses to a cause of action for damages based on negligence. Possible defenses include the following:

① The accountant was not negligent.

② If the accountant was negligent, this negligence was not the proximate cause of the client's losses.

③ The client was negligent (depending on whether state law allows contributory negligence as a defense).

Unaudited Financial Statements. Sometimes accountants are hired to prepare unaudited financial statements. (A

---

[1] The word *defalcation* originated in the fifteenth century. Its roots are two Latin words that loosely translate to "a lopping off" or "a cutting off."

financial statement is considered unaudited if no proce-dures have been used to verify its accuracy or if insufficient procedures have been used to justify the contents.) Accountants may be subject to liability for failing, in accor-dance with standard accounting procedures, to delineate a balance sheet as unaudited. An accountant will also be held liable for failure to disclose to a client facts or circumstances that give reason to believe that misstatements have been made or that a fraud has been committed.

Attorney's Duty of Care. The conduct of attorneys is gov-erned by rules established by each state and by the American Bar Association's Code of Professional Responsibility and Model Rules of Professional Conduct. All attorneys owe a duty to provide competent and diligent representation. In judging an attorney's performance, the standard used will normally be that of a reasonably compe-tent general practitioner of ordinary skill, experience, and capacity. If the attorney holds himself or herself out as hav-ing expertise in a special area of law, the standard is that of a reasonably competent specialist of ordinary skill, experi-ence, and capacity in that area of the law. Attorneys are required to be familiar with well-settled principles of law applicable to a case and to discover law that can be found through a reasonable amount of research. The lawyer also must investigate and discover facts that could materially affect the client's legal rights.

When an attorney fails to exercise reasonable care and professional judgment, he or she breaches the duty of care. The plaintiff must then prove that the breach actually caused him or her some injury. ● **EXAMPLE #1** John Jones, an attorney, allows the statute of limitations to lapse on the claim of Karen Anderson, a client. Jones can be held liable for **malpractice** (professional negligence) because Anderson can no longer file a cause of action in this case and has lost a potential award of damages. ●

Traditionally, to establish causation, the client normally had to show that "but for" the attorney's negligence, the client would not have suffered the injury. In recent years, however, several courts have held that plaintiffs in malprac-tice cases only need show that the defendant's negligence was a "substantial factor" in causing the plaintiff's injury.

PROFESSIONALS' LIABILITY FOR FRAUD

Actual fraud and constructive fraud present two different circumstances under which an accountant may be found liable. Recall from Chapter 10 that fraud, or misrepresenta-tion, consists of the following elements:

① A misrepresentation of a material fact has occurred.

② There exists an intent to deceive.

③ The innocent party has justifiably relied on the misrepresentation.

④ For damages, the innocent party must have been injured.

A professional may be held liable for *actual fraud* when he or she intentionally misstates a material fact to mislead his or her client and the client justifiably relies on the mis-stated fact to his or her injury. A material fact is one that a reasonable person would consider important in deciding whether to act. In contrast, a professional may be held liable for *constructive fraud* whether or not he or she acted with fraudulent intent. ● **EXAMPLE #2** In conducting an audit of National Computing Company (NCC), Paula, the auditor, accepts the explanations of Ron, an NCC officer, regarding certain financial irregularities, despite evidence that contra-dicts those explanations and indicates that the irregularities may be illegal. Paula's conduct could be characterized as an intentional failure to perform a duty in reckless disregard of the consequences of such a failure. This would constitute gross negligence and could be held to be constructive fraud. ● Both actual and constructive fraud are potential sources of legal liability under which a client can bring an action against an accountant or other professional.

Auditors' Liability to Third Parties

Traditionally, an accountant or other professional did not owe any duty to a third person with whom he or she had no direct contractual relationship—that is, to any person not in *privity of contract* with the professional. A professional's duty was only to his or her client. Violations of statutory laws, fraud, and other intentional or reckless acts of wrong-doing were the only exceptions to this general rule.

Today, numerous third parties—including investors, shareholders, creditors, corporate managers and directors, regulatory agencies, and others—rely on professional opin-ions, such as those of auditors, when making decisions. In view of this extensive reliance, many courts have all but abandoned the privity requirement in regard to account-ants' liability to third parties.

In this section, we focus on the potential liability of audi-tors to third parties. Understanding an auditor's common law liability to third parties is critical, because often, when a business fails, its independent auditor (accountant) may be one of the few potentially solvent defendants. The majority of courts now hold that auditors can be held liable to third parties for negligence, but the standard for the imposition of this liability varies. There are generally three different views of accountants' liability to third parties, each of which we discuss next.

THE *ULTRAMARES* RULE

The traditional rule regarding an accountant's liability to third parties was enunciated by Chief Judge Benjamin Cardozo in *Ultramares Corp. v. Touche,* a case decided in 1931.[2] In *Ultramares,* Fred Stern & Company (Stern) hired the public accounting firm of Touche, Niven & Company (Touche) to review Stern's financial records and prepare a balance sheet for the year ending December 31, 1923.[3] Touche prepared the balance sheet and supplied Stern with thirty-two certified copies. According to the certified balance sheet, Stern had a net worth (assets less liabilities) of $1,070,715.26. In reality, however, Stern was insolvent—the company's records had been falsified by Stern's insiders to reflect a positive net worth. In reliance on the certified balance sheets, a lender, Ultramares Corporation, loaned substantial amounts to Stern. After Stern was declared bankrupt, Ultramares brought an action against Touche for negligence in an attempt to recover damages.

The New York Court of Appeals (that state's highest court) refused to impose liability on the accountants and concluded that they owed a duty of care only to those persons for whose "primary benefit" the statements were intended. In this case, Stern was the only person for whose primary benefit the statements were intended. The court held that in the absence of privity or a relationship "so close as to approach that of privity," a party could not recover from an accountant.

The court's requirement of privity or near privity has since been referred to as the *Ultramares* rule, or the New York rule. The rule was restated and somewhat modified in a 1985 New York case, *Credit Alliance Corp. v. Arthur Andersen & Co.*[4] In that case, the court held that if a third

---

[2] 255 N.Y. 170, 174 N.E. 441 (1931).

[3] A *balance sheet* is often relied on by banks, creditors, stockholders, purchasers, or sellers as a basis for making decisions relating to a company's business.

[4] 65 N.Y.2d 536, 483 N.E.2d 110 (1985): A "relationship sufficiently intimate to be equated with privity" is sufficient for a third party to sue another's accountant for negligence.

party has a sufficiently close relationship or nexus (link or connection) with an accountant, then the *Ultramares* privity requirement may be satisfied even if no accountant-client relationship is established. The rule enunciated in *Credit Alliance* is often referred to as the "near privity" rule. Only a minority of states have adopted this rule of accountants' liability to third parties.

THE *RESTATEMENT* RULE

In the past several years, the *Ultramares* rule has been severely criticized. Auditors perform much of their work for use by persons who are not parties to the contract. Thus, it is asserted that they owe a duty to these third parties. Consequently, there has been an erosion of the *Ultramares* rule, and accountants have been exposed to potential liability to third parties.

The majority of courts have adopted the position taken by the *Restatement (Second) of Torts,* which states that accountants are subject to liability for negligence not only to their clients but also to *foreseen,* or *known,* users—or classes of users—of their reports or financial statements. Under Section 552(2) of the *Restatement (Second) of Torts,* an accountant's liability extends to those persons for whose benefit and guidance the accountant "intends to supply the information or knows that the recipient intends to supply it" and to those persons whom the accountant "intends the information to influence or knows that the recipient so intends." ● **EXAMPLE #3** Steve, an accountant, prepares a financial statement for Tech Software, Inc., a client, knowing that the client will submit that statement to First National Bank to secure a loan. If Steve makes negligent misstatements or omissions in the statement, he may be held liable by the bank because he knew that the bank would rely on his work product when deciding whether to make the loan. ●

The following case involved an application of the *Restatement* rule.

CASE 31.1 **Stroud v. Arthur Andersen & Co.**

Supreme Court of Oklahoma, 2001.
2001 OK 76,
37 P.3d 783.

FACTS Steve Stroud built Insurance Company of the Prairie States (ICOPS) into one of the largest providers of crop insurance in the United States. Stroud Crop, Inc. (SCI), was the general managing agent and operator of ICOPS. Stroud was

the primary owner of both companies, and his property served as the collateral for the firms' debts. SCI hired Arthur Andersen & Company to audit its financial statements for 1988 through 1992,[a] and ICOPS engaged Andersen to audit

---

a. A *financial statement* is a written statement that shows an individual's or a business's actual or anticipated financial position, the results of operations, cash flow, and changes in financial position that relate to a specific period of time, on the basis of GAAP.

(Continued)

CASE 31.1—Continued

its statements for 1989 through 1993. During the 1990s, SCI and ICOPS lost their economic viability. Stroud and others filed a suit in an Oklahoma state court against Andersen, alleging, among other things, that its audits had negligently understated SCI's liabilities by more than $3 million and failed to identify material weaknesses in SCI's internal accounting system.**b** The plaintiffs asserted that they had relied on these audits to make business decisions that caused SCI's economic losses. Andersen responded in part that it owed nothing to Stroud, who had not been its client. The court awarded damages to the plaintiffs, and Andersen appealed to a state intermediate appellate court, which reversed this judgment. The plaintiffs appealed to the Oklahoma Supreme Court.

b. Under GAAS, a *material weakness* is "a reportable condition in which the design or operation of one or more internal control components does not reduce to a relatively low level the risk that errors or irregularities in amounts that would be material in relation to the financial statements being audited may occur and not be detected within a timely period by employees in the normal course of performing their assigned functions."

ISSUE Should Andersen be held liable to Stroud?

REASON The court stated, "The common law remains in full force in Oklahoma unless a statute explicitly provides to the contrary." Further, the court held that the common law principle embraced by the *Restatement* was "decisive." Because Andersen knew that Stroud was using his personal assets as collateral for the debts of the two companies, he "fell within the ambit of that group of persons to whom Andersen owed a duty of care."

DECISION The Oklahoma Supreme Court vacated the opinion of the lower appellate court and reinstated the judgment of the trial court. The state supreme court applied the *Restatement (Second) of Torts* rule to uphold the award of damages to Stroud, a third party who Andersen knew would rely on its audits and who did rely on them, to his detriment.

FOR CRITICAL ANALYSIS—Social Consideration
Under the Restatement *rule, is there anyone else to whom the auditor in this case might have been held liable?*

LIABILITY TO REASONABLY FORESEEABLE USERS

A small minority of courts hold accountants liable to any users whose reliance on an accountant's statements or reports was *reasonably foreseeable*. This standard has been criticized as extending liability too far. ● **EXAMPLE #4** In *Raritan River Steel Co. v. Cherry, Bekaert & Holland*, the North Carolina Supreme Court stated that "in fairness accountants should not be liable in circumstances where they are unaware of the use to which their opinions will be put. Instead, their liability should be commensurate with those persons or classes of persons whom they know will rely on their work. With such knowledge the auditor can, through purchase of liability insurance, setting fees, and adopting other protective measures appropriate to the risk, prepare accordingly."[5] ●

It is the view of the majority of the courts that the *Restatement's* approach is the more reasonable one because it allows accountants to control their exposure to liability. Liability is "fixed by the accountants' particular knowledge at the moment the audit is published," not by the foreseeability of the harm that might occur to a third party after the report is released.[6]

Even the California courts, which for several years relied on reasonable foreseeability as the standard for determining an auditor's liability to third parties, have changed their position. In a 1992 case, the California Supreme Court held

that an accountant "owes no general duty of care regarding the conduct of an audit to persons other than the client." The court went on to say that if third parties rely on an auditor's opinion, "there is no liability even though the [auditor] should reasonably have foreseen such a possibility."[7]

Liability of Attorneys to Third Parties

Like accountants, attorneys may be held liable under the common law to third parties who rely on legal opinions to their detriment. Generally, an attorney is not liable to a nonclient unless there is fraud (or malicious conduct) by the attorney. The liability principles stated in Section 552 of the *Restatement (Second) of Torts*, however, may apply to attorneys just as they may apply to accountants.

The Sarbanes-Oxley Act of 2002

As mentioned in this chapter's introduction (and discussed in Chapter 27), in 2002 Congress enacted the Sarbanes-Oxley Act, which became effective on August 29, 2002. The act imposes a number of strict requirements on both domestic and foreign public accounting firms that provide auditing services to companies, or "issuers," whose securities are sold to public investors. The act defines the term *issuer* as a com-

[5] 322 N.C. 200, 367 S.E.2d 609 (1988).
[6] *Bethlehem Steel Corp. v. Ernst & Whinney*, 822 S.W.2d 592 (1991).

[7] *Bily v. Arthur Young & Co.*, 3 Cal.4th 370, 834 P.2d 745, 11 Cal.Rptr.2d 51 (1992).

pany that has securities that are registered under Section 12 of the Securities Exchange Act of 1934, that is required to file reports under Section 15(d) of the 1934 act, or that files—or has filed—a registration statement that has not yet become effective under the Securities Act of 1933.

THE PUBLIC COMPANY ACCOUNTING OVERSIGHT BOARD

Among other things, the Sarbanes-Oxley Act calls for a greater degree of government oversight over public accounting practices. To this end, the act created the Public Company Accounting Oversight Board, which reports to the Securities and Exchange Commission. The board con-

sists of a chair and four other members. The purpose of the board is to oversee the audit of public companies that are subject to securities laws in order to protect public investors and to ensure that public accounting firms comply with the provisions of the Sarbanes-Oxley Act.

APPLICABILITY TO PUBLIC ACCOUNTING FIRMS

Titles I and II of the act set forth the key provisions relating to the duties of the new oversight board and the requirements relating to public accounting firms—defined by the act as firms and associated persons that are "engaged in the practice of public accounting or preparing or issuing audit reports." We summarize these provisions in Exhibit 31–1.

EXHIBIT 31–1 KEY PROVISIONS OF THE SARBANES-OXLEY ACT OF 2002 RELATING TO PUBLIC ACCOUNTING FIRMS

DUTIES OF THE PUBLIC COMPANY ACCOUNTING OVERSIGHT BOARD

Title I of the Sarbanes-Oxley Act of 2002 states that the duties of the Public Company Accounting Oversight Board are as follows:

- Generally, to oversee the audit of companies ("issuers") whose securities are sold to public investors in order to protect the interests of investors and further the public interest.
- To register public accounting firms that prepare audit reports for issuers. (A nonregistered firm is prohibited from preparing, or participating in the preparation of, an audit report with respect to an issuer.)
- To establish or adopt standards relating to the preparation of audit reports for issuers.
- To enforce compliance with the Sarbanes-Oxley Act by inspecting registered public accounting firms (RPAFs) and by investigating and disciplining, by appropriate sanctions, firms that violate the act's provisions. (Sanctions range from a temporary or permanent suspension to civil penalties that can be as high as $15 million for intentional violations.)
- To perform any other duties necessary or appropriate to promote high professional standards among RPAFs and improve the quality of audit services offered by those firms.

AUDITOR INDEPENDENCE

To help ensure that auditors remain independent of the firms that they audit, Title II of the Sarbanes-Oxley Act does the following:

- Makes it unlawful for RPAFs to contemporaneously perform both audit and nonaudit services. Nonaudit services include the following:
  1. Bookkeeping or other services related to the accounting records or financial statements of the audit client.
  2. Financial information systems design and implementation.
  3. Appraisal or valuation services.
  4. Fairness opinions.
  5. Management functions.
  6. Broker or dealer, investment adviser, or investment banking services.
- Requires preapproval for most auditing services from the issuer's audit committee.
- Prohibits RPAFs from providing audit services to an issuer if either the lead audit partner or the audit partner responsible for reviewing the audit has provided such services to the issuer in each of the prior five years.
- Requires RPAFs to make timely reports to the audit committees of the issuers, indicating all critical accounting policies and practices to be used; all alternative treatments of financial information within generally accepted accounting principles that have been discussed with the issuer's management officials, the ramifications of the use of such alternative treatments, and the treatment preferred by the auditor; and other material written communications between the auditor and the issuer's management.
- Makes it unlawful for an RPAF to provide auditing services to an issuer if the issuer's chief executive officer, chief financial officer, chief accounting officer, or controller was previously employed by the auditor and participated in any capacity in the audit of the issuer during the one-year period preceding the date that the audit began.

DOCUMENT DESTRUCTION

- The Sarbanes-Oxley Act also prohibits the destruction or falsification of records with the intent to obstruct or influence a federal investigation or in relation to bankruptcy proceedings.
- Violation of this provision can result in a fine, imprisonment for up to twenty years, or both.

(Provisions of the act that are more directly concerned with corporate fraud and the responsibilities of corporate officers and directors were listed and described in Exhibit 27–1 in Chapter 27.)

Liability of Accountants under Securities Laws

Both civil and criminal liability may be imposed on accountants under the Securities Act of 1933 and the Securities Exchange Act of 1934.[8]

LIABILITY UNDER THE SECURITIES ACT OF 1933

The Securities Act of 1933 requires registration statements to be filed with the Securities and Exchange Commission (SEC) prior to an offering of securities (see Chapter 27).[9] Accountants frequently prepare and certify (attest to the accuracy of) the issuer's financial statements that are included in the registration statement.

---

[8] Other potential sources of civil and criminal liability that may be imposed on accountants and other professionals include provisions of the Racketeer Influenced and Corrupt Organizations Act (RICO). RICO is discussed in Chapter 6.

[9] Many securities and transactions are expressly exempted from the 1933 act.

Liability under Section 11. Section 11 of the Securities Act of 1933 imposes civil liability on accountants for misstatements and omissions of material facts in registration statements. Therefore, an accountant may be found liable if he or she prepared any financial statements included in the registration statement that "contained an untrue statement of a material fact or omitted to state a material fact required to be stated therein or necessary to make the statements therein not misleading."[10]

Liability to Purchasers of Securities. Under Section 11, an accountant's liability for a misstatement or omission of a material fact in a registration statement extends to anyone who acquires a security covered by the registration statement. A purchaser of a security need only demonstrate that he or she has suffered a loss on the security. Proof of reliance on the materially false statement or misleading omission is not ordinarily required. Nor is there a requirement of privity between the accountant and the security purchasers.

Under Section 11, clearly an accountant may be liable to those who buy stock in an initial public offering, or IPO purchasers. The question in the following case is whether an accountant's liability can extend to those who buy stock later, or so-called aftermarket buyers.

---

[10] 15 U.S.C. Section 77k(a).

CASE 31.2   Lee v. Ernst & Young, LLP[a]

United States Court of Appeals, Eighth Circuit, 2002. 294 F.3d 969.

FACTS Summit Medical Systems, Inc., a corporation headquartered in Minneapolis, Minnesota, sells "clinical outcomes" medical database software and related products and services. Summit made an initial public offering (IPO) of stock in 1995 and a second public offering the next year. In 1997, Summit announced that it had been improperly recognizing revenues and restated its financial results dating back to 1994, showing an 11 percent cumulative shortfall. Jong Lee and other Summit shareholders filed a suit in a federal district court against the corporation's accounting firm, Ernst & Young, LLP (E&Y), and others. The investors alleged that the registration statement for the 1995 IPO contained materially false and misleading statements about Summit's financial status and

---

a. *LLP* is an abbreviation for *limited liability partnership*. LLPs were discussed in Chapter 24.

accounting practices, in violation of Section 11 of the Securities Act of 1933. The court held that only those who had bought stock in the 1995 IPO had standing to sue E&Y. Because none of the plaintiffs had bought their stock at that time, the court dismissed the complaint. The shareholders appealed to the U.S. Court of Appeals for the Eighth Circuit.

ISSUE Did the plaintiffs have standing to sue E&Y?

DECISION Yes. The U.S. Court of Appeals for the Eighth Circuit reversed the lower court's dismissal of the plaintiffs' complaint and remanded the case for further proceedings. The appellate court held that standing to pursue a claim against an accounting firm under Section 11 exists for aftermarket buyers who can demonstrate that the shares they bought can be traced to an allegedly false registration statement.

REASON The court pointed out that Section 12(2) "expressly requires privity between the issuer and the purchaser of the security at issue. Section 11, by contrast, has no comparable language—it simply refers to 'any person acquir-

CASE 31.2—Continued

ing such security,' with 'such security' referring to a security registered under the registration statement alleged to be defective." Therefore, the court concluded, Section 11 "is broad enough to encompass some aftermarket purchasers, subject, of course, to the long-recognized requirement that the plaintiff must directly trace his or her security to the allegedly defective registration statement at issue." The court also noted that in calculating the damages, "[i]t would be unnecessary to limit the price to no more than the price

offered to the public [which the courts generally do] if the cause of action were limited to participants in the initial public offering. Similarly, [Section] 11(g)—which expressly caps the maximum amount recoverable to the price offered to the public—would likewise be superfluous."

FOR CRITICAL ANALYSIS—Ethical Consideration
Does holding E&Y liable to aftermarket purchasers extend the liability of accountants too far? Why or why not?

The Due Diligence Standard. Section 11 imposes a duty on accountants to use **due diligence** in the preparation of financial statements included in the filed registration statements. After a purchaser has proved a loss on the security, the accountant bears the burden of showing that he or she exercised due diligence in the preparation of the financial statements. To avoid liability, the accountant must show that he or she had, "after reasonable investigation, reasonable grounds to believe and did believe, at the time such part of the registration statement became effective, that the statements therein were true and that there was no omission of a material fact required to be stated therein or necessary to make the statements therein not misleading."[11] Further, the failure to follow GAAP and GAAS is also proof of a lack of due diligence.

In particular, the due diligence standard places a burden on accountants to verify information furnished by a corporation's officers and directors. The burden of proving due diligence requires an accountant to demonstrate that he or she is free from negligence or fraud. Merely asking questions is not always sufficient to satisfy the requirement of due diligence. ● EXAMPLE #5 In *Escott v. BarChris Construction*

Corp.,[12] accountants were held liable for failing to detect danger signals in documents furnished by corporate officers that, under GAAS, required further investigation under the circumstances. ●

Defenses to Liability. Besides proving that he or she has acted with due diligence, an accountant can raise the following defenses to Section 11 liability:

① There were no misstatements or omissions.

② The misstatements or omissions were not of material facts.

③ The misstatements or omissions had no causal connection to the plaintiff's loss.

④ The plaintiff purchaser invested in the securities knowing of the misstatements or omissions.

Another defense is that an alleged misstatement or omission was not part of a financial statement that the accountant prepared or certified. Whether an accountant prepared or certified a particular statement is not always as obvious as it might seem, as illustrated by the following case.

---

[11] 15 U.S.C. Section 77k(b)(3).

[12] 283 F.Supp. 643 (S.D.N.Y. 1968).

CASE 31.3 Endo v. Arthur Andersen & Co.

United States Court of Appeals,
Seventh Circuit, 1999.
163 F.3d 463.
**http://www.findlaw.com/casecode/
courts/7th.html**[a]

---

a. This is a page, within the FindLaw Web site, that provides access to some of the opinions of the U.S. Court of Appeals for the Seventh Circuit. In the "Select Year" box, choose "1999." Then in the "Select Month" box, select "January" and click on "Search." When that page opens, scroll down the list of cases to the *Endo* case. Click on the case name to access the opinion.

FACTS Arthur Andersen & Company audited the financial statements of Fruit of the Loom, Inc. (FOL), for 1985. The statements included a footnote that said FOL was contesting, in federal court, $105 million in deficiencies assessed by the Internal Revenue Service (IRS). The footnote warned that the ultimate payment to the IRS could, with interest, exceed $105 million. This warning did not appear in FOL's 1986 financial statements, which were audited by Ernst & Young. In 1987, FOL made a stock offering that required the firm to

(Continued)

CASE 31.3—Continued

disclose its 1985 financial statements. FOL asked Andersen to consent to a republication of its 1985 report without the warning in the footnote. Andersen checked with Ernst & Young, which certified that nothing had been discovered to warrant changing the data in the 1985 statements. Andersen consented to the republication. Within a year, FOL was ordered to pay the IRS more than $105 million. The price of the FOL stock dropped by 33 percent. Investors who lost money filed a suit in a federal district court against Andersen and others, alleging in part that omitting the warning from the footnote in the republished report violated Section 11 of the Securities Act of 1933. The court granted a summary judgment in Andersen's favor. The plaintiffs appealed to the U.S. Court of Appeals for the Seventh Circuit.

ISSUE Did Andersen's omission of the footnote in the republished report constitute a violation of the Securities Act of 1933?

DECISION No. The U.S. Court of Appeals for the Seventh Circuit affirmed the judgment of the lower court. The appellate court concluded that the omitted warning was a past

prediction about a future event about which Andersen's successor had more current information.

REASON The court stated that a reasonable investor would expect "data for periods prior to the hiring of [the current] auditor to be audited by a former auditor" and current data, including estimates of tax liability, to be audited by the current auditor. "[A]n accountant's liability for misleading information in a registration statement is limited to the portion of any financial statements which purports to have been prepared or certified by him." Footnotes are part of financial statements, but the footnotes in the documents accompanying the stock offering were the responsibility of Ernst & Young, the current auditor, not Andersen, the former auditor. "Nor would any reasonable investor have thought otherwise."**b**

FOR CRITICAL ANALYSIS—Social Consideration
If the court had held that old audits could be republished only with unrevised footnotes, what would happen to the documents that accompany stock offerings?

---

b. The investors also filed a suit against Ernst & Young, which was settled out of court.

Liability under Section 12(2). Section 12(2) of the Securities Act of 1933 imposes civil liability for fraud in relation to offerings or sales of securities.[13] Liability is based on the communication to an investor, whether orally or in the written prospectus, of an untrue statement or the omission of a material fact.

Before 1994, some courts applied Section 12(2) to accountants who *aided and abetted* the seller or the offeror of the securities in violating Section 12(2). In jurisdictions that applied Section 12(2) to accountants for aiding and abetting, the accountant might have been liable if he or she knew, or should have known, that an untrue statement or omission of material fact existed in the offer or sale. In light of the United States Supreme Court's decision in *Central Bank of Denver, N.A. v. First Interstate Bank of Denver, N.A.*[14] regarding liability for aiding and abetting under Section 10(b), accountants are unlikely to be held liable in the future, in suits by private individuals, for aiding and abetting their clients' Section 12(2) violations.

Penalties and Sanctions for Violations. Those who purchase securities and suffer harm as a result of a false or

omitted statement, or some other violation, may bring a suit in a federal court to recover their losses and other damages. The U.S. Department of Justice brings criminal actions against those who commit willful violations. The penalties include fines up to $10,000, imprisonment up to five years, or both. The SEC is authorized to seek an injunction against a willful violator to prevent further violations. The SEC can also ask a court to grant other relief, such as an order to a violator to refund profits derived from an illegal transaction.

LIABILITY UNDER THE SECURITIES EXCHANGE ACT OF 1934

Under Sections 18 and 10(b) of the Securities Exchange Act of 1934 and Rule 10b-5 of the SEC, an accountant may be found liable for fraud. A plaintiff has a substantially heavier burden of proof under the 1934 act than under the 1933 act. Unlike the 1933 act, which provides that an accountant must prove due diligence to escape liability, the 1934 act relieves an accountant from liability if the accountant acted in "good faith."

Liability under Section 18. Section 18 of the 1934 act imposes civil liability on an accountant who makes or causes to be made in any application, report, or document

---

[13] 15 U.S.C. Section 77l.
[14] 511 U.S. 164, 114 S.Ct. 1439, 128 L.Ed.2d 119 (1994).

a statement that at the time and in light of the circumstances was false or misleading with respect to any material fact.[15] Under Section 18, a court also has the discretion to assess reasonable costs, including attorneys' fees, against accountants.[16] Sellers and purchasers may maintain a cause of action "within one year after the discovery of the facts constituting the cause of action and within three years after such cause of action accrued."[17]

The Narrow Scope of Section 18 Liability. Section 18 liability is narrow in that it applies only to applications, reports, documents, and registration statements filed with the SEC. This remedy is further limited in that it applies only to sellers and purchasers. Under Section 18, a seller or purchaser must prove one of the following:

① That the false or misleading statement affected the price of the security.

② That the purchaser or seller relied on the false or misleading statement in making the purchase or sale and was not aware of the inaccuracy of the statement.

The Good Faith Defense. Even if a purchaser or seller proves these two elements, an accountant can be exonerated of liability by proving good faith in the preparation of the financial statement. To demonstrate good faith, an accountant must show that he or she had no knowledge that the financial statement was false or misleading. Acting in good faith requires the total absence of an intention on the part of the accountant to seek an unfair advantage over, or to defraud, another party. Proving a lack of intent to deceive, manipulate, or defraud is frequently referred to as proving a lack of *scienter* (knowledge on the part of a misrepresenting party that material facts have been misrepresented or omitted with an intent to deceive).

Demonstrating the Absence of Good Faith. The absence of good faith can be demonstrated not only by proof of *scienter* but also by the accountant's reckless conduct and gross negligence. (Note that "mere" negligence in the preparation of a financial statement does not constitute liability under the 1934 act. This differs from provisions of the 1933 act, under which an accountant is liable for all negligent actions.) In addition to the good faith defense, accountants have available as a defense the buyer's or seller's knowledge that the financial statement was false or misleading.

Liability under Section 10(b) and SEC Rule 10b-5. The Securities Exchange Act of 1934 further subjects accountants to potential legal liability in its antifraud provisions. Section 10(b) of the 1934 act and SEC Rule 10b-5 contain the antifraud provisions.

Section 10(b) of the 1934 act makes it unlawful for any person, including accountants, to use, in connection with the purchase or sale of any security, any manipulative or deceptive device or contrivance in contravention of SEC rules and regulations.[18] Rule 10b-5 further makes it unlawful for any person, by use of any means or instrumentality of interstate commerce, to do the following:

① Employ any device, scheme, or artifice to defraud.

② Make any untrue statement of a material fact or omit to state a material fact necessary to make the statements made, in light of the circumstances, not misleading.

③ Engage in any act, practice, or course of business that operates or would operate as a fraud or deceit on any person, in connection with the purchase or sale of any security.[19]

The Scope of Accountants' Liability under Section 10(b) and SEC Rule 10b-5. Accountants may be held liable only to sellers or purchasers under Section 10(b) and Rule 10b-5. The scope of these antifraud provisions is extremely wide. Privity is not necessary for a recovery. Under these provisions, an accountant may be found liable not only for fraudulent misstatements of material facts in written material filed with the SEC but also for any fraudulent oral statements or omissions made in connection with the purchase or sale of any security.

Requirements for Recovering Damages. To recover from an accountant under the antifraud provisions of the 1934 act, a plaintiff must, in addition to establishing status as a purchaser or seller, prove *scienter,* a fraudulent action or deception, reliance, materiality, and causation. A plaintiff who fails to establish these elements cannot recover damages from an accountant under Section 10(b) or Rule 10b-5.

THE PRIVATE SECURITIES LITIGATION REFORM ACT OF 1995

The Private Securities Litigation Reform Act of 1995 made some changes to the potential liability of accountants and other professionals in securities fraud cases.

---

15 15 U.S.C. Section 78r(a).
16 15 U.S.C. Section 78r(a).
17 15 U.S.C. Section 78r(c).

---

18 15 U.S.C. Section 78j(b).
19 17 C.F.R. Section 240.10b-5.

A New Statutory Obligation. Among other things, the act imposed a new statutory obligation on accountants. An auditor must use adequate procedures in an audit to detect any illegal acts of the company being audited. If something illegal is detected, the auditor must disclose it to the company's board of directors, the audit committee, or the SEC, depending on the circumstances.[20]

Scope of Liability. In terms of liability, the 1995 act provides that in most situations, a party is liable only for that proportion of damages for which he or she is responsible.[21] ● EXAMPLE #6 If an accountant actually participated in defrauding investors, he or she could be liable for the entire loss. If the accountant was not aware of the fraud, however, his or her liability could be proportionately less.●

Aiding and Abetting. The act also states that aiding and abetting a violation of the Securities Exchange Act of 1934 is a violation in itself. The SEC can enforce this provision by seeking an injunction or money damages against any person who knowingly aids and abets primary violators of the securities law. An accountant aids and abets when she or he is generally aware that she or he is participating in an activity that is improper and knowingly assists the activity. Silence may constitute aiding.
● EXAMPLE #7 Smith & Jones, an accounting firm, performs an audit for ABC Sales Company that is so inadequate as to constitute gross negligence. ABC uses the materials provided by Smith & Jones as part of a scheme to defraud investors. When the scheme is uncovered, the SEC can bring an action against Smith & Jones for aiding and abetting on the ground that the firm knew or should have known of the material misrepresentations that were in its audit and on which investors were likely to rely.●

POTENTIAL CRIMINAL LIABILITY OF ACCOUNTANTS

An accountant may be found criminally liable for violations of the Securities Act of 1933, the Securities Exchange Act of 1934, the Internal Revenue Code, and both state and federal criminal codes.

Liability under Securities Laws. Under both the 1933 act and the 1934 act, accountants may be subject to criminal penalties for *willful* violations—imprisonment of up to five years and/or a fine of up to $10,000 under the 1933 act and up to ten years and $100,000 under the 1934 act. Under the

Sarbanes-Oxley Act of 2002, for a securities filing that is accompanied by an accountant's false or misleading certified audit statement, the accountant may be fined up to $5 million, imprisoned up to twenty years, or both.

Liability under the Internal Revenue Code. The Internal Revenue Code makes aiding or assisting in the preparation of a false tax return a felony punishable by a fine of $100,000 ($500,000 in the case of a corporation) and imprisonment for up to three years.[22] Those who prepare tax returns for others may also face liability under the Internal Revenue Code. Note that a person does not have to be an accountant to be subject to liability for tax-preparer penalties. The Internal Revenue Code defines a tax preparer as any person who prepares for compensation, or who employs one or more persons to prepare for compensation, all or a substantial portion of a tax return or a claim for a tax refund.[23]

Under Section 6694,[24] the Internal Revenue Code imposes on the tax preparer a penalty of $250 per return for negligent understatement of the client's tax liability and a penalty of $1,000 for willful understatement of tax liability or reckless or intentional disregard of rules or regulations. A tax preparer may also be subject to penalties for failing to furnish the taxpayer with a copy of the return, failing to sign the return, or failing to furnish the appropriate tax identification numbers.[25]

In addition, the Internal Revenue Code imposes a penalty of $1,000 per document for aiding and abetting an individual's understatement of tax liability (the penalty is increased to $10,000 in corporate cases).[26] The tax preparer's liability is limited to one penalty per taxpayer per tax year. If this penalty is imposed, no penalty can be imposed under Section 6694 with respect to the same document.

Working Papers

Performing an audit for a client involves an accumulation of **working papers**—the various documents used and developed during the audit. These include notes, computations, memoranda, copies, and other papers that make up the work product of an accountant's services to a client. Under the common law, which in this instance has been codified in a number of states, working papers remain the accountant's

[20] 15 U.S.C. Section 78j-1.
[21] 15 U.S.C. Section 78u-4(g).

[22] 26 U.S.C. Section 7206(2).
[23] 26 U.S.C. Section 7701(a)(36).
[24] 26 U.S.C. Section 6694.
[25] 26 U.S.C. Section 6695.
[26] 26 U.S.C. Section 6701.

property. It is important for accountants to retain such records in the event that they need to defend against lawsuits for negligence or other actions in which their competence is challenged. But because an accountant's working papers reflect the client's financial situation, the client has a right of access to them. (On a client's request, an accountant must return to the client any of the client's records or journals, and failure to do so may result in liability.)

The client must give permission before working papers can be transferred to another accountant. The contents of working papers may not be disclosed without the client's permission or a valid court order. Disclosure will constitute a breach of the accountant's fiduciary duty to the client, and the client may initiate a malpractice suit on the ground of unauthorized disclosure. The accountant's best defense would be that the client gave permission for the papers' release.

Under Section 802(a)(1) of the Sarbanes-Oxley Act of 2002, accountants are required, in some circumstances, to maintain working papers relating to an audit or review for five years from the end of the fiscal period in which the audit or review was concluded. A knowing violation of this requirement will subject the accountant to a fine, imprisonment for up to ten years, or both.

Confidentiality and Privilege

Professionals are constrained by the ethical tenets of their professions to keep all communications with their clients confidential. The confidentiality of attorney-client communications is also protected by law, which confers a privilege on such communications. This privilege is granted because of the need for full disclosure to the attorney of the facts of a client's case. To encourage frankness, confidential attorney-client communications relating to representation are normally held in strictest confidence and safeguarded by statute. The attorney and his or her employees may not discuss the client's case with anyone—even under court order—without the client's permission. The client holds the privilege, and only the client may waive it. ● **EXAMPLE #8** Jane consults with Larry, an attorney, regarding her potential liability in an upcoming lawsuit. Jane discusses the suit with some of her co-workers and friends. By disclosing

what is otherwise privileged information to someone outside the privilege, Jane has waived it.●

In a few states, accountant-client communications are privileged by state statute. In these states, accountant-client communications may not be revealed even in court or in court-sanctioned proceedings without the client's permission. The majority of states, however, abide by the common law, which provides that, if a court so orders, an accountant must disclose information about his or her client to the court. Physicians and other professionals may similarly be compelled to disclose in court information given to them in confidence by patients or clients.

Professional-client communications—other than those between an attorney and his or her client—are not privileged under federal law. In cases involving federal law, state-provided rights to confidentiality of accountant-client communications are not recognized. ● **EXAMPLE #9** Greg, an accountant, has a client, Mary, who is involved in a case brought in a federal court against Mary by the Internal Revenue Service claiming that she filed false federal tax returns. In that case, in response to a court order, Greg must provide the information sought.●

Limiting Professionals' Liability

Accountants (and other professionals) can limit their liability to some extent by disclaiming it. Depending on the circumstances, a disclaimer that does not meet certain requirements will not be effective, and in some situations, a disclaimer may not be effective at all.

Professionals may be able to limit their liability for the misconduct of other professionals with whom they work by organizing their business as a professional corporation (P.C.) or a limited liability partnership (LLP). In some states, a professional who is a member of a P.C. is not personally liable for a co-member's misconduct unless he or she participated in it or supervised the member who acted wrongly. The innocent professional is liable only to the extent of his or her interest in the assets of the firm. This is also true for professionals who are partners in an LLP. P.C.s were discussed in detail in Chapter 25. LLPs were covered in Chapter 24.

Terms and Concepts

defalcation 651
due diligence 657
generally accepted accounting
   principles (GAAP) 651

generally accepted auditing
   standards (GAAS) 651

malpractice 652
working papers 660

| Chapter Summary | **Professional Liability** |

COMMON LAW LIABILITY	
Liability to Client (See pages 651–652.)	1. *Breach of contract*—An accountant or other professional who fails to perform according to his or her contractual obligations can be held liable for breach of contract and resulting damages. 2. *Negligence*—An accountant or other professional, in performance of his or her duties, must use the care, knowledge, and judgment generally used by professionals in the same or similar circumstances. Failure to do so is negligence. An accountant's violation of generally accepted accounting principles or generally accepted auditing standards is *prima facie* evidence of negligence. An accountant who reveals confidential information or the contents of working papers without the client's permission or a court order can be held liable for malpractice. 3. *Fraud*—Actual intent to misrepresent a material fact to a client, when the client relies on the misrepresentation, is fraud. Gross negligence in performance of duties is constructive fraud.
Liability to Third Parties (See pages 652–654.)	An accountant may be liable for negligence to any third person the accountant knows or should have known will benefit from the accountant's work. The standard for imposing this liability varies, but generally courts follow one of the following three rules: 1. *Ultramares rule*—Liability will be imposed only if the accountant is in privity, or near privity, with the third party. 2. *Restatement rule*—Liability will be imposed only if the third party's reliance is foreseen, or known, or if the third party is among a class of foreseen, or known, users. The majority of courts adopt this rule. 3. *"Reasonably foreseeable user" rule*—Liability will be imposed if the third party's use was reasonably foreseeable.
STATUTORY LIABILITY	
Sarbanes-Oxley Act of 2002 (See pages 654–656.)	See Exhibit 31–1 on page 655 for the duties of the Public Company Accounting Oversight Board and the provisions of the act on auditor independence. Additionally, under Section 802(a)(1) of the act, accountants are required, in some circumstances, to maintain working papers relating to an audit or review for five years from the end of the fiscal period in which the audit or review was concluded. A knowing violation of this requirement will subject the accountant to a fine, imprisonment for up to ten years, or both.
Securities Act of 1933, Section 11 (See pages 656–658.)	An accountant who makes a false statement or omits a material fact in audited financial statements required for registration of securities under the law may be liable to anyone who acquires securities covered by the registration statement. The accountant's defense is basically the use of due diligence and the reasonable belief that the work was complete and correct. The burden of proof is on the accountant. Willful violations of this act may be subject to criminal penalties.
Securities Act of 1933, Section 12(2) (See page 658.)	In some jurisdictions, an accountant may be liable for aiding and abetting the seller or offeror of securities when a prospectus or communication presented to an investor contained an untrue statement or omission of material fact. To be liable, the accountant must have known, or at least should have known, that an untrue statement or omission of material fact existed in the offer to sell the security.
Securities Exchange Act of 1934, Sections 10(b) and 18 (See pages 658–659.)	Accountants are held liable for false and misleading applications, reports, and documents required under the act. The burden is on the plaintiff, and the accountant has numerous defenses, including good faith and lack of knowledge that what was submitted was false. Willful violations of this act may be subject to criminal penalties.

Chapter Summary	Professional Liability—Continued
Internal Revenue Code (See page 660.)	1. Aiding or assisting in the preparation of a false tax return is a felony. Aiding and abetting an individual's understatement of tax liability is a separate crime. 2. Tax preparers who negligently or willfully understate a client's tax liability or who recklessly or intentionally disregard Internal Revenue Code regulations are subject to criminal penalties. 3. Tax preparers who fail to provide a taxpayer with a copy of the return, fail to sign the return, or fail to furnish the appropriate tax identification numbers may also be subject to criminal penalties.
Confidentiality and Privilege (See page 661.)	The confidentiality of attorney-client communications is privileged—that is, the attorney may not discuss the client's case with anyone, even under court order, without the client's permission. In general, other professional-client communications are not privileged and can be disclosed under court order. In a few states accountant-client communications are privileged, but the federal government does not recognize this privilege.

For Review

① Under what common law theories may professionals be liable to clients?

② What are the rules concerning an auditor's liability to third parties?

③ How might an accountant violate federal securities laws?

④ What crimes might an accountant commit under the Internal Revenue Code?

⑤ What constrains professionals to keep communications with their clients confidential?

Questions and Case Problems

31–1. *Ultramares* Rule. Larkin, Inc., retains Howard Perkins to manage its books and prepare its financial statements. Perkins, a certified public accountant, lives in Indiana and practices there. After twenty years, Perkins has become a bit bored with generally accepted accounting principles and has become creative in his accounting methods. Now, though, Perkins has a problem, as he is being sued by Molly Tucker, one of Larkin's creditors. Tucker alleges that Perkins either knew or should have known that Larkin's financial statements would be distributed to various individuals. Furthermore, she asserts that these financial statements were negligently prepared and seriously inaccurate. What are the consequences of Perkins's failure to adopt generally accepted accounting principles? Under the traditional *Ultramares* rule, can Tucker recover damages from Perkins? Explain.

31–2. Accountant's Liability to Third Parties and Public Policy. The accounting firm of Goldman, Walters, Johnson & Co. prepared financial statements for Lucy's Fashions, Inc. After reviewing the various financial statements, Happydays State Bank agreed to loan Lucy's Fashions $35,000 for expansion. When Lucy's Fashions declared bankruptcy under Chapter 11 six months later, Happydays State Bank promptly filed an action against Goldman, Walters, Johnson & Co., alleging negligent preparation of financial statements. Assuming that the court has abandoned the *Ultramares* approach, what is the result? What are the policy reasons for holding accountants liable to third parties with whom they are not in privity?

31–3. Accountant's Liability under Rule 10b-5. In early 1995, Bennett, Inc., offered a substantial number of new common shares to the public. Harvey Helms had a long-standing interest in Bennett because his grandfather had once been president of the company. On receiving a prospectus prepared and distributed by Bennett, Helms was dismayed by the pessimism it embodied. Helms decided to delay purchasing stock in the company. Later, Helms asserted that the prospectus prepared by the accountants was overly pessimistic and contained materially misleading statements. Discuss fully how successful Helms would be in bringing a cause of action under Rule 10b-5 against the accountants of Bennett, Inc.

31–4. Accountant's Liability to Third Parties. Toro Co. was a major supplier of equipment and credit to Summit Power

Equipment Distributors. Toro required audited reports from Summit to evaluate the distributor's financial condition. Summit supplied Toro with reports prepared by Krouse, Kern & Co., an accounting firm. The reports allegedly contained mistakes and omissions regarding Summit's financial condition. According to Toro, it extended and renewed large amounts of credit to Summit in reliance on the audited reports. Summit was unable to repay these amounts, and Toro brought a negligence action against the accounting firm and the individual accountants. Evidence produced at the trial showed that Krouse knew that the reports it furnished to Summit were to be used by Summit to induce Toro to extend credit, but no evidence was produced to show either a contractual relationship between Krouse and Toro or a link between these companies evidencing Krouse's understanding of Toro's actual reliance on the reports. The relevant state law follows the *Ultramares* rule. What was the result? [*Toro Co. v. Krouse, Kern & Co.,* 827 F.2d 155 (7th Cir. 1987)]

31–5. Accountant's Liability under Rule 10b-5. The accounting firm of Arthur Young & Co. was employed by DMI Furniture, Inc., to conduct a review of an audit prepared by Brown, Kraft & Co., certified public accountants, for Gillespie Furniture Co. DMI planned to purchase Gillespie and wished to determine its net worth. Arthur Young, by letter, advised DMI that Brown, Kraft had performed a high-quality audit and that Gillespie's inventory on the audit dates was fairly stated on the general ledger. Allegedly as a result of these representations, DMI went forward with its purchase of Gillespie. Subsequently, DMI charged Brown, Kraft & Co., Arthur Young, and Gillespie's former owners with violations of Section 10(b) of the Securities Exchange Act and SEC Rule 10b-5. DMI complained that Arthur Young's review had proved to be materially inaccurate and misleading, primarily because the inventory reflected in the balance sheet was grossly overstated. Arthur Young was charged "with acting recklessly in failing to detect, and thus failing to disclose, material omissions and reckless conduct on the part of Brown, Kraft, and in making affirmative misstatements in its letter" to DMI. Did DMI have a valid cause of action under either Section 10(b) or Rule 10b-5? Discuss. [*DMI Furniture, Inc. v. Brown, Kraft & Co.,* 644 F.Supp. 1517 (C.D.Cal. 1986)]

31–6. Attorney-Client Privilege. John and Christine Powell invested in a hotel-condominium development project. When legal problems with the project arose, the attorney representing the Powells was given access to certain documents and correspondence between the project developer, H. E. F. Partnership (HEF), and HEF's own legal counsel. When the project failed, the Powells sued HEF and others involved with the development scheme. In preparation for trial, the Powells sought discovery (see Chapter 2) of the documents and correspondence that HEF had released to them earlier. HEF refused to release the documents, alleging that they were confidential communications and protected under the attorney-client privilege. The Powells filed a motion with the court to compel discovery. How should the court rule on the motion to compel? Explain. [*Powell v. H.E.F. Partnership,* 835 F.Supp. 762 (D.Vt. 1993)]

31–7. Attorney's Duty of Care. Five members of the Hendry family owned property in Arlington, Virginia. When a dispute arose with a developer, the family hired attorney Francis Pelland to represent them. The mother wanted to continue to live in a house on the property. The son and the daughter wanted to preserve the trees on the property. The best interest of the two grandchildren was to maximize the property's long-term value. Pelland advised the family to settle with the developer for $1.5 million, which they did. Unhappy with this result, the Hendrys filed a suit in a federal district court against Pelland for breach of fiduciary duty, seeking in part a refund of the legal fees they had paid. On what basis might the court rule in the Hendrys' favor? Is there any basis on which a court could rule in Pelland's favor? [*Hendry v. Pelland,* 73 F.3d 397 (D.C.Cir. 1996)]

31–8. Accountant's Liability to Third Parties. In June 1993, Sparkomatic Corp. agreed to negotiate a sale of its Kenco Engineering division to Williams Controls, Inc. At the end of July, Sparkomatic asked its accountants, Parente, Randolph, Orlando, Carey & Associates, to audit Kenco's financial statements for the previous three years and to certify interim and closing balance sheets to be included with the closing documents for the sale. All of the parties knew that these documents would serve as a basis for setting the sale price. Within a few days, Williams signed an Asset Purchase Agreement that promised access to Parente's records with respect to Kenco. The sale closed in mid-August. In September, Williams was given the financial statements for Kenco's previous three years and the interim and closing balance sheets, all of which were certified by Parente. Williams's accountant found no errors in the closing balance sheet but did not review any of the other documents. The parties set a final purchase price. Later, however, Williams filed a suit in a federal district court against Parente, claiming negligent misrepresentation, among other things, in connection with Parente's preparation of the financial documents. Parente responded with a motion for summary judgment, asserting that the parties lacked privity. Under the *Restatement (Second) of Torts,* Section 552, how should the court rule? Explain. [*Williams Controls, Inc. v. Parente, Randolph, Orlando, Carey & Associates,* 39 F.Supp.2d 517 (M.D.Pa. 1999)]

CASE PROBLEM WITH SAMPLE ANSWER

31–9. In 1995, JTD Health Systems, Inc., hired Tammy Heiby as accounting coordinator. Apparently overwhelmed by the position, Heiby failed to make payroll tax payments to the Internal Revenue Service (IRS) in 1995 and 1996. Heiby tried to hide this failure by falsifying journal entries and writing three checks, manually, out of sequence, totaling $1.7 million, and payable to a bank, from JTD's cash account (to dispose of excess funds that should have been paid in taxes). JTD hired Pricewaterhouse Coopers, LLP, to review JTD's internal accounting procedures and audit JTD's financial statements for 1995. Coopers's inexperienced auditor was aware that the cash account had not been balanced in months and knew about the checks but never questioned them. The auditor instead mistakenly explained that the unbalanced account was due to changes in Medicaid/Medicare procedures and recommended no further investigation. In 1996, the IRS asked JTD to pay the unpaid taxes, plus interest and penalties. JTD filed a suit in an Ohio state court against Coopers, alleging negligence and breach of contract. Should Coopers be held liable to JTD on these grounds? Why or why not? [*JTD Health Systems, Inc. v. Pricewaterhouse Coopers, LLP*, 141 Ohio App.3d 280, 750 N.E.2d 1177 (Ohio App. 3 Dist. 2001)]

◗ To view a sample answer for this case problem, go to this book's Web site at **http://fundamentals.westbuslaw.com** and click on "Interactive Study Center."

31–10. Accountant's Liability under the Private Securities Litigation Reform Act. Solucorp Industries, Ltd., a corporation headquartered in New York, develops and markets products for use in environmental clean-ups. Solucorp's financial statements for the six months ending December 31, 1997, recognized $1.09 million in license fees payable by Smart International, Ltd. The fees comprised about 50 percent of Solucorp's revenue for the period. At the time, however, the parties had a license agreement only "in principle," and Smart had made only one payment of $150,000. Glenn Ohlhauser, an accountant asked to audit the statements, objected to the inclusion of the fees. In February 1998, Solucorp showed Ohlhauser a license agreement backdated to September 1997 but refused to provide any financial information about Smart. Ohlhauser issued an unqualified opinion on the 1997 statements, which were included with forms filed with the Securities and Exchange Commission (SEC). The SEC filed a suit in a federal district court against Ohlhauser and others. What might be the basis, in the Private Securities Litigation Reform Act, for the SEC's suit against Ohlhauser? What might be Ohlhauser's defense? Discuss. [*Securities and Exchange Commission v. Solucorp Industries, Ltd.*, 197 F.Supp.2d 4 (S.D.N.Y. 2002)]

A QUESTION OF ETHICS AND SOCIAL RESPONSIBILITY

31–11. Crawford, a certified public accountant, prepared a financial statement for Erps Construction Co., which was seeking a loan from the First National Bank of Bluefield. Crawford knew at the time he prepared the statement that the bank would rely on the statement in making its decision on whether to extend credit to Erps. The loan was made, and Erps defaulted. The bank sued Crawford, alleging that he had been professionally negligent in preparing the financial statement, on which the bank had relied in determining whether to give the construction company a loan. Crawford defended against the suit by asserting that he could not be liable to the bank because of lack of privity. The trial court ruled that in the absence of contractual privity between the parties, the bank could not recover from the accountant. On appeal, the appellate court adopted the rule enunciated by the *Restatement (Second) of Torts* in regard to a professional's liability to third parties. [*First National Bank of Bluefield v. Crawford*, 386 S.E.2d 310 (W.Va. 1989)]

1. What is the standard of an accountant's liability to third parties under the *Restatement (Second) of Torts?* What ethical reasoning underlies this standard?

2. Do you think that the standard of liability under the *Restatement* adequately balances the rights of accountants and the rights of third parties? Can you think of a fairer standard?

3. A few courts have adopted the principle that accountants should be liable for negligence to all persons who use and rely on their work products, provided that this use and reliance was foreseeable by the accountants at the time they prepared the documents relied on. Does such a standard of liability impose too great a burden on accountants and accounting firms? Why or why not?

VIDEO QUESTION

31–12. Go to this text's Web site at **http://fundamentals.westbuslaw.com** and click on "Video Questions." Select "Chapter 31" and view the video titled *Accountant's Liability.* Then answer the following questions:

1. Should Ray prepare a financial statement that values a list of assets provided by the advertising firm without verifying that the firm actually owns these assets?

2. Discuss whether Ray is "in privity" with the company interested in buying Laura's advertising firm.

3. Under the *Ultramares* rule, to whom does Ray owe a duty?

4. Assume that Laura in the video did not tell Ray that she intended to give the financial statement to the potential acquiror. Would this fact change Ray's liability under the *Ultramares* rule?

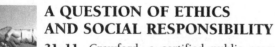

PROFESSIONAL LIABILITY

For updated links to resources available on the Web, as well as other materials, visit this text's Web site at

http://fundamentals.westbuslaw.com

The Web site for the Financial Accounting Standards Board can be found at

http://www.fasb.org

For information on the accounting profession, including links to the Sarbanes-Oxley Act of 2002 and articles on its impact on the accounting profession, go to the Web site of the American Institute of Certified Public Accountants at

http://www.aicpa.org

Paul R. Rice, a law professor at American University's Washington College of Law, maintains a Web site containing a large number of articles on attorney-client privilege. Go to

http://www.acprivilege.com

Online Legal Research

Go to the *Fundamentals of Business Law* home page at **http://fundamentals. westbuslaw.com**. Select "Interactive Study Center" and then click on "Chapter 31." There you will find the following Internet research exercises that you can perform to learn more about topics covered in this chapter.

Activity 31-1: LEGAL PERSPECTIVE—The Sarbanes-Oxley Act of 2002
Activity 31-2: MANAGEMENT PERSPECTIVE—Avoiding Legal Liability

Before the Test

Go to the *Fundamentals of Business Law* home page at **http://fundamentals. westbuslaw.com**. Click on "Interactive Quizzes." You will find at least twenty interactive questions relating to this chapter.

Westlaw® Campus

If your textbook provided for a subscription to Westlaw® Campus, or if you have otherwise purchased access to the Westlaw Campus database, you can access any of the cases presented or cited in this chapter by using your Westlaw Campus account.

KPMG, LLP v. Securities and Exchange Commission

INTRODUCTION

In Chapter 31, we explained that in performing their services, accountants must comply with generally accepted auditing standards (GAAS). In this *Focus on Legal Reasoning,* we examine *KPMG, LLP v. Securities and Exchange Commission,*[1] a decision concerned with "present and future" violations of GAAS.

CASE BACKGROUND

In January 1995, to launch a separate entity to provide financial and business consulting services, KPMG, LLP (then known as KPMG Peat Marwick, LLP), entered into an agreement with KPMG BayMark, LLC (BayMark), and its subsidiaries, known as KPMG BayMark

1. 289 F.3d 109 (D.C.Cir. 2002).

Strategies (Strategies). As part of the agreement, KPMG lent $100,000 to each of BayMark's founders, including Edward Olson. Strategies subsequently entered into an agreement with PORTA, a KPMG client. Under this agreement, Olson was made PORTA's president and chief operating officer and Strategies was to be paid a fee contingent in part on PORTA's earnings.

In 1997, the SEC determined that KPMG violated SEC Rule 2-02(b) of Regulation S-X.[2] This rule mandates compliance with GAAS, which require accountants to be independent from their clients. The SEC found that Rule 302 of the American Institute of Certified Public Accountants (AICPA) proscribed the contingent fee, and that

2. 17 C.F.R. Section 210.2-02.

this fee and the Olson loan impaired KPMG's independence. The SEC also concluded that KPMG caused PORTA to violate Section 13(a) of the Securities Exchange Act of 1934 and SEC Rule 13a-1, which require reports to be certified by *independent* public accountants.[3]

The SEC issued an order to KPMG to "cease and desist" from committing present or future violations of Rule 2-02, or causing present or future violations of Section 13(a), by having any transaction, interest, or relationship that impairs its independence. KPMG asked the U.S. Court of Appeals for the District of Columbia Circuit to review the order, arguing in part that it was "overbroad."

3. 15 U.S.C. Section 78m(a) and 17 C.F.R. Section 240.13a-1.

MAJORITY OPINION

ROGERS, Circuit Judge:

* * * *

KPMG contends that the cease-and-desist order is overbroad because it bears no reasonable relation to the violations found. * * *

Section 21C of [the Securities Exchange Act] authorizes the entry of a cease-and-desist order to prohibit "*any* future violation of the same provision" found to have been violated in the instant case. The provisions at issue are Rule 2-02(b) of Regulation S-X, Section 13(a) of the Exchange Act, and Rule 13a-1 * * *. There is, consequently, no "sweeping order to obey the law" as KPMG contends, because the terms of the order are limited to these provisions. Further, the [Securities and Exchange] Commission stated that the order "extends only to violative acts the threat of which in the future is indicated because of their similarity or relation to those [past] unlawful acts." The order thus extends only to a subset of the violations comprehended by the rules and statutory provisions involved, namely those that are independence related. By concluding that the seriousness of KPMG's misconduct, combined with the flaws in its mode of assessing independence, created a serious risk of future independence-impairing relationships beyond the two circumstances at issue, the Commission justified an order aimed at preventing violations flowing from a broader array of independence impairments than the precise ones found. In so doing, it cannot be said that the order has no reasonable relation to the unlawful practices found to exist. * * *

Neither is there any requirement on the part of the Commission to tailor its order more narrowly to specific types of violations of the provisions involved. The "any future violation" language in Section 21C makes this clear and the "reasonable relationship" requirement does not impose such a limit. As the [United States] Supreme Court observed in [*Federal Trade Commission*] *v. Ruberoid Co.,* 343 U.S. 470, 72 S.Ct. 800, 96 L.Ed. 1081 (1952), cease-and-desist authority is "not limited to prohibiting the illegal practice in the precise form in which it is found to have existed in the past. If the Commission is to attain the objectives Congress envisioned, it cannot be required to confine its road block to the narrow lane the transgressor has traveled; it must be allowed effectively to close all roads to the prohibited goal, so that its order may not be by-passed with impunity." What KPMG would appear to suggest is required—namely an order so narrow that in the absence of copy-cat violations there would be no possibility of a violation of the order—ignores the expansive language used by Congress. Given the Congressional purpose of empowering the Commission to curb a wider range of securities violations in an effort to combat recidivism, the Commission could reasonably interpret Section 21C as empowering it to issue orders limited only by the specific provisions of law or regulations found to have been violated.

Consequently, the record belies KPMG's contentions that the order bears no reasonable relation to the violations found * * *. The judgment underlying the Commission's decision that the independence violations were of an order of seriousness that

(Continued)

KPMG failed to appreciate is the type of agency expertise to which courts defer.

* * * *

Accordingly, * * * [w]e * * * reject KPMG's contentions that the order is overbroad[.] * * * We therefore deny KPMG's petition for review.

DISSENTING OPINION
RANDOLPH, Circuit Judge, dissenting:

* * * *

The SEC's contingent fee finding was clearly erroneous. On its face, AICPA's Rule 302 covers not all services * * * , but only professional services. The SEC's interpretation of the rule receives no deference because we have no hint that Congress intended the SEC to fill in gaps left by AICPA. It would be another thing entirely if the SEC had its own rule on contingent fees, but all the agency has is its general requirement that accountants be independent.

* * * *

In light of the SEC's errors in finding a contingent fee arrangement * * * , the cease and desist order cannot be sustained. We should have vacated the order and sent the case back so the SEC could decide whether it still wants to issue the order without [this leg] of the table.

LEGAL REASONING AND ANALYSIS

1 **Legal Reasoning.** On what point do the majority and dissent disagree in the KPMG case? With whom do you agree, and why?

2 **Legal Analysis.** The majority cites, in its opinion, *Federal Trade Commission v. Ruberoid Co.*, 343 U.S. 470, 72 S.Ct. 800, 96 L.Ed. 1081 (1952) (see the *Accessing the Internet* feature at the end of Chapter 2 for instructions on how to access opinions of the Supreme Court of the United States). How do the facts, issues, and holdings in that case compare to the facts and issues in the KPMG case? Does the principle for which the *Ruberoid* case is cited support the position of the majority in the KPMG case?

3 **Social Consideration.** Should liability in this case be extended to anyone beyond KPMG? Why or why not? If so, to whom?

4 **Implications for Accountants.** What does the holding in this case say to accountants who want to actively participate in the management of a client's firm?

5 **Case Briefing Assignment.** Using the guidelines for briefing cases given in Appendix A of this text, brief the KPMG case.

This text's Web site, at **http://fundamentals.westbuslaw.com**, offers links to West's Court Case Updates, as well as to other online research sources. You can also locate court cases at the Web sites listed in the *Accessing the Internet* section at the end of Chapter 2.

The AICPA maintains a Web site, at **http://www.aicpa.org/yellow/index.htm**, that contains links to other sites related to auditing and accounting, including some of those by or concerning Federal Reserve banks, securities exchanges, state and federal governments, and state CPA associations.

APPENDIX A

How to Brief Cases and Analyze Case Problems

How to Brief Cases

To fully understand the law with respect to business, you need to be able to read and understand court decisions. To make this task easier, you can use a method of case analysis that is called *briefing*. There is a fairly standard procedure that you can follow when you "brief" any court case. You must first read the case opinion carefully. When you feel you understand the case, you can prepare a brief of it.

Although the format of the brief may vary, typically it will present the essentials of the case under headings such as those listed below.

1. **Citation.** Give the full citation for the case, including the name of the case, the date it was decided, and the court that decided it.

2. **Facts.** Briefly indicate (a) the reasons for the lawsuit; (b) the identity and arguments of the plaintiff(s) and defendant(s), respectively; and (c) the lower court's decision—if appropriate.

3. **Issue.** Concisely phrase, in the form of a question, the essential issue before the court. (If more than one issue is involved, you may have two—or even more—questions here.)

4. **Decision.** Indicate here—with a "yes" or "no," if possible—the court's answer to the question (or questions) in the *Issue* section above.

5. **Reason.** Summarize as briefly as possible the reasons given by the court for its decision (or decisions) and the case or statutory law relied on by the court in arriving at its decision.

For an example of the format used in briefing cases, refer back to the briefed version of the sample court case that was presented in the appendix following Chapter 1 in Exhibit 1A–3.

How to Analyze Case Problems

In addition to learning how to brief cases, students of business law also find it helpful to know how to analyze case problems. Part of the study of business law usually involves analyzing case problems, such as those included in this text at the end of each chapter.

For each case problem in this book, we provide the relevant background and facts of the lawsuit and the issue before the court. When you are assigned one of these problems, your job will be to determine how the court should decide the issue and why. In other words, you will need to engage in legal analysis and reasoning. Here we offer some suggestions on how to make this task less daunting. We begin by presenting a sample problem:

> While Janet Lawson, a famous pianist, was shopping in Quality Market, she slipped and fell on a wet floor in one of the aisles. The floor had recently been mopped by one of the store's employees, but there were no signs warning customers that the floor in that area was wet. As a result of the fall, Lawson injured her right arm and was unable to perform piano concerts for the next six months. Had she been able to perform the scheduled concerts, she would have earned approximately $60,000 over that period of time. Lawson sued Quality Market for this amount, plus another $10,000 in medical expenses. She claimed that the store's failure to warn customers of the wet floor constituted negligence and therefore the market was liable for her injuries. Will the court agree with Lawson? Discuss.

UNDERSTAND THE FACTS

This may sound obvious, but before you can analyze or apply the relevant law to a specific set of facts, you must clearly understand those facts. In other words, you should read through the case problem carefully and more than once, if necessary, to make sure you understand the identity of the plaintiff(s) and defendant(s) in the case and the progression of events that led to the lawsuit.

In the sample case just given, the identity of the parties is fairly obvious. Janet Lawson is the one bringing the suit; therefore, she is the plaintiff. Quality Market, against whom she is bringing the suit, is the defendant. Some of the case problems you work on may have multiple plaintiffs or defendants. Often, it is helpful to use abbreviations for the parties. To indicate a reference to a plaintiff, for example, the pi symbol—π—is often used, and a defendant is denoted by a delta—Δ—a triangle.

The events leading to the lawsuit are also fairly straightforward. Lawson slipped and fell on a wet floor, and she contends that Quality Market should be liable for her injuries because it was negligent in not posting a sign warning customers of the wet floor.

When you are working on case problems, realize that the facts should be accepted as they are given. For example, in our sample problem, it should be accepted that the floor was wet and that there was no sign. In other words, avoid making conjectures, such as "Maybe the floor wasn't too wet," or "Maybe an employee was getting a sign to put up," or "Maybe someone stole the sign." Questioning the facts as they are presented only adds confusion to your analysis.

LEGAL ANALYSIS AND REASONING

Once you understand the facts given in the case problem, you can begin to analyze the case. The IRAC method is a helpful tool to use in the legal analysis and reasoning process. IRAC is an acronym for Issue, Rule, Application, Conclusion. Applying this method to our sample problem would involve the following steps:

1. First, you need to decide what legal **issue** is involved in the case. In our sample case, the basic issue is whether Quality Market's failure to warn customers of the wet floor constituted negligence. As discussed in Chapter 4, negligence is a *tort*—a civil wrong. In a tort lawsuit, the plaintiff seeks to be compensated for another's wrongful act. A defendant will be deemed negligent if he or she breached a duty of care owed to the plaintiff and the breach of that duty caused the plaintiff to suffer harm.

2. Once you have identified the issue, the next step is to determine what **rule of law** applies to the issue. To make this determination, you will want to review carefully the text of the chapter in which the problem

appears to find the relevant rule of law. Our sample case involves the tort of negligence, covered in Chapter 4. The applicable rule of law is the tort law principle that business owners owe a duty to exercise reasonable care to protect their customers ("business invitees"). Reasonable care, in this context, includes either removing—or warning customers of—*foreseeable* risks about which the owner *knew* or *should have known*. Business owners need not warn customers of "open and obvious" risks, however. If a business owner breaches this duty of care (fails to exercise the appropriate degree of care toward customers), and the breach of duty causes a customer to be injured, the business owner will be liable to the customer for the customer's injuries.

3. The next—and usually the most difficult—step in analyzing case problems is the **application** of the relevant rule of law to the specific facts of the case you are studying. In our sample problem, applying the tort law principle just discussed presents few difficulties. An employee of the store had mopped the floor in the aisle where Lawson slipped and fell, but no sign was present indicating that the floor was wet. That a customer might fall on a wet floor is clearly a foreseeable risk. Therefore, the failure to warn customers about the wet floor was a breach of the duty of care owed by the business owner to the store's customers.

4. Once you have completed step 3 in the IRAC method, you should be ready to draw your **conclusion**. In our sample case, Quality Market is liable to Lawson for her injuries, because the market's breach of its duty of care caused Lawson's injuries.

The fact patterns in the case problems presented in this text are not always as simple as those presented in our sample problem. Often, for example, there may be more than one plaintiff or defendant. There also may be more than one issue involved in a case and more than one applicable rule of law. Furthermore, in some case problems the facts may indicate that the general rule of law should not apply. For example, suppose a store employee advised Lawson not to walk on the floor in the aisle because it was wet, but Lawson decided to walk on it anyway. This fact could alter the outcome of the case because the store could then raise the defense of assumption of risk (see Chapter 4). Nonetheless, a careful review of the chapter should always provide you with the knowledge you need to analyze the problem thoroughly and arrive at accurate conclusions.

APPENDIX B
The Constitution of the United States

PREAMBLE

We the People of the United States, in Order to form a more perfect Union, establish Justice, insure domestic Tranquility, provide for the common defence, promote the general Welfare, and secure the Blessings of Liberty to ourselves and our Posterity, do ordain and establish this Constitution for the United States of America.

ARTICLE I

Section 1. All legislative Powers herein granted shall be vested in a Congress of the United States, which shall consist of a Senate and House of Representatives.

Section 2. The House of Representatives shall be composed of Members chosen every second Year by the People of the several States, and the Electors in each State shall have the Qualifications requisite for Electors of the most numerous Branch of the State Legislature.

No Person shall be a Representative who shall not have attained to the Age of twenty five Years, and been seven Years a Citizen of the United States, and who shall not, when elected, be an Inhabitant of that State in which he shall be chosen.

Representatives and direct Taxes shall be apportioned among the several States which may be included within this Union, according to their respective Numbers, which shall be determined by adding to the whole Number of free Persons, including those bound to Service for a Term of Years, and excluding Indians not taxed, three fifths of all other Persons. The actual Enumeration shall be made within three Years after the first Meeting of the Congress of the United States, and within every subsequent Term of ten Years, in such Manner as they shall by Law direct. The Number of Representatives shall not exceed one for every thirty Thousand, but each State shall have at Least one Representative; and until such enumeration shall be made, the State of New Hampshire shall be entitled to chuse three, Massachusetts eight, Rhode Island and Providence Plantations one, Connecticut five, New York six, New Jersey four, Pennsylvania eight, Delaware one, Maryland six, Virginia ten, North Carolina five, South Carolina five, and Georgia three.

When vacancies happen in the Representation from any State, the Executive Authority thereof shall issue Writs of Election to fill such Vacancies.

The House of Representatives shall chuse their Speaker and other Officers; and shall have the sole Power of Impeachment.

Section 3. The Senate of the United States shall be composed of two Senators from each State, chosen by the Legislature thereof, for six Years; and each Senator shall have one Vote.

Immediately after they shall be assembled in Consequence of the first Election, they shall be divided as equally as may be into three Classes. The Seats of the Senators of the first Class shall be vacated at the Expiration of the second Year, of the second Class at the Expiration of the fourth Year, and of the third Class at the Expiration of the sixth Year, so that one third may be chosen every second Year; and if Vacancies happen by Resignation, or otherwise, during the Recess of the Legislature of any State, the Executive thereof may make temporary Appointments until the next Meeting of the Legislature, which shall then fill such Vacancies.

No Person shall be a Senator who shall not have attained to the Age of thirty Years, and been nine Years a Citizen of the United States, and who shall not, when elected, be an Inhabitant of that State for which he shall be chosen.

The Vice President of the United States shall be President of the Senate, but shall have no Vote, unless they be equally divided.

The Senate shall chuse their other Officers, and also a President pro tempore, in the Absence of the Vice President, or when he shall exercise the Office of President of the United States.

The Senate shall have the sole Power to try all Impeachments. When sitting for that Purpose, they shall be on Oath or Affirmation. When the President of the United States is tried, the Chief Justice shall preside: And no Person shall be convicted without the Concurrence of two thirds of the Members present.

Judgment in Cases of Impeachment shall not extend further than to removal from Office, and disqualification to hold and enjoy any Office of honor, Trust, or Profit under the United States: but the Party convicted shall nevertheless be liable and subject to Indictment, Trial, Judgment, and Punishment, according to Law.

Section 4. The Times, Places and Manner of holding Elections for Senators and Representatives, shall be prescribed in each State by the Legislature thereof; but the Congress may at any time by Law make or alter such Regulations, except as to the Places of chusing Senators.

The Congress shall assemble at least once in every Year, and such Meeting shall be on the first Monday in December, unless they shall by Law appoint a different Day.

Section 5. Each House shall be the Judge of the Elections, Returns, and Qualifications of its own Members, and a Majority of each shall constitute a Quorum to do Business; but a smaller Number may adjourn from day to day, and may be authorized to compel the Attendance of absent Members, in such Manner, and under such Penalties as each House may provide.

Each House may determine the Rules of its Proceedings, punish its Members for disorderly Behavior, and, with the Concurrence of two thirds, expel a Member.

Each House shall keep a Journal of its Proceedings, and from time to time publish the same, excepting such Parts as may in their Judgment require Secrecy; and the Yeas and Nays of the Members of either House on any question shall, at the Desire of one fifth of those Present, be entered on the Journal.

Neither House, during the Session of Congress, shall, without the Consent of the other, adjourn for more than three days, nor to any other Place than that in which the two Houses shall be sitting.

Section 6. The Senators and Representatives shall receive a Compensation for their Services, to be ascertained by Law, and paid out of the Treasury of the United States. They shall in all Cases, except Treason, Felony and Breach of the Peace, be privileged from Arrest during their Attendance at the Session of their respective Houses, and in going to and returning from the same; and for any Speech or Debate in either House, they shall not be questioned in any other Place.

No Senator or Representative shall, during the Time for which he was elected, be appointed to any civil Office under the Authority of the United States, which shall have been created, or the Emoluments whereof shall have been increased during such time; and no Person holding any Office under the United States, shall be a Member of either House during his Continuance in Office.

Section 7. All Bills for raising Revenue shall originate in the House of Representatives; but the Senate may propose or concur with Amendments as on other Bills.

Every Bill which shall have passed the House of Representatives and the Senate, shall, before it become a Law, be presented to the President of the United States; If he approve he shall sign it, but if not he shall return it, with his Objections to the House in which it shall have originated, who shall enter the Objections at large on their Journal, and proceed to reconsider it. If after such Reconsideration two thirds of that House shall agree to pass the Bill, it shall be sent together with the Objections, to the other House, by which it shall likewise be reconsidered, and if approved by two thirds of that House, it shall become a Law.

But in all such Cases the Votes of both Houses shall be determined by Yeas and Nays, and the Names of the Persons voting for and against the Bill shall be entered on the Journal of each House respectively. If any Bill shall not be returned by the President within ten Days (Sundays excepted) after it shall have been presented to him, the Same shall be a Law, in like Manner as if he had signed it, unless the Congress by their Adjournment prevent its Return in which Case it shall not be a Law.

Every Order, Resolution, or Vote, to which the Concurrence of the Senate and House of Representatives may be necessary (except on a question of Adjournment) shall be presented to the President of the United States; and before the Same shall take Effect, shall be approved by him, or being disapproved by him, shall be repassed by two thirds of the Senate and House of Representatives, according to the Rules and Limitations prescribed in the Case of a Bill.

Section 8. The Congress shall have Power To lay and collect Taxes, Duties, Imposts and Excises, to pay the Debts and provide for the common Defence and general Welfare of the United States; but all Duties, Imposts and Excises shall be uniform throughout the United States;

To borrow Money on the credit of the United States;

To regulate Commerce with foreign Nations, and among the several States, and with the Indian Tribes;

To establish an uniform Rule of Naturalization, and uniform Laws on the subject of Bankruptcies throughout the United States;

To coin Money, regulate the Value thereof, and of foreign Coin, and fix the Standard of Weights and Measures;

To provide for the Punishment of counterfeiting the Securities and current Coin of the United States;

To establish Post Offices and post Roads;

To promote the Progress of Science and useful Arts, by securing for limited Times to Authors and Inventors the exclusive Right to their respective Writings and Discoveries;

To constitute Tribunals inferior to the supreme Court;

To define and punish Piracies and Felonies committed on the high Seas, and Offenses against the Law of Nations;

To declare War, grant Letters of Marque and Reprisal, and make Rules concerning Captures on Land and Water;

To raise and support Armies, but no Appropriation of Money to that Use shall be for a longer Term than two Years;

To provide and maintain a Navy;

To make Rules for the Government and Regulation of the land and naval Forces;

To provide for calling forth the Militia to execute the Laws of the Union, suppress Insurrections and repel Invasions;

To provide for organizing, arming, and disciplining, the Militia, and for governing such Part of them as may be employed in the Service of the United States, reserving to the States respectively, the Appointment of the Officers, and the Authority of training the Militia according to the discipline prescribed by Congress;

To exercise exclusive Legislation in all Cases whatsoever, over such District (not exceeding ten Miles square) as may, by Cession of particular States, and the Acceptance of Congress, become the Seat of the Government of the United States, and to exercise like Authority over all Places purchased by the Consent of the Legislature of the State in which the Same shall be, for the Erection of Forts, Magazines, Arsenals, dock-Yards, and other needful Buildings;—And

To make all Laws which shall be necessary and proper for carrying into Execution the foregoing Powers, and all other Powers vested by this Constitution in the Government of the United States, or in any Department or Officer thereof.

Section 9. The Migration or Importation of such Persons as any of the States now existing shall think proper to admit, shall not be prohibited by the Congress prior to the Year one thousand eight hundred and eight, but a Tax or duty may be imposed on such Importation, not exceeding ten dollars for each Person.

The privilege of the Writ of Habeas Corpus shall not be suspended, unless when in Cases of Rebellion or Invasion the public Safety may require it.

No Bill of Attainder or ex post facto Law shall be passed.

No Capitation, or other direct, Tax shall be laid, unless in Proportion to the Census or Enumeration herein before directed to be taken.

No Tax or Duty shall be laid on Articles exported from any State.

No Preference shall be given by any Regulation of Commerce or Revenue to the Ports of one State over those of another: nor shall Vessels bound to, or from, one State be obliged to enter, clear, or pay Duties in another.

No Money shall be drawn from the Treasury, but in Consequence of Appropriations made by Law; and a regular Statement and Account of the Receipts and Expenditures of all public Money shall be published from time to time.

No Title of Nobility shall be granted by the United States: And no Person holding any Office of Profit or Trust under them, shall, without the Consent of the Congress, accept of any present, Emolument, Office, or Title, of any kind whatever, from any King, Prince, or foreign State.

Section 10. No State shall enter into any Treaty, Alliance, or Confederation; grant Letters of Marque and Reprisal; coin Money; emit Bills of Credit; make any Thing but gold and silver Coin a Tender in Payment of Debts; pass any Bill of Attainder, ex post facto Law, or Law impairing the Obligation of Contracts, or grant any Title of Nobility.

No State shall, without the Consent of the Congress, lay any Imposts or Duties on Imports or Exports, except what may be absolutely necessary for executing its inspection Laws: and the net Produce of all Duties and Imposts, laid by any State on Imports or Exports, shall be for the Use of the Treasury of the United States; and all such Laws shall be subject to the Revision and Controul of the Congress.

No State shall, without the Consent of Congress, lay any Duty of Tonnage, keep Troops, or Ships of War in time of Peace, enter into any Agreement or Compact with another State, or with a foreign Power, or engage in War, unless actually invaded, or in such imminent Danger as will not admit of delay.

ARTICLE II

Section 1. The executive Power shall be vested in a President of the United States of America. He shall hold his Office during the Term of four Years, and, together with the Vice President, chosen for the same Term, be elected, as follows:

Each State shall appoint, in such Manner as the Legislature thereof may direct, a Number of Electors, equal to the whole Number of Senators and Representatives to which the State may be entitled in the Congress; but no Senator or Representative, or Person holding an Office of Trust or Profit under the United States, shall be appointed an Elector.

The Electors shall meet in their respective States, and vote by Ballot for two Persons, of whom one at least shall not be an Inhabitant of the same State with themselves. And they shall make a List of all the Persons voted for, and of the Number of Votes for each; which List they shall sign and certify, and transmit sealed to the Seat of the Government of the United States, directed to the President of the Senate. The President of the Senate shall, in the Presence of the Senate and House of Representatives, open all the Certificates, and the Votes shall then be counted. The Person having the greatest Number of Votes shall be the President, if such Number be a Majority of the whole Number of Electors appointed; and if there be more than one who have such Majority, and have an equal Number of Votes, then the House of Representatives shall immediately chuse by Ballot one of them for President; and if no Person have a Majority, then from the five highest on the List the said House shall in like Manner chuse the President. But in chusing the President, the Votes shall be taken by States, the Representation from each State having one Vote; A quorum for this Purpose shall consist of a Member or Members from two thirds of the States, and a Majority of all the States shall be necessary to a Choice. In every Case, after the Choice of the President, the Person having the greater Number of Votes of the Electors shall be the Vice President. But if there should remain two or more who have equal Votes, the Senate shall chuse from them by Ballot the Vice President.

The Congress may determine the Time of chusing the Electors, and the Day on which they shall give their Votes; which Day shall be the same throughout the United States.

No person except a natural born Citizen, or a Citizen of the United States, at the time of the Adoption of this Constitution, shall be eligible to the Office of President; neither shall any Person be eligible to that Office who shall not have attained to the Age of thirty five Years, and been fourteen Years a Resident within the United States.

In Case of the Removal of the President from Office, or of his Death, Resignation or Inability to discharge the Powers and Duties of the said Office, the same shall devolve on the Vice President, and the Congress may by Law provide for the Case of Removal, Death, Resignation or Inability, both of the President and Vice President, declaring what Officer shall then act as

President, and such Officer shall act accordingly, until the Disability be removed, or a President shall be elected.

The President shall, at stated Times, receive for his Services, a Compensation, which shall neither be increased nor diminished during the Period for which he shall have been elected, and he shall not receive within that Period any other Emolument from the United States, or any of them.

Before he enter on the Execution of his Office, he shall take the following Oath or Affirmation: "I do solemnly swear (or affirm) that I will faithfully execute the Office of President of the United States, and will to the best of my Ability, preserve, protect and defend the Constitution of the United States."

Section 2.   The President shall be Commander in Chief of the Army and Navy of the United States, and of the Militia of the several States, when called into the actual Service of the United States; he may require the Opinion, in writing, of the principal Officer in each of the executive Departments, upon any Subject relating to the Duties of their respective Offices, and he shall have Power to grant Reprieves and Pardons for Offenses against the United States, except in Cases of Impeachment.

He shall have Power, by and with the Advice and Consent of the Senate to make Treaties, provided two thirds of the Senators present concur; and he shall nominate, and by and with the Advice and Consent of the Senate, shall appoint Ambassadors, other public Ministers and Consuls, Judges of the supreme Court, and all other Officers of the United States, whose Appointments are not herein otherwise provided for, and which shall be established by Law; but the Congress may by Law vest the Appointment of such inferior Officers, as they think proper, in the President alone, in the Courts of Law, or in the Heads of Departments.

The President shall have Power to fill up all Vacancies that may happen during the Recess of the Senate, by granting Commissions which shall expire at the End of their next Session.

Section 3.   He shall from time to time give to the Congress Information of the State of the Union, and recommend to their Consideration such Measures as he shall judge necessary and expedient; he may, on extraordinary Occasions, convene both Houses, or either of them, and in Case of Disagreement between them, with Respect to the Time of Adjournment, he may adjourn them to such Time as he shall think proper; he shall receive Ambassadors and other public Ministers; he shall take Care that the Laws be faithfully executed, and shall Commission all the Officers of the United States.

Section 4.   The President, Vice President and all civil Officers of the United States, shall be removed from Office on Impeachment for, and Conviction of, Treason, Bribery, or other high Crimes and Misdemeanors.

ARTICLE III

Section 1.   The judicial Power of the United States, shall be vested in one supreme Court, and in such inferior Courts as the Congress may from time to time ordain and establish. The Judges, both of the supreme and inferior Courts, shall hold their Offices during good Behaviour, and shall, at stated Times, receive for their Services a Compensation, which shall not be diminished during their Continuance in Office.

Section 2.   The judicial Power shall extend to all Cases, in Law and Equity, arising under this Constitution, the Laws of the United States, and Treaties made, or which shall be made, under their Authority;—to all Cases affecting Ambassadors, other public Ministers and Consuls;—to all Cases of admiralty and maritime Jurisdiction;—to Controversies to which the United States shall be a Party;—to Controversies between two or more States;—between a State and Citizens of another State;—between Citizens of different States;—between Citizens of the same State claiming Lands under Grants of different States, and between a State, or the Citizens thereof, and foreign States, Citizens or Subjects.

In all Cases affecting Ambassadors, other public Ministers and Consuls, and those in which a State shall be a Party, the supreme Court shall have original Jurisdiction. In all the other Cases before mentioned, the supreme Court shall have appellate Jurisdiction, both as to Law and Fact, with such Exceptions, and under such Regulations as the Congress shall make.

The Trial of all Crimes, except in Cases of Impeachment, shall be by Jury; and such Trial shall be held in the State where the said Crimes shall have been committed; but when not committed within any State, the Trial shall be at such Place or Places as the Congress may by Law have directed.

Section 3.   Treason against the United States, shall consist only in levying War against them, or, in adhering to their Enemies, giving them Aid and Comfort. No Person shall be convicted of Treason unless on the Testimony of two Witnesses to the same overt Act, or on Confession in open Court.

The Congress shall have Power to declare the Punishment of Treason, but no Attainder of Treason shall work Corruption of Blood, or Forfeiture except during the Life of the Person attainted.

ARTICLE IV

Section 1.   Full Faith and Credit shall be given in each State to the public Acts, Records, and judicial Proceedings of every other State. And the Congress may by general Laws prescribe the Manner in which such Acts, Records and Proceedings shall be proved, and the Effect thereof.

Section 2.   The Citizens of each State shall be entitled to all Privileges and Immunities of Citizens in the several States.

A Person charged in any State with Treason, Felony, or other Crime, who shall flee from Justice, and be found in another State, shall on Demand of the executive Authority of the State from which he fled, be delivered up, to be removed to the State having Jurisdiction of the Crime.

No Person held to Service or Labour in one State, under the Laws thereof, escaping into another, shall, in Consequence of any Law or Regulation therein, be discharged from such Service or Labour, but shall be delivered up on Claim of the Party to whom such Service or Labour may be due.

Section 3.   New States may be admitted by the Congress into this Union; but no new State shall be formed or erected within the Jurisdiction of any other State; nor any State be formed by the Junction of two or more States, or Parts of States, without the Consent of the Legislatures of the States concerned as well as of the Congress.

The Congress shall have Power to dispose of and make all needful Rules and Regulations respecting the Territory or other Property belonging to the United States; and nothing in this Constitution shall be so construed as to Prejudice any Claims of the United States, or of any particular State.

Section 4. The United States shall guarantee to every State in this Union a Republican Form of Government, and shall protect each of them against Invasion; and on Application of the Legislature, or of the Executive (when the Legislature cannot be convened) against domestic Violence.

ARTICLE V

The Congress, whenever two thirds of both Houses shall deem it necessary, shall propose Amendments to this Constitution, or, on the Application of the Legislatures of two thirds of the several States, shall call a Convention for proposing Amendments, which, in either Case, shall be valid to all Intents and Purposes, as part of this Constitution, when ratified by the Legislatures of three fourths of the several States, or by Conventions in three fourths thereof, as the one or the other Mode of Ratification may be proposed by the Congress; Provided that no Amendment which may be made prior to the Year One thousand eight hundred and eight shall in any Manner affect the first and fourth Clauses in the Ninth Section of the first Article; and that no State, without its Consent, shall be deprived of its equal Suffrage in the Senate.

ARTICLE VI

All Debts contracted and Engagements entered into, before the Adoption of this Constitution shall be as valid against the United States under this Constitution, as under the Confederation.

This Constitution, and the Laws of the United States which shall be made in Pursuance thereof; and all Treaties made, or which shall be made, under the Authority of the United States, shall be the supreme Law of the Land; and the Judges in every State shall be bound thereby, any Thing in the Constitution or Laws of any State to the Contrary notwithstanding.

The Senators and Representatives before mentioned, and the Members of the several State Legislatures, and all executive and judicial Officers, both of the United States and of the several States, shall be bound by Oath or Affirmation, to support this Constitution; but no religious Test shall ever be required as a Qualification to any Office or public Trust under the United States.

ARTICLE VII

The Ratification of the Conventions of nine States shall be sufficient for the Establishment of this Constitution between the States so ratifying the Same.

AMENDMENT I [1791]

Congress shall make no law respecting an establishment of religion, or prohibiting the free exercise thereof; or abridging the freedom of speech, or of the press; or the right of the people peaceably to assembly, and to petition the Government for a redress of grievances.

AMENDMENT II [1791]

A well regulated Militia, being necessary to the security of a free State, the right of the people to keep and bear Arms, shall not be infringed.

AMENDMENT III [1791]

No Soldier shall, in time of peace be quartered in any house, without the consent of the Owner, nor in time of war, but in a manner to be prescribed by law.

AMENDMENT IV [1791]

The right of the people to be secure in their persons, houses, papers, and effects, against unreasonable searches and seizures, shall not be violated, and no Warrants shall issue, but upon probable cause, supported by Oath or affirmation, and particularly describing the place to be searched, and the persons or things to be seized.

AMENDMENT V [1791]

No person shall be held to answer for a capital, or otherwise infamous crime, unless on a presentment or indictment of a Grand Jury, except in cases arising in the land or naval forces, or in the Militia, when in actual service in time of War or public danger; nor shall any person be subject for the same offence to be twice put in jeopardy of life or limb; nor shall be compelled in any criminal case to be a witness against himself, nor be deprived of life, liberty, or property, without due process of law; nor shall private property be taken for public use, without just compensation.

AMENDMENT VI [1791]

In all criminal prosecutions, the accused shall enjoy the right to a speedy and public trial, by an impartial jury of the State and district wherein the crime shall have been committed, which district shall have been previously ascertained by law, and to be informed of the nature and cause of the accusation; to be confronted with the witnesses against him; to have compulsory process for obtaining witnesses in his favor, and to have the Assistance of Counsel for his defence.

AMENDMENT VII [1791]

In Suits at common law, where the value in controversy shall exceed twenty dollars, the right of trial by jury shall be preserved, and no fact tried by jury, shall be otherwise re-examined in any Court of the United States, than according to the rules of the common law.

AMENDMENT VIII [1791]

Excessive bail shall not be required, nor excessive fines imposed, nor cruel and unusual punishments inflicted.

AMENDMENT IX [1791]

The enumeration in the Constitution, of certain rights, shall not be construed to deny or disparage others retained by the people.

AMENDMENT X [1791]

The powers not delegated to the United States by the Constitution, nor prohibited by it to the States, are reserved to the States respectively, or to the people.

AMENDMENT XI [1798]

The Judicial power of the United States shall not be construed to extend to any suit in law or equity, commenced or prosecuted against one of the United States by Citizens of another State, or by Citizens or Subjects of any Foreign State.

AMENDMENT XII [1804]

The Electors shall meet in their respective states, and vote by ballot for President and Vice-President, one of whom, at least, shall not be an inhabitant of the same state with themselves; they shall name in their ballots the person voted for as President, and in distinct ballots the person voted for as Vice-President, and they shall make distinct lists of all persons voted for as President, and of all persons voted for as Vice-President, and of the number of votes for each, which lists they shall sign and certify, and transmit sealed to the seat of the government of the United States, directed to the President of the Senate;—The President of the Senate shall, in the presence of the Senate and House of Representatives, open all the certificates and the votes shall then be counted;—The person having the greatest number of votes for President, shall be the President, if such number be a majority of the whole number of Electors appointed; and if no person have such majority, then from the persons having the highest numbers not exceeding three on the list of those voted for as President, the House of Representatives shall choose immediately, by ballot, the President. But in choosing the President, the votes shall be taken by states, the representation from each state having one vote; a quorum for this purpose shall consist of a member or members from two-thirds of the states, and a majority of all states shall be necessary to a choice. And if the House of Representatives shall not choose a President whenever the right of choice shall devolve upon them, before the fourth day of March next following, then the Vice-President shall act as President, as in the case of the death or other constitutional disability of the President.—The person having the greatest number of votes as Vice-President, shall be the Vice-President, if such number be a majority of the whole number of Electors appointed, and if no person have a majority, then from the two highest numbers on the list, the Senate shall choose the Vice-President; a quorum for the purpose shall consist of two-thirds of the whole number of Senators, and a majority of the whole number shall be necessary to a choice. But no person constitutionally ineligible to the office of President shall be eligible to that of Vice-President of the United States.

AMENDMENT XIII [1865]

Section 1.   Neither slavery nor involuntary servitude, except as a punishment for crime whereof the party shall have been duly convicted, shall exist within the United States, or any place subject to their jurisdiction.

Section 2.   Congress shall have power to enforce this article by appropriate legislation.

AMENDMENT XIV [1868]

Section 1.   All persons born or naturalized in the United States, and subject to the jurisdiction thereof, are citizens of the United States and of the State wherein they reside. No State shall make or enforce any law which shall abridge the privileges or immunities of citizens of the United States; nor shall any State deprive any person of life, liberty, or property, without due process of law; nor deny to any person within its jurisdiction the equal protection of the laws.

Section 2.   Representatives shall be apportioned among the several States according to their respective numbers, counting the whole number of persons in each State, excluding Indians not taxed. But when the right to vote at any election for the choice of electors for President and Vice President of the United States, Representatives in Congress, the Executive and Judicial officers of a State, or the members of the Legislature thereof, is denied to any of the male inhabitants of such State, being twenty-one years of age, and citizens of the United States, or in any way abridged, except for participation in rebellion, or other crime, the basis of representation therein shall be reduced in the proportion which the number of such male citizens shall bear to the whole number of male citizens twenty-one years of age in such State.

Section 3.   No person shall be a Senator or Representative in Congress, or elector of President and Vice President, or hold any office, civil or military, under the United States, or under any State, who having previously taken an oath, as a member of Congress, or as an officer of the United States, or as a member of any State legislature, or as an executive or judicial officer of any State, to support the Constitution of the United States, shall have engaged in insurrection or rebellion against the same, or given aid or comfort to the enemies thereof. But Congress may by a vote of two-thirds of each House, remove such disability.

Section 4.   The validity of the public debt of the United States, authorized by law, including debts incurred for payment of pensions and bounties for services in suppressing insurrection or rebellion, shall not be questioned. But neither the United States nor any State shall assume or pay any debt or obligation incurred in aid of insurrection or rebellion against the United States, or any claim for the loss or emancipation of any slave; but all such debts, obligations and claims shall be held illegal and void.

Section 5.   The Congress shall have power to enforce, by appropriate legislation, the provisions of this article.

AMENDMENT XV [1870]

Section 1.   The right of citizens of the United States to vote shall not be denied or abridged by the United States or by any State on account of race, color, or previous condition of servitude.

Section 2.   The Congress shall have power to enforce this article by appropriate legislation.

Amendment XVI [1913]

The Congress shall have power to lay and collect taxes on incomes, from whatever source derived, without apportionment among the several States, and without regard to any census or enumeration.

Amendment XVII [1913]

Section 1. The Senate of the United States shall be composed of two Senators from each State, elected by the people thereof, for six years; and each Senator shall have one vote. The electors in each State shall have the qualifications requisite for electors of the most numerous branch of the State legislatures.

Section 2. When vacancies happen in the representation of any State in the Senate, the executive authority of such State shall issue writs of election to fill such vacancies: *Provided*, That the legislature of any State may empower the executive thereof to make temporary appointments until the people fill the vacancies by election as the legislature may direct.

Section 3. This amendment shall not be so construed as to affect the election or term of any Senator chosen before it becomes valid as part of the Constitution.

Amendment XVIII [1919]

Section 1. After one year from the ratification of this article the manufacture, sale, or transportation of intoxicating liquors within, the importation thereof into, or the exportation thereof from the United States and all territory subject to the jurisdiction thereof for beverage purposes is hereby prohibited.

Section 2. The Congress and the several States shall have concurrent power to enforce this article by appropriate legislation.

Section 3. This article shall be inoperative unless it shall have been ratified as an amendment to the Constitution by the legislatures of the several States, as provided in the Constitution, within seven years from the date of the submission hereof to the States by the Congress.

Amendment XIX [1920]

Section 1. The right of citizens of the United States to vote shall not be denied or abridged by the United States or by any State on account of sex.

Section 2. Congress shall have power to enforce this article by appropriate legislation.

Amendment XX [1933]

Section 1. The terms of the President and Vice President shall end at noon on the 20th day of January, and the terms of Senators and Representatives at noon on the 3d day of January, of the years in which such terms would have ended if this article had not been ratified; and the terms of their successors shall then begin.

Section 2. The Congress shall assemble at least once in every year, and such meeting shall begin at noon on the 3d day of January, unless they shall by law appoint a different day.

Section 3. If, at the time fixed for the beginning of the term of the President, the President elect shall have died, the Vice President elect shall become President. If the President shall not have been chosen before the time fixed for the beginning of his term, or if the President elect shall have failed to qualify, then the Vice President elect shall act as President until a President shall have qualified; and the Congress may by law provide for the case wherein neither a President elect nor a Vice President elect shall have qualified, declaring who shall then act as President, or the manner in which one who is to act shall be selected, and such person shall act accordingly until a President or Vice President shall have qualified.

Section 4. The Congress may by law provide for the case of the death of any of the persons from whom the House of Representatives may choose a President whenever the right of choice shall have devolved upon them, and for the case of the death of any of the persons from whom the Senate may choose a Vice President whenever the right of choice shall have devolved upon them.

Section 5. Sections 1 and 2 shall take effect on the 15th day of October following the ratification of this article.

Section 6. This article shall be inoperative unless it shall have been ratified as an amendment to the Constitution by the legislatures of three-fourths of the several States within seven years from the date of its submission.

Amendment XXI [1933]

Section 1. The eighteenth article of amendment to the Constitution of the United States is hereby repealed.

Section 2. The transportation or importation into any State, Territory, or possession of the United States for delivery or use therein of intoxicating liquors, in violation of the laws thereof, is hereby prohibited.

Section 3. This article shall be inoperative unless it shall have been ratified as an amendment to the Constitution by conventions in the several States, as provided in the Constitution, within seven years from the date of the submission hereof to the States by the Congress.

Amendment XXII [1951]

Section 1. No person shall be elected to the office of the President more than twice, and no person who has held the office of President, or acted as President, for more than two years of a term to which some other person was elected President shall be elected to the office of President more than once. But this Article shall not apply to any person holding the office of President when this Article was proposed by the Congress, and shall not prevent any person who may be holding the office of President, or acting as President, during the term within which this Article becomes operative from holding the office of President or acting as President during the remainder of such term.

Section 2. This article shall be inoperative unless it shall have been ratified as an amendment to the Constitution by the legislatures of three-fourths of the several States within seven years from the date of its submission to the States by the Congress.

Amendment XXIII [1961]

Section 1. The District constituting the seat of Government of the United States shall appoint in such manner as the Congress may direct:

A number of electors of President and Vice President equal to the whole number of Senators and Representatives in Congress to which the District would be entitled if it were a State, but in no event more than the least populous state; they shall be in addition to those appointed by the states, but they shall be considered, for the purposes of the election of President and Vice President, to be electors appointed by a state; and they shall meet in the District and perform such duties as provided by the twelfth article of amendment.

Section 2. The Congress shall have power to enforce this article by appropriate legislation.

Amendment XXIV [1964]

Section 1. The right of citizens of the United States to vote in any primary or other election for President or Vice President, for electors for President or Vice President, or for Senator or Representative in Congress, shall not be denied or abridged by the United States, or any State by reason of failure to pay any poll tax or other tax.

Section 2. The Congress shall have power to enforce this article by appropriate legislation.

Amendment XXV [1967]

Section 1. In case of the removal of the President from office or of his death or resignation, the Vice President shall become President.

Section 2. Whenever there is a vacancy in the office of the Vice President, the President shall nominate a Vice President who shall take office upon confirmation by a majority vote of both Houses of Congress.

Section 3. Whenever the President transmits to the President pro tempore of the Senate and the Speaker of the House of Representatives his written declaration that he is unable to discharge the powers and duties of his office, and until he transmits to them a written declaration to the contrary, such powers and duties shall be discharged by the Vice President as Acting President.

Section 4. Whenever the Vice President and a majority of either the principal officers of the executive departments or of such other body as Congress may by law provide, transmit to the President pro tempore of the Senate and the Speaker of the House of Representatives their written declaration that the President is unable to discharge the powers and duties of his office, the Vice President shall immediately assume the powers and duties of the office as Acting President.

Thereafter, when the President transmits to the President pro tempore of the Senate and the Speaker of the House of Representatives his written declaration that no inability exists, he shall resume the powers and duties of his office unless the Vice President and a majority of either the principal officers of the executive department or of such other body as Congress may by law provide, transmit within four days to the President pro tempore of the Senate and the Speaker of the House of Representatives their written declaration that the President is unable to discharge the powers and duties of his office. Thereupon Congress shall decide the issue, assembling within forty-eight hours for that purpose if not in session. If the Congress, within twenty-one days after receipt of the latter written declaration, or, if Congress is not in session, within twenty-one days after Congress is required to assemble, determines by two-thirds vote of both Houses that the President is unable to discharge the powers and duties of his office, the Vice President shall continue to discharge the same as Acting President; otherwise, the President shall resume the powers and duties of his office.

Amendment XXVI [1971]

Section 1. The right of citizens of the United States, who are eighteen years of age or older, to vote shall not be denied or abridged by the United States or by any State on account of age.

Section 2. The Congress shall have power to enforce this article by appropriate legislation.

Amendment XXVII [1992]

No law, varying the compensation for the services of the Senators and Representatives, shall take effect, until an election of Representatives shall have intervened.

APPENDIX C
The Uniform Commercial Code (Excerpts)

Article 1
GENERAL PROVISIONS

Part 1 Short Title, Construction, Application and Subject Matter of the Act

§ 1–101. Short Title.

This Act shall be known and may be cited as Uniform Commercial Code.

§ 1–102. Purposes; Rules of Construction; Variation by Agreement.

(1) This Act shall be liberally construed and applied to promote its underlying purposes and policies.

(2) Underlying purposes and policies of this Act are

(a) to simplify, clarify and modernize the law governing commercial transactions;

(b) to permit the continued expansion of commercial practices through custom, usage and agreement of the parties;

(c) to make uniform the law among the various jurisdictions.

(3) The effect of provisions of this Act may be varied by agreement, except as otherwise provided in this Act and except that the obligations of good faith, diligence, reasonableness and care prescribed by this Act may not be disclaimed by agreement but the parties may by agreement determine the standards by which the performance of such obligations is to be measured if such standards are not manifestly unreasonable.

(4) The presence in certain provisions of this Act of the words "unless otherwise agreed" or words of similar import does not imply that the effect of other provisions may not be varied by agreement under subsection (3).

(5) In this Act unless the context otherwise requires

(a) words in the singular number include the plural, and in the plural include the singular;

(b) words of the masculine gender include the feminine and the neuter, and when the sense so indicates words of the neuter gender may refer to any gender.

§ 1–103. Supplementary General Principles of Law Applicable.

Unless displaced by the particular provisions of this Act, the principles of law and equity, including the law merchant and the law relative to capacity to contract, principal and agent, estoppel, fraud, misrepresentation, duress, coercion, mistake, bankruptcy, or other validating or invalidating cause shall supplement its provisions.

§ 1–104. Construction Against Implicit Repeal.

This Act being a general act intended as a unified coverage of its subject matter, no part of it shall be deemed to be impliedly repealed by subsequent legislation if such construction can reasonably be avoided.

§ 1–105. Territorial Application of the Act; Parties' Power to Choose Applicable Law.

(1) Except as provided hereafter in this section, when a transaction bears a reasonable relation to this state and also to another state or nation the parties may agree that the law either of this state or of such other state or nation shall govern their rights and duties. Failing such agreement this Act applies to transactions bearing an appropriate relation to this state.

(2) Where one of the following provisions of this Act specifies the applicable law, that provision governs and a contrary agreement is effective only to the extent permitted by the law (including the conflict of laws rules) so specified:

Rights of creditors against sold goods. Section 2–402.

Applicability of the Article on Leases. Sections 2A–105 and 2A–106.

Applicability of the Article on Bank Deposits and Collections. Section 4–102.

Governing law in the Article on Funds Transfers. Section 4A–507.

Letters of Credit, Section 5–116.

Bulk sales subject to the Article on Bulk Sales. Section 6–103.

Applicability of the Article on Investment Securities. Section 8–106.

Law governing perfection, the effect of perfection or nonperfection, and the priority of security interests and agricultural liens. Sections 9–301 through 9–307.

As amended in 1972, 1987, 1988, 1989, 1994, 1995, and 1999.

§ 1–106. Remedies to Be Liberally Administered.

(1) The remedies provided by this Act shall be liberally administered to the end that the aggrieved party may be put in as good a position as if the other party had fully performed but neither consequential or special nor penal damages may be had except as specifically provided in this Act or by other rule of law.

(2) Any right or obligation declared by this Act is enforceable by action unless the provision declaring it specifies a different and limited effect.

§ 1–107. Waiver or Renunciation of Claim or Right After Breach.

Any claim or right arising out of an alleged breach can be discharged in whole or in part without consideration by a written waiver or renunciation signed and delivered by the aggrieved party.

§ 1–108. Severability.

If any provision or clause of this Act or application thereof to any person or circumstances is held invalid, such invalidity shall not affect other provisions or applications of the Act which can be given effect without the invalid provision or application, and to this end the provisions of this Act are declared to be severable.

§ 1–109. Section Captions.

Section captions are parts of this Act.

Part 2 General Definitions and Principles of Interpretation

§ 1–201. General Definitions.

Subject to additional definitions contained in the subsequent Articles of this Act which are applicable to specific Articles or Parts thereof, and unless the context otherwise requires, in this Act:

(1) "Action" in the sense of a judicial proceeding includes recoupment, counterclaim, set-off, suit in equity and any other proceedings in which rights are determined.

(2) "Aggrieved party" means a party entitled to resort to a remedy.

(3) "Agreement" means the bargain of the parties in fact as found in their language or by implication from other circumstances including course of dealing or usage of trade or course of performance as provided in this Act (Sections 1–205 and 2–208). Whether an agreement has legal consequences is determined by the provisions of this Act, if applicable; otherwise by the law of contracts (Section 1–103). (Compare "Contract".)

(4) "Bank" means any person engaged in the business of banking.

(5) "Bearer" means the person in possession of an instrument, document of title, or certificated security payable to bearer or indorsed in blank.

(6) "Bill of lading" means a document evidencing the receipt of goods for shipment issued by a person engaged in the business of transporting or forwarding goods, and includes an airbill. "Airbill" means a document serving for air transportation as a bill of lading does for marine or rail transportation, and includes an air consignment note or air waybill.

(7) "Branch" includes a separately incorporated foreign branch of a bank.

(8) "Burden of establishing" a fact means the burden of persuading the triers of fact that the existence of the fact is more probable than its non-existence.

(9) "Buyer in ordinary course of business" means a person that buys goods in good faith, without knowledge that the sale violates the rights of another person in the goods, and in the ordinary course from a person, other than a pawnbroker, in the business of selling goods of that kind. A person buys goods in the ordinary course if the sale to the person comports with the usual or customary practices in the kind of business in which the seller is engaged or with the seller's own usual or customary practices. A person that sells oil, gas, or other minerals at the wellhead or minehead is a person in the business of selling goods of that kind. A buyer in ordinary course of business may buy for cash, by exchange of other property, or on secured or unsecured credit, and may acquire goods or documents of title under a pre-existing contract for sale. Only a buyer that takes possession of the goods or has a right to recover the goods from the seller under Article 2 may be a buyer in ordinary course of business. A person that acquires goods in a transfer in bulk or as security for or in total or partial satisfaction of a money debt is not a buyer in ordinary course of business.

(10) "Conspicuous": A term or clause is conspicuous when it is so written that a reasonable person against whom it is to operate ought to have noticed it. A printed heading in capitals (as: NON-NEGOTIABLE BILL OF LADING) is conspicuous. Language in the body of a form is "conspicuous" if it is in larger or other contrasting type or color. But in a telegram any stated term is "conspicuous". Whether a term or clause is "conspicuous" or not is for decision by the court.

(11) "Contract" means the total legal obligation which results from the parties' agreement as affected by this Act and any other applicable rules of law. (Compare "Agreement".)

(12) "Creditor" includes a general creditor, a secured creditor, a lien creditor and any representative of creditors, including an assignee for the benefit of creditors, a trustee in bankruptcy, a receiver in equity and an executor or administrator of an insolvent debtor's or assignor's estate.

(13) "Defendant" includes a person in the position of defendant in a cross-action or counterclaim.

(14) "Delivery" with respect to instruments, documents of title, chattel paper, or certificated securities means voluntary transfer of possession.

(15) "Document of title" includes bill of lading, dock warrant, dock receipt, warehouse receipt or order for the delivery of goods, and also any other document which in the regular course of business or financing is treated as adequately evidencing that the person in possession of it is entitled to receive, hold and dispose of the document and the goods it covers. To be a document of title a document must purport to be issued by or addressed to a bailee and purport to cover goods in the bailee's possession which are either identified or are fungible portions of an identified mass.

(16) "Fault" means wrongful act, omission or breach.

(17) "Fungible" with respect to goods or securities means goods or securities of which any unit is, by nature or usage of trade, the equivalent of any other like unit. Goods which are not fungible shall be deemed fungible for the purposes of this Act to the extent that under a particular agreement or document unlike units are treated as equivalents.

(18) "Genuine" means free of forgery or counterfeiting.

(19) "Good faith" means honesty in fact in the conduct or transaction concerned.

(20) "Holder" with respect to a negotiable instrument, means the person in possession if the instrument is payable to bearer or, in the cases of an instrument payable to an identified person, if the identified person is in possession. "Holder" with respect to a document of title means the person in possession if the goods are deliverable to bearer or to the order of the person in possession.

(21) To "honor" is to pay or to accept and pay, or where a credit so engages to purchase or discount a draft complying with the terms of the credit.

(22) "Insolvency proceedings" includes any assignment for the benefit of creditors or other proceedings intended to liquidate or rehabilitate the estate of the person involved.

(23) A person is "insolvent" who either has ceased to pay his debts in the ordinary course of business or cannot pay his debts as they become due or is insolvent within the meaning of the federal bankruptcy law.

(24) "Money" means a medium of exchange authorized or adopted by a domestic or foreign government and includes a monetary unit of account established by an intergovernmental organization or by agreement between two or more nations.

(25) A person has "notice" of a fact when

(a) he has actual knowledge of it; or

(b) he has received a notice or notification of it; or

(c) from all the facts and circumstances known to him at the time in question he has reason to know that it exists.

A person "knows" or has "knowledge" of a fact when he has actual knowledge of it. "Discover" or "learn" or a word or phrase of similar import refers to knowledge rather than to reason to know. The time and circumstances under which a notice or notification may cease to be effective are not determined by this Act.

(26) A person "notifies" or "gives" a notice or notification to another by taking such steps as may be reasonably required to inform the other in ordinary course whether or not such other actually comes to know of it. A person "receives" a notice or notification when

(a) it comes to his attention; or

(b) it is duly delivered at the place of business through which the contract was made or at any other place held out by him as the place for receipt of such communications.

(27) Notice, knowledge or a notice or notification received by an organization is effective for a particular transaction from the time when it is brought to the attention of the individual conducting that transaction, and in any event from the time when it would have been brought to his attention if the organization had exercised due diligence. An organization exercises due diligence if it maintains reasonable routines for communicating significant information to the person conducting the transaction and there is reasonable compliance with the routines. Due diligence does not require an individual acting for the organization to communicate information unless such communication is part of his regular duties or unless he has reason to know of the transaction and that the transaction would be materially affected by the information.

(28) "Organization" includes a corporation, government or governmental subdivision or agency, business trust, estate, trust, partnership or association, two or more persons having a joint or common interest, or any other legal or commercial entity.

(29) "Party", as distinct from "third party", means a person who has engaged in a transaction or made an agreement within this Act.

(30) "Person" includes an individual or an organization (See Section 1–102).

(31) "Presumption" or "presumed" means that the trier of fact must find the existence of the fact presumed unless and until evidence is introduced which would support a finding of its non-existence.

(32) "Purchase" includes taking by sale, discount, negotiation, mortgage, pledge, lien, issue or re-issue, gift or any other voluntary transaction creating an interest in property.

(33) "Purchaser" means a person who takes by purchase.

(34) "Remedy" means any remedial right to which an aggrieved party is entitled with or without resort to a tribunal.

(35) "Representative" includes an agent, an officer of a corporation or association, and a trustee, executor or administrator of an estate, or any other person empowered to act for another.

(36) "Rights" includes remedies.

(37) "Security interest" means an interest in personal property or fixtures which secures payment or performance of an obligation. The term also includes any interest of a consignor and a buyer of accounts, chattel paper, a payment intangible, or a promissory note in a transaction that is subject to Article 9. The special property interest of a buyer of goods on identification of those goods to a contract for sale under Section 2–401 is not a "security interest", but a buyer may also acquire a "security interest" by complying with Article 9. Except as otherwise provided in Section 2–505, the right of a seller or lessor of goods under Article 2 or 2A to retain or acquire possession of the goods is not a "security interest", but a seller or lessor may also acquire a "security interest" by complying with Article 9. The retention or reservation of title by a seller of goods notwithstanding shipment or delivery to the buyer (Section 2–401) is limited in effect to a reservation of a "security interest".

Whether a transaction creates a lease or security interest is determined by the facts of each case; however, a transaction creates a security interest if the consideration the lessee is to pay the lessor for the right to possession and use of the goods is an obligation for the term of the lease not subject to termination by the lessee, and

(a) the original term of the lease is equal to or greater than the remaining economic life of the goods,

(b) the lessee is bound to renew the lease for the remaining economic life of the goods or is bound to become the owner of the goods,

(c) the lessee has an option to renew the lease for the remaining economic life of the goods for no additional consideration or nominal additional consideration upon compliance with the lease agreement, or

(d) the lessee has an option to become the owner of the goods for no additional consideration or nominal additional consideration upon compliance with the lease agreement.

A transaction does not create a security interest merely because it provides that

(a) the present value of the consideration the lessee is obligated to pay the lessor for the right to possession and use of the goods is substantially equal to or is greater than the fair market value of the goods at the time the lease is entered into,

(b) the lessee assumes risk of loss of the goods, or agrees to pay taxes, insurance, filing, recording, or registration fees, or service or maintenance costs with respect to the goods,

(c) the lessee has an option to renew the lease or to become the owner of the goods,

(d) the lessee has an option to renew the lease for a fixed rent that is equal to or greater than the reasonably predictable fair market rent for the use of the goods for the term of the renewal at the time the option is to be performed, or

(e) the lessee has an option to become the owner of the goods for a fixed price that is equal to or greater than the reasonably predictable fair market value of the goods at the time the option is to be performed.

For purposes of this subsection (37):

(x) Additional consideration is not nominal if (i) when the option to renew the lease is granted to the lessee the rent is stated to be the fair market rent for the use of the goods for the term of the renewal determined at the time the option is to be performed, or (ii) when the option to become the owner of the goods is granted to the lessee the price is stated to be the fair market value of the goods determined at the time the option is to be performed. Additional consideration is nominal if it is less than the lessee's reasonably predictable cost of performing under the lease agreement if the option is not exercised;

(y) "Reasonably predictable" and "remaining economic life of the goods" are to be determined with reference to the facts and circumstances at the time the transaction is entered into; and

(z) "Present value" means the amount as of a date certain of one or more sums payable in the future, discounted to the date certain. The discount is determined by the interest rate specified by the parties if the rate is not manifestly unreasonable at the time the transaction is entered into; otherwise, the discount is determined by a commercially reasonable rate that takes into account the facts and circumstances of each case at the time the transaction was entered into.

(38) "Send" in connection with any writing or notice means to deposit in the mail or deliver for transmission by any other usual means of communication with postage or cost of transmission provided for and properly addressed and in the case of an instrument to an address specified thereon or otherwise agreed, or if there be none to any address reasonable under the circumstances. The receipt of any writing or notice within the time at which it would have arrived if properly sent has the effect of a proper sending.

(39) "Signed" includes any symbol executed or adopted by a party with present intention to authenticate a writing.

(40) "Surety" includes guarantor.

(41) "Telegram" includes a message transmitted by radio, teletype, cable, any mechanical method of transmission, or the like.

(42) "Term" means that portion of an agreement which relates to a particular matter.

(43) "Unauthorized" signature means one made without actual, implied or apparent authority and includes a forgery.

(44) "Value". Except as otherwise provided with respect to negotiable instruments and bank collections (Sections 3–303, 4–210 and 4–211) a person gives "value" for rights if he acquires them

(a) in return for a binding commitment to extend credit or for the extension of immediately available credit whether or not drawn upon and whether or not a chargeback is provided for in the event of difficulties in collection; or

(b) as security for or in total or partial satisfaction of a pre-existing claim; or

(c) by accepting delivery pursuant to a preexisting contract for purchase; or

(d) generally, in return for any consideration sufficient to support a simple contract.

(45) "Warehouse receipt" means a receipt issued by a person engaged in the business of storing goods for hire.

(46) "Written" or "writing" includes printing, typewriting or any other intentional reduction to tangible form.

§1–202. Prima Facie Evidence by Third Party Documents.

A document in due form purporting to be a bill of lading, policy or certificate of insurance, official weigher's or inspector's certificate, consular invoice, or any other document authorized or required by the contract to be issued by a third party shall be prima facie evidence of its own authenticity and genuineness and of the facts stated in the document by the third party.

§ 1–203. Obligation of Good Faith.

Every contract or duty within this Act imposes an obligation of good faith in its performance or enforcement.

§ 1–204. Time; Reasonable Time; "Seasonably".

(1) Whenever this Act requires any action to be taken within a reasonable time, any time which is not manifestly unreasonable may be fixed by agreement.

(2) What is a reasonable time for taking any action depends on the nature, purpose and circumstances of such action.

(3) An action is taken "seasonably" when it is taken at or within the time agreed or if no time is agreed at or within a reasonable time.

§ 1–205. Course of Dealing and Usage of Trade.

(1) A course of dealing is a sequence of previous conduct between the parties to a particular transaction which is fairly to be regarded as establishing a common basis of understanding for interpreting their expressions and other conduct.

(2) A usage of trade is any practice or method of dealing having such regularity of observance in a place, vocation or trade as to justify an expectation that it will be observed with respect to the transaction in question. The existence and scope of such a usage are to be proved as facts. If it is established that such a usage is embodied in a written trade code or similar writing the interpretation of the writing is for the court.

(3) A course of dealing between parties and any usage of trade in the vocation or trade in which they are engaged or of which they are or should be aware give particular meaning to and supplement or qualify terms of an agreement.

(4) The express terms of an agreement and an applicable course of dealing or usage of trade shall be construed wherever reasonable as consistent with each other; but when such construction is unreasonable express terms control both course of dealing and usage of trade and course of dealing controls usage trade.

(5) An applicable usage of trade in the place where any part of performance is to occur shall be used in interpreting the agreement as to that part of the performance.

(6) Evidence of a relevant usage of trade offered by one party is not admissible unless and until he has given the other party such notice as the court finds sufficient to prevent unfair surprise to the latter.

§ 1–206. Statute of Frauds for Kinds of Personal Property Not Otherwise Covered.

(1) Except in the cases described in subsection (2) of this section a contract for the sale of personal property is not enforceable by way of action or defense beyond five thousand dollars in amount or value of

remedy unless there is some writing which indicates that a contract for sale has been made between the parties at a defined or stated price, reasonably identifies the subject matter, and is signed by the party against whom enforcement is sought or by his authorized agent.

(2) Subsection (1) of this section does not apply to contracts for the sale of goods (Section 2–201) nor of securities (Section 8–113) nor to security agreements (Section 9–203).

As amended in 1994.

§ 1–207. Performance or Acceptance Under Reservation of Rights.

(1) A party who with explicit reservation of rights performs or promises performance or assents to performance in a manner demanded or offered by the other party does not thereby prejudice the rights reserved. Such words as "without prejudice", "under protest" or the like are sufficient.

(2) Subsection (1) does not apply to an accord and satisfaction.

As amended in 1990.

§ 1–208. Option to Accelerate at Will.

A term providing that one party or his successor in interest may accelerate payment or performance or require collateral or additional collateral "at will" or "when he deems himself insecure" or in words of similar import shall be construed to mean that he shall have power to do so only if he in good faith believes that the prospect of payment or performance is impaired. The burden of establishing lack of good faith is on the party against whom the power has been exercised.

§ 1–209. Subordinated Obligations.

An obligation may be issued as subordinated to payment of another obligation of the person obligated, or a creditor may subordinate his right to payment of an obligation by agreement with either the person obligated or another creditor of the person obligated. Such a subordination does not create a security interest as against either the common debtor or a subordinated creditor. This section shall be construed as declaring the law as it existed prior to the enactment of this section and not as modifying it. Added 1966.

Note: *This new section is proposed as an optional provision to make it clear that a subordination agreement does not create a security interest unless so intended.*

Article 2
SALES

Part 1 Short Title, General Construction and Subject Matter

§ 2–101. Short Title.

This Article shall be known and may be cited as Uniform Commercial Code—Sales.

§ 2–102. Scope; Certain Security and Other Transactions Excluded From This Article.

Unless the context otherwise requires, this Article applies to transactions in goods; it does not apply to any transaction which although in the form of an unconditional contract to sell or present sale is intended to operate only as a security transaction nor does this Article impair or repeal any statute regulating sales to consumers, farmers or other specified classes of buyers.

§ 2–103. Definitions and Index of Definitions.

(1) In this Article unless the context otherwise requires

(a) "Buyer" means a person who buys or contracts to buy goods.

(b) "Good faith" in the case of a merchant means honesty in fact and the observance of reasonable commercial standards of fair dealing in the trade.

(c) "Receipt" of goods means taking physical possession of them.

(d) "Seller" means a person who sells or contracts to sell goods.

(2) Other definitions applying to this Article or to specified Parts thereof, and the sections in which they appear are:

"Acceptance". Section 2–606.
"Banker's credit". Section 2–325.
"Between merchants". Section 2–104.
"Cancellation". Section 2–106(4).
"Commercial unit". Section 2–105.
"Confirmed credit". Section 2–325.
"Conforming to contract". Section 2–106.
"Contract for sale". Section 2–106.
"Cover". Section 2–712.
"Entrusting". Section 2–403.
"Financing agency". Section 2–104.
"Future goods". Section 2–105.
"Goods". Section 2–105.
"Identification". Section 2–501.
"Installment contract". Section 2–612.
"Letter of Credit". Section 2–325.
"Lot". Section 2–105.
"Merchant". Section 2–104.
"Overseas". Section 2–323.
"Person in position of seller". Section 2–707.
"Present sale". Section 2–106.
"Sale". Section 2–106.
"Sale on approval". Section 2–326.
"Sale or return". Section 2–326.
"Termination". Section 2–106.

(3) The following definitions in other Articles apply to this Article:

"Check". Section 3–104.
"Consignee". Section 7–102.
"Consignor". Section 7–102.
"Consumer goods". Section 9–109.
"Dishonor". Section 3–507.
"Draft". Section 3–104.

(4) In addition Article 1 contains general definitions and principles of construction and interpretation applicable throughout this Article.

As amended in 1994 and 1999.

§ 2–104. Definitions: "Merchant"; "Between Merchants"; "Financing Agency".

(1) "Merchant" means a person who deals in goods of the kind or otherwise by his occupation holds himself out as having knowledge or skill peculiar to the practices or goods involved in the transaction or to whom such knowledge or skill may be attributed by his employment of an agent or broker or other intermediary who by his occupation holds himself out as having such knowledge or skill.

(2) "Financing agency" means a bank, finance company or other

person who in the ordinary course of business makes advances against goods or documents of title or who by arrangement with either the seller or the buyer intervenes in ordinary course to make or collect payment due or claimed under the contract for sale, as by purchasing or paying the seller's draft or making advances against it or by merely taking it for collection whether or not documents of title accompany the draft. "Financing agency" includes also a bank or other person who similarly intervenes between persons who are in the position of seller and buyer in respect to the goods (Section 2–707).

(3) "Between merchants" means in any transaction with respect to which both parties are chargeable with the knowledge or skill of merchants.

§ 2–105. Definitions: Transferability; "Goods"; "Future" Goods; "Lot"; "Commercial Unit".

(1) "Goods" means all things (including specially manufactured goods) which are movable at the time of identification to the contract for sale other than the money in which the price is to be paid, investment securities (Article 8) and things in action. "Goods" also includes the unborn young of animals and growing crops and other identified things attached to realty as described in the section on goods to be severed from realty (Section 2–107).

(2) Goods must be both existing and identified before any interest in them can pass. Goods which are not both existing and identified are "future" goods. A purported present sale of future goods or of any interest therein operates as a contract to sell.

(3) There may be a sale of a part interest in existing identified goods.

(4) An undivided share in an identified bulk of fungible goods is sufficiently identified to be sold although the quantity of the bulk is not determined. Any agreed proportion of such a bulk or any quantity thereof agreed upon by number, weight or other measure may to the extent of the seller's interest in the bulk be sold to the buyer who then becomes an owner in common.

(5) "Lot" means a parcel or a single article which is the subject matter of a separate sale or delivery, whether or not it is sufficient to perform the contract.

(6) "Commercial unit" means such a unit of goods as by commercial usage is a single whole for purposes of sale and division of which materially impairs its character or value on the market or in use. A commercial unit may be a single article (as a machine) or a set of articles (as a suite of furniture or an assortment of sizes) or a quantity (as a bale, gross, or carload) or any other unit treated in use or in the relevant market as a single whole.

§ 2–106. Definitions: "Contract"; "Agreement"; "Contract for Sale"; "Sale"; "Present Sale"; "Conforming" to Contract; "Termination"; "Cancellation".

(1) In this Article unless the context otherwise requires "contract" and "agreement" are limited to those relating to the present or future sale of goods. "Contract for sale" includes both a present sale of goods and a contract to sell goods at a future time. A "sale" consists in the passing of title from the seller to the buyer for a price (Section 2–401). A "present sale" means a sale which is accomplished by the making of the contract.

(2) Goods or conduct including any part of a performance are "conforming" or conform to the contract when they are in accordance with the obligations under the contract.

(3) "Termination" occurs when either party pursuant to a power created by agreement or law puts an end to the contract otherwise than for its breach. On "termination" all obligations which are still execu-

tory on both sides are discharged but any right based on prior breach or performance survives.

(4) "Cancellation" occurs when either party puts an end to the contract for breach by the other and its effect is the same as that of "termination" except that the cancelling party also retains any remedy for breach of the whole contract or any unperformed balance.

§ 2–107. Goods to Be Severed From Realty: Recording.

(1) A contract for the sale of minerals or the like (including oil and gas) or a structure or its materials to be removed from realty is a contract for the sale of goods within this Article if they are to be severed by the seller but until severance a purported present sale thereof which is not effective as a transfer of an interest in land is effective only as a contract to sell.

(2) A contract for the sale apart from the land of growing crops or other things attached to realty and capable of severance without material harm thereto but not described in subsection (1) or of timber to be cut is a contract for the sale of goods within this Article whether the subject matter is to be severed by the buyer or by the seller even though it forms part of the realty at the time of contracting, and the parties can by identification effect a present sale before severance.

(3) The provisions of this section are subject to any third party rights provided by the law relating to realty records, and the contract for sale may be executed and recorded as a document transferring an interest in land and shall then constitute notice to third parties of the buyer's rights under the contract for sale.

As amended in 1972.

Part 2 Form, Formation and Readjustment of Contract

§ 2–201. Formal Requirements; Statute of Frauds.

(1) Except as otherwise provided in this section a contract for the sale of goods for the price of $500 or more is not enforceable by way of action or defense unless there is some writing sufficient to indicate that a contract for sale has been made between the parties and signed by the party against whom enforcement is sought or by his authorized agent or broker. A writing is not insufficient because it omits or incorrectly states a term agreed upon but the contract is not enforceable under this paragraph beyond the quantity of goods shown in such writing.

(2) Between merchants if within a reasonable time a writing in confirmation of the contract and sufficient against the sender is received and the party receiving it has reason to know its contents, its satisfies the requirements of subsection (1) against such party unless written notice of objection to its contents is given within ten days after it is received.

(3) A contract which does not satisfy the requirements of subsection (1) but which is valid in other respects is enforceable

> (a) if the goods are to be specially manufactured for the buyer and are not suitable for sale to others in the ordinary course of the seller's business and the seller, before notice of repudiation is received and under circumstances which reasonably indicate that the goods are for the buyer, has made either a substantial beginning of their manufacture or commitments for their procurement; or

> (b) if the party against whom enforcement is sought admits in his pleading, testimony or otherwise in court that a contract

for sale was made, but the contract is not enforceable under this provision beyond the quantity of goods admitted; or

(c) with respect to goods for which payment has been made and accepted or which have been received and accepted (Sec. 2–606).

§ 2–202. Final Written Expression: Parol or Extrinsic Evidence.

Terms with respect to which the confirmatory memoranda of the parties agree or which are otherwise set forth in a writing intended by the parties as a final expression of their agreement with respect to such terms as are included therein may not be contradicted by evidence of any prior agreement or of a contemporaneous oral agreement but may be explained or supplemented

(a) by course of dealing or usage of trade (Section 1–205) or by course of performance (Section 2–208); and

(b) by evidence of consistent additional terms unless the court finds the writing to have been intended also as a complete and exclusive statement of the terms of the agreement.

§ 2–203. Seals Inoperative.

The affixing of a seal to a writing evidencing a contract for sale or an offer to buy or sell goods does not constitute the writing a sealed instrument and the law with respect to sealed instruments does not apply to such a contract or offer.

§ 2–204. Formation in General.

(1) A contract for sale of goods may be made in any manner sufficient to show agreement, including conduct by both parties which recognizes the existence of such a contract.

(2) An agreement sufficient to constitute a contract for sale may be found even though the moment of its making is undetermined.

(3) Even though one or more terms are left open a contract for sale does not fail for indefiniteness if the parties have intended to make a contract and there is a reasonably certain basis for giving an appropriate remedy.

§ 2–205. Firm Offers.

An offer by a merchant to buy or sell goods in a signed writing which by its terms gives assurance that it will be held open is not revocable, for lack of consideration, during the time stated or if no time is stated for a reasonable time, but in no event may such period of irrevocability exceed three months; but any such term of assurance on a form supplied by the offeree must be separately signed by the offeror.

§ 2–206. Offer and Acceptance in Formation of Contract.

(1) Unless otherwise unambiguously indicated by the language or circumstances

(a) an offer to make a contract shall be construed as inviting acceptance in any manner and by any medium reasonable in the circumstances;

(b) an order or other offer to buy goods for prompt or current shipment shall be construed as inviting acceptance either by a prompt promise to ship or by the prompt or current shipment of conforming or nonconforming goods, but such a shipment of non-conforming goods does not constitute an acceptance if the seller seasonably notifies the buyer that the shipment is offered only as an accommodation to the buyer.

(2) Where the beginning of a requested performance is a reasonable mode of acceptance an offeror who is not notified of acceptance within a reasonable time may treat the offer as having lapsed before acceptance.

§ 2–207. Additional Terms in Acceptance or Confirmation.

(1) A definite and seasonable expression of acceptance or a written confirmation which is sent within a reasonable time operates as an acceptance even though it states terms additional to or different from those offered or agreed upon, unless acceptance is expressly made conditional on assent to the additional or different terms.

(2) The additional terms are to be construed as proposals for addition to the contract. Between merchants such terms become part of the contract unless:

(a) the offer expressly limits acceptance to the terms of the offer;

(b) they materially alter it; or

(c) notification of objection to them has already been given or is given within a reasonable time after notice of them is received.

(3) Conduct by both parties which recognizes the existence of a contract is sufficient to establish a contract for sale although the writings of the parties do not otherwise establish a contract. In such case the terms of the particular contract consist of those terms on which the writings of the parties agree, together with any supplementary terms incorporated under any other provisions of this Act.

§ 2–208. Course of Performance or Practical Construction.

(1) Where the contract for sale involves repeated occasions for performance by either party with knowledge of the nature of the performance and opportunity for objection to it by the other, any course of performance accepted or acquiesced in without objection shall be relevant to determine the meaning of the agreement.

(2) The express terms of the agreement and any such course of performance, as well as any course of dealing and usage of trade, shall be construed whenever reasonable as consistent with each other; but when such construction is unreasonable, express terms shall control course of performance and course of performance shall control both course of dealing and usage of trade (Section 1–205).

(3) Subject to the provisions of the next section on modification and waiver, such course of performance shall be relevant to show a waiver or modification of any term inconsistent with such course of performance.

§ 2–209. Modification, Rescission and Waiver.

(1) An agreement modifying a contract within this Article needs no consideration to be binding.

(2) A signed agreement which excludes modification or rescission except by a signed writing cannot be otherwise modified or rescinded, but except as between merchants such a requirement on a form supplied by the merchant must be separately signed by the other party.

(3) The requirements of the statute of frauds section of this Article (Section 2–201) must be satisfied if the contract as modified is within its provisions.

(4) Although an attempt at modification or rescission does not satisfy the requirements of subsection (2) or (3) it can operate as a waiver.

(5) A party who has made a waiver affecting an executory portion of the contract may retract the waiver by reasonable notification received by the other party that strict performance will be required of any term waived, unless the retraction would be unjust in view of a material change of position in reliance on the waiver.

§ 2–210. Delegation of Performance; Assignment of Rights.

(1) A party may perform his duty through a delegate unless otherwise agreed or unless the other party has a substantial interest in having his original promisor perform or control the acts required by the contract. No delegation of performance relieves the party delegating of any duty to perform or any liability for breach.

(2) Except as otherwise provided in Section 9–406, unless otherwise agreed, all rights of either seller or buyer can be assigned except where the assignment would materially change the duty of the other party, or increase materially the burden or risk imposed on him by his contract, or impair materially his chance of obtaining return performance. A right to damages for breach of the whole contract or a right arising out of the assignor's due performance of his entire obligation can be assigned despite agreement otherwise.

(3) The creation, attachment, perfection, or enforcement of a security interest in the seller's interest under a contract is not a transfer that materially changes the duty of or increases materially the burden or risk imposed on the buyer or impairs materially the buyer's chance of obtaining return performance within the purview of subsection (2) unless, and then only to the extent that, enforcement actually results in a delegation of material performance of the seller. Even in that event, the creation, attachment, perfection, and enforcement of the security interest remain effective, but (i) the seller is liable to the buyer for damages caused by the delegation to the extent that the damages could not reasonably by prevented by the buyer, and (ii) a court having jurisdiction may grant other appropriate relief, including cancellation of the contract for sale or an injunction against enforcement of the security interest or consummation of the enforcement.

(4) Unless the circumstnaces indicate the contrary a prohibition of assignment of "the contract" is to be construed as barring only the delegation to the assignes of the assignor's performance.

(5) An assignment of "the contract" or of "all my rights under the contract" or an assignment in similar general terms is an assignment of rights and unless the language or the circumstances (as in an assignment for security) indicate the contrary, it is a delegation of performance of the duties of the assignor and its acceptance by the assignee constitutes a promise by him to perform those duties. This promise is enforceable by either the assignor or the other party to the original contract.

(6) The other party may treat any assignment which delegates performance as creating reasonable grounds for insecurity and may without prejudice to his rights against the assignor demand assurances from the assignee (Section 2–609).

As amended in 1999.

Part 3 General Obligation and Construction of Contract

§ 2–301. General Obligations of Parties.

The obligation of the seller is to transfer and deliver and that of the buyer is to accept and pay in accordance with the contract.

§ 2–302. Unconscionable Contract or Clause.

(1) If the court as a matter of law finds the contract or any clause of the contract to have been unconscionable at the time it was made the court may refuse to enforce the contract, or it may enforce the remainder of the contract without the unconscionable clause, or it may so limit the application of any unconscionable clause as to avoid any unconscionable result.

(2) When it is claimed or appears to the court that the contract or any clause thereof may be unconscionable the parties shall be afforded a reasonable opportunity to present evidence as to its commercial setting, purpose and effect to aid the court in making the determination.

§ 2–303. Allocations or Division of Risks.

Where this Article allocates a risk or a burden as between the parties "unless otherwise agreed", the agreement may not only shift the allocation but may also divide the risk or burden.

§ 2–304. Price Payable in Money, Goods, Realty, or Otherwise.

(1) The price can be made payable in money or otherwise. If it is payable in whole or in part in goods each party is a seller of the goods which he is to transfer.

(2) Even though all or part of the price is payable in an interest in realty the transfer of the goods and the seller's obligations with reference to them are subject to this Article, but not the transfer of the interest in realty or the transferor's obligations in connection therewith.

§ 2–305. Open Price Term.

(1) The parties if they so intend can conclude a contract for sale even though the price is not settled. In such a case the price is a reasonable price at the time for delivery if

(a) nothing is said as to price; or

(b) the price is left to be agreed by the parties and they fail to agree; or

(c) the price is to be fixed in terms of some agreed market or other standard as set or recorded by a third person or agency and it is not so set or recorded.

(2) A price to be fixed by the seller or by the buyer means a price for him to fix in good faith.

(3) When a price left to be fixed otherwise than by agreement of the parties fails to be fixed through fault of one party the other may at his option treat the contract as cancelled or himself fix a reasonable price.

(4) Where, however, the parties intend not to be bound unless the price be fixed or agreed and it is not fixed or agreed there is no contract. In such a case the buyer must return any goods already received or if unable so to do must pay their reasonable value at the time of delivery and the seller must return any portion of the price paid on account.

§ 2–306. Output, Requirements and Exclusive Dealings.

(1) A term which measures the quantity by the output of the seller or the requirements of the buyer means such actual output or requirements as may occur in good faith, except that no quantity unreasonably disproportionate to any stated estimate or in the absence of a stated estimate to any normal or otherwise comparable prior output or requirements may be tendered or demanded.

(2) A lawful agreement by either the seller or the buyer for exclusive dealing in the kind of goods concerned imposes unless otherwise agreed an obligation by the seller to use best efforts to supply the goods and by the buyer to use best efforts to promote their sale.

§ 2–307. Delivery in Single Lot or Several Lots.

Unless otherwise agreed all goods called for by a contract for sale must be tendered in a single delivery and payment is due only on such tender but where the circumstances give either party the right to make or demand delivery in lots the price if it can be apportioned may be demanded for each lot.

§ 2–308. Absence of Specified Place for Delivery.

Unless otherwise agreed

(a) the place for delivery of goods is the seller's place of business or if he has none his residence; but

(b) in a contract for sale of identified goods which to the knowledge of the parties at the time of contracting are in some other place, that place is the place for their delivery; and

(c) documents of title may be delivered through customary banking channels.

§ 2–309. Absence of Specific Time Provisions; Notice of Termination.

(1) The time for shipment or delivery or any other action under a contract if not provided in this Article or agreed upon shall be a reasonable time.

(2) Where the contract provides for successive performances but is indefinite in duration it is valid for a reasonable time but unless otherwise agreed may be terminated at any time by either party.

(3) Termination of a contract by one party except on the happening of an agreed event requires that reasonable notification be received by the other party and an agreement dispensing with notification is invalid if its operation would be unconscionable.

§ 2–310. Open Time for Payment or Running of Credit; Authority to Ship Under Reservation.

Unless otherwise agreed

(a) payment is due at the time and place at which the buyer is to receive the goods even though the place of shipment is the place of delivery; and

(b) if the seller is authorized to send the goods he may ship them under reservation, and may tender the documents of title, but the buyer may inspect the goods after their arrival before payment is due unless such inspection is inconsistent with the terms of the contract (Section 2–513); and

(c) if delivery is authorized and made by way of documents of title otherwise than by subsection (b) then payment is due at the time and place at which the buyer is to receive the documents regardless of where the goods are to be received; and

(d) where the seller is required or authorized to ship the goods on credit the credit period runs from the time of shipment but post-dating the invoice or delaying its dispatch will correspondingly delay the starting of the credit period.

§ 2–311. Options and Cooperation Respecting Performance.

(1) An agreement for sale which is otherwise sufficiently definite (subsection (3) of Section 2–204) to be a contract is not made invalid by the fact that it leaves particulars of performance to be specified by one of the parties. Any such specification must be made in good faith and within limits set by commercial reasonableness.

(2) Unless otherwise agreed specifications relating to assortment of the goods are at the buyer's option and except as otherwise provided in subsections (1)(c) and (3) of Section 2–319 specifications or arrangements relating to shipment are at the seller's option.

(3) Where such specification would materially affect the other party's performance but is not seasonably made or where one party's cooperation is necessary to the agreed performance of the other but is not seasonably forthcoming, the other party in addition to all other remedies

(a) is excused for any resulting delay in his own performance; and

(b) may also either proceed to perform in any reasonable manner or after the time for a material part of his own performance treat the failure to specify or to cooperate as a breach by failure to deliver or accept the goods.

§ 2–312. Warranty of Title and Against Infringement; Buyer's Obligation Against Infringement.

(1) Subject to subsection (2) there is in a contract for sale a warranty by the seller that

(a) the title conveyed shall be good, and its transfer rightful; and

(b) the goods shall be delivered free from any security interest or other lien or encumbrance of which the buyer at the time of contracting has no knowledge.

(2) A warranty under subsection (1) will be excluded or modified only by specific language or by circumstances which give the buyer reason to know that the person selling does not claim title in himself or that he is purporting to sell only such right or title as he or a third person may have.

(3) Unless otherwise agreed a seller who is a merchant regularly dealing in goods of the kind warrants that the goods shall be delivered free of the rightful claim of any third person by way of infringement or the like but a buyer who furnishes specifications to the seller must hold the seller harmless against any such claim which arises out of compliance with the specifications.

§ 2–313. Express Warranties by Affirmation, Promise, Description, Sample.

(1) Express warranties by the seller are created as follows:

(a) Any affirmation of fact or promise made by the seller to the buyer which relates to the goods and becomes part of the basis of the bargain creates an express warranty that the goods shall conform to the affirmation or promise.

(b) Any description of the goods which is made part of the basis of the bargain creates an express warranty that the goods shall conform to the description.

(c) Any sample or model which is made part of the basis of the bargain creates an express warranty that the whole of the goods shall conform to the sample or model.

(2) It is not necessary to the creation of an express warranty that the seller use formal words such as "warrant" or "guarantee" or that he have a specific intention to make a warranty, but an affirmation merely of the value of the goods or a statement purporting to be merely the seller's opinion or commendation of the goods does not create a warranty.

§ 2–314. Implied Warranty: Merchantability; Usage of Trade.

(1) Unless excluded or modified (Section 2–316), a warranty that the goods shall be merchantable is implied in a contract for their sale if the seller is a merchant with respect to goods of that kind. Under this section the serving for value of food or drink to be consumed either on the premises or elsewhere is a sale.

(2) Goods to be merchantable must be at least such as

(a) pass without objection in the trade under the contract description; and

(b) in the case of fungible goods, are of fair average quality within the description; and

(c) are fit for the ordinary purposes for which such goods are used; and

(d) run, within the variations permitted by the agreement, of even kind, quality and quantity within each unit and among all units involved; and

(e) are adequately contained, packaged, and labeled as the agreement may require; and

(f) conform to the promises or affirmations of fact made on the container or label if any.

(3) Unless excluded or modified (Section 2–316) other implied warranties may arise from course of dealing or usage of trade.

§ 2–315. Implied Warranty: Fitness for Particular Purpose.

Where the seller at the time of contracting has reason to know any particular purpose for which the goods are required and that the buyer is relying on the seller's skill or judgment to select or furnish suitable goods, there is unless excluded or modified under the next section an implied warranty that the goods shall be fit for such purpose.

§ 2–316. Exclusion or Modification of Warranties.

(1) Words or conduct relevant to the creation of an express warranty and words or conduct tending to negate or limit warranty shall be construed wherever reasonable as consistent with each other; but subject to the provisions of this Article on parol or extrinsic evidence (Section 2–202) negation or limitation is inoperative to the extent that such construction is unreasonable.

(2) Subject to subsection (3), to exclude or modify the implied warranty of merchantability or any part of it the language must mention merchantability and in case of a writing must be conspicuous, and to exclude or modify any implied warranty of fitness the exclusion must be by a writing and conspicuous. Language to exclude all implied warranties of fitness is sufficient if it states, for example, that "There are no warranties which extend beyond the description on the face hereof."

(3) Notwithstanding subsection (2)

(a) unless the circumstances indicate otherwise, all implied warranties are excluded by expressions like "as is", "with all faults" or other language which in common understanding calls the buyer's attention to the exclusion of warranties and makes plain that there is no implied warranty; and

(b) when the buyer before entering into the contract has examined the goods or the sample or model as fully as he desired or has refused to examine the goods there is no implied warranty with regard to defects which an examination ought in the circumstances to have revealed to him; and

(c) an implied warranty can also be excluded or modified by course of dealing or course of performance or usage of trade.

(4) Remedies for breach of warranty can be limited in accordance with the provisions of this Article on liquidation or limitation of damages and on contractual modification of remedy (Sections 2–718 and 2–719).

§ 2–317. Cumulation and Conflict of Warranties Express or Implied.

Warranties whether express or implied shall be construed as consistent with each other and as cumulative, but if such construction is unreasonable the intention of the parties shall determine which warranty is dominant. In ascertaining that intention the following rules apply:

(a) Exact or technical specifications displace an inconsistent sample or model or general language of description.

(b) A sample from an existing bulk displaces inconsistent general language of description.

(c) Express warranties displace inconsistent implied warranties other than an implied warranty of fitness for a particular purpose.

§ 2–318. Third Party Beneficiaries of Warranties Express or Implied.

Note: If this Act is introduced in the Congress of the United States this section should be omitted. (States to select one alternative.)

Alternative A

A seller's warranty whether express or implied extends to any natural person who is in the family or household of his buyer or who is a guest in his home if it is reasonable to expect that such person may use, consume or be affected by the goods and who is injured in person by breach of the warranty. A seller may not exclude or limit the operation of this section.

Alternative B

A seller's warranty whether express or implied extends to any natural person who may reasonably be expected to use, consume or be affected by the goods and who is injured in person by breach of the warranty. A seller may not exclude or limit the operation of this section.

Alternative C

A seller's warranty whether express or implied extends to any person who may reasonably be expected to use, consume or be affected by the goods and who is injured by breach of the warranty. A seller may not exclude or limit the operation of this section with respect to injury to the person of an individual to whom the warranty extends.

As amended 1966.

§ 2–319. F.O.B. and F.A.S. Terms.

(1) Unless otherwise agreed the term F.O.B. (which means "free on board") at a named place, even though used only in connection with the stated price, is a delivery term under which

(a) when the term is F.O.B. the place of shipment, the seller must at that place ship the goods in the manner provided in this Article (Section 2–504) and bear the expense and risk of putting them into the possession of the carrier; or

(b) when the term is F.O.B. the place of destination, the seller must at his own expense and risk transport the goods to that place and there tender delivery of them in the manner provided in this Article (Section 2–503);

(c) when under either (a) or (b) the term is also F.O.B. vessel, car or other vehicle, the seller must in addition at his own expense and risk load the goods on board. If the term is F.O.B. vessel the buyer must name the vessel and in an appropriate case the seller must comply with the provisions of this Article on the form of bill of lading (Section 2–323).

(2) Unless otherwise agreed the term F.A.S. vessel (which means "free alongside") at a named port, even though used only in connection with the stated price, is a delivery term under which the seller must

(a) at his own expense and risk deliver the goods alongside the vessel in the manner usual in that port or on a dock designated and provided by the buyer; and

(b) obtain and tender a receipt for the goods in exchange for which the carrier is under a duty to issue a bill of lading.

(3) Unless otherwise agreed in any case falling within subsection (1)(a) or (c) or subsection (2) the buyer must seasonably give any needed instructions for making delivery, including when the term is F.A.S. or F.O.B. the loading berth of the vessel and in an appropriate case its name and sailing date. The seller may treat the failure of needed instructions as a failure of cooperation under this Article (Section 2–311). He may also at his option move the goods in any reasonable manner preparatory to delivery or shipment.

(4) Under the term F.O.B. vessel or F.A.S. unless otherwise agreed the buyer must make payment against tender of the required documents and the seller may not tender nor the buyer demand delivery of the goods in substitution for the documents.

§ 2–320. C.I.F. and C. & F. Terms.

(1) The term C.I.F. means that the price includes in a lump sum the cost of the goods and the insurance and freight to the named destination. The term C. & F. or C.F. means that the price so includes cost and freight to the named destination.

(2) Unless otherwise agreed and even though used only in connection with the stated price and destination, the term C.I.F. destination or its equivalent requires the seller at his own expense and risk to

(a) put the goods into the possession of a carrier at the port for shipment and obtain a negotiable bill or bills of lading covering the entire transportation to the named destination; and

(b) load the goods and obtain a receipt from the carrier (which may be contained in the bill of lading) showing that the freight has been paid or provided for; and

(c) obtain a policy or certificate of insurance, including any war risk insurance, of a kind and on terms then current at the port of shipment in the usual amount, in the currency of the contract, shown to cover the same goods covered by the bill of lading and providing for payment of loss to the order of the buyer or for the account of whom it may concern; but the seller may add to the price the amount of the premium for any such war risk insurance; and

(d) prepare an invoice of the goods and procure any other documents required to effect shipment or to comply with the contract; and

(e) forward and tender with commercial promptness all the documents in due form and with any indorsement necessary to perfect the buyer's rights.

(3) Unless otherwise agreed the term C. & F. or its equivalent has the same effect and imposes upon the seller the same obligations and risks as a C.I.F. term except the obligation as to insurance.

(4) Under the term C.I.F. or C. & F. unless otherwise agreed the buyer must make payment against tender of the required documents and the seller may not tender nor the buyer demand delivery of the goods in substitution for the documents.

§ 2–321. C.I.F. or C. & F.: "Net Landed Weights"; "Payment on Arrival"; Warranty of Condition on Arrival.

Under a contract containing a term C.I.F. or C. & F.

(1) Where the price is based on or is to be adjusted according to "net landed weights", "delivered weights", "out turn" quantity or quality or the like, unless otherwise agreed the seller must reason-

ably estimate the price. The payment due on tender of the documents called for by the contract is the amount so estimated, but after final adjustment of the price a settlement must be made with commercial promptness.

(2) An agreement described in subsection (1) or any warranty of quality or condition of the goods on arrival places upon the seller the risk of ordinary deterioration, shrinkage and the like in transportation but has no effect on the place or time of identification to the contract for sale or delivery or on the passing of the risk of loss.

(3) Unless otherwise agreed where the contract provides for payment on or after arrival of the goods the seller must before payment allow such preliminary inspection as is feasible; but if the goods are lost delivery of the documents and payment are due when the goods should have arrived.

§ 2–322. Delivery "Ex-Ship".

(1) Unless otherwise agreed a term for delivery of goods "ex-ship" (which means from the carrying vessel) or in equivalent language is not restricted to a particular ship and requires delivery from a ship which has reached a place at the named port of destination where goods of the kind are usually discharged.

(2) Under such a term unless otherwise agreed

(a) the seller must discharge all liens arising out of the carriage and furnish the buyer with a direction which puts the carrier under a duty to deliver the goods; and

(b) the risk of loss does not pass to the buyer until the goods leave the ship's tackle or are otherwise properly unloaded.

§ 2–323. Form of Bill of Lading Required in Overseas Shipment; "Overseas".

(1) Where the contract contemplates overseas shipment and contains a term C.I.F. or C. & F. or F.O.B. vessel, the seller unless otherwise agreed must obtain a negotiable bill of lading stating that the goods have been loaded on board or, in the case of a term C.I.F. or C. & F., received for shipment.

(2) Where in a case within subsection (1) a bill of lading has been issued in a set of parts, unless otherwise agreed if the documents are not to be sent from abroad the buyer may demand tender of the full set; otherwise only one part of the bill of lading need be tendered. Even if the agreement expressly requires a full set

(a) due tender of a single part is acceptable within the provisions of this Article on cure of improper delivery (subsection (1) of Section 2–508); and

(b) even though the full set is demanded, if the documents are sent from abroad the person tendering an incomplete set may nevertheless require payment upon furnishing an indemnity which the buyer in good faith deems adequate.

(3) A shipment by water or by air or a contract contemplating such shipment is "overseas" insofar as by usage of trade or agreement it is subject to the commercial, financing or shipping practices characteristic of international deep water commerce.

§ 2–324. "No Arrival, No Sale" Term.

Under a term "no arrival, no sale" or terms of like meaning, unless otherwise agreed,

(a) the seller must properly ship conforming goods and if they arrive by any means he must tender them on arrival but he assumes no obligation that the goods will arrive unless he has caused the non-arrival; and

(b) where without fault of the seller the goods are in part lost or have so deteriorated as no longer to conform to the contract or arrive after the contract time, the buyer may proceed as if there had been casualty to identified goods (Section 2–613).

§ 2–325. "Letter of Credit" Term; "Confirmed Credit".

(1) Failure of the buyer seasonably to furnish an agreed letter of credit is a breach of the contract for sale.

(2) The delivery to seller of a proper letter of credit suspends the buyer's obligation to pay. If the letter of credit is dishonored, the seller may on seasonable notification to the buyer require payment directly from him.

(3) Unless otherwise agreed the term "letter of credit" or "banker's credit" in a contract for sale means an irrevocable credit issued by a financing agency of good repute and, where the shipment is overseas, of good international repute. The term "confirmed credit" means that the credit must also carry the direct obligation of such an agency which does business in the seller's financial market.

§ 2–326. Sale on Approval and Sale or Return; Rights of Creditors.

(1) Unless otherwise agreed, if delivered goods may be returned by the buyer even though they conform to the contract, the transaction is

(a) a "sale on approval" if the goods are delivered primarily for use, and

(b) a "sale or return" if the goods are delivered primarily for resale.

(2) Goods held on approval are not subject to the claims of the buyer's creditors until acceptance; goods held on sale or return are subject to such claims while in the buyer's possession.

(3) Any "or return" term of a contract for sale is to be treated as a separate contract for sale within the statute of frauds section of this Article (Section 2–201) and as contradicting the sale aspect of the contract within the provisions of this Article or on parol or extrinsic evidence (Section 2–202).

As amended in 1999.

§ 2–327. Special Incidents of Sale on Approval and Sale or Return.

(1) Under a sale on approval unless otherwise agreed

(a) although the goods are identified to the contract the risk of loss and the title do not pass to the buyer until acceptance; and

(b) use of the goods consistent with the purpose of trial is not acceptance but failure seasonably to notify the seller of election to return the goods is acceptance, and if the goods conform to the contract acceptance of any part is acceptance of the whole; and

(c) after due notification of election to return, the return is at the seller's risk and expense but a merchant buyer must follow any reasonable instructions.

(2) Under a sale or return unless otherwise agreed

(a) the option to return extends to the whole or any commercial unit of the goods while in substantially their original condition, but must be exercised seasonably; and

(b) the return is at the buyer's risk and expense.

§ 2–328. Sale by Auction.

(1) In a sale by auction if goods are put up in lots each lot is the subject of a separate sale.

(2) A sale by auction is complete when the auctioneer so announces by the fall of the hammer or in other customary manner. Where a bid is made while the hammer is falling in acceptance of a prior bid the auctioneer may in his discretion reopen the bidding or declare the goods sold under the bid on which the hammer was falling.

(3) Such a sale is with reserve unless the goods are in explicit terms put up without reserve. In an auction with reserve the auctioneer may withdraw the goods at any time until he announces completion of the sale. In an auction without reserve, after the auctioneer calls for bids on an article or lot, that article or lot cannot be withdrawn unless no bid is made within a reasonable time. In either case a bidder may retract his bid until the auctioneer's announcement of completion of the sale, but a bidder's retraction does not revive any previous bid.

(4) If the auctioneer knowingly receives a bid on the seller's behalf or the seller makes or procures such as bid, and notice has not been given that liberty for such bidding is reserved, the buyer may at his option avoid the sale or take the goods at the price of the last good faith bid prior to the completion of the sale. This subsection shall not apply to any bid at a forced sale.

Part 4 Title, Creditors and Good Faith Purchasers

§ 2–401. Passing of Title; Reservation for Security; Limited Application of This Section.

Each provision of this Article with regard to the rights, obligations and remedies of the seller, the buyer, purchasers or other third parties applies irrespective of title to the goods except where the provision refers to such title. Insofar as situations are not covered by the other provisions of this Article and matters concerning title became material the following rules apply:

(1) Title to goods cannot pass under a contract for sale prior to their identification to the contract (Section 2–501), and unless otherwise explicitly agreed the buyer acquires by their identification a special property as limited by this Act. Any retention or reservation by the seller of the title (property) in goods shipped or delivered to the buyer is limited in effect to a reservation of a security interest. Subject to these provisions and to the provisions of the Article on Secured Transactions (Article 9), title to goods passes from the seller to the buyer in any manner and on any conditions explicitly agreed on by the parties.

(2) Unless otherwise explicitly agreed title passes to the buyer at the time and place at which the seller completes his performance with reference to the physical delivery of the goods, despite any reservation of a security interest and even though a document of title is to be delivered at a different time or place; and in particular and despite any reservation of a security interest by the bill of lading

(a) if the contract requires or authorizes the seller to send the goods to the buyer but does not require him to deliver them at destination, title passes to the buyer at the time and place of shipment; but

(b) if the contract requires delivery at destination, title passes on tender there.

(3) Unless otherwise explicitly agreed where delivery is to be made without moving the goods,

(a) if the seller is to deliver a document of title, title passes at the time when and the place where he delivers such documents; or

(b) if the goods are at the time of contracting already identified and no documents are to be delivered, title passes at the time and place of contracting.

(4) A rejection or other refusal by the buyer to receive or retain the goods, whether or not justified, or a justified revocation of acceptance revests title to the goods in the seller. Such revesting occurs by operation of law and is not a "sale".

§ 2–402. Rights of Seller's Creditors Against Sold Goods.

(1) Except as provided in subsections (2) and (3), rights of unsecured creditors of the seller with respect to goods which have been identified to a contract for sale are subject to the buyer's rights to recover the goods under this Article (Sections 2–502 and 2–716).

(2) A creditor of the seller may treat a sale or an identification of goods to a contract for sale as void if as against him a retention of possession by the seller is fraudulent under any rule of law of the state where the goods are situated, except that retention of possession in good faith and current course of trade by a merchant-seller for a commercially reasonable time after a sale or identification is not fraudulent.

(3) Nothing in this Article shall be deemed to impair the rights of creditors of the seller

(a) under the provisions of the Article on Secured Transactions (Article 9); or

(b) where identification to the contract or delivery is made not in current course of trade but in satisfaction of or as security for a pre-existing claim for money, security or the like and is made under circumstances which under any rule of law of the state where the goods are situated would apart from this Article constitute the transaction a fraudulent transfer or voidable preference.

§ 2–403. Power to Transfer; Good Faith Purchase of Goods; "Entrusting".

(1) A purchaser of goods acquires all title which his transferor had or had power to transfer except that a purchaser of a limited interest acquires rights only to the extent of the interest purchased. A person with voidable title has power to transfer a good title to a good faith purchaser for value. When goods have been delivered under a transaction of purchase the purchaser has such power even though

(a) the transferor was deceived as to the identity of the purchaser, or

(b) the delivery was in exchange for a check which is later dishonored, or

(c) it was agreed that the transaction was to be a "cash sale", or

(d) the delivery was procured through fraud punishable as larcenous under the criminal law.

(2) Any entrusting of possession of goods to a merchant who deals in goods of that kind gives him power to transfer all rights of the entruster to a buyer in ordinary course of business.

(3) "Entrusting" includes any delivery and any acquiescence in retention of possession regardless of any condition expressed between the parties to the delivery or acquiescence and regardless of whether the procurement of the entrusting or the possessor's disposition of the goods have been such as to be larcenous under the criminal law.

(4) The rights of other purchasers of goods and of lien creditors are governed by the Articles on Secured Transactions (Article 9), Bulk Transfers (Article 6) and Documents of Title (Article 7).
As amended in 1988.

Part 5 Performance

§ 2–501. Insurable Interest in Goods; Manner of Identification of Goods.

(1) The buyer obtains a special property and an insurable interest in goods by identification of existing goods as goods to which the contract refers even though the goods so identified are non-conforming and he has an option to return or reject them. Such identification can be made at any time and in any manner explicitly agreed to by the parties. In the absence of explicit agreement identification occurs

(a) when the contract is made if it is for the sale of goods already existing and identified;

(b) if the contract is for the sale of future goods other than those described in paragraph (c), when goods are shipped, marked or otherwise designated by the seller as goods to which the contract refers;

(c) when the crops are planted or otherwise become growing crops or the young are conceived if the contract is for the sale of unborn young to be born within twelve months after contracting or for the sale of crops to be harvested within twelve months or the next normal harvest season after contracting whichever is longer.

(2) The seller retains an insurable interest in goods so long as title to or any security interest in the goods remains in him and where the identification is by the seller alone he may until default or insolvency or notification to the buyer that the identification is final substitute other goods for those identified.

(3) Nothing in this section impairs any insurable interest recognized under any other statute or rule of law.

§ 2–502. Buyer's Right to Goods on Seller's Insolvency.

(1) Subject to subsections (2) and (3) and even though the goods have not been shipped a buyer who has paid a part or all of the price of goods in which he has a special property under the provisions of the immediately preceding section may on making and keeping good a tender of any unpaid portion of their price recover them from the seller if:

(a) in the case of goods bought for personal, family, or household purposes, the seller repudiates or fails to deliver as required by the contract; or

(b) in all cases, the seller becomes insolvent within ten days after receipt of the first installment on their price.

(2) The buyer's right to recover the goods under subsection (1)(a) vests upon acquisition of a special property, even if the seller had not then repudiated or failed to deliver.

(3) If the identification creating his special property has been made by the buyer he acquires the right to recover the goods only if they conform to the contract for sale.
As amended in 1999.

§ 2–503. Manner of Seller's Tender of Delivery.

(1) Tender of delivery requires that the seller put and hold conforming goods at the buyer's disposition and give the buyer any notification reasonably necessary to enable him to take delivery. The manner, time and place for tender are determined by the agreement and this Article, and in particular

(a) tender must be at a reasonable hour, and if it is of goods they must be kept available for the period reasonably necessary to enable the buyer to take possession; but

(b) unless otherwise agreed the buyer must furnish facilities reasonably suited to the receipt of the goods.

(2) Where the case is within the next section respecting shipment tender requires that the seller comply with its provisions.

(3) Where the seller is required to deliver at a particular destination tender requires that he comply with subsection (1) and also in any appropriate case tender documents as described in subsections (4) and (5) of this section.

(4) Where goods are in the possession of a bailee and are to be delivered without being moved

    (a) tender requires that the seller either tender a negotiable document of title covering such goods or procure acknowledgment by the bailee of the buyer's right to possession of the goods; but

    (b) tender to the buyer of a non-negotiable document of title or of a written direction to the bailee to deliver is sufficient tender unless the buyer seasonably objects, and receipt by the bailee of notification of the buyer's rights fixes those rights as against the bailee and all third persons; but risk of loss of the goods and of any failure by the bailee to honor the non-negotiable document of title or to obey the direction remains on the seller until the buyer has had a reasonable time to present the document or direction, and a refusal by the bailee to honor the document or to obey the direction defeats the tender.

(5) Where the contract requires the seller to deliver documents

    (a) he must tender all such documents in correct form, except as provided in this Article with respect to bills of lading in a set (subsection (2) of Section 2–323); and

    (b) tender through customary banking channels is sufficient and dishonor of a draft accompanying the documents constitutes non-acceptance or rejection.

§ 2–504. Shipment by Seller.

Where the seller is required or authorized to send the goods to the buyer and the contract does not require him to deliver them at a particular destination, then unless otherwise agreed he must

    (a) put the goods in the possession of such a carrier and make such a contract for their transportation as may be reasonable having regard to the nature of the goods and other circumstances of the case; and

    (b) obtain and promptly deliver or tender in due form any document necessary to enable the buyer to obtain possession of the goods or otherwise required by the agreement or by usage of trade; and

    (c) promptly notify the buyer of the shipment.

Failure to notify the buyer under paragraph (c) or to make a proper contract under paragraph (a) is a ground for rejection only if material delay or loss ensues.

§ 2–505. Seller's Shipment under Reservation.

(1) Where the seller has identified goods to the contract by or before shipment:

    (a) his procurement of a negotiable bill of lading to his own order or otherwise reserves in him a security interest in the goods. His procurement of the bill to the order of a financing agency or of the buyer indicates in addition only the seller's expectation of transferring that interest to the person named.

    (b) a non-negotiable bill of lading to himself or his nominee reserves possession of the goods as security but except in a case

of conditional delivery (subsection (2) of Section 2–507) a non-negotiable bill of lading naming the buyer as consignee reserves no security interest even though the seller retains possession of the bill of lading.

(2) When shipment by the seller with reservation of a security interest is in violation of the contract for sale it constitutes an improper contract for transportation within the preceding section but impairs neither the rights given to the buyer by shipment and identification of the goods to the contract nor the seller's powers as a holder of a negotiable document.

§ 2–506. Rights of Financing Agency.

(1) A financing agency by paying or purchasing for value a draft which relates to a shipment of goods acquires to the extent of the payment or purchase and in addition to its own rights under the draft and any document of title securing it any rights of the shipper in the goods including the right to stop delivery and the shipper's right to have the draft honored by the buyer.

(2) The right to reimbursement of a financing agency which has in good faith honored or purchased the draft under commitment to or authority from the buyer is not impaired by subsequent discovery of defects with reference to any relevant document which was apparently regular on its face.

§ 2–507. Effect of Seller's Tender; Delivery on Condition.

(1) Tender of delivery is a condition to the buyer's duty to accept the goods and, unless otherwise agreed, to his duty to pay for them. Tender entitles the seller to acceptance of the goods and to payment according to the contract.

(2) Where payment is due and demanded on the delivery to the buyer of goods or documents of title, his right as against the seller to retain or dispose of them is conditional upon his making the payment due.

§ 2–508. Cure by Seller of Improper Tender or Delivery; Replacement.

(1) Where any tender or delivery by the seller is rejected because non-conforming and the time for performance has not yet expired, the seller may seasonably notify the buyer of his intention to cure and may then within the contract time make a conforming delivery.

(2) Where the buyer rejects a non-conforming tender which the seller had reasonable grounds to believe would be acceptable with or without money allowance the seller may if he seasonably notifies the buyer have a further reasonable time to substitute a conforming tender.

§ 2–509. Risk of Loss in the Absence of Breach.

(1) Where the contract requires or authorizes the seller to ship the goods by carrier

    (a) if it does not require him to deliver them at a particular destination, the risk of loss passes to the buyer when the goods are duly delivered to the carrier even though the shipment is under reservation (Section 2–505); but

    (b) if it does require him to deliver them at a particular destination and the goods are there duly tendered while in the possession of the carrier, the risk of loss passes to the buyer when the goods are there duly so tendered as to enable the buyer to take delivery.

(2) Where the goods are held by a bailee to be delivered without being moved, the risk of loss passes to the buyer

(a) on his receipt of a negotiable document of title covering the goods; or

(b) on acknowledgment by the bailee of the buyer's right to possession of the goods; or

(c) after his receipt of a non-negotiable document of title or other written direction to deliver, as provided in subsection (4)(b) of Section 2–503.

(3) In any case not within subsection (1) or (2), the risk of loss passes to the buyer on his receipt of the goods if the seller is a merchant; otherwise the risk passes to the buyer on tender of delivery.

(4) The provisions of this section are subject to contrary agreement of the parties and to the provisions of this Article on sale on approval (Section 2–327) and on effect of breach on risk of loss (Section 2–510).

§ 2–510. Effect of Breach on Risk of Loss.

(1) Where a tender or delivery of goods so fails to conform to the contract as to give a right of rejection the risk of their loss remains on the seller until cure or acceptance.

(2) Where the buyer rightfully revokes acceptance he may to the extent of any deficiency in his effective insurance coverage treat the risk of loss as having rested on the seller from the beginning.

(3) Where the buyer as to conforming goods already identified to the contract for sale repudiates or is otherwise in breach before risk of their loss has passed to him, the seller may to the extent of any deficiency in his effective insurance coverage treat the risk of loss as resting on the buyer for a commercially reasonable time.

§ 2–511. Tender of Payment by Buyer; Payment by Check.

(1) Unless otherwise agreed tender of payment is a condition to the seller's duty to tender and complete any delivery.

(2) Tender of payment is sufficient when made by any means or in any manner current in the ordinary course of business unless the seller demands payment in legal tender and gives any extension of time reasonably necessary to procure it.

(3) Subject to the provisions of this Act on the effect of an instrument on an obligation (Section 3–310), payment by check is conditional and is defeated as between the parties by dishonor of the check on due presentment.

As amended in 1994.

§ 2–512. Payment by Buyer Before Inspection.

(1) Where the contract requires payment before inspection non-conformity of the goods does not excuse the buyer from so making payment unless

(a) the non-conformity appears without inspection; or

(b) despite tender of the required documents the circumstances would justify injunction against honor under this Act (Section 5–109(b)).

(2) Payment pursuant to subsection (1) does not constitute an acceptance of goods or impair the buyer's right to inspect or any of his remedies.

As amended in 1995.

§ 2–513. Buyer's Right to Inspection of Goods.

(1) Unless otherwise agreed and subject to subsection (3), where goods are tendered or delivered or identified to the contract for sale, the buyer has a right before payment or acceptance to inspect them at any reasonable place and time and in any reasonable manner. When the seller is required or authorized to send the goods to the buyer, the inspection may be after their arrival.

(2) Expenses of inspection must be borne by the buyer but may be recovered from the seller if the goods do not conform and are rejected.

(3) Unless otherwise agreed and subject to the provisions of this Article on C.I.F. contracts (subsection (3) of Section 2–321), the buyer is not entitled to inspect the goods before payment of the price when the contract provides

(a) for delivery "C.O.D." or on other like terms; or

(b) for payment against documents of title, except where such payment is due only after the goods are to become available for inspection.

(4) A place or method of inspection fixed by the parties is presumed to be exclusive but unless otherwise expressly agreed it does not postpone identification or shift the place for delivery or for passing the risk of loss. If compliance becomes impossible, inspection shall be as provided in this section unless the place or method fixed was clearly intended as an indispensable condition failure of which avoids the contract.

§ 2–514. When Documents Deliverable on Acceptance; When on Payment.

Unless otherwise agreed documents against which a draft is drawn are to be delivered to the drawee on acceptance of the draft if it is payable more than three days after presentment; otherwise, only on payment.

§ 2–515. Preserving Evidence of Goods in Dispute.

In furtherance of the adjustment of any claim or dispute

(a) either party on reasonable notification to the other and for the purpose of ascertaining the facts and preserving evidence has the right to inspect, test and sample the goods including such of them as may be in the possession or control of the other; and

(b) the parties may agree to a third party inspection or survey to determine the conformity or condition of the goods and may agree that the findings shall be binding upon them in any subsequent litigation or adjustment.

Part 6 Breach, Repudiation and Excuse

§ 2–601. Buyer's Rights on Improper Delivery.

Subject to the provisions of this Article on breach in installment contracts (Section 2–612) and unless otherwise agreed under the sections on contractual limitations of remedy (Sections 2–718 and 2–719), if the goods or the tender of delivery fail in any respect to conform to the contract, the buyer may

(a) reject the whole; or

(b) accept the whole; or

(c) accept any commercial unit or units and reject the rest.

§ 2–602. Manner and Effect of Rightful Rejection.

(1) Rejection of goods must be within a reasonable time after their delivery or tender. It is ineffective unless the buyer seasonably notifies the seller.

(2) Subject to the provisions of the two following sections on rejected goods (Sections 2–603 and 2–604),

(a) after rejection any exercise of ownership by the buyer with respect to any commercial unit is wrongful as against the seller; and

(b) if the buyer has before rejection taken physical possession of goods in which he does not have a security interest under the provisions of this Article (subsection (3) of Section 2–711), he is under a duty after rejection to hold them with reasonable care at the seller's disposition for a time sufficient to permit the seller to remove them; but

(c) the buyer has no further obligations with regard to goods rightfully rejected.

(3) The seller's rights with respect to goods wrongfully rejected are governed by the provisions of this Article on Seller's remedies in general (Section 2–703).

§ 2–603. Merchant Buyer's Duties as to Rightfully Rejected Goods.

(1) Subject to any security interest in the buyer (subsection (3) of Section 2–711), when the seller has no agent or place of business at the market of rejection a merchant buyer is under a duty after rejection of goods in his possession or control to follow any reasonable instructions received from the seller with respect to the goods and in the absence of such instructions to make reasonable efforts to sell them for the seller's account if they are perishable or threaten to decline in value speedily. Instructions are not reasonable if on demand indemnity for expenses is not forthcoming.

(2) When the buyer sells goods under subsection (1), he is entitled to reimbursement from the seller or out of the proceeds for reasonable expenses of caring for and selling them, and if the expenses include no selling commission then to such commission as is usual in the trade or if there is none to a reasonable sum not exceeding ten per cent on the gross proceeds.

(3) In complying with this section the buyer is held only to good faith and good faith conduct hereunder is neither acceptance nor conversion nor the basis of an action for damages.

§ 2–604. Buyer's Options as to Salvage of Rightfully Rejected Goods.

Subject to the provisions of the immediately preceding section on perishables if the seller gives no instructions within a reasonable time after notification of rejection the buyer may store the rejected goods for the seller's account or reship them to him or resell them for the seller's account with reimbursement as provided in the preceding section. Such action is not acceptance or conversion.

§ 2–605. Waiver of Buyer's Objections by Failure to Particularize.

(1) The buyer's failure to state in connection with rejection a particular defect which is ascertainable by reasonable inspection precludes him from relying on the unstated defect to justify rejection or to establish breach

(a) where the seller could have cured it if stated seasonally; or

(b) between merchants when the seller has after rejection made a request in writing for a full and final written statement of all defects on which the buyer proposes to rely.

(2) Payment against documents made without reservation of rights precludes recovery of the payment for defects apparent on the face of the documents.

§ 2–606. What Constitutes Acceptance of Goods.

(1) Acceptance of goods occurs when the buyer

(a) after a reasonable opportunity to inspect the goods signifies to the seller that the goods are conforming or that he will take or retain them in spite of their nonconformity; or

(b) fails to make an effective rejection (subsection (1) of Section 2–602), but such acceptance does not occur until the buyer has had a reasonable opportunity to inspect them; or

(c) does any act inconsistent with the seller's ownership; but if such act is wrongful as against the seller it is an acceptance only if ratified by him.

(2) Acceptance of a part of any commercial unit is acceptance of that entire unit.

§ 2–607. Effect of Acceptance; Notice of Breach; Burden of Establishing Breach After Acceptance; Notice of Claim or Litigation to Person Answerable Over.

(1) The buyer must pay at the contract rate for any goods accepted.

(2) Acceptance of goods by the buyer precludes rejection of the goods accepted and if made with knowledge of a non-conformity cannot be revoked because of it unless the acceptance was on the reasonable assumption that the non-conformity would be seasonably cured but acceptance does not of itself impair any other remedy provided by this Article for non-conformity.

(3) Where a tender has been accepted

(a) the buyer must within a reasonable time after he discovers or should have discovered any breach notify the seller of breach or be barred from any remedy; and

(b) if the claim is one for infringement or the like (subsection (3) of Section 2–312) and the buyer is sued as a result of such a breach he must so notify the seller within a reasonable time after he receives notice of the litigation or be barred from any remedy over for liability established by the litigation.

(4) The burden is on the buyer to establish any breach with respect to the goods accepted.

(5) Where the buyer is sued for breach of a warranty or other obligation for which his seller is answerable over

(a) he may give his seller written notice of the litigation. If the notice states that the seller may come in and defend and that if the seller does not do so he will be bound in any action against him by his buyer by any determination of fact common to the two litigations, then unless the seller after seasonable receipt of the notice does come in and defend he is so bound.

(b) if the claim is one for infringement or the like (subsection (3) of Section 2–312) the original seller may demand in writing that his buyer turn over to him control of the litigation including settlement or else be barred from any remedy over and if he also agrees to bear all expense and to satisfy any adverse judgment, then unless the buyer after seasonable receipt of the demand does turn over control the buyer is so barred.

(6) The provisions of subsections (3), (4) and (5) apply to any obligation of a buyer to hold the seller harmless against infringement or the like (subsection (3) of Section 2–312).

§ 2–608. Revocation of Acceptance in Whole or in Part.

(1) The buyer may revoke his acceptance of a lot or commercial unit whose non-conformity substantially impairs its value to him if he has accepted it

(a) on the reasonable assumption that its nonconformity would be cured and it has not been seasonably cured; or

(b) without discovery of such non-conformity if his acceptance was reasonably induced either by the difficulty of discovery before acceptance or by the seller's assurances.

(2) Revocation of acceptance must occur within a reasonable time after the buyer discovers or should have discovered the ground for it and before any substantial change in condition of the goods which is not caused by their own defects. It is not effective until the buyer notifies the seller of it.

(3) A buyer who so revokes has the same rights and duties with regard to the goods involved as if he had rejected them.

§ 2–609. Right to Adequate Assurance of Performance.

(1) A contract for sale imposes an obligation on each party that the other's expectation of receiving due performance will not be impaired. When reasonable grounds for insecurity arise with respect to the performance of either party the other may in writing demand adequate assurance of due performance and until he receives such assurance may if commercially reasonable suspend any performance for which he has not already received the agreed return.

(2) Between merchants the reasonableness of grounds for insecurity and the adequacy of any assurance offered shall be determined according to commercial standards.

(3) Acceptance of any improper delivery or payment does not prejudice the party's right to demand adequate assurance of future performance.

(4) After receipt of a justified demand failure to provide within a reasonable time not exceeding thirty days such assurance of due performance as is adequate under the circumstances of the particular case is a repudiation of the contract.

§ 2–610. Anticipatory Repudiation.

When either party repudiates the contract with respect to a performance not yet due the loss of which will substantially impair the value of the contract to the other, the aggrieved party may

(a) for a commercially reasonable time await performance by the repudiating party; or

(b) resort to any remedy for breach (Section 2–703 or Section 2–711), even though he has notified the repudiating party that he would await the latter's performance and has urged retraction; and

(c) in either case suspend his own performance or proceed in accordance with the provisions of this Article on the seller's right to identify goods to the contract notwithstanding breach or to salvage unfinished goods (Section 2–704).

§ 2–611. Retraction of Anticipatory Repudiation.

(1) Until the repudiating party's next performance is due he can retract his repudiation unless the aggrieved party has since the repudiation cancelled or materially changed his position or otherwise indicated that he considers the repudiation final.

(2) Retraction may be by any method which clearly indicates to the aggrieved party that the repudiating party intends to perform, but must include any assurance justifiably demanded under the provisions of this Article (Section 2–609).

(3) Retraction reinstates the repudiating party's rights under the contract with due excuse and allowance to the aggrieved party for any delay occasioned by the repudiation.

§ 2–612. "Installment Contract"; Breach.

(1) An "installment contract" is one which requires or authorizes the delivery of goods in separate lots to be separately accepted, even though the contract contains a clause "each delivery is a separate contract" or its equivalent.

(2) The buyer may reject any installment which is non-conforming if the non-conformity substantially impairs the value of that installment and cannot be cured or if the non-conformity is a defect in the required documents; but if the non-conformity does not fall within subsection (3) and the seller gives adequate assurance of its cure the buyer must accept that installment.

(3) Whenever non-conformity or default with respect to one or more installments substantially impairs the value of the whole contract there is a breach of the whole. But the aggrieved party reinstates the contract if he accepts a non-conforming installment without seasonably notifying of cancellation or if he brings an action with respect only to past installments or demands performance as to future installments.

§ 2–613. Casualty to Identified Goods.

Where the contract requires for its performance goods identified when the contract is made, and the goods suffer casualty without fault of either party before the risk of loss passes to the buyer, or in a proper case under a "no arrival, no sale" term (Section 2–324) then

(a) if the loss is total the contract is avoided; and

(b) if the loss is partial or the goods have so deteriorated as no longer to conform to the contract the buyer may nevertheless demand inspection and at his option either treat the contract as voided or accept the goods with due allowance from the contract price for the deterioration or the deficiency in quantity but without further right against the seller.

§ 2–614. Substituted Performance.

(1) Where without fault of either party the agreed berthing, loading, or unloading facilities fail or an agreed type of carrier becomes unavailable or the agreed manner of delivery otherwise becomes commercially impracticable but a commercially reasonable substitute is available, such substitute performance must be tendered and accepted.

(2) If the agreed means or manner of payment fails because of domestic or foreign governmental regulation, the seller may withhold or stop delivery unless the buyer provides a means or manner of payment which is commercially a substantial equivalent. If delivery has already been taken, payment by the means or in the manner provided by the regulation discharges the buyer's obligation unless the regulation is discriminatory, oppressive or predatory.

§ 2–615. Excuse by Failure of Presupposed Conditions.

Except so far as a seller may have assumed a greater obligation and subject to the preceding section on substituted performance:

(a) Delay in delivery or non-delivery in whole or in part by a seller who complies with paragraphs (b) and (c) is not a breach of his duty under a contract for sale if performance as agreed has been made impracticable by the occurrence of a contingency the nonoccurrence of which was a basic assumption on which the contract was made or by compliance in good faith with any applicable foreign or domestic governmental regulation or order whether or not it later proves to be invalid.

(b) Where the causes mentioned in paragraph (a) affect only a part of the seller's capacity to perform, he must allocate production and deliveries among his customers but may at his option include regular customers not then under contract as well as his own requirements for further manufacture. He may so allocate in any manner which is fair and reasonable.

(c) The seller must notify the buyer seasonably that there will be delay or non-delivery and, when allocation is required under paragraph (b), of the estimated quota thus made available for the buyer.

§ 2–616. Procedure on Notice Claiming Excuse.

(1) Where the buyer receives notification of a material or indefinite delay or an allocation justified under the preceding section he may by written notification to the seller as to any delivery concerned, and where the prospective deficiency substantially impairs the value of the whole contract under the provisions of this Article relating to breach of installment contracts (Section 2–612), then also as to the whole,

> (a) terminate and thereby discharge any unexecuted portion of the contract; or
>
> (b) modify the contract by agreeing to take his available quota in substitution.

(2) If after receipt of such notification from the seller the buyer fails so to modify the contract within a reasonable time not exceeding thirty days the contract lapses with respect to any deliveries affected.

(3) The provisions of this section may not be negated by agreement except in so far as the seller has assumed a greater obligation under the preceding section.

Part 7 Remedies

§ 2–701. Remedies for Breach of Collateral Contracts Not Impaired.

Remedies for breach of any obligation or promise collateral or ancillary to a contract for sale are not impaired by the provisions of this Article.

§ 2–702. Seller's Remedies on Discovery of Buyer's Insolvency.

(1) Where the seller discovers the buyer to be insolvent he may refuse delivery except for cash including payment for all goods theretofore delivered under the contract, and stop delivery under this Article (Section 2–705).

(2) Where the seller discovers that the buyer has received goods on credit while insolvent he may reclaim the goods upon demand made within ten days after the receipt, but if misrepresentation of solvency has been made to the particular seller in writing within three months before delivery the ten day limitation does not apply. Except as provided in this subsection the seller may not base a right to reclaim goods on the buyer's fraudulent or innocent misrepresentation of solvency or of intent to pay.

(3) The seller's right to reclaim under subsection (2) is subject to the rights of a buyer in ordinary course or other good faith purchaser under this Article (Section 2–403). Successful reclamation of goods excludes all other remedies with respect to them.

§ 2–703. Seller's Remedies in General.

Where the buyer wrongfully rejects or revokes acceptance of goods or fails to make a payment due on or before delivery or repudiates with respect to a part or the whole, then with respect to any goods directly affected and, if the breach is of the whole contract (Section 2–612), then also with respect to the whole undelivered balance, the aggrieved seller may

(a) withhold delivery of such goods;

(b) stop delivery by any bailee as hereafter provided (Section 2–705);

(c) proceed under the next section respecting goods still unidentified to the contract;

(d) resell and recover damages as hereafter provided (Section 2–706);

(e) recover damages for non-acceptance (Section 2–708) or in a proper case the price (Section 2–709);

(f) cancel.

§ 2–704. Seller's Right to Identify Goods to the Contract Notwithstanding Breach or to Salvage Unfinished Goods.

(1) An aggrieved seller under the preceding section may

> (a) identify to the contract conforming goods not already identified if at the time he learned of the breach they are in his possession or control;
>
> (b) treat as the subject of resale goods which have demonstrably been intended for the particular contract even though those goods are unfinished.

(2) Where the goods are unfinished an aggrieved seller may in the exercise of reasonable commercial judgment for the purposes of avoiding loss and of effective realization either complete the manufacture and wholly identify the goods to the contract or cease manufacture and resell for scrap or salvage value or proceed in any other reasonable manner.

§ 2–705. Seller's Stoppage of Delivery in Transit or Otherwise.

(1) The seller may stop delivery of goods in the possession of a carrier or other bailee when he discovers the buyer to be insolvent (Section 2–702) and may stop delivery of carload, truckload, planeload or larger shipments of express or freight when the buyer repudiates or fails to make a payment due before delivery or if for any other reason the seller has a right to withhold or reclaim the goods.

(2) As against such buyer the seller may stop delivery until

> (a) receipt of the goods by the buyer; or
>
> (b) acknowledgment to the buyer by any bailee of the goods except a carrier that the bailee holds the goods for the buyer; or
>
> (c) such acknowledgment to the buyer by a carrier by reshipment or as warehouseman; or
>
> (d) negotiation to the buyer of any negotiable document of title covering the goods.

(3) (a) To stop delivery the seller must so notify as to enable the bailee by reasonable diligence to prevent delivery of the goods.

> (b) After such notification the bailee must hold and deliver the goods according to the directions of the seller but the seller is liable to the bailee for any ensuing charges or damages.
>
> (c) If a negotiable document of title has been issued for goods the bailee is not obliged to obey a notification to stop until surrender of the document.
>
> (d) A carrier who has issued a non-negotiable bill of lading is not obliged to obey a notification to stop received from a person other than the consignor.

§ 2–706. Seller's Resale Including Contract for Resale.

(1) Under the conditions stated in Section 2–703 on seller's remedies, the seller may resell the goods concerned or the undelivered balance thereof. Where the resale is made in good faith and in a commercially reasonable manner the seller may recover the difference between the resale price and the contract price together with any incidental damages allowed under the provisions of this Article (Section 2–710), but less expenses saved in consequence of the buyer's breach.

(2) Except as otherwise provided in subsection (3) or unless otherwise agreed resale may be at public or private sale including sale by way of one or more contracts to sell or of identification to an existing contract of the seller. Sale may be as a unit or in parcels and at any time and place and on any terms but every aspect of the sale including the method, manner, time, place and terms must be commercially reasonable. The resale must be reasonably identified as referring to the broken contract, but it is not necessary that the goods be in existence or that any or all of them have been identified to the contract before the breach.

(3) Where the resale is at private sale the seller must give the buyer reasonable notification of his intention to resell.

(4) Where the resale is at public sale

(a) only identified goods can be sold except where there is a recognized market for a public sale of futures in goods of the kind; and

(b) it must be made at a usual place or market for public sale if one is reasonably available and except in the case of goods which are perishable or threaten to decline in value speedily the seller must give the buyer reasonable notice of the time and place of the resale; and

(c) if the goods are not to be within the view of those attending the sale the notification of sale must state the place where the goods are located and provide for their reasonable inspection by prospective bidders; and

(d) the seller may buy.

(5) A purchaser who buys in good faith at a resale takes the goods free of any rights of the original buyer even though the seller fails to comply with one or more of the requirements of this section.

(6) The seller is not accountable to the buyer for any profit made on any resale. A person in the position of a seller (Section 2–707) or a buyer who has rightfully rejected or justifiably revoked acceptance must account for any excess over the amount of his security interest, as hereinafter defined (subsection (3) of Section 2–711).

§ 2–707. "Person in the Position of a Seller".

(1) A "person in the position of a seller" includes as against a principal an agent who has paid or become responsible for the price of goods on behalf of his principal or anyone who otherwise holds a security interest or other right in goods similar to that of a seller.

(2) A person in the position of a seller may as provided in this Article withhold or stop delivery (Section 2–705) and resell (Section 2–706) and recover incidental damages (Section 2–710).

§ 2–708. Seller's Damages for Non-Acceptance or Repudiation.

(1) Subject to subsection (2) and to the provisions of this Article with respect to proof of market price (Section 2–723), the measure of damages for non-acceptance or repudiation by the buyer is the difference between the market price at the time and place for tender and the unpaid contract price together with any incidental damages provided in this Article (Section 2–710), but less expenses saved in consequence of the buyer's breach.

(2) If the measure of damages provided in subsection (1) is inadequate to put the seller in as good a position as performance would have done then the measure of damages is the profit (including reasonable overhead) which the seller would have made from full performance by the buyer, together with any incidental damages provided in this Article (Section 2–710), due allowance for costs reasonably incurred and due credit for payments or proceeds of resale.

§ 2–709. Action for the Price.

(1) When the buyer fails to pay the price as it becomes due the seller may recover, together with any incidental damages under the next section, the price

(a) of goods accepted or of conforming goods lost or damaged within a commercially reasonable time after risk of their loss has passed to the buyer; and

(b) of goods identified to the contract if the seller is unable after reasonable effort to resell them at a reasonable price or the circumstances reasonably indicate that such effort will be unavailing.

(2) Where the seller sues for the price he must hold for the buyer any goods which have been identified to the contract and are still in his control except that if resale becomes possible he may resell them at any time prior to the collection of the judgment. The net proceeds of any such resale must be credited to the buyer and payment of the judgment entitles him to any goods not resold.

(3) After the buyer has wrongfully rejected or revoked acceptance of the goods or has failed to make a payment due or has repudiated (Section 2–610), a seller who is held not entitled to the price under this section shall nevertheless be awarded damages for non-acceptance under the preceding section.

§ 2–710. Seller's Incidental Damages.

Incidental damages to an aggrieved seller include any commercially reasonable charges, expenses or commissions incurred in stopping delivery, in the transportation, care and custody of goods after the buyer's breach, in connection with return or resale of the goods or otherwise resulting from the breach.

§ 2–711. Buyer's Remedies in General; Buyer's Security Interest in Rejected Goods.

(1) Where the seller fails to make delivery or repudiates or the buyer rightfully rejects or justifiably revokes acceptance then with respect to any goods involved, and with respect to the whole if the breach goes to the whole contract (Section 2–612), the buyer may cancel and whether or not he has done so may in addition to recovering so much of the price as has been paid

(a) "cover" and have damages under the next section as to all the goods affected whether or not they have been identified to the contract; or

(b) recover damages for non-delivery as provided in this Article (Section 2–713).

(2) Where the seller fails to deliver or repudiates the buyer may also

(a) if the goods have been identified recover them as provided in this Article (Section 2–502); or

(b) in a proper case obtain specific performance or replevy the goods as provided in this Article (Section 2–716).

(3) On rightful rejection or justifiable revocation of acceptance a buyer has a security interest in goods in his possession or control for any payments made on their price and any expenses reasonably incurred in their inspection, receipt, transportation, care and custody and may hold such goods and resell them in like manner as an aggrieved seller (Section 2–706).

§ 2–712. "Cover"; Buyer's Procurement of Substitute Goods.

(1) After a breach within the preceding section the buyer may "cover" by making in good faith and without unreasonable delay any reasonable purchase of or contract to purchase goods in substitution for those due from the seller.

(2) The buyer may recover from the seller as damages the difference between the cost of cover and the contract price together with any incidental or consequential damages as hereinafter defined (Section 2–715), but less expenses saved in consequence of the seller's breach.

(3) Failure of the buyer to effect cover within this section does not bar him from any other remedy.

§ 2–713. Buyer's Damages for Non-Delivery or Repudiation.

(1) Subject to the provisions of this Article with respect to proof of market price (Section 2–723), the measure of damages for non-delivery or repudiation by the seller is the difference between the market price at the time when the buyer learned of the breach and the contract price together with any incidental and consequential damages provided in this Article (Section 2–715), but less expenses saved in consequence of the seller's breach.

(2) Market price is to be determined as of the place for tender or, in cases of rejection after arrival or revocation of acceptance, as of the place of arrival.

§ 2–714. Buyer's Damages for Breach in Regard to Accepted Goods.

(1) Where the buyer has accepted goods and given notification (subsection (3) of Section 2–607) he may recover as damages for any non-conformity of tender the loss resulting in the ordinary course of events from the seller's breach as determined in any manner which is reasonable.

(2) The measure of damages for breach of warranty is the difference at the time and place of acceptance between the value of the goods accepted and the value they would have had if they had been as warranted, unless special circumstances show proximate damages of a different amount.

(3) In a proper case any incidental and consequential damages under the next section may also be recovered.

§ 2–715. Buyer's Incidental and Consequential Damages.

(1) Incidental damages resulting from the seller's breach include expenses reasonably incurred in inspection, receipt, transportation and care and custody of goods rightfully rejected, any commercially reasonable charges, expenses or commissions in connection with effecting cover and any other reasonable expense incident to the delay or other breach.

(2) Consequential damages resulting from the seller's breach include

(a) any loss resulting from general or particular requirements and needs of which the seller at the time of contracting had reason to know and which could not reasonably be prevented by cover or otherwise; and

(b) injury to person or property proximately resulting from any breach of warranty.

§ 2–716. Buyer's Right to Specific Performance or Replevin.

(1) Specific performance may be decreed where the goods are unique or in other proper circumstances.

(2) The decree for specific performance may include such terms and conditions as to payment of the price, damages, or other relief as the court may deem just.

(3) The buyer has a right of replevin for goods identified to the contract if after reasonable effort he is unable to effect cover for such goods or the circumstances reasonably indicate that such effort will be unavailing or if the goods have been shipped under reservation and satisfaction of the security interest in them has been made or tendered. In the case of goods bought for personal, family, or household purposes, the buyer's right of replevin vests upon acquisition of a special property, even if the seller had not then repudiated or failed to deliver.

As amended in 1999.

§ 2–717. Deduction of Damages From the Price.

The buyer on notifying the seller of his intention to do so may deduct all or any part of the damages resulting from any breach of the contract from any part of the price still due under the same contract.

§ 2–718. Liquidation or Limitation of Damages; Deposits.

(1) Damages for breach by either party may be liquidated in the agreement but only at an amount which is reasonable in the light of the anticipated or actual harm caused by the breach, the difficulties of proof of loss, and the inconvenience or nonfeasibility of otherwise obtaining an adequate remedy. A term fixing unreasonably large liquidated damages is void as a penalty.

(2) Where the seller justifiably withholds delivery of goods because of the buyer's breach, the buyer is entitled to restitution of any amount by which the sum of his payments exceeds

(a) the amount to which the seller is entitled by virtue of terms liquidating the seller's damages in accordance with subsection (1), or

(b) in the absence of such terms, twenty per cent of the value of the total performance for which the buyer is obligated under the contract or $500, whichever is smaller.

(3) The buyer's right to restitution under subsection (2) is subject to offset to the extent that the seller establishes

(a) a right to recover damages under the provisions of this Article other than subsection (1), and

(b) the amount or value of any benefits received by the buyer directly or indirectly by reason of the contract.

(4) Where a seller has received payment in goods their reasonable value or the proceeds of their resale shall be treated as payments for the purposes of subsection (2); but if the seller has notice of the buyer's breach before reselling goods received in part performance, his resale is subject to the conditions laid down in this Article on resale by an aggrieved seller (Section 2–706).

§ 2–719. Contractual Modification or Limitation of Remedy.

(1) Subject to the provisions of subsections (2) and (3) of this section and of the preceding section on liquidation and limitation of damages,

(a) the agreement may provide for remedies in addition to or in substitution for those provided in this Article and may limit or alter the measure of damages recoverable under this Article, as by limiting the buyer's remedies to return of the goods and repayment of the price or to repair and replacement of nonconforming goods or parts; and

(b) resort to a remedy as provided is optional unless the remedy is expressly agreed to be exclusive, in which case it is the sole remedy.

(2) Where circumstances cause an exclusive or limited remedy to fail of its essential purpose, remedy may be had as provided in this Act.

(3) Consequential damages may be limited or excluded unless the limitation or exclusion is unconscionable. Limitation of consequential

damages for injury to the person in the case of consumer goods is prima facie unconscionable but limitation of damages where the loss is commercial is not.

§ 2–720. Effect of "Cancellation" or "Rescission" on Claims for Antecedent Breach.

Unless the contrary intention clearly appears, expressions of "cancellation" or "rescission" of the contract or the like shall not be construed as a renunciation or discharge of any claim in damages for an antecedent breach.

§ 2–721. Remedies for Fraud.

Remedies for material misrepresentation or fraud include all remedies available under this Article for non-fraudulent breach. Neither rescission or a claim for rescission of the contract for sale nor rejection or return of the goods shall bar or be deemed inconsistent with a claim for damages or other remedy.

§ 2–722. Who Can Sue Third Parties for Injury to Goods.

Where a third party so deals with goods which have been identified to a contract for sale as to cause actionable injury to a party to that contract

(a) a right of action against the third party is in either party to the contract for sale who has title to or a security interest or a special property or an insurable interest in the goods; and if the goods have been destroyed or converted a right of action is also in the party who either bore the risk of loss under the contract for sale or has since the injury assumed that risk as against the other;

(b) if at the time of the injury the party plaintiff did not bear the risk of loss as against the other party to the contract for sale and there is no arrangement between them for disposition of the recovery, his suit or settlement is, subject to his own interest, as a fiduciary for the other party to the contract;

(c) either party may with the consent of the other sue for the benefit of whom it may concern.

§ 2–723. Proof of Market Price: Time and Place.

(1) If an action based on anticipatory repudiation comes to trial before the time for performance with respect to some or all of the goods, any damages based on market price (Section 2–708 or Section 2–713) shall be determined according to the price of such goods prevailing at the time when the aggrieved party learned of the repudiation.

(2) If evidence of a price prevailing at the times or places described in this Article is not readily available the price prevailing within any reasonable time before or after the time described or at any other place which in commercial judgment or under usage of trade would serve as a reasonable substitute for the one described may be used, making any proper allowance for the cost of transporting the goods to or from such other place.

(3) Evidence of a relevant price prevailing at a time or place other than the one described in this Article offered by one party is not admissible unless and until he has given the other party such notice as the court finds sufficient to prevent unfair surprise.

§ 2–724. Admissibility of Market Quotations.

Whenever the prevailing price or value of any goods regularly bought and sold in any established commodity market is in issue, reports in official publications or trade journals or in newspapers or periodicals of general circulation published as the reports of such market shall be admissible in evidence. The circumstances of the preparation of such a report may be shown to affect its weight but not its admissibility.

§ 2–725. Statute of Limitations in Contracts for Sale.

(1) An action for breach of any contract for sale must be commenced within four years after the cause of action has accrued. By the original agreement the parties may reduce the period of limitation to not less than one year but may not extend it.

(2) A cause of action accrues when the breach occurs, regardless of the aggrieved party's lack of knowledge of the breach. A breach of warranty occurs when tender of delivery is made, except that where a warranty explicitly extends to future performance of the goods and discovery of the breach must await the time of such performance the cause of action accrues when the breach is or should have been discovered.

(3) Where an action commenced within the time limited by subsection (1) is so terminated as to leave available a remedy by another action for the same breach such other action may be commenced after the expiration of the time limited and within six months after the termination of the first action unless the termination resulted from voluntary discontinuance or from dismissal for failure or neglect to prosecute.

(4) This section does not alter the law on tolling of the statute of limitations nor does it apply to causes of action which have accrued before this Act becomes effective.

Article 2 Amendments (Excerpts)[1]

Part 1 Short Title, General Construction and Subject Matter

* * * *

§ 2–103. Definitions and Index of Definitions.

(1) In this article unless the context otherwise requires

* * * *

(b) "Conspicuous", with reference to a term, means so written, displayed, or presented that a reasonable person against which it is to operate ought to have noticed it. A term in an electronic record intended to evoke a response by an electronic agent is conspicuous if it is presented in a form that would enable a reasonably configured electronic agent to take it into account or react to it without review of the record by an individual. Whether a term is "conspicuous" or not is a decision for the court. Conspicuous terms include the following:

(i) for a person:

(A) a heading in capitals equal to or greater in size than the surrounding text, or in contrasting type, font, or color to the surrounding text of the same or lesser size and;

---

1. Additions and new wording are underlined. What follows represents only selected changes made by the 2003 amendments. Although the National Conference of Commissioners on Uniform State Laws and the American Law Institute approved the amendments in May of 2003, as of this writing, they have not as yet been adopted by any state.

(B) language in the body of a record or display in larger type than the surrounding text, or in contrasting type, font, or color to the surrounding text of the same size, or set off from surrounding text of the same size by symbols or other marks that call attention to the language; and

(ii) for a person or an electronic agent, a term that is so placed in a record or display that the person or electronic agent cannot proceed without taking action with respect to the particular term.

(c) "Consumer" means an individual who buys or contracts to buy goods that, at the time of contracting, are intended by the individual to be used primarily for personal, family, or household purposes.

(d) "Consumer contract" means a contract between a merchant seller and a consumer.

* * * *

(j) "Good faith" means honesty in fact and the observance of reasonable commercial standards of fair dealing.

(k) "Goods" means all things that are movable at the time of identification to a contract for sale. The term includes future goods, specially manufactured goods, the unborn young of animals, growing crops, and other identified things attached to realty as described in Section 2–107. The term does not include information, the money in which the price is to be paid, investment securities under Article 8, the subject matter of foreign exchange transactions, and choses in action.

* * * *

(m) "Record" means information that is inscribed on a tangible medium or that is stored in an electronic or other medium and is retrievable in perceivable form.

(n) "Remedial promise" means a promise by the seller to repair or replace the goods or to refund all or part of the price upon the happening of a specified event.

* * * *

(p) "Sign" means, with present intent to authenticate or adopt a record,

(i) to execute or adopt a tangible symbol; or

(ii) to attach to or logically associate with the record an electronic sound, symbol, or process.

* * * *

Part 2 Form, Formation, Terms and Readjustment of Contract; Electronic Contracting

§ 2–201. Formal Requirements; Statute of Frauds.

(1) A contract for the sale of goods for the price of $5,000 or more is not enforceable by way of action or defense unless there is some record sufficient to indicate that a contract for sale has been made between the parties and signed by the party against which enforcement is sought or by the party's authorized agent or broker. A record is not insufficient because it omits or incorrectly states a term agreed upon but the contract is not enforceable under this subsection beyond the quantity of goods shown in the record.

(2) Between merchants if within a reasonable time a record in confirmation of the contract and sufficient against the sender is received and the party receiving it has reason to know its contents, it satisfies the requirements of subsection (1) against the recipient unless notice of objection to its contents is given in a record within 10 days after it is received.

(3) A contract which does not satisfy the requirements of subsection (1) but which is valid in other respects is enforceable

(a) if the goods are to be specially manufactured for the buyer and are not suitable for sale to others in the ordinary course of the seller's business and the seller, before notice of repudiation is received and under circumstances which reasonably indicate that the goods are for the buyer, has made either a substantial beginning of their manufacture or commitments for their procurement; or

(b) if the party against which enforcement is sought admits in the party's pleading, or in the party's testimony or otherwise under oath that a contract for sale was made, but the contract is not enforceable under this paragraph beyond the quantity of goods admitted; or

(c) with respect to goods for which payment has been made and accepted or which have been received and accepted (Sec. 2–606).

(4) A contract that is enforceable under this section is not rendered unenforceable merely because it is not capable of being performed within one year or any other applicable period after its making.

* * * *

§ 2–207. Terms of Contract; Effect of Confirmation.

Subject to Section 2–202, if (i) conduct by both parties recognizes the existence of a contract although their records do not otherwise establish a contract, (ii) a contract is formed by an offer and acceptance, or (iii) a contract formed in any manner is confirmed by a record that contains terms additional to or different from those in the contract being confirmed, the terms of the contract, are:

(a) terms that appear in the records of both parties;

(b) terms, whether in a record or not, to which both parties agree; and

(c) terms supplied or incorporated under any provision of this Act.

* * * *

Part 3 General Obligation and Construction of Contract

* * * *

§ 2–312. Warranty of Title and Against Infringement; Buyer's Obligation Against Infringement.

(1) Subject to subsection (3) there is in a contract for sale a warranty by the seller that

(a) the title conveyed shall be, good and its transfer rightful and shall not, unreasonably expose the buyer to litigation because of any colorable claim to or interest in the goods; and

(b) the goods shall be delivered free from any security interest or other lien or encumbrance of which the buyer at the time of contracting has no knowledge.

(2) Unless otherwise agreed a seller that is a merchant regularly dealing in goods of the kind warrants that the goods shall be delivered free of the rightful claim of any third person by way of infringement or the like but a buyer that furnishes specifications to the seller must hold the seller harmless against any such claim that arises out of compliance with the specifications.

(3) A warranty under this section may be disclaimed or modified only by specific language or by circumstances that give the buyer reason to know that the seller does not claim title, that the seller is purporting to sell only the right or title as the seller or a third person may have, or that the seller is selling subject to any claims of infringement or the like.

§ 2–313. Express Warranties by Affirmation, Promise, Description, Sample; Remedial Promise.

(1) In this section, "immediate buyer" means a buyer that enters into a contract with the seller.

*   *   *   *

(4) Any remedial promise made by the seller to the immediate buyer creates an obligation that the promise will be performed upon the happening of the specified event.

§ 2–313A. Obligation to Remote Purchaser Created by Record Packaged with or Accompanying Goods.

(1) In this section:

    (a) "Immediate buyer" means a buyer that enters into a contract with the seller.

    (b) "Remote purchaser" means a person that buys or leases goods from an immediate buyer or other person in the normal chain of distribution.

(2) This section applies only to new goods and goods sold or leased as new goods in a transaction of purchase in the normal chain of distribution.

(3) If in a record packaged with or accompanying the goods the seller makes an affirmation of fact or promise that relates to the goods, provides a description that relates to the goods, or makes a remedial promise, and the seller reasonably expects the record to be, and the record is, furnished to the remote purchaser, the seller has an obligation to the remote purchaser that:

    (a) the goods will conform to the affirmation of fact, promise or description unless a reasonable person in the position of the remote purchaser would not believe that the affirmation of fact, promise or description created an obligation; and

    (b) the seller will perform the remedial promise.

(4) It is not necessary to the creation of an obligation under this section that the seller use formal words such as "warrant" or "guarantee" or that the seller have a specific intention to undertake an obligation, but an affirmation merely of the value of the goods or a statement purporting to be merely the seller's opinion or commendation of the goods does not create an obligation.

(5) The following rules apply to the remedies for breach of an obligation created under this section:

    (a) The seller may modify or limit the remedies available to the remote purchaser if the modification or limitation is furnished to the remote purchaser no later than the time of purchase or if the modification or limitation is contained in the record that contains the affirmation of fact, promise or description.

    (b) Subject to a modification or limitation of remedy, a seller in breach is liable for incidental or consequential damages under Section 2–715, but not for lost profits.

    (c) The remote purchaser may recover as damages for breach of a seller's obligation arising under subsection (2) the loss resulting in the ordinary course of events as determined in any reasonable manner.

(5) An obligation that is not a remedial promise is breached if the goods did not conform to the affirmation of fact, promise or description creating the obligation when the goods left the seller's control.

§ 2–313B. Obligation to Remote Purchaser Created by Communication to the Public.

(1) In this section:

    (a) "Immediate buyer" means a buyer that enters into a contract with the seller.

    (b) "Remote purchaser" means a person that buys or leases goods from an immediate buyer or other person in the normal chain of distribution.

(2) This section applies only to new goods and goods sold or leased as new goods in a transaction of purchase in the normal chain of distribution.

(3) If in an advertisement or a similar communication to the public a seller makes an affirmation of fact or promise that relates to the goods, provides a description that relates to the goods, or makes a remedial promise, and the remote purchaser enters into a transaction of purchase with knowledge of and with the expectation that the goods will conform to the affirmation of fact, promise, or description, or that the seller will perform the remedial promise, the seller has an obligation to the remote purchaser that:

    (a) the goods will conform to the affirmation of fact, promise or description unless a reasonable person in the position of the remote purchaser would not believe that the affirmation of fact, promise or description created an obligation; and

    (b) the seller will perform the remedial promise.

(4) It is not necessary to the creation of an obligation under this section that the seller use formal words such as "warrant" or "guarantee" or that the seller have a specific intention to undertake an obligation, but an affirmation merely of the value of the goods or a statement purporting to be merely the seller's opinion or commendation of the goods does not create an obligation.

(5) The following rules apply to the remedies for breach of an obligation created under this section:

    (a) The seller may modify or limit the remedies available to the remote purchaser if the modification or limitation is furnished to the remote purchaser no later than the time of purchase. The modification or limitation may be furnished as part of the communication that contains the affirmation of fact, promise or description.

    (b) Subject to a modification or limitation of remedy, a seller in breach is liable for incidental or consequential damages under Section 2–715, but not for lost profits.

    (c) The remote purchaser may recover as damages for breach of a seller's obligation arising under subsection (2) the loss resulting in the ordinary course of events as determined in any reasonable manner.

(6) An obligation that is not a remedial promise is breached if the goods did not conform to the affirmation of fact, promise or description creating the obligation when the goods left the seller's control.

*   *   *   *

§ 2–316. Exclusion or Modification of Warranties.

* * * *

(2) Subject to subsection (3), to exclude or modify the implied warranty of merchantability or any part of it in a consumer contract the language must be in a record, be conspicuous, and state "The seller undertakes no responsibility for the quality of the goods except as otherwise provided in this contract," and in any other contract the language must mention merchantability and in case of a record must be conspicuous. Subject to subsection (3), to exclude or modify the implied warranty of fitness the exclusion must be in a record and be conspicuous. Language to exclude all implied warranties of fitness in a consumer contract must state "The seller assumes no responsibility that the goods will be fit for any particular purpose for which you may be buying these goods, except as otherwise provided in the contract," and in any other contract the language is sufficient if it states, for example, that "There are no warranties that extend beyond the description on the face hereof." Language that satisfies the requirements of this subsection for the exclusion and modification of a warranty in a consumer contract also satisfies the requirements for any other contract.

(3) Notwithstanding subsection (2):

(a) unless the circumstances indicate otherwise, all implied warranties are excluded by expressions like "as is", "with all faults" or other language which in common understanding calls the buyer's attention to the exclusion of warranties, makes plain that there is no implied warranty, and in a consumer contract evidenced by a record is set forth conspicuously in the record; and

(b) when the buyer before entering into the contract has examined the goods or the sample or model as fully as desired or has refused to examine the goods after a demand by the seller there is no implied warranty with regard to defects which an examination ought in the circumstances to have revealed to the buyer; and

(c) an implied warranty can also be excluded or modified by course of dealing or course of performance or usage of trade.

* * * *

§ 2–318. Third Party Beneficiaries of Warranties and Obligations.

(1) In this section:

(a) "Immediate buyer" means a buyer that enters into a contract with the seller.

(b) "Remote purchaser" means a person that buys or leases goods from an immediate buyer or other person in the normal chain of distribution.

Alternative A to subsection (2)

(2) A seller's warranty to an immediate buyer, whether express or implied, a seller's remedial promise to an immediate buyer, or a seller's obligation to a remote purchaser under Section 2–313A or 2–313B extends to any natural person who is in the family or household of the immediate buyer or the remote purchaser or who is a guest in the home of either if it is reasonable to expect that the person may use, consume or be affected by the goods and who is injured in person by breach of the warranty, remedial promise or obligation. A seller may not exclude or limit the operation of this section.

Alternative B to subsection (2)

(2) A seller's warranty to an immediate buyer, whether express or implied, a seller's remedial promise to an immediate buyer, or a seller's obligation to a remote purchaser under Section 2–313A or 2–313B extends to any natural person who may reasonably be expected to use, consume or be affected by the goods and who is injured in person by breach of the warranty, remedial promise or obligation. A seller may not exclude or limit the operation of this section.

Alternative C to subsection (2)

(2) A seller's warranty to an immediate buyer, whether express or implied, a seller's remedial promise to an immediate buyer, or a seller's obligation to a remote purchaser under Section 2–313A or 2–313B extends to any person that may reasonably be expected to use, consume or be affected by the goods and that is injured by breach of the warranty, remedial promise or obligation. A seller may not exclude or limit the operation of this section with respect to injury to the person of an individual to whom the warranty, remedial promise or obligation extends.

* * * *

Part 5 Performance

* * * *

§ 2–502. Buyer's Right to Goods on Seller's Insolvency.

(1) Subject to subsections (2) and (3) and even though the goods have not been shipped a buyer that has paid a part or all of the price of goods in which the buyer has a special property under the provisions of the immediately preceding section may on making and keeping good a tender of any unpaid portion of their price recover them from the seller if:

(a) in the case of goods bought by a consumer, the seller repudiates or fails to deliver as required by the contract; or

(b) in all cases, the seller becomes insolvent within ten days after receipt of the first installment on their price.

(2) The buyer's right to recover the goods under subsection (1) vests upon acquisition of a special property, even if the seller had not then repudiated or failed to deliver.

(3) If the identification creating the special property has been made by the buyer, the buyer acquires the right to recover the goods only if they conform to the contract for sale.

* * * *

§ 2–508. Cure by Seller of Improper Tender or Delivery; Replacement.

(1) Where the buyer rejects goods or a tender of delivery under Section 2–601 or 2–612 or, except in a consumer contract, justifiably revokes acceptance under Section 2–608(1)(b) and the agreed time for performance has not expired, a seller that has performed in good faith, upon seasonable notice to the buyer and at the seller's own expense, may cure the breach of contract by making a conforming tender of delivery within the agreed time. The seller shall compensate the buyer for all of the buyer's reasonable expenses caused by the seller's breach of contract and subsequent cure.

(2) Where the buyer rejects goods or a tender of delivery under Section 2–601 or 2–612 or except in a consumer contract justifiably revokes acceptance under Section 2–608(1)(b) and the agreed time for performance has expired, a seller that has performed in good faith, upon seasonable notice to the buyer and at the seller's own expense, may cure the breach of contract, if the cure is appropriate and timely under the

circumstances, by making a tender of conforming goods. The seller shall compensate the buyer for all of the buyer's reasonable expenses caused by the seller's breach of contract and subsequent cure.

§ 2–509. Risk of Loss in the Absence of Breach.

(1) Where the contract requires or authorizes the seller to ship the goods by carrier

(a) if it does not require the seller to deliver them at a particular destination, the risk of loss passes to the buyer when the goods are delivered to the carrier even though the shipment is under reservation (Section 2–505); but

(b) if it does require the seller to deliver them at a particular destination and the goods are there tendered while in the possession of the carrier, the risk of loss passes to the buyer when the goods are there so tendered as to enable the buyer to take delivery.

(2) Where the goods are held by a bailee to be delivered without being moved, the risk of loss passes to the buyer

(a) on the buyer's receipt of a negotiable document of title covering the goods; or

(b) on acknowledgment by the bailee to the buyer of the buyer's right to possession of the goods; or

(c) after the buyer's receipt of a non-negotiable document of title or other direction to deliver in a record, as provided in subsection (4)(b) of Section 2–503.

(3) In any case not within subsection (1) or (2), the risk of loss passes to the buyer on the buyer's receipt of the goods.

(4) The provisions of this section are subject to contrary agreement of the parties and to the provisions of this Article on sale on approval (Section 2–327) and on effect of breach on risk of loss (Section 2–510).

* * * *

§ 2–513. Buyer's Right to Inspection of Goods.

* * * *

(3) Unless otherwise agreed, the buyer is not entitled to inspect the goods before payment of the price when the contract provides

(a) for delivery on terms that under applicable course of performance, course of dealing, or usage of trade are interpreted to preclude inspection before payment; or

(b) for payment against documents of title, except where such payment is due only after the goods are to become available for inspection.

* * * *

Part 6 Breach, Repudiation and Excuse

* * * *

§ 2–605. Waiver of Buyer's Objections by Failure to Particularize.

(1) The buyer's failure to state in connection with rejection a particular defect or in connection with revocation of acceptance a defect that justifies revocation precludes the buyer from relying on the unstated defect to justify rejection or revocation of acceptance if the defect is ascertainable by reasonable inspection

(a) where the seller had a right to cure the defect and could have cured it if stated seasonably; or

(b) between merchants when the seller has after rejection made a request in a record for a full and final statement in record form of all defects on which the buyer proposes to rely.

(2) A buyer's payment against documents tendered to the buyer made without reservation of rights precludes recovery of the payment for defects apparent on the face of the documents.

* * * *

§ 2–607. Effect of Acceptance; Notice of Breach; Burden of Establishing Breach After Acceptance; Notice of Claim or Litigation to Person Answerable Over.

* * * *

(3) Where a tender has been accepted

(a) the buyer must within a reasonable time after the buyer discovers or should have discovered any breach notify the seller. However, failure to give timely notice bars the buyer from a remedy only to the extent that the seller is prejudiced by the failure and

(b) if the claim is one for infringement or the like (subsection (3) of Section 2–312) and the buyer is sued as a result of such a breach the buyer must so notify the seller within a reasonable time after the buyer receives notice of the litigation or be barred from any remedy over for liability established by the litigation.

* * * *

§ 2–608. Revocation of Acceptance in Whole or in Part.

* * * *

(4) If a buyer uses the goods after a rightful rejection or justifiable revocation of acceptance, the following rules apply:

(a) Any use by the buyer which is unreasonable under the circumstances is wrongful as against the seller and is an acceptance only if ratified by the seller.

(b) Any use of the goods which is reasonable under the circumstances is not wrongful as against the seller and is not an acceptance, but in an appropriate case the buyer shall be obligated to the seller for the value of the use to the buyer.

* * * *

§ 2–612. "Installment Contract"; Breach.

* * * *

(2) The buyer may reject any installment which is non-conforming if the non-conformity substantially impairs the value of that installment to the buyer or if the non-conformity is a defect in the required documents; but if the non-conformity does not fall within subsection (3) and the seller gives adequate assurance of its cure the buyer must accept that installment.

(3) Whenever non-conformity or default with respect to one or more installments substantially impairs the value of the whole contract there is a breach of the whole. But the aggrieved party reinstates the contract if the party accepts a non-conforming installment without seasonably notifying of cancellation or if the party brings an action with respect only to past installments or demands performance as to future installments.

* * * *

Part 7 Remedies

§ 2–702. Seller's Remedies on Discovery of Buyer's Insolvency.

*   *   *   *

(2) Where the seller discovers that the buyer has received goods on credit while insolvent the seller may reclaim the goods upon demand made within a reasonable time after the buyer's receipt of the goods. Except as provided in this subsection the seller may not base a right to reclaim goods on the buyer's fraudulent or innocent misrepresentation of solvency or of intent to pay.

*   *   *   *

§ 2–703. Seller's Remedies in General.

(1) A breach of contract by the buyer includes the buyer's wrongful rejection or wrongful attempt to revoke acceptance of goods, wrongful failure to perform a contractual obligation, failure to make a payment when due, and repudiation.

(2) If the buyer is in breach of contract the seller, to the extent provided for by this Act or other law, may:

    (a) withhold delivery of the goods;

    (b) stop delivery of the goods under Section 2–705;

    (c) proceed under Section 2–704 with respect to goods unidentified to the contract or unfinished;

    (d) reclaim the goods under Section 2–507(2) or 2–702(2);

    (e) require payment directly from the buyer under Section 2–325(c);

    (f) cancel;

    (g) resell and recover damages under Section 2–706;

    (h) recover damages for nonacceptance or repudiation under Section 2–708(1);

    (i) recover lost profits under Section 2–708(2);

    (j) recover the price under Section 2–709;

    (k) obtain specific performance under Section 2–716;

    (l) recover liquidated damages under Section 2–718;

    (m) in other cases, recover damages in any manner that is reasonable under the circumstances.

(3) If a buyer becomes insolvent, the seller may:

    (a) withhold delivery under Section 2–702(1);

    (b) stop delivery of the goods under Section 2–705;

    (c) reclaim the goods under Section 2–702(2).

*   *   *   *

§ 2–705. Seller's Stoppage of Delivery in Transit or Otherwise.

(1) The seller may stop delivery of goods in the possession of a carrier or other bailee when the seller discovers the buyer to be insolvent (Section 2–702) or when the buyer repudiates or fails to make a payment due before delivery or if for any other reason the seller has a right to withhold or reclaim the goods.

*   *   *   *

§ 2–706. Seller's Resale Including Contract for Resale.

(1) In an appropriate case involving breach by the buyer, the seller may resell the goods concerned or the undelivered balance thereof. Where

the resale is made in good faith and in a commercially reasonable manner the seller may recover the difference between the contract price and the resale price together with any incidental or consequential damages allowed under the provisions of this Article (Section 2–710), but less expenses saved in consequence of the buyer's breach.

*   *   *   *

§ 2–708. Seller's Damages for Non-Acceptance or Repudiation.

(1) Subject to subsection (2) and to the provisions of this Article with respect to proof of market price (Section 2–723)

    (a) the measure of damages for non-acceptance by the buyer is the difference between the contract price and the market price at the time and place for tender together with any incidental or consequential damages provided in this Article (Section 2–710), but less expenses saved in consequence of the buyer's breach; and

    (b) the measure of damages for repudiation by the buyer is the difference between the contract price and the market price at the place for tender at the expiration of a commercially reasonable time after the seller learned of the repudiation, but no later than the time stated in paragraph (a), together with any incidental or consequential damages provided in this Article (Section 2–710), but less expenses saved in consequence of the buyer's breach.

(2) If the measure of damages provided in subsection (1) or in Section 2–706 is inadequate to put the seller in as good a position as performance would have done then the measure of damages is the profit (including reasonable overhead) which the seller would have made from full performance by the buyer, together with any incidental or consequential damages provided in this Article (Section 2–710).

§ 2–709. Action for the Price.

(1) When the buyer fails to pay the price as it becomes due the seller may recover, together with any incidental or consequential damages under the next section, the price

    (a) of goods accepted or of conforming goods lost or damaged within a commercially reasonable time after risk of their loss has passed to the buyer; and

    (b) of goods identified to the contract if the seller is unable after reasonable effort to resell them at a reasonable price or the circumstances reasonably indicate that such effort will be unavailing.

*   *   *   *

§ 2–710. Seller's Incidental and Consequential Damages.

(1) Incidental damages to an aggrieved seller include any commercially reasonable charges, expenses or commissions incurred in stopping delivery, in the transportation, care and custody of goods after the buyer's breach, in connection with return or resale of the goods or otherwise resulting from the breach.

(2) Consequential damages resulting from the buyer's breach include any loss resulting from general or particular requirements and needs of which the buyer at the time of contracting had reason to know and which could not reasonably be prevented by resale or otherwise.

(3) In a consumer contract, a seller may not recover consequential damages from a consumer.

*   *   *   *

§ 2–711. Buyer's Remedies in General; Buyer's Security Interest in Rejected Goods.

(1) A breach of contract by the seller includes the seller's wrongful failure to deliver or to perform a contractual obligation, making of a nonconforming tender of delivery or performance, and repudiation.

(2) If a seller is in breach of contract under subsection (1) the buyer, to the extent provided for by this Act or other law, may:

(a) in the case of rightful cancellation, rightful rejection or justifiable revocation of acceptance recover so much of the price as has been paid;

(b) deduct damages from any part of the price still due under Section 2–717;

(c) cancel;

(d) cover and have damages under Section 2–712 as to all goods affected whether or not they have been identified to the contract;

(e) recover damages for non-delivery or repudiation under Section 2–713;

(f) recover damages for breach with regard to accepted goods or breach with regard to a remedial promise under Section 2–714;

(g) recover identified goods under Section 2–502;

(h) obtain specific performance or obtain the goods by replevin or similar remedy under Section 7–716;

(i) recover liquidated damages under Section 2–718;

(j) in other cases, recover damages in any manner that is reasonable under the circumstances.

(3) On rightful rejection or justifiable revocation of acceptance a buyer has a security interest in goods in the buyer's possession or control for any payments made on their price and any expenses reasonably incurred in their inspection, receipt, transportation, care and custody and may hold such goods and resell them in like manner as an aggrieved seller (Section 2–706).

*   *   *   *

§ 2–713. Buyer's Damages for Non-Delivery or Repudiation.

(1) Subject to the provisions of this Article with respect to proof of market price (Section 2–723), if the seller wrongfully fails to deliver or repudiates or the buyer rightfully rejects or justifiably revokes acceptance

(a) the measure of damages in the case of wrongful failure to deliver by the seller or rightful rejection or justifiable revocation of acceptance by the buyer is the difference between the market price at the time for tender under the contract and the contract price together with any incidental or consequential damages provided in this Article (Section 2–715), but less expenses saved in consequence of the seller's breach; and

(b) the measure of damages for repudiation by the seller is the difference between the market price at the expiration of a commercially reasonable time after the buyer learned of the repudiation, but no later than the time stated in paragraph (a), and the contract price together with any incidental or consequential damages provided in this Article (Section 2–715), less expenses saved in consequence of the seller's breach.

*   *   *   *

§ 2–725. Statute of Limitations in Contracts for Sale.

(1) Except as otherwise provided in this section, an action for breach of any contract for sale must be commenced within the later of four years after the right of action has accrued under subsection (2) or (3) or one year after the breach was or should have been discovered, but no longer than five years after the right of action accrued. By the original agreement the parties may reduce the period of limitation to not less than one year but may not extend it. However, in a consumer contract, the period of limitation may not be reduced.

(2) Except as otherwise provided in subsection (3), the following rules apply:

(a) Except as otherwise provided in this subsection, a right of action for breach of a contract accrues when the breach occurs, even if the aggrieved party did not have knowledge of the breach.

(b) For breach of a contract by repudiation, a right of action accrues at the earlier of when the aggrieved party elects to treat the repudiation as a breach or when a commercially reasonable time for awaiting performance has expired.

(c) For breach of a remedial promise, a right of action accrues when the remedial promise is not performed when performance is due.

(d) In an action by a buyer against a person that is answerable over to the buyer for a claim asserted against the buyer, the buyer's right of action against the person answerable over accrues at the time the claim was originally asserted against the buyer.

(3) If a breach of a warranty arising under Section 2–312, 2–313(2), 2–314, or 2–315, or a breach of an obligation, other than a remedial promise, arising under Section 2–313A or 2–313B, is claimed the following rules apply:

(a) Except as otherwise provided in paragraph (c), a right of action for breach of a warranty arising under Section 2–313(2), 2–314 or 2–315 accrues when the seller has tendered delivery to the immediate buyer, as defined in Section 2–313, and has completed performance of any agreed installation or assembly of the goods.

(b) Except as otherwise provided in paragraph (c), a right of action for breach of an obligation other than a remedial promise arising under Section 2–313A or 2–313B accrues when the remote purchaser, as defined in sections 2–313A and 2–313B, receives the goods.

(c) Where a warranty arising under Section 2–313(2) or an obligation, other than a remedial promise, arising under 2–313A or 2–313B explicitly extends to future performance of the goods and discovery of the breach must await the time for performance the right of action accrues when the immediate buyer as defined in Section 2–313 or the remote purchaser as defined in Sections 2–313A and 2–313B discovers or should have discovered the breach.

(d) A right of action for breach of warranty arising under Section 2–312 accrues when the aggrieved party discovers or should have discovered the breach. However, an action for breach of the warranty of non-infringement may not be commenced more than six years after tender of delivery of the goods to the aggrieved party.

*   *   *   *

Article 2A
LEASES

Part 1 General Provisions

§ 2A–101. Short Title.

This Article shall be known and may be cited as the Uniform Commercial Code—Leases.

§ 2A–102. Scope.

This Article applies to any transaction, regardless of form, that creates a lease.

§ 2A–103. Definitions and Index of Definitions.

(1) In this Article unless the context otherwise requires:

(a) "Buyer in ordinary course of business" means a person who in good faith and without knowledge that the sale to him [or her] is in violation of the ownership rights or security interest or leasehold interest of a third party in the goods buys in ordinary course from a person in the business of selling goods of that kind but does not include a pawnbroker. "Buying" may be for cash or by exchange of other property or on secured or unsecured credit and includes receiving goods or documents of title under a pre-existing contract for sale but does not include a transfer in bulk or as security for or in total or partial satisfaction of a money debt.

(b) "Cancellation" occurs when either party puts an end to the lease contract for default by the other party.

(c) "Commercial unit" means such a unit of goods as by commercial usage is a single whole for purposes of lease and division of which materially impairs its character or value on the market or in use. A commercial unit may be a single article, as a machine, or a set of articles, as a suite of furniture or a line of machinery, or a quantity, as a gross or carload, or any other unit treated in use or in the relevant market as a single whole.

(d) "Conforming" goods or performance under a lease contract means goods or performance that are in accordance with the obligations under the lease contract.

(e) "Consumer lease" means a lease that a lessor regularly engaged in the business of leasing or selling makes to a lessee who is an individual and who takes under the lease primarily for a personal, family, or household purpose [, if the total payments to be made under the lease contract, excluding payments for options to renew or buy, do not exceed $_____].

(f) "Fault" means wrongful act, omission, breach, or default.

(g) "Finance lease" means a lease with respect to which:

(i) the lessor does not select, manufacture or supply the goods;

(ii) the lessor acquires the goods or the right to possession and use of the goods in connection with the lease; and

(iii) one of the following occurs:

(A) the lessee receives a copy of the contract by which the lessor acquired the goods or the right to possession and use of the goods before signing the lease contract;

(B) the lessee's approval of the contract by which the lessor acquired the goods or the right to possession and use of the goods is a condition to effectiveness of the lease contract;

(C) the lessee, before signing the lease contract, receives an accurate and complete statement designating the promises and warranties, and any disclaimers of warranties, limitations or modifications of remedies, or liquidated damages, including those of a third party, such as the manufacturer of the goods, provided to the lessor by the person supplying the goods in connection with or as part of the contract by which the lessor acquired the goods or the right to possession and use of the goods; or

(D) if the lease is not a consumer lease, the lessor, before the lessee signs the lease contract, informs the lessee in writing (a) of the identity of the person supplying the goods to the lessor, unless the lessee has selected that person and directed the lessor to acquire the goods or the right to possession and use of the goods from that person, (b) that the lessee is entitled under this Article to any promises and warranties, including those of any third party, provided to the lessor by the person supplying the goods in connection with or as part of the contract by which the lessor acquired the goods or the right to possession and use of the goods, and (c) that the lessee may communicate with the person supplying the goods to the lessor and receive an accurate and complete statement of those promises and warranties, including any disclaimers and limitations of them or of remedies.

(h) "Goods" means all things that are movable at the time of identification to the lease contract, or are fixtures (Section 2A–309), but the term does not include money, documents, instruments, accounts, chattel paper, general intangibles, or minerals or the like, including oil and gas, before extraction. The term also includes the unborn young of animals.

(i) "Installment lease contract" means a lease contract that authorizes or requires the delivery of goods in separate lots to be separately accepted, even though the lease contract contains a clause "each delivery is a separate lease" or its equivalent.

(j) "Lease" means a transfer of the right to possession and use of goods for a term in return for consideration, but a sale, including a sale on approval or a sale or return, or retention or creation of a security interest is not a lease. Unless the context clearly indicates otherwise, the term includes a sublease.

(k) "Lease agreement" means the bargain, with respect to the lease, of the lessor and the lessee in fact as found in their language or by implication from other circumstances including course of dealing or usage of trade or course of performance as provided in this Article. Unless the context clearly indicates otherwise, the term includes a sublease agreement.

(l) "Lease contract" means the total legal obligation that results from the lease agreement as affected by this Article and any other applicable rules of law. Unless the context clearly indicates otherwise, the term includes a sublease contract.

(m) "Leasehold interest" means the interest of the lessor or the lessee under a lease contract.

(n) "Lessee" means a person who acquires the right to possession and use of goods under a lease. Unless the context clearly indicates otherwise, the term includes a sublessee.

(o) "Lessee in ordinary course of business" means a person who in good faith and without knowledge that the lease to him [or her] is in violation of the ownership rights or security interest or leasehold interest of a third party in the goods, leases in ordinary course from a person in the business of selling or leasing goods of that kind but does not include a pawnbroker. "Leasing" may be for cash or by exchange of other property or on secured or unsecured credit and includes receiving goods or documents of title under a pre-existing lease contract but does not include a transfer in bulk or as security for or in total or partial satisfaction of a money debt.

(p) "Lessor" means a person who transfers the right to possession and use of goods under a lease. Unless the context clearly indicates otherwise, the term includes a sublessor.

(q) "Lessor's residual interest" means the lessor's interest in the goods after expiration, termination, or cancellation of the lease contract.

(r) "Lien" means a charge against or interest in goods to secure payment of a debt or performance of an obligation, but the term does not include a security interest.

(s) "Lot" means a parcel or a single article that is the subject matter of a separate lease or delivery, whether or not it is sufficient to perform the lease contract.

(t) "Merchant lessee" means a lessee that is a merchant with respect to goods of the kind subject to the lease.

(u) "Present value" means the amount as of a date certain of one or more sums payable in the future, discounted to the date certain. The discount is determined by the interest rate specified by the parties if the rate was not manifestly unreasonable at the time the transaction was entered into; otherwise, the discount is determined by a commercially reasonable rate that takes into account the facts and circumstances of each case at the time the transaction was entered into.

(v) "Purchase" includes taking by sale, lease, mortgage, security interest, pledge, gift, or any other voluntary transaction creating an interest in goods.

(w) "Sublease" means a lease of goods the right to possession and use of which was acquired by the lessor as a lessee under an existing lease.

(x) "Supplier" means a person from whom a lessor buys or leases goods to be leased under a finance lease.

(y) "Supply contract" means a contract under which a lessor buys or leases goods to be leased.

(z) "Termination" occurs when either party pursuant to a power created by agreement or law puts an end to the lease contract otherwise than for default.

(2) Other definitions applying to this Article and the sections in which they appear are:

"Accessions". Section 2A–310(1).
"Construction mortgage". Section 2A–309(1)(d).
"Encumbrance". Section 2A–309(1)(e).
"Fixtures". Section 2A–309(1)(a).
"Fixture filing". Section 2A–309(1)(b).
"Purchase money lease". Section 2A–309(1)(c).

(3) The following definitions in other Articles apply to this Article:

"Accounts". Section 9–106.
"Between merchants". Section 2–104(3).
"Buyer". Section 2–103(1)(a).
"Chattel paper". Section 9–105(1)(b).

"Consumer goods". Section 9–109(1).
"Document". Section 9–105(1)(f).
"Entrusting". Section 2–403(3).
"General intangibles". Section 9–106.
"Good faith". Section 2–103(1)(b).
"Instrument". Section 9–105(1)(i).
"Merchant". Section 2–104(1).
"Mortgage". Section 9–105(1)(j).
"Pursuant to commitment". Section 9–105(1)(k).
"Receipt". Section 2–103(1)(c).
"Sale". Section 2–106(1).
"Sale on approval". Section 2–326.
"Sale or return". Section 2–326.
"Seller". Section 2–103(1)(d).

(4) In addition Article 1 contains general definitions and principles of construction and interpretation applicable throughout this Article.

As amended in 1990 and 1999.

§ 2A–104. Leases Subject to Other Law.

(1) A lease, although subject to this Article, is also subject to any applicable:

(a) certificate of title statute of this State: (list any certificate of title statutes covering automobiles, trailers, mobile homes, boats, farm tractors, and the like);

(b) certificate of title statute of another jurisdiction (Section 2A–105); or

(c) consumer protection statute of this State, or final consumer protection decision of a court of this State existing on the effective date of this Article.

(2) In case of conflict between this Article, other than Sections 2A–105, 2A–304(3), and 2A–305(3), and a statute or decision referred to in subsection (1), the statute or decision controls.

(3) Failure to comply with an applicable law has only the effect specified therein.

As amended in 1990.

§ 2A–105. Territorial Application of Article to Goods Covered by Certificate of Title.

Subject to the provisions of Sections 2A–304(3) and 2A–305(3), with respect to goods covered by a certificate of title issued under a statute of this State or of another jurisdiction, compliance and the effect of compliance or noncompliance with a certificate of title statute are governed by the law (including the conflict of laws rules) of the jurisdiction issuing the certificate until the earlier of (a) surrender of the certificate, or (b) four months after the goods are removed from that jurisdiction and thereafter until a new certificate of title is issued by another jurisdiction.

§ 2A–106. Limitation on Power of Parties to Consumer Lease to Choose Applicable Law and Judicial Forum.

(1) If the law chosen by the parties to a consumer lease is that of a jurisdiction other than a jurisdiction in which the lessee resides at the time the lease agreement becomes enforceable or within 30 days thereafter or in which the goods are to be used, the choice is not enforceable.

(2) If the judicial forum chosen by the parties to a consumer lease is a forum that would not otherwise have jurisdiction over the lessee, the choice is not enforceable.

§ 2A–107. Waiver or Renunciation of Claim or Right After Default.

Any claim or right arising out of an alleged default or breach of warranty may be discharged in whole or in part without consideration by a written waiver or renunciation signed and delivered by the aggrieved party.

§ 2A–108. Unconscionability.

(1) If the court as a matter of law finds a lease contract or any clause of a lease contract to have been unconscionable at the time it was made the court may refuse to enforce the lease contract, or it may enforce the remainder of the lease contract without the unconscionable clause, or it may so limit the application of any unconscionable clause as to avoid any unconscionable result.

(2) With respect to a consumer lease, if the court as a matter of law finds that a lease contract or any clause of a lease contract has been induced by unconscionable conduct or that unconscionable conduct has occurred in the collection of a claim arising from a lease contract, the court may grant appropriate relief.

(3) Before making a finding of unconscionability under subsection (1) or (2), the court, on its own motion or that of a party, shall afford the parties a reasonable opportunity to present evidence as to the setting, purpose, and effect of the lease contract or clause thereof, or of the conduct.

(4) In an action in which the lessee claims unconscionability with respect to a consumer lease:

(a) If the court finds unconscionability under subsection (1) or (2), the court shall award reasonable attorney's fees to the lessee.

(b) If the court does not find unconscionability and the lessee claiming unconscionability has brought or maintained an action he [or she] knew to be groundless, the court shall award reasonable attorney's fees to the party against whom the claim is made.

(c) In determining attorney's fees, the amount of the recovery on behalf of the claimant under subsections (1) and (2) is not controlling.

§ 2A–109. Option to Accelerate at Will.

(1) A term providing that one party or his [or her] successor in interest may accelerate payment or performance or require collateral or additional collateral "at will" or "when he [or she] deems himself [or herself] insecure" or in words of similar import must be construed to mean that he [or she] has power to do so only if he [or she] in good faith believes that the prospect of payment or performance is impaired.

(2) With respect to a consumer lease, the burden of establishing good faith under subsection (1) is on the party who exercised the power; otherwise the burden of establishing lack of good faith is on the party against whom the power has been exercised.

Part 2 Formation and Construction of Lease Contract

§ 2A–201. Statute of Frauds.

(1) A lease contract is not enforceable by way of action or defense unless:

(a) the total payments to be made under the lease contract, excluding payments for options to renew or buy, are less than $1,000; or

(b) there is a writing, signed by the party against whom enforcement is sought or by that party's authorized agent, sufficient to indicate that a lease contract has been made between the parties and to describe the goods leased and the lease term.

(2) Any description of leased goods or of the lease term is sufficient and satisfies subsection (1)(b), whether or not it is specific, if it reasonably identifies what is described.

(3) A writing is not insufficient because it omits or incorrectly states a term agreed upon, but the lease contract is not enforceable under subsection (1)(b) beyond the lease term and the quantity of goods shown in the writing.

(4) A lease contract that does not satisfy the requirements of subsection (1), but which is valid in other respects, is enforceable:

(a) if the goods are to be specially manufactured or obtained for the lessee and are not suitable for lease or sale to others in the ordinary course of the lessor's business, and the lessor, before notice of repudiation is received and under circumstances that reasonably indicate that the goods are for the lessee, has made either a substantial beginning of their manufacture or commitments for their procurement;

(b) if the party against whom enforcement is sought admits in that party's pleading, testimony or otherwise in court that a lease contract was made, but the lease contract is not enforceable under this provision beyond the quantity of goods admitted; or

(c) with respect to goods that have been received and accepted by the lessee.

(5) The lease term under a lease contract referred to in subsection (4) is:

(a) if there is a writing signed by the party against whom enforcement is sought or by that party's authorized agent specifying the lease term, the term so specified;

(b) if the party against whom enforcement is sought admits in that party's pleading, testimony, or otherwise in court a lease term, the term so admitted; or

(c) a reasonable lease term.

§ 2A–202. Final Written Expression: Parol or Extrinsic Evidence.

Terms with respect to which the confirmatory memoranda of the parties agree or which are otherwise set forth in a writing intended by the parties as a final expression of their agreement with respect to such terms as are included therein may not be contradicted by evidence of any prior agreement or of a contemporaneous oral agreement but may be explained or supplemented:

(a) by course of dealing or usage of trade or by course of performance; and

(b) by evidence of consistent additional terms unless the court finds the writing to have been intended also as a complete and exclusive statement of the terms of the agreement.

§ 2A–203. Seals Inoperative.

The affixing of a seal to a writing evidencing a lease contract or an offer to enter into a lease contract does not render the writing a sealed instrument and the law with respect to sealed instruments does not apply to the lease contract or offer.

§ 2A–204. Formation in General.

(1) A lease contract may be made in any manner sufficient to show agreement, including conduct by both parties which recognizes the existence of a lease contract.

(2) An agreement sufficient to constitute a lease contract may be found although the moment of its making is undetermined.

(3) Although one or more terms are left open, a lease contract does not fail for indefiniteness if the parties have intended to make a lease contract and there is a reasonably certain basis for giving an appropriate remedy.

§ 2A–205. Firm Offers.

An offer by a merchant to lease goods to or from another person in a signed writing that by its terms gives assurance it will be held open is not revocable, for lack of consideration, during the time stated or, if no time is stated, for a reasonable time, but in no event may the period of irrevocability exceed 3 months. Any such term of assurance on a form supplied by the offeree must be separately signed by the offeror.

§ 2A–206. Offer and Acceptance in Formation of Lease Contract.

(1) Unless otherwise unambiguously indicated by the language or circumstances, an offer to make a lease contract must be construed as inviting acceptance in any manner and by any medium reasonable in the circumstances.

(2) If the beginning of a requested performance is a reasonable mode of acceptance, an offeror who is not notified of acceptance within a reasonable time may treat the offer as having lapsed before acceptance.

§ 2A–207. Course of Performance or Practical Construction.

(1) If a lease contract involves repeated occasions for performance by either party with knowledge of the nature of the performance and opportunity for objection to it by the other, any course of performance accepted or acquiesced in without objection is relevant to determine the meaning of the lease agreement.

(2) The express terms of a lease agreement and any course of performance, as well as any course of dealing and usage of trade, must be construed whenever reasonable as consistent with each other; but if that construction is unreasonable, express terms control course of performance, course of performance controls both course of dealing and usage of trade, and course of dealing controls usage of trade.

(3) Subject to the provisions of Section 2A–208 on modification and waiver, course of performance is relevant to show a waiver or modification of any term inconsistent with the course of performance.

§ 2A–208. Modification, Rescission and Waiver.

(1) An agreement modifying a lease contract needs no consideration to be binding.

(2) A signed lease agreement that excludes modification or rescission except by a signed writing may not be otherwise modified or rescinded, but, except as between merchants, such a requirement on a form supplied by a merchant must be separately signed by the other party.

(3) Although an attempt at modification or rescission does not satisfy the requirements of subsection (2), it may operate as a waiver.

(4) A party who has made a waiver affecting an executory portion of a lease contract may retract the waiver by reasonable notification received by the other party that strict performance will be required of any term waived, unless the retraction would be unjust in view of a material change of position in reliance on the waiver.

§ 2A–209. Lessee under Finance Lease as Beneficiary of Supply Contract.

(1) The benefit of the supplier's promises to the lessor under the supply contract and of all warranties, whether express or implied, including those of any third party provided in connection with or as part of the supply contract, extends to the lessee to the extent of the lessee's leasehold interest under a finance lease related to the supply contract, but is subject to the terms warranty and of the supply contract and all defenses or claims arising therefrom.

(2) The extension of the benefit of supplier's promises and of warranties to the lessee (Section 2A–209(1)) does not: (i) modify the rights and obligations of the parties to the supply contract, whether arising therefrom or otherwise, or (ii) impose any duty or liability under the supply contract on the lessee.

(3) Any modification or rescission of the supply contract by the supplier and the lessor is effective between the supplier and the lessee unless, before the modification or rescission, the supplier has received notice that the lessee has entered into a finance lease related to the supply contract. If the modification or rescission is effective between the supplier and the lessee, the lessor is deemed to have assumed, in addition to the obligations of the lessor to the lessee under the lease contract, promises of the supplier to the lessor and warranties that were so modified or rescinded as they existed and were available to the lessee before modification or rescission.

(4) In addition to the extension of the benefit of the supplier's promises and of warranties to the lessee under subsection (1), the lessee retains all rights that the lessee may have against the supplier which arise from an agreement between the lessee and the supplier or under other law.

As amended in 1990.

§ 2A–210. Express Warranties.

(1) Express warranties by the lessor are created as follows:

(a) Any affirmation of fact or promise made by the lessor to the lessee which relates to the goods and becomes part of the basis of the bargain creates an express warranty that the goods will conform to the affirmation or promise.

(b) Any description of the goods which is made part of the basis of the bargain creates an express warranty that the goods will conform to the description.

(c) Any sample or model that is made part of the basis of the bargain creates an express warranty that the whole of the goods will conform to the sample or model.

(2) It is not necessary to the creation of an express warranty that the lessor use formal words, such as "warrant" or "guarantee," or that the lessor have a specific intention to make a warranty, but an affirmation merely of the value of the goods or a statement purporting to be merely the lessor's opinion or commendation of the goods does not create a warranty.

§ 2A–211. Warranties Against Interference and Against Infringement; Lessee's Obligation Against Infringement.

(1) There is in a lease contract a warranty that for the lease term no person holds a claim to or interest in the goods that arose from an act

or omission of the lessor, other than a claim by way of infringement or the like, which will interfere with the lessee's enjoyment of its leasehold interest.

(2) Except in a finance lease there is in a lease contract by a lessor who is a merchant regularly dealing in goods of the kind a warranty that the goods are delivered free of the rightful claim of any person by way of infringement or the like.

(3) A lessee who furnishes specifications to a lessor or a supplier shall hold the lessor and the supplier harmless against any claim by way of infringement or the like that arises out of compliance with the specifications.

§ 2A–212. Implied Warranty of Merchantability.

(1) Except in a finance lease, a warranty that the goods will be merchantable is implied in a lease contract if the lessor is a merchant with respect to goods of that kind.

(2) Goods to be merchantable must be at least such as

(a) pass without objection in the trade under the description in the lease agreement;

(b) in the case of fungible goods, are of fair average quality within the description;

(c) are fit for the ordinary purposes for which goods of that type are used;

(d) run, within the variation permitted by the lease agreement, of even kind, quality, and quantity within each unit and among all units involved;

(e) are adequately contained, packaged, and labeled as the lease agreement may require; and

(f) conform to any promises or affirmations of fact made on the container or label.

(3) Other implied warranties may arise from course of dealing or usage of trade.

§ 2A–213. Implied Warranty of Fitness for Particular Purpose.

Except in a finance of lease, if the lessor at the time the lease contract is made has reason to know of any particular purpose for which the goods are required and that the lessee is relying on the lessor's skill or judgment to select or furnish suitable goods, there is in the lease contract an implied warranty that the goods will be fit for that purpose.

§ 2A–214. Exclusion or Modification of Warranties.

(1) Words or conduct relevant to the creation of an express warranty and words or conduct tending to negate or limit a warranty must be construed wherever reasonable as consistent with each other; but, subject to the provisions of Section 2A–202 on parol or extrinsic evidence, negation or limitation is inoperative to the extent that the construction is unreasonable.

(2) Subject to subsection (3), to exclude or modify the implied warranty of merchantability or any part of it the language must mention "merchantability", be by a writing, and be conspicuous. Subject to subsection (3), to exclude or modify any implied warranty of fitness the exclusion must be by a writing and be conspicuous. Language to exclude all implied warranties of fitness is sufficient if it is in writing, is conspicuous and states, for example, "There is no warranty that the goods will be fit for a particular purpose".

(3) Notwithstanding subsection (2), but subject to subsection (4),

(a) unless the circumstances indicate otherwise, all implied warranties are excluded by expressions like "as is" or "with all faults"

or by other language that in common understanding calls the lessee's attention to the exclusion of warranties and makes plain that there is no implied warranty, if in writing and conspicuous;

(b) if the lessee before entering into the lease contract has examined the goods or the sample or model as fully as desired or has refused to examine the goods, there is no implied warranty with regard to defects that an examination ought in the circumstances to have revealed; and

(c) an implied warranty may also be excluded or modified by course of dealing, course of performance, or usage of trade.

(4) To exclude or modify a warranty against interference or against infringement (Section 2A–211) or any part of it, the language must be specific, be by a writing, and be conspicuous, unless the circumstances, including course of performance, course of dealing, or usage of trade, give the lessee reason to know that the goods are being leased subject to a claim or interest of any person.

§ 2A–215. Cumulation and Conflict of Warranties Express or Implied.

Warranties, whether express or implied, must be construed as consistent with each other and as cumulative, but if that construction is unreasonable, the intention of the parties determines which warranty is dominant. In ascertaining that intention the following rules apply:

(a) Exact or technical specifications displace an inconsistent sample or model or general language of description.

(b) A sample from an existing bulk displaces inconsistent general language of description.

(c) Express warranties displace inconsistent implied warranties other than an implied warranty of fitness for a particular purpose.

§ 2A–216. Third-Party Beneficiaries of Express and Implied Warranties.

Alternative A

A warranty to or for the benefit of a lessee under this Article, whether express or implied, extends to any natural person who is in the family or household of the lessee or who is a guest in the lessee's home if it is reasonable to expect that such person may use, consume, or be affected by the goods and who is injured in person by breach of the warranty. This section does not displace principles of law and equity that extend a warranty to or for the benefit of a lessee to other persons. The operation of this section may not be excluded, modified, or limited, but an exclusion, modification, or limitation of the warranty, including any with respect to rights and remedies, effective against the lessee is also effective against any beneficiary designated under this section.

Alternative B

A warranty to or for the benefit of a lessee under this Article, whether express or implied, extends to any natural person who may reasonably be expected to use, consume, or be affected by the goods and who is injured in person by breach of the warranty. This section does not displace principles of law and equity that extend a warranty to or for the benefit of a lessee to other persons. The operation of this section may not be excluded, modified, or limited, but an exclusion, modification, or limitation of the warranty, including any with respect to rights and remedies, effective against the lessee is also effective against the beneficiary designated under this section.

Alternative C

A warranty to or for the benefit of a lessee under this Article, whether express or implied, extends to any person who may reasonably be expected to use, consume, or be affected by the goods and who is injured by breach of the warranty. The operation of this section may not be excluded, modified, or limited with respect to injury to the person of an individual to whom the warranty extends, but an exclusion, modification, or limitation of the warranty, including any with respect to rights and remedies, effective against the lessee is also effective against the beneficiary designated under this section.

§ 2A–217. Identification.

Identification of goods as goods to which a lease contract refers may be made at any time and in any manner explicitly agreed to by the parties. In the absence of explicit agreement, identification occurs:

(a) when the lease contract is made if the lease contract is for a lease of goods that are existing and identified;

(b) when the goods are shipped, marked, or otherwise designated by the lessor as goods to which the lease contract refers, if the lease contract is for a lease of goods that are not existing and identified; or

(c) when the young are conceived, if the lease contract is for a lease of unborn young of animals.

§ 2A–218. Insurance and Proceeds.

(1) A lessee obtains an insurable interest when existing goods are identified to the lease contract even though the goods identified are nonconforming and the lessee has an option to reject them.

(2) If a lessee has an insurable interest only by reason of the lessor's identification of the goods, the lessor, until default or insolvency or notification to the lessee that identification is final, may substitute other goods for those identified.

(3) Notwithstanding a lessee's insurable interest under subsections (1) and (2), the lessor retains an insurable interest until an option to buy has been exercised by the lessee and risk of loss has passed to the lessee.

(4) Nothing in this section impairs any insurable interest recognized under any other statute or rule of law.

(5) The parties by agreement may determine that one or more parties have an obligation to obtain and pay for insurance covering the goods and by agreement may determine the beneficiary of the proceeds of the insurance.

§ 2A–219. Risk of Loss.

(1) Except in the case of a finance lease, risk of loss is retained by the lessor and does not pass to the lessee. In the case of a finance lease, risk of loss passes to the lessee.

(2) Subject to the provisions of this Article on the effect of default on risk of loss (Section 2A–220), if risk of loss is to pass to the lessee and the time of passage is not stated, the following rules apply:

(a) If the lease contract requires or authorizes the goods to be shipped by carrier

(i) and it does not require delivery at a particular destination, the risk of loss passes to the lessee when the goods are duly delivered to the carrier; but

(ii) if it does require delivery at a particular destination and the goods are there duly tendered while in the possession of the carrier, the risk of loss passes to the lessee when the goods are there duly so tendered as to enable the lessee to take delivery.

(b) If the goods are held by a bailee to be delivered without being moved, the risk of loss passes to the lessee on acknowledgment by the bailee of the lessee's right to possession of the goods.

(c) In any case not within subsection (a) or (b), the risk of loss passes to the lessee on the lessee's receipt of the goods if the lessor, or, in the case of a finance lease, the supplier, is a merchant; otherwise the risk passes to the lessee on tender of delivery.

§ 2A–220. Effect of Default on Risk of Loss.

(1) Where risk of loss is to pass to the lessee and the time of passage is not stated:

(a) If a tender or delivery of goods so fails to conform to the lease contract as to give a right of rejection, the risk of their loss remains with the lessor, or, in the case of a finance lease, the supplier, until cure or acceptance.

(b) If the lessee rightfully revokes acceptance, he [or she], to the extent of any deficiency in his [or her] effective insurance coverage, may treat the risk of loss as having remained with the lessor from the beginning.

(2) Whether or not risk of loss is to pass to the lessee, if the lessee as to conforming goods already identified to a lease contract repudiates or is otherwise in default under the lease contract, the lessor, or, in the case of a finance lease, the supplier, to the extent of any deficiency in his [or her] effective insurance coverage may treat the risk of loss as resting on the lessee for a commercially reasonable time.

§ 2A–221. Casualty to Identified Goods.

If a lease contract requires goods identified when the lease contract is made, and the goods suffer casualty without fault of the lessee, the lessor or the supplier before delivery, or the goods suffer casualty before risk of loss passes to the lessee pursuant to the lease agreement or Section 2A–219, then:

(a) if the loss is total, the lease contract is avoided; and

(b) if the loss is partial or the goods have so deteriorated as to no longer conform to the lease contract, the lessee may nevertheless demand inspection and at his [or her] option either treat the lease contract as avoided or, except in a finance lease that is not a consumer lease, accept the goods with due allowance from the rent payable for the balance of the lease term for the deterioration or the deficiency in quantity but without further right against the lessor.

Part 3 Effect of Lease Contract

§ 2A–301. Enforceability of Lease Contract.

Except as otherwise provided in this Article, a lease contract is effective and enforceable according to its terms between the parties, against purchasers of the goods and against creditors of the parties.

§ 2A–302. Title to and Possession of Goods.

Except as otherwise provided in this Article, each provision of this Article applies whether the lessor or a third party has title to the goods, and whether the lessor, the lessee, or a third party has possession of the goods, notwithstanding any statute or rule of law that possession or the absence of possession is fraudulent.

§ 2A–303. Alienability of Party's Interest Under Lease Contract or of Lessor's Residual Interest in Goods; Delegation of Performance; Transfer of Rights.

(1) As used in this section, "creation of a security interest" includes the sale of a lease contract that is subject to Article 9, Secured Transactions, by reason of Section 9–109(a)(3).

(2) Except as provided in subsections (3) and Section 9–407, a provision in a lease agreement which (i) prohibits the voluntary or involuntary transfer, including a transfer by sale, sublease, creation or enforcement of a security interest, or attachment, levy, or other judicial process, of an interest of a party under the lease contract or of the lessor's residual interest in the goods, or (ii) makes such a transfer an event of default, gives rise to the rights and remedies provided in subsection (4), but a transfer that is prohibited or is an event of default under the lease agreement is otherwise effective.

(3) A provision in a lease agreement which (i) prohibits a transfer of a right to damages for default with respect to the whole lease contract or of a right to payment arising out of the transferor's due performance of the transferor's entire obligation, or (ii) makes such a transfer an event of default, is not enforceable, and such a transfer is not a transfer that materially impairs the propsect of obtaining return performance by, materially changes the duty of, or materially increases the burden or risk imposed on, the other party to the lease contract within the purview of subsection (4).

(4) Subject to subsection (3) and Section 9–407:

    (a) if a transfer is made which is made an event of default under a lease agreement, the party to the lease contract not making the transfer, unless that party waives the default or otherwise agrees, has the rights and remedies described in Section 2A–501(2);

    (b) if paragraph (a) is not applicable and if a transfer is made that (i) is prohibited under a lease agreement or (ii) materially impairs the prospect of obtaining return performance by, materially changes the duty of, or materially increases the burden or risk imposed on, the other party to the lease contract, unless the party not making the transfer agrees at any time to the transfer in the lease contract or otherwise, then, except as limited by contract, (i) the transferor is liable to the party not making the transfer for damages caused by the transfer to the extent that the damages could not reasonably be prevented by the party not making the transfer and (ii) a court having jurisdiction may grant other appropriate relief, including cancellation of the lease contract or an injunction against the transfer.

(5) A transfer of "the lease" or of "all my rights under the lease", or a transfer in similar general terms, is a transfer of rights and, unless the language or the circumstances, as in a transfer for security, indicate the contrary, the transfer is a delegation of duties by the transferor to the transferee. Acceptance by the transferee constitutes a promise by the transferee to perform those duties. The promise is enforceable by either the transferor or the other party to the lease contract.

(6) Unless otherwise agreed by the lessor and the lessee, a delegation of performance does not relieve the transferor as against the other party of any duty to perform or of any liability for default.

(7) In a consumer lease, to prohibit the transfer of an interest of a party under the lease contract or to make a transfer an event of default, the language must be specific, by a writing, and conspicuous.

As amended in 1990 and 1999.

§ 2A–304. Subsequent Lease of Goods by Lessor.

(1) Subject to Section 2A–303, a subsequent lessee from a lessor of goods under an existing lease contract obtains, to the extent of the leasehold interest transferred, the leasehold interest in the goods that the lessor had or had power to transfer, and except as provided in subsection (2) and Section 2A–527(4), takes subject to the existing lease contract. A lessor with voidable title has power to transfer a good leasehold interest to a good faith subsequent lessee for value,

but only to the extent set forth in the preceding sentence. If goods have been delivered under a transaction of purchase the lessor has that power even though:

    (a) the lessor's transferor was deceived as to the identity of the lessor;

    (b) the delivery was in exchange for a check which is later dishonored;

    (c) it was agreed that the transaction was to be a "cash sale"; or

    (d) the delivery was procured through fraud punishable as larcenous under the criminal law.

(2) A subsequent lessee in the ordinary course of business from a lessor who is a merchant dealing in goods of that kind to whom the goods were entrusted by the existing lessee of that lessor before the interest of the subsequent lessee became enforceable against that lessor obtains, to the extent of the leasehold interest transferred, all of that lessor's and the existing lessee's rights to the goods, and takes free of the existing lease contract.

(3) A subsequent lessee from the lessor of goods that are subject to an existing lease contract and are covered by a certificate of title issued under a statute of this State or of another jurisdiction takes no greater rights than those provided both by this section and by the certificate of title statute.

As amended in 1990.

§ 2A–305. Sale or Sublease of Goods by Lessee.

(1) Subject to the provisions of Section 2A–303, a buyer or sublessee from the lessee of goods under an existing lease contract obtains, to the extent of the interest transferred, the leasehold interest in the goods that the lessee had or had power to transfer, and except as provided in subsection (2) and Section 2A–511(4), takes subject to the existing lease contract. A lessee with a voidable leasehold interest has power to transfer a good leasehold interest to a good faith buyer for value or a good faith sublessee for value, but only to the extent set forth in the preceding sentence. When goods have been delivered under a transaction of lease the lessee has that power even though:

    (a) the lessor was deceived as to the identity of the lessee;

    (b) the delivery was in exchange for a check which is later dishonored; or

    (c) the delivery was procured through fraud punishable as larcenous under the criminal law.

(2) A buyer in the ordinary course of business or a sublessee in the ordinary course of business from a lessee who is a merchant dealing in goods of that kind to whom the goods were entrusted by the lessor obtains, to the extent of the interest transferred, all of the lessor's and lessee's rights to the goods, and takes free of the existing lease contract.

(3) A buyer or sublessee from the lessee of goods that are subject to an existing lease contract and are covered by a certificate of title issued under a statute of this State or of another jurisdiction takes no greater rights than those provided both by this section and by the certificate of title statute.

§ 2A–306. Priority of Certain Liens Arising by Operation of Law.

If a person in the ordinary course of his [or her] business furnishes services or materials with respect to goods subject to a lease contract, a lien upon those goods in the possession of that person given by statute or rule of law for those materials or services takes priority over any interest of the lessor or lessee under the lease contract or this Article unless the lien is created by statute and the statute provides otherwise or unless the lien is created by rule of law and the rule of law provides otherwise.

§ 2A–307. Priority of Liens Arising by Attachment or Levy on, Security Interests in, and Other Claims to Goods.

(1) Except as otherwise provided in Section 2A–306, a creditor of a lessee takes subject to the lease contract.

(2) Except as otherwise provided in subsection (3) and in Sections 2A–306 and 2A–308, a creditor of a lessor takes subject to the lease contract unless the creditor holds a lien that attached to the goods before the lease contract became enforceable.

(3) Except as otherwise provided in Sections 9–317, 9–321, and 9–323, a lessee takes a leasehold interest subject to a security interest held by a creditor of the lessor.

As amended in 1990 and 1999.

§ 2A–308. Special Rights of Creditors.

(1) A creditor of a lessor in possession of goods subject to a lease contract may treat the lease contract as void if as against the creditor retention of possession by the lessor is fraudulent under any statute or rule of law, but retention of possession in good faith and current course of trade by the lessor for a commercially reasonable time after the lease contract becomes enforceable is not fraudulent.

(2) Nothing in this Article impairs the rights of creditors of a lessor if the lease contract (a) becomes enforceable, not in current course of trade but in satisfaction of or as security for a pre-existing claim for money, security, or the like, and (b) is made under circumstances which under any statute or rule of law apart from this Article would constitute the transaction a fraudulent transfer or voidable preference.

(3) A creditor of a seller may treat a sale or an identification of goods to a contract for sale as void if as against the creditor retention of possession by the seller is fraudulent under any statute or rule of law, but retention of possession of the goods pursuant to a lease contract entered into by the seller as lessee and the buyer as lessor in connection with the sale or identification of the goods is not fraudulent if the buyer bought for value and in good faith.

§ 2A–309. Lessor's and Lessee's Rights When Goods Become Fixtures.

(1) In this section:

(a) goods are "fixtures" when they become so related to particular real estate that an interest in them arises under real estate law;

(b) a "fixture filing" is the filing, in the office where a mortgage on the real estate would be filed or recorded, of a financing statement covering goods that are or are to become fixtures and conforming to the requirements of Section 9–502(a) and (b);

(c) a lease is a "purchase money lease" unless the lessee has possession or use of the goods or the right to possession or use of the goods before the lease agreement is enforceable;

(d) a mortgage is a "construction mortgage" to the extent it secures an obligation incurred for the construction of an improvement on land including the acquisition cost of the land, if the recorded writing so indicates; and

(e) "encumbrance" includes real estate mortgages and other liens on real estate and all other rights in real estate that are not ownership interests.

(2) Under this Article a lease may be of goods that are fixtures or may continue in goods that become fixtures, but no lease exists under this Article of ordinary building materials incorporated into an improvement on land.

(3) This Article does not prevent creation of a lease of fixtures pursuant to real estate law.

(4) The perfected interest of a lessor of fixtures has priority over a conflicting interest of an encumbrancer or owner of the real estate if:

(a) the lease is a purchase money lease, the conflicting interest of the encumbrancer or owner arises before the goods become fixtures, the interest of the lessor is perfected by a fixture filing before the goods become fixtures or within ten days thereafter, and the lessee has an interest of record in the real estate or is in possession of the real estate; or

(b) the interest of the lessor is perfected by a fixture filing before the interest of the encumbrancer or owner is of record, the lessor's interest has priority over any conflicting interest of a predecessor in title of the encumbrancer or owner, and the lessee has an interest of record in the real estate or is in possession of the real estate.

(5) The interest of a lessor of fixtures, whether or not perfected, has priority over the conflicting interest of an encumbrancer or owner of the real estate if:

(a) the fixtures are readily removable factory or office machines, readily removable equipment that is not primarily used or leased for use in the operation of the real estate, or readily removable replacements of domestic appliances that are goods subject to a consumer lease, and before the goods become fixtures the lease contract is enforceable; or

(b) the conflicting interest is a lien on the real estate obtained by legal or equitable proceedings after the lease contract is enforceable; or

(c) the encumbrancer or owner has consented in writing to the lease or has disclaimed an interest in the goods as fixtures; or

(d) the lessee has a right to remove the goods as against the encumbrancer or owner. If the lessee's right to remove terminates, the priority of the interest of the lessor continues for a reasonable time.

(6) Notwithstanding paragraph (4)(a) but otherwise subject to subsections (4) and (5), the interest of a lessor of fixtures, including the lessor's residual interest, is subordinate to the conflicting interest of an encumbrancer of the real estate under a construction mortgage recorded before the goods become fixtures if the goods become fixtures before the completion of the construction. To the extent given to refinance a construction mortgage, the conflicting interest of an encumbrancer of the real estate under a mortgage has this priority to the same extent as the encumbrancer of the real estate under the construction mortgage.

(7) In cases not within the preceding subsections, priority between the interest of a lessor of fixtures, including the lessor's residual interest, and the conflicting interest of an encumbrancer or owner of the real estate who is not the lessee is determined by the priority rules governing conflicting interests in real estate.

(8) If the interest of a lessor of fixtures, including the lessor's residual interest, has priority over all conflicting interests of all owners

and encumbrancers of the real estate, the lessor or the lessee may (i) on default, expiration, termination, or cancellation of the lease agreement but subject to the agreement and this Article, or (ii) if necessary to enforce other rights and remedies of the lessor or lessee under this Article, remove the goods from the real estate, free and clear of all conflicting interests of all owners and encumbrancers of the real estate, but the lessor or lessee must reimburse any encumbrancer or owner of the real estate who is not the lessee and who has not otherwise agreed for the cost of repair of any physical injury, but not for any diminution in value of the real estate caused by the absence of the goods removed or by any necessity of replacing them. A person entitled to reimbursement may refuse permission to remove until the party seeking removal gives adequate security for the performance of this obligation.

(9) Even though the lease agreement does not create a security interest, the interest of a lessor of fixtures, including the lessor's residual interest, is perfected by filing a financing statement as a fixture filing for leased goods that are or are to become fixtures in accordance with the relevant provisions of the Article on Secured Transactions (Article 9).

As amended in 1990 and 1999.

§ 2A–310. Lessor's and Lessee's Rights When Goods Become Accessions.

(1) Goods are "accessions" when they are installed in or affixed to other goods.

(2) The interest of a lessor or a lessee under a lease contract entered into before the goods became accessions is superior to all interests in the whole except as stated in subsection (4).

(3) The interest of a lessor or a lessee under a lease contract entered into at the time or after the goods became accessions is superior to all subsequently acquired interests in the whole except as stated in subsection (4) but is subordinate to interests in the whole existing at the time the lease contract was made unless the holders of such interests in the whole have in writing consented to the lease or disclaimed an interest in the goods as part of the whole.

(4) The interest of a lessor* or a lessee under a lease contract described in subsection (2) or (3) is subordinate to the interest of

  (a) a buyer in the ordinary course of business or a lessee in the ordinary course of business of any interest in the whole acquired after the goods became accessions; or

  (b) a creditor with a security interest in the whole perfected before the lease contract was made to the extent that the creditor makes subsequent advances without knowledge of the lease contract.

(5) When under subsections (2) or (3) and (4) a lessor or a lessee of accessions holds an interest that is superior to all interests in the whole, the lessor or the lessee may (a) on default, expiration, termination, or cancellation of the lease contract by the other party but subject to the provisions of the lease contract and this Article, or (b) if necessary to enforce his [or her] other rights and remedies under this Article, remove the goods from the whole, free and clear of all interests in the whole, but he [or she] must reimburse any holder of an interest in the whole who is not the lessee and who has not otherwise agreed for the cost of repair of any physical injury but not for any diminution in value of the whole caused by the absence of the goods removed or by any necessity for replacing them. A person entitled to reimbursement may refuse permission to remove until the party seeking removal gives adequate security for the performance of this obligation.

§ 2A–311. Priority Subject to Subordination.

Nothing in this Article prevents subordination by agreement by any person entitled to priority.

As added in 1990.

Part 4 Performance of Lease Contract: Repudiated, Substituted and Excused

§ 2A–401. Insecurity: Adequate Assurance of Performance.

(1) A lease contract imposes an obligation on each party that the other's expectation of receiving due performance will not be impaired.

(2) If reasonable grounds for insecurity arise with respect to the performance of either party, the insecure party may demand in writing adequate assurance of due performance. Until the insecure party receives that assurance, if commercially reasonable the insecure party may suspend any performance for which he [or she] has not already received the agreed return.

(3) A repudiation of the lease contract occurs if assurance of due performance adequate under the circumstances of the particular case is not provided to the insecure party within a reasonable time, not to exceed 30 days after receipt of a demand by the other party.

(4) Between merchants, the reasonableness of grounds for insecurity and the adequacy of any assurance offered must be determined according to commercial standards.

(5) Acceptance of any nonconforming delivery or payment does not prejudice the aggrieved party's right to demand adequate assurance of future performance.

§ 2A–402. Anticipatory Repudiation.

If either party repudiates a lease contract with respect to a performance not yet due under the lease contract, the loss of which performance will substantially impair the value of the lease contract to the other, the aggrieved party may:

(a) for a commercially reasonable time, await retraction of repudiation and performance by the repudiating party;

(b) make demand pursuant to Section 2A–401 and await assurance of future performance adequate under the circumstances of the particular case; or

(c) resort to any right or remedy upon default under the lease contract or this Article, even though the aggrieved party has notified the repudiating party that the aggrieved party would await the repudiating party's performance and assurance and has urged retraction. In addition, whether or not the aggrieved party is pursuing one of the foregoing remedies, the aggrieved party may suspend performance or, if the aggrieved party is the lessor, proceed in accordance with the provisions of this Article on the lessor's right to identify goods to the lease contract notwithstanding default or to salvage unfinished goods (Section 2A–524).

§ 2A–403. Retraction of Anticipatory Repudiation.

(1) Until the repudiating party's next performance is due, the repudiating party can retract the repudiation unless, since the repudiation, the aggrieved party has cancelled the lease contract or materially changed the aggrieved party's position or otherwise indicated that the aggrieved party considers the repudiation final.

(2) Retraction may be by any method that clearly indicates to the aggrieved party that the repudiating party intends to perform under

the lease contract and includes any assurance demanded under Section 2A–401.

(3) Retraction reinstates a repudiating party's rights under a lease contract with due excuse and allowance to the aggrieved party for any delay occasioned by the repudiation.

§ 2A–404. Substituted Performance.

(1) If without fault of the lessee, the lessor and the supplier, the agreed berthing, loading, or unloading facilities fail or the agreed type of carrier becomes unavailable or the agreed manner of delivery otherwise becomes commercially impracticable, but a commercially reasonable substitute is available, the substitute performance must be tendered and accepted.

(2) If the agreed means or manner of payment fails because of domestic or foreign governmental regulation:

(a) the lessor may withhold or stop delivery or cause the supplier to withhold or stop delivery unless the lessee provides a means or manner of payment that is commercially a substantial equivalent; and

(b) if delivery has already been taken, payment by the means or in the manner provided by the regulation discharges the lessee's obligation unless the regulation is discriminatory, oppressive, or predatory.

§ 2A–405. Excused Performance.

Subject to Section 2A–404 on substituted performance, the following rules apply:

(a) Delay in delivery or nondelivery in whole or in part by a lessor or a supplier who complies with paragraphs (b) and (c) is not a default under the lease contract if performance as agreed has been made impracticable by the occurrence of a contingency the nonoccurrence of which was a basic assumption on which the lease contract was made or by compliance in good faith with any applicable foreign or domestic governmental regulation or order, whether or not the regulation or order later proves to be invalid.

(b) If the causes mentioned in paragraph (a) affect only part of the lessor's or the supplier's capacity to perform, he [or she] shall allocate production and deliveries among his [or her] customers but at his [or her] option may include regular customers not then under contract for sale or lease as well as his [or her] own requirements for further manufacture. He [or she] may so allocate in any manner that is fair and reasonable.

(c) The lessor seasonably shall notify the lessee and in the case of a finance lease the supplier seasonably shall notify the lessor and the lessee, if known, that there will be delay or nondelivery and, if allocation is required under paragraph (b), of the estimated quota thus made available for the lessee.

§ 2A–406. Procedure on Excused Performance.

(1) If the lessee receives notification of a material or indefinite delay or an allocation justified under Section 2A–405, the lessee may by written notification to the lessor as to any goods involved, and with respect to all of the goods if under an installment lease contract the value of the whole lease contract is substantially impaired (Section 2A–510):

(a) terminate the lease contract (Section 2A–505(2)); or

(b) except in a finance lease that is not a consumer lease, modify the lease contract by accepting the available quota in substitution, with due allowance from the rent payable for the balance of the lease term for the deficiency but without further right against the lessor.

(2) If, after receipt of a notification from the lessor under Section 2A–405, the lessee fails so to modify the lease agreement within a reasonable time not exceeding 30 days, the lease contract lapses with respect to any deliveries affected.

§ 2A–407. Irrevocable Promises: Finance Leases.

(1) In the case of a finance lease that is not a consumer lease the lessee's promises under the lease contract become irrevocable and independent upon the lessee's acceptance of the goods.

(2) A promise that has become irrevocable and independent under subsection (1):

(a) is effective and enforceable between the parties, and by or against third parties including assignees of the parties, and

(b) is not subject to cancellation, termination, modification, repudiation, excuse, or substitution without the consent of the party to whom the promise runs.

(3) This section does not affect the validity under any other law of a covenant in any lease contract making the lessee's promises irrevocable and independent upon the lessee's acceptance of the goods.

As amended in 1990.

Part 5 Default

A. In General

§ 2A–501. Default: Procedure.

(1) Whether the lessor or the lessee is in default under a lease contract is determined by the lease agreement and this Article.

(2) If the lessor or the lessee is in default under the lease contract, the party seeking enforcement has rights and remedies as provided in this Article and, except as limited by this Article, as provided in the lease agreement.

(3) If the lessor or the lessee is in default under the lease contract, the party seeking enforcement may reduce the party's claim to judgment, or otherwise enforce the lease contract by self-help or any available judicial procedure or nonjudicial procedure, including administrative proceeding, arbitration, or the like, in accordance with this Article.

(4) Except as otherwise provided in Section 1–106(1) or this Article or the lease agreement, the rights and remedies referred to in subsections (2) and (3) are cumulative.

(5) If the lease agreement covers both real property and goods, the party seeking enforcement may proceed under this Part as to the goods, or under other applicable law as to both the real property and the goods in accordance with that party's rights and remedies in respect of the real property, in which case this Part does not apply.

As amended in 1990.

§ 2A–502. Notice After Default.

Except as otherwise provided in this Article or the lease agreement, the lessor or lessee in default under the lease contract is not entitled to notice of default or notice of enforcement from the other party to the lease agreement.

§ 2A–503. Modification or Impairment of Rights and Remedies.

(1) Except as otherwise provided in this Article, the lease agreement may include rights and remedies for default in addition to or in substitution for those provided in this Article and may limit or alter the measure of damages recoverable under this Article.

(2) Resort to a remedy provided under this Article or in the lease agreement is optional unless the remedy is expressly agreed to be exclusive. If circumstances cause an exclusive or limited remedy to fail of its essential purpose, or provision for an exclusive remedy is unconscionable, remedy may be had as provided in this Article.

(3) Consequential damages may be liquidated under Section 2A–504, or may otherwise be limited, altered, or excluded unless the limitation, alteration, or exclusion is unconscionable. Limitation, alteration, or exclusion of consequential damages for injury to the person in the case of consumer goods is prima facie unconscionable but limitation, alteration, or exclusion of damages where the loss is commercial is not prima facie unconscionable.

(4) Rights and remedies on default by the lessor or the lessee with respect to any obligation or promise collateral or ancillary to the lease contract are not impaired by this Article.

As amended in 1990.

§ 2A–504. Liquidation of Damages.

(1) Damages payable by either party for default, or any other act or omission, including indemnity for loss or diminution of anticipated tax benefits or loss or damage to lessor's residual interest, may be liquidated in the lease agreement but only at an amount or by a formula that is reasonable in light of the then anticipated harm caused by the default or other act or omission.

(2) If the lease agreement provides for liquidation of damages, and such provision does not comply with subsection (1), or such provision is an exclusive or limited remedy that circumstances cause to fail of its essential purpose, remedy may be had as provided in this Article.

(3) If the lessor justifiably withholds or stops delivery of goods because of the lessee's default or insolvency (Section 2A–525 or 2A–526), the lessee is entitled to restitution of any amount by which the sum of his [or her] payments exceeds:

(a) the amount to which the lessor is entitled by virtue of terms liquidating the lessor's damages in accordance with subsection (1); or

(b) in the absence of those terms, 20 percent of the then present value of the total rent the lessee was obligated to pay for the balance of the lease term, or, in the case of a consumer lease, the lesser of such amount or $500.

(4) A lessee's right to restitution under subsection (3) is subject to offset to the extent the lessor establishes:

(a) a right to recover damages under the provisions of this Article other than subsection (1); and

(b) the amount or value of any benefits received by the lessee directly or indirectly by reason of the lease contract.

§ 2A–505. Cancellation and Termination and Effect of Cancellation, Termination, Rescission, or Fraud on Rights and Remedies.

(1) On cancellation of the lease contract, all obligations that are still executory on both sides are discharged, but any right based on prior default or performance survives, and the cancelling party also retains any remedy for default of the whole lease contract or any unperformed balance.

(2) On termination of the lease contract, all obligations that are still executory on both sides are discharged but any right based on prior default or performance survives.

(3) Unless the contrary intention clearly appears, expressions of "cancellation," "rescission," or the like of the lease contract may not be construed as a renunciation or discharge of any claim in damages for an antecedent default.

(4) Rights and remedies for material misrepresentation or fraud include all rights and remedies available under this Article for default.

(5) Neither rescission nor a claim for rescission of the lease contract nor rejection or return of the goods may bar or be deemed inconsistent with a claim for damages or other right or remedy.

§ 2A–506. Statute of Limitations.

(1) An action for default under a lease contract, including breach of warranty or indemnity, must be commenced within 4 years after the cause of action accrued. By the original lease contract the parties may reduce the period of limitation to not less than one year.

(2) A cause of action for default accrues when the act or omission on which the default or breach of warranty is based is or should have been discovered by the aggrieved party, or when the default occurs, whichever is later. A cause of action for indemnity accrues when the act or omission on which the claim for indemnity is based is or should have been discovered by the indemnified party, whichever is later.

(3) If an action commenced within the time limited by subsection (1) is so terminated as to leave available a remedy by another action for the same default or breach of warranty or indemnity, the other action may be commenced after the expiration of the time limited and within 6 months after the termination of the first action unless the termination resulted from voluntary discontinuance or from dismissal for failure or neglect to prosecute.

(4) This section does not alter the law on tolling of the statute of limitations nor does it apply to causes of action that have accrued before this Article becomes effective.

§ 2A–507. Proof of Market Rent: Time and Place.

(1) Damages based on market rent (Section 2A–519 or 2A–528) are determined according to the rent for the use of the goods concerned for a lease term identical to the remaining lease term of the original lease agreement and prevailing at the times specified in Sections 2A–519 and 2A–528.

(2) If evidence of rent for the use of the goods concerned for a lease term identical to the remaining lease term of the original lease agreement and prevailing at the times or places described in this Article is not readily available, the rent prevailing within any reasonable time before or after the time described or at any other place or for a different lease term which in commercial judgment or under usage of trade would serve as a reasonable substitute for the one described may be used, making any proper allowance for the difference, including the cost of transporting the goods to or from the other place.

(3) Evidence of a relevant rent prevailing at a time or place or for a lease term other than the one described in this Article offered by one party is not admissible unless and until he [or she] has given the other party notice the court finds sufficient to prevent unfair surprise.

(4) If the prevailing rent or value of any goods regularly leased in any established market is in issue, reports in official publications or trade journals or in newspapers or periodicals of general circulation published as the reports of that market are admissible in evidence. The circumstances of the preparation of the report may be shown to affect its weight but not its admissibility.

As amended in 1990.

B. Default by Lessor

§ 2A–508. Lessee's Remedies.

(1) If a lessor fails to deliver the goods in conformity to the lease contract (Section 2A–509) or repudiates the lease contract (Section 2A–402), or a lessee rightfully rejects the goods (Section 2A–509) or justifiably revokes acceptance of the goods (Section 2A–517), then with respect to any goods involved, and with respect to all of the goods if under an installment lease contract the value of the whole lease contract is substantially impaired (Section 2A–510), the lessor is in default under the lease contract and the lessee may:

　　(a) cancel the lease contract (Section 2A–505(1));

　　(b) recover so much of the rent and security as has been paid and is just under the circumstances;

　　(c) cover and recover damages as to all goods affected whether or not they have been identified to the lease contract (Sections 2A–518 and 2A–520), or recover damages for nondelivery (Sections 2A–519 and 2A–520);

　　(d) exercise any other rights or pursue any other remedies provided in the lease contract.

(2) If a lessor fails to deliver the goods in conformity to the lease contract or repudiates the lease contract, the lessee may also:

　　(a) if the goods have been identified, recover them (Section 2A–522); or

　　(b) in a proper case, obtain specific performance or replevy the goods (Section 2A–521).

(3) If a lessor is otherwise in default under a lease contract, the lessee may exercise the rights and pursue the remedies provided in the lease contract, which may include a right to cancel the lease, and in Section 2A–519(3).

(4) If a lessor has breached a warranty, whether express or implied, the lessee may recover damages (Section 2A–519(4)).

(5) On rightful rejection or justifiable revocation of acceptance, a lessee has a security interest in goods in the lessee's possession or control for any rent and security that has been paid and any expenses reasonably incurred in their inspection, receipt, transportation, and care and custody and may hold those goods and dispose of them in good faith and in a commercially reasonable manner, subject to Section 2A–527(5).

(6) Subject to the provisions of Section 2A–407, a lessee, on notifying the lessor of the lessee's intention to do so, may deduct all or any part of the damages resulting from any default under the lease contract from any part of the rent still due under the same lease contract.

As amended in 1990.

§ 2A–509. Lessee's Rights on Improper Delivery; Rightful Rejection.

(1) Subject to the provisions of Section 2A–510 on default in installment lease contracts, if the goods or the tender or delivery fail in any respect to conform to the lease contract, the lessee may reject or accept the goods or accept any commercial unit or units and reject the rest of the goods.

(2) Rejection of goods is ineffective unless it is within a reasonable time after tender or delivery of the goods and the lessee seasonably notifies the lessor.

§ 2A–510. Installment Lease Contracts: Rejection and Default.

(1) Under an installment lease contract a lessee may reject any delivery that is nonconforming if the nonconformity substantially impairs the value of that delivery and cannot be cured or the nonconformity is a defect in the required documents; but if the nonconformity does not fall within subsection (2) and the lessor or the supplier gives adequate assurance of its cure, the lessee must accept that delivery.

(2) Whenever nonconformity or default with respect to one or more deliveries substantially impairs the value of the installment lease contract as a whole there is a default with respect to the whole. But, the aggrieved party reinstates the installment lease contract as a whole if the aggrieved party accepts a nonconforming delivery without seasonably notifying of cancellation or brings an action with respect only to past deliveries or demands performance as to future deliveries.

§ 2A–511. Merchant Lessee's Duties as to Rightfully Rejected Goods.

(1) Subject to any security interest of a lessee (Section 2A–508(5)), if a lessor or a supplier has no agent or place of business at the market of rejection, a merchant lessee, after rejection of goods in his [or her] possession or control, shall follow any reasonable instructions received from the lessor or the supplier with respect to the goods. In the absence of those instructions, a merchant lessee shall make reasonable efforts to sell, lease, or otherwise dispose of the goods for the lessor's account if they threaten to decline in value speedily. Instructions are not reasonable if on demand indemnity for expenses is not forthcoming.

(2) If a merchant lessee (subsection (1)) or any other lessee (Section 2A–512) disposes of goods, he [or she] is entitled to reimbursement either from the lessor or the supplier or out of the proceeds for reasonable expenses of caring for and disposing of the goods and, if the expenses include no disposition commission, to such commission as is usual in the trade, or if there is none, to a reasonable sum not exceeding 10 percent of the gross proceeds.

(3) In complying with this section or Section 2A–512, the lessee is held only to good faith. Good faith conduct hereunder is neither acceptance or conversion nor the basis of an action for damages.

(4) A purchaser who purchases in good faith from a lessee pursuant to this section or Section 2A–512 takes the goods free of any rights of the lessor and the supplier even though the lessee fails to comply with one or more of the requirements of this Article.

§ 2A–512. Lessee's Duties as to Rightfully Rejected Goods.

(1) Except as otherwise provided with respect to goods that threaten to decline in value speedily (Section 2A–511) and subject to any security interest of a lessee (Section 2A–508(5)):

　　(a) the lessee, after rejection of goods in the lessee's possession, shall hold them with reasonable care at the lessor's or the supplier's disposition for a reasonable time after the lessee's seasonable notification of rejection;

　　(b) if the lessor or the supplier gives no instructions within a reasonable time after notification of rejection, the lessee may store the rejected goods for the lessor's or the supplier's account or ship them to the lessor or the supplier or dispose of them for the lessor's or the supplier's account with reimbursement in the manner provided in Section 2A–511; but

(c) the lessee has no further obligations with regard to goods rightfully rejected.

(2) Action by the lessee pursuant to subsection (1) is not acceptance or conversion.

§ 2A–513. Cure by Lessor of Improper Tender or Delivery; Replacement.

(1) If any tender or delivery by the lessor or the supplier is rejected because nonconforming and the time for performance has not yet expired, the lessor or the supplier may seasonably notify the lessee of the lessor's or the supplier's intention to cure and may then make a conforming delivery within the time provided in the lease contract.

(2) If the lessee rejects a nonconforming tender that the lessor or the supplier had reasonable grounds to believe would be acceptable with or without money allowance, the lessor or the supplier may have a further reasonable time to substitute a conforming tender if he [or she] seasonably notifies the lessee.

§ 2A–514. Waiver of Lessee's Objections.

(1) In rejecting goods, a lessee's failure to state a particular defect that is ascertainable by reasonable inspection precludes the lessee from relying on the defect to justify rejection or to establish default:

(a) if, stated seasonably, the lessor or the supplier could have cured it (Section 2A–513); or

(b) between merchants if the lessor or the supplier after rejection has made a request in writing for a full and final written statement of all defects on which the lessee proposes to rely.

(2) A lessee's failure to reserve rights when paying rent or other consideration against documents precludes recovery of the payment for defects apparent on the face of the documents.

§ 2A–515. Acceptance of Goods.

(1) Acceptance of goods occurs after the lessee has had a reasonable opportunity to inspect the goods and

(a) the lessee signifies or acts with respect to the goods in a manner that signifies to the lessor or the supplier that the goods are conforming or that the lessee will take or retain them in spite of their nonconformity; or

(b) the lessee fails to make an effective rejection of the goods (Section 2A–509(2)).

(2) Acceptance of a part of any commercial unit is acceptance of that entire unit.

§ 2A–516. Effect of Acceptance of Goods; Notice of Default; Burden of Establishing Default after Acceptance; Notice of Claim or Litigation to Person Answerable Over.

(1) A lessee must pay rent for any goods accepted in accordance with the lease contract, with due allowance for goods rightfully rejected or not delivered.

(2) A lessee's acceptance of goods precludes rejection of the goods accepted. In the case of a finance lease, if made with knowledge of a nonconformity, acceptance cannot be revoked because of it. In any other case, if made with knowledge of a nonconformity, acceptance cannot be revoked because of it unless the acceptance was on the reasonable assumption that the nonconformity would be seasonably

cured. Acceptance does not of itself impair any other remedy provided by this Article or the lease agreement for nonconformity.

(3) If a tender has been accepted:

(a) within a reasonable time after the lessee discovers or should have discovered any default, the lessee shall notify the lessor and the supplier, if any, or be barred from any remedy against the party notified;

(b) except in the case of a consumer lease, within a reasonable time after the lessee receives notice of litigation for infringement or the like (Section 2A–211) the lessee shall notify the lessor or be barred from any remedy over for liability established by the litigation; and

(c) the burden is on the lessee to establish any default.

(4) If a lessee is sued for breach of a warranty or other obligation for which a lessor or a supplier is answerable over the following apply:

(a) The lessee may give the lessor or the supplier, or both, written notice of the litigation. If the notice states that the person notified may come in and defend and that if the person notified does not do so that person will be bound in any action against that person by the lessee by any determination of fact common to the two litigations, then unless the person notified after seasonable receipt of the notice does come in and defend that person is so bound.

(b) The lessor or the supplier may demand in writing that the lessee turn over control of the litigation including settlement if the claim is one for infringement or the like (Section 2A–211) or else be barred from any remedy over. If the demand states that the lessor or the supplier agrees to bear all expense and to satisfy any adverse judgment, then unless the lessee after seasonable receipt of the demand does turn over control the lessee is so barred.

(5) Subsections (3) and (4) apply to any obligation of a lessee to hold the lessor or the supplier harmless against infringement or the like (Section 2A–211).

As amended in 1990.

§ 2A–517. Revocation of Acceptance of Goods.

(1) A lessee may revoke acceptance of a lot or commercial unit whose nonconformity substantially impairs its value to the lessee if the lessee has accepted it:

(a) except in the case of a finance lease, on the reasonable assumption that its nonconformity would be cured and it has not been seasonably cured; or

(b) without discovery of the nonconformity if the lessee's acceptance was reasonably induced either by the lessor's assurances or, except in the case of a finance lease, by the difficulty of discovery before acceptance.

(2) Except in the case of a finance lease that is not a consumer lease, a lessee may revoke acceptance of a lot or commercial unit if the lessor defaults under the lease contract and the default substantially impairs the value of that lot or commercial unit to the lessee.

(3) If the lease agreement so provides, the lessee may revoke acceptance of a lot or commercial unit because of other defaults by the lessor.

(4) Revocation of acceptance must occur within a reasonable time after the lessee discovers or should have discovered the ground for it and before any substantial change in condition of the goods which is not caused by the nonconformity. Revocation is not effective until the lessee notifies the lessor.

(5) A lessee who so revokes has the same rights and duties with

regard to the goods involved as if the lessee had rejected them. As amended in 1990.

§ 2A–518. Cover; Substitute Goods.

(1) After a default by a lessor under the lease contract of the type described in Section 2A–508(1), or, if agreed, after other default by the lessor, the lessee may cover by making any purchase or lease of or contract to purchase or lease goods in substitution for those due from the lessor.

(2) Except as otherwise provided with respect to damages liquidated in the lease agreement (Section 2A–504) or otherwise determined pursuant to agreement of the parties (Sections 1–102(3) and 2A–503), if a lessee's cover is by lease agreement substantially similar to the original lease agreement and the new lease agreement is made in good faith and in a commercially reasonable manner, the lessee may recover from the lessor as damages (i) the present value, as of the date of the commencement of the term of the new lease agreement, of the rent under the new lease agreement applicable to that period of the new lease term which is comparable to the then remaining term of the original lease agreement minus the present value as of the same date of the total rent for the then remaining lease term of the original lease agreement, and (ii) any incidental or consequential damages, less expenses saved in consequence of the lessor's default.

(3) If a lessee's cover is by lease agreement that for any reason does not qualify for treatment under subsection (2), or is by purchase or otherwise, the lessee may recover from the lessor as if the lessee had elected not to cover and Section 2A–519 governs. As amended in 1990.

§ 2A–519. Lessee's Damages for Non-Delivery, Repudiation, Default, and Breach of Warranty in Regard to Accepted Goods.

(1) Except as otherwise provided with respect to damages liquidated in the lease agreement (Section 2A–504) or otherwise determined pursuant to agreement of the parties (Sections 1–102(3) and 2A–503), if a lessee elects not to cover or a lessee elects to cover and the cover is by lease agreement that for any reason does not qualify for treatment under Section 2A–518(2), or is by purchase or otherwise, the measure of damages for non-delivery or repudiation by the lessor or for rejection or revocation of acceptance by the lessee is the present value, as of the date of the default, of the then market rent minus the present value as of the same date of the original rent, computed for the remaining lease term of the original lease agreement, together with incidental and consequential damages, less expenses saved in consequence of the lessor's default.

(2) Market rent is to be determined as of the place for tender or, in cases of rejection after arrival or revocation of acceptance, as of the place of arrival.

(3) Except as otherwise agreed, if the lessee has accepted goods and given notification (Section 2A–516(3)), the measure of damages for non-conforming tender or delivery or other default by a lessor is the loss resulting in the ordinary course of events from the lessor's default as determined in any manner that is reasonable together with incidental and consequential damages, less expenses saved in consequence of the lessor's default.

(4) Except as otherwise agreed, the measure of damages for breach of warranty is the present value at the time and place of acceptance of the difference between the value of the use of the goods accepted and the value if they had been as warranted for the lease term, unless special circumstances show proximate damages of a different amount,

together with incidental and consequential damages, less expenses saved in consequence of the lessor's default or breach of warranty. As amended in 1990.

§ 2A–520. Lessee's Incidental and Consequential Damages.

(1) Incidental damages resulting from a lessor's default include expenses reasonably incurred in inspection, receipt, transportation, and care and custody of goods rightfully rejected or goods the acceptance of which is justifiably revoked, any commercially reasonable charges, expenses or commissions in connection with effecting cover, and any other reasonable expense incident to the default.

(2) Consequential damages resulting from a lessor's default include:

(a) any loss resulting from general or particular requirements and needs of which the lessor at the time of contracting had reason to know and which could not reasonably be prevented by cover or otherwise; and

(b) injury to person or property proximately resulting from any breach of warranty.

§ 2A–521. Lessee's Right to Specific Performance or Replevin.

(1) Specific performance may be decreed if the goods are unique or in other proper circumstances.

(2) A decree for specific performance may include any terms and conditions as to payment of the rent, damages, or other relief that the court deems just.

(3) A lessee has a right of replevin, detinue, sequestration, claim and delivery, or the like for goods identified to the lease contract if after reasonable effort the lessee is unable to effect cover for those goods or the circumstances reasonably indicate that the effort will be unavailing.

§ 2A–522. Lessee's Right to Goods on Lessor's Insolvency.

(1) Subject to subsection (2) and even though the goods have not been shipped, a lessee who has paid a part or all of the rent and security for goods identified to a lease contract (Section 2A–217) on making and keeping good a tender of any unpaid portion of the rent and security due under the lease contract may recover the goods identified from the lessor if the lessor becomes insolvent within 10 days after receipt of the first installment of rent and security.

(2) A lessee acquires the right to recover goods identified to a lease contract only if they conform to the lease contract.

C. Default by Lessee

§ 2A–523. Lessor's Remedies.

(1) If a lessee wrongfully rejects or revokes acceptance of goods or fails to make a payment when due or repudiates with respect to a part or the whole, then, with respect to any goods involved, and with respect to all of the goods if under an installment lease contract the value of the whole lease contract is substantially impaired (Section 2A–510), the lessee is in default under the lease contract and the lessor may:

(a) cancel the lease contract (Section 2A–505(1));

(b) proceed respecting goods not identified to the lease contract (Section 2A–524);

(c) withhold delivery of the goods and take possession of goods previously delivered (Section 2A–525);

(d) stop delivery of the goods by any bailee (Section 2A–526);

(e) dispose of the goods and recover damages (Section 2A–527), or retain the goods and recover damages (Section 2A–528), or in a proper case recover rent (Section 2A–529)

(f) exercise any other rights or pursue any other remedies provided in the lease contract.

(2) If a lessor does not fully exercise a right or obtain a remedy to which the lessor is entitled under subsection (1), the lessor may recover the loss resulting in the ordinary course of events from the lessee's default as determined in any reasonable manner, together with incidental damages, less expenses saved in consequence of the lessee's default.

(3) If a lessee is otherwise in default under a lease contract, the lessor may exercise the rights and pursue the remedies provided in the lease contract, which may include a right to cancel the lease. In addition, unless otherwise provided in the lease contract:

(a) if the default substantially impairs the value of the lease contract to the lessor, the lessor may exercise the rights and pursue the remedies provided in subsections (1) or (2); or

(b) if the default does not substantially impair the value of the lease contract to the lessor, the lessor may recover as provided in subsection (2).

As amended in 1990.

§ 2A–524. Lessor's Right to Identify Goods to Lease Contract.

(1) After default by the lessee under the lease contract of the type described in Section 2A–523(1) or 2A–523(3)(a) or, if agreed, after other default by the lessee, the lessor may:

(a) identify to the lease contract conforming goods not already identified if at the time the lessor learned of the default they were in the lessor's or the supplier's possession or control; and

(b) dispose of goods (Section 2A–527(1)) that demonstrably have been intended for the particular lease contract even though those goods are unfinished.

(2) If the goods are unfinished, in the exercise of reasonable commercial judgment for the purposes of avoiding loss and of effective realization, an aggrieved lessor or the supplier may either complete manufacture and wholly identify the goods to the lease contract or cease manufacture and lease, sell, or otherwise dispose of the goods for scrap or salvage value or proceed in any other reasonable manner.

As amended in 1990.

§ 2A–525. Lessor's Right to Possession of Goods.

(1) If a lessor discovers the lessee to be insolvent, the lessor may refuse to deliver the goods.

(2) After a default by the lessee under the lease contract of the type described in Section 2A–523(1) or 2A–523(3)(a) or, if agreed, after other default by the lessee, the lessor has the right to take possession of the goods. If the lease contract so provides, the lessor may require the lessee to assemble the goods and make them available to the lessor at a place to be designated by the lessor which is reasonably convenient to both parties. Without removal, the lessor may render unusable any goods employed in trade or business, and may dispose of goods on the lessee's premises (Section 2A–527).

(3) The lessor may proceed under subsection (2) without judicial process if that can be done without breach of the peace or the lessor may proceed by action.

As amended in 1990.

§ 2A–526. Lessor's Stoppage of Delivery in Transit or Otherwise.

(1) A lessor may stop delivery of goods in the possession of a carrier or other bailee if the lessor discovers the lessee to be insolvent and may stop delivery of carload, truckload, planeload, or larger shipments of express or freight if the lessee repudiates or fails to make a payment due before delivery, whether for rent, security or otherwise under the lease contract, or for any other reason the lessor has a right to withhold or take possession of the goods.

(2) In pursuing its remedies under subsection (1), the lessor may stop delivery until

(a) receipt of the goods by the lessee;

(b) acknowledgment to the lessee by any bailee of the goods, except a carrier, that the bailee holds the goods for the lessee; or

(c) such an acknowledgment to the lessee by a carrier via reshipment or as warehouseman.

(3) (a) To stop delivery, a lessor shall so notify as to enable the bailee by reasonable diligence to prevent delivery of the goods.

(b) After notification, the bailee shall hold and deliver the goods according to the directions of the lessor, but the lessor is liable to the bailee for any ensuing charges or damages.

(c) A carrier who has issued a nonnegotiable bill of lading is not obliged to obey a notification to stop received from a person other than the consignor.

§ 2A–527. Lessor's Rights to Dispose of Goods.

(1) After a default by a lessee under the lease contract of the type described in Section 2A–523(1) or 2A–523(3)(a) or after the lessor refuses to deliver or takes possession of goods (Section 2A–525 or 2A–526), or, if agreed, after other default by a lessee, the lessor may dispose of the goods concerned or the undelivered balance thereof by lease, sale, or otherwise.

(2) Except as otherwise provided with respect to damages liquidated in the lease agreement (Section 2A–504) or otherwise determined pursuant to agreement of the parties (Sections 1–102(3) and 2A–503), if the disposition is by lease agreement substantially similar to the original lease agreement and the new lease agreement is made in good faith and in a commercially reasonable manner, the lessor may recover from the lessee as damages (i) accrued and unpaid rent as of the date of the commencement of the term of the new lease agreement, (ii) the present value, as of the same date, of the total rent for the then remaining lease term of the original lease agreement minus the present value, as of the same date, of the rent under the new lease agreement applicable to that period of the new lease term which is comparable to the then remaining term of the original lease agreement, and (iii) any incidental damages allowed under Section 2A–530, less expenses saved in consequence of the lessee's default.

(3) If the lessor's disposition is by lease agreement that for any reason does not qualify for treatment under subsection (2), or is by sale or otherwise, the lessor may recover from the lessee as if the lessor had elected not to dispose of the goods and Section 2A–528 governs.

(4) A subsequent buyer or lessee who buys or leases from the lessor in good faith for value as a result of a disposition under this section takes the goods free of the original lease contract and any rights of the original lessee even though the lessor fails to comply with one or more of the requirements of this Article.

(5) The lessor is not accountable to the lessee for any profit made on any disposition. A lessee who has rightfully rejected or justifiably revoked acceptance shall account to the lessor for any excess over the amount of the lessee's security interest (Section 2A–508(5)).

As amended in 1990.

§ 2A–528. Lessor's Damages for Non-acceptance, Failure to Pay, Repudiation, or Other Default.

(1) Except as otherwise provided with respect to damages liquidated in the lease agreement (Section 2A–504) or otherwise determined pursuant to agreement of the parties (Section 1–102(3) and 2A–503), if a lessor elects to retain the goods or a lessor elects to dispose of the goods and the disposition is by lease agreement that for any reason does not qualify for treatment under Section 2A–527(2), or is by sale or otherwise, the lessor may recover from the lessee as damages for a default of the type described in Section 2A–523(1) or 2A–523(3)(a), or if agreed, for other default of the lessee, (i) accrued and unpaid rent as of the date of the default if the lessee has never taken possession of the goods, or, if the lessee has taken possession of the goods, as of the date the lessor repossesses the goods or an earlier date on which the lessee makes a tender of the goods to the lessor, (ii) the present value as of the date determined under clause (i) of the total rent for the then remaining lease term of the original lease agreement minus the present value as of the same date of the market rent as the place where the goods are located computed for the same lease term, and (iii) any incidental damages allowed under Section 2A–530, less expenses saved in consequence of the lessee's default.

(2) If the measure of damages provided in subsection (1) is inadequate to put a lessor in as good a position as performance would have, the measure of damages is the present value of the profit, including reasonable overhead, the lessor would have made from full performance by the lessee, together with any incidental damages allowed under Section 2A–530, due allowance for costs reasonably incurred and due credit for payments or proceeds of disposition.

As amended in 1990.

§ 2A–529. Lessor's Action for the Rent.

(1) After default by the lessee under the lease contract of the type described in Section 2A–523(1) or 2A–523(3)(a) or, if agreed, after other default by the lessee, if the lessor complies with subsection (2), the lessor may recover from the lessee as damages:

   (a) for goods accepted by the lessee and not repossessed by or tendered to the lessor, and for conforming goods lost or damaged within a commercially reasonable time after risk of loss passes to the lessee (Section 2A–219), (i) accrued and unpaid rent as of the date of entry of judgment in favor of the lessor (ii) the present value as of the same date of the rent for the then remaining lease term of the lease agreement, and (iii) any incidental damages allowed under Section 2A–530, less expenses saved in consequence of the lessee's default; and

   (b) for goods identified to the lease contract if the lessor is unable after reasonable effort to dispose of them at a reasonable price or the circumstances reasonably indicate that effort will be unavailing, (i) accrued and unpaid rent as of the date of entry of judgment in favor of the lessor, (ii) the present value as of the same date of the rent for the then remaining lease term of the lease agreement, and (iii) any incidental damages allowed under Section 2A–530, less expenses saved in consequence of the lessee's default.

(2) Except as provided in subsection (3), the lessor shall hold for the lessee for the remaining lease term of the lease agreement any goods that have been identified to the lease contract and are in the lessor's control.

(3) The lessor may dispose of the goods at any time before collection of the judgment for damages obtained pursuant to subsection (1). If the disposition is before the end of the remaining lease term of the lease

agreement, the lessor's recovery against the lessee for damages is governed by Section 2A–527 or Section 2A–528, and the lessor will cause an appropriate credit to be provided against a judgment for damages to the extent that the amount of the judgment exceeds the recovery available pursuant to Section 2A–527 or 2A–528.

(4) Payment of the judgment for damages obtained pursuant to subsection (1) entitles the lessee to the use and possession of the goods not then disposed of for the remaining lease term of and in accordance with the lease agreement.

(5) After default by the lessee under the lease contract of the type described in Section 2A–523(1) or Section 2A–523(3)(a) or, if agreed, after other default by the lessee, a lessor who is held not entitled to rent under this section must nevertheless be awarded damages for non-acceptance under Sections 2A–527 and 2A–528.

As amended in 1990.

§ 2A–530. Lessor's Incidental Damages.

Incidental damages to an aggrieved lessor include any commercially reasonable charges, expenses, or commissions incurred in stopping delivery, in the transportation, care and custody of goods after the lessee's default, in connection with return or disposition of the goods, or otherwise resulting from the default.

§ 2A–531. Standing to Sue Third Parties for Injury to Goods.

(1) If a third party so deals with goods that have been identified to a lease contract as to cause actionable injury to a party to the lease contract (a) the lessor has a right of action against the third party, and (b) the lessee also has a right of action against the third party if the lessee:

   (i) has a security interest in the goods;

   (ii) has an insurable interest in the goods; or

   (iii) bears the risk of loss under the lease contract or has since the injury assumed that risk as against the lessor and the goods have been converted or destroyed.

(2) If at the time of the injury the party plaintiff did not bear the risk of loss as against the other party to the lease contract and there is no arrangement between them for disposition of the recovery, his [or her] suit or settlement, subject to his [or her] own interest, is as a fiduciary for the other party to the lease contract.

(3) Either party with the consent of the other may sue for the benefit of whom it may concern.

§ 2A–532. Lessor's Rights to Residual Interest.

In addition to any other recovery permitted by this Article or other law, the lessor may recover from the lessee an amount that will fully compensate the lessor for any loss of or damage to the lessor's residual interest in the goods caused by the default of the lessee.

As added in 1990.

Revised Article 3
NEGOTIABLE INSTRUMENTS

Part 1 General Provisions and Definitions

§ 3–101. Short Title.

This Article may be cited as Uniform Commercial Code–Negotiable Instruments.

§ 3–102. Subject Matter.

(a) This Article applies to negotiable instruments. It does not apply to money, to payment orders governed by Article 4A, or to securities governed by Article 8.

(b) If there is conflict between this Article and Article 4 or 9, Articles 4 and 9 govern.

(c) Regulations of the Board of Governors of the Federal Reserve System and operating circulars of the Federal Reserve Banks supersede any inconsistent provision of this Article to the extent of the inconsistency.

§ 3–103. Definitions.

(a) In this Article:

(1) "Acceptor" means a drawee who has accepted a draft.

(2) "Drawee" means a person ordered in a draft to make payment.

(3) "Drawer" means a person who signs or is identified in a draft as a person ordering payment.

(4) "Good faith" means honesty in fact and the observance of reasonable commercial standards of fair dealing.

(5) "Maker" means a person who signs or is identified in a note as a person undertaking to pay.

(6) "Order" means a written instruction to pay money signed by the person giving the instruction. The instruction may be addressed to any person, including the person giving the instruction, or to one or more persons jointly or in the alternative but not in succession. An authorization to pay is not an order unless the person authorized to pay is also instructed to pay.

(7) "Ordinary care" in the case of a person engaged in business means observance of reasonable commercial standards, prevailing in the area in which the person is located, with respect to the business in which the person is engaged. In the case of a bank that takes an instrument for processing for collection or payment by automated means, reasonable commercial standards do not require the bank to examine the instrument if the failure to examine does not violate the bank's prescribed procedures and the bank's procedures do not vary unreasonably from general banking usage not disapproved by this Article or Article 4.

(8) "Party" means a party to an instrument.

(9) "Promise" means a written undertaking to pay money signed by the person undertaking to pay. An acknowledgment of an obligation by the obligor is not a promise unless the obligor also undertakes to pay the obligation.

(10) "Prove" with respect to a fact means to meet the burden of establishing the fact (Section 1–201(8)).

(11) "Remitter" means a person who purchases an instrument from its issuer if the instrument is payable to an identified person other than the purchaser.

(b) [Other definitions' section references deleted.]

(c) [Other definitions' section references deleted.]

(d) In addition, Article 1 contains general definitions and principles of construction and interpretation applicable throughout this Article.

§ 3–104. Negotiable Instrument.

(a) Except as provided in subsections (c) and (d), "negotiable instrument" means an unconditional promise or order to pay a fixed amount of money, with or without interest or other charges described in the promise or order, if it:

(1) is payable to bearer or to order at the time it is issued or first comes into possession of a holder;

(2) is payable on demand or at a definite time; and

(3) does not state any other undertaking or instruction by the person promising or ordering payment to do any act in addition to the payment of money, but the promise or order may contain (i) an undertaking or power to give, maintain, or protect collateral to secure payment, (ii) an authorization or power to the holder to confess judgment or realize on or dispose of collateral, or (iii) a waiver of the benefit of any law intended for the advantage or protection of an obligor.

(b) "Instrument" means a negotiable instrument.

(c) An order that meets all of the requirements of subsection (a), except paragraph (1), and otherwise falls within the definition of "check" in subsection (f) is a negotiable instrument and a check.

(d) A promise or order other than a check is not an instrument if, at the time it is issued or first comes into possession of a holder, it contains a conspicuous statement, however expressed, to the effect that the promise or order is not negotiable or is not an instrument governed by this Article.

(e) An instrument is a "note" if it is a promise and is a "draft" if it is an order. If an instrument falls within the definition of both "note" and "draft," a person entitled to enforce the instrument may treat it as either.

(f) "Check" means (i) a draft, other than a documentary draft, payable on demand and drawn on a bank or (ii) a cashier's check or teller's check. An instrument may be a check even though it is described on its face by another term, such as "money order."

(g) "Cashier's check" means a draft with respect to which the drawer and drawee are the same bank or branches of the same bank.

(h) "Teller's check" means a draft drawn by a bank (i) on another bank, or (ii) payable at or through a bank.

(i) "Traveler's check" means an instrument that (i) is payable on demand, (ii) is drawn on or payable at or through a bank, (iii) is designated by the term "traveler's check" or by a substantially similar term, and (iv) requires, as a condition to payment, a countersignature by a person whose specimen signature appears on the instrument.

(j) "Certificate of deposit" means an instrument containing an acknowledgment by a bank that a sum of money has been received by the bank and a promise by the bank to repay the sum of money. A certificate of deposit is a note of the bank.

§ 3–105. Issue of Instrument.

(a) "Issue" means the first delivery of an instrument by the maker or drawer, whether to a holder or nonholder, for the purpose of giving rights on the instrument to any person.

(b) An unissued instrument, or an unissued incomplete instrument that is completed, is binding on the maker or drawer, but nonissuance is a defense. An instrument that is conditionally issued or is issued for a special purpose is binding on the maker or drawer, but failure of the condition or special purpose to be fulfilled is a defense.

(c) "Issuer" applies to issued and unissued instruments and means a maker or drawer of an instrument.

§ 3–106. Unconditional Promise or Order.

(a) Except as provided in this section, for the purposes of Section 3–104(a), a promise or order is unconditional unless it states (i) an express condition to payment, (ii) that the promise or order is subject to or governed by another writing, or (iii) that rights or obligations with respect to the promise or order are stated in another writing. A reference to another writing does not of itself make the promise or order conditional.

(b) A promise or order is not made conditional (i) by a reference to another writing for a statement of rights with respect to collateral, prepayment, or acceleration, or (ii) because payment is limited to resort to a particular fund or source.

(c) If a promise or order requires, as a condition to payment, a countersignature by a person whose specimen signature appears on the promise or order, the condition does not make the promise or order conditional for the purposes of Section 3–104(a). If the person whose specimen signature appears on an instrument fails to countersign the instrument, the failure to countersign is a defense to the obligation of the issuer, but the failure does not prevent a transferee of the instrument from becoming a holder of the instrument.

(d) If a promise or order at the time it is issued or first comes into possession of a holder contains a statement, required by applicable statutory or administrative law, to the effect that the rights of a holder or transferee are subject to claims or defenses that the issuer could assert against the original payee, the promise or order is not thereby made conditional for the purposes of Section 3–104(a); but if the promise or order is an instrument, there cannot be a holder in due course of the instrument.

§ 3–107. Instrument Payable in Foreign Money.

Unless the instrument otherwise provides, an instrument that states the amount payable in foreign money may be paid in the foreign money or in an equivalent amount in dollars calculated by using the current bank-offered spot rate at the place of payment for the purchase of dollars on the day on which the instrument is paid.

§ 3–108. Payable on Demand or at Definite Time.

(a) A promise or order is "payable on demand" if it (i) states that it is payable on demand or at sight, or otherwise indicates that it is payable at the will of the holder, or (ii) does not state any time of payment.

(b) A promise or order is "payable at a definite time" if it is payable on elapse of a definite period of time after sight or acceptance or at a fixed date or dates or at a time or times readily ascertainable at the time the promise or order is issued, subject to rights of (i) prepayment, (ii) acceleration, (iii) extension at the option of the holder, or (iv) extension to a further definite time at the option of the maker or acceptor or automatically upon or after a specified act or event.

(c) If an instrument, payable at a fixed date, is also payable upon demand made before the fixed date, the instrument is payable on demand until the fixed date and, if demand for payment is not made before that date, becomes payable at a definite time on the fixed date.

§ 3–109. Payable to Bearer or to Order.

(a) A promise or order is payable to bearer if it:

(1) states that it is payable to bearer or to the order of bearer or otherwise indicates that the person in possession of the promise or order is entitled to payment;

(2) does not state a payee; or

(3) states that it is payable to or to the order of cash or otherwise indicates that it is not payable to an identified person.

(b) A promise or order that is not payable to bearer is payable to order if it is payable (i) to the order of an identified person or (ii) to

an identified person or order. A promise or order that is payable to order is payable to the identified person.

(c) An instrument payable to bearer may become payable to an identified person if it is specially indorsed pursuant to Section 3–205(a). An instrument payable to an identified person may become payable to bearer if it is indorsed in blank pursuant to Section 3–205(b).

§ 3–110. Identification of Person to Whom Instrument Is Payable.

(a) The person to whom an instrument is initially payable is determined by the intent of the person, whether or not authorized, signing as, or in the name or behalf of, the issuer of the instrument. The instrument is payable to the person intended by the signer even if that person is identified in the instrument by a name or other identification that is not that of the intended person. If more than one person signs in the name or behalf of the issuer of an instrument and all the signers do not intend the same person as payee, the instrument is payable to any person intended by one or more of the signers.

(b) If the signature of the issuer of an instrument is made by automated means, such as a check-writing machine, the payee of the instrument is determined by the intent of the person who supplied the name or identification of the payee, whether or not authorized to do so.

(c) A person to whom an instrument is payable may be identified in any way, including by name, identifying number, office, or account number. For the purpose of determining the holder of an instrument, the following rules apply:

(1) If an instrument is payable to an account and the account is identified only by number, the instrument is payable to the person to whom the account is payable. If an instrument is payable to an account identified by number and by the name of a person, the instrument is payable to the named person, whether or not that person is the owner of the account identified by number.

(2) If an instrument is payable to:

(i) a trust, an estate, or a person described as trustee or representative of a trust or estate, the instrument is payable to the trustee, the representative, or a successor of either, whether or not the beneficiary or estate is also named;

(ii) a person described as agent or similar representative of a named or identified person, the instrument is payable to the represented person, the representative, or a successor of the representative;

(iii) a fund or organization that is not a legal entity, the instrument is payable to a representative of the members of the fund or organization; or

(iv) an office or to a person described as holding an office, the instrument is payable to the named person, the incumbent of the office, or a successor to the incumbent.

(d) If an instrument is payable to two or more persons alternatively, it is payable to any of them and may be negotiated, discharged, or enforced by any or all of them in possession of the instrument. If an instrument is payable to two or more persons not alternatively, it is payable to all of them and may be negotiated, discharged, or enforced only by all of them. If an instrument payable to two or more persons is ambiguous as to whether it is payable to the persons alternatively, the instrument is payable to the persons alternatively.

§ 3–111. Place of Payment.

Except as otherwise provided for items in Article 4, an instrument is payable at the place of payment stated in the instrument. If no place of payment is stated, an instrument is payable at the address of the drawee or maker stated in the instrument. If no address is stated, the place of payment is the place of business of the drawee or maker. If a drawee or maker has more than one place of business, the place of payment is any place of business of the drawee or maker chosen by the person entitled to enforce the instrument. If the drawee or maker has no place of business, the place of payment is the residence of the drawee or maker.

§ 3–112. Interest.

(a) Unless otherwise provided in the instrument, (i) an instrument is not payable with interest, and (ii) interest on an interest-bearing instrument is payable from the date of the instrument.

(b) Interest may be stated in an instrument as a fixed or variable amount of money or it may be expressed as a fixed or variable rate or rates. The amount or rate of interest may be stated or described in the instrument in any manner and may require reference to information not contained in the instrument. If an instrument provides for interest, but the amount of interest payable cannot be ascertained from the description, interest is payable at the judgment rate in effect at the place of payment of the instrument and at the time interest first accrues.

§ 3–113. Date of Instrument.

(a) An instrument may be antedated or postdated. The date stated determines the time of payment if the instrument is payable at a fixed period after date. Except as provided in Section 4–401(c), an instrument payable on demand is not payable before the date of the instrument.

(b) If an instrument is undated, its date is the date of its issue or, in the case of an unissued instrument, the date it first comes into possession of a holder.

§ 3–114. Contradictory Terms of Instrument.

If an instrument contains contradictory terms, typewritten terms prevail over printed terms, handwritten terms prevail over both, and words prevail over numbers.

§ 3–115. Incomplete Instrument.

(a) "Incomplete instrument" means a signed writing, whether or not issued by the signer, the contents of which show at the time of signing that it is incomplete but that the signer intended it to be completed by the addition of words or numbers.

(b) Subject to subsection (c), if an incomplete instrument is an instrument under Section 3–104, it may be enforced according to its terms if it is not completed, or according to its terms as augmented by completion. If an incomplete instrument is not an instrument under Section 3–104, but, after completion, the requirements of Section 3–104 are met, the instrument may be enforced according to its terms as augmented by completion.

(c) If words or numbers are added to an incomplete instrument without authority of the signer, there is an alteration of the incomplete instrument under Section 3–407.

(d) The burden of establishing that words or numbers were added to an incomplete instrument without authority of the signer is on the person asserting the lack of authority.

§ 3–116. Joint and Several Liability; Contribution.

(a) Except as otherwise provided in the instrument, two or more persons who have the same liability on an instrument as makers, drawers, acceptors, indorsers who indorse as joint payees, or anomalous indorsers are jointly and severally liable in the capacity in which they sign.

(b) Except as provided in Section 3–419(e) or by agreement of the affected parties, a party having joint and several liability who pays the instrument is entitled to receive from any party having the same joint and several liability contribution in accordance with applicable law.

(c) Discharge of one party having joint and several liability by a person entitled to enforce the instrument does not affect the right under subsection (b) of a party having the same joint and several liability to receive contribution from the party discharged.

§ 3–117. Other Agreements Affecting Instrument.

Subject to applicable law regarding exclusion of proof of contemporaneous or previous agreements, the obligation of a party to an instrument to pay the instrument may be modified, supplemented, or nullified by a separate agreement of the obligor and a person entitled to enforce the instrument, if the instrument is issued or the obligation is incurred in reliance on the agreement or as part of the same transaction giving rise to the agreement. To the extent an obligation is modified, supplemented, or nullified by an agreement under this section, the agreement is a defense to the obligation.

§ 3–118. Statute of Limitations.

(a) Except as provided in subsection (e), an action to enforce the obligation of a party to pay a note payable at a definite time must be commenced within six years after the due date or dates stated in the note or, if a due date is accelerated, within six years after the accelerated due date.

(b) Except as provided in subsection (d) or (e), if demand for payment is made to the maker of a note payable on demand, an action to enforce the obligation of a party to pay the note must be commenced within six years after the demand. If no demand for payment is made to the maker, an action to enforce the note is barred if neither principal nor interest on the note has been paid for a continuous period of 10 years.

(c) Except as provided in subsection (d), an action to enforce the obligation of a party to an unaccepted draft to pay the draft must be commenced within three years after dishonor of the draft or 10 years after the date of the draft, whichever period expires first.

(d) An action to enforce the obligation of the acceptor of a certified check or the issuer of a teller's check, cashier's check, or traveler's check must be commenced within three years after demand for payment is made to the acceptor or issuer, as the case may be.

(e) An action to enforce the obligation of a party to a certificate of deposit to pay the instrument must be commenced within six years after demand for payment is made to the maker, but if the instrument states a due date and the maker is not required to pay before that date, the six-year period begins when a demand for payment is in effect and the due date has passed.

(f) An action to enforce the obligation of a party to pay an accepted draft, other than a certified check, must be commenced (i) within six years after the due date or dates stated in the draft or acceptance if the obligation of the acceptor is payable at a definite time, or (ii) within six years after the date of the acceptance if the obligation of the acceptor is payable on demand.

(g) Unless governed by other law regarding claims for indemnity or contribution, an action (i) for conversion of an instrument, for money had and received, or like action based on conversion, (ii) for breach of warranty, or (iii) to enforce an obligation, duty, or right arising under this Article and not governed by this section must be commenced within three years after the [cause of action] accrues.

§ 3–119. Notice of Right to Defend Action.

In an action for breach of an obligation for which a third person is answerable over pursuant to this Article or Article 4, the defendant may give the third person written notice of the litigation, and the person notified may then give similar notice to any other person who is answerable over. If the notice states (i) that the person notified may come in and defend and (ii) that failure to do so will bind the person notified in an action later brought by the person giving the notice as to any determination of fact common to the two litigations, the person notified is so bound unless after seasonable receipt of the notice the person notified does come in and defend.

Part 2 Negotiation, Transfer, and Indorsement

§ 3–201. Negotiation.

(a) "Negotiation" means a transfer of possession, whether voluntary or involuntary, of an instrument by a person other than the issuer to a person who thereby becomes its holder.

(b) Except for negotiation by a remitter, if an instrument is payable to an identified person, negotiation requires transfer of possession of the instrument and its indorsement by the holder. If an instrument is payable to bearer, it may be negotiated by transfer of possession alone.

§ 3–202. Negotiation Subject to Rescission.

(a) Negotiation is effective even if obtained (i) from an infant, a corporation exceeding its powers, or a person without capacity, (ii) by fraud, duress, or mistake, or (iii) in breach of duty or as part of an illegal transaction.

(b) To the extent permitted by other law, negotiation may be rescinded or may be subject to other remedies, but those remedies may not be asserted against a subsequent holder in due course or a person paying the instrument in good faith and without knowledge of facts that are a basis for rescission or other remedy.

§ 3–203. Transfer of Instrument; Rights Acquired by Transfer.

(a) An instrument is transferred when it is delivered by a person other than its issuer for the purpose of giving to the person receiving delivery the right to enforce the instrument.

(b) Transfer of an instrument, whether or not the transfer is a negotiation, vests in the transferee any right of the transferor to enforce the instrument, including any right as a holder in due course, but the transferee cannot acquire rights of a holder in due course by a transfer, directly or indirectly, from a holder in due course if the transferee engaged in fraud or illegality affecting the instrument.

(c) Unless otherwise agreed, if an instrument is transferred for value and the transferee does not become a holder because of lack of indorsement by the transferor, the transferee has a specifically enforceable right to the unqualified indorsement of the transferor, but negotiation of the instrument does not occur until the indorsement is made.

(d) If a transferor purports to transfer less than the entire instrument, negotiation of the instrument does not occur. The transferee obtains no rights under this Article and has only the rights of a partial assignee.

§ 3–204. Indorsement.

(a) "Indorsement" means a signature, other than that of a signer as maker, drawer, or acceptor, that alone or accompanied by other words is made on an instrument for the purpose of (i) negotiating the instrument, (ii) restricting payment of the instrument, or (iii) incurring indorser's liability on the instrument, but regardless of the intent of the signer, a signature and its accompanying words is an indorsement unless the accompanying words, terms of the instrument, place of the signature, or other circumstances unambiguously indicate that the signature was made for a purpose other than indorsement. For the purpose of determining whether a signature is made on an instrument, a paper affixed to the instrument is a part of the instrument.

(b) "Indorser" means a person who makes an indorsement.

(c) For the purpose of determining whether the transferee of an instrument is a holder, an indorsement that transfers a security interest in the instrument is effective as an unqualified indorsement of the instrument.

(d) If an instrument is payable to a holder under a name that is not the name of the holder, indorsement may be made by the holder in the name stated in the instrument or in the holder's name or both, but signature in both names may be required by a person paying or taking the instrument for value or collection.

§ 3–205. Special Indorsement; Blank Indorsement; Anomalous Indorsement.

(a) If an indorsement is made by the holder of an instrument, whether payable to an identified person or payable to bearer, and the indorsement identifies a person to whom it makes the instrument payable, it is a "special indorsement." When specially indorsed, an instrument becomes payable to the identified person and may be negotiated only by the indorsement of that person. The principles stated in Section 3–110 apply to special indorsements.

(b) If an indorsement is made by the holder of an instrument and it is not a special indorsement, it is a "blank indorsement." When indorsed in blank, an instrument becomes payable to bearer and may be negotiated by transfer of possession alone until specially indorsed.

(c) The holder may convert a blank indorsement that consists only of a signature into a special indorsement by writing, above the signature of the indorser, words identifying the person to whom the instrument is made payable.

(d) "Anomalous indorsement" means an indorsement made by a person who is not the holder of the instrument. An anomalous indorsement does not affect the manner in which the instrument may be negotiated.

§ 3–206. Restrictive Indorsement.

(a) An indorsement limiting payment to a particular person or otherwise prohibiting further transfer or negotiation of the instrument is not effective to prevent further transfer or negotiation of the instrument.

(b) An indorsement stating a condition to the right of the indorsee to receive payment does not affect the right of the indorsee to enforce the instrument. A person paying the instrument or taking it for value or collection may disregard the condition, and the rights and liabilities of that person are not affected by whether the condition has been fulfilled.

(c) If an instrument bears an indorsement (i) described in Section 4–201(b), or (ii) in blank or to a particular bank using the words "for deposit," "for collection," or other words indicating a purpose of having the instrument collected by a bank for the indorser or for a particular account, the following rules apply:

(1) A person, other than a bank, who purchases the instrument when so indorsed converts the instrument unless the amount paid for the instrument is received by the indorser or applied consistently with the indorsement.

(2) A depositary bank that purchases the instrument or takes it for collection when so indorsed converts the instrument unless the amount paid by the bank with respect to the instrument is received by the indorser or applied consistently with the indorsement.

(3) A payor bank that is also the depositary bank or that takes the instrument for immediate payment over the counter from a person other than a collecting bank converts the instrument unless the proceeds of the instrument are received by the indorser or applied consistently with the indorsement.

(4) Except as otherwise provided in paragraph (3), a payor bank or intermediary bank may disregard the indorsement and is not liable if the proceeds of the instrument are not received by the indorser or applied consistently with the indorsement.

(d) Except for an indorsement covered by subsection (c), if an instrument bears an indorsement using words to the effect that payment is to be made to the indorsee as agent, trustee, or other fiduciary for the benefit of the indorser or another person, the following rules apply:

(1) Unless there is notice of breach of fiduciary duty as provided in Section 3–307, a person who purchases the instrument from the indorsee or takes the instrument from the indorsee for collection or payment may pay the proceeds of payment or the value given for the instrument to the indorsee without regard to whether the indorsee violates a fiduciary duty to the indorser.

(2) A subsequent transferee of the instrument or person who pays the instrument is neither given notice nor otherwise affected by the restriction in the indorsement unless the transferee or payor knows that the fiduciary dealt with the instrument or its proceeds in breach of fiduciary duty.

(e) The presence on an instrument of an indorsement to which this section applies does not prevent a purchaser of the instrument from becoming a holder in due course of the instrument unless the purchaser is a converter under subsection (c) or has notice or knowledge of breach of fiduciary duty as stated in subsection (d).

(f) In an action to enforce the obligation of a party to pay the instrument, the obligor has a defense if payment would violate an indorsement to which this section applies and the payment is not permitted by this section.

§ 3–207. Reacquisition.

Reacquisition of an instrument occurs if it is transferred to a former holder, by negotiation or otherwise. A former holder who reacquires the instrument may cancel indorsements made after the reacquirer first became a holder of the instrument. If the cancellation causes the instrument to be payable to the reacquirer or to bearer, the reacquirer may negotiate the instrument. An indorser whose indorsement is canceled is discharged, and the discharge is effective against any subsequent holder.

Part 3 Enforcement of Instruments

§ 3–301. Person Entitled to Enforce Instrument.

"Person entitled to enforce" an instrument means (i) the holder of the instrument, (ii) a nonholder in possession of the instrument who has the rights of a holder, or (iii) a person not in possession of the instrument who is entitled to enforce the instrument pursuant to Section 3–309 or 3–418(d). A person may be a person entitled to enforce the instrument even though the person is not the owner of the instrument or is in wrongful possession of the instrument.

§ 3–302. Holder in Due Course.

(a) Subject to subsection (c) and Section 3–106(d), "holder in due course" means the holder of an instrument if:

(1) the instrument when issued or negotiated to the holder does not bear such apparent evidence of forgery or alteration or is not otherwise so irregular or incomplete as to call into question its authenticity; and

(2) the holder took the instrument (i) for value, (ii) in good faith, (iii) without notice that the instrument is overdue or has been dishonored or that there is an uncured default with respect to payment of another instrument issued as part of the same series, (iv) without notice that the instrument contains an unauthorized signature or has been altered, (v) without notice of any claim to the instrument described in Section 3–306, and (vi) without notice that any party has a defense or claim in recoupment described in Section 3–305(a).

(b) Notice of discharge of a party, other than discharge in an insolvency proceeding, is not notice of a defense under subsection (a), but discharge is effective against a person who became a holder in due course with notice of the discharge. Public filing or recording of a document does not of itself constitute notice of a defense, claim in recoupment, or claim to the instrument.

(c) Except to the extent a transferor or predecessor in interest has rights as a holder in due course, a person does not acquire rights of a holder in due course of an instrument taken (i) by legal process or by purchase in an execution, bankruptcy, or creditor's sale or similar proceeding, (ii) by purchase as part of a bulk transaction not in ordinary course of business of the transferor, or (iii) as the successor in interest to an estate or other organization.

(d) If, under Section 3–303(a)(1), the promise of performance that is the consideration for an instrument has been partially performed, the holder may assert rights as a holder in due course of the instrument only to the fraction of the amount payable under the instrument equal to the value of the partial performance divided by the value of the promised performance.

(e) If (i) the person entitled to enforce an instrument has only a security interest in the instrument and (ii) the person obliged to pay the instrument has a defense, claim in recoupment, or claim to the instrument that may be asserted against the person who granted the security interest, the person entitled to enforce the instrument may assert rights as a holder in due course only to an amount payable under the instrument which, at the time of enforcement of the instrument, does not exceed the amount of the unpaid obligation secured.

(f) To be effective, notice must be received at a time and in a manner that gives a reasonable opportunity to act on it.

(g) This section is subject to any law limiting status as a holder in due course in particular classes of transactions.

§ 3–303. Value and Consideration.

(a) An instrument is issued or transferred for value if:

(1) the instrument is issued or transferred for a promise of performance, to the extent the promise has been performed;

(2) the transferee acquires a security interest or other lien in the instrument other than a lien obtained by judicial proceeding;

(3) the instrument is issued or transferred as payment of, or as security for, an antecedent claim against any person, whether or not the claim is due;

(4) the instrument is issued or transferred in exchange for a negotiable instrument; or

(5) the instrument is issued or transferred in exchange for the incurring of an irrevocable obligation to a third party by the person taking the instrument.

(b) "Consideration" means any consideration sufficient to support a simple contract. The drawer or maker of an instrument has a defense if the instrument is issued without consideration. If an instrument is issued for a promise of performance, the issuer has a defense to the extent performance of the promise is due and the promise has not been performed. If an instrument is issued for value as stated in subsection (a), the instrument is also issued for consideration.

§ 3–304. Overdue Instrument.

(a) An instrument payable on demand becomes overdue at the earliest of the following times:

(1) on the day after the day demand for payment is duly made;

(2) if the instrument is a check, 90 days after its date; or

(3) if the instrument is not a check, when the instrument has been outstanding for a period of time after its date which is unreasonably long under the circumstances of the particular case in light of the nature of the instrument and usage of the trade.

(b) With respect to an instrument payable at a definite time the following rules apply:

(1) If the principal is payable in installments and a due date has not been accelerated, the instrument becomes overdue upon default under the instrument for nonpayment of an installment, and the instrument remains overdue until the default is cured.

(2) If the principal is not payable in installments and the due date has not been accelerated, the instrument becomes overdue on the day after the due date.

(3) If a due date with respect to principal has been accelerated, the instrument becomes overdue on the day after the accelerated due date.

(c) Unless the due date of principal has been accelerated, an instrument does not become overdue if there is default in payment of interest but no default in payment of principal.

§ 3–305. Defenses and Claims in Recoupment.

(a) Except as stated in subsection (b), the right to enforce the obligation of a party to pay an instrument is subject to the following:

(1) a defense of the obligor based on (i) infancy of the obligor to the extent it is a defense to a simple contract, (ii) duress, lack of legal capacity, or illegality of the transaction which, under other law, nullifies the obligation of the obligor, (iii) fraud that induced the obligor to sign the instrument with neither knowledge nor reasonable opportunity to learn of its character or its essential terms, or (iv) discharge of the obligor in insolvency proceedings;

(2) a defense of the obligor stated in another section of this Article or a defense of the obligor that would be available if the person entitled to enforce the instrument were enforcing a right to payment under a simple contract; and

(3) a claim in recoupment of the obligor against the original payee of the instrument if the claim arose from the transaction that gave rise to the instrument; but the claim of the obligor may be asserted against a transferee of the instrument only to reduce the amount owing on the instrument at the time the action is brought.

(b) The right of a holder in due course to enforce the obligation of a party to pay the instrument is subject to defenses of the obligor stated in subsection (a)(1), but is not subject to defenses of the obligor stated in subsection (a)(2) or claims in recoupment stated in subsection (a)(3) against a person other than the holder.

(c) Except as stated in subsection (d), in an action to enforce the obligation of a party to pay the instrument, the obligor may not assert against the person entitled to enforce the instrument a defense, claim in recoupment, or claim to the instrument (Section 3–306) of another person, but the other person's claim to the instrument may be asserted by the obligor if the other person is joined in the action and personally asserts the claim against the person entitled to enforce the instrument. An obligor is not obliged to pay the instrument if the person seeking enforcement of the instrument does not have rights of a holder in due course and the obligor proves that the instrument is a lost or stolen instrument.

(d) In an action to enforce the obligation of an accommodation party to pay an instrument, the accommodation party may assert against the person entitled to enforce the instrument any defense or claim in recoupment under subsection (a) that the accommodated party could assert against the person entitled to enforce the instrument, except the defenses of discharge in insolvency proceedings, infancy, and lack of legal capacity.

§ 3–306. Claims to an Instrument.

A person taking an instrument, other than a person having rights of a holder in due course, is subject to a claim of a property or possessory right in the instrument or its proceeds, including a claim to rescind a negotiation and to recover the instrument or its proceeds. A person having rights of a holder in due course takes free of the claim to the instrument.

§ 3–307. Notice of Breach of Fiduciary Duty.

(a) In this section:

(1) "Fiduciary" means an agent, trustee, partner, corporate officer or director, or other representative owing a fiduciary duty with respect to an instrument.

(2) "Represented person" means the principal, beneficiary, partnership, corporation, or other person to whom the duty stated in paragraph (1) is owed.

(b) If (i) an instrument is taken from a fiduciary for payment or collection or for value, (ii) the taker has knowledge of the fiduciary status of the fiduciary, and (iii) the represented person makes a claim to the instrument or its proceeds on the basis that the transaction of the fiduciary is a breach of fiduciary duty, the following rules apply:

(1) Notice of breach of fiduciary duty by the fiduciary is notice of the claim of the represented person.

(2) In the case of an instrument payable to the represented person or the fiduciary as such, the taker has notice of the breach of fiduciary duty if the instrument is (i) taken in payment of or as security for a debt known by the taker to be the personal debt of the fiduciary, (ii) taken in a transaction known by the taker to be

for the personal benefit of the fiduciary, or (iii) deposited to an account other than an account of the fiduciary, as such, or an account of the represented person.

(3) If an instrument is issued by the represented person or the fiduciary as such, and made payable to the fiduciary personally, the taker does not have notice of the breach of fiduciary duty unless the taker knows of the breach of fiduciary duty.

(4) If an instrument is issued by the represented person or the fiduciary as such, to the taker as payee, the taker has notice of the breach of fiduciary duty if the instrument is (i) taken in payment of or as security for a debt known by the taker to be the personal debt of the fiduciary, (ii) taken in a transaction known by the taker to be for the personal benefit of the fiduciary, or (iii) deposited to an account other than an account of the fiduciary, as such, or an account of the represented person.

§ 3–308. Proof of Signatures and Status as Holder in Due Course.

(a) In an action with respect to an instrument, the authenticity of, and authority to make, each signature on the instrument is admitted unless specifically denied in the pleadings. If the validity of a signature is denied in the pleadings, the burden of establishing validity is on the person claiming validity, but the signature is presumed to be authentic and authorized unless the action is to enforce the liability of the purported signer and the signer is dead or incompetent at the time of trial of the issue of validity of the signature. If an action to enforce the instrument is brought against a person as the undisclosed principal of a person who signed the instrument as a party to the instrument, the plaintiff has the burden of establishing that the defendant is liable on the instrument as a represented person under Section 3–402(a).

(b) If the validity of signatures is admitted or proved and there is compliance with subsection (a), a plaintiff producing the instrument is entitled to payment if the plaintiff proves entitlement to enforce the instrument under Section 3–301, unless the defendant proves a defense or claim in recoupment. If a defense or claim in recoupment is proved, the right to payment of the plaintiff is subject to the defense or claim, except to the extent the plaintiff proves that the plaintiff has rights of a holder in due course which are not subject to the defense or claim.

§ 3–309. Enforcement of Lost, Destroyed, or Stolen Instrument.

(a) A person not in possession of an instrument is entitled to enforce the instrument if (i) the person was in possession of the instrument and entitled to enforce it when loss of possession occurred, (ii) the loss of possession was not the result of a transfer by the person or a lawful seizure, and (iii) the person cannot reasonably obtain possession of the instrument because the instrument was destroyed, its whereabouts cannot be determined, or it is in the wrongful possession of an unknown person or a person that cannot be found or is not amenable to service of process.

(b) A person seeking enforcement of an instrument under subsection (a) must prove the terms of the instrument and the person's right to enforce the instrument. If that proof is made, Section 3–308 applies to the case as if the person seeking enforcement had produced the instrument. The court may not enter judgment in favor of the person seeking enforcement unless it finds that the person required to pay the instrument is adequately protected against loss that might occur by reason of a claim by another person to enforce the instrument. Adequate protection may be provided by any reasonable means.

§ 3–310. Effect of Instrument on Obligation for Which Taken.

(a) Unless otherwise agreed, if a certified check, cashier's check, or teller's check is taken for an obligation, the obligation is discharged to the same extent discharge would result if an amount of money equal to the amount of the instrument were taken in payment of the obligation. Discharge of the obligation does not affect any liability that the obligor may have as an indorser of the instrument.

(b) Unless otherwise agreed and except as provided in subsection (a), if a note or an uncertified check is taken for an obligation, the obligation is suspended to the same extent the obligation would be discharged if an amount of money equal to the amount of the instrument were taken, and the following rules apply:

(1) In the case of an uncertified check, suspension of the obligation continues until dishonor of the check or until it is paid or certified. Payment or certification of the check results in discharge of the obligation to the extent of the amount of the check.

(2) In the case of a note, suspension of the obligation continues until dishonor of the note or until it is paid. Payment of the note results in discharge of the obligation to the extent of the payment.

(3) Except as provided in paragraph (4), if the check or note is dishonored and the obligee of the obligation for which the instrument was taken is the person entitled to enforce the instrument, the obligee may enforce either the instrument or the obligation. In the case of an instrument of a third person which is negotiated to the obligee by the obligor, discharge of the obligor on the instrument also discharges the obligation.

(4) If the person entitled to enforce the instrument taken for an obligation is a person other than the obligee, the obligee may not enforce the obligation to the extent the obligation is suspended. If the obligee is the person entitled to enforce the instrument but no longer has possession of it because it was lost, stolen, or destroyed, the obligation may not be enforced to the extent of the amount payable on the instrument, and to that extent the obligee's rights against the obligor are limited to enforcement of the instrument.

(c) If an instrument other than one described in subsection (a) or (b) is taken for an obligation, the effect is (i) that stated in subsection (a) if the instrument is one on which a bank is liable as maker or acceptor, or (ii) that stated in subsection (b) in any other case.

§ 3–311. Accord and Satisfaction by Use of Instrument.

(a) If a person against whom a claim is asserted proves that (i) that person in good faith tendered an instrument to the claimant as full satisfaction of the claim, (ii) the amount of the claim was unliquidated or subject to a bona fide dispute, and (iii) the claimant obtained payment of the instrument, the following subsections apply.

(b) Unless subsection (c) applies, the claim is discharged if the person against whom the claim is asserted proves that the instrument or an accompanying written communication contained a conspicuous statement to the effect that the instrument was tendered as full satisfaction of the claim.

(c) Subject to subsection (d), a claim is not discharged under subsection (b) if either of the following applies:

(1) The claimant, if an organization, proves that (i) within a reasonable time before the tender, the claimant sent a conspicuous statement to the person against whom the claim is asserted that communications concerning disputed debts, including an instrument tendered as full satisfaction of a debt, are to be sent to a designated person, office, or place, and (ii) the

instrument or accompanying communication was not received by that designated person, office, or place.

(2) The claimant, whether or not an organization, proves that within 90 days after payment of the instrument, the claimant tendered repayment of the amount of the instrument to the person against whom the claim is asserted. This paragraph does not apply if the claimant is an organization that sent a statement complying with paragraph (1)(i).

(d) A claim is discharged if the person against whom the claim is asserted proves that within a reasonable time before collection of the instrument was initiated, the claimant, or an agent of the claimant having direct responsibility with respect to the disputed obligation, knew that the instrument was tendered in full satisfaction of the claim.

§ 3–312. Lost, Destroyed, or Stolen Cashier's Check, Teller's Check, or Certified Check.*

(a) In this section:

(1) "Check" means a cashier's check, teller's check, or certified check.

(2) "Claimant" means a person who claims the right to receive the amount of a cashier's check, teller's check, or certified check that was lost, destroyed, or stolen.

(3) "Declaration of loss" means a written statement, made under penalty of perjury, to the effect that (i) the declarer lost possession of a check, (ii) the declarer is the drawer or payee of the check, in the case of a certified check, or the remitter or payee of the check, in the case of a cashier's check or teller's check, (iii) the loss of possession was not the result of a transfer by the declarer or a lawful seizure, and (iv) the declarer cannot reasonably obtain possession of the check because the check was destroyed, its whereabouts cannot be determined, or it is in the wrongful possession of an unknown person or a person that cannot be found or is not amenable to service of process.

(4) "Obligated bank" means the issuer of a cashier's check or teller's check or the acceptor of a certified check.

(b) A claimant may assert a claim to the amount of a check by a communication to the obligated bank describing the check with reasonable certainty and requesting payment of the amount of the check, if (i) the claimant is the drawer or payee of a certified check or the remitter or payee of a cashier's check or teller's check, (ii) the communication contains or is accompanied by a declaration of loss of the claimant with respect to the check, (iii) the communication is received at a time and in a manner affording the bank a reasonable time to act on it before the check is paid, and (iv) the claimant provides reasonable identification if requested by the obligated bank. Delivery of a declaration of loss is a warranty of the truth of the statements made in the declaration. If a claim is asserted in compliance with this subsection, the following rules apply:

(1) The claim becomes enforceable at the later of (i) the time the claim is asserted, or (ii) the 90th day following the date of the check, in the case of a cashier's check or teller's check, or the 90th day following the date of the acceptance, in the case of a certified check.

(2) Until the claim becomes enforceable, it has no legal effect and the obligated bank may pay the check or, in the case of a teller's check, may permit the drawee to pay the check. Payment to a person entitled to enforce the check discharges all liability of the obligated bank with respect to the check.

(3) If the claim becomes enforceable before the check is presented for payment, the obligated bank is not obliged to pay the check.

(4) When the claim becomes enforceable, the obligated bank becomes obliged to pay the amount of the check to the claimant if payment of the check has not been made to a person entitled to enforce the check. Subject to Section 4–302(a)(1), payment to the claimant discharges all liability of the obligated bank with respect to the check.

(c) If the obligated bank pays the amount of a check to a claimant under subsection (b)(4) and the check is presented for payment by a person having rights of a holder in due course, the claimant is obliged to (i) refund the payment to the obligated bank if the check is paid, or (ii) pay the amount of the check to the person having rights of a holder in due course if the check is dishonored.

(d) If a claimant has the right to assert a claim under subsection (b) and is also a person entitled to enforce a cashier's check, teller's check, or certified check which is lost, destroyed, or stolen, the claimant may assert rights with respect to the check either under this section or Section 3–309.

Added in 1991.

Part 4 Liability of Parties

§ 3–401. Signature.

(a) A person is not liable on an instrument unless (i) the person signed the instrument, or (ii) the person is represented by an agent or representative who signed the instrument and the signature is binding on the represented person under Section 3–402.

(b) A signature may be made (i) manually or by means of a device or machine, and (ii) by the use of any name, including a trade or assumed name, or by a word, mark, or symbol executed or adopted by a person with present intention to authenticate a writing.

§ 3–402. Signature by Representative.

(a) If a person acting, or purporting to act, as a representative signs an instrument by signing either the name of the represented person or the name of the signer, the represented person is bound by the signature to the same extent the represented person would be bound if the signature were on a simple contract. If the represented person is bound, the signature of the representative is the "authorized signature of the represented person" and the represented person is liable on the instrument, whether or not identified in the instrument.

(b) If a representative signs the name of the representative to an instrument and the signature is an authorized signature of the represented person, the following rules apply:

(1) If the form of the signature shows unambiguously that the signature is made on behalf of the represented person who is identified in the instrument, the representative is not liable on the instrument.

(2) Subject to subsection (c), if (i) the form of the signature does not show unambiguously that the signature is made in a representative capacity or (ii) the represented person is not identified in the instrument, the representative is liable on the instrument to a holder in due course that took the instrument without notice that the representative was not intended to be liable on the instrument. With respect to any other person, the representative is liable on the instrument unless the representative proves that the original parties did not intend the representative to be liable on the instrument.

(c) If a representative signs the name of the representative as drawer of a check without indication of the representative status and the check is payable from an account of the represented person who is identified on the check, the signer is not liable on the check if the signature is an authorized signature of the represented person.

§ 3–403. Unauthorized Signature.

(a) Unless otherwise provided in this Article or Article 4, an unauthorized signature is ineffective except as the signature of the unauthorized signer in favor of a person who in good faith pays the instrument or takes it for value. An unauthorized signature may be ratified for all purposes of this Article.

(b) If the signature of more than one person is required to constitute the authorized signature of an organization, the signature of the organization is unauthorized if one of the required signatures is lacking.

(c) The civil or criminal liability of a person who makes an unauthorized signature is not affected by any provision of this Article which makes the unauthorized signature effective for the purposes of this Article.

§ 3–404. Impostors; Fictitious Payees.

(a) If an impostor, by use of the mails or otherwise, induces the issuer of an instrument to issue the instrument to the impostor, or to a person acting in concert with the impostor, by impersonating the payee of the instrument or a person authorized to act for the payee, an indorsement of the instrument by any person in the name of the payee is effective as the indorsement of the payee in favor of a person who, in good faith, pays the instrument or takes it for value or for collection.

(b) If (i) a person whose intent determines to whom an instrument is payable (Section 3–110(a) or (b)) does not intend the person identified as payee to have any interest in the instrument, or (ii) the person identified as payee of an instrument is a fictitious person, the following rules apply until the instrument is negotiated by special indorsement:

(1) Any person in possession of the instrument is its holder.

(2) An indorsement by any person in the name of the payee stated in the instrument is effective as the indorsement of the payee in favor of a person who, in good faith, pays the instrument or takes it for value or for collection.

(c) Under subsection (a) or (b), an indorsement is made in the name of a payee if (i) it is made in a name substantially similar to that of the payee or (ii) the instrument, whether or not indorsed, is deposited in a depositary bank to an account in a name substantially similar to that of the payee.

(d) With respect to an instrument to which subsection (a) or (b) applies, if a person paying the instrument or taking it for value or for collection fails to exercise ordinary care in paying or taking the instrument and that failure substantially contributes to loss resulting from payment of the instrument, the person bearing the loss may recover from the person failing to exercise ordinary care to the extent the failure to exercise ordinary care contributed to the loss.

§ 3–405. Employer's Responsibility for Fraudulent Indorsement by Employee.

(a) In this section:

(1) "Employee" includes an independent contractor and employee of an independent contractor retained by the employer.

(2) "Fraudulent indorsement" means (i) in the case of an instrument payable to the employer, a forged indorsement purporting to

be that of the employer, or (ii) in the case of an instrument with respect to which the employer is the issuer, a forged indorsement purporting to be that of the person identified as payee.

(3) "Responsibility" with respect to instruments means authority (i) to sign or indorse instruments on behalf of the employer, (ii) to process instruments received by the employer for bookkeeping purposes, for deposit to an account, or for other disposition, (iii) to prepare or process instruments for issue in the name of the employer, (iv) to supply information determining the names or addresses of payees of instruments to be issued in the name of the employer, (v) to control the disposition of instruments to be issued in the name of the employer, or (vi) to act otherwise with respect to instruments in a responsible capacity. "Responsibility" does not include authority that merely allows an employee to have access to instruments or blank or incomplete instrument forms that are being stored or transported or are part of incoming or outgoing mail, or similar access.

(b) For the purpose of determining the rights and liabilities of a person who, in good faith, pays an instrument or takes it for value or for collection, if an employer entrusted an employee with responsibility with respect to the instrument and the employee or a person acting in concert with the employee makes a fraudulent indorsement of the instrument, the indorsement is effective as the indorsement of the person to whom the instrument is payable if it is made in the name of that person. If the person paying the instrument or taking it for value or for collection fails to exercise ordinary care in paying or taking the instrument and that failure substantially contributes to loss resulting from the fraud, the person bearing the loss may recover from the person failing to exercise ordinary care to the extent the failure to exercise ordinary care contributed to the loss.

(c) Under subsection (b), an indorsement is made in the name of the person to whom an instrument is payable if (i) it is made in a name substantially similar to the name of that person or (ii) the instrument, whether or not indorsed, is deposited in a depositary bank to an account in a name substantially similar to the name of that person.

§ 3–406. Negligence Contributing to Forged Signature or Alteration of Instrument.

(a) A person whose failure to exercise ordinary care substantially contributes to an alteration of an instrument or to the making of a forged signature on an instrument is precluded from asserting the alteration or the forgery against a person who, in good faith, pays the instrument or takes it for value or for collection.

(b) Under subsection (a), if the person asserting the preclusion fails to exercise ordinary care in paying or taking the instrument and that failure substantially contributes to loss, the loss is allocated between the person precluded and the person asserting the preclusion according to the extent to which the failure of each to exercise ordinary care contributed to the loss.

(c) Under subsection (a), the burden of proving failure to exercise ordinary care is on the person asserting the preclusion. Under subsection (b), the burden of proving failure to exercise ordinary care is on the person precluded.

§ 3–407. Alteration.

(a) "Alteration" means (i) an unauthorized change in an instrument that purports to modify in any respect the obligation of a party, or (ii) an unauthorized addition of words or numbers or other change to an incomplete instrument relating to the obligation of a party.

(b) Except as provided in subsection (c), an alteration fraudulently made discharges a party whose obligation is affected by the alteration unless that party assents or is precluded from asserting the alteration. No other alteration discharges a party, and the instrument may be enforced according to its original terms.

(c) A payor bank or drawee paying a fraudulently altered instrument or a person taking it for value, in good faith and without notice of the alteration, may enforce rights with respect to the instrument (i) according to its original terms, or (ii) in the case of an incomplete instrument altered by unauthorized completion, according to its terms as completed.

§ 3–408. Drawee Not Liable on Unaccepted Draft.

A check or other draft does not of itself operate as an assignment of funds in the hands of the drawee available for its payment, and the drawee is not liable on the instrument until the drawee accepts it.

§ 3–409. Acceptance of Draft; Certified Check.

(a) "Acceptance" means the drawee's signed agreement to pay a draft as presented. It must be written on the draft and may consist of the drawee's signature alone. Acceptance may be made at any time and becomes effective when notification pursuant to instructions is given or the accepted draft is delivered for the purpose of giving rights on the acceptance to any person.

(b) A draft may be accepted although it has not been signed by the drawer, is otherwise incomplete, is overdue, or has been dishonored.

(c) If a draft is payable at a fixed period after sight and the acceptor fails to date the acceptance, the holder may complete the acceptance by supplying a date in good faith.

(d) "Certified check" means a check accepted by the bank on which it is drawn. Acceptance may be made as stated in subsection (a) or by a writing on the check which indicates that the check is certified. The drawee of a check has no obligation to certify the check, and refusal to certify is not dishonor of the check.

§ 3–410. Acceptance Varying Draft.

(a) If the terms of a drawee's acceptance vary from the terms of the draft as presented, the holder may refuse the acceptance and treat the draft as dishonored. In that case, the drawee may cancel the acceptance.

§ 3–407. Alteration.

(a) "Alteration" means (i) an unauthorized change in an instrument that purports to modify in any respect the obligation of a party, or (ii) an unauthorized addition of words or numbers or other change to an incomplete instrument relating to the obligation of a party.

(b) Except as provided in subsection (c), an alteration fraudulently made discharges a party whose obligation is affected by the alteration unless that party assents or is precluded from asserting the alteration. No other alteration discharges a party, and the instrument may be enforced according to its original terms.

(c) A payor bank or drawee paying a fraudulently altered instrument or a person taking it for value, in good faith and without notice of the alteration, may enforce rights with respect to the instrument (i) according to its original terms, or (ii) in the case of an incomplete instrument altered by unauthorized completion, according to its terms as completed.

§ 3–408. Drawee Not Liable on Unaccepted Draft.

A check or other draft does not of itself operate as an assignment of funds in the hands of the drawee available for its payment, and the drawee is not liable on the instrument until the drawee accepts it.

§ 3–409. Acceptance of Draft; Certified Check.

(a) "Acceptance" means the drawee's signed agreement to pay a draft as presented. It must be written on the draft and may consist of the drawee's signature alone. Acceptance may be made at any time and becomes effective when notification pursuant to instructions is given or the accepted draft is delivered for the purpose of giving rights on the acceptance to any person.

(b) A draft may be accepted although it has not been signed by the drawer, is otherwise incomplete, is overdue, or has been dishonored.

(c) If a draft is payable at a fixed period after sight and the acceptor fails to date the acceptance, the holder may complete the acceptance by supplying a date in good faith.

(d) "Certified check" means a check accepted by the bank on which it is drawn. Acceptance may be made as stated in subsection (a) or by a writing on the check which indicates that the check is certified. The drawee of a check has no obligation to certify the check, and refusal to certify is not dishonor of the check.

§ 3–410. Acceptance Varying Draft.

(a) If the terms of a drawee's acceptance vary from the terms of the draft as presented, the holder may refuse the acceptance and treat the draft as dishonored. In that case, the drawee may cancel the acceptance.

(b) The terms of a draft are not varied by an acceptance to pay at a particular bank or place in the United States, unless the acceptance states that the draft is to be paid only at that bank or place.

(c) If the holder assents to an acceptance varying the terms of a draft, the obligation of each drawer and indorser that does not expressly assent to the acceptance is discharged.

§ 3–411. Refusal to Pay Cashier's Checks, Teller's Checks, and Certified Checks.

(a) In this section, "obligated bank" means the acceptor of a certified check or the issuer of a cashier's check or teller's check bought from the issuer.

(b) If the obligated bank wrongfully (i) refuses to pay a cashier's check or certified check, (ii) stops payment of a teller's check, or (iii) refuses to pay a dishonored teller's check, the person asserting the right to enforce the check is entitled to compensation for expenses and loss of interest resulting from the nonpayment and may recover consequential damages if the obligated bank refuses to pay after receiving notice of particular circumstances giving rise to the damages.

(c) Expenses or consequential damages under subsection (b) are not recoverable if the refusal of the obligated bank to pay occurs because (i) the bank suspends payments, (ii) the obligated bank asserts a claim or defense of the bank that it has reasonable grounds to believe is available against the person entitled to enforce the instrument, (iii) the obligated bank has a reasonable doubt whether the person demanding payment is the person entitled to enforce the instrument, or (iv) payment is prohibited by law.

§ 3–412. Obligation of Issuer of Note or Cashier's Check.

The issuer of a note or cashier's check or other draft drawn on the drawer is obliged to pay the instrument (i) according to its terms at the time it was issued or, if not issued, at the time it first came into possession of a holder, or (ii) if the issuer signed an incomplete instrument, according to its terms when completed, to the extent stated in Sections 3–115 and 3–407. The obligation is owed to a person entitled to enforce the instrument or to an indorser who paid the instrument under Section 3–415.

§ 3–413. Obligation of Acceptor.

(a) The acceptor of a draft is obliged to pay the draft (i) according to its terms at the time it was accepted, even though the acceptance states that the draft is payable "as originally drawn" or equivalent terms, (ii) if the acceptance varies the terms of the draft, according to the terms of the draft as varied, or (iii) if the acceptance is of a draft that is an incomplete instrument, according to its terms when completed, to the extent stated in Sections 3–115 and 3–407. The obligation is owed to a person entitled to enforce the draft or to the drawer or an indorser who paid the draft under Section 3–414 or 3–415.

(b) If the certification of a check or other acceptance of a draft states the amount certified or accepted, the obligation of the acceptor is that amount. If (i) the certification or acceptance does not state an amount, (ii) the amount of the instrument is subsequently raised, and (iii) the instrument is then negotiated to a holder in due course, the obligation of the acceptor is the amount of the instrument at the time it was taken by the holder in due course.

§ 3–414. Obligation of Drawer.

(a) This section does not apply to cashier's checks or other drafts drawn on the drawer.

(b) If an unaccepted draft is dishonored, the drawer is obliged to pay the draft (i) according to its terms at the time it was issued or, if not issued, at the time it first came into possession of a holder, or (ii) if the drawer signed an incomplete instrument, according to its terms when completed, to the extent stated in Sections 3–115 and 3–407. The obligation is owed to a person entitled to enforce the draft or to an indorser who paid the draft under Section 3–415.

(c) If a draft is accepted by a bank, the drawer is discharged, regardless of when or by whom acceptance was obtained.

(d) If a draft is accepted and the acceptor is not a bank, the obligation of the drawer to pay the draft if the draft is dishonored by the acceptor is the same as the obligation of an indorser under Section 3–415(a) and (c).

(e) If a draft states that it is drawn "without recourse" or otherwise disclaims liability of the drawer to pay the draft, the drawer is not liable under subsection (b) to pay the draft if the draft is not a check. A disclaimer of the liability stated in subsection (b) is not effective if the draft is a check.

(f) If (i) a check is not presented for payment or given to a depositary bank for collection within 30 days after its date, (ii) the drawee suspends payments after expiration of the 30-day period without paying the check, and (iii) because of the suspension of payments, the drawer is deprived of funds maintained with the drawee to cover payment of the check, the drawer to the extent deprived of funds may discharge its obligation to pay the check by assigning to the person entitled to enforce the check the rights of the drawer against the drawee with respect to the funds.

§ 3–415. Obligation of Indorser.

(a) Subject to subsections (b), (c), and (d) and to Section 3–419(d), if an instrument is dishonored, an indorser is obliged to pay the amount due on the instrument (i) according to the terms of the instrument at the time it was indorsed, or (ii) if the indorser indorsed an incomplete instrument, according to its terms when completed, to the extent stated in Sections 3–115 and 3–407. The obligation of the indorser is owed to a person entitled to enforce the instrument or to a subsequent indorser who paid the instrument under this section.

(b) If an indorsement states that it is made "without recourse" or otherwise disclaims liability of the indorser, the indorser is not liable under subsection (a) to pay the instrument.

(c) If notice of dishonor of an instrument is required by Section 3–503 and notice of dishonor complying with that section is not given to an indorser, the liability of the indorser under subsection (a) is discharged.

(d) If a draft is accepted by a bank after an indorsement is made, the liability of the indorser under subsection (a) is discharged.

(e) If an indorser of a check is liable under subsection (a) and the check is not presented for payment, or given to a depositary bank for collection, within 30 days after the day the indorsement was made, the liability of the indorser under subsection (a) is discharged.

As amended in 1993.

§ 3–416. Transfer Warranties.

(a) A person who transfers an instrument for consideration warrants to the transferee and, if the transfer is by indorsement, to any subsequent transferee that:

(1) the warrantor is a person entitled to enforce the instrument;

(2) all signatures on the instrument are authentic and authorized;

(3) the instrument has not been altered;

(4) the instrument is not subject to a defense or claim in recoupment of any party which can be asserted against the warrantor; and

(5) the warrantor has no knowledge of any insolvency proceeding commenced with respect to the maker or acceptor or, in the case of an unaccepted draft, the drawer.

(b) A person to whom the warranties under subsection (a) are made and who took the instrument in good faith may recover from the warrantor as damages for breach of warranty an amount equal to the loss suffered as a result of the breach, but not more than the amount of the instrument plus expenses and loss of interest incurred as a result of the breach.

(c) The warranties stated in subsection (a) cannot be disclaimed with respect to checks. Unless notice of a claim for breach of warranty is given to the warrantor within 30 days after the claimant has reason to know of the breach and the identity of the warrantor, the liability of the warrantor under subsection (b) is discharged to the extent of any loss caused by the delay in giving notice of the claim.

(d) A [cause of action] for breach of warranty under this section accrues when the claimant has reason to know of the breach.

§ 3–417. Presentment Warranties.

(a) If an unaccepted draft is presented to the drawee for payment or acceptance and the drawee pays or accepts the draft, (i) the person obtaining payment or acceptance, at the time of presentment, and (ii) a previous transferor of the draft, at the time of transfer, warrant to the drawee making payment or accepting the draft in good faith that:

(1) the warrantor is, or was, at the time the warrantor transferred the draft, a person entitled to enforce the draft or authorized to obtain payment or acceptance of the draft on behalf of a person entitled to enforce the draft;

(2) the draft has not been altered; and

(3) the warrantor has no knowledge that the signature of the drawer of the draft is unauthorized.

(b) A drawee making payment may recover from any warrantor damages for breach of warranty equal to the amount paid by the drawee less the amount the drawee received or is entitled to receive from the drawer because of the payment. In addition, the drawee is entitled to compensation for expenses and loss of interest resulting from the breach. The right of the drawee to recover damages under this subsection is not affected by any failure of the drawee to exercise ordinary care in making payment. If the drawee accepts the draft, breach of warranty is a defense to the obligation of the acceptor. If the acceptor makes payment with respect to the draft, the acceptor is entitled to recover from any warrantor for breach of warranty the amounts stated in this subsection.

(c) If a drawee asserts a claim for breach of warranty under subsection (a) based on an unauthorized indorsement of the draft or an alteration of the draft, the warrantor may defend by proving that the indorsement is effective under Section 3–404 or 3–405 or the drawer is precluded under Section 3–406 or 4–406 from asserting against the drawee the unauthorized indorsement or alteration.

(d) If (i) a dishonored draft is presented for payment to the drawer or an indorser or (ii) any other instrument is presented for payment to a party obliged to pay the instrument, and (iii) payment is received, the following rules apply:

(1) The person obtaining payment and a prior transferor of the instrument warrant to the person making payment in good faith that the warrantor is, or was, at the time the warrantor transferred the instrument, a person entitled to enforce the instrument or authorized to obtain payment on behalf of a person entitled to enforce the instrument.

(2) The person making payment may recover from any warrantor for breach of warranty an amount equal to the amount paid plus expenses and loss of interest resulting from the breach.

(e) The warranties stated in subsections (a) and (d) cannot be disclaimed with respect to checks. Unless notice of a claim for breach of warranty is given to the warrantor within 30 days after the claimant has reason to know of the breach and the identity of the warrantor, the liability of the warrantor under subsection (b) or (d) is discharged to the extent of any loss caused by the delay in giving notice of the claim.

(f) A [cause of action] for breach of warranty under this section accrues when the claimant has reason to know of the breach.

§ 3–418. Payment or Acceptance by Mistake.

(a) Except as provided in subsection (c), if the drawee of a draft pays or accepts the draft and the drawee acted on the mistaken belief that (i) payment of the draft had not been stopped pursuant to Section 4–403 or (ii) the signature of the drawer of the draft was authorized, the drawee may recover the amount of the draft from the person to whom or for whose benefit payment was made or, in the case of acceptance, may revoke the acceptance. Rights of the drawee under this subsection are not affected by failure of the drawee to exercise ordinary care in paying or accepting the draft.

(b) Except as provided in subsection (c), if an instrument has been paid or accepted by mistake and the case is not covered by subsec-

tion (a), the person paying or accepting may, to the extent permitted by the law governing mistake and restitution, (i) recover the payment from the person to whom or for whose benefit payment was made or (ii) in the case of acceptance, may revoke the acceptance.

(c) The remedies provided by subsection (a) or (b) may not be asserted against a person who took the instrument in good faith and for value or who in good faith changed position in reliance on the payment or acceptance. This subsection does not limit remedies provided by Section 3–417 or 4–407.

(d) Notwithstanding Section 4–215, if an instrument is paid or accepted by mistake and the payor or acceptor recovers payment or revokes acceptance under subsection (a) or (b), the instrument is deemed not to have been paid or accepted and is treated as dishonored, and the person from whom payment is recovered has rights as a person entitled to enforce the dishonored instrument.

§ 3–419. Instruments Signed for Accommodation.

(a) If an instrument is issued for value given for the benefit of a party to the instrument ("accommodated party") and another party to the instrument ("accommodation party") signs the instrument for the purpose of incurring liability on the instrument without being a direct beneficiary of the value given for the instrument, the instrument is signed by the accommodation party "for accommodation."

(b) An accommodation party may sign the instrument as maker, drawer, acceptor, or indorser and, subject to subsection (d), is obliged to pay the instrument in the capacity in which the accommodation party signs. The obligation of an accommodation party may be enforced notwithstanding any statute of frauds and whether or not the accommodation party receives consideration for the accommodation.

(c) A person signing an instrument is presumed to be an accommodation party and there is notice that the instrument is signed for accommodation if the signature is an anomalous indorsement or is accompanied by words indicating that the signer is acting as surety or guarantor with respect to the obligation of another party to the instrument. Except as provided in Section 3–605, the obligation of an accommodation party to pay the instrument is not affected by the fact that the person enforcing the obligation had notice when the instrument was taken by that person that the accommodation party signed the instrument for accommodation.

(d) If the signature of a party to an instrument is accompanied by words indicating unambiguously that the party is guaranteeing collection rather than payment of the obligation of another party to the instrument, the signer is obliged to pay the amount due on the instrument to a person entitled to enforce the instrument only if (i) execution of judgment against the other party has been returned unsatisfied, (ii) the other party is insolvent or in an insolvency proceeding, (iii) the other party cannot be served with process, or (iv) it is otherwise apparent that payment cannot be obtained from the other party.

(e) An accommodation party who pays the instrument is entitled to reimbursement from the accommodated party and is entitled to enforce the instrument against the accommodated party. An accommodated party who pays the instrument has no right of recourse against, and is not entitled to contribution from, an accommodation party.

§ 3–420. Conversion of Instrument.

(a) The law applicable to conversion of personal property applies to instruments. An instrument is also converted if it is taken by transfer, other than a negotiation, from a person not entitled to enforce the instrument or a bank makes or obtains payment with respect to the instrument for a person not entitled to enforce the instrument or receive payment. An action for conversion of an instrument may not be brought by (i) the issuer or acceptor of the instrument or (ii) a payee or indorsee who did not receive delivery of the instrument either directly or through delivery to an agent or a co-payee.

(b) In an action under subsection (a), the measure of liability is presumed to be the amount payable on the instrument, but recovery may not exceed the amount of the plaintiff's interest in the instrument.

(c) A representative, other than a depositary bank, who has in good faith dealt with an instrument or its proceeds on behalf of one who was not the person entitled to enforce the instrument is not liable in conversion to that person beyond the amount of any proceeds that it has not paid out.

Part 5 Dishonor

§ 3–501. Presentment.

(a) "Presentment" means a demand made by or on behalf of a person entitled to enforce an instrument (i) to pay the instrument made to the drawee or a party obliged to pay the instrument or, in the case of a note or accepted draft payable at a bank, to the bank, or (ii) to accept a draft made to the drawee.

(b) The following rules are subject to Article 4, agreement of the parties, and clearing-house rules and the like:

(1) Presentment may be made at the place of payment of the instrument and must be made at the place of payment if the instrument is payable at a bank in the United States; may be made by any commercially reasonable means, including an oral, written, or electronic communication; is effective when the demand for payment or acceptance is received by the person to whom presentment is made; and is effective if made to any one of two or more makers, acceptors, drawees, or other payors.

(2) Upon demand of the person to whom presentment is made, the person making presentment must (i) exhibit the instrument, (ii) give reasonable identification and, if presentment is made on behalf of another person, reasonable evidence of authority to do so, and (. . .) sign a receipt on the instrument for any payment made or surrender the instrument if full payment is made.

(3) Without dishonoring the instrument, the party to whom presentment is made may (i) return the instrument for lack of a necessary indorsement, or (ii) refuse payment or acceptance for failure of the presentment to comply with the terms of the instrument, an agreement of the parties, or other applicable law or rule.

(4) The party to whom presentment is made may treat presentment as occurring on the next business day after the day of presentment if the party to whom presentment is made has established a cut-off hour not earlier than 2 P.M. for the receipt and processing of instruments presented for payment or acceptance and presentment is made after the cut-off hour.

§ 3–502. Dishonor.

(a) Dishonor of a note is governed by the following rules:

(1) If the note is payable on demand, the note is dishonored if presentment is duly made to the maker and the note is not paid on the day of presentment.

(2) If the note is not payable on demand and is payable at or through a bank or the terms of the note require presentment, the note is dishonored if presentment is duly made and the note is not paid on the day it becomes payable or the day of presentment, whichever is later.

(3) If the note is not payable on demand and paragraph (2) does not apply, the note is dishonored if it is not paid on the day it becomes payable.

(b) Dishonor of an unaccepted draft other than a documentary draft is governed by the following rules:

(1) If a check is duly presented for payment to the payor bank otherwise than for immediate payment over the counter, the check is dishonored if the payor bank makes timely return of the check or sends timely notice of dishonor or nonpayment under Section 4–301 or 4–302, or becomes accountable for the amount of the check under Section 4–302.

(2) If a draft is payable on demand and paragraph (1) does not apply, the draft is dishonored if presentment for payment is duly made to the drawee and the draft is not paid on the day of presentment.

(3) If a draft is payable on a date stated in the draft, the draft is dishonored if (i) presentment for payment is duly made to the drawee and payment is not made on the day the draft becomes payable or the day of presentment, whichever is later, or (ii) presentment for acceptance is duly made before the day the draft becomes payable and the draft is not accepted on the day of presentment.

(4) If a draft is payable on elapse of a period of time after sight or acceptance, the draft is dishonored if presentment for acceptance is duly made and the draft is not accepted on the day of presentment.

(c) Dishonor of an unaccepted documentary draft occurs according to the rules stated in subsection (b)(2), (3), and (4), except that payment or acceptance may be delayed without dishonor until no later than the close of the third business day of the drawee following the day on which payment or acceptance is required by those paragraphs.

(d) Dishonor of an accepted draft is governed by the following rules:

(1) If the draft is payable on demand, the draft is dishonored if presentment for payment is duly made to the acceptor and the draft is not paid on the day of presentment.

(2) If the draft is not payable on demand, the draft is dishonored if presentment for payment is duly made to the acceptor and payment is not made on the day it becomes payable or the day of presentment, whichever is later.

(e) In any case in which presentment is otherwise required for dishonor under this section and presentment is excused under Section 3–504, dishonor occurs without presentment if the instrument is not duly accepted or paid.

(f) If a draft is dishonored because timely acceptance of the draft was not made and the person entitled to demand acceptance consents to a late acceptance, from the time of acceptance the draft is treated as never having been dishonored.

§ 3–503. Notice of Dishonor.

(a) The obligation of an indorser stated in Section 3–415(a) and the obligation of a drawer stated in Section 3–414(d) may not be enforced unless (i) the indorser or drawer is given notice of dishonor of the instrument complying with this section or (ii) notice of dishonor is excused under Section 3–504(b).

(b) Notice of dishonor may be given by any person; may be given by any commercially reasonable means, including an oral, written, or electronic communication; and is sufficient if it reasonably identifies the instrument and indicates that the instrument has been dishonored or has not been paid or accepted. Return of an instrument given to a bank for collection is sufficient notice of dishonor.

(c) Subject to Section 3–504(c), with respect to an instrument taken for collection by a collecting bank, notice of dishonor must be given (i) by the bank before midnight of the next banking day following the banking day on which the bank receives notice of dishonor of the instrument, or (ii) by any other person within 30 days following the day on which the person receives notice of dishonor. With respect to any other instrument, notice of dishonor must be given within 30 days following the day on which dishonor occurs.

§ 3–504. Excused Presentment and Notice of Dishonor.

(a) Presentment for payment or acceptance of an instrument is excused if (i) the person entitled to present the instrument cannot with reasonable diligence make presentment, (ii) the maker or acceptor has repudiated an obligation to pay the instrument or is dead or in insolvency proceedings, (iii) by the terms of the instrument presentment is not necessary to enforce the obligation of indorsers or the drawer, (iv) the drawer or indorser whose obligation is being enforced has waived presentment or otherwise has no reason to expect or right to require that the instrument be paid or accepted, or (v) the drawer instructed the drawee not to pay or accept the draft or the drawee was not obligated to the drawer to pay the draft.

(b) Notice of dishonor is excused if (i) by the terms of the instrument notice of dishonor is not necessary to enforce the obligation of a party to pay the instrument, or (ii) the party whose obligation is being enforced waived notice of dishonor. A waiver of presentment is also a waiver of notice of dishonor.

(c) Delay in giving notice of dishonor is excused if the delay was caused by circumstances beyond the control of the person giving the notice and the person giving the notice exercised reasonable diligence after the cause of the delay ceased to operate.

§ 3–505. Evidence of Dishonor.

(a) The following are admissible as evidence and create a presumption of dishonor and of any notice of dishonor stated:

   (1) a document regular in form as provided in subsection (b) which purports to be a protest;

   (2) a purported stamp or writing of the drawee, payor bank, or presenting bank on or accompanying the instrument stating that acceptance or payment has been refused unless reasons for the refusal are stated and the reasons are not consistent with dishonor;

   (3) a book or record of the drawee, payor bank, or collecting bank, kept in the usual course of business which shows dishonor, even if there is no evidence of who made the entry.

(b) A protest is a certificate of dishonor made by a United States consul or vice consul, or a notary public or other person authorized to administer oaths by the law of the place where dishonor occurs. It may be made upon information satisfactory to that person. The protest must identify the instrument and certify either that present-

ment has been made or, if not made, the reason why it was not made, and that the instrument has been dishonored by nonacceptance or nonpayment. The protest may also certify that notice of dishonor has been given to some or all parties.

Part 6 Discharge and Payment

§ 3–601. Discharge and Effect of Discharge.

(a) The obligation of a party to pay the instrument is discharged as stated in this Article or by an act or agreement with the party which would discharge an obligation to pay money under a simple contract.

(b) Discharge of the obligation of a party is not effective against a person acquiring rights of a holder in due course of the instrument without notice of the discharge.

§ 3–602. Payment.

(a) Subject to subsection (b), an instrument is paid to the extent payment is made (i) by or on behalf of a party obliged to pay the instrument, and (ii) to a person entitled to enforce the instrument. To the extent of the payment, the obligation of the party obliged to pay the instrument is discharged even though payment is made with knowledge of a claim to the instrument under Section 3–306 by another person.

(b) The obligation of a party to pay the instrument is not discharged under subsection (a) if:

   (1) a claim to the instrument under Section 3–306 is enforceable against the party receiving payment and (i) payment is made with knowledge by the payor that payment is prohibited by injunction or similar process of a court of competent jurisdiction, or (ii) in the case of an instrument other than a cashier's check, teller's check, or certified check, the party making payment accepted, from the person having a claim to the instrument, indemnity against loss resulting from refusal to pay the person entitled to enforce the instrument; or

   (2) the person making payment knows that the instrument is a stolen instrument and pays a person it knows is in wrongful possession of the instrument.

§ 3–603. Tender of Payment.

(a) If tender of payment of an obligation to pay an instrument is made to a person entitled to enforce the instrument, the effect of tender is governed by principles of law applicable to tender of payment under a simple contract.

(b) If tender of payment of an obligation to pay an instrument is made to a person entitled to enforce the instrument and the tender is refused, there is discharge, to the extent of the amount of the tender, of the obligation of an indorser or accommodation party having a right of recourse with respect to the obligation to which the tender relates.

(c) If tender of payment of an amount due on an instrument is made to a person entitled to enforce the instrument, the obligation of the obligor to pay interest after the due date on the amount tendered is discharged. If presentment is required with respect to an instrument and the obligor is able and ready to pay on the due date at every place of payment stated in the instrument, the obligor is deemed to have made tender of payment on the due date to the person entitled to enforce the instrument.

§ 3–604. Discharge by Cancellation or Renunciation.

(a) A person entitled to enforce an instrument, with or without consideration, may discharge the obligation of a party to pay the instrument (i) by an intentional voluntary act, such as surrender of the instrument to the party, destruction, mutilation, or cancellation of the instrument, cancellation or striking out of the party's signature, or the addition of words to the instrument indicating discharge, or (ii) by agreeing not to sue or otherwise renouncing rights against the party by a signed writing.

(b) Cancellation or striking out of an indorsement pursuant to subsection (a) does not affect the status and rights of a party derived from the indorsement.

§ 3–605. Discharge of Indorsers and Accommodation Parties.

(a) In this section, the term "indorser" includes a drawer having the obligation described in Section 3–414(d).

(b) Discharge, under Section 3–604, of the obligation of a party to pay an instrument does not discharge the obligation of an indorser or accommodation party having a right of recourse against the discharged party.

(c) If a person entitled to enforce an instrument agrees, with or without consideration, to an extension of the due date of the obligation of a party to pay the instrument, the extension discharges an indorser or accommodation party having a right of recourse against the party whose obligation is extended to the extent the indorser or accommodation party proves that the extension caused loss to the indorser or accommodation party with respect to the right of recourse.

(d) If a person entitled to enforce an instrument agrees, with or without consideration, to a material modification of the obligation of a party other than an extension of the due date, the modification discharges the obligation of an indorser or accommodation party having a right of recourse against the person whose obligation is modified to the extent the modification causes loss to the indorser or accommodation party with respect to the right of recourse. The loss suffered by the indorser or accommodation party as a result of the modification is equal to the amount of the right of recourse unless the person enforcing the instrument proves that no loss was caused by the modification or that the loss caused by the modification was an amount less than the amount of the right of recourse.

(e) If the obligation of a party to pay an instrument is secured by an interest in collateral and a person entitled to enforce the instrument impairs the value of the interest in collateral, the obligation of an indorser or accommodation party having a right of recourse against the obligor is discharged to the extent of the impairment. The value of an interest in collateral is impaired to the extent (i) the value of the interest is reduced to an amount less than the amount of the right of recourse of the party asserting discharge, or (ii) the reduction in value of the interest causes an increase in the amount by which the amount of the right of recourse exceeds the value of the interest. The burden of proving impairment is on the party asserting discharge.

(f) If the obligation of a party is secured by an interest in collateral not provided by an accommodation party and a person entitled to enforce the instrument impairs the value of the interest in collateral, the obligation of any party who is jointly and severally liable with respect to the secured obligation is discharged to the extent the impairment causes the party asserting discharge to pay more than that party would have been obliged to pay, taking into account rights of contribution, if impairment had not occurred. If the party asserting discharge is an accommodation party not entitled to discharge under subsection (e), the party is deemed to have a right to contribution based on joint and several liability rather than a right to reimbursement. The burden of proving impairment is on the party asserting discharge.

(g) Under subsection (e) or (f), impairing value of an interest in collateral includes (i) failure to obtain or maintain perfection or recordation of the interest in collateral, (ii) release of collateral without substitution of collateral of equal value, (iii) failure to perform a duty to preserve the value of collateral owed, under Article 9 or other law, to a debtor or surety or other person secondarily liable, or (iv) failure to comply with applicable law in disposing of collateral.

(h) An accommodation party is not discharged under subsection (c), (d), or (e) unless the person entitled to enforce the instrument knows of the accommodation or has notice under Section 3–419(c) that the instrument was signed for accommodation.

(i) A party is not discharged under this section if (i) the party asserting discharge consents to the event or conduct that is the basis of the discharge, or (ii) the instrument or a separate agreement of the party provides for waiver of discharge under this section either specifically or by general language indicating that parties waive defenses based on suretyship or impairment of collateral.

ADDENDUM TO REVISED ARTICLE 3

Notes to Legislative Counsel

1. If revised Article 3 is adopted in your state, the reference in Section 2–511 to Section 3–802 should be changed to Section 3–310.

2. If revised Article 3 is adopted in your state and the Uniform Fiduciaries Act is also in effect in your state, you may want to consider amending Uniform Fiduciaries Act § 9 to conform to Section 3–307(b)(2)(iii) and (4)(iii). See Official Comment 3 to Section 3–307.

Revised Article 4
BANK DEPOSITS AND COLLECTIONS

Part 1 General Provisions and Definitions

§ 4–101. Short Title.

This Article may be cited as Uniform Commercial Code—Bank Deposits and Collections.

As amended in 1990.

§ 4–102. Applicability.

(a) To the extent that items within this Article are also within Articles 3 and 8, they are subject to those Articles. If there is conflict, this Article governs Article 3, but Article 8 governs this Article.

(b) The liability of a bank for action or non-action with respect to an item handled by it for purposes of presentment, payment, or collection is governed by the law of the place where the bank is located. In the case of action or non-action by or at a branch or separate office of a bank, its liability is governed by the law of the place where the branch or separate office is located.

§ 4–103. Variation by Agreement; Measure of Damages; Action Constituting Ordinary Care.

(a) The effect of the provisions of this Article may be varied by agreement, but the parties to the agreement cannot disclaim a bank's responsibility for its lack of good faith or failure to exercise ordinary care or limit the measure of damages for the lack or failure. However, the parties may determine by agreement the standards by which the bank's responsibility is to be measured if those standards are not manifestly unreasonable.

(b) Federal Reserve regulations and operating circulars, clearing-house rules, and the like have the effect of agreements under subsection (a), whether or not specifically assented to by all parties interested in items handled.

(c) Action or non-action approved by this Article or pursuant to Federal Reserve regulations or operating circulars is the exercise of ordinary care and, in the absence of special instructions, action or non-action consistent with clearing-house rules and the like or with a general banking usage not disapproved by this Article, is prima facie the exercise of ordinary care.

(d) The specification or approval of certain procedures by this Article is not disapproval of other procedures that may be reasonable under the circumstances.

(e) The measure of damages for failure to exercise ordinary care in handling an item is the amount of the item reduced by an amount that could not have been realized by the exercise of ordinary care. If there is also bad faith it includes any other damages the party suffered as a proximate consequence.

As amended in 1990.

§ 4–104. Definitions and Index of Definitions.

(a) In this Article, unless the context otherwise requires:

(1) "Account" means any deposit or credit account with a bank, including a demand, time, savings, passbook, share draft, or like account, other than an account evidenced by a certificate of deposit;

(2) "Afternoon" means the period of a day between noon and midnight;

(3) "Banking day" means the part of a day on which a bank is open to the public for carrying on substantially all of its banking functions;

(4) "Clearing house" means an association of banks or other payors regularly clearing items;

(5) "Customer" means a person having an account with a bank or for whom a bank has agreed to collect items, including a bank that maintains an account at another bank;

(6) "Documentary draft" means a draft to be presented for acceptance or payment if specified documents, certificated securities (Section 8–102) or instructions for uncertificated securities (Section 8–102), or other certificates, statements, or the like are to be received by the drawee or other payor before acceptance or payment of the draft;

(7) "Draft" means a draft as defined in Section 3–104 or an item, other than an instrument, that is an order;

(8) "Drawee" means a person ordered in a draft to make payment;

(9) "Item" means an instrument or a promise or order to pay money handled by a bank for collection or payment. The term does not include a payment order governed by Article 4A or a credit or debit card slip;

(10) "Midnight deadline" with respect to a bank is midnight on its next banking day following the banking day on which it receives the relevant item or notice or from which the time for taking action commences to run, whichever is later;

(11) "Settle" means to pay in cash, by clearing-house settlement, in a charge or credit or by remittance, or otherwise as agreed. A settlement may be either provisional or final;

(12) "Suspends payments" with respect to a bank means that it has been closed by order of the supervisory authorities, that a public officer has been appointed to take it over, or that it ceases or refuses to make payments in the ordinary course of business.

(b) [Other definitions' section references deleted.]

(c) [Other definitions' section references deleted.]

(d) In addition, Article 1 contains general definitions and principles of construction and interpretation applicable throughout this Article.

§ 4–105. "Bank"; "Depositary Bank"; "Payor Bank"; "Intermediary Bank"; "Collecting Bank"; "Presenting Bank".

In this Article:

(1) "Bank" means a person engaged in the business of banking, including a savings bank, savings and loan association, credit union, or trust company;

(2) "Depositary bank" means the first bank to take an item even though it is also the payor bank, unless the item is presented for immediate payment over the counter;

(3) "Payor bank" means a bank that is the drawee of a draft;

(4) "Intermediary bank" means a bank to which an item is transferred in course of collection except the depositary or payor bank;

(5) "Collecting bank" means a bank handling an item for collection except the payor bank;

(6) "Presenting bank" means a bank presenting an item except a payor bank.

§ 4–106. Payable Through or Payable at Bank: Collecting Bank.

(a) If an item states that it is "payable through" a bank identified in the item, (i) the item designates the bank as a collecting bank and does not by itself authorize the bank to pay the item, and (ii) the item may be presented for payment only by or through the bank.

Alternative A

(b) If an item states that it is "payable at" a bank identified in the item, the item is equivalent to a draft drawn on the bank.

Alternative B

(b) If an item states that it is "payable at" a bank identified in the item, (i) the item designates the bank as a collecting bank and does not by itself authorize the bank to pay the item, and (ii) the item may be presented for payment only by or through the bank.

(c) If a draft names a nonbank drawee and it is unclear whether a bank named in the draft is a co-drawee or a collecting bank, the bank is a collecting bank.

As added in 1990.

§ 4–107. Separate Office of Bank.

A branch or separate office of a bank is a separate bank for the purpose of computing the time within which and determining the place at or to which action may be taken or notices or orders shall be given under this Article and under Article 3.

As amended in 1962 and 1990.

§ 4–108. Time of Receipt of Items.

(a) For the purpose of allowing time to process items, prove balances, and make the necessary entries on its books to determine its position for the day, a bank may fix an afternoon hour of 2 P.M. or later as a cutoff hour for the handling of money and items and the making of entries on its books.

(b) An item or deposit of money received on any day after a cutoff hour so fixed or after the close of the banking day may be treated as being received at the opening of the next banking day.

As amended in 1990.

§ 4–109. Delays.

(a) Unless otherwise instructed, a collecting bank in a good faith effort to secure payment of a specific item drawn on a payor other than a bank, and with or without the approval of any person involved, may waive, modify, or extend time limits imposed or permitted by this [act] for a period not exceeding two additional banking days without discharge of drawers or indorsers or liability to its transferor or a prior party.

(b) Delay by a collecting bank or payor bank beyond time limits prescribed or permitted by this [act] or by instructions is excused if (i) the delay is caused by interruption of communication or computer facilities, suspension of payments by another bank, war, emergency conditions, failure of equipment, or other circumstances beyond the control of the bank, and (ii) the bank exercises such diligence as the circumstances require.

§ 4–110. Electronic Presentment.

(a) "Agreement for electronic presentment" means an agreement, clearing-house rule, or Federal Reserve regulation or operating circular, providing that presentment of an item may be made by transmission of an image of an item or information describing the item ("presentment notice") rather than delivery of the item itself. The agreement may provide for procedures governing retention, presentment, payment, dishonor, and other matters concerning items subject to the agreement.

(b) Presentment of an item pursuant to an agreement for presentment is made when the presentment notice is received.

(c) If presentment is made by presentment notice, a reference to "item" or "check" in this Article means the presentment notice unless the context otherwise indicates.

As added in 1990.

§ 4–111. Statute of Limitations.

An action to enforce an obligation, duty, or right arising under this Article must be commenced within three years after the [cause of action] accrues.

As added in 1990.

Part 2 Collection of Items: Depositary and Collecting Banks

§ 4–201. Status of Collecting Bank as Agent and Provisional Status of Credits; Applicability of Article; Item Indorsed "Pay Any Bank".

(a) Unless a contrary intent clearly appears and before the time that a settlement given by a collecting bank for an item is or becomes final, the bank, with respect to an item, is an agent or sub-agent of the owner of the item and any settlement given for the item is provisional. This provision applies regardless of the form of indorsement or lack of indorsement and even though credit given for the item is subject to immediate withdrawal as of right or is in fact withdrawn; but the continuance of ownership of an item by its owner and any rights of the owner to proceeds of the item are subject to rights of a collecting bank, such as those resulting from outstanding advances on the item and rights of recoupment or setoff. If an item is handled by banks for purposes of presentment, payment, collection, or return, the relevant provisions of this Article apply even though action of the parties clearly establishes that a particular bank has purchased the item and is the owner of it.

(b) After an item has been indorsed with the words "pay any bank" or the like, only a bank may acquire the rights of a holder until the item has been:

(1) returned to the customer initiating collection; or

(2) specially indorsed by a bank to a person who is not a bank.

As amended in 1990.

§ 4–202. Responsibility for Collection or Return; When Action Timely.

(a) A collecting bank must exercise ordinary care in:

(1) presenting an item or sending it for presentment;

(2) sending notice of dishonor or nonpayment or returning an item other than a documentary draft to the bank's transferor after learning that the item has not been paid or accepted, as the case may be;

(3) settling for an item when the bank receives final settlement; and

(4) notifying its transferor of any loss or delay in transit within a reasonable time after discovery thereof.

(b) A collecting bank exercises ordinary care under subsection (a) by taking proper action before its midnight deadline following receipt of an item, notice, or settlement. Taking proper action within a reasonably longer time may constitute the exercise of ordinary care, but the bank has the burden of establishing timeliness.

(c) Subject to subsection (a)(1), a bank is not liable for the insolvency, neglect, misconduct, mistake, or default of another bank or person or for loss or destruction of an item in the possession of others or in transit.

As amended in 1990.

§ 4–203. Effect of Instructions.

Subject to Article 3 concerning conversion of instruments (Section 3–420) and restrictive indorsements (Section 3–206), only a collecting bank's transferor can give instructions that affect the bank or constitute notice to it, and a collecting bank is not liable to prior parties for any action taken pursuant to the instructions or in accordance with any agreement with its transferor.

§ 4–204. Methods of Sending and Presenting; Sending Directly to Payor Bank.

(a) A collecting bank shall send items by a reasonably prompt method, taking into consideration relevant instructions, the nature of the item, the number of those items on hand, the cost of collection involved, and the method generally used by it or others to present those items.

(b) A collecting bank may send:

    (1) an item directly to the payor bank;

    (2) an item to a nonbank payor if authorized by its transferor; and

    (3) an item other than documentary drafts to a nonbank payor, if authorized by Federal Reserve regulation or operating circular, clearing-house rule, or the like.

(c) Presentment may be made by a presenting bank at a place where the payor bank or other payor has requested that presentment be made.

As amended in 1990.

§ 4–205. Depositary Bank Holder of Unindorsed Item.

If a customer delivers an item to a depositary bank for collection:

(1) the depositary bank becomes a holder of the item at the time it receives the item for collection if the customer at the time of delivery was a holder of the item, whether or not the customer indorses the item, and, if the bank satisfies the other requirements of Section 3–302, it is a holder in due course; and

(2) the depositary bank warrants to collecting banks, the payor bank or other payor, and the drawer that the amount of the item was paid to the customer or deposited to the customer's account.

As amended in 1990.

§ 4–206. Transfer Between Banks.

Any agreed method that identifies the transferor bank is sufficient for the item's further transfer to another bank.

As amended in 1990.

§ 4–207. Transfer Warranties.

(a) A customer or collecting bank that transfers an item and receives a settlement or other consideration warrants to the transferee and to any subsequent collecting bank that:

    (1) the warrantor is a person entitled to enforce the item;

    (2) all signatures on the item are authentic and authorized;

    (3) the item has not been altered;

    (4) the item is not subject to a defense or claim in recoupment (Section 3–305(a)) of any party that can be asserted against the warrantor; and

    (5) the warrantor has no knowledge of any insolvency proceeding commenced with respect to the maker or acceptor or, in the case of an unaccepted draft, the drawer.

(b) If an item is dishonored, a customer or collecting bank transferring the item and receiving settlement or other consideration is obliged to pay the amount due on the item (i) according to the terms of the item at the time it was transferred, or (ii) if the transfer was of an incomplete item, according to its terms when completed as stated in Sections 3–115 and 3–407. The obligation of a transferor is owed to the transferee and to any subsequent collecting bank that takes the item in good faith. A transferor cannot disclaim its obligation under this subsection by an indorsement stating that it is made "without recourse" or otherwise disclaiming liability.

(c) A person to whom the warranties under subsection (a) are made and who took the item in good faith may recover from the warrantor as damages for breach of warranty an amount equal to the loss suffered as a result of the breach, but not more than the amount of the item plus expenses and loss of interest incurred as a result of the breach.

(d) The warranties stated in subsection (a) cannot be disclaimed with respect to checks. Unless notice of a claim for breach of warranty is given to the warrantor within 30 days after the claimant has reason to know of the breach and the identity of the warrantor, the warrantor is discharged to the extent of any loss caused by the delay in giving notice of the claim.

(e) A cause of action for breach of warranty under this section accrues when the claimant has reason to know of the breach.

As amended in 1990.

§ 4–208. Presentment Warranties.

(a) If an unaccepted draft is presented to the drawee for payment or acceptance and the drawee pays or accepts the draft, (i) the person obtaining payment or acceptance, at the time of presentment, and (ii) a previous transferor of the draft, at the time of transfer, warrant to the drawee that pays or accepts the draft in good faith that:

    (1) the warrantor is, or was, at the time the warrantor transferred the draft, a person entitled to enforce the draft or authorized to obtain payment or acceptance of the draft on behalf of a person entitled to enforce the draft;

    (2) the draft has not been altered; and

    (3) the warrantor has no knowledge that the signature of the purported drawer of the draft is unauthorized.

(b) A drawee making payment may recover from a warrantor damages for breach of warranty equal to the amount paid by the drawee less the amount the drawee received or is entitled to receive from the drawer because of the payment. In addition, the drawee is entitled to compensation for expenses and loss of interest resulting from the breach. The right of the drawee to recover damages under this subsection is not affected by any failure of the drawee to exercise ordinary care in making payment. If the drawee accepts the draft (i) breach of warranty is a defense to the obligation of the acceptor, and (ii) if the acceptor makes payment with respect to the draft, the acceptor is entitled to recover from a warrantor for breach of warranty the amounts stated in this subsection.

(c) If a drawee asserts a claim for breach of warranty under subsection (a) based on an unauthorized indorsement of the draft or an alteration of the draft, the warrantor may defend by proving that the indorsement is effective under Section 3–404 or 3–405 or the drawer is precluded under Section 3–406 or 4–406 from asserting against the drawee the unauthorized indorsement or alteration.

(d) If (i) a dishonored draft is presented for payment to the drawer or an indorser or (ii) any other item is presented for payment to a party obliged to pay the item, and the item is paid, the person obtaining payment and a prior transferor of the item warrant to the person making payment in good faith that the warrantor is, or was, at the time the warrantor transferred the item, a person entitled to enforce the item or authorized to obtain payment on behalf of a person entitled to enforce the item. The person making payment may recover from any warrantor for breach of warranty an amount equal to the amount paid plus expenses and loss of interest resulting from the breach.

(e) The warranties stated in subsections (a) and (d) cannot be disclaimed with respect to checks. Unless notice of a claim for breach of warranty is given to the warrantor within 30 days after the claimant has reason to know of the breach and the identity of the warrantor, the warrantor is discharged to the extent of any loss caused by the delay in giving notice of the claim.

(f) A cause of action for breach of warranty under this section accrues when the claimant has reason to know of the breach.

As amended in 1990.

§ 4–209. Encoding and Retention Warranties.

(a) A person who encodes information on or with respect to an item after issue warrants to any subsequent collecting bank and to the payor bank or other payor that the information is correctly encoded. If the customer of a depositary bank encodes, that bank also makes the warranty.

(b) A person who undertakes to retain an item pursuant to an agreement for electronic presentment warrants to any subsequent collecting bank and to the payor bank or other payor that retention and presentment of the item comply with the agreement. If a customer of a depositary bank undertakes to retain an item, that bank also makes this warranty.

(c) A person to whom warranties are made under this section and who took the item in good faith may recover from the warrantor as damages for breach of warranty an amount equal to the loss suffered as a result of the breach, plus expenses and loss of interest incurred as a result of the breach.

As added in 1990.

§ 4–210. Security Interest of Collecting Bank in Items, Accompanying Documents and Proceeds.

(a) A collecting bank has a security interest in an item and any accompanying documents or the proceeds of either:

(1) in case of an item deposited in an account, to the extent to which credit given for the item has been withdrawn or applied;

(2) in case of an item for which it has given credit available for withdrawal as of right, to the extent of the credit given, whether or not the credit is drawn upon or there is a right of charge-back; or

(3) if it makes an advance on or against the item.

(b) If credit given for several items received at one time or pursuant to a single agreement is withdrawn or applied in part, the security interest remains upon all the items, any accompanying documents or the proceeds of either. For the purpose of this section, credits first given are first withdrawn.

(c) Receipt by a collecting bank of a final settlement for an item is a realization on its security interest in the item, accompanying documents, and proceeds. So long as the bank does not receive final settlement for the item or give up possession of the item or accompanying documents for purposes other than collection, the security interest continues to that extent and is subject to Article 9, but:

(1) no security agreement is necessary to make the security interest enforceable (Section 9–203(1)(a));

(2) no filing is required to perfect the security interest; and

(3) the security interest has priority over conflicting perfected security interests in the item, accompanying documents, or proceeds.

As amended in 1990 and 1999.

§ 4–211. When Bank Gives Value for Purposes of Holder in Due Course.

For purposes of determining its status as a holder in due course, a bank has given value to the extent it has a security interest in an item, if the bank otherwise complies with the requirements of Section 3–302 on what constitutes a holder in due course.

As amended in 1990.

§ 4–212. Presentment by Notice of Item Not Payable by, Through, or at Bank; Liability of Drawer or Indorser.

(a) Unless otherwise instructed, a collecting bank may present an item not payable by, through, or at a bank by sending to the party to accept or pay a written notice that the bank holds the item for acceptance or payment. The notice must be sent in time to be received on or before the day when presentment is due and the bank must meet any requirement of the party to accept or pay under Section 3–501 by the close of the bank's next banking day after it knows of the requirement.

(b) If presentment is made by notice and payment, acceptance, or request for compliance with a requirement under Section 3–501 is not received by the close of business on the day after maturity or, in the case of demand items, by the close of business on the third banking day after notice was sent, the presenting bank may treat the item as dishonored and charge any drawer or indorser by sending it notice of the facts.

As amended in 1990.

§ 4–213. Medium and Time of Settlement by Bank.

(a) With respect to settlement by a bank, the medium and time of settlement may be prescribed by Federal Reserve regulations or circulars, clearing-house rules, and the like, or agreement. In the absence of such prescription:

(1) the medium of settlement is cash or credit to an account in a Federal Reserve bank of or specified by the person to receive settlement; and

(2) the time of settlement is:

(i) with respect to tender of settlement by cash, a cashier's check, or teller's check, when the cash or check is sent or delivered;

(ii) with respect to tender of settlement by credit in an account in a Federal Reserve Bank, when the credit is made;

(iii) with respect to tender of settlement by a credit or debit to an account in a bank, when the credit or debit is made or, in the case of tender of settlement by authority to charge an account, when the authority is sent or delivered; or

(iv) with respect to tender of settlement by a funds transfer, when payment is made pursuant to Section 4A–406(a) to the person receiving settlement.

(b) If the tender of settlement is not by a medium authorized by subsection (a) or the time of settlement is not fixed by subsection (a), no settlement occurs until the tender of settlement is accepted by the person receiving settlement.

(c) If settlement for an item is made by cashier's check or teller's check and the person receiving settlement, before its midnight deadline:

(1) presents or forwards the check for collection, settlement is final when the check is finally paid; or

(2) fails to present or forward the check for collection, settlement is final at the midnight deadline of the person receiving settlement.

(d) If settlement for an item is made by giving authority to charge the account of the bank giving settlement in the bank receiving settlement, settlement is final when the charge is made by the bank receiving settlement if there are funds available in the account for the amount of the item.

As amended in 1990.

§ 4–214. Right of Charge-Back or Refund; Liability of Collecting Bank: Return of Item.

(a) If a collecting bank has made provisional settlement with its customer for an item and fails by reason of dishonor, suspension of payments by a bank, or otherwise to receive settlement for the item which is or becomes final, the bank may revoke the settlement given by it, charge back the amount of any credit given for the item to its customer's account, or obtain refund from its customer, whether or not it is able to return the item, if by its midnight deadline or within a longer reasonable time after it learns the facts it returns the item or sends notification of the facts. If the return or notice is delayed beyond the bank's midnight deadline or a longer reasonable time after it learns the facts, the bank may revoke the settlement, charge back the credit, or obtain refund from its customer, but it is liable for any loss resulting from the delay. These rights to revoke, charge back, and obtain refund terminate if and when a settlement for the item received by the bank is or becomes final.

(b) A collecting bank returns an item when it is sent or delivered to the bank's customer or transferor or pursuant to its instructions.

(c) A depositary bank that is also the payor may charge back the amount of an item to its customer's account or obtain refund in accordance with the section governing return of an item received by a payor bank for credit on its books (Section 4–301).

(d) The right to charge back is not affected by:

(1) previous use of a credit given for the item; or

(2) failure by any bank to exercise ordinary care with respect to the item, but a bank so failing remains liable.

(e) A failure to charge back or claim refund does not affect other rights of the bank against the customer or any other party.

(f) If credit is given in dollars as the equivalent of the value of an item payable in foreign money, the dollar amount of any charge-back or refund must be calculated on the basis of the bank-offered spot rate for the foreign money prevailing on the day when the person entitled to the charge-back or refund learns that it will not receive payment in ordinary course.

As amended in 1990.

§ 4–215. Final Payment of Item by Payor Bank; When Provisional Debits and Credits Become Final; When Certain Credits Become Available for Withdrawal.

(a) An item is finally paid by a payor bank when the bank has first done any of the following:

(1) paid the item in cash;

(2) settled for the item without having a right to revoke the settlement under statute, clearing-house rule, or agreement; or

(3) made a provisional settlement for the item and failed to revoke the settlement in the time and manner permitted by statute, clearing-house rule, or agreement.

(b) If provisional settlement for an item does not become final, the item is not finally paid.

(c) If provisional settlement for an item between the presenting and payor banks is made through a clearing house or by debits or credits in an account between them, then to the extent that provisional debits or credits for the item are entered in accounts between the presenting and payor banks or between the presenting and successive prior collecting banks seriatim, they become final upon final payment of the item by the payor bank.

(d) If a collecting bank receives a settlement for an item which is or becomes final, the bank is accountable to its customer for the amount of the item and any provisional credit given for the item in an account with its customer becomes final.

(e) Subject to (i) applicable law stating a time for availability of funds and (ii) any right of the bank to apply the credit to an obligation of the customer, credit given by a bank for an item in a customer's account becomes available for withdrawal as of right:

(1) if the bank has received a provisional settlement for the item, when the settlement becomes final and the bank has had a reasonable time to receive return of the item and the item has not been received within that time;

(2) if the bank is both the depositary bank and the payor bank, and the item is finally paid, at the opening of the bank's second banking day following receipt of the item.

(f) Subject to applicable law stating a time for availability of funds and any right of a bank to apply a deposit to an obligation of the depositor, a deposit of money becomes available for withdrawal as of right at the opening of the bank's next banking day after receipt of the deposit.

As amended in 1990.

§ 4–216. Insolvency and Preference.

(a) If an item is in or comes into the possession of a payor or collecting bank that suspends payment and the item has not been finally paid, the item must be returned by the receiver, trustee, or agent in charge of the closed bank to the presenting bank or the closed bank's customer.

(b) If a payor bank finally pays an item and suspends payments without making a settlement for the item with its customer or the presenting bank which settlement is or becomes final, the owner of the item has a preferred claim against the payor bank.

(c) If a payor bank gives or a collecting bank gives or receives a provisional settlement for an item and thereafter suspends payments, the suspension does not prevent or interfere with the settlement's becoming final if the finality occurs automatically upon the lapse of certain time or the happening of certain events.

(d) If a collecting bank receives from subsequent parties settlement for an item, which settlement is or becomes final and the bank suspends payments without making a settlement for the item with its customer which settlement is or becomes final, the owner of the item has a preferred claim against the collecting bank.

As amended in 1990.

Part 3 Collection of Items: Payor Banks

§ 4–301. Deferred Posting; Recovery of Payment by Return of Items; Time of Dishonor; Return of Items by Payor Bank.

(a) If a payor bank settles for a demand item other than a documentary draft presented otherwise than for immediate payment over the counter before midnight of the banking day of receipt, the payor bank may revoke the settlement and recover the settlement if, before it has made final payment and before its midnight deadline, it

(1) returns the item; or

(2) sends written notice of dishonor or nonpayment if the item is unavailable for return.

(b) If a demand item is received by a payor bank for credit on its books, it may return the item or send notice of dishonor and may revoke any credit given or recover the amount thereof withdrawn by its customer, if it acts within the time limit and in the manner specified in subsection (a).

(c) Unless previous notice of dishonor has been sent, an item is dishonored at the time when for purposes of dishonor it is returned or notice sent in accordance with this section.

(d) An item is returned:

(1) as to an item presented through a clearing house, when it is delivered to the presenting or last collecting bank or to the clearing house or is sent or delivered in accordance with clearing-house rules; or

(2) in all other cases, when it is sent or delivered to the bank's customer or transferor or pursuant to instructions.

As amended in 1990.

§ 4–302. Payor Bank's Responsibility for Late Return of Item.

(a) If an item is presented to and received by a payor bank, the bank is accountable for the amount of:

(1) a demand item, other than a documentary draft, whether properly payable or not, if the bank, in any case in which it is not also the depositary bank, retains the item beyond midnight of the banking day of receipt without settling for it or, whether or not it is also the depositary bank, does not pay or return the item or send notice of dishonor until after its midnight deadline; or

(2) any other properly payable item unless, within the time allowed for acceptance or payment of that item, the bank either accepts or pays the item or returns it and accompanying documents.

(b) The liability of a payor bank to pay an item pursuant to subsection (a) is subject to defenses based on breach of a presentment warranty (Section 4–208) or proof that the person seeking enforcement of the liability presented or transferred the item for the purpose of defrauding the payor bank.

As amended in 1990.

§ 4–303. When Items Subject to Notice, Stop-Payment Order, Legal Process, or Setoff; Order in Which Items May Be Charged or Certified.

(a) Any knowledge, notice, or stop-payment order received by, legal process served upon, or setoff exercised by a payor bank comes too late to terminate, suspend, or modify the bank's right or duty to pay an item or to charge its customer's account for the item if the knowledge, notice, stop-payment order, or legal process is received or served and a reasonable time for the bank to act thereon expires or the setoff is exercised after the earliest of the following:

(1) the bank accepts or certifies the item;

(2) the bank pays the item in cash;

(3) the bank settles for the item without having a right to revoke the settlement under statute, clearing-house rule, or agreement;

(4) the bank becomes accountable for the amount of the item under Section 4–302 dealing with the payor bank's responsibility for late return of items; or

(5) with respect to checks, a cutoff hour no earlier than one hour after the opening of the next banking day after the banking day on which the bank received the check and no later than the close of that next banking day or, if no cutoff hour is fixed, the close of the next banking day after the banking day on which the bank received the check.

(b) Subject to subsection (a), items may be accepted, paid, certified, or charged to the indicated account of its customer in any order.

As amended in 1990.

Part 4 Relationship Between Payor Bank and Its Customer

§ 4–401. When Bank May Charge Customer's Account.

(a) A bank may charge against the account of a customer an item that is properly payable from the account even though the charge creates an overdraft. An item is properly payable if it is authorized by the customer and is in accordance with any agreement between the customer and bank.

(b) A customer is not liable for the amount of an overdraft if the customer neither signed the item nor benefited from the proceeds of the item.

(c) A bank may charge against the account of a customer a check that is otherwise properly payable from the account, even though payment was made before the date of the check, unless the customer has given notice to the bank of the postdating describing the check with reasonable certainty. The notice is effective for the period stated in Section 4–403(b) for stop-payment orders, and must be received at such time and in such manner as to afford the bank a reasonable opportunity to act on it before the bank takes any action with respect to the check described in Section 4–303. If a bank charges against the account of a customer a check before the date stated in the notice of postdating, the bank is liable for damages for the loss resulting from its act. The loss may include damages for dishonor of subsequent items under Section 4–402.

(d) A bank that in good faith makes payment to a holder may charge the indicated account of its customer according to:

(1) the original terms of the altered item; or

(2) the terms of the completed item, even though the bank knows the item has been completed unless the bank has notice that the completion was improper.

As amended in 1990.

§ 4–402. Bank's Liability to Customer for Wrongful Dishonor; Time of Determining Insufficiency of Account.

(a) Except as otherwise provided in this Article, a payor bank wrongfully dishonors an item if it dishonors an item that is properly payable, but a bank may dishonor an item that would create an overdraft unless it has agreed to pay the overdraft.

(b) A payor bank is liable to its customer for damages proximately caused by the wrongful dishonor of an item. Liability is limited to actual damages proved and may include damages for an arrest or prosecution of the customer or other consequential damages. Whether any consequential damages are proximately caused by the wrongful dishonor is a question of fact to be determined in each case.

(c) A payor bank's determination of the customer's account balance on which a decision to dishonor for insufficiency of available funds is based may be made at any time between the time the item is received by the payor bank and the time that the payor bank returns the item or gives notice in lieu of return, and no more than one determination need be made. If, at the election of the payor bank, a subsequent balance determination is made for the purpose of reevaluating the bank's decision to dishonor the item, the account balance at that time is determinative of whether a dishonor for insufficiency of available funds is wrongful.

As amended in 1990.

§ 4–403. Customer's Right to Stop Payment; Burden of Proof of Loss.

(a) A customer or any person authorized to draw on the account if there is more than one person may stop payment of any item drawn on the customer's account or close the account by an order to the bank describing the item or account with reasonable certainty received at a time and in a manner that affords the bank a reasonable opportunity to act on it before any action by the bank with respect to the item described in Section 4–303. If the signature of more than one person is required to draw on an account, any of these persons may stop payment or close the account.

(b) A stop-payment order is effective for six months, but it lapses after 14 calendar days if the original order was oral and was not confirmed in writing within that period. A stop-payment order may be renewed for additional six-month periods by a writing given to the bank within a period during which the stop-payment order is effective.

(c) The burden of establishing the fact and amount of loss resulting from the payment of an item contrary to a stop-payment order or order to close an account is on the customer. The loss from payment of an item contrary to a stop-payment order may include damages for dishonor of subsequent items under Section 4–402.

As amended in 1990.

§ 4–404. Bank Not Obliged to Pay Check More Than Six Months Old.

A bank is under no obligation to a customer having a checking account to pay a check, other than a certified check, which is presented more than six months after its date, but it may charge its customer's account for a payment made thereafter in good faith.

§ 4–405. Death or Incompetence of Customer.

(a) A payor or collecting bank's authority to accept, pay, or collect an item or to account for proceeds of its collection, if otherwise effective, is not rendered ineffective by incompetence of a customer of either bank existing at the time the item is issued or its collection is undertaken if the bank does not know of an adjudication of incompetence. Neither death nor incompetence of a customer revokes the authority to accept, pay, collect, or account until the bank knows of the fact of death or of an adjudication of incompetence and has reasonable opportunity to act on it.

(b) Even with knowledge, a bank may for 10 days after the date of death pay or certify checks drawn on or before the date unless ordered to stop payment by a person claiming an interest in the account.

As amended in 1990.

§ 4–406. Customer's Duty to Discover and Report Unauthorized Signature or Alteration.

(a) A bank that sends or makes available to a customer a statement of account showing payment of items for the account shall either return or make available to the customer the items paid or provide information in the statement of account sufficient to allow the customer reasonably to identify the items paid. The statement of account provides sufficient information if the item is described by item number, amount, and date of payment.

(b) If the items are not returned to the customer, the person retaining the items shall either retain the items or, if the items are destroyed, maintain the capacity to furnish legible copies of the items until the expiration of seven years after receipt of the items. A customer may request an item from the bank that paid the item, and that bank must provide in a reasonable time either the item or, if the item has been destroyed or is not otherwise obtainable, a legible copy of the item.

(c) If a bank sends or makes available a statement of account or items pursuant to subsection (a), the customer must exercise reasonable promptness in examining the statement or the items to determine whether any payment was not authorized because of an alteration of an item or because a purported signature by or on behalf of the customer was not authorized. If, based on the statement or items provided, the customer should reasonably have discovered the unauthorized payment, the customer must promptly notify the bank of the relevant facts.

(d) If the bank proves that the customer failed, with respect to an item, to comply with the duties imposed on the customer by subsection (c), the customer is precluded from asserting against the bank:

(1) the customer's unauthorized signature or any alteration on the item, if the bank also proves that it suffered a loss by reason of the failure; and

(2) the customer's unauthorized signature or alteration by the same wrongdoer on any other item paid in good faith by the bank if the payment was made before the bank received notice from the customer of the unauthorized signature or alteration and after the customer had been afforded a reasonable period of time, not exceeding 30 days, in which to examine the item or statement of account and notify the bank.

(e) If subsection (d) applies and the customer proves that the bank failed to exercise ordinary care in paying the item and that the failure substantially contributed to loss, the loss is allocated between the customer precluded and the bank asserting the preclusion according to the extent to which the failure of the customer to comply with subsection (c) and the failure of the bank to exercise ordinary care contributed to the loss. If the customer proves that the bank did not pay the item in good faith, the preclusion under subsection (d) does not apply.

(f) Without regard to care or lack of care of either the customer or the bank, a customer who does not within one year after the statement or items are made available to the customer (subsection (a)) discover and report the customer's unauthorized signature on or any alteration on the item is precluded from asserting against the bank the unauthorized signature or alteration. If there is a preclusion under this subsection, the payor bank may not recover for breach of warranty under Section 4–208 with respect to the unauthorized signature or alteration to which the preclusion applies.

As amended in 1990.

§ 4–407. Payor Bank's Right to Subrogation on Improper Payment.

If a payor has paid an item over the order of the drawer or maker to stop payment, or after an account has been closed, or otherwise under circumstances giving a basis for objection by the drawer or maker, to prevent unjust enrichment and only to the extent necessary to prevent loss to the bank by reason of its payment of the item, the payor bank is subrogated to the rights

(1) of any holder in due course on the item against the drawer or maker;

(2) of the payee or any other holder of the item against the drawer or maker either on the item or under the transaction out of which the item arose; and

(3) of the drawer or maker against the payee or any other holder of the item with respect to the transaction out of which the item arose.

As amended in 1990.

Part 5 Collection of Documentary Drafts

§ 4–501. Handling of Documentary Drafts; Duty to Send for Presentment and to Notify Customer of Dishonor.

A bank that takes a documentary draft for collection shall present or send the draft and accompanying documents for presentment and, upon learning that the draft has not been paid or accepted in due course, shall seasonably notify its customer of the fact even though it may have discounted or bought the draft or extended credit available for withdrawal as of right.

As amended in 1990.

§ 4–502. Presentment of "On Arrival" Drafts.

If a draft or the relevant instructions require presentment "on arrival", "when goods arrive" or the like, the collecting bank need not present until in its judgment a reasonable time for arrival of the goods has expired. Refusal to pay or accept because the goods have not arrived is not dishonor; the bank must notify its transferor of the refusal but need not present the draft again until it is instructed to do so or learns of the arrival of the goods.

§ 4–503. Responsibility of Presenting Bank for Documents and Goods; Report of Reasons for Dishonor; Referee in Case of Need.

Unless otherwise instructed and except as provided in Article 5, a bank presenting a documentary draft:

(1) must deliver the documents to the drawee on acceptance of the draft if it is payable more than three days after presentment, otherwise, only on payment; and

(2) upon dishonor, either in the case of presentment for acceptance or presentment for payment, may seek and follow instructions from any referee in case of need designated in the draft or, if the presenting bank does not choose to utilize the referee's services, it must use diligence and good faith to ascertain the reason for dishonor, must notify its transferor of the dishonor and of the results of its effort to ascertain the reasons therefor, and must request instructions.

However, the presenting bank is under no obligation with respect to goods represented by the documents except to follow any reasonable instructions seasonably received; it has a right to reimbursement for any expense incurred in following instructions and to prepayment of or indemnity for those expenses.

As amended in 1990.

§ 4–504. Privilege of Presenting Bank to Deal With Goods; Security Interest for Expenses.

(a) A presenting bank that, following the dishonor of a documentary draft, has seasonably requested instructions but does not receive them within a reasonable time may store, sell, or otherwise deal with the goods in any reasonable manner.

(b) For its reasonable expenses incurred by action under subsection (a) the presenting bank has a lien upon the goods or their proceeds, which may be foreclosed in the same manner as an unpaid seller's lien.

As amended in 1990.

Article 4A
FUNDS TRANSFERS

Part 1 Subject Matter and Definitions

§ 4A–101. Short Title.

This Article may be cited as Uniform Commercial Code—Funds Transfers.

§ 4A–102. Subject Matter.

Except as otherwise provided in Section 4A–108, this Article applies to funds transfers defined in Section 4A–104.

§ 4A–103. Payment Order–Definitions.

(a) In this Article:

(1) "Payment order" means an instruction of a sender to a receiving bank, transmitted orally, electronically, or in writing, to pay, or to cause another bank to pay, a fixed or determinable amount of money to a beneficiary if:

(i) the instruction does not state a condition to payment to the beneficiary other than time of payment,

(ii) the receiving bank is to be reimbursed by debiting an account of, or otherwise receiving payment from, the sender, and

(iii) the instruction is transmitted by the sender directly to the receiving bank or to an agent, funds-transfer system, or communication system for transmittal to the receiving bank.

(2) "Beneficiary" means the person to be paid by the beneficiary's bank.

(3) "Beneficiary's bank" means the bank identified in a payment order in which an account of the beneficiary is to be credited pursuant to the order or which otherwise is to make payment to the beneficiary if the order does not provide for payment to an account.

(4) "Receiving bank" means the bank to which the sender's instruction is addressed.

(5) "Sender" means the person giving the instruction to the receiving bank.

(b) If an instruction complying with subsection (a)(1) is to make more than one payment to a beneficiary, the instruction is a separate payment order with respect to each payment.

(c) A payment order is issued when it is sent to the receiving bank.

§ 4A–104. Funds Transfer–Definitions.

In this Article:

(a) "Funds transfer" means the series of transactions, beginning with the originator's payment order, made for the purpose of making payment to the beneficiary of the order. The term includes any payment order issued by the originator's bank or an intermediary bank intended to carry out the originator's payment order. A funds transfer is completed by acceptance by the beneficiary's bank of a payment order for the benefit of the beneficiary of the originator's payment order.

(b) "Intermediary bank" means a receiving bank other than the originator's bank or the beneficiary's bank.

(c) "Originator" means the sender of the first payment order in a funds transfer.

(d) "Originator's bank" means (i) the receiving bank to which the payment order of the originator is issued if the originator is not a bank, or (ii) the originator if the originator is a bank.

§ 4A–105. Other Definitions.

(a) In this Article:

(1) "Authorized account" means a deposit account of a customer in a bank designated by the customer as a source of payment of payment orders issued by the customer to the bank. If a customer does not so designate an account, any account of the customer is an authorized account if payment of a payment order from that account is not inconsistent with a restriction on the use of that account.

(2) "Bank" means a person engaged in the business of banking and includes a savings bank, savings and loan association, credit union, and trust company. A branch or separate office of a bank is a separate bank for purposes of this Article.

(3) "Customer" means a person, including a bank, having an account with a bank or from whom a bank has agreed to receive payment orders.

(4) "Funds-transfer business day" of a receiving bank means the part of a day during which the receiving bank is open for the receipt, processing, and transmittal of payment orders and cancellations and amendments of payment orders.

(5) "Funds-transfer system" means a wire transfer network, automated clearing house, or other communication system of a clearing house or other association of banks through which a payment order by a bank may be transmitted to the bank to which the order is addressed.

(6) "Good faith" means honesty in fact and the observance of reasonable commercial standards of fair dealing.

(7) "Prove" with respect to a fact means to meet the burden of establishing the fact (Section 1–201(8)).

(b) Other definitions applying to this Article and the sections in which they appear are:

"Acceptance"	Section 4A–209
"Beneficiary"	Section 4A–103
"Beneficiary's bank"	Section 4A–103
"Executed"	Section 4A–301
"Execution date"	Section 4A–301
"Funds transfer"	Section 4A–104
"Funds-transfer system rule"	Section 4A–501
"Intermediary bank"	Section 4A–104
"Originator"	Section 4A–104
"Originator's bank"	Section 4A–104
"Payment by beneficiary's bank to beneficiary"	Section 4A–405
"Payment by originator to beneficiary"	Section 4A–406
"Payment by sender to receiving bank"	Section 4A–403
"Payment date"	Section 4A–401
"Payment order"	Section 4A–103
"Receiving bank"	Section 4A–103
"Security procedure"	Section 4A–201
"Sender"	Section 4A–103

(c) The following definitions in Article 4 apply to this Article:

"Clearing house"	Section 4–104
"Item"	Section 4–104
"Suspends payments"	Section 4–104

(d) In addition, Article 1 contains general definitions and principles of construction and interpretation applicable throughout this Article.

§ 4A–106. Time Payment Order Is Received.

(a) The time of receipt of a payment order or communication cancelling or amending a payment order is determined by the rules applicable to receipt of a notice stated in Section 1–201(27). A receiving bank may fix a cut-off time or times on a funds-transfer business day for the receipt and processing of payment orders and communications cancelling or amending payment orders. Different cut-off times may apply to payment orders, cancellations, or amendments, or to different categories of payment orders, cancellations, or amendments. A cut-off time may apply to senders generally or different cut-off times may apply to different senders or categories of payment orders. If a payment order or communication cancelling or amending a payment order is received after the close of a funds-transfer business day or after the appropriate cut-off time on a funds-transfer business day, the receiving bank may treat the payment order or communication as received at the opening of the next funds-transfer business day.

(b) If this Article refers to an execution date or payment date or states a day on which a receiving bank is required to take action, and the date or day does not fall on a funds-transfer business day, the next day that is a funds-transfer business day is treated as the date or day stated, unless the contrary is stated in this Article.

§ 4A–107. Federal Reserve Regulations and Operating Circulars.

Regulations of the Board of Governors of the Federal Reserve System and operating circulars of the Federal Reserve Banks supersede any inconsistent provision of this Article to the extent of the inconsistency.

§ 4A–108. Exclusion of Consumer Transactions Governed by Federal Law.

This Article does not apply to a funds transfer any part of which is governed by the Electronic Fund Transfer Act of 1978 (Title XX, Public Law 95–630, 92 Stat. 3728, 15 U.S.C. § 1693 et seq.) as amended from time to time.

Part 2 Issue and Acceptance of Payment Order

§ 4A–201. Security Procedure.

"Security procedure" means a procedure established by agreement of a customer and a receiving bank for the purpose of (i) verifying that a payment order or communication amending or cancelling a payment order is that of the customer, or (ii) detecting error in the transmission or the content of the payment order or communication. A security procedure may require the use of algorithms or other codes, identifying words or numbers, encryption, callback procedures, or similar security devices. Comparison of a signature on a payment order or communication with an authorized specimen signature of the customer is not by itself a security procedure.

§ 4A–202. Authorized and Verified Payment Orders.

(a) A payment order received by the receiving bank is the authorized order of the person identified as sender if that person authorized the order or is otherwise bound by it under the law of agency.

(b) If a bank and its customer have agreed that the authenticity of payment orders issued to the bank in the name of the customer as sender will be verified pursuant to a security procedure, a payment order received by the receiving bank is effective as the order of the customer, whether or not authorized, if (i) the security procedure is a commercially reasonable method of providing security against unauthorized payment orders, and (ii) the bank proves that it accepted the payment order in good faith and in compliance with the security procedure and any written agreement or instruction of the customer restricting acceptance of payment orders issued in the name of the customer. The bank is not required to follow an instruction that violates a written agreement with the customer or notice of which is not received at a time and in a manner affording the bank a reasonable opportunity to act on it before the payment order is accepted.

(c) Commercial reasonableness of a security procedure is a question of law to be determined by considering the wishes of the customer expressed to the bank, the circumstances of the customer known to the bank, including the size, type, and frequency of payment orders normally issued by the customer to the bank, alternative security procedures offered to the customer, and security procedures in general use by customers and receiving banks similarly situated. A security procedure is deemed to be commercially reasonable if (i) the security procedure was chosen by the customer after the bank offered, and the customer refused, a security procedure that was commercially reasonable for that customer, and (ii) the customer expressly agreed in writing to be bound by any payment order, whether or not authorized, issued in its name and accepted by the bank in compliance with the security procedure chosen by the customer.

(d) The term "sender" in this Article includes the customer in whose name a payment order is issued if the order is the authorized order of the customer under subsection (a), or it is effective as the order of the customer under subsection (b).

(e) This section applies to amendments and cancellations of payment orders to the same extent it applies to payment orders.

(f) Except as provided in this section and in Section 4A–203(a)(1), rights and obligations arising under this section or Section 4A–203 may not be varied by agreement.

§ 4A–203. Unenforceability of Certain Verified Payment Orders.

(a) If an accepted payment order is not, under Section 4A–202(a), an authorized order of a customer identified as sender, but is effective as an order of the customer pursuant to Section 4A–202(b), the following rules apply:

(1) By express written agreement, the receiving bank may limit the extent to which it is entitled to enforce or retain payment of the payment order.

(2) The receiving bank is not entitled to enforce or retain payment of the payment order if the customer proves that the order was not caused, directly or indirectly, by a person (i) entrusted at any time with duties to act for the customer with respect to payment orders or the security procedure, or (ii) who obtained access to transmitting facilities of the customer or who obtained, from a source controlled by the customer and without authority of the receiving bank, information facilitating breach of the security procedure, regardless of how the information was obtained or whether the customer was at fault. Information includes any access device, computer software, or the like.

(b) This section applies to amendments of payment orders to the same extent it applies to payment orders.

§ 4A–204. Refund of Payment and Duty of Customer to Report with Respect to Unauthorized Payment Order.

(a) If a receiving bank accepts a payment order issued in the name of its customer as sender which is (i) not authorized and not effective as the order of the customer under Section 4A–202, or (ii) not enforceable, in whole or in part, against the customer under Section 4A–203, the bank shall refund any payment of the payment order received from the customer to the extent the bank is not entitled to enforce payment and shall pay interest on the refundable amount calculated from the date the bank received payment to the date of the refund. However, the customer is not entitled to interest from the bank on the amount to be refunded if the customer fails to exercise ordinary care to determine that the order was not authorized by the customer and to notify the bank of the relevant facts within a reasonable time not exceeding 90 days after the date the customer received notification from the bank that the order was accepted or that the customer's account was debited with respect to the order. The bank is not entitled to any recovery from the customer on account of a failure by the customer to give notification as stated in this section.

(b) Reasonable time under subsection (a) may be fixed by agreement as stated in Section 1–204(1), but the obligation of a receiving bank to refund payment as stated in subsection (a) may not otherwise be varied by agreement.

§ 4A–205. Erroneous Payment Orders.

(a) If an accepted payment order was transmitted pursuant to a security procedure for the detection of error and the payment order (i) erroneously instructed payment to a beneficiary not intended by the sender,

(ii) erroneously instructed payment in an amount greater than the amount intended by the sender, or (iii) was an erroneously transmitted duplicate of a payment order previously sent by the sender, the following rules apply:

(1) If the sender proves that the sender or a person acting on behalf of the sender pursuant to Section 4A–206 complied with the security procedure and that the error would have been detected if the receiving bank had also complied, the sender is not obliged to pay the order to the extent stated in paragraphs (2) and (3).

(2) If the funds transfer is completed on the basis of an erroneous payment order described in clause (i) or (iii) of subsection (a), the sender is not obliged to pay the order and the receiving bank is entitled to recover from the beneficiary any amount paid to the beneficiary to the extent allowed by the law governing mistake and restitution.

(3) If the funds transfer is completed on the basis of a payment order described in clause (ii) of subsection (a), the sender is not obliged to pay the order to the extent the amount received by the beneficiary is greater than the amount intended by the sender. In that case, the receiving bank is entitled to recover from the beneficiary the excess amount received to the extent allowed by the law governing mistake and restitution.

(b) If (i) the sender of an erroneous payment order described in subsection (a) is not obliged to pay all or part of the order, and (ii) the sender receives notification from the receiving bank that the order was accepted by the bank or that the sender's account was debited with respect to the order, the sender has a duty to exercise ordinary care, on the basis of information available to the sender, to discover the error with respect to the order and to advise the bank of the relevant facts within a reasonable time, not exceeding 90 days, after the bank's notification was received by the sender. If the bank proves that the sender failed to perform that duty, the sender is liable to the bank for the loss the bank proves it incurred as a result of the failure, but the liability of the sender may not exceed the amount of the sender's order.

(c) This section applies to amendments to payment orders to the same extent it applies to payment orders.

§ 4A–206. Transmission of Payment Order through Funds-Transfer or Other Communication System.

(a) If a payment order addressed to a receiving bank is transmitted to a funds-transfer system or other third party communication system for transmittal to the bank, the system is deemed to be an agent of the sender for the purpose of transmitting the payment order to the bank. If there is a discrepancy between the terms of the payment order transmitted to the system and the terms of the payment order transmitted by the system to the bank, the terms of the payment order of the sender are those transmitted by the system. This section does not apply to a funds-transfer system of the Federal Reserve Banks.

(b) This section applies to cancellations and amendments to payment orders to the same extent it applies to payment orders.

§ 4A–207. Misdescription of Beneficiary.

(a) Subject to subsection (b), if, in a payment order received by the beneficiary's bank, the name, bank account number, or other identification of the beneficiary refers to a nonexistent or unidentifiable person or account, no person has rights as a beneficiary of the order and acceptance of the order cannot occur.

(b) If a payment order received by the beneficiary's bank identifies the beneficiary both by name and by an identifying or bank account number and the name and number identify different persons, the following rules apply:

(1) Except as otherwise provided in subsection (c), if the beneficiary's bank does not know that the name and number refer to different persons, it may rely on the number as the proper identification of the beneficiary of the order. The beneficiary's bank need not determine whether the name and number refer to the same person.

(2) If the beneficiary's bank pays the person identified by name or knows that the name and number identify different persons, no person has rights as beneficiary except the person paid by the beneficiary's bank if that person was entitled to receive payment from the originator of the funds transfer. If no person has rights as beneficiary, acceptance of the order cannot occur.

(c) If (i) a payment order described in subsection (b) is accepted, (ii) the originator's payment order described the beneficiary inconsistently by name and number, and (iii) the beneficiary's bank pays the person identified by number as permitted by subsection (b)(1), the following rules apply:

(1) If the originator is a bank, the originator is obliged to pay its order.

(2) If the originator is not a bank and proves that the person identified by number was not entitled to receive payment from the originator, the originator is not obliged to pay its order unless the originator's bank proves that the originator, before acceptance of the originator's order, had notice that payment of a payment order issued by the originator might be made by the beneficiary's bank on the basis of an identifying or bank account number even if it identifies a person different from the named beneficiary. Proof of notice may be made by any admissible evidence. The originator's bank satisfies the burden of proof if it proves that the originator, before the payment order was accepted, signed a writing stating the information to which the notice relates.

(d) In a case governed by subsection (b)(1), if the beneficiary's bank rightfully pays the person identified by number and that person was not entitled to receive payment from the originator, the amount paid may be recovered from that person to the extent allowed by the law governing mistake and restitution as follows:

(1) If the originator is obliged to pay its payment order as stated in subsection (c), the originator has the right to recover.

(2) If the originator is not a bank and is not obliged to pay its payment order, the originator's bank has the right to recover.

§ 4A–208. Misdescription of Intermediary Bank or Beneficiary's Bank.

(a) This subsection applies to a payment order identifying an intermediary bank or the beneficiary's bank only by an identifying number.

(1) The receiving bank may rely on the number as the proper identification of the intermediary or beneficiary's bank and need not determine whether the number identifies a bank.

(2) The sender is obliged to compensate the receiving bank for any loss and expenses incurred by the receiving bank as a result of its reliance on the number in executing or attempting to execute the order.

(b) This subsection applies to a payment order identifying an inter-mediary bank or the beneficiary's bank both by name and an identi-fying number if the name and number identify different persons.

(1) If the sender is a bank, the receiving bank may rely on the number as the proper identification of the intermediary or bene-ficiary's bank if the receiving bank, when it executes the sender's order, does not know that the name and number identify differ-ent persons. The receiving bank need not determine whether the name and number refer to the same person or whether the num-ber refers to a bank. The sender is obliged to compensate the receiving bank for any loss and expenses incurred by the receiv-ing bank as a result of its reliance on the number in executing or attempting to execute the order.

(2) If the sender is not a bank and the receiving bank proves that the sender, before the payment order was accepted, had notice that the receiving bank might rely on the number as the proper identification of the intermediary or beneficiary's bank even if it identifies a person different from the bank identified by name, the rights and obligations of the sender and the receiving bank are governed by subsection (b)(1), as though the sender were a bank. Proof of notice may be made by any admis-sible evidence. The receiving bank satisfies the burden of proof if it proves that the sender, before the payment order was accepted, signed a writing stating the information to which the notice relates.

(3) Regardless of whether the sender is a bank, the receiving bank may rely on the name as the proper identification of the interme-diary or beneficiary's bank if the receiving bank, at the time it exe-cutes the sender's order, does not know that the name and number identify different persons. The receiving bank need not determine whether the name and number refer to the same person.

(4) If the receiving bank knows that the name and number identify different persons, reliance on either the name or the number in executing the sender's payment order is a breach of the obligation stated in Section 4A–302(a)(1).

§ 4A–209. Acceptance of Payment Order.

(a) Subject to subsection (d), a receiving bank other than the bene-ficiary's bank accepts a payment order when it executes the order.

(b) Subject to subsections (c) and (d), a beneficiary's bank accepts a payment order at the earliest of the following times:

(1) When the bank (i) pays the beneficiary as stated in Section 4A–405(a) or 4A–405(b), or (ii) notifies the beneficiary of receipt of the order or that the account of the beneficiary has been credited with respect to the order unless the notice indi-cates that the bank is rejecting the order or that funds with respect to the order may not be withdrawn or used until receipt of payment from the sender of the order;

(2) When the bank receives payment of the entire amount of the sender's order pursuant to Section 4A–403(a)(1) or 4A–403(a)(2); or

(3) The opening of the next funds-transfer business day of the bank following the payment date of the order if, at that time, the amount of the sender's order is fully covered by a with-drawable credit balance in an authorized account of the sender or the bank has otherwise received full payment from the sender, unless the order was rejected before that time or is

rejected within (i) one hour after that time, or (ii) one hour after the opening of the next business day of the sender fol-lowing the payment date if that time is later. If notice of rejec-tion is received by the sender after the payment date and the authorized account of the sender does not bear interest, the bank is obliged to pay interest to the sender on the amount of the order for the number of days elapsing after the payment date to the day the sender receives notice or learns that the order was not accepted, counting that day as an elapsed day. If the withdrawable credit balance during that period falls below the amount of the order, the amount of interest payable is reduced accordingly.

(c) Acceptance of a payment order cannot occur before the order is received by the receiving bank. Acceptance does not occur under subsection (b)(2) or (b)(3) if the beneficiary of the payment order does not have an account with the receiving bank, the account has been closed, or the receiving bank is not permitted by law to receive credits for the beneficiary's account.

(d) A payment order issued to the originator's bank cannot be accepted until the payment date if the bank is the beneficiary's bank, or the execution date if the bank is not the beneficiary's bank. If the originator's bank executes the originator's payment order before the execution date or pays the beneficiary of the originator's payment order before the payment date and the payment order is subsequently cancelled pursuant to Section 4A–211(b), the bank may recover from the beneficiary any payment received to the extent allowed by the law governing mistake and restitution.

§ 4A–210. Rejection of Payment Order.

(a) A payment order is rejected by the receiving bank by a notice of rejection transmitted to the sender orally, electronically, or in writing. A notice of rejection need not use any particular words and is suffi-cient if it indicates that the receiving bank is rejecting the order or will not execute or pay the order. Rejection is effective when the notice is given if transmission is by a means that is reasonable in the circumstances. If notice of rejection is given by a means that is not reasonable, rejection is effective when the notice is received. If an agreement of the sender and receiving bank establishes the means to be used to reject a payment order, (i) any means complying with the agreement is reasonable and (ii) any means not complying is not rea-sonable unless no significant delay in receipt of the notice resulted from the use of the noncomplying means.

(b) This subsection applies if a receiving bank other than the benefi-ciary's bank fails to execute a payment order despite the existence on the execution date of a withdrawable credit balance in an authorized account of the sender sufficient to cover the order. If the sender does not receive notice of rejection of the order on the execution date and the authorized account of the sender does not bear interest, the bank is obliged to pay interest to the sender on the amount of the order for the number of days elapsing after the execution date to the earlier of the day the order is cancelled pursuant to Section 4A–211(d) or the day the sender receives notice or learns that the order was not executed, count-ing the final day of the period as an elapsed day. If the withdrawable credit balance during that period falls below the amount of the order, the amount of interest is reduced accordingly.

(c) If a receiving bank suspends payments, all unaccepted payment orders issued to it are are deemed rejected at the time the bank sus-pends payments.

(d) Acceptance of a payment order precludes a later rejection of the order. Rejection of a payment order precludes a later acceptance of the order.

§ 4A–211. Cancellation and Amendment of Payment Order.

(a) A communication of the sender of a payment order cancelling or amending the order may be transmitted to the receiving bank orally, electronically, or in writing. If a security procedure is in effect between the sender and the receiving bank, the communication is not effective to cancel or amend the order unless the communication is verified pursuant to the security procedure or the bank agrees to the cancellation or amendment.

(b) Subject to subsection (a), a communication by the sender cancelling or amending a payment order is effective to cancel or amend the order if notice of the communication is received at a time and in a manner affording the receiving bank a reasonable opportunity to act on the communication before the bank accepts the payment order.

(c) After a payment order has been accepted, cancellation or amendment of the order is not effective unless the receiving bank agrees or a funds-transfer system rule allows cancellation or amendment without agreement of the bank.

> (1) With respect to a payment order accepted by a receiving bank other than the beneficiary's bank, cancellation or amendment is not effective unless a conforming cancellation or amendment of the payment order issued by the receiving bank is also made.

> (2) With respect to a payment order accepted by the beneficiary's bank, cancellation or amendment is not effective unless the order was issued in execution of an unauthorized payment order, or because of a mistake by a sender in the funds transfer which resulted in the issuance of a payment order (i) that is a duplicate of a payment order previously issued by the sender, (ii) that orders payment to a beneficiary not entitled to receive payment from the originator, or (iii) that orders payment in an amount greater than the amount the beneficiary was entitled to receive from the originator. If the payment order is cancelled or amended, the beneficiary's bank is entitled to recover from the beneficiary any amount paid to the beneficiary to the extent allowed by the law governing mistake and restitution.

(d) An unaccepted payment order is cancelled by operation of law at the close of the fifth funds-transfer business day of the receiving bank after the execution date or payment date of the order.

(e) A cancelled payment order cannot be accepted. If an accepted payment order is cancelled, the acceptance is nullified and no person has any right or obligation based on the acceptance. Amendment of a payment order is deemed to be cancellation of the original order at the time of amendment and issue of a new payment order in the amended form at the same time.

(f) Unless otherwise provided in an agreement of the parties or in a funds-transfer system rule, if the receiving bank, after accepting a payment order, agrees to cancellation or amendment of the order by the sender or is bound by a funds-transfer system rule allowing cancellation or amendment without the bank's agreement, the sender, whether or not cancellation or amendment is effective, is liable to the bank for any loss and expenses, including reasonable attorney's fees, incurred by the bank as a result of the cancellation or amendment or attempted cancellation or amendment.

(g) A payment order is not revoked by the death or legal incapacity of the sender unless the receiving bank knows of the death or of an adjudication of incapacity by a court of competent jurisdiction and has reasonable opportunity to act before acceptance of the order.

(h) A funds-transfer system rule is not effective to the extent it conflicts with subsection (c)(2).

§ 4A–212. Liability and Duty of Receiving Bank Regarding Unaccepted Payment Order.

If a receiving bank fails to accept a payment order that it is obliged by express agreement to accept, the bank is liable for breach of the agreement to the extent provided in the agreement or in this Article, but does not otherwise have any duty to accept a payment order or, before acceptance, to take any action, or refrain from taking action, with respect to the order except as provided in this Article or by express agreement. Liability based on acceptance arises only when acceptance occurs as stated in Section 4A–209, and liability is limited to that provided in this Article. A receiving bank is not the agent of the sender or beneficiary of the payment order it accepts, or of any other party to the funds transfer, and the bank owes no duty to any party to the funds transfer except as provided in this Article or by express agreement.

Part 3 Execution of Sender's Payment Order by Receiving Bank

§ 4A–301. Execution and Execution Date.

(a) A payment order is "executed" by the receiving bank when it issues a payment order intended to carry out the payment order received by the bank. A payment order received by the beneficiary's bank can be accepted but cannot be executed.

(b) "Execution date" of a payment order means the day on which the receiving bank may properly issue a payment order in execution of the sender's order. The execution date may be determined by instruction of the sender but cannot be earlier than the day the order is received and, unless otherwise determined, is the day the order is received. If the sender's instruction states a payment date, the execution date is the payment date or an earlier date on which execution is reasonably necessary to allow payment to the beneficiary on the payment date.

§ 4A–302. Obligations of Receiving Bank in Execution of Payment Order.

(a) Except as provided in subsections (b) through (d), if the receiving bank accepts a payment order pursuant to Section 4A–209(a), the bank has the following obligations in executing the order:

> (1) The receiving bank is obliged to issue, on the execution date, a payment order complying with the sender's order and to follow the sender's instructions concerning (i) any intermediary bank or funds-transfer system to be used in carrying out the funds transfer, or (ii) the means by which payment orders are to be transmitted in the funds transfer. If the originator's bank issues a payment order to an intermediary bank, the originator's bank is obliged to instruct the intermediary bank according to the instruction of the originator. An intermediary bank in the funds transfer is similarly bound by an instruction given to it by the sender of the payment order it accepts.

> (2) If the sender's instruction states that the funds transfer is to be carried out telephonically or by wire transfer or otherwise indicates that the funds transfer is to be carried out by the most expeditious means, the receiving bank is obliged to transmit its payment order by the most expeditious available means, and to

instruct any intermediary bank accordingly. If a sender's instruction states a payment date, the receiving bank is obliged to transmit its payment order at a time and by means reasonably necessary to allow payment to the beneficiary on the payment date or as soon thereafter as is feasible.

(b) Unless otherwise instructed, a receiving bank executing a payment order may (i) use any funds-transfer system if use of that system is reasonable in the circumstances, and (ii) issue a payment order to the beneficiary's bank or to an intermediary bank through which a payment order conforming to the sender's order can expeditiously be issued to the beneficiary's bank if the receiving bank exercises ordinary care in the selection of the intermediary bank. A receiving bank is not required to follow an instruction of the sender designating a funds-transfer system to be used in carrying out the funds transfer if the receiving bank, in good faith, determines that it is not feasible to follow the instruction or that following the instruction would unduly delay completion of the funds transfer.

(c) Unless subsection (a)(2) applies or the receiving bank is otherwise instructed, the bank may execute a payment order by transmitting its payment order by first class mail or by any means reasonable in the circumstances. If the receiving bank is instructed to execute the sender's order by transmitting its payment order by a particular means, the receiving bank may issue its payment order by the means stated or by any means as expeditious as the means stated.

(d) Unless instructed by the sender, (i) the receiving bank may not obtain payment of its charges for services and expenses in connection with the execution of the sender's order by issuing a payment order in an amount equal to the amount of the sender's order less the amount of the charges, and (ii) may not instruct a subsequent receiving bank to obtain payment of its charges in the same manner.

§ 4A–303. Erroneous Execution of Payment Order.

(a) A receiving bank that (i) executes the payment order of the sender by issuing a payment order in an amount greater than the amount of the sender's order, or (ii) issues a payment order in execution of the sender's order and then issues a duplicate order, is entitled to payment of the amount of the sender's order under Section 4A–402(c) if that subsection is otherwise satisfied. The bank is entitled to recover from the beneficiary of the erroneous order the excess payment received to the extent allowed by the law governing mistake and restitution.

(b) A receiving bank that executes the payment order of the sender by issuing a payment order in an amount less than the amount of the sender's order is entitled to payment of the amount of the sender's order under Section 4A–402(c) if (i) that subsection is otherwise satisfied and (ii) the bank corrects its mistake by issuing an additional payment order for the benefit of the beneficiary of the sender's order. If the error is not corrected, the issuer of the erroneous order is entitled to receive or retain payment from the sender of the order it accepted only to the extent of the amount of the erroneous order. This subsection does not apply if the receiving bank executes the sender's payment order by issuing a payment order in an amount less than the amount of the sender's order for the purpose of obtaining payment of its charges for services and expenses pursuant to instruction of the sender.

(c) If a receiving bank executes the payment order of the sender by issuing a payment order to a beneficiary different from the beneficiary of the sender's order and the funds transfer is completed on the basis of that error, the sender of the payment order that was erroneously executed and all previous senders in the funds transfer are not obliged to pay the payment orders they issued. The issuer of the erroneous order is entitled to recover from the beneficiary of the order the payment received to the extent allowed by the law governing mistake and restitution.

§ 4A–304. Duty of Sender to Report Erroneously Executed Payment Order.

If the sender of a payment order that is erroneously executed as stated in Section 4A–303 receives notification from the receiving bank that the order was executed or that the sender's account was debited with respect to the order, the sender has a duty to exercise ordinary care to determine, on the basis of information available to the sender, that the order was erroneously executed and to notify the bank of the relevant facts within a reasonable time not exceeding 90 days after the notification from the bank was received by the sender. If the sender fails to perform that duty, the bank is not obliged to pay interest on any amount refundable to the sender under Section 4A–402(d) for the period before the bank learns of the execution error. The bank is not entitled to any recovery from the sender on account of a failure by the sender to perform the duty stated in this section.

§ 4A–305. Liability for Late or Improper Execution or Failure to Execute Payment Order.

(a) If a funds transfer is completed but execution of a payment order by the receiving bank in breach of Section 4A–302 results in delay in payment to the beneficiary, the bank is obliged to pay interest to either the originator or the beneficiary of the funds transfer for the period of delay caused by the improper execution. Except as provided in subsection (c), additional damages are not recoverable.

(b) If execution of a payment order by a receiving bank in breach of Section 4A–302 results in (i) noncompletion of the funds transfer, (ii) failure to use an intermediary bank designated by the originator, or (iii) issuance of a payment order that does not comply with the terms of the payment order of the originator, the bank is liable to the originator for its expenses in the funds transfer and for incidental expenses and interest losses, to the extent not covered by subsection (a), resulting from the improper execution. Except as provided in subsection (c), additional damages are not recoverable.

(c) In addition to the amounts payable under subsections (a) and (b), damages, including consequential damages, are recoverable to the extent provided in an express written agreement of the receiving bank.

(d) If a receiving bank fails to execute a payment order it was obliged by express agreement to execute, the receiving bank is liable to the sender for its expenses in the transaction and for incidental expenses and interest losses resulting from the failure to execute. Additional damages, including consequential damages, are recoverable to the extent provided in an express written agreement of the receiving bank, but are not otherwise recoverable.

(e) Reasonable attorney's fees are recoverable if demand for compensation under subsection (a) or (b) is made and refused before an action is brought on the claim. If a claim is made for breach of an agreement under subsection (d) and the agreement does not provide for damages, reasonable attorney's fees are recoverable if demand for compensation under subsection (d) is made and refused before an action is brought on the claim.

(f) Except as stated in this section, the liability of a receiving bank under subsections (a) and (b) may not be varied by agreement.

Part 4 Payment

§ 4A–401. Payment Date.

"Payment date" of a payment order means the day on which the amount of the order is payable to the beneficiary by the beneficiary's bank. The payment date may be determined by instruction of the sender but cannot be earlier than the day the order is received by the beneficiary's bank and, unless otherwise determined, is the day the order is received by the beneficiary's bank.

§ 4A–402. Obligation of Sender to Pay Receiving Bank.

(a) This section is subject to Sections 4A–205 and 4A–207.

(b) With respect to a payment order issued to the beneficiary's bank, acceptance of the order by the bank obliges the sender to pay the bank the amount of the order, but payment is not due until the payment date of the order.

(c) This subsection is subject to subsection (e) and to Section 4A–303. With respect to a payment order issued to a receiving bank other than the beneficiary's bank, acceptance of the order by the receiving bank obliges the sender to pay the bank the amount of the sender's order. Payment by the sender is not due until the execution date of the sender's order. The obligation of that sender to pay its payment order is excused if the funds transfer is not completed by acceptance by the beneficiary's bank of a payment order instructing payment to the beneficiary of that sender's payment order.

(d) If the sender of a payment order pays the order and was not obliged to pay all or part of the amount paid, the bank receiving payment is obliged to refund payment to the extent the sender was not obliged to pay. Except as provided in Sections 4A–204 and 4A–304, interest is payable on the refundable amount from the date of payment.

(e) If a funds transfer is not completed as stated in subsection (c) and an intermediary bank is obliged to refund payment as stated in subsection (d) but is unable to do so because not permitted by applicable law or because the bank suspends payments, a sender in the funds transfer that executed a payment order in compliance with an instruction, as stated in Section 4A–302(a)(1), to route the funds transfer through that intermediary bank is entitled to receive or retain payment from the sender of the payment order that it accepted. The first sender in the funds transfer that issued an instruction requiring routing through that intermediary bank is subrogated to the right of the bank that paid the intermediary bank to refund as stated in subsection (d).

(f) The right of the sender of a payment order to be excused from the obligation to pay the order as stated in subsection (c) or to receive refund under subsection (d) may not be varied by agreement.

§ 4A–403. Payment by Sender to Receiving Bank.

(a) Payment of the sender's obligation under Section 4A–402 to pay the receiving bank occurs as follows:

(1) If the sender is a bank, payment occurs when the receiving bank receives final settlement of the obligation through a Federal Reserve Bank or through a funds-transfer system.

(2) If the sender is a bank and the sender (i) credited an account of the receiving bank with the sender, or (ii) caused an account of the receiving bank in another bank to be credited, payment

occurs when the credit is withdrawn or, if not withdrawn, at midnight of the day on which the credit is withdrawable and the receiving bank learns of that fact.

(3) If the receiving bank debits an account of the sender with the receiving bank, payment occurs when the debit is made to the extent the debit is covered by a withdrawable credit balance in the account.

(b) If the sender and receiving bank are members of a funds-transfer system that nets obligations multilaterally among participants, the receiving bank receives final settlement when settlement is complete in accordance with the rules of the system. The obligation of the sender to pay the amount of a payment order transmitted through the funds-transfer system may be satisfied, to the extent permitted by the rules of the system, by setting off and applying against the sender's obligation the right of the sender to receive payment from the receiving bank of the amount of any other payment order transmitted to the sender by the receiving bank through the funds-transfer system. The aggregate balance of obligations owed by each sender to each receiving bank in the funds-transfer system may be satisfied, to the extent permitted by the rules of the system, by setting off and applying against that balance the aggregate balance of obligations owed to the sender by other members of the system. The aggregate balance is determined after the right of setoff stated in the second sentence of this subsection has been exercised.

(c) If two banks transmit payment orders to each other under an agreement that settlement of the obligations of each bank to the other under Section 4A–402 will be made at the end of the day or other period, the total amount owed with respect to all orders transmitted by one bank shall be set off against the total amount owed with respect to all orders transmitted by the other bank. To the extent of the setoff, each bank has made payment to the other.

(d) In a case not covered by subsection (a), the time when payment of the sender's obligation under Section 4A–402(b) or 4A–402(c) occurs is governed by applicable principles of law that determine when an obligation is satisfied.

§ 4A–404. Obligation of Beneficiary's Bank to Pay and Give Notice to Beneficiary.

(a) Subject to Sections 4A–211(e), 4A–405(d), and 4A–405(e), if a beneficiary's bank accepts a payment order, the bank is obliged to pay the amount of the order to the beneficiary of the order. Payment is due on the payment date of the order, but if acceptance occurs on the payment date after the close of the funds-transfer business day of the bank, payment is due on the next funds-transfer business day. If the bank refuses to pay after demand by the beneficiary and receipt of notice of particular circumstances that will give rise to consequential damages as a result of nonpayment, the beneficiary may recover damages resulting from the refusal to pay to the extent the bank had notice of the damages, unless the bank proves that it did not pay because of a reasonable doubt concerning the right of the beneficiary to payment.

(b) If a payment order accepted by the beneficiary's bank instructs payment to an account of the beneficiary, the bank is obliged to notify the beneficiary of receipt of the order before midnight of the next funds-transfer business day following the payment date. If the payment order does not instruct payment to an account of the beneficiary, the bank is required to notify the beneficiary only if notice is required by the order. Notice may be given by first class mail or any other means reasonable in the circumstances. If the bank fails to give the required notice, the bank is obliged to pay interest to the beneficiary on the amount of the payment order from the day notice should have been given until the day the beneficiary learned of receipt of the payment order by the bank. No other damages are recoverable. Reasonable attorney's fees are also recoverable if demand for interest is made and refused before an action is brought on the claim.

(c) The right of a beneficiary to receive payment and damages as stated in subsection (a) may not be varied by agreement or a funds-transfer system rule. The right of a beneficiary to be notified as stated in subsection (b) may be varied by agreement of the beneficiary or by a funds-transfer system rule if the beneficiary is notified of the rule before initiation of the funds transfer.

§ 4A–405. Payment by Beneficiary's Bank to Beneficiary.

(a) If the beneficiary's bank credits an account of the beneficiary of a payment order, payment of the bank's obligation under Section 4A–404(a) occurs when and to the extent (i) the beneficiary is notified of the right to withdraw the credit, (ii) the bank lawfully applies the credit to a debt of the beneficiary, or (iii) funds with respect to the order are otherwise made available to the beneficiary by the bank.

(b) If the beneficiary's bank does not credit an account of the beneficiary of a payment order, the time when payment of the bank's obligation under Section 4A–404(a) occurs is governed by principles of law that determine when an obligation is satisfied.

(c) Except as stated in subsections (d) and (e), if the beneficiary's bank pays the beneficiary of a payment order under a condition to payment or agreement of the beneficiary giving the bank the right to recover payment from the beneficiary if the bank does not receive payment of the order, the condition to payment or agreement is not enforceable.

(d) A funds-transfer system rule may provide that payments made to beneficiaries of funds transfers made through the system are provisional until receipt of payment by the beneficiary's bank of the payment order it accepted. A beneficiary's bank that makes a payment that is provisional under the rule is entitled to refund from the beneficiary if (i) the rule requires that both the beneficiary and the originator be given notice of the provisional nature of the payment before the funds transfer is initiated, (ii) the beneficiary, the beneficiary's bank, and the originator's bank agreed to be bound by the rule, and (iii) the beneficiary's bank did not receive payment of the payment order that it accepted. If the beneficiary is obliged to refund payment to the beneficiary's bank, acceptance of the payment order by the beneficiary's bank is nullified and no payment by the originator of the funds transfer to the beneficiary occurs under Section 4A–406.

(e) This subsection applies to a funds transfer that includes a payment order transmitted over a funds-transfer system that (i) nets obligations multilaterally among participants, and (ii) has in effect a loss-sharing agreement among participants for the purpose of providing funds necessary to complete settlement of the obligations of one or more participants that do not meet their settlement obligations. If the beneficiary's bank in the funds transfer accepts a payment order and the system fails to complete settlement pursuant to its rules with respect to any payment order in the funds transfer, (i) the acceptance by the beneficiary's bank is nullified and no person has any right or obligation based on the acceptance, (ii) the beneficiary's bank is entitled to recover payment from the beneficiary, (iii) no payment by the originator to the beneficiary occurs under Section 4A–406, and (iv) subject to Section 4A–402(e), each sender in the funds transfer is excused from its obligation to pay its payment order under Section 4A–402(c) because the funds transfer has not been completed.

§ 4A–406. Payment by Originator to Beneficiary; Discharge of Underlying Obligation.

(a) Subject to Sections 4A–211(e), 4A–405(d), and 4A–405(e), the originator of a funds transfer pays the beneficiary of the originator's payment order (i) at the time a payment order for the benefit of the beneficiary is accepted by the beneficiary's bank in the funds transfer and (ii) in an amount equal to the amount of the order accepted by the beneficiary's bank, but not more than the amount of the originator's order.

(b) If payment under subsection (a) is made to satisfy an obligation, the obligation is discharged to the same extent discharge would result from payment to the beneficiary of the same amount in money, unless (i) the payment under subsection (a) was made by a means prohibited by the contract of the beneficiary with respect to the obligation, (ii) the beneficiary, within a reasonable time after receiving notice of receipt of the order by the beneficiary's bank, notified the originator of the beneficiary's refusal of the payment, (iii) funds with respect to the order were not withdrawn by the beneficiary or applied to a debt of the beneficiary, and (iv) the beneficiary would suffer a loss that could reasonably have been avoided if payment had been made by a means complying with the contract. If payment by the originator does not result in discharge under this section, the originator is subrogated to the rights of the beneficiary to receive payment from the beneficiary's bank under Section 4A–404(a).

(c) For the purpose of determining whether discharge of an obligation occurs under subsection (b), if the beneficiary's bank accepts a payment order in an amount equal to the amount of the originator's payment order less charges of one or more receiving banks in the funds transfer, payment to the beneficiary is deemed to be in the amount of the originator's order unless upon demand by the beneficiary the originator does not pay the beneficiary the amount of the deducted charges.

(d) Rights of the originator or of the beneficiary of a funds transfer under this section may be varied only by agreement of the originator and the beneficiary.

Part 5 M\iscellaneous Provisions

§ 4A–501. Variation by Agreement and Effect of Funds-Transfer System Rule.

(a) Except as otherwise provided in this Article, the rights and obligations of a party to a funds transfer may be varied by agreement of the affected party.

(b) "Funds-transfer system rule" means a rule of an association of banks (i) governing transmission of payment orders by means of a funds-transfer system of the association or rights and obligations with respect to those orders, or (ii) to the extent the rule governs rights and obligations between banks that are parties to a funds transfer in which a Federal Reserve Bank, acting as an intermediary bank, sends a payment order to the beneficiary's bank. Except as otherwise provided in this Article, a funds-transfer system rule governing rights and obligations between participating banks using the system may be effective even if the rule conflicts with this Article and indirectly affects another party to the funds transfer who does not consent to the rule. A funds-transfer system rule may also govern rights and obligations of parties other than participating banks using the system to the extent stated in Sections 4A–404(c), 4A–405(d), and 4A–507(c).

§ 4A–502. Creditor Process Served on Receiving Bank; Setoff by Beneficiary's Bank.

(a) As used in this section, "creditor process" means levy, attachment, garnishment, notice of lien, sequestration, or similar process issued by or on behalf of a creditor or other claimant with respect to an account.

(b) This subsection applies to creditor process with respect to an authorized account of the sender of a payment order if the creditor process is served on the receiving bank. For the purpose of determining rights with respect to the creditor process, if the receiving bank accepts the payment order the balance in the authorized account is deemed to be reduced by the amount of the payment order to the extent the bank did not otherwise receive payment of the order, unless the creditor process is served at a time and in a manner affording the bank a reasonable opportunity to act on it before the bank accepts the payment order.

(c) If a beneficiary's bank has received a payment order for payment to the beneficiary's account in the bank, the following rules apply:

(1) The bank may credit the beneficiary's account. The amount credited may be set off against an obligation owed by the beneficiary to the bank or may be applied to satisfy creditor process served on the bank with respect to the account.

(2) The bank may credit the beneficiary's account and allow withdrawal of the amount credited unless creditor process with respect to the account is served at a time and in a manner affording the bank a reasonable opportunity to act to prevent withdrawal.

(3) If creditor process with respect to the beneficiary's account has been served and the bank has had a reasonable opportunity to act on it, the bank may not reject the payment order except for a reason unrelated to the service of process.

(d) Creditor process with respect to a payment by the originator to the beneficiary pursuant to a funds transfer may be served only on the beneficiary's bank with respect to the debt owed by that bank to the beneficiary. Any other bank served with the creditor process is not obliged to act with respect to the process.

§ 4A–503. Injunction or Restraining Order with Respect to Funds Transfer.

For proper cause and in compliance with applicable law, a court may restrain (i) a person from issuing a payment order to initiate a funds transfer, (ii) an originator's bank from executing the payment order of the originator, or (iii) the beneficiary's bank from releasing funds to the beneficiary or the beneficiary from withdrawing the funds. A court may not otherwise restrain a person from issuing a payment order, paying or receiving payment of a payment order, or otherwise acting with respect to a funds transfer.

§ 4A–504. Order in Which Items and Payment Orders May Be Charged to Account; Order of Withdrawals from Account.

(a) If a receiving bank has received more than one payment order of the sender or one or more payment orders and other items that are payable from the sender's account, the bank may charge the sender's account with respect to the various orders and items in any sequence.

(b) In determining whether a credit to an account has been withdrawn by the holder of the account or applied to a debt of the holder of the account, credits first made to the account are first withdrawn or applied.

§ 4A–505. Preclusion of Objection to Debit of Customer's Account.

If a receiving bank has received payment from its customer with respect to a payment order issued in the name of the customer as sender and accepted by the bank, and the customer received notification reasonably identifying the order, the customer is precluded from asserting that the bank is not entitled to retain the payment unless the customer notifies the bank of the customer's objection to the payment within one year after the notification was received by the customer.

§ 4A–506. Rate of Interest.

(a) If, under this Article, a receiving bank is obliged to pay interest with respect to a payment order issued to the bank, the amount payable may be determined (i) by agreement of the sender and receiving bank, or (ii) by a funds-transfer system rule if the payment order is transmitted through a funds-transfer system.

(b) If the amount of interest is not determined by an agreement or rule as stated in subsection (a), the amount is calculated by multiplying the applicable Federal Funds rate by the amount on which interest is payable, and then multiplying the product by the number of days for which interest is payable. The applicable Federal Funds rate is the average of the Federal Funds rates published by the Federal Reserve Bank of New York for each of the days for which interest is payable divided by 360. The Federal Funds rate for any day on which a published rate is not available is the same as the published rate for the next preceding day for which there is a published rate. If a receiving bank that accepted a payment order is required to refund payment to the sender of the order because the funds transfer was not completed, but the failure to complete was not due to any fault by the bank, the interest payable is reduced by a percentage equal to the reserve requirement on deposits of the receiving bank.

§ 4A–507. Choice of Law.

(a) The following rules apply unless the affected parties otherwise agree or subsection (c) applies:

(1) The rights and obligations between the sender of a payment order and the receiving bank are governed by the law of the jurisdiction in which the receiving bank is located.

(2) The rights and obligations between the beneficiary's bank and the beneficiary are governed by the law of the jurisdiction in which the beneficiary's bank is located.

(3) The issue of when payment is made pursuant to a funds transfer by the originator to the beneficiary is governed by the law of the jurisdiction in which the beneficiary's bank is located.

(b) If the parties described in each paragraph of subsection (a) have made an agreement selecting the law of a particular jurisdiction to govern rights and obligations between each other, the law of that jurisdiction governs those rights and obligations, whether or not the payment order or the funds transfer bears a reasonable relation to that jurisdiction.

(c) A funds-transfer system rule may select the law of a particular jurisdiction to govern (i) rights and obligations between participating banks with respect to payment orders transmitted or processed through the system, or (ii) the rights and obligations of some or all parties to a funds transfer any part of which is carried out by means of the system. A choice of law made pursuant to clause (i) is binding on participating banks. A choice of law made pursuant to clause (ii) is binding on the originator, other sender, or a receiving bank having notice that the funds-transfer system might be used in the funds transfer and of the choice of law by the system when the originator, other sender, or receiving bank issued or accepted a payment order. The beneficiary of a funds transfer is bound by the choice of law if, when the funds transfer is initiated, the beneficiary has notice that the funds-transfer system might be used in the funds transfer and of the choice of law by the system. The law of a jurisdiction selected pursuant to this subsection may govern, whether or not that law bears a reasonable relation to the matter in issue.

(d) In the event of inconsistency between an agreement under subsection (b) and a choice-of-law rule under subsection (c), the agreement under subsection (b) prevails.

(e) If a funds transfer is made by use of more than one funds-transfer system and there is inconsistency between choice-of-law rules of the systems, the matter in issue is governed by the law of the selected jurisdiction that has the most significant relationship to the matter in issue.

Revised Article 9
SECURED TRANSACTIONS

Part 1 General Provisions

[Subpart 1. Short Title, Definitions, and General Concepts]

§ 9–101. Short Title.

This article may be cited as Uniform Commercial Code—Secured Transactions.

§ 9–102. Definitions and Index of Definitions.

(a) In this article:

(1) "Accession" means goods that are physically united with other goods in such a manner that the identity of the original goods is not lost.

(2) "Account", except as used in "account for", means a right to payment of a monetary obligation, whether or not earned by performance, (i) for property that has been or is to be sold, leased, licensed, assigned, or otherwise disposed of, (ii) for services rendered or to be rendered, (iii) for a policy of insurance issued or to be issued, (iv) for a secondary obligation incurred or to be incurred, (v) for energy provided or to be provided, (vi) for the use or hire of a vessel under a charter or other contract, (vii) arising out of the use of a credit or charge card or information contained on or for use with the card, or (viii) as winnings in a lottery or other game of chance operated or sponsored by a State, governmental unit of a State, or person licensed or authorized to operate the game by a State or governmental unit of a State. The term includes health-care insurance receivables. The term does

not include (i) rights to payment evidenced by chattel paper or an instrument, (ii) commercial tort claims, (iii) deposit accounts, (iv) investment property, (v) letter-of-credit rights or letters of credit, or (vi) rights to payment for money or funds advanced or sold, other than rights arising out of the use of a credit or charge card or information contained on or for use with the card.

(3) "Account debtor" means a person obligated on an account, chattel paper, or general intangible. The term does not include persons obligated to pay a negotiable instrument, even if the instrument constitutes part of chattel paper.

(4) "Accounting", except as used in "accounting for", means a record:

(A) authenticated by a secured party;

(B) indicating the aggregate unpaid secured obligations as of a date not more than 35 days earlier or 35 days later than the date of the record; and

(C) identifying the components of the obligations in reasonable detail.

(5) "Agricultural lien" means an interest, other than a security interest, in farm products:

(A) which secures payment or performance of an obligation for:

(i) goods or services furnished in connection with a debtor's farming operation; or

(ii) rent on real property leased by a debtor in connection with its farming operation;

(B) which is created by statute in favor of a person that:

(i) in the ordinary course of its business furnished goods or services to a debtor in connection with a debtor's farming operation; or

(ii) leased real property to a debtor in connection with the debtor's farming operation; and

(C) whose effectiveness does not depend on the person's possession of the personal property.

(6) "As-extracted collateral" means:

(A) oil, gas, or other minerals that are subject to a security interest that:

(i) is created by a debtor having an interest in the minerals before extraction; and

(ii) attaches to the minerals as extracted; or

(B) accounts arising out of the sale at the wellhead or minehead of oil, gas, or other minerals in which the debtor had an interest before extraction.

(7) "Authenticate" means:

(A) to sign; or

(B) to execute or otherwise adopt a symbol, or encrypt or similarly process a record in whole or in part, with the present intent of the authenticating person to identify the person and adopt or accept a record.

(8) "Bank" means an organization that is engaged in the business of banking. The term includes savings banks, savings and loan associations, credit unions, and trust companies.

(9) "Cash proceeds" means proceeds that are money, checks, deposit accounts, or the like.

(10) "Certificate of title" means a certificate of title with respect to which a statute provides for the security interest in question to be indicated on the certificate as a condition or result of the security interest's obtaining priority over the rights of a lien creditor with respect to the collateral.

(11) "Chattel paper" means a record or records that evidence both a monetary obligation and a security interest in specific goods, a security interest in specific goods and software used in the goods, a security interest in specific goods and license of software used in the goods, a lease of specific goods, or a lease of specific goods and license of software used in the goods. In this paragraph, "monetary obligation" means a monetary obligation secured by the goods or owed under a lease of the goods and includes a monetary obligation with respect to software used in the goods. The term does not include (i) charters or other contracts involving the use or hire of a vessel or (ii) records that evidence a right to payment arising out of the use of a credit or charge card or information contained on or for use with the card. If a transaction is evidenced by records that include an instrument or series of instruments, the group of records taken together constitutes chattel paper.

(12) "Collateral" means the property subject to a security interest or agricultural lien. The term includes:

(A) proceeds to which a security interest attaches;

(B) accounts, chattel paper, payment intangibles, and promissory notes that have been sold; and

(C) goods that are the subject of a consignment.

(13) "Commercial tort claim" means a claim arising in tort with respect to which:

(A) the claimant is an organization; or

(B) the claimant is an individual and the claim:

(i) arose in the course of the claimant's business or profession; and

(ii) does not include damages arising out of personal injury to or the death of an individual.

(14) "Commodity account" means an account maintained by a commodity intermediary in which a commodity contract is carried for a commodity customer.

(15) "Commodity contract" means a commodity futures contract, an option on a commodity futures contract, a commodity option, or another contract if the contract or option is:

(A) traded on or subject to the rules of a board of trade that has been designated as a contract market for such a contract pursuant to federal commodities laws; or

(B) traded on a foreign commodity board of trade, exchange, or market, and is carried on the books of a commodity intermediary for a commodity customer.

(16) "Commodity customer" means a person for which a commodity intermediary carries a commodity contract on its books.

(17) "Commodity intermediary" means a person that:

(A) is registered as a futures commission merchant under federal commodities law; or

(B) in the ordinary course of its business provides clearance or settlement services for a board of trade that has been designated as a contract market pursuant to federal commodities law.

(18) "Communicate" means:

(A) to send a written or other tangible record;

(B) to transmit a record by any means agreed upon by the persons sending and receiving the record; or

(C) in the case of transmission of a record to or by a filing office, to transmit a record by any means prescribed by filing-office rule.

(19) "Consignee" means a merchant to which goods are delivered in a consignment.

(20) "Consignment" means a transaction, regardless of its form, in which a person delivers goods to a merchant for the purpose of sale and:

(A) the merchant:

(i) deals in goods of that kind under a name other than the name of the person making delivery;

(ii) is not an auctioneer; and

(iii) is not generally known by its creditors to be substantially engaged in selling the goods of others;

(B) with respect to each delivery, the aggregate value of the goods is $1,000 or more at the time of delivery;

(C) the goods are not consumer goods immediately before delivery; and

(D) the transaction does not create a security interest that secures an obligation.

(21) "Consignor" means a person that delivers goods to a consignee in a consignment.

(22) "Consumer debtor" means a debtor in a consumer transaction.

(23) "Consumer goods" means goods that are used or bought for use primarily for personal, family, or household purposes.

(24) "Consumer-goods transaction" means a consumer transaction in which:

(A) an individual incurs an obligation primarily for personal, family, or household purposes; and

(B) a security interest in consumer goods secures the obligation.

(25) "Consumer obligor" means an obligor who is an individual and who incurred the obligation as part of a transaction entered into primarily for personal, family, or household purposes.

(26) "Consumer transaction" means a transaction in which (i) an individual incurs an obligation primarily for personal, family, or household purposes, (ii) a security interest secures the obligation, and (iii) the collateral is held or acquired primarily for personal, family, or household purposes. The term includes consumer-goods transactions.

(27) "Continuation statement" means an amendment of a financing statement which:

(A) identifies, by its file number, the initial financing statement to which it relates; and

(B) indicates that it is a continuation statement for, or that it is filed to continue the effectiveness of, the identified financing statement.

(28) "Debtor" means:

(A) a person having an interest, other than a security interest or other lien, in the collateral, whether or not the person is an obligor;

(B) a seller of accounts, chattel paper, payment intangibles, or promissory notes; or

(C) a consignee.

(29) "Deposit account" means a demand, time, savings, passbook, or similar account maintained with a bank. The term does not include investment property or accounts evidenced by an instrument.

(30) "Document" means a document of title or a receipt of the type described in Section 7–201(2).

(31) "Electronic chattel paper" means chattel paper evidenced by a record or records consisting of information stored in an electronic medium.

(32) "Encumbrance" means a right, other than an ownership interest, in real property. The term includes mortgages and other liens on real property.

(33) "Equipment" means goods other than inventory, farm products, or consumer goods.

(34) "Farm products" means goods, other than standing timber, with respect to which the debtor is engaged in a farming operation and which are:

(A) crops grown, growing, or to be grown, including:

(i) crops produced on trees, vines, and bushes; and

(ii) aquatic goods produced in aquacultural operations;

(B) livestock, born or unborn, including aquatic goods produced in aquacultural operations;

(C) supplies used or produced in a farming operation; or

(D) products of crops or livestock in their unmanufactured states.

(35) "Farming operation" means raising, cultivating, propagating, fattening, grazing, or any other farming, livestock, or aquacultural operation.

(36) "File number" means the number assigned to an initial financing statement pursuant to Section 9–519(a).

(37) "Filing office" means an office designated in Section 9–501 as the place to file a financing statement.

(38) "Filing-office rule" means a rule adopted pursuant to Section 9–526.

(39) "Financing statement" means a record or records composed of an initial financing statement and any filed record relating to the initial financing statement.

(40) "Fixture filing" means the filing of a financing statement covering goods that are or are to become fixtures and satisfying Section 9–502(a) and (b). The term includes the filing of a financing statement covering goods of a transmitting utility which are or are to become fixtures.

(41) "Fixtures" means goods that have become so related to particular real property that an interest in them arises under real property law.

(42) "General intangible" means any personal property, including things in action, other than accounts, chattel paper, commercial tort claims, deposit accounts, documents, goods, instruments, investment property, letter-of-credit rights, letters of credit, money, and oil, gas, or other minerals before extraction. The term includes payment intangibles and software.

(43) "Good faith" means honesty in fact and the observance of reasonable commercial standards of fair dealing.

(44) "Goods" means all things that are movable when a security interest attaches. The term includes (i) fixtures, (ii) standing timber that is to be cut and removed under a conveyance or contract for sale, (iii) the unborn young of animals, (iv) crops grown, growing, or to be grown, even if the crops are produced on trees, vines, or bushes, and (v) manufactured homes. The term also includes a computer program embedded in goods and any supporting information provided in connection with a transaction relating to the program if (i) the program is associated with the goods in such a manner that it customarily is considered part of the goods, or (ii) by becoming the owner of the goods, a person acquires a right to use the program in connection with the goods. The term does not include a computer program embedded in goods that consist solely of the medium in which the program is embedded. The term also does not include accounts, chattel paper, commercial tort claims, deposit accounts, documents, general intangibles, instruments, investment property, letter-of-credit rights, letters of credit, money, or oil, gas, or other minerals before extraction.

(45) "Governmental unit" means a subdivision, agency, department, county, parish, municipality, or other unit of the government of the United States, a State, or a foreign country. The term includes an organization having a separate corporate existence if the organization is eligible to issue debt on which interest is exempt from income taxation under the laws of the United States.

(46) "Health-care-insurance receivable" means an interest in or claim under a policy of insurance which is a right to payment of a monetary obligation for health-care goods or services provided.

(47) "Instrument" means a negotiable instrument or any other writing that evidences a right to the payment of a monetary obligation, is not itself a security agreement or lease, and is of a type that in ordinary course of business is transferred by delivery with any necessary indorsement or assignment. The term does not include (i) investment property, (ii) letters of credit, or (iii) writings that evidence a right to payment arising out of the use of a credit or charge card or information contained on or for use with the card.

(48) "Inventory" means goods, other than farm products, which:

(A) are leased by a person as lessor;

(B) are held by a person for sale or lease or to be furnished under a contract of service;

(C) are furnished by a person under a contract of service; or

(D) consist of raw materials, work in process, or materials used or consumed in a business.

(49) "Investment property" means a security, whether certificated or uncertificated, security entitlement, securities account, commodity contract, or commodity account.

(50) "Jurisdiction of organization", with respect to a registered organization, means the jurisdiction under whose law the organization is organized.

(51) "Letter-of-credit right" means a right to payment or performance under a letter of credit, whether or not the beneficiary

has demanded or is at the time entitled to demand payment or performance. The term does not include the right of a beneficiary to demand payment or performance under a letter of credit.

(52) "Lien creditor" means:

(A) a creditor that has acquired a lien on the property involved by attachment, levy, or the like;

(B) an assignee for benefit of creditors from the time of assignment;

(C) a trustee in bankruptcy from the date of the filing of the petition; or

(D) a receiver in equity from the time of appointment.

(53) "Manufactured home" means a structure, transportable in one or more sections, which, in the traveling mode, is eight body feet or more in width or 40 body feet or more in length, or, when erected on site, is 320 or more square feet, and which is built on a permanent chassis and designed to be used as a dwelling with or without a permanent foundation when connected to the required utilities, and includes the plumbing, heating, air-conditioning, and electrical systems contained therein. The term includes any structure that meets all of the requirements of this paragraph except the size requirements and with respect to which the manufacturer voluntarily files a certification required by the United States Secretary of Housing and Urban Development and complies with the standards established under Title 42 of the United States Code.

(54) "Manufactured-home transaction" means a secured transaction:

(A) that creates a purchase-money security interest in a manufactured home, other than a manufactured home held as inventory; or

(B) in which a manufactured home, other than a manufactured home held as inventory, is the primary collateral.

(55) "Mortgage" means a consensual interest in real property, including fixtures, which secures payment or performance of an obligation.

(56) "New debtor" means a person that becomes bound as debtor under Section 9–203(d) by a security agreement previously entered into by another person.

(57) "New value" means (i) money, (ii) money's worth in property, services, or new credit, or (iii) release by a transferee of an interest in property previously transferred to the transferee. The term does not include an obligation substituted for another obligation.

(58) "Noncash proceeds" means proceeds other than cash proceeds.

(59) "Obligor" means a person that, with respect to an obligation secured by a security interest in or an agricultural lien on the collateral, (i) owes payment or other performance of the obligation, (ii) has provided property other than the collateral to secure payment or other performance of the obligation, or (iii) is otherwise accountable in whole or in part for payment or other performance of the obligation. The term does not include issuers or nominated persons under a letter of credit.

(60) "Original debtor", except as used in Section 9–310(c), means a person that, as debtor, entered into a security agreement

to which a new debtor has become bound under Section 9–203(d).

(61) "Payment intangible" means a general intangible under which the account debtor's principal obligation is a monetary obligation.

(62) "Person related to", with respect to an individual, means:

(A) the spouse of the individual;

(B) a brother, brother-in-law, sister, or sister-in-law of the individual;

(C) an ancestor or lineal descendant of the individual or the individual's spouse; or

(D) any other relative, by blood or marriage, of the individual or the individual's spouse who shares the same home with the individual.

(63) "Person related to", with respect to an organization, means:

(A) a person directly or indirectly controlling, controlled by, or under common control with the organization;

(B) an officer or director of, or a person performing similar functions with respect to, the organization;

(C) an officer or director of, or a person performing similar functions with respect to, a person described in subparagraph (A);

(D) the spouse of an individual described in subparagraph (A), (B), or (C); or

(E) an individual who is related by blood or marriage to an individual described in subparagraph (A), (B), (C), or (D) and shares the same home with the individual.

(64) "Proceeds", except as used in Section 9–609(b), means the following property:

(A) whatever is acquired upon the sale, lease, license, exchange, or other disposition of collateral;

(B) whatever is collected on, or distributed on account of, collateral;

(C) rights arising out of collateral;

(D) to the extent of the value of collateral, claims arising out of the loss, nonconformity, or interference with the use of, defects or infringement of rights in, or damage to, the collateral; or

(E) to the extent of the value of collateral and to the extent payable to the debtor or the secured party, insurance payable by reason of the loss or nonconformity of, defects or infringement of rights in, or damage to, the collateral.

(65) "Promissory note" means an instrument that evidences a promise to pay a monetary obligation, does not evidence an order to pay, and does not contain an acknowledgment by a bank that the bank has received for deposit a sum of money or funds.

(66) "Proposal" means a record authenticated by a secured party which includes the terms on which the secured party is willing to accept collateral in full or partial satisfaction of the obligation it secures pursuant to Sections 9–620, 9–621, and 9–622.

(67) "Public-finance transaction" means a secured transaction in connection with which:

(A) debt securities are issued;

(B) all or a portion of the securities issued have an initial stated maturity of at least 20 years; and

(C) the debtor, obligor, secured party, account debtor or other person obligated on collateral, assignor or assignee of a secured obligation, or assignor or assignee of a security interest is a State or a governmental unit of a State.

(68) "Pursuant to commitment", with respect to an advance made or other value given by a secured party, means pursuant to the secured party's obligation, whether or not a subsequent event of default or other event not within the secured party's control has relieved or may relieve the secured party from its obligation.

(69) "Record", except as used in "for record", "of record", "record or legal title", and "record owner", means information that is inscribed on a tangible medium or which is stored in an electronic or other medium and is retrievable in perceivable form.

(70) "Registered organization" means an organization organized solely under the law of a single State or the United States and as to which the State or the United States must maintain a public record showing the organization to have been organized.

(71) "Secondary obligor" means an obligor to the extent that:

(A) the obligor's obligation is secondary; or

(B) the obligor has a right of recourse with respect to an obligation secured by collateral against the debtor, another obligor, or property of either.

(72) "Secured party" means:

(A) a person in whose favor a security interest is created or provided for under a security agreement, whether or not any obligation to be secured is outstanding;

(B) a person that holds an agricultural lien;

(C) a consignor;

(D) a person to which accounts, chattel paper, payment intangibles, or promissory notes have been sold;

(E) a trustee, indenture trustee, agent, collateral agent, or other representative in whose favor a security interest or agricultural lien is created or provided for; or

(F) a person that holds a security interest arising under Section 2–401, 2–505, 2–711(3), 2A–508(5), 4–210, or 5–118.

(73) "Security agreement" means an agreement that creates or provides for a security interest.

(74) "Send", in connection with a record or notification, means:

(A) to deposit in the mail, deliver for transmission, or transmit by any other usual means of communication, with postage or cost of transmission provided for, addressed to any address reasonable under the circumstances; or

(B) to cause the record or notification to be received within the time that it would have been received if properly sent under subparagraph (A).

(75) "Software" means a computer program and any supporting information provided in connection with a transaction relating to the program. The term does not include a computer program that is included in the definition of goods.

(76) "State" means a State of the United States, the District of Columbia, Puerto Rico, the United States Virgin Islands, or any territory or insular possession subject to the jurisdiction of the United States.

(77) "Supporting obligation" means a letter-of-credit right or secondary obligation that supports the payment or performance of an account, chattel paper, a document, a general intangible, an instrument, or investment property.

(78) "Tangible chattel paper" means chattel paper evidenced by a record or records consisting of information that is inscribed on a tangible medium.

(79) "Termination statement" means an amendment of a financing statement which:

(A) identifies, by its file number, the initial financing statement to which it relates; and

(B) indicates either that it is a termination statement or that the identified financing statement is no longer effective.

(80) "Transmitting utility" means a person primarily engaged in the business of:

(A) operating a railroad, subway, street railway, or trolley bus;

(B) transmitting communications electrically, electromagnetically, or by light;

(C) transmitting goods by pipeline or sewer; or

(D) transmitting or producing and transmitting electricity, steam, gas, or water.

(b) The following definitions in other articles apply to this article:

"Applicant."	Section 5–102
"Beneficiary."	Section 5–102
"Broker."	Section 8–102
"Certificated security."	Section 8–102
"Check."	Section 3–104
"Clearing corporation."	Section 8–102
"Contract for sale."	Section 2–106
"Customer."	Section 4–104
"Entitlement holder."	Section 8–102
"Financial asset."	Section 8–102
"Holder in due course."	Section 3–302
"Issuer" (with respect to a letter of credit or letter-of-credit right).	Section 5–102
"Issuer" (with respect to a security).	Section 8–201
"Lease."	Section 2A–103
"Lease agreement."	Section 2A–103
"Lease contract."	Section 2A–103
"Leasehold interest."	Section 2A–103
"Lessee."	Section 2A–103
"Lessee in ordinary course of business."	Section 2A–103
"Lessor."	Section 2A–103
"Lessor's residual interest."	Section 2A–103
"Letter of credit."	Section 5–102
"Merchant."	Section 2–104
"Negotiable instrument."	Section 3–104
"Nominated person."	Section 5–102

(c) Article 1 contains general definitions and principles of construction and interpretation applicable throughout this article.

Amended in 1999 and 2000.

§ 9–103. Purchase-Money Security Interest; Application of Payments; Burden of Establishing.

(a) In this section:

(1) "purchase-money collateral" means goods or software that secures a purchase-money obligation incurred with respect to that collateral; and

(2) "purchase-money obligation" means an obligation of an obligor incurred as all or part of the price of the collateral or for value given to enable the debtor to acquire rights in or the use of the collateral if the value is in fact so used.

(b) A security interest in goods is a purchase-money security interest:

(1) to the extent that the goods are purchase-money collateral with respect to that security interest;

(2) if the security interest is in inventory that is or was purchase-money collateral, also to the extent that the security interest secures a purchase-money obligation incurred with respect to other inventory in which the secured party holds or held a purchase-money security interest; and

(3) also to the extent that the security interest secures a purchase-money obligation incurred with respect to software in which the secured party holds or held a purchase-money security interest.

(c) A security interest in software is a purchase-money security interest to the extent that the security interest also secures a purchase-money obligation incurred with respect to goods in which the secured party holds or held a purchase-money security interest if:

(1) the debtor acquired its interest in the software in an integrated transaction in which it acquired an interest in the goods; and

(2) the debtor acquired its interest in the software for the principal purpose of using the software in the goods.

(d) The security interest of a consignor in goods that are the subject of a consignment is a purchase-money security interest in inventory.

(e) In a transaction other than a consumer-goods transaction, if the extent to which a security interest is a purchase-money security interest depends on the application of a payment to a particular obligation, the payment must be applied:

(1) in accordance with any reasonable method of application to which the parties agree;

(2) in the absence of the parties' agreement to a reasonable method, in accordance with any intention of the obligor manifested at or before the time of payment; or

(3) in the absence of an agreement to a reasonable method and a timely manifestation of the obligor's intention, in the following order:

(A) to obligations that are not secured; and

(B) if more than one obligation is secured, to obligations secured by purchase-money security interests in the order in which those obligations were incurred.

(f) In a transaction other than a consumer-goods transaction, a purchase-money security interest does not lose its status as such, even if:

(1) the purchase-money collateral also secures an obligation that is not a purchase-money obligation;

(2) collateral that is not purchase-money collateral also secures the purchase-money obligation; or

(3) the purchase-money obligation has been renewed, refinanced, consolidated, or restructured.

(g) In a transaction other than a consumer-goods transaction, a secured party claiming a purchase-money security interest has the burden of establishing the extent to which the security interest is a purchase-money security interest.

(h) The limitation of the rules in subsections (e), (f), and (g) to transactions other than consumer-goods transactions is intended to leave to the court the determination of the proper rules in consumer-goods transactions. The court may not infer from that limitation the nature of the proper rule in consumer-goods transactions and may continue to apply established approaches.

§ 9–104. Control of Deposit Account.

(a) A secured party has control of a deposit account if:

(1) the secured party is the bank with which the deposit account is maintained;

(2) the debtor, secured party, and bank have agreed in an authenticated record that the bank will comply with instructions originated by the secured party directing disposition of the funds in the deposit account without further consent by the debtor; or

(3) the secured party becomes the bank's customer with respect to the deposit account.

(b) A secured party that has satisfied subsection (a) has control, even if the debtor retains the right to direct the disposition of funds from the deposit account.

§ 9–105. Control of Electronic Chattel Paper.

A secured party has control of electronic chattel paper if the record or records comprising the chattel paper are created, stored, and assigned in such a manner that:

(1) a single authoritative copy of the record or records exists which is unique, identifiable and, except as otherwise provided in paragraphs (4), (5), and (6), unalterable;

(2) the authoritative copy identifies the secured party as the assignee of the record or records;

(3) the authoritative copy is communicated to and maintained by the secured party or its designated custodian;

(4) copies or revisions that add or change an identified assignee of the authoritative copy can be made only with the participation of the secured party;

(5) each copy of the authoritative copy and any copy of a copy is readily identifiable as a copy that is not the authoritative copy; and

(6) any revision of the authoritative copy is readily identifiable as an authorized or unauthorized revision.

§ 9–106. Control of Investment Property.

(a) A person has control of a certificated security, uncertificated security, or security entitlement as provided in Section 8–106.

(b) A secured party has control of a commodity contract if:

(1) the secured party is the commodity intermediary with which the commodity contract is carried; or

(2) the commodity customer, secured party, and commodity intermediary have agreed that the commodity intermediary will apply any value distributed on account of the commodity contract as directed by the secured party without further consent by the commodity customer.

(c) A secured party having control of all security entitlements or commodity contracts carried in a securities account or commodity account has control over the securities account or commodity account.

§ 9–107. Control of Letter-of-Credit Right.

A secured party has control of a letter-of-credit right to the extent of any right to payment or performance by the issuer or any nominated person if the issuer or nominated person has consented to an assignment of proceeds of the letter of credit under Section 5–114(c) or otherwise applicable law or practice.

§ 9–108. Sufficiency of Description.

(a) Except as otherwise provided in subsections (c), (d), and (e), a description of personal or real property is sufficient, whether or not it is specific, if it reasonably identifies what is described.

(b) Except as otherwise provided in subsection (d), a description of collateral reasonably identifies the collateral if it identifies the collateral by:

(1) specific listing;

(2) category;

(3) except as otherwise provided in subsection (e), a type of collateral defined in [the Uniform Commercial Code];

(4) quantity;

(5) computational or allocational formula or procedure; or

(6) except as otherwise provided in subsection (c), any other method, if the identity of the collateral is objectively determinable.

(c) A description of collateral as "all the debtor's assets" or "all the debtor's personal property" or using words of similar import does not reasonably identify the collateral.

(d) Except as otherwise provided in subsection (e), a description of a security entitlement, securities account, or commodity account is sufficient if it describes:

(1) the collateral by those terms or as investment property; or

(2) the underlying financial asset or commodity contract.

(e) A description only by type of collateral defined in [the Uniform Commercial Code] is an insufficient description of:

(1) a commercial tort claim; or

(2) in a consumer transaction, consumer goods, a security entitlement, a securities account, or a commodity account.

[Subpart 2. Applicability of Article]

§ 9–109. Scope.

(a) Except as otherwise provided in subsections (c) and (d), this article applies to:

(1) a transaction, regardless of its form, that creates a security interest in personal property or fixtures by contract;

(2) an agricultural lien;

(3) a sale of accounts, chattel paper, payment intangibles, or promissory notes;

(4) a consignment;

(5) a security interest arising under Section 2–401, 2–505, 2–711(3), or 2A–508(5), as provided in Section 9–110; and

(6) a security interest arising under Section 4–210 or 5–118.

(b) The application of this article to a security interest in a secured obligation is not affected by the fact that the obligation is itself secured by a transaction or interest to which this article does not apply.

(c) This article does not apply to the extent that:

(1) a statute, regulation, or treaty of the United States preempts this article;

(2) another statute of this State expressly governs the creation, perfection, priority, or enforcement of a security interest created by this State or a governmental unit of this State;

(3) a statute of another State, a foreign country, or a governmental unit of another State or a foreign country, other than a statute generally applicable to security interests, expressly governs creation, perfection, priority, or enforcement of a security interest created by the State, country, or governmental unit; or

(4) the rights of a transferee beneficiary or nominated person under a letter of credit are independent and superior under Section 5–114.

(d) This article does not apply to:

(1) a landlord's lien, other than an agricultural lien;

(2) a lien, other than an agricultural lien, given by statute or other rule of law for services or materials, but Section 9–333 applies with respect to priority of the lien;

(3) an assignment of a claim for wages, salary, or other compensation of an employee;

(4) a sale of accounts, chattel paper, payment intangibles, or promissory notes as part of a sale of the business out of which they arose;

(5) an assignment of accounts, chattel paper, payment intangibles, or promissory notes which is for the purpose of collection only;

(6) an assignment of a right to payment under a contract to an assignee that is also obligated to perform under the contract;

(7) an assignment of a single account, payment intangible, or promissory note to an assignee in full or partial satisfaction of a preexisting indebtedness;

(8) a transfer of an interest in or an assignment of a claim under a policy of insurance, other than an assignment by or to a health-care provider of a health-care-insurance receivable and any subsequent assignment of the right to payment, but Sections 9–315 and 9–322 apply with respect to proceeds and priorities in proceeds;

(9) an assignment of a right represented by a judgment, other than a judgment taken on a right to payment that was collateral;

(10) a right of recoupment or set-off, but:

(A) Section 9–340 applies with respect to the effectiveness of rights of recoupment or set-off against deposit accounts; and

(B) Section 9–404 applies with respect to defenses or claims of an account debtor;

(11) the creation or transfer of an interest in or lien on real property, including a lease or rents thereunder, except to the extent that provision is made for:

(A) liens on real property in Sections 9–203 and 9–308;

(B) fixtures in Section 9–334;

(C) fixture filings in Sections 9–501, 9–502, 9–512, 9–516, and 9–519; and

(D) security agreements covering personal and real property in Section 9–604;

(12) an assignment of a claim arising in tort, other than a commercial tort claim, but Sections 9–315 and 9–322 apply with respect to proceeds and priorities in proceeds; or

(13) an assignment of a deposit account in a consumer transaction, but Sections 9–315 and 9–322 apply with respect to proceeds and priorities in proceeds.

§ 9–110. Security Interests Arising under Article 2 or 2A.

A security interest arising under Section 2–401, 2–505, 2–711(3), or 2A–508(5) is subject to this article. However, until the debtor obtains possession of the goods:

(1) the security interest is enforceable, even if Section 9–203(b)(3) has not been satisfied;

(2) filing is not required to perfect the security interest;

(3) the rights of the secured party after default by the debtor are governed by Article 2 or 2A; and

(4) the security interest has priority over a conflicting security interest created by the debtor.

Part 2 Effectiveness of Security Agreement; Attachment of Security Interest; Rights of Parties to Security Agreement

[Subpart 1. Effectiveness and Attachment]

§ 9–201. General Effectiveness of Security Agreement.

(a) Except as otherwise provided in [the Uniform Commercial Code], a security agreement is effective according to its terms between the parties, against purchasers of the collateral, and against creditors.

(b) A transaction subject to this article is subject to any applicable rule of law which establishes a different rule for consumers and [insert reference to (i) any other statute or regulation that regulates the rates, charges, agreements, and practices for loans, credit sales, or other extensions of credit and (ii) any consumer-protection statute or regulation].

(c) In case of conflict between this article and a rule of law, statute, or regulation described in subsection (b), the rule of law, statute, or regulation controls. Failure to comply with a statute or regulation described in subsection (b) has only the effect the statute or regulation specifies.

(d) This article does not:

(1) validate any rate, charge, agreement, or practice that violates a rule of law, statute, or regulation described in subsection (b); or

(2) extend the application of the rule of law, statute, or regulation to a transaction not otherwise subject to it.

§ 9–202. Title to Collateral Immaterial.

Except as otherwise provided with respect to consignments or sales of accounts, chattel paper, payment intangibles, or promissory notes, the provisions of this article with regard to rights and obligations apply whether title to collateral is in the secured party or the debtor.

§ 9–203. Attachment and Enforceability of Security Interest; Proceeds; Supporting Obligations; Formal Requisites.

(a) A security interest attaches to collateral when it becomes enforceable against the debtor with respect to the collateral, unless an agreement expressly postpones the time of attachment.

(b) Except as otherwise provided in subsections (c) through (i), a security interest is enforceable against the debtor and third parties with respect to the collateral only if:

(1) value has been given;

(2) the debtor has rights in the collateral or the power to transfer rights in the collateral to a secured party; and

(3) one of the following conditions is met:

(A) the debtor has authenticated a security agreement that provides a description of the collateral and, if the security interest covers timber to be cut, a description of the land concerned;

(B) the collateral is not a certificated security and is in the possession of the secured party under Section 9–313 pursuant to the debtor's security agreement;

(C) the collateral is a certificated security in registered form and the security certificate has been delivered to the secured party under Section 8–301 pursuant to the debtor's security agreement; or

(D) the collateral is deposit accounts, electronic chattel paper, investment property, or letter-of-credit rights, and the secured party has control under Section 9–104, 9–105, 9–106, or 9–107 pursuant to the debtor's security agreement.

(c) Subsection (b) is subject to Section 4–210 on the security interest of a collecting bank, Section 5–118 on the security interest of a letter-of-credit issuer or nominated person, Section 9–110 on a security interest arising under Article 2 or 2A, and Section 9–206 on security interests in investment property.

(d) A person becomes bound as debtor by a security agreement entered into by another person if, by operation of law other than this article or by contract:

(1) the security agreement becomes effective to create a security interest in the person's property; or

(2) the person becomes generally obligated for the obligations of the other person, including the obligation secured under the

security agreement, and acquires or succeeds to all or substantially all of the assets of the other person.

(e) If a new debtor becomes bound as debtor by a security agreement entered into by another person:

(1) the agreement satisfies subsection (b)(3) with respect to existing or after-acquired property of the new debtor to the extent the property is described in the agreement; and

(2) another agreement is not necessary to make a security interest in the property enforceable.

(f) The attachment of a security interest in collateral gives the secured party the rights to proceeds provided by Section 9–315 and is also attachment of a security interest in a supporting obligation for the collateral.

(g) The attachment of a security interest in a right to payment or performance secured by a security interest or other lien on personal or real property is also attachment of a security interest in the security interest, mortgage, or other lien.

(h) The attachment of a security interest in a securities account is also attachment of a security interest in the security entitlements carried in the securities account.

(i) The attachment of a security interest in a commodity account is also attachment of a security interest in the commodity contracts carried in the commodity account.

§ 9–204. After-Acquired Property; Future Advances.

(a) Except as otherwise provided in subsection (b), a security agreement may create or provide for a security interest in after-acquired collateral.

(b) A security interest does not attach under a term constituting an after-acquired property clause to:

(1) consumer goods, other than an accession when given as additional security, unless the debtor acquires rights in them within 10 days after the secured party gives value; or

(2) a commercial tort claim.

(c) A security agreement may provide that collateral secures, or that accounts, chattel paper, payment intangibles, or promissory notes are sold in connection with, future advances or other value, whether or not the advances or value are given pursuant to commitment.

§ 9–205. Use or Disposition of Collateral Permissible.

(a) A security interest is not invalid or fraudulent against creditors solely because:

(1) the debtor has the right or ability to:

(A) use, commingle, or dispose of all or part of the collateral, including returned or repossessed goods;

(B) collect, compromise, enforce, or otherwise deal with collateral;

(C) accept the return of collateral or make repossessions; or

(D) use, commingle, or dispose of proceeds; or

(2) the secured party fails to require the debtor to account for proceeds or replace collateral.

(b) This section does not relax the requirements of possession if attachment, perfection, or enforcement of a security interest depends upon possession of the collateral by the secured party.

§ 9–206. Security Interest Arising in Purchase or Delivery of Financial Asset.

(a) A security interest in favor of a securities intermediary attaches to a person's security entitlement if:

(1) the person buys a financial asset through the securities intermediary in a transaction in which the person is obligated to pay the purchase price to the securities intermediary at the time of the purchase; and

(2) the securities intermediary credits the financial asset to the buyer's securities account before the buyer pays the securities intermediary.

(b) The security interest described in subsection (a) secures the person's obligation to pay for the financial asset.

(c) A security interest in favor of a person that delivers a certificated security or other financial asset represented by a writing attaches to the security or other financial asset if:

(1) the security or other financial asset:

(A) in the ordinary course of business is transferred by delivery with any necessary indorsement or assignment; and

(B) is delivered under an agreement between persons in the business of dealing with such securities or financial assets; and

(2) the agreement calls for delivery against payment.

(d) The security interest described in subsection (c) secures the obligation to make payment for the delivery.

[Subpart 2. Rights and Duties]

§ 9–207. Rights and Duties of Secured Party Having Possession or Control of Collateral.

(a) Except as otherwise provided in subsection (d), a secured party shall use reasonable care in the custody and preservation of collateral in the secured party's possession. In the case of chattel paper or an instrument, reasonable care includes taking necessary steps to preserve rights against prior parties unless otherwise agreed.

(b) Except as otherwise provided in subsection (d), if a secured party has possession of collateral:

(1) reasonable expenses, including the cost of insurance and payment of taxes or other charges, incurred in the custody, preservation, use, or operation of the collateral are chargeable to the debtor and are secured by the collateral;

(2) the risk of accidental loss or damage is on the debtor to the extent of a deficiency in any effective insurance coverage;

(3) the secured party shall keep the collateral identifiable, but fungible collateral may be commingled; and

(4) the secured party may use or operate the collateral:

(A) for the purpose of preserving the collateral or its value;

(B) as permitted by an order of a court having competent jurisdiction; or

(C) except in the case of consumer goods, in the manner and to the extent agreed by the debtor.

(c) Except as otherwise provided in subsection (d), a secured party having possession of collateral or control of collateral under Section 9–104, 9–105, 9–106, or 9–107:

(1) may hold as additional security any proceeds, except money or funds, received from the collateral;

(2) shall apply money or funds received from the collateral to reduce the secured obligation, unless remitted to the debtor; and

(3) may create a security interest in the collateral.

(d) If the secured party is a buyer of accounts, chattel paper, payment intangibles, or promissory notes or a consignor:

(1) subsection (a) does not apply unless the secured party is entitled under an agreement:

(A) to charge back uncollected collateral; or

(B) otherwise to full or limited recourse against the debtor or a secondary obligor based on the nonpayment or other default of an account debtor or other obligor on the collateral; and

(2) subsections (b) and (c) do not apply.

§ 9–208. Additional Duties of Secured Party Having Control of Collateral.

(a) This section applies to cases in which there is no outstanding secured obligation and the secured party is not committed to make advances, incur obligations, or otherwise give value.

(b) Within 10 days after receiving an authenticated demand by the debtor:

(1) a secured party having control of a deposit account under Section 9–104(a)(2) shall send to the bank with which the deposit account is maintained an authenticated statement that releases the bank from any further obligation to comply with instructions originated by the secured party;

(2) a secured party having control of a deposit account under Section 9–104(a)(3) shall:

(A) pay the debtor the balance on deposit in the deposit account; or

(B) transfer the balance on deposit into a deposit account in the debtor's name;

(3) a secured party, other than a buyer, having control of electronic chattel paper under Section 9–105 shall:

(A) communicate the authoritative copy of the electronic chattel paper to the debtor or its designated custodian;

(B) if the debtor designates a custodian that is the designated custodian with which the authoritative copy of the electronic chattel paper is maintained for the secured party, communicate to the custodian an authenticated record releasing the designated custodian from any further obligation to comply with instructions originated by the secured party and instructing the custodian to comply with instructions originated by the debtor; and

(C) take appropriate action to enable the debtor or its designated custodian to make copies of or revisions to the authoritative copy which add or change an identified assignee of the authoritative copy without the consent of the secured party;

(4) a secured party having control of investment property under Section 8–106(d)(2) or 9–106(b) shall send to the securities intermediary or commodity intermediary with which the security entitlement or commodity contract is maintained an authenticated record that releases the securities intermediary or commodity

intermediary from any further obligation to comply with entitlement orders or directions originated by the secured party; and

(5) a secured party having control of a letter-of-credit right under Section 9–107 shall send to each person having an unfulfilled obligation to pay or deliver proceeds of the letter of credit to the secured party an authenticated release from any further obligation to pay or deliver proceeds of the letter of credit to the secured party.

§ 9–209. Duties of Secured Party If Account Debtor Has Been Notified of Assignment.

(a) Except as otherwise provided in subsection (c), this section applies if:

(1) there is no outstanding secured obligation; and

(2) the secured party is not committed to make advances, incur obligations, or otherwise give value.

(b) Within 10 days after receiving an authenticated demand by the debtor, a secured party shall send to an account debtor that has received notification of an assignment to the secured party as assignee under Section 9–406(a) an authenticated record that releases the account debtor from any further obligation to the secured party.

(c) This section does not apply to an assignment constituting the sale of an account, chattel paper, or payment intangible.

§ 9–210. Request for Accounting; Request Regarding List of Collateral or Statement of Account.

(a) In this section:

(1) "Request" means a record of a type described in paragraph (2), (3), or (4).

(2) "Request for an accounting" means a record authenticated by a debtor requesting that the recipient provide an accounting of the unpaid obligations secured by collateral and reasonably identifying the transaction or relationship that is the subject of the request.

(3) "Request regarding a list of collateral" means a record authenticated by a debtor requesting that the recipient approve or correct a list of what the debtor believes to be the collateral securing an obligation and reasonably identifying the transaction or relationship that is the subject of the request.

(4) "Request regarding a statement of account" means a record authenticated by a debtor requesting that the recipient approve or correct a statement indicating what the debtor believes to be the aggregate amount of unpaid obligations secured by collateral as of a specified date and reasonably identifying the transaction or relationship that is the subject of the request.

(b) Subject to subsections (c), (d), (e), and (f), a secured party, other than a buyer of accounts, chattel paper, payment intangibles, or promissory notes or a consignor, shall comply with a request within 14 days after receipt:

(1) in the case of a request for an accounting, by authenticating and sending to the debtor an accounting; and

(2) in the case of a request regarding a list of collateral or a request regarding a statement of account, by authenticating and sending to the debtor an approval or correction.

(c) A secured party that claims a security interest in all of a particular type of collateral owned by the debtor may comply with a request regarding a list of collateral by sending to the debtor an authenticated record including a statement to that effect within 14 days after receipt.

(d) A person that receives a request regarding a list of collateral, claims no interest in the collateral when it receives the request, and claimed an interest in the collateral at an earlier time shall comply with the request within 14 days after receipt by sending to the debtor an authenticated record:

(1) disclaiming any interest in the collateral; and

(2) if known to the recipient, providing the name and mailing address of any assignee of or successor to the recipient's interest in the collateral.

(e) A person that receives a request for an accounting or a request regarding a statement of account, claims no interest in the obligations when it receives the request, and claimed an interest in the obligations at an earlier time shall comply with the request within 14 days after receipt by sending to the debtor an authenticated record:

(1) disclaiming any interest in the obligations; and

(2) if known to the recipient, providing the name and mailing address of any assignee of or successor to the recipient's interest in the obligations.

(f) A debtor is entitled without charge to one response to a request under this section during any six-month period. The secured party may require payment of a charge not exceeding $25 for each additional response.

As amended in 1999.

Part 3 Perfection and Priority

[Subpart 1. Law Governing Perfection and Priority]

§ 9–301. Law Governing Perfection and Priority of Security Interests.

Except as otherwise provided in Sections 9–303 through 9–306, the following rules determine the law governing perfection, the effect of perfection or nonperfection, and the priority of a security interest in collateral:

(1) Except as otherwise provided in this section, while a debtor is located in a jurisdiction, the local law of that jurisdiction governs perfection, the effect of perfection or nonperfection, and the priority of a security interest in collateral.

(2) While collateral is located in a jurisdiction, the local law of that jurisdiction governs perfection, the effect of perfection or nonperfection, and the priority of a possessory security interest in that collateral.

(3) Except as otherwise provided in paragraph (4), while negotiable documents, goods, instruments, money, or tangible chattel paper is located in a jurisdiction, the local law of that jurisdiction governs:

(A) perfection of a security interest in the goods by filing a fixture filing;

(B) perfection of a security interest in timber to be cut; and

(C) the effect of perfection or nonperfection and the priority of a nonpossessory security interest in the collateral.

(4) The local law of the jurisdiction in which the wellhead or minehead is located governs perfection, the effect of perfection or nonperfection, and the priority of a security interest in as-extracted collateral.

§ 9–302. Law Governing Perfection and Priority of Agricultural Liens.

While farm products are located in a jurisdiction, the local law of that jurisdiction governs perfection, the effect of perfection or nonperfection, and the priority of an agricultural lien on the farm products.

§ 9–303. Law Governing Perfection and Priority of Security Interests in Goods Covered by a Certificate of Title.

(a) This section applies to goods covered by a certificate of title, even if there is no other relationship between the jurisdiction under whose certificate of title the goods are covered and the goods or the debtor.

(b) Goods become covered by a certificate of title when a valid application for the certificate of title and the applicable fee are delivered to the appropriate authority. Goods cease to be covered by a certificate of title at the earlier of the time the certificate of title ceases to be effective under the law of the issuing jurisdiction or the time the goods become covered subsequently by a certificate of title issued by another jurisdiction.

(c) The local law of the jurisdiction under whose certificate of title the goods are covered governs perfection, the effect of perfection or nonperfection, and the priority of a security interest in goods covered by a certificate of title from the time the goods become covered by the certificate of title until the goods cease to be covered by the certificate of title.

§ 9–304. Law Governing Perfection and Priority of Security Interests in Deposit Accounts.

(a) The local law of a bank's jurisdiction governs perfection, the effect of perfection or nonperfection, and the priority of a security interest in a deposit account maintained with that bank.

(b) The following rules determine a bank's jurisdiction for purposes of this part:

(1) If an agreement between the bank and the debtor governing the deposit account expressly provides that a particular jurisdiction is the bank's jurisdiction for purposes of this part, this article, or [the Uniform Commercial Code], that jurisdiction is the bank's jurisdiction.

(2) If paragraph (1) does not apply and an agreement between the bank and its customer governing the deposit account expressly provides that the agreement is governed by the law of a particular jurisdiction, that jurisdiction is the bank's jurisdiction.

(3) If neither paragraph (1) nor paragraph (2) applies and an agreement between the bank and its customer governing the deposit account expressly provides that the deposit account is maintained at an office in a particular jurisdiction, that jurisdiction is the bank's jurisdiction.

(4) If none of the preceding paragraphs applies, the bank's jurisdiction is the jurisdiction in which the office identified in an account statement as the office serving the customer's account is located.

(5) If none of the preceding paragraphs applies, the bank's jurisdiction is the jurisdiction in which the chief executive office of the bank is located.

§ 9–305. Law Governing Perfection and Priority of Security Interests in Investment Property.

(a) Except as otherwise provided in subsection (c), the following rules apply:

(1) While a security certificate is located in a jurisdiction, the local law of that jurisdiction governs perfection, the effect of perfection or nonperfection, and the priority of a security interest in the certificated security represented thereby.

(2) The local law of the issuer's jurisdiction as specified in Section 8–110(d) governs perfection, the effect of perfection or nonperfection, and the priority of a security interest in an uncertificated security.

(3) The local law of the securities intermediary's jurisdiction as specified in Section 8–110(e) governs perfection, the effect of perfection or nonperfection, and the priority of a security interest in a security entitlement or securities account.

(4) The local law of the commodity intermediary's jurisdiction governs perfection, the effect of perfection or nonperfection, and the priority of a security interest in a commodity contract or commodity account.

(b) The following rules determine a commodity intermediary's jurisdiction for purposes of this part:

(1) If an agreement between the commodity intermediary and commodity customer governing the commodity account expressly provides that a particular jurisdiction is the commodity intermediary's jurisdiction for purposes of this part, this article, or [the Uniform Commercial Code], that jurisdiction is the commodity intermediary's jurisdiction.

(2) If paragraph (1) does not apply and an agreement between the commodity intermediary and commodity customer governing the commodity account expressly provides that the agreement is governed by the law of a particular jurisdiction, that jurisdiction is the commodity intermediary's jurisdiction.

(3) If neither paragraph (1) nor paragraph (2) applies and an agreement between the commodity intermediary and commodity customer governing the commodity account expressly provides that the commodity account is maintained at an office in a particular jurisdiction, that jurisdiction is the commodity intermediary's jurisdiction.

(4) If none of the preceding paragraphs applies, the commodity intermediary's jurisdiction is the jurisdiction in which the office identified in an account statement as the office serving the commodity customer's account is located.

(5) If none of the preceding paragraphs applies, the commodity intermediary's jurisdiction is the jurisdiction in which the chief executive office of the commodity intermediary is located.

(c) The local law of the jurisdiction in which the debtor is located governs:

(1) perfection of a security interest in investment property by filing;

(2) automatic perfection of a security interest in investment property created by a broker or securities intermediary; and

(3) automatic perfection of a security interest in a commodity contract or commodity account created by a commodity intermediary.

§ 9–306. Law Governing Perfection and Priority of Security Interests in Letter-of-Credit Rights.

(a) Subject to subsection (c), the local law of the issuer's jurisdiction or a nominated person's jurisdiction governs perfection, the effect of perfection or nonperfection, and the priority of a security interest in a letter-of-credit right if the issuer's jurisdiction or nominated person's jurisdiction is a State.

(b) For purposes of this part, an issuer's jurisdiction or nominated person's jurisdiction is the jurisdiction whose law governs the liability of the issuer or nominated person with respect to the letter-of-credit right as provided in Section 5–116.

(c) This section does not apply to a security interest that is perfected only under Section 9–308(d).

§ 9–307. Location of Debtor.

(a) In this section, "place of business" means a place where a debtor conducts its affairs.

(b) Except as otherwise provided in this section, the following rules determine a debtor's location:

(1) A debtor who is an individual is located at the individual's principal residence.

(2) A debtor that is an organization and has only one place of business is located at its place of business.

(3) A debtor that is an organization and has more than one place of business is located at its chief executive office.

(c) Subsection (b) applies only if a debtor's residence, place of business, or chief executive office, as applicable, is located in a jurisdiction whose law generally requires information concerning the existence of a nonpossessory security interest to be made generally available in a filing, recording, or registration system as a condition or result of the security interest's obtaining priority over the rights of a lien creditor with respect to the collateral. If subsection (b) does not apply, the debtor is located in the District of Columbia.

(d) A person that ceases to exist, have a residence, or have a place of business continues to be located in the jurisdiction specified by subsections (b) and (c).

(e) A registered organization that is organized under the law of a State is located in that State.

(f) Except as otherwise provided in subsection (i), a registered organization that is organized under the law of the United States and a branch or agency of a bank that is not organized under the law of the United States or a State are located:

(1) in the State that the law of the United States designates, if the law designates a State of location;

(2) in the State that the registered organization, branch, or agency designates, if the law of the United States authorizes the registered organization, branch, or agency to designate its State of location; or

(3) in the District of Columbia, if neither paragraph (1) nor paragraph (2) applies.

(g) A registered organization continues to be located in the jurisdiction specified by subsection (e) or (f) notwithstanding:

(1) the suspension, revocation, forfeiture, or lapse of the registered organization's status as such in its jurisdiction of organization; or

(2) the dissolution, winding up, or cancellation of the existence of the registered organization.

(h) The United States is located in the District of Columbia.

(i) A branch or agency of a bank that is not organized under the law of the United States or a State is located in the State in which the branch or agency is licensed, if all branches and agencies of the bank are licensed in only one State.

(j) A foreign air carrier under the Federal Aviation Act of 1958, as amended, is located at the designated office of the agent upon which service of process may be made on behalf of the carrier.

(k) This section applies only for purposes of this part.

[Subpart 2. Perfection]

§ 9–308. When Security Interest or Agricultural Lien Is Perfected; Continuity of Perfection.

(a) Except as otherwise provided in this section and Section 9–309, a security interest is perfected if it has attached and all of the applicable requirements for perfection in Sections 9–310 through 9–316 have been satisfied. A security interest is perfected when it attaches if the applicable requirements are satisfied before the security interest attaches.

(b) An agricultural lien is perfected if it has become effective and all of the applicable requirements for perfection in Section 9–310 have been satisfied. An agricultural lien is perfected when it becomes effective if the applicable requirements are satisfied before the agricultural lien becomes effective.

(c) A security interest or agricultural lien is perfected continuously if it is originally perfected by one method under this article and is later perfected by another method under this article, without an intermediate period when it was unperfected.

(d) Perfection of a security interest in collateral also perfects a security interest in a supporting obligation for the collateral.

(e) Perfection of a security interest in a right to payment or performance also perfects a security interest in a security interest, mortgage, or other lien on personal or real property securing the right.

(f) Perfection of a security interest in a securities account also perfects a security interest in the security entitlements carried in the securities account.

(g) Perfection of a security interest in a commodity account also perfects a security interest in the commodity contracts carried in the commodity account.

Legislative Note: Any statute conflicting with subsection (e) must be made expressly subject to that subsection.

§ 9–309. Security Interest Perfected upon Attachment.

The following security interests are perfected when they attach:

(1) a purchase-money security interest in consumer goods, except as otherwise provided in Section 9–311(b) with respect to consumer goods that are subject to a statute or treaty described in Section 9–311(a);

(2) an assignment of accounts or payment intangibles which does not by itself or in conjunction with other assignments to the same assignee transfer a significant part of the assignor's outstanding accounts or payment intangibles;

(3) a sale of a payment intangible;

(4) a sale of a promissory note;

(5) a security interest created by the assignment of a health-care-insurance receivable to the provider of the health-care goods or services;

(6) a security interest arising under Section 2–401, 2–505, 2–711(3), or 2A–508(5), until the debtor obtains possession of the collateral;

(7) a security interest of a collecting bank arising under Section 4–210;

(8) a security interest of an issuer or nominated person arising under Section 5–118;

(9) a security interest arising in the delivery of a financial asset under Section 9–206(c);

(10) a security interest in investment property created by a broker or securities intermediary;

(11) a security interest in a commodity contract or a commodity account created by a commodity intermediary;

(12) an assignment for the benefit of all creditors of the transferor and subsequent transfers by the assignee thereunder; and

(13) a security interest created by an assignment of a beneficial interest in a decedent's estate; and

(14) a sale by an individual of an account that is a right to payment of winnings in a lottery or other game of chance.

§ 9–310. When Filing Required to Perfect Security Interest or Agricultural Lien; Security Interests and Agricultural Liens to Which Filing Provisions Do Not Apply.

(a) Except as otherwise provided in subsection (b) and Section 9–312(b), a financing statement must be filed to perfect all security interests and agricultural liens.

(b) The filing of a financing statement is not necessary to perfect a security interest:

(1) that is perfected under Section 9–308(d), (e), (f), or (g);

(2) that is perfected under Section 9–309 when it attaches;

(3) in property subject to a statute, regulation, or treaty described in Section 9–311(a);

(4) in goods in possession of a bailee which is perfected under Section 9–312(d)(1) or (2);

(5) in certificated securities, documents, goods, or instruments which is perfected without filing or possession under Section 9–312(e), (f), or (g);

(6) in collateral in the secured party's possession under Section 9–313;

(7) in a certificated security which is perfected by delivery of the security certificate to the secured party under Section 9–313;

(8) in deposit accounts, electronic chattel paper, investment property, or letter-of-credit rights which is perfected by control under Section 9–314;

(9) in proceeds which is perfected under Section 9–315; or

(10) that is perfected under Section 9–316.

(c) If a secured party assigns a perfected security interest or agricultural lien, a filing under this article is not required to continue the perfected status of the security interest against creditors of and transferees from the original debtor.

§ 9–311. Perfection of Security Interests in Property Subject to Certain Statutes, Regulations, and Treaties.

(a) Except as otherwise provided in subsection (d), the filing of a financing statement is not necessary or effective to perfect a security interest in property subject to:

(1) a statute, regulation, or treaty of the United States whose requirements for a security interest's obtaining priority over the rights of a lien creditor with respect to the property preempt Section 9–310(a);

(2) [list any certificate-of-title statute covering automobiles, trailers, mobile homes, boats, farm tractors, or the like, which provides for a security interest to be indicated on the certificate as a condition or result of perfection, and any non-Uniform Commercial Code central filing statute]; or

(3) a certificate-of-title statute of another jurisdiction which provides for a security interest to be indicated on the certificate as a condition or result of the security interest's obtaining priority over the rights of a lien creditor with respect to the property.

(b) Compliance with the requirements of a statute, regulation, or treaty described in subsection (a) for obtaining priority over the rights of a lien creditor is equivalent to the filing of a financing statement under this article. Except as otherwise provided in subsection (d) and Sections 9–313 and 9–316(d) and (e) for goods covered by a certificate of title, a security interest in property subject to a statute, regulation, or treaty described in subsection (a) may be perfected only by compliance with those requirements, and a security interest so perfected remains perfected notwithstanding a change in the use or transfer of possession of the collateral.

(c) Except as otherwise provided in subsection (d) and Section 9–316(d) and (e), duration and renewal of perfection of a security interest perfected by compliance with the requirements prescribed by a statute, regulation, or treaty described in subsection (a) are governed by the statute, regulation, or treaty. In other respects, the security interest is subject to this article.

(d) During any period in which collateral subject to a statute specified in subsection (a)(2) is inventory held for sale or lease by a person or leased by that person as lessor and that person is in the business of selling goods of that kind, this section does not apply to a security interest in that collateral created by that person.

Legislative Note: This Article contemplates that perfection of a security interest in goods covered by a certificate of title occurs upon receipt by appropriate State officials of a properly tendered application for a certificate of title on which the security interest is to be indicated, without a relation back to an earlier time. States whose certificate-of-title statutes provide for perfection at a different time or contain a relation-back provision should amend the statutes accordingly.

§ 9–312. Perfection of Security Interests in Chattel Paper, Deposit Accounts, Documents, Goods Covered by Documents, Instruments, Investment Property, Letter-of-Credit Rights, and Money; Perfection by Permissive Filing; Temporary Perfection without Filing or Transfer of Possession.

(a) A security interest in chattel paper, negotiable documents, instruments, or investment property may be perfected by filing.

(b) Except as otherwise provided in Section 9–315(c) and (d) for proceeds:

(1) a security interest in a deposit account may be perfected only by control under Section 9–314;

(2) and except as otherwise provided in Section 9–308(d), a security interest in a letter-of-credit right may be perfected only by control under Section 9–314; and

(3) a security interest in money may be perfected only by the secured party's taking possession under Section 9–313.

(c) While goods are in the possession of a bailee that has issued a negotiable document covering the goods:

(1) a security interest in the goods may be perfected by perfecting a security interest in the document; and

(2) a security interest perfected in the document has priority over any security interest that becomes perfected in the goods by another method during that time.

(d) While goods are in the possession of a bailee that has issued a nonnegotiable document covering the goods, a security interest in the goods may be perfected by:

(1) issuance of a document in the name of the secured party;

(2) the bailee's receipt of notification of the secured party's interest; or

(3) filing as to the goods.

(e) A security interest in certificated securities, negotiable documents, or instruments is perfected without filing or the taking of possession for a period of 20 days from the time it attaches to the extent that it arises for new value given under an authenticated security agreement.

(f) A perfected security interest in a negotiable document or goods in possession of a bailee, other than one that has issued a negotiable document for the goods, remains perfected for 20 days without filing if the secured party makes available to the debtor the goods or documents representing the goods for the purpose of:

(1) ultimate sale or exchange; or

(2) loading, unloading, storing, shipping, transshipping, manufacturing, processing, or otherwise dealing with them in a manner preliminary to their sale or exchange.

(g) A perfected security interest in a certificated security or instrument remains perfected for 20 days without filing if the secured party delivers the security certificate or instrument to the debtor for the purpose of:

(1) ultimate sale or exchange; or

(2) presentation, collection, enforcement, renewal, or registration of transfer.

(h) After the 20-day period specified in subsection (e), (f), or (g) expires, perfection depends upon compliance with this article.

§ 9–313. When Possession by or Delivery to Secured Party Perfects Security Interest without Filing.

(a) Except as otherwise provided in subsection (b), a secured party may perfect a security interest in negotiable documents, goods, instruments, money, or tangible chattel paper by taking possession of the collateral. A secured party may perfect a security interest in certificated securities by taking delivery of the certificated securities under Section 8–301.

(b) With respect to goods covered by a certificate of title issued by this State, a secured party may perfect a security interest in the goods by taking possession of the goods only in the circumstances described in Section 9–316(d).

(c) With respect to collateral other than certificated securities and goods covered by a document, a secured party takes possession of collateral in the possession of a person other than the debtor, the secured party, or a lessee of the collateral from the debtor in the ordinary course of the debtor's business, when:

(1) the person in possession authenticates a record acknowledging that it holds possession of the collateral for the secured party's benefit; or

(2) the person takes possession of the collateral after having authenticated a record acknowledging that it will hold possession of collateral for the secured party's benefit.

(d) If perfection of a security interest depends upon possession of the collateral by a secured party, perfection occurs no earlier than the time the secured party takes possession and continues only while the secured party retains possession.

(e) A security interest in a certificated security in registered form is perfected by delivery when delivery of the certificated security occurs under Section 8–301 and remains perfected by delivery until the debtor obtains possession of the security certificate.

(f) A person in possession of collateral is not required to acknowledge that it holds possession for a secured party's benefit.

(g) If a person acknowledges that it holds possession for the secured party's benefit:

(1) the acknowledgment is effective under subsection (c) or Section 8–301(a), even if the acknowledgment violates the rights of a debtor; and

(2) unless the person otherwise agrees or law other than this article otherwise provides, the person does not owe any duty to the secured party and is not required to confirm the acknowledgment to another person.

(h) A secured party having possession of collateral does not relinquish possession by delivering the collateral to a person other than the debtor or a lessee of the collateral from the debtor in the ordinary course of the debtor's business if the person was instructed before the delivery or is instructed contemporaneously with the delivery:

(1) to hold possession of the collateral for the secured party's benefit; or

(2) to redeliver the collateral to the secured party.

(i) A secured party does not relinquish possession, even if a delivery under subsection (h) violates the rights of a debtor. A person to which collateral is delivered under subsection (h) does not owe any duty to the secured party and is not required to confirm the delivery to another person unless the person otherwise agrees or law other than this article otherwise provides.

§ 9–314. Perfection by Control.

(a) A security interest in investment property, deposit accounts, letter-of-credit rights, or electronic chattel paper may be perfected by control of the collateral under Section 9–104, 9–105, 9–106, or 9–107.

(b) A security interest in deposit accounts, electronic chattel paper, or letter-of-credit rights is perfected by control under Section 9–104, 9–105, or 9–107 when the secured party obtains control and remains perfected by control only while the secured party retains control.

(c) A security interest in investment property is perfected by control under Section 9–106 from the time the secured party obtains control and remains perfected by control until:

(1) the secured party does not have control; and

(2) one of the following occurs:

(A) if the collateral is a certificated security, the debtor has or acquires possession of the security certificate;

(B) if the collateral is an uncertificated security, the issuer has registered or registers the debtor as the registered owner; or

(C) if the collateral is a security entitlement, the debtor is or becomes the entitlement holder.

§ 9–315. Secured Party's Rights on Disposition of Collateral and in Proceeds.

(a) Except as otherwise provided in this article and in Section 2–403(2):

(1) a security interest or agricultural lien continues in collateral notwithstanding sale, lease, license, exchange, or other disposition thereof unless the secured party authorized the disposition free of the security interest or agricultural lien; and

(2) a security interest attaches to any identifiable proceeds of collateral.

(b) Proceeds that are commingled with other property are identifiable proceeds:

(1) if the proceeds are goods, to the extent provided by Section 9–336; and

(2) if the proceeds are not goods, to the extent that the secured party identifies the proceeds by a method of tracing, including application of equitable principles, that is permitted under law other than this article with respect to commingled property of the type involved.

(c) A security interest in proceeds is a perfected security interest if the security interest in the original collateral was perfected.

(d) A perfected security interest in proceeds becomes unperfected on the 21st day after the security interest attaches to the proceeds unless:

(1) the following conditions are satisfied:

(A) a filed financing statement covers the original collateral;

(B) the proceeds are collateral in which a security interest may be perfected by filing in the office in which the financing statement has been filed; and

(C) the proceeds are not acquired with cash proceeds;

(2) the proceeds are identifiable cash proceeds; or

(3) the security interest in the proceeds is perfected other than under subsection (c) when the security interest attaches to the proceeds or within 20 days thereafter.

(e) If a filed financing statement covers the original collateral, a security interest in proceeds which remains perfected under subsection (d)(1) becomes unperfected at the later of:

(1) when the effectiveness of the filed financing statement lapses under Section 9–515 or is terminated under Section 9–513; or

(2) the 21st day after the security interest attaches to the proceeds.

§ 9–316. Continued Perfection of Security Interest Following Change in Governing Law.

(a) A security interest perfected pursuant to the law of the jurisdiction designated in Section 9–301(1) or 9–305(c) remains perfected until the earliest of:

(1) the time perfection would have ceased under the law of that jurisdiction;

(2) the expiration of four months after a change of the debtor's location to another jurisdiction; or

(3) the expiration of one year after a transfer of collateral to a person that thereby becomes a debtor and is located in another jurisdiction.

(b) If a security interest described in subsection (a) becomes perfected under the law of the other jurisdiction before the earliest time or event described in that subsection, it remains perfected thereafter. If the security interest does not become perfected under the law of the other jurisdiction before the earliest time or event, it becomes unperfected and is deemed never to have been perfected as against a purchaser of the collateral for value.

(c) A possessory security interest in collateral, other than goods covered by a certificate of title and as-extracted collateral consisting of goods, remains continuously perfected if:

(1) the collateral is located in one jurisdiction and subject to a security interest perfected under the law of that jurisdiction;

(2) thereafter the collateral is brought into another jurisdiction; and

(3) upon entry into the other jurisdiction, the security interest is perfected under the law of the other jurisdiction.

(d) Except as otherwise provided in subsection (e), a security interest in goods covered by a certificate of title which is perfected by any method under the law of another jurisdiction when the goods become covered by a certificate of title from this State remains perfected until the security interest would have become unperfected under the law of the other jurisdiction had the goods not become so covered.

(e) A security interest described in subsection (d) becomes unperfected as against a purchaser of the goods for value and is deemed never to have been perfected as against a purchaser of the goods for value if the applicable requirements for perfection under Section 9–311(b) or 9–313 are not satisfied before the earlier of:

(1) the time the security interest would have become unperfected under the law of the other jurisdiction had the goods not become covered by a certificate of title from this State; or

(2) the expiration of four months after the goods had become so covered.

(f) A security interest in deposit accounts, letter-of-credit rights, or investment property which is perfected under the law of the bank's jurisdiction, the issuer's jurisdiction, a nominated person's jurisdiction, the securities intermediary's jurisdiction, or the commodity intermediary's jurisdiction, as applicable, remains perfected until the earlier of:

(1) the time the security interest would have become unperfected under the law of that jurisdiction; or

(2) the expiration of four months after a change of the applicable jurisdiction to another jurisdiction.

(g) If a security interest described in subsection (f) becomes perfected under the law of the other jurisdiction before the earlier of the time or the end of the period described in that subsection, it remains perfected thereafter. If the security interest does not become perfected under the law of the other jurisdiction before the earlier of that time or the end of

that period, it becomes unperfected and is deemed never to have been perfected as against a purchaser of the collateral for value.

[Subpart 3. Priority]

§ 9–317. Interests That Take Priority over or Take Free of Security Interest or Agricultural Lien.

(a) A security interest or agricultural lien is subordinate to the rights of:

(1) a person entitled to priority under Section 9–322; and

(2) except as otherwise provided in subsection (e), a person that becomes a lien creditor before the earlier of the time:

(A) the security interest or agricultural lien is perfected; or

(B) one of the conditions specified in Section 9–203(b)(3) is met and a financing statement covering the collateral is filed.

(b) Except as otherwise provided in subsection (e), a buyer, other than a secured party, of tangible chattel paper, documents, goods, instruments, or a security certificate takes free of a security interest or agricultural lien if the buyer gives value and receives delivery of the collateral without knowledge of the security interest or agricultural lien and before it is perfected.

(c) Except as otherwise provided in subsection (e), a lessee of goods takes free of a security interest or agricultural lien if the lessee gives value and receives delivery of the collateral without knowledge of the security interest or agricultural lien and before it is perfected.

(d) A licensee of a general intangible or a buyer, other than a secured party, of accounts, electronic chattel paper, general intangibles, or investment property other than a certificated security takes free of a security interest if the licensee or buyer gives value without knowledge of the security interest and before it is perfected.

(e) Except as otherwise provided in Sections 9–320 and 9–321, if a person files a financing statement with respect to a purchase-money security interest before or within 20 days after the debtor receives delivery of the collateral, the security interest takes priority over the rights of a buyer, lessee, or lien creditor which arise between the time the security interest attaches and the time of filing.

As amended in 2000.

§ 9–318. No Interest Retained in Right to Payment That Is Sold; Rights and Title of Seller of Account or Chattel Paper with Respect to Creditors and Purchasers.

(a) A debtor that has sold an account, chattel paper, payment intangible, or promissory note does not retain a legal or equitable interest in the collateral sold.

(b) For purposes of determining the rights of creditors of, and purchasers for value of an account or chattel paper from, a debtor that has sold an account or chattel paper, while the buyer's security interest is unperfected, the debtor is deemed to have rights and title to the account or chattel paper identical to those the debtor sold.

§ 9–319. Rights and Title of Consignee with Respect to Creditors and Purchasers.

(a) Except as otherwise provided in subsection (b), for purposes of determining the rights of creditors of, and purchasers for value of goods from, a consignee, while the goods are in the possession of the consignee, the consignee is deemed to have rights and title to the goods identical to those the consignor had or had power to transfer.

(b) For purposes of determining the rights of a creditor of a consignee, law other than this article determines the rights and title of a consignee while goods are in the consignee's possession if, under this part, a perfected security interest held by the consignor would have priority over the rights of the creditor.

§ 9–320. Buyer of Goods.

(a) Except as otherwise provided in subsection (e), a buyer in ordinary course of business, other than a person buying farm products from a person engaged in farming operations, takes free of a security interest created by the buyer's seller, even if the security interest is perfected and the buyer knows of its existence.

(b) Except as otherwise provided in subsection (e), a buyer of goods from a person who used or bought the goods for use primarily for personal, family, or household purposes takes free of a security interest, even if perfected, if the buyer buys:

    (1) without knowledge of the security interest;

    (2) for value;

    (3) primarily for the buyer's personal, family, or household purposes; and

    (4) before the filing of a financing statement covering the goods.

(c) To the extent that it affects the priority of a security interest over a buyer of goods under subsection (b), the period of effectiveness of a filing made in the jurisdiction in which the seller is located is governed by Section 9–316(a) and (b).

(d) A buyer in ordinary course of business buying oil, gas, or other minerals at the wellhead or minehead or after extraction takes free of an interest arising out of an encumbrance.

(e) Subsections (a) and (b) do not affect a security interest in goods in the possession of the secured party under Section 9–313.

§ 9–321. Licensee of General Intangible and Lessee of Goods in Ordinary Course of Business.

(a) In this section, "licensee in ordinary course of business" means a person that becomes a licensee of a general intangible in good faith, without knowledge that the license violates the rights of another person in the general intangible, and in the ordinary course from a person in the business of licensing general intangibles of that kind. A person becomes a licensee in the ordinary course if the license to the person comports with the usual or customary practices in the kind of business in which the licensor is engaged or with the licensor's own usual or customary practices.

(b) A licensee in ordinary course of business takes its rights under a nonexclusive license free of a security interest in the general intangible created by the licensor, even if the security interest is perfected and the licensee knows of its existence.

(c) A lessee in ordinary course of business takes its leasehold interest free of a security interest in the goods created by the lessor, even if the security interest is perfected and the lessee knows of its existence.

§ 9–322. Priorities among Conflicting Security Interests in and Agricultural Liens on Same Collateral.

(a) Except as otherwise provided in this section, priority among conflicting security interests and agricultural liens in the same collateral is determined according to the following rules:

    (1) Conflicting perfected security interests and agricultural liens rank according to priority in time of filing or perfection. Priority dates from the earlier of the time a filing covering the collateral is first made or the security interest or agricultural lien is first perfected, if there is no period thereafter when there is neither filing nor perfection.

    (2) A perfected security interest or agricultural lien has priority over a conflicting unperfected security interest or agricultural lien.

    (3) The first security interest or agricultural lien to attach or become effective has priority if conflicting security interests and agricultural liens are unperfected.

(b) For the purposes of subsection (a)(1):

    (1) the time of filing or perfection as to a security interest in collateral is also the time of filing or perfection as to a security interest in proceeds; and

    (2) the time of filing or perfection as to a security interest in collateral supported by a supporting obligation is also the time of filing or perfection as to a security interest in the supporting obligation.

(c) Except as otherwise provided in subsection (f), a security interest in collateral which qualifies for priority over a conflicting security interest under Section 9–327, 9–328, 9–329, 9–330, or 9–331 also has priority over a conflicting security interest in:

    (1) any supporting obligation for the collateral; and

    (2) proceeds of the collateral if:

        (A) the security interest in proceeds is perfected;

        (B) the proceeds are cash proceeds or of the same type as the collateral; and

        (C) in the case of proceeds that are proceeds of proceeds, all intervening proceeds are cash proceeds, proceeds of the same type as the collateral, or an account relating to the collateral.

(d) Subject to subsection (e) and except as otherwise provided in subsection (f), if a security interest in chattel paper, deposit accounts, negotiable documents, instruments, investment property, or letter-of-credit rights is perfected by a method other than filing, conflicting perfected security interests in proceeds of the collateral rank according to priority in time of filing.

(e) Subsection (d) applies only if the proceeds of the collateral are not cash proceeds, chattel paper, negotiable documents, instruments, investment property, or letter-of-credit rights.

(f) Subsections (a) through (e) are subject to:

    (1) subsection (g) and the other provisions of this part;

    (2) Section 4–210 with respect to a security interest of a collecting bank;

    (3) Section 5–118 with respect to a security interest of an issuer or nominated person; and

    (4) Section 9–110 with respect to a security interest arising under Article 2 or 2A.

(g) A perfected agricultural lien on collateral has priority over a conflicting security interest in or agricultural lien on the same collateral if the statute creating the agricultural lien so provides.

§ 9–323. Future Advances.

(a) Except as otherwise provided in subsection (c), for purposes of determining the priority of a perfected security interest under Section

9–322(a)(1), perfection of the security interest dates from the time an advance is made to the extent that the security interest secures an advance that:

(1) is made while the security interest is perfected only:

(A) under Section 9–309 when it attaches; or

(B) temporarily under Section 9–312(e), (f), or (g); and

(2) is not made pursuant to a commitment entered into before or while the security interest is perfected by a method other than under Section 9–309 or 9–312(e), (f), or (g).

(b) Except as otherwise provided in subsection (c), a security interest is subordinate to the rights of a person that becomes a lien creditor to the extent that the security interest secures an advance made more than 45 days after the person becomes a lien creditor unless the advance is made:

(1) without knowledge of the lien; or

(2) pursuant to a commitment entered into without knowledge of the lien.

(c) Subsections (a) and (b) do not apply to a security interest held by a secured party that is a buyer of accounts, chattel paper, payment intangibles, or promissory notes or a consignor.

(d) Except as otherwise provided in subsection (e), a buyer of goods other than a buyer in ordinary course of business takes free of a security interest to the extent that it secures advances made after the earlier of:

(1) the time the secured party acquires knowledge of the buyer's purchase; or

(2) 45 days after the purchase.

(e) Subsection (d) does not apply if the advance is made pursuant to a commitment entered into without knowledge of the buyer's purchase and before the expiration of the 45-day period.

(f) Except as otherwise provided in subsection (g), a lessee of goods, other than a lessee in ordinary course of business, takes the leasehold interest free of a security interest to the extent that it secures advances made after the earlier of:

(1) the time the secured party acquires knowledge of the lease; or

(2) 45 days after the lease contract becomes enforceable.

(g) Subsection (f) does not apply if the advance is made pursuant to a commitment entered into without knowledge of the lease and before the expiration of the 45-day period.

As amended in 1999.

§ 9–324. Priority of Purchase-Money Security Interests.

(a) Except as otherwise provided in subsection (g), a perfected purchase-money security interest in goods other than inventory or livestock has priority over a conflicting security interest in the same goods, and, except as otherwise provided in Section 9–327, a perfected security interest in its identifiable proceeds also has priority, if the purchase-money security interest is perfected when the debtor receives possession of the collateral or within 20 days thereafter.

(b) Subject to subsection (c) and except as otherwise provided in subsection (g), a perfected purchase-money security interest in inventory has priority over a conflicting security interest in the same inventory, has priority over a conflicting security interest in chattel paper or an instrument constituting proceeds of the inventory and in pro-

ceeds of the chattel paper, if so provided in Section 9–330, and, except as otherwise provided in Section 9–327, also has priority in identifiable cash proceeds of the inventory to the extent the identifiable cash proceeds are received on or before the delivery of the inventory to a buyer, if:

(1) the purchase-money security interest is perfected when the debtor receives possession of the inventory;

(2) the purchase-money secured party sends an authenticated notification to the holder of the conflicting security interest;

(3) the holder of the conflicting security interest receives the notification within five years before the debtor receives possession of the inventory; and

(4) the notification states that the person sending the notification has or expects to acquire a purchase-money security interest in inventory of the debtor and describes the inventory.

(c) Subsections (b)(2) through (4) apply only if the holder of the conflicting security interest had filed a financing statement covering the same types of inventory:

(1) if the purchase-money security interest is perfected by filing, before the date of the filing; or

(2) if the purchase-money security interest is temporarily perfected without filing or possession under Section 9–312(f), before the beginning of the 20-day period thereunder.

(d) Subject to subsection (e) and except as otherwise provided in subsection (g), a perfected purchase-money security interest in livestock that are farm products has priority over a conflicting security interest in the same livestock, and, except as otherwise provided in Section 9–327, a perfected security interest in their identifiable proceeds and identifiable products in their unmanufactured states also has priority, if:

(1) the purchase-money security interest is perfected when the debtor receives possession of the livestock;

(2) the purchase-money secured party sends an authenticated notification to the holder of the conflicting security interest;

(3) the holder of the conflicting security interest receives the notification within six months before the debtor receives possession of the livestock; and

(4) the notification states that the person sending the notification has or expects to acquire a purchase-money security interest in livestock of the debtor and describes the livestock.

(e) Subsections (d)(2) through (4) apply only if the holder of the conflicting security interest had filed a financing statement covering the same types of livestock:

(1) if the purchase-money security interest is perfected by filing, before the date of the filing; or

(2) if the purchase-money security interest is temporarily perfected without filing or possession under Section 9–312(f), before the beginning of the 20-day period thereunder.

(f) Except as otherwise provided in subsection (g), a perfected purchase-money security interest in software has priority over a conflicting security interest in the same collateral, and, except as otherwise provided in Section 9–327, a perfected security interest in its identifiable proceeds also has priority, to the extent that the purchase-money security interest in the goods in which the software was acquired for use has priority in the goods and proceeds of the goods under this section.

(g) If more than one security interest qualifies for priority in the same collateral under subsection (a), (b), (d), or (f):

(1) a security interest securing an obligation incurred as all or part of the price of the collateral has priority over a security interest securing an obligation incurred for value given to enable the debtor to acquire rights in or the use of collateral; and

(2) in all other cases, Section 9–322(a) applies to the qualifying security interests.

§ 9–325. Priority of Security Interests in Transferred Collateral.

(a) Except as otherwise provided in subsection (b), a security interest created by a debtor is subordinate to a security interest in the same collateral created by another person if:

(1) the debtor acquired the collateral subject to the security interest created by the other person;

(2) the security interest created by the other person was perfected when the debtor acquired the collateral; and

(3) there is no period thereafter when the security interest is unperfected.

(b) Subsection (a) subordinates a security interest only if the security interest:

(1) otherwise would have priority solely under Section 9–322(a) or 9–324; or

(2) arose solely under Section 2–711(3) or 2A–508(5).

§ 9–326. Priority of Security Interests Created by New Debtor.

(a) Subject to subsection (b), a security interest created by a new debtor which is perfected by a filed financing statement that is effective solely under Section 9–508 in collateral in which a new debtor has or acquires rights is subordinate to a security interest in the same collateral which is perfected other than by a filed financing statement that is effective solely under Section 9–508.

(b) The other provisions of this part determine the priority among conflicting security interests in the same collateral perfected by filed financing statements that are effective solely under Section 9–508. However, if the security agreements to which a new debtor became bound as debtor were not entered into by the same original debtor, the conflicting security interests rank according to priority in time of the new debtor's having become bound.

§ 9–327. Priority of Security Interests in Deposit Account.

The following rules govern priority among conflicting security interests in the same deposit account:

(1) A security interest held by a secured party having control of the deposit account under Section 9–104 has priority over a conflicting security interest held by a secured party that does not have control.

(2) Except as otherwise provided in paragraphs (3) and (4), security interests perfected by control under Section 9–314 rank according to priority in time of obtaining control.

(3) Except as otherwise provided in paragraph (4), a security interest held by the bank with which the deposit account is maintained has priority over a conflicting security interest held by another secured party.

(4) A security interest perfected by control under Section 9–104(a)(3) has priority over a security interest held by the bank with which the deposit account is maintained.

§ 9–328. Priority of Security Interests in Investment Property.

The following rules govern priority among conflicting security interests in the same investment property:

(1) A security interest held by a secured party having control of investment property under Section 9–106 has priority over a security interest held by a secured party that does not have control of the investment property.

(2) Except as otherwise provided in paragraphs (3) and (4), conflicting security interests held by secured parties each of which has control under Section 9–106 rank according to priority in time of:

(A) if the collateral is a security, obtaining control;

(B) if the collateral is a security entitlement carried in a securities account and:

(i) if the secured party obtained control under Section 8–106(d)(1), the secured party's becoming the person for which the securities account is maintained;

(ii) if the secured party obtained control under Section 8–106(d)(2), the securities intermediary's agreement to comply with the secured party's entitlement orders with respect to security entitlements carried or to be carried in the securities account; or

(iii) if the secured party obtained control through another person under Section 8–106(d)(3), the time on which priority would be based under this paragraph if the other person were the secured party; or

(C) if the collateral is a commodity contract carried with a commodity intermediary, the satisfaction of the requirement for control specified in Section 9–106(b)(2) with respect to commodity contracts carried or to be carried with the commodity intermediary.

(3) A security interest held by a securities intermediary in a security entitlement or a securities account maintained with the securities intermediary has priority over a conflicting security interest held by another secured party.

(4) A security interest held by a commodity intermediary in a commodity contract or a commodity account maintained with the commodity intermediary has priority over a conflicting security interest held by another secured party.

(5) A security interest in a certificated security in registered form which is perfected by taking delivery under Section 9–313(a) and not by control under Section 9–314 has priority over a conflicting security interest perfected by a method other than control.

(6) Conflicting security interests created by a broker, securities intermediary, or commodity intermediary which are perfected without control under Section 9–106 rank equally.

(7) In all other cases, priority among conflicting security interests in investment property is governed by Sections 9–322 and 9–323.

§ 9–329. Priority of Security Interests in Letter-of-Credit Right.

The following rules govern priority among conflicting security interests in the same letter-of-credit right:

(1) A security interest held by a secured party having control of the letter-of-credit right under Section 9–107 has priority to the extent of its control over a conflicting security interest held by a secured party that does not have control.

(2) Security interests perfected by control under Section 9–314 rank according to priority in time of obtaining control.

§ 9–330. Priority of Purchaser of Chattel Paper or Instrument.

(a) A purchaser of chattel paper has priority over a security interest in the chattel paper which is claimed merely as proceeds of inventory subject to a security interest if:

> (1) in good faith and in the ordinary course of the purchaser's business, the purchaser gives new value and takes possession of the chattel paper or obtains control of the chattel paper under Section 9–105; and

> (2) the chattel paper does not indicate that it has been assigned to an identified assignee other than the purchaser.

(b) A purchaser of chattel paper has priority over a security interest in the chattel paper which is claimed other than merely as proceeds of inventory subject to a security interest if the purchaser gives new value and takes possession of the chattel paper or obtains control of the chattel paper under Section 9–105 in good faith, in the ordinary course of the purchaser's business, and without knowledge that the purchase violates the rights of the secured party.

(c) Except as otherwise provided in Section 9–327, a purchaser having priority in chattel paper under subsection (a) or (b) also has priority in proceeds of the chattel paper to the extent that:

> (1) Section 9–322 provides for priority in the proceeds; or

> (2) the proceeds consist of the specific goods covered by the chattel paper or cash proceeds of the specific goods, even if the purchaser's security interest in the proceeds is unperfected.

(d) Except as otherwise provided in Section 9–331(a), a purchaser of an instrument has priority over a security interest in the instrument perfected by a method other than possession if the purchaser gives value and takes possession of the instrument in good faith and without knowledge that the purchase violates the rights of the secured party.

(e) For purposes of subsections (a) and (b), the holder of a purchase-money security interest in inventory gives new value for chattel paper constituting proceeds of the inventory.

(f) For purposes of subsections (b) and (d), if chattel paper or an instrument indicates that it has been assigned to an identified secured party other than the purchaser, a purchaser of the chattel paper or instrument has knowledge that the purchase violates the rights of the secured party.

§ 9–331. Priority of Rights of Purchasers of Instruments, Documents, and Securities under Other Articles; Priority of Interests in Financial Assets and Security Entitlements under Article 8.

(a) This article does not limit the rights of a holder in due course of a negotiable instrument, a holder to which a negotiable document of title has been duly negotiated, or a protected purchaser of a security. These holders or purchasers take priority over an earlier security interest, even if perfected, to the extent provided in Articles 3, 7, and 8.

(b) This article does not limit the rights of or impose liability on a person to the extent that the person is protected against the assertion of a claim under Article 8.

(c) Filing under this article does not constitute notice of a claim or defense to the holders, or purchasers, or persons described in subsections (a) and (b).

§ 9–332. Transfer of Money; Transfer of Funds from Deposit Account.

(a) A transferee of money takes the money free of a security interest unless the transferee acts in collusion with the debtor in violating the rights of the secured party.

(b) A transferee of funds from a deposit account takes the funds free of a security interest in the deposit account unless the transferee acts in collusion with the debtor in violating the rights of the secured party.

§ 9–333. Priority of Certain Liens Arising by Operation of Law.

(a) In this section, "possessory lien" means an interest, other than a security interest or an agricultural lien:

> (1) which secures payment or performance of an obligation for services or materials furnished with respect to goods by a person in the ordinary course of the person's business;

> (2) which is created by statute or rule of law in favor of the person; and

> (3) whose effectiveness depends on the person's possession of the goods.

(b) A possessory lien on goods has priority over a security interest in the goods unless the lien is created by a statute that expressly provides otherwise.

§ 9–334. Priority of Security Interests in Fixtures and Crops.

(a) A security interest under this article may be created in goods that are fixtures or may continue in goods that become fixtures. A security interest does not exist under this article in ordinary building materials incorporated into an improvement on land.

(b) This article does not prevent creation of an encumbrance upon fixtures under real property law.

(c) In cases not governed by subsections (d) through (h), a security interest in fixtures is subordinate to a conflicting interest of an encumbrancer or owner of the related real property other than the debtor.

(d) Except as otherwise provided in subsection (h), a perfected security interest in fixtures has priority over a conflicting interest of an encumbrancer or owner of the real property if the debtor has an interest of record in or is in possession of the real property and:

> (1) the security interest is a purchase-money security interest;

> (2) the interest of the encumbrancer or owner arises before the goods become fixtures; and

> (3) the security interest is perfected by a fixture filing before the goods become fixtures or within 20 days thereafter.

(e) A perfected security interest in fixtures has priority over a conflicting interest of an encumbrancer or owner of the real property if:

> (1) the debtor has an interest of record in the real property or is in possession of the real property and the security interest:

(A) is perfected by a fixture filing before the interest of the encumbrancer or owner is of record; and

(B) has priority over any conflicting interest of a predecessor in title of the encumbrancer or owner;

(2) before the goods become fixtures, the security interest is perfected by any method permitted by this article and the fixtures are readily removable:

(A) factory or office machines;

(B) equipment that is not primarily used or leased for use in the operation of the real property; or

(C) replacements of domestic appliances that are consumer goods;

(3) the conflicting interest is a lien on the real property obtained by legal or equitable proceedings after the security interest was perfected by any method permitted by this article; or

(4) the security interest is:

(A) created in a manufactured home in a manufactured-home transaction; and

(B) perfected pursuant to a statute described in Section 9–311(a)(2).

(f) A security interest in fixtures, whether or not perfected, has priority over a conflicting interest of an encumbrancer or owner of the real property if:

(1) the encumbrancer or owner has, in an authenticated record, consented to the security interest or disclaimed an interest in the goods as fixtures; or

(2) the debtor has a right to remove the goods as against the encumbrancer or owner.

(g) The priority of the security interest under paragraph (f)(2) continues for a reasonable time if the debtor's right to remove the goods as against the encumbrancer or owner terminates.

(h) A mortgage is a construction mortgage to the extent that it secures an obligation incurred for the construction of an improvement on land, including the acquisition cost of the land, if a recorded record of the mortgage so indicates. Except as otherwise provided in subsections (e) and (f), a security interest in fixtures is subordinate to a construction mortgage if a record of the mortgage is recorded before the goods become fixtures and the goods become fixtures before the completion of the construction. A mortgage has this priority to the same extent as a construction mortgage to the extent that it is given to refinance a construction mortgage.

(i) A perfected security interest in crops growing on real property has priority over a conflicting interest of an encumbrancer or owner of the real property if the debtor has an interest of record in or is in possession of the real property.

(j) Subsection (i) prevails over any inconsistent provisions of the following statutes:

[List here any statutes containing provisions inconsistent with subsection (i).]

Legislative Note: States that amend statutes to remove provisions inconsistent with subsection (i) need not enact subsection (j).

§ 9–335. Accessions.

(a) A security interest may be created in an accession and continues in collateral that becomes an accession.

(b) If a security interest is perfected when the collateral becomes an accession, the security interest remains perfected in the collateral.

(c) Except as otherwise provided in subsection (d), the other provisions of this part determine the priority of a security interest in an accession.

(d) A security interest in an accession is subordinate to a security interest in the whole which is perfected by compliance with the requirements of a certificate-of-title statute under Section 9–311(b).

(e) After default, subject to Part 6, a secured party may remove an accession from other goods if the security interest in the accession has priority over the claims of every person having an interest in the whole.

(f) A secured party that removes an accession from other goods under subsection (e) shall promptly reimburse any holder of a security interest or other lien on, or owner of, the whole or of the other goods, other than the debtor, for the cost of repair of any physical injury to the whole or the other goods. The secured party need not reimburse the holder or owner for any diminution in value of the whole or the other goods caused by the absence of the accession removed or by any necessity for replacing it. A person entitled to reimbursement may refuse permission to remove until the secured party gives adequate assurance for the performance of the obligation to reimburse.

§ 9–336. Commingled Goods.

(a) In this section, "commingled goods" means goods that are physically united with other goods in such a manner that their identity is lost in a product or mass.

(b) A security interest does not exist in commingled goods as such. However, a security interest may attach to a product or mass that results when goods become commingled goods.

(c) If collateral becomes commingled goods, a security interest attaches to the product or mass.

(d) If a security interest in collateral is perfected before the collateral becomes commingled goods, the security interest that attaches to the product or mass under subsection (c) is perfected.

(e) Except as otherwise provided in subsection (f), the other provisions of this part determine the priority of a security interest that attaches to the product or mass under subsection (c).

(f) If more than one security interest attaches to the product or mass under subsection (c), the following rules determine priority:

(1) A security interest that is perfected under subsection (d) has priority over a security interest that is unperfected at the time the collateral becomes commingled goods.

(2) If more than one security interest is perfected under subsection (d), the security interests rank equally in proportion to the value of the collateral at the time it became commingled goods.

§ 9–337. Priority of Security Interests in Goods Covered by Certificate of Title.

If, while a security interest in goods is perfected by any method under the law of another jurisdiction, this State issues a certificate of title that does not show that the goods are subject to the security interest or contain a statement that they may be subject to security interests not shown on the certificate:

(1) a buyer of the goods, other than a person in the business of selling goods of that kind, takes free of the security interest if the buyer gives value and receives delivery of the goods after issuance of the certificate and without knowledge of the security interest; and

(2) the security interest is subordinate to a conflicting security interest in the goods that attaches, and is perfected under Section 9–311(b), after issuance of the certificate and without the conflicting secured party's knowledge of the security interest.

§ 9–338. Priority of Security Interest or Agricultural Lien Perfected by Filed Financing Statement Providing Certain Incorrect Information.

If a security interest or agricultural lien is perfected by a filed financing statement providing information described in Section 9–516(b)(5) which is incorrect at the time the financing statement is filed:

(1) the security interest or agricultural lien is subordinate to a conflicting perfected security interest in the collateral to the extent that the holder of the conflicting security interest gives value in reasonable reliance upon the incorrect information; and

(2) a purchaser, other than a secured party, of the collateral takes free of the security interest or agricultural lien to the extent that, in reasonable reliance upon the incorrect information, the purchaser gives value and, in the case of chattel paper, documents, goods, instruments, or a security certificate, receives delivery of the collateral.

§ 9–339. Priority Subject to Subordination.

This article does not preclude subordination by agreement by a person entitled to priority.

[Subpart 4. Rights of Bank]

§ 9–340. Effectiveness of Right of Recoupment or Set-Off against Deposit Account.

(a) Except as otherwise provided in subsection (c), a bank with which a deposit account is maintained may exercise any right of recoupment or set-off against a secured party that holds a security interest in the deposit account.

(b) Except as otherwise provided in subsection (c), the application of this article to a security interest in a deposit account does not affect a right of recoupment or set-off of the secured party as to a deposit account maintained with the secured party.

(c) The exercise by a bank of a set-off against a deposit account is ineffective against a secured party that holds a security interest in the deposit account which is perfected by control under Section 9–104(a)(3), if the set-off is based on a claim against the debtor.

§ 9–341. Bank's Rights and Duties with Respect to Deposit Account.

Except as otherwise provided in Section 9–340(c), and unless the bank otherwise agrees in an authenticated record, a bank's rights and duties with respect to a deposit account maintained with the bank are not terminated, suspended, or modified by:

(1) the creation, attachment, or perfection of a security interest in the deposit account;

(2) the bank's knowledge of the security interest; or

(3) the bank's receipt of instructions from the secured party.

§ 9–342. Bank's Right to Refuse to Enter into or Disclose Existence of Control Agreement.

This article does not require a bank to enter into an agreement of the kind described in Section 9–104(a)(2), even if its customer so requests or directs. A bank that has entered into such an agreement is not required to confirm the existence of the agreement to another person unless requested to do so by its customer.

Part 4   Rights of Third Parties

§ 9–401. Alienability of Debtor's Rights.

(a) Except as otherwise provided in subsection (b) and Sections 9–406, 9–407, 9–408, and 9–409, whether a debtor's rights in collateral may be voluntarily or involuntarily transferred is governed by law other than this article.

(b) An agreement between the debtor and secured party which prohibits a transfer of the debtor's rights in collateral or makes the transfer a default does not prevent the transfer from taking effect.

§ 9–402. Secured Party Not Obligated on Contract of Debtor or in Tort.

The existence of a security interest, agricultural lien, or authority given to a debtor to dispose of or use collateral, without more, does not subject a secured party to liability in contract or tort for the debtor's acts or omissions.

§ 9–403. Agreement Not to Assert Defenses against Assignee.

(a) In this section, "value" has the meaning provided in Section 3–303(a).

(b) Except as otherwise provided in this section, an agreement between an account debtor and an assignor not to assert against an assignee any claim or defense that the account debtor may have against the assignor is enforceable by an assignee that takes an assignment:

(1) for value;

(2) in good faith;

(3) without notice of a claim of a property or possessory right to the property assigned; and

(4) without notice of a defense or claim in recoupment of the type that may be asserted against a person entitled to enforce a negotiable instrument under Section 3–305(a).

(c) Subsection (b) does not apply to defenses of a type that may be asserted against a holder in due course of a negotiable instrument under Section 3–305(b).

(d) In a consumer transaction, if a record evidences the account debtor's obligation, law other than this article requires that the record include a statement to the effect that the rights of an assignee are subject to claims or defenses that the account debtor could assert against the original obligee, and the record does not include such a statement:

(1) the record has the same effect as if the record included such a statement; and

(2) the account debtor may assert against an assignee those claims and defenses that would have been available if the record included such a statement.

(e) This section is subject to law other than this article which establishes a different rule for an account debtor who is an individual and who incurred the obligation primarily for personal, family, or household purposes.

(f) Except as otherwise provided in subsection (d), this section does not displace law other than this article which gives effect to an agreement by an account debtor not to assert a claim or defense against an assignee.

§ 9–404. Rights Acquired by Assignee; Claims and Defenses against Assignee.

(a) Unless an account debtor has made an enforceable agreement not to assert defenses or claims, and subject to subsections (b) through (e), the rights of an assignee are subject to:

(1) all terms of the agreement between the account debtor and assignor and any defense or claim in recoupment arising from the transaction that gave rise to the contract; and

(2) any other defense or claim of the account debtor against the assignor which accrues before the account debtor receives a notification of the assignment authenticated by the assignor or the assignee.

(b) Subject to subsection (c) and except as otherwise provided in subsection (d), the claim of an account debtor against an assignor may be asserted against an assignee under subsection (a) only to reduce the amount the account debtor owes.

(c) This section is subject to law other than this article which establishes a different rule for an account debtor who is an individual and who incurred the obligation primarily for personal, family, or household purposes.

(d) In a consumer transaction, if a record evidences the account debtor's obligation, law other than this article requires that the record include a statement to the effect that the account debtor's recovery against an assignee with respect to claims and defenses against the assignor may not exceed amounts paid by the account debtor under the record, and the record does not include such a statement, the extent to which a claim of an account debtor against the assignor may be asserted against an assignee is determined as if the record included such a statement.

(e) This section does not apply to an assignment of a health-care-insurance receivable.

§ 9–405. Modification of Assigned Contract.

(a) A modification of or substitution for an assigned contract is effective against an assignee if made in good faith. The assignee acquires corresponding rights under the modified or substituted contract. The assignment may provide that the modification or substitution is a breach of contract by the assignor. This subsection is subject to subsections (b) through (d).

(b) Subsection (a) applies to the extent that:

(1) the right to payment or a part thereof under an assigned contract has not been fully earned by performance; or

(2) the right to payment or a part thereof has been fully earned by performance and the account debtor has not received notification of the assignment under Section 9–406(a).

(c) This section is subject to law other than this article which establishes a different rule for an account debtor who is an individual and who incurred the obligation primarily for personal, family, or household purposes.

(d) This section does not apply to an assignment of a health-care-insurance receivable.

§ 9–406. Discharge of Account Debtor; Notification of Assignment; Identification and Proof of Assignment; Restrictions on Assignment of Accounts, Chattel Paper, Payment Intangibles, and Promissory Notes Ineffective.

(a) Subject to subsections (b) through (i), an account debtor on an account, chattel paper, or a payment intangible may discharge its obligation by paying the assignor until, but not after, the account debtor receives a notification, authenticated by the assignor or the assignee, that the amount due or to become due has been assigned and that payment is to be made to the assignee. After receipt of the notification, the account debtor may discharge its obligation by paying the assignee and may not discharge the obligation by paying the assignor.

(b) Subject to subsection (h), notification is ineffective under subsection (a):

(1) if it does not reasonably identify the rights assigned;

(2) to the extent that an agreement between an account debtor and a seller of a payment intangible limits the account debtor's duty to pay a person other than the seller and the limitation is effective under law other than this article; or

(3) at the option of an account debtor, if the notification notifies the account debtor to make less than the full amount of any installment or other periodic payment to the assignee, even if:

(A) only a portion of the account, chattel paper, or payment intangible has been assigned to that assignee;

(B) a portion has been assigned to another assignee; or

(C) the account debtor knows that the assignment to that assignee is limited.

(c) Subject to subsection (h), if requested by the account debtor, an assignee shall seasonably furnish reasonable proof that the assignment has been made. Unless the assignee complies, the account debtor may discharge its obligation by paying the assignor, even if the account debtor has received a notification under subsection (a).

(d) Except as otherwise provided in subsection (e) and Sections 2A–303 and 9–407, and subject to subsection (h), a term in an agreement between an account debtor and an assignor or in a promissory note is ineffective to the extent that it:

(1) prohibits, restricts, or requires the consent of the account debtor or person obligated on the promissory note to the assignment or transfer of, or the creation, attachment, perfection, or enforcement of a security interest in, the account, chattel paper, payment intangible, or promissory note; or

(2) provides that the assignment or transfer or the creation, attachment, perfection, or enforcement of the security interest may give rise to a default, breach, right of recoupment, claim,

defense, termination, right of termination, or remedy under the account, chattel paper, payment intangible, or promissory note.

(e) Subsection (d) does not apply to the sale of a payment intangible or promissory note.

(f) Except as otherwise provided in Sections 2A–303 and 9–407 and subject to subsections (h) and (i), a rule of law, statute, or regulation that prohibits, restricts, or requires the consent of a government, governmental body or official, or account debtor to the assignment or transfer of, or creation of a security interest in, an account or chattel paper is ineffective to the extent that the rule of law, statute, or regulation:

(1) prohibits, restricts, or requires the consent of the government, governmental body or official, or account debtor to the assignment or transfer of, or the creation, attachment, perfection, or enforcement of a security interest in the account or chattel paper; or

(2) provides that the assignment or transfer or the creation, attachment, perfection, or enforcement of the security interest may give rise to a default, breach, right of recoupment, claim, defense, termination, right of termination, or remedy under the account or chattel paper.

(g) Subject to subsection (h), an account debtor may not waive or vary its option under subsection (b)(3).

(h) This section is subject to law other than this article which establishes a different rule for an account debtor who is an individual and who incurred the obligation primarily for personal, family, or household purposes.

(i) This section does not apply to an assignment of a health-care-insurance receivable.

(j) This section prevails over any inconsistent provisions of the following statutes, rules, and regulations:

[List here any statutes, rules, and regulations containing provisions inconsistent with this section.]

Legislative Note: States that amend statutes, rules, and regulations to remove provisions inconsistent with this section need not enact subsection (j).

As amended in 1999 and 2000.

§ 9–407. Restrictions on Creation or Enforcement of Security Interest in Leasehold Interest or in Lessor's Residual Interest.

(a) Except as otherwise provided in subsection (b), a term in a lease agreement is ineffective to the extent that it:

(1) prohibits, restricts, or requires the consent of a party to the lease to the assignment or transfer of, or the creation, attachment, perfection, or enforcement of a security interest in an interest of a party under the lease contract or in the lessor's residual interest in the goods; or

(2) provides that the assignment or transfer or the creation, attachment, perfection, or enforcement of the security interest may give rise to a default, breach, right of recoupment, claim, defense, termination, right of termination, or remedy under the lease.

(b) Except as otherwise provided in Section 2A–303(7), a term described in subsection (a)(2) is effective to the extent that there is:

(1) a transfer by the lessee of the lessee's right of possession or use of the goods in violation of the term; or

(2) a delegation of a material performance of either party to the lease contract in violation of the term.

(c) The creation, attachment, perfection, or enforcement of a security interest in the lessor's interest under the lease contract or the lessor's residual interest in the goods is not a transfer that materially impairs the lessee's prospect of obtaining return performance or materially changes the duty of or materially increases the burden or risk imposed on the lessee within the purview of Section 2A–303(4) unless, and then only to the extent that, enforcement actually results in a delegation of material performance of the lessor.

As amended in 1999.

§ 9–408. Restrictions on Assignment of Promissory Notes, Health-Care-Insurance Receivables, and Certain General Intangibles Ineffective.

(a) Except as otherwise provided in subsection (b), a term in a promissory note or in an agreement between an account debtor and a debtor which relates to a health-care-insurance receivable or a general intangible, including a contract, permit, license, or franchise, and which term prohibits, restricts, or requires the consent of the person obligated on the promissory note or the account debtor to, the assignment or transfer of, or creation, attachment, or perfection of a security interest in, the promissory note, health-care-insurance receivable, or general intangible, is ineffective to the extent that the term:

(1) would impair the creation, attachment, or perfection of a security interest; or

(2) provides that the assignment or transfer or the creation, attachment, or perfection of the security interest may give rise to a default, breach, right of recoupment, claim, defense, termination, right of termination, or remedy under the promissory note, health-care-insurance receivable, or general intangible.

(b) Subsection (a) applies to a security interest in a payment intangible or promissory note only if the security interest arises out of a sale of the payment intangible or promissory note.

(c) A rule of law, statute, or regulation that prohibits, restricts, or requires the consent of a government, governmental body or official, person obligated on a promissory note, or account debtor to the assignment or transfer of, or creation of a security interest in, a promissory note, health-care-insurance receivable, or general intangible, including a contract, permit, license, or franchise between an account debtor and a debtor, is ineffective to the extent that the rule of law, statute, or regulation:

(1) would impair the creation, attachment, or perfection of a security interest; or

(2) provides that the assignment or transfer or the creation, attachment, or perfection of the security interest may give rise to a default, breach, right of recoupment, claim, defense, termination, right of termination, or remedy under the promissory note, health-care-insurance receivable, or general intangible.

(d) To the extent that a term in a promissory note or in an agreement between an account debtor and a debtor which relates to a health-care-insurance receivable or general intangible or a rule of law, statute, or regulation described in subsection (c) would be effective under law other than this article but is ineffective under subsection (a) or (c), the creation, attachment, or perfection of a security interest in the promissory note, health-care-insurance receivable, or general intangible:

(1) is not enforceable against the person obligated on the promissory note or the account debtor;

(2) does not impose a duty or obligation on the person obligated on the promissory note or the account debtor;

(3) does not require the person obligated on the promissory note or the account debtor to recognize the security interest, pay or render performance to the secured party, or accept payment or performance from the secured party;

(4) does not entitle the secured party to use or assign the debtor's rights under the promissory note, health-care-insurance receivable, or general intangible, including any related information or materials furnished to the debtor in the transaction giving rise to the promissory note, health-care-insurance receivable, or general intangible;

(5) does not entitle the secured party to use, assign, possess, or have access to any trade secrets or confidential information of the person obligated on the promissory note or the account debtor; and

(6) does not entitle the secured party to enforce the security interest in the promissory note, health-care-insurance receivable, or general intangible.

(e) This section prevails over any inconsistent provisions of the following statutes, rules, and regulations:

[List here any statutes, rules, and regulations containing provisions inconsistent with this section.]

Legislative Note: States that amend statutes, rules, and regulations to remove provisions inconsistent with this section need not enact subsection (e).

As amended in 1999.

§ 9–409. Restrictions on Assignment of Letter-of-Credit Rights Ineffective.

(a) A term in a letter of credit or a rule of law, statute, regulation, custom, or practice applicable to the letter of credit which prohibits, restricts, or requires the consent of an applicant, issuer, or nominated person to a beneficiary's assignment of or creation of a security interest in a letter-of-credit right is ineffective to the extent that the term or rule of law, statute, regulation, custom, or practice:

(1) would impair the creation, attachment, or perfection of a security interest in the letter-of-credit right; or

(2) provides that the assignment or the creation, attachment, or perfection of the security interest may give rise to a default, breach, right of recoupment, claim, defense, termination, right of termination, or remedy under the letter-of-credit right.

(b) To the extent that a term in a letter of credit is ineffective under subsection (a) but would be effective under law other than this article or a custom or practice applicable to the letter of credit, to the transfer of a right to draw or otherwise demand performance under the letter of credit, or to the assignment of a right to proceeds of the letter of credit, the creation, attachment, or perfection of a security interest in the letter-of-credit right:

(1) is not enforceable against the applicant, issuer, nominated person, or transferee beneficiary;

(2) imposes no duties or obligations on the applicant, issuer, nominated person, or transferee beneficiary; and

(3) does not require the applicant, issuer, nominated person, or transferee beneficiary to recognize the security interest, pay or render performance to the secured party, or accept payment or other performance from the secured party.

As amended in 1999.

Part 5 Filing

[Subpart 1. Filing Office; Contents and Effectiveness of Financing Statement]

§ 9–501. Filing Office.

(a) Except as otherwise provided in subsection (b), if the local law of this State governs perfection of a security interest or agricultural lien, the office in which to file a financing statement to perfect the security interest or agricultural lien is:

(1) the office designated for the filing or recording of a record of a mortgage on the related real property, if:

(A) the collateral is as-extracted collateral or timber to be cut; or

(B) the financing statement is filed as a fixture filing and the collateral is goods that are or are to become fixtures; or

(2) the office of [ ] [or any office duly authorized by [ ]], in all other cases, including a case in which the collateral is goods that are or are to become fixtures and the financing statement is not filed as a fixture filing.

(b) The office in which to file a financing statement to perfect a security interest in collateral, including fixtures, of a transmitting utility is the office of [ ]. The financing statement also constitutes a fixture filing as to the collateral indicated in the financing statement which is or is to become fixtures.

Legislative Note: The State should designate the filing office where the brackets appear. The filing office may be that of a governmental official (e.g., the Secretary of State) or a private party that maintains the State's filing system.

§ 9–502. Contents of Financing Statement; Record of Mortgage as Financing Statement; Time of Filing Financing Statement.

(a) Subject to subsection (b), a financing statement is sufficient only if it:

(1) provides the name of the debtor;

(2) provides the name of the secured party or a representative of the secured party; and

(3) indicates the collateral covered by the financing statement.

(b) Except as otherwise provided in Section 9–501(b), to be sufficient, a financing statement that covers as-extracted collateral or timber to be cut, or which is filed as a fixture filing and covers goods that are or are to become fixtures, must satisfy subsection (a) and also:

(1) indicate that it covers this type of collateral;

(2) indicate that it is to be filed [for record] in the real property records;

(3) provide a description of the real property to which the collateral is related [sufficient to give constructive notice of a mortgage

under the law of this State if the description were contained in a record of the mortgage of the real property]; and

(4) if the debtor does not have an interest of record in the real property, provide the name of a record owner.

(c) A record of a mortgage is effective, from the date of recording, as a financing statement filed as a fixture filing or as a financing statement covering as-extracted collateral or timber to be cut only if:

(1) the record indicates the goods or accounts that it covers;

(2) the goods are or are to become fixtures related to the real property described in the record or the collateral is related to the real property described in the record and is as-extracted collateral or timber to be cut;

(3) the record satisfies the requirements for a financing statement in this section other than an indication that it is to be filed in the real property records; and

(4) the record is [duly] recorded.

(d) A financing statement may be filed before a security agreement is made or a security interest otherwise attaches.

Legislative Note: Language in brackets is optional. Where the State has any special recording system for real property other than the usual grantor-grantee index (as, for instance, a tract system or a title registration or Torrens system) local adaptations of subsection (b) and Section 9–519(d) and (e) may be necessary. See, e.g., Mass. Gen. Laws Chapter 106, Section 9–410.

§ 9–503. Name of Debtor and Secured Party.

(a) A financing statement sufficiently provides the name of the debtor:

(1) if the debtor is a registered organization, only if the financing statement provides the name of the debtor indicated on the public record of the debtor's jurisdiction of organization which shows the debtor to have been organized;

(2) if the debtor is a decedent's estate, only if the financing statement provides the name of the decedent and indicates that the debtor is an estate;

(3) if the debtor is a trust or a trustee acting with respect to property held in trust, only if the financing statement:

(A) provides the name specified for the trust in its organic documents or, if no name is specified, provides the name of the settlor and additional information sufficient to distinguish the debtor from other trusts having one or more of the same settlors; and

(B) indicates, in the debtor's name or otherwise, that the debtor is a trust or is a trustee acting with respect to property held in trust; and

(4) in other cases:

(A) if the debtor has a name, only if it provides the individual or organizational name of the debtor; and

(B) if the debtor does not have a name, only if it provides the names of the partners, members, associates, or other persons comprising the debtor.

(b) A financing statement that provides the name of the debtor in accordance with subsection (a) is not rendered ineffective by the absence of:

(1) a trade name or other name of the debtor; or

(2) unless required under subsection (a)(4)(B), names of partners, members, associates, or other persons comprising the debtor.

(c) A financing statement that provides only the debtor's trade name does not sufficiently provide the name of the debtor.

(d) Failure to indicate the representative capacity of a secured party or representative of a secured party does not affect the sufficiency of a financing statement.

(e) A financing statement may provide the name of more than one debtor and the name of more than one secured party.

§ 9–504. Indication of Collateral.

A financing statement sufficiently indicates the collateral that it covers if the financing statement provides:

(1) a description of the collateral pursuant to Section 9–108; or

(2) an indication that the financing statement covers all assets or all personal property.

As amended in 1999.

§ 9–505. Filing and Compliance with Other Statutes and Treaties for Consignments, Leases, Other Bailments, and Other Transactions.

(a) A consignor, lessor, or other bailor of goods, a licensor, or a buyer of a payment intangible or promissory note may file a financing statement, or may comply with a statute or treaty described in Section 9–311(a), using the terms "consignor", "consignee", "lessor", "lessee", "bailor", "bailee", "licensor", "licensee", "owner", "registered owner", "buyer", "seller", or words of similar import, instead of the terms "secured party" and "debtor".

(b) This part applies to the filing of a financing statement under subsection (a) and, as appropriate, to compliance that is equivalent to filing a financing statement under Section 9–311(b), but the filing or compliance is not of itself a factor in determining whether the collateral secures an obligation. If it is determined for another reason that the collateral secures an obligation, a security interest held by the consignor, lessor, bailor, licensor, owner, or buyer which attaches to the collateral is perfected by the filing or compliance.

§ 9–506. Effect of Errors or Omissions.

(a) A financing statement substantially satisfying the requirements of this part is effective, even if it has minor errors or omissions, unless the errors or omissions make the financing statement seriously misleading.

(b) Except as otherwise provided in subsection (c), a financing statement that fails sufficiently to provide the name of the debtor in accordance with Section 9–503(a) is seriously misleading.

(c) If a search of the records of the filing office under the debtor's correct name, using the filing office's standard search logic, if any, would disclose a financing statement that fails sufficiently to provide the name of the debtor in accordance with Section 9–503(a), the name provided does not make the financing statement seriously misleading.

(d) For purposes of Section 9–508(b), the "debtor's correct name" in subsection (c) means the correct name of the new debtor.

§ 9–507. Effect of Certain Events on Effectiveness of Financing Statement.

(a) A filed financing statement remains effective with respect to collateral that is sold, exchanged, leased, licensed, or otherwise disposed of and in which a security interest or agricultural lien continues, even if the secured party knows of or consents to the disposition.

(b) Except as otherwise provided in subsection (c) and Section 9–508, a financing statement is not rendered ineffective if, after the financing statement is filed, the information provided in the financing statement becomes seriously misleading under Section 9–506.

(c) If a debtor so changes its name that a filed financing statement becomes seriously misleading under Section 9–506:

(1) the financing statement is effective to perfect a security interest in collateral acquired by the debtor before, or within four months after, the change; and

(2) the financing statement is not effective to perfect a security interest in collateral acquired by the debtor more than four months after the change, unless an amendment to the financing statement which renders the financing statement not seriously misleading is filed within four months after the change.

§ 9–508. Effectiveness of Financing Statement If New Debtor Becomes Bound by Security Agreement.

(a) Except as otherwise provided in this section, a filed financing statement naming an original debtor is effective to perfect a security interest in collateral in which a new debtor has or acquires rights to the extent that the financing statement would have been effective had the original debtor acquired rights in the collateral.

(b) If the difference between the name of the original debtor and that of the new debtor causes a filed financing statement that is effective under subsection (a) to be seriously misleading under Section 9–506:

(1) the financing statement is effective to perfect a security interest in collateral acquired by the new debtor before, and within four months after, the new debtor becomes bound under Section 9B–203(d); and

(2) the financing statement is not effective to perfect a security interest in collateral acquired by the new debtor more than four months after the new debtor becomes bound under Section 9–203(d) unless an initial financing statement providing the name of the new debtor is filed before the expiration of that time.

(c) This section does not apply to collateral as to which a filed financing statement remains effective against the new debtor under Section 9–507(a).

§ 9–509. Persons Entitled to File a Record.

(a) A person may file an initial financing statement, amendment that adds collateral covered by a financing statement, or amendment that adds a debtor to a financing statement only if:

(1) the debtor authorizes the filing in an authenticated record or pursuant to subsection (b) or (c); or

(2) the person holds an agricultural lien that has become effective at the time of filing and the financing statement covers only collateral in which the person holds an agricultural lien.

(b) By authenticating or becoming bound as debtor by a security agreement, a debtor or new debtor authorizes the filing of an initial financing statement, and an amendment, covering:

(1) the collateral described in the security agreement; and

(2) property that becomes collateral under Section 9–315(a)(2), whether or not the security agreement expressly covers proceeds.

(c) By acquiring collateral in which a security interest or agricultural lien continues under Section 9–315(a)(1), a debtor authorizes the filing of an initial financing statement, and an amendment, covering the collateral and property that becomes collateral under Section 9–315(a)(2).

(d) A person may file an amendment other than an amendment that adds collateral covered by a financing statement or an amendment that adds a debtor to a financing statement only if:

(1) the secured party of record authorizes the filing; or

(2) the amendment is a termination statement for a financing statement as to which the secured party of record has failed to file or send a termination statement as required by Section 9–513(a) or (c), the debtor authorizes the filing, and the termination statement indicates that the debtor authorized it to be filed.

(e) If there is more than one secured party of record for a financing statement, each secured party of record may authorize the filing of an amendment under subsection (d).

As amended in 2000.

§ 9–510. Effectiveness of Filed Record.

(a) A filed record is effective only to the extent that it was filed by a person that may file it under Section 9–509.

(b) A record authorized by one secured party of record does not affect the financing statement with respect to another secured party of record.

(c) A continuation statement that is not filed within the six-month period prescribed by Section 9–515(d) is ineffective.

§ 9–511. Secured Party of Record.

(a) A secured party of record with respect to a financing statement is a person whose name is provided as the name of the secured party or a representative of the secured party in an initial financing statement that has been filed. If an initial financing statement is filed under Section 9–514(a), the assignee named in the initial financing statement is the secured party of record with respect to the financing statement.

(b) If an amendment of a financing statement which provides the name of a person as a secured party or a representative of a secured party is filed, the person named in the amendment is a secured party of record. If an amendment is filed under Section 9–514(b), the assignee named in the amendment is a secured party of record.

(c) A person remains a secured party of record until the filing of an amendment of the financing statement which deletes the person.

§ 9–512. Amendment of Financing Statement.

[Alternative A]

(a) Subject to Section 9–509, a person may add or delete collateral covered by, continue or terminate the effectiveness of, or, subject to subsection (e), otherwise amend the information provided in, a financing statement by filing an amendment that:

(1) identifies, by its file number, the initial financing statement to which the amendment relates; and

(2) if the amendment relates to an initial financing statement filed [or recorded] in a filing office described in Section 9–501(a)(1), provides the information specified in Section 9–502(b).

[Alternative B]

(a) Subject to Section 9–509, a person may add or delete collateral covered by, continue or terminate the effectiveness of, or, subject to subsection (e), otherwise amend the information provided in, a financing statement by filing an amendment that:

(1) identifies, by its file number, the initial financing statement to which the amendment relates; and

(2) if the amendment relates to an initial financing statement filed [or recorded] in a filing office described in Section 9–501(a)(1), provides the date [and time] that the initial financing statement was filed [or recorded] and the information specified in Section 9–502(b).

[End of Alternatives]

(b) Except as otherwise provided in Section 9–515, the filing of an amendment does not extend the period of effectiveness of the financing statement.

(c) A financing statement that is amended by an amendment that adds collateral is effective as to the added collateral only from the date of the filing of the amendment.

(d) A financing statement that is amended by an amendment that adds a debtor is effective as to the added debtor only from the date of the filing of the amendment.

(e) An amendment is ineffective to the extent it:

(1) purports to delete all debtors and fails to provide the name of a debtor to be covered by the financing statement; or

(2) purports to delete all secured parties of record and fails to provide the name of a new secured party of record.

Legislative Note: States whose real-estate filing offices require additional information in amendments and cannot search their records by both the name of the debtor and the file number should enact Alternative B to Sections 9–512(a), 9–518(b), 9–519(f), and 9–522(a).

§ 9–513. Termination Statement.

(a) A secured party shall cause the secured party of record for a financing statement to file a termination statement for the financing statement if the financing statement covers consumer goods and:

(1) there is no obligation secured by the collateral covered by the financing statement and no commitment to make an advance, incur an obligation, or otherwise give value; or

(2) the debtor did not authorize the filing of the initial financing statement.

(b) To comply with subsection (a), a secured party shall cause the secured party of record to file the termination statement:

(1) within one month after there is no obligation secured by the collateral covered by the financing statement and no commitment to make an advance, incur an obligation, or otherwise give value; or

(2) if earlier, within 20 days after the secured party receives an authenticated demand from a debtor.

(c) In cases not governed by subsection (a), within 20 days after a secured party receives an authenticated demand from a debtor, the secured party shall cause the secured party of record for a financing statement to send to the debtor a termination statement for the financing statement or file the termination statement in the filing office if:

(1) except in the case of a financing statement covering accounts or chattel paper that has been sold or goods that are the subject of a consignment, there is no obligation secured by the collateral covered by the financing statement and no commitment to make an advance, incur an obligation, or otherwise give value;

(2) the financing statement covers accounts or chattel paper that has been sold but as to which the account debtor or other person obligated has discharged its obligation;

(3) the financing statement covers goods that were the subject of a consignment to the debtor but are not in the debtor's possession; or

(4) the debtor did not authorize the filing of the initial financing statement.

(d) Except as otherwise provided in Section 9–510, upon the filing of a termination statement with the filing office, the financing statement to which the termination statement relates ceases to be effective. Except as otherwise provided in Section 9–510, for purposes of Sections 9–519(g), 9–522(a), and 9–523(c), the filing with the filing office of a termination statement relating to a financing statement that indicates that the debtor is a transmitting utility also causes the effectiveness of the financing statement to lapse.

As amended in 2000.

§ 9–514. Assignment of Powers of Secured Party of Record.

(a) Except as otherwise provided in subsection (c), an initial financing statement may reflect an assignment of all of the secured party's power to authorize an amendment to the financing statement by providing the name and mailing address of the assignee as the name and address of the secured party.

(b) Except as otherwise provided in subsection (c), a secured party of record may assign of record all or part of its power to authorize an amendment to a financing statement by filing in the filing office an amendment of the financing statement which:

(1) identifies, by its file number, the initial financing statement to which it relates;

(2) provides the name of the assignor; and

(3) provides the name and mailing address of the assignee.

(c) An assignment of record of a security interest in a fixture covered by a record of a mortgage which is effective as a financing statement filed as a fixture filing under Section 9–502(c) may be made only by an assignment of record of the mortgage in the manner provided by law of this State other than [the Uniform Commercial Code].

§ 9–515. Duration and Effectiveness of Financing Statement; Effect of Lapsed Financing Statement.

(a) Except as otherwise provided in subsections (b), (e), (f), and (g), a filed financing statement is effective for a period of five years after the date of filing.

(b) Except as otherwise provided in subsections (e), (f), and (g), an initial financing statement filed in connection with a public-finance transaction or manufactured-home transaction is effective for a period of 30 years after the date of filing if it indicates that it is filed in connection with a public-finance transaction or manufactured-home transaction.

(c) The effectiveness of a filed financing statement lapses on the expiration of the period of its effectiveness unless before the lapse a continuation statement is filed pursuant to subsection (d). Upon lapse, a financing statement ceases to be effective and any security interest or agricultural lien that was perfected by the financing statement becomes unperfected, unless the security interest is perfected otherwise. If the security interest or agricultural lien becomes unperfected upon lapse, it is deemed never to have been perfected as against a purchaser of the collateral for value.

(d) A continuation statement may be filed only within six months before the expiration of the five-year period specified in subsection (a) or the 30-year period specified in subsection (b), whichever is applicable.

(e) Except as otherwise provided in Section 9–510, upon timely filing of a continuation statement, the effectiveness of the initial financing statement continues for a period of five years commencing on the day on which the financing statement would have become ineffective in the absence of the filing. Upon the expiration of the five-year period, the financing statement lapses in the same manner as provided in subsection (c), unless, before the lapse, another continuation statement is filed pursuant to subsection (d). Succeeding continuation statements may be filed in the same manner to continue the effectiveness of the initial financing statement.

(f) If a debtor is a transmitting utility and a filed financing statement so indicates, the financing statement is effective until a termination statement is filed.

(g) A record of a mortgage that is effective as a financing statement filed as a fixture filing under Section 9–502(c) remains effective as a financing statement filed as a fixture filing until the mortgage is released or satisfied of record or its effectiveness otherwise terminates as to the real property.

§ 9–516. What Constitutes Filing; Effectiveness of Filing.

(a) Except as otherwise provided in subsection (b), communication of a record to a filing office and tender of the filing fee or acceptance of the record by the filing office constitutes filing.

(b) Filing does not occur with respect to a record that a filing office refuses to accept because:

(1) the record is not communicated by a method or medium of communication authorized by the filing office;

(2) an amount equal to or greater than the applicable filing fee is not tendered;

(3) the filing office is unable to index the record because:

(A) in the case of an initial financing statement, the record does not provide a name for the debtor;

(B) in the case of an amendment or correction statement, the record:

(i) does not identify the initial financing statement as required by Section 9–512 or 9–518, as applicable; or

(ii) identifies an initial financing statement whose effectiveness has lapsed under Section 9–515;

(C) in the case of an initial financing statement that provides the name of a debtor identified as an individual or an amendment that provides a name of a debtor identified as an individual which was not previously provided in the financing statement to which the record relates, the record does not identify the debtor's last name; or

(D) in the case of a record filed [or recorded] in the filing office described in Section 9–501(a)(1), the record does not provide a sufficient description of the real property to which it relates;

(4) in the case of an initial financing statement or an amendment that adds a secured party of record, the record does not provide a name and mailing address for the secured party of record;

(5) in the case of an initial financing statement or an amendment that provides a name of a debtor which was not previously provided in the financing statement to which the amendment relates, the record does not:

(A) provide a mailing address for the debtor;

(B) indicate whether the debtor is an individual or an organization; or

(C) if the financing statement indicates that the debtor is an organization, provide:

(i) a type of organization for the debtor;

(ii) a jurisdiction of organization for the debtor; or

(iii) an organizational identification number for the debtor or indicate that the debtor has none;

(6) in the case of an assignment reflected in an initial financing statement under Section 9–514(a) or an amendment filed under Section 9–514(b), the record does not provide a name and mailing address for the assignee; or

(7) in the case of a continuation statement, the record is not filed within the six-month period prescribed by Section 9–515(d).

(c) For purposes of subsection (b):

(1) a record does not provide information if the filing office is unable to read or decipher the information; and

(2) a record that does not indicate that it is an amendment or identify an initial financing statement to which it relates, as required by Section 9–512, 9–514, or 9–518, is an initial financing statement.

(d) A record that is communicated to the filing office with tender of the filing fee, but which the filing office refuses to accept for a reason other than one set forth in subsection (b), is effective as a filed record except as against a purchaser of the collateral which gives value in reasonable reliance upon the absence of the record from the files.

§ 9–517. Effect of Indexing Errors.

The failure of the filing office to index a record correctly does not affect the effectiveness of the filed record.

§ 9–518. Claim Concerning Inaccurate or Wrongfully Filed Record.

(a) A person may file in the filing office a correction statement with respect to a record indexed there under the person's name if the person believes that the record is inaccurate or was wrongfully filed.

[Alternative A]

(b) A correction statement must:

(1) identify the record to which it relates by the file number assigned to the initial financing statement to which the record relates;

(2) indicate that it is a correction statement; and

(3) provide the basis for the person's belief that the record is inaccurate and indicate the manner in which the person believes the record should be amended to cure any inaccuracy or provide the basis for the person's belief that the record was wrongfully filed.

[Alternative B]

(b) A correction statement must:

(1) identify the record to which it relates by:

(A) the file number assigned to the initial financing statement to which the record relates; and

(B) if the correction statement relates to a record filed [or recorded] in a filing office described in Section 9–501(a)(1), the date [and time] that the initial financing statement was filed [or recorded] and the information specified in Section 9–502(b);

(2) indicate that it is a correction statement; and

(3) provide the basis for the person's belief that the record is inaccurate and indicate the manner in which the person believes the record should be amended to cure any inaccuracy or provide the basis for the person's belief that the record was wrongfully filed.

[End of Alternatives]

(c) The filing of a correction statement does not affect the effectiveness of an initial financing statement or other filed record.

Legislative Note: States whose real-estate filing offices require additional information in amendments and cannot search their records by both the name of the debtor and the file number should enact Alternative B to Sections 9–512(a), 9–518(b), 9–519(f), and 9–522(a).

[Subpart 2. Duties and Operation of Filing Office]

§ 9–519. Numbering, Maintaining, and Indexing Records; Communicating Information Provided in Records.

(a) For each record filed in a filing office, the filing office shall:

(1) assign a unique number to the filed record;

(2) create a record that bears the number assigned to the filed record and the date and time of filing;

(3) maintain the filed record for public inspection; and

(4) index the filed record in accordance with subsections (c), (d), and (e).

(b) A file number [assigned after January 1, 2002,] must include a digit that:

(1) is mathematically derived from or related to the other digits of the file number; and

(2) aids the filing office in determining whether a number communicated as the file number includes a single-digit or transpositional error.

(c) Except as otherwise provided in subsections (d) and (e), the filing office shall:

(1) index an initial financing statement according to the name of the debtor and index all filed records relating to the initial financing statement in a manner that associates with one another an initial financing statement and all filed records relating to the initial financing statement; and

(2) index a record that provides a name of a debtor which was not previously provided in the financing statement to which the record relates also according to the name that was not previously provided.

(d) If a financing statement is filed as a fixture filing or covers as-extracted collateral or timber to be cut, [it must be filed for record and] the filing office shall index it:

(1) under the names of the debtor and of each owner of record shown on the financing statement as if they were the mortgagors under a mortgage of the real property described; and

(2) to the extent that the law of this State provides for indexing of records of mortgages under the name of the mortgagee, under the name of the secured party as if the secured party were the mortgagee thereunder, or, if indexing is by description, as if the financing statement were a record of a mortgage of the real property described.

(e) If a financing statement is filed as a fixture filing or covers as-extracted collateral or timber to be cut, the filing office shall index an assignment filed under Section 9–514(a) or an amendment filed under Section 9–514(b):

(1) under the name of the assignor as grantor; and

(2) to the extent that the law of this State provides for indexing a record of the assignment of a mortgage under the name of the assignee, under the name of the assignee.

[Alternative A]

(f) The filing office shall maintain a capability:

(1) to retrieve a record by the name of the debtor and by the file number assigned to the initial financing statement to which the record relates; and

(2) to associate and retrieve with one another an initial financing statement and each filed record relating to the initial financing statement.

[Alternative B]

(f) The filing office shall maintain a capability:

(1) to retrieve a record by the name of the debtor and:

(A) if the filing office is described in Section 9–501(a)(1), by the file number assigned to the initial financing statement to which the record relates and the date [and time] that the record was filed [or recorded]; or

(B) if the filing office is described in Section 9–501(a)(2), by the file number assigned to the initial financing statement to which the record relates; and

(2) to associate and retrieve with one another an initial financing statement and each filed record relating to the initial financing statement.

[End of Alternatives]

(g) The filing office may not remove a debtor's name from the index until one year after the effectiveness of a financing statement naming the debtor lapses under Section 9–515 with respect to all secured parties of record.

(h) The filing office shall perform the acts required by subsections (a) through (e) at the time and in the manner prescribed by filing-office rule, but not later than two business days after the filing office receives the record in question.

[(i) Subsection[s] [(b)] [and] [(h)] do[es] not apply to a filing office described in Section 9–501(a)(1).]

Legislative Notes:

1. States whose filing offices currently assign file numbers that include a verification number, commonly known as a "check digit," or can implement this requirement before the effective date of this Article should omit the bracketed language in subsection (b).

2. In States in which writings will not appear in the real property records and indices unless actually recorded the bracketed language in subsection (d) should be used.

3. States whose real-estate filing offices require additional information in amendments and cannot search their records by both the name of the debtor and the file number should enact Alternative B to Sections 9–512(a), 9–518(b), 9–519(f), and 9–522(a).

4. A State that elects not to require real-estate filing offices to comply with either or both of subsections (b) and (h) may adopt an applicable variation of subsection (i) and add "Except as otherwise provided in subsection (i)," to the appropriate subsection or subsections.

§ 9–520. Acceptance and Refusal to Accept Record.

(a) A filing office shall refuse to accept a record for filing for a reason set forth in Section 9–516(b) and may refuse to accept a record for filing only for a reason set forth in Section 9–516(b).

(b) If a filing office refuses to accept a record for filing, it shall communicate to the person that presented the record the fact of and reason for the refusal and the date and time the record would have been filed had the filing office accepted it. The communication must be made at the time and in the manner prescribed by filing-office rule but [, in the case of a filing office described in Section 9–501(a)(2),] in no event more than two business days after the filing office receives the record.

(c) A filed financing statement satisfying Section 9–502(a) and (b) is effective, even if the filing office is required to refuse to accept it for filing under subsection (a). However, Section 9–338 applies to a filed financing statement providing information described in Section 9–516(b)(5) which is incorrect at the time the financing statement is filed.

(d) If a record communicated to a filing office provides information that relates to more than one debtor, this part applies as to each debtor separately.

Legislative Note: A State that elects not to require real-property filing offices to comply with subsection (b) should include the bracketed language.

§ 9–521. Uniform Form of Written Financing Statement and Amendment.

(a) A filing office that accepts written records may not refuse to accept a written initial financing statement in the following form and format except for a reason set forth in Section 9–516(b):

[NATIONAL UCC FINANCING STATEMENT (FORM UCC1)(REV. 7/29/98)]

[NATIONAL UCC FINANCING STATEMENT ADDENDUM (FORM UCC1Ad)(REV. 07/29/98)]

(b) A filing office that accepts written records may not refuse to accept a written record in the following form and format except for a reason set forth in Section 9–516(b):

[NATIONAL UCC FINANCING STATEMENT AMENDMENT (FORM UCC3)(REV. 07/29/98)]

[NATIONAL UCC FINANCING STATEMENT AMENDMENT ADDENDUM (FORM UCC3Ad)(REV. 07/29/98)]

§ 9–522. Maintenance and Destruction of Records.

[Alternative A]

(a) The filing office shall maintain a record of the information provided in a filed financing statement for at least one year after the effectiveness of the financing statement has lapsed under Section 9–515 with respect to all secured parties of record. The record must be retrievable by using the name of the debtor and by using the file number assigned to the initial financing statement to which the record relates.

[Alternative B]

(a) The filing office shall maintain a record of the information provided in a filed financing statement for at least one year after the effectiveness of the financing statement has lapsed under Section 9–515 with respect to all secured parties of record. The record must be retrievable by using the name of the debtor and:

> (1) if the record was filed [or recorded] in the filing office described in Section 9–501(a)(1), by using the file number assigned to the initial financing statement to which the record relates and the date [and time] that the record was filed [or recorded]; or

> (2) if the record was filed in the filing office described in Section 9–501(a)(2), by using the file number assigned to the initial financing statement to which the record relates.

[End of Alternatives]

(b) Except to the extent that a statute governing disposition of public records provides otherwise, the filing office immediately may destroy any written record evidencing a financing statement. However, if the filing office destroys a written record, it shall maintain another record of the financing statement which complies with subsection (a).

Legislative Note: States whose real-estate filing offices require additional information in amendments and cannot search their records by both the name of the debtor and the file number should enact Alternative B to Sections 9–512(a), 9–518(b), 9–519(f), and 9–522(a).

§ 9–523. Information from Filing Office; Sale or License of Records.

(a) If a person that files a written record requests an acknowledgment of the filing, the filing office shall send to the person an image of the record showing the number assigned to the record pursuant to Section 9–519(a)(1) and the date and time of the filing of the record. However, if the person furnishes a copy of the record to the filing office, the filing office may instead:

> (1) note upon the copy the number assigned to the record pursuant to Section 9–519(a)(1) and the date and time of the filing of the record; and

(2) send the copy to the person.

(b) If a person files a record other than a written record, the filing office shall communicate to the person an acknowledgment that provides:

(1) the information in the record;

(2) the number assigned to the record pursuant to Section 9–519(a)(1); and

(3) the date and time of the filing of the record.

(c) The filing office shall communicate or otherwise make available in a record the following information to any person that requests it:

(1) whether there is on file on a date and time specified by the filing office, but not a date earlier than three business days before the filing office receives the request, any financing statement that:

(A) designates a particular debtor [or, if the request so states, designates a particular debtor at the address specified in the request];

(B) has not lapsed under Section 9–515 with respect to all secured parties of record; and

(C) if the request so states, has lapsed under Section 9–515 and a record of which is maintained by the filing office under Section 9–522(a);

(2) the date and time of filing of each financing statement; and

(3) the information provided in each financing statement.

(d) In complying with its duty under subsection (c), the filing office may communicate information in any medium. However, if requested, the filing office shall communicate information by issuing [its written certificate] [a record that can be admitted into evidence in the courts of this State without extrinsic evidence of its authenticity].

(e) The filing office shall perform the acts required by subsections (a) through (d) at the time and in the manner prescribed by filing-office rule, but not later than two business days after the filing office receives the request.

(f) At least weekly, the [insert appropriate official or governmental agency] [filing office] shall offer to sell or license to the public on a nonexclusive basis, in bulk, copies of all records filed in it under this part, in every medium from time to time available to the filing office.

Legislative Notes:

1. States whose filing office does not offer the additional service of responding to search requests limited to a particular address should omit the bracketed language in subsection (c)(1)(A).

2. A State that elects not to require real-estate filing offices to comply with either or both of subsections (e) and (f) should specify in the appropriate subsection(s) only the filing office described in Section 9–501(a)(2).

§ 9–524. Delay by Filing Office.

Delay by the filing office beyond a time limit prescribed by this part is excused if:

(1) the delay is caused by interruption of communication or computer facilities, war, emergency conditions, failure of equipment, or other circumstances beyond control of the filing office; and

(2) the filing office exercises reasonable diligence under the circumstances.

§ 9–525. Fees.

(a) Except as otherwise provided in subsection (e), the fee for filing and indexing a record under this part, other than an initial financing statement of the kind described in subsection (b), is [the amount specified in subsection (c), if applicable, plus]:

(1) $[X] if the record is communicated in writing and consists of one or two pages;

(2) $[2X] if the record is communicated in writing and consists of more than two pages; and

(3) $[½X] if the record is communicated by another medium authorized by filing-office rule.

(b) Except as otherwise provided in subsection (e), the fee for filing and indexing an initial financing statement of the following kind is [the amount specified in subsection (c), if applicable, plus]:

(1) $_____ if the financing statement indicates that it is filed in connection with a public-finance transaction;

(2) $_____ if the financing statement indicates that it is filed in connection with a manufactured-home transaction.

[Alternative A]

(c) The number of names required to be indexed does not affect the amount of the fee in subsections (a) and (b).

[Alternative B]

(c) Except as otherwise provided in subsection (e), if a record is communicated in writing, the fee for each name more than two required to be indexed is $_____.

[End of Alternatives]

(d) The fee for responding to a request for information from the filing office, including for [issuing a certificate showing] [communicating] whether there is on file any financing statement naming a particular debtor, is:

(1) $_____ if the request is communicated in writing; and

(2) $_____ if the request is communicated by another medium authorized by filing-office rule.

(e) This section does not require a fee with respect to a record of a mortgage which is effective as a financing statement filed as a fixture filing or as a financing statement covering as-extracted collateral or timber to be cut under Section 9–502(c). However, the recording and satisfaction fees that otherwise would be applicable to the record of the mortgage apply.

Legislative Notes:

1. To preserve uniformity, a State that places the provisions of this section together with statutes setting fees for other services should do so without modification.

2. A State should enact subsection (c), Alternative A, and omit the bracketed language in subsections (a) and (b) unless its indexing system entails a substantial additional cost when indexing additional names.

As amended in 2000.

§ 9–526. Filing-Office Rules.

(a) The [insert appropriate governmental official or agency] shall adopt and publish rules to implement this article. The filing-office rules must be[:

(1)] consistent with this article[; and

(2) adopted and published in accordance with the [insert any applicable state administrative procedure act]].

(b) To keep the filing-office rules and practices of the filing office in harmony with the rules and practices of filing offices in other jurisdictions that enact substantially this part, and to keep the technology used by the filing office compatible with the technology used by filing offices in other jurisdictions that enact substantially this part, the [insert appropriate governmental official or agency], so far as is consistent with the purposes, policies, and provisions of this article, in adopting, amending, and repealing filing-office rules, shall:

(1) consult with filing offices in other jurisdictions that enact substantially this part; and

(2) consult the most recent version of the Model Rules promulgated by the International Association of Corporate Administrators or any successor organization; and

(3) take into consideration the rules and practices of, and the technology used by, filing offices in other jurisdictions that enact substantially this part.

§ 9–527. Duty to Report.

The [insert appropriate governmental official or agency] shall report [annually on or before _____] to the [Governor and Legislature] on the operation of the filing office. The report must contain a statement of the extent to which:

(1) the filing-office rules are not in harmony with the rules of filing offices in other jurisdictions that enact substantially this part and the reasons for these variations; and

(2) the filing-office rules are not in harmony with the most recent version of the Model Rules promulgated by the International Association of Corporate Administrators, or any successor organization, and the reasons for these variations.

Part 6 Default

[Subpart 1. Default and Enforcement of Security Interest]

§ 9–601. Rights after Default; Judicial Enforcement; Consignor or Buyer of Accounts, Chattel Paper, Payment Intangibles, or Promissory Notes.

(a) After default, a secured party has the rights provided in this part and, except as otherwise provided in Section 9–602, those provided by agreement of the parties. A secured party:

(1) may reduce a claim to judgment, foreclose, or otherwise enforce the claim, security interest, or agricultural lien by any available judicial procedure; and

(2) if the collateral is documents, may proceed either as to the documents or as to the goods they cover.

(b) A secured party in possession of collateral or control of collateral under Section 9–104, 9–105, 9–106, or 9–107 has the rights and duties provided in Section 9–207.

(c) The rights under subsections (a) and (b) are cumulative and may be exercised simultaneously.

(d) Except as otherwise provided in subsection (g) and Section 9–605, after default, a debtor and an obligor have the rights provided in this part and by agreement of the parties.

(e) If a secured party has reduced its claim to judgment, the lien of any levy that may be made upon the collateral by virtue of an execution based upon the judgment relates back to the earliest of:

(1) the date of perfection of the security interest or agricultural lien in the collateral;

(2) the date of filing a financing statement covering the collateral; or

(3) any date specified in a statute under which the agricultural lien was created.

(f) A sale pursuant to an execution is a foreclosure of the security interest or agricultural lien by judicial procedure within the meaning of this section. A secured party may purchase at the sale and thereafter hold the collateral free of any other requirements of this article.

(g) Except as otherwise provided in Section 9–607(c), this part imposes no duties upon a secured party that is a consignor or is a buyer of accounts, chattel paper, payment intangibles, or promissory notes.

§ 9–602. Waiver and Variance of Rights and Duties.

Except as otherwise provided in Section 9–624, to the extent that they give rights to a debtor or obligor and impose duties on a secured party, the debtor or obligor may not waive or vary the rules stated in the following listed sections:

(1) Section 9–207(b)(4)(C), which deals with use and operation of the collateral by the secured party;

(2) Section 9–210, which deals with requests for an accounting and requests concerning a list of collateral and statement of account;

(3) Section 9–607(c), which deals with collection and enforcement of collateral;

(4) Sections 9–608(a) and 9–615(c) to the extent that they deal with application or payment of noncash proceeds of collection, enforcement, or disposition;

(5) Sections 9–608(a) and 9–615(d) to the extent that they require accounting for or payment of surplus proceeds of collateral;

(6) Section 9–609 to the extent that it imposes upon a secured party that takes possession of collateral without judicial process the duty to do so without breach of the peace;

(7) Sections 9–610(b), 9–611, 9–613, and 9–614, which deal with disposition of collateral;

(8) Section 9–615(f), which deals with calculation of a deficiency or surplus when a disposition is made to the secured party, a person related to the secured party, or a secondary obligor;

(9) Section 9–616, which deals with explanation of the calculation of a surplus or deficiency;

(10) Sections 9–620, 9–621, and 9–622, which deal with acceptance of collateral in satisfaction of obligation;

(11) Section 9–623, which deals with redemption of collateral;

(12) Section 9–624, which deals with permissible waivers; and

(13) Sections 9–625 and 9–626, which deal with the secured party's liability for failure to comply with this article.

§ 9–603. Agreement on Standards Concerning Rights and Duties.

(a) The parties may determine by agreement the standards measuring the fulfillment of the rights of a debtor or obligor and the duties of a secured party under a rule stated in Section 9–602 if the standards are not manifestly unreasonable.

(b) Subsection (a) does not apply to the duty under Section 9–609 to refrain from breaching the peace.

§ 9–604. Procedure If Security Agreement Covers Real Property or Fixtures.

(a) If a security agreement covers both personal and real property, a secured party may proceed:

(1) under this part as to the personal property without prejudicing any rights with respect to the real property; or

(2) as to both the personal property and the real property in accordance with the rights with respect to the real property, in which case the other provisions of this part do not apply.

(b) Subject to subsection (c), if a security agreement covers goods that are or become fixtures, a secured party may proceed:

(1) under this part; or

(2) in accordance with the rights with respect to real property, in which case the other provisions of this part do not apply.

(c) Subject to the other provisions of this part, if a secured party holding a security interest in fixtures has priority over all owners and encumbrancers of the real property, the secured party, after default, may remove the collateral from the real property.

(d) A secured party that removes collateral shall promptly reimburse any encumbrancer or owner of the real property, other than the debtor, for the cost of repair of any physical injury caused by the removal. The secured party need not reimburse the encumbrancer or owner for any diminution in value of the real property caused by the absence of the goods removed or by any necessity of replacing them. A person entitled to reimbursement may refuse permission to remove until the secured party gives adequate assurance for the performance of the obligation to reimburse.

§ 9–605. Unknown Debtor or Secondary Obligor

A secured party does not owe a duty based on its status as secured party:

(1) to a person that is a debtor or obligor, unless the secured party knows:

(A) that the person is a debtor or obligor;

(B) the identity of the person; and

(C) how to communicate with the person; or

(2) to a secured party or lienholder that has filed a financing statement against a person, unless the secured party knows:

(A) that the person is a debtor; and

(B) the identity of the person.

§ 9–606. Time of Default for Agricultural Lien.

For purposes of this part, a default occurs in connection with an agricultural lien at the time the secured party becomes entitled to enforce the lien in accordance with the statute under which it was created.

§ 9–607. Collection and Enforcement by Secured Party.

(a) If so agreed, and in any event after default, a secured party:

(1) may notify an account debtor or other person obligated on collateral to make payment or otherwise render performance to or for the benefit of the secured party;

(2) may take any proceeds to which the secured party is entitled under Section 9–315;

(3) may enforce the obligations of an account debtor or other person obligated on collateral and exercise the rights of the debtor with respect to the obligation of the account debtor or other person obligated on collateral to make payment or otherwise render performance to the debtor, and with respect to any property that secures the obligations of the account debtor or other person obligated on the collateral;

(4) if it holds a security interest in a deposit account perfected by control under Section 9–104(a)(1), may apply the balance of the deposit account to the obligation secured by the deposit account; and

(5) if it holds a security interest in a deposit account perfected by control under Section 9–104(a)(2) or (3), may instruct the bank to pay the balance of the deposit account to or for the benefit of the secured party.

(b) If necessary to enable a secured party to exercise under subsection (a)(3) the right of a debtor to enforce a mortgage nonjudicially, the secured party may record in the office in which a record of the mortgage is recorded:

(1) a copy of the security agreement that creates or provides for a security interest in the obligation secured by the mortgage; and

(2) the secured party's sworn affidavit in recordable form stating that:

(A) a default has occurred; and

(B) the secured party is entitled to enforce the mortgage nonjudicially.

(c) A secured party shall proceed in a commercially reasonable manner if the secured party:

(1) undertakes to collect from or enforce an obligation of an account debtor or other person obligated on collateral; and

(2) is entitled to charge back uncollected collateral or otherwise to full or limited recourse against the debtor or a secondary obligor.

(d) A secured party may deduct from the collections made pursuant to subsection (c) reasonable expenses of collection and enforcement, including reasonable attorney's fees and legal expenses incurred by the secured party.

(e) This section does not determine whether an account debtor, bank, or other person obligated on collateral owes a duty to a secured party.

As amended in 2000.

§ 9–608. Application of Proceeds of Collection or Enforcement; Liability for Deficiency and Right to Surplus.

(a) If a security interest or agricultural lien secures payment or performance of an obligation, the following rules apply:

(1) A secured party shall apply or pay over for application the cash proceeds of collection or enforcement under Section 9–607 in the following order to:

(A) the reasonable expenses of collection and enforcement and, to the extent provided for by agreement and not prohibited by law, reasonable attorney's fees and legal expenses incurred by the secured party;

(B) the satisfaction of obligations secured by the security interest or agricultural lien under which the collection or enforcement is made; and

(C) the satisfaction of obligations secured by any subordinate security interest in or other lien on the collateral subject to the security interest or agricultural lien under which the collection or enforcement is made if the secured party receives an authenticated demand for proceeds before distribution of the proceeds is completed.

(2) If requested by a secured party, a holder of a subordinate security interest or other lien shall furnish reasonable proof of the interest or lien within a reasonable time. Unless the holder complies, the secured party need not comply with the holder's demand under paragraph (1)(C).

(3) A secured party need not apply or pay over for application noncash proceeds of collection and enforcement under Section 9–607 unless the failure to do so would be commercially unreasonable. A secured party that applies or pays over for application noncash proceeds shall do so in a commercially reasonable manner.

(4) A secured party shall account to and pay a debtor for any surplus, and the obligor is liable for any deficiency.

(b) If the underlying transaction is a sale of accounts, chattel paper, payment intangibles, or promissory notes, the debtor is not entitled to any surplus, and the obligor is not liable for any deficiency.

As amended in 2000.

§ 9–609. Secured Party's Right to Take Possession after Default.

(a) After default, a secured party:

(1) may take possession of the collateral; and

(2) without removal, may render equipment unusable and dispose of collateral on a debtor's premises under Section 9–610.

(b) A secured party may proceed under subsection (a):

(1) pursuant to judicial process; or

(2) without judicial process, if it proceeds without breach of the peace.

(c) If so agreed, and in any event after default, a secured party may require the debtor to assemble the collateral and make it available to the secured party at a place to be designated by the secured party which is reasonably convenient to both parties.

§ 9–610. Disposition of Collateral after Default.

(a) After default, a secured party may sell, lease, license, or otherwise dispose of any or all of the collateral in its present condition or following any commercially reasonable preparation or processing.

(b) Every aspect of a disposition of collateral, including the method, manner, time, place, and other terms, must be commercially reasonable. If commercially reasonable, a secured party may dispose of collateral by public or private proceedings, by one or more contracts, as a unit or in parcels, and at any time and place and on any terms.

(c) A secured party may purchase collateral:

(1) at a public disposition; or

(2) at a private disposition only if the collateral is of a kind that is customarily sold on a recognized market or the subject of widely distributed standard price quotations.

(d) A contract for sale, lease, license, or other disposition includes the warranties relating to title, possession, quiet enjoyment, and the like which by operation of law accompany a voluntary disposition of property of the kind subject to the contract.

(e) A secured party may disclaim or modify warranties under subsection (d):

(1) in a manner that would be effective to disclaim or modify the warranties in a voluntary disposition of property of the kind subject to the contract of disposition; or

(2) by communicating to the purchaser a record evidencing the contract for disposition and including an express disclaimer or modification of the warranties.

(f) A record is sufficient to disclaim warranties under subsection (e) if it indicates "There is no warranty relating to title, possession, quiet enjoyment, or the like in this disposition" or uses words of similar import.

§ 9–611. Notification before Disposition of Collateral.

(a) In this section, "notification date" means the earlier of the date on which:

(1) a secured party sends to the debtor and any secondary obligor an authenticated notification of disposition; or

(2) the debtor and any secondary obligor waive the right to notification.

(b) Except as otherwise provided in subsection (d), a secured party that disposes of collateral under Section 9–610 shall send to the persons specified in subsection (c) a reasonable authenticated notification of disposition.

(c) To comply with subsection (b), the secured party shall send an authenticated notification of disposition to:

(1) the debtor;

(2) any secondary obligor; and

(3) if the collateral is other than consumer goods:

(A) any other person from which the secured party has received, before the notification date, an authenticated notification of a claim of an interest in the collateral;

(B) any other secured party or lienholder that, 10 days before the notification date, held a security interest in or other lien on the collateral perfected by the filing of a financing statement that:

(i) identified the collateral;

(ii) was indexed under the debtor's name as of that date; and

(iii) was filed in the office in which to file a financing statement against the debtor covering the collateral as of that date; and

(C) any other secured party that, 10 days before the notification date, held a security interest in the collateral perfected by compliance with a statute, regulation, or treaty described in Section 9–311(a).

(d) Subsection (b) does not apply if the collateral is perishable or threatens to decline speedily in value or is of a type customarily sold on a recognized market.

(e) A secured party complies with the requirement for notification prescribed by subsection (c)(3)(B) if:

(1) not later than 20 days or earlier than 30 days before the notification date, the secured party requests, in a commercially reasonable manner, information concerning financing statements indexed under the debtor's name in the office indicated in subsection (c)(3)(B); and

(2) before the notification date, the secured party:

(A) did not receive a response to the request for information; or

(B) received a response to the request for information and sent an authenticated notification of disposition to each secured party or other lienholder named in that response whose financing statement covered the collateral.

§ 9–612. Timeliness of Notification before Disposition of Collateral.

(a) Except as otherwise provided in subsection (b), whether a notification is sent within a reasonable time is a question of fact.

(b) In a transaction other than a consumer transaction, a notification of disposition sent after default and 10 days or more before the earliest time of disposition set forth in the notification is sent within a reasonable time before the disposition.

§ 9–613. Contents and Form of Notification before Disposition of Collateral: General.

Except in a consumer-goods transaction, the following rules apply:

(1) The contents of a notification of disposition are sufficient if the notification:

(A) describes the debtor and the secured party;

(B) describes the collateral that is the subject of the intended disposition;

(C) states the method of intended disposition;

(D) states that the debtor is entitled to an accounting of the unpaid indebtedness and states the charge, if any, for an accounting; and

(E) states the time and place of a public disposition or the time after which any other disposition is to be made.

(2) Whether the contents of a notification that lacks any of the information specified in paragraph (1) are nevertheless sufficient is a question of fact.

(3) The contents of a notification providing substantially the information specified in paragraph (1) are sufficient, even if the notification includes:

(A) information not specified by that paragraph; or

(B) minor errors that are not seriously misleading.

(4) A particular phrasing of the notification is not required.

(5) The following form of notification and the form appearing in Section 9–614(3), when completed, each provides sufficient information:

NOTIFICATION OF DISPOSITION OF COLLATERAL

To: [*Name of debtor, obligor, or other person to which the notification is sent*]

From: [*Name, address, and telephone number of secured party*]

Name of Debtor(s): [*Include only if debtor(s) are not an addressee*]

[*For a public disposition:*]

We will sell [or lease or license, *as applicable*] the [*describe collateral*] [to the highest qualified bidder] in public as follows:

Day and Date: _____

Time: _____

Place: _____

[*For a private disposition:*]

We will sell [or lease or license, *as applicable*] the [*describe collateral*] privately sometime after [*day and date*].

You are entitled to an accounting of the unpaid indebtedness secured by the property that we intend to sell [or lease or license, *as applicable*] [for a charge of $_____]. You may request an accounting by calling us at [*telephone number*].

[End of Form]

As amended in 2000.

§ 9–614. Contents and Form of Notification before Disposition of Collateral: Consumer-Goods Transaction.

In a consumer-goods transaction, the following rules apply:

(1) A notification of disposition must provide the following information:

(A) the information specified in Section 9–613(1);

(B) a description of any liability for a deficiency of the person to which the notification is sent;

(C) a telephone number from which the amount that must be paid to the secured party to redeem the collateral under Section 9–623 is available; and

(D) a telephone number or mailing address from which additional information concerning the disposition and the obligation secured is available.

(2) A particular phrasing of the notification is not required.

(3) The following form of notification, when completed, provides sufficient information:

[*Name and address of secured party*]

[*Date*]

NOTICE OF OUR PLAN TO SELL PROPERTY

[*Name and address of any obligor who is also a debtor*]

Subject: [*Identification of Transaction*]

We have your [*describe collateral*], because you broke promises in our agreement.

[*For a public disposition:*]

We will sell [*describe collateral*] at public sale. A sale could include a lease or license. The sale will be held as follows:

Date: _____

Time: _____

Place: _____

You may attend the sale and bring bidders if you want.

[*For a private disposition:*]

We will sell [*describe collateral*] at private sale sometime after [*date*]. A sale could include a lease or license.

The money that we get from the sale (after paying our costs) will reduce the amount you owe. If we get less money than you owe, you [will or will not, *as applicable*] still owe us the difference. If we get more money than you owe, you will get the extra money, unless we must pay it to someone else.

You can get the property back at any time before we sell it by paying us the full amount you owe (not just the past due payments), including our expenses. To learn the exact amount you must pay, call us at [telephone number].

If you want us to explain to you in writing how we have figured the amount that you owe us, you may call us at [telephone number] [or write us at [secured party's address]] and request a written explanation. [We will charge you $_____ for the explanation if we sent you another written explanation of the amount you owe us within the last six months.]

If you need more information about the sale call us at [telephone number] [or write us at [secured party's address]].

We are sending this notice to the following other people who have an interest in [describe collateral] or who owe money under your agreement:

[Names of all other debtors and obligors, if any]

[End of Form]

(4) A notification in the form of paragraph (3) is sufficient, even if additional information appears at the end of the form.

(5) A notification in the form of paragraph (3) is sufficient, even if it includes errors in information not required by paragraph (1), unless the error is misleading with respect to rights arising under this article.

(6) If a notification under this section is not in the form of paragraph (3), law other than this article determines the effect of including information not required by paragraph (1).

§ 9–615. Application of Proceeds of Disposition; Liability for Deficiency and Right to Surplus.

(a) A secured party shall apply or pay over for application the cash proceeds of disposition under Section 9–610 in the following order to:

(1) the reasonable expenses of retaking, holding, preparing for disposition, processing, and disposing, and, to the extent provided for by agreement and not prohibited by law, reasonable attorney's fees and legal expenses incurred by the secured party;

(2) the satisfaction of obligations secured by the security interest or agricultural lien under which the disposition is made;

(3) the satisfaction of obligations secured by any subordinate security interest in or other subordinate lien on the collateral if:

(A) the secured party receives from the holder of the subordinate security interest or other lien an authenticated demand for proceeds before distribution of the proceeds is completed; and

(B) in a case in which a consignor has an interest in the collateral, the subordinate security interest or other lien is senior to the interest of the consignor; and

(4) a secured party that is a consignor of the collateral if the secured party receives from the consignor an authenticated demand for proceeds before distribution of the proceeds is completed.

(b) If requested by a secured party, a holder of a subordinate security interest or other lien shall furnish reasonable proof of the interest or lien within a reasonable time. Unless the holder does so, the secured party need not comply with the holder's demand under subsection (a)(3).

(c) A secured party need not apply or pay over for application noncash proceeds of disposition under Section 9–610 unless the failure to do so would be commercially unreasonable. A secured party that applies or pays over for application noncash proceeds shall do so in a commercially reasonable manner.

(d) If the security interest under which a disposition is made secures payment or performance of an obligation, after making the payments and applications required by subsection (a) and permitted by subsection (c):

(1) unless subsection (a)(4) requires the secured party to apply or pay over cash proceeds to a consignor, the secured party shall account to and pay a debtor for any surplus; and

(2) the obligor is liable for any deficiency.

(e) If the underlying transaction is a sale of accounts, chattel paper, payment intangibles, or promissory notes:

(1) the debtor is not entitled to any surplus; and

(2) the obligor is not liable for any deficiency.

(f) The surplus or deficiency following a disposition is calculated based on the amount of proceeds that would have been realized in a disposition complying with this part to a transferee other than the secured party, a person related to the secured party, or a secondary obligor if:

(1) the transferee in the disposition is the secured party, a person related to the secured party, or a secondary obligor; and

(2) the amount of proceeds of the disposition is significantly below the range of proceeds that a complying disposition to a person other than the secured party, a person related to the secured party, or a secondary obligor would have brought.

(g) A secured party that receives cash proceeds of a disposition in good faith and without knowledge that the receipt violates the rights of the holder of a security interest or other lien that is not subordinate to the security interest or agricultural lien under which the disposition is made:

(1) takes the cash proceeds free of the security interest or other lien;

(2) is not obligated to apply the proceeds of the disposition to the satisfaction of obligations secured by the security interest or other lien; and

(3) is not obligated to account to or pay the holder of the security interest or other lien for any surplus.

As amended in 2000.

§ 9–616. Explanation of Calculation of Surplus or Deficiency.

(a) In this section:

(1) "Explanation" means a writing that:

(A) states the amount of the surplus or deficiency;

(B) provides an explanation in accordance with subsection (c) of how the secured party calculated the surplus or deficiency;

(C) states, if applicable, that future debits, credits, charges, including additional credit service charges or interest, rebates, and expenses may affect the amount of the surplus or deficiency; and

(D) provides a telephone number or mailing address from which additional information concerning the transaction is available.

(2) "Request" means a record:

(A) authenticated by a debtor or consumer obligor;

(B) requesting that the recipient provide an explanation; and

(C) sent after disposition of the collateral under Section 9–610.

(b) In a consumer-goods transaction in which the debtor is entitled to a surplus or a consumer obligor is liable for a deficiency under Section 9–615, the secured party shall:

(1) send an explanation to the debtor or consumer obligor, as applicable, after the disposition and:

(A) before or when the secured party accounts to the debtor and pays any surplus or first makes written demand on the consumer obligor after the disposition for payment of the deficiency; and

(B) within 14 days after receipt of a request; or

(2) in the case of a consumer obligor who is liable for a deficiency, within 14 days after receipt of a request, send to the consumer obligor a record waiving the secured party's right to a deficiency.

(c) To comply with subsection (a)(1)(B), a writing must provide the following information in the following order:

(1) the aggregate amount of obligations secured by the security interest under which the disposition was made, and, if the amount reflects a rebate of unearned interest or credit service charge, an indication of that fact, calculated as of a specified date:

(A) if the secured party takes or receives possession of the collateral after default, not more than 35 days before the secured party takes or receives possession; or

(B) if the secured party takes or receives possession of the collateral before default or does not take possession of the collateral, not more than 35 days before the disposition;

(2) the amount of proceeds of the disposition;

(3) the aggregate amount of the obligations after deducting the amount of proceeds;

(4) the amount, in the aggregate or by type, and types of expenses, including expenses of retaking, holding, preparing for disposition, processing, and disposing of the collateral, and attorney's fees secured by the collateral which are known to the secured party and relate to the current disposition;

(5) the amount, in the aggregate or by type, and types of credits, including rebates of interest or credit service charges, to which the obligor is known to be entitled and which are not reflected in the amount in paragraph (1); and

(6) the amount of the surplus or deficiency.

(d) A particular phrasing of the explanation is not required. An explanation complying substantially with the requirements of subsection (a) is sufficient, even if it includes minor errors that are not seriously misleading.

(e) A debtor or consumer obligor is entitled without charge to one response to a request under this section during any six-month period in which the secured party did not send to the debtor or consumer obligor an explanation pursuant to subsection (b)(1). The secured party may require payment of a charge not exceeding $25 for each additional response.

§ 9–617. Rights of Transferee of Collateral.

(a) A secured party's disposition of collateral after default:

(1) transfers to a transferee for value all of the debtor's rights in the collateral;

(2) discharges the security interest under which the disposition is made; and

(3) discharges any subordinate security interest or other subordinate lien [other than liens created under [cite acts or statutes providing for liens, if any, that are not to be discharged]].

(b) A transferee that acts in good faith takes free of the rights and interests described in subsection (a), even if the secured party fails to comply with this article or the requirements of any judicial proceeding.

(c) If a transferee does not take free of the rights and interests described in subsection (a), the transferee takes the collateral subject to:

(1) the debtor's rights in the collateral;

(2) the security interest or agricultural lien under which the disposition is made; and

(3) any other security interest or other lien.

§ 9–618. Rights and Duties of Certain Secondary Obligors.

(a) A secondary obligor acquires the rights and becomes obligated to perform the duties of the secured party after the secondary obligor:

(1) receives an assignment of a secured obligation from the secured party;

(2) receives a transfer of collateral from the secured party and agrees to accept the rights and assume the duties of the secured party; or

(3) is subrogated to the rights of a secured party with respect to collateral.

(b) An assignment, transfer, or subrogation described in subsection (a):

(1) is not a disposition of collateral under Section 9–610; and

(2) relieves the secured party of further duties under this article.

§ 9–619. Transfer of Record or Legal Title.

(a) In this section, "transfer statement" means a record authenticated by a secured party stating:

(1) that the debtor has defaulted in connection with an obligation secured by specified collateral;

(2) that the secured party has exercised its post-default remedies with respect to the collateral;

(3) that, by reason of the exercise, a transferee has acquired the rights of the debtor in the collateral; and

(4) the name and mailing address of the secured party, debtor, and transferee.

(b) A transfer statement entitles the transferee to the transfer of record of all rights of the debtor in the collateral specified in the statement in any official filing, recording, registration, or certificate-of-title system covering the collateral. If a transfer statement is presented with the applicable fee and request form to the official or office responsible for maintaining the system, the official or office shall:

(1) accept the transfer statement;

(2) promptly amend its records to reflect the transfer; and

(3) if applicable, issue a new appropriate certificate of title in the name of the transferee.

(c) A transfer of the record or legal title to collateral to a secured party under subsection (b) or otherwise is not of itself a disposition of collateral under this article and does not of itself relieve the secured party of its duties under this article.

§ 9–620. Acceptance of Collateral in Full or Partial Satisfaction of Obligation; Compulsory Disposition of Collateral.

(a) Except as otherwise provided in subsection (g), a secured party may accept collateral in full or partial satisfaction of the obligation it secures only if:

(1) the debtor consents to the acceptance under subsection (c);

(2) the secured party does not receive, within the time set forth in subsection (d), a notification of objection to the proposal authenticated by:

(A) a person to which the secured party was required to send a proposal under Section 9–621; or

(B) any other person, other than the debtor, holding an interest in the collateral subordinate to the security interest that is the subject of the proposal;

(3) if the collateral is consumer goods, the collateral is not in the possession of the debtor when the debtor consents to the acceptance; and

(4) subsection (e) does not require the secured party to dispose of the collateral or the debtor waives the requirement pursuant to Section 9–624.

(b) A purported or apparent acceptance of collateral under this section is ineffective unless:

(1) the secured party consents to the acceptance in an authenticated record or sends a proposal to the debtor; and

(2) the conditions of subsection (a) are met.

(c) For purposes of this section:

(1) a debtor consents to an acceptance of collateral in partial satisfaction of the obligation it secures only if the debtor agrees to the terms of the acceptance in a record authenticated after default; and

(2) a debtor consents to an acceptance of collateral in full satisfaction of the obligation it secures only if the debtor agrees to the terms of the acceptance in a record authenticated after default or the secured party:

(A) sends to the debtor after default a proposal that is unconditional or subject only to a condition that collateral not in the possession of the secured party be preserved or maintained;

(B) in the proposal, proposes to accept collateral in full satisfaction of the obligation it secures; and

(C) does not receive a notification of objection authenticated by the debtor within 20 days after the proposal is sent.

(d) To be effective under subsection (a)(2), a notification of objection must be received by the secured party:

(1) in the case of a person to which the proposal was sent pursuant to Section 9–621, within 20 days after notification was sent to that person; and

(2) in other cases:

(A) within 20 days after the last notification was sent pursuant to Section 9–621; or

(B) if a notification was not sent, before the debtor consents to the acceptance under subsection (c).

(e) A secured party that has taken possession of collateral shall dispose of the collateral pursuant to Section 9–610 within the time specified in subsection (f) if:

(1) 60 percent of the cash price has been paid in the case of a purchase-money security interest in consumer goods; or

(2) 60 percent of the principal amount of the obligation secured has been paid in the case of a non-purchase-money security interest in consumer goods.

(f) To comply with subsection (e), the secured party shall dispose of the collateral:

(1) within 90 days after taking possession; or

(2) within any longer period to which the debtor and all secondary obligors have agreed in an agreement to that effect entered into and authenticated after default.

(g) In a consumer transaction, a secured party may not accept collateral in partial satisfaction of the obligation it secures.

§ 9–621. Notification of Proposal to Accept Collateral.

(a) A secured party that desires to accept collateral in full or partial satisfaction of the obligation it secures shall send its proposal to:

(1) any person from which the secured party has received, before the debtor consented to the acceptance, an authenticated notification of a claim of an interest in the collateral;

(2) any other secured party or lienholder that, 10 days before the debtor consented to the acceptance, held a security interest in or other lien on the collateral perfected by the filing of a financing statement that:

(A) identified the collateral;

(B) was indexed under the debtor's name as of that date; and

(C) was filed in the office or offices in which to file a financing statement against the debtor covering the collateral as of that date; and

(3) any other secured party that, 10 days before the debtor consented to the acceptance, held a security interest in the collateral perfected by compliance with a statute, regulation, or treaty described in Section 9–311(a).

(b) A secured party that desires to accept collateral in partial satisfaction of the obligation it secures shall send its proposal to any secondary obligor in addition to the persons described in subsection (a).

§ 9–622. Effect of Acceptance of Collateral.

(a) A secured party's acceptance of collateral in full or partial satisfaction of the obligation it secures:

(1) discharges the obligation to the extent consented to by the debtor;

(2) transfers to the secured party all of a debtor's rights in the collateral;

(3) discharges the security interest or agricultural lien that is the subject of the debtor's consent and any subordinate security interest or other subordinate lien; and

(4) terminates any other subordinate interest.

(b) A subordinate interest is discharged or terminated under subsection (a), even if the secured party fails to comply with this article.

§ 9–623. Right to Redeem Collateral.

(a) A debtor, any secondary obligor, or any other secured party or lienholder may redeem collateral.

(b) To redeem collateral, a person shall tender:

(1) fulfillment of all obligations secured by the collateral; and

(2) the reasonable expenses and attorney's fees described in Section 9–615(a)(1).

(c) A redemption may occur at any time before a secured party:

(1) has collected collateral under Section 9–607;

(2) has disposed of collateral or entered into a contract for its disposition under Section 9–610; or

(3) has accepted collateral in full or partial satisfaction of the obligation it secures under Section 9–622.

§ 9–624. Waiver.

(a) A debtor or secondary obligor may waive the right to notification of disposition of collateral under Section 9–611 only by an agreement to that effect entered into and authenticated after default.

(b) A debtor may waive the right to require disposition of collateral under Section 9–620(e) only by an agreement to that effect entered into and authenticated after default.

(c) Except in a consumer-goods transaction, a debtor or secondary obligor may waive the right to redeem collateral under Section 9–623 only by an agreement to that effect entered into and authenticated after default.

[Subpart 2. Noncompliance with Article]

§ 9–625. Remedies for Secured Party's Failure to Comply with Article.

(a) If it is established that a secured party is not proceeding in accordance with this article, a court may order or restrain collection, enforcement, or disposition of collateral on appropriate terms and conditions.

(b) Subject to subsections (c), (d), and (f), a person is liable for damages in the amount of any loss caused by a failure to comply with this article. Loss caused by a failure to comply may include loss resulting from the debtor's inability to obtain, or increased costs of, alternative financing.

(c) Except as otherwise provided in Section 9–628:

(1) a person that, at the time of the failure, was a debtor, was an obligor, or held a security interest in or other lien on the collateral may recover damages under subsection (b) for its loss; and

(2) if the collateral is consumer goods, a person that was a debtor or a secondary obligor at the time a secured party failed to comply with this part may recover for that failure in any event an amount not less than the credit service charge plus 10 percent of the principal amount of the obligation or the time-price differential plus 10 percent of the cash price.

(d) A debtor whose deficiency is eliminated under Section 9–626 may recover damages for the loss of any surplus. However, a debtor

or secondary obligor whose deficiency is eliminated or reduced under Section 9–626 may not otherwise recover under subsection (b) for noncompliance with the provisions of this part relating to collection, enforcement, disposition, or acceptance.

(e) In addition to any damages recoverable under subsection (b), the debtor, consumer obligor, or person named as a debtor in a filed record, as applicable, may recover $500 in each case from a person that:

(1) fails to comply with Section 9–208;

(2) fails to comply with Section 9–209;

(3) files a record that the person is not entitled to file under Section 9–509(a);

(4) fails to cause the secured party of record to file or send a termination statement as required by Section 9–513(a) or (c);

(5) fails to comply with Section 9–616(b)(1) and whose failure is part of a pattern, or consistent with a practice, of noncompliance; or

(6) fails to comply with Section 9–616(b)(2).

(f) A debtor or consumer obligor may recover damages under subsection (b) and, in addition, $500 in each case from a person that, without reasonable cause, fails to comply with a request under Section 9–210. A recipient of a request under Section 9–210 which never claimed an interest in the collateral or obligations that are the subject of a request under that section has a reasonable excuse for failure to comply with the request within the meaning of this subsection.

(g) If a secured party fails to comply with a request regarding a list of collateral or a statement of account under Section 9–210, the secured party may claim a security interest only as shown in the list or statement included in the request as against a person that is reasonably misled by the failure.

As amended in 2000.

§ 9–626. Action in Which Deficiency or Surplus Is in Issue.

(a) In an action arising from a transaction, other than a consumer transaction, in which the amount of a deficiency or surplus is in issue, the following rules apply:

(1) A secured party need not prove compliance with the provisions of this part relating to collection, enforcement, disposition, or acceptance unless the debtor or a secondary obligor places the secured party's compliance in issue.

(2) If the secured party's compliance is placed in issue, the secured party has the burden of establishing that the collection, enforcement, disposition, or acceptance was conducted in accordance with this part.

(3) Except as otherwise provided in Section 9–628, if a secured party fails to prove that the collection, enforcement, disposition, or acceptance was conducted in accordance with the provisions of this part relating to collection, enforcement, disposition, or acceptance, the liability of a debtor or a secondary obligor for a deficiency is limited to an amount by which the sum of the secured obligation, expenses, and attorney's fees exceeds the greater of:

(A) the proceeds of the collection, enforcement, disposition, or acceptance; or

(B) the amount of proceeds that would have been realized had the noncomplying secured party proceeded in accordance with the provisions of this part relating to collection, enforcement, disposition, or acceptance.

(4) For purposes of paragraph (3)(B), the amount of proceeds that would have been realized is equal to the sum of the secured obligation, expenses, and attorney's fees unless the secured party proves that the amount is less than that sum.

(5) If a deficiency or surplus is calculated under Section 9–615(f), the debtor or obligor has the burden of establishing that the amount of proceeds of the disposition is significantly below the range of prices that a complying disposition to a person other than the secured party, a person related to the secured party, or a secondary obligor would have brought.

(b) The limitation of the rules in subsection (a) to transactions other than consumer transactions is intended to leave to the court the determination of the proper rules in consumer transactions. The court may not infer from that limitation the nature of the proper rule in consumer transactions and may continue to apply established approaches.

§ 9–627. Determination of Whether Conduct Was Commercially Reasonable.

(a) The fact that a greater amount could have been obtained by a collection, enforcement, disposition, or acceptance at a different time or in a different method from that selected by the secured party is not of itself sufficient to preclude the secured party from establishing that the collection, enforcement, disposition, or acceptance was made in a commercially reasonable manner.

(b) A disposition of collateral is made in a commercially reasonable manner if the disposition is made:

(1) in the usual manner on any recognized market;

(2) at the price current in any recognized market at the time of the disposition; or

(3) otherwise in conformity with reasonable commercial practices among dealers in the type of property that was the subject of the disposition.

(c) A collection, enforcement, disposition, or acceptance is commercially reasonable if it has been approved:

(1) in a judicial proceeding;

(2) by a bona fide creditors' committee;

(3) by a representative of creditors; or

(4) by an assignee for the benefit of creditors.

(d) Approval under subsection (c) need not be obtained, and lack of approval does not mean that the collection, enforcement, disposition, or acceptance is not commercially reasonable.

§ 9–628. Nonliability and Limitation on Liability of Secured Party; Liability of Secondary Obligor.

(a) Unless a secured party knows that a person is a debtor or obligor, knows the identity of the person, and knows how to communicate with the person:

(1) the secured party is not liable to the person, or to a secured party or lienholder that has filed a financing statement against the person, for failure to comply with this article; and

(2) the secured party's failure to comply with this article does not affect the liability of the person for a deficiency.

(b) A secured party is not liable because of its status as secured party:

(1) to a person that is a debtor or obligor, unless the secured party knows:

(A) that the person is a debtor or obligor;

(B) the identity of the person; and

(C) how to communicate with the person; or

(2) to a secured party or lienholder that has filed a financing statement against a person, unless the secured party knows:

(A) that the person is a debtor; and

(B) the identity of the person.

(c) A secured party is not liable to any person, and a person's liability for a deficiency is not affected, because of any act or omission arising out of the secured party's reasonable belief that a transaction is not a consumer-goods transaction or a consumer transaction or that goods are not consumer goods, if the secured party's belief is based on its reasonable reliance on:

(1) a debtor's representation concerning the purpose for which collateral was to be used, acquired, or held; or

(2) an obligor's representation concerning the purpose for which a secured obligation was incurred.

(d) A secured party is not liable to any person under Section 9–625(c)(2) for its failure to comply with Section 9–616.

(e) A secured party is not liable under Section 9–625(c)(2) more than once with respect to any one secured obligation.

Part 7 Transition

§ 9–701. Effective Date.

This [Act] takes effect on July 1, 2001.

§ 9–702. Savings Clause.

(a) Except as otherwise provided in this part, this [Act] applies to a transaction or lien within its scope, even if the transaction or lien was entered into or created before this [Act] takes effect.

(b) Except as otherwise provided in subsection (c) and Sections 9–703 through 9–709:

(1) transactions and liens that were not governed by [former Article 9], were validly entered into or created before this [Act] takes effect, and would be subject to this [Act] if they had been entered into or created after this [Act] takes effect, and the rights, duties, and interests flowing from those transactions and liens remain valid after this [Act] takes effect; and

(2) the transactions and liens may be terminated, completed, consummated, and enforced as required or permitted by this [Act] or by the law that otherwise would apply if this [Act] had not taken effect.

(c) This [Act] does not affect an action, case, or proceeding commenced before this [Act] takes effect.

As amended in 2000.

§ 9–703. Security Interest Perfected before Effective Date.

(a) A security interest that is enforceable immediately before this [Act] takes effect and would have priority over the rights of a person that becomes a lien creditor at that time is a perfected security interest under this [Act] if, when this [Act] takes effect, the applicable requirements for enforceability and perfection under this [Act] are satisfied without further action.

(b) Except as otherwise provided in Section 9–705, if, immediately before this [Act] takes effect, a security interest is enforceable and would have priority over the rights of a person that becomes a lien creditor at that time, but the applicable requirements for enforceability or perfection under this [Act] are not satisfied when this [Act] takes effect, the security interest:

(1) is a perfected security interest for one year after this [Act] takes effect;

(2) remains enforceable thereafter only if the security interest becomes enforceable under Section 9–203 before the year expires; and

(3) remains perfected thereafter only if the applicable requirements for perfection under this [Act] are satisfied before the year expires.

§ 9–704. Security Interest Unperfected before Effective Date.

A security interest that is enforceable immediately before this [Act] takes effect but which would be subordinate to the rights of a person that becomes a lien creditor at that time:

(1) remains an enforceable security interest for one year after this [Act] takes effect;

(2) remains enforceable thereafter if the security interest becomes enforceable under Section 9–203 when this [Act] takes effect or within one year thereafter; and

(3) becomes perfected:

(A) without further action, when this [Act] takes effect if the applicable requirements for perfection under this [Act] are satisfied before or at that time; or

(B) when the applicable requirements for perfection are satisfied if the requirements are satisfied after that time.

§ 9–705. Effectiveness of Action Taken before Effective Date.

(a) If action, other than the filing of a financing statement, is taken before this [Act] takes effect and the action would have resulted in priority of a security interest over the rights of a person that becomes a lien creditor had the security interest become enforceable before this [Act] takes effect, the action is effective to perfect a security interest that attaches under this [Act] within one year after this [Act] takes effect. An attached security interest becomes unperfected one year after this [Act] takes effect unless the security interest becomes a perfected security interest under this [Act] before the expiration of that period.

(b) The filing of a financing statement before this [Act] takes effect is effective to perfect a security interest to the extent the filing would satisfy the applicable requirements for perfection under this [Act].

(c) This [Act] does not render ineffective an effective financing statement that, before this [Act] takes effect, is filed and satisfies the applicable requirements for perfection under the law of the jurisdiction governing perfection as provided in [former Section 9–103]. However, except as otherwise provided in subsections (d) and (e) and Section 9–706, the financing statement ceases to be effective at the earlier of:

(1) the time the financing statement would have ceased to be effective under the law of the jurisdiction in which it is filed; or

(2) June 30, 2006.

(d) The filing of a continuation statement after this [Act] takes effect does not continue the effectiveness of the financing statement filed before this [Act] takes effect. However, upon the timely filing of a continuation statement after this [Act] takes effect and in accordance with the law of the jurisdiction governing perfection as provided in Part 3, the effectiveness of a financing statement filed in the same office in that jurisdiction before this [Act] takes effect continues for the period provided by the law of that jurisdiction.

(e) Subsection (c)(2) applies to a financing statement that, before this [Act] takes effect, is filed against a transmitting utility and satisfies the applicable requirements for perfection under the law of the jurisdiction governing perfection as provided in [former Section 9–103] only to the extent that Part 3 provides that the law of a jurisdiction other than the jurisdiction in which the financing statement is filed governs perfection of a security interest in collateral covered by the financing statement.

(f) A financing statement that includes a financing statement filed before this [Act] takes effect and a continuation statement filed after this [Act] takes effect is effective only to the extent that it satisfies the requirements of Part 5 for an initial financing statement.

§ 9–706. When Initial Financing Statement Suffices to Continue Effectiveness of Financing Statement.

(a) The filing of an initial financing statement in the office specified in Section 9–501 continues the effectiveness of a financing statement filed before this [Act] takes effect if:

(1) the filing of an initial financing statement in that office would be effective to perfect a security interest under this [Act];

(2) the pre-effective-date financing statement was filed in an office in another State or another office in this State; and

(3) the initial financing statement satisfies subsection (c).

(b) The filing of an initial financing statement under subsection (a) continues the effectiveness of the pre-effective-date financing statement:

(1) if the initial financing statement is filed before this [Act] takes effect, for the period provided in [former Section 9–403] with respect to a financing statement; and

(2) if the initial financing statement is filed after this [Act] takes effect, for the period provided in Section 9–515 with respect to an initial financing statement.

(c) To be effective for purposes of subsection (a), an initial financing statement must:

(1) satisfy the requirements of Part 5 for an initial financing statement;

(2) identify the pre-effective-date financing statement by indicating the office in which the financing statement was filed and providing the dates of filing and file numbers, if any, of the financing statement and of the most recent continuation statement filed with respect to the financing statement; and

(3) indicate that the pre-effective-date financing statement remains effective.

§ 9–707. Amendment of Pre-Effective-Date Financing Statement.

(a) In this section, "Pre-effective-date financing statement" means a financing statement filed before this [Act] takes effect.

(b) After this [Act] takes effect, a person may add or delete collateral covered by, continue or terminate the effectiveness of, or otherwise amend the information provided in, a pre-effective-date financing statement only in accordance with the law of the jurisdiction governing perfection as provided in Part 3. However, the effectiveness of a pre-effective-date financing statement also may be terminated in accordance with the law of the jurisdiction in which the financing statement is filed.

(c) Except as otherwise provided in subsection (d), if the law of this State governs perfection of a security interest, the information in a pre-effective-date financing statement may be amended after this [Act] takes effect only if:

(1) the pre-effective-date financing statement and an amendment are filed in the office specified in Section 9–501;

(2) an amendment is filed in the office specified in Section 9–501 concurrently with, or after the filing in that office of, an initial financing statement that satisfies Section 9–706(c); or

(3) an initial financing statement that provides the information as amended and satisfies Section 9–706(c) is filed in the office specified in Section 9–501.

(d) If the law of this State governs perfection of a security interest, the effectiveness of a pre-effective-date financing statement may be continued only under Section 9–705(d) and (f) or 9–706.

(e) Whether or not the law of this State governs perfection of a security interest, the effectiveness of a pre-effective-date financing statement filed in this State may be terminated after this [Act] takes effect by filing a termination statement in the office in which the pre-effective-date financing statement is filed, unless an initial financing statement that satisfies Section 9–706(c) has been filed in the office specified by the law of the jurisdiction governing perfection as provided in Part 3 as the office in which to file a financing statement.

As amended in 2000.

§ 9–708. Persons Entitled to File Initial Financing Statement or Continuation Statement.

A person may file an initial financing statement or a continuation statement under this part if:

(1) the secured party of record authorizes the filing; and

(2) the filing is necessary under this part:

(A) to continue the effectiveness of a financing statement filed before this [Act] takes effect; or

(B) to perfect or continue the perfection of a security interest.

As amended in 2000.

§ 9–709. Priority.

(a) This [Act] determines the priority of conflicting claims to collateral. However, if the relative priorities of the claims were established before this [Act] takes effect, [former Article 9] determines priority.

(b) For purposes of Section 9–322(a), the priority of a security interest that becomes enforceable under Section 9–203 of this [Act] dates from the time this [Act] takes effect if the security interest is perfected under this [Act] by the filing of a financing statement before this [Act] takes effect which would not have been effective to perfect the security interest under [former Article 9]. This subsection does not apply to conflicting security interests each of which is perfected by the filing of such a financing statement.

As amended in 2000.

APPENDIX D
Spanish Equivalents for Important Legal Terms in English

Abandoned property: bienes abandonados
Acceptance: aceptación; consentimiento; acuerdo
Acceptor: aceptante
Accession: toma de posesión; aumento; accesión
Accommodation indorser: avalista de favor
Accommodation party: firmante de favor
Accord: acuerdo; convenio; arregio
Accord and satisfaction: transacción ejecutada
Act of state doctrine: doctrina de acto de gobierno
Administrative law: derecho administrativo
Administrative process: procedimiento o metódo administrativo
Administrator: administrador (-a)
Adverse possession: posesión de hecho susceptible de proscripción adquisitiva
Affirmative action: acción afirmativa
Affirmative defense: defensa afirmativa
After-acquired property: bienes adquiridos con posterioridad a un hecho dado
Agency: mandato; agencia
Agent: mandatorio; agente; representante
Agreement: convenio; acuerdo; contrato
Alien corporation: empresa extranjera
Allonge: hojas adicionales de endosos
Answer: contestación de la demande; alegato
Anticipatory repudiation: anuncio previo de las partes de su imposibilidad de cumplir con el contrato
Appeal: apelación; recurso de apelación
Appellate jurisdiction: jurisdicción de apelaciones
Appraisal right: derecho de valuación
Arbitration: arbitraje
Arson: incendio intencional

Articles of partnership: contrato social
Artisan's lien: derecho de retención que ejerce al artesano
Assault: asalto; ataque; agresión
Assignment of rights: transmisión; transferencia; cesión
Assumption of risk: no resarcimiento por exposición voluntaria al peligro
Attachment: auto judicial que autoriza el embargo; embargo

Bailee: depositario
Bailment: depósito; constitución en depósito
Bailor: depositante
Bankruptcy trustee: síndico de la quiebra
Battery: agresión; física
Bearer: portador; tenedor
Bearer instrument: documento al portador
Bequest or legacy: legado (de bienes muebles)
Bilateral contract: contrato bilateral
Bill of lading: conocimiento de embarque; carta de porte
Bill of Rights: declaración de derechos
Binder: póliza de seguro provisoria; recibo de pago a cuenta del precio
Blank indorsement: endoso en blanco
Blue sky laws: leyes reguladoras del comercio bursátil
Bond: título de crédito; garantía; caución
Bond indenture: contrato de emisión de bonos; contrato del ampréstito
Breach of contract: incumplimiento de contrato
Brief: escrito; resumen; informe
Burglary: violación de domicilio
Business judgment rule: regla de juicio comercial
Business tort: agravio comercial

Case law: ley de casos; derecho casuístico
Cashier's check: cheque de caja
Causation in fact: causalidad en realidad
Cease-and-desist order: orden para cesar y desistir
Certificate of deposit: certificado de depósito
Certified check: cheque certificado
Charitable trust: fideicomiso para fines benéficos
Chattel: bien mueble
Check: cheque
Chose in action: derecho inmaterial; derecho de acción
Civil law: derecho civil
Close corporation: sociedad de un solo accionista o de un grupo restringido de accionistas
Closed shop: taller agremiado (emplea solamente a miembros de un gremio)
Closing argument: argumento al final
Codicil: codicilo
Collateral: guarantía; bien objeto de la guarantía real
Comity: cortesía; cortesía entre naciones
Commercial paper: instrumentos negociables; documentos a valores commerciales
Common law: derecho consuetudinario; derecho común; ley común
Common stock: acción ordinaria
Comparative negligence: negligencia comparada
Compensatory damages: daños y perjuicios reales o compensatorios
Concurrent conditions: condiciones concurrentes
Concurrent jurisdiction: competencia concurrente de varios tribunales para entender en una misma causa
Concurring opinion: opinión concurrente
Condition: condición

797

Condition precedent: condición suspensiva

Condition subsequent: condición resolutoria

Confiscation: confiscación

Confusion: confusión; fusión

Conglomerate merger: fusión de firmas que operan en distintos mercados

Consent decree: acuerdo entre las partes aprobado por un tribunal

Consequential damages: daños y perjuicios indirectos

Consideration: consideración; motivo; contraprestación

Consolidation: consolidación

Constructive delivery: entrega simbólica

Constructive trust: fideicomiso creado por aplicación de la ley

Consumer protection law: ley para proteger el consumidor

Contract: contrato

Contract under seal: contrato formal o sellado

Contributory negligence: negligencia de la parte actora

Conversion: usurpación; conversión de valores

Copyright: derecho de autor

Corporation: sociedad anónima; corporación; persona juridica

Co-sureties: cogarantes

Counterclaim: reconvención; contrademanda

Counteroffer: contraoferta

Course of dealing: curso de transacciones

Course of performance: curso de cumplimiento

Covenant: pacto; garantía; contrato

Covenant not to sue: pacto or contrato a no demandar

Covenant of quiet enjoyment: garantía del uso y goce pacífico del inmueble

Creditors' composition agreement: concordato preventivo

Crime: crimen; delito; contravención

Criminal law: derecho penal

Cross-examination: contrainterrogatorio

Cure: cura; cuidado; derecho de remediar un vicio contractual

Customs receipts: recibos de derechos aduaneros

Damages: daños; indemnización por daños y perjuicios

Debit card: tarjeta de dé bito

Debtor: deudor

Debt securities: seguridades de deuda

Deceptive advertising: publicidad engañosa

Deed: escritura; título; acta translativa de domino

Defamation: difamación

Delegation of duties: delegación de obligaciones

Demand deposit: depósito a la vista

Depositions: declaración de un testigo fuera del tribunal

Devise: legado; deposición testamentaria (bienes inmuebles)

Directed verdict: veredicto según orden del juez y sin participación activa del jurado

Direct examination: interrogatorio directo; primer interrogatorio

Disaffirmance: repudiación; renuncia; anulación

Discharge: descargo; liberación; cumplimiento

Disclosed principal: mandante revelado

Discovery: descubrimiento; producción de la prueba

Dissenting opinion: opinión disidente

Dissolution: disolución; terminación

Diversity of citizenship: competencia de los tribunales federales para entender en causas cuyas partes intervinientes son cuidadanos de distintos estados

Divestiture: extinción premature de derechos reales

Dividend: dividendo

Docket: orden del día; lista de causas pendientes

Domestic corporation: sociedad local

Draft: orden de pago; letrade cambio

Drawee: girado; beneficiario

Drawer: librador

Duress: coacción; violencia

Easement: servidumbre

Embezzlement: desfalco; malversación

Eminent domain: poder de expropiación

Employment discrimination: discriminación en el empleo

Entrepreneur: empresario

Environmental law: ley ambiental

Equal dignity rule: regla de dignidad egual

Equity security: tipo de participación en una sociedad

Estate: propiedad; patrimonio; derecho

Estop: impedir; prevenir

Ethical issue: cuestión ética

Exclusive jurisdiction: competencia exclusiva

Exculpatory clause: cláusula eximente

Executed contract: contrato ejecutado

Execution: ejecución; cumplimiento

Executor: albacea

Executory contract: contrato aún no completamente consumado

Executory interest: derecho futuro

Express contract: contrato expreso

Expropriation: expropriación

Federal question: caso federal

Fee simple: pleno dominio; dominio absoluto

Fee simple absolute: dominio absoluto

Fee simple defeasible: dominio sujeta a una condición resolutoria

Felony: crimen; delito grave

Fictitious payee: beneficiario ficticio

Fiduciary: fiduciaro

Firm offer: oferta en firme

Fixture: inmueble por destino, incorporación a anexación

Floating lien: gravamen continuado

Foreign corporation: sociedad extranjera; U.S. sociedad constituída en otro estado

Forgery: falso; falsificación

Formal contract: contrato formal

Franchise: privilegio; franquicia; concesión

Franchisee: persona que recibe una concesión

Franchisor: persona que vende una concesión

Fraud: fraude; dolo; engaño

Future interest: bien futuro

Garnishment: embargo de derechos

General partner: socio comanditario

General warranty deed: escritura translativa de domino con garantía de título

Gift: donación

Gift *causa mortis:* donación por causa de muerte

Gift *inter vivos:* donación entre vivos

Good faith: buena fe

Good faith purchaser: comprador de buena fe

Holder: tenedor por contraprestación

Holder in due course: tenedor legítimo

Holographic will: testamento ológrafico

Homestead exemption laws: leyes que exceptúan las casas de familia de ejecución por duedas generales

Horizontal merger: fusión horizontal

Identification: identificación
Implied-in-fact contract: contrato implícito en realidad
Implied warranty: guarantía implícita
Implied warranty of merchantability: garantía implícita de vendibilidad
Impossibility of performance: imposibilidad de cumplir un contrato
Imposter: imposter
Incidental beneficiary: beneficiario incidental; beneficiario secundario
Incidental damages: daños incidentales
Indictment: auto de acusación; acusación
Indorsee: endorsatario
Indorsement: endoso
Indorser: endosante
Informal contract: contrato no formal; contrato verbal
Information: acusación hecha por el ministerio público
Injunction: mandamiento; orden de no innovar
Innkeeper's lien: derecho de retención que ejerce el posadero
Installment contract: contrato de pago en cuotas
Insurable interest: interés asegurable
Intended beneficiary: beneficiario destinado
Intentional tort: agravio; cuasi-delito intencional
International law: derecho internacional
Interrogatories: preguntas escritas sometidas por una parte a la otra o a un testigo
Inter vivos **trust:** fideicomiso entre vivos
Intestacy laws: leyes de la condición de morir intestado
Intestate: intestado
Investment company: compañía de inversiones
Issue: emisión

Joint tenancy: derechos conjuntos en un bien inmueble en favor del beneficiario sobreviviente
Judgment *n.o.v.*: juicio no obstante veredicto
Judgment rate of interest: interés de juicio
Judicial process: acto de procedimiento; proceso jurídico
Judicial review: revisión judicial
Jurisdiction: jurisdicción

Larceny: robo; hurto
Law: derecho; ley; jurisprudencia

Lease: contrato de locación; contrato de alquiler
Leasehold estate: bienes forales
Legal rate of interest: interés legal
Legatee: legatario
Letter of credit: carta de crédito
Levy: embargo; comiso
Libel: libelo; difamación escrita
Life estate: usufructo
Limited partner: comanditario
Limited partnership: sociedad en comandita
Liquidation: liquidación; realización
Lost property: objetos perdidos

Majority opinion: opinión de la mayoría
Maker: persona que realiza u ordena; librador
Mechanic's lien: gravamen de constructor
Mediation: mediación; intervención
Merger: fusión
Mirror image rule: fallo de reflejo
Misdemeanor: infracción; contravención
Mislaid property: bienes extraviados
Mitigation of damages: reducción de daños
Mortgage: hipoteca
Motion to dismiss: excepción parentoria
Mutual fund: fondo mutual

Negotiable instrument: instrumento negociable
Negotiation: negociación
Nominal damages: daños y perjuicios nominales
Novation: novación
Nuncupative will: testamento nuncupativo

Objective theory of contracts: teoria objetiva de contratos
Offer: oferta
Offeree: persona que recibe una oferta
Offeror: oferente
Order instrument: instrumento o documento a la orden
Original jurisdiction: jurisdicción de primera instancia
Output contract: contrato de producción

Parol evidence rule: regla relativa a la prueba oral
Partially disclosed principal: mandante revelado en parte
Partnership: sociedad colectiva; asociación; asociación de participación
Past consideration: causa o contraprestación anterior
Patent: patente; privilegio
Pattern or practice: muestra o práctica

Payee: beneficiario de un pago
Penalty: pena; penalidad
Per capita: por cabeza
Perfection: perfeción
Performance: cumplimiento; ejecución
Personal defenses: excepciones personales
Personal property: bienes muebles
Per stirpes: por estirpe
Plea bargaining: regateo por un alegato
Pleadings: alegatos
Pledge: prenda
Police powers: poders de policia y de prevención del crimen
Policy: póliza
Positive law: derecho positivo; ley positiva
Possibility of reverter: posibilidad de reversión
Precedent: precedente
Preemptive right: derecho de prelación
Preferred stock: acciones preferidas
Premium: recompensa; prima
Presentment warranty: garantía de presentación
Price discrimination: discriminación en los precios
Principal: mandante; principal
Privity: nexo jurídico
Privity of contract: relación contractual
Probable cause: causa probable
Probate: verificación; verificación del testamento
Probate court: tribunal de sucesiones y tutelas
Proceeds: resultados; ingresos
Profit: beneficio; utilidad; lucro
Promise: promesa
Promisee: beneficiario de una promesa
Promisor: promtente
Promissory estoppel: impedimento promisorio
Promissory note: pagaré; nota de pago
Promoter: promotor; fundador
Proximate cause: causa inmediata o próxima
Proxy: apoderado; poder
Punitive, or exemplary, damages: daños y perjuicios punitivos o ejemplares

Qualified indorsement: endoso con reservas
Quasi contract: contrato tácito o implícito
Quitclaim deed: acto de transferencia de una propiedad por finiquito, pero sin ninguna garantía sobre la validez del título transferido

Ratification: ratificación
Real property: bienes inmuebles
Reasonable doubt: duda razonable
Rebuttal: refutación
Recognizance: promesa; compromiso; reconocimiento
Recording statutes: leyes estatales sobre registros oficiales
Redress: reporacín
Reformation: rectificación; reforma; corrección
Rejoinder: dúplica; contrarréplica
Release: liberación; renuncia a un derecho
Remainder: substitución; reversión
Remedy: recurso; remedio; reparación
Replevin: acción reivindicatoria; reivindicación
Reply: réplica
Requirements contract: contrato de suministro
Rescission: rescisión
Res judicata: cosa juzgada; res judicata
Respondeat superior: responsabilidad del mandante o del maestro
Restitution: restitución
Restrictive indorsement: endoso restrictivo
Resulting trust: fideicomiso implícito
Reversion: reversión; sustitución
Revocation: revocación; derogación
Right of contribution: derecho de contribución
Right of reimbursement: derecho de reembolso
Right of subrogation: derecho de subrogación
Right-to-work law: ley de libertad de trabajo
Robbery: robo
Rule 10b-5: Regla 10b-5

Sale: venta; contrato de compreventa
Sale on approval: venta a ensayo; venta sujeta a la aprobación del comprador
Sale or return: venta con derecho de devolución
Sales contract: contrato de compraventa; boleto de compraventa
Satisfaction: satisfacción; pago
Scienter: a sabiendas
S corporation: S corporación
Secured party: acreedor garantizado
Secured transaction: transacción garantizada
Securities: volares; titulos; seguridades
Security agreement: convenio de seguridad

Security interest: interés en un bien dado en garantía que permite a quien lo detenta venderlo en caso de incumplimiento
Service mark: marca de identificación de servicios
Shareholder's derivative suit: acción judicial entablada por un accionista en nombre de la sociedad
Signature: firma; rúbrica
Slander: difamación oral; calumnia
Sovereign immunity: immunidad soberana
Special indorsement: endoso especial; endoso a la orden de una person en particular
Specific performance: ejecución precisa, según los términos del contrato
Spendthrift trust: fideicomiso para pródigos
Stale check: cheque vencido
Stare decisis: acatar las decisiones, observar los precedentes
Statutory law: derecho estatutario; derecho legislado; derecho escrito
Stock: acciones
Stock warrant: certificado para la compra de acciones
Stop-payment order: orden de suspensión del pago de un cheque dada por el librador del mismo
Strict liability: responsabilidad unconditional
Summary judgment: fallo sumario

Tangible property: bienes corpóreos
Tenancy at will: inguilino por tiempo indeterminado (según la voluntad del propietario)
Tenancy by sufferance: posesión por tolerancia
Tenancy by the entirety: locación conyugal conjunta
Tenancy for years: inguilino por un término fijo
Tenancy in common: specie de copropiedad indivisa
Tender: oferta de pago; oferta de ejecución
Testamentary trust: fideicomiso testamentario
Testator: testador (-a)
Third party beneficiary contract: contrato para el beneficio del tercero-beneficiario
Tort: agravio; cuasi-delito
Totten trust: fideicomiso creado por un depósito bancario

Trade acceptance: letra de cambio aceptada
Trademark: marca registrada
Trade name: nombre comercial; razón social
Traveler's check: cheque del viajero
Trespass to land: ingreso no authorizado a las tierras de otro
Trespass to personal property: violación de los derechos posesorios de un tercero con respecto a bienes muebles
Trust: fideicomiso; trust

Ultra vires: ultra vires; fuera de la facultad (de una sociedad anónima)
Unanimous opinion: opinión unámine
Unconscionable contract or clause: contrato leonino; cláusula leonino
Underwriter: subscriptor; asegurador
Unenforceable contract: contrato que no se puede hacer cumplir
Unilateral contract: contrato unilateral
Union shop: taller agremiado; empresa en la que todos los empleados son miembros del gremio o sindicato
Universal defenses: defensas legitimas o legales
Usage of trade: uso comercial
Usury: usura

Valid contract: contrato válido
Venue: lugar; sede del proceso
Vertical merger: fusión vertical de empresas
Voidable contract: contrato anulable
Void contract: contrato nulo; contrato inválido, sin fuerza legal
Voir dire: examen preliminar de un testigo a jurado por el tribunal para determinar su competencia
Voting trust: fideicomiso para ejercer el derecho de voto

Waiver: renuncia; abandono
Warranty of habitability: garantía de habitabilidad
Watered stock: acciones diluídos; capital inflado
White-collar crime: crimen administrativo
Writ of attachment: mandamiento de ejecución; mandamiento de embargo
Writ of *certiorari*: auto de avocación; auto de certiorari
Writ of execution: auto ejecutivo; mandamiento de ejecutión
Writ of mandamus: auto de mandamus; mandamiento; orden judicial

Glossary

A

Abandoned property Property with which the owner has voluntarily parted, with no intention of recovering it.

Acceptance A voluntary act by the offeree that shows assent, or agreement, to the terms of an offer; may consist of words or conduct.

Acceptor A drawee that promises to pay an instrument when the instrument is presented later for payment.

Accession Occurs when an individual adds value to personal property by either labor or materials. In some situations, a person may acquire ownership rights in another's property through accession.

Accord and satisfaction An agreement for payment (or other performance) between two parties, one of whom has a right of action against the other. After the payment has been accepted or other performance has been made, the "accord and satisfaction" is complete and the obligation is discharged.

Accredited investors In the context of securities offerings, sophisticated investors, such as banks, insurance companies, investment companies, the issuer's executive officers and directors, and persons whose income or net worth exceeds certain limits.

Actionable Capable of serving as the basis of a lawsuit.

Actual malice Real and demonstrable evil intent. In a defamation suit, a statement made about a public figure normally must be made with actual malice (with either knowledge of its falsity or a reckless disregard of the truth) for liability to be incurred.

Adhesion contract A "standard form" contract, such as that between a large retailer and a consumer, in which the stronger party dictates the terms.

Adjudicate To render a judicial decision. In the administrative process, the proceeding in which an administrative law judge hears and decides on issues that arise when an administrative agency charges a person or a firm with violating a law or regulation enforced by the agency.

Administrative agency A federal or state government agency established to perform a specific function. Administrative agencies are authorized by legislative acts to make and enforce rules to administer and enforce the acts.

Administrative law The body of law created by administrative agencies (in the form of rules, regulations, orders, and decisions) in order to carry out their duties and responsibilities.

Administrative process The procedure used by administrative agencies in the administration of law.

Administrator One who is appointed by a court to handle the probate (disposition) of a person's estate if that person dies intestate (without a valid will) or if the executor named in the will cannot serve.

Adverse possession The acquisition of title to real property by occupying it openly, without the consent of the owner, for a period of time specified by a state statute. The occupation must be actual, open, notorious, exclusive, and in opposition to all others, including the owner.

Affirmative action Job-hiring and admissions policies that give special consideration to members of protected classes in an effort to overcome present effects of past discrimination.

After-acquired property Property of the debtor that is acquired after the execution of a security agreement.

Agency A relationship between two parties in which one party (the agent) agrees to represent or act for the other (the principal).

Agreement A meeting of two or more minds in regard to the terms of a contract; usually broken down into two events—an offer by one party to form a contract, and an acceptance of the offer by the person to whom the offer is made.

Alien corporation A designation in the United States for a corporation formed in another country but doing business in the United States.

Alienation In real property law, a term used to define the process of transferring land out of one's possession (thus "alienating" the land from oneself).

Alternative dispute resolution (ADR) The resolution of disputes in ways other than those involved in the traditional judicial process. Negotiation, mediation, and arbitration are forms of ADR.

Answer Procedurally, a defendant's response to the plaintiff's complaint.

Anticipatory repudiation An assertion or action by a party indicating that he or she will not perform an obligation that the party is contractually obligated to perform at a future time.

Appraisal right The right of a dissenting shareholder, if he or she objects to an extraordinary transaction of the corporation (such as a merger or consolidation), to have his or her shares appraised and to be paid the fair value of his or her shares by the corporation.

Appropriation In tort law, the use by one person of another person's name, likeness, or other identifying characteristic without permission and for the benefit of the user.

Arbitration The settling of a dispute by submitting it to a disinterested third party (other than a court), who renders a decision that is (usually) legally binding.

Arbitration clause A clause in a contract that provides that, in case of a dispute, the parties will submit the dispute to arbitration rather than litigate the dispute in court.

Arson The malicious burning of another's dwelling. Some statutes have expanded this to include any real property regardless of ownership and the destruction of property by other means—for example, by explosion.

Articles of incorporation The document filed with the appropriate governmental agency, usually the secretary of state, when a business is incorporated; state statutes usually prescribe what kind of information must be contained in the articles of incorporation.

Articles of organization The document filed with a designated state official by which a limited liability company is formed.

Articles of partnership A written agreement that sets forth each partner's rights and obligations with respect to the partnership.

Artisan's lien A possessory lien given to a person who has made improvements and added value to another person's personal property as security for payment for services performed.

Assault Any word or action intended to make another person fearful of immediate physical harm; a reasonably believable threat.

Assignee A party to whom the rights under a contract are transferred, or assigned.

Assignment The act of transferring to another all or part of one's rights arising under a contract.

Assignor A party who transfers (assigns) his or her rights under a contract to another party (called the assignee).

Assumption of risk A defense against negligence that can be used when the plaintiff is aware of a danger and voluntarily assumes the risk of injury from that danger.

Attachment In the context of secured transactions, the process by which a security interest in the property of another becomes enforceable. In the context of judicial liens, a court-ordered seizure and taking into custody of property prior to the securing of a judgment for a past-due debt.

Automated clearinghouse (ACH) An electronic banking system used to transfer payments and settle accounts.

Automatic stay In bankruptcy proceedings, the suspension of virtually all litigation and other action by creditors against the debtor or the debtor's property; the stay is effective the moment the debtor files a petition in bankruptcy.

Award In the context of litigation, the amount of money awarded to a plaintiff in a civil lawsuit as damages. In the context of arbitration, the arbitrator's decision.

B

Bailee One to whom goods are entrusted by a bailor. Under the UCC, a party who, by a bill of lading, warehouse receipt, or other document of title, acknowledges possession of goods and contracts.

Bailment A situation in which the personal property of one person (a bailor) is entrusted to another (a bailee), who is obligated to return the bailed property to the bailor or dispose of it as directed.

Bailor One who entrusts goods to a bailee.

Bankruptcy court A federal court of limited jurisdiction that handles only bankruptcy proceedings. Bankruptcy proceedings are governed by federal bankruptcy law.

Battery The unprivileged, intentional touching of another.

Bearer A person in the possession of an instrument payable to bearer or indorsed in blank.

Bearer instrument Any instrument that is not payable to a specific person, including instruments payable to the bearer or to "cash."

Bequest A gift by will of personal property (from the verb—to bequeath).

Beyond a reasonable doubt The standard of proof used in criminal cases. If there is any reasonable doubt that a criminal defendant did not commit the crime with which he or she has been charged, then the verdict must be "not guilty."

Bilateral contract A type of contract that arises when a promise is given in exchange for a return promise.

Bill of Rights The first ten amendments to the U.S. Constitution.

Binder A written, temporary insurance policy.

Binding authority Any source of law that a court must follow when deciding a case. Binding authorities include constitutions, statutes, and regulations that govern the issue being decided, as well as court decisions that are controlling precedents within the jurisdiction.

Blue laws State or local laws that prohibit the performance of certain types of commercial activities on Sunday.

Blue sky laws State laws that regulate the offer and sale of securities.

Bona fide occupational qualification (BFOQ) Identifiable characteristics reasonably necessary to the normal operation of a particular business. These characteristics can include gender, national origin, and religion, but not race.

Bond A certificate that evidences a corporate (or government) debt. It is a security that involves no ownership interest in the issuing entity.

Bond indenture A contract between the issuer of a bond and the bondholder.

Bounty payment A reward (payment) given to a person or persons who perform a certain service—such as informing legal authorities of illegal actions.

Breach of contract The failure, without legal excuse, of a promisor to perform the obligations of a contract.

Brief A formal legal document submitted by the attorney for the appellant or the appellee (in answer to the appellant's brief) to an appellate court when a case is appealed. The appellant's brief outlines the facts and issues of the case, the judge's rulings or jury's findings that should be reversed or modified, the applicable law, and the arguments on the client's behalf.

Browse-wrap terms Terms and conditions of use that are presented to an Internet user at the time certain products, such as software, are being downloaded but that need not be agreed to (by clicking "I agree," for example) before being able to install or use the product.

Burglary The unlawful entry into a building with the intent to commit a felony. (Some state statutes expand this to include the intent to commit any crime.)

Business ethics Ethics in a business context; a consensus of what constitutes right or wrong behavior in the world of business and the application of moral principles to situations that arise in a business setting.

Business invitees Those people, such as customers or clients, who are invited onto business premises by the owner of those premises for business purposes.

Business judgment rule A rule that immunizes corporate management from liability for actions that result in corporate losses or damages if the actions are undertaken in good faith and are within both the power of the corporation and the authority of management to make.

Business necessity A defense to allegations of employment discrimination in which the employer demonstrates that an employment practice that discriminates against members of a protected class is related to job performance.

Business tort The wrongful interference with another's business rights.

Bylaws A set of governing rules adopted by a corporation or other association.

C

Case law The rules of law announced in court decisions. Case law includes the aggregate of reported cases that interpret judicial precedents, statutes, regulations, and constitutional provisions.

Cashier's check A check drawn by a bank on itself.

Categorical imperative A concept developed by the philosopher Immanuel Kant as an ethical guideline for behavior. In deciding whether an action is right or wrong, or desirable or undesirable, a person should evaluate the action in terms of what would happen if everybody else in the same situation, or category, acted the same way.

Causation in fact An act or omission without which an event would not have occurred.

Certificate of deposit (CD) A note of a bank in which a bank acknowledges a receipt of money from a party and promises to repay the money, with interest, to the party on a certain date.

Certificate of incorporation The primary document that evidences corporate existence (referred to as articles of incorporation in some states).

Certificate of limited partnership The basic document filed with a designated state official by which a limited partnership is formed.

Certified check A check that has been accepted by the bank on which it is drawn. Essentially, the bank, by certifying (accepting) the check, promises to pay the check at the time the check is presented.

Charging order In partnership law, an order granted by a court to a judgment creditor that entitles the creditor to attach profits or assets of a partner on the dissolution of the partnership.

Charitable trust A trust in which the property held by a trustee must be used for a charitable purpose, such as the advancement of health, education, or religion.

Chattel All forms of personal property.

Check A draft drawn by a drawer ordering the drawee bank or financial institution to pay a certain amount of money to the holder on demand.

Choice-of-language clause A clause in a contract designating the official language by which the contract will be interpreted in the event of a future disagreement over the contract's terms.

Choice-of-law clause A clause in a contract designating the law (such as the law of a particular state or nation) that will govern the contract.

Chose in action A right that can be enforced in court to recover a debt or to obtain damages.

Citation A reference to a publication in which a legal authority—such as a statute or a court decision—or other source can be found.

Civil law The branch of law dealing with the definition and enforcement of all private or public rights, as opposed to criminal matters.

Civil law system A system of law derived from that of the Roman Empire and based on a code rather than case law; the predominant system of law in the nations of continental Europe and the nations that were once their colonies. In the United States, Louisiana is the only state that has a civil law system.

Clearinghouse A system or place where banks exchange checks and drafts drawn on each other and settle daily balances.

Click-on agreement   This occurs when a buyer, completing a transaction on a computer, is required to indicate his or her assent to be bound by the terms of an offer by clicking on a button that says, for example, "I agree." Sometimes referred to as a *click-on license* or a *click-wrap agreement.*

Close corporation   A corporation whose shareholders are limited to a small group of persons, often including only family members. The rights of shareholders of a close corporation usually are restricted regarding the transfer of shares to others.

Closed shop   A firm that requires union membership by its workers as a condition of employment. The closed shop was made illegal by the Labor-Management Relations Act of 1947.

Codicil   A written supplement or modification to a will. A codicil must be executed with the same formalities as a will.

Collateral   Under Article 9 of the UCC, the property subject to a security interest, including accounts and chattel paper that have been sold.

Collateral promise   A secondary promise that is ancillary (subsidiary) to a principal transaction or primary contractual relationship, such as a promise made by one person to pay the debts of another if the latter fails to perform. A collateral promise normally must be in writing to be enforceable.

Collecting bank   Any bank handling an item for collection, except the payor bank.

Commerce clause   The provision in Article I, Section 8, of the U.S. Constitution that gives Congress the power to regulate interstate commerce.

Commingle   To mix together. In corporate law, if personal and corporate interests are commingled to the extent that the corporation has no separate identity, a court may "pierce the corporate veil" and expose the shareholders to personal liability.

Common carrier   An owner of a truck, railroad, airline, ship, or other vehicle who is licensed to offer transportation services to the public, generally in return for compensation or a payment.

Common law   That body of law developed from custom or judicial decisions in English and U.S. courts, not attributable to a legislature.

Common stock   Shares of ownership in a corporation that give the owner of the stock a proportionate interest in the corporation with regard to control, earnings, and net assets; shares of common stock are lowest in priority with respect to payment of dividends and distribution of the corporation's assets upon dissolution.

Community property   A form of concurrent ownership of property in which each spouse technically owns an undivided one-half interest in property acquired during the marriage. This form of joint ownership occurs in only ten states and Puerto Rico.

Comparative negligence   A theory in tort law under which the liability for injuries resulting from negligent acts is shared by all parties who were negligent (including the injured party), on the basis of each person's proportionate negligence.

Compensatory damages   A money award equivalent to the actual value of injuries or damages sustained by the aggrieved party.

Complaint   The pleading made by a plaintiff alleging wrongdoing on the part of the defendant; the document that, when filed with a court, initiates a lawsuit.

Computer crime   Any act that is directed against computers and computer parts, that uses computers as instruments of crime, or that involves computers and constitutes abuse.

Concurrent conditions   Conditions in a contract that must occur or be performed at the same time; they are mutually dependent. No obligations arise until these conditions are simultaneously performed.

Concurrent jurisdiction   Jurisdiction that exists when two different courts have the power to hear a case. For example, some cases can be heard in a federal or a state court.

Condemnation   The process of taking private property for public use through the government's power of eminent domain.

Condition   A qualification, provision, or clause in a contractual agreement, the occurrence of which creates, suspends, or terminates the obligations of the contracting parties.

Condition precedent   A condition in a contract that must be met before a party's promise becomes absolute.

Condition subsequent   A condition in a contract that operates to terminate a party's absolute promise to perform.

Confession of judgment   The act of a debtor in permitting a judgment to be entered against him or her by a creditor, for an agreed sum, without the institution of legal proceedings.

Confusion   The mixing together of goods belonging to two or more owners so that the separately owned goods cannot be identified.

Consent   Voluntary agreement to a proposition or an act of another. A concurrence of wills.

Consequential damages   Special damages that compensate for a loss that is not direct or immediate (for example, lost profits). The special damages must have been reasonably foreseeable at the time the breach or injury occurred in order for the plaintiff to collect them.

Consideration   Generally, the value given in return for a promise. The consideration, which must be present to make the contract legally binding, must be something of legally sufficient value and bargained for.

Consignment   A transaction in which an owner of goods (the consignor) delivers the goods to another (the consignee) for the consignee to sell. The consignee pays the consignor for the goods when they are sold by the consignee.

Consolidation   A contractual and statutory process in which two or more corporations join to become a completely new corporation. The original corporations cease to exist, and the new corporation acquires all their assets and liabilities.

Constitutional law   Law based on the U.S. Constitution and the constitutions of the various states.

Constructive delivery   An act equivalent to the actual, physical delivery of property that cannot be physically delivered because of difficulty or impossibility; for example, the transfer of a key to a safe constructively delivers the contents of the safe.

Constructive eviction   A form of eviction that occurs when a landlord fails to perform adequately any of the undertakings (such as providing heat in the winter) required by the lease, thereby making the tenant's further use and enjoyment of the property exceedingly difficult or impossible.

Constructive trust   An equitable trust that is imposed in the interests of fairness and justice when someone wrongfully holds legal title to property. A court may require the owner to hold the property in trust for the person or persons who rightfully should own the property.

Consumer-debtor   An individual whose debts are primarily consumer debts (debts for purchases made primarily for personal or household use).

Continuation statement   A statement that, if filed within six months prior to the expiration date of the original financing statement, continues the perfection of the original security interest for another five years. The perfection of a security interest can be continued in the same manner indefinitely.

Contract   An agreement that can be enforced in court; formed by two or more parties who agree to perform or to refrain from performing some act now or in the future.

Contractual capacity   The threshold mental capacity required by the law for a party who enters into a contract to be bound by that contract.

Contributory negligence   A theory in tort law under which a complaining party's own negligence contributed to or caused his or her injuries. Contributory negligence is an absolute bar to recovery in a minority of jurisdictions.

Conversion   The wrongful taking, using, or retaining possession of personal property that belongs to another.

Conveyance   The transfer of a title to land from one person to another by deed; a document (such as a deed) by which an interest in land is transferred from one person to another.

Copyright   The exclusive right of "authors" to publish, print, or sell an intellectual production for a statutory period of time. A copyright has the same monopolistic nature as a patent or trademark, but it differs in that it applies exclusively to works of art, literature, and other works of authorship (including computer programs).

Corporate charter   The document issued by a state agency or authority (usually the secretary of state) that grants a corporation legal existence and the right to function.

Corporate social responsibility   The concept that corporations can and should act ethically and be accountable to society for their actions.

Corporation   A legal entity formed in compliance with statutory requirements. The entity is distinct from its shareholders-owners.

Cost-benefit analysis   A decision-making technique that involves weighing the costs of a given action against the benefits of the action.

Co-surety   A joint surety; a person who assumes liability jointly with another surety for the payment of an obligation.

Counterclaim   A claim made by a defendant in a civil lawsuit that in effect sues the plaintiff.

Counteroffer   An offeree's response to an offer in which the offeree rejects the original offer and at the same time makes a new offer.

Course of dealing   Prior conduct between parties to a contract that establishes a common basis for their understanding.

Course of performance   The conduct that occurs under the terms of a particular agreement; such conduct indicates what the parties to an agreement intended it to mean.

Covenant not to sue   An agreement to substitute a contractual obligation for some other type of legal action based on a valid claim.

Cover   Under the UCC, a remedy of the buyer that allows the buyer or lessee, on the seller's or lessor's breach, to purchase the goods from another seller or lessor and substitute them for the goods due under the contract. If the cost of cover exceeds the cost of the contract goods, the breaching seller or lessor will be liable to the buyer or lessee for the difference. In obtaining cover, the buyer or lessee must act in good faith and without unreasonable delay.

Cram-down provision   A provision of the Bankruptcy Code that allows a court to confirm a debtor's Chapter 11 reorganization plan even though only one class of creditors has accepted it. To exercise the court's right under this provision, the court must demonstrate that the plan does not discriminate unfairly against any creditors and is fair and equitable.

Creditors' composition agreement   An agreement formed between a debtor and his or her creditors in which the creditors agree to accept a lesser sum than that owed by the debtor in full satisfaction of the debt.

Crime   A wrong against society proclaimed in a statute and, if committed, punishable by society through fines and/or imprisonment—and, in some cases, death.

Criminal law   Law that defines and governs actions that constitute crimes. Generally, criminal law has to do with wrongful actions committed against society for which society demands redress.

Cure   The right of a party who tenders nonconforming performance to correct his or her performance within the contract period [UCC 3–508].

Cyber crime   A crime that occurs online, in the virtual community of the Internet, as opposed to the physical world.

Cyber mark   A trademark in cyberspace.

Cybernotary   A legally recognized certification authority that issues the keys for digital signatures, identifies their owners, certifies their validity, and serves as a repository for public keys.

Cybersquatting   Registering a domain name that is the same as, or confusingly similar to, the trademark of another. Often involves an attempt to sell the domain name back to the trademark's owner.

Cyber stalker   A person who commits the crime of stalking in cyberspace. Generally, stalking consists of harassing a person and putting that person in reasonable fear for his or her safety or the safety of the person's immediate family.

Cyber terrorist   A hacker whose purpose is to exploit a target computer for a serious impact, such as corrupting a program to sabotage a business.

Cyber tort   A tort committed in cyberspace.

D

Damages   Money sought as a remedy for a breach of contract or for a tortious act.

Debit card   A plastic card that allows the bearer to transfer funds to a merchant's account, provided that the bearer authorizes the transfer by providing personal identification.

Debtor   Under Article 9 of the UCC, a debtor is any party who owes payment or performance of a secured obligation, whether or not the party actually owns or has rights in the collateral.

Debtor in possession (DIP)   In Chapter 11 bankruptcy proceedings, a debtor who is allowed to continue in possession of the estate in property (the business) and to continue business operations.

Deed   A document by which title to property (usually real property) is passed.

Defalcation   The misuse of funds.

Defamation   Anything published or publicly spoken that causes injury to another's good name, reputation, or character.

Default   The failure to observe a promise or discharge an obligation. The term is commonly used to mean the failure to pay a debt when it is due.

Default judgment   A judgment entered by a court against a defendant who has failed to appear in court to answer or defend against the plaintiff's claim.

Defendant   One against whom a lawsuit is brought; the accused person in a criminal proceeding.

Defense   That which a defendant offers and alleges in an action or suit as a reason why the plaintiff should not recover or establish what he or she seeks.

Deficiency judgment   A judgment against a debtor for the amount of a debt remaining unpaid after collateral has been repossessed and sold.

Delegatee   A party to whom contractual obligations are transferred, or delegated.

Delegation of duties   The act of transferring to another all or part of one's duties arising under a contract.

Delegator   A party who transfers (delegates) her or his obligations under a contract to another party (called the delegatee).

Depositary bank   The first bank to receive a check for payment.

Deposition   The testimony of a party to a lawsuit or a witness taken under oath before a trial.

Destination contract   A contract for the sale of goods in which the seller is required or authorized to ship the goods by carrier and deliver them at a particular destination. The seller assumes liability for any losses or damage to the goods until they are tendered at the destination specified in the contract.

Devise   To make a gift of real property by will.

Devisee   One designated in a will to receive a gift of real property.

Digital cash   Funds contained on computer software, in the form of secure programs stored on microchips and other computer devices.

Disaffirmance   The legal avoidance, or setting aside, of a contractual obligation.

Discharge   The termination of an obligation. In contract law, discharge occurs when the parties have fully performed their contractual obligations or when events, conduct of the parties, or operation of the law releases the parties from performance. In bankruptcy proceedings, the extinction of the debtor's dischargeable debts.

Disclosed principal   A principal whose identity is known to a third party at the time the agent makes a contract with the third party.

Discovery   A phase in the litigation process during which the opposing parties may obtain information from each other and from third parties prior to trial.

Disparagement of property   An economically injurious falsehood made about another's product or property. A general term for torts that are more specifically referred to as slander of quality or slander of title.

Disparate-impact discrimination   A form of employment discrimination that results from certain employer practices or procedures that, although not discriminatory on their face, have a discriminatory effect.

Disparate-treatment discrimination   A form of employment discrimination that results when an employer intentionally discriminates against employees who are members of protected classes.

Dissolution   The formal disbanding of a partnership or a corporation. It can take place by (1) acts of the partners or, in a corporation, of the shareholders and board of directors; (2) the death of a partner; (3) the expiration of a time period stated in a partnership agreement or a certificate of incorporation; or (4) judicial decree.

Distributed network   A network that can be used by persons located (distributed) around the country or the globe to share computer files.

Diversity of citizenship   Under Article III, Section 2, of the Constitution, a basis for federal court jurisdiction over a lawsuit between (1) citizens of different states, (2) a foreign country and citizens of a state or of different states, or (3) citizens of a state and citizens or subjects of a foreign country. The amount in controversy must be more than $75,000 before a federal court can take jurisdiction in such cases.

Dividend   A distribution to corporate shareholders of corporate profits or income, disbursed in proportion to the number of shares held.

Docket   The list of cases entered on a court's calendar and thus scheduled to be heard by the court.

Document of title   Paper exchanged in the regular course of business that evidences the right to possession of goods (for example, a bill of lading or a warehouse receipt).

Domain name   The last part of an Internet address, such as "westlaw.com." The top level (the part of the name to the right of the period) represents the type of entity that operates the site ("com" is an abbreviation for "commercial"). The second level (the part of the name to the left of the period) is chosen by the entity.

Domestic corporation   In a given state, a corporation that does business in, and is organized under the law of, that state.

Dominion   Ownership rights in property, including the right to possess and control the property.

Dormant commerce clause   An implied aspect of the Constitution's commerce clause, which grants the national government the exclusive authority to regulate interstate commerce. The implied doctrine is that the states do *not* have the right to regulate interstate commerce.

Double jeopardy   A situation occurring when a person is tried twice for the same criminal offense; prohibited by the Fifth Amendment to the Constitution.

Draft   Any instrument drawn on a drawee (such as a bank) that orders the drawee to pay a certain sum of money, usually to a third party (the payee), on demand or at a definite future time.

Dram shop act   A state statute that imposes liability on the owners of bars and taverns, as well as those who serve alcoholic drinks to the public, for injuries resulting from accidents caused by intoxicated persons when the sellers or servers of alcoholic drinks contributed to the intoxication.

Drawee   The party that is ordered to pay a draft or check. With a check, a financial institution is always the drawee.

Drawer   The party that initiates a draft (such as a check), thereby ordering the drawee to pay.

Due diligence   A required standard of care that certain professionals, such as accountants, must meet to avoid liability for securities violations. Under securities law, an accountant will be deemed to have exercised due diligence if he or she followed generally accepted accounting principles and generally accepted auditing standards and had, "after reasonable investigation, reasonable grounds to believe and did believe, at the time such part of the registration statement became effective, that the statements therein were true and that there was no omission of a material fact required to be stated therein or necessary to make the statements therein not misleading."

Due process clause   The provisions of the Fifth and Fourteenth Amendments to the Constitution that guarantee that no person shall be deprived of life, liberty, or property without due process of law. Similar clauses are found in most state constitutions.

Duress   Unlawful pressure brought to bear on a person, causing the person to perform an act that he or she would not otherwise perform.

Duty of care   The duty of all persons, as established by tort law, to exercise a reasonable amount of care in their dealings with others. Failure to exercise due care, which is normally determined by the "reasonable person standard," constitutes the tort of negligence.

E

E-contract   A contract that is formed electronically.

Early neutral case evaluation   A form of alternative dispute resolution in which a neutral third party evaluates the strengths and weakness of the disputing parties' positions; the evaluator's opinion forms the basis for negotiating a settlement.

Easement   A nonpossessory right to use another's property in a manner established by either express or implied agreement.

Electronic fund transfer (EFT)   A transfer of funds with the use of an electronic terminal, a telephone, a computer, or magnetic tape.

E-money   Prepaid funds recorded on a computer or a card (such as a smart card or a stored-value card).

Emancipation   In regard to minors, the act of being freed from parental control; occurs when a child's parent or legal guardian relinquishes the legal right to exercise control over the child. Normally, a minor who leaves home to support himself or herself is considered emancipated.

Embezzlement   The fraudulent appropriation of money or other property by a person to whom the money or property has been entrusted.

Eminent domain   The power of a government to take land for public use from private citizens for just compensation.

Employment at will   A common law doctrine under which either party may terminate an employment relationship at any time for any reason, unless a contract specifies otherwise.

Employment discrimination   Treating employees or job applicants unequally on the basis of race, color, national origin, religion, gender, age, or disability; prohibited by federal statutes.

Enabling legislation   A statute enacted by Congress that authorizes the creation of an administrative agency and specifies the name, composition, purpose, functions, and powers of the agency being created.

Entrapment   In criminal law, a defense in which the defendant claims that he or she was induced by a public official—usually an undercover agent or police officer—to commit a crime that he or she would otherwise not have committed.

Equal dignity rule   In most states, a rule stating that express authority given to an agent must be in writing if the contract to be made on behalf of the principal is required to be in writing.

Equal protection clause   The provision in the Fourteenth Amendment to the Constitution that guarantees that no state will "deny to any person within its jurisdiction the equal protection of the laws." This clause mandates that the state governments treat similarly situated individuals in a similar manner.

Equitable principles and maxims   General propositions or principles of law that have to do with fairness (equity).

E-signature   An electronic sound, symbol, or process attached to or logically associated with a record and executed or adopted by a person with the intent to sign the record, according to the Uniform Electronic Transactions Act.

Establishment clause   The provision in the First Amendment to the Constitution that prohibits Congress from creating any law "respecting an establishment of religion."

Estate in property   In bankruptcy proceedings, all of the debtor's legal and equitable interests in property presently held, wherever located, together with certain jointly owned property, property transferred in transactions voidable by the trustee, proceeds and profits from the property of the estate, and certain property interests to which the debtor becomes entitled within 180 days after filing for bankruptcy.

Estopped   Barred, impeded, or precluded.

Estray statute   A statute defining finders' rights in property when the true owners are unknown.

Ethical reasoning   A reasoning process in which an individual links his or her moral convictions or ethical standards to the particular situation at hand.

Ethics   Moral principles and values applied to social behavior.

Eviction   A landlord's act of depriving a tenant of possession of the leased premises.

Exclusionary rule   In criminal procedure, a rule under which any evidence that is obtained in violation of the accused's constitutional rights guaranteed by the Fourth, Fifth, and Sixth Amendments, as well as any evidence derived from illegally obtained evidence, will not be admissible in court.

Exclusive jurisdiction   Jurisdiction that exists when a case can be heard only in a particular court or type of court.

Exclusive-dealing contract   An agreement under which a seller forbids a buyer to purchase products from the seller's competitors.

Exculpatory clause   A clause that releases a contractual party from liability in the event of monetary or physical injury, no matter who is at fault.

Executed contract   A contract that has been completely performed by both parties.

Execution   An action to carry into effect the directions in a court decree or judgment.

Executive agency   An administrative agency within the executive branch of government. At the federal level, executive agencies are those within the cabinet departments.

Executor   A person appointed by a testator to see that his or her will is administered appropriately.

Executory contract   A contract that has not as yet been fully performed.

Executory interest   A future interest, held by a person other than the grantor, that or begins some time after the termination of the preceding estate.

Express contract   A contract in which the terms of the agreement are fully and explicitly stated in words, oral or written.

Express warranty A seller's or lessor's oral or written promise, ancillary to an underlying sales or lease agreement, as to the quality, description, or performance of the goods being sold or leased.

Extension clause A clause in a time instrument that allows the instrument's date of maturity to be extended into the future.

F

Family limited liability partnership (FLLP) A type of limited liability partnership owned by family members or fiduciaries of family members.

Federal form of government A system of government in which the states form a union and the sovereign power is divided between a central government and the member states.

Federal question A question that pertains to the U.S. Constitution, acts of Congress, or treaties. A federal question provides a basis for federal jurisdiction.

Federal Reserve System A network of twelve central banks, located around the country and headed by the Federal Reserve Board of Governors. Most banks in the United States have Federal Reserve accounts.

Fee simple An absolute form of property ownership entitling the property owner to use, possess, or dispose of the property as he or she chooses during his or her lifetime. On death, the interest in the property descends to the owner's heirs.

Fee simple absolute An ownership interest in land in which the owner has the greatest possible aggregation of rights, privileges, and power. Ownership in fee simple absolute is limited absolutely to a person and his or her heirs.

Fee simple defeasible An ownership interest in real property that can be taken away (by the prior grantor) on the occurrence or nonoccurrence of a specified event.

Felony A crime—such as arson, murder, rape, or robbery—that carries the most severe sanctions, usually ranging from one year in a state or federal prison to the forfeiture of one's life.

Fictitious payee A payee on a negotiable instrument whom the maker or drawer does not intend to have an interest in the instrument. Indorsements by fictitious payees are not treated as unauthorized under Article 3 of the UCC.

Fiduciary As a noun, a person having a duty created by his or her undertaking to act primarily for another's benefit in matters connected with the undertaking. As an adjective, a relationship founded upon trust and confidence.

Filtering software A computer program that includes a pattern through which data are passed. When designed to block access to certain Web sites, the pattern blocks the retrieval of a site whose URL or key words are on a list within the program.

Financing statement A document prepared by a secured creditor and filed with the appropriate state or local official to give notice to the public that the creditor claims an interest in collateral belonging to the debtor named in the statement. The financing statement must contain the addresses of both the debtor and the creditor, and describe the collateral by type or item.

Firm offer An offer (by a merchant) that is irrevocable without consideration for a period of time (not longer than three months). A firm offer by a merchant must be in writing and must be signed by the offeror.

Fixture A thing that was once personal property but that has become attached to real property in such a way that it takes on the characteristics of real property and becomes part of that real property.

Floating lien A security interest in proceeds, after-acquired property, or property purchased under a line of credit (or all three); a security interest in collateral that is retained even when the collateral changes in character, classification, or location.

Foreign corporation In a given state, a corporation that does business in the state without being incorporated therein.

Foreign exchange market A worldwide system in which foreign currencies are bought and sold.

Forgery The fraudulent making or altering of any writing in a way that changes the legal rights and liabilities of another.

Formal contract A contract that by law requires for its validity a specific form, such as executed under seal.

Forum-selection clause A provision in a contract designating the court, jurisdiction, or tribunal that will decide any disputes arising under the contract.

Franchise Any arrangement in which the owner of a trademark, trade name, or copyright licenses another to use that trademark, trade name, or copyright, under specified conditions or limitations, in the selling of goods and services.

Franchisee One receiving a license to use another's (the franchisor's) trademark, trade name, or copyright in the sale of goods and services.

Franchisor One licensing another (the franchisee) to use his or her trademark, trade name, or copyright in the sale of goods or services.

Fraudulent misrepresentation (fraud) Any misrepresentation, either by misstatement or omission of a material fact, knowingly made with the intention of deceiving another and on which a reasonable person would and does rely to his or her detriment.

Free exercise clause The provision in the First Amendment to the Constitution that prohibits Congress from making any law "prohibiting the free exercise" of religion.

Fungible goods Goods that are alike by physical nature, by agreement, or by trade usage. Examples of fungible goods are wheat and oil that are identical in type and quality.

Future interest An interest in real property that is not at present possessory but will or may become possessory in the future.

G

Garnishment A legal process used by a creditor to collect a debt by seizing property of the debtor (such as wages) that is being held by a third party (such as the debtor's employer).

General partner In a limited partnership, a partner who assumes responsibility for the management of the partnership and liability for all partnership debts.

Generally accepted accounting principles (GAAP) The conventions, rules, and procedures necessary to define accepted accounting practices at a particular time. The source of the principles is the Federal Accounting Standards Board.

Generally accepted auditing standards (GAAS) Standards concerning an auditor's professional qualities and the judgment exercised by him or her in the performance of an examination and report. The source of the standards is the American Institute of Certified Public Accountants.

Gift Any voluntary transfer of property made without consideration, past or present.

Gift *causa mortis* A gift made in contemplation of death. If the donor does not die of that ailment, the gift is revoked.

Gift *inter vivos* A gift made during one's lifetime and not in contemplation of imminent death, in contrast to a gift *causa mortis*.

Good faith purchaser A purchaser who buys without notice of any circumstance that would put a person of ordinary prudence on inquiry as to whether the seller has valid title to the goods being sold.

Good Samaritan statute A state statute that provides that persons who rescue or provide emergency services to others in peril—unless they do so recklessly, thus causing further harm—cannot be sued for negligence.

Grand jury A group of citizens called to decide, after hearing the state's evidence, whether a reasonable basis (probable cause) exists for believing that a crime has been committed and whether a trial ought to be held.

Guarantor A person who agrees to satisfy the debt of another (the debtor) only after the principal debtor defaults; a guarantor's liability is thus secondary.

H

Hacker A person who uses one computer to break into another.

Holder Any person in the possession of an instrument drawn, issued, or indorsed to him or her, to his or her order, to bearer, or in blank.

Holder in due course (HDC) A holder who acquires a negotiable instrument for value; in good faith; and without notice that the instrument is overdue, that it has been dishonored, that any person has a defense against it or a claim to it, or that the instrument contains unauthorized signatures, alterations, or is so irregular or incomplete as to call into question its authenticity.

Holographic will A will written entirely in the signer's handwriting and usually not witnessed.

Homestead exemption A law permitting a debtor to retain the family home, either in its entirety or up to a specified dollar amount, free from the claims of unsecured creditors or trustees in bankruptcy.

Hot-cargo agreement An agreement in which employers voluntarily agree with unions not to handle, use, or deal in nonunion-produced goods of other employers; a type of secondary boycott explicitly prohibited by the Labor-Management Reporting and Disclosure Act of 1959.

I

Identification In a sale of goods, the express designation of the goods provided for in the contract.

Identity theft Occurs when a person steals another's identifying information—such as a name, date of birth, or Social Security number—and uses the information to access the victim's financial resources.

Implied warranty A warranty that the law derives by implication or inference from the nature of the transaction or the relative situation or circumstances of the parties.

Implied warranty of fitness for a particular purpose A warranty that goods sold or leased are fit for a particular purpose. The warranty arises when any seller or lessor knows the particular purpose for which a buyer or lessee will use the goods and knows that the buyer or lessee is relying on the skill and judgment of the seller or lessor to select suitable goods.

Implied warranty of habitability An implied promise by a landlord that rented residential premises are fit for human habitation—that is, in a condition that is safe and suitable for people to live in.

Implied warranty of merchantability A warranty that goods being sold or leased are reasonably fit for the general purpose for which they are sold or leased, are properly packaged and labeled, and are of proper quality. The warranty automatically arises in every sale or lease of goods made by a merchant who deals in goods of the kind sold or leased.

Implied-in-fact contract A contract formed in whole or in part from the conduct of the parties (as opposed to an express contract).

Impossibility of performance A doctrine under which a party to a contract is relieved of his or her duty to perform when performance becomes impossible or totally impracticable (through no fault of either party).

Imposter One who, by use of the mails, telephone, or personal appearance, induces a maker or drawer to issue an instrument in the name of an impersonated payee. Indorsements by imposters are not treated as unauthorized under Article 3 of the UCC.

Incidental beneficiary A third party who incidentally benefits from a contract but whose benefit was not the reason the contract was formed; an incidental beneficiary has no rights in a contract and cannot sue to have the contract enforced.

Incidental damages Damages resulting from a breach of contract, including all reasonable expenses incurred because of the breach.

Independent contractor One who works for, and receives payment from, an employer but whose working conditions and methods are not controlled by the employer. An independent contractor is not an employee but may be an agent.

Independent regulatory agency An administrative agency that is not considered part of the government's executive branch and is not subject to the authority of the president. Independent agency officials cannot be removed without cause.

Indictment (pronounced in-*dyte*-ment) A charge by a grand jury that a named person has committed a crime.

Indorsee The person to whom a negotiable instrument is transferred by indorsement.

Indorsement A signature placed on an instrument for the purpose of transferring one's ownership rights in the instrument.

Indorser A person who transfers an instrument by signing (indorsing) it and delivering it to another person.

Informal contract A contract that does not require a specified form or formality in order to be valid.

Information A formal accusation or complaint (without an indictment) issued in certain types of actions by a law enforcement officer, such as a prosecutor.

Innkeeper's lien A possessory lien placed on the luggage of hotel guests for hotel charges that remain unpaid.

Insider trading The purchase or sale of securities on the basis of "inside information" (information that has not been made available to the public) in violation of a duty owed to the company whose stock is being traded.

Insolvent Under the UCC, a term describing a person who ceases to pay "his debts in the ordinary course of business or cannot pay his debts as they become due or is insolvent within the meaning of federal bankruptcy law" [UCC 1–201(23)].

Installment contract Under the UCC, a contract that requires or authorizes delivery in two or more separate lots to be accepted and paid for separately.

Insurable interest An interest either in a person's life or well-being or in property that is sufficiently substantial that insuring against injury to (or the death of) the person or against damage to the property does not amount to a mere wagering (betting) contract.

Insurance A contract in which, for a stipulated consideration, one party agrees to compensate the other for loss on a specific subject by a specified peril.

Integrated contract A written contract that constitutes the final expression of the parties' agreement. If a contract is integrated, evidence extraneous to the contract that contradicts or alters the meaning of the contract in any way is inadmissible.

Intellectual property Property resulting from intellectual, creative processes. Patents, trademarks, and copyrights are examples of intellectual property.

Intended beneficiary A third party for whose benefit a contract is formed; an intended beneficiary can sue the promisor if such a contract is breached.

Intentional tort A wrongful act knowingly committed.

Inter vivos **trust** A trust created by the grantor (settlor) and effective during the grantor's lifetime; a trust not established by a will.

Intermediary bank Any bank to which an item is transferred in the course of collection, except the depositary or payor bank.

International law The law that governs relations among nations. National laws, customs, treaties, and international conferences and organizations are generally considered to be the most important sources of international law.

International organization In international law, a term that generally refers to an organization composed mainly of nations and usually established by treaty. The United States is a member of more than one hundred multilateral and bilateral organizations, including at least twenty through the United Nations.

Interrogatories A series of written questions for which written answers are prepared and then signed under oath by a party to a lawsuit, usually with the assistance of the party's attorney.

Intestacy laws State statutes that specify how property will be distributed when a person dies intestate (without a valid will); also called statutes of descent and distribution.

Intestate As a noun, one who has died without having created a valid will; as an adjective, the state of having died without a will.

Investment company A company that acts on behalf of many smaller shareholders-owners by buying a large portfolio of securities and professionally managing that portfolio.

J

Joint tenancy The joint ownership of property by two or more co-owners of property in which each co-owner owns an undivided portion of the property. On the death of one of the joint tenants, his or her interest automatically passes to the surviving joint tenants.

Joint and several liability In partnership law, a doctrine under which a plaintiff may sue, and collect a judgment from, one or more of the partners separately (severally, or individually) or all of the partners together (jointly). This is true even if one of the partners sued did not participate in, ratify, or know about whatever it was that gave rise to the cause of action.

Joint liability Shared liability. In partnership law, partners incur joint liability for partnership obligations and debts. For example, if a third party sues a partner on a partnership debt, the partner has the right to insist that the other partners be sued with him or her.

Judicial review The process by which a court decides on the constitutionality of legislative enactments and actions of the executive branch.

Jurisdiction The authority of a court to hear and decide a specific action.

Jurisprudence The science or philosophy of law.

Justiciable (pronounced jus-*tish*-a-bul) controversy A controversy that is not hypothetical or academic but real and substantial; a requirement that must be satisfied before a court will hear a case.

L

Larceny The wrongful taking and carrying away of another person's personal property with the intent to permanently deprive the owner of the property. Some states classify larceny as either grand or petit, depending on the property's value.

Law A body of enforceable rules governing relationships among individuals and between individuals and their society.

Lease In real property law, a contract by which the owner of real property (the landlord, or lessor) grants to a person (the tenant, or lessee) an exclusive right to use and possess the property, usually for a specified period of time, in return for rent or some other form of payment.

Lease agreement An agreement in which one person (the lessor) agrees to transfer the right to the possession and use of property to another person (the lessee) in exchange for rental payments; a lease.

Leasehold estate An estate in realty held by a tenant under a lease. In every leasehold estate, the tenant has a qualified right to possess and/or use the land.

Legacy A gift of personal property under a will.

Legatee One designated in a will to receive a gift of personal property.

Lessee A person who acquires the right to the possession and use of another's property in exchange for rental payments.

Lessor A person who sells the right to the possession and use of property to another in exchange for rental payments.

Levy The obtaining of money by legal process through the seizure and sale of property, usually done after a writ of execution has been issued.

Libel Defamation in written form.

License A revocable right or privilege of a person to come onto another person's land.

Lien (pronounced *leen*) An encumbrance on specific property to satisfy a debt or protect a claim for payment of a debt.

Life estate An interest in land that exists only for the duration of the life of some person, usually the holder of the estate.

Limited liability company (LLC) A hybrid form of business enterprise that offers the limited liability of the coporation but the tax advantages of a partnership.

Limited liability limited partnership (LLLP) A type of limited partnership in which the liability of all of the partners, including general partners, is limited to the amount of their investments.

Limited liability partnership (LLP) A form of partnership that allows professionals to enjoy the tax benefits of a partnership while avoiding personal liability for the malpractice of other partners.

Limited partner In a limited partnership, a partner who contributes capital to the partnership but has no right to participate in the management and operation of the business. The limited partner assumes no liability for partnership debts beyond the capital contributed.

Limited partnership A partnership consisting of one or more general partners (who manage the business and are liable to the full extent of their personal assets for debts of the partnership) and one or more limited partners (who contribute only assets and are liable only to the extent of their contributions).

Liquidated damages An amount, stipulated in the contract, that the parties to a contract believe to be a reasonable estimation of the damages that will occur in the event of a breach.

Liquidation In regard to corporations, the process by which corporate assets are converted into cash and distributed among creditors and shareholders according to specific rules of preference. In regard to bankruptcy, the sale of all of the nonexempt assets of a debtor and the distribution of the proceeds to the debtor's creditors. Chapter 7 of the Bankruptcy Code provides for liquidation bankruptcy proceedings.

Litigation The process of resolving a dispute through the court system.

Long arm statute A state statute that permits a state to obtain personal jurisdiction over nonresident defendants. A defendant must have certain "minimum contacts" with that state for the statute to apply.

Lost property Property with which the owner has involuntarily parted and then cannot find or recover.

M

Mailbox rule A rule providing that an acceptance of an offer becomes effective on dispatch (on being placed in a mailbox), if mail is, expressly or impliedly, an authorized means of communication of acceptance to the offeror.

Maker One who promises to pay a certain sum to the holder of a promissory note or certificate of deposit (CD).

Malpractice Professional misconduct or the lack of the requisite degree of skill as a professional. Negligence—the failure to exercise due care—on the part of a professional, such as a physician or an attorney, is commonly referred to as malpractice.

Mechanic's lien A statutory lien on the real property of another, created to ensure payment for work performed and materials furnished in the repair or improvement of real property, such as a building.

Mediation A method of settling disputes outside of court by using the services of a neutral third party, who acts as a communicating agent between the parties and assists the parties in negotiating a settlement.

Member The term used to designate a person who has an ownership interest in a limited liability company.

Merchant A person who is engaged in the purchase and sale of goods. Under the UCC, a person who deals in goods of the kind involved in the sales contract; for further definitions, see UCC 2–104.

Merger A contractual and statutory process in which one corporation (the surviving corporation) acquires all of the assets and liabilities of another corporation (the merged corporation). The shareholders of the merged corporation receive either payment for their shares or shares in the surviving corporation.

Mini-trial A private proceeding in which each party to a dispute argues its position before the other side and vice versa. A neutral third party may be present and act as an adviser if the parties fail to reach an agreement.

Minimum wage The lowest wage, either by government regulation or union contract, that an employer may pay an hourly worker.

Mirror image rule A common law rule that requires, for a valid contractual agreement, that the terms of the offeree's acceptance adhere exactly to the terms of the offeror's offer.

Misdemeanor A lesser crime than a felony, punishable by a fine or imprisonment for up to one year in other than a state or federal penitentiary.

Mislaid property Property with which the owner has voluntarily parted and then cannot find or recover.

Mitigation of damages A rule requiring a plaintiff to have done whatever was reasonable to minimize the damages caused by the defendant.

Money laundering Falsely reporting income that has been obtained through criminal activity as income obtained through a legitimate business enterprise—in effect, "laundering" the "dirty money."

Moral minimum The minimum degree of ethical behavior expected of a business firm, which is usually defined as compliance with the law.

Mortgagee Under a mortgage agreement, the creditor who takes a security interest in the debtor's property.

Mortgagor Under a mortgage agreement, the debtor who gives the creditor a security interest in the debtor's property in return for a mortgage loan.

Motion for a directed verdict In a jury trial, a motion for the judge to take the decision out of the hands of the jury and direct a verdict for the moving party on the ground that the other party has not produced sufficient evidence to support his or her claim.

Motion for a new trial A motion asserting that the trial was so fundamentally flawed (because of error, newly discovered evidence, prejudice, or other reason) that a new trial is necessary to prevent a miscarriage of justice.

Motion for judgment *n.o.v.* A motion requesting the court to grant judgment in favor of the party making the motion on the ground that the jury verdict against him or her was unreasonable and erroneous.

Motion for judgment on the pleadings A motion by either party to a lawsuit at the close of the pleadings requesting the court to decide the issue solely on the pleadings without proceeding to trial. The motion will be granted only if no facts are in dispute.

Motion for summary judgment A motion requesting the court to enter a judgment without proceeding to trial. The motion can be based on evidence outside the pleadings and will be granted only if no facts are in dispute.

Motion to dismiss A pleading in which a defendant asserts that the plaintiff's claim fails to state a cause of action (that is, has no basis in law) or that there are other grounds on which a suit should be dismissed.

Mutual fund A specific type of investment company that continually buys or sells to investors shares of ownership in a portfolio.

N

National law Law that pertains to a particular nation (as opposed to international law).

Natural law The belief that government and the legal system should reflect universal moral and ethical principles that are inherent in human nature. The natural law school is the oldest and one of the most significant schools of legal thought.

Necessaries Necessities required for life, such as food, shelter, clothing, and medical attention; may include whatever is believed to be necessary to maintain a person's standard of living or financial and social status.

Negligence The failure to exercise the standard of care that a reasonable person would exercise in similar circumstances.

Negligence *per se* An act (or failure to act) in violation of a statutory requirement.

Negotiable instrument A signed writing that contains an unconditional promise or order to pay an exact sum of money, on demand or at an exact future time, to a specific person or order, or to bearer.

Negotiation In regard to dispute settlement, a process in which parties attempt to settle their dispute informally, with or without attorneys to represent them. In regard to instruments, the transfer of an instrument in such a way that the transferee (the person to whom the instrument is transferred) becomes a holder.

Newsgroup A discussion group operated according to certain Internet formats and rules. Like a bulletin board, a newsgroup is a location to which participants go to read and post messages.

No-par shares Corporate shares that have no face value—that is, no specific dollar amount is printed on their face.

Nominal damages A small monetary award (often one dollar) granted to a plaintiff when no actual damage was suffered.

Notary public A public official authorized to attest to the authenticity of signatures.

Novation The substitution, by agreement, of a new contract for an old one, with the rights under the old one being terminated. Typically, there is a substitution of a new person who is responsible for the contract and the removal of an original party's rights and duties under the contract.

Nuisance A common law doctrine under which persons may be held liable for using their property in a manner that unreasonably interferes with others' rights to use or enjoy their own property.

Nuncupative will An oral will (often called a deathbed will) made before witnesses; usually limited to transfers of personal property.

O

Objective theory of contracts A theory under which the intent to form a contract will be judged by outward, objective facts (what the party said when entering into the contract, how the party acted or appeared, and the circumstances surrounding the transaction) as interpreted by a reasonable person, rather than by the party's own secret, subjective intentions.

Offer A promise or commitment to perform or refrain from performing some specified act in the future.

Offeree A person to whom an offer is made.

Offeror A person who makes an offer.

Online dispute resolution (ODR) The resolution of a dispute in cyberspace.

Operating agreement In a limited liability company, an agreement in which the members set forth the details of how the business will be managed and operated. State statutes typically give the members wide latitude in deciding for themselves the rules that will govern their organization.

Optimum profits The amount of profits that a business can make and still act ethically, as opposed to maximum profits, defined as the amount of profits a firm can make if it is willing to disregard ethical concerns.

Option contract A contract under which the offeror cannot revoke his or her offer for a stipulated time period, and the offeree can accept or reject the offer during this period without fear that the offer will be made to another person. The offeree must give consideration for the option (the irrevocable offer) to be enforceable.

Order for relief A court's grant of assistance to a complainant. In bankruptcy proceedings, the order relieves the debtor of the immediate obligation to pay the debts listed in the bankruptcy petition.

Order instrument A negotiable instrument that is payable "to the order of an identified person" or "to an identified person or order."

Output contract An agreement in which a seller agrees to sell and a buyer agrees to buy all or up to a stated amount of what the seller produces.

Overdraft A check written on a checking account in which there are insufficient funds to cover the amount of the check.

P

Panel An arbitrator, or arbitrators, appointed to make a decision regarding a domain name complaint in an online dispute resolution proceeding governed by the policy and rules of the Internet Corporation for Assigned Names and Numbers (ICANN). An ICANN-approved dispute resolution service provider appoints the panelists.

Par-value shares Corporate shares that have a specific face value, or formal cash-in value, written on them, such as one dollar.

Parol evidence rule A substantive rule of contracts under which a court will not receive into evidence the parties' prior negotiations, prior agreements, or contemporaneous oral agreements if that evidence contradicts or varies the terms of the parties' written contract.

Partially disclosed principal A principal whose identity is unknown by a third person, but the third person knows that the agent is or may be acting for a principal at the time the agent and the third person form a contract.

Partnering agreement An agreement between a seller and a buyer who frequently do business with each other on the terms and conditions that will apply to all subsequently formed electronic contracts.

Partnership An agreement by two or more persons to carry on, as co-owners, a business for profit.

Past consideration An act done before the contract is made, which ordinarily, by itself, cannot be consideration for a later promise to pay for the act.

Patent A government grant that gives an inventor the exclusive right or privilege to make, use, or sell his or her invention for a limited time period. The word patent usually refers to some invention and designates either the instrument by which patent rights are evidenced or the patent itself.

Payee A person to whom an instrument is made payable.

Payor bank The bank on which a check is drawn (the drawee bank).

Peer-to-peer (P2P) networking A technology that allows Internet users to access files on other users' computers.

Penalty A sum inserted into a contract, not as a measure of compensation for its breach but rather as punishment for a default. The agreement as to the amount will not be enforced, and recovery will be limited to actual damages.

Per capita A Latin term meaning "per person." In the law governing estate distribution, a method of distributing the property of an intestate's estate in which each heir in a certain class (such as grandchildren) receives an equal share.

Per stirpes A Latin term meaning "by the roots." In the law governing estate distribution, a method of distributing an intestate's estate in which each heir in a certain class (such as grandchildren) takes the share to which his or her deceased ancestor (such as a mother or father) would have been entitled.

Perfection The legal process by which secured parties protect themselves against the claims of third parties who may wish to have their debts satisfied out of the same collateral; usually accomplished by the filing of a financing statement with the appropriate government official.

Performance In contract law, the fulfillment of one's duties arising under a contract with another; the normal way of discharging one's contractual obligations.

Periodic tenancy A lease interest in land for an indefinite period involving payment of rent at fixed intervals, such as week to week, month to month, or year to year.

Personal defenses Defenses that can be used to avoid payment to an ordinary holder of a negotiable instrument but not a holder in due course (HDC) or a holder with the rights of an HDC.

Personal property   Property that is movable; any property that is not real property.

Persuasive authority   Any legal authority or source of law that a court may look to for guidance but on which it need not rely in making its decision. Persuasive authorities include cases from other jurisdictions and secondary sources of law.

Petition in bankruptcy   The document that is filed with a bankruptcy court to initiate bankruptcy proceedings. The official forms required for a petition in bankruptcy must be completed accurately, sworn to under oath, and signed by the debtor.

Petty offense   In criminal law, the least serious kind of criminal offense, such as a traffic or building-code violation.

Piercing the corporate veil   An action in which a court disregards the corporate entity and holds the shareholders personally liable for corporate debts and obligations.

Plaintiff   One who initiates a lawsuit.

Plea bargaining   The process by which a criminal defendant and the prosecutor in a criminal case work out a mutually satisfactory disposition of the case, subject to court approval; usually involves the defendant's pleading guilty to a lesser offense in return for a lighter sentence.

Pleadings   Statements made by the plaintiff and the defendant in a lawsuit that detail the facts, charges, and defenses involved in the litigation; the complaint and answer are part of the pleadings.

Pledge   A common law security device (retained in Article 9 of the UCC) in which personal property is turned over to the creditor as security for the payment of a debt and retained by the creditor until the debt is paid.

Police powers   Powers possessed by states as part of their inherent sovereignty. These powers may be exercised to protect or promote the public order, health, safety, morals, and general welfare.

Policy   In insurance law, a contract between the insurer and the insured in which, for a stipulated consideration, the insurer agrees to compensate the insured for loss on a specific subject by a specified peril.

Positive law   The body of conventional, or written, law of a particular society at a particular point in time.

Power of attorney   A written document, which is usually notarized, authorizing another to act as one's agent; can be special (permitting the agent to do specified acts only) or general (permitting the agent to transact all business for the principal).

Precedent   A court decision that furnishes an example or authority for deciding subsequent cases involving identical or similar facts.

Predatory behavior   Business behavior that is undertaken with the intention of unlawfully driving competitors out of the market.

Preemption   A doctrine under which certain federal laws preempt, or take precedence over, conflicting state or local laws.

Preemptive rights   Rights held by shareholders that entitle them to purchase newly issued shares of a corporation's stock, equal in percentage to shares presently held, before the stock is offered to any outside buyers. Preemptive rights enable shareholders to maintain their proportionate ownership and voice in the corporation.

Preference   In bankruptcy proceedings, property transfers or payments made by the debtor that favor (give preference to) one creditor over others. The bankruptcy trustee is allowed to recover payments made both voluntarily and involuntarily to one creditor in preference over another.

Preferred stock   Classes of stock that have priority over common stock both as to payment of dividends and distribution of assets upon the corporation's dissolution.

Premium   In insurance law, the price paid by the insured for insurance protection for a specified period of time.

Prenuptial agreement   An agreement made before marriage that defines each partner's ownership rights in the other partner's property. Prenuptial agreements must be in writing to be enforceable.

Presentment   The act of presenting an instrument to the party liable on the instrument to collect payment; presentment also occurs when a person presents an instrument to a drawee for acceptance.

Presentment warranties   Implied warranties, made by any person who presents an instrument for payment or acceptance, that (1) the person

obtaining payment or acceptance is entitled to enforce the instrument or is authorized to obtain payment or acceptance on behalf of a person who is entitled to enforce the instrument, (2) the instrument has not been altered, and (3) the person obtaining payment or acceptance has no knowledge that the signature of the drawer of the instrument is unauthorized.

Prima facie **case**   A case in which the plaintiff has produced sufficient evidence of his or her conclusion that the case can go to to a jury; a case in which the evidence compels the plaintiff's conclusion if the defendant produces no evidence to disprove it.

Primary source of law   A document that establishes the law on a particular issue, such as a constitution, a statute, an administrative rule, or a court decision.

Principal   In agency law, a person who agrees to have another, called the agent, act on his or her behalf.

Principle of rights   The principle that human beings have certain fundamental rights (to life, freedom, and the pursuit of happiness, for example). Those who adhere to this "rights theory" believe that a key factor in determining whether a business decision is ethical is how that decision affects the rights of others. These others include the firm's owners, its employees, the consumers of its products or services, its suppliers, the community in which it does business, and society as a whole.

Privilege   In tort law, the ability to act contrary to another person's right without that person's having legal redress for such acts. Privilege may be raised as a defense to defamation.

Privity of contract   The relationship that exists between the promisor and the promisee of a contract.

Probable cause   Reasonable grounds to believe the existence of facts warranting certain actions, such as the search or arrest of a person.

Probate court   A state court of limited jurisdiction that conducts proceedings relating to the settlement of a deceased person's estate.

Procedural law   Law that establishes the methods of enforcing the rights established by substantive law.

Proceeds   Under Article 9 of the UCC, whatever is received when the collateral is sold or otherwise disposed of, such as by exchange.

Product liability   The legal liability of manufacturers, sellers, and lessors of goods to consumers, users, and bystanders for injuries or damages that are caused by the goods.

Profit   In real property law, the right to enter upon and remove things from the property of another (for example, the right to enter onto a person's land and remove sand and gravel therefrom).

Promise   A declaration that something either will or will not happen in the future.

Promisee   A person to whom a promise is made.

Promisor   A person who makes a promise.

Promissory estoppel   A doctrine that applies when a promisor makes a clear and definite promise on which the promisee justifiably relies; such a promise is binding if justice will be better served by the enforcement of the promise.

Promissory note   A written promise made by one person (the maker) to pay a fixed sum of money to another person (the payee or a subsequent holder) on demand or on a specified date.

Promoter   A person who takes the preliminary steps in organizing a corporation, including (usually) issuing a prospectus, procuring stock subscriptions, making contract purchases, securing a corporate charter, and the like.

Property   Legally protected rights and interests in anything with an ascertainable value that is subject to ownership.

Prospectus   A document required by federal or state securities laws that describes the financial operations of the corporation, thus allowing investors to make informed decisions.

Protected class   A group of persons protected by specific laws because of the group's defining characteristics. Under laws prohibiting employment discrimination, these characteristics include race, color, religion, national origin, gender, age, and disability.

Proximate cause   Legal cause; exists when the connection between an act and an injury is strong enough to justify imposing liability.

Proxy   In corporation law, a written agreement between a stockholder and another under which the stockholder authorizes the other to vote the stockholder's shares in a certain manner.

Puffery A salesperson's often exaggerated claims concerning the quality of property offered for sale. Such claims involve opinions rather than facts and are not considered to be legally binding promises or warranties.

Punitive damages Money damages that may be awarded to a plaintiff to punish the defendant and deter future similar conduct.

Purchase-money security interest (PMSI) A security interest that arises when a seller or lender extends credit for part or all of the purchase price of goods purchased by a buyer.

Q

Qualified indorsement An indorsement on a negotiable instrument in which the indorser disclaims any contract liability on the instrument; the notation "without recourse" is commonly used to create a qualified indorsement.

Quasi contract A fictional contract imposed on parties by a court in the interests of fairness and justice; usually, quasi contracts are imposed to avoid the unjust enrichment of one party at the expense of another.

Quitclaim deed A deed intended to pass any title, interest, or claim that the grantor may have in the property but not warranting that such title is valid. A quitclaim deed offers the least amount of protection against defects in the title.

Quorum The number of members of a decision-making body that must be present before business may be transacted.

R

Ratification The act of accepting and giving legal force to an obligation that previously was not enforceable.

Real property Land and everything attached to it, such as foliage and buildings.

Reasonable person standard The standard of behavior expected of a hypothetical "reasonable person." The standard against which negligence is measured and that must be observed to avoid liability for negligence.

Receiver In a corporate dissolution, a court-appointed person who winds up corporate affairs and liquidates corporate assets.

Record Information that is inscribed in either a tangible medium or stored in an electronic or other medium and that is retrievable, according to the Uniform Electronic Transactions Act. The Uniform Computer Information Transaction Act uses *record* instead of *writing*.

Recording statutes Statutes that allow deeds, mortgages, and other real property transactions be recorded so as to provide notice to future purchasers or creditors of an existing claim on the property.

Red herring A preliminary prospectus that can be distributed to potential investors after the registration statement (for a securities offering) has been filed with the Securities and Exchange Commission. The name derives from the red legend printed across the prospectus stating that the registration has been filed but has not become effective.

Reformation A court-ordered correction of a written contract so that it reflects the true intentions of the parties.

Regulation E A set of rules issued by the Federal Reserve System's Board of Governors to protect users of electronic fund transfer systems.

Regulation Z A set of rules promulgated by the Federal Reserve Board to implement the provisions of the Truth-in-Lending Act.

Release A contract in which one party forfeits the right to pursue a legal claim against the other party.

Remainder A future interest in property held by a person other than the original owner.

Remedy The relief given to an innocent party to enforce a right or compensate for the violation of a right.

Replevin (pronounced ruh-*pleh*-vin) An action to recover specific goods in the hands of a party who is wrongfully withholding them from the other party.

Reply Procedurally, a plaintiff's response to a defendant's answer.

Requirements contract An agreement in which a buyer agrees to purchase and the seller agrees to sell all or up to a stated amount of what the buyer needs or requires.

Res ipsa loquitur (pronounced *rays ihp*-suh *low*-kwuh-duhr) A doctrine under which negligence may be inferred simply because an event occurred, if it is the type of event that would not occur in the absence of negligence. Literally, the term means "the facts speak for themselves."

Rescission (pronounced reh-*sih*-zhen) A remedy whereby a contract is canceled and the parties are returned to the positions they occupied before the contract was made; may be effected through the mutual consent of the parties, by their conduct, or by court decree.

Respondeat superior (pronounced ree-*spahn*-dee-uht soo-*peer*-ee-your) In Latin, "Let the master respond." A doctrine under which a principal or an employer is held liable for the wrongful acts committed by agents or employees while acting within the scope of their agency or employment.

Restitution An equitable remedy under which a person is restored to his or her original position prior to loss or injury, or placed in the position he or she would have been in had the breach not occurred.

Restrictive indorsement Any indorsement on a negotiable instrument that requires the indorsee to comply with certain instructions regarding the funds involved. A restrictive indorsement does not prohibit the further negotiation of the instrument.

Resulting trust An implied trust arising from the conduct of the parties. A trust in which a party holds the actual legal title to another's property but only for that person's benefit.

Retained earnings The portion of a corporation's profits that has not been paid out as dividends to shareholders.

Reversionary interest A future interest in property retained by the original owner.

Revocation In contract law, the withdrawal of an offer by an offeror; unless the offer is irrevocable, it can be revoked at any time prior to acceptance without liability.

Right of contribution The right of a co-surety who pays more than his or her proportionate share on a debtor's default to recover the excess paid from other co-sureties.

Right of first refusal The right to purchase personal or real property—such as corporate shares or real estate—before the property is offered for sale to others.

Right of reimbursement The legal right of a person to be restored, repaid, or indemnified for costs, expenses, or losses incurred or expended on behalf of another.

Right of subrogation The right of a person to stand in the place of (be substituted for) another, giving the substituted party the same legal rights that the original party had.

Right-to-work law A state law providing that employees are not to be required to join a union as a condition of obtaining or retaining employment.

Risk A prediction concerning potential loss based on known and unknown factors.

Risk management Planning that is undertaken to protect one's interest should some event threaten to undermine its security. In the context of insurance, risk management involves transferring certain risks from the insured to the insurance company.

Robbery The act of forcefully and unlawfully taking personal property of any value from another; force or intimidation is usually necessary for an act of theft to be considered a robbery.

Rule of four A rule of the United States Supreme Court under which the Court will not issue a writ of *certiorari* unless at least four justices approve of the decision to issue the writ.

Rulemaking The process undertaken by an administrative agency when formally adopting a new regulation or amending an old one. Rulemaking involves notifying the public of a proposed rule or change and receiving and considering the public's comments.

S

S corporation A close business corporation that has met certain requirements as set out by the Internal Revenue Code and thus qualifies for special income-tax treatment. Essentially, an S corporation is taxed the same as a partnership, but its owners enjoy the privilege of limited liability.

Sale The passing of title from the seller to the buyer for a price.

Sale on approval A type of conditional sale in which the buyer may take the goods on a trial basis. The sale becomes absolute only when the buyer approves of (or is satisfied with) the goods being sold.

Sale or return A type of conditional sale in which title and possession pass from the seller to the buyer; however, the buyer retains the option to return the goods during a specified period even though the goods conform to the contract.

Sales contract A contract for the sale of goods under which the ownership of goods is transferred from a seller to a buyer for a price.

Scienter (pronounced sy-*en*-ter) Knowledge by the misrepresenting party that material facts have been falsely represented or omitted with an intent to deceive.

Search warrant An order granted by a public authority, such as a judge, that authorizes law enforcement personnel to search particular premises or property.

Seasonably Within a specified time period, or, if no period is specified, within a reasonable time.

SEC Rule 10b-5 A rule of the Securities and Exchange Commission that makes it unlawful, in connection with the purchase or sale of any security, to make any untrue statement of a material fact or to omit a material fact if such omission causes the statement to be misleading.

Secondary boycott A union's refusal to work for, purchase from, or handle the products of a secondary employer, with whom the union has no dispute, for the purpose of forcing that employer to stop doing business with the primary employer, with whom the union has a labor dispute.

Secondary source of law A publication that summarizes or interprets the law, such as a legal encyclopedia, a legal treatise, or an article in a law review.

Secured party A lender, seller, or any other person in whose favor there is a security interest, including a person to whom accounts or chattel paper has been sold.

Secured transaction Any transaction in which the payment of a debt is guaranteed, or secured, by personal property owned by the debtor or in which the debtor has a legal interest.

Security Generally, a stock certificate, bond, note, debenture, warrant, or other document given as evidence of an ownership interest in a corporation or as a promise of repayment by a corporation.

Security agreement An agreement that creates or provides for a security interest between the debtor and a secured party.

Security interest Any interest "in personal property or fixtures which secures payment or performance of an obligation" [UCC 1–201(37)].

Self-defense The legally recognized privilege to protect one's self or property against injury by another. The privilege of self-defense protects only acts that are reasonably necessary to protect one's self or property.

Self-incrimination The giving of testimony that may subject the testifier to criminal prosecution. The Fifth Amendment to the Constitution protects against self-incrimination by providing that no person "shall be compelled in any criminal case to be a witness against himself."

Seniority system In regard to employment relationships, a system in which those who have worked longest for the company are first in line for promotions, salary increases, and other benefits; they are also the last to be laid off if the work force must be reduced.

Service mark A mark used in the sale or the advertising of services, such as to distinguish the services of one person from the services of others. Titles, character names, and other distinctive features of radio and television programs may be registered as service marks.

Sexual harassment In the employment context, the granting of job promotions or other benefits in return for sexual favors or language or conduct that is so sexually offensive that it creates a hostile working environment.

Shareholder's derivative suit A suit brought by a shareholder to enforce a corporate cause of action against a third person.

Shelter principle The principle that the holder of a negotiable instrument who cannot qualify as a holder in due course (HDC), but who derives his or her title through an HDC, acquires the rights of an HDC.

Shipment contract A contract for the sale of goods in which the seller is required or authorized to ship the goods by carrier. The buyer assumes liability for any losses or damage to the goods after they are delivered to the carrier.

Short-form merger A merger between a subsidiary corporation and a parent corporation that owns at least 90 percent of the outstanding shares of each class of stock issued by the subsidiary corporation. Short-form mergers can be accomplished without the approval of the shareholders of either corporation.

Shrink-wrap agreement An agreement whose terms are expressed inside a box in which goods are packaged. Sometimes called a *shrink-wrap license.*

Signature Under the UCC, "any symbol executed or adopted by a party with a present intention to authenticate a writing."

Slander Defamation in oral form.

Slander of quality (trade libel) The publication of false information about another's product, alleging that it is not what its seller claims.

Slander of title The publication of a statement that denies or casts doubt upon another's legal ownership of any property, causing financial loss to that property's owner.

Small claims courts Special courts in which parties may litigate small claims (usually, claims involving $5,000 or less). Attorneys are not required in small claims courts, and in many states attorneys are not allowed to represent the parties.

Smart card A card containing a microprocessor that permits storage of funds via security programming, can communicate with other computers, and does not require online authorization for fund transfers.

Sole proprietorship The simplest form of business, in which the owner is the business; the owner reports business income on his or her personal income tax return and is legally responsible for all debts and obligations incurred by the business.

Spam Bulk, unsolicited ("junk") e-mail.

Special indorsement An indorsement on an instrument that indicates the specific person to whom the indorser intends to make the instrument payable; that is, it names the indorsee.

Specific performance An equitable remedy requiring exactly the performance that was specified in a contract; usually granted only when money damages would be an inadequate remedy and the subject matter of the contract is unique (for example, real property).

Spendthrift trust A trust created to protect the beneficiary from spending all the money to which he or she is entitled. Only a certain portion of the total amount is given to the beneficiary at any one time, and most states prohibit creditors from attaching assets of the trust.

Stale check A check, other than a certified check, that is presented for payment more than six months after its date.

Standing to sue The requirement that an individual must have a sufficient stake in a controversy before he or she can bring a lawsuit. The plaintiff must demonstrate that he or she either has been injured or threatened with injury.

Stare decisis (pronounced *ster*-ay dih-*si*-ses) A common law doctrine under which judges are obligated to follow the precedents established in prior decisions.

Statute of Frauds A state statute under which certain types of contracts must be in writing to be enforceable.

Statute of limitations A federal or state statute setting the maximum time period during which a certain action can be brought or certain rights enforced.

Statute of repose Basically, a statute of limitations that is not dependent on the happening of a cause of action. Statutes of repose generally begin to run at an earlier date and run for a longer period of time than statutes of limitations.

Statutory law The body of law enacted by legislative bodies (as opposed to constitutional law, administrative law, or case law).

Stock An equity (ownership) interest in a corporation, measured in units of shares.

Stock certificate A certificate issued by a corporation evidencing the ownership of a specified number of shares in the corporation.

Stock warrant A certificate that grants the owner the option to buy a given number of shares of stock, usually within a set time period.

Stop-payment order An order by a bank customer to his or her bank not to pay or certify a certain check.

Strict liability Liability regardless of fault. In tort law, strict liability may be imposed on defendants in cases involving abnormally dangerous activities, dangerous animals, or defective products.

Sublease A lease executed by the lessee of real estate to a third person, conveying the same interest that the lessee enjoys but for a shorter term than that held by the lessee.

Substantive law Law that defines, describes, regulates, and creates legal rights and obligations.

Summary jury trial (SJT) A method of settling disputes in which a trial is held, but the jury's verdict is not binding. The verdict acts only as a guide to both sides in reaching an agreement during the mandatory negotiations that immediately follow the summary jury trial.

Summons A document informing a defendant that a legal action has been commenced against him or her and that the defendant must appear in court on a certain date to answer the plaintiff's complaint. The document is delivered by a sheriff or any other person so authorized.

Supremacy clause The provision in Article VI of the Constitution that provides that the Constitution, laws, and treaties of the United States are "the supreme Law of the Land." Under this clause, state and local laws that directly conflict with federal law will be rendered invalid.

Surety A person, such as a cosigner on a note, who agrees to be primarily responsible for the debt of another.

Suretyship An express contract in which a third party to a debtor-creditor relationship (the surety) promises to be primarily responsible for the debtor's obligation.

Symbolic speech Nonverbal conduct that expresses opinions or thoughts about a subject. Symbolic speech is protected under the First Amendment's guarantee of freedom of speech.

T

Taking The taking of private property by the government for public use. Under the Fifth Amendment to the Constitution, the government may not take private property for public use without "just compensation."

Tangible property Property that has physical existence and can be distinguished by the senses of touch, sight, and so on. A car is tangible property; a patent right is intangible property.

Target corporation The corporation to be acquired in a corporate takeover; a corporation to whose shareholders a tender offer is submitted.

Tenancy at sufferance A type of tenancy under which one who, after rightfully being in possession of leased premises, continues (wrongfully) to occupy the property after the lease has been terminated. The tenant has no rights to possess the property and occupies it only because the person entitled to evict the tenant has not done so.

Tenancy at will A type of tenancy under which either party can terminate the tenancy without notice; usually arises when a tenant who has been under a tenancy for years retains possession, with the landlord's consent, after the tenancy for years has terminated.

Tenancy by the entirety The joint ownership of property by a husband and wife. Neither party can transfer his or her interest in the property without the consent of the other.

Tenancy for years A type of tenancy under which property is leased for a specified period of time, such as a month, a year, or a period of years.

Tenancy in common Co-ownership of property in which each party owns an undivided interest that passes to his or her heirs at death.

Tender An unconditional offer to perform an obligation by a person who is ready, willing, and able to do so.

Tender offer An offer to purchase made by one company directly to the shareholders of another (target) company; often referred to as a "takeover bid."

Testamentary trust A trust that is created by will and therefore does not take effect until the death of the testator.

Testator One who makes and executes a will.

Third party beneficiary One for whose benefit a promise is made in a contract but who is not a party to the contract.

Tippee A person who receives inside information.

Tombstone ad An advertisement, historically in a format resembling a tombstone, of a securities offering. The ad informs potential investors of where and how they may obtain a prospectus.

Tort A civil wrong not arising from a breach of contract. A breach of a legal duty that proximately causes harm or injury to another.

Tortfeasor One who commits a tort.

Totten trust A trust created by the deposit of a person's own money in his or her own name as a trustee for another. It is a tentative trust, revocable at will until the depositor dies or completes the gift in his or her lifetime by some unequivocal act or declaration.

Trade acceptance A draft that is drawn by a seller of goods ordering the buyer to pay a specified sum of money to the seller, usually at a stated time in the future. The buyer accepts the draft by signing the face of the draft, thus creating an enforceable obligation to pay the draft when it comes due. On a trade acceptance, the seller is both the drawer and the payee.

Trade dress The image and overall appearance of a product—for example, the distinctive decor, menu, layout, and style of service of a particular restaurant. Basically, trade dress is subject to the same protection as trademarks.

Trade libel The publication of false information about another's product, alleging it is not what its seller claims; also referred to as slander of quality.

Trade name A term that is used to indicate part or all of a business's name and that is directly related to the business's reputation and goodwill. Trade names are protected under the common law (and under trademark law, if the name is the same as the firm's trademarked property).

Trade secrets Information or processes that give a business an advantage over competitors who do not know the information or processes.

Trademark A distinctive mark, motto, device, or implement that a manufacturer stamps, prints, or otherwise affixes to the goods it produces so that they may be identified on the market and their origins made known. Once a trademark is established (under the common law or through registration), the owner is entitled to its exclusive use.

Transfer warranties Implied warranties, made by any person who transfers an instrument for consideration to subsequent transferees and holders who take the instrument in good faith, that (1) the transferor is entitled to enforce the instrument, (2) all signatures are authentic and authorized, (3) the instrument has not been altered, (4) the instrument is not subject to a defense or claim of any party that can be asserted against the transferor, and (5) the transferor has no knowledge of any insolvency proceedings against the maker, the acceptor, or the drawer of the instrument.

Traveler's check A check that is payable on demand, drawn on or payable through a bank, and designated as a traveler's check.

Treaty An agreement formed between two or more independent nations.

Trespass to land The entry onto, above, or below the surface of land owned by another without the owner's permission or legal authorization.

Trespass to personal property The unlawful taking or harming of another's personal property; interference with another's right to the exclusive possession of his or her personal property.

Trust An arrangement in which title to property is held by one person (a trustee) for the benefit of another (a beneficiary).

Trust indorsement An indorsement for the benefit of the indorser or a third person; also known as an agency indorsement. The indorsement results in legal title vesting in the original indorsee.

U

U.S. trustee A government official who performs certain administrative tasks that a bankruptcy judge would otherwise have to perform.

Ultra vires (pronounced *uhl-trah vye-reez*) A Latin term meaning "beyond the powers"; in corporate law, acts of a corporation that are beyond its express and implied powers to undertake.

Unconscionable (pronounced *un-kon-shun-uh-bul*) **contract (or unconscionable clause)** A contract or clause that is void on the basis of public policy because one party, as a result of his or her disproportionate bargaining power, is forced to accept terms that are unfairly burdensome and that unfairly benefit the dominating party.

Underwriter In insurance law, the insurer, or the one assuming a risk in return for the payment of a premium.

Undisclosed principal A principal whose identity is unknown by a third person, and the third person has no knowledge that the agent is acting for a principal at the time the agent and the third person form a contract.

Unenforceable contract A valid contract rendered unenforceable by some statute or law.

Unilateral contract A contract that results when an offer can only be accepted by the offeree's performance.

Union shop A place of employment in which all workers, once employed, must become union members within a specified period of time as a condition of their continued employment.

Universal defenses Defenses that are valid against all holders of a negotiable instrument, including holders in due course (HDCs) and holders with the rights of HDCs.

Unreasonably dangerous product In product liability, a product that is defective to the point of threatening a consumer's health and safety. A product will be considered unreasonably dangerous if it is dangerous beyond the expectation of the ordinary consumer or if a less dangerous alternative was economically feasible for the manufacturer, but the manufacturer failed to produce it.

Usage of trade Any practice or method of dealing having such regularity of observance in a place, vocation, or trade as to justify an expectation that it will be observed with respect to the transaction in question.

Usury   Charging an illegal rate of interest.

Utilitarianism   An approach to ethical reasoning in which ethically correct behavior is not related to any absolute ethical or moral values but to an evaluation of the consequences of a given action on those who will be affected by it. In utilitarian reasoning, a "good" decision is one that results in the greatest good for the greatest number of people affected by the decision.

V

Valid contract   A contract that results when elements necessary for contract formation (agreement, consideration, legal purpose, and contractual capacity) are present.

Venue (pronounced *ven*-yoo)   The geographical district in which an action is tried and from which the jury is selected.

Vesting   The creation of an absolute or unconditional right or power.

Void contract   A contract having no legal force or binding effect.

Voidable contract   A contract that may be legally avoided (canceled, or annulled) at the option of one of the parties.

Voir dire (pronounced vwahr-*deehr*)   An Old French phrase meaning "to speak the truth." In jury trials, the phrase refers to the process in which the attorneys question prospective jurors to determine whether they are biased or have any connection with a party of the action or with a prospective witness.

Voting trust   An agreement (trust contract) under which legal title to shares of corporate stock is transferred to a trustee who is authorized by the shareholders to vote the shares on their behalf.

W

Warranty deed   A deed in which the grantor guarantees to the grantee that the grantor has title to the property conveyed in the deed, that there are no encumbrances on the property other than what the grantor has represented, and that the grantee will enjoy quiet possession of the property; a deed that provides the greatest amount of protection for the grantee.

Watered stock   Shares of stock issued by a corporation for which the corporation receives, as payment, less than the stated value of the shares.

Whistleblowing   An employee's disclosure to government, the press, or upper-management authorities that the employer is engaged in unsafe or illegal activities.

White-collar crime   Nonviolent crime committed by individuals or corporations to obtain a personal or business advantage.

Will   An instrument directing what is to be done with the testator's property upon his or her death, made by the testator and revocable during his or her lifetime. No interests in the testator's property pass until the testator dies.

Winding up   The second of two stages involved in the termination of a partnership or corporation. Once the firm is dissolved, it continues to exist legally until the process of winding up all business affairs (collecting and distributing the firm's assets) is complete.

Workers' compensation laws   State statutes establishing an administrative procedure for compensating workers' injuries that arise out of—or in the course of—their employment, regardless of fault.

Working papers   The various documents used and developed by an accountant during an audit. Working papers include notes, computations, memoranda, copies, and other papers that make up the work product of an accountant's services to a client.

Workout   An out-of-court agreement between a debtor and his or her creditors in which the parties work out a payment plan or schedule under which the debtor's debts can be discharged.

Writ of attachment   A court's order, prior to a trial to collect a debt, directing the sheriff or other officer to seize nonexempt property of the debtor; if the creditor prevails at trial, the seized property can be sold to satisfy the judgment.

Writ of *certiorari* (pronounced sur-shee-uh-*rah*-ree)   A writ from a higher court asking the lower court for the record of a case.

Writ of execution   A court's order, after a judgment has been entered against the debtor, directing the sheriff to seize (levy) and sell any of the debtor's nonexempt real or personal property. The proceeds of the sale are used to pay off the judgment, accrued interest, and costs of the sale; any surplus is paid to the debtor.

Wrongful discharge   An employer's termination of an employee's employment in violation of an employment contract or laws that protect employees.

Table of Cases

The titles of cases presented within the chapter text or in the *Focus on Legal Reasoning* features are in bold type. The titles of cases otherwise cited or discussed are in roman type.

Index